T0229690

VMware
Certified Professional Test Prep

VMware Certified Professional Test Prep

Merle Ilgenfritz, VCP, VCI
John Ilgenfritz, VCP, VCI

Technical editors
John Powell and Steven Baca, VCP, VCI

CRC Press is an imprint of the
Taylor & Francis Group, an **informa** business
AN AUERBACH BOOK

Auerbach Publications
Taylor & Francis Group
6000 Broken Sound Parkway NW, Suite 300
Boca Raton, FL 33487-2742

International Standard Book Number-13: 978-1-4200-6599-2 (hbk)

Library of Congress Cataloging-in-Publication Data

Ilgenfritz, Merle.
VMware certified professional test prep / Merle Ilgenfritz, John Ilgenfritz.
p. cm.
Includes bibliographical references and index.
ISBN 978-1-4200-6599-2 (alk. paper)
1. Electronic data processing personnel--Certification. 2. Virtual computer systems--Examinations--Study guides. 3. VMware. I. Ilgenfritz, John. II. Title.

QA76.3.I56 2009
005.4'3--dc22 2008037138

Visit the Taylor & Francis Web site at
http://www.taylorandfrancis.com

and the Auerbach Web site at
http://www.auerbach-publications.com

About the Authors

Merle Ilgenfritz has 15 years extensive experience training corporate clients at colleges, universities, private technical training institutions and vendor training sites. He is a VMware Certified Professional (VCP) and VMware Certified Instructor (VCI).

He also is a Sun Certified Instructor and has written Sun hardware and Solaris 10 administration courses for Sun Education. He participated in the development of the Solaris 10 Certification exams and has taught over 80 different customer and internal courses at their training sites across the world. Merle has taught over 160 different Microsoft/Unix based courses over the years as well.

Merle currently lives in Crossville, TN with his wife Ann Marie and their three children: Joel, Matt and Jaclyn.

John Ilgenfritz has been involved with information technology for over 17 years. He spent several years working as a systems administrator maintaining Windows and UNIX/Linux servers.

For 7 years, he worked as a Software Engineer involved with support and development of Enterprise Network Systems Management and ITIL Service Level Management software.

John is an A+ Certified Technician and Microsoft Certified Systems Engineer. He is also a VMware Certified Professional (VCP) and VMware Certified Instructor (VCI.)

He currently resides in Pittsburgh, PA with his wife Tina, daughter Jessica and son Seth.

About the Technical Editors

John Powell has been in the computer industry for more than 15 years working primarily in the Unix environment. He is a certified Solaris System Administrator and has developed and delivered high-quality training in the hardware and administration space. John has also developed and professionally voiced a multitude of web-based courses. He currently resides in Las Vegas with his wife and daughter.

Steven Baca is a Certified Instructor for VMware and a VMware Certified Professional (VCP). He also is a certified instructor for Sun Microsystems and Symantec focusing on the areas of Clustering and System Administration. Currently Steven resides in Omaha Nebraska with his wife and six kids. When he is not working, he enjoys his time with his family.

Table of Contents

Acknowledgments

The authors would like to give special thanks over the years to all of the students that provided some of the VMware certified instructors on the VMTN that answered our questions concerning the products covered in this book. VMware is a first rate company and provides many useful resources. Merle gives a special thanks to Hay Buddy for all of his help and technical feedback. I owe you a box of good cigars!

We would also like to thank our two technical editors for all of their hard work on this book. Their feedback was instrumental in keeping us on the right track!

Preface

Preparing to take a certification test can be a daunting task for many individuals. The fear of not passing combined with the magnitude of information that you are required to know can cause many people to "blank out" during the test. Most of their anxiety is caused by their perceived lack of preparation.

In preparing to write this book, we decided to write the content of this book to help you, the reader to understand the topics that VMware says you must know in order to be a VMware Certified professional. We have used many of the real world examples that we use when teaching the materials to our students to help illustrate the use of the various virtualization technologies.

We also realize that many of you will not have access to the resources that you would need to practice using the software. We have included over 700 screenshots of the various programs to walk you through the interface and help you understand where you go to configure the resources controlled by the programs.

We realized that some of you might have already taken the VCP test but were looking for information about the latest release of the software. This book covers the ESX 3.0.x thru ESX 3.5.x releases. Questions on the VCP test cover those releases.

We also wrote this book to experienced administrators by providing solutions to many of the common "gotchas" that could cause problems in your environment.

Each chapter has questions at the end of the chapter that cover the important concepts covered in the text. We did not want to write a "brain dump" book but instead provide you with practical information to help you pass the VCP test and provide you with a resource that you could use at work.

Good luck on the test!

Merle and John Ilgenfritz

Chapter 1

VMware Certified Professional Test Requirements

What you should expect to learn:

- What you need to do to prepare for taking the VMware Certified Professional (VCP) Exam on VMware ESX Server 3.5 and Virtual Center 2.5
- How to sign up for the VMware educational courses to help prepare you for the test
- How to sign up for the test

Official Web Resource

The best place to start to see if VMware has made any changes to their certification requirements is the VMware Certified Professional website:

http://mylearn1.vmware.com/portals/certification/

The website contains the links to the latest certification information you will need in preparing to take the VCP exam. If you have a VCP certification on the ESX 2.x product it will not expire but it does not certify you for the ESX 3.5 and VirtualCenter 2.5 software. You must pass the exam for the newer product to be considered certified.

The VCP exam on VMware ESX Server 3.5 and Virtual Center 2.5 was made available on March 1st, 2008. If you passed the VCP exam on the ESX 3.0.x and VirtualCenter 2.0 software you would not need to take the VCP exam on VMware ESX Server 3.5 and Virtual Center 2.5 exam.

If you attended qualifying ESX 3.0.x classes and did not take the 3.0.x test before March 1st, 2008 then you should do self study and get hands on experience in the ESX 3.5 and VirtualCenter 2.5 software before attempting the new exam. VMware offers a What's New e-learning offering as well as a What's New class but they will not be required for those attempting the exam. If you still have questions about the exam you can contact VMware at: certification@vmware.com

Certification Requirements

In order to be able to pass the VCP310 – VMware Certified Professional on VI3 exam you should have:

- Attended at least one qualifying certified VMware class

- Hands on experience with the product
- Technical skills supporting hardware, networking resources, SAN resources and supported OS's used in conjunction with the ESX 3.5 and VirtualCenter 2.5 software.

VMware Sanctioned Classes

VMware requires that if you have not attended any prior courses then you must attend either the four day VMware Infrastructure 3: Install and Configure course or the four day VMware Infrastructure 3: Deploy, Secure and Analyze course before you can take the VCP exam. If you would like to get all the information contained in both of these four day courses in one five day format then you should take the VMware Infrastructure 3: Fast Track Program course. It is a high-intensity class but it does not provide all of the information needed to successfully pass the exam. You will also receive a voucher for taking the exam if you attend the Fast Track class.

The course data sheets containing class details can be accessed at:

- VMware Infrastructure 3: What's New V 3.5 (self-paced online):
  http://mylearn.vmware.com/mgrReg/courses.cfm?ui=www&a=one&id_subject=3694
- VMware Infrastructure 3: Install and Configure V3.5:
  http://mylearn.vmware.com/descriptions/EDU%20DATASHEET%20VI3.5%20InstallAndConfigure3.pdf
- VMware Infrastructure 3: Deploy, Secure and Analyze V3.5:
  http://mylearn1.vmware.com/descriptions/EDU%20DATASHEET%20VI3%20DeploySecureAnalyze12.pdf
- VMware Infrastructure 3: Fast Track Program V3.5:
  http://mylearn.vmware.com/descriptions/EDU%20DATASHEET%20VI35%20FastTrack1.pdf
- VMware Class locations and links to the schedules at the training locations page is at:
  http://mylearn1.vmware.com/mgrreg/locations.cfm?ui=www

Prerequisite Skills: Hardware, SAN, Windows OS, Linux OS and Supported Guest OS's

A good understanding of your ESX 3.5 server hardware will be helpful when taking the VCP test. You should have a basic understanding of how the major components in a system work and how the ESX 3.5 software will interact with them. Specifically you should know how the software interacts with:

- The processors
- The memory subsystem
- The physical networking ports

- The internal and attached storage devices
- Configuration of the server's BIOS
- Configuration of the server's host bus adapters

Being familiar with the ESX 3.5 server and the supporting infrastructure and how it operates will make supporting the virtual infrastructure much easier. It will also help you with test questions that pertain to the physical configuration and operations of the hardware. The hardware listed on the VMware Hardware Compatibility Lists will have additional documentation on the associated vendor's website and are updated frequently:

- I/O Compatibility Guide For ESX Server 3.5 and ESXi: http://www.vmware.com/pdf/vi35_io_guide.pdf
- Systems Compatibility Guide for ESX Server 3.5 and ESXi: http://www.vmware.com/pdf/vi35_systems_guide.pdf
- Storage/SAN Compatibility Guide for ESX Server 3.5 and ESXi: http://www.vmware.com/pdf/vi35_san_guide.pdf

You should have a good understanding of how your network is configured and how the server interacts with network resources. The test questions that deal with networking require that you understand how the physical ports are being used by the server and how they connect to the physical network as well as how they interact with the virtual machines. If you don't have much networking experience, you might want to search for some online tutorial on networking basics or pick up one of the networking basics books at your local bookstore.

A good understanding of SAN and storage concepts will also help you with storage based questions. There are multiple ways of accessing storage resources and many ways to misconfigure the server so that it won't be able to use those resources.

Every server has a finite amount of resources. This means that every server can be configured in an over-committed state. An over-committed state is when the server cannot provide the resources that have been promised to the VMs. This can be due to limited resources or due to configuration settings that have been set for the VM that prevent the VM from using the resources. Resources can be CPU time, memory, I/O bandwidth and networking bandwidth.

You need to know the minimum requirements and the maximum configuration parameters supported by the ESX 3.5 software. Without a clear understanding of the capabilities of the software and how it interacts with the various virtual infrastructure resources you will not be able to answer many of the configuration based questions as well as deal with performance based issues at work.

For more information about the configuration maximum values see the VMware Configuration Maximums for VMware Infrastructure 3 doc at:

http://www.vmware.com/pdf/vi3_35/esx_3/r35/vi3_35_25_config_max.pdf

You will also need to have basic Windows operating system administration skills to answer the VirtualCenter based questions since it only runs in a Windows environment. Basic Linux command line administration skills are helpful to support the ESX 3.5 server but are not needed for the test. It is also helpful to have a good understanding of the operating systems that you will support running in your virtual machines. This will help you when troubleshooting VM issues in your virtual infrastructure.

The VMware Certified Professional Blueprint Outline document can be acquired at:

http://mylearn1.vmware.com/lcms/mL_faq/1714/VCP3.5Blueprint.PDF

This book provides information on all of the topics listed in the VMware Certified Professional Blueprint Outline document plus additional in-depth information not required for the exam. VMware does not require that you know every Command Line Interface (CLI) command for everything that can be done in the Graphical User Interface (GUI) to pass the exam. This book will provide many of those commands as well as insight to how the GUI actions or CLI commands edit the appropriate files in the ESX 3.5 server.

This guideline specifies that you should focus your preparation in the following areas:

- Understand VMware Products
- Differentiate Among VMware Products
- Understand the Architecture of the ESX Server
- Install and Configure the ESX Server
- Operate and Manage the ESX Server
- Configure Networking Under the ESX Server
- Set the ESX Server Resource Allocation Policies
- Administer Virtual Machines Under the ESX Server
- Monitor and Tune the ESX Server
- Configure Clustering Between the ESX Server Virtual Machines
- Troubleshoot the ESX Server

After Attending the Course

It will be much easier to pass the exam if you've gained a good amount of hands on experience. Give yourself at least a month to absorb all the information in the classes and documentation by using the product.

Testing Details

To sign up for the VCP310 – VMware Certified Professional on VI3 exam, go to the Pearson VUE website:

http://www.pearsonvue.com/vmware/

This link contains information to find a testing center that is convenient for you and the procedure to sign up for the exam online. There are over 3500 exam centers worldwide. There is also a toll free number on the website to set up a test session appointment so you can take the exam. The exam code is VCP-310.

Test Cost

The exam costs $175.00 (USD). You want to make sure you arrive at least 20 minutes early. If you are late you will not be given any additional time.

The test is 90 minutes in length. You will be given an additional 30 minutes if you live in a country where English is not the primary language. There are 75 questions on the exam and the questions are either:

- Multiple choice
- Scenario-based descriptions are followed by multiple choice questions

After You Pass the Exam

Four to six weeks after you successfully complete the exam, you will receive your certification kit and be issued a certificate indicating that you have achieved your VMware Certified Professional status, your personal registered VCP number and a login code to access the VCP website. You will also be able to use the VCP logo on your business cards, letterheads, and/or website. You will also receive an individual copy of VMware's Workstation product for your own personal use.

External References

The VMware Certified Professional Website:

http://mylearn1.vmware.com/portals/certification/

VMware Infrastructure 3: What's New V 3.5 (self-paced online):

http://mylearn.vmware.com/mgrReg/courses.cfm?ui=www&a=one&id_subject=3694

VMware Infrastructure 3: Install and Configure V3.5:

http://mylearn.vmware.com/descriptions/EDU%20DATASHEET%20VI3.5%20InstallAndConfigure3.pdf

VMware Infrastructure 3: Deploy, Secure and Analyze V3.5:

http://mylearn1.vmware.com/descriptions/EDU%20DATASHEET%20VI3%20DeploySecureAnalyze12.pdf

VMware Infrastructure 3: Fast Track Program V3.5:

http://mylearn.vmware.com/descriptions/EDU%20DATASHEET%20VI35%20FastTrack1.pdf

Certified Professional Blueprint Outline:

http://mylearn1.vmware.com/lcms/mL_faq/1714/VCP3.5Blueprint.PDF

VMware Class locations Webpage:

http://mylearn1.vmware.com/mgrreg/locations.cfm?ui=www

Pearson Vue Website:

http://www.pearsonvue.com/vmware/

VMware Infrastructure 3 Documentation:

http://www.vmware.com/support/pubs/vi_pubs.html

The VMware ESX 3.5 and ESX 3i Documentation Page:

http://www.vmware.com/support/pubs/vi_pubs.html

ESX Server 3.5 and VirtualCenter 2.5 Release Notes:

http://www.vmware.com/support/vi3/doc/vi3_esx35_vc25_rel_notes.html

Chapter 2

Overview of VMware Products and Technologies

After reading this chapter you should expect to learn:

- How Virtualization and the Virtual Infrastructure works
- Creating virtual hardware by abstracting physical hardware using the hypervisor
- Overview of the products (price vs. performance, capabilities, hosted vs. bare metal)
- VMware ESX 3.5
- VMware ESXi
- VMware VirtualCenter
- VMware Server
- VMware Workstation
- VMware Fusion
- VMware ACE
- Virtual Desktop Infrastructure (VDI)
- VMware Converter 3.x
- VMware Player
- Virtual Appliances
- VMware Lab Manager
- VMware Site Recovery Manager

What Is Virtualization?

Virtualization in context with computer technology can be defined as the abstraction of the hardware resources. In other words, virtualization hides the underlying hardware architecture from the resources wanting to use them.

In a traditional computer environment we may have hundreds of physical servers providing many of the services that our organization needs. We access these services typically from a client system. The services run in an operating system that has been designed to be able to recognize and utilize the various physical hardware components in the servers. The servers have access to internal and possibly external storage devices to store the applications and data needed to make the services work and be useful. The servers are connected to the clients and possibly other servers through a physical network infrastructure. All of these components must be configured properly and must be compatible with the services in order for us to gain value from their use.

The skills and knowledge needed to manage all of these resources is immense. Not all products are compatible with your physical resources. Even the operating systems are not going to run on all computers so care must be given to make sure that the products are properly configured and compatible with the other physical resources and applications in your physical infrastructure.

Physical and Virtual Infrastructure Differences

There are a number of distinct differences between a physical infrastructure and a virtual infrastructure. When we compare physical server requirements to a virtual environment, we shall see that there are many additional issues in deploying an operating system and its applications on the physical hardware. Virtualization eliminates many of these deployment issues. Virtualization also makes the task of maintenance much easier to accomplish as well.

The operating systems on a physical server must be able to access all of the physical resources in your computer to take full advantages of its capabilities. These physical resources are accessed using device drivers which are programs that the operating system uses to communicate, access and control the physical hardware in the computer. If the operating system does not have the correct device drivers then it will not be able to properly use the associated hardware. Most system administrators would agree that keeping the drivers up to date can be a daunting task. Some organizations are reluctant to update these drivers in their environment without proper testing. Bugs in the hardware drivers can cause your operating system and applications to not function properly.

Keeping the hardware drivers or the firmware, which is directly installed into the hardware, up to date is important to eliminate any "bugs" which are difficult to troubleshoot. The VMkernel, which is installed on your ESX 3.5 server, eliminates the problems associated with device drivers through virtualization. The operating systems communicate with a virtual device driver which communicates with the VMkernel. This hides the underlying hardware from the virtual machines.

It is important that the ESX 3.5 server software is able to recognize every piece of hardware during the power on self-test (POST) and have the correct drivers for the devices. That is why it is important that you only use devices on VMware's Hardware Compatibility List (HCL).

In a physical server, the operating system makes a request to access a physical CPU or core. The main difference in a virtual environment is that the VMs do not have direct access to the CPUs. Instead they make requests to the vCPUs virtual device driver which in turn communicates to the VMkernel scheduler. The scheduler determines what physical CPU resource will handle the request. This process will allow the VMkernel to load balance the requests per the VMs CPU settings across the available resources.

The memory resources in a physical server are managed typically by a memory management unit (MMU). The MMU is either embedded in the processor or on its chip. It handles the memory requests in the system. Operating systems access memory locations in a virtual fashion. These virtual memory addresses are translated to actual physical addresses in the memory subsystems. In the virtual environment, VMs cannot directly request memory locations. This is virtualized away by the VMkernel memory management components. Using various memory management techniques that will be covered later in this book, the VMkernel is able to utilize the available physical memory and distribute it amongst the VMs based on memory resource settings in the VMs.

The networking resources in a physical system are based on the number and type of NICs in the server. In a physical environment, the operating systems have total access to all of those resources. If the resources are under-utilized, they cannot be used by another system.

In the virtual environment the networking resources in the physical server are managed by the VMkernel and allocated to the various VMs through virtual switches and virtual device drivers that reside within them. The system's total network throughput, subsequently, can be more fully utilized.

I/O device resources in a physical environment are utilized by only one OS. Just like with networking devices, if they are not fully utilized the resources are wasted since no other system can use them.

In the virtual environment the I/O device resources in the physical server are managed by the VMkernel and allocated to the various VMs through virtual device drivers. The systems total I/O throughput then can be more fully utilized. Storage devices can be local to the system, on the SAN, or on the network and be accessed by the VMs. The virtual machine disks are encapsulated files accessible to the virtualization product. They are easily moved or copied. This allows for many new exciting possibilities in disaster recovery scenarios as well as making the backup of the VMs a simple process.

VMware Product Overview

We will examine the various VMware products to understand how they would be best applied into your virtual infrastructure. We will look at the uses of each product and compare the products to determine which might be better for configurations where the primary issue is performance, availability, remote management, pricing value or security.

VMware ESX 3.5

VMware's ESX 3.5 server is the company's flagship product. ESX is a datacenter grade server designed to facilitate a stable virtualized environment where significant cost savings can be realized in a short time frame, thus providing a return on investment (ROI) that can be monitored and measured against existing service level agreements (SLAs). An SLA is used to define a level of service in a service contract. The primary purpose of the ESX 3.5 server software is to provide a virtual machine (VM) access to the physical resources necessary that will be needed by the guest operating systems running within the VM. The ESX 3.5 server's ability to do this is contained within a proprietary kernel called the VMkernel.

One of the functions of any kernel is to provide low level access to the physical computer's hardware so that once an operating system is running, the kernel will be able to perform basic functions such as writing to the hard disk or accessing the internet via a network card which is installed inside the computer. Examples of kernels in use today are Microsoft's ntkernel, the Linux kernel and Sun Microsystems's genunix kernel to name a few. These kernels were designed to provide a single operating system access to the hardware. In contrast, the VMkernel was designed from its conception to be a highly efficient kernel responsible for scheduling CPU time, disk I/O, memory access and networking concurrently for several virtual machines running various operating systems.

The ESX 3.5 server is installed onto the "bare metal" of the machine and is therefore known as an unhosted application. It is considered unhosted because it does not require an already installed and running operating system to act as its host. Because of this, VMware must provide the needed hardware drivers in order for the VMkernel to function properly. Third party vendors who wish to have their hardware used by an ESX 3.5 server need to have their products certified by VMware in order to be a supported device. This testing is a necessary requirement for the proper functionality of the ESX 3.5 server as the VMkernel assumes it is running on supported hardware.

Running the hypervisor on the "bare metal" instead of in a host's operating system is done with the VMware Workstation, VMware Fusion, VMware Player or VMware Server software which provides for much better performance for the guest VMs. The guest operating systems can communicate directly with the VMkernel to access the hardware instead of interacting with the virtualization software in the host operating system and having it access the hardware. The VMkernel is specially designed to provide direct hardware access in an optimized manner.

Familiarity with using a Linux distribution will prove to be helpful in working with an ESX server. The VMkernel virtualizes a running instance of Red Hat Enterprise Linux (RHEL) 3 Update 6 during the RHEL boot process. This Red Hat virtual machine is known as the service console. The service console is frequently referred to as the console operating system (COS). It is created and configured at installation time of the ESX 3.5 server. VMware removed the components within RHEL that were not needed for the proper functioning of the ESX server. This was done to improve both stability and security.

To download a copy of the VMware ESX 3.5 software, go to:

http://www.vmware.com/products/vi/esx

The VMware ESX 3.5 documentation is located at:

http://www.vmware.com/support/pubs/vi_pubs.html

VMware ESXi

With the release of ESXi, VMware is moving towards rapid deployment of their ESX servers. This is achieved by adding a hardware integrated hypervisor within a firmware chip in a physical server. This new ESXi server only requires a 32 MB footprint contained on an onboard firmware chip. The small size is achieved by only needing to provide the VMkernel. Third party vendors that ship their servers with this ESXi chip already installed within the motherboard will allow the customer to simply power on the server. Once the VMkernel boots, the customer will be able to quickly add the new ESXi server into the existing VI3 virtualized infrastructure and simply move existing VMs to the new ESXi server or quickly deploy new VMs to this server.

This is made possible as the console operating system has been removed from the contents contained in the on-board firmware chip. A separate VM running the service console can be used, if needed, to further administer the ESXi server. Aside from the rapid deployment capability offered by ESXi, not running a service console means additional security out of the box. An ESX server administrator will not have to be concerned about securing a service console that does not exist. In addition, not having a console operating system also translates into additional power consumption savings as an ESXi server can easily operate without any physical disks. Fewer physical devices mean more stability and less downtime due to hardware failures.

ESXi server supports the Common Information Model (CIM), an open standard for managing elements in an IT environment. CIM allows agent-free monitoring of an ESXi server and is an industry standard. Patch management will be possible via VMware Update Manager. In environments where VMware Update Manager is not present, an update utility will also be provided. The update process for an ESXi server is simply an entire replacement of the firmware image. These updates will be less frequent as the majority of patches for an ESX server are patches specifically for the console operating system which will not be present in the ESXi server. With less power usage, no installation required stronger, security and built in CIM management capabilities, ESXi is true plug-n-play server hardware.

To download a copy of the VMware ESXi software, go to:

http://www.vmware.com/products/vi/esx/esx3i

The VMware ESXi documentation is located at:

http://www.vmware.com/support/pubs/vi_pubs.html

VMware VirtualCenter 2.x

At the core of maintaining your virtualized IT infrastructure is VMware's VirtualCenter (VC) management server. Rapidly provision new VMs with VCs cloning and template functionality. With the ability to clone a VM, an administrator can quickly and rapidly provide an identical copy of a VM for testing purposes such as applying the latest service packs to ensure the successful application of the patch. In addition to cloning, VC can be used to create a VM that will serve as a master image for future VMs. This master image VM can be cloned or converted easily to a template. The template functionality makes rapid server provisioning possible and ensures a consistent replicated image, thus reducing the possibility of introducing unknown configurations in the virtualized IT environment.

Also provided with VC is VM snapshot capabilities. A snapshot is a point-in-time image of a VM. Both the filesystem and memory state of a VM are preserved with a snapshot. Such snapshots are easily and quickly activated via VC's snapshot manager. Snapshots are a simple and convenient method for testing configuration changes, development and testing work or evaluating beta software.

Troubleshooting assistance is provided by VC. An administrator can monitor the status of VMs, ESX servers, networking and storage components from within the VC graphical user interface (GUI). This interface is accessible by using VMware's virtual infrastructure (VI) client. If a VM, ESX server or VMware cluster experiences a fault or degradation in performance, the VC GUI will provide easily identifiable icons to alert a change in the elements status. Service level agreements (SLAs) can be monitored from within VC via the performance monitoring charts. These charts are stored in the VC database (MS SQL server or Oracle) and provide historical trend data. The performance charts are customizable and offer analysis on numerous statistical metrics. If additional analysis is needed, VC performance charts can be exported to MS Excel.

VC provides an administrator the ability to configure VMware high availability (HA) clusters. HA clusters enable the restarting of VMs in the event of a physical ESX failing or if isolated in the event of a network failure or misconfiguration. These VMs can be restarted on another ESX server that has spare capacity within the HA cluster.

VC supports ROI by offering distributed resource scheduling (DRS) clusters. In a DRS cluster, VC can optimize physical ESX servers by balancing CPU and memory workloads across each ESX server in the DRS cluster. This ensures that an ESX server in the cluster will not be under heavy utilization while other ESX servers in the cluster are only being lightly used. Therefore, VC will prevent such a situation from occurring which, if allowed, could degrade the performance of individual VMs running on the over utilized server.

To download a copy of the VMware VirtualCenter 2.x software, go to:

http://www.vmware.com/products/vi/vc

The VMware VirtualCenter 2.x documentation is located at:

http://www.vmware.com/support/pubs/vi_pubs.html

VMware Server

VMware has made it possible to experience virtualization without requiring any additional financial investment. Their free VMware Server product provides an introduction to the world of x86 virtual machines. The product is designed to run on a server that is already configured with either the Windows or Linux operating systems. Servers that run a single operating system are susceptible to heavily utilizing one resource such as memory, while lightly utilizing other resources such as CPU or network bandwidth. Therefore a bottleneck occurring on one resource limits the full potential of all available resources.

VMware Server provides a cost effective means of resolving this imbalanced utilization of resources by allowing multiple VMs to concurrently run on top of a Windows or Linux server. Further cost savings can be immediately realized since an existing server can be transformed into a virtualization server, thereby eliminating the need to purchase additional hardware. VMware Server's ability to run within an existing operating system enables it to benefit from the underlying operating systems hardware support. This leveraging of existing hardware support reduces the time and configuration by IT administrators and allows VMware Server to be quickly deployed by companies of any size. It also allows servers that are not on the VMware Hardware Compatibility Lists to be used to create, use and test virtual machines.

Administrators with little virtualization experience can use VMware Server in conjunction with the numerous VMs available at the VMware appliance marketplace to quickly introduce virtualization. Additionally, the product supports virtualizing 64-bit guest operating systems, including Windows,

Linux and Solaris. Experimental support is provided for both two-processor virtual Symmetrical Multi Processing (SMP) and Intel's Virtualization Technology (VT). The VT technology is designed to enhance software based virtualization products through the use of new processor enhancements. By optimizing the way the processor interacts with virtual environment the performance overhead can be reduced and the VMs can run at a much higher performance level.

VMware Server can use VMs created with Microsoft Virtual Server and Symantec LiveState Recovery images. Management of VMware Server can be achieved using VirtualCenter 1.4. A user friendly remote console tool is included allowing access to the desktop of guest operating systems running within the VMs.

To download a copy of the VMware Server software, go to:

http://www.vmware.com/download/server

The VMware Server documentation is located at:

http://www.vmware.com/support/pubs/server_pubs.html

VMware Workstation

The Workstation product from VMware was first introduced more than eight years ago. Now in its sixth generation, it is an industry leading desktop virtualization application. VMware Workstation can be installed on Windows or Linux based computers. The range of target users is broad. Technology enthusiasts will find it appealing as a means to simultaneously run more than one operating system on their desktops or laptops.

For businesses, VMware Workstation offers software developers, support engineers, QA staff, and sales personnel a tool that reduces costs, enables collaboration and can demonstrate the value of a software product to potential customers.

The list of product features is impressive. Users can take snapshots in order to preserve the memory and file system state of a VM. At any time, a user can revert back to a snapshot easily and quickly using the snapshot manager tool. Software developers and support engineers can improve their productivity with Workstation's ability to record and play video files. These files are recordings that capture all changes to a VM over a period of time. Software debugging, customer problem recreation, sales presentations and classroom training can be enhanced as well with the new video record and playback feature.

VMware Workstation supports configuring multi-tier application servers with its Teams feature. Users can build several networked VMs that are isolated from the physical network. Building multiple VMs is easy as well with the VMware Cloning tool. This tool can be used to build baseline images allowing rapid deployment of new VMs. The deployment of new VMs can be further enhanced with the VMware ACE Option Pack available for Workstation. Assured Computing Environment (ACE) is used to create secure mobile VMs used on portable devices such as laptops and USB thumb drives.

To download a copy of the VMware Workstation 6.x software, go to:

http://www.vmware.com/products/ws

The VMware Workstation 6.x documentation is located at:

http://www.vmware.com/support/pubs/ws_pubs.html

VMware Fusion

VMware's Fusion product allows users running the Intel based Mac operating system to run virtual machines and guest operating system just like the VMware Workstation product does. Over 60 different guest operating systems are supported with the Fusion product. The Mac X OS is not supported as a VM due to licensing constraints. Virtual appliances can also be used with this product. There are over 550 virtual appliances available from the VMware website for download and evaluation.

The product also supports both 32 bit and 64 bit guests and the virtual machines can have multiple processors configured because the product supports the Intel Core Duo chips found in the latest Mac's. This will allow you to build your VMs with this product and migrate the VMs to any of the supported products that support their configuration. This includes VMware Workstation 6.0, VMware Player 2.0 and ACE 2.0.

Installation of the product is easy since it installs as any application would in the Mac OS. You can get a 30 day evaluation copy from the VMware website. If you decide to purchase the product you will need to remove the evaluation copy before installing the full licensed release on your Mac. The guest operating systems use the host operating system to communicate to the host's hardware drivers, USB 2.0 is supported in the guest VMs as well as using your Mac's DVD drive to burn CD's and DVD's from your virtual machines.

For individuals that use PCs at work but have a Mac at home this product will make it easy for you to use your VMs in both environments. A virtual machine is comprised of encapsulated files. Since many of the VMware products support USB devices you could put the VM files on a USB thumb drive or USB external drive and use it with both products seamlessly.

For more information about the product or to get an evaluation copy, go to the VMware Fusion support page at:

http://www.vmware.com/products/fusion/support.html

To get the VMware Fusion documentation, go to:

http://www.vmware.com/support/pubs/fusion_pubs.html

VMware ACE 2.x

The ACE 2.x software provides a secure way to deploy platform independent virtual machines. The advantage of this deployment is that enterprises can deploy a VM that can be easily transported home with the user. The ACE 2.x VM is useful in the following scenarios:

- Virtual Laptops
- Legacy OS Support

- Sandbox Environments
- Training and Education Environments

Virtual Laptops

Many organizations today are faced with the daunting task of managing their employee desktops. Hardware costs and the support of the operating systems and applications can drain the overall IT budget. Many organizations are looking for ways to reduce costs and to give employees flexibility in hours by allowing them to work from home. The ACE 2.x product provides a solution to these issues.

The ACE 2.x software can create secure virtual machines that easily deployed as a "virtual laptop" and can be put on a USB thumb drive and easily transported between the office and home. The virtual laptop VM can be accessed by using either the VMware Workstation or VMware Player products.

Legacy OS Support

Many applications that still are in use today were created many years ago and cannot be ported to the latest operating systems. This could be because the company that created it is no longer in business and the source code is no longer available. It could also be because the software won't run correctly on the newer processors. In any event, the application still provides a useful function in the organization. By creating a VM using the legacy OS, running the application from within it and using the ACE 2.x software to securely deploy it, the application could still be used on current systems in the virtualized environment. The older hardware could then be retired freeing up useful space for newer systems.

Sandbox Environments

Many applications provide sensitive information that an organization would not want to be made available to anyone outside of the organization. If an employee needs to access those applications the ACE 2.x client software and the ACE 2.x Management Server software provide methods to control access to those resources.

The "virtual sandbox" can provide the following security controls:

- User authentication using Active Directory or LDAP
- User and group access control to allow only certain user or groups to access the ACE 2.x resources
- SSL and HTTPS security when connecting to the centralized ACE 2.x Management Server
- Enhanced security options to access the built-in security databases
- Control of removable devices under the ACE 2.x client's operation
- Control from which networks the clients can access the enterprise resources from

Training and Education Environments

Many schools and technical training institutions face an ever changing learning environment. Maintaining the hardware, software, applications, and network and storage resources in the education environment is a challenging task. The ACE 2.x software allows the students to access a "virtual computer" complete with all of the applications and class files needed for their courses deployed in a secure manner. The students can be issued their own personal ACE 2.x client for the duration of the class. It could be taken to the home or dorm and run from their personal system. The ACE 2.x product eliminates the high maintenance costs of trying to reuse the same classroom environments multiple times in the same day.

For more information about the ACE 2.x product or to get an evaluation copy, go to the VMware ACE 2.x Support Page at:

http://www.vmware.com/products/ace/

To get the VMware ACE 2.x documentation, go to:

http://www.vmware.com/support/pubs/ace_pubs.html

Virtual Desktop Infrastructure (VDI)

Administration of desktops remains a top priority of IT departments. The complexity of modern operating systems and applications combined with internet connectivity can overwhelm administrators and support staff reducing productivity. Maintenance of desktop and laptop hardware can be compounded by compatibility issues, device hardware failures and lost or stolen laptops. In some industrial work environments, excessive dirt and dust may make operating a modern computer difficult or impossible.

To solve such issues, VMware introduced its Virtual Desktop Infrastructure (VDI). Using its industry proven, enterprise grade ESX 3.5 and ESXi servers, VMware's VDI can significantly reduce the complexity of desktop management. VDI supports the application of golden images that serve as a common configuration for desktops and laptops. A template of the golden image can be used to efficiently deploy VMs. A template can be converted to a running VM, updated, and then converted back to a template. This process of template updating increases productivity and decreases risks of desktop misconfiguration.

Essential in addressing security concerns, the VMs are stored and operated from ESX servers running within the data center. This allows administrators further control by enabling quick backups and timely patch management updates. A time savings can be realized as troubleshooting of local desktops can be performed instead of time spent traveling to remote sites.

Upgrading desktop hardware is less demanding and expensive. End users can use last generation hardware, re-purposed computers or thin clients due to applications running within the VMs instead of the local machines. Fast network interface cards (NIC) combined with a fast network infrastructure enhances end user experience. Some environments, due to environmental circumstances, (inserted commas) can benefit from the enclosed architecture that thin clients provide. VDI is a good solution for large call centers as well. In such an environment, end users typically require the exact same set of applications accessing database servers. ESX 3.5 Server's internal virtual switching can reduce physical network bandwidth usage and increase database access times. Workloads of large numbers of VM desktops can be balanced using ESX 3.5 server's distributed resource scheduler (DRS).

To learn more about VMware's VDI solution, visit:

http://www.vmware.com/products/vdi/

VMware Converter 3.x

Making the decision to virtualize the data center requires careful analysis and research. Once the decision to virtualize has been made, proper planning to virtualize existing physical servers is the next step. Converting physical machines to virtual machines is commonly referred to as P2V (Physical to Virtual). The task of building virtual machines to replace physical machines can be a time consuming process. An administrator may chose to manually install a supported operating system into a VM and recreate a physical machine application by application. Critical to this process is attention to detail as a misconfiguration in a Windows registry or UNIX configuration file can introduce instability into the VM.

With VMware's Converter, the server recreation step of Windows operating systems can be fully automated. Converter can be installed in one of the following operating systems:

- Windows NT4 SP4+
- Windows XP
- Windows 2000
- Windows 2003
- Windows XP 64-bit
- Windows 2003 64-bit

There are two editions of Converter, Starter and Enterprise. Converter Starter can be downloaded for free. With Converter Starter, local cloning of the physical machine where Converter is installed is possible. Converting a running machine is commonly referred to as hot cloning. When performing a hot local clone with Converter Starter, the local machine is required to be powered on and running one of the supported versions of Windows. The ability to clone a remotely running machine is limited to standalone virtual machines (GSX Server, VMware Server, VMware Workstation and VMware Player,) as destination target types. From the Converter Starter console window, it is only possible to view a single conversion process at a time.

VMware Converter Enterprise allows the scheduling of multiple simultaneous conversion processes. The status of these can be observed from the Converter Enterprise console window. These conversions can take place locally or remotely. Conversion can take place as either hot cloning or cold cloning. Cold cloning involves the physical machine being powered on with the VMware Converter Enterprise Boot CD used to start the cloning process. This form of conversion is used if hot cloning is not possible or desired.

The following can be converted using VMware Converter 3.x:

- Microsoft Windows Operating system-based only system images from Symantec Backup Exec System Recovery (formerly source system images LiveState recovery)
- Norton Ghost versions 9 or higher
- Microsoft Virtual PC 7 and higher
- Microsoft Virtual Server
- VMware Consolidated Backup (VCB) images of virtual machines

Integration with VirtualCenter 2.x and ESX 3.5 is available. With Converter Starter, exporting of local machines directly into VirtualCenter is supported. Converter Enterprise supports exporting local and remote machines directly into VirtualCenter 2.x. Converter Enterprise is included as part of the support and subscription for VirtualCenter Management Server.

To download a copy of the VMware Converter 3.x software, go to:

http://www.vmware.com/products/converter

The VMware Converter 3.x documentation is located at:

http://www.vmware.com/support/pubs/converter_pubs.html

VMware Player

IT departments that have a VI3 virtualized environment typically grant access to centrally managed VMs to authorized IT support staff. Access to common virtual machine images located in a shared storage may be beneficial for end users whose job functions are outside of the IT department. In such cases, these users can utilize these VM images with the free VMware Player product. Operating a pre-built VM created by VMware Workstation, VMware Server or VMware ESX Server, as well as Microsoft virtual machines and Symantec LiveState Recovery disks is quick and easy. End users can run multiple operating systems on the same PC at the same time. This eliminates the time installing guest operating systems, applying service packs, installing and configuring applications.

A VM running inside VMware Player can share data between the VM guest operating system and the host operating system running Player.

The following guest operating systems can be used:

- 32-bit Windows, Linux, NetWare, or Solaris x86
- 64-bit Windows, Linux, NetWare, or Solaris x86

Multiple operating systems can be running on the same physical machine without the need to reboot. VMware Player is limited in that virtual hardware cannot be added or removed from virtual machines. The creation of virtual machines using Player is not possible.

The ability to test various software configurations, evaluate support patches and beta software quickly and easily using existing VMs makes VMware Player a useful addition to virtualized environments.

To download a copy of the VMware Player 2.x software, go to:

http://www.vmware.com/products/player/

The VMware Player 2.x documentation is located at:

http://www.vmware.com/support/pubs/player_pubs.html

Virtual Appliances

IT Support staff spend valuable time when tasked with installing unfamiliar operating systems and applications. Enterprise grade applications typically require advanced knowledge of the underlying operating system to ensure stability and maximum application performance. VMware has designed its Virtual Appliance Marketplace to address these problems. At the Virtual Appliance Marketplace, users will find hundreds of pre-built, optimally configured virtual machines to use. These virtual machines are referred to as virtual appliances and are formatted and distributed using the Open Virtual Format (OVF). OVF is a platform independent format for distributing virtual machines that provides the freedom of deployment on the virtualization platform of their choice.

These appliances can be downloaded from the VMware Virtual Appliances Marketplace webpage at:

http://www.vmware.com/appliances/

They are organized into categories which are:

- Administration
- App/Web Server
- Communications
- Community Contributed
- Content/Collaboration
- Database
- Eval Appliances
- Networking
- Operating Systems
- Production Ready Appliances
- Security
- Other Appliances

Once the download completes, the user simply can start the virtual appliance within VMware Player, Workstation or on an ESX server and be operational in minutes instead of hours or days. This process can significantly reduce the time traditionally spent installing and configuring operating systems and applications. Additionally, Independent Software Vendors (ISV) building their virtual appliances have the in-house knowledge to properly secure the appliance. IT departments leveraging the appliance marketplace can increase productivity while successfully deploying optimized and secure virtual machines.

VMware Lab Manager

Software developers are typically challenged with acquiring the proper hardware needed to create a testing environment for their applications. However, acquiring the hardware is only one step towards meeting the goal of creating a test environment. Properly configuring the hardware is another major obstacle. This step often consumes valuable development hours from the project and can also require assistance from IT administrators. The IT administrators often have higher priorities than configuring test and development environments thus delaying the development project even further.

VMware created Lab Manager as a solution to these types of problems that occur during the development cycle of a project. With Lab Manager, a software development group can create VMs that are custom tailored to meet their needs. These VMs can be stored in a dedicated shared storage library and cataloged based on organizational requirements. A software developer can log into the Lab Manager server, select a predefined environment, for example, an MS Active Directory setup that includes MS SQL and Exchange servers and with just a few clicks of the mouse, rapidly deploy the set of VMs and begin their development and testing work without the aid of IT administrators.

With the network fencing technology, VMware Lab Manager enables multiple developers to deploy the same library configuration without any duplicate MAC addresses, IP addresses or security ID conflicts. With Lab Manager, it is just as easy to tear down a setup as it is to build it. This flexibility allows developers to increase the number of configurations their software can support. If a bug is discovered during development, the setup where the bug was found can be suspended, saved and shared with other development members and groups. These capabilities can lead to quicker development times, reduced costs and few bugs in the released software.

Support and Quality Assure (QA) professionals can also benefit from using Lab Manager. QA testers can share the environments where software defects were discovered with the development group. Support personnel can research customer issues and work with development to further identify the root cause of the issue.

For more information about the VMware Lab Manager product or to get an evaluation copy, go to the VMware Lab Manager Support Page at:

http://www.vmware.com/products/labmanager/

To get the VMware Lab Manager documentation, go to:

http://www.vmware.com/support/pubs/labmanager_pubs.html

VMware Site Recovery Manager

VMware has announced in March, 2008 that they will be releasing a new product called VMware Site Recovery Manager. There might be some test questions on this new product latter on in the year. At the time of this books release we don't have any additional information.

For more information on our website as to how this will be added to the test (if at all) please refer to our website at:

http://www.vcpprep.com/errata.html

External References

The Roadmap to Virtual Infrastructure: Practical Implementation Strategies:

http://download3.vmware.com/elq/pdf/wp_roadmaptovirtualinfrastructure.pdf

VMware Products Download Page:

http://www.vmware.com/products/

VMware Infrastructure 3 Documentation:

http://www.vmware.com/support/pubs/vi_pubs.html

The ESX Server 3 Datasheet:

http://www.vmware.com/files/pdf/esx_datasheet.pdf

The ESX Server 3i Datasheet:

http://www.vmware.com/files/pdf/esx_server3i_datasheet.pdf

VMware VirtualCenter 2.5 Documentation Page:

http://www.vmware.com/support/pubs/vi_pubs.html

The VMware Server Documentation Page:

http://www.vmware.com/support/pubs/server_pubs.html

The VMware Workstation 6.x Documentation Page:

http://www.vmware.com/support/pubs/ws_pubs.html

VMware Fusion Documentation Page:

http://www.vmware.com/support/pubs/fusion_pubs.html

VMware ACE 2.x Documentation Page:

http://www.vmware.com/support/pubs/ace_pubs.html

VDI -- A New Desktop Strategy Whitepaper:

http://www.vmware.com/pdf/vdi_strategy.pdf

The VMware Converter 3.x Documentation Page:

http://www.vmware.com/support/pubs/converter_pubs.html

The VMware Player 2.x Documentation Page:

http://www.vmware.com/support/pubs/player_pubs.html

What are the Benefits of Deploying Virtual Appliances?:

http://www.vmware.com/appliances/deploy/why.html

The VMware Lab Manager Documentation Page:

http://www.vmware.com/support/pubs/labmanager_pubs.html

Sample Test Questions

1. Which of the following is not true of the VMware Server product?

a. It can support VMs with multiple processors

b. It can support virtual switches with VLAN capabilities

c. It uses the hardware drivers in the host OS

d. It can be managed using VirtualCenter 1.4

e. It can support up to 2-4 VMs per core

2. Licenses are not required for which of the following products?

a. ESX 3.5 standalone servers

b. VirtualCenter 2.x managing multiple servers

c. VMware Player

d. VMware High Availability

e. VMware VMotion

f. VMware Server

g. VMware SMP

h. VMware Fusion

3. The only product that supports the creation of templates is the ESX 3.5 Server software.

a. True

b. False

4. Which of the following products support USB devices in the guest OS's that they will run inside of a VM?

a. VMware Workstation

b. ESX 3.5 Server

c. VMware Server

d. VMware Player

e. VMware Fusion

5. The VMware ACE 2.x product is used in conjunction with which of the following products?

a. ESXi Server and ESX 3.5 Server

b. VirtualCenter 1.4

c. VirtualCenter 2.x

d. VMware Player, VMware Server and VMware Fusion

e. VMware Player, VMware Workstation and ACE 2.x Management Server

f. VMware Lab Manager

6. A new virtual disk can be added to virtual machines running on the VMware Player product.

a. True

b. False

7. Which product will allow you to create and run virtual machines on the Mac OS?

a. VMware Workstation

b. ESX 3.5 Server

c. VMware Server

d. VMware Player

e. VMware Fusion

8. Which kernel is used by the ESX 3.5 server?

a. Genunix

b. Ntkernel

c. Vmkcore

d. VMkernel

e. Linux

9. VMware Server would be a better choice over ESX 3.5 in which of the following situations?

a. When maximum scalability is important

b. When maximum performance is important

c. When a departmental project must keep its costs as low as possible

d. When load balancing the I/O to the SAN is important

e. When trying to connect to storage resources with a non-supported HBA

f. When migrating running VMs is important

10. The ACE 2.x software allows you to create and securely deploy a VM to a USB 2.0 thumb drive.

a. True

b. False

11. ESX 3.5 uses which OS for its console operating system?

a. SUSE Linux

b. Open Solaris

c. Red Hat Core

d. Fedora

e. Red Hat Enterprise 3

12. How many hard drives are required to operate an ESXi server?

a. 4

b. 0

c. 2

d. 1

e. 3

13. Without additional configuration, which of the following monitoring technologies does an ESXi server support?

a. SNMP

b. Ethereal

c. CIM

d. RDP

e. VNC

14. VirtualCenter enables administrators the capability to do which of the following?

a. Cloning

b. Partitioning

c. Templates

d. Transparent memory sharing

e. Optimized mouse drivers

15. Which of the following can the VirtualCenter snapshot manager perform?

a. Schedule snapshot events

b. Generate VM bookmarks

c. Create a filesystem consistent VM image

d. Modify templates e. apply system patches

16. What Operating Systems can VMware Server be installed on?

a. Solaris machine

b. Windows machine

c. HPUX machine

d. Linux machine

e. AIX machine

17. VMware Server supports SMP in the following configuration?

a. Two-way

b. Eight-way

c. Does not support SMP

d. One-way

e. Six-way

18. ACE can be used to do which of the following?

a. Create VMs

b. Secure an ESX server

c. Add SMP

d. Secure a VirtualCenter server

e. Add hardware devices

19. The VMware Player Product can be used to build new VMs.

a. True

b. False

20. A virtual machine can communicate directly with the network interfaces in an ESXi server?

a. True

b. False

21. Which of the following does the VMkernel manage access to the physical CPUs?

a. the VMs operating system's processor driver

b. the VMs operating system's memory driver

c. the ntkernel

d. the genunix kernel

e. the VMkernel's scheduler

22. Virtualization of the VM disk resources allows which of the following?

a. Easy replication of the VMs operating system files

b. Easy replication of virtualized data disks

c. Easy relocation of the virtual disks to a different storage device

d. Locating the disks on shared network storage

e. Locating the virtual disk files on a SAN

23. Virtual Machines have direct access to SAN storage.

a. True

b. False

24. Virtual Appliances are physical devices that can run several virtual machines simultaneously.

a. True

b. False

25. Which of the following is not possible with VMware Server?

a. Managed by VirtualCenter

b. Create and restore multiple snapshots

c. VMotion

d. VLANs

e. SAN storage

26. VMware Converter Starter supports how many simultaneous conversions?

a. 2

b. 1

c. 4

d. 8

e. 5

27. Cold cloning is a function only of VMware Converter Enterprise?

a. True

b. False

28. VMware ACE provides features to configure which of the following?

a. Security policies

b. Expiration dates

c. Network Access

d. Virtual SMP

e. SSH

29. VMware Converter is available as which of the following?

a. Converter Advanced

b. Converter Enterprise

c. Converter Unlicensed

d. Converter Basic

e. Converter Starter

30. Using Workstation 6.x allows users to do which of the following?

a. Operate virtual machines on the MAC operating system

b. Integrate with ACE Option Pack

c. Create a video recording of a virtual machine

d. Set copy protection policies

e. Dynamic resource management

31. Which of the following two is not a function of VirtualCenter?

a. Cloning

b. Memory management

c. Templating

d. Disk I/O management

e. VMotion

32. All virtual appliances are free of change.

a. True

b. False

Sample Test Solutions

1. Which of the following is not true of the VMware Server product?

a. It can support VMs with multiple processors

b. It can support virtual switches with VLAN capabilities

c. It uses the hardware drivers in the host OS

d. It can be managed using VirtualCenter 1.4

e. It can support up to 2-4 VMs per core

Answer: b - ESX 3.5 supports virtual switches with VLAN capabilities, VMware Server does not.

2. Licenses are not required for which of the following products?

a. ESX 3.5 standalone servers

b. VirtualCenter 2.x managing multiple servers

c. VMware Player

d. VMware High Availability

e. VMware VMotion

f. VMware Server

g. VMware SMP

h. VMware Fusion

Answer: c & f

3. Is the only product that supports the creation of templates the ESX 3.5 Server software?

a. True

b. False

Answer: b - A standalone ESX 3.5 server cannot create a template. You must build one using VirtualCenter.

4. Which of the following products support USB devices in the guest OS's that they will run inside of a VM?

a. VMware Workstation

b. ESX 3.5 Server

c. VMware Server

d. VMware Player

e. VMware Fusion

Answer: a, c, d & e

5. The VMware ACE 2.x product is used in conjunction with which of the following products?

a. ESXi Server and ESX 3.5 Server

b. VirtualCenter 1.4

c. VirtualCenter 2.x

d. VMware Player, VMware Server and VMware Fusion

e. VMware Player, VMware Workstation and ACE 2.x Management Server

f. VMware Lab Manager

Answer: e

6. The VMware Player Product can add a new virtual disk to virtual machines.

a. True

b. False

Answer: b

7. Which product will allow you to create and run virtual machines on the Mac OS?

a. VMware Workstation

b. ESX 3.5 Server

c. VMware Server

d. VMware Player

e. VMware Fusion

Answer: e

8. Which kernel is used by the ESX 3.5 server?

a. Genunix

b. Ntkernel

c. Vmkcore

d. VMkernel

e. Linux

Answer: d

9. VMware Server would be a better choice over ESX 3.5 in which of the following situations?

a. When maximum scalability is important

b. When maximum performance is important

c. When a departmental project must keep its costs down as low as possible

d. When load balancing the I/O load to the SAN is important

e. When trying to connect to storage resources with a non-supported HBA

f. When migrating running VMs is important

Answer: c & e: VMware Server is a free product and it uses the drivers from the host OS that don't have to be on the Hardware Compatibility List.

10. The ACE 2.x software allows you to create and securely deploy a VM to a USB 2.0 thumb drive?

a. True

b. False

Answer: a

11. ESX 3.5 uses which OS for its console operating system?

a. SUSE Linux

b. open Solaris

c. Red Hat Core

d. Fedora

e. Red Hat Enterprise 3

Answer: e

12. How many hard drives are required to operate an ESXi server?

a. 4

b. 0

c. 2

d. 1

e. 3

Answer: b

13. Without additional configuration, which of the following monitoring technologies does an ESXi server support out of the box?

a. SNMP

b. Ethereal

c. CIM

d. RDP

e. VNC

Answer: c

14. VirtualCenter enables administrators the capability to do which of the following?

a. Cloning

b. Partitioning

c. Templates

d. Transparent memory sharing

e. Optimized mouse drivers

Answer: a & c

15. The VirtualCenter snapshot manager can?

a. Schedule snapshot events

b. Generate VM bookmarks

c. Create a filesystem consistent VM image

d. Modify templates

e. Apply system patches

Answer: c – that product cannot do any of the other tasks

16. VMware Server can be installed on a?

a. Solaris machine

b. Windows machine

c. HPUX machine

d. Linux machine

e. AIX machine

Answer: b & d

17. VMware Server supports SMP in the following configuration?

a. Two-way

b. Eight-way

c. Does not support SMP

d. One-way

e. Six-way

Answer: a

18. ACE can be used to do which of the following?

a. Create VMs

b. Secure an ESX server

c. Add SMP

d. Secure a VirtualCenter server

e. Add hardware devices

Answer: a

19. The VMware Player Product can be used to build new VMs.

a. True

b. False

Answer: b

20. A virtual machine can communicate directly with the network interfaces in an ESXi server?

a. True

b. False

Answer: b - In an ESXi Server or ESX 3.5 server the VMs communicate with the network interfaces via the VMkernel

21. The VMkernel manages access to the physical CPUs with?

a. The VMs operating system's processor driver

b. The VMs operating system's memory driver

c. The ntkernel

d. The genunix kernel

e. The VMkernel's scheduler

Answer: e – The VMkernel's scheduler allocates vCPUs to the VMs as they request access to them provided they are available and can meet the vCPU resource requirements of the virtual machine.

22. Virtualization of the VM disk resources allows which of the following?

a. Easy replication of the VMs operating system files

b. Easy replication of virtualized data disks

c. Easy relocation of the virtual disks to a different storage device

d. Locating the disks on shared network storage

e. Locating the virtual disk files on a SAN

Answer: all of the above – virtualization of the disks used by the VM provides all of these benefits

23. Virtual Machines have direct access to SAN storage?

a. True

b. False

Answer: b - Virtual machines see their storage as local SCSI hard drives regardless of the virtual hard disk physical location. All disk I/O is delegated via the VMkernel.

24. Virtual Appliances are physical devices that can run several virtual machines simultaneously?

a. True

b. False

Answer: b - Virtual Appliances are pre-built virtual machines and are downloadable from the VMware Virtual Marketplace.

25. Which of the following is not possible with VMware Server?

a. Managed by VirtualCenter

b. Create and restore multiple snapshots

c. VMotion

d. VLANs

e. SAN storage

Answer: b, c, d - VMware server allows a single snapshot per virtual machine. VMotion and VLANS are only possible with ESX 3.5 and ESXi servers.

26. VMware Converter Starter supports how many simultaneous conversions?

a. 2

b. 1

c. 4

d. 8

e. 5

Answer: b - Converter Starter is the free version of VMware Converter and allows a single conversion at a time. VMware Converter Enterprise supports multiple simultaneous conversions.

27. Cold cloning is a function only of VMware Converter Enterprise?

a. True

b. False

Answer: a - VMware Converter Enterprise provides a boot CD that can be used to clone a physical machine without the operating system of the machine being operational. VMware Converter Starter supports hot cloning only.

28. VMware ACE provides features to configure which of the following?

a. Security policies

b. Expiration dates

c. Network Access

d. Virtual SMP

e. SSH

Answer: a, b, c - VMware ACE allows IT security administrators the ability to set security policies such as authentication, expiration dates of the virtual machines and limitations on network access.

29. VMware Converter is available as which of the following?

a. Converter Advanced

b. Converter Enterprise

c. Converter Unlicensed

d. Converter Basic

e. Converter Starter

Answer: - VMware Converter is available in two versions, Converter Starter and Converter Enterprise.

30. Using Workstation 6.x allows users to do which of the following?

a. Operate virtual machines on the MAC operating system

b. Integrate with ACE Option Pack

c. Create a video recording of a virtual machine

d. Set copy protection policies

e. Dynamic resource management

Answer: b, c - VMware Workstation 6.x allows users enhanced virtual machine security setting with the integration of VMware ACE via the ACE Option Pack. Workstation 6.x also allows user to record virtual machine sessions for playback at a later time.

31. Which of the following two is not a function of VirtualCenter?

a. Cloning

b. Memory management

c. Templating

d. Disk I/O management

e. VMotion

Answer: b & d - VirtualCenter provides the ability to create templates, clone and VMotion virtual machines. ESX 3.5 and ESXi manage both memory and disk resources.

32. Are all virtual appliances are free of change?

a. True

b. False

Answer: b - Virtual appliances are created by ISVs and technology enthusiasts. Some virtual appliances are 30-day evaluation virtual machines provide by vendors requiring a fee to extend the use of the appliance. Other appliances are based on open source software and are free of charge.

Chapter 3

ESX 3.5 Server Installation

What you should expect to learn:

- Install the VMware ESX 3.5 Server software
- Post Installation Configuration
- Upgrading from ESX 2.x to ESX 3.5
- Troubleshooting common ESX 3.5 server installation problems

Planning an ESX 3.5 Server Software Installation

This module will discuss the procedure to do an install of the ESX 3.5 software. Before we can do an install we need to determine how we want to integrate the ESX 3.5 server into our environment. We must determine any potential issues that the install might encounter as well as any issues about integrating the ESX 3.5 server into the existing environment.

Some of the issues we must address are:

- Is the physical server that we plan on using to install the ESX 3.5 server software and its components supported on the Hardware Compatibility Lists (HCL)?
- How much processing power will be needed to run the ESX 3.5 server software, all the guest operating systems installed in the Virtual Machines (VMs), and all the applications running in the VMs?
- How much memory will be needed to run the ESX 3.5 server software, all the guest operating systems installed in the Virtual Machines (VMs), and all of the applications running in the VMs?
- What disk(s) are to be used to install the files needed to boot and run the ESX 3.5 server software?
- What storage device(s) will be used to store the VM files?
- What storage device(s) will be used to store the software ISO images that are to be used for software installations?
- What network interfaces are available on the ESX 3.5 server?
- How is this server to be integrated into the existing network infrastructure?
- What license keys will be required to support the VMs installed on this ESX 3.5 server?
- What security requirements are needed to be maintained when accessing the ESX 3.5 server?
- Is this to be a stand-alone ESX 3.5 server that will be directly administered or will it be put under the VirtualCenter 2.5 software's control so that it can be administered with other ESX 3.5 servers?

With proper planning the installation and configuration of the ESX 3.5 server should not be a daunting task. Too little planning can cause issues and a lot of reconfigurations later on as you realize that the configuration is lacking in providing either the proper performance, availability, or security required by your organization.

Pre-installation Requirements

Before installing the ESX 3.5 server software onto your server you must determine if the server contains the required and supported hardware necessary to support the ESX 3.5 server software. VMware updates on a regular basis their Hardware Compatibility List (HCL) guides. Prior to installation, you should download the following guides:

- Systems Compatibility Guide for ESX Server 3.5 and ESXi Server 3.5:
  http://www.VMware.com/pdf/vi35_systems_guide.pdf
- I/O Compatibility Guide for ESX Server 3.5 and ESXi Server 3.5:
  http://www.VMware.com/pdf/vi35_io_guide.pdf
- Storage/SAN Compatibility Guide for ESX Server 3.5 and ESXi Server 3.5:
  http://www.VMware.com/pdf/vi35_san_guide.pdf

There are two additional HCL guides that will be discussed in a later chapter but are not needed for the installation and deployment of the ESX 3.5 server software:

- Backup Software Compatibility Guide for ESX Server 3.5 and ESXi Server 3.5
- VMware ESX Server Supported Hardware Lifecycle Management Agents

Systems Compatibility Guide for ESX 3.5

The Systems Compatibility Guide for ESX 3.5 contains the list of currently supported:

- Servers
- Guest Operating Systems
- Qualified Hardware Lifecycle Management Application
- VMotion Processor Compatibility Requirements

If the server you plan to use is not in the Systems Compatibility Guide, VMware is not required to provide support for that server. Use the Systems Compatibility Guide to determine which servers should be purchased and are best suited for VMware software. Some of the servers that are supported for the ESX 2.5 server software are not yet qualified to run the ESX 3.5 software. So if you plan to upgrade from ESX 2.5 to ESX 3.5 you should still check the HCL to see if your system is listed.

CPU Requirements

Your server must have as a minimum at least two processors (sockets). Many of the servers listed in the Systems Compatibility Guide for ESX Server 3.5 and ESXi Server 3.5 can be purchased from the vendor in single socket configurations. You must have at least 2 sockets to meet licensing requirements. Also be aware that you will not be able to run any 64 bit guest operating systems if the processors in the server are 32 bit processors. The minimum recommended CPU speed for ESX 3.0, ESX 3.01, ESX 3.02 and ESX 3.5 software with or without Virtual SMP is 1500 MHz.

Maximum CPU Configurations

The maximum supported processor configuration in an ESX 3.5 server with single cores per socket with Hyperthreading is 16 sockets. This would give you a maximum of 16 cores and 32 threads.

The maximum supported processor configuration in an ESX 3.5 server with single cores per socket without Hyperthreading is 16 sockets. This would give you a maximum of 16 cores and 16 threads.

The maximum supported processor configuration in an ESX 3.5 server with dual cores per socket with Hyperthreading is 8 sockets. This would give you a maximum of 16 cores and 32 threads.

The maximum supported processor configuration in an ESX 3.5 server with dual cores per socket without Hyperthreading is 16 sockets. This would give you a maximum of 32 cores and 32 threads.

The maximum supported processor configuration in an ESX 3.5 server with quad cores per socket with Hyperthreading is 8 sockets. This would give you a maximum of 32 cores and *64 threads.

NOTE: The maximum supported logical processors supported on an ESX 3.5.x server at the release of this book is 32.

Each virtual machine may be configured with one, two or four virtual CPUs (vCPUs). The maximum supported total of vCPUs running in VMs on an ESX 3.5 server is 128. You are also limited to up to eight vCPUs per core.

For example you cannot have a mixture of single and multi vCPU virtual machines that exceed a combined total of 128 vCPUs per ESX server.

Memory Requirements

The minimum amount of RAM required is 1 GB. The maximum amount of RAM supported in an ESX 3.5 server is 256 GB. The service console will reserve 272 MB of RAM by default. The maximum amount of RAM that can be configured for the service console is 800 MB.

I/O Compatibility Guide For ESX 3.5

The I/O Compatibility Guide for ESX 3.5 contains supported:

- Storage I/O Drivers and Devices

- Network I/O Drivers and Devices

You should confirm that all of your internal (on the motherboard) or I/O cards are listed as supported in the I/O Compatibility Guide for ESX 3.5. Usually the vendor will have a detailed list on the website describing the internal I/O controllers for your server.

Network Interfaces

The minimum number of network interfaces required by the ESX 3.5 server is one. VMware best practices recommend at least four physical network interfaces. For the virtual machines, create a NIC team using two network interfaces and create a second NIC team using two more network interfaces for the service console and VMotion network. The VMotion port must be a Gbit Ethernet port. The second NIC team, configure it with only one active adapter for the service console, the other NIC configured as a standby. The service console standby port would be the active port for VMotion and the service console active port would serve as the standby port for VMotion. Place the VMotion and service console ports on the same vSwitch. For more information about ESX networking concepts, please refer to Chapter 4 - ESX 3.x Server Networking Configurations. For more information about VMotion, please refer to Chapter 13 – Virtual Machine Migration.

The total combination of NICs supported is 32 on an ESX 3.5 server. The server can support (by type) up to 26 e100 (100 Mbit) NICs. It can support up to 32 e1000 (1 Gbit) NICs or up to 20 Broadcom (1 Gbit) NICs.

Storage Interfaces and Disks

The ESX 3.5 server software supports IDE, SCSI, Fibre Channel or iSCSI controllers to access disk devices. SATA controllers and disks are supported only for the installation of the ESX 3.5 server operating system, but not for a VMFS file system.

NOTE: New with ESX 3.5 U1 are supported Dual SATA Controllers on the HCL; also, if SATA drives are in an array in the SAN Compatibility Guide matrix, they would be supported for use.

There can be up to 16 SCSI/FC HBAs installed in your ESX 3.5 server. iSCSI support is new with the ESX 3.0 release.

You can have up to two iSCSI HBAs installed in your ESX 3.5 server. The iSCSI HBA is known as an iSCSI hardware initiator or also known as the TCP/IP Offload Engine (TOE). Gbit Ethernet NICs can be used with the iSCSI software initiator. You can only have one iSCSI software initiator per ESX 3.5 server. Multipathing can be achieved using two Gbit NICs that are NIC teamed with the proper routing set up on your network. This will be covered in more detail in Chapter 5 - ESX 3.x Server Storage Configurations.

You must decide what disk(s) that you want to configure during the installation process to store the ESX 3.5 server boot files as well as the other critical operational files that the server needs in order to run. The main decision you will need to make is whether to install the files on one of the internal (also known as local) disks or on your fiber channel or iSCSI SAN.

When you connect an ESX 3.5 server to your SAN, up to 256 fiber channel LUNs on the SAN can be identified by the server, post install. It can also identify up to 256 LUNs on an iSCSI SAN. So you must know exactly what disk(s) you are going to use to install the software to before starting the installation process. Only 128 LUNs in the range of 0 through 127 is supported by the ESX 3.5 server during the installation process. So make sure your boot disk is identified using a LUN in that range, or the install may fail.

The first step to configure the boot device starts by configuring your server's BIOS to boot to the proper disk. Some servers have multiple internal drives, so if that is the case you must configure the BIOS to boot off of the internal drive that you will install the ESX 3.5 server software on.

If you want to boot off of the SAN then you need to configure the BIOS to use the FC or iSCSI HBA as its boot controller. You must also configure the HBA to boot off of the correct LUN on the SAN. Don't forget to disable the IDE controller if the server has one.

Acquiring the ESX 3.5 Installation Software

The ESX 3.5 Installation Software can be downloaded from the VMware website at:

http://www.VMware.com/download/vi/

You can evaluate the ESX 3.5 Server product for 60 days at no cost before purchasing the appropriate licenses for the server.

Starting the Installation Process

After you have downloaded the software and created a CD with it, insert the installation CD for the ESX 3.5 server software into your CD/DVD drive and reboot the system. The system will use the BIOS settings to determine the boot drive. If you had a different operating system previously installed then you should set the server boot order so that the server will boot from the CD/DVD drive first and then boot from the boot drive.

The First Install Screen

After the system runs the Power On Self Test (POST) and boots off of the CD you will get the first installation screen (See Figure 3.1). If you want to use a GUI interface during the installation process, hit enter or wait until the one minute timeout period is over and it will automatically continue the process. If you want to do the installation process in a text only mode then type "esx text" without the double quotes at the boot: prompt. This mode is useful if you are connected to your server via a serial connect that only supports an ASCII text interface.

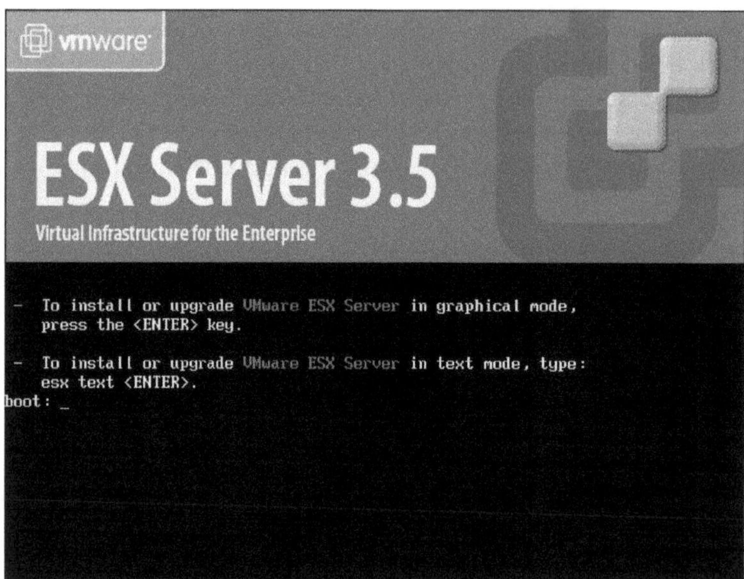

Figure 3.1 First Install Screen

The CD Media Test Screen

The next screen, Figure 3.2, will prompt you to test your installation media.

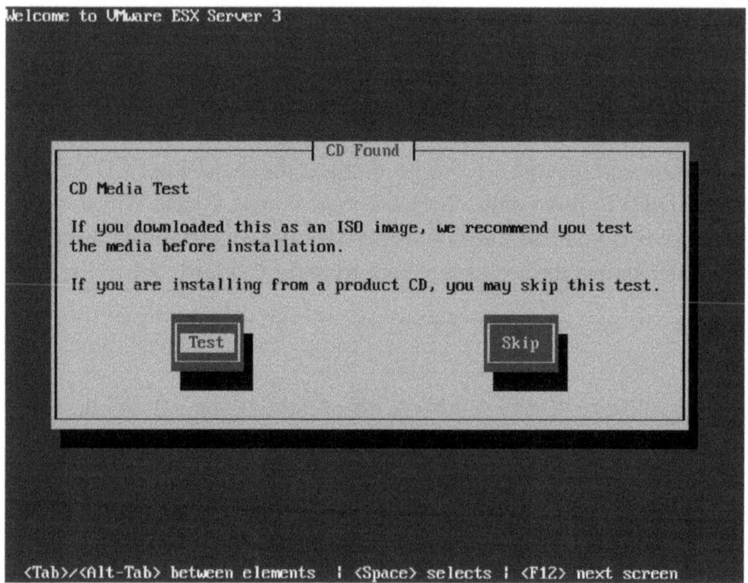

Figure 3.2 CD Media Test Screen

If this is the first time you have used this CD then you should run the test to make sure that all of the files on the disc are ok. If you have done this on the disc before then select the Skip button to move on to the next screen. The Media Test is useful if installing off of an ISO ripped image from a CD, especially when installing multiple servers off the same ISO image.

The Welcome Screen

The next screen in the installation process is the Welcome Screen (See Figure 3.3).

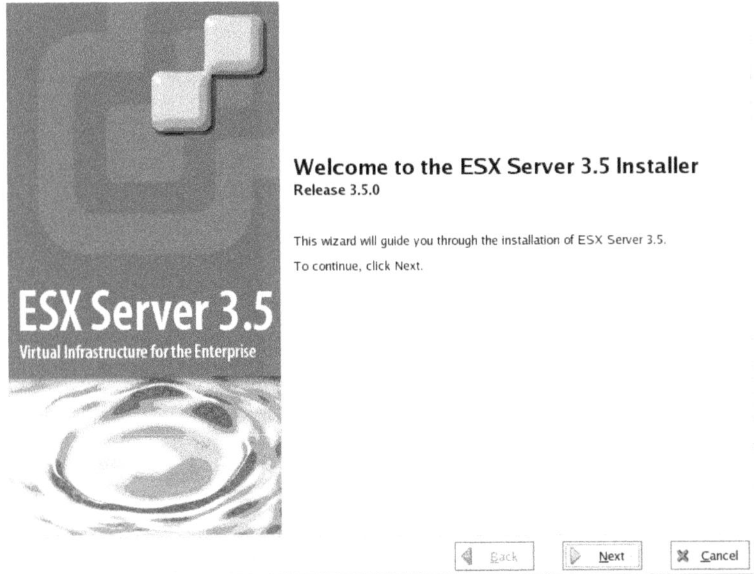

Figure 3.3 The Welcome Screen

This will start the installation wizard to install the ESX 3.5 Server software. Select the Next button to continue.

The Select Keyboard Screen

The next screen, Figure 3.4, will allow you to select the keyboard that you are using on your ESX 3.5 server.

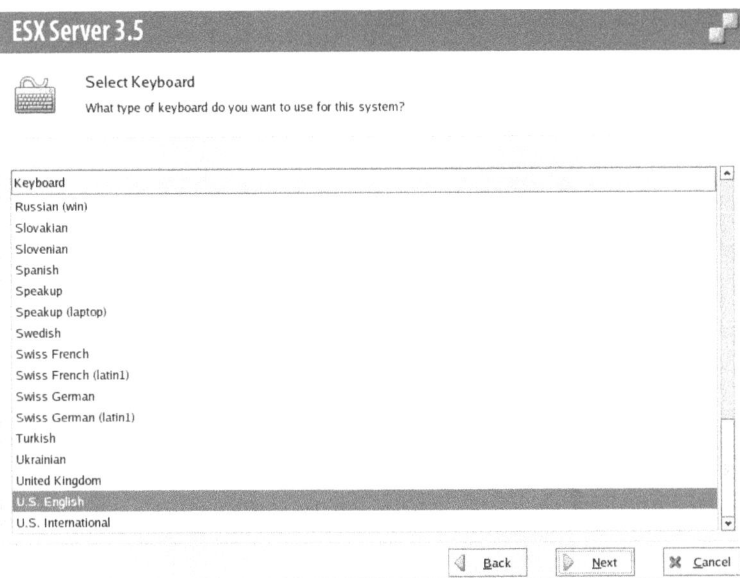

Figure 3.4 The Select Keyboard Screen

Select the appropriate keyboard and select the Next button to continue.

The Select Mouse Screen

The next screen, Figure 3.5, allows you to select the mouse that you are using on your ESX 3.5 server.

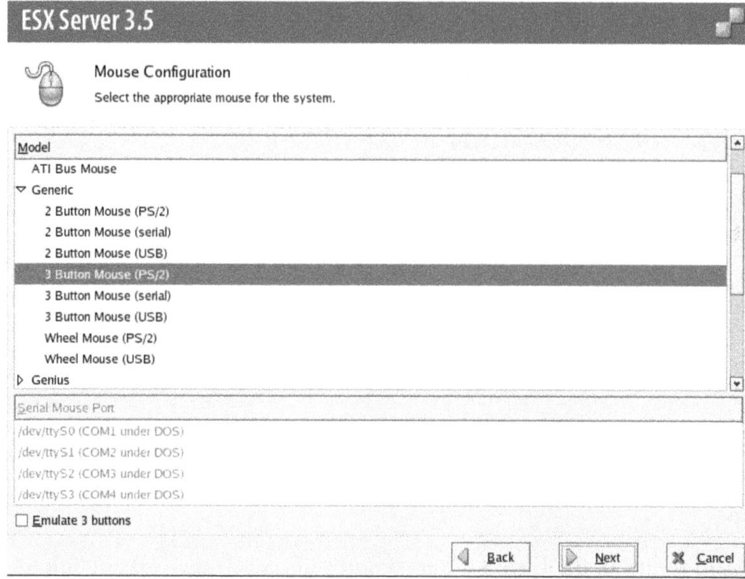

Figure 3.5 The Select Mouse Screen

Select the appropriate mouse and select the Next button to continue.

NOTE: Auto-detect is used by the installer here, thus manual selection of mouse type is unnecessary.

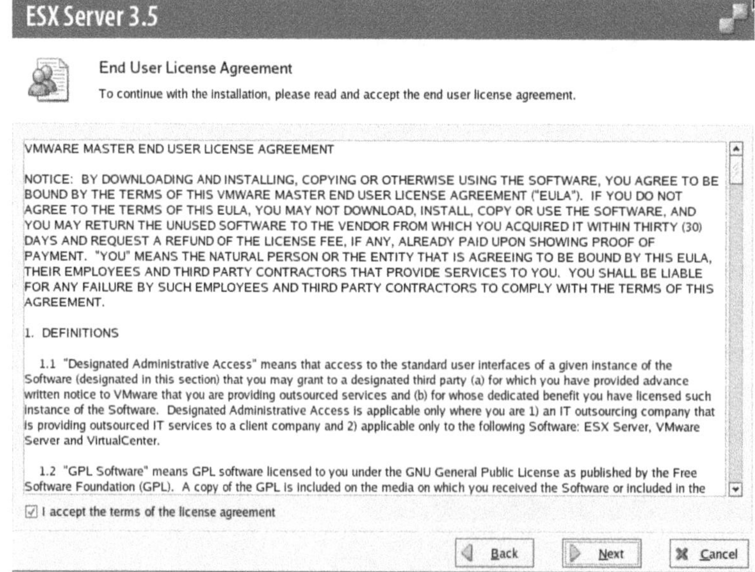

Figure 3.6 The End User License Agreement Screen

The End User License Agreement Screen

The next screen, Figure 3.6, will require that you accept the terms of the license agreement for the ESX 3.5 server software.

Select the check box after you have read the agreement and select the Next button to continue.

The Internal Disk is Unreadable Pop-up Message

The next thing that you will see are pop-up messages if your internal disk(s) or SAN disk(s) are unreadable, meaning that a VMFS file system is not on the drive.

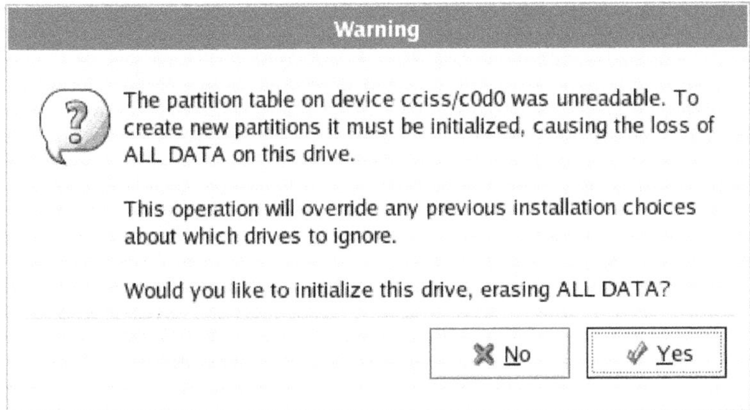

Figure 3.7 The Internal Disk is Unreadable Pop-up Message

This warning refers to a device known as cciss/c0d0. The device cciss is the name of the SCSI device driver for this particular type of server. The reference to c0d0 refers to controller 0 disk 0. This happens to be the drive that is to be used for this example. Be aware that some servers will use a different controller than controller 0 for its internal boot drive.

Select the Yes button if you want to use the drive to install the ESX 3.5 server software and select the No button if you don't.

The SAN Disk is Unreadable Pop-up Message

SAN drives (known as LUNs) will have a designation in the warning message of sda, sdb, sdc etc. If the boot process was able to identify any LUNs on your SAN, you will be prompted for all SAN LUNs that are visible to the ESX 3.5 server at boot time. If you are not using the SAN LUNs for this server or don't want to get these messages during the install process then you should disconnect the cabling from the server that connects it to the SAN. Do not select any LUNs if you are unsure if you are to use them, because the installation process will overwrite any existing data on them.

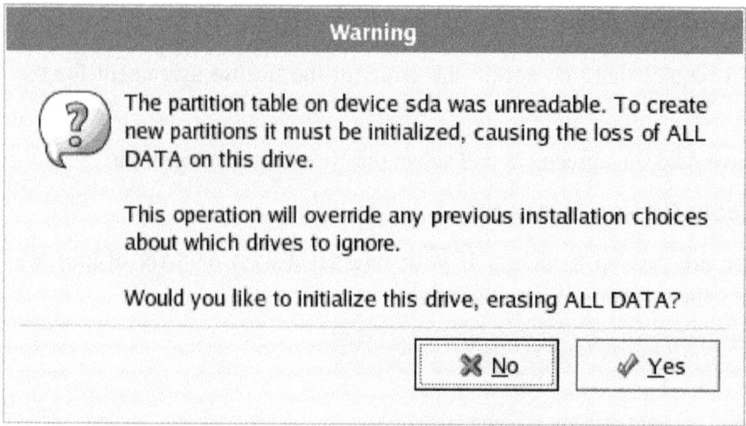

Figure 3.8 The SAN Disk is Unreadable Pop-up Message

Select the Yes button if you want to use the drive to install the ESX 3.5 server software and select the No button if you don't.

Disk Space Requirements For Installation Partitions

The next thing we need to look at is how we should partition the boot drive. The installation process can automatically partition the drive for you or you can manually partition it if you want to.

The Partition Options Screen

The next screen you will see is the Partitions Options Screen. If you want the software to automatically partition your boot drive then leave the radio button selected at the default of Recommended. Be sure that the drive that you wish to install the software is selected in the drop down menu (sometimes another drive is listed there!) Select the check box below the drop down menu if the drive had a previous installation on it and you want to retain the VMs and support files from that previous install.

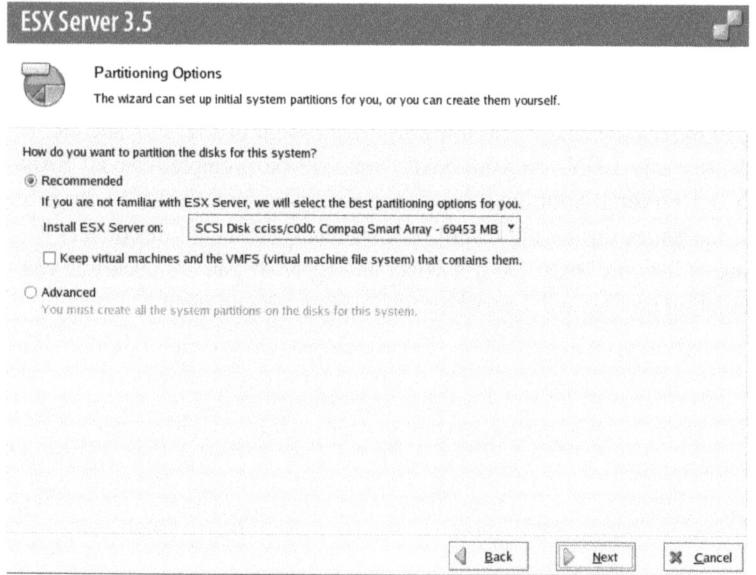

Figure 3.9 The Partition Options Screen

Select the Advanced radio button if you want to manually partition the disk. If you plan on manually partitioning your disk be aware that there are recommended sizes and locations when partitioning your disks.

The ESX 3.5 server local boot drive requires three specific partitions in order for it to function properly. The three partitions are:

- /boot
- swap
- /

Also at least one local or remote VMFS file system partition must be created and one local or remote vmkcore partition is required to provide storage space for core dumps for technical support.

/boot Partition

The /boot partition should be at least 100 MB in size and if located on a SAN LUN ensure that only the ESX server being installed can access the LUN. If this is not done, then it may be possible for another server to corrupt the boot LUN. It contains the various files needed to boot the system including the Grand Unified Bootloader (GRUB) boot loader program. It should use the ext3 file system type to support logging. This technology speeds the boot process after a system failure.

Swap Partition

The swap partition needs to be set using the swap file system type and needs to be at least 544 MB in size (twice the default size of memory allocated to the service console). The minimum allowed value is 100 MB. The maximum size needed would be 1.6 GB (twice the maximum size of memory that can be allocated to the service console).

The / File System

The root file system should be set using the ext3 file system and is recommended to be at least 5 GB in size. If you plan on running any of the supported 3rd party applications that directly run on the ESX 3.5 server you should make the partition bigger to support those additional software packages.

VMFS3 File System

The VMFS3 file system is used to store your virtual machine files, ISO images and VM templates files. The recommended size is at least 1.1 GB. The location for these files can be on any local disk or SAN LUN that can be seen by the ESX 3.5 server installation process. At least one VMFS partition needs to be created but it does not need to be on the boot drive. IDE drives cannot be used for VMFS3 file systems.

vmkcore Partition

The vmkcore partition needs to be at least 100 MB in size and can be located on either the local disk or remote SAN storage. This partition is used to store core dumps to be used by VMware's technical support department.

The following file systems are optional file systems that can be created during the installation process.

/home File System

The /home file system should be set using the ext3 file system and can be used to store users personal files. The recommended size is at least 512 MB.

/tmp File System

The /tmp file system should be set using the ext3 file system and is used to store temporary files. Be aware that a reboot of the ESX 3.5 server will delete any files located in this file system. The recommended minimum size is at least 1 GB.

/var/log File System

The /var/log file system should be set using the ext3 file system and is used to store log files. It is good practice to have the /var/log file system assigned to its own partition. If this file system is located on the same partition as the root file system, it may eventually utilize all of the free space due to log files dynamically increasing in size. If this situation occurs, the ESX server may become unstable when there is no available free space on the root partition.

NOTE: In ESX 3, /var/log is defined as a separate partition 2 GB in size, by the auto-partitioner. It should be 2.5 GB if using this server for Scripted Install, as /var is the location for the copy of ESX software.

If you choose to manually partition the disk(s), you should select the advanced options radio button and set the partitions to at least the required sizes. Once all of the selections have been made, select the Next button to continue the installation process.

The installation will display a Warning dialog box stating that all partitions will be removed on the drive, in this installation, the drive is cciss/c0d0. If this is the correct drive to perform a fresh installation, confirm the removal of the partitions by selecting the Yes button.

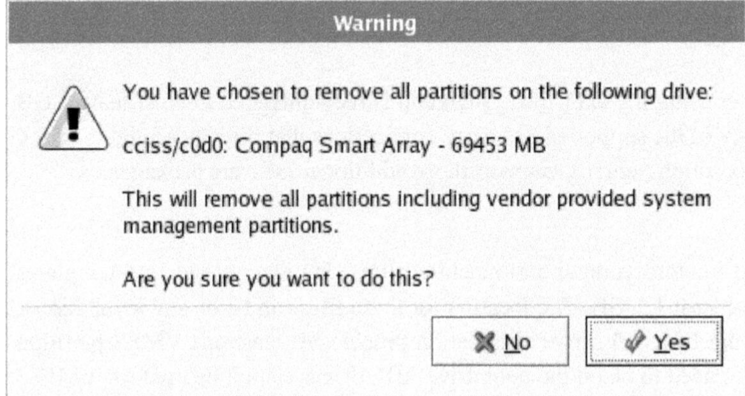

Figure 3.10 Warning Dialog Box

The Partition Disks Screen

After the disk(s) are partitioned, you will see a summary of the partition information.

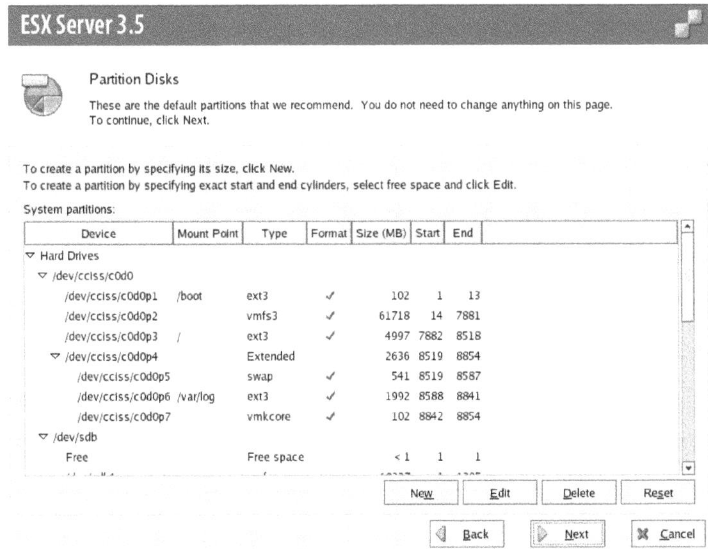

Figure 3.11 The Partition Summary Screen

You can create additional partitions, edit existing partitions, delete existing partitions or reset the complete partition table back to its original state (in case you need to start over.) Select the Next button to continue with the installation of the software.

The Advanced Options Screen

The next screen allows you to choose the disk that you will boot from or if you want to boot from another partition. It also allows you to set custom boot options. Typically you use the defaults on this screen.

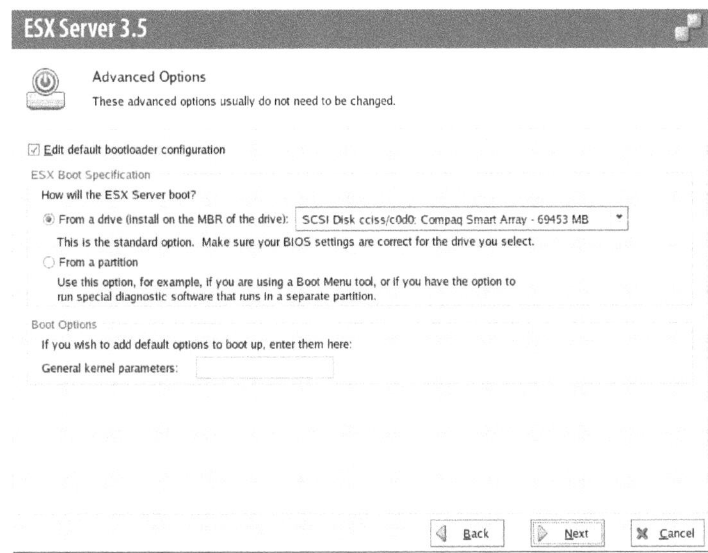

Figure 3.12 The Advanced Options Screen

Be sure to verify that the drive you want to boot from is the drive you are installing the /boot partition on. If it is not the correct drive to boot from, select the check box next to "Edit default bootloader configuration" as shown in Figure 3.12. Doing so will cause the installation to display the warning message as shown in Figure 3.13. Click the Cancel button if it is not necessary to change the bootloader location. For this installation, it was necessary to change the bootloader location. The OK button is selected to continue.

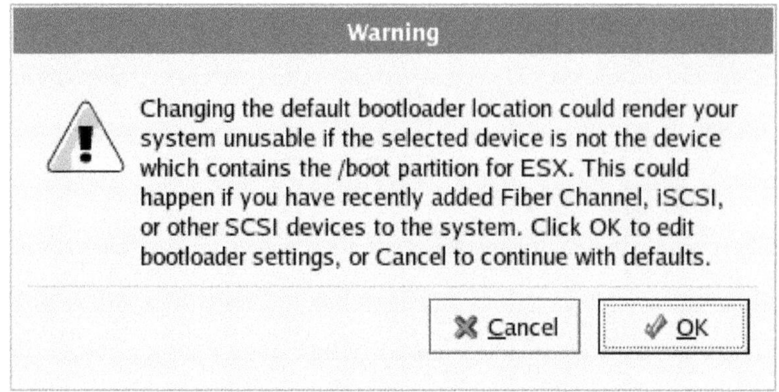

Figure 3.13 Changing The Default Bootloader Location

Configuring the Network Connection

The next screen will allow you to set the service console's network settings.

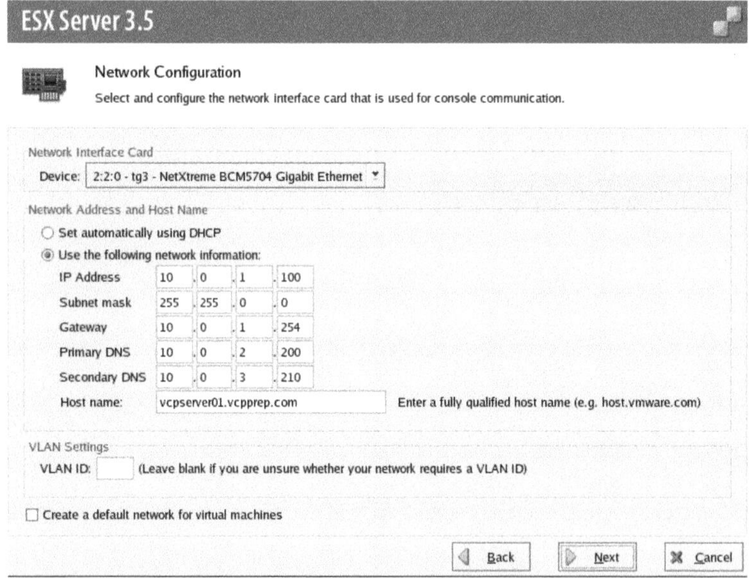

Figure 3.14 The Network Configuration Screen

Choosing the Right NIC

The top dropdown menu of the Network Configuration screen allows you to choose which physical NIC you want to use for the service console. The choices will include all physical ports that were discovered during POST by the ESX 3.5 server boot process. Each entry in the drop down menu will include a brief description of the interface proceeded by a number that identifies its location as enumerated by the boot process.

In the Figure 3.14 example the number listed was 2:2:0 (and then a brief hardware description of the NIC). The numbers identifies the port in this manner:

PCI BUS NUMBER: DEVICE ON THE BUS: INSTANCE ON THE DEVICE

The first number 2 identifies this device as being located on PCI Bus 2. Many of the newer servers have multiple I/O controllers to load balance the PCI bus throughput. The I/O controller chips can also have multiple PCI buses on them. The probing order of the devices in the server during POST determines the PCI bus order. Your vendor should be able to provide you with that information as to what devices are located on which PCI bus.

The second number 2 identifies the device as being the second device (on PCI bus 2). Many vendors mix internal devices with PCI card slots, so don't assume all internal devices are on the first PCI bus and the external one (in the card slots) are on the higher numbered buses. You must get the probing order information from the vendor to determine how their architecture is probed during the boot process. Most new servers will only have as many devices on a bus as it can handle if all devices are operating at their full potential. For example, since an Enhanced PCI (ePCI) card operating at 66 MHz can provide 270 Mbytes/sec data throughput and if the server I/O controller PCI bus is rated to handle a total throughput of 1.2 Gbytes per second then the bus could handle 4 devices operating with a full load:

4 X 270 Mbytes/sec = 1080 Mbytes/sec < 1200 Mbytes/sec (1.2 Gbytes/sec)

The third number 0 identifies the device as being the 0 instance (which is the first instance) on the device. If you installed a NIC card with four ports on it then port 0 would be listed as instance 0 on that device, port 1 as instance 1 and so on.

Setting IP Addressing, Host Name, VLAN

The next thing that needs to be configured is the IP address for the ESX 3.5 server's service console network port. You can choose whether it is to be configured via DHCP or if you will set it manually. Choose the appropriate radio button to make this selection.

If you choose to manually set the IP address configuration, you can supply the service console port's IP address, netmask, gateway, primary and secondary DNS server's IP addresses and the ESX 3.5 server's fully qualified domain name (FQDN).

If the service console port is to be configured on a specific VLAN (IEEE 802.1q) you can set it in the VLAN-ID box. VLAN's will be discussed in more detail later in this book.

There is also a check box to configure a default network for virtual machines. This option will create a default port group for virtual machines. This check box is selected by default. This default setting is not recommended for high security installations because the virtual machines will share the same physical port as the service console unless you otherwise configure them to a different port.

After you have confirmed that all of your settings are correct (and it will save you a lot of time later if you catch any mistakes in this window) then you click on the Next button to continue.

Setting the ESX 3.5 Server's Time Zone

The next screen you will see allows you to set the time zone for the ESX 3.5 server.

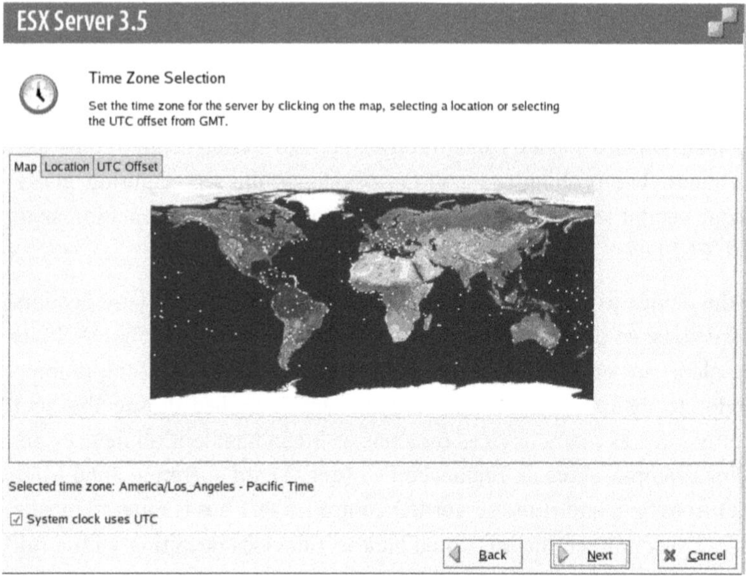

Figure 3.15 The Time Zone Selection Screen – Map Tab

This screen allows you to set the ESX 3.5 server's time zone using any of the three methods available by selecting the appropriate tab. The three methods are:

1. Setting the time zone using a map. Select a location close to the ESX 3.5 server's location. Figure 3.15 shows this screen.

2. Setting the time zone using a location. The location tab will reveal a list of cities and you should select a city in the ESX 3.5 server's time zone. Figure 3.16 shows this screen.

3. Setting the time zone using a UTC (coordinated universal time) offset from Greenwich Mean Time (GMT). The UTC tab will reveal a list of offsets. The offset for the U.S Eastern time zone is -5 hours from GMT. Figure 3.17 shows this screen.

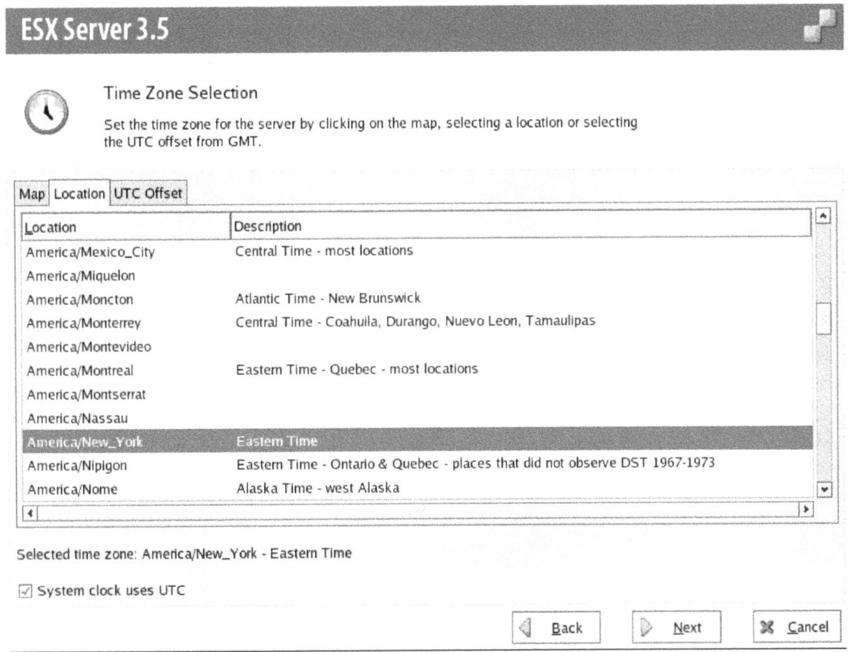

Figure 3.16 The Time Zone Selection Screen – Location Tab

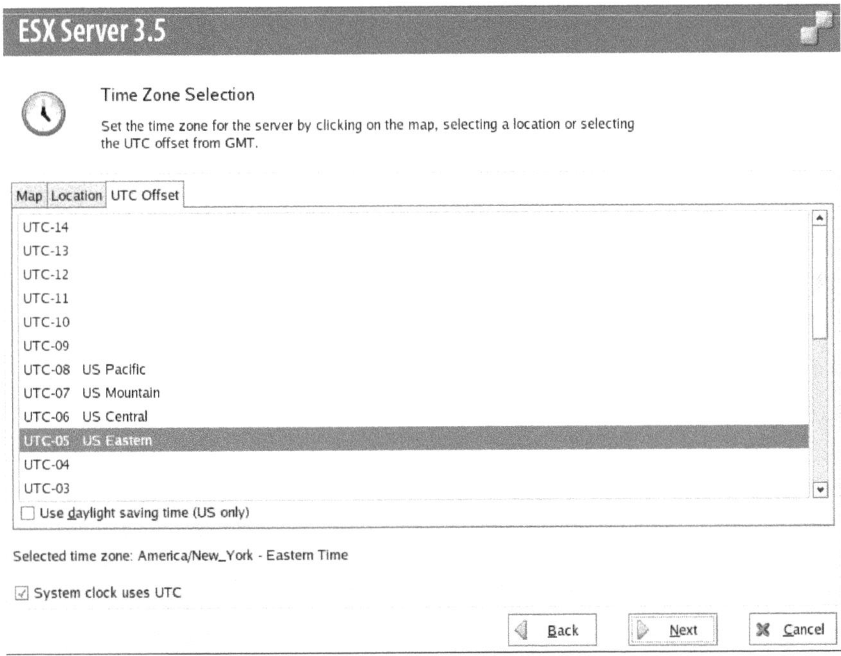

Figure 3.17 The Time Zone Selection Screen – UTC Offset Tab

After selecting the time zone for the ESX 3.5 server you can select the use UTC check box. The advantage of this setting is that the server's log entries will be referenced using UTC time instead of the local time zone which makes it easier to determine the exact time an event occurred. Imagine reviewing events on a large number of ESX 3.5 servers in many time zones. You would have to factor in each servers location and time zone in order to determine (in reference to your time zone) when an event occurred. You can also set the server to use Daylight Savings Time if appropriate. After you have made your selections click on the Next button.

NOTE: At the time of this writing, there is a bug in the current version of VI Client (VIC), 2.5, that if UTC is selected during the interactive install, not the check box, but in the tab, that using the VI Client to configure NTP through the VI Client GUI will fail. NTP configuration from the CLI, by creating/modifying the NTP config files is unaffected. This is only a VIC related bug if UTC time zone is chosen; the current solution is to choose the time zone Europe/London (Dublin) during the interactive install.

Setting the ESX 3.5 Server's Root Password

The next screen will allow you to set the root (super-user) password. Figure 3.18 shows this screen.

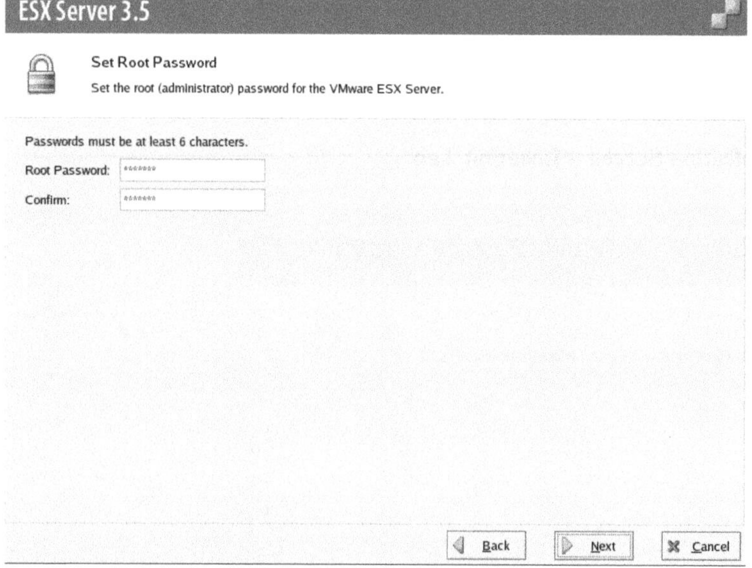

Figure 3.18 The Set Root Password Screen

The root account is equivalent to the Administrator account in a Windows based system. This account can run any command on the ESX 3.5 server and change any setting, so it is important to use a strong password to prevent unauthorized access to the server. Using mixed case and numeric or special characters will help create a stronger (harder to guess) password. The root password must have at least 6 characters and the installation process will not warn you of a weak password. You must put the password in twice and the entries need to match in order to set the password. The password can be changed later by the root account if needed.

The About to Install Screen

The last screen before installation begins is the About to Install screen. Figure 3.19 shows this screen.

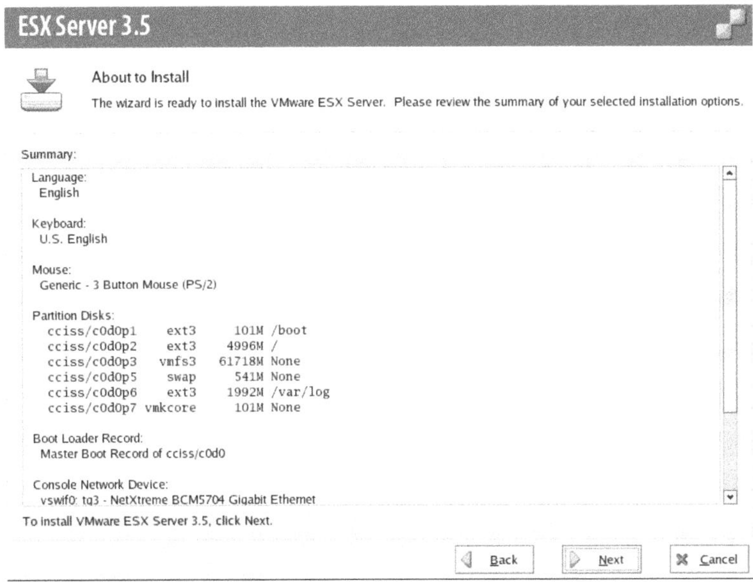

Figure 3.19 The About To Install Screen

This screen contains a summary of your previous configuration selections. It is wise to review these settings and to select the back button to navigate back and fix any errors that could cause a misconfiguration of your server. Once you are satisfied with the configuration, select the Next button to continue. The installation process will now begin. Notice the service console port is referenced as vswif0. This will be covered in detail in the next chapter.

The Installing Packages Screen

The next screen will show the progress of the server installation software. Figure 3.20 shows this screen.

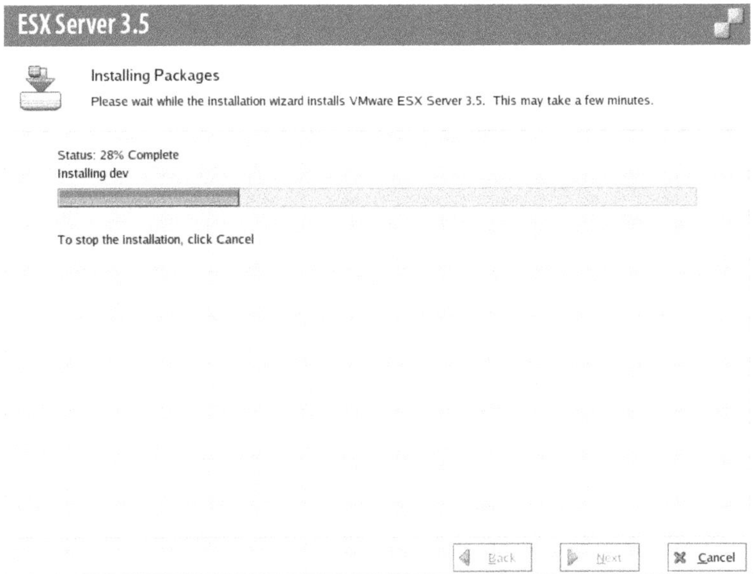

Figure 3.20 The Installing Packages Screen

You cancel the installation at any time by pressing the Cancel button.

The ESX Server 3 Installer Complete Screen

After the installation completes you will see the ESX Server 3 Installer Complete screen,

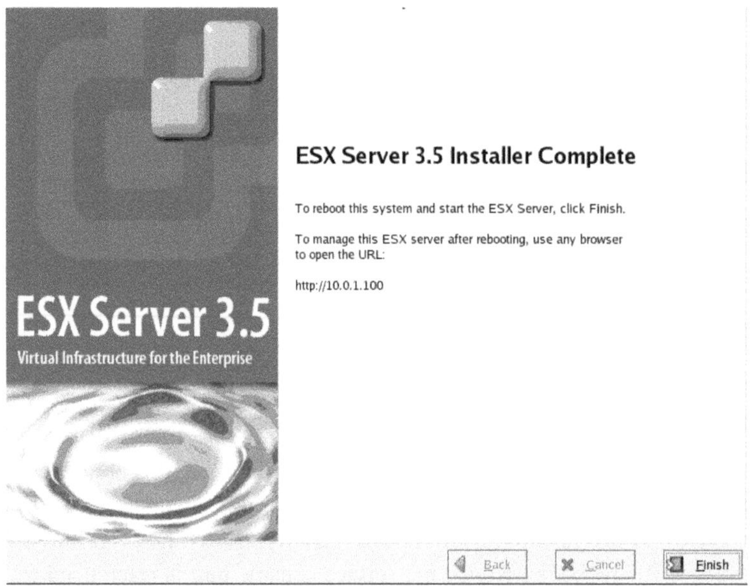

Figure 3.21 The ESX Server 3 Installer Complete Screen

By selecting the Finish button the server will reboot and start the Apache Web server service. This screen contains the http link showing the IP address to access the ESX 3.5 server via a web browser after the server reboots. You should verify that the web client can connect to the web server on the newly installed ESX 3.5 server.

The ESX 3.5 Server GRUB Screen

Once rebooted, the ESX server will then display the GRUB menu as shown in Figure 3.22. GRUB enables the ESX 3.5 system to be booted. Choose the "VMware ESX Server" option to boot the ESX server for normal operation. This is the default. Choose "VMware ESX Server (debug mode)" when experiencing system startup problems. If the system will not boot in either the default or debug mode, it may be necessary to choose the "Service Console Only (troubleshooting mode)". This mode will load the ESX service console without the VMkernel and may provide access to the system files for further analysis.

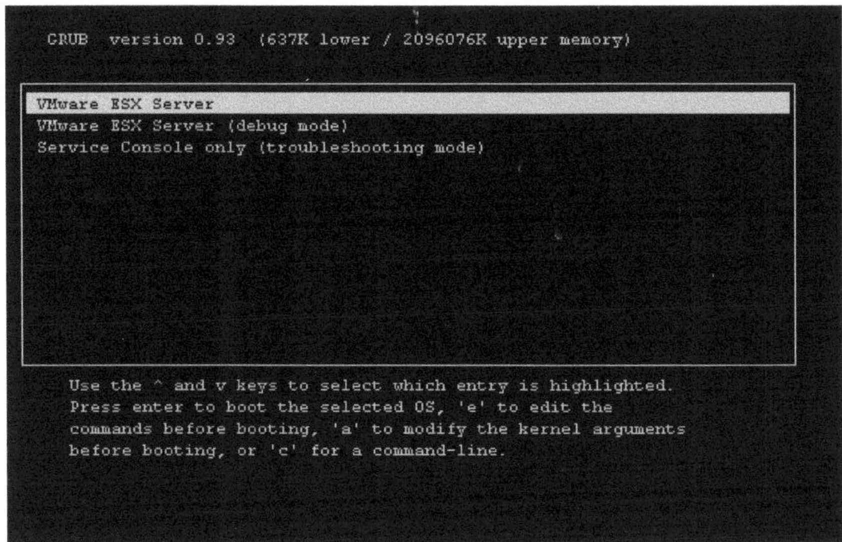

Figure 3.22 The ESX 3.5 Server GRUB Screen

The ESX server loads and initializes several system components and services when booting. The status of individual system components and services is displayed while the system boots up as shown in Figure 3.23. This provides useful feedback when troubleshooting faulty components or services.

```
                 VMware ESX Server 3 Service Console
                 Press 'I' to enter interactive startup.
Configuring kernel parameters:                                [  OK  ]
Setting clock  (utc): Tue Jan  8 08:20:54 GMT-5 2008          [  OK  ]
Loading default keymap (us):                                  [  OK  ]
Setting hostname vcpserver01.vcpprep.com:                     [  OK  ]
Initializing USB controller (usb-uhci):                       [  OK  ]
Initializing USB controller (ehci-hcd):                       [  OK  ]
Mounting USB filesystem:                                      [  OK  ]
Initializing USB HID interface:                               [  OK  ]
Initializing USB keyboard:                                    [  OK  ]
Initializing USB mouse:                                       [  OK  ]
Checking root filesystem
/: clean, 58518/640000 files, 332026/1279175 blocks
                                                              [  OK  ]
Remounting root filesystem in read-write mode:                [  OK  ]
Activating swap partitions:                                   [  OK  ]
Finding module dependencies:                                  [  OK  ]
Checking filesystems
/boot: clean, 33/26104 files, 29882/104391 blocks
/var/log: clean, 25/255488 files, 16263/510055 blocks
                                                              [  OK  ]
Mounting local filesystems:                                   [  OK  ]
Saving boot_                                                  [  OK  ]
Mounting local filesystems:
```

Figure 3.23 ESX 3.5 Server System Components And Services

The ESX 3.5 Server Console Screen

If you view the ESX 3.5 server's physical console (or access it via its remote management port if it has one) you should see information as shown in Figure 3.24.

```
VMware ESX Server version 3.5.0

vcpserver01.vcpprep.com (10.0.1.100)

To manage this ESX Server, use any browser to open the URL:

http://10.0.1.100/

To open the ESX Server console, press Alt-F1.
To return to this screen, press Alt-F11.
```

Figure 3.24 The ESX 3.5 Server Physical Console Screen

The physical console screen will contain the ESX 3.5 server version number, the FQDN, the service console port IP address, and the http link to access it via a web connection. It should also give the directions on how to access the service console directly via the command line.

Connecting to the ESX 3.5 Server via the VI Client

After installation there are three ways to access the service console on the ESX 3.5 server.

1. Using the command line interface (CLI)
2. Using the VI Client GUI software
3. Using the Web Client browser based interface

The CLI Interface

The CLI can be accessed either directly on the physical console (which would be by using the keyboard and monitor connected to the server) or by using a remote CLI utility through a remote management port.

The ESX 3.5 service console is protected by a firewall and the root account cannot login remotely by default from the command line. This security feature can be disabled by logging into the physical console and editing the /etc/ssh/sshd_config file.

There is a line in the sshd_config file that reads: PermitRootLogin no

Change that line to read: PermitRootLogin yes

Save the file and execute the command to restart the sshd service: service sshd restart

Now you will be able to login remotely as the root account. Be aware that this does not allow you to track who is logging in as root. The default configuration does not allow remote root logins, so a user would have to login as a non root account and use the su – command to switch from their non root account to the root account. They would also have to correctly enter the root account password.

The popular freeware utility PuTTy which was written and maintained by Simon Tatham, provides a CLI client that can use SSH (Secure Shell), telnet, rlogin and raw TCP protocols to access a remote host as shown in Figure 3.25. It is available for a number of different operating systems. It can be downloaded from the developer's website at: http://www.chiark.greenend.org.uk/~sgtatham/putty/

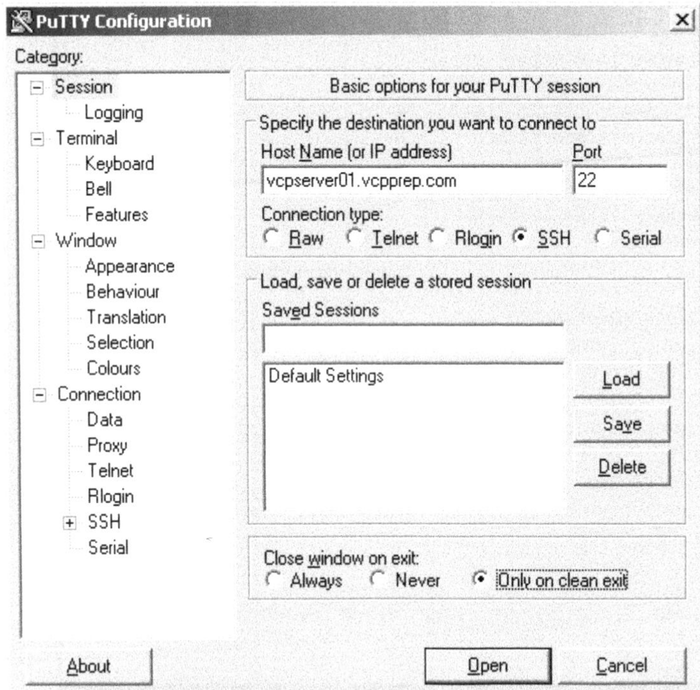

Figure 3.25 The PuTTy GUI Interface

The VMware Infrastructure (VI) Client Download Link

Once the ESX 3.5 Server software has been installed and the server has been rebooted the Apache web server service will be started by default. If you launch a web browser you will see the screen shown in Figure 3.26.

VMware ESX Server 3

Welcome

Getting Started

If you need to access this host remotely, use the following program to install VMware Infrastructure client software. After running the installer, start the client and log in to this host.

- Download VMware Infrastructure Client

To streamline your IT operations with VMware Infrastructure, use the following program to install VirtualCenter Server. VirtualCenter Server will help you consolidate and optimize workload distribution across ESX Server hosts, reduce new system deployment time from weeks to seconds, monitor your virtual computing environment around the clock, avoid service disruptions due to planned hardware maintenance or unexpected failure, centralize access control, and automate system administration tasks.

- Download VMware VirtualCenter Server

If you need more help, please refer to our documentation library:

- VMware Infrastructure 3 Documentation

For Administrators

VMware Infrastructure Web Access

VMware Infrastructure Web Access streamlines remote desktop deployment by allowing you to organize and share virtual machines using ordinary web browser URLs.

Log in to Web Access

Web-Based Datastore Browser

Use your web browser to find and download files (for example, virtual machine and virtual disk files).

Browse datastores in this host's inventory

ESX Server Scripted Installer

This browser-based utility allows you to automate host provisioning.

Log in to the Scripted Installer

For Developers

VMware Infrastructure SDK

The VMware Infrastructure SDK package contains interface definitions, detailed documentation and sample code to help you write your own management programs.

Download the SDK

- Browse objects managed by this host

Figure 3.26 The VMware ESX 3.5 Welcome Screen

There is a link to download the VI Client software on this webpage. The VI Client will only install on windows based systems. If you want to connect using another operating system besides Windows then you need to connect via the CLI or the Web Client. There is also a link to use the ESX Server Scripted Installer. This allows the configuration of unattended installation files by using the web browser interface utility. In order to use this utility, the ESX server host requires the following configuration modifications:

Step 1.

First log into the service console of the ESX server that will be used to create the unattended installation files.

Step 2.

Using a command line editor such as VI or Nano, open the following file:

/usr/lib/VMware/webAccess/tomcat/apache-tomcat-5.5.17/webapps/ui/WEB-INF/struts-config.xml

Step 3.

Find the following line as shown below.

<action path="/scriptedInstall" type="org.apache.struts.actions.ForwardAction" parameter="/WEB-INF/jsp/scriptedInstall/disabled.jsp" />

Step 4.

This line needs to be commented out using Hypertext Markup Language (HTML) comments as follows:

<!-- <action path="/scriptedInstall" type="org.apache.struts.actions.ForwardAction" parameter="/WEB-INF/jsp/scriptedInstall/disabled.jsp" /> -->

Step 5.

Next, find the following line:

<action path="/scriptedInstall" type="com.VMware.webcenter.scripted.ProcessAction">

Step 6.

There will be an HTML comment line just before this line. The comment line will need to be deleted. The comment line appears as follows:

<!--

Step 7.

By removing this comment line, the following lines will be enabled:

<action path="/scriptedInstall" type="com.VMware.webcenter.scripted.ProcessAction">

<forward name="scriptedInstall.form1" path="/WEB-INF/jsp/scriptedInstall/form1.jsp" />

<forward name="scriptedInstall.form2" path="/WEB-INF/jsp/scriptedInstall/form2.jsp" />

<forward name="scriptedInstall.form3" path="/WEB-INF/jsp/scriptedInstall/form3.jsp" />

<forward name="scriptedInstall.form4" path="/WEB-INF/jsp/scriptedInstall/form4.jsp" />

<forward name="scriptedInstall.form5" path="/WEB-INF/jsp/scriptedInstall/form5.jsp" />

<forward name="scriptedInstall.form6" path="/WEB-INF/jsp/scriptedInstall/form6.jsp" />

<forward name="scriptedInstall.form7" path="/WEB-INF/jsp/scriptedInstall/form7.jsp" />

</action>

Step 8.

Delete the following HTML closing comment line:

-->

Step 9.

Next, save the file and close it.

Step 10.

The last step to enable the Scripted Install utility is to perform the following command from within the service console:

service VMware-webAccess restart

This causes the Apache service to re-read its configuration file, which has been modified, so the enablement changes will be applied, and the Scripted Install interface can be accessed on this ESX server.

Now, when clicking the link to access the Scripted Install utility, the web page will be displayed that will walk you through the creation of the unattended installation file. Several options are available to use the new unattended installation file, such as using a local CDROM drive, local floppy drive or using a Preboot Execution Environment (PXE) server. If using the local CDROM method, place the ESX 3.5 installation CDROM into the CDROM drive and allow it to boot to the first installation screen where the choice of a graphical or text mode install is presented. On this screen, the following line is displayed at the bottom of the screen:

boot:

The following depicts the command entered at the "boot:" line when accessing a unattended installation file that has been saved on an NFS server:

esx ks=nfs:MyNFS_SERVER:/file_dir/install_script.cfg ksdevice=eth1

In the above command, "MyNFS_SERVER" is the hostname or IP address of the NFS server where the unattended installation file is located. The "/file_dir" is the directory on the NFS server where the unattended installation file is located and "/install_script.cfg" is the name of the file to use. "eth1" is the interface used on the ESX server to connect to the NFS server. This will launch and execute the unattended installation.

After installing and running the VI Client on your Windows based system you will see the Login GUI as shown on Figure 3.27.

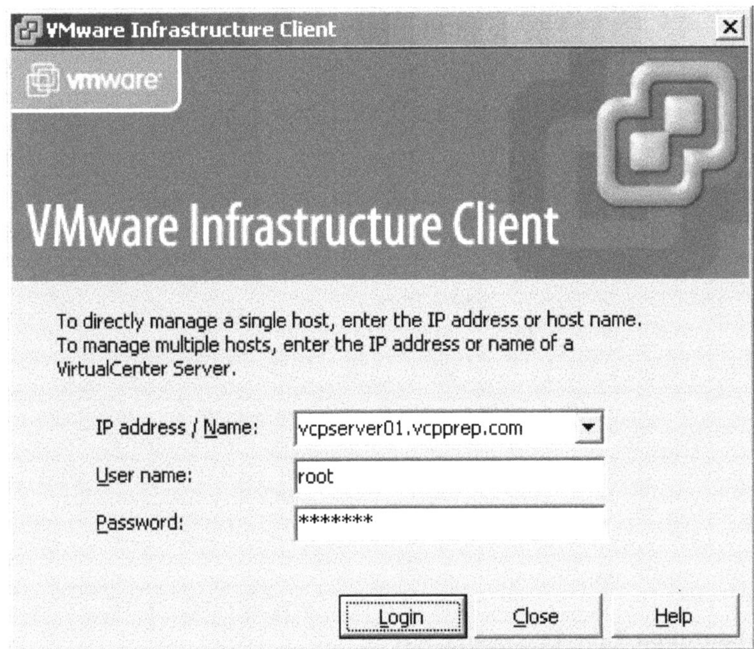

Figure 3.27 The VI Client Login Interface

You must enter a valid account that exists on that ESX 3.5 server and enter the correct password in order to use the VI Client software.

The Configuration Tab

When you select the Configuration tab in the VI Client interface, it provides general information on the configuration of the ESX 3.5 server.

ESX 3.5 Server Processor Configuration

In the Hardware box there is a link to the Processor configuration information. For example, in Figure 3.28 shows the ESX 3.5 server's processor model type, processor speed, the number of physical processors and how many cores are on each processor (socket). It also shows if Hyperthreading is available and the total number of logical CPUs that are in the server. The link also shows the vendor and model information of the server.

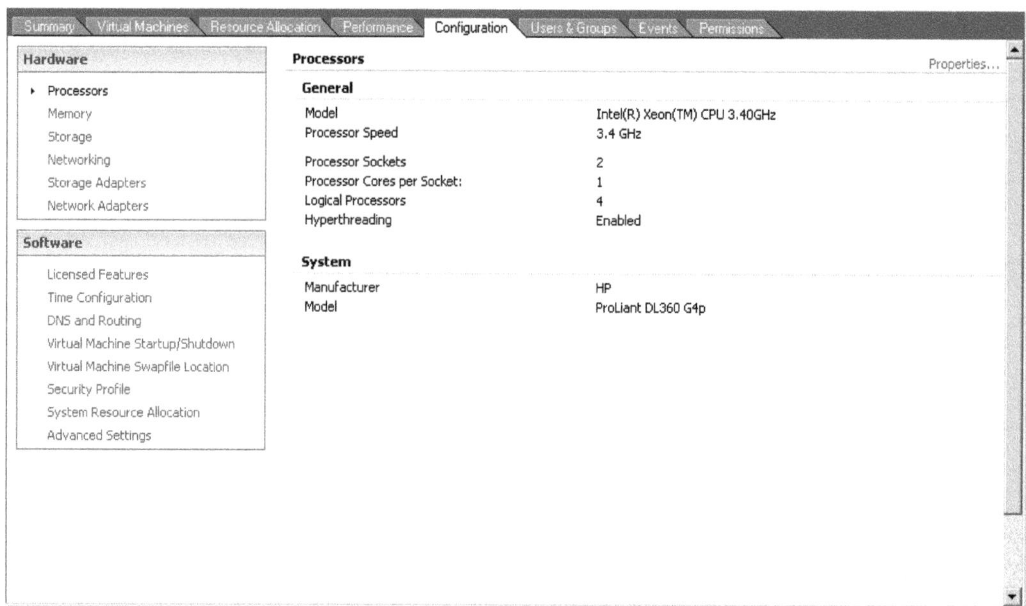

Figure 3.28 The VI Client Configuration Tab - Processors Screen

ESX 3.5 Server memory configuration information can be found by clicking on the Memory link in the hardware box in the Configuration tab as shown in Figure 3.29.

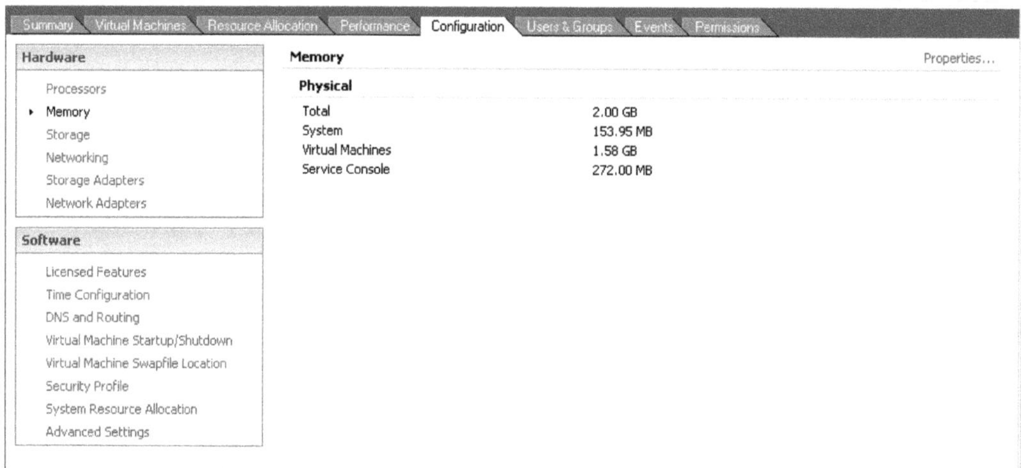

Figure 3.29 The VI Client Configuration Tab Memory Screen

Other Hardware Configuration Links

The Hardware Box also has links to display the current datastores that can be accessed by the ESX 3.5 server as well as the networking configuration of the server. It also has links to display the storage and network adapters. We will explore these links in later chapters.

Other Software Configuration Links

The Software box contains links to configure the server's licenses as well as DNS and routing configurations, virtual machine startup and shutdown settings, security and resource allocation settings and some advanced settings. We will explore these links later in the book as well.

Other VI Client Tabs

The other tabs in the VI Client interface (which will be explored later in this book) are:

- Summary
- Virtual Machines
- Resource Allocation
- Performance
- Users & Groups
- Events
- Permissions

The Web Client Interface

The third interface to access the service console is the web client interface. You can log into it from an internet browser from a system that has network access to the ESX 3.5 server's service console port. You can use either the FQDN or IP address of that port. Figure 3.30 shows an example of this screen.

Figure 3.30 The Web Client Login Interface

You must log in with a user account that is configured on that particular ESX 3.5 server. The web client interface provides an alternative to the VI Client. The interface does not allow you to do all of the functions that the VI Client provides however. You will be limited by permissions granted to the account you are using to access the server.

Licensing

After the ESX 3.5 software has been installed the next thing that needs to be done is to configure the licenses that provide the server with what it is allowed to support.

Installing Licenses

To configure the ESX 3.5 server for licensing you need to access the Configuration tab in the VI Client interface and select the Licensed Features link in the Software box as shown in Figure 3.31.

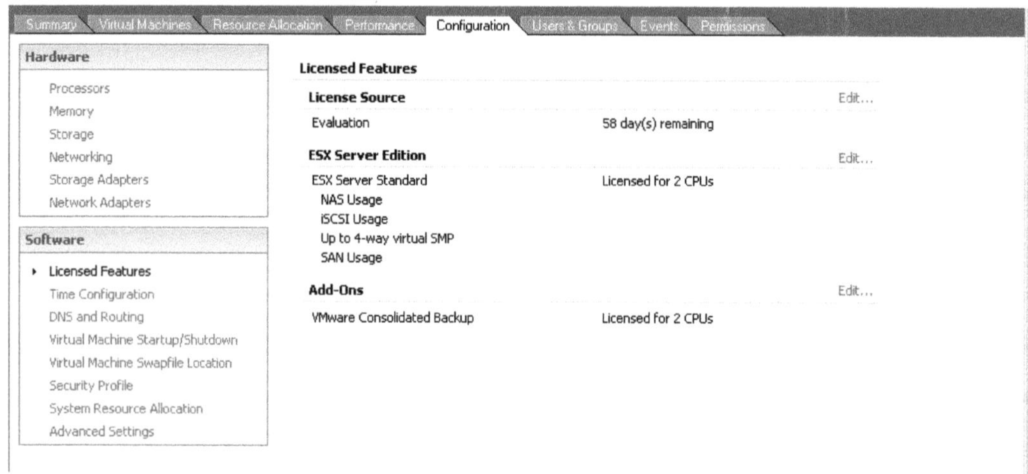

Figure 3.31 The Configuration Tab Licensed Features Link

Licensing is available in two modes:

- Single-host licensing mode – each ESX 3.5 server uses it's own license file
- Centralized licensing mode – a centralized license server provides floating licenses to any server that is configured to use it

Single-host and centralized licensing modes can be combined within the same virtualized environment. Such a configuration is referred to as mixed licensing.

ESX 3.5 Editions

ESX 3.5 is available in three separate editions, VI Foundation, VI Standard and VI Enterprise.

VI Foundation

The VI Foundation edition operates in either single-host or centralized modes. This edition targets configurations that do not require fault tolerant or load balancing capabilities. Quality assurance and test and development environments typically do not require these capabilities and may find the VI Foundation edition to be appropriate. The following details the features supported by this edition:

- VMware Update Manager
- VMware Consolidate Backup (VCB)
- Virtual Center Management Agent

- Guided Consolidation (Requires purchase of VirtualCenter)
- VMFS
- Remote CLI
- Virtual Symmetric Multi Processing (SMP)
- The ability to be managed by the VI Client and VirtualCenter in either evaluation or production mode

VI Foundation does not provide the following features:

- VMware VMotion, DRS and HA

These can be obtained as Add-ons.

VI Standard

The VI Standard edition provides all the features available in the VI Foundation edition. It differs in that it also provides High Availability (HA) functionality. Therefore, it is an appropriate edition for environments requiring the additional capabilities of fail over of ESX 3.5 servers.

VI Standard does not provide the following features:

- VMware VMotion, DRS

These can be obtained as Add-ons.

VI Enterprise

The VI Enterprise edition offers all of the features provided by the Standard edition. This is the edition often used within datacenters in a production environment. It adds the load balancing capabilities missing in the VI Foundation and VI Standard editions. The VMotion feature of the VI Enterprise edition allows system administrators to schedule downtime in production environments by re-assigning virtual machines off of a ESX host to other ESX 3.5 servers. This allows for maintenance to be performed on the ESX host during normal business hours without disruption of operations. The Distributed Resource Scheduler (DRS) is provided in the VI Enterprise edition. DRS uses the VMotion technology to re-assign virtual machines to ESX hosts when necessary to efficiently load balance memory and CPU resources for a group of ESX 3.5 servers.

Purchasing Licenses

The licensing for the ESX 3.5 server software is based on a per-processor basis and is sold in increments of two. A processor is considered to be a physical processor placed into a socket on the system board. The number of cores per socket does not matter, only the number of physical sockets. All the features listed for each of the ESX 3.5 editions are licensed on a per socket basis. It is not possible to partially license an ESX system. In other words, if the server has 4 sockets, you cannot purchase just two ESX licenses and still use the server. Four licenses will need to be purchased on such a system. Therefore, if purchasing a group of 20 ESX server systems each containing four sockets on the system board, a total of 80 ESX licenses will need to be purchased. If VMotion is to occur on all 20 ESX hosts, then 80 VMotion licenses will need to be purchased. 80 DRS licenses will need to be purchased if utilizing DRS on each ESX host. A fail over configuration that only encompasses 4 of these ESX hosts would only require 16 HA licenses.

Enabling Licensed Features

To configure the ESX 3.5 server to use a host based license you must select the Configuration tab in the VI Client GUI and select the Licensed Features link in the Software box. Then you must select the top edit link on the right of the screen. This will bring up the License Sources window as shown in Figure 3.32.

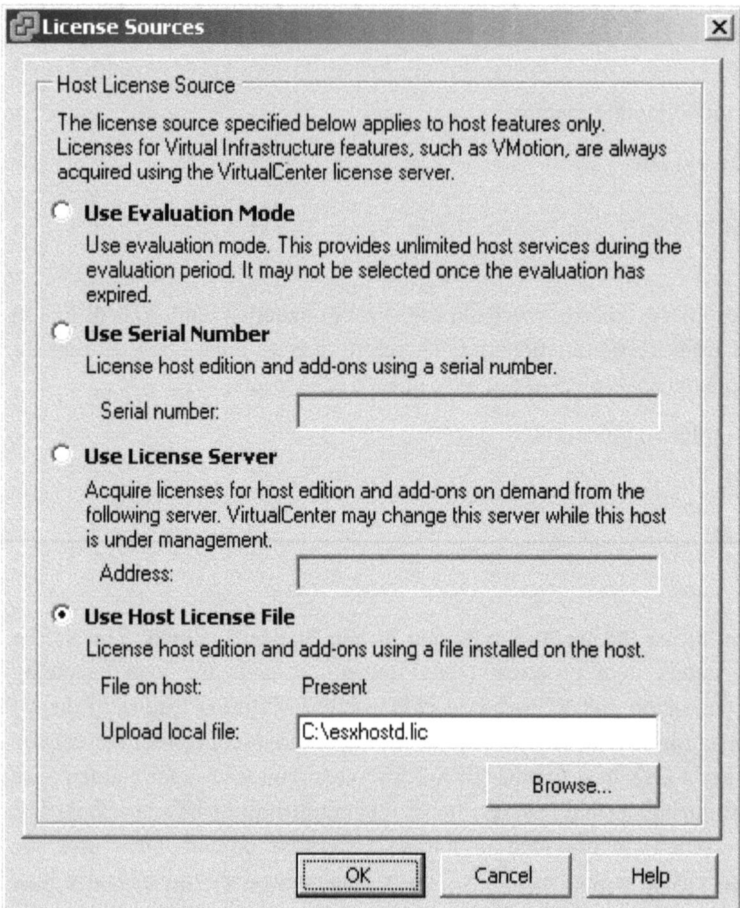

Figure 3.32 The License Sources Window

The top radio button in Figure 3.32 can be selected to use the new evaluation mode. This allows the use of the ESX 3.5 server for 60 days. Once the 60 days has expired, licensing will need to be acquired.

The serial number selection is used with ESXi servers, not with ESX 3.5 servers. Enter the serial number obtained from VMware to enable licensing for the ESXi server.

The use of a license server is possible when a VirtualCenter server is configured within the virtualized environment. It is used to configure the ESX 3.5 server to use a license server. Installation and configuration of the License server will be covered in Chapter 6 – VirtualCenter 2.5.

Select the bottom radio button and either enter the full path to your single-host license file or click on the browse button and navigate to it. This will allow you to configure the ESX 3.5 server to use the single-host license file. Once you have selected the correct host based license file select the OK button to close the window.

Setting the License Type

To set what type of license the server will use you must click on the Configuration tab in the VI Client GUI and select the Licensed Features link in the Software box. Then you must select the middle edit link on the right of the screen. This will bring up the ESX Server Edition dialog box as shown in Figure 3.33.

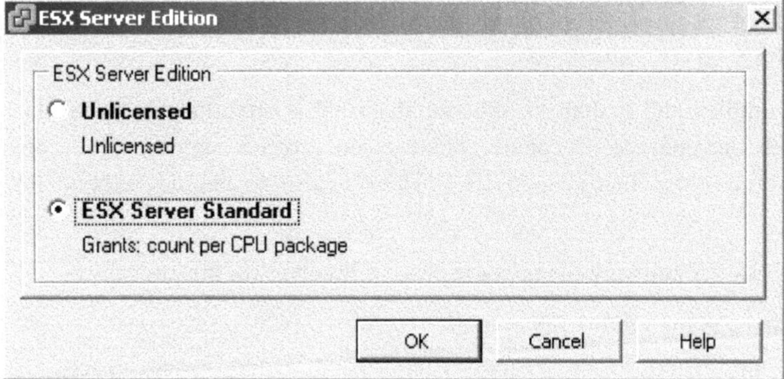

Figure 3.33 The ESX Server Edition Dialog Box

The license edition being used is ESX Server Standard as shown in Figure 3.33.

Configured ESX 3.5 Licenses

Figure 3.34 shows an example of licenses configured on an ESX 3.5 server. Notice that the ESX Server Edition section lists the available features that this server is licensed to support.

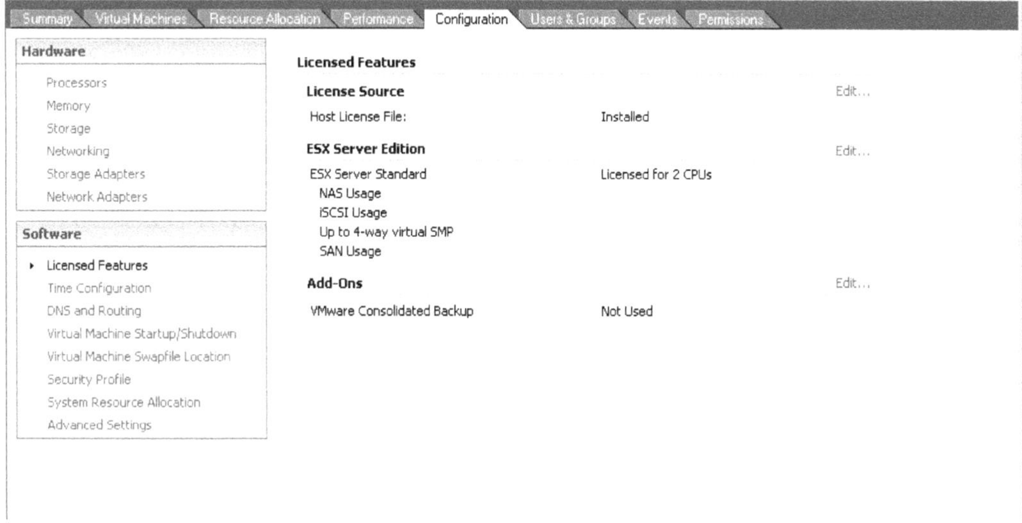

Figure 3.34 Configured Licensed Features

Upgrading from ESX 2.x to ESX 3.5

If your server has the ESX 2.x software installed on it you can also do an upgrade instead of a fresh installation. You should download the latest release of the Installation and Upgrade Guide at:

http://www.VMware.com/support/pubs/vi_pubs.html

It contains all of the latest information to migrate from one of the earlier versions of the software to the latest version including all of the issues with the software that could cause the process to fail.

If you are running the 1.x version of Virtual Center then you should refer to the Installation and Upgrade Guide as well. Virtual Center must be upgraded first before any of your ESX servers are upgraded to support the newest ESX server features.

The upgrade process is rather complex and is done in specific stages. It is important that you plan carefully before proceeding with the upgrade procedure. There is no upgrade support if you are running a version of the ESX server older than version 2.1.1. There is also no upgrade support for versions 2.3 and 2.5.0.

If you are currently running the ESX 2.x software the upgrade process involves (in this order):

1. Upgrading the vmfs-2 file systems to the vmfs-3 file system

2. Upgrading the virtual machine file structures

3. Upgrading the VMware Tools running in the VM's.

It is important that you upgrade your resources in this same order for the upgrade to be successful.

Configuring the Network Time Protocol Service

After installation, it is recommended to configure the ESX 3.5 servers to use a Network Time Protocol (NTP) server to synchronize the server's time and date settings to a consistent common time source. By having a consistent time across ESX hosts, troubleshooting is enhanced by having accurate time/date stamps in system log files across ESX hosts. Guest operating systems running inside virtual machines can have their system time synchronized to the system time of the ESX hosts they are operating on. This is an important configuration as it allows consistent task scheduling and accurate performance statistics to be recorded when the ESX 3.5 host is under the management of a VirtualCenter server.

To synchronize the ESX 3.5 host with a NTP server, click the Configuration tab then select the Time Configuration link within the Software section of the VI Client. Next, select the Properties link in the upper right hand of the screen as shown in Figure 3.35.

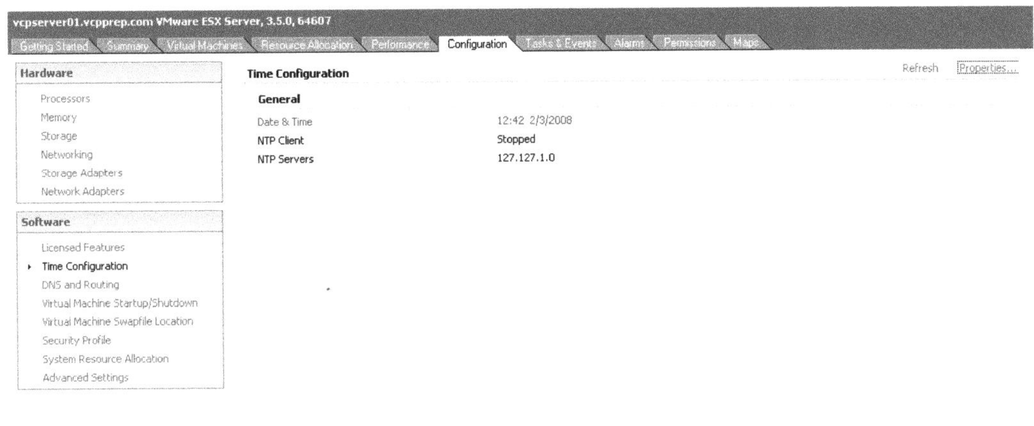

Figure 3.35 Default Time Configuration Screen

In order to activate the NTP client on the ESX 3.5 host, select the check box next to NTP Client Enabled within the NTP Configuration section as shown in Figure 3.36. The NTP client uses port 123 over UDP. Firewall settings may need to be adjusted to allow NTP communication. Select the OK button to enable the NTP client.

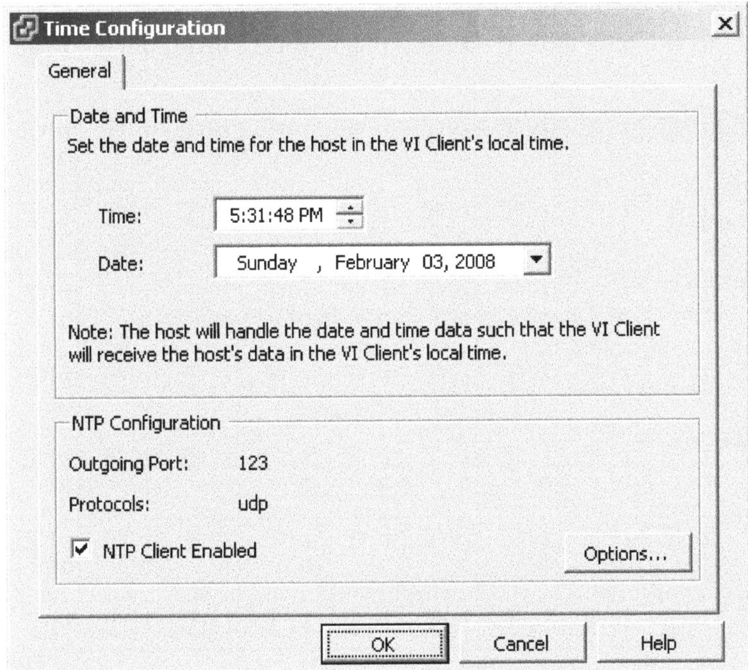

Figure 3.36 Time Configuration Dialog Box

The NTP client is now running as shown in Figure 3.37.

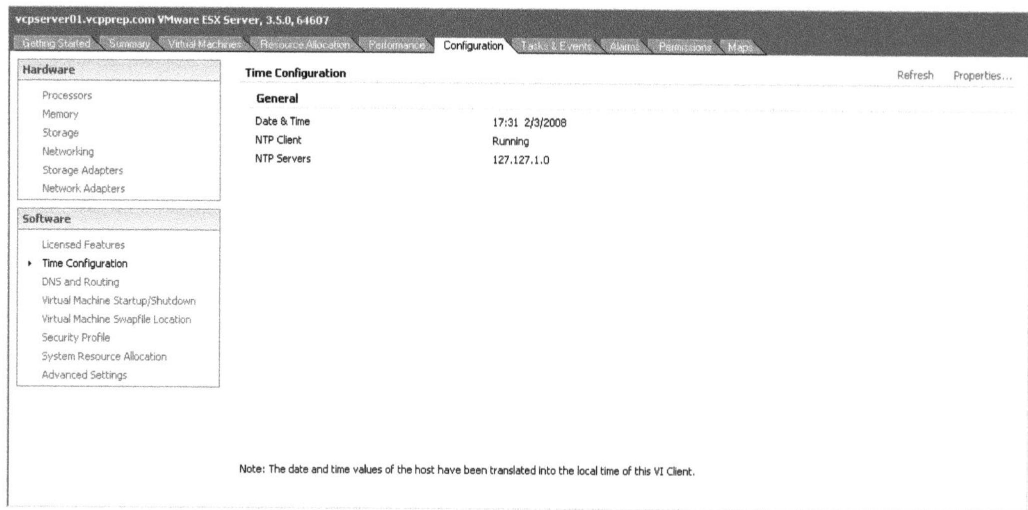

Figure 3.37 Time Configuration Screen NTP Client Enabled

To specify a NTP server, select the Properties link in the upper right hand of the screen to once again open the Time Configuration dialog box. Opening this dialog box a second time is necessary in order to configure a NTP server. If you try to set a NTP server the first time you access this dialog box, it will generate an error as the NTP client will first need to be running prior to configure the NTP server. To configure the NTP server, select the Options button within the NTP Configuration section of the Time Configuration dialog box. This will open the NTP Daemon (ntpd) Options dialog box as shown in Figure 3.38.

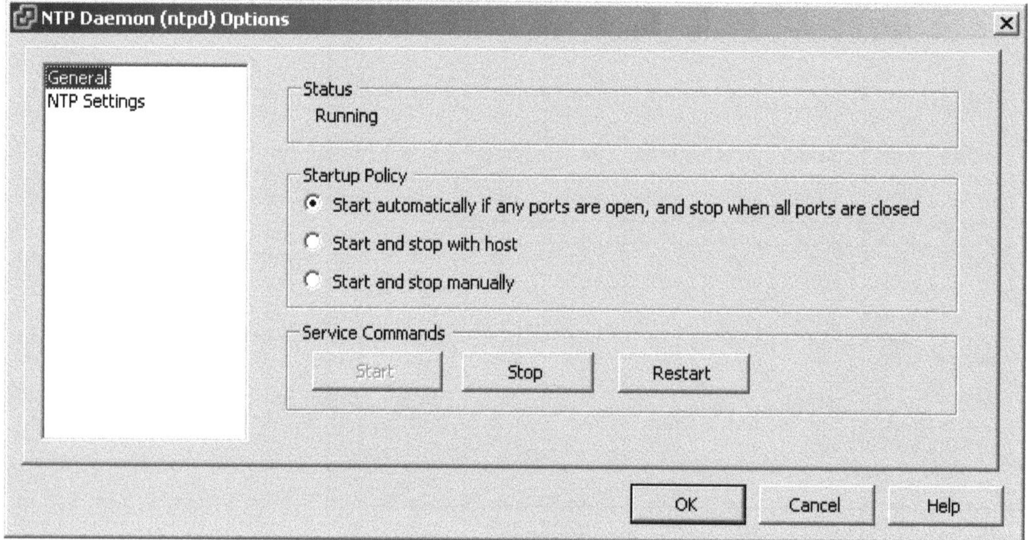

Figure 3.38 NTP Daemon Dialog Box General Settings

The General option displays the current status of the NTP daemon (ntpd). It is possible to set the following startup policies for the NTP daemon:

- Start automatically if any ports are open, and stop when all ports are closed. This may be a useful policy in a test and development environment.

- Start and stop with host. This may be a useful policy if utilizing more than one NTP server. One of the two NTP servers may only be accessible outside of a firewall while the other is located inside of the firewall. In this case, having the NTP daemon starting with the host allows it to synchronize its time regardless of firewall settings.
- Start and stop manually. This is a useful setting when writing a script. The script may need to manually control the activation of the NTP daemon.

The NTP Settings option is used to add NTP servers. Select the Add button as shown in Figure 3.39.

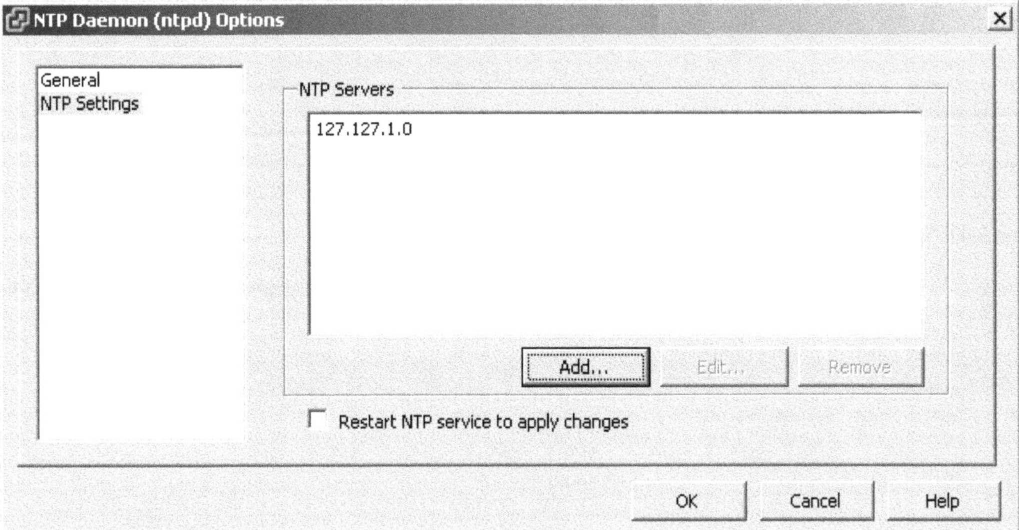

Figure 3.39 NTP Daemon Dialog Box NTP Settings

Enter the IP address of the NTP server as shown in Figure 3.40.

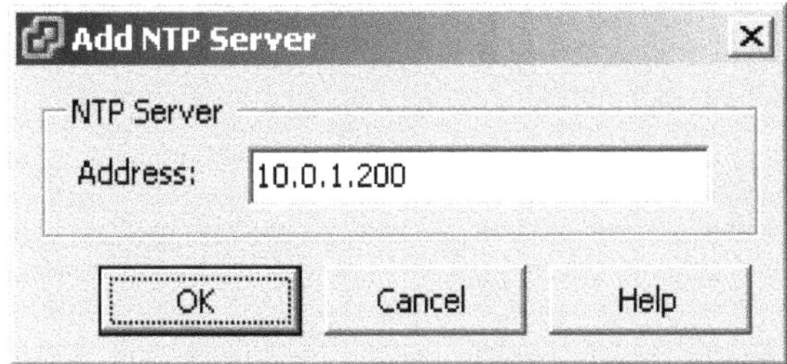

Figure 3.40 Add NTP Server Dialog Box

Select the check box next to "Restart NTP service to apply changes" and click the OK button as shown in Figure 3.41.

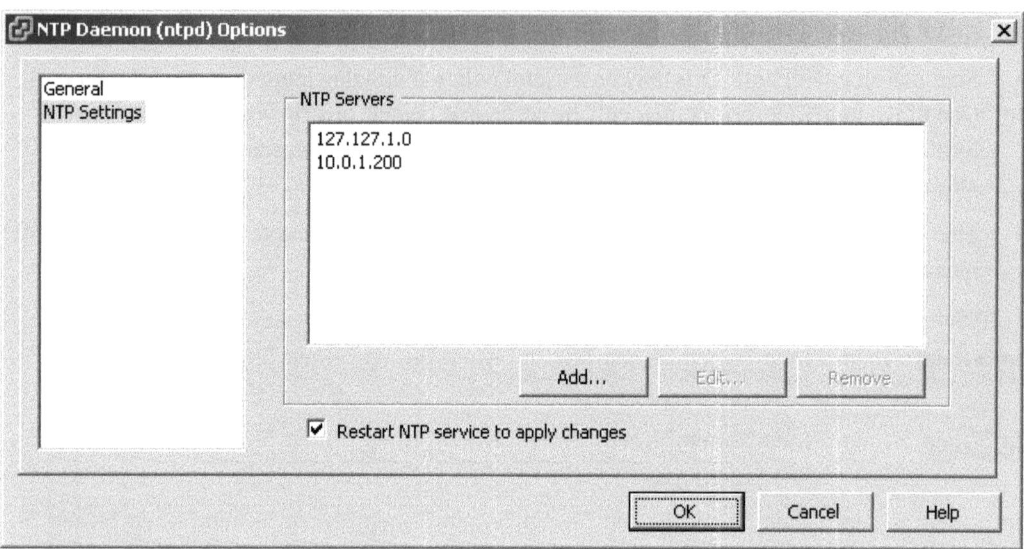

Figure 3.41 NTP Server Added Dialog Box

The new NTP server is now configured and is displayed in the Time Configuration screen of the VI Client as shown in Figure 3.42.

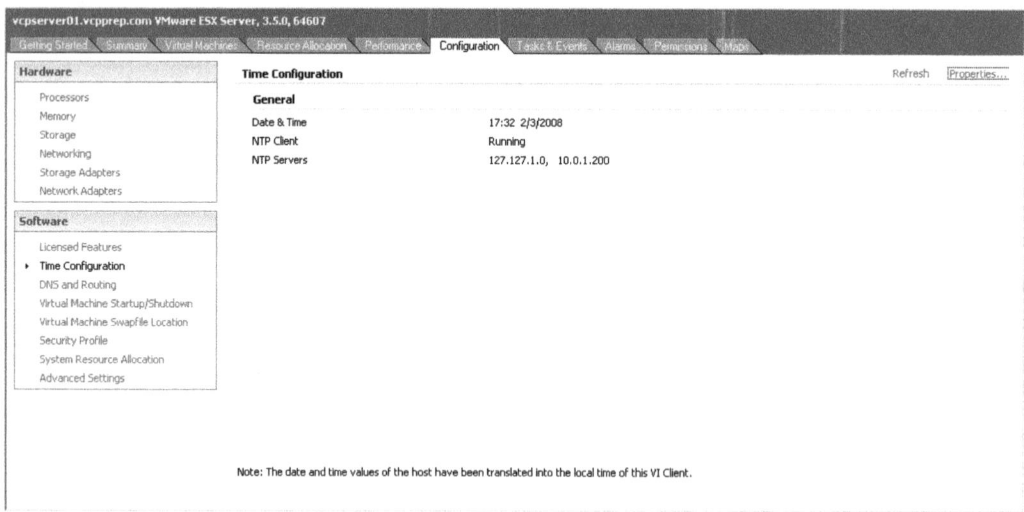

Figure 3.42 NTP Server Added Dialog Box

ESXi Installable Installation

There are two editions of ESXi. The embedded version resides on firmware located on the server's system board. This version does not require an installation process. All that is required is to power on the server and set the initial configuration settings once it has booted. The other edition is ESXi installable. This edition requires an installation process to be performed.

The ESXi installable version is available from VMware's website at the following location:

http://www.VMware.com/download/vi/

If downloading the ESXi installable edition from VMware's website, the downloaded image will need to be transferred to a CD/DVD disk. Configure the server's to boot from the ESXi installable media loaded in the server's CD/ROM drive if necessary by modifying the server's boot order within the BIOS settings. The server will then begin to load as shown in Figure 3.43.

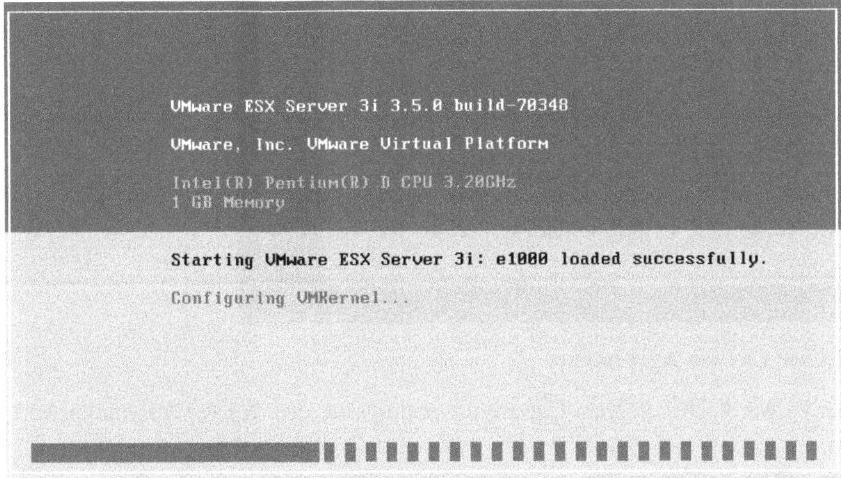

Figure 3.43 ESXi Boot From CD Media

NOTE: In Figure 3.43, the product is referred to as ESX Server 3i. At the time of this writing, VMware changed the name of the product to ESXi. The product will be referred to as ESXi throughout this book.

The installer will then present a menu to choose either to cancel the install, repair an existing installation or to install a new system. Press Enter to install a new ESXi system as shown in Figure 3.44.

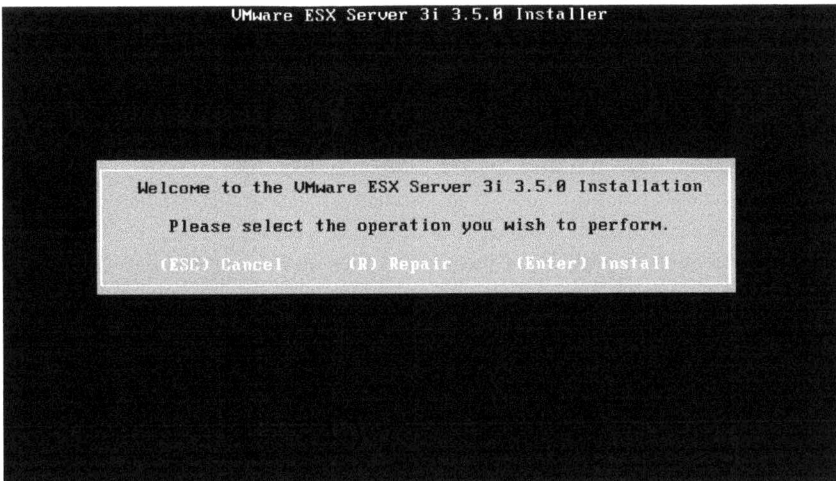

Figure 3.44 ESXi Install Menu

The installer will present the End User License Agreement (EULA). Pressing F11 to accept the license agreement will continue the installation as shown in Figure 3.45.

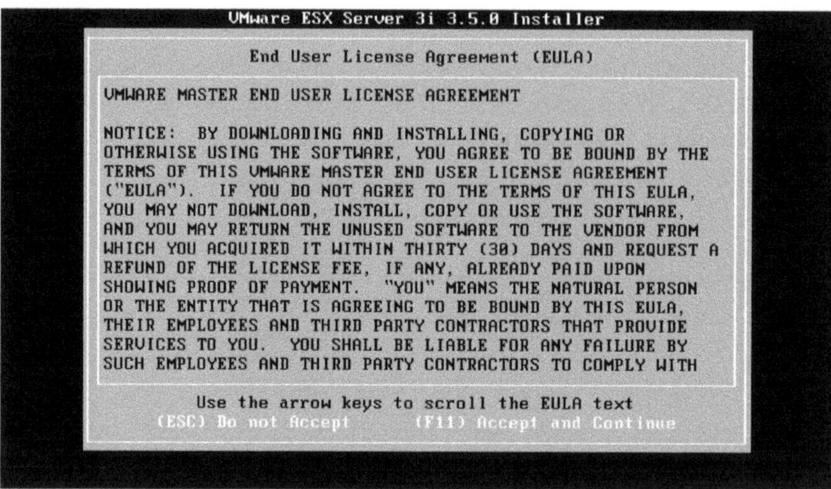

Figure 3.45 ESXi End User License Agreement

Figure 3.46 displays the Select A Disk screen. Choose the appropriate disk for the installation and press Enter to continue.

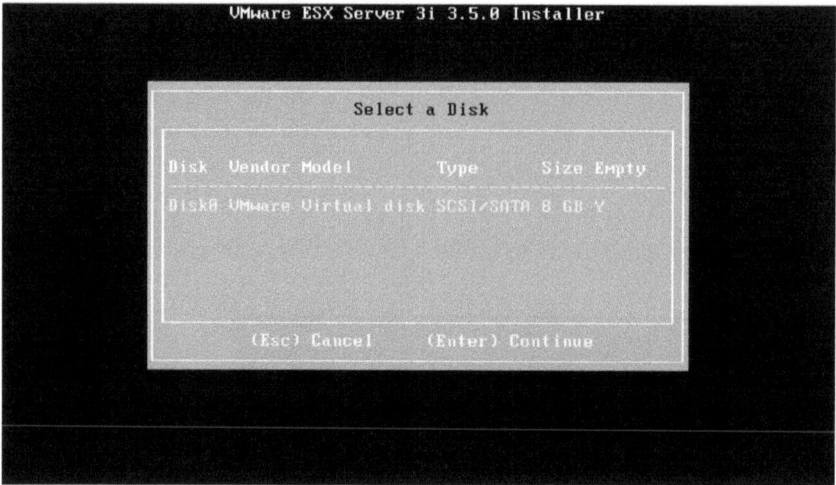

Figure 3.46 ESXi Select A Disk

The ESXi installer is now ready to begin installing the installation files on the selected disk as shown in Figure 3.47. Modifications to the previous installation choices can be performed if necessary by using the Backspace key. The installation can be canceled by pressing the Esc key. To begin installing the files press the F11 key.

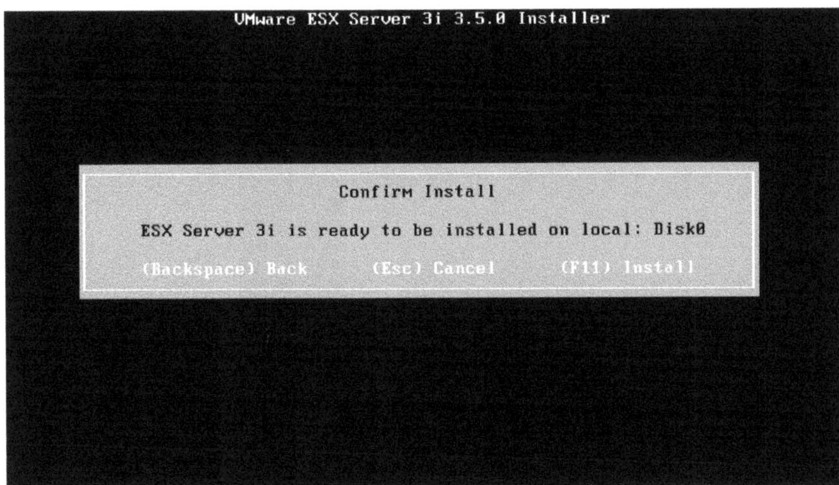

Figure 3.47 ESXi Confirm Install Screen

As shown in Figure 3.48, the ESXi installer will display its progress as it proceeds to install the installation media. On modern systems, this is a relatively fast installation process.

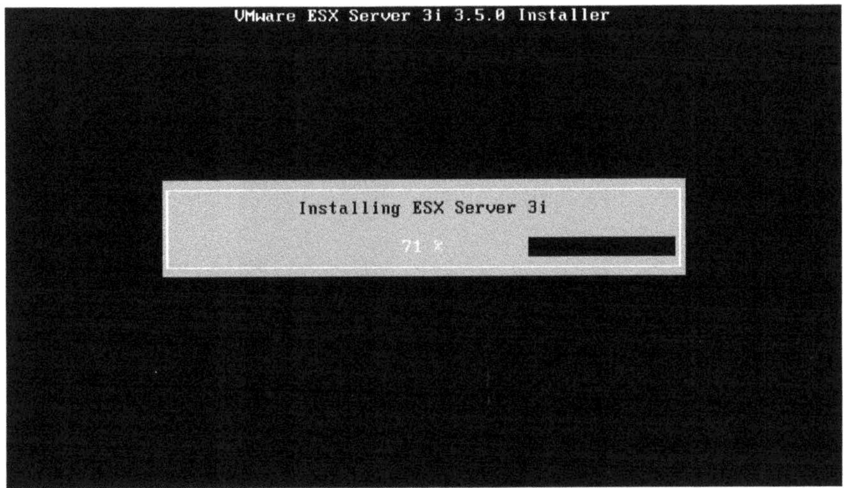

Figure 3.48 ESXi Installation Progress

The installation will display the Installation Complete screen as shown in Figure 3.49. The ESXi server can operate for 60 days in evaluation mode. The license can be configured from within the VI Client interface.

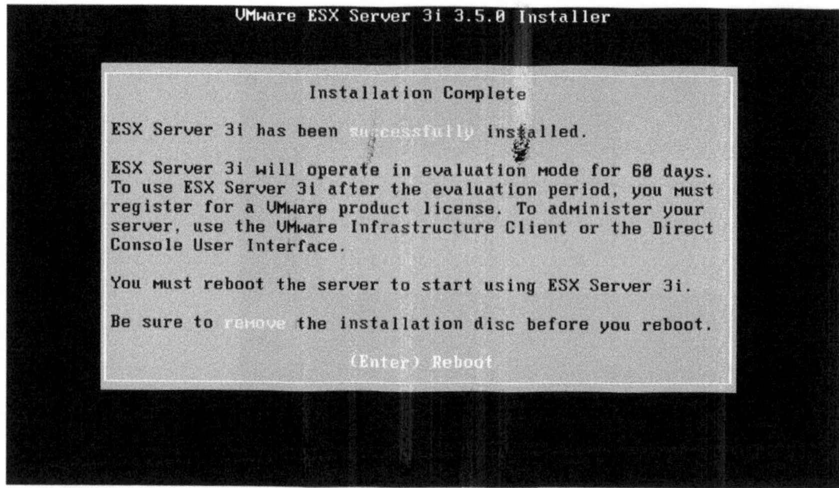

Figure 3.49 ESXi Installation Complete Screen

The ESXi system will need to be rebooted as shown in Figure 3.50 before being placed into operation.

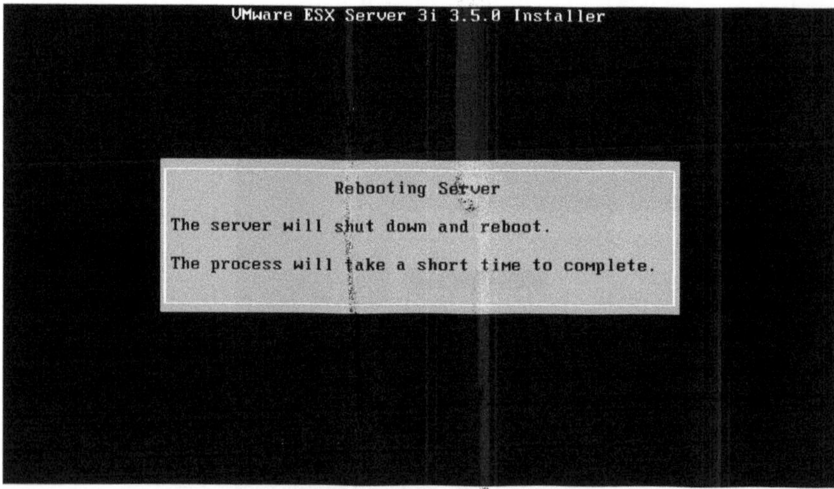

Figure 3.50 ESXi Reboot after Installation

As the ESXi system is initialized, the VMkernel will be loaded along with several system components and services as shown in Figure 3.51.

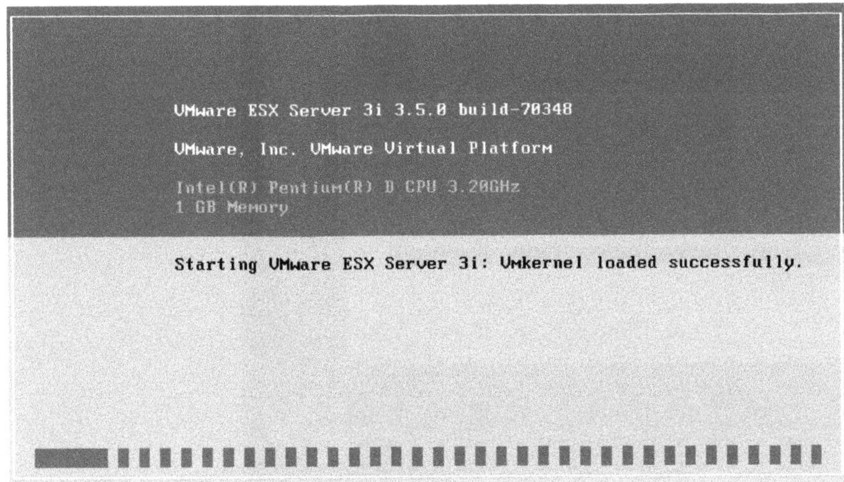

Figure 3.51 Starting the ESXi System

Figure 3.52 displays the completed boot screen of the ESXi server. The ESXi server can obtain an IP address via DHCP or a static IP address can be assigned.

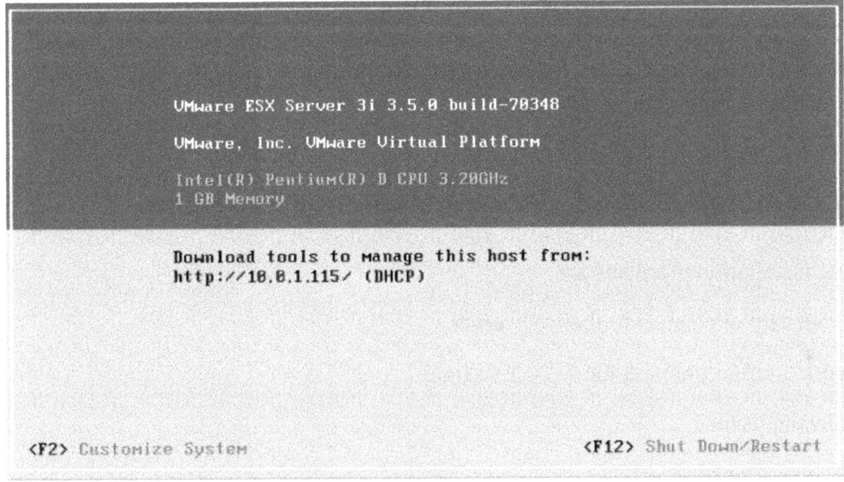

Figure 3.52 ESXi System Console Screen

It is also important to set a password for the system to increase the server's security level. This can be achieved by pressing the F2 key to customize the system. As shown in Figure 3.53, the ESX administrator can assign a root password by typing the password in once then once more to confirm the password.

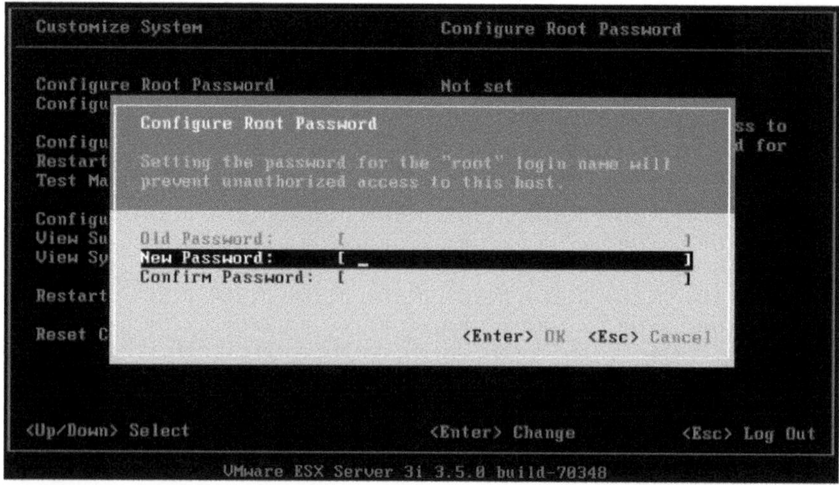

Figure 3.53 ESXi Root Password

There are other customization options that can be performed by pressing the F2 key and entering the customization screen. The DNS and default gateway can be configured. Tests can be performed as well to verify the system's IP connectivity. Once the DNS default gateway and IP connectivity have been confirmed, the ESXi system is ready to be placed into operation. The system can be managed either by using the Remote Command Line Interface (RCLI) or the VI Client. Both of these management tools will be discussed later in this book.

Troubleshooting Common ESX 3.5 Server Installation Problems

Common ESX 3.5 server installation problems are:

- The WebUI client cannot connect to the web server
- Incorrect network configuration on the ESX 3.5 server
- NTP synchronization issues
- ESX 3.5 server boot problems

WebUI Client Cannot Connect to Web Server

By default, the installation process sets up and configures the Apache Tomcat web server service on the ESX 3.5 server. This service allows remote users to connect to the service console via a web browser. If you cannot connect to the server via a web browser check whether or not the web server service is running. You can use these commands to stop, start, restart and check the status of the apache web service on a 3.5 ESX server:

[root@vcpserver01 rc5.d]# service VMware-webAccess stop

Stopping VMware ESX Server webAccess: VMware ESX Server webAccess [OK]

[root@vcpserver01 rc5.d]# service VMware-webAccess start

Starting VMware ESX Server webAccess: VMware ESX Server webAccess [OK] [root@vcpserver01 rc5.d]# service VMware-webAccess restart

Stopping VMware ESX Server webAccess: VMware ESX Server webAccess [FAILED]

Starting VMware ESX Server webAccess: VMware ESX Server webAccess [OK]

[root@vcpserver01 rc5.d]# service VMware-webAccess status

webAccess (pid 2391) is running...

Incorrect Network Configuration on the ESX 3.5 server

Try to ping the ESX 3.5 server:

[root@vcpserver01 rc5.d]# ping [put your ESX 3.5 servers IP address here]

If there is no response check the following configuration files:

- /etc/hosts
- /etc/sysconfig/network
- /etc/sysconfig/network-scripts/ifcfg-vswif0
- /etc/resolv.conf)

Check the following to determine if it was configured with the correct network settings:

- IP Address
- Netmask
- DNS Server(s)
- Service Console VLAN Configuration

NTP Synchronization Issues

In many environments, all resources on the network must have their time and date settings synced to the organization's "network time". This is usually done using the Network Time Protocol. You can check your configuration using the GUI.

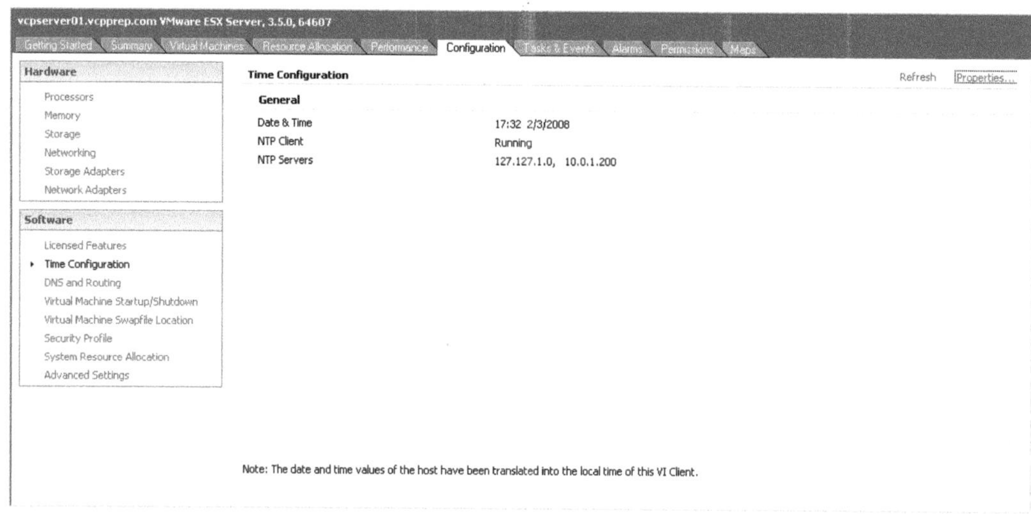

Figure 3.54 Time Configuration Screen NTP Client

Or you can edit the NTP configuration files:

/etc/ntp.conf

server 1.2.3.4 server 2.3.4.5 server 3.4.5.6

Then update the /etc/ntp.conf file as shown below:

server 127.127.1.0 # local clock fudge 127.127.1.0 stratum 10

The ESX 3.5 Server Does not Boot Properly

After the installation of the ESX 3.5 software is installed, the boot process and any associated errors with the boot process are logged. Two useful log files contain information pertaining to boot problems. They are:

- /var/log/boot.log
- /var/log/VMware/hostd.log

You should also examine the system and application logs found in /var/log. Look for entries that include alert, critical, error, failed and warning entries.

/var/log/boot.log

The /var/log/boot.log looks like this:

Feb 3 05:12:25 vcpserver01 VMware: Saving VMware ESX Server configuration succeeded

Feb 3 05:12:32 vcpserver01 gpm: gpm shutdown succeeded

Feb 3 05:12:32 vcpserver01 sshd: sshd -TERM succeeded

Feb 3 05:12:32 vcpserver01 xinetd: xinetd shutdown succeeded

Feb 3 05:12:32 vcpserver01 crond: crond shutdown succeeded

Feb 3 05:12:33 vcpserver01 dd: 1+0 records in

Feb 3 05:12:33 vcpserver01 dd: 1+0 records out

Feb 3 05:12:33 vcpserver01 random: Saving random seed: succeeded

Feb 3 05:14:47 vcpserver01 syslog: syslogd startup succeeded

Feb 3 05:14:47 vcpserver01 syslog: klogd startup succeeded

Feb 3 05:14:47 vcpserver01 irqbalance: irqbalance startup succeeded

Feb 3 05:14:48 vcpserver01 ipmi: failed

Feb 3 05:14:48 vcpserver01 random: Initializing random numb

/var/log/VMware/hostd.log

The /var/log/VMware/hostd.log looks like this:

Log for VMware ESX Server, pid=1321, version=3.5.0, build=build-64607, option=Release, section=2

[2008-02-03 05:18:27.116 'App' 3076432800 info] Current working directory: /var/log/VMware

[2008-02-03 05:18:27.117 'BaseLibs' 3076432800 info] HOSTINFO: Seeing Intel CPU, numCoresPerCPU 1 numThreadsPerCore 2.

[2008-02-03 05:18:27.123 'BaseLibs' 3076432800 info] HOSTINFO: This machine has 2 physical CPUS, 2 total cores, and 4 logical CPUs.

[2008-02-03 05:18:27.123 'Handle checker' 3076432800 info] Setting system limit of 2048

[2008-02-03 05:18:27.123 'Handle checker' 3076432800 info] Set system limit to 2048

[2008-02-03 05:18:27.126 'App' 3076432800 info] Trying blklistsvc

[2008-02-03 05:18:27.130 'BlklistsvcPlugin' 3076432800 info] Block List Service Plugin initialized

[2008-02-03 05:18:27.130 'App' 3076432800 info] Trying cimsvc

[2008-02-03 05:18:27.130 'App' 3076432800 info] Trying directorysvc

[2008-02-03 05:18:27.138 'DirectorysvcPlugin' 3076432800 info] Plugin initialized

[2008-02-03 05:18:27.138 'App' 3076432800 info] Trying hostsvc

[2008-02-03 05:18:27.165 'HostsvcPlugin' 3076432800 info] Storage data synchronization policy set to invalidate_change

[2008-02-03 05:18:27.174 'Vmfs2UpgradeModeLock' 3076432800 info] [Init] undoAttempts(15), timeoutMsec(2000)

[2008-02-03 05:18:27.251 'HostsvcPlugin' 3076432800 info] Resource pool configuration: /etc/VMware/hostd/pools.xml

[2008-02-03 05:18:27.343 'HostsvcPlugin' 3076432800 info] Datastore auto-refresh is disabled.

[2008-02-03 05:18:27.344 'Hostsvc::DatastoreSystem' 3076432800 info] Datastore alias configuration file is

/etc/VMware/hostd/datastores.xml

[2008-02-03 05:18:27.367 'Hostsvc::AutoStartManager' 3076432800 info] VM autostart configuration: /etc/VMware/hostd/vmAutoStart.xml

[2008-02-03 05:18:42.137 'FirewallSystem' 3076432800 error] Failed to update service ntpd: vim.fault.PlatformConfigFault

External References

VMware Infrastructure 3 Documentation:

http://www.VMware.com/support/pubs/vi_pubs.html

ESX Server 3 Installation Guide:

http://www.VMware.com/pdf/vi3_35/esx_3/r35/vi3_35_25_installation_guide.pdf

Systems Compatibility Guide for ESX Server 3.5 and ESXi Server 3.5:

http://www.VMware.com/pdf/vi35_systems_guide.pdf

I/O Compatibility Guide for ESX Server 3.5 and ESXi Server 3.5:

http://www.VMware.com/pdf/vi35_io_guide.pdf

Storage/SAN Compatibility Guide for ESX Server 3.5 and ESXi Server 3.5:

http://www.VMware.com/pdf/vi35_san_guide.pdf

Pricing, Packaging and Licensing Overview:

http://www.VMware.com/pdf/vi_pricing.pdf

PuTTy Download Page:

http://www.chiark.greenend.org.uk/~sgtatham/putty/

Sample Test Questions

1. How many LUNs can the ESX 3.5 server recognize during the installation process?

a. 64

b. 128

c. 256

d. 512

2. What type of drives can you install the ESX 3.5 server boot drive partitions to?

a. SATA

b. SCSI

c. IDE

d. Fiber Channel

e. USB

3. What are the only file systems not recognized as a "raw LUN" during the installation process?

a. UFS

b. FAT32

c. EXT2

d. VMFS-2

e. NTFS

f. EXT3

g. VMFS-3

4. Which of the following is supported to allow the ESX 3.5 server to boot from the SAN?

a. Fiber Channel HBA

b. iSCSI HBA

c. iSCSI software initiator

d. InfiniBand HBA

5. What is the default amount of memory allocated to the service console by the installation process?

a. 100 MB

b. 200 MB

c. 272 MB

d. 512 MB

e. 1024 MB

6. What ESX 3.5 Server License Type allows the ESX 3.5 server to access SAN resources?

a. Unlicensed

b. ESX Server Starter

c. ESX Server Limited Edition

d. ESX Server Standard

e. ESX Server Ultimate Release

7. How large does the /boot file system need to be if put into its own partition?

a. 100 MB

b. 272 MB

c. 512 MB

d. 1024 MB

e. 2560 MB

8. What is the minimum amount of memory required for an ESX 3.5 server installation?

a. 100 MB

b. 272 MB

c. 512 MB

d. 1024 MB

e. 2560 MB

9. What is the minimum amount of characters required for the root account password during installation?

a. 0

b. 1

c. 3

d. 6

e. 8

10. What is the minimum number of processors required for an ESX 3.5 server install?

a. 1

b. 2

c. 3

d. 4

11. What are the three ways you can set the time zone on an ESX 3.5 server during the installation process?

a. Using the current year/date/hours/minutes/seconds on your watch

b. Using the Time Zone Map tab

c. Using the Time Zone Location tab

d. Using the Time Zone UTC tab

e. Using the Time Zone offset from UTC tab

f. Using the current year/date/hours/minutes/seconds from a NTP server

12. What features cannot be used with host based licensing?

a. 4-way SMP

b. VMotion

c. VMware HA

d. iSCSI SAN

e. VMware DRS

f. NFS

g. VMware Consolidated Backup

13. How many LUNs can an ESX 3.5 server see after installation on a Fiber Channel SAN?

a. 127

b. 128

c. 255

d. 256

e. 512

14. Which partition is used to store core dumps that can be used by technical support?

a. swap

b. /coredump

c. /vmcore

d. /kernel

e. /vmkcore

15. How many Ethernet adapters are required to do an ESX 3.5 installation?

a. 0

b. 1

c. 2

d. 3

16. If you partition the disk(s) manually during installation, what is the recommended size for the swap partition assuming that the default amount of memory is to be assigned to the service console?

a. 100 MB

b. 256 MB

c. 272 MB

d. 512 MB

e. 544 MB

17. Which file system is not required to be put in its own partition during the installation process?

a. /

b. /boot

c. swap

d. /var/log

e. /vmkcore

18. During installation which of the following will cause the ESX 3.5 server not to see any devices on the SAN?

a. If all of the SAN HBA's are disconnected on the ESX

b. If the server uses a ESX host based Server Starter type license

c. If all of the LUN's on the SAN have been zoned or masked making them invisible to the ESX 3.5

server

d. If all of the LUNs are labeled as LUN 127 or higher

19. What is the minimum size of the VMFS-3 file system?

a. 272 MB

b. 256 MB

c. 512 MB

d. 1024 MB

e. 1100 MB

20. The service console should be put on a VLAN during installation.

a. True

b. False

21. Which methods allow you login remotely as the root account after installation?

a. CLI

b. VI Client

c. Web client

22. What types of disks do not support the VMFS3 file system?

a. SCSI

b. IDE

c. Fiber Channel

d. SATA

Sample Test Solutions

1. How many LUNs can the ESX 3.5 server recognize during the installation process?

a. 64

b. 128

c. 256

d. 512

Answer: b - LUNs 0 through 127 can be seen during the install process.

2. What type of drives can you install the ESX 3.5 server boot drive partitions to?

a. SATA

b. SCSI

c. IDE

d. Fiber Channel

e. USB

Answer: b, c and d

3. What are the only file systems not recognized as a "raw LUN" during the installation process?

a. UFS

b. FAT32

c. EXT2

d. VMFS-2

e. NTFS

f. EXT3

g. VMFS-3

Answer: d and g

4. Which of the following is supported to allow the ESX 3.5 server to boot from the SAN?

a. Fiber Channel HBA

b. iSCSI HBA

c. iSCSI software initiator

d. InfiniBand HBA

Answer: a and b

5. What is the default amount of memory allocated to the service console by the installation process?

a. 100 MB

b. 200 MB

c. 272 MB

d. 512 MB

e. 1024 MB

Answer: c

6. What ESX 3.5 Server License Type allows the ESX 3.5 server to access SAN resources?

a. Unlicensed

b. ESX Server Starter

c. ESX Server Limited Edition

d. ESX Server Standard

e. ESX Server Ultimate Release

Answer: d

7. How large does the /boot file system need to be if out into its own partition?

a. 100 MB

b. 272 MB

c. 512 MB

d. 1024 MB

e. 2560 MB

Answer: a

8. What is the minimum amount of memory required for an ESX 3.5 server installation?

a. 100 MB

b. 272 MB

c. 512 MB

d. 1024 MB

e. 2560 MB

Answer: d

9. What is the minimum amount of characters required for the root account password during installation?

a. 0

b. 1

c. 3

d. 6

e. 8

Answer: d

10. What is the minimum number of processors required for an ESX 3.5 server install?

a. 1

b. 2

c. 3

d. 4

Answer: b

11. What are the three ways you can set the time zone on an ESX 3.5 server during the installation process?

a. Using the current year/date/hours/minutes/seconds on your watch

b. Using the Time Zone Map tab

c. Using the Time Zone Location tab

d. Using the Time Zone UTC tab

e. Using the Time Zone offset from UTC tab

f. Using the current year/date/hours/minutes/seconds from a NTP server

Answer: b, c & d - NTP can be configured after the installation process

12. What features cannot be used using host based licensing?

a. 4-way SMP

b. VMotion

c. VMware HA

d. iSCSI SAN

e. VMware DRS

f. NFS

g. VMware Consolidated Backup

Answer: b, c & e

13. How many LUNs can an ESX 3.5 server see after installation on a Fiber Channel SAN?

a. 127

b. 128

c. 255

d. 256

e. 512

Answer: d

14. Which partition is used to store core dumps that can be used by technical support?

a. swap

b. /coredump

c. /vmcore

d. /kernel

e. /vmkcore

Answer: e

15. How many Ethernet adapters are required to do an ESX 3.5 installation?

a. 0

b. 1

c. 2

d. 3

Answer: b

16. If you partition the disk(s) manually during installation, what is the recommended size for the swap partition assuming that the default amount of memory is to be assigned to the service console?

a. 100 MB

b. 256 MB

c. 272 MB

d. 512 MB

e. 544 MB

Answer: e

17. Which file system is not required to be put in its own partition during the installation process?

a. /

b. /boot

c. swap

d. /var/log

e. /vmkcore

Answer: d

18. During installation which of the following will cause the ESX 3.5 server not to see any devices on the SAN?

a. If all of the SAN HBA's are disconnected on the ESX

b. If the server uses a ESX host based Server Starter type license

c. If all of the LUN's on the SAN have been zoned or masked making them invisible to the ESX 3.5 server

d. If all of the LUNs are labeled as LUN 127 or higher

Answer: a & c – The license type does not prevent the ESX server to see the SAN devices during installation and LUNs 128 and higher are not supported by the ESX 3.5 server during installation.

19. What is the minimum size of the VMFS-3 file system?

a. 272 MB

b. 256 MB

c. 512 MB

d. 1024 MB

e. 1100 MB

Answer: e

20. The service console should be put on a VLAN during installation.

a. True

b. False

Answer: a

21. Which methods allow you login remotely as the root account after installation?

a. CLI

b. VI Client

c. Web client

Answer: b & c

22. What types of disks do not support the VMFS3 file system?

a. SCSI

b. IDE

c. Fiber Channel

d. SATA

Answer: b & d

Chapter 4

ESX 3.5 Server Networking Configurations

After reading this chapter you should be able to complete the following tasks:

- Identify physical NICs within the ESX server
- Create virtual switches (vSwitch)
- Set the number of ports on a virtual switch
- Set security policies on a virtual switch
- Control outbound traffic
- Configure fail over policies
- Configure load balancing policies
- Create a NIC team
- Configure physical NIC speed and duplex settings
- Utilize virtual switch call out boxes
- Remove a physical NIC from a virtual switch
- Create a service console port
- Create a VMkernel port
- Create a virtual machine port group
- Assign VLAN IDs
- Override virtual switch settings
- Use the command line to display virtual switch settings
- Use the command line to unlink and link physical NICs to virtual switches
- Configure active and standby physical NICs

Physical NICs in an ESX 3.5 Server

To communicate with other resources in the virtual infrastructure an ESX 3.5 server must have at least one supported Network Interface Controller (NIC). A physical NIC is referred to as an uplink port. The network controllers provide network access to the server for remote management purposes as well as network access for the virtual machines. The network ports can be either embedded (on-board) or installed cards. You must only use supported NICs that are listed in the latest VMware hardware compatibility guides.

For more information about supported servers view the Systems Compatibility Guide For ESX Server 3.5 and ESXi version 3.5:

http://www.vmware.com/pdf/vi35_systems_guide.pdf

For more information about supported NICs view the I/O Compatibility Guide For ESX Server 3.5 and ESXi version 3.5:

http://www.vmware.com/pdf/vi35_io_guide.pdf

During the installation process a physical NIC is chosen to provide service console access. Reference Figure 3.14 The Network Configuration Screen in Chapter 3 – ESX 3.5 Server Installation to review the installation screen where the service console NIC is configured. Figure 4.1 shows how to display the server's physical NIC information in the VI Client GUI once the ESX 3.5 server installation has been completed.

Figure 4.1 Network Adapters Configuration

By selecting the Configuration tab and the Network Adapter link in the Hardware section you can examine the NICs identified by POST during the booting of the ESX 3.5 server. Each physical NIC will be displayed with the name vmnic and numbered sequentially. The probing order of the hardware determines which physical NIC is given the vmnic0 designation.

In Figure 4.1 you will also see the following information:

- NIC speed and duplex setting
- Negotiation setting (Auto Negotiate is the default)
- The name of the virtual switch the vmnic is linked to. In Figure 4.1, vmnic0 is linked to the vSwitch0 virtual switch. A NIC can only be assigned to one vSwitch at a time.

- Observed IP ranges - this column depicts what the VMkernel observes as available IP ranges. View this information as just a suggestion from the VMkernel as it can be helpful when creating virtual machine port groups.
- Wake on LAN Supported - This column states whether or not the physical NIC card supports the Wake on LAN technology. Wake on LAN allows the ESX server to be placed in standby mode which is a new feature in the ESX 3.5 server product. It can also be used by the new Distributed Power Management (DPM) feature as well.

It is also possible to display PCI slot location from within the service console by using the lspci command as follows:

```
[root@vcpserver01 root]# lspci

00:00.0 Host bridge: ServerWorks CNB20-HE Host Bridge (rev 32)

00:00.1 Host bridge: ServerWorks CNB20-HE Host Bridge

00:00.2 Host bridge: ServerWorks CNB20-HE Host Bridge

00:03.0 VGA compatible controller: ATI Technologies Inc Rage XL (rev 27)

00:04.0 RAID bus controller: Compaq Computer Corporation Smart Array 5i/532 (rev 01)

00:05.0 System peripheral: Compaq Computer Corporation: Unknown device b203 (rev 01)

00:05.2 System peripheral: Compaq Computer Corporation: Unknown device b204 (rev 01)

00:0f.0 ISA bridge: ServerWorks CSB5 South Bridge (rev 93)

00:0f.1 IDE interface: ServerWorks CT8 mainboard (rev 93)

00:0f.2 USB Controller: ServerWorks OSB4/CSB5 OHCI USB Controller (rev 05)

00:0f.3 Host bridge: ServerWorks GCLE Host Bridge

00:11.0 Host bridge: ServerWorks: Unknown device 0101 (rev 05)

00:11.2 Host bridge: ServerWorks: Unknown device 0101 (rev 05)

01:02.0 Ethernet controller: Broadcom Corporation NetXtreme BCM5703 Gigabit Ethernet (rev 02)

04:02.0 Ethernet controller: Broadcom Corporation NetXtreme BCM5703 Gigabit Ethernet (rev 02)
```

You can obtain NIC port information using the service console ethtool as follows:

```
[root@vcpserver01 root]# ethtool vmnic0

Settings for vmnic0:

Supported ports: [ MII ]

Supported link modes: 10baseT/Half 10baseT/Full

100baseT/Half 100baseT/Full

1000baseT/Half 1000baseT/Full

Supports auto-negotiation: Yes
```

Advertised link modes: 10baseT/Half 10baseT/Full

100baseT/Half 100baseT/Full

1000baseT/Half 1000baseT/Full

Advertised auto-negotiation: Yes

Speed: 1000Mb/s

Duplex: Full

Port: Twisted Pair

PHYAD: 1

Transceiver: internal

Auto-negotiation: on

Supports Wake-on: g

Wake-on: g

Current message level: 0x000000ff (255)

Link detected: yes

The server can support (by type) up to 26 e100 (100 Mbit) NICs. It can support up to 32 e1000 (1 Gbit) NICs or up to 20 Broadcom (1 Gbit) NICs.

Virtual Switches

Virtual switches facilitate the connection between the ESX 3.5 server's virtual networks and the physical switched network. The idea here is that a virtual switch is the software representation of a hardware switch. The controller of the virtual switch operations is the VMkernel. As such, the VMkernel requires CPU cycles to conduct its virtual switching functionality. Depending on the workloads of applications running within virtual machines, contention for CPU cycles may arise that directly affect the performance of virtual machine network Input/Output (I/O). We will discuss the performance aspects of virtualization in chapter 11 - Resource Optimization. As discussed later in this chapter, user settings can affect the VMkernel and how it controls network traffic. Specifically, setting that influences how the VMkernel directs the flow of outbound traffic, enforcement of security policies, load balancing methods and more. These user settings are dependent upon the type of virtual switch to be configured. Virtual switches are commonly categorized in the following three configurations:

- Internal Virtual Switch - This is a virtual switch that does not have a physical uplink port attached to it. This type of virtual switch is useful when keeping unnecessary traffic off of the physical network. Another use for an internal vSwitch is to put the network transmissions of protected applications off of the physical wire. By configuring a virtual machine to only access an internal vSwitch you in effect are putting all of its network traffic "off the wire". Internal vSwitches also are very useful for isolating traffic in a test and development environment.

- Virtual Switch with one physical NIC uplink port - This is simply a virtual switch that is configured with a single physical uplink port attached to it. The downside to such a configuration is that there is no fail over capabilities in the event the single physical NIC fails.
- Virtual Switch with more than one physical NIC uplink port - This type of virtual switch configuration is referred to as a NIC team. A virtual switch configured with multiple physical uplink ports provides for fail over and load balancing capabilities. We will discuss NIC teams later in this chapter.

In some aspects, physical and virtual switches are similar. For example, both physical and virtual switches look up the destination of each frame when it is received. However, the VMkernel does not build its Content Addressable Memory (CAM) table from directly observable traffic; hence, it is more secure than its physical counterpart. There are several common capabilities of physical Ethernet switches that are not provided by virtual switches.

Protocol Support on Virtual Switches

Not all network protocols are supported in the virtual infrastructure. We will examine the following protocols to see if they are or are not supported and the interaction of the protocols with the virtual switch technology:

- Spanning Tree Protocol (STP)
- VLAN Trunking Protocol (VTP)
- Dynamic Trunking Protocol (DTP)
- Inter-Switch Linking Protocol (ISL)
- Port Aggregation Control Protocol (PAgP)
- Link Aggregation Control Protocol (LACP)
- Cisco Discovery Protocol (CDP)

Spanning Tree Protocol

Virtual switches do not support the use of the Spanning Tree Protocol (STP). Nor do they need to as virtual switches are configured in a single tier topology. Redundant loops are not possible within the same virtual switch. STP is used in physical switched networks to avoid redundant network loops. Such loops if they exist can cause broadcast packets to endlessly traverse the network causing the available bandwidth to be consumed. STP can place a switch port in one of the following five states:

- blocking
- listening
- learning
- forwarding
- disabled

STP initially places a port in the blocking state, then the listening state followed by the learning state. Approximately 30 seconds is spent in total while transitioning between the listening and learning states. Fifteen seconds for each state. The learning state allows the switch port to discover which MAC addresses live off the port. If STP discovers a redundant loop, the port will be placed into blocking mode.

As we will see later in this chapter, it is possible to have multiple physical NICs linked to one virtual switch for load balancing and network fail over. In such a configuration, it is possible to have more than one of the physical NICs coming from the ESX server connected to the same physical Ethernet switch. This could cause a problem when STP is configured on those ports as the physical switch may see the same MAC address being received on two different switch ports. STP may place one of the ports in blocking mode in an attempt to prevent a redundant loop. If one of the ports is being used by the standby NIC on the ESX server and a fail over occurs, the fail over port may already be in a blocking state. This would introduce network latency to the virtual machines during ESX NIC fail over.

To alleviate this problem, either disable STP on the physical Ethernet switch ports that are connected to the ESX server or place these ports on the physical switch in PortFast mode. PortFast does not disable STP. It is typically used on Ethernet switch ports that are connected to a single end node, such as a workstation or server not performing any routing functions. These end nodes are often referred to as leaf nodes. Since a leaf node is typically not going to introduce a network loop, PortFast mode can be used on these ports as it will skip the initial blocking, listening and learning states and go directly to the forwarding state.

VLAN Trunking Protocol and Dynamic Trunking Protocol

Some widely used trunking protocols such as VLAN Trunking Protocol (VTP) and Dynamic Trunking Protocol (DTP) are not supported on virtual switches. Cisco's VTP is a proprietary layer 2 messaging protocol used to share VLAN information between switches. Typical administrative tasks such as adding, deleting and renaming VLANs throughout the network can be performed to reduce network administration. DTP is also a Cisco proprietary layer 2 protocol used to establish a trunking link between two switches. Trunk links are used to enable Virtual Local Area Network (VLAN) traffic across physical switches. Multiple VLANs can be used over the same trunk port. The trunk port adds a VLAN ID tag to identify which VLAN the Ethernet frame is a associated with. DTP, if so configured, can automatically establish trunking ports.

Inter-Switch Linking Protocol

It is also not possible to link two virtual switches together using Inter-Switch Linking protocol (ISL). ISL is another Cisco proprietary protocol. It operates at the Data Link layer of the Open Systems Interconnection (OSI) reference model and is used as an encapsulation method for the transport of VLAN traffic. Virtual switches do support the use of the IEEE 802.1q standard, often referred to as VLAN tagging. 802.1q will allow a virtual switch to tag an Ethernet frame prior to being sent upstream to the physical switched port. However, 802.1q does not link two virtual switches together. The only method available to link two virtual switches together is by configuring a virtual machine with two virtual NICs, often referred to as a multi-homed configuration. Each virtual NIC can be linked to one of the two virtual switches. For example, a virtual machine running an operating system such as Linux can act as a bridge between the two virtual switches.

Port Aggregation Control Protocol and Link Aggregation Control Protocol

Virtual switches do not support Port Aggregation Control Protocol (PAgP). This protocol is used when defining Fast EtherChannel capable ports. EtherChannel is used to aggregate several ports to create a logical Ethernet link providing higher bandwidth and fault tolerance. PAgP packets can be used on physical switches to allow the automatic forming of EtherChannel links. The Link Aggregation Control Protocol (LACP) is similar to PAgP in that it is used to form the creation of channel links. It is also not available on virtual switches.

We can use the service console CLI or the VI Client GUI to gather information about the current virtual switch configurations. Figure 4.2 shows the virtual switch configurations. It can be accessed by selecting the Networking link in the Hardware section.

Figure 4.2 Networking Configuration

The virtual switch information displayed in Figure 4.2 shows that currently only one vSwitch is configured on the server. The vSwitch label is vSwitch0. This virtual switch was created during the ESX server's installation. Virtual switches when created are numbered sequentially. Therefore the next virtual switch created will have the label of vSwitch1 and so on. We can see that vSwitch0 is using vmnic0 and that the NIC is configured to operate at 1,000 Mbits/sec using a Full Duplex connection. The virtual switch contains one port labeled "Service Console". This port is created during the ESX 3.5 server installation and is used as the management interface. Service console ports are denoted as vswif#. As with virtual switches, vswif ports are numbered starting with 0 (zero) and sequentially numbered thereafter.

Virtual Switch Properties

When a new virtual switch is created, by default it is given 64 ports. Of these 64 ports, only 56 are usable ports. There are 8 ports created for every virtual switch that are exclusively used by the VMkernel for management purposes. Since these 8 additional ports are not displayed in the GUI and are not usable by the ESX administrator, it is correct to say there are 56 ports available for every new virtual switch. However, these 8 additional ports can be seen by issuing the esxcfg-vswitch command from the ESX server's CLI as follows:

[root@vcpserver01 root]# esxcfg-vswitch -l

Switch Name Num Ports Used Ports Configured Ports MTU Uplinks

vSwitch0 64 5 64 1500 vmnic0

PortGroup Name VLAN ID Used Ports Uplinks

Service Console 0 1 vmnic0

In the "Num Ports" column in the output of the esxcfg-vswitch command, there are 64 ports displayed for vSwitch0.

You can access the virtual switch configuration within the VI Client by selecting the Properties link to the right of the vSwitch information. Figure 4.3 shows the Properties window for vSwitch0.

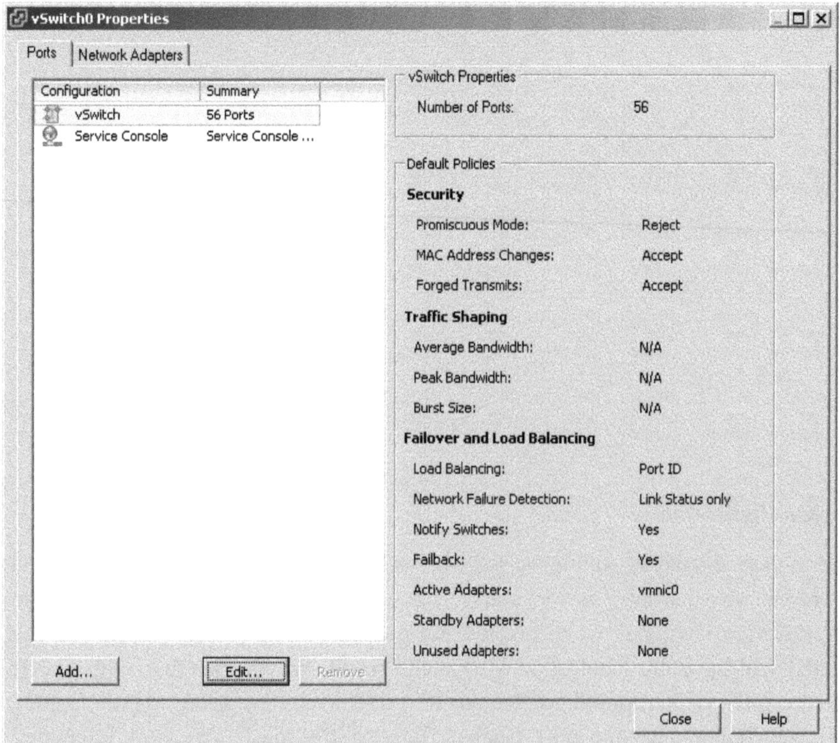

Figure 4.3 Virtual Switch Properties Dialog Box

By clicking on the vSwitch icon in the Configuration column within the Ports tab as shown in Figure 4.3, you can display the current virtual switch configuration information for the vSwitch. The right hand pane displays the vSwitch Properties section where the available number of ports is shown. The Default Policies section displays the virtual switches default settings. These default settings can be modified by selecting the Edit button as shown in Figure 4.3.

Selecting the Edit button will launch the vSwitch Properties dialog box as shown in Figure 4.4. There are four configuration tabs in this dialog box that can be used to modify the default settings of the virtual switch. In Figure 4.4, the General tab is displayed. By selecting the drop down menu you can configure the vSwitch with as few as 8 available ports up to as many as 1016 ports. Modifying the value will require that the ESX server be rebooted in order for the change to take affect. As mentioned earlier, 56 ports is the default available ports when creating a virtual switch from the VI Client. This number of ports should be sufficient in most cases. A virtual switch port whether used or not requires the use of system resources for each port. Only select a higher value of virtual switch ports if needed in order to avoid wasting unnecessary system resources.

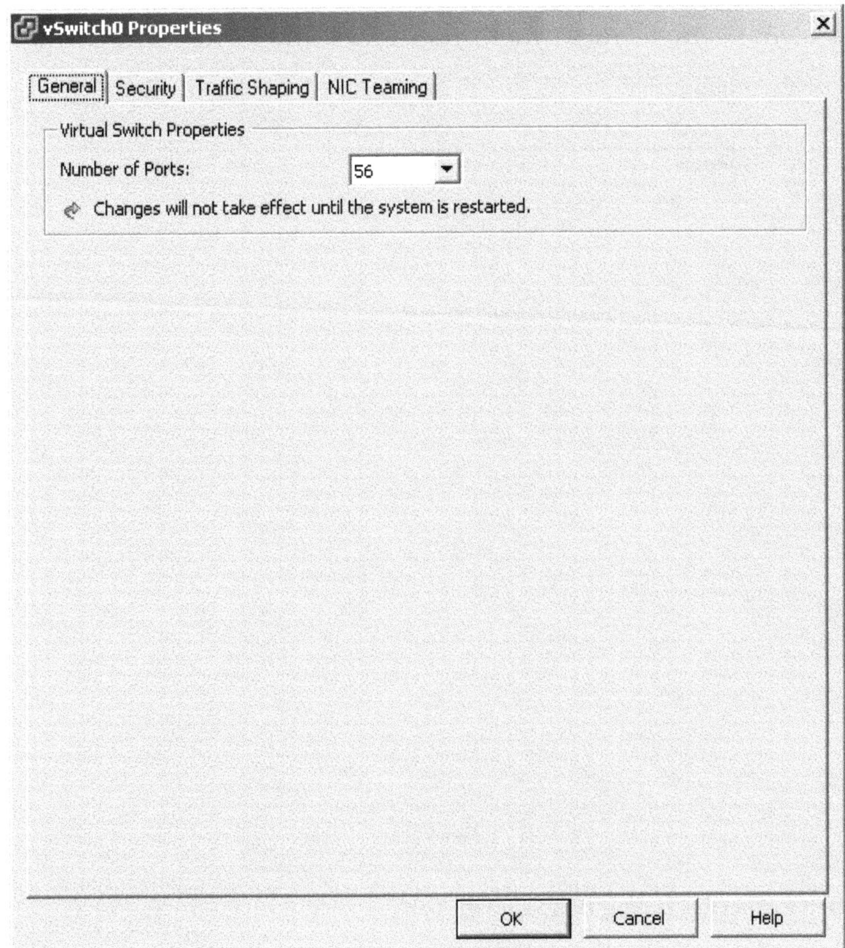

Figure 4.4 Virtual Switch Properties Dialog Box General Tab

Creating a virtual switch from the service console CLI allows the ESX administrator to set a value other than the default of 56 ports. The esxcfg-vswitch command can be used to create virtual switches. The number of ports can be selected as well during the creation of the virtual switch as follows: [root@vcpserver01 root]# esxcfg-vswitch -a vSwitch1:24

This command will create a virtual switch labeled "vSwitch1" with 24 available ports.

The Security tab as shown in Figure 4.5 allows an ESX administrator to set security policies for the virtual switch. The settings are:

- Promiscuous Mode

- MAC Address Changes
- Forged Transmits

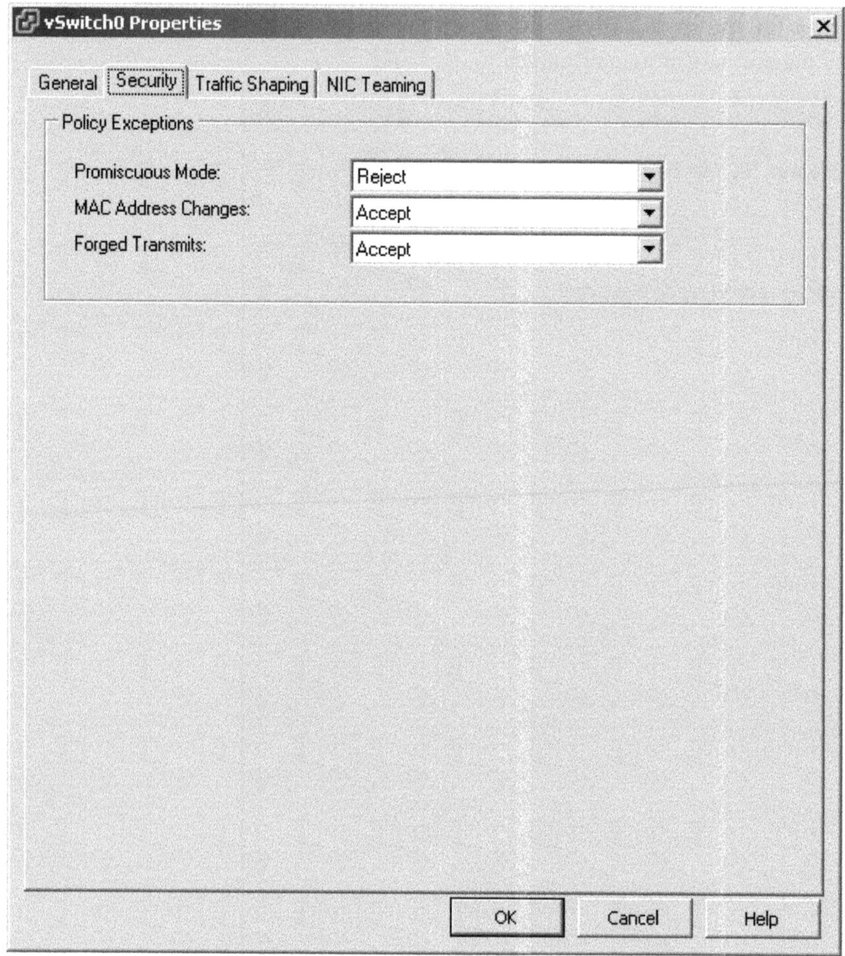

Figure 4.5 Virtual Switch Properties Dialog Box Security Tab

Promiscuous Mode

These settings allow a higher level of control over certain security vulnerabilities for virtual machines than is possible with physical machines. For example, suppose we have two identical Linux systems in use, one is a physical machine while the other is a virtual machine. If an attacker is able to gain root access to our physical Linux system, this would not only jeopardize this system but other systems on the network as well. Root access on a Linux/UNIX system is the equivalent to the Administrator account on a Windows system. Once root access is obtained on our physical system, the attacker could place the system's physical NIC into promiscuous mode. This mode allows a NIC to receive all traffic on the network that it can see. This is often referred to as snooping the network.

In contrast, if our virtual Linux box was attacked and root access was obtained, the attacker could still place the virtual NIC in promiscuous mode. However, as we can see in Figure 4.5, the default for a virtual switch is to reject promiscuous mode. This setting instructs the VMkernel to drop any packets to a virtual NIC that do not contain that virtual NICs MAC address. Thus preventing the attacker from snooping the network. There are times when changing the promiscuous mode value to accept is useful. An example of this would be if an ESX administrator is performing intrusion detection or vulnerability tests on the network

MAC Address Changes

A virtual machine's NIC is assigned a unique MAC address by the VMkernel. This value can be modified either by the ESX administrator via the virtual machine properties dialog box or the virtual machines configuration file. In chapter 7 - Virtual Machines, we will discuss virtual machine settings in more detail. When a virtual machine is powered on, the MAC address of it's virtual NIC(s) is considered the source MAC address. In other words, the MAC address assigned at the time the virtual machine was powered on. Operating systems can allow modification of MAC addresses. When a MAC address has been changed from within the guest operating system, this new MAC address becomes the effective MAC address.

By default, the VMkernel accepts the modification of MAC addresses from the source MAC address to the effective MAC address. The MAC Address Changes setting will allow a guest operating system that has altered it's source MAC address within a virtual machine to receive frames for the effective MAC address. The default setting of accept allows MAC impersonation to occur. If this default behavior is undesirable, it should be sent to reject. However, this setting is useful for some load balancing and test and development configurations.

Forged Transmits

Forged Transmits allows the transmission of frames from a guest operating system using a different MAC address other than the source MAC address (i.e. the effective MAC address.) This setting is set to accept by default. One common use of this setting is with Microsoft Network Load Balancing (NLB.) NLB is used to load balance network requests across a group of servers, for example, database or web servers. NLB is available in all versions of Windows Server 2003. It tricks the switch into sending frames for a given MAC address (the NLB cluster MAC address) to all stations on the subnet. This is accomplished by spoofing the source MAC address in the Address Resolution Replies (ARP) replies. NLB can be configured in either unicast or multicast mode.

When using unicast mode, it is necessary to set both MAC address changes and forged transmits to accept as well as disable switch notification. One of the uses for switch notification is in fault tolerant configurations. Enabling this setting will notify the physical switch when a fail over occurs to a standby uplink port. The notification consists of sending an ARP request in order to notify the switch that the virtual NIC MAC addresses will now be sent to a different port on the physical switch. This process can reduce network latency during a fail over event. However, doing so will break an NLB cluster as the ARP will now expose the source MAC address of each virtual machine in the NLB cluster. VMware recommends using multicast mode instead. An ARP entry for the multicast MAC address of the NLB cluster will need to be added to the ARP table of the switch. The benefit of using Multicast mode is that it places less of a load on the network switches.

Traffic Shaping Policy

It may be necessary at some time to decrease the allowed network bandwidth of a virtual machine. The need may arise in situations where a rogue application whether deliberate or not is saturating the physical uplink port NIC. It may also be necessary to limit network bandwidth or simulate limited network bandwidth in a test and development environment. In such cases, the traffic shaping policy as shown in Figure 4.6 can be utilized to accomplish this.

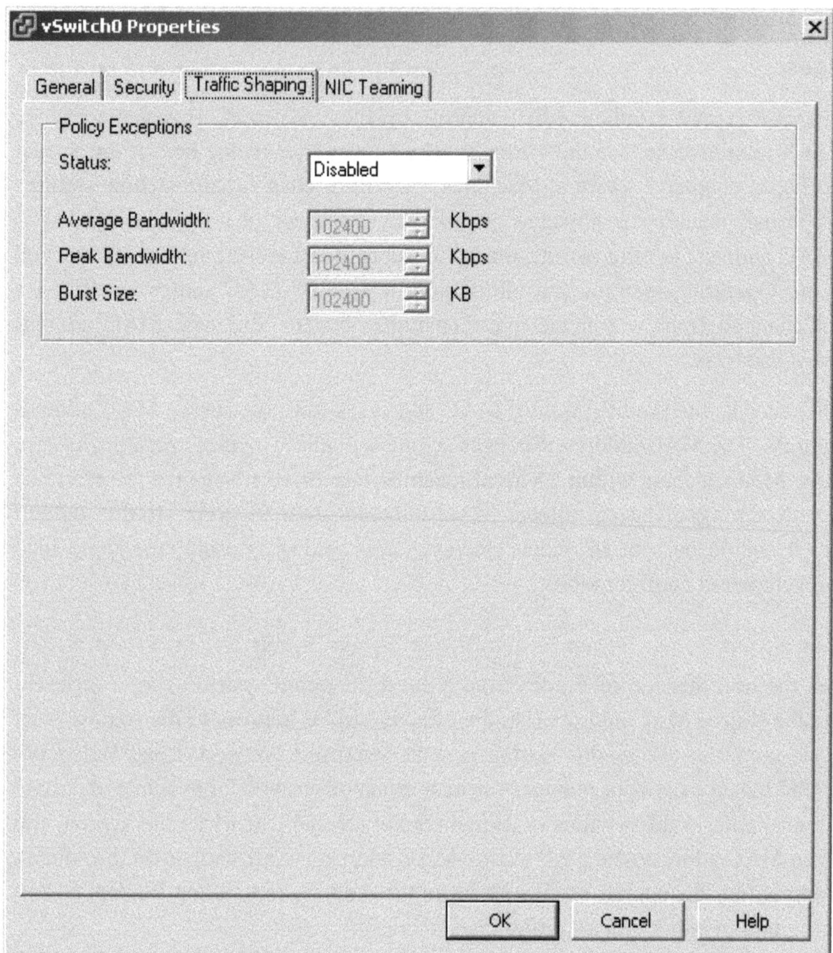

Figure 4.6 Virtual Switch Properties Dialog Box Traffic Shaping Tab

The default setting for traffic shaping is disabled for the virtual switch. Select the Status drop down box and set it to Enabled to configure the traffic shaping policy. Within computing environments in general, there are two primary methods to implement traffic shaping, leaky bucket and token bucket. With the leaky bucket algorithm, a hard limit on the transmission rate is set. VMware uses the token bucket algorithm. In this method, a certain amount of burst traffic is allowed imposing a limit on the average data transmission. The following are the configurable settings:

- Average Bandwidth (Kbps) - This is the allowed average load. This load is determined by the number of bits per second allowed to traverse the virtual switch averaged over a period of time.
- Peak Bandwidth (Kbps) - This value sets the maximum number of bits allowed in a burst. If a burst is larger than this setting the packets are queued and transmitted later. However, once

the queue becomes full, all incoming packets will be dropped.

- Burst Size (KB) - This is the maximum bandwidth capacity a virtual switch can handle. Note, this is the only value out of the three traffic shaping policy settings that is set in Kilo Bytes. Once this value is reached, incoming packets are queued. If the queue becomes full, all incoming packets will be dropped.

NIC Teaming

A NIC team is formed by associating more than one physical NIC port to a virtual switch. Creating a NIC team will be discussed later in this chapter. The NIC teaming tab shown in Figure 4.7 allows for several types of configuration options as follows:

- Load Balancing
- Network Failover Detection
- Notify Switches
- Failback
- Failover Order

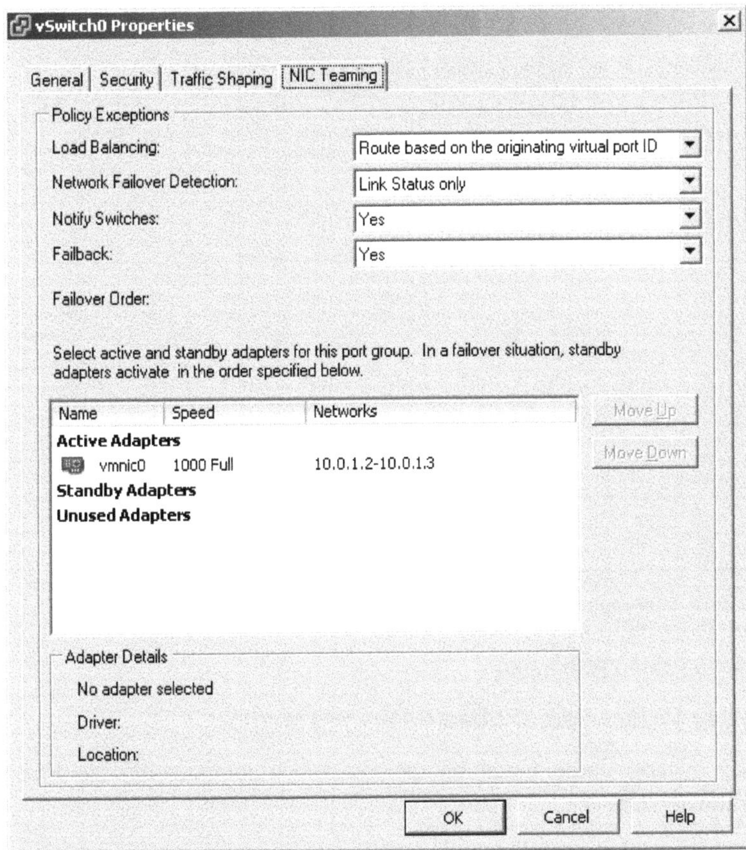

Figure 4.7 Virtual Switch Properties Dialog Box NIC Teaming Tab

Load Balancing

Load Balancing can be performed using the following methods as shown in Figure 4.8:

- Route based on the originating virtual port ID (Default)
- Route based on IP hash
- Route based on source MAC hash
- Use explicit failover order

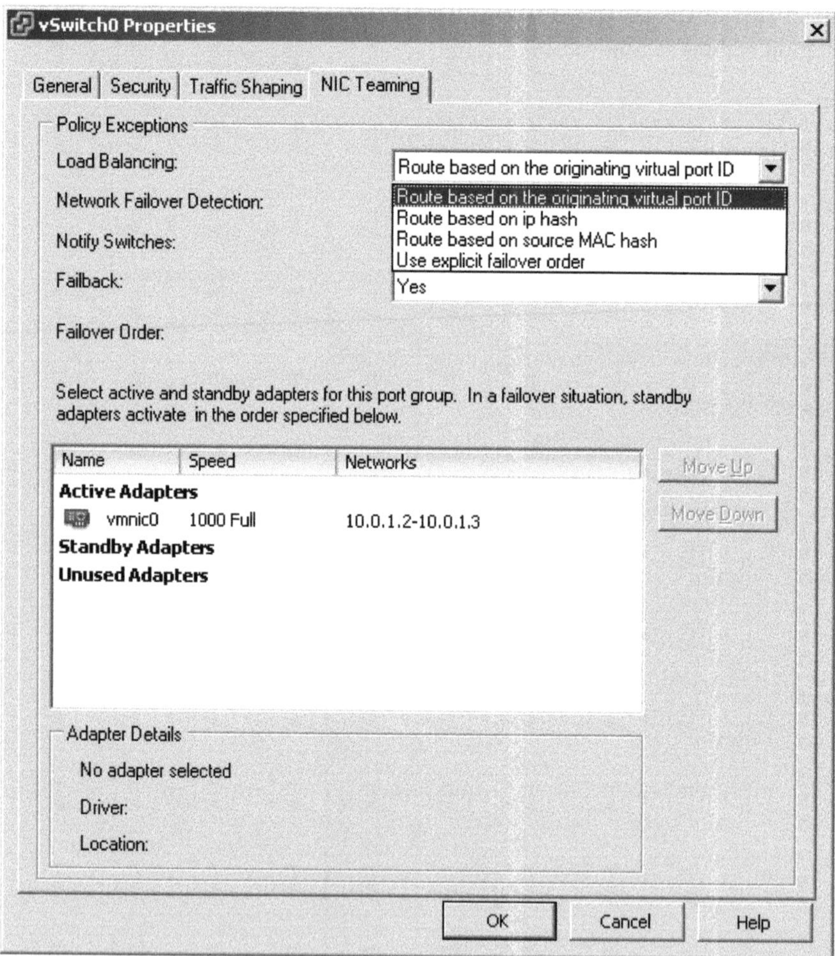

Figure 4.8 Virtual Switch Properties Load Balancing

Route Based on the Originating Virtual Port ID Load Balancing Method

With the default load balancing method, route based on originating virtual port ID, the load distribution is calculated in the following manner:

virtual port ID number % number of physical NIC ports in the ESX server equals the physical NIC port to use

In the above expression, the % is the modulo operator where we are finding the remainder. So if we have a virtual port ID of 4 and 3 physical NICs in the system numbered 0, 1 and 2, the VMkernel will send the packet out of the second uplink adapter, adapter number 1 as follows.

4 % 3 = 1

This method of load balancing more closely resembles load distribution in that the calculation will always be the same unless one of the values in the calculation changes. Virtual port IDs change when a virtual NIC is disconnected and reconnected to the virtual switch or when the virtual machine is powered off then back on. The calculation would also change if one of the physical ports went down. Otherwise the same physical NIC is used repeatedly for a given virtual NIC. This method incurs little overhead from the VMkernel as it only needs to plug the virtual port ID into the calculation in order to send the network traffic.

Route Based on IP Hash

With the route based on IP hash method, the same algorithm is used as before. With one exception, instead of using the virtual port ID number in the calculation, now the VMkernel will instead use a hash value generated from the source and destination IP address of the packet being sent. In this case, a virtual machine configured as a web server for example, would potentially be able to send packets using all physical NICs configured on the virtual switch. This is possible due to the potential of having a different destination address for the packets. This method is useful for circumstances where it is necessary to meet service level agreements (SLAs), such as is often the case with service providers in a web hosting environment. Note though that this method places an additional load on the ESX server's CPU(s) due to the VMkernel having to interrogate each packet when determining the IP addresses used to create the hash value.

Route Based on Source MAC Hash

Using route based on source MAC hash is once again similar to the previous two methods in that it utilizes the same algorithm. In this method, a hash value generated from the least significant byte (LSB) of the MAC address is used instead of the virtual port ID. The down side to this method is that the MAC address doesn't change when disconnecting and reconnecting the virtual NIC to the virtual switch. It also does not change when the virtual machine is powered off and on. Therefore, the same virtual NIC will utilize the same physical NIC for network traffic unless the MAC address changes or a physical NIC fails. In addition, if multiple virtual NICs happen to have the same LSB, then they will all use the same uplink port.

Explicit Failover Order

Using an explicit failover order simply uses the physical NIC that is listed at the top of the active adapters list. In Figure 4.8, there is only one active adapter therefore the Move Up and Move Down buttons are disabled. When there are multiple active adapters as we will see later on in this chapter, these two buttons can be used to move a physical NIC up or down in the list.

Network Failover Detection

As depicted in Figure 4.9, two options exist for network failover detection:

- Link Status Only

- Beacon Probing

Link Status Only

With link status only, the ESX 3.5 server simply checks to see whether or not the status of the physical NIC is up or down. A failure is detected if the link is detected as being down. The limitation of this method of failure detection is that it only see either the ESX's physical NIC or the switch port connected to the ESX physical NIC. Upstream failures cannot be detected. This method is more useful when using it in conjunction with link state tracking. Link state tracking is available on some Cisco switches and allows upstream failures to be detected. When an upstream failure is detected, the downstream links can be disabled all the way to the ESX server.

Beacon Probing

Beacon probing will cause the ESX server to send a 62 byte beacon probe packet about every 10 seconds. This method is similar to a traceroute. It attempts to detect upstream failures or mis-configurations in the switched environment by transmitting the beacon packet to another physical NIC in the NIC team. This method requires two active NICs as one physical NIC sends the beacon probe and another receives it. In order for a two active adapter NIC team to have fail over ability, this method of failure detection requires a third physical NIC configured as a standby NIC.

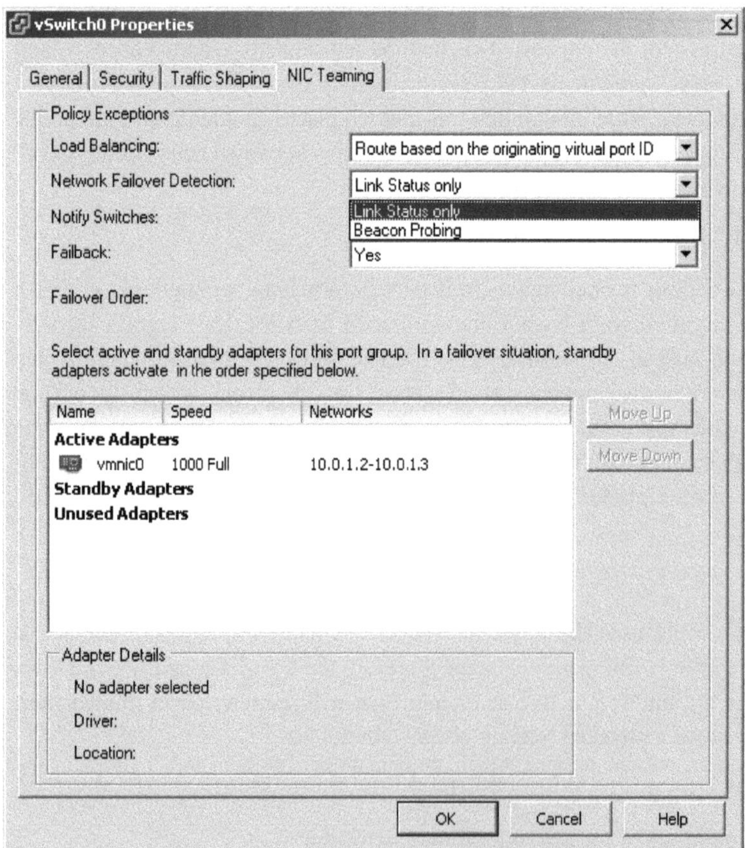

Figure 4.9 Virtual Switch Properties Network Failure Detection

Notify Switches

The notify switches option allows the ESX administrator to control whether or not the physical switch attached to the ESX server is notified via an ARP packet that a fail over event has occurred. Setting this value to Yes will send the ARP packet thereby updating the physical switch's forwarding tables. This behavior can reduce latency during a fail over event. Note however, if using Microsoft NLB, this setting should be set to No. Setting it to No will allow the NLB cluster to continue to function properly as the physical switch will not be able to obtain the individual MAC addresses of the virtual machines in the NLB cluster.

Failback

The failback option controls the rolling behavior of physical NICs in the team that go down and then come back up. For example, with this option set to yes (the default) when the active NIC in the team goes down, the ESX server will begin transmitting packets out the standby NIC. If the physical NIC that failed once again becomes available, the ESX server will begin sending packets out the original active NIC. When this option is set to No and the original active NIC goes down, the standby NIC begins transferring packets and will continue to do so even if the original physical NIC is placed back online.

NIC Teams

A physical NIC can only be assigned exclusively to a single virtual switch at any given time. However, it is possible to have more than one physical NIC assigned to a single virtual switch. Such a configuration is known as a NIC team. The advantage of NIC teaming is that it provides load balancing and fail over capabilities to all of the virtual machines connected to the virtual switch. The NIC teaming tab as shown previously in Figure 4.7, has options that can be set to configure load balancing and fail over order within a NIC team. The following steps can be used to configure a NIC team.

To configure a virtual switch for NIC teaming follow this procedure:

Step 1. Click on the virtual switch Properties link shown in Figure 4.2 to launch the Properties window as shown in Figure 4.10.

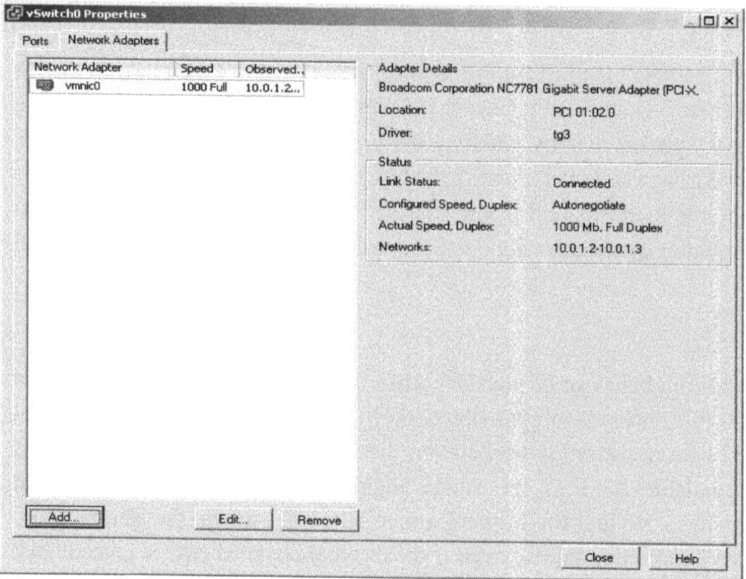

Figure 4.10 Add a Network Adapter To A Virtual Switch

In this example we have selected vSwitch0 and we can see that it is currently configured with one vmnic. The adapter configuration information is displayed to the right of this screen. To add additional physical NICs to this vSwitch click on the Add button on the bottom left of the window to continue.

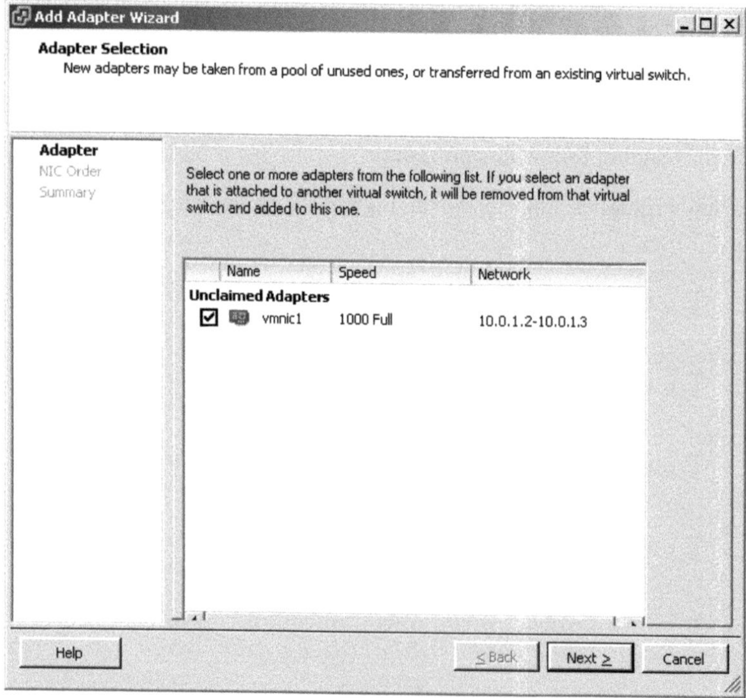

Figure 4.11 Select Network Adapter to Add

Step 2. The Add Adapter Wizard will now launch and display any unclaimed (unused) adapters as shown in Figure 4.11. If more than one adapter is available click in the check box to select the NICs that you want to team on the vSwitch.

Click on the Next button to continue.

Step 3. The next screen in the wizard allows you to determine the failover order as shown in Figure 4.12.

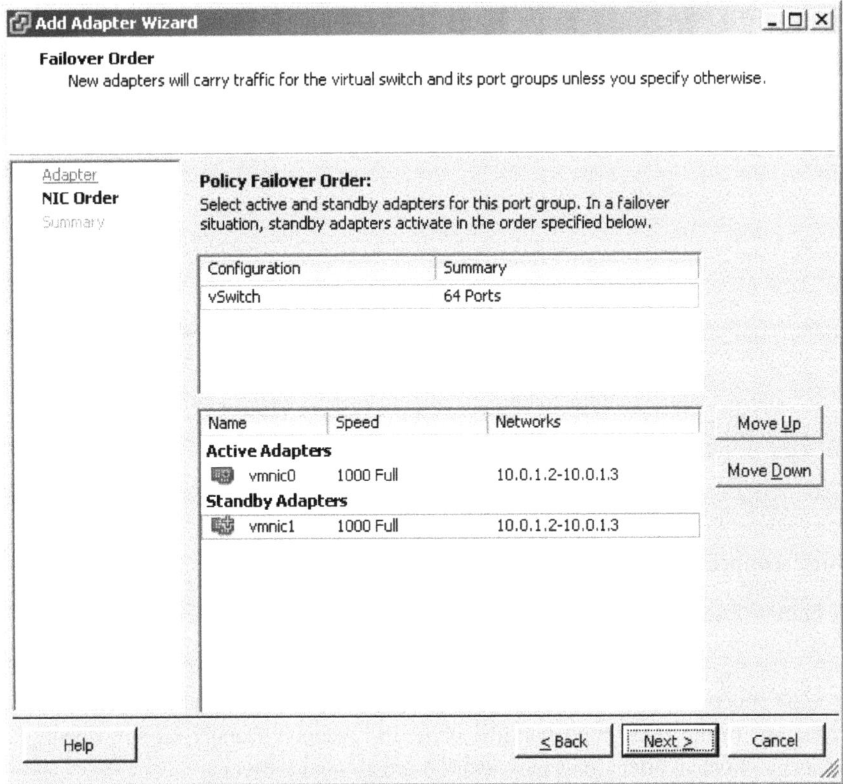

Figure 4.12 Active or Standby Network Adapter

In Figure 4.12, this NIC team will be configured only for fail over purposes. It consists of two NICs, vmnic0 and vmnic1. Since vmnic0 is set as the only active NIC in the team, vmnic1 will serve as the standby NIC and is only activated if vmnic0 experiences a network connectivity failure. As mentioned previously in this chapter, link failure detection is based on link status (optionally with link state tracking) or beacon probes. If additional physical NICs are available, multiple active and standby NICs can be configured in a NIC team. This is accomplished by selecting the appropriate NIC and using the Move Up or Move Down buttons to either place a NIC as active or standby. Once the appropriate active and standby NIC configuration is set, click on the next button to continue.

Step 4. Figure 4.13 shows the summary screen for the wizard.

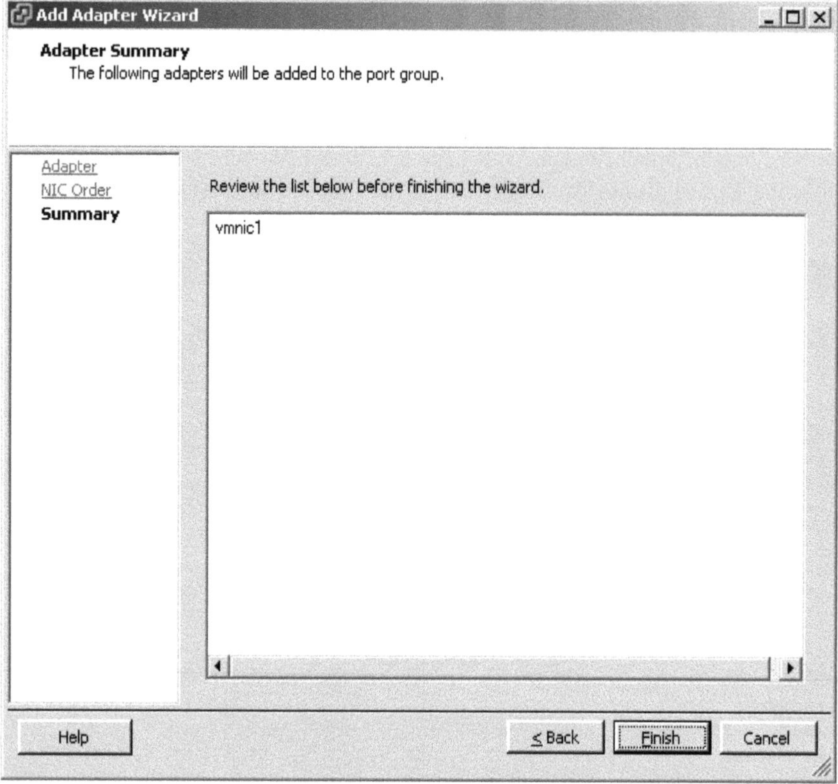

Figure 4.13 Add Network Adapter Summary Dialog Box

You can select the back button if necessary to make changes or click on the Finish button to complete the process.

Figure 4.14 now displays the second adapter within the Network Adapters tab. Select a physical NIC to display adapter information. In the right hand window pane, the Adapter Details section displays the vendor information for the physical NIC along with it's PCI location and driver.

To improve your fault tolerance using NIC teaming do the following:

- Using ports on different NIC cards. Then a single card can't be the point of failure.
- Using two different vendor NICs within a team. This is done so that in the event a driver corruption occurs, it would only affect one of the NICs in the team.
- Placing each NIC in the team on a separate PCI bus (if the server has two multiple buses) to guard against PCI bus failure. A common way to achieve this type of configuration is to utilize an onboard NIC injunction with a NIC placed into a PCI slot.

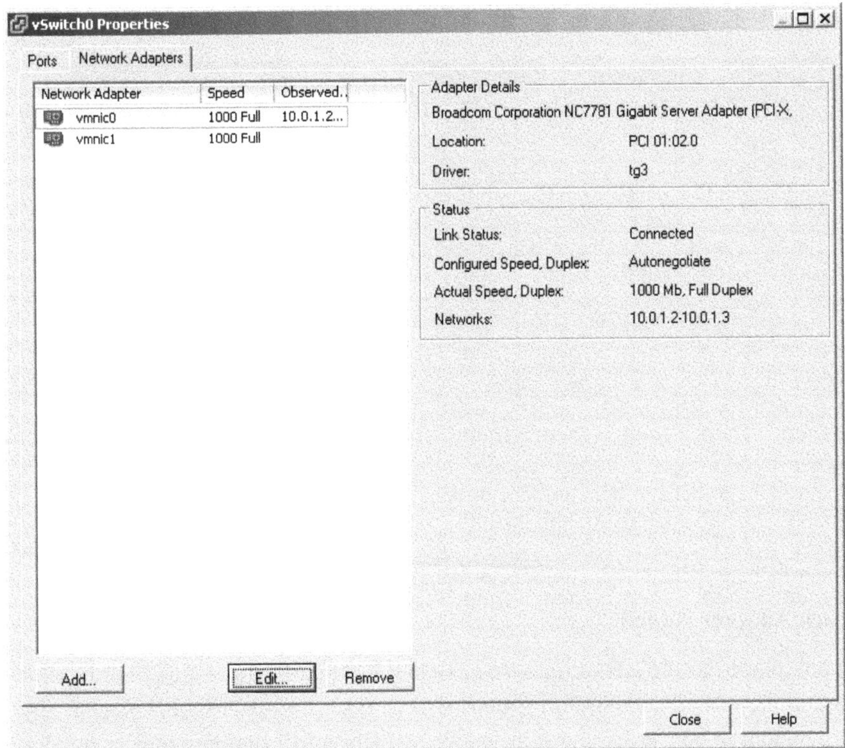

Figure 4.14 Edit Network Adapter

The Status section in the right hand window pane displays the NIC status along with it's configured speed and duplex settings. The default setting for a physical NIC is autonegotiate. Some physical NICs and physical switch port combinations may not automatically negotiate the optimum speed and duplex settings. If this is the case, select the NIC from the list of NICs with the Adapters tab and click on the Edit button. The dialog box in Figure 4.15 will be displayed and can be used to manually set the appropriate speed and duplex settings of the NIC. Be sure that the physical NIC port on the ESX host and the physical switch port are set to the same setting, or there will be limited or no connectivity on the link.

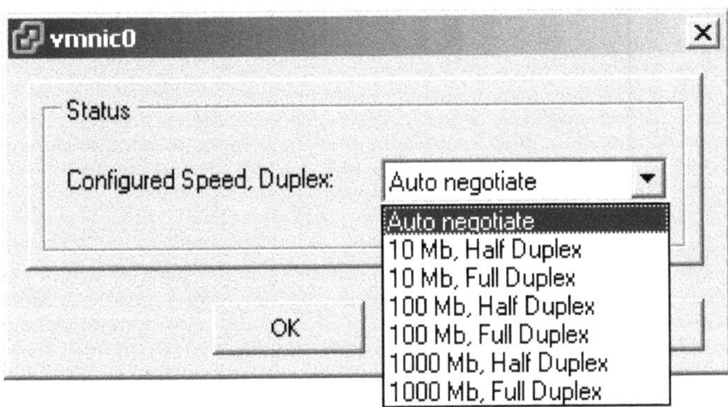

Figure 4.15 Network Adapter Speed and Duplex Settings

The VI Client network settings screen displays the vSwitch0 virtual switch now configured as a NIC team as shown in Figure 4.16.

Figure 4.16 New Network Adapter Added

The rectangular shaped box placed to the left of the virtual switch in Figure 4.16 is a call out box for the port groups contained in the virtual switch. Port groups will be discussed later in this chapter. By selecting this call out box, a dialog box is displayed as shown in Figure 4.17 that provides as a quick method of reviewing the settings defined within the virtual switch without having to open the virtual switch properties dialog box.

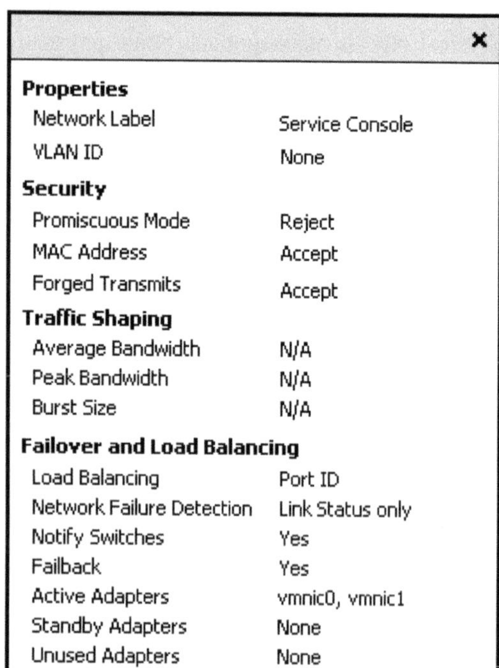

Properties	
Network Label	Service Console
VLAN ID	None
Security	
Promiscuous Mode	Reject
MAC Address	Accept
Forged Transmits	Accept
Traffic Shaping	
Average Bandwidth	N/A
Peak Bandwidth	N/A
Burst Size	N/A
Failover and Load Balancing	
Load Balancing	Port ID
Network Failure Detection	Link Status only
Notify Switches	Yes
Failback	Yes
Active Adapters	vmnic0, vmnic1
Standby Adapters	None
Unused Adapters	None

Figure 4.17 Port or Port Group Information Pop Up Box

The call out boxes to the right of the virtual switch are available for each physical NIC in the team. Select the call out box to display the Cisco Discovery Protocol (CDP) information as shown in Figure 4.18. CDP is used in Cisco switched networks so that switches can share information about themselves to each other. This is done by sending advertisement broadcasts that occur once every minute. The call out box displays information for the physical switch port connected to the virtual switch's physical NIC. The Cisco switch displays information such as its hardware platform, software version, device ID and timeout value. CDP has the following four possible modes:

- Down - This mode disables CDP
- Listen - This mode only enables the ESX server to detect and display the connected Cisco switch port information
- Advertise - This mode sends ESX server information to the Cisco switch but does not detect or display Cisco switch information
- Both - This mode performs all the functionality of both the Listen and Advertise modes

By default, an ESX 3.5 server is in CDP listen mode. However, note that if using either Advertise or Both modes, the ESX server will display to the Cisco switch its uplink name, hostname and ESX build number. This could be a potential security risk if an attacker is able to discover the ESX build number as it allows an attacker to know if there are any known vulnerabilities with that particular build number.

To display the current CDP mode for a virtual switch, from the service console command line, use the esxcfg-vswitch command. The following is an example of obtaining the CDP mode of vSwitch0:

```
[root@vcpserver01 root]# esxcfg-vswitch -b vSwitch0
listen
```

To change the CDP mode to use the Both mode for vSwitch0, issue the following command:

```
esxcfg-vswitch -B both vSwitch0
```

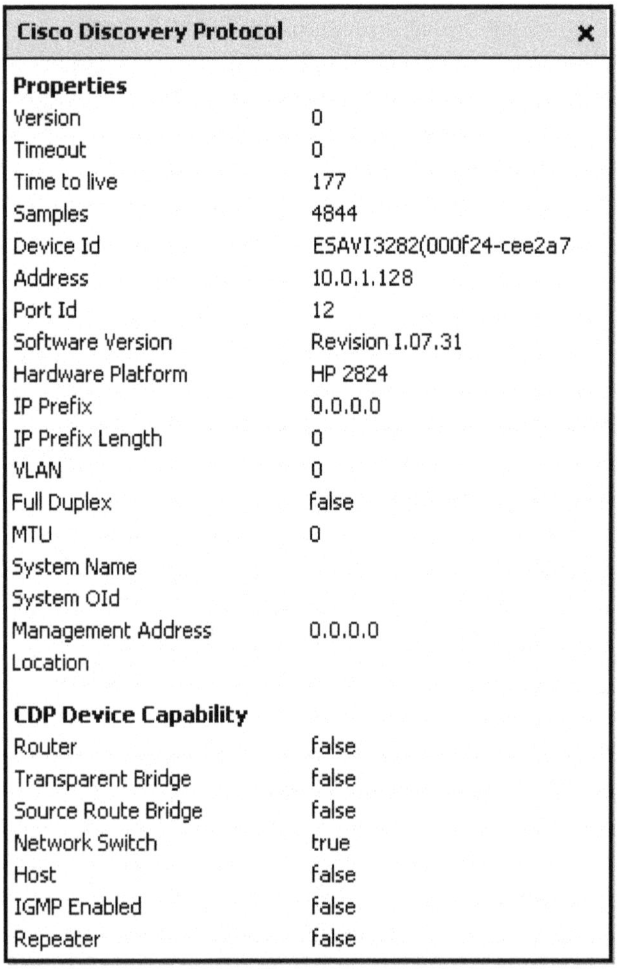

Cisco Discovery Protocol	
Properties	
Version	0
Timeout	0
Time to live	177
Samples	4844
Device Id	ESAVI3282(000f24-cee2a7
Address	10.0.1.128
Port Id	12
Software Version	Revision I.07.31
Hardware Platform	HP 2824
IP Prefix	0.0.0.0
IP Prefix Length	0
VLAN	0
Full Duplex	false
MTU	0
System Name	
System OId	
Management Address	0.0.0.0
Location	
CDP Device Capability	
Router	false
Transparent Bridge	false
Source Route Bridge	false
Network Switch	true
Host	false
IGMP Enabled	false
Repeater	false

Figure 4.18 Virtual Switch Cisco Discovery Protocol Information Pop Up Box

In order to remove (unlink) a physical NIC from a virtual switch using the VI Client, select the NIC from the Network Adapters tab and click on the Remove button as shown in Figure 4.19.

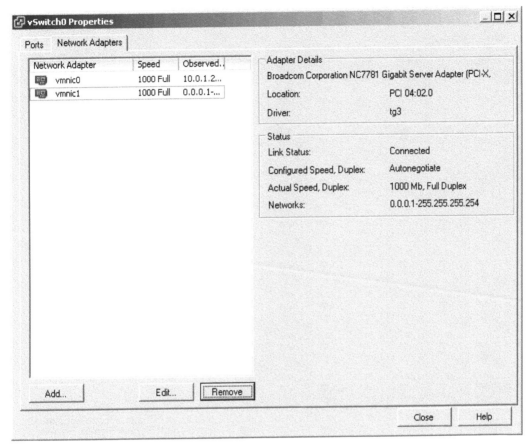

Figure 4.19 Select Network Adapter to Remove From Virtual Switch

The Confirm Remove dialog box is displayed as shown in Figure 4.20. To remove the NIC from the team select the Yes button.

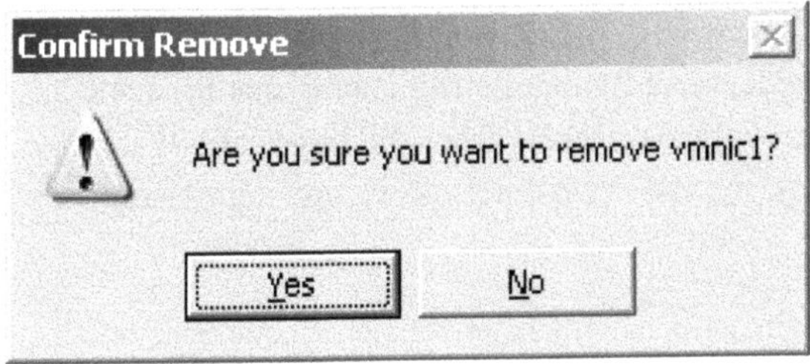

Figure 4.20 Confirm Network Adapter Removal from Virtual Switch

The NIC has been removed as shown in Figure 4.21. We will see later in this chapter how to link a physical NIC to a virtual switch and unlink the physical NIC using the service console CLI. Knowing how to perform these operations using the CLI is very useful when scripting such operations in a test and development environment or when creating unattended installation files as discussed in Chapter 3 – ESX 3.5 Server Installation.

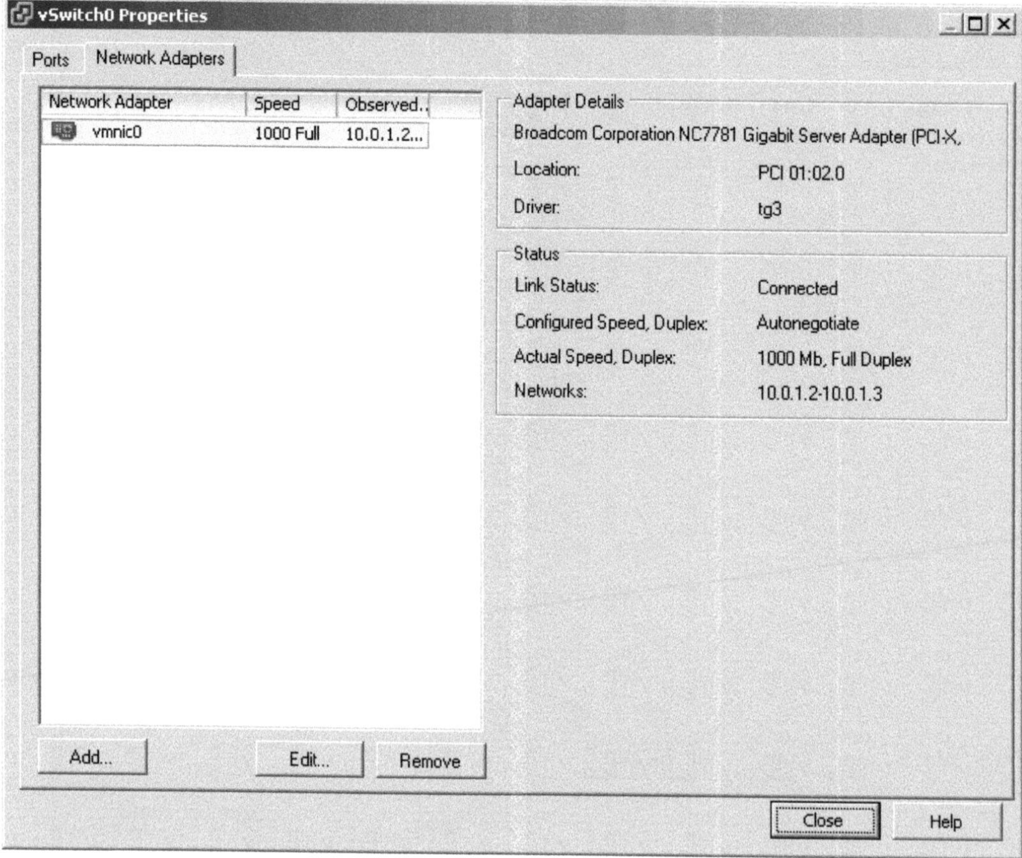

Figure 4.21 Network Adapter Removed from Virtual Switch

Reverse Teaming

An ESX 3.5 server does not act as a router. When it sends packets out of a physical NIC, it will only receive the corresponding packets on the same physical NIC. It will not forward packets to other physical NICs within the team. This is referred to as Reverse Teaming. The idea is that the ESX 3.5 server will prevent virtual machines from receiving duplicate packets from the physical NICs in the team. Reverse teaming is performed automatically by the VMkernel. It is not administratively configurable.

Virtual Switch Connection Types

Virtual switches, like their physical counterparts have switch ports available for use. Physical switches can have different types of ports such as access ports and trunk ports. Virtual switches too have different types of ports. There are three connection types of virtual switch ports:

- Service console port
- VMkernel port
- Virtual machine port groups

Service Console Port

A service console port is created during the installation of the ESX server. It connects a virtual switch to the service console management interface. During the installation process, vSwitch0 is the virtual switch that contains the service console port that provides access to the physical network. For security reasons, it is good practice to assign the service console physical NIC(s) to a private network. This is ideal as physical separation makes attacks against the management service console more difficult. If this is not possible, at least try to place the service console port within its own VLAN to isolate its management traffic.

For fault tolerant purposes, place the service console port on a virtual switch that is configured as a NIC team. Each NIC in the team should be connected to a separate physical switch to avoid a single point of failure, but same broadcast domain. If a NIC team configuration is not possible, a second service console port can be created on another virtual switch to provide redundancy. In such a configuration, try once again to at least place the service console it its own VLAN and be sure to connect the physical NICs being utilized by each service console port to a separate physical switch.

Service console ports are displayed with the VI Client and the service console CLI with a vswif designation. The service console port created during the installation of the ESX server was placed on vSwitch0 and is identified as vswif0. Any additional service console ports on virtual switches on the server will be numbered sequentially (i.e. vswif1, vswif2, etc.) The service console uses its own separate TCP/IP stack. As a result, it uses its own routing table. The ping command so commonly used is available from the service console to identify IP connectivity issues. To view the service console's routing table, issue either the netstat or route commands as follows:

[root@vcpserver01 root]# netstat -rn

Kernel IP routing table

Destination Gateway Genmask Flags MSS Window irtt Iface

10.0.1.0 0.0.0.0 255.255.255.0 U 0 0 0 vswif0

10.0.2.0 0.0.0.0 255.255.0.0 U 0 0 0 vswif0

0.0.0.0 10.0.1.1 0.0.0.0 UG 0 0 0 vswif0

Executing the "route -n" command produces the exact same output as the above "netstat -rn" command.

VMkernel Port

A VMkernel port is used for several purposes. VMware's VMotion technology allows a powered on virtual machine to be reassigned to another ESX 3.5 server without being powered off. In order for the VMotion process to occur, one of the configuration requirements is the virtual switch that the virtual machine is connected to must be configured with a VMkernel port. The VMkernel port must be enabled for VMotion and only one VMkernel port per ESX 3.5 server can be enabled for VMotion.

VMkernel ports can also be used when the ESX 3.5 server is accessing IP based storage, such as iSCSI SANs and NFS servers. The VMkernel itself contains its own TCP/IP stack that is separate from the service console's TCP/IP stack. The VMkernel also has its own routing table. The esxcfg-route command can be used as follows to display the VMkernel routing table:

[root@vcpserver01 root]# esxcfg-route

VMkernel default gateway is 10.0.1.1

[root@vcpserver01 root]# esxcfg-route -l

VMkernel Routes:

Network Netmask Gateway

10.0.1.0 255.255.255.0 Local Subnet

default 0.0.0.0 10.0.1.1

In addition, the following command can be issued to view the VMkernel routing information:

cat /proc/vmware/net/tcpip/ifconfig

The cat command can be used to display the contents of files. The /proc filesystem contains files that represent the current state of the system. By using the /proc filesystem. both system users and programs can see the kernel's view of the system.

Virtual Machine Port Groups

This port type is used to connect a virtual machine to a virtual switch. The virtual machine must have a virtual NIC configured to be able to connect to a virtual switch. Virtual machine port groups when created do not get assigned a number of ports. The virtual switch itself is assigned a number of ports. What determines how many virtual ports are within a virtual machine port group is simply the number of virtual machine virtual NICs connected to the port group. If the maximum number of virtual ports are already in use on the virtual switch, a virtual machine's NIC will not be able to connect to the virtual switch.

To create a virtual machine port group, from within the VI Client's Configuration tab, select the Networking link from within the Hardware section. Then select the Add Networking link in the upper right hand corner of the screen. This will launch the Add Network Wizard as shown in Figure 4.22.

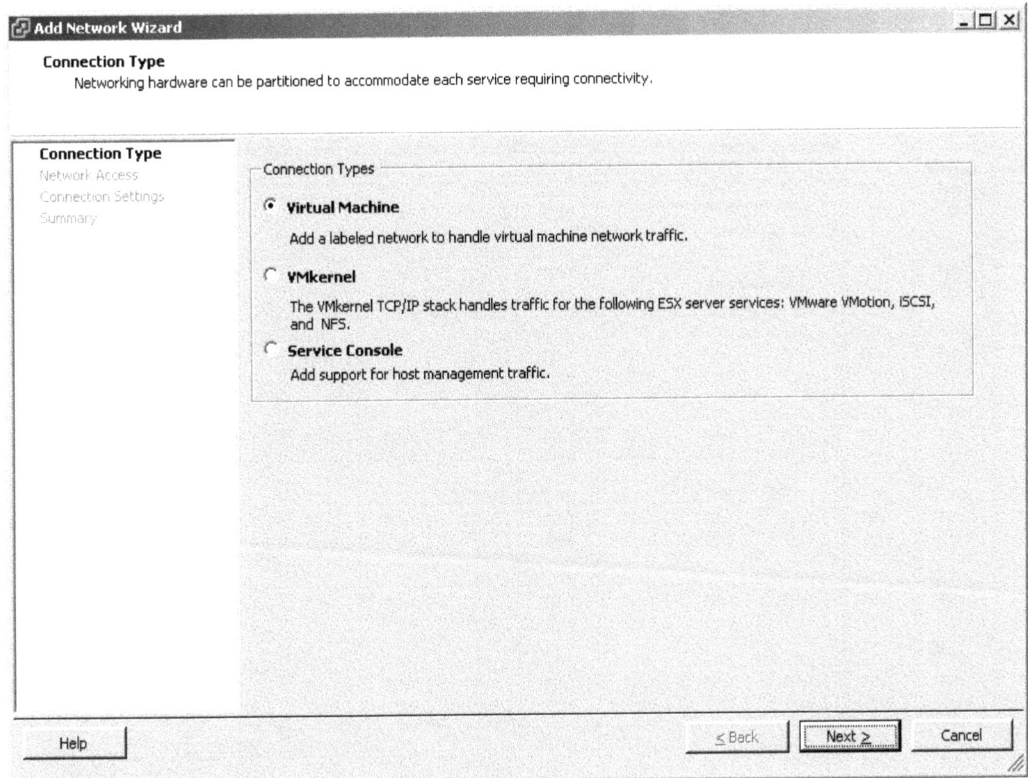

Figure 4.22 Add Virtual Machine Port Group

From this dialog box, all three of the available connection types can be created. The process for creating any of the three connection types is very similar. With the exception that with a service console connection type, the port can be assigned an IP address, subnet mask and default gateway or have these settings obtained via Dynamic Host Configuration Protocol (DHCP). A VMkernel port must have it's IP settings manually assigned, DHCP is not an option. The VMkernel port can also be set to enable VMotion. We will discuss VMotion and how to configure it in chapter 13 - Virtual Machine Migration. The configuration of a virtual machine port group does not require IP settings since virtual machine NICs are attached to the port group. The virtual machine's NIC has a MAC address auto-assigned to it by the VMkernel, while a VM's guest operating system is where the IP address is assigned, either statically by the guest's administrator, or via DHCP.

To configure the virtual machine port group, select the Virtual Machine connection type then select the Next button.

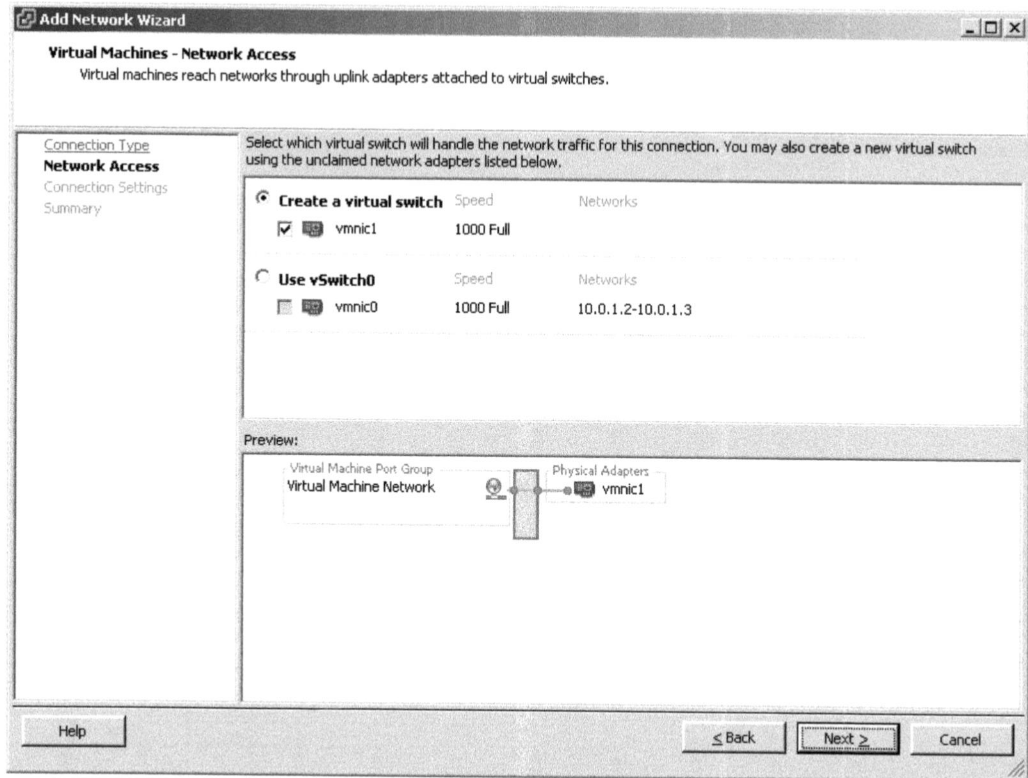

Figure 4.23 Select Uplink Network Adapter for Virtual Machine Port Group

Select the physical NIC to use for the virtual switch. In Figure 4.23, vmnic1 is selected. Click the Next button to continue.

The connection settings for the virtual machine port group need to be configured. Within the Port Group Properties section, assign the port group a case-sensitive network label as shown in Figure 4.24. The network label assigned to the virtual machine port group in Figure 4.24 is "VM Production Network". A Virtual Local Area Network (VLAN) ID can be set as well, in this example, the VLAN ID is set to 107.

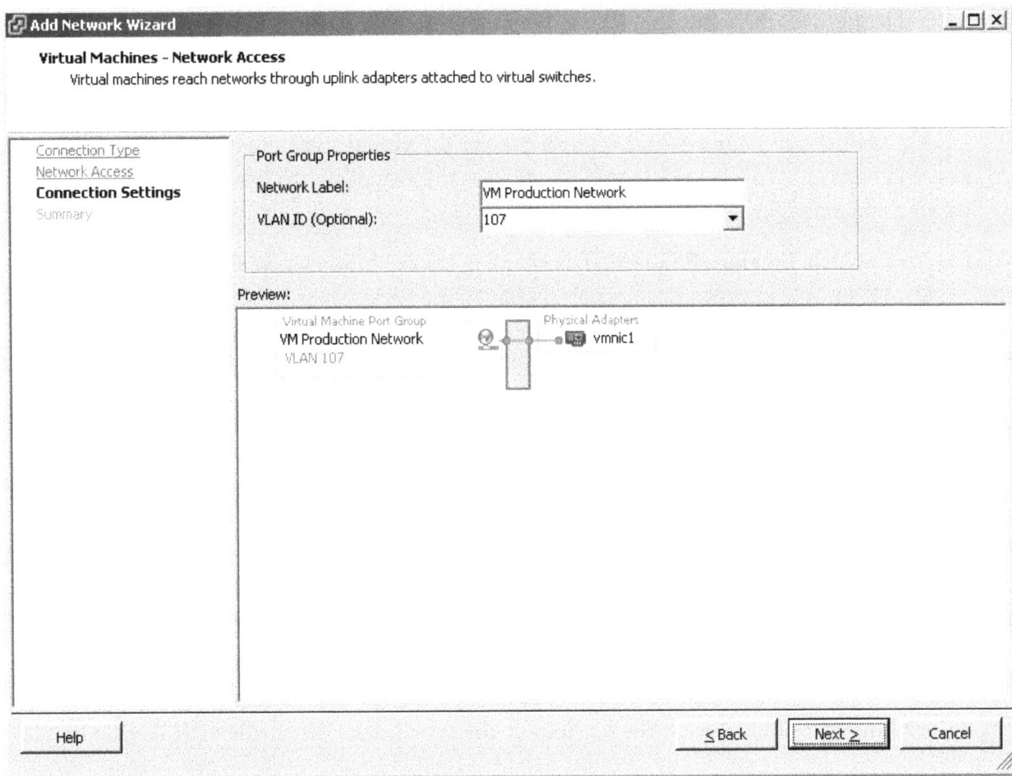

Figure 4.24 Configure Network Label and VLAN Settings

VLANs are very beneficial in switched networks as they provide a means to isolate network traffic. When a server or workstation is operating within a VLAN, each packet transmitted is tagged with a VLAN ID. The VLAN ID is stripped from the packet upon being received. Different types of VLANs can be used. The following is a list of some of the ways VLANs can be implemented:

- MAC address-based - Members of the VLAN are grouped by designated MAC addresses
- Protocol-based - VLAN members based on OSI layer 3 or higher IP protocols
- Policy-based - Members of policy based VLANs are determined by Quality Of Service (QOS) bits used to classify network traffic
- Port-based - This is the most common method of VLAN membership. A group of ports are assigned a specific VLAN ID. A VLAN member simply depends on whether or not a server or workstation is connected to a switched port assigned to a VLAN.

An ESX 3.5 server supports the following VLAN modes:

- VLAN Guest Tagging (VGT) - In VGT mode, a virtual machine can be a part of several VLANs simultaneously. This is accomplished by configuring the guest operating system with an 802.1q VLAN trunking driver inside the virtual machine. This is useful if a physical machine that participated in several VLANs is converted to a virtual machine. The downside is that if the networking card within the ESX 3.5 server does not support VLAN hardware acceleration, then the VMkernel will be taxed with additional CPU cycles when performing

VLAN tagging for the network packets. When this mode is used, VLAN ID 4095 should be assigned to the virtual machine port group.

- Virtual Switch Tagging (VST) - A virtual machine port or port group can be assigned a VLAN as shown in Figure 4.24. Doing so enables the virtual switch to tag and untag packets sent and received. This is known as VST mode as the virtual switch is responsible for tagging and untagging the packets.
- External Switch Tagging (EST) - EST is simply a configuration where the ESX server does not VLAN tag any packets. Each physical NIC on the ESX server, attached to a port on the physical switch can potentially be a member of a different VLAN if port-based VLAN is implemented on the physical switch. In such a configuration, the ESX server is only able to participate in as many VLANs as there are physical NICs in the ESX server.

The valid VLAN range for a virtual switch is between 1-4094 inclusive. VLAN ID 1 is commonly used as a native VLAN ID for Cisco switched environments. Native VLANs transport untagged packets and is often used for switch management purposes. An ESX 3.5 server will drop native VLAN packets. Other switch vendors may use another VLAN ID number for their native VLAN. It is important to know the native VLAN being used in the physical switched environment in order to avoid assigning this VLAN ID to virtual switches. As mentioned previously, VLAN ID 4095 is used specifically for VGT mode. VLAN ID 0 is typically reserved for user priority data and is not used by ESX servers. If a VLAN ID is modified on a virtual switch, the new VLAN ID is used immediately. There is no need to restart the ESX server services or the server itself for the new VLAN ID to take effect.

To complete creating the virtual machine port group, select the Finish button as shown in Figure 4.25.

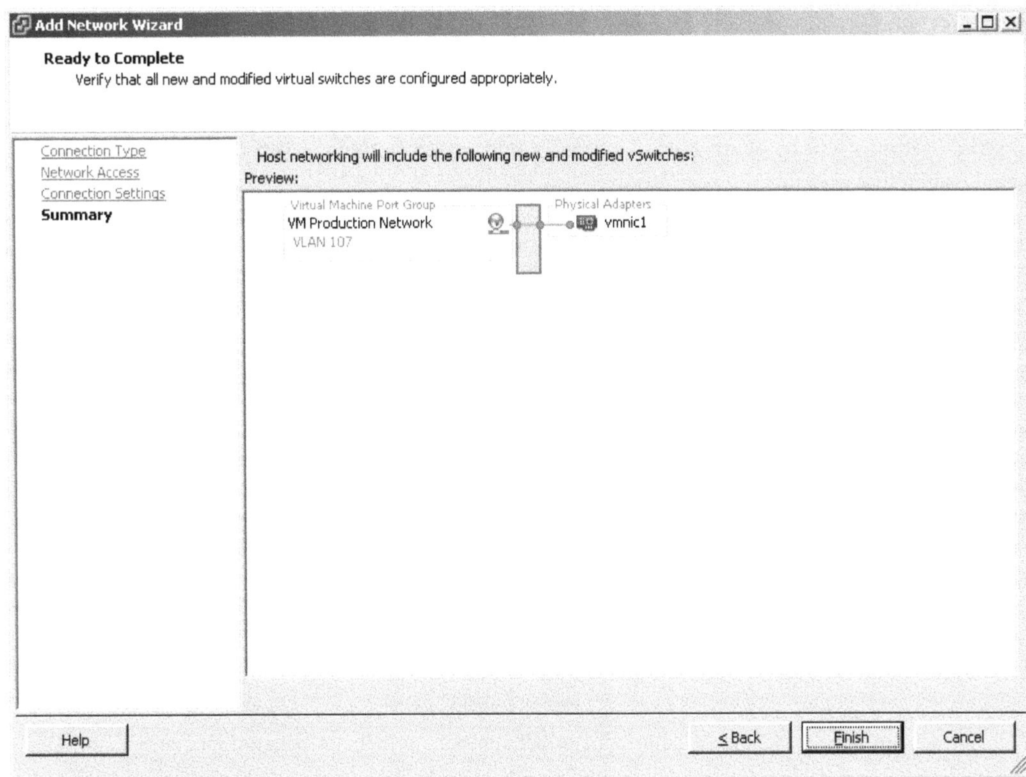

Figure 4.25 Virtual Machine Port Group Ready To Complete Dialog Box

The newly created virtual port group is now displayed within the VI Client Networking screen as shown in Figure 4.26. The process of creating the "VM Production Network" virtual port group also created a new virtual switch named vSwitch1. As previously mentioned, virtual switches are named sequentially, vSwitch0, vSwitch1, vSwitch2, and so forth.

Figure 4.26 New Virtual Machine Port Group Added

Port Group Configurations

The virtual port and port groups within a virtual switch contain the same properties as does a virtual switch. An important point about these properties that are set at the port or port groups level is the virtual switch settings will be overridden. To modify port group settings, select the Properties link for the virtual switch that contains the port group.

The following steps display the "VM Production Network" port group settings. The vSwitch1 properties link has been selected launching the dialog box for the vSwitch1 properties as shown in Figure 4.27. Select the "VM Production Network" port group from within the Ports tab and click on the Edit button.

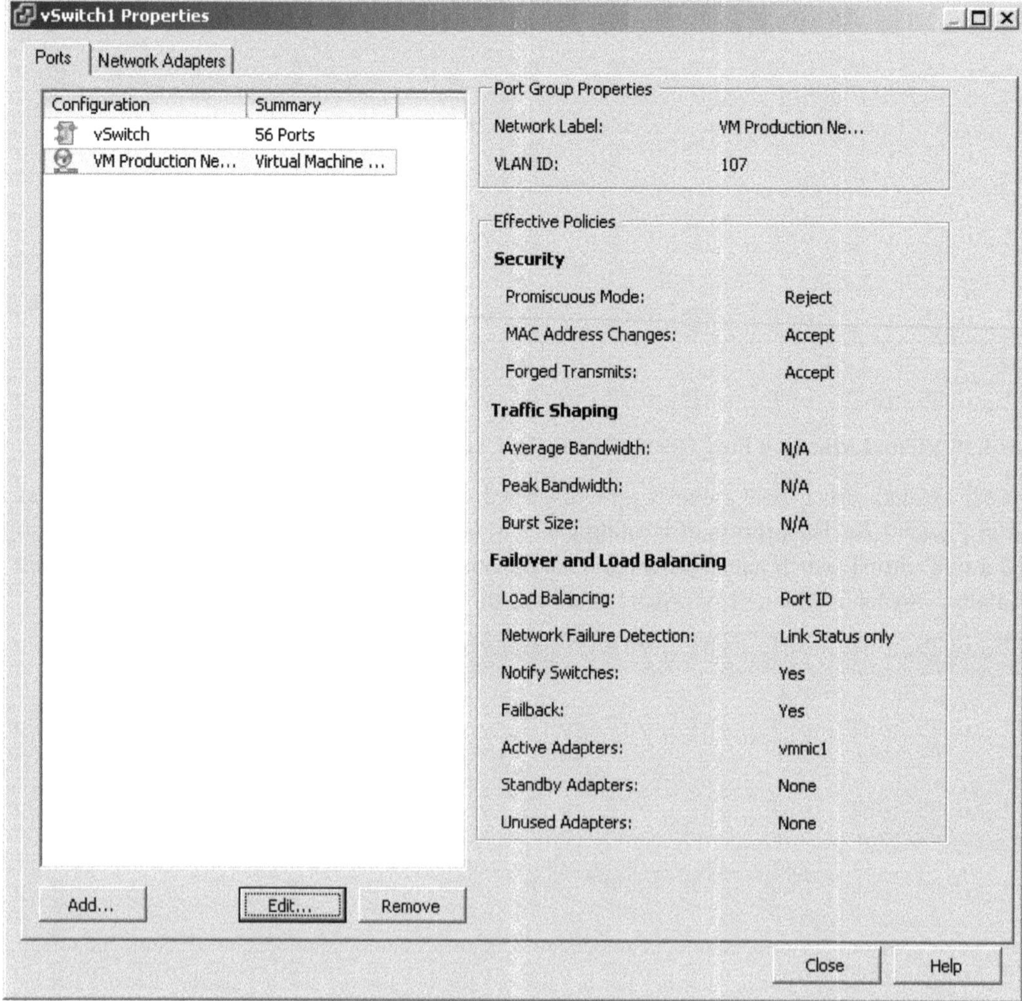

Figure 4.27 Edit Virtual Machine Port Group

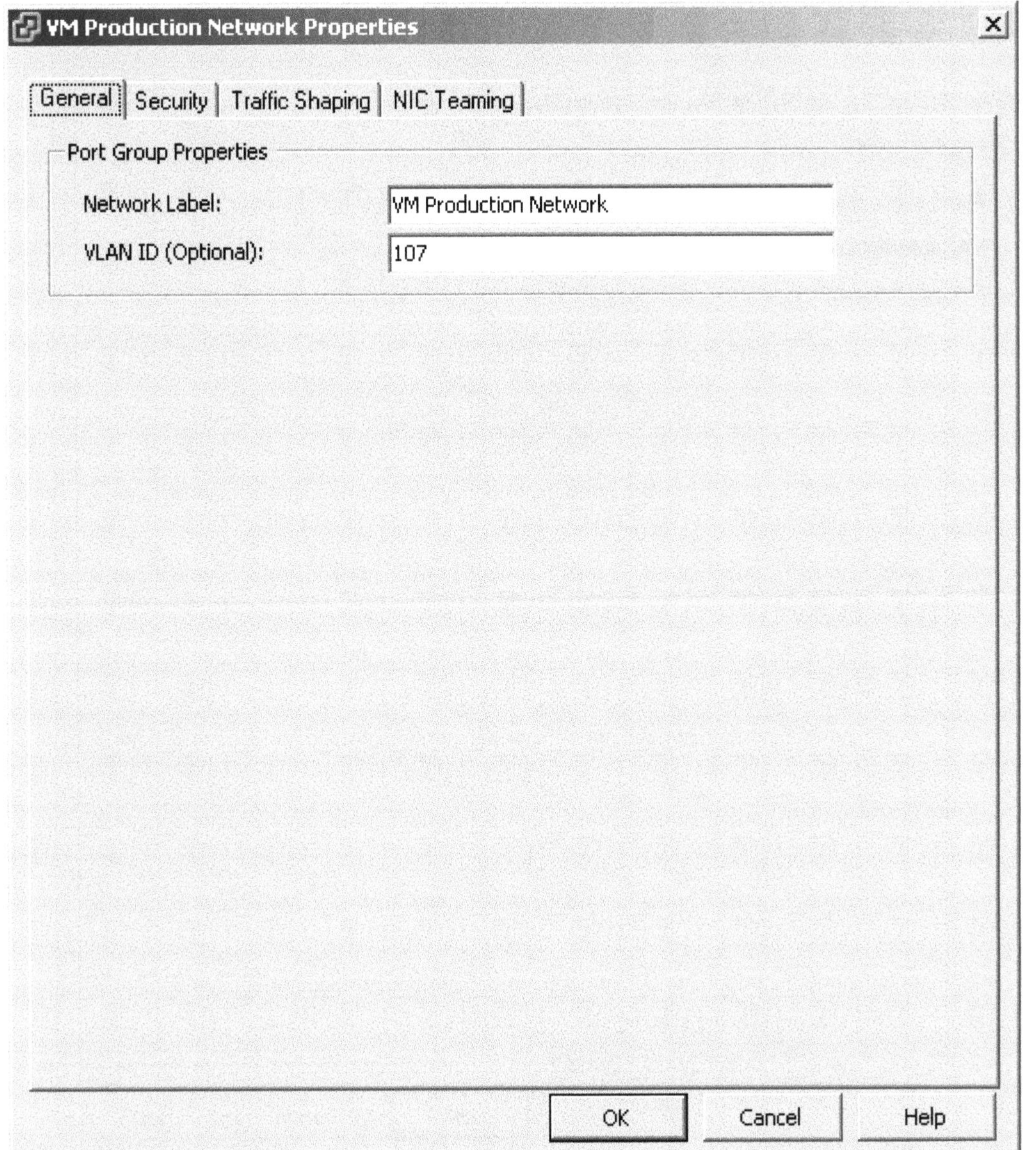

Figure 4.28 Virtual Machine Port Group General Tab

The General tab displays the port group label and VLAN ID settings. Both labels and VLAN IDs can be modified by entering the new values in the corresponding text fields. Next, select the Security tab as shown in Figure 4.28.

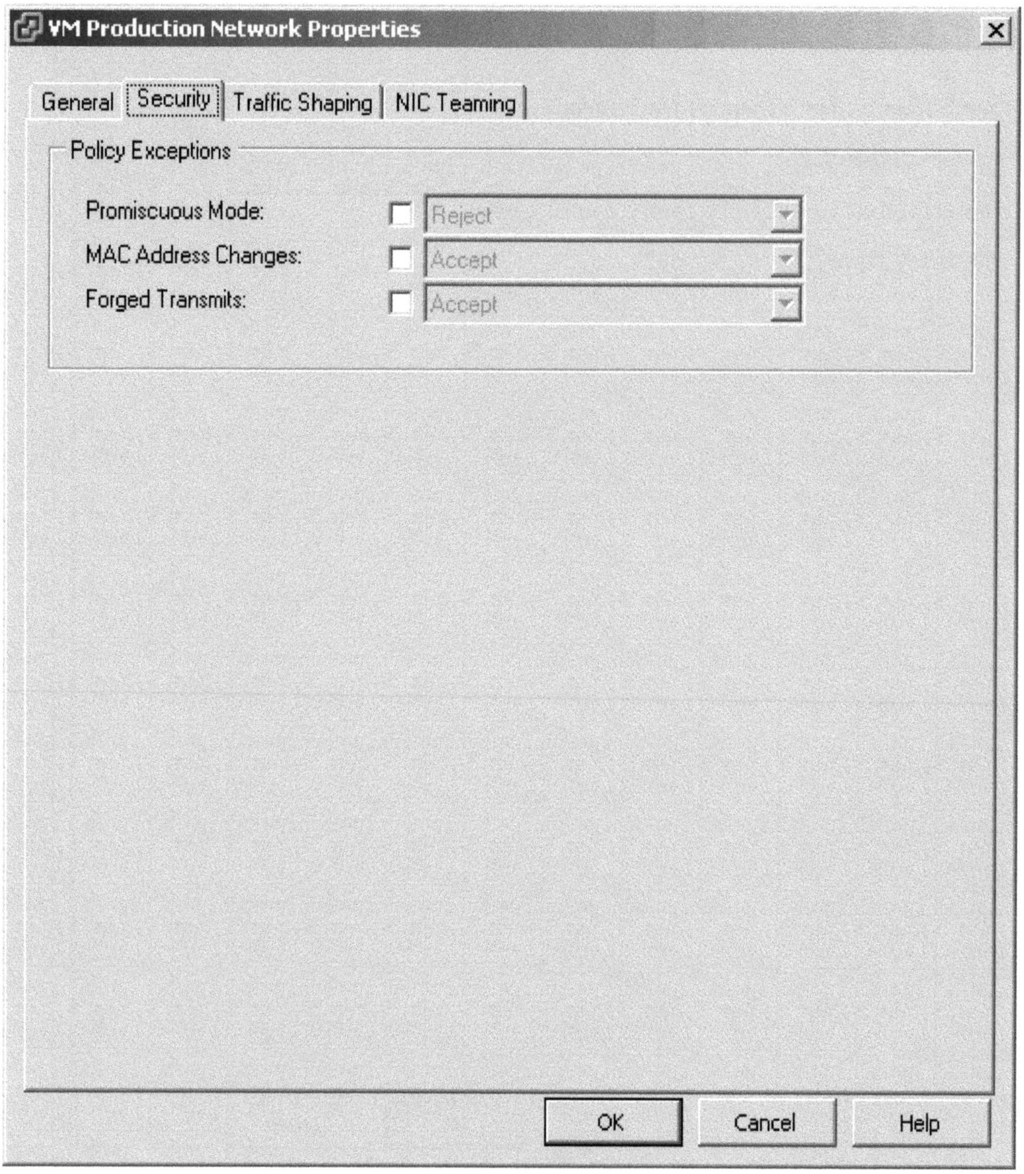

Figure 4.29 Virtual Machine Port Group Security Tab

As shown in Figure 4.29, the port group settings are ghosted out. Unlike the virtual switch settings, some of the port or port group settings require placing a check in the check box to make a modification.

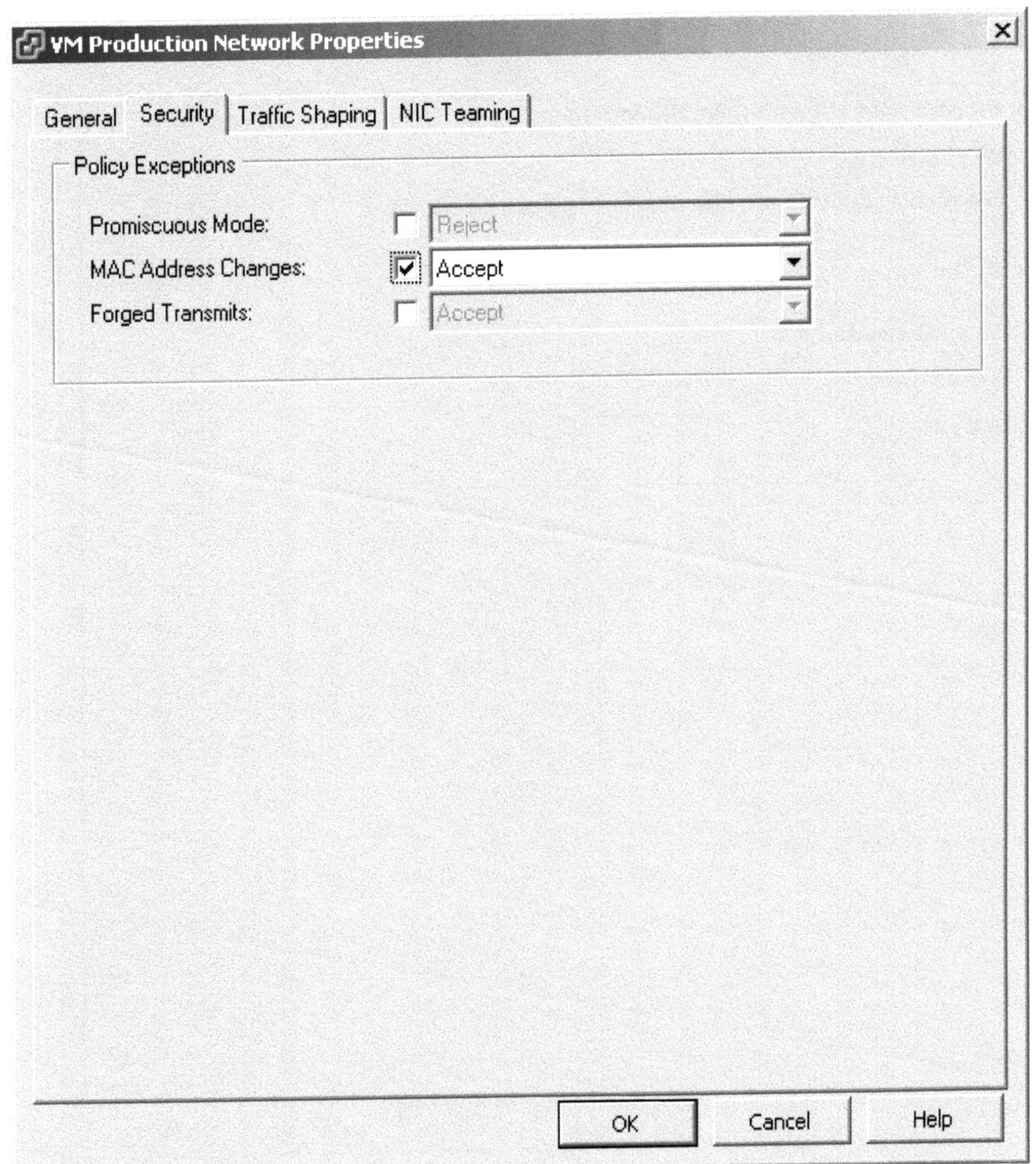

Figure 4.30 Virtual Machine Port Group Security Tab Enable MAC Address Changes

By placing a check in the check box, a setting becomes un-ghosted and can be modified as shown in Figure 4.30.

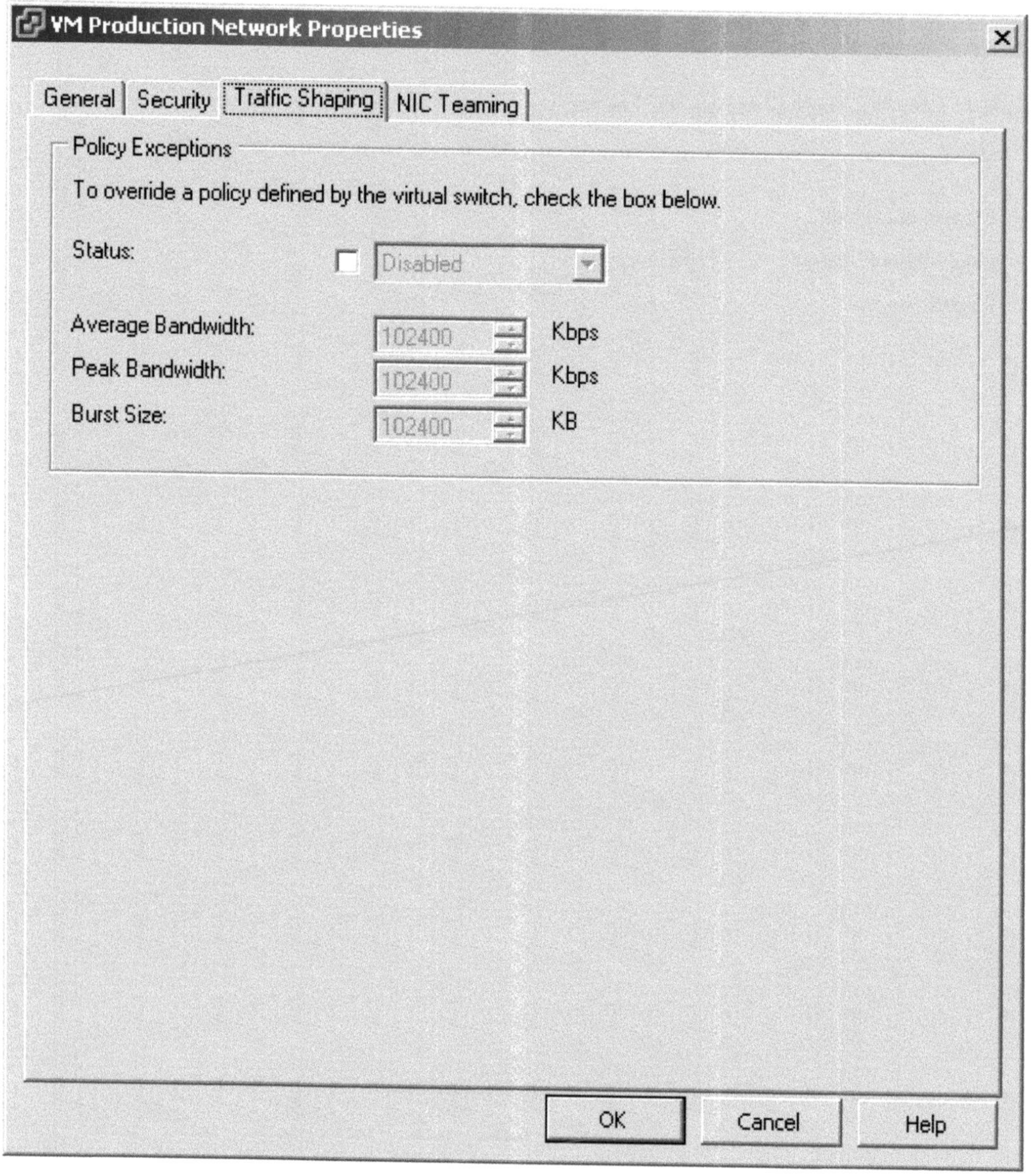

VM Production Network Properties

General | Security | Traffic Shaping | NIC Teaming

Policy Exceptions

To override a policy defined by the virtual switch, check the box below.

Status: Disabled

Average Bandwidth: 102400 Kbps

Peak Bandwidth: 102400 Kbps

Burst Size: 102400 KB

OK | Cancel | Help

Figure 4.31 Virtual Machine Port Group Traffic Shaping Tab

To continue, select the Traffic Shaping tab as shown in Figure 4.31. Once again, the check boxes need to be selected to modify a setting.

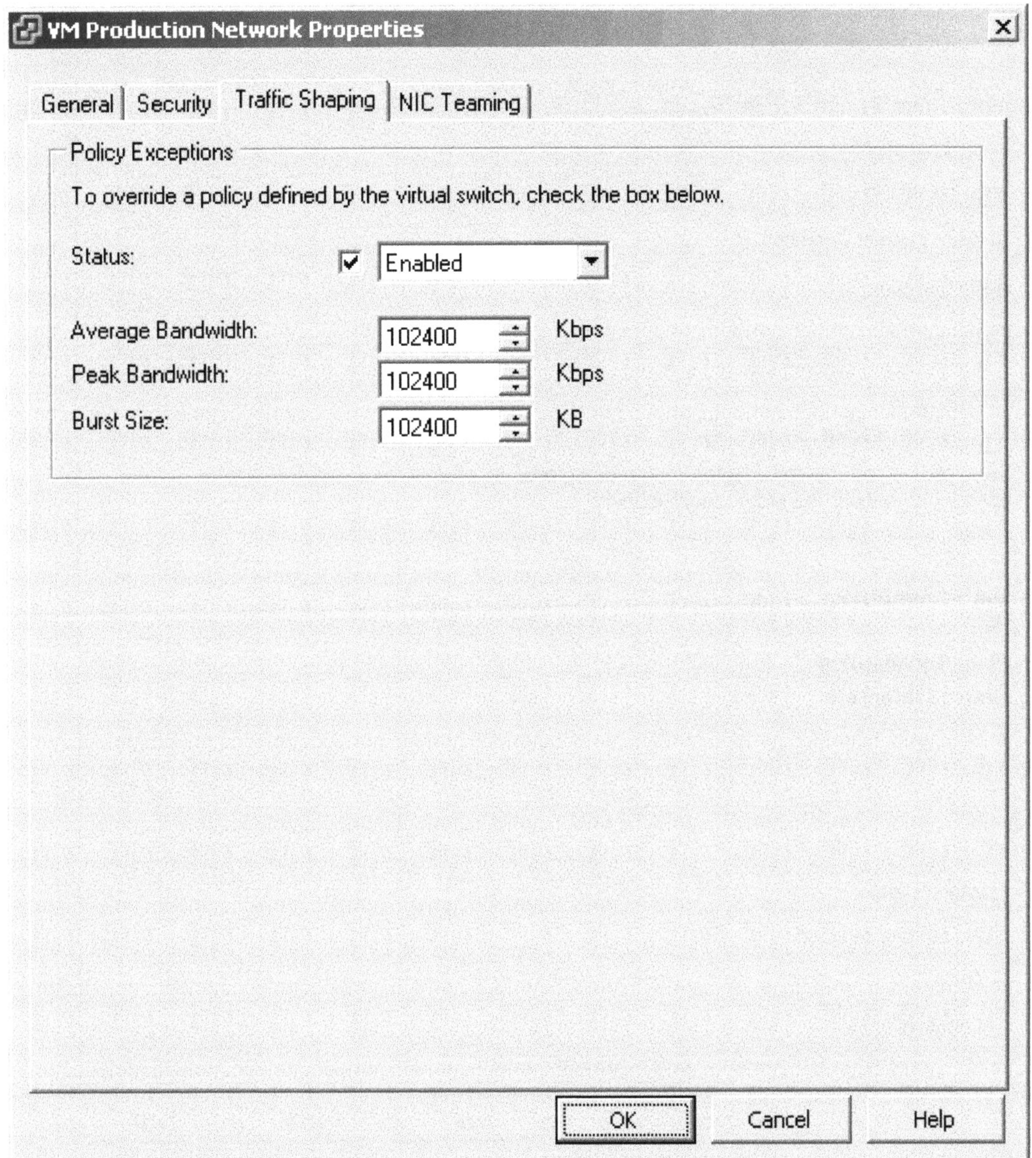

Figure 4.32 Virtual Machine Port Group Enable Traffic Shaping

As with virtual switches, Traffic Shaping is disabled by default. Place a check in the Status check box as shown in Figure 4.32 and select the drop down box to select the Enabled option. The three settings, Average Bandwidth, Peak Bandwidth and Burst Size apply to each NIC specifically attached to the virtual machine port group rather than to all virtual NICs attached to the virtual switch collectively.

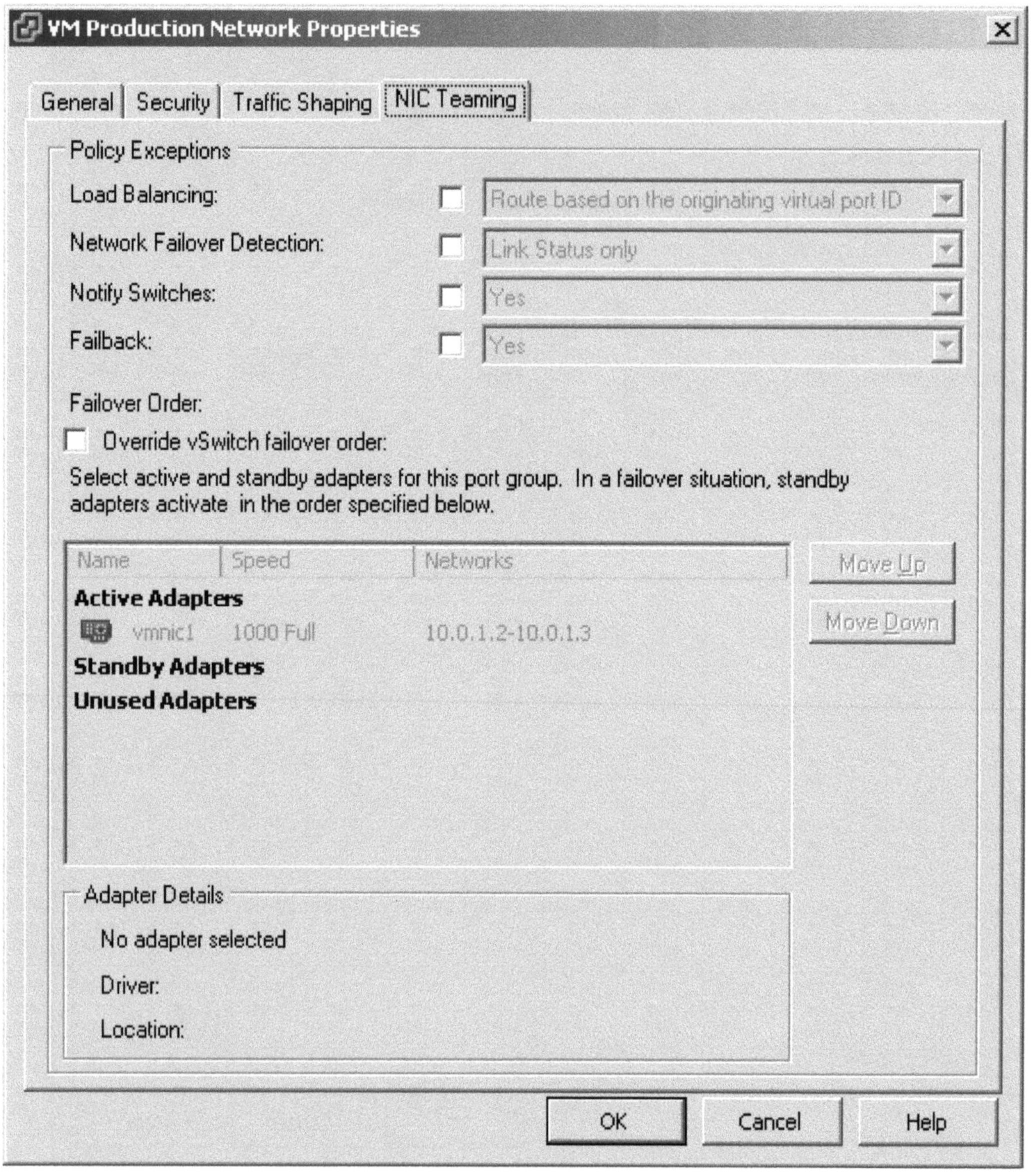

Figure 4.33 Virtual Machine Port Group NIC Teaming Tab

Load balancing, network failover detection, notify switches and failback settings can be set specifically for each port or port group configured on a virtual switch as shown in Figure 4.33.

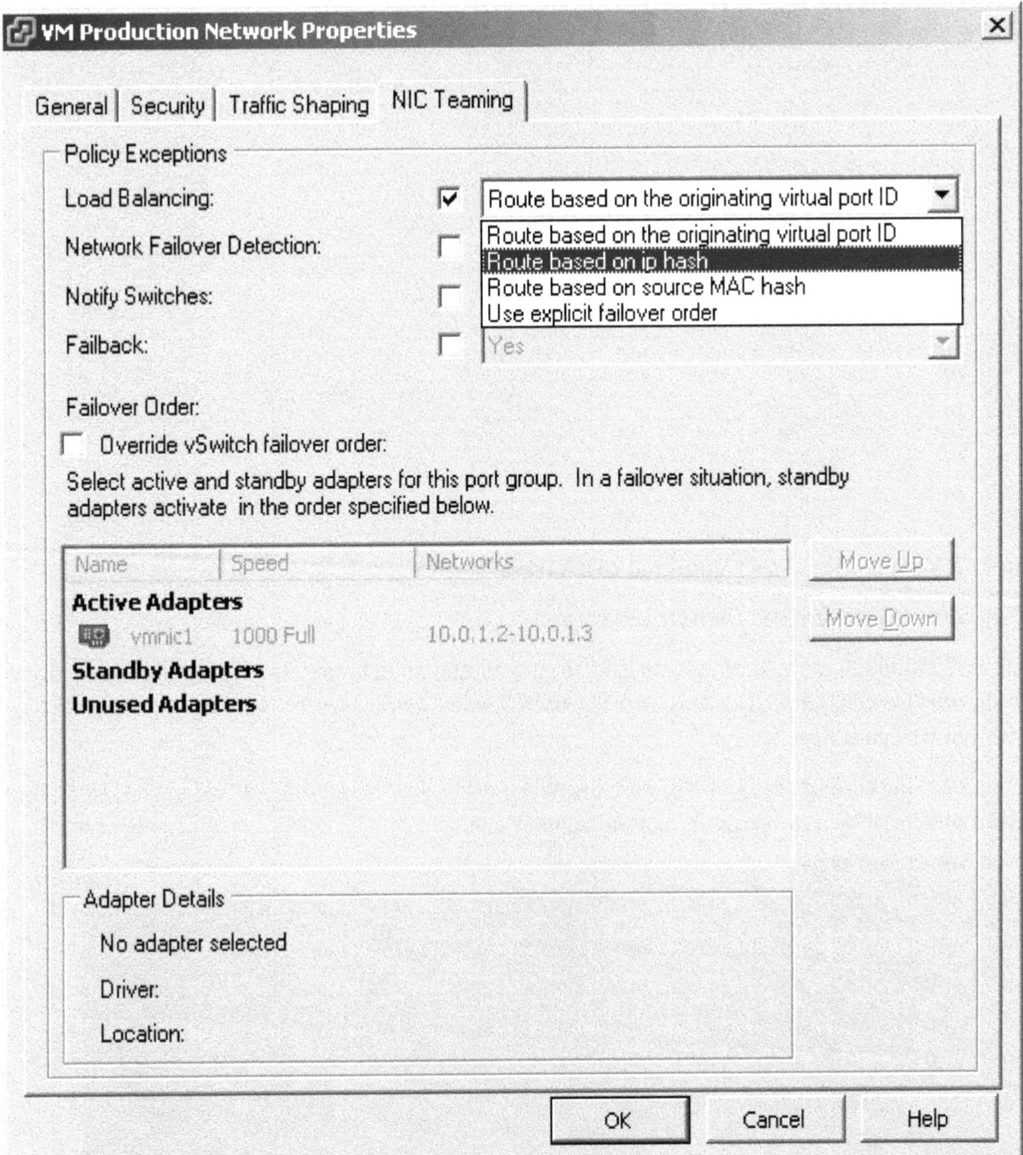

Figure 4.34 Virtual Machine Port Group Load Balancing

The same load balancing options available for virtual switches are available for port or port groups. Once again, place a check in the appropriate check box to modify a setting as shown in Figure 4.34.

Note that if a port or port group is configured in a NIC team and a different physical NIC is used for both the active and standby adapter then is set for the virtual switch, only the virtual switch settings are displayed from within the VI Client.

Figure 4.35 displays vSwitch1 with multiple virtual machines attached to "VM Production Network" virtual machine port group. We will see in chapter 7 - Virtual Machines, how to connect a virtual machine to a virtual switch.

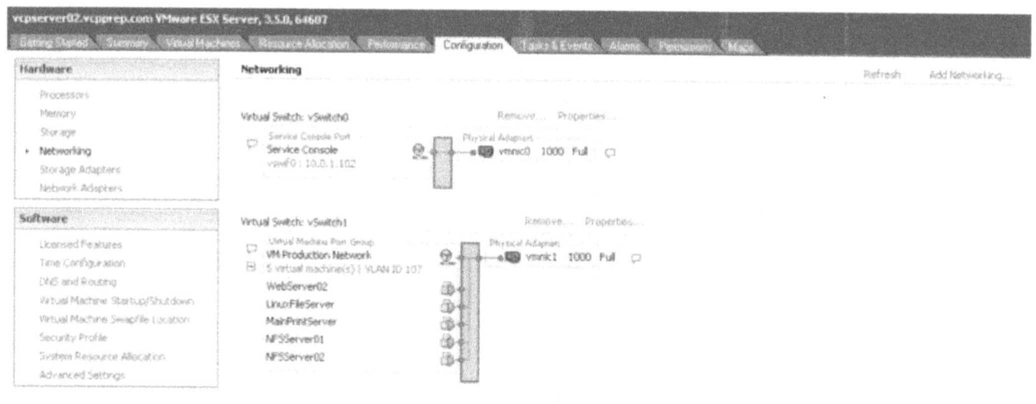

Figure 4.35 Virtual Machines Connected to a Virtual Switch

CLI Physical NIC to Virtual Switch Linking

Linking and unlinking a physical NIC to and from a virtual switch can also be accomplished from within the service console's CLI. This is often useful when automatically building virtual switches from custom written scripts.

In Figure 4.36, the current physical NICs are displayed using the "esxcfg-nics -l" command. Note, the command switch "-l" is a lowercase L, not the number one.

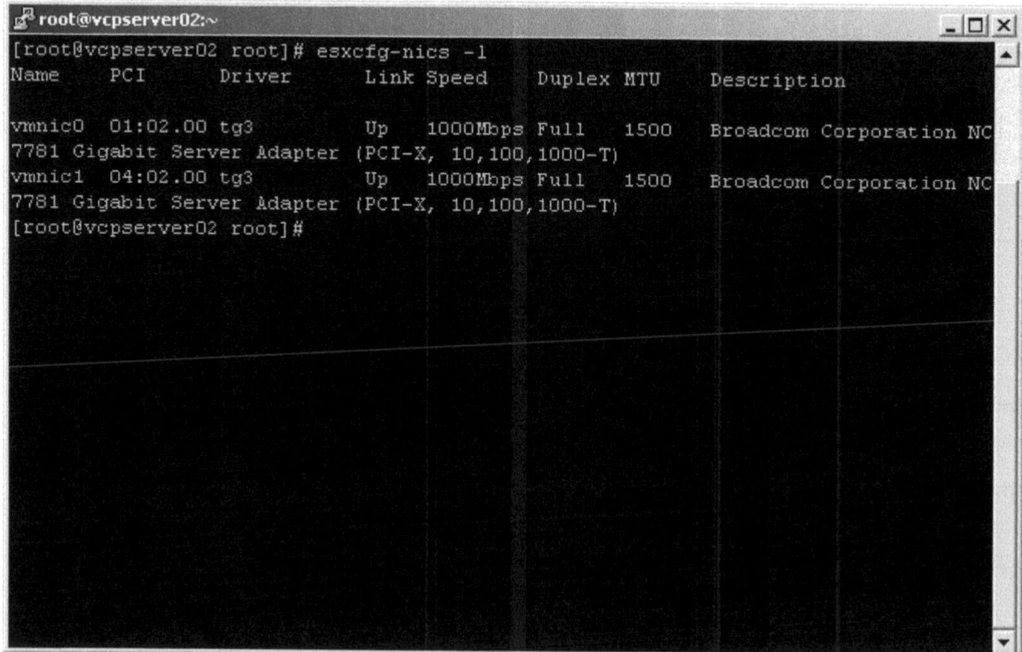

Figure 4.36 The esxcfg-nics Command

To display which physical NIC is attached to which virtual switch, invoke the "esxcfg-vswitch -l" command as shown in Figure 4.37. Note, the command switch "-l" is a lowercase L, not the number one. We can see that vmnic0 is linked to vSwitch0 and vmnic1 is linked to vSwitch1.

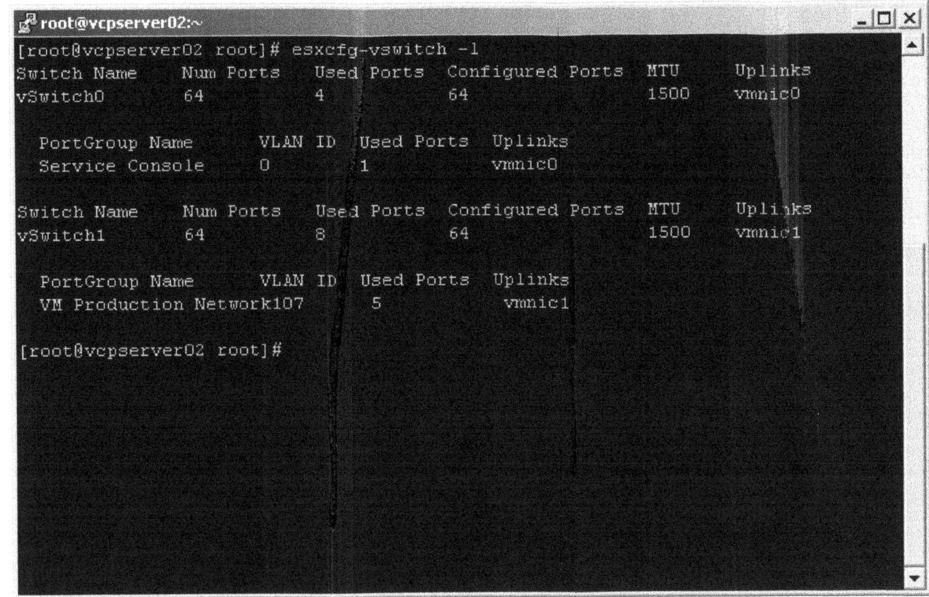

Figure 4.37 The esxcfg-vswitch Command

To unlink vmnic1 from vSwitch1, issue the "esxcfg-vswitch -U vmnic1 vSwitch1" command as shown in Figure 4.38.

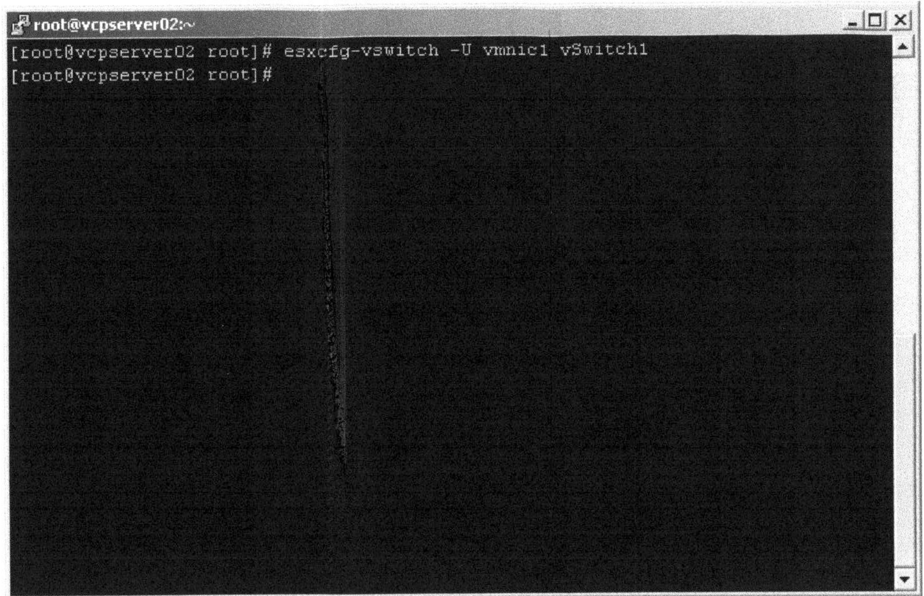

Figure 4.38 Using The esxcfg-vswitch Command To Disconnect Network Adapter

To display the current physical NIC to virtual switch mapping, invoke the "esxcfg-vswitch -l" as shown in Figure 4.39. We can see now that vSwitch1 no longer has vmnic1 attached to it as there is no listing under the uplinks column.

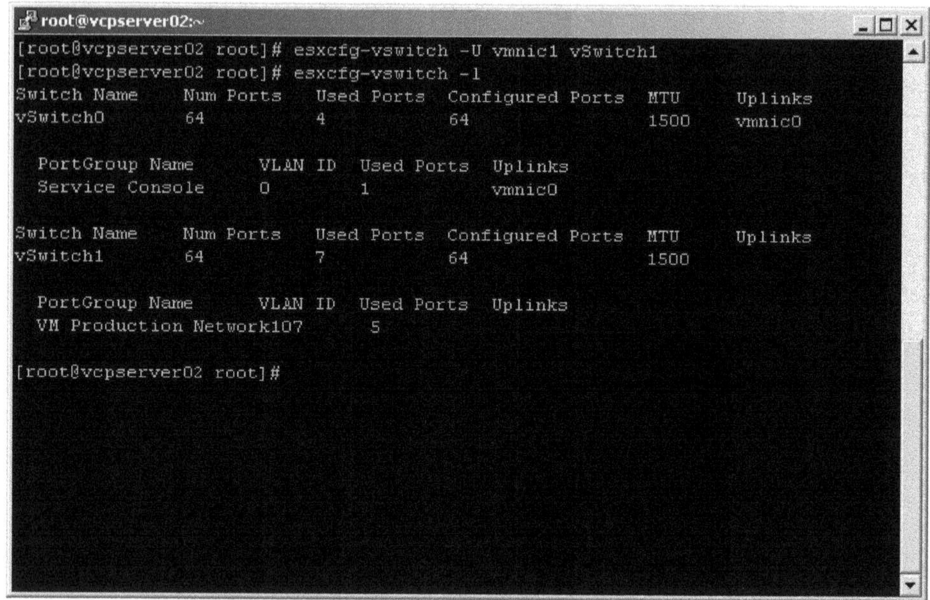

Figure 4.39 Modified Virtual Switch To Network Adapter Configuration

To create a NIC team on vSwitch0 by linking vmnic1 to it, issue the "esxcfg-vswitch -L vmnic1 vSwitch0" as shown in Figure 4.40.

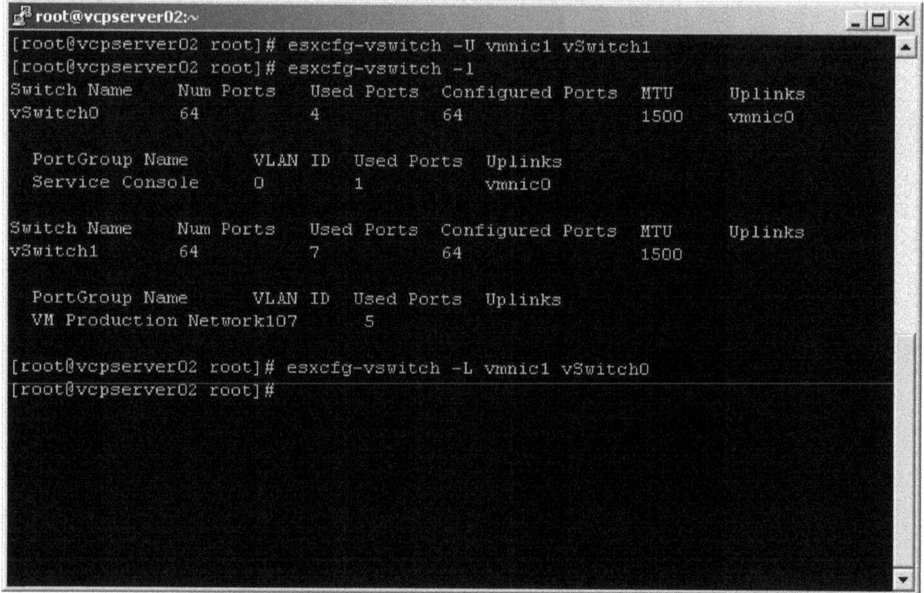

Figure 4.40 Using The esxcfg-vswitch Command to Connect Network Adapter

Using the "esxcfg-vswitch -l" command as shown in Figure 4.41 to display the updated virtual switch to physical NIC mapping. Under the uplinks column, vmnic0 and vmnic1 are now linked to vSwitch0.

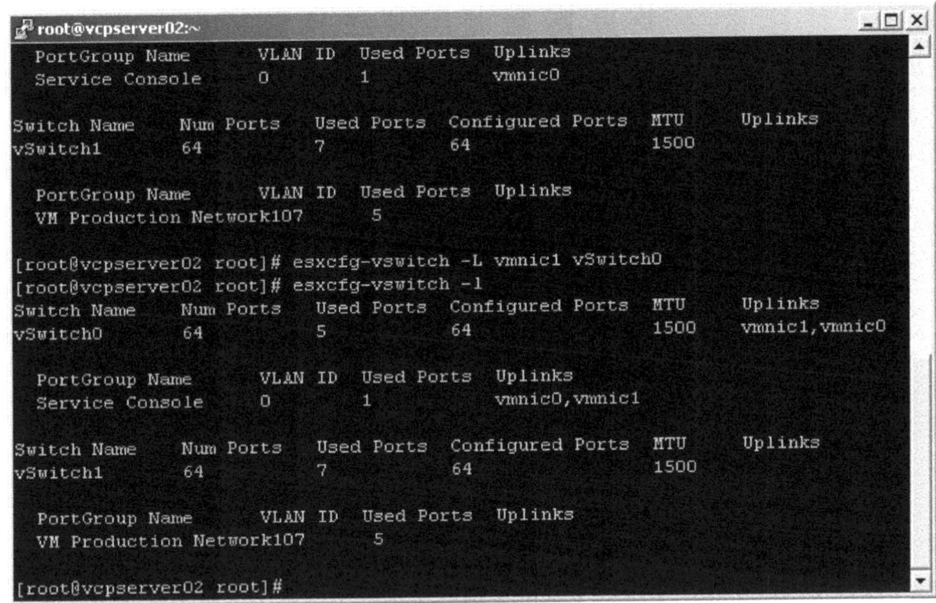

```
root@vcpserver02:~
  PortGroup Name       VLAN ID  Used Ports  Uplinks
  Service Console      0        1           vmnic0

Switch Name     Num Ports   Used Ports  Configured Ports  MTU     Uplinks
vSwitch1        64          7           64                1500

  PortGroup Name       VLAN ID  Used Ports  Uplinks
  VM Production Network107      5

[root@vcpserver02 root]# esxcfg-vswitch -L vmnic1 vSwitch0
[root@vcpserver02 root]# esxcfg-vswitch -l
Switch Name     Num Ports   Used Ports  Configured Ports  MTU     Uplinks
vSwitch0        64          5           64                1500    vmnic1,vmnic0

  PortGroup Name       VLAN ID  Used Ports  Uplinks
  Service Console      0        1           vmnic0,vmnic1

Switch Name     Num Ports   Used Ports  Configured Ports  MTU     Uplinks
vSwitch1        64          7           64                1500

  PortGroup Name       VLAN ID  Used Ports  Uplinks
  VM Production Network107      5

[root@vcpserver02 root]#
```

Figure 4.41 New Virtual Switch to Network Adapter Configuration

Network services can be restarted if needed from the command line by issuing the "service network restart" command as shown in Figure 4.42.

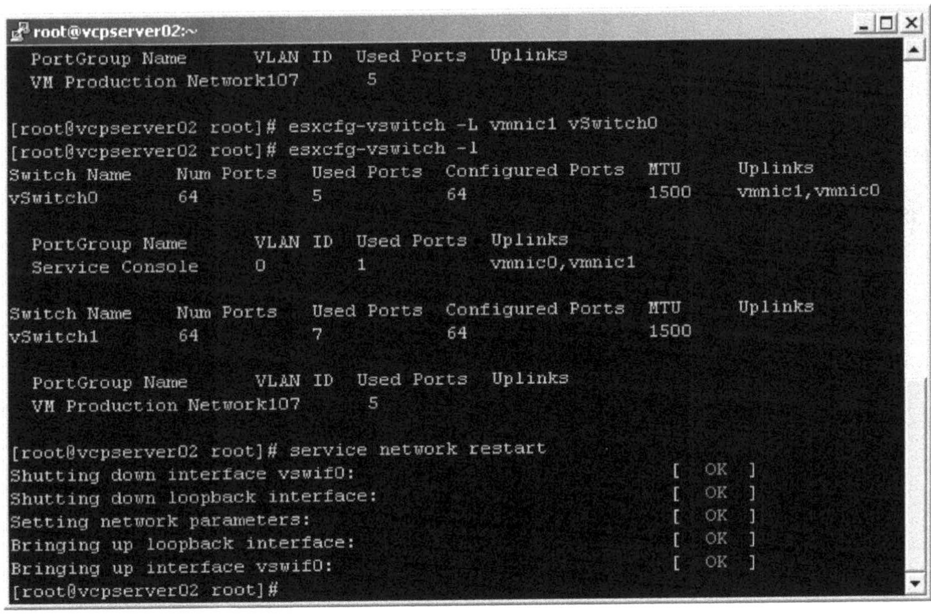

```
root@vcpserver02:~
  PortGroup Name       VLAN ID  Used Ports  Uplinks
  VM Production Network107      5

[root@vcpserver02 root]# esxcfg-vswitch -L vmnic1 vSwitch0
[root@vcpserver02 root]# esxcfg-vswitch -l
Switch Name     Num Ports   Used Ports  Configured Ports  MTU     Uplinks
vSwitch0        64          5           64                1500    vmnic1,vmnic0

  PortGroup Name       VLAN ID  Used Ports  Uplinks
  Service Console      0        1           vmnic0,vmnic1

Switch Name     Num Ports   Used Ports  Configured Ports  MTU     Uplinks
vSwitch1        64          7           64                1500

  PortGroup Name       VLAN ID  Used Ports  Uplinks
  VM Production Network107      5

[root@vcpserver02 root]# service network restart
Shutting down interface vswif0:                           [  OK  ]
Shutting down loopback interface:                         [  OK  ]
Setting network parameters:                               [  OK  ]
Bringing up loopback interface:                           [  OK  ]
Bringing up interface vswif0:                             [  OK  ]
[root@vcpserver02 root]#
```

Figure 4.42 Restart the Network Service

Figure 4.43 displays vSwitch0 now in a NIC team configuration with physical NICs vmnic0 and vmnic1. We can also see that vSwitch1 is now an internal virtual switch due to having no physical adapters attached to it.

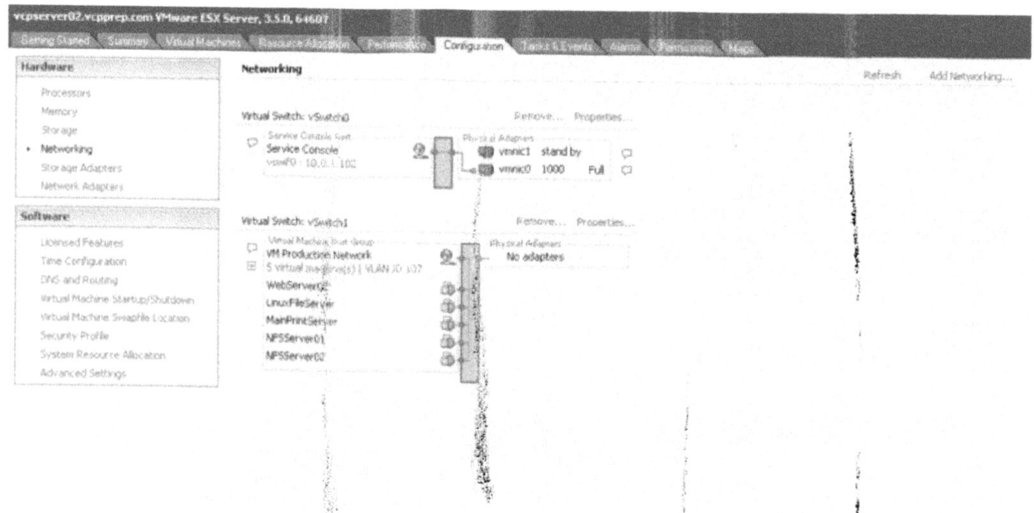

Figure 4.43 Internal Only Virtual Switch

Setting Active, Standby and Unused Physical NICs

Using the CLI commands to unlink the vmnic1 adapter from vSwitch1 and linking it to vSwitch0 set the vmnic1 adapter in standby mode. Standby mode is not shown from within the CLI. The VI Client displays this status as shown in Figure 4.43. The following describes how to set a physical NIC from standby mode to active mode.

Once again, open up the virtual switch properties by selecting the properties link for the virtual switch. In Figure 4.44, the properties dialog box for vSwitch0 is displayed. We are going to modify the service console port NIC team by selecting the Service Console from within the Ports tab and selecting edit as shown in Figure 4.44.

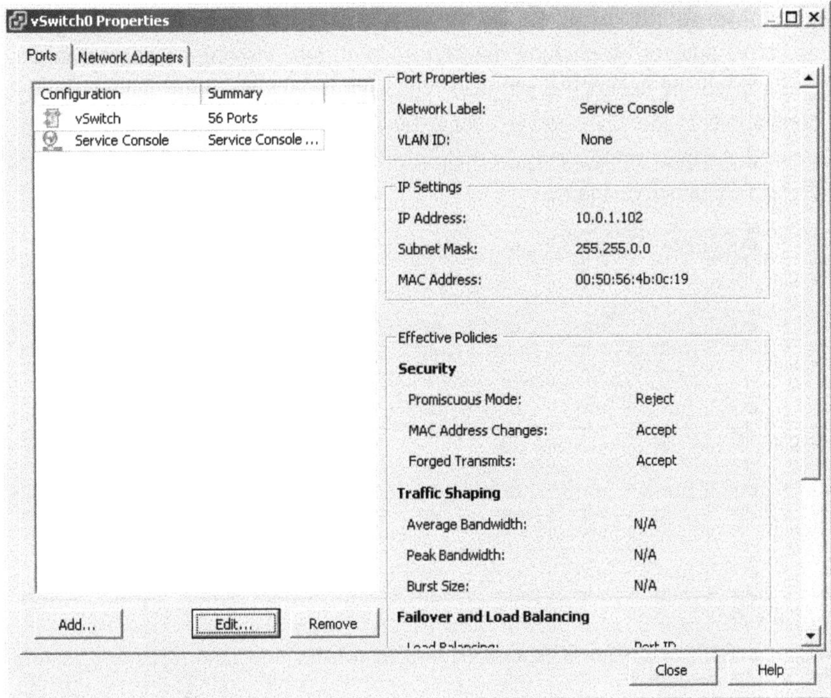

Figure 4.44 The Service Console Port

A warning dialog box is displayed as shown in Figure 4.45 because we are attempting to modify the service console. Incorrectly modifying the service console port can prevent further remote access to the ESX 3.5 server. Since we are just going to promote a physical NIC from standby to active status, select the "Continue to modify this connection" option to continue.

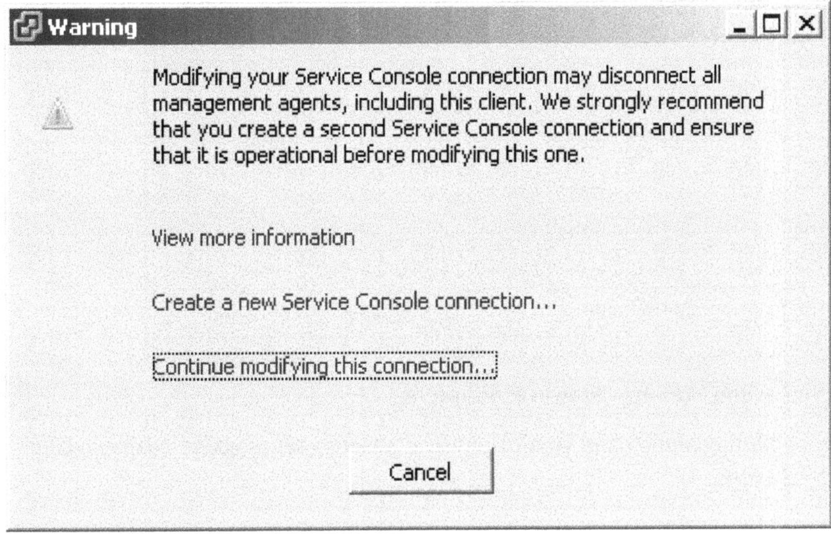

Figure 4.45 Warning Modifying Service Console Port

Select the NIC Teaming tab as shown in Figure 4.46. Selecting the vmnic1 adapter under the Standby

Adapters section allows the physical NIC to be moved to either an unused adapter by clicking the Move Down button or an active adapter by clicking the Move Up button. Moving an adapter under the Unused Adapters section might be useful if a physical NIC fails or is performing inconsistently possibly due to driver corruption. If the ESX server cannot be placed into maintenance mode and powered off, then the Unused Adapter option may be helpful. The Move Up button is selected in Figure 4.46 to promote vmnic1 to an active adapter.

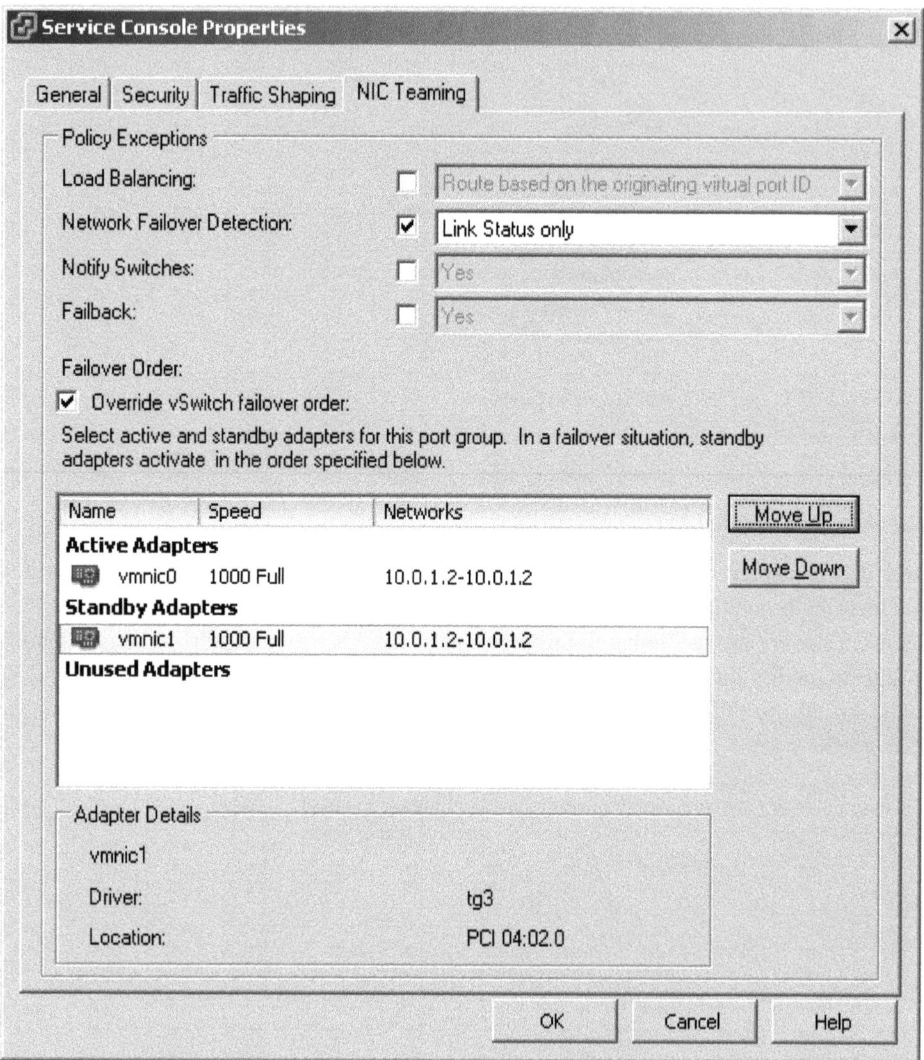

Figure 4.46 Modified Active and Standby Network Adapters

Figure 4.46 now displays both the vmnic0 and vmnic1 physical adapters set as active adapters. Click the OK button to save the changes.

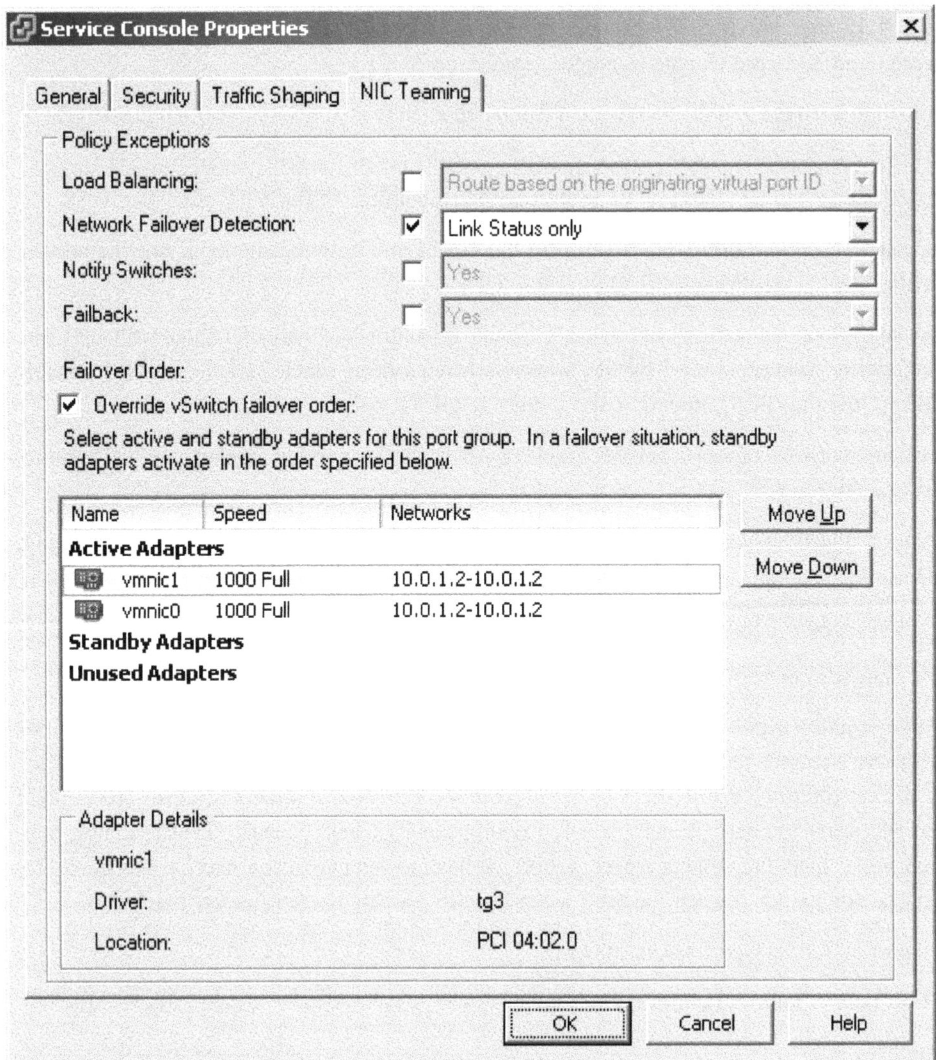

Figure 4.47 Modified Active and Standby Network Adapters

Troubleshooting Common Virtual Infrastructure Network Problems

We will now examine some of the common networking issues and how to troubleshoot them:

Mis-configured Firewall Settings

Often, networking issues can be attributed to mis-configured firewall settings. The following is a list of the ESX 3.5 server and VirtualCenter 2.5 ports used to communicate with various components:

Ports Used

22 - SSH access to service console.

80 - HTTP access to web servers. Access to this port is redirected to port 443 (SSL). (Incoming TCP)

443 - HTTPS, SSL connection for Web Access, VI Client access to ESX Server or VirtualCenter, VMware Converter and VMware Update Manager. (Incoming TCP)

902 - Communication between ESX 3.5 servers, VirtualCenter Server to ESX Server. (Incoming TCP, Outgoing UDP)

903 - VM Console access via VI Client or VI Web Access. (Incoming TCP)

2049 - Connection to NFS storage devices used by the VMkernel networking stack not the service console networking stack. (Incoming TCP, Outgoing UDP)

2050-2250, and 8042-8045 - Traffic between ESX Server hosts for VMware HA (also utilizes EMC Automated Availability Manager) used by the VMkernel networking stack, not the service console networking stack. (Outgoing TCP, Incoming and Outgoing UDP)

3260 - Connection to iSCSI storage devices made from both the service console and VMkernel networking stacks. (Outgoing TCP)

8000 - Incoming requests from VMotion used by the VMkernel networking stack. (Incoming, Outgoing TCP)

27000 - License transactions from ESX Server to the License Server. (Incoming, Outgoing TCP)

27010 - License transactions from the License Server. (Incoming, Outgoing TCP)

If the ESX 3.5 server and VirtualCenter 2.5 servers require access through a firewall, verify that all of the ports listed above are able to pass through an external firewall if needed. ESX uses the iptables application for packet filtering. While the VI Client provides a means to open and close pre-defined ports, it may be necessary to enable ports not listed within the VI Client Security Profile dialog box. This is common when installing management agents or backup agents in the service console. The following is a list of commands that can be used when troubleshooting the service console firewall:

Open or close a port on the service console firewall:

esxcfg-firewall -o "port", "protocol", "direction", "name"

"port" - Port number

"protocol" - tcp or udp

"direction" - in or out

"name" - Name of service

For example:

esxcfg-firewall -o 1221,tcp,in,jmi

This command will assign the label jmi as open port number 1221 for incoming TCP connections. This can be verified running the following command:

esxcfg-firewall -q

This newly opened port will appear at the end of the output as follows:

NOTE: All but the end of the command output has been truncated.

Opened ports:

jmi : port 1221 tcp.in

A port can be closed by issuing the following command:

esxcfg-firewall -c 1221,tcp,in

Critical Services Not Running

Critical functionality in the ESX 3.5 and VirtualCenter 2.5 products require that certain services be running and configured properly for your environment. The following commands can be used to check the status of a service and enable or disable a service:

Available services can be identified using the following command:

esxcfg-firewall -s

Known services: activeDirectorKerberos caARCserve CIMHttpServer CIMHttpsServer CIMSLP commvaultDynamic

commvaultStatic ftpClient ftpServer kerberos LDAP LDAPS legatoNetWorker LicenseClient nfsClient nisClient ntpClient

smbClient snmpd sshClient sshServer swISCSIClient symantecBackupExec symantecNetBackup telnetClient TSM

updateManager VCB vncServer vpxHeartbeats

Query Service Status

esxcfg-firewall -q "service name"

Enable Service

esxcfg-firewall -e "service name"

Disable Service

esxcfg-firewall -d "service name"

Changes made with the "esxcfg-firewall" commands will place entries within the main ESX configuration file, /etc/vmware/esx.conf. These entries are denoted by lines starting with "/firewall". Firewall modifications are logged in the following file, /var/log/vmware/esxcfg-firewall.log

Firewall configuration changes are effective immediately. The ESX server will flush the firewall rules from memory and rebuild the rules without requiring a system reboot.

Capturing Network Traffic

It is often important to capture traffic off of the network when troubleshooting network related issues. A useful tool available from within the service console is tcpdump. The following example depicts the command used to capture ARP requests. Arp requests are initiated each time a virtual machine is powered on.

NOTE: The port or port group that tcpdump is run on must be placed in promiscuous mode before running tcpdump.

tcpdump -i vswif0 arp

tcpdump: listening on vswif0

01:19:51.416504 arp who-has webserver01.vcpprep.com (0:4:91:27:70:30) tell ilo-vcpserver01.vcpprep.com

01:21:35.696713 arp reply webserver01.vcpprep.com is-at 0:4:91:27:70:30

This command can be used to record network traffic over a period. The following command is used to capture ARP packets to a file named arppackets.cap:

tcpdump -i vswif0 -w arppackets.cap arp

To stop the above trace enter Ctrl+c. To read the captured data, perform the following command:

tcmpdump -r arppackets.cap

Cannot Connect to the Service Console

When testing service console connectivity, perform a simple ping test as follows:

ping 10.0.1.2

This tests connectivity using the service console's own TCP/IP stack. When testing VMkernel connectivity, issue the following command:

vmkping 10.0.1.2

This tests connectivity using the VMkernel's own TCP/IP stack.

VMkernel routing should be inspected if the VMkernel port(s) are experiencing difficulty connecting to IP storage. Since VMware does not support VMotion over different subnets, the VMkernel route table would not be applicable in a VMotion situation; checking that each GB port on source and target server is on the SAME subnet would suffice. The following commands can be used to check the routing table of the VMkernel:

esxcfg-route -l

and

cat /proc/vmware/net/tcpip/ifconfig

It is important to know that the VMkernel only has one single routing table that is used. Therefore, if multiple VMkernel ports are configured on different virtual switches, it may initially seem that this design will be optimum for load balancing. A problem would occur if both of these VMkernel ports were on the same subnet. If this is the case, the first physical NIC in the routing table would be used to send all network traffic onto the physical network while the second physical NIC listed in the routing table would not be used. Due to this routing table issue, it is good design to place VMkernel ports on separate subnets.

Service Console

Routing tables used in the service console can be checked with the following commands:

- route -n

- netstat -rn

It is useful to know which files the service console utilizes for its networking services. The service console configuration files should be inspected when troubleshooting network issues. The following files should be reviewed:

- /etc/sysconfig/network - This file contains the useful information such as the gateway and hostname for the service console.
- /etc/sysconfig/network-scripts/ifcfg-vswif0 - This file contains useful information such as the MAC address, IP address and netmask information about the service console. It also contains the ONBOOT parameter, which is set to "yes" by default; when a service console port is disabled, it is set to "no". Attempting to reconfigure the vswif0 interface with an ifconfig command will thus yield a 'no such device' error message, until the interface is RE-enabled.
- /etc/resolv.conf - This file contains the DNS configuration of the service console.
- /etc/nsswitch.conf - This file lists the order in which the service console will resolve hostnames.
- / etc/hosts - This file contains the list of IP to hostname mappings.

The nslookup command issued within the service console can be used to resolve host name resolutions. DNS resolution needs to be fully functional. An ESX server should be able to resolve hostnames using both the Fully Qualified Domain Name (FQDN) or via the short host name (i.e. hostname without the domain name.) Also, both forward and backwards name lookups is needed.

NIC Teaming

When configuring NIC teaming, there is no issue with using both Port ID based and MAC hash based load balancing methods when the physical NICs in the team are connected to two separate physical switches. Load balancing using the IP hash method should not be used when the physical NICs in the team are connected to two separate physical switches. The reason for this is that link aggregation is required on the physical switch ports. Most switches do not support link aggregation of ports across multiple physical switches.

External References

The VMware ESX 3.5 and ESXi version 3.5 Documentation Page:

http://www.vmware.com/support/pubs/vi_pubs.html

ESX Server 3 Installation Guide - ESX Server 3.5 and VirtualCenter 2.5:

http://vmware.com/pdf/vi3_35/esx_3/r35/vi3_35_25_installation_guide.pdf

Upgrade Guide - ESX Server 3.5, ESXi version 3.5 and VirtualCenter 2.5:

http://vmware.com/pdf/vi3_35/esx_3/r35/vi3_35_25_upgrade_guide.pdf

Basic System Administration Guide - ESX Server 3.5, ESXi version 3.5 and Virtual

Center 2.5:

http://vmware.com/pdf/vi3_35/esx_3/r35/vi3_35_25_admin_guide.pdf

ESX Server 3 Configuration Guide - ESX Server 3.5 and VirtualCenter 2.5:

http://vmware.com/pdf/vi3_35/esx_3/r35/vi3_35_25_3_server_config.pdf

VMware Virtual Networking Concepts:

http://www.vmware.com/files/pdf/virtual_networking_concepts.pdf

Networking Performance in Multiple VMs:

http://www.vmware.com/pdf/Multi-VM_Network_Performance.pdf

Configuration Maximums for VMware Infrastructure 3:

http://vmware.com/pdf/vi3_35/esx_3/r35/vi3_35_25_config_max.pdf

ESX Server 3.5 and VirtualCenter 2.5 Release Notes:

http://www.vmware.com/support/vi3/doc/vi3_esx35_vc25_rel_notes.html

Sample Test Questions

1. You want to create a new virtual machine on your ESX 3.5 server. When you try to configure it, you get an error telling you that there are not enough virtual ports available on the virtual switch that you want to connect it to. What is the maximum number of usable virtual ports available on a virtual switch?

a. 8

b. 16

c. 56

d. 256

e. 512

f. 1016

g. 1024

h. unlimited

2. You are called to troubleshoot a problem that a coworker has with his ESX 3.5 server that has 3 physical NICs. The coworker is trying to configure one of the physical NICs on the server but the process is failing. After examining the configuration of the NIC you confirm that it is already assigned to vSwitch1. Which of the following is the reason why they can't assign the NIC to the new vSwitch?

a. The physical NIC is not connected to an Ethernet cable

b. The physical NIC is connected to the wrong type of CAT cable

c. A physical NIC can only be assigned to a single vSwitch

d. The NIC's duplex setting is incorrect

e. The physical switch will not support this type of physical NIC

3. The network administrator in your organization wants to know how you are configuring certain network protocols on your virtual infrastructure. Which of the following protocols is supported on vSwitches?

a. VLAN Trunking Protocol

b. Spanning Tree Protocol

c. Dynamic Trunking Protocol

d. Cisco Discovery Protocol

e. All of the above

f. None of the above

4. You are demonstrating the ESX 3.5 server product to a potential customer and they ask you how to configure the four types of vSwitch ports. Which of the following cannot be configured using the Add Networking wizard?

a. Uplink port

b. Service console port

c. VMkernel port

d. Virtual machine port groups

e. None of the above

5. You determine that one of the applications needs to be available as much as possible so you configure the vSwitch that the VM uses with NIC teaming. You are concerned that you haven't configured the Failover policy to suit the VMs requirements. Which of the following is a true statement about the Failover policy?

a. Only one of the adapters can be active at a time.

b. Only two of the adapters can be active at a time.

c. Up to eight adapters can be active at a time.

d. Only even number of adapters can be active at a time.

e. All of the adapters can be active at a time.

6. You are examining a vSwitch on your ESX 3.5 server and discover it has multiple VMkernel ports. What is a VMkernel port used for?

a. To manage NIC teaming on the vSwitch.

b. To configure and manage VMotion support on the VMs connected to the vSwitch.

c. To configure and manage NFSv3 shared resources that the ESX 3.5 server is configured to access.

d. To configure and manage fibre SAN shared resources that the ESX 3.5 server is configured to access.

e. To configure and manage an iSCSI software initiator connecting to an iSCSI SAN that the ESX 3.5 server is configured to access.

f. To configure and manage the internal firewall ports that the ESX 3.5 server is configured to access.

7. You have been called into troubleshoot a customer that is having no access to the VM that runs an application they need to use for work. When you try to connect remotely with the VI Client directly to the ESX 3.5 server you discover that the systems network ports are not responding. You decide to connect directly to the service console port and discover that it too is not responding. You then connect to the servers ALOM port and discover that the ESX 3.5 server is indeed up and running. After logging into the root account, what command would you first run to determine the current state of all network ports on the server?

a. ifconfig -a

b. ping - to try to connect to a remote server

c. esxcfg-nics -l

d. esxnics-config -l

e. rup

8. You have an ESX 3.5 server that has a high number of configured virtual ports and you are concerned about running out of available ports. What is the minimum number of usable ports that a vSwitch can be configured to have.

a. 1

b. 2

c. 4

d. 8

e. 16

9. You are called in to troubleshoot a connection problem with a stand-alone ESX 3.5 server. The customer cannot connect to the server using the VI Client. You ping the server's IP address and determine it is responding. You connect to the service console via the serial connection on the remote management port. You determine that the server's firewall has been mis-configured. What port needs to be open in order for the VI Client to be able to connect to it?

a. 22

b. 80

b. 443

c. 902

d. 903

e. 2049

10. You are examining a vSwitch configuration to determine if it has NIC teaming configured. NIC teaming requires multiple:

a. vSwitches

b. Port group ports

c. VMkernel ports

d. Port 22 configured in the firewall

e. Uplink ports

11. You are required to provide more security for the applications for one of the departments in your company. They require that you set up an intrusion detection VM to monitor the network traffic going in and out of the VMs running their applications. Which of the following settings should you set to provide them with that capability?

a. Intrusion Control Policy

b. Traffic Shaping Policy

c. Promiscuous Mode

d. Forged Transmits

e. MAC Address Changes

12. You want to provide a specific VM with the ability to be part of multiple VLANs on your physical network infrastructure. By setting the virtual machine port group with VLAN ID 4095 it gives the VM access to multiple VLANs using which of the following?

a. VLAN Broadcast Policy

b. VLAN Guest Tagging Mode

c. VLAN Unicast Mode

d. Virtual Switch Tagging

e. External Switch Tagging

13. You are called in to monitor and configure network I/O bandwidth on the VMs running on a newly configured ESX 3.5 server. After evaluating the performance requirements you notice that certain VMs are not being controlled through the traffic shaping policy. Why is that?

a. Traffic shaping is done only at the vSwitch level

b. You are also running the HA product which does not support traffic shaping

c. Traffic shaping is turned off by default

d. The VMs operating systems don't support traffic shaping

e. The Peak Bandwidth is set in Mbps at a value too low to allow the VMs to meet their needs.

14. A customer has contacted you with a complaint that two of their VMs can communicate with each other but for security reasons they are not supposed to be able to do that. You examine the VMs and notice that they are next to each other. When VMs are connected to the same port group on the same vSwitch they are____?

a. routed to each other using the physical switch configuration

b. routed to each other based on the operating systems configuration in each VM

c. routed to each other locally by use of the VMkernel

d. not routed to each other via the vSwitch by default

e. not ever routed to each other via the vSwitch

15. Which of the following load balancing methods is the default for an ESX 3.5 server?

a. Route based on the originating virtual port ID

b. Route based on IP hash

c. Route based on source MAC hash

d. Use explicit failover order

16. Operators of a company's virtualized web servers contact the ESX system administrator reporting a noticeable reduction in network performance. The ESX administrator has not modified anything on the ESX server but has recently upgraded the previous Ethernet switch that was connected to the ESX server. The new switch has been configured with the exact settings as the older replaced switch. Which of the following might the ESX system administrator check first as a possible root cause?

a. Faulty switch port

b. Bad network cable

c. Bad forwarding tables

d. Speed and duplex settings

e. Routing tables

17. The default behavior within a NIC team when a NIC has failed is to do which of the following?

a. Unload the NIC driver using the vmkload-module command

b. Promote all remaining NICs in the team to active status

c. Send an SNMP trap

d. Suspend virtual network traffic until NIC is placed in inactive status

e. Notify physical switch using an ARP packet

18. Virtual machines obtain their MAC addresses from which of the following?

a. VMkernel

b. Virtual Switches

c. Service Console

d. Port Group

e. NIC Team

19. Which of the following is not an attribute of a port group?

a. Label

b. VLAN ID

c. IP Address

d. Subnet Mask

e. Number of ports

20. An ESX system administrator is not successful when attempting to connect to the ESX server via the VI Client. Needing to verify which physical NIC is linked to a virtual switch, which of the following commands can be performed on the service console to obtain this information?

a. esxcfg-advcfg -u

b. esxcfg-vnics -a

c. esxcfg-vmhbadevs -n

d. esxcfg-vlink -l

e. esxcfg-vswitch -l

Sample Test Solutions

1. You want to create a new virtual machine on your ESX 3.5 server. When you try to configure it, you get an error telling you that there are not enough virtual ports available on the virtual switch that you want to connect it to. What is the maximum number of usable virtual ports available on a virtual switch?

a. 8

b. 16

c. 56

d. 256

e. 512

f. 1016

g. 1024

h. unlimited

***Answer:** f - there are 1024 ports on a single virtual switch but 8 of them cannot be used. They are dedicated for the VMkernel's use.*

2. You are called to troubleshoot a problem that a coworker has with his ESX 3.5 server that has 3 physical NICs. The coworker is trying to configure one of the physical NICs on the server but the process is failing. After examining the configuration of the NIC you confirm that it is already assigned to vSwitch1. Which of the following is the reason why they can't assign the NIC to the new vSwitch?

a. The physical NIC is not connected to an Ethernet cable

b. The physical NIC is connected to the wrong type of CAT cable

c. A physical NIC can only be assigned to a single vSwitch

d. The NIC's duplex setting is incorrect

e. The physical switch will not support this type of physical NIC

***Answer:** c - all of the other answers will not cause the NIC to be assigned to a new vSwitch*

3. The network administrator in your organization wants to know how you are configuring certain network protocols on your virtual infrastructure. Which of the following protocols is supported on vSwitches?

a. VLAN Trunking Protocol

b. Spanning Tree Protocol

c. Dynamic Trunking Protocol

d. Cisco Discovery Protocol

e. All of the above

f. None of the above

Answer: d - none of the other protocols are supported on vSwitches.

4. You are demonstrating the ESX 3.5 server product to a potential customer and they ask you how to configure the four types of vSwitch ports. Which of the following cannot be configured using the Add Networking wizard?

a. Uplink port

b. Service console port

c. VMkernel port

d. Virtual machine port groups

e. None of the above

Answer: a - the uplink port is configured when the vSwitch is originally created or if the vSwitch is configured for NIC teaming.

5. You determine that one of the applications needs to be available as much as possible so you configure the vSwitch that the VM uses with NIC teaming. You are concerned that you haven't configured the Failover policy to suite the VMs requirements. Which of the following is a true statement about the Failover policy?

a. Only one of the adapters can be active at a time.

b. Only two of the adapters can be active at a time.

c. Up to eight adapters can be active at a time.

d. Only even number of adapters can be active at a time.

e. All of the adapters can be active at a time.

Answer: a - One of the other adapters can be configured to become the active adapter if the primary adapter fails. This allows you to control the failover order of the NICs.

6. You are examining a vSwitch on your ESX 3.5 server and discover it has multiple VMkernel ports. What is a VMkernel port used for?

a. To manage NIC teaming on the vSwitch.

b. To configure and manage VMotion support on the VMs connected to the vSwitch.

c. To configure and manage NFSv3 shared resources that the ESX 3.5 server is configured to access.

d. To configure and manage fibre SAN shared resources that the ESX 3.5 server is configured to access.

e. To configure and manage an iSCSI software initiator connecting to an iSCSI SAN that the ESX 3.5

server is configured to access.

f. To configure and manage the internal firewall ports that the ESX 3.5 server is configured to access.

Answer: b, c, & e - A VMkernel port is used when configuring VMotion, NFS or iSCSI connections.

7. You have been called into troubleshoot a customer that is having no access to the VM that runs an application they need to use for work. When you try to connect remotely with the VI Client directly to the ESX 3.5 server you discover that the systems network ports are not responding. You decide to connect directly to the service console port and discover that it too is not responding. You then connect to the servers ALOM port and discover that the ESX 3.5 server is indeed up and running. After logging into the root account, what command would you first run to determine the current state of all network ports on the server?

a. ifconfig -a

b. ping - to try to connect to a remote server

c. esxcfg-nics -l

d. esxnics-config -l

e. rup

Answer: c - The esxcfg-nics -l command will identify what NICS are in the system.

8. You have an ESX 3.5 server that has a high number of configured virtual ports and you are concerned about running out of available ports. What is the minimum number of usable ports that a vSwitch can be configured to have.

a. 1

b. 2

c. 4

d. 8

e. 16

Answer: d - 8 usable ports is the smallest port configuration supported. By changing some of the existing vSwitches from the default configuration of 56 usable ports to a number slightly more than it is using, you can free up ports for additional vSwitches.

9. You are called in to troubleshoot a connection problem with a stand-alone ESX 3.5 server. The customer cannot connect to the server using the VI Client. You ping the server's IP address and determine it is responding. You connect to the service console via the serial connection on the remote management port. You determine that the server's firewall has been mis-configured. What port needs to be open in order for the VI Client to be able to connect to it?

a. 22

b. 80

b. 443

c. 902

d. 903

e. 2049

Answer: b - Port 443 is used for HTTPS, SSL connection for Web Access, VI Client access to ESX Server or VirtualCenter, VMware Converter and VMware Update Manager. Port 22 is used for SSH access to service console. Port 80 is used for HTTP access to web servers. Access to this port is redirected to port 443 (SSL). Port 902 is used for Communication between ESX 3.5 servers on Incoming TCP and Outgoing UDP transmissions and VC Server to ESX Server in its inventory. Port 903 is used for VM Console access via VI Client or VI Web Access on Incoming TCP. Port 2049 is used for connection to NFS storage devices used by the VMkernel networking stack not the service console networking stack on Incoming TCP and Outgoing UDP transmissions.

10. You are examining a vSwitch configuration to determine if it has NIC teaming configured. NIC teaming requires multiple:

a. vSwitches

b. Port group ports

c. VMkernel ports

d. Port 22 configured in the firewall

e. Uplink ports

Answer: e - The process of connecting a vSwitch to a physical NIC creates an uplink port on the vSwitch. NIC teaming requires two or more physical NICS. Therefore you would see two or more uplink ports on the vSwitch.

11. You are required to provide more security for the applications for one of the departments in your company. They require that you set up an intrusion detection VM to monitor the network traffic going in and out of the VMs running their applications. Which of the following settings should you set to provide them with that capability?

a. Intrusion Control Policy

b. Traffic Shaping Policy

c. Promiscuous Mode

d. Forged Transmits

e. MAC Address Changes

Answer: c - Promiscuous Mode allows the network to be "snooped". Network intrusion detection VMs would usually require that ability on the vSwitch or port groups connecting to the VMs that

you wanted to monitor.

12. You want to provide a specific VM with the ability to be part of multiple VLANs on your physical network infrastructure. By setting the virtual machine port group with VLAN ID 4095 it gives the VM access to multiple VLANs using which of the following?

a. VLAN Broadcast Policy

b. VLAN Guest Tagging Mode

c. VLAN Unicast Mode

d. Virtual Switch Tagging

e. External Switch Tagging

Answer: b - In VGT mode, a virtual machine can be a part of several VLANs simultaneously.

13. You are called in to monitor and configure network I/O bandwidth on the VMs running on a newly configured ESX 3.5 server. After evaluating the performance requirements you notice that certain VMs are not being controlled through the traffic shaping policy. Why is that?

a. Traffic shaping is done only at the vSwitch level

b. You are also running the HA product which does not support traffic shaping

c. Traffic shaping is turned off by default

d. The VMs operating systems don't support traffic shaping

e. The Peak Bandwidth is set in Mbps at a value too low to allow the VMs to meet their needs.

Answer: c - Traffic shaping must be turned on and configured. All of the other options are false options.

14. A customer has contacted you with a complaint that two of their VMs can communicate with each other but for security reasons they are not supposed to be able to do that. You examine the VMs and notice that they are next to each other. When VMs are connected to the same port group on the same vSwitch they are____?

a. routed to each other using the physical switch configuration

b. routed to each other based on the operating systems configuration in each VM

c. routed to each other locally by use of the VMkernel

d. not routed to each other via the vSwitch by default

e. not ever routed to each other via the vSwitch

Answer: c- VMs on the same port group on the same vSwitch are routed to all VMs on the same vSwitch

15. Which of the following load balancing methods is the default for an ESX 3.5 server?

a. Route based on the originating virtual port ID

b. Route based on IP hash

c. Route based on source MAC hash

d. Use explicit failover order

Answer: a - Route based on the originating virtual port ID is the default as it incurs little overhead to perform its load distribution algorithm.

16. Operators of a company's virtualized web servers contact the ESX system administrator reporting a noticeable reduction in network performance. The ESX administrator has not modified anything on the ESX server but has recently upgraded the previous Ethernet switch that was connected to the ESX server. The new switch has been configured with the exact settings as the older replaced switch. Which of the following might the ESX system administrator check first as a possible root cause?

a. Faulty switch port

b. Bad network cable

c. Bad forwarding tables

d. Speed and duplex settings

e. Routing tables

Answer: d - By default, ESX servers will use autonegotiation to determine their speed and duplex settings. Not all physical NICs and physical switch ports autonegotiate properly. It may be possible that the connection has been set at a lower speed or an improper duplex setting. In such cases, it is important to manually set the speed and duplex settings appropriately.

17. The default behavior within a NIC team when a NIC has failed is to do which of the following?

a. Unload the NIC driver using the vmkload-module command

b. Promote all remaining NICs in the team to active status

c. Send an SNMP trap

d. Suspend virtual network traffic until NIC is placed in inactive status

e. Notify physical switch using an ARP packet

Answer: e - When a fail over event occurs within a NIC team, the standby adapter will notify the physical switch by sending an ARP packet to the physical switch so that the switch can properly update it's forwarding tables.

18. Virtual machines obtain their MAC addresses from which of the following?

a. VMkernel

b. Virtual Switches

c. Service Console

d. Port Group

e. NIC Team

Answer: a - Virtual NICs obtained their MAC addresses from the VMkernel. A virtual machine's MAC address can be changed from within the edit settings dialog box for the virtual machine.

19. Which of the following is not an attribute of a port group?

a. Label

b. VLAN ID

c. IP Address

d. Subnet Mask

e. Number of ports

Answer: c and d - Virtual switch port groups are not assigned an IP address or a subnet mask. Virtual switch ports have these attributes. Virtual switch attributes include a label, VLAN ID and number of ports.

20. An ESX system administrator is not successful when attempting to connect to the ESX server via the VI Client. Needing to verify which physical NIC is linked to a virtual switch, which of the following commands can be performed on the service console to obtain this information?

a. esxcfg-advcfg -u

b. esxcfg-vnics -a

c. esxcfg-vmhbadevs -n

d. esxcfg-vlink -l

e. esxcfg-vswitch -l

Answer: e - esxcfg-vswitch -l will display the physical NIC to virtual switch mappings.

Chapter 5

ESX 3.5 Server Storage Configurations

After reading this chapter you should expect to learn:

- What are the available storage options in VI3
- What is a SCSI datastore
- What is a Fibre Channel datastore
- What is an iSCSI datastore
- What is a NAS/NFS datastore
- What is storage multipathing
- What are the differences of the various RAID levels
- What is a VMFS
- How to increase the size of a VMFS
- How to boot an ESX 3.5 server from a SAN
- What is a Raw Device Mapping file
- Troubleshooting common storage infrastructure problems

What Are the Available Storage Options for Your Virtual Infrastructure?

Storage is a vital component of virtualization in the data center. Successful virtualization deployments require proper planning of storage requirements and a solid understanding of VMware's Virtual Machine File System (VMFS). The choice of storage may comprise of one or more storage technologies to obtain the necessary performance, functionality and scalability typically needed in modern data centers.

When making a purchase or installation decision be aware that to the ESX 3.5 server software your storage can be either:

- Local
- Private
- Shared

Local Storage

Local storage would be located either internal in your ESX 3.5 or directly attached to it. In other words the server directly controls access to the data on these disks using its own internal host bus adapters (HBA). No other server would control access to the storage space on a local storage device. Local storage is appropriate for standalone ESX 3.5 servers providing virtualization for a small number of virtual machines. Standalone ESX 3.5 servers are a good fit for small workgroup environments, development and testing labs and proof of concept projects.

Private Storage

Data centers typically require solutions that go beyond the local storage capacity found in standalone ESX 3.5 servers. VMware's VI3 can take advantage of storage area networks (SANs). Remote storage devices are made accessible to ESX 3.5 servers within a SAN implementation. Several SAN solutions are available in IT environments.

Private storage would be located on either a fibre channel or iSCSI SAN or on a NFS server. The storage space would be configured to allow only one ESX 3.5 server to access the data that it stores. These three remote storage technologies can be configured to hide the storage space from other servers.

Shared Storage

Shared storage can be located on fibre channel SANs, iSCSI SANs or on a NFS server. Although the service console can access FTP (File Transfer Protocol) and SMB (Server Message Block) / CIFS (Common Internet File System) based storage, these cannot be used by ESX 3.5 servers to operate virtual machines.

The ESX 3.5 server and Virtual Center 2.x features that require the use of shared storage are:

- VMotion
- DRS
- HA
- VCB

In Figure 5.1, ESX Server A has exclusive access to the two private LUNs in the storage array. Exclusive access can be implemented with the use of hard zoning done at the fibre channel switch along with masking at the storage processor level. Fibre channel, zoning and masking will be discussed later in this chapter. The path ESX Server A uses leaves its HBA (Host Bus Adapter) and traverses through the switch to the top storage processor located on the top of the storage array. These two private LUNs would not be able to be used with any of the VMware technologies that require the VMs to be on shared storage. Both ESX Server A and B have access to the public LUN as seen by the dotted lines accessing the public LUN through the bottom storage processor.

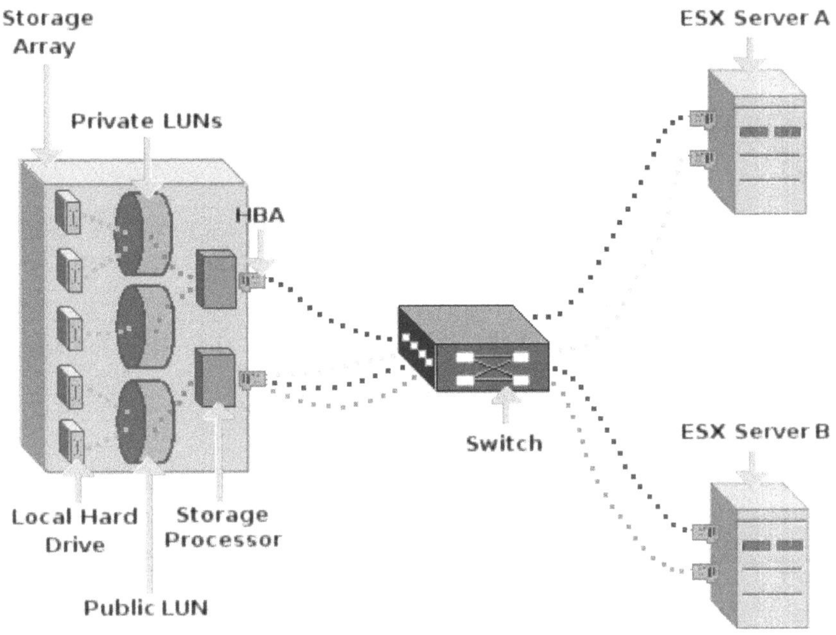

Figure 5.1 Public and Private LUNs

IDE Storage Devices

The numerous storage options available to be used in your virtual infrastructure offer a wide range of choices in both price and performance. IDE (Integrated Drive Electronics) hard disks are common inexpensive storage components. A VMware's ESX 3.5 server can use these drives when installed within the server. IDE drives are supported only as a means to store the ESX 3.5 server's boot installation files. VMware does not support the use of IDE drives formatted with VMFS in order to store virtual machines. The drives can however be used to store the ESX 3.5's service console files.

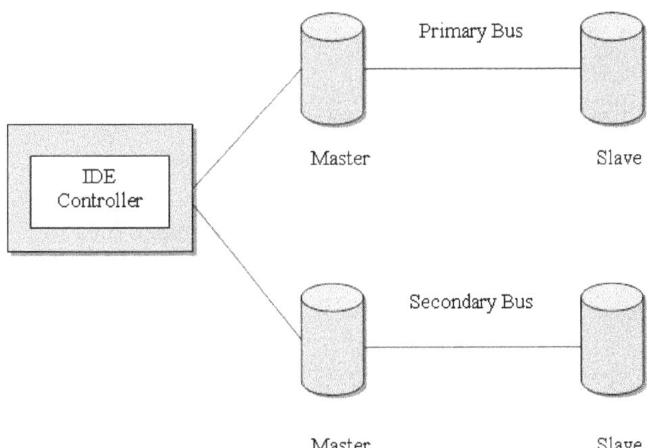

Figure 5.2 IDE Bus Configuration

The IDE controller as shown in Figure 5.2 manages a primary and secondary bus. Each of these buses supports up to two drives for a total of up to four drives. One is identified as the master drive and the other is identified as the slave drive. The supported cable length is minimal for IDE buses, so the drives are installed internally to the server enclosure.

NOTE: IDE RAID and SATA RAID are not supported for use with the VMFS file system.

SCSI Storage Devices

VMware requires the use of SCSI (Small Computer System Interface) hard disks, formatted with the virtual machine file system when storing virtual machines locally. These drives can be installed within the ESX 3.5 server or as directly attached storage devices.

SCSI drives can provide better performance than IDE drives although SCSI controllers and drives typically cost more than IDE controllers and drives.

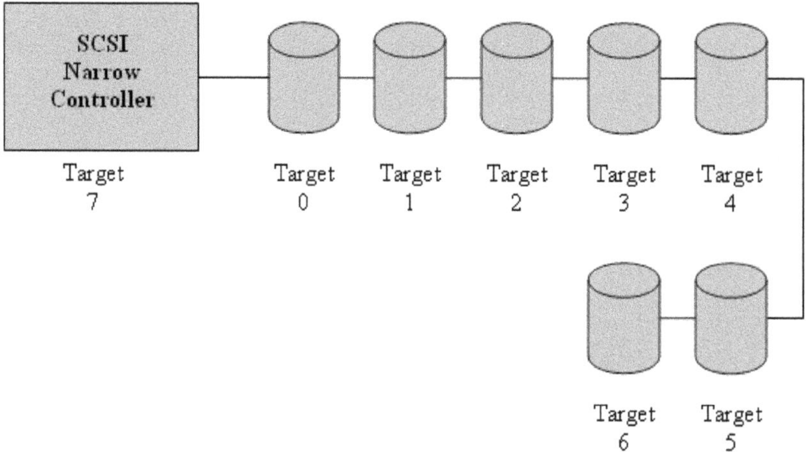

Figure 5.3 SCSI Bus Configuration

It is good practice to have at least two SCSI drives in a server as shown in Figure 5.3. This is done so that the SCSI drives can be placed in a mirror (RAID 1) configuration if the motherboard supports it. RAID configurations will be discussed later in this chapter.

SCSI storage devices can be used as an ESX 3.5 server datastore. You can store the following:

- VM state files
- International Organization for Standardization 9660 (ISO) image files. ISO image files typically use a .iso file extension
- VM templates (if using VirtualCenter)

Fibre Channel Storage Devices

Fibre Channel (FC) is a commonly deployed SAN solution. The FC protocol is used to embed the SCSI protocol commands, transmitted as light pulses across fiber optic cabling and routed via FC switches. This configuration is referred to as the fibre switched fabric. What makes FC so popular is its performance, reliability, scalability and security. Its fast performance is due to its high bandwidth capabilities. Reliability is achieved when the switched fabric employs the use of redundant high speed fibre channel switches.

Additional FC switches can be added when needed to scale out the switched fabric. Due to the sensitive nature of light, security is strong as it is virtually impossible to tap into the light signal without a noticeable disruption in service occurring.

Fibre Channel storage devices can be used as an ESX 3.5 server datastore. You can store the following:

- VM state files
- ISO image (.iso) files
- VM templates (if using VirtualCenter)

Another benefit of using Fibre Channel storage devices is that the FC protocol supports the use of SCSI protocol commands. The ESX 3.5 server can use the same commands on both FC drives and SCSI drives.

ESX 3.5 servers are connected to the FC SAN with the use of HBAs that provide the proper fiber optic connections needed to attach to FC switches. The VMkernel controls the flow of disk I/O from the virtual machines and passes it onto the switched fabric via the HBAs. The data flows across the fabric, routed through the ports on the FC switch to its final destination, the remote FC storage array as shown in Figure 5.4.

Fibre Channel Storage Arrays

Storage arrays contain numerous high speed, large capacity hard drives. Access to these hard drives is controlled by devices known as storage processors (SPs). Storage processors behave similar to CPUs within a computer by providing management of the SCSI commands it receives on the fabric for requests to read and write data on the drives it manages.

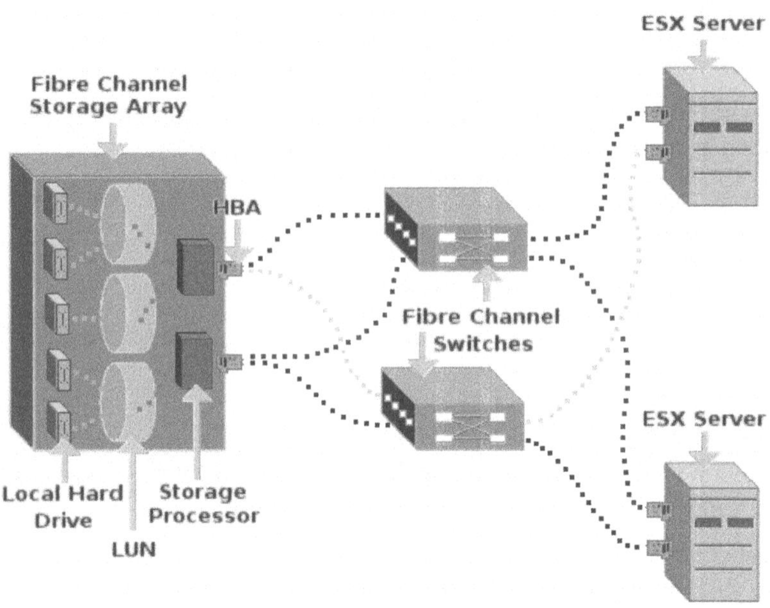

Figure 5.4 Fibre Channel SAN Configuration

Storage processors also handle the RAID calculations needed to store data in a volume on the array. They are also responsible for the data recovery process if a drive fails in the array. The load from these requests can be spread if multiple SPs are configured in the array. This configuration also provides failover capabilities as well. It would pose a significant problem, if any server connected to the switched fabric could use any piece of storage visible to it. Multiple servers writing data to the same storage space with different file systems could lead to data corruption and or significant data loss. Proper zoning and masking within a fibre channel switch fabric can prevent such data corruption situations from occurring and will be discussed later in this chapter.

For an up to date listing of all supported SAN storage devices refer to the ESX 3.5 Storage/SAN Compatibility Guide:

http://www.vmware.com/pdf/vi35_san_guide.pdf

Fibre Channel Storage LUNs

The SAN administrator using software provided by the storage array vendor may need to provide a piece of storage larger than the capacity of any single drive housed in the array. To provide larger pieces of storage, SAN administrators typically combine two or more hard drives in a storage array in a configuration known as a LUN (Logical Unit Number). As the name implies, these LUNs are assigned an identification number. LUN numbers are presented to servers or groups of servers within the switched fabric. Figure 5.5 shows an example of a storage array with four LUNs configured on it.

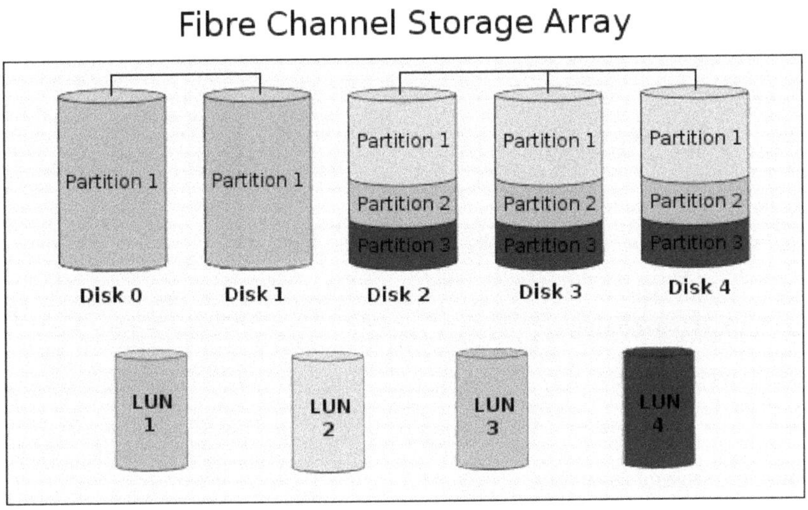

Figure 5.5 Fibre Channel Storage Array LUN Assignments

In this example, LUN 1 consists of disk 0 and disk 1. These two drives each contain a single partition (also known as a slice) and are configured as a mirrored set (RAID 1). LUN 2 consists of three drives configured in a striped set with parity (RAID 5). LUN 2 uses partition 1 on disks 2, 3, and 4 and occupies 1/2 of the total available drive space. LUN 3 consists of each partition 2, occupying 1/4 of the total drive space within the RAID 5 configuration of disks 2, 3, and 4. LUN 4 consists of each partition 3, occupying the remaining 1/4 of the total drive space within the RAID 5 configuration of disks 2, 3, and 4. It is important to note that a SAN administrator can configure numerous drive configurations that the storage device supports within a single storage array. Both the ESX and SAN administrators should properly plan storage considerations to ensure acceptable performance vs. ease of management when designing the storage solution. Several virtual machines can operate from a single LUN. It is necessary to consider the individual application workloads of the virtual machines when assigning virtual machines to a LUN.

Fibre Channel Zoning

To prevent data loss and corruption from occurring, a switched fabric can be configured in such a way as to limit which storage arrays a server can access. SAN administrators impose these restrictions by way of FC zones. A zone enforces access policies within a FC switch in several different ways.

Fibre Channel Hard Zoning

Hard zoning can be setup by using the FC switch to configure the fibre channel fabric so that only a specific port or ports can communicate data to each other. An example of this is shown in Figure 5.6. Only the ports connected with the dotted lines are permitted to communicate with one another.

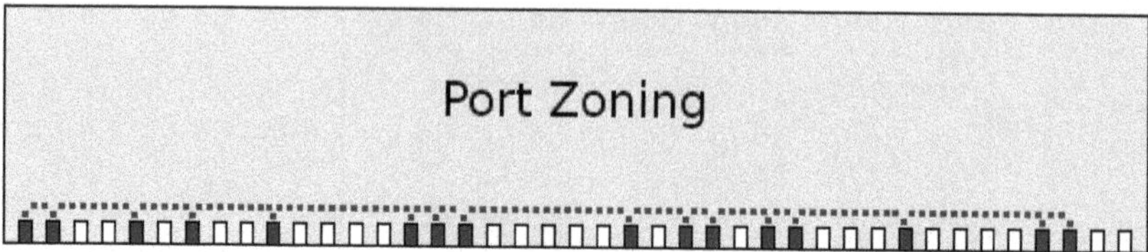

Figure 5.6 Fibre Channel SAN Hard Zoning

Hard zoning provides the following benefits:

- Improved security
- Improved control of the storage resources
- Centralized management of the zoning capabilities on the SAN

Improved security

In order for unauthorized access to occur, it would first be necessary for the attacker to obtain physical access to the switch fabric then disconnect and reconnect another cable to the port without being noticed. This method of zoning is preferred when strong security is desired. Hard zoning is often referred to as port zoning.

Improved Control of the Storage Resources

Hard zoning provides a way to hide LUNs from servers that shouldn't access those resources. This allows the SAN administrator to control which servers access a particular storage array. Controlling access can assure maximum throughput for an ESX 3.5 server that needs it due to high I/O requirements of their VM's applications.

Centralized Management of the Zoning Ccapabilities on the SAN

The other benefit of hard zoning is that the SAN administrator can control all access at the switch level which centralizes the management of the SAN fabric. In large organizations this simplifies the process of controlling access to resources.

For example:

The ESX 3.5 server administrator would make a request to the SAN storage administrator for a LUN that is 20 GB in size and is configured with a certain storage configuration of RAID level and stripe size (we will discuss these issues later in the chapter.) The SAN administrator builds the required LUN. Implementation of the zone within the fabric can be performed to allow only that particular ESX 3.5 server to see the LUN. The storage array containing that LUN might have other LUNs that are visible to other servers as well.

Zoning can also be implemented as soft zones. Soft zones work by using a unique identification number known as a WWN (World Wide Name).

A WWN is assigned to each port within the switched fabric. Within the FC switch, a soft zone is configured with a listing of WWNs that are allowed to communicate with each other. In Figure 5.7, HBAs on the switched fabric can communicate with WWN number 1, 2 or 3 by simply using the WWN number when making a storage request.

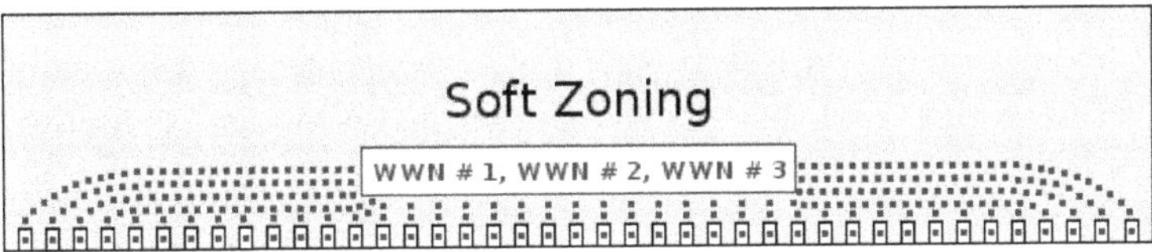

Figure 5.7 Fibre Channel SAN Soft Zoning

Soft zoning is less secure than hard zoning. All that is required for an unauthorized server to access a piece of storage is for that server to have the WWN of the storage array. Once the WWN is known, the request can be made to access the storage from any port on the fibre channel switch. The FC switch will then pass the data through if the WWN is on the list for that soft zone. Soft zoning is also referred to as WWN zoning.

Fibre Channel Storage LUN Sizing

Communication between the ESX and SAN administrators is essential. SAN administrators may at first be surprised when an ESX administrator requests unusually large LUN sizes. The SAN administrator may be accustomed to creating LUNs for physical servers. In such situations, there typically is a one to one relationship. One physical server assigned to a single LUN. Physical servers often use LUNs as additional data storage repositories. The size of these LUNs is typically under 100 GB. SAN administrators may become reluctant when an ESX administrator requests large LUNs reaching 500 GB in size or greater along with having multiple ESX servers being granted access to the same LUN.

iSCSI Devices

iSCSI is the Internet SCSI protocol used to transport the SCSI protocol across local or wide area networks. iSCSI utilizes the widely used TCP/IP (Transmission Control Protocol/Internet Protocol) protocol to transfer SCSI commands to storage arrays within a SAN. The popularity of iSCSI is mainly due to its ability to take advantage of existing switched Ethernet networks as shown in Figure 5.8. This reduces the learning curve for existing ESX and network administrators who typically are well versed in Ethernet based TCP/IP networks. Due to iSCSI not requiring organizations to purchase expensive specialized switches as is the requirement for fibre channel SANs, a significant cost savings combined with little training needed to implement iSCSI has increased its appeal as a SAN solution in modern data centers.

A system on the network that accesses an iSCSI storage device is referred to as an iSCSI initiator. iSCSI storage devices are referred to as iSCSI targets. iSCSI targets can be used as ESX 3.5 server datastores. You can store the following:

- VM state files
- .iso images
- VM templates (if using VirtualCenter)

iSCSI targets support access to raw LUNs via RDM (Raw Device Mappings) and the ability to VMotion virtual machines. RDM is discussed later in this chapter and VMotion is discussed in chapter 13 - Virtual Machine Migration.

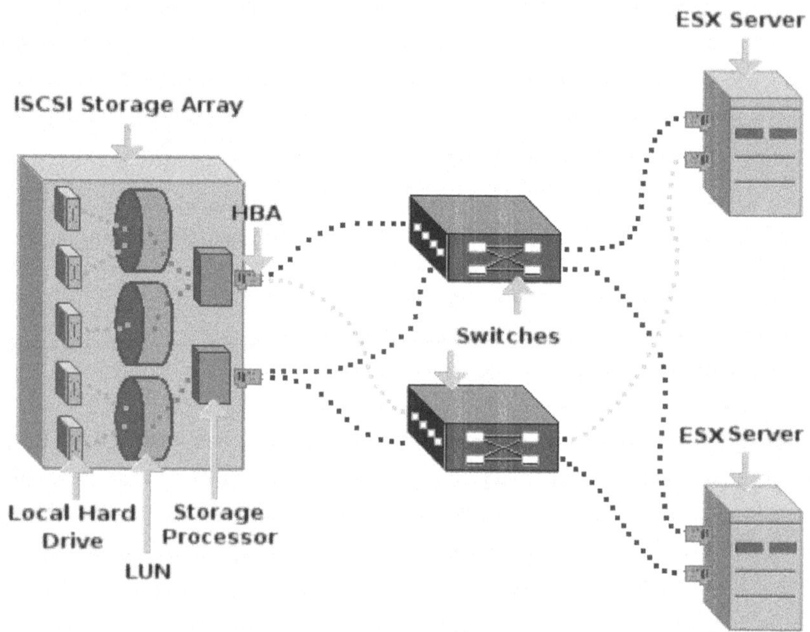

Figure 5.8 ISCSI SAN Configuration

The ESX 3.5 server product can be configured with either a software or hardware based iSCSI initiator.

iSCSI Software Initiators

Out of the box, ESX 3.5 servers can be configured with an iSCSI software initiator. When operating as an iSCSI software initiator, the ESX 3.5 server can communicate with iSCSI targets. With the iSCSI software initiator, the vmkiscsid daemon is used in the service console to login and authenticate to the iSCSI target. Requests can then be made to discover within the iSCSI storage arrays the LUNs that are being presented to the ESX 3.5 server. This initiator is fully supported and can be configured to connect to a wide variety of iSCSI targets.

Only one iSCSI software adapter can be configured per ESX server. The iSCSI software adapter is always assigned the device identifier of vmhba32.

An iSCSI software initiator uses a 1,000 Mbit ethernet adapter in the ESX 3.5 server to emulate an iSCSI HBA. An iSCSI software initiator provides the following iSCSI functions:

- iSCSI initiatior (based on the Cisco iSCSI driver)
- TCP/IP
- NIC driver

NOTE: The iSCSI functionality follows the Cisco iSCSI Initiator Common Reference.

Configuring the iSCSI Software Initiator

The iSCSI software initiator requires additional networking configurations to work properly. A service console and VMkernel port on a virtual switch that contains an uplink port that has connectivity to the subnet where the iSCSI target is located is required. Refer to Chapter 4 - Networking for further information on configuring virtual switches and connection types. Once the network configurations have been implemented, an ESX administrator needs to perform the following steps to implement the iSCSI software initiator:

Step 1. Select the Configuration tab and click on the Networking link as shown in Figure 5.9. Review the configuration to verify that a VMkernel port has been configured for the iSCSI software initiator to use. You need to add this type of port if it has not already been configured. In Figure 5.9, the VMkernel port is located on vSwitch0 and has the port label of iSCSIa02. The VMkernel port needs a different IP address than the service console. Both the service console and VMkernel ports need to access the iSCSI target(s). Therefore, either both of these ports can be on the same subnet as the iSCSI target(s) or routing will need to be correctly implemented within the network. It is not necessary to have both the service console port and VMkernel port configured on the same virtual switch.

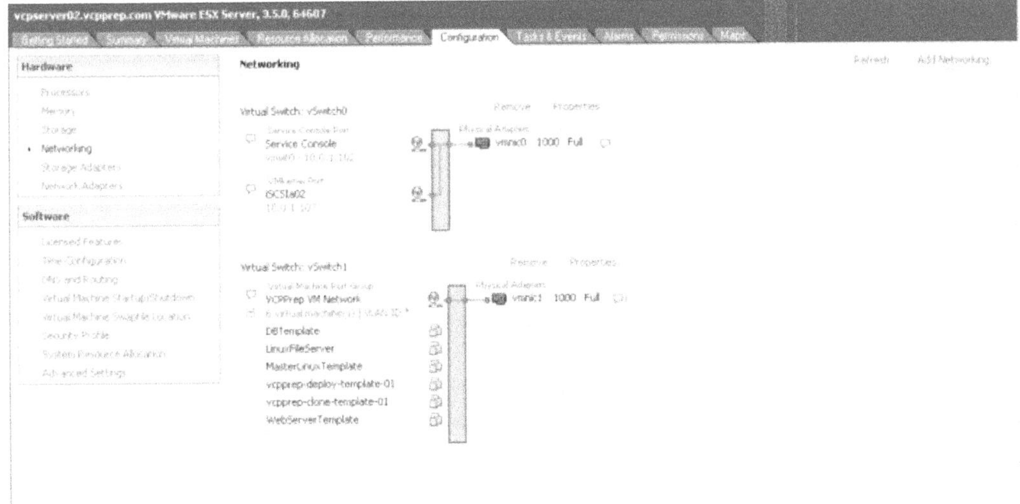

Figure 5.9 iSCSI Networking Requirements

Step 2. To enable the ESX 3.5 server firewall to allow iSCSI communication of port 3260, you must click on the Security Profile link in the lower left of the Software box as shown in Figure 5.10.

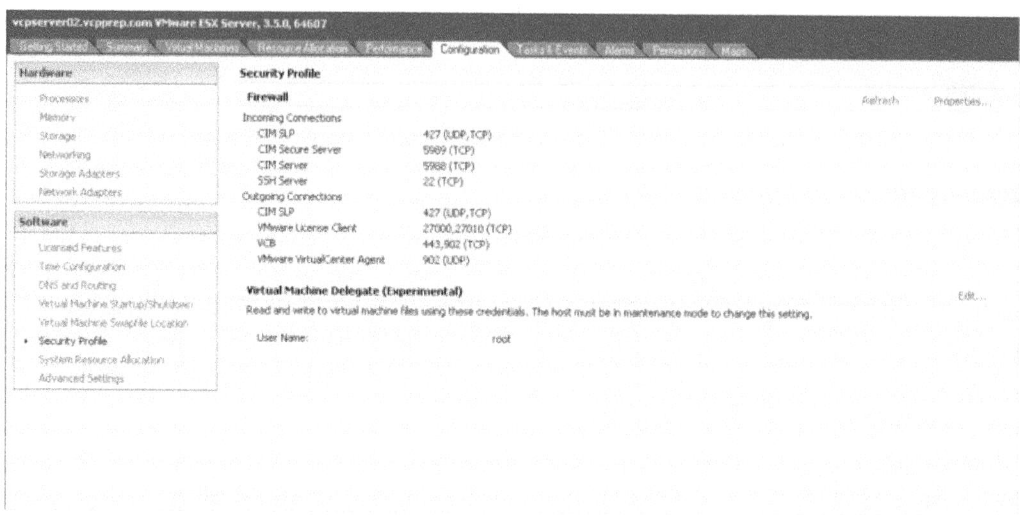

Figure 5.10 iSCSI Firewall Default Settings

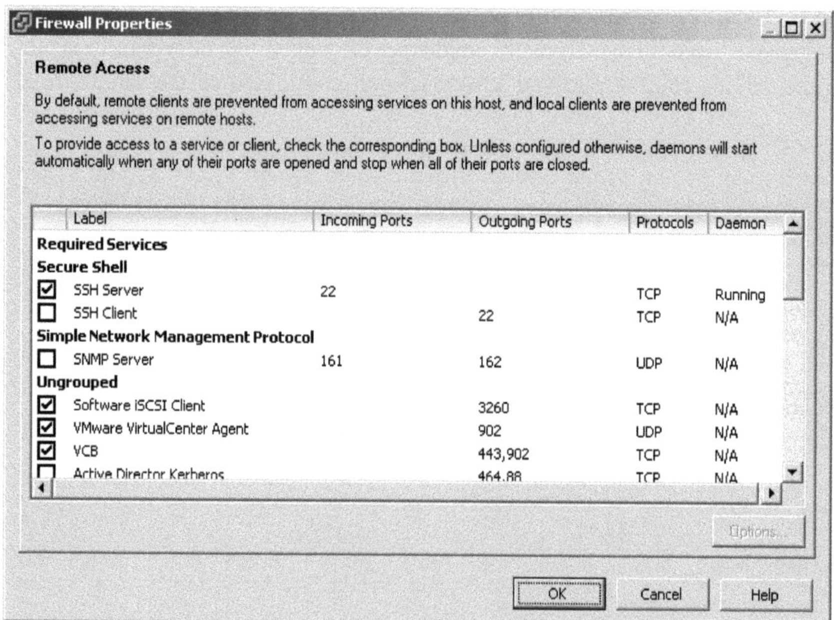

Figure 5.11 Firewall Properties To Enable iSCSI Software Client

Step 3. Click on the Properties link in the upper right to bring up the Firewall Properties window as shown in Figure 5.11.Click in the check box to enable the Software iSCSI Client. Click on the OK button to continue.

Step 4. You should now see that the Software iSCSI Client is enabled as shown in Figure 5.12. If it doesn't display that, click on the Refresh link in the upper right to refresh the display.

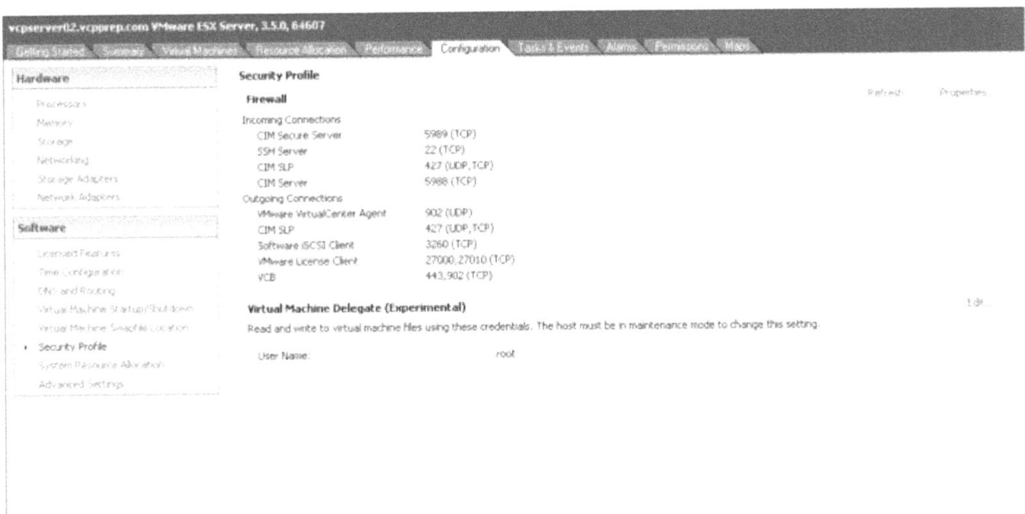

Figure 5.12 Firewall Enabled For iSCSI Software Client

CLI NOTE: From the CLI you can query the software iSCSI Client service to view its current setting by executing the following command:

 # esxcfg-firewall –q swISCSIClient

Service swISCSIClient is blocked.

CLI NOTE: If you get a Service swISCSIClient is blocked message you can enable it using this CLI command:

 # esxcfg-firewall –e swISCSIClient

Service swISCSIClient is enabled.

CLI NOTE: If you are still having problems connecting you can disable the firewall using the following CLI command:

 # /etc/init.d/iptables stop

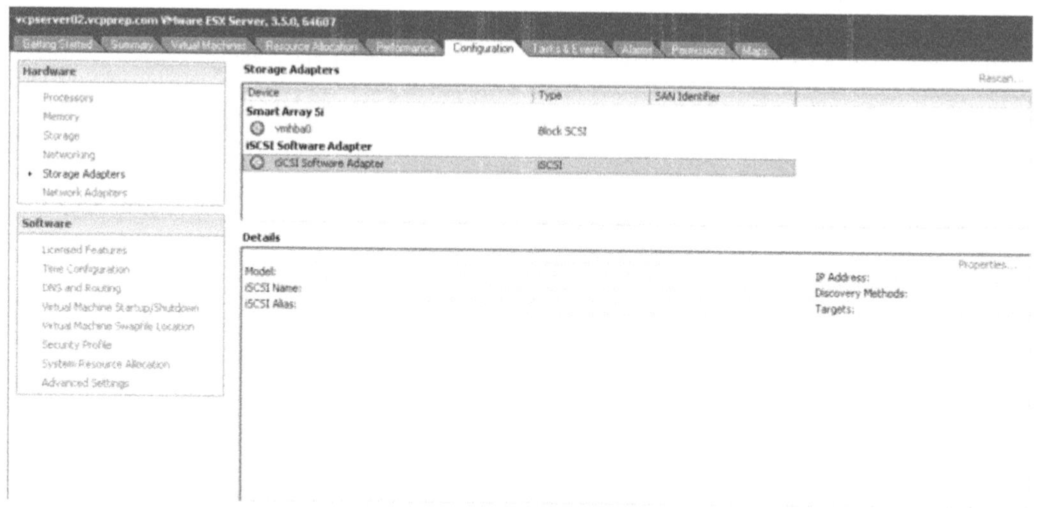

Figure 5.13 iSCSI Software Initiator Adapter

Step 5. You can now click on the Storage Adapters link in the Hardware box to see the iSCSI Software Adapter as shown in Figure 5.13. Clicking on the adapter will display its details. Notice that there is no information displayed yet.

Step 6. Click on the iSCSI Software Adapter Properties link in the lower right of the screen. This will open the Properties window as shown in Figure 5.14.

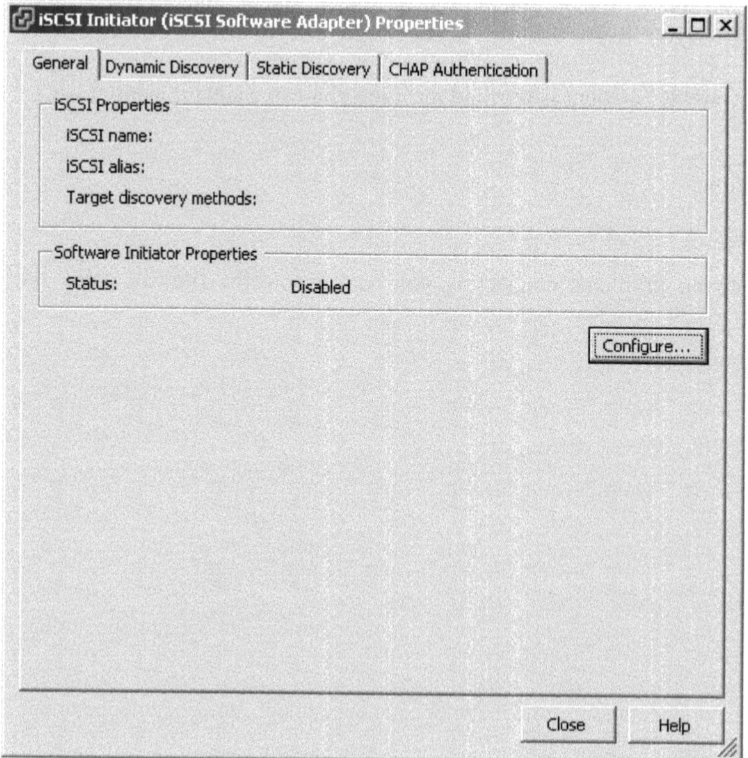

Figure 5.14 iSCSI Software Initiator General Tab

The iSCSI software initiator is currently disabled.

CLI NOTE: To determine if the iSCSI software adapter is enabled or disabled from the command line execute the following command:

 # esxcfg-swiscsi –q

Software iSCSI is disabled

Click on the "Configure…" button to open the General Properties window as shown in Figure 5.15.

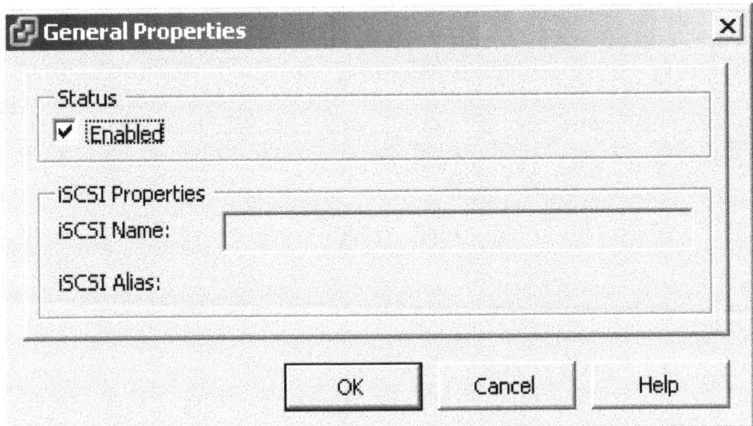

Figure 5.15 iSCSI Software Initiator Enabled Check Box

Click in the Enabled check box to activate the iSCSI software initiator. Click on the OK button to continue.

CLI NOTE: To enable the iSCSI software adapter from the command line execute the following command:

 # esxcfg-swiscsi –e

Enabling software iSCSI

...

Module load of iscsi_mod succeeded.

The ESX 3.5 server will build an iSCSI Qualified Name for the iSCSI software initiator as shown in Figure 5.16.

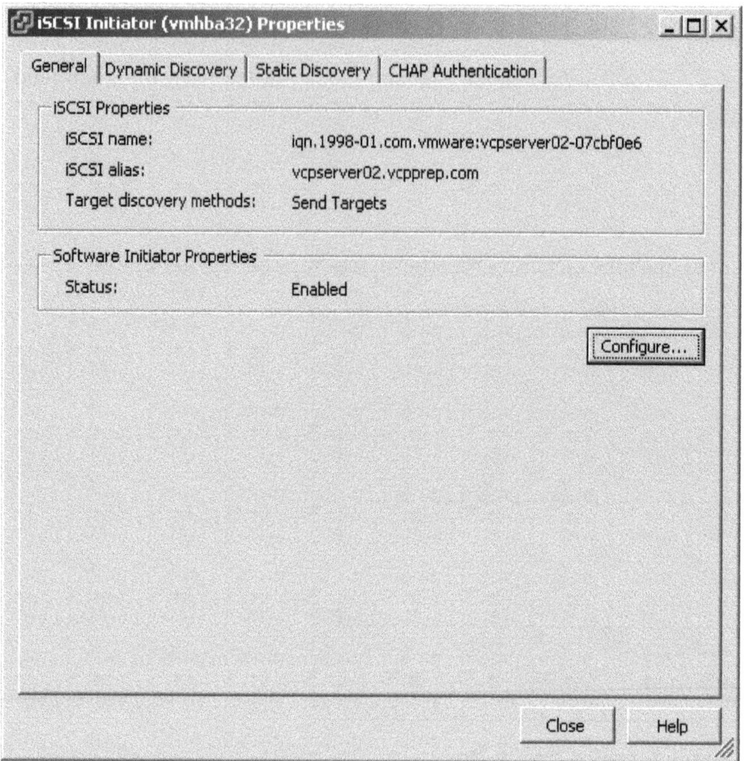

Figure 5.16 iSCSI Software Initiator Enabled

CLI NOTE: To view the iSCSI name and alias from the command line execute the following commands:

 # vmkiscsi-tool –I –l vmhba32

iSCSI Node Name: iqn.1998-01.com.vmware:vcpserver02-07cbf0e6

 # vmkiscsi-tool -k –l vmhba32

iSCSI Node Alias: server02.vcpprep.com

It is important to understand the syntax of the assigned IQN. Using the IQN assigned in Figure 5.16, the description of the syntax is as follows:

iqn.1998-01.com.vmware:vcpserver02-07cbf0e6

- iqn - stands for iSCSI Qualified Name
- .1998-01 – is the year and month the creator of the IQN registered their domain name
- .com.vmware - is the reverse DNS name assigned to the creator of the IQN
- vcpserver02-07cbf0e6 – is the unique alias name that is automatically generated by the iSCSI vendor. In this case, the iSCSI vendor is VMware. The alias name defaults to the name of the ESX host system.

The iSCSI target is provisioned its own unique IP address as well. This step is performed when the network configuration for the iSCSI software initiator is performed. Careful IP planning should be done to ensure that the iSCSI software initiator does not experience service disruptions. Any such disruptions such as accidental cable disconnections, layer 2 switch misconfiguration or inadequate IP provisioning can cause virtual machine disk I/O failure for VMs that are accessing their virtual hard disks on an iSCSI storage array.

Target Discovery Methods

Two iSCSI target discovery methods are available. The Static configuration method is available to iSCSI hardware initiators. iSCSI hardware initiators are discussed later in this chapter. The discovery method available to iSCSI software initiators is the Send Targets method. The Send Targets method will query the iSCSI target for all LUNs that the ESX 3.5 server has permission to access. This process will populate the "Discovery Tab" with any available LUNs discovered during the Send Targets discovery process. The following depicts the configuration process of the Send Targets discovery method.

Step 1. Click on the Dynamic Discovery tab as shown in Figure 5.17.

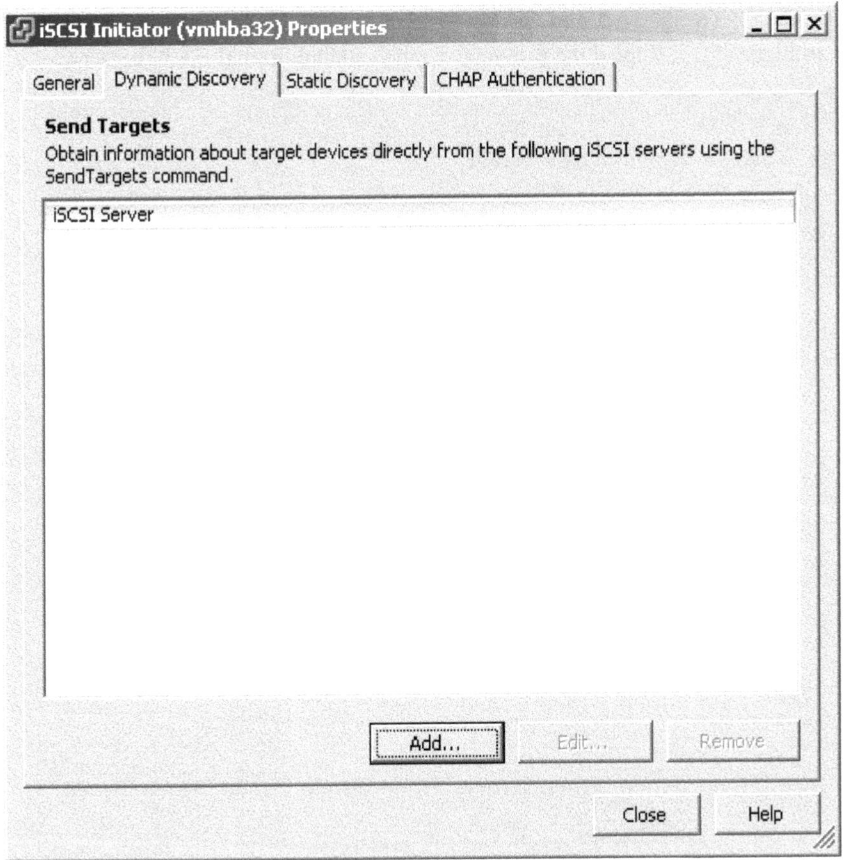

Figure 5.17 iSCSI Initiator Dynamic Discovery Tab

Click on the Add Button to continue.

Step 2. Enter the iSCSI Send Targets Server IP Address as shown in Figure 5.18. This information is often obtained by contacting the SAN administrator.

Add Send Targets Server
Send Targets
iSCSI Server: 10 . 0 . 1 . 240
Port: 3260
Authentication may need to be configured before a session can be established with any discovered targets.
OK
Cancel
Help

Figure 5.18 iSCSI Initiator Add Send Targets Server

The default port that iSCSI communicates over the network is 3260. Enter the port number and click on the OK button to continue. You should now see the iSCSI server displayed in the Dynamic Discovery tab as shown in Figure 5.19. Repeat the previous steps to add additional iSCSI servers.

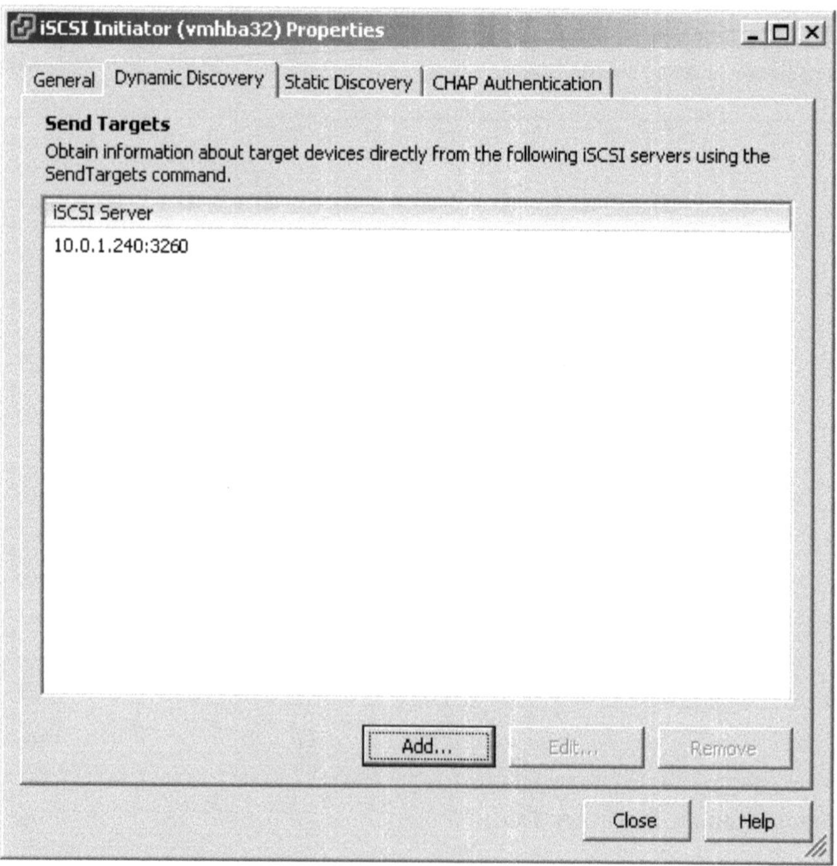

Figure 5.19 iSCSI Initiator ISCSI Server Added

CLI NOTE: To set the target IP address for the vmhba32 adapter (the software iSCSI initiator) execute the following command:

 # vmkiscsi-tool -D -a 10.0.1.240 vmhba32

CLI NOTE: To list the targets found execute the following command:

 # vmkiscsi-tool –T –l vmhba32

NAME : iqn.2006-01.com.openfiler:vol2.remvol2

ALIAS :

DISCOVERY METHOD FLAGS : 0

SEND TARGETS DISCOVERY SETTABLE : 0

SEND TARGETS DISCOVERY ENABLED : 0

Portal 0 : 10.0.1.240:3260

NAME : iqn.2006-01.com.openfiler:vol1.remvol1

ALIAS :

DISCOVERY METHOD FLAGS : 0

SEND TARGETS DISCOVERY SETTABLE : 0

SEND TARGETS DISCOVERY ENABLED : 0

Portal 0 : 10.0.1.240:3260

NAME : iqn.2006-01.com.openfiler:vol3.remvol3

ALIAS :

DISCOVERY METHOD FLAGS : 0

SEND TARGETS DISCOVERY SETTABLE : 0

SEND TARGETS DISCOVERY ENABLED : 0

Portal 0 : 10.0.1.240:3260

CLI NOTE: To rescan for storage devices on vmhba32 execute the following command:

 # esxcfg-rescan vmhba32

The Static Discovery Method

The Static Discovery method is not supported with iSCSI software initiators. The Static Discovery tab will not display any information as shown in Figure 5.20 if there are no hardware based initiators in the server. Hardware initiators are discussed later in this chapter.

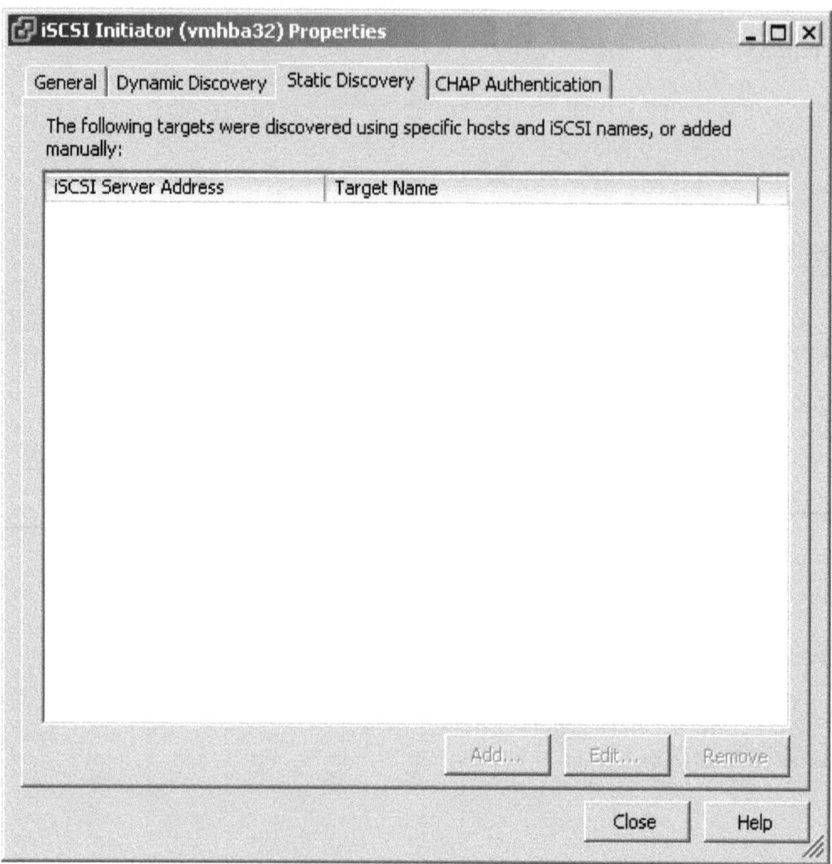

Figure 5.20 iSCSI Initiator Static Discovery Tab

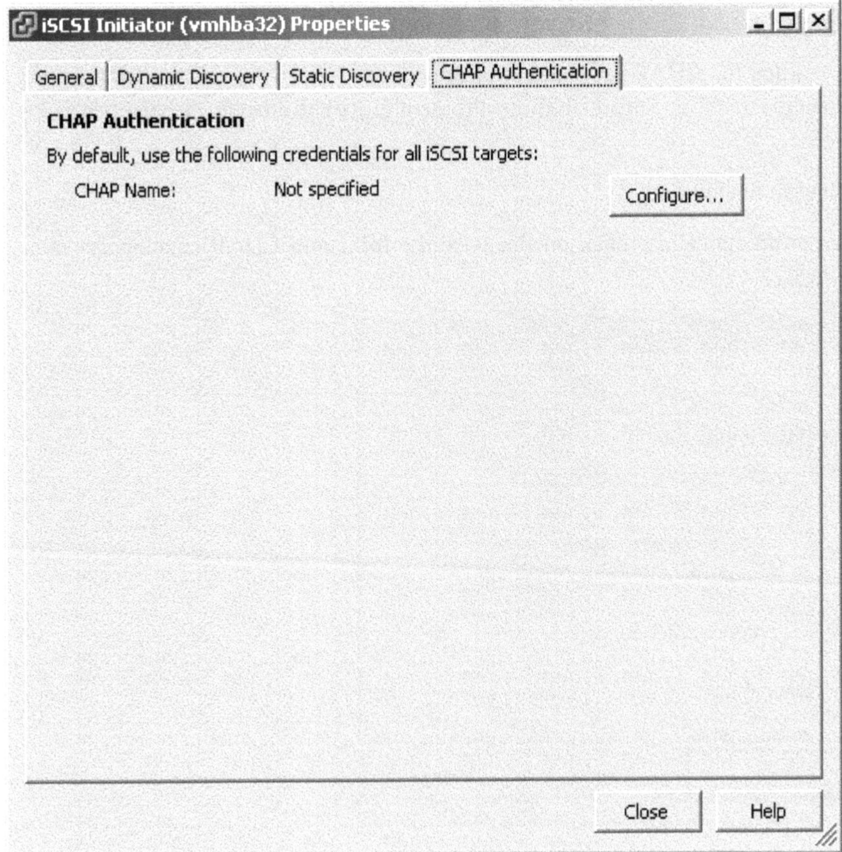

Figure 5.21 iSCSI Initiator CHAP Authentication Tab

CHAP Authentication

Step 1. To set the only ESX 3.5 server supported iSCSI authentication method, click on the Chap Authentication tab as shown in Figure 5.21.

Challenge Handshake Authentication Protocol (CHAP) is commonly used in iSCSI implementations. VMware uses a unidirectional CHAP method that works in the following sequence:

1. The iSCSI initiator requests access to the iSCSI target storage device.

2. The iSCSI target creates a hash value obtained by generating a random number and its ID number.

3. The iSCSI target then transmits this hash value to the iSCSI initiator.

4. The iSCSI target then uses the hash value it just sent to the iSCSI initiator and combines it with its CHAP password to form a new hash value.

5. The iSCSI initiator receives the original hash value and combines it with its CHAP password to create a new hash value.

6. The iSCSI initiator then transmits this new hash value to the iSCSI target.

7. The iSCSI target then compares the hash value it received from the initiator with its hash value

generated in step 4 and grants access if these two hash values are the same.

This method eliminates sending the CHAP password in clear text. The ESX 3.5 servers do not support other authentication protocols such as Secure Remote Protocol (SRP), Kerberos or methods using public keys.

Click on the Configure button to continue.

Step 2. To enable CHAP Authentication, click on the "Use the following CHAP credentials" radio button as shown in Figure 5.22.

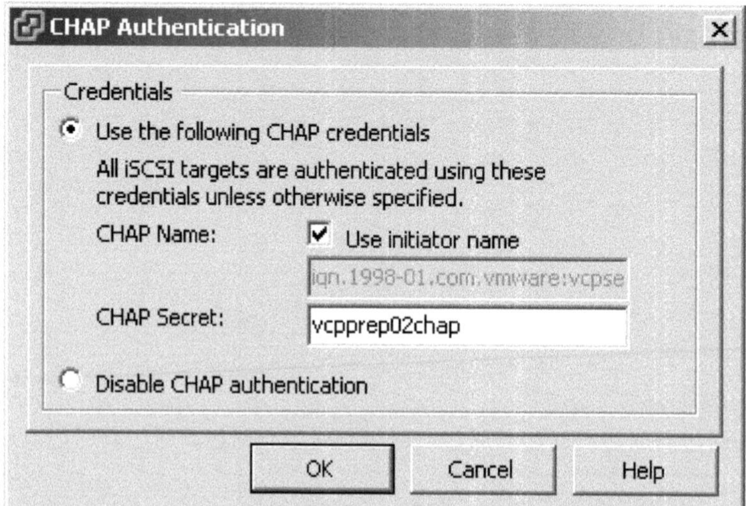

Figure 5.22 iSCSI Initiator CHAP Authentication Credentials

If you do not want to use the assigned IQN, click on the Use initiator name check box and enter a name of your choosing. Be sure to follow the iSCSI guidelines for naming iSCSI resources.

For more information on iSCSI naming guidelines, refer to:

http://www.ietf.org/rfc/rfc3720.txt

You can enter the CHAP secret value. ESX 3.5 server only supports one CHAP secret per initiator. This means that only one CHAP secret can be defined per ESX 3.5 server if using the software initiator as only one software initiator can be defined per ESX 3.5 host. Therefore this value needs to be the same on all resources that are to communicate with each other. Enabling CHAP does not affect existing iSCSI sessions. If CHAP is disabled, iSCSI sessions that were using CHAP prior to it being disabled continue to use CHAP until either the ESX host is rebooted or the storage system ends the iSCSI session.

Click on the OK button to continue.

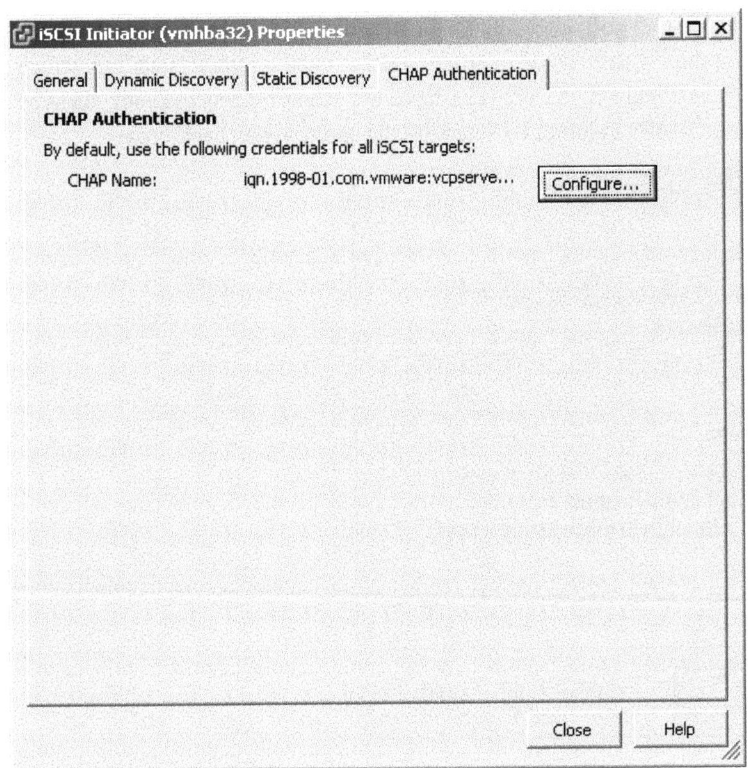

Figure 5.23 iSCSI Initiator CHAP Authentication Enabled

The Chap Authentication tab will now display information showing that the feature is enabled as shown in Figure 5.23.

Click on the close button to return to the Storage adapters screen as shown in Figure 5.24.

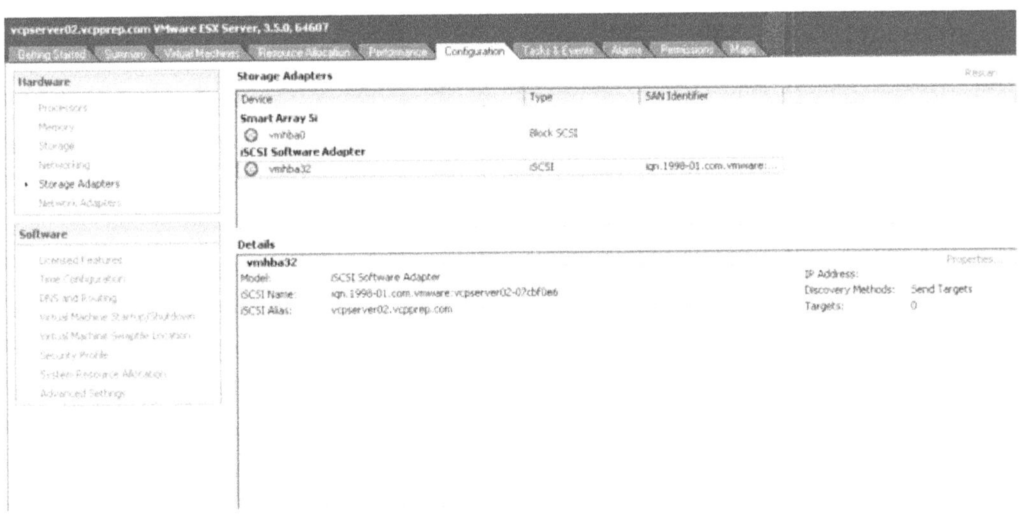

Figure 5.24 iSCSI Software Adapter Details View

The Details section now shows the iSCSI software initiator's configuration information. To have the ESX 3.5 server communicate with the iSCSi SAN devices you need to click on the Rescan link which will bring up the window shown in Figure 5.25. You can have the scanning process look for new storage devices and to look for new VMFS volumes by selecting the appropriate check boxes.

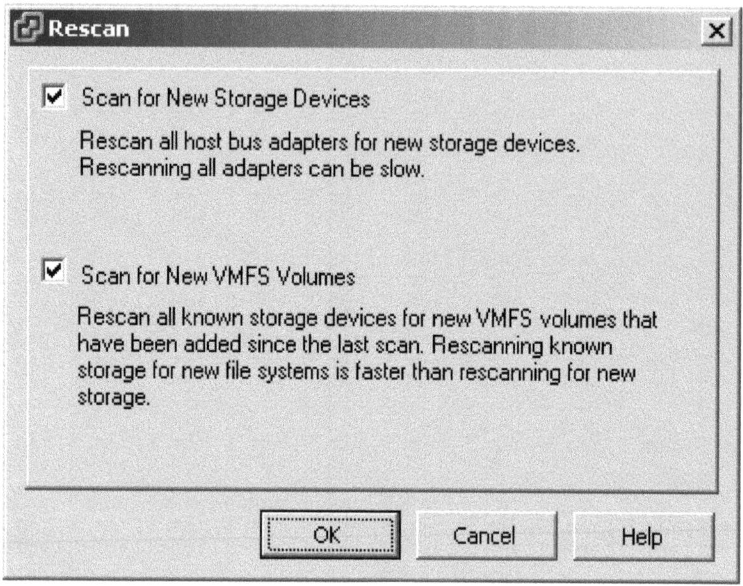

Figure 5.25 iSCSI Software Initiator Rescan

Click on the OK button to continue.

Figure 5.26 shows the newly discovered iSCSI SAN resources.

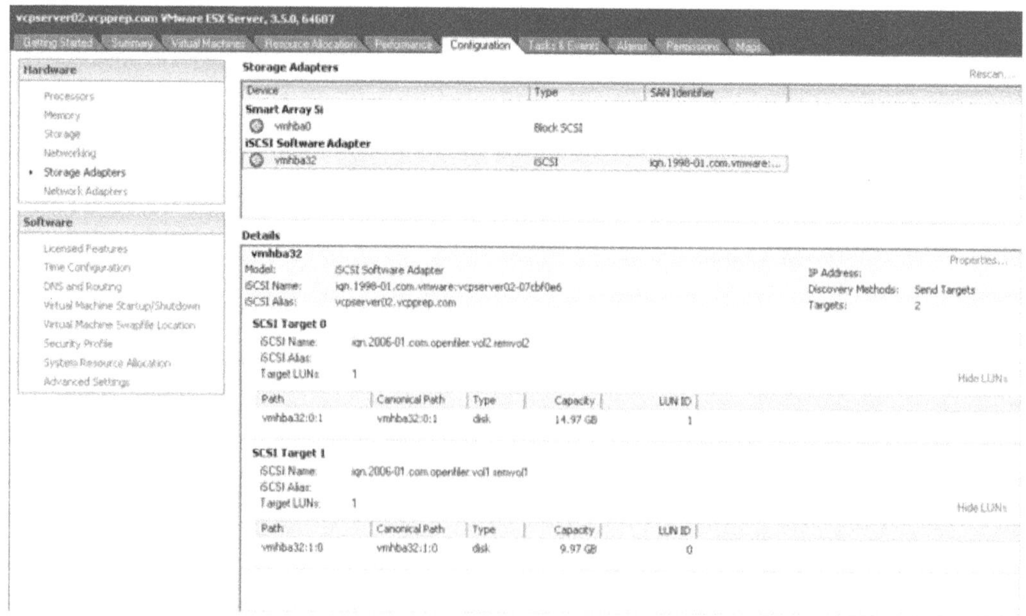

Figure 5.26 iSCSI Software Initiator Discovered LUNs

You can click on the Hide LUNs links if you have a lot of LUNs to list.

iSCSI Hardware Initiators

An iSCSI hardware initiator also known as an iSCSI host bus adapter (HBA) provides the ESX 3.5 server with the ability to connect via TCP/IP to iSCSI storage devices. The iSCSI HBAs have on board circuitry to make the connections and query the iSCSI storage devices. Hardware initiators utilize TOE (TCP Offload Engine) technology providing the benefit of a reduced workload on the ESX server. This is a benefit unique to hardware initiators as the software initiator requires additional processing by the VMkernel. This processing of the TCP/IP stack performed by the hardware initiator typically results in improved performance over the software initiator when accessing an iSCSI storage target. ESX 3.5 servers can be configured with a maximum of two hardware initiators. In such a configuration, it is possible to configure multiple paths to a iSCSI target to provide fail over capabilities. Multipathing is discussed later in this chapter.

As mentioned previously in the Targets Discovery Methods section, there are two iSCSI target discovery methods available. iSCSI hardware initiators can use the Send Targets method as well as the Static configuration method. The Static configuration method is only available to iSCSI hardware initiators. The Static Discovery tab as shown previously in Figure 5.20, is used only when a hardware initiator is present in the system. By selecting the Add button within the Static Discovery tab, the ESX administrator can enter the IP address, port number and iSCSI target name manually. This method of discovery when compared to the Send Targets method requires knowledge of the iSCSI target name. The Send Targets method can be used when this information is not known at the time of configuration. Send Targets often adds only a little additional time to discover iSCSI targets and is a commonly used discovery method.

For the most up to date list of supported iSCSI HBAs consult the VI 3.5 I/O Compatibility Guide:

http://www.vmware.com/pdf/vi35_io_guide.pdf

For the most up to date list of supported iSCSI storage arrays consult the VI 3.5 Storage/SAN Compatibility Guide:

http://www.vmware.com/pdf/vi35_san_guide.pdf

Configuring iSCSI Hardware Initiators

Configuring an iSCSI HBA with an ESX 3.5 server is very similar to configuring the iSCSI software initiator. A hardware initiator however does not require a VMkernel port as does the software initiator. The iSCSI HBA should be installed into the ESX 3.5 server per the vendor's instructions. Drivers for supported iSCSI HBA cards are included with the ESX 3.5 system. After the system boots, log in with the VI Client and click on the Configuration tab and then click on the Storage Adapters link. You should see the iSCSI HBA listed there. Click on the storage adapter's Properties link which will bring up the iSCSI Initiator Properties screen dialog box. Continue the configuration as you would a software initiator with the exception that unlike the software initiator, the hardware initiator can optionally use the Static Discovery Method.

Advanced Settings

To alleviate bottlenecks when the iSCSI storage resource has a high I/O load you can set the maximum queue depths setting. For example on a QLogic 4050 HBA connect into the service console and examine the */etc/vmware/esx.conf* file. Find the device name in this file.

It should look something like this:

/device/001:02:0/vmkname = "vmhba3"

Add the following line after the device name:

/device/001:02:0/options = "ql4xmaxqdepth=nn"

Be sure to refer to your iSCSI HBA vendor's documentation for the appropriate values.

NAS/NFS Networked Based Storage

Network Attached Storage (NAS) is storage that is accessible over the network instead of on an attached bus to the server. Two of the most popular NAS technologies are:

- Common Internet File System (CIFS) - also known as Server Message Block (SMB)
- Network Files System (NFS)

NFS is the only supported network attached storage (NAS) technology currently supported by the ESX 3.5 server product. NFS was created in 1984 by Sun Microsystems, Inc. NFS makes it simple to share files across the network. Support for NFS datastores is a new feature since the release of the ESX 3.0 server product.

NFS uses a simple client/server configuration and setting up each is fairly simple. The benefit of NFS is that it hides the underlying structure of the directory that is shared out from the client. In other words, if the files reside on a third extended file system (ext3), Unix File System (UFS) or Zettabyte File System (ZFS), the client can still access the files even if the operating system that it is using does not support that file system. NFS has gone through some changes over the years. NFSv2 was released in 1989 and is described in RFC 1094 and was implemented widely in Unix environments.

In 1995 NFSv3 was released and described in RFC 1813. The improvements over NFSv2 were:

- Support for larger files
- Support for enhanced file attributes
- Enhanced file access methods
- Better file transfer speeds with larger files

NFS supports both User Datagram Protocol (UDP) and Transmission Control Protocol (TCP). ESX 3.5 servers support NFSv3 over TCP only. This is important to note because a newer version of NFS was released in 2000. NFSv4 was originally described in RFC 3010 and later revised in 2003 in RFC 3510. NFSv4 provides additional capabilities and controls that NFSv3. NFSv4 supports enhanced client side access controls. It allows the NFS administrator to set a NFS shared directory to accept clients connecting with one of the 3 supported NFS versions.

For example:

An NFS administrator could share a directory so that clients connecting with NFSv2, NFSv3 and

NFSv4 protocols are allowed to connect to that directory. But they could also share another directory allowing **only** NFSv4 clients to connect. This is an important issue since Sun Microsystems Solaris 10 and most new distributions of Linux now support NFSv4. You need to make sure that the NFS server administrator is allowing NFSv3 clients to connect or you will not have access to your NFS datastore.

NFS Datastores

Using a shared directory on a NFS server provides the ESX 3.5 with the following features and benefits:

- NFS datastores are persistent across reboots. The VMkernel is responsible to reconnect to the shared resource
- VM state files can be stored in a NFS datastore
- ISO (.iso) images can be stored in a NFS datastore
- NFS datastores support Dynamic Resizing
- NFS datastores leverage VMware NIC teaming and load balancing policies for path management
- You can backup a NFS target using the ESX Ranger product to backup VMFS to NFS
- In the ESX 3.5 server the NFS datastores are mounted to /vmfs/volumes/datastore_name (where "datastore_name" is the name of the NFS datastore) for a consistent datastore location on the ESX 3.5 server
- Multiple ESX 3.5 servers can share the same NFS datastore
- VMotion is supported on VMs that have their VM state files on a NFS datastore
- If you use ISO images on NFS datastores it prevents VMotion failure due to "hardware CD-ROM connected errors"
- HA is supported using a NFS datastore
- DRS is supported using a NFS datastore
- VMware snapshots are supported using a NFS datastore

NOTE: As of ESX Server 3.5, update 1, VCB can be used to backup VMs located on a NFS datastore.

Configuring the ESX 3.5 Server To Use A NFS Datastore

The steps to configure your ESX server to use a NFS datastore are:

You must create a VMkernel port so that the VMkernel can make the connection and mount the shared NFS directory. Figure 5.27 shows that this server has a VMkernel port configured with the IP address of 10.0.1.250. Refer to chapter 4 - Networking for information on how to create a VMkernel port.

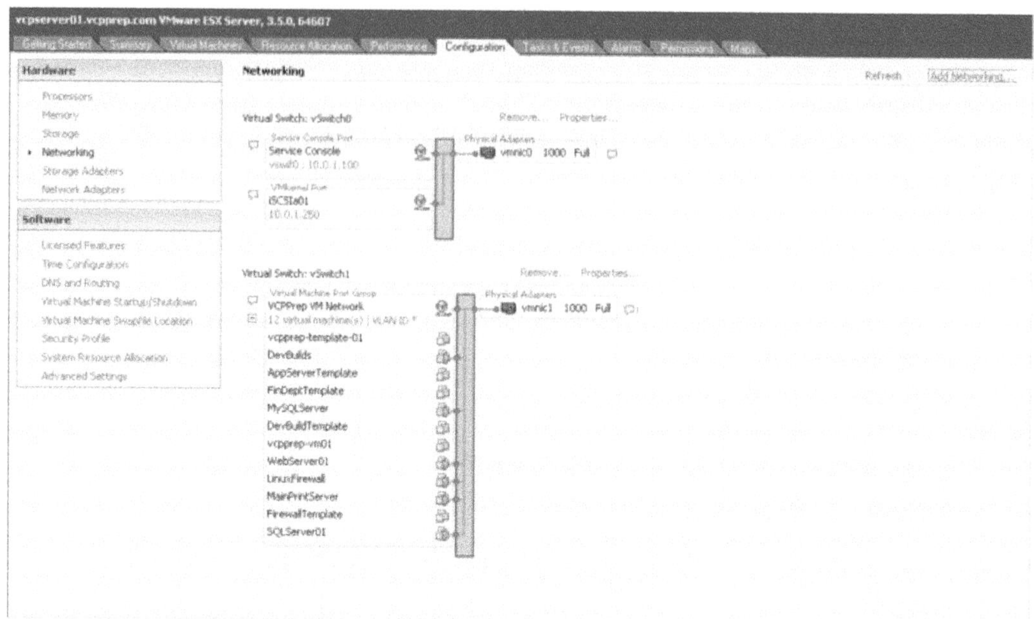

Figure 5.27 NFS Datastore Networking Requirements

Step 1. Select the Storage link in the Hardware box and click on the Add Storage link in the upper right of the screen to continue as shown in Figure 5.28.

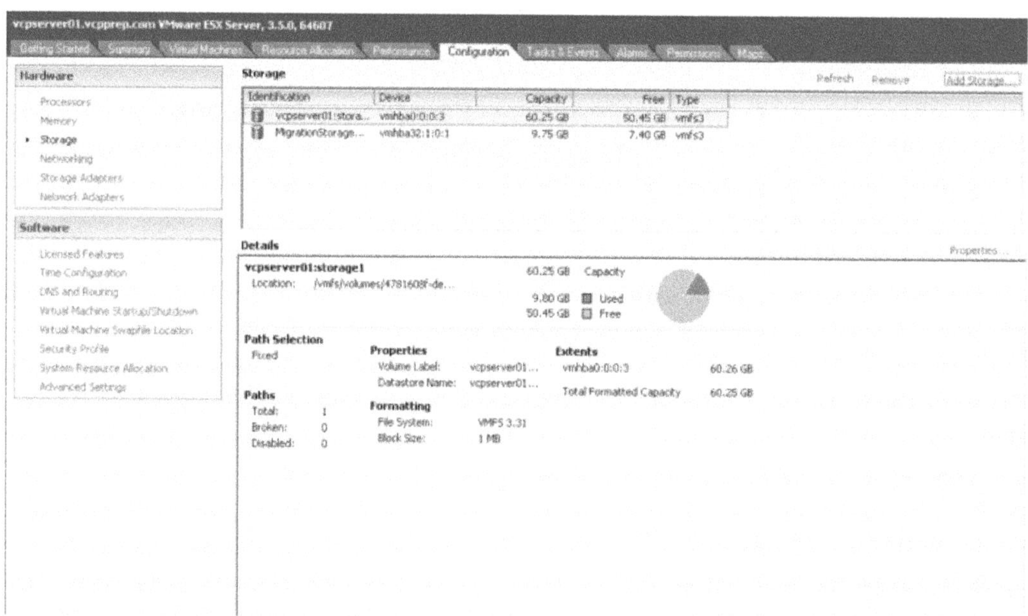

Figure 5.28 Add Storage Link

The Add Storage Wizard window will now appear as shown in Figure 5.29.

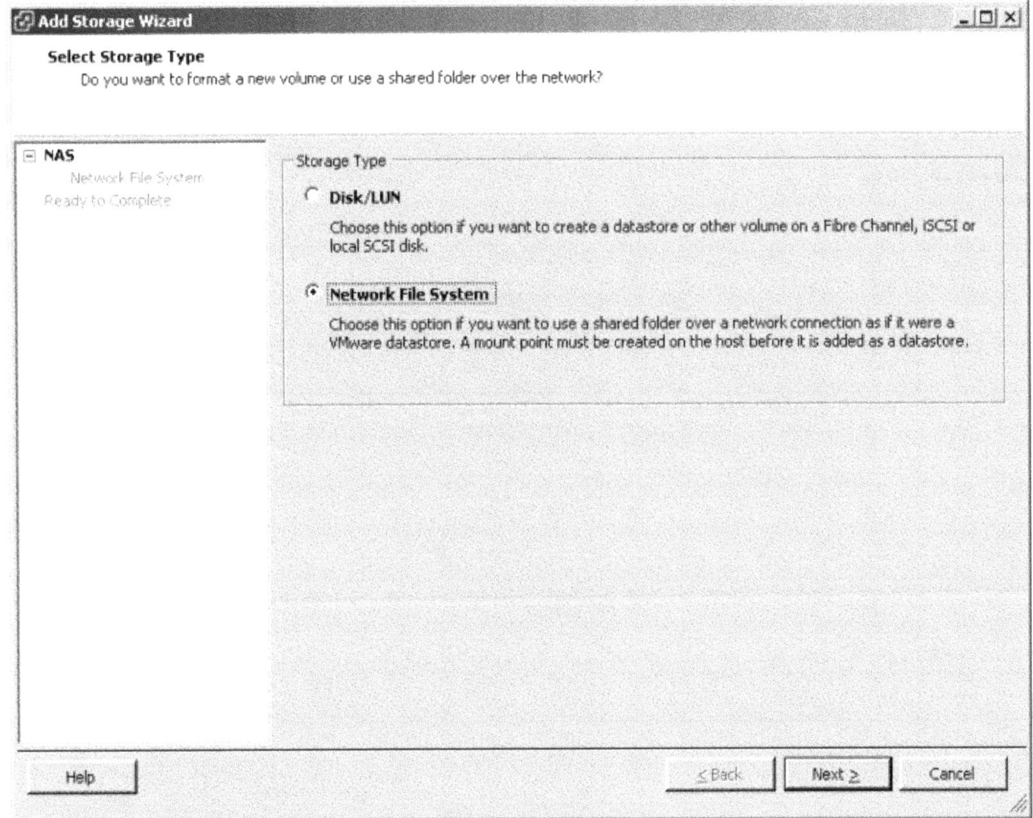

Figure 5.29 Add Storage Wizard Network File System

Step 2. Select the Network File System radio button and click Next to continue. As mentioned in the Add Storage Wizard dialog box, an NFS server must already be properly configured prior to completing the Add Storage Wizard.

Step 3. Enter the IP address of the NFS server you wish to connect to. You also input the directory that is shared on the NFS server and what you want to call this datastore as shown in Figure 5.30.

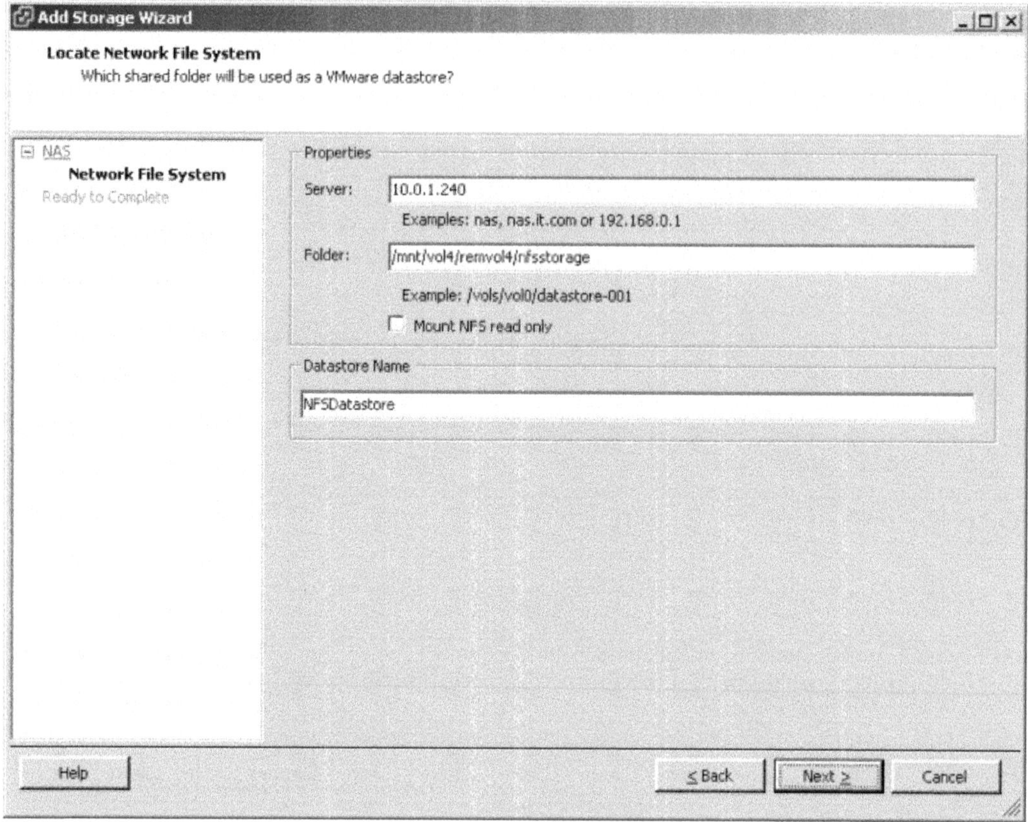

Figure 5.30 Add Storage Wizard Locate Network File System

If the NFS shared directory is configured as read/write and you want the ESX 3.5 server to only access it as "read only" then click on the "Mount NFS read only" check box. Click on the Next button to continue.

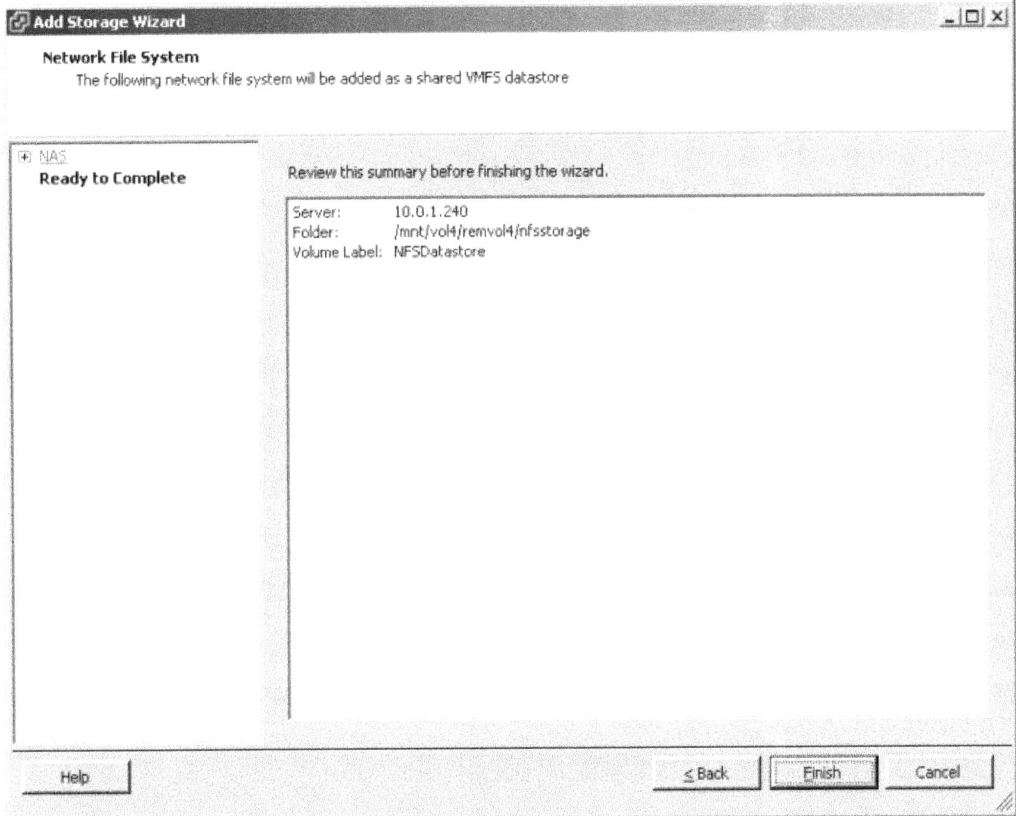

Figure 5.31 Add Storage Wizard Network File System Ready To Complete

Step 4. A summary of your settings are listed in the next screen. Click Finish to complete the NFS datastore configuration as shown in Figure 5.31.

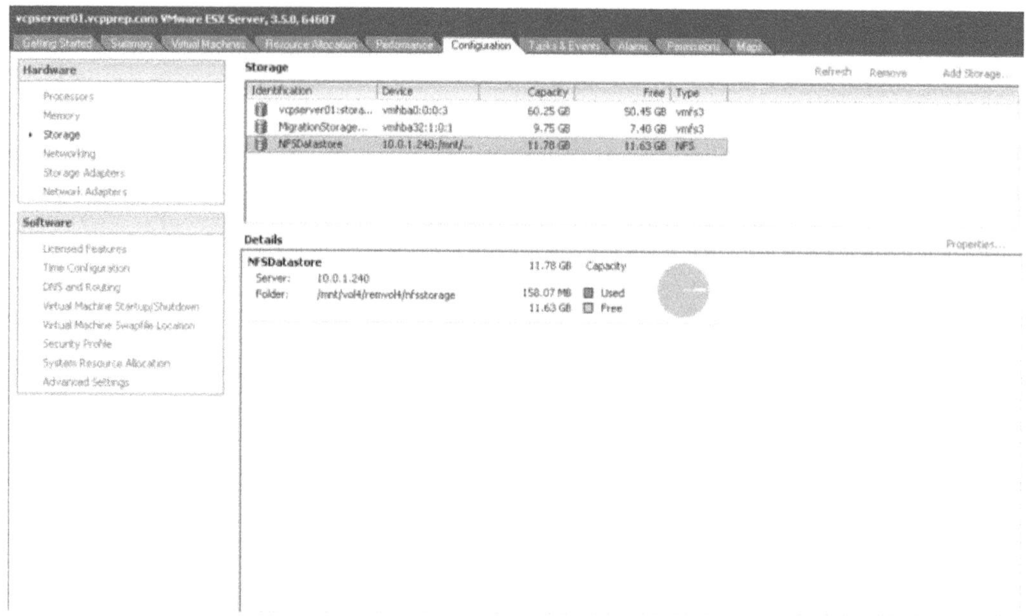

Figure 5.32 New Network File System Datastore Added

The newly added NFS datastore can be displayed within the configuration tab of the VI Client as shown is Figure 5.32.

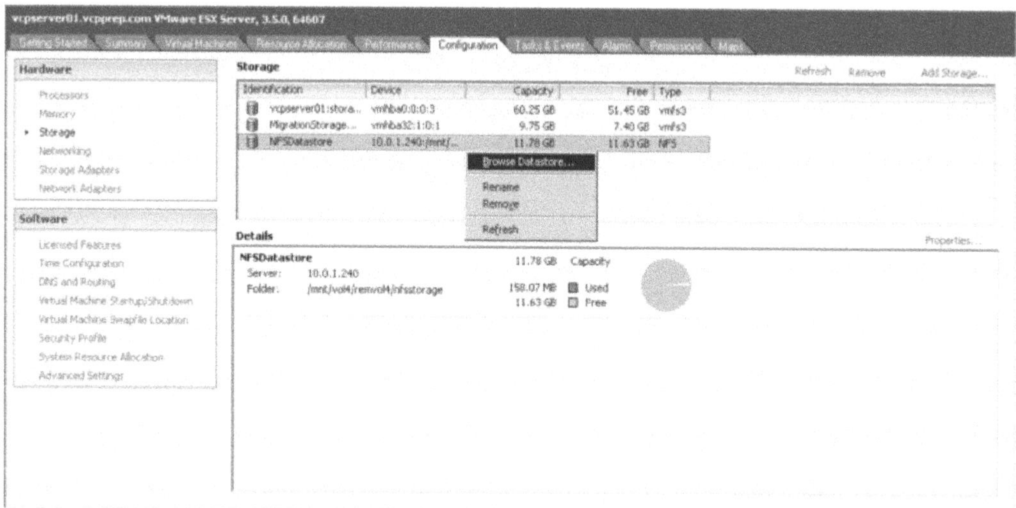

Figure 5.33 Browse Datastore Menu Option

The contents of any datastore can be displayed from the VI Client by performing the following steps:

1. Select the datastore in the list of datastores
2. Click on it with the right mouse button
3. Select Browse Datastore from the pop up menu as shown in Figure 5.33.

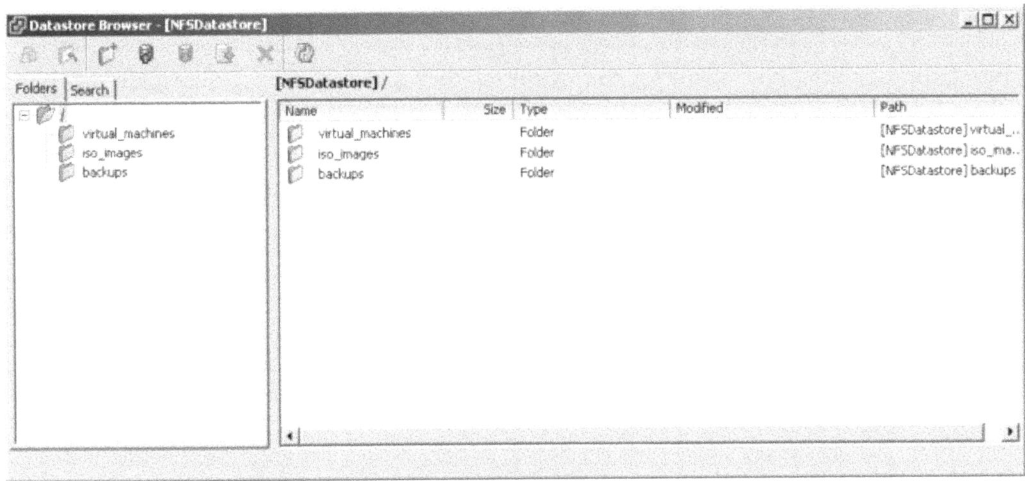

Figure 5.34 Datastore Browser Dialog Box

The contents of the datastore will be displayed as shown in Figure 5.34. You can upload files to a datastore and download files from a datastore. You can also move files from one datastore to another and delete files from a datastore. The ability to perform such file operations from the VI Client can make ESX administration tasks easier to perform.

Advanced NFS Datastore Settings

NFSv2 and NVSv3 do not include procedures for opening or closing resources on a remote server. The VMkernel uses the special Mount protocol to mount a file system and create a file handle to access a file on it as well as unmounting the file system when it is no longer required.

By default an ESX 3.5 server can connect to up to 8 NFS datastores. This value can be set to up to 32 NFS datastores maximum by setting the NFS.MaxVolumes parameter via the VI Client.

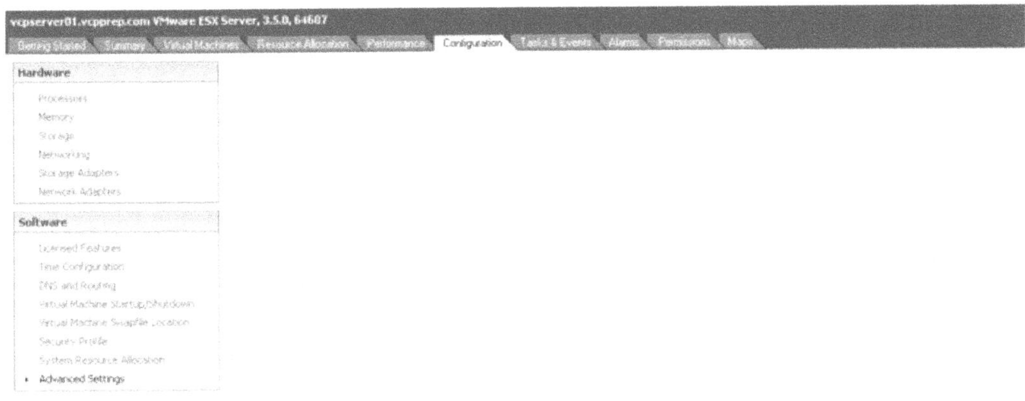

Figure 5.35 Advanced Settings Link

Step 1. Click on the Advanced Settings link in the Software Box as shown in Figure 5.35.

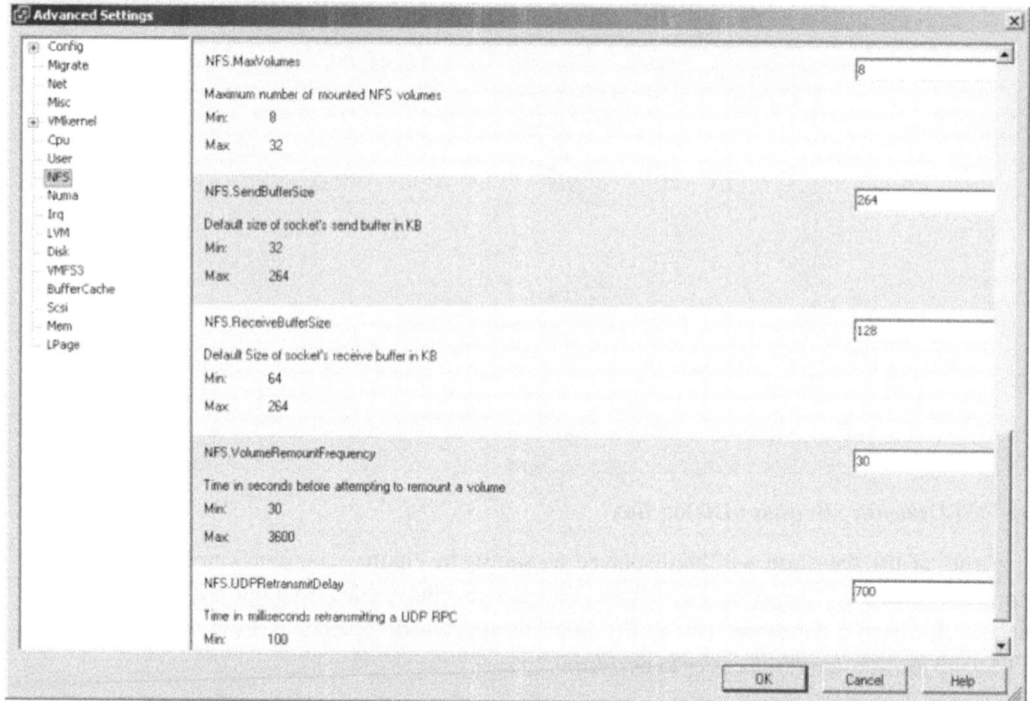

Figure 5.36 Advanced Settings For NFS

Step 2. Change the defaults settings for NFS by clicking on NFS in the left pane and setting the individual settings in the right pane as shown in Figure 5.36.

CLI NOTE: To view the current value for the maximum amount of NFS datastores on the ESX 3.5 server execute the following CLI command:

 # esxcfg-advcfg -g /NFS/MaxVolumes

Value of MaxVolumes is 8

CLI NOTE: To change the maximum value of NFS datastores on the ESX 3.5 server execute the following CLI command:

 # esxcfg-advcfg -s 32 /NFS/MaxVolumes

Value of MaxVolumes is 32

ESX 3.5 Server LUN Configuration

Once a LUN has been configured on the SAN storage array and presented to an ESX 3.5 server, the following steps must be taken using the VI Client for the LUN to be used:

Step 1. Select the Configuration tab, within the Hardware pane, select "Storage (SCSI, SAN, and NFS). Doing so, will load the Storage information in the right window pane. This will show you the currently configured datastores on the ESX 3.5 server.

CLI NOTE: Use the esxcfg-vmhbadevs command to see which LUNs are available to an ESX host:

 # esxcfg-vmhbadevs

Step 2. Select the "Add Storage..." link.

Step 3. In the Add Storage dialog box, there are two choices, Disk/LUN and Network File System as shown in Figure 5.37.

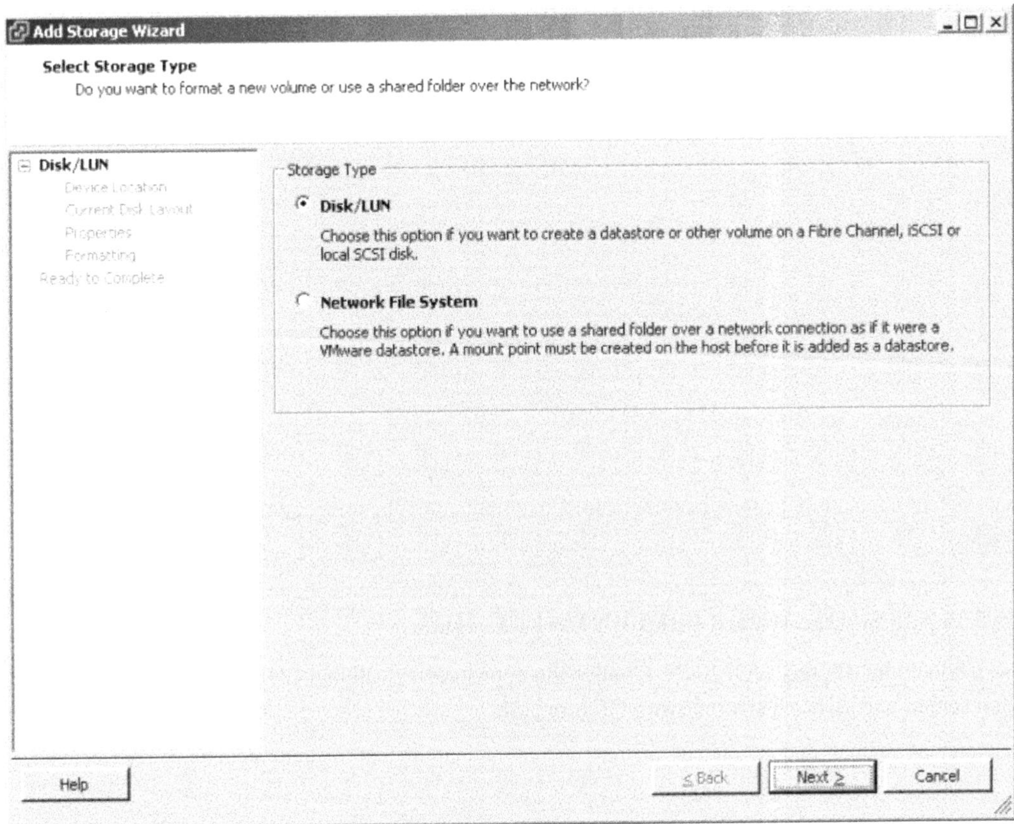

Figure 5.37 Add Storage Wizard Disk/LUN

Choose Disk/LUN to create a datastore on a Fibre Channel LUN, iSCSI LUN or on the local SCSI disk then click the Next button.

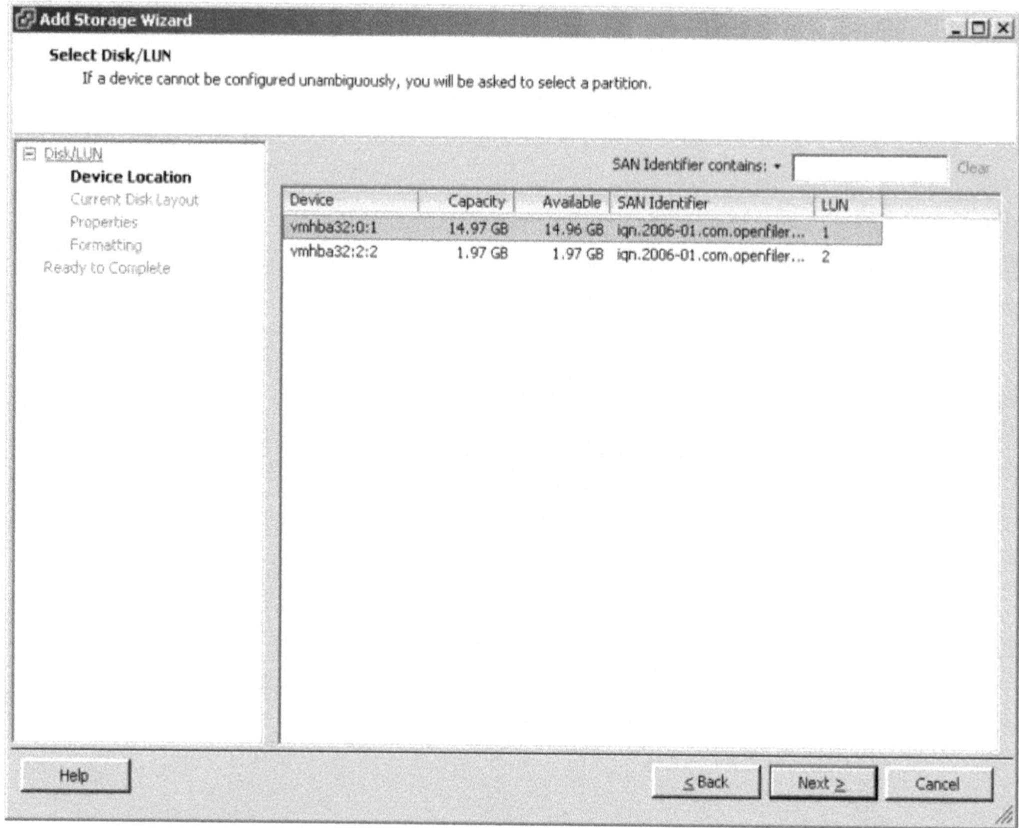

Figure 5.38 Add Storage Wizard Disk/LUN Device Location

Step 4. Choose the desired SAN LUN. Choose the appropriate available LUN in the device location selection screen and click Next as shown in Figure 5.38.

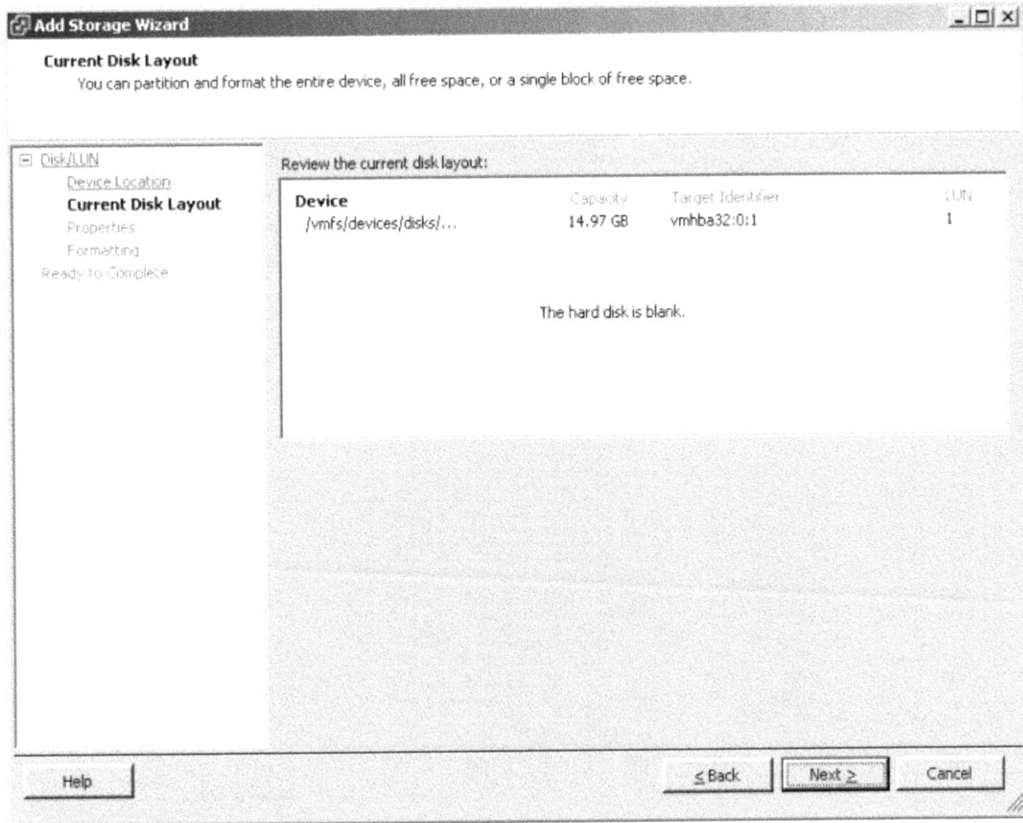

Figure 5.39 Add Storage Wizard Disk/LUN Current Disk Layout

Step 5. Review the current disk layout. Verify the current disk layout is appropriate as shown in Figure 5.39 and select Next.

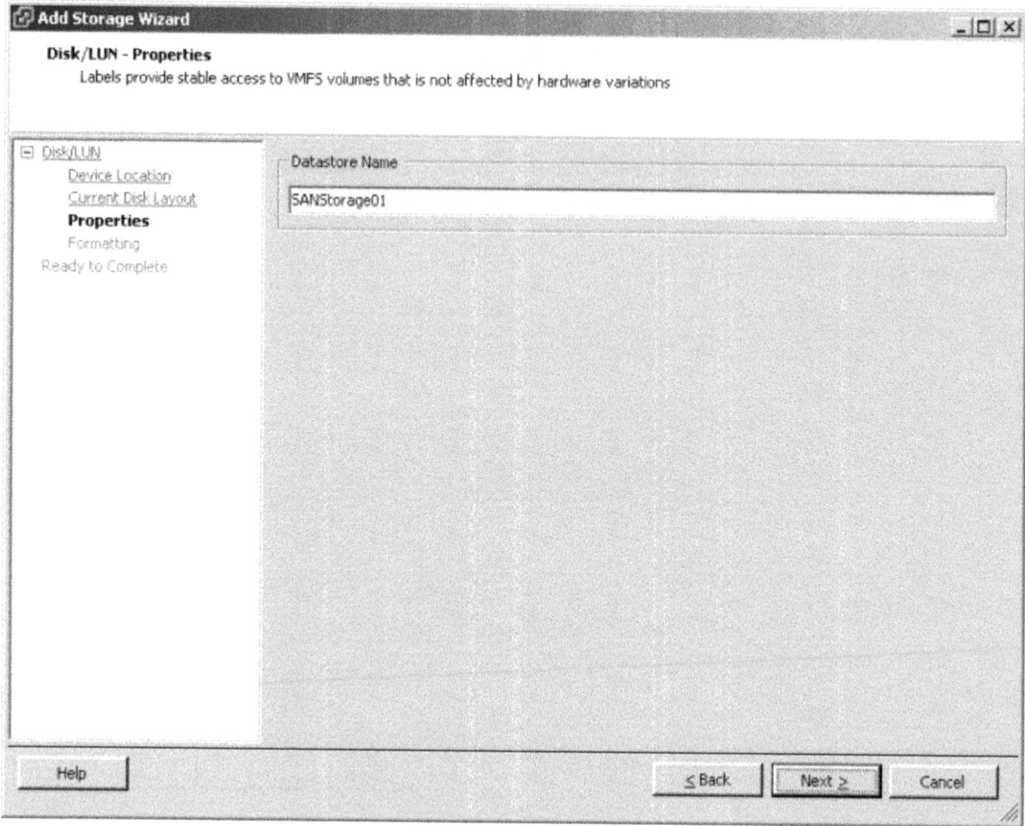

Figure 5.40 Add Storage Wizard Disk/LUN Datastore Name

Step 6. Give the datastore a descriptive name as shown in Figure 5.40. The datastore name should reflect the intended purpose of the storage. This helps to reduce possible confusion when the datastore is managed by multiple ESX server administrators. The label should also NOT contain spaces; special characters, such as underscores (_), hyphens (-) are acceptable, for the label to have a consecutive string of characters.

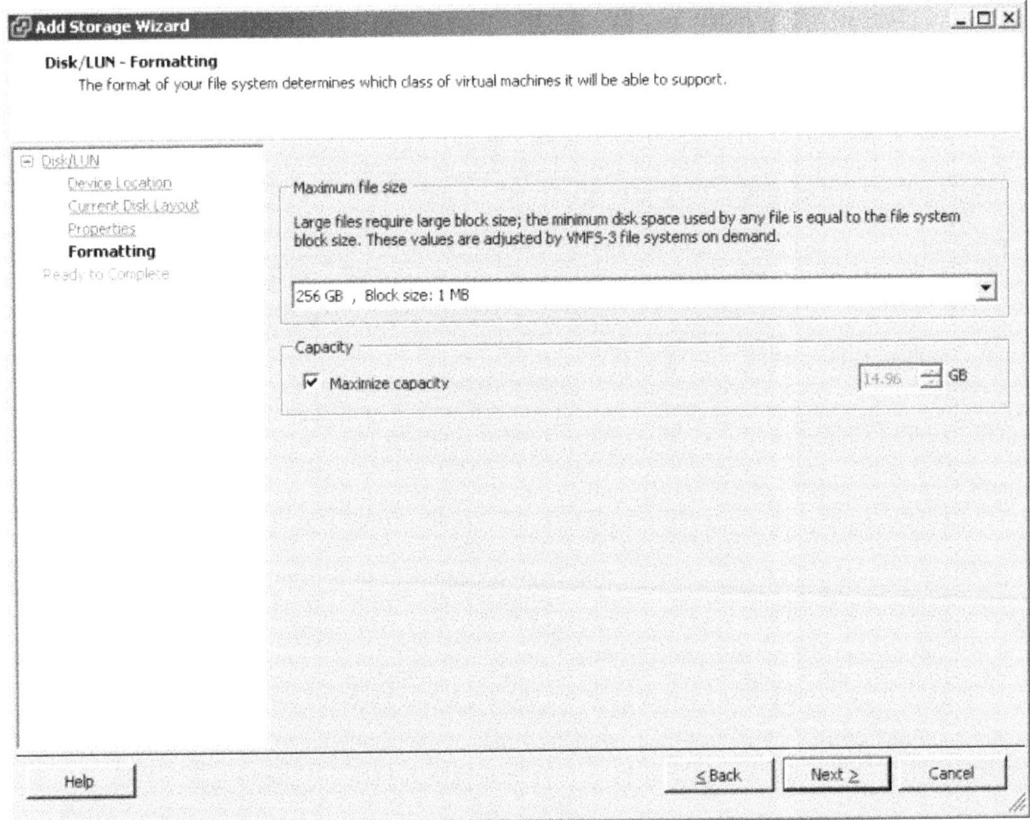

Figure 5.41 Add Storage Wizard Disk/LUN Formatting

Step 7. Choose appropriate format of the file system as shown in Figure 5.41. Knowing in advance the type of virtual machines that will make use of the storage helps to properly configure the LUN. For example, if a virtual machine configured as a database server is to use the LUN and the database file will grow over 256 GB, the default block size of 1 MB will need to be modified due to a 1 MB block size for the file system having a maximum VMFS file system size of 256 GB.

Step 8. (Optional) Different maximum block sizes can be used.

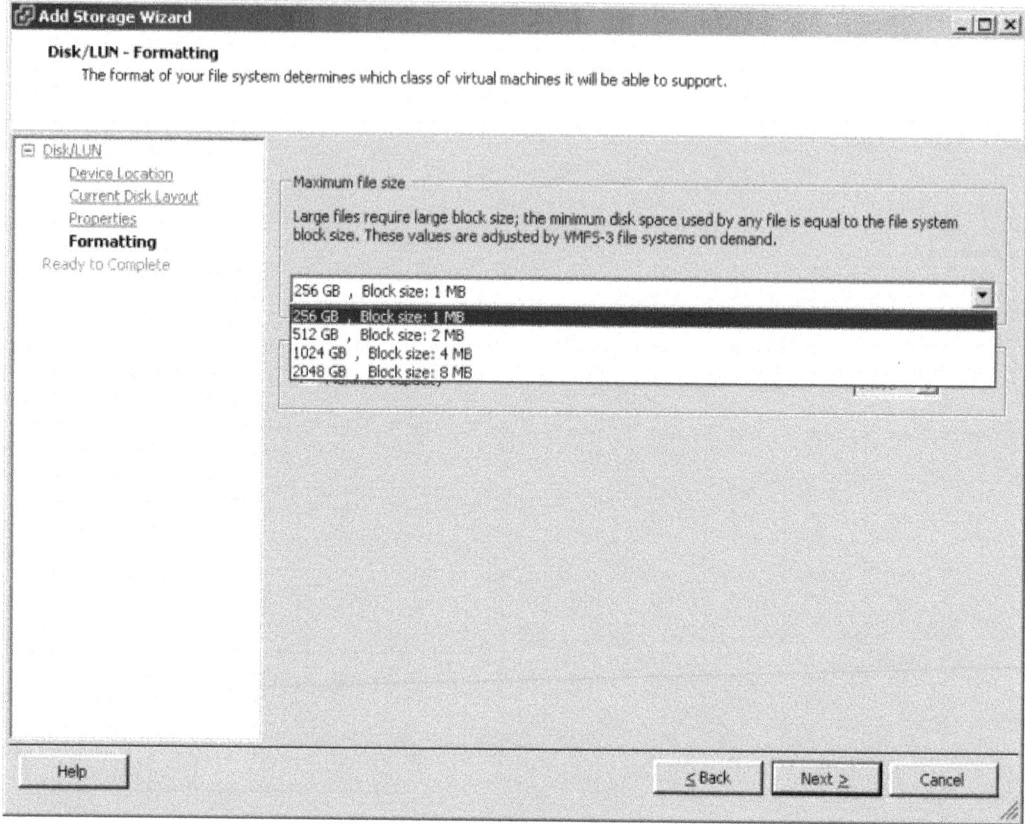

Figure 5.42 Add Storage Wizard Disk/LUN Formatting List

Click the drop down box as shown in Figure 5.42 to choose a larger block size **only** if a file system size greater than 256 GB is required. Click Next after making the appropriate choice.

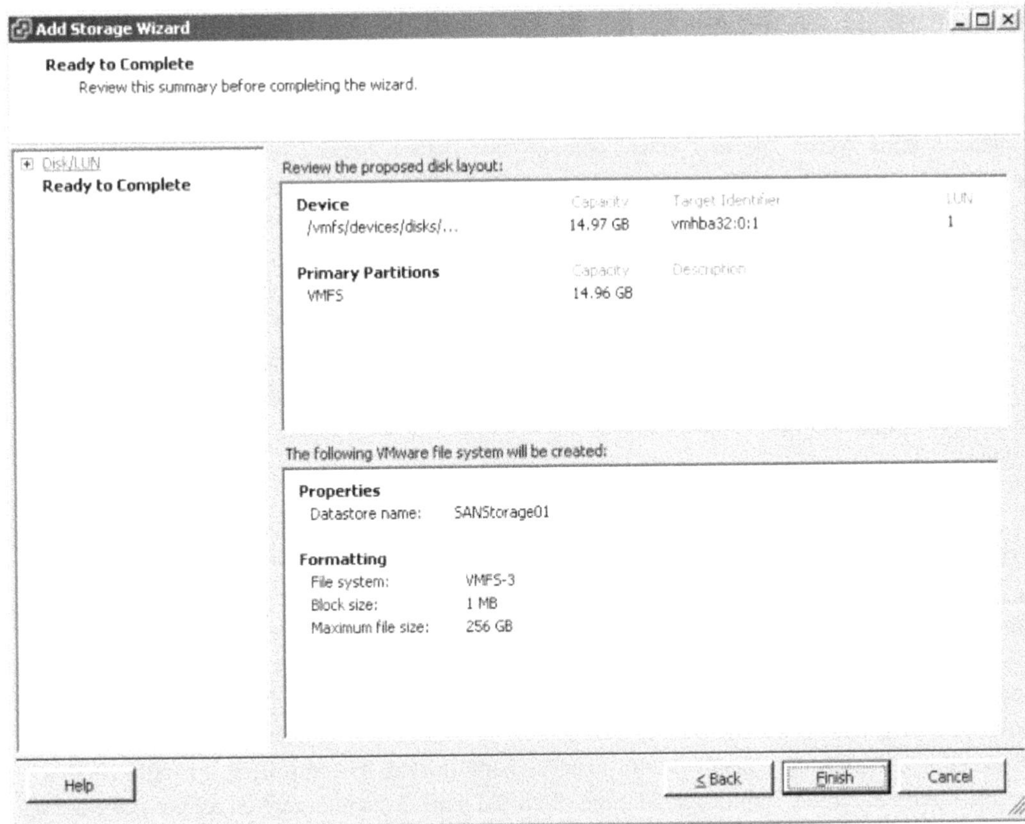

Figure 5.43 Add Storage Wizard Disk/LUN Ready To Complete

Step 9. Review the final storage attributes that were selected during the Add Storage wizard process as shown in Figure 5.43. If any changes need to be made, select the "Back" button and make the appropriate changes. Click Finish to complete adding new storage.

ESX 3.5 Server Storage Block And File System Sizes

It is possible to add a total of 31 extents to an existing LUN. The original LUN is considered extent number one. Thus, a VMFS volume can span a total of 32 extents. An extent can be configured with the following block sizes:

- 1 MB block size allows a maximum of 256 GB per extent size
- 2 MB block size allows a maximum of 512 GB per extent size
- 4 MB block size allows a maximum of 1024 GB (1 TB) per extent size
- 8 MB block size allows a maximum of 2048 GB (2 TB) per extent size

With an 8 MB block size, an extent can be a maximum of 2 TB. 32 extents, each configured with an 8 MB block size, offer a VMFS a maximum capacity of 64 TB. The maximum file size supported on a VMFS volume is 2 TB. This limitation is set at the VMFS extent level. In other words, since an extent is limited to 2 TB, a file greater than 2 TB is not supported as even though the VMFS volume can span multiple extents, the individual files on the extents do not span across extents.

The first extent holds the metadata for all of the other extents in the VMFS volume. Metadata is data about data. In other words, the first extent contains information needed for the VMFS volume to properly access and use the additional spanned LUNs. In the event that the first extent becomes corrupted, without proper backups or RAID levels in place, access to the remaining extents within the VMFS volume may not be possible. Extents should be used in situations where additional storage is needed and virtual machines placed on a LUN that is almost filled to capacity cannot be powered off. These virtual machines, when scheduled for downtime, can be moved to a larger, newly created LUN and the spanned VMFS volume can be deleted and reused as needed. Conversely, the NEW storage VMotion technology, a feature of the ESX Server 3.5 release, could be used to move a powered on VM's files to larger storage. Storage VMotion is discussed in Chapter 13 – Virtual Machine Migration.

Multipathing

Virtual machine state files can be stored on storage formatted as VMFS or NFS. All guest operating systems running within a virtual machine see their hard disks as local SCSI drives regardless of where the virtual hard disk files physically reside. A virtual machine that has its hard disk files stored locally (i.e. on a SCSI disk within the ESX server), isn't likely to experience connection problems accessing the drives. Unless there is a mechanical error with the hard disks or its controllers, it is unlikely that a SCSI cable failure internally will occur. Storage of virtual hard disks remotely on a FC SAN exposes virtual machines to potential physical cabling problems, misconfigured or failed FC switches, FC switch port(s) and FC storage arrays. Any disruption with the virtual machines disk I/O can cause loss of data or failure of the guest operating system running within the VM. ESX servers can provide fault tolerance by using multiple HBAs. Each HBA card should be configured with a separate physical path to the FC storage array. Having multiple physical paths to a storage array is known as multipathing and at a minimum should provide at least an N+1 (Need + 1) configuration.

ESX servers provide two multipathing policies, the fixed path policy (also called the preferred path) and the most recently used (MRU) policy. During the initial discovery process of the LUN, ESX servers can automatically detect the correct multipathing policy to use if the storage array is a supported device.

Supported storage arrays are documented in VMware's VI 3.5 Storage/SAN Compatibility Guide located at:

http://www.vmware.com/pdf/vi35_san_guide.pdf

Modifying Multipathing Policies

The following steps demonstrate modifying the path configuration from MRU to Fixed:

Step 1. Select the appropriate datastore:

Step 2. Click the "Manage Paths..." button and select the "Manage Paths" button to modify the multipathing policy settings as shown in Figure 5.44.

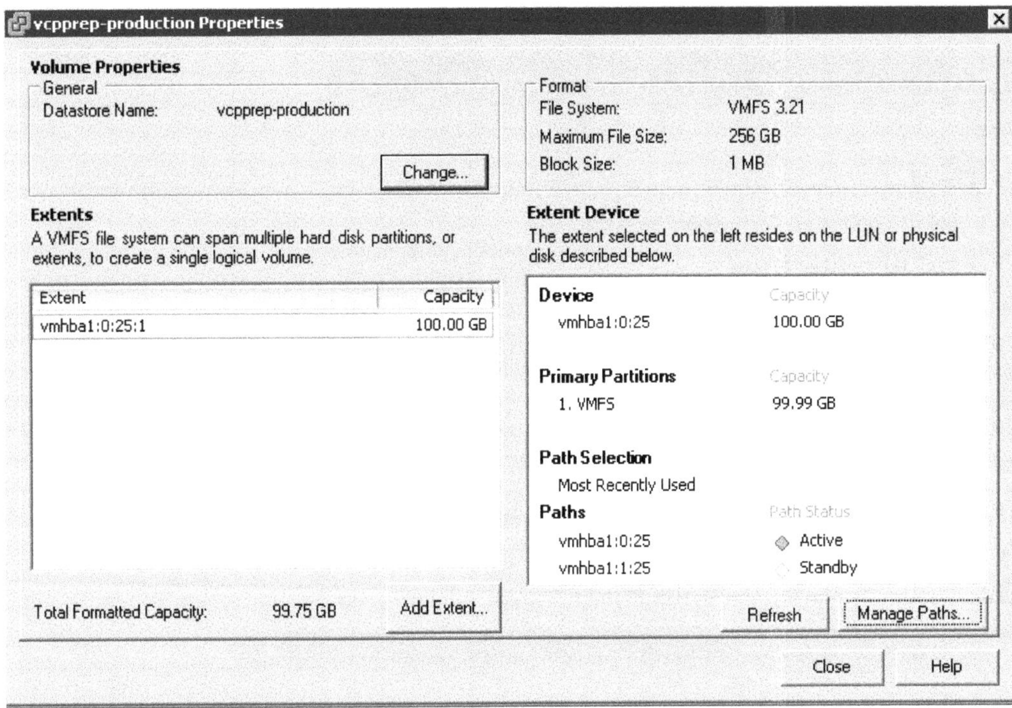

Figure 5.44 Select Manage Paths Button

Step 3. Selecting the "Change..." button will enable the multipathing policy to be altered as shown in Figure 5.45.

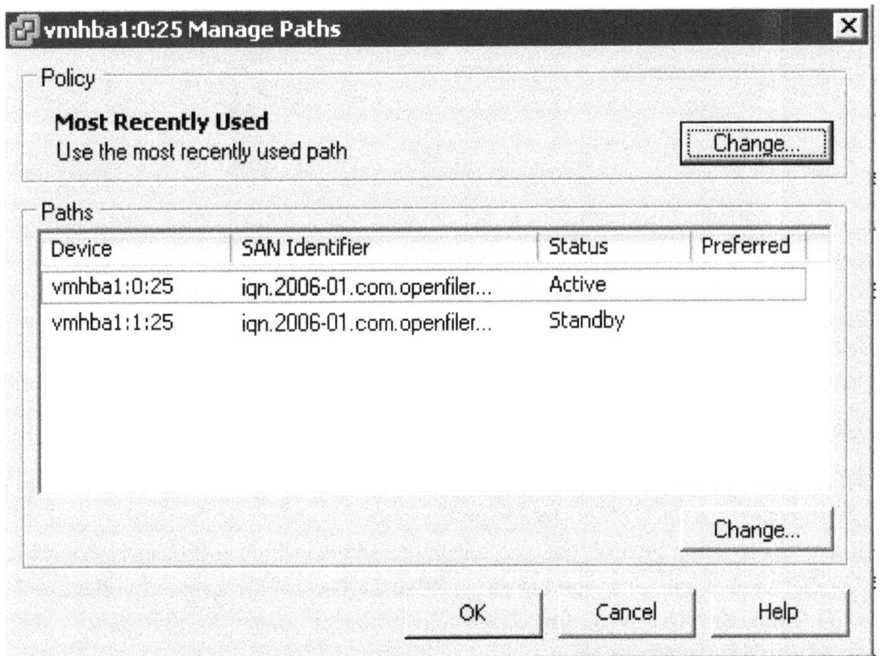

Figure 5.45 Select Change Button Within Policy Section

Step 4. In the pop-up dialog box, select "Fixed" as shown in Figure 5.46.

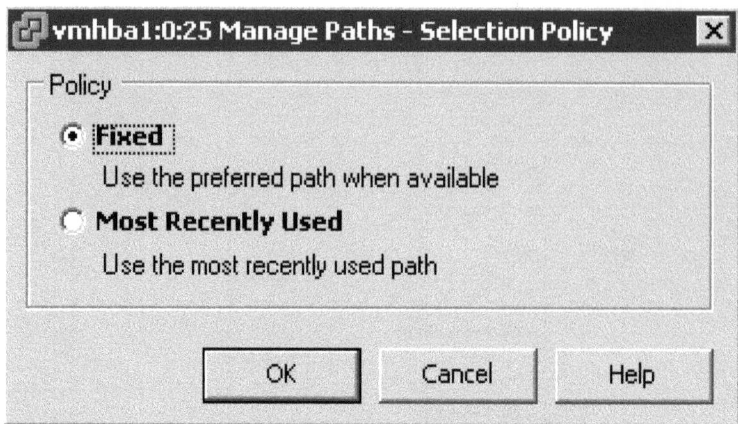

Figure 5.46 Manage Paths Selection Policy Dialog Box

Step 5. The effective path policy is now set to "Fixed" as shown in Figure 5.47. Note, the preferred path is denoted by displaying an asterisk in the Preferred column.

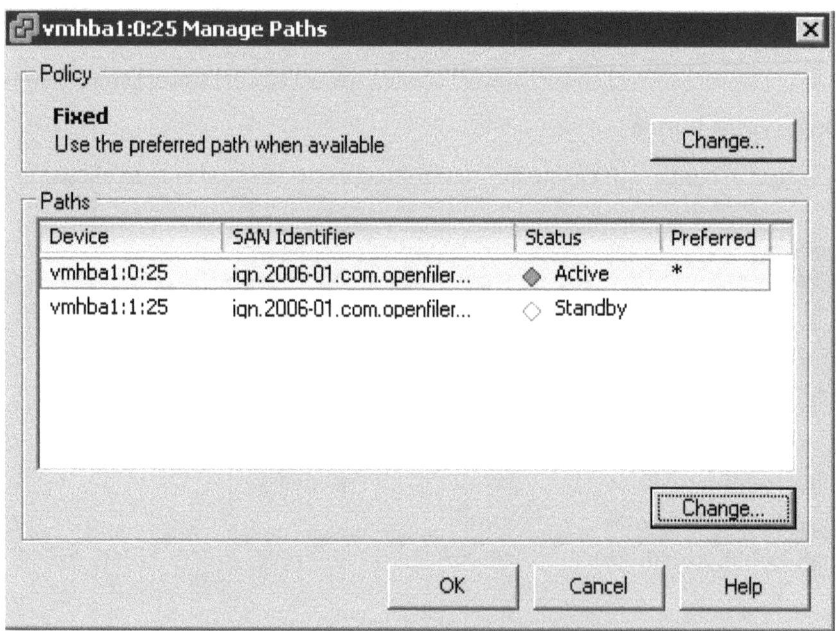

Figure 5.47 Select Change Button Within Paths Section

Fixed path is the default for active/active storage arrays. An active/active storage array is able to process disk I/O simultaneously via each of its storage processors. This increases the performance of the storage array. In data centers that have virtualized database servers writing to FC storage arrays for example, disk I/O performance will be a high priority. Active/Active storage arrays are often used to meet high disk I/O demands. The price for active/active storage arrays is high due to the performance gain of two active storage processors.

The fixed path policy is implemented by setting the preferred path to the storage array. In the event that a storage processor on the storage array fails for example, an ESX 3.5 server will use an alternative path to access the LUN. When the failed storage processor is back in service, the fixed path policy will automatically switch back over to using the preferred path. To modify the preferred path, select an HBA in the Device column and click the "Change..." button in the Paths section as shown in Figure 5.47.

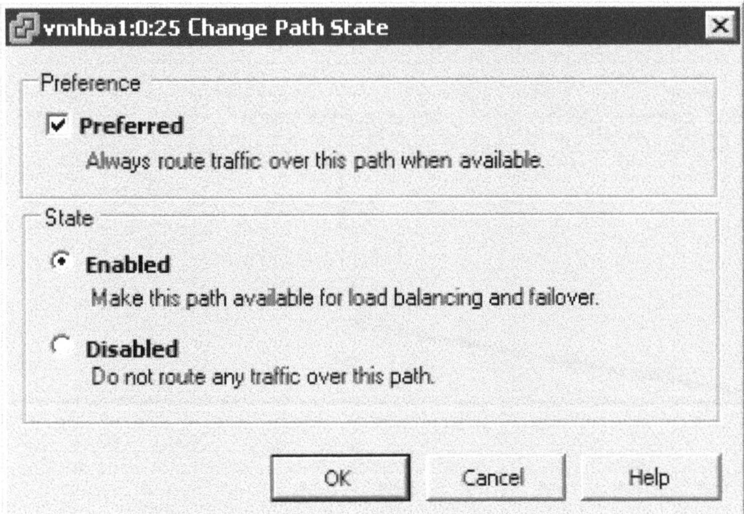

Figure 5.48 Change Path State Dialog Box

The preferred path is set by clicking in the check box next to the Preferred option in the Preference section as shown in Figure 5.48. In addition, a path can be enabled or disabled by selecting the desired option within the State section. Disabling a path may be useful during SAN reconfiguration tasks or when testing fail over conditions.

Path Thrashing

In data centers where disk I/O is less demanding, SAN administrators may chose active/passive storage arrays. These devices allow for only one storage processor at a time to be used for writing data to a LUN. Active/Passive storage devices offer lower performance than their active/active counterparts. MRU is the default path policy with supported active/passive storage arrays. When the current active path to the storage processor fails on an active/passive array, the ESX 3.5 with MRU configured as the path policy for that LUN, will use the alternate path. When the failed path returns to service, the ESX 3.5 server will not automatically switch back to using the previous HBA. This is the desired behavior to avoid a situation known as path thrashing.

Path thrashing, sometimes referred to as LUN thrashing, can occur when using an active/passive storage array when the ESX 3.5 server is configured using the fixed path policy. Typically, only one storage processor on an active/passive storage array has ownership of a LUN. A time delay is incurred when switching ownership of the LUN between these two storage processors. Let's take a look at a configuration that can cause path thrashing.

In Figure 5.49, one ESX 3.5 server is using the Fixed policy with an Active/Passive storage array.

ESX 1 is configured with HBA 1 as its preferred path. HBA 1 is actively using storage processor 1 to access LUN 15. In this simple scenario, there are no problems with path thrashing.

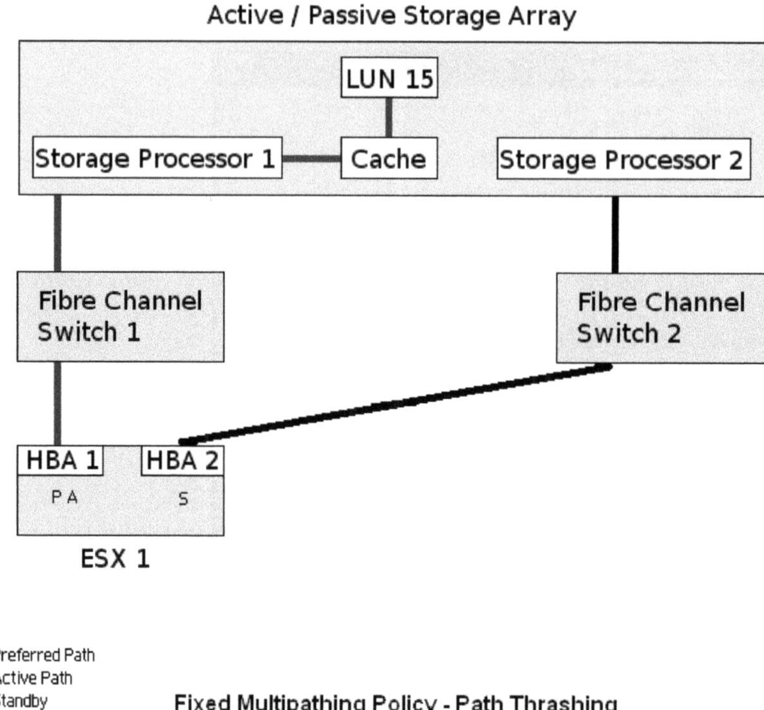

Figure 5.49 Fixed Policy With Active/Passive Storage Array

Storage processor 1 now experiences a problem and can no longer service requests to LUN 15 as shown in Figure 5.50. ESX 1 can no longer access the LUN 15 through this path and fails over to its secondary path.

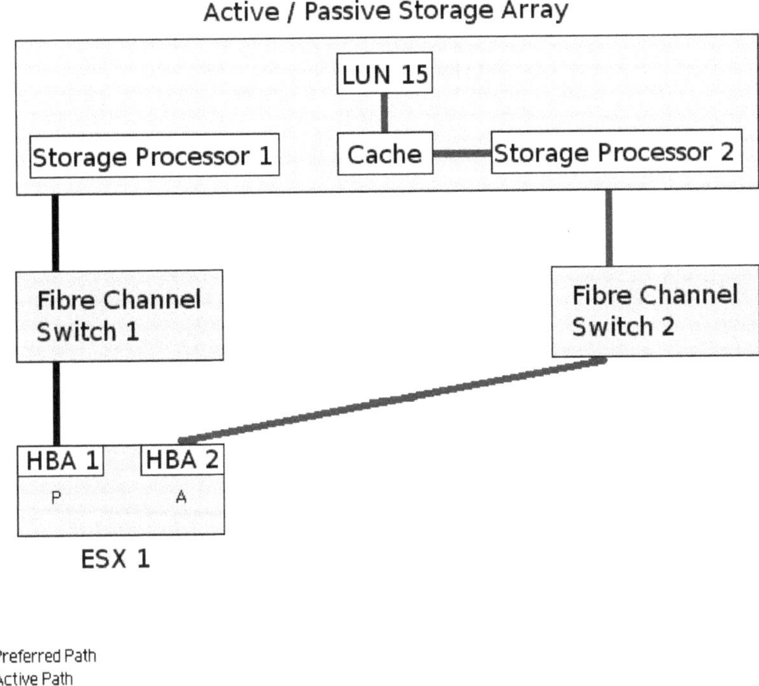

Figure 5.50 Fixed Policy Failover With Active/Passive Storage Array

HBA 2 is now the active path used to access storage processor 2. In this simple scenario, path thrashing does not take place as only a single fail over event occurred. If storage processor 1 would resume service and then fail within a minute, then resume again and continue such a recover/failure cycle, this could cause path thrashing to occur. In this unlikely event, the active/passive storage array would spend the majority of time transferring ownership of LUN 15. The reason being that the ESX 1 server is set with Fixed path policy so when it senses that storage processor 1 is once again available, it begins sending disk I/O down the path to storage processor 1. This could result in little to no data being written to LUN 15 due to the continuous transferring of LUN ownership between the two storage processors. This would be considered path thrashing. A faulty HBA or fibre channel switched port that became active and inactive repeatedly could also cause path thrashing.

This next scenario is more likely to occur then the previous scenario. In this next scenario as shown in Figure 5.51, there are two ESX servers set to Fixed policy with an Active/Passive storage array. ESX 1 is configured with HBA 1 to access the storage array via storage processor 1 and a failover path of HBA 2 to storage processor 2. ESX 2 is configured with HBA 2 to access the storage array via storage processor 2 and a failover path of HBA 1 to storage processor 1.

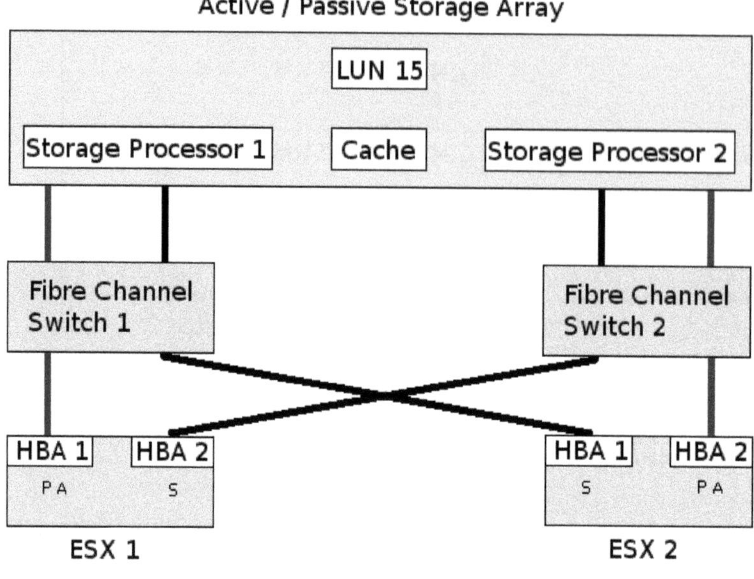

Figure 5.51 Two ESX Servers Using Fixed Policy With Active/Passive Storage Array

In the configuration shown in Figure 5.52, when these two ESX 3.5 servers attempt to access the Active/Passive storage array, path thrashing will occur. Each ESX 3.5 server is configured to use a different fixed path to a different storage processor on the storage array. As a result, the storage processors continuously switch ownership of the cache. This results in path thrashing as once again, little or no data will be written to LUN 15 due to storage processors spending the majority of their time switching ownership of the LUN.

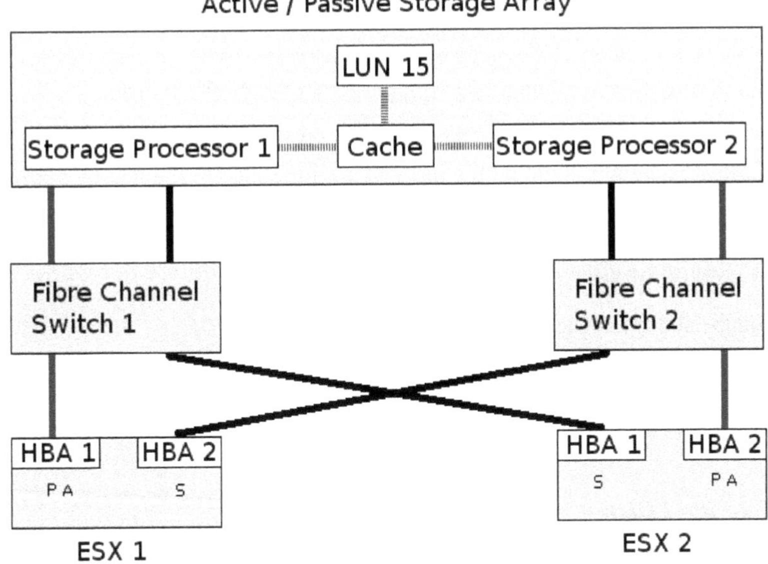

Figure 5.52 Two ESX Servers Using Fixed Policy With Active/Passive Storage Array Resulting In Path Thrashing

In a typical fail over event, a switched fabric can take up to one minute to stabilize. This can cause virtual machine guest operating systems to time out when attempting to access their virtual hard disks. It may be helpful to configure guest operating systems with longer disk access time out values.

Also note, if the detected array is not supported, it is treated as an active/active storage array. This may cause path thrashing to occur if the storage array is actually active/passive and the ESX 3.5 servers are configured with a Fixed path policy. Consult VMware's compatibility guides to ensure supported hardware is used.

Storage Considerations And Planning

Planning an ESX 3.5 server deployment requires knowledge of storage maximums to properly design and provide for the desired disk I/O performance. The following are the ESX 3.5 storage maximums:

- Maximum number of paths per LUN is 32.
- Maximum number of targets per HBA is 15.
- Maximum number of total paths is 1024.

- Maximum HBAs per system is 16.
- Maximum LUNs per system is 256. LUN numbers in the range of 0-255.

These maximum values for LUNs, HBAs, targets and paths can help in making decisions when designing a virtualization storage solution along with preparing for the VCP exam.

Placement of your virtual machine state files on either a VMFS or NFS datastore can directly affect the performance of the applications contained in the VM. Performance is affected by many factors:

- If the VM is located on a SCSI, Fibre Channel SAN, iSCSI SAN or NFS datastore
- The RAID level of the LUN that the VMFS is located on
- The load on the storage device containing the VM
- The total throughput of the storage devices on the device path to the VM

Let's examine some of the issues that you need to consider before locating your VM in your virtual infrastructure.

RAID Level Of Storage LUNs

RAID stands for any of the following:

- Redundant Array of Independent Drives
- Redundant Array of Independent Disks
- Redundant Array of Inexpensive Drives
- Redundant Array of Inexpensive Disks

The concept of RAID was developed in the late 1970s to provide an alternative to tape storage and its slow performance at the time. The term RAID was defined in 1987 by David A. Patterson, Garth A. Gibson and Randy Katz at the University of California, Berkeley. They published a paper in 1988 that defined different levels of RAID which originally were defined as:

- First level: mirrored drives
- Second level: Hamming code used for error correction
- Third level: single check disk per group
- Fourth level: independent reads and writes
- Fifth level: spread data/parity over all drives

Additional levels were defined later and hardware vendors implement the levels using different methods. Let's explore the various RAID levels.

RAID 0 Striping

Raid 0 was not one of the original levels defined. The data is broken up into smaller parts and written as a data stripe to each disk.

RAID 0 doesn't actually meet part of the definition of RAID because it isn't redundant in any way. In other words, the data gets placed on the disks with no additional data redundancy so it is not fault tolerant. If you lose access to the data on any of the disks in the LUN you cannot recover it. The more disks you have in your RAID 0 volume will raise the chances that one will fail causing the whole LUN to fail. RAID 0 also doesn't implement any kind of error checking either. If a stripe is not written correctly the data will be corrupted in that stripe and the stripe cannot be recovered.

RAID 0 requires a minimum of two disks. The main benefit of RAID 0 is to give better performance. The greater number of disks in the RAID 0 LUN will result in faster performance. Data is written to the disks in a reconfigured amount known as a stripe or also known as a fragment. Most modern storage arrays support different stripe sizes and the total amount of data stored in parallel at one time is defined as the stripe width.

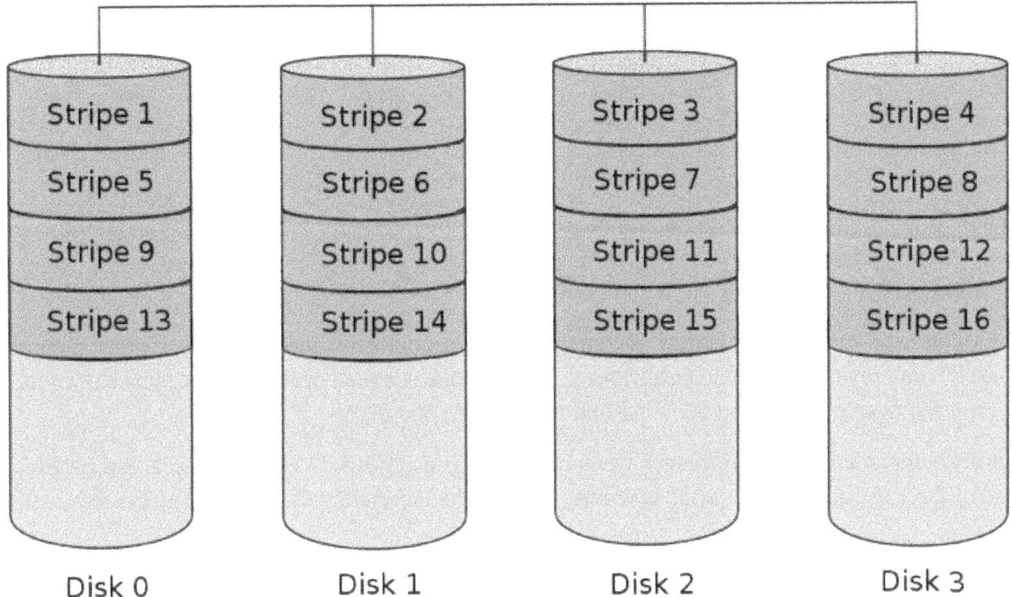

Figure 5.53 RAID 0 - Striping

Writing the data in parallel to multiple disks greatly improves performance. In the example in Figure 5.53 the file is broken into smaller fragments (stripes) and is written to the disks in parallel. All 16 stripes represent this one file. RAID 0 is best suited for configurations where performance is important and costs need to be kept as low as possible. RAID 0 has no redundancy so the total size of all disks in a RAID 0 LUN are usable for data. All disks should be the same size since the usable space for writing files will be equal to the smallest disk in the LUN.

RAID 1 - Mirroring

RAID 1 requires two disks. A data stripe written to the first disk is also written to the second disk thus providing redundancy. In the example in Figure 5.54 the first stripe of data (1) is also written to the second mirrored disk. The next stripe of data is stripe 2 and is written to both disks and so on.

The advantage to using RAID 1 is that either disk can fail and you can still access the data on the surviving disk because there is a complete set of stripes on either disk.

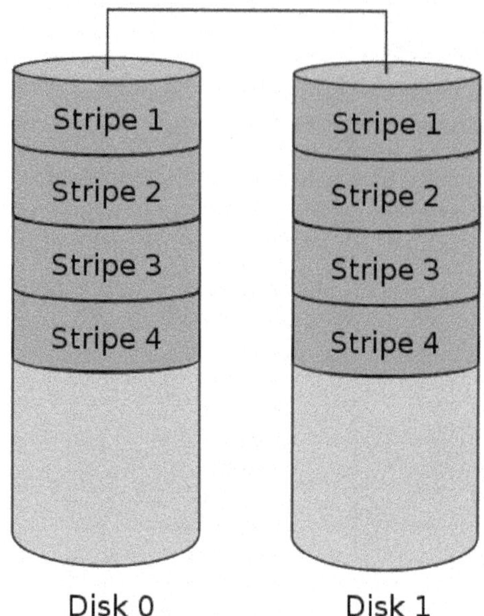

Figure 5.54 RAID 1 - Mirroring

RAID 1 when used with multi-threaded operating systems or multi-threaded applications that support "split seeks" can provide faster read performance. A split seek is a read operation that pulls half of the stripes for a file from one disk and the other half from the second disk.

There is a small reduction in performance when doing writes using RAID 1. RAID 1 does not perform any kind of error checking. If the stripe is written to the disks incorrectly there is no way to recover it.

RAID 2 – Hamming Code

RAID 2 uses bit level striping using a linear error-correcting code for data protection. This error-correction technique was named after its inventor Richard Hamming. RAID 2 doesn't use parity, stripping or mirroring. Instead, RAID 2 splits the data at the bit level and spreads it across some of the disks and some of the redundancy disks in the LUN. Hamming code is a form of error correcting code (ECC) that uses the actual data written to the data disks and using the Hamming code algorithm calculates redundancy data at the same time and writes that ECC data to the redundancy disks in the LUN. The ECC data is compared to the actual data to determine if there are any errors caused by the write process.

The value of this RAID level is that it is able to fix single bit errors on the fly. Today's ECC memory systems use the same technology.

The downside is that the calculation of the ECC data and verification of it causes poor performance during writes.

RAID 2 didn't see much commercial success and was rarely used in commercial applications due to the performance issues. It also used expensive HBAs and required many redundancy disks.

RAID 3 – Single Parity Disk

RAID 3 uses striped disks for data and one disk designated for parity data to provide the volume with a single disk fault tolerance. This RAID level was not supported much by the hardware vendors. The main reason for the lack of support is that it usually cannot service multiple requests for data. In Figure 5.55 when the disks are being accessed to read the lighter stripes it cannot read the darker stripes until the first read request has been completed. Because of this feature performance was not as good as the other levels.

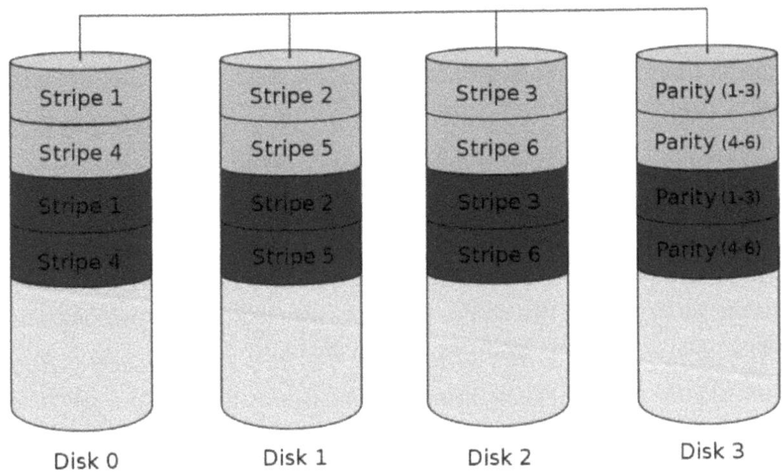

Figure 5.55 RAID 3 – Single Parity Disk

RAID 4 – Independent Reads/Writes

RAID 4 uses striping like RAID 3 but instead of striping at the byte level as RAID 3 does it stripes at the block level. A minimum of three disks are needed for a RAID 4 LUN. RAID 4 uses parity to provide data protection like RAID 5 does but it does not distribute it instead all parity data is put on one disk.

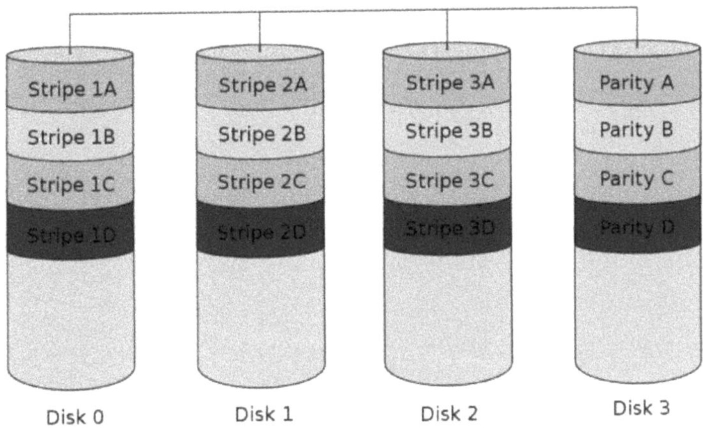

Figure 5.56 RAID 4 – Independent Reads/Writes

When a read request has been made to read stripe 1B on disk 0 as shown in Figure 5.56 and a simultaneous read request for block 1D on disk 0 is made the request for 1D will have to wait until the first request has been completed.

The data in a RAID 4 LUN is protected with parity information on each stripe so the LUN can survive a single disk failure. The missing data on the failed disk in each stripe can be recovered using the parity information generated for each stripe. Performance however will be reduced until the failed drive is replaced.

RAID 4 performance also benefits from having more disks in the LUN and the overhead to provide redundancy is equal to one disk in the LUN.

RAID 5 –Parity Across All Disks

RAID 5 uses distributed parity across the disks and requires a minimum of three disks in the LUN. Distributed parity is accomplished by writing data to all of the disks in the LUN except one and calculating parity data to be stored in the remaining disk for that stripe. On the next stripe the last data disk on the previous stripe gets the parity data for that stripe. The parity data therefore is distributed to all disks after a number of stripes equal to the total number of disks in the LUN.

In Figure 5.57 the first stripe of data (the "a" stripe) gets written simultaneously to disks 0, 1 and 2. A parity calculation is done and that data is also written at the same time to disk 3. This parity data now protects the "a" stripe if either disk 0, 1 or 2 fails.

The next stripe "b" now needs to be written. The disk that had the previous parity data (in this case disk 3) now gets the first data stripe (in this case stripe 1b). Disk 0 gets the second data stripe (2b) and disk 1 gets the third data stripe (3b). Parity data is then put on disk 2 (parity b) and so on. This method of distributing parity provides a benefit not found in RAID 4 which is that since RAID 5 has its parity data distributed across all disks instead of just one as in RAID 4, it gets better performance when a disk fails and it is being repaired after the disk has been replaced.

RAID 5 has poor performance when there are many writes which are smaller than the capacity of a single stripe. Parity must be updated on each write requiring a read-modify-write sequence for both the data block and the parity block. RAID 5 performance does benefit from having more disks in the LUN and the overhead to provide redundancy (using parity) is equal to one disk in the LUN.

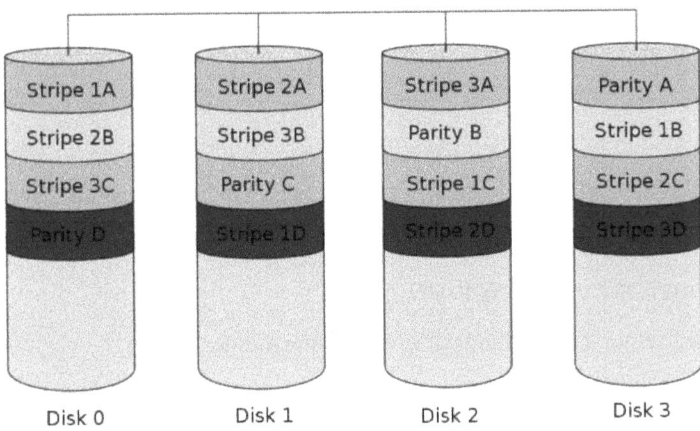

Figure 5.57 RAID 5 –Parity Across All Disks

RAID 5 LUNs can survive a single disk failure because the remaining disks can be used to rebuild the missing data in a stripe. The failed disk will need to be replaced as soon as possible because performance will be greatly diminished in this degraded state.

RAID 1+0 - Mirrored Set In A Striped Set

While not one of the originally defined RAID levels, RAID 1+0 combines the speed of striping with the redundancy of mirroring. This level has the highest storage costs of all commonly used RAID levels.

RAID 1+0 requires a minimum of four disks. All RAID 1+0 LUNs must use an even number of disks. It can survive multiple disk failures provided no one mirror has both disks failed at the same time.

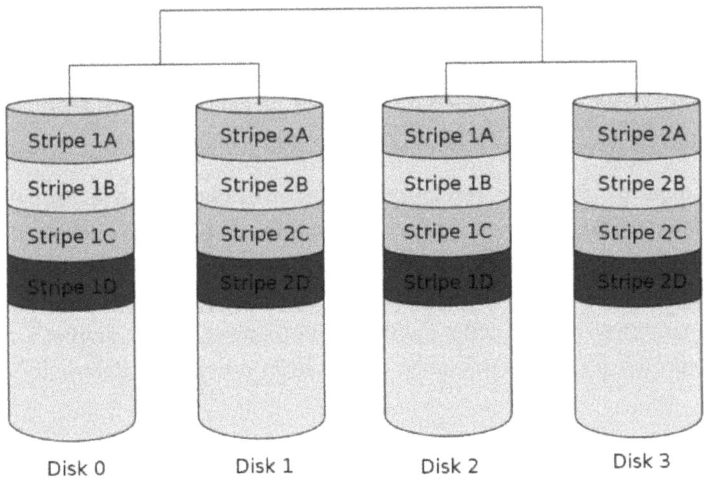

Figure 5.58 RAID 1 + 0 – Mirrored Set in a Striped Set

In Figure 5.58 the first stripe of data (stripe a) goes on disk 0 (1A) and disk 1 (2A). Those blocks of data are also mirrored to disks 2 and 3 respectively (stripes 1A and 2A). Each additional strip is mirrored as well. The performance gain of striping is gained as well as having redundancy. The downside is that like RAID 1 there must be twice as many disks in the LUN to provide data redundancy.

Additional RAID Levels

There are many more RAID levels that have been defined; here are a few of the more popular ones:

- RAID 0+1: Striped sets in a mirrored set
- RAID 5+0: Striping across distributed parity RAID systems
- RAID 5+1: Mirror striped set with distributed parity (also known as RAID 53)
- RAID 6: Striped set with dual distributed parity

I/O Bus Capacities

Every I/O bus technology has a maximum throughput and cannot process more data across the bus than that limit. It is possible to configure your I/O buses with more resources attached to it than the I/O bus can provide bandwidth for. This becomes a performance bottleneck.

There are a number of tools available that can help you determine exactly how much bandwidth each of your VMs is using. You will however need a good understanding of the limitations of all of the devices used to store your VM state files if you want to troubleshoot I/O bottlenecks. These tools will be covered in Chapter 16 – Monitoring and Alerting.

SCSI Bus Performance

Since 1986 when the standard was first published, the SCSI technology has greatly improved performance through a number of releases:

- SCSI-1
- SCSI-2
- SCSI-3

SCSI-1

The first defined SCSI bus used a narrow 8-bit bus which operated at 5 MHz bus speed and provided only 5 MB/sec bandwidth. Single-ended transmission mode was supported using passive termination. The Bus used a 50-pin connector and supported 8 devices on the bus known as targets. You could not have two devices on the bus assigned to the same target number at the same time. If you did the bus wouldn't function properly. The targets were assigned a number from 0 through 7 with target 6 or 7 usually assigned to the SCSI controller. Passive termination was used to provide an electronic "end point" to the SCSI bus.

SCSI-2

Originally released in 1990 but not formally adopted until 1994 the SCSI-2 standard provided many improvements over the SCSI-1 standard. It provided additional SCSI commands to enable additional capabilities between the SCSI controller (also known as the SCSI HBA) and the SCSI devices.

These enhancements are:

- Implementation of a Wide SCSI bus which increased the bus to 16 bits and later to 32 bits. This increased the data throughput on the bus significantly. The SCSI-2 standard was designed to be backwards compatible with the SCSI-1 standard
- Implementation of the Fast SCSI protocol which doubled the speed of the bus to 10 MHz and later to 20 MHz to provide speeds up to 40 MB/sec
- 16 devices supported on the Wide SCSI bus as shown in Figure 5.59
- SCSI-2 implemented active termination that allows more reliable termination of the SCSI bus
- Implementation of differential signaling which was later renamed to high-voltage differential. This provided a better signal strength to provide a longer cable length in the SCSI bus
- The SCSI-2 specification defined higher-density connections using an 80-pin connector
- The introduction of command queuing which allows multiple outstanding simultaneous requests between devices on the bus
- The introduction of additional SCSI command sets that support the use of SCSI CD-ROMs devices, removable media and scanners

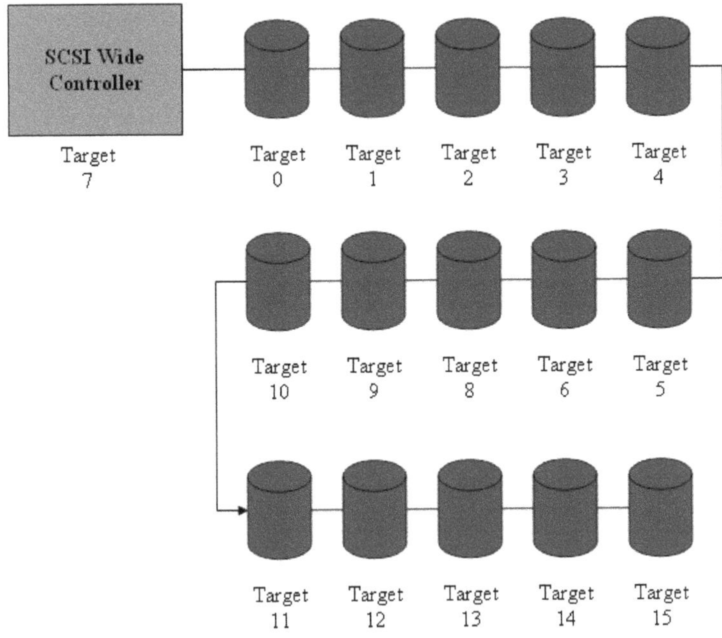

Figure 5.59 Wide SCSI Bus Configuration

SCSI-3

The SCSI-3 standard was broken into multiple standards and development on the standard started in

1993 and continues to be refined. The improvements to the SCSI architecture as implemented by the various SCSI-3 standards are too numerous for the scope of this book but can be summarized as:

- SCSI-3 Interlocked Protocol (SIP) to provide parallel device configurations. This was later improved upon with the SCSI(-3) Parallel Interface - 2, (SPI-2) standard
- Faster data transfer speeds were attained using bus speeds up to 40 MHz
- A new implementation of Low voltage differential or LVD signaling which was needed to run the higher bus speeds
- Single Connector Attachment Connectors (SCA-2) which provided power and the bus connection all in one connector
- Very High Density Cable Interconnect (VHDCI) which provides 68-pins on the connector but packaged in a smaller form factor
- Implementation of SCSI(-3) Parallel Interface - 4 (SPI-4) which defines Ultra 160 and Ultra 320 capabilities. Resulting in 160 MB/sec and 320 MB/sec bus performance.
- Better signal strength allowing cabling up to 25 meters in length

Fibre Channel Bus Performance

In 1994 the American National Standards Institute (ANSI) approved the Fibre Channel standard. Later updates to the protocol provided higher bus speeds and the ability to connect to SCSI devices. The fibre channel fabric allows more devices to be configured on it than a SCSI bus can have. An ESX 3.5 server can access up to 256 LUNs in the FC fabric. The Disk.MaxLun parameter can be changed to reduce the number of LUNs scanned which could improve LUN discovery speed. Not all FC HBA's are supported in an ESX 3.5 server. You should look at the VMware I/O Compatibility Guide to verify that the HBA you want to use is supported.

Over the years new fibre channel standards have been created and their performance has increased. Be aware that not all of these standards are currently supported in an ESX 3.5 server.

- 1 Gigabit Fibre Channel (1GFC) has a line rate of 1.0625 Gbit/s and a throughput of 100 MByte/s.
- 2 Gigabit Fibre Channel (2GFC) has a line rate of 2.125 Gbit/s and a throughput of 200 MByte/s
- 4 Gigabit Fibre Channel (4GFC) has a line rate of 4.25 Gbit/s and a throughput of 400 MByte/s
- 8 Gigabit Fibre Channel (8GFC) has a line rate of 8.5 Gbit/s and a throughput of 800 MByte/s.
- 10 Gigabit Fibre Channel (10GFC) has a line rate of 10.51875 Gbit/s and a throughput of 1,000 MByte/s.
- 20 Gigabit Fibre Channel (20GFC) has a line rate of 10.52 Gbit/s and a throughput of 2,000 MByte/s.

The fibre channel HBAs communicate with the fibre channel arrays by using lasers to pulse the FC signal over glass-based fibre wires. The attenuation (also known as signal loss) is significantly lower than SCSI signals over a copper wire. Multimode fibre supports cable lengths up to 500 meters and single mode fibre cables support signals up to 10 kilometers.

For more information about the Fibre Channel technology visit the following websites:

- Fibre Channel Industry Association (FCIA) website: http://www.fibrechannel.org/
- FC standards (T11) - INCITS technical committee: http://www.t11.org/index.html
- University of New Hampshire Fibre Channel Tutorial: http://www.iol.unh.edu/services/testing/fc/training/tutorials/fc_tutorial.php

iSCSI Bus Performance

iSCSI bus performance is greatly dependent on the throughput of the network it is connected to. The following can help increase your iSCSI datastore data performance:

- Use only supported iSCSI HBAs. Refer to the VMware I/O Compatibility Guide for the latest listing of supported HBAs.
- VMware does not support using 100 MB NICs as an iSCSI software initiator. iSCSI software initiators must be supported gigabit NICs.
- Make sure you set the iSCSI interface to full duplex or configured to negotiate at full duplex.
- Put you iSCSI resources on an isolated network. This will reduce the chance of too many resources overwhelming the available bandwidth and will provide better security.

To improve availability of the iSCSI LUN:

- Try to use two iSCSI hardware initiators when possible in an ESX 3.5 server. This will automatically configure the server for multipathing if both initiators are routed and connected to the LUN through different IP addresses and are connected to different storage processors on the same iSCSI storage device.
- If using an iSCSI software initiator, multipathing can be achieved by creating a virtual switch that is connected to multiple physical NICs. Do not use that virtual switch for any other purposes to ensure isolation from the other network resources.
- Consider setting the failover policy from the default of most recently used (MRU) to the fixed path policy.

Some other considerations for your iSCSI infrastructure:

- You cannot mix hardware and software iSCSI initiators on the same ESX 3.5 server.
- VMware does not support DHCP for iSCSI connections on an ESX 3.5 server so use static IP addresses for initiators.
- The iSCSI technology is based on RFC 3720 which defines that the default port to use is port 3260. You must make sure that your firewalls are configured to allow communications on the iSCSI network to pass through on this port.
- Microsoft Clustering Service (MSCS) not supported for iSCSI.

NFS Bus Performance

NFS performance is affected by the following issues:

- Poor network connectivity. Try to use gigabit NICs when possible to increase bandwidth.
- Contention on the network. Try to isolate the NFS resources to an isolated network. This will also increase security of the resources.
- The underlying storage performance that the NFS shared directory is placed on. The read and write speeds are impacted by slow storage devices housing the NFS shared directory. Try to use faster drives or RAID to increase the performance when possible.
- The underlying file system that the NFS shared directory is placed on. Some of the older file systems don't perform as well as the latest ones. Benchmarking is important to determine performance gains.
- The load put on the NFS server. If the server provides multiple NFS shared directories, examine its CPU load, memory load and I/O and network loads to determine if it is able to meet the workload demand placed on it.

The VMware File System

Virtual machines consist of a set of files (known as state files) that hold the configuration and file system state of the VM. The encapsulation of virtual hardware as a set of files is essential in providing the many benefits virtualization has to offer. In chapter 7, we will examine each of the files of a virtual machine in detail. The performance of a virtual machine depends a great deal on access to its virtual hard disk files. The physical location of the virtual hard disk file is an important decision when planning virtual machine deployments. Refer to the "Storage Considerations and Planning" section of this chapter for more information on the physical placement of virtual machine files. The virtual hard disk file consumes the majority of storage space of all the virtual machine files. Multiple servers having file access to different virtual hard disk files at the same time may be problematic for conventional file systems where a single server has exclusive read-write access to the file system. VMware has created its own file system solution to address the unique storage needs of a virtualized data center.

Virtual Machine File System (VMFS) is designed to optimize the storage and management of virtual machines. Deploying virtual machines on a VMFS offers the following benefits:

- Reduces virtual machine administration
- Enables rapid provisioning of virtual machines
- Supports VMware High Availability (HA) clusters
- Supports VMware Distributed Resource Scheduler (DRS) clusters
- Supports VMware VMotion technology

Virtual machine administration is made easier with the use of VMFS. An ESX administrator can place a request for a large 2 TB LUN to the SAN administrator. The LUN can then be formatted as a VMFS volume and a large number of virtual machines can be rapidly provisioned and stored as needed without any additional interaction with the SAN administrator. Should the original 2 TB LUN become insufficient and additional storage space is required, VMware supports spanning a VMFS volume across different LUNs without the need to reboot ESX servers or virtual machines currently accessing the VMFS volume. Dynamic VMFS volume expansion eliminates downtime and reduces administration overhead. Understanding the limitations of VMFS volume spanning is necessary for proper implementation.

VMFS is supported on an entire LUN, not individual partitions of a LUN; for example, a LUN partitioned into 3 slices, and a VMFS created on each partition, each VMFS being presented to a separate ESX Server is not supported. A single LUN that contains a VMFS volume is referred to as an extent. Each extent has a maximum size limit of 2 TB. VMFS can span a total of 32 extents to create a maximum VMFS volume size of 64 TB. The first extent created when spanning a VMFS volume across multiple LUNs is called the master extent. The master extent contains the metadata for all extents. If the master extent is lost or corrupted, data loss could occur for the entire VMFS volume.

The use of multiple extents with VMFS should be limited to a few circumstances. For example, when running out of disk space on a LUN as mentioned earlier and when enhanced performance gains can be realized by spreading the disk I/O load among LUNs with specific characteristics that enhance applications running within VMs while accessing these LUNs through multiple physical paths. Refer to the Configuring ESX 3.5 Storage Extents section later in this chapter for the steps to create an extent.

VMFS is a high performance clustered file system. VMware supports a maximum of 32 ESX 3.5 servers simultaneously accessing a VMFS volume. While a virtual machine is powered on, VMFS places a file lock on the virtual machine files. This prevents other ESX 3.5 servers accessing the same VMFS volume from potentially causing file corruption. File locking is referred to as distributed lock management. It is implemented within the VMkernel which moves the point of control from the SAN to the ESX 3.5 servers further reducing SAN administration management. VMware's VMotion, DRS and HA technologies require multiple ESX 3.5 servers to have simultaneous access to a file system. VMFS enables each of these through its clustering capabilities.

VMFS Metadata

The amount of disk spaced required to store the metadata is pre-allocated and only changes with the block size of the datastore as follows:

- 1 MB block = 626 MB metadata
- 2 MB block = 694 MB metadata
- 4 MB block = 832 MB metadata
- 8 MB block = 856 MB metadata

VMFS metadata updates occur when making the following modifications to files:

- Permissions
- Ownership
- Moving a file

- Renaming a file
- Accessing the creation and modification times
- Opening a file
- Closing a file

In order for the metadata updates to occur, non-persistent SCSI-2 reservations are used to lock the entire LUN. When there are a large number of virtual machines on a single LUN, SCSI reservation conflicts can occur due to performing too many VMFS metadata updates simultaneously. The Advanced Settings configuration screen within the VI Client can be used to increase the scsi.ConflictRetries value. This setting won't resolve misconfiguration problems, such as improperly configured storage arrays. It just generates a longer retry period to obtain a SCSI reservation.

Using non-VMware aware tools can cause excessive SCSI reservations as well. For example, using the service console cp command to copy large virtual hard disk files will initiate a SCSI reservation after a few megabytes are written to disk. Instead, using the VMware vmkfstools command will cause a non-persistent SCSI reservation to occur and then it will quickly be released once the file has been created and use file locks to copy the remaining data.

The output of the vmkfstools –P CLI command will show the following VMFS metadata information:

- Block size
- Number of extents
- Volume capacity
- VMFS version
- Label
- VMFS UUID

CLI NOTE: Information about the VMFS volume is stored in the metadata for the volume. You can access this metadata information

 # vmkfstools –P –h MyVMFS

- The -P option is used to read the metadata
- The -h option is used to print output in KB, MB or GB instead of bytes
- MyVMFS in this example is the VMFS volume label

The following shows the output of this command on an ESX 3.5 server named vcpserver02:

[root@vcpserver02 root]# vmkfstools -P -h /vmfs/volumes/SANLUN01

VMFS-3.31 file system spanning 1 partitions.

File system label (if any): SANLUN01

Mode: public

Capacity 14G, 14G available, file block size 1.0M

UUID: 47b5ba90-0a226742-5102-000bcdcb4aaf

Partitions spanned (on "lvm"):

vmhba32:0:1:1

Early adopters of virtualization may have a mix of VMFS versions in use. ESX 2.x servers use VMFS version 2. VMFS-2 is a flat file system without the capability of creating a directory structure. ESX Server 2.x servers cannot read or write to VMFS-3 volumes. ESX 3.5 servers are able to read data from VMFS-2 volumes but are unable to write data to a VMFS-2 volume. ESX 3.5 servers use VMFS version 3. VMFS-3 has added the capability of creating a directory structure in the file system. As a most noticeable feature, it introduced directory structure in the file system. Older versions of ESX Server cannot read or write VMFS3 volumes. The default location of virtual machine files has changed from VMFS-2 to VMFS-3. With a VMFS-3 volume as the chosen datastore, the virtual machine configuration files and virtual disk(s) are located by default in the VMFS partition.

To Create A VMFS Volume Using The CLI

A VMFS volume can also be created using the CLI.

CLI NOTE: To create a VMFS volume, use the following command:

 # vmkfstools –C vmfs2|vmfs3 -S label vmhba#:#:#:#

- The –C specifies the type of VMFS volume to create
- The –S specifies a simple name that references the VMFS volume
- The vmhba format is instance:target:LUN:partition

A UUID which is a unique hexadecimal value will be created for the VMFS volume.

Configuring ESX 3.5 Storage Extents

A LUN that at first thought appeared to be large enough to accommodate virtual machine files may in time become full. Additional storage when needed can be requested at any time and provided to virtual machines without any downtime imposed on the virtual machines. This can be accomplished with the use of extents. An extent is an additional LUN provided by the SAN administrator and presented to the ESX server. The ESX administrator can use this additional LUN to span an existing VMFS volume that has become full.

The following are the steps needed to configure an additional extent:

Step1. Select the Storage Link in the Hardware box and if needed click the Refresh link to access newly available storage. The LUNs available to the ESX 3.5 server will be listed in the Storage section as shown in Figure 5.60.

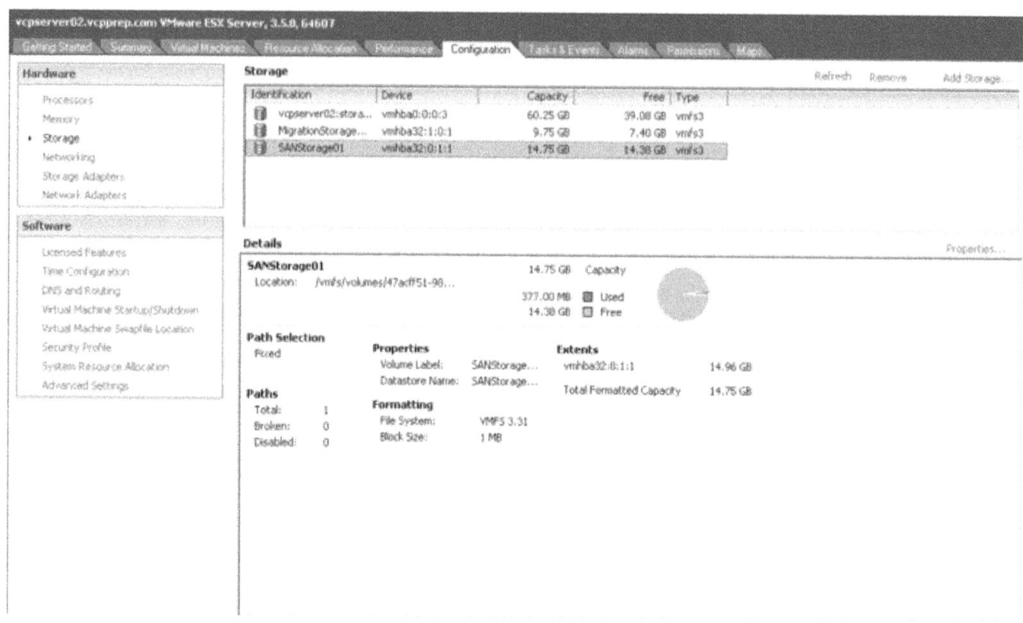

Figure 5.60 Select Datastore Storage To Extend

Step 2. Select the LUN that needs to be spanned and you will see its properties in the Details section of the screen. Click on the Properties link to continue.

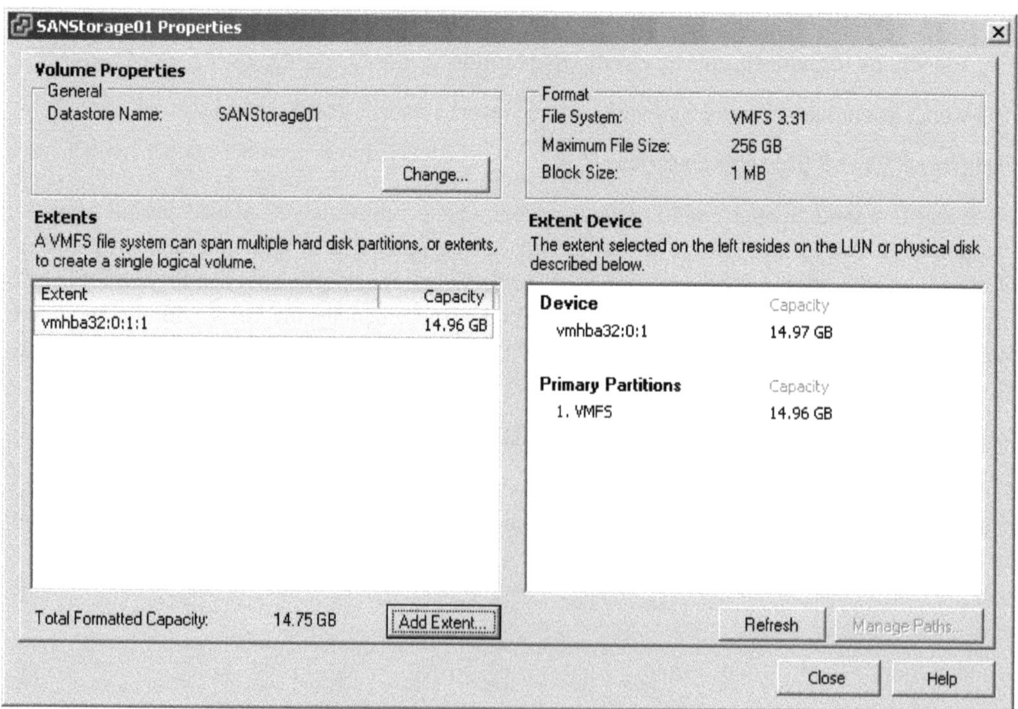

Figure 5.61 Datastore Properties Dialog Box

Step 3. In the Properties window you can see that the VMFS volume has one extent vmhba32:0:1:1

and has a capacity of 14.96 GB. To add an extent click on the Add Extent button as shown in Figure 5.61.

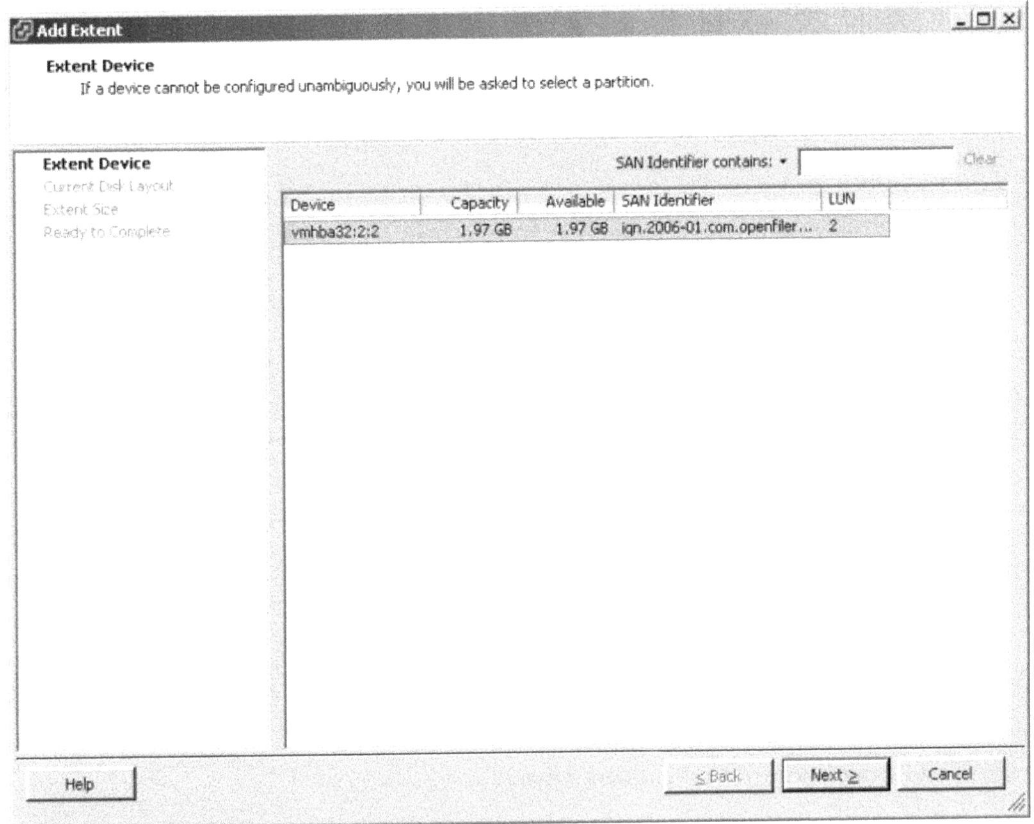

Figure 5.62 Add Extent Wizard Select Device

Step 4. Select the appropriate LUN that will serve as the additional extent as shown in Figure 5.62. Click on the Next button to continue.

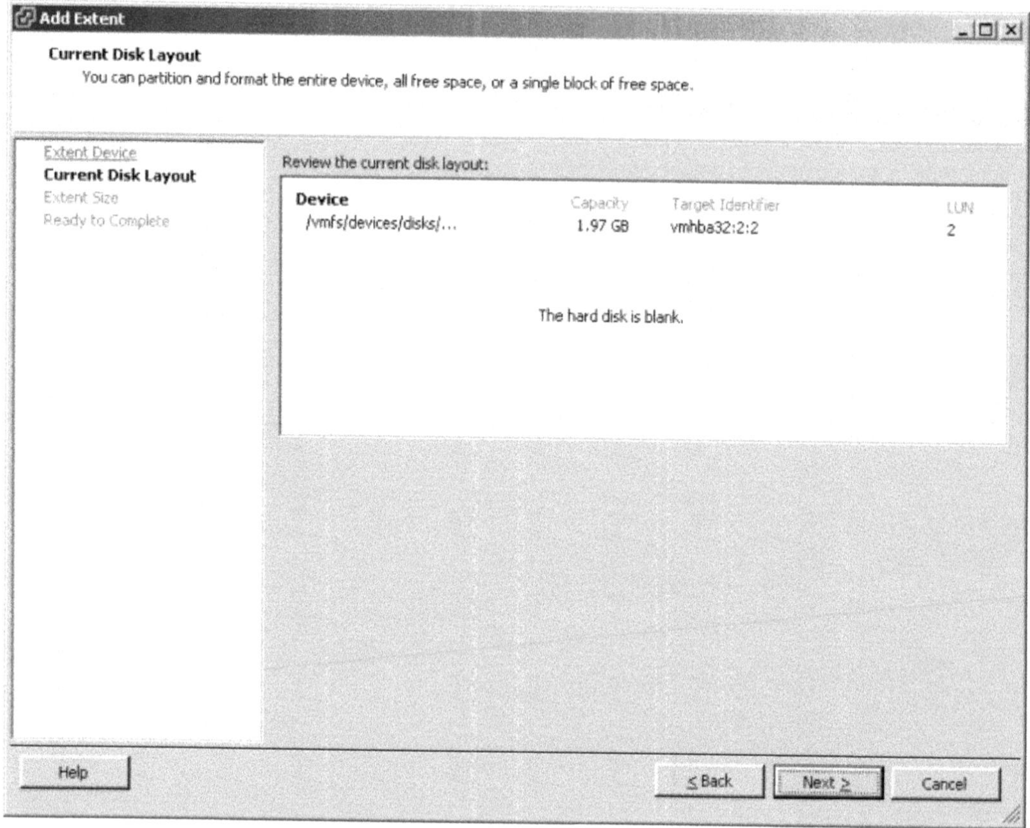

Figure 5.63 Add Extent Wizard Current Disk Layout

Step 5. Verify the current disk layout is appropriate as shown in Figure 5.63 and click Next to continue.

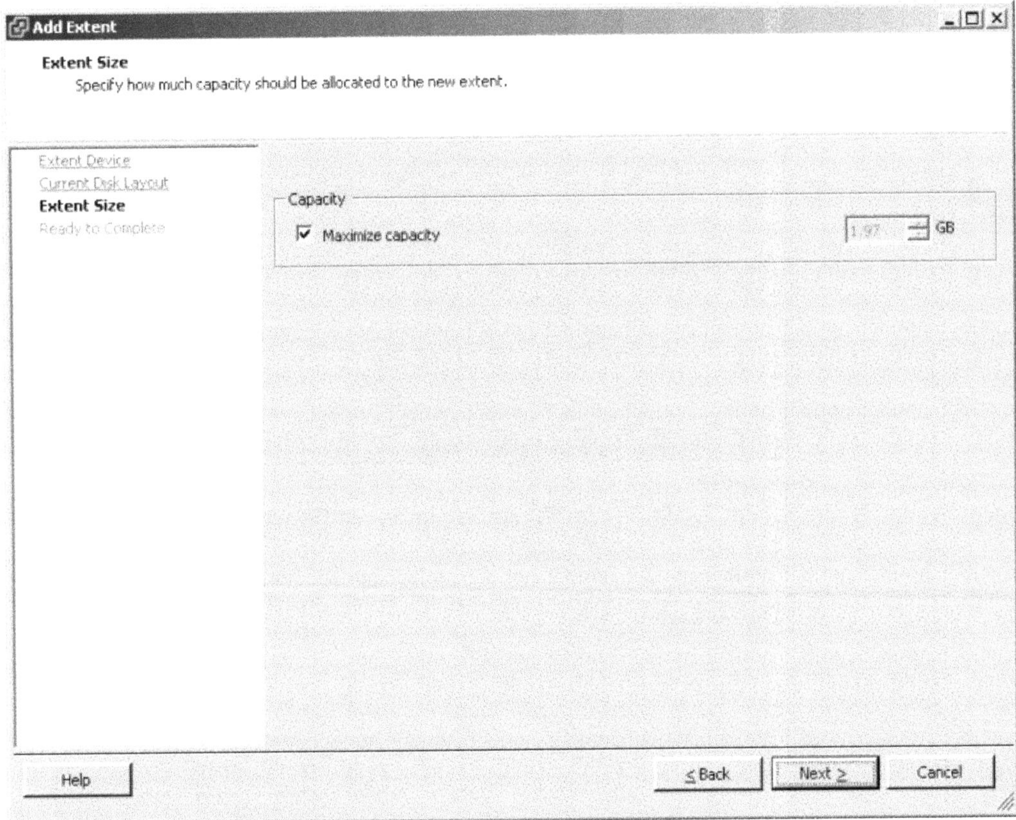

Figure 5.64 Add Extent Wizard Extent Size

Step 6. Choose how much of the new extent should be allocated as shown in Figure 5.64.

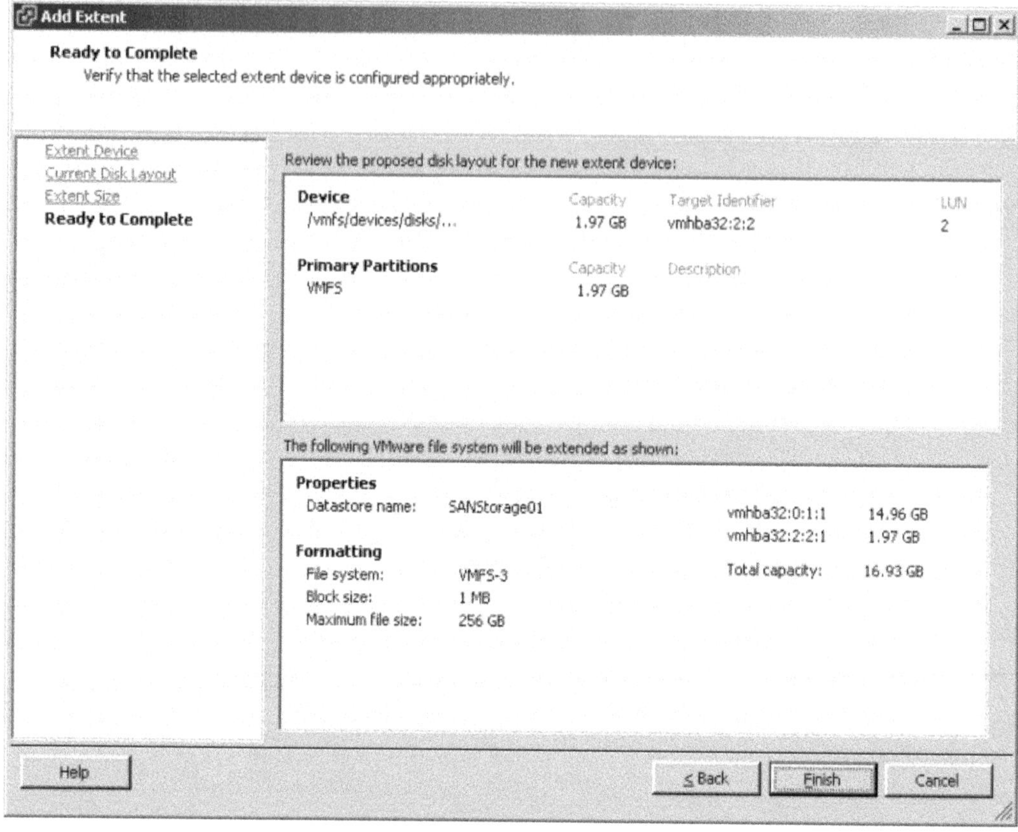

Figure 5.65 Add Extent Wizard Ready to Complete

Step 7. Review the extent configuration as shown in Figure 5.65. Verify that the final disk layout is correct and click “Finish”.

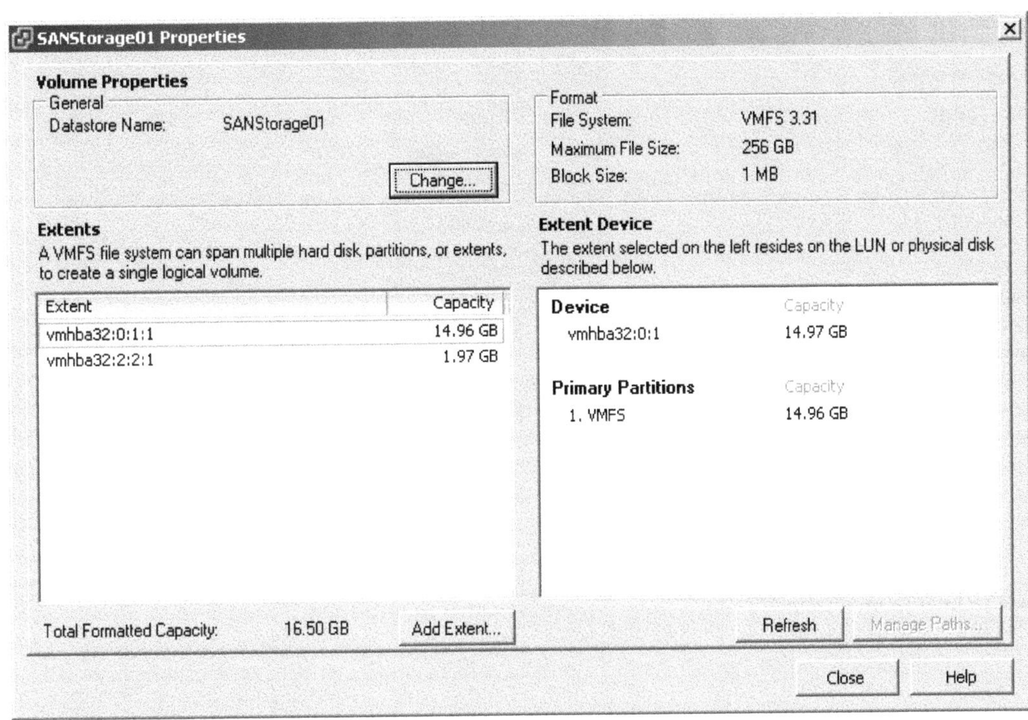

Figure 5.66 Datastore Properties Dialog Box Extent Added

As shown in Figure 5.66, the second extent has been added as listed under the Extent column as vmhba32:2:2:1 with the capacity of 1.97 GB.

To modify the datastore name, select the Change button within the General section of the storage properties dialog box. The datastore properties window is displayed as shown in Figure 5.67.

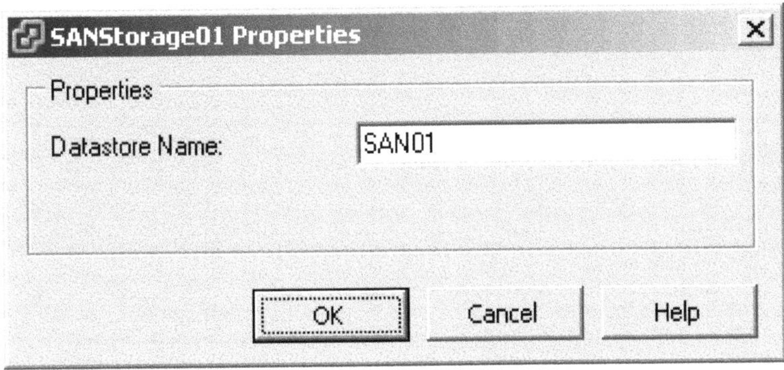

Figure 5.67 Change Datastore Name Dialog Box

The name of the datastore can be modified by entering a new name and selecting the OK button as shown in Figure 5.67.

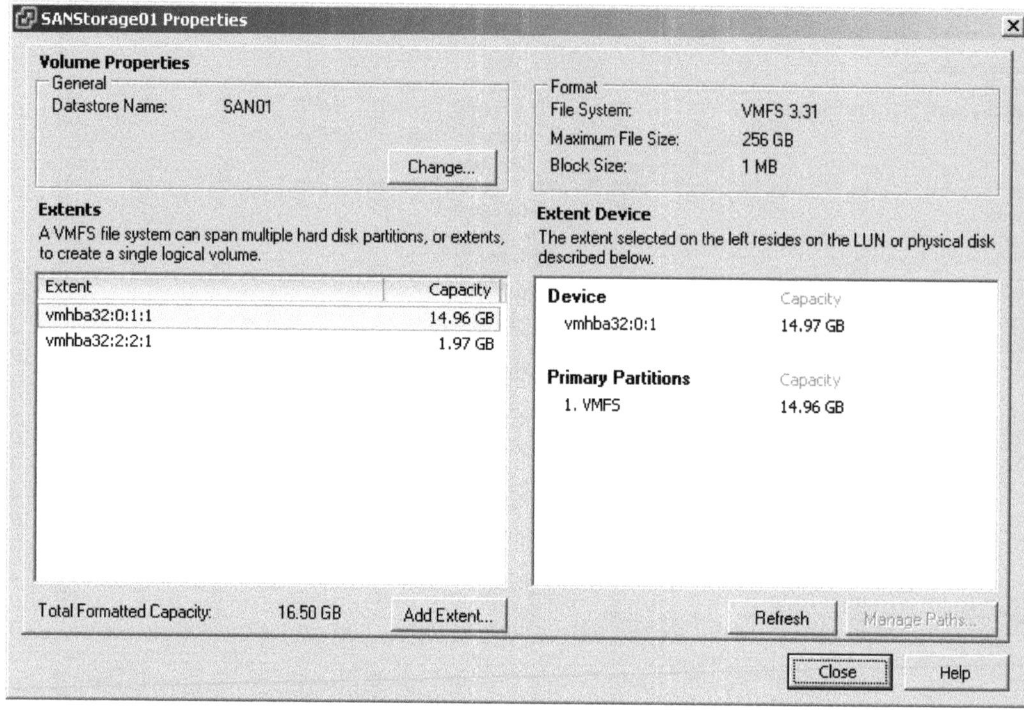

Figure 5.68 Datastore Properties Dialog Box Select Close Button

Confirm the datastore name has been modified as shown in Figure 5.68 and select the Close button.

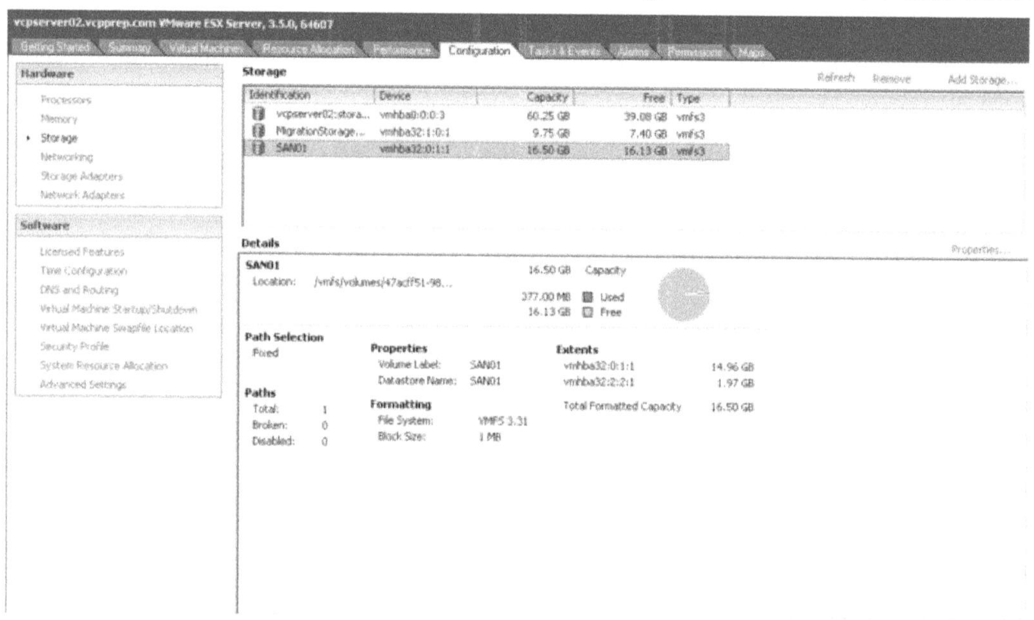

Figure 5.69 Datastore Details View With New Extent Added

The new datastore name is displayed within the Configuration Tab as shown in Figure 5.69. We can also confirm within the Details window that the VMFS volume now has two extents with a storage capacity of 16.50 GB.

CLI NOTE: You can use the `vmkfstools` command w/ "-Z" option to extend a VMFS volume.

 # vmkfstools –Z vmhba1:0:03:1 vmhba1:0:11:1

Be aware that any data on vmhba1:0:03:1 will be destroyed as it is merged with vmhba1:0:11:1.

To Remove an Extent

It is not possible to remove a single extent once it has been added. It is necessary to remove the entire VMFS volume including all extents. Therefore, prior to deleting a VMFS volume, first create backups of all data. Deleting a VMFS volume destroys all data on all extents in the VMFS volume.

RDM - Raw Device Mapping

Raw Device Mapping (RDM) files are used to access raw LUNs. A raw LUN is a NON-VMFS formatted LUN. RDM files are stored on a VMFS volume using local storage, FC SAN or iSCSI SAN storage. They can also be stored on NFS storage. RDM files work similar to a shortcut file in Windows or a symbolic link in Linux/UNIX operating systems as shown in Figure 5.70.

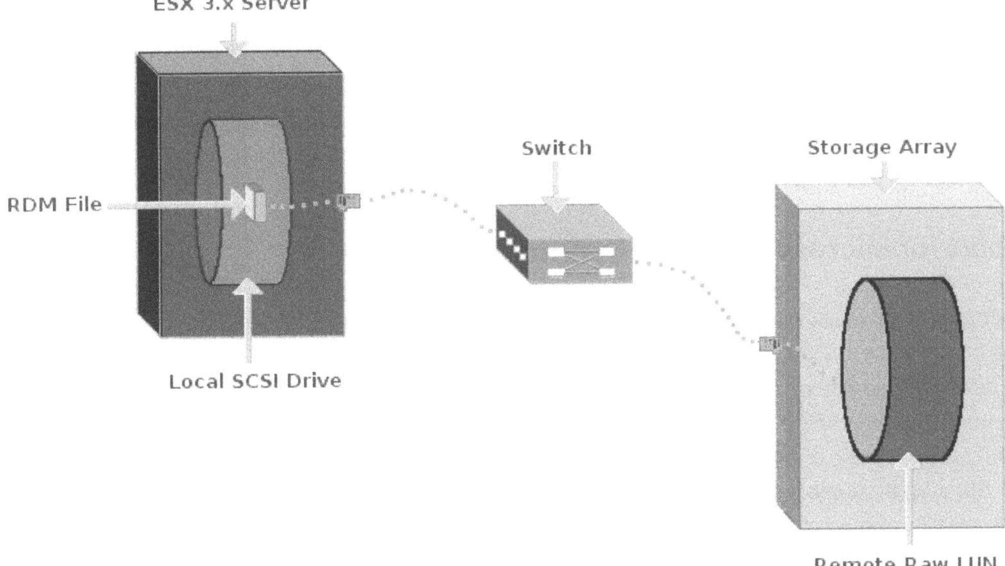

Figure 5.70 RDM access to raw LUN

The metadata stored in a RDM file contains important information such as the location of the raw LUN along with the locking state of the mapped device. The RDM file supports dynamic name resolution in the event that the path to the raw LUN changes. Another useful feature of RDM files is user friendly persistent names. For example, if the location of the RDM file is vmfs/localvolume/rawlun.vmdk, the ESX administrator can refer to the RDM file as rawlun.vmdk.

This eliminates the need to refer to a raw LUN by its device name such as vmhba2:1:4 as was required in earlier versions of ESX server. The ESX administrator can choose between two RDM modes, virtual or physical compatibility modes.

Virtual Compatibility Mode

Virtual compatibility mode allows the RDM file to work similar to a virtual hard disk file. An ESX administrator would choose this mode when using VMware's snapshot capability. Another common use of virtual compatibility mode is when using MSCS (Microsoft Cluster Service) to cluster two virtual machines hosted on one ESX 3.5 server. This type of cluster is known as a cluster in a box (CIB). The cluster requires each VM to be configured with at least two virtual hard disks. One virtual disk is used as a shared data disk and the other for the quorum disk. The quorum disk is used to store the cluster log file. When both the data and quorum disks are placed on a local drive within the ESX 3.5 server, an RDM file is not required. When these disks are located on remote storage, an RDM file in virtual compatibility mode is required.

Physical Compatibility Mode

Physical compatibility mode is used to enable lower level access to the raw LUN for applications that require it. An ESX administrator would choose this mode for example, to allow the guest operating system running within a virtual machine the ability to utilize SAN software to take snapshots of the raw LUN. During the virtualization of some physical servers, it may be desired to leave existing raw LUNs as is. Once the physical server has been virtualized, an RDM file can be created to access the raw LUN. This reduces physical to virtual conversion time and reduces the number of potential errors. In physical mode, all SCSI commands except the REPORT LUN command are virtualized. The REPORT LUN command is not virtualized so that the VMkernel can isolate the LUN from the VM utilizing the RDM file. Physical compatibility mode is often used when the physical server that has been virtualized is a database server and the raw LUN contains the data for the server.

Support for Microsoft Cluster Service

Another use of physical compatibility mode is in clustering Microsoft server virtual machines not located on the same ESX 3.5 server. Virtual machines located on different ESX servers configured in a MSCS cluster are referred to as CAB (Cluster Across Boxes). When the two virtual machines are configured, it is recommended to use a RDM set to physical compatibility mode to access both the data and quorum disks. However, virtual compatibility mode is supported. The quorum disk requires native file system support access. Physical compatibility mode for the RDM file is a requirement when a virtual machine is operating in a MSCS cluster with a physical machine.

For additional information in configuring virtual machines in a MSCS cluster, refer to Chapter 15 – High Availability and the Setup for Microsoft Cluster Service guide located at:

http://www.vmware.com/pdf/vi3_vm_and_mscs.pdf

Booting From the SAN

ESX 3.5 blade servers are more likely to be configured to boot from a remote SAN as some blade servers are sold without any local SCSI drives. Without local storage, these diskless blade servers have the benefit of typically being less expensive. They can be loaded with extra hardware such as additional NICs and still run cooler without internal storage. Another benefit with booting from SAN is simplification of backups. Existing SAN backup procedures can be used to provide full backups of the ESX 3.5 service console to meet DR (Disaster Recovery) requirements.

To configure booting an ESX 3.5 server from a remote SAN, the SAN administrator will first need to ensure proper SAN zoning and masking of the LUN that is to be used to hold the boot installation. Each boot LUN should only be seen by its own ESX 3.5 server.

The following list should be considered prior to configuring boot from SAN:

- RDMs are supported with boot from SAN configurations when using a ESX 3.5 server. RDMs are not supported when booting an ESX 2.5.x server from SAN.
- Booting from a Fibre Channel storage array is supported.
- Booting from a iSCSI storage array when the ESX 3.5 server is configured with a hardware initiator is supported. The software initiator is not supported when booting from a SAN LUN.
- Booting from a NAS device is not supported.
- Ensure the HBA BIOS for your HBA Fibre Channel card is enabled and properly configured to access the remote SAN boot LUN. The BIOS of the HBA card must set the Fibre Channel card as the boot controller device.
- The HBA Fibre Channel card should be inserted into the lowest PCI bus and slot number. Doing so enables quick detection of the HBA as their drivers scan the HBAs in ascending PCI bus and slot numbers. This is the scanning method regardless of the corresponding virtual machine's HBA number.
- Active/Passive storage arrays are only supported if the storage processor whose WWN is specified in the HBA BIOS is active when booting from the storage array.
- Connection from the ESX 3.5 server to the remote FC SAN boot LUN must be through a switch fabric topology. Directly connecting to the FC storage array without FC switches is not supported. Fibre Channel arbitrated loop connections are not supported either.

The use of scripted installations in conjunction with ESX Server boot from SAN configurations requires steps to prevent unintentional loss of data. Refer to the VMware knowledge base article 1540 at:

http://www.vmware.com/support/kb/enduser/std_adp.php?p_faqid=1540.

For additional configuration information, refer to the SAN System Design and Deployment Guide located at:

http://www.vmware.com/pdf/vi3_san_design_deploy.pdf

Troubleshooting Common Storage Infrastructure Problems

Fibre Channel Storage

If the ESX 3.5 server is unable to communicate to the fibre channel storage array, verify with the SAN administrator that the proper zoning and masking is in place within the SAN environment. Masking is commonly performed only at the storage processor level of the storage array. However, it is possible using the Advanced Setting link from within the VI Client Configuration tab to mask LUNs from the ESX 3.5 server. Verify the proper LUNs if any are being masked via the Advanced Settings option Disk.MaskLUNs. Only one active path to a fibre channel storage device is used. It is necessary to ensure that the correct VMkernel LUN address is being used. The LUN address information is displayed within the device column of the VI Client Configuration tab under the Storage link. Path fail over policy information can be verified by using the esxcfg-mpath command as follows:

[root@vcpserver01 root]# esxcfg-mpath -l

Disk vmhba1:0:08 /dev/sdb (15236MB) has 1 paths and policy of Most Recently Used

FC 3:1.0 270000e07a1467d0<->800802e3000ca753 vmhba1:0:08 On active preferred

Disk vmhba0:0:0 /dev/cciss/c0d0 (78525MB) has 1 paths and policy of Fixed

Local 0:4.0 vmhba0:0:0 On active preferred

Disk vmhba1:0:09 /dev/sdc (3015MB) has 1 paths and policy of Most Recently Used

FC 3:1.0 270000e07a1467d0<->800802e3000ca753 vmhba1:0:09 On active preferred

RAID Controller (SCSI-3) vmhba1:0:0 (0MB) has 1 paths and policy of Most Recently Used

FC 3:1.0 270000e07a1467d0<->800802e3000ca753 vmhba1:0:0 On active preferred

Disk vmhba32:0:1 /dev/sde (4048MB) has 1 paths and policy of Fixed

iScsi sw iqn.1998-01.com.vmware:vcpserver01-08caf0e6<->iqn.2006-01.com.openfiler:vol1.remvol1 vmhba32:0:1 On active preferred

Disk vmhba1:0:10 /dev/sdc (20230MB) has 1 paths and policy of Most Recently Used

FC 3:1.0 270000e07a1467d0<->800802e3000ca753 vmhba1:0:10 On active preferred

iSCSI Storage

It may be necessary to create a second service console port if the default service console port has been placed on a separate isolated subnet or within a VLAN that prevents it from communicating to the iSCSI target device. Other items to check include proper CHAP credentials are being used along with the correct IP address, port and iSCSI target name when configuring the target method. If a firewall is involved in the communication between the ESX 3.5 host and the iSCSI target, verify that the iSCSI port being used (by default, port 3260) is open within the firewall. It is important to verify that there is IP connectivity from the ESX 3.5 server to the iSCSI target device. Use the ping command from within the service console CLI to verify service console connectivity if using a software initiator. A vmkping test can be used to verify proper IP connectivity from the VMkernel TCP/IP stack as follows:

```
[root@vcpserver01 root]# vmkping 10.0.1.240
PING 10.0.1.240 (10.0.1.240): 56 data bytes
64 bytes from 10.0.1.240: icmp_seq=0 ttl=64 time=0.445 ms
64 bytes from 10.0.1.240: icmp_seq=1 ttl=64 time=0.268 ms
64 bytes from 10.0.1.240: icmp_seq=2 ttl=64 time=0.264 ms
--- 10.0.1.240 ping statistics ---
3 packets transmitted, 3 packets received, 0% packet loss
round-trip min/avg/max = 0.264/0.326/0.445 ms
```

NFS Storage

NFS depends on a correctly configured VMkernel port when accessing NFS storage. Verify that the VMkernel port is either on the same subnet as the NFS server or that the correct routing is available within the network environment. During configuration of the NFS server, the NFS server needs to be configured with the no_root_squash option so that the ESX 3.5 server can establish a successful connection (though the delegate user account, vimuser, with User ID (UID) 12 / Group ID (GID) 20 can be used instead if the default root_squash option is required due to SOX compliance standards.) The NFS server is required to support connections using NFS version 3 over TCP. In addition, a vmkping test should be performed to check VMkernel IP connectivity between the ESX 3.5 server and the NFS server. Also verify that the proper IP address or Fully Qualified Domain Name (FQDN) and NFS share name are being used by the ESX 3.5 system.

External References

VMware ESX 3.5 Documentation Page:

http://www.vmware.com/support/pubs/vi_pages/vi_pubs_35.html

VMware ESXi Server version 3.5 Embedded and VirtualCenter 2.5 Page:

http://www.vmware.com/support/pubs/vi_pages/vi_pubs_35_3i_e.html

VMware ESXi Server version 3.5 Installable and VirtualCenter 2.5 Page:

http://www.vmware.com/support/pubs/vi_pages/vi_pubs_35_3i_i.html

iSCSI SAN Configuration Guide - ESX Server 3.5, ESXi version 3.5 and VirtualCenter 2.5:

http://vmware.com/pdf/vi3_35/esx_3/r35/vi3_35_25_iscsi_san_cfg.pdf

iSCSI Naming Guidelines:

http://www.ietf.org/rfc/rfc3720.txt

VI 3.5 Storage/SAN Compatibility Guide:

http://www.vmware.com/pdf/vi35_san_guide.pdf

Fibre Channel SAN Configuration Guide - ESX Server 3.5, ESXi Server version 3.5 and VirtualCenter 2.5:

http://vmware.com/pdf/vi3_35/esx_3/r35/vi3_35_25_san_cfg.pdf

SAN System Design and Deployment Guide:

http://www.vmware.com/pdf/vi3_san_design_deploy.pdf

I/O Compatibility Guide For ESX Server 3.5 and ESXi Server version 3.5:

http://www.vmware.com/pdf/vi35_io_guide.pdf

Configuration Maximums for VMware 3.5 Infrastructure:

http://vmware.com/pdf/vi3_35/esx_3/r35/vi3_35_25_config_max.pdf

Moving Virtual Disks to or from ESX Server:

http://kb.vmware.com/selfservice/microsites/search.do?language=en_US&cmd=displayKC&externalI d=900

SAN System Design and Deployment Guide:

http://www.vmware.com/pdf/vi3_san_design_deploy.pdf

iSCSI , NAS and IP Storage Configuration for VMware ESX Server:

http://download3.vmware.com/vmworld/2006/tac9722.pdf

ESX Server Raw Device Mapping:

http://pubs.vmware.com/vi301/server_config/wwhelp/wwhimpl/common/html/wwhelp.htm?context=s erver_config&file=sc_adv_storage.12.2.html

VMFS information link:

http://www.vmware.com/products/vi/esx/vmfs.html

Cisco iSCSI Initiator Command Reference:

http://www.cuddletech.com/articles/iscsi/ar01s07.html

Fibre Channel Industry Association (FCIA) Website:

http://www.fibrechannel.org/

FC standards(T11) - INCITS technical committee:

http://www.t11.org/index.html

University of New Hampshire Fibre Channel Tutorial:

http://www.iol.unh.edu/services/testing/fc/training/tutorials/fc_tutorial.php

Going Enterprise - setup your FC4 iSCSI target in 5 minutes:

http://fedoranews.org/mediawiki/index.php/Going_Enterprise_-
_setup_your_FC4_iSCSI_target_in_5_minutes

Setup for Microsoft Cluster Service Guide:

http://www.vmware.com/pdf/vi3_vm_and_mscs.pdf

Sample Test Questions

1. A member of your security department is concerned about the authentication process over the network when the iSCSI storage array is accessed from your ESX server. Which of the following authentication security protocols does VMware support in its iSCSI implementation?

a. Encrypted Key Exchange (EKE)

b. Challenge Handshake Authentication Protocol (CHAP)

c. Hashed Message Authentication Code (HMAC)

d. IP Security (IPsec)

e. Kerberos

f. Secure Remote Protocol (SRP)

g. Advanced Encryption Standard (AES)

2. Operators of virtual machines running on an ESX 3.5 server notify the ESX administrator that performance in their virtual machines is significantly degraded. These virtual machines are all located on the same FC active/passive storage array. Which of the following can cause this poor performance to occur?

a. The LUN is masked from the ESX 3.5 server

b. The ESX 3.5 server has been removed from the proper FC zone

c. The incorrect multipathing policy is being used

d. The default gateway for the service console has been improperly configured

e. The "Virtual Machine Startup / Shutdown" order has been modified

3. You have been called into a meeting to discover why applications seem to be running slowly on multiple VMs within your organization. After doing some research on the current configuration of the ESX servers containing the VMs in question, you have discovered that someone has configured 26 ESX servers to access the same VMFS on your SCSI SAN storage array. How many servers at most should be configured to access the VMFS volume at the same time?

a. 10

b. 20

c. 32

d. 25

e. 34

4. After requesting a LUN from the SAN administrator, you rescan the iSCSI HBA and are able to now see the new LUN. You decide to build the VMFS volume using the default of 1 MB block size. What can be stored in this VMFS volume?

a. Service console configuration files

b. Virtual machine state files

c. ISO images

d. NFS shared files

e. Virtual machine template files

5. After several attempts, the ESX 3.5 server is unsuccessful in accessing the remote SCSI array. Proper network connectivity to the iSCSI array has been confirmed. All iSCSI hardware is properly working. The SAN administrator suggests checking that the iSCSI target ID is correct. Which of the following contains the proper syntax for iSCSI initiators and targets?

a. World_Wide_Name(WWN).iSCSI_alias_name

b. iqn.ip-address.reversed_domain_name.iSCSI_alias_name

c. iqn.year-mo.reversed_domain_name:unique_name

d. iSCSI.ip-address.domain_name:iSCSI_alias.name

e. iqn.ip-address.domain_name:iSCSI_alias.name

6. A junior administrator is having difficulty connecting to a NFS shared directory on your network. You contact the NFS server administrator and they tell you that they are running the latest version of NFS on the server and you should be able to connect. What version of the NFS protocol is supported for an ESX server to create a NFS datastore?

a. NFSv1

b. NFSv2

c. NFSv3

d. NFSv4

e. NFSv5

7. Security policies at a company require iSCSI disk I/O to be secured. Separate isolated iSCSI networks have been configured. Which of the following technologies can an ESX 3.5 server employ to further secure iSCSI traffic?

a. SSL

b. Unidirectional CHAP

c. Kerberos

d. Bidirectional CHAP

e. RSA

8. Your database application needs a lot of storage space for the database files. You need to allocate some disk space and create a VMFS to store your database VM's disk files. A VMFS can be as large as which of the following?

a. 16 GB

b. 512 GB

c. 1 TB

d. 16 TB

e. 64 TB

f. 512 TB

9. The storage policy at a company states that the iSCSI SAN LUN size is limited to 20 GB with only one virtual machine accessing a LUN. How many iSCSI LUNs can the ESX 3.5 server connect to?

a. 64

b. 128

c. 254

d. 255

e. 256

f. 512

10. Your ESX 3.5 server is configured with 4 FC HBAs connected to a FC SAN. A database virtual machine is accessing a raw LUN on the FC SAN. What must you do to configure the ESX 3.5 server to see multiple paths to the FC SAN?

a. Set the mpath variable to "TRUE" in the /etc/msetpath.conf file

b. Create a virtual switch attached to the appropriate subnet

c. Nothing, the ESX 3.5 server will automatically detect multipath to the FC SAN

d. Configure four virtual network cards in the database virtual machine

e. Set the VMkernel port to autodetect in the /etc/autodetect.path file

11.You are trying to connect to your iSCSI server but you believe one of your firewalls is blocking access to it. The ESX 3.5 server uses which of the following TCP ports to communicate with the iSCSI storage device?

a. 2330

b. 2660

c. 3260

d. 3620

e. 6200

12. You are tasked with setting up the storage for your virtual infrastructure at work. You are trying to determine if you should create a few large LUNs and put a VMFS on each of them or build many LUNS each with a VMFS on them for better disk performance. What is the maximum number of VMFS volumes supported on one ESX 3.5 server?

a. 32

b. 64

c. 128

d. 255

e. 256

13. A blade server is purchased and is to be used as an ESX 3.5 server. The blade does not contain any local hard disk storage. Which of the following are not supported when configuring the blade server to boot from SAN?

a. NFS share

b. iSCSI hardware initiator

c. Fibre Channel HBA

d. iSCSI software initiator

e. CIFS share

14. An ESX 3.5 server is having a problem discovering LUNs on a FC active/active storage array that the SAN administrator has made available to the server. Which of the following can cause the LUNs not to be discovered by the ESX 3.5 server?

a. Improper configuration of the /usr/share/zoneinfo files

b. The LUNs have been administratively masked on the ESX 3.5 server

c. The LUNs are configured with VMFS version 2

d. The virtual switches on the ESX 3.5 server do not have a VMkernel port configured

e. Port numbers 902 and 903 are not open on the ESX 3.5 server

15. You are called to investigate an issue with a VM in which the administrator is trying to build a virtual disk and the software is not allowing the disk to be built. Which of the following could prevent the virtual disk from being built?

a. The administrator doesn't have the privileges to add a virtual disk

b. The virtual disk is larger than 256 GB and the VMFS that the disk is trying to be built on was built using the default file size limit

c. The operating system doesn't support a disk that large

d. The VMFS doesn't have enough free space to add the disk file

e. The administrator is using VMplayer to add the virtual hard disk.

16. The SAN administrator configures 5 LUNs on the iSCSI storage array and presents these LUNs to an ESX 3.5 server that is not configured with iSCSI HBA cards. The full path to the LUNs are given to the ESX administrator but the LUNs are not successfully discovered. Which of the following can cause the LUNs to not be discovered?

a. Static discovery method is being used

b. The iSCSI TOE cards need configured

c. The service console port is not able to connect to the iSCSI array

d. Only one iSCSI LUN can be presented at a time

e. The VMkernel port is not configured correctly

17. A CAB (Cluster Across Boxes) is needed using MSCS (Microsoft Cluster Service). Which of the following is required to successfully configure the cluster?

a. Gigabit Ethernet

b. NIC teaming

c. RDM

d. Promiscuous mode set to reject

e. Set rolling failover to Yes

18. SAN backups are required for a company's DR (Disaster Recovery) strategy. To meet DR requirements, a raw LUN that the ESX 3.5 server uses is to be backed up using software provided by the SAN vendor. How must the ESX administrator configure access to this raw LUN to fulfill DR requirements?

a. By setting the block size to 8 MB

b. By placing the RDM in physical compatibility mode

c. By having the raw LUN presented as LUN # 0

d. By placing the RDM in virtual compatibility mode

e. By spanning the LUN with at least two extents

19. During the virtualization planning phase, a company identified the needed functionality to support their business. VMware's VMFS enables the company to utilize which of the following?

a. HA clusters

b. NFS storage

c. DRS clusters

d. Remote Console Access

e. Virtual Machines ACLs (Access Control Lists)

20. A virtualization proof of concept project is proposed to the IT department. The ESX administrator is tasked with creating a VMFS LUN for the project. The LUN is created and presented to the ESX 3.5 server. Which of the following would prevent the VMFS volume from being created?

a. The LUN is located on an iSCSI storage array

b. There is only one HBA card present in the ESX 3.5 server

c. The LUN is 500 MB in size

d. The LUN is located on a FC active/active storage array

e. There is only one network adapter present in the ESX 3.5 server

21. A high priority Windows 2003 virtual machine that cannot be powered off requires a second virtual hard disk to be added. The ESX 3.5 server where the LUN used to store this virtual machine is out of free space. What is the feature that supports spanning VMFS volumes across multiple LUNs?

a. LVM (Logical Volume Manager)

b. Hot migration

c. Active/Active storage arrays

d. VMFS sub block architecture

e. VMFS SCSI reservations

22. A SAN administrator is concerned about security within the FC SAN environment and requires the WWPN (World Wide Port Number) used by all servers connected to the SAN. Which of the following will the ESX server administrator not need to give to the SAN administrator?

a. WWPN of each FC HBA configured in the ESX 3.5 servers

b. iSCSI Qualified Name of each iSCSI HBA configured in the ESX 3.5 servers

c. The IP address of all the NICs configured in the ESX 3.5 servers

d. UUID number of the local storage devices configured in the ESX 3.5 servers

e. The virtual SCSI HBA configured in each virtual machine running on all ESX 3.5 servers

23. Only one SAN administrator is employed at a company. There is concern that virtualization will place too much of a work load on the SAN administrator. In which of the following ways can VMFS reduce the management tasks of a SAN administrator?

a. By having the ability to store several virtual machines on the same LUN

b. By supporting the use of multiple extents to create VMFS volumes

c. By allowing up to 32 ESX 3.5 servers accessing the same LUN simultaneously

d. By allowing the use of short-lived SCSI reservations

e. By supporting VMFS version 2 volumes as read-only

24. Each VMFS volume contains data about the data that is to be stored on the volume. This data is referred to as metadata. During the updating of the metadata on both Fibre Channel and iSCSI storage arrays, which of the following is not used?

a. FC HBAs

b. SCSI Reservations

c. iSCSI HBAs

e. iSCSI software initiator

f. FC Switches

25. VMware VMFS requirements are being followed as part of a large scale virtualization deployment. The storage system engineers responsible for successfully meeting VMware's storage requirements for VMFS must not implement which of the following?

a. Configure the FC storage array to allow a maximum of 32 ESX 3.5 servers access to the VMFS volume

b. Create the VMFS volume spanning a maximum of 32 extents

c. Configure an ESX 3.5 server to connect to the same LUN in the FC storage array with more than 1 HBA

d. Create a 200 GB VMFS volume

e. Configure two VMFS volumes per LUN

26. The backup administrator is researching options to perform backups of the virtual machines. VMware Consolidated Backup is not being used at this time. Which of the following cannot be used as part of the backup solution?

a. VMFS partition on the local SCSI drive within the ESX 3.5 server

b. Remote NFS share

c. Fibre Channel storage LUN

d. Fibre Channel connected tape device

e. iSCSI storage LUN

27. A standalone ESX 3.5 server is attached to a FC SAN via two HBAs. One HBA is a Emulex and the other is a Qlogic. The ESX 3.5 server is having problems connecting to the target. Which of the following is not a supported configuration?

a. Emulex HBAs are not supported

b. Having two different vendor HBAs accessing the same target is not supported

c. Qlogic HBAs are not supported

d. Two HBAs in the same ESX 3.5 server is not supported

e. Standalone ESX 3.5 servers accessing FC SAN storage is not supported

28. A failure of a FC switch occurred within the FC switch fabric. Although the correct multipathing policy was configured on the ESX 3.5 server which has two HBAs, the ESX 3.5 server did not fail over to the second HBA. Which of the following can cause this to occur?

a. FC active/active storage device was being used with Fixed policy

b. Different LUN numbers were presented to each of the two HBAs in the ESX 3.5 server c. Only one service console port was configured on the ESX 3.5 server

d. The VirtualCenter service was not running

e. The HA cluster was improperly configured

29. Both iSCSI and FC storage arrays are being used in a VI3 environment. An N+1 (Need + 1) configuration is required per service level agreement requirements. The ESX administrator can implement which of the following fail over solutions from the ESX 3.5 server?

a. Fixed policy

b. HA cluster

c. MRU policy

d. Multipathing software running within the virtual machines

e. Multiple NICs when using the iSCSI software initiator

30. The SAN administrator inquires about the maximum number of paths to a LUN the ESX 3.5 server supports. The ESX administrator correctly answers the SAN administrator's question with the following response?

a. 32

b. 16

c. 8

d. 4

e. 2

31. You are asked to configure storage for the storage and operation of 10 new virtual machines. Which of the following storage types can be used to accomplish this task?

a. Fibre Channel storage

b. FTP storage

c. CIFS share

d. iSCSI storage

e. NFS server

32. Performance degradation is occurring on a remote storage LUN. Your SAN administrator suspects excessive SCSI reservations may be the root cause. Which types of VMFS metadata updates issue SCSI reservations against the entire LUN?

a. Permissions

b. Ownership

c. Moving a file

d. Renaming a file

e. Accessing the creation and modification times

33. A database server has just been virtualized. The raw LUN that the database server uses was not virtualized. Which of the following allows the newly virtualized database access to the raw LUN?

a. Modification of the /etc/ssh/sshd_config to allow root access

b. RDM file in physical compatibility mode

c. A second service console port configured with the correct default gateway

d. RDM file in virtual compatibility mode

e. RDM file in independent mode

34. A Linux/UNIX administrator recently created 10 NFS servers to be used as remote storage for all the ESX 3.5 virtualization servers. In order for a single ESX 3.5 server to access all NFS servers, which of the following must be done?

a. Open up firewall port 3260

b. Configure NFS servers on the same subnet as the ESX 3.5 servers

c. Increase the NFS.MaxVolumes setting within the Advanced Settings dialog box to 10

d. This can't be done, 8 NFS mounts is the maximum limit

e. Ensure the NFS server accepts only NFS version 4

35. While logged into the ESX 3.5 server's service console, an ESX administrator decides to read the metadata of a VMFS volume with the label of MyVMFS. Which of the following commands can be used to accomplish this task?

a. esxcfg-vmhbadevs

b. esxcfg-firewall –q swISCSIClient

c. esxcfg-rescan vmhba40

d. vmkfstools –P –h MyVMFS

e. esxcfg-advcfg -g /NFS/MaxVolumes

36. The SAN administrator has configured and presented a new iSCSI LUN to your ESX 3.5 server. Using the iSCSI software initiator, you are unable to discover this new LUN. Which of the following daemon can prevent the new LUN from being discovered?

a. vmware-authd

b. vmware-hostd

c. vmkiscsid

d. smbd

e. snmpd

Sample Test Solutions

1. A member of your security department is concerned about the authentication process over the network when the iSCSI storage array is accessed from your ESX server. Which of the following authentication security protocols does VMware support in its iSCSI implementation?

a. Encrypted Key Exchange (EKE)

b. Challenge Handshake Authentication Protocol (CHAP)

c. Hashed Message Authentication Code (HMAC)

d. IP Security (IPsec)

e. Kerberos

f. Secure Remote Protocol (SRP)

g. Advanced Encryption Standard (AES)

Answer: b – VMware only currently supports CHAP for authentication between the ESX server and the iSCSI storage resources. Refer to the VMware whitepaper – Configuring iSCSI in a VMware ESX Server 3 Environment.

2. Operators of virtual machines running on an ESX 3.5 server notify the ESX administrator that performance in their virtual machines is significantly degraded. These virtual machines are all located on the same FC active/passive storage array. Which of the following can cause this poor performance to occur?

a. The LUN is masked from the ESX 3.5 server

b. The ESX 3.5 server has been removed from the proper FC zone

c. The incorrect multipathing policy is being used

d. The default gateway for the service console has been improperly configured

e. The "Virtual Machine Startup / Shutdown" order has been modified

Answer: c - Since the virtual machine operators can successfully access their virtual machine desktops, both LUN masking and the FC zone are set correctly. If they were not, access to the LUNs where these virtual machines reside would not be possible. The service console default gateway is not used to access FC storage arrays. Modification of the "Virtual Machine Startup / Shutdown" order can be used to determine the order of startup of virtual machines when an ESX 3.5 server is powered on. It has no affect on performance of running virtual machines. Improperly setting the multipathing policy can greatly impact performance of virtual machines. When using active/passive FC storage arrays, it is recommended to use the MRU (Most Recently Used) multipathing policy to avoid path thrashing.

3. You have been called into a meeting to discover why applications seem to be running slowly on multiple VMs within your organization. After doing some research on the current configuration of the ESX servers containing the VMs in question, you have discovered that someone has configured 26 ESX servers to access the same VMFS volume on you iSCSI SAN storage array. How many servers at most should be configured to access that VMFS at the same time?

a. 10

b. 20

c. 32

d. 15

e. 16

Answer: c - By using short-lived SCSI reservations multiple ESX 3.5 servers can access the same LUN at a time while preventing the metadata from becoming out of sync. A maximum of 32 ESX 3.5 servers can simultaneously access a VMFS volume.

4. You are asked to create a VMFS volume on a FC storage array. The VMFS volume is created with the default block size of 1 MB. What can be stored in this VMFS volume?

a. Service console configuration files

b. Virtual machine state files

c. ISO images

d. NFS shared files

e. Virtual machine template files

Answer: b, c, e – The service console files are stored in various locations on ext3 file systems configured during installation and a VMFS volume cannot be shared on the network using NFS.

5. After several attempts, the ESX 3.5 server is unsuccessful in accessing the remote iSCSI array. Proper network connectivity to the iSCSI array has been confirmed. All iSCSI hardware is properly working. The SAN administrator suggests checking that the iSCSI target ID is correct. Which of the following contains the proper syntax for iSCSI initiators and targets?

a. World_Wide_Name(WWN).iSCSI_alias_name

b. iqn.ip-address.reversed_domain_name.iSCSI_alias_name

c. iqn.year-mo.reversed_domain_name:unique_name

d. iSCSI.ip-address.domain_name:iSCSI_alias.name

e. iqn.ip-address.domain_name:iSCSI_alias.name

Answer: c –This is specified in the RFC 3720.

6. A junior administrator is having difficulty connecting to a NFS shared directory on your network. You contact the NFS server administrator and they tell you that they are running the latest version of NFS on the server and you should be able to connect. What version of the NFS protocol is supported for an ESX server to create a NFS datastore?

a. NFSv1

b. NFSv2

c. NFSv3

d. NFSv4

e. NFSv5

Answer: c – The latest version of the NFS protocol is NFS version 4 which is not currently supported. ESX 3.5 supports datastores only on NFS version 3 servers. NFSv4 servers can set the shared directory to support NFSv2, NFSv3 and NFSv4 clients. See RFC 3530 for more NFSv4 information.

7. Security policies at a company require iSCSI disk I/O to be secured. Separate isolated iSCSI networks have been configured. Which of the following technologies can an ESX 3.5 server employ to further secure iSCSI traffic?

a. SSL

b. Unidirectional CHAP

c. Kerberos

d. Bidirectional CHAP

e. RSA

Answer: b - SSL, Kerberos and RSA or not supported with iSCSI disk I/O. Unidirectional CHAP authentication is the only supported because bidirectional CHAP authentication would require the server and the storage array to authenticate the connection which puts additional overhead on the ESX 3.5 server.

Also only one set of authentication credentials can be currently maintained by an ESX 3.5 server – see the Configuring iSCSI in a VMware Server 3 Environment document.

8. Your database application needs a lot of storage space for the database files. You need to allocate some disk space and create a VMFS to store your database VM's disk files. A VMFS can be as large as which of the following?

a. 16 GB

b. 512 GB

c. 1 TB

d. 16 TB

e. 64 TB

f. 512 TB

Answer: e – There is a 2 TB limit on LUN size, but 32 LUNS can be joined together as extents making 64 TB the maximum size for a VMFS.

9. The storage policy at a company states that the iSCSI SAN LUN size is limited to 20 with only one virtual machine accessing a LUN. How many iSCSI LUNs can the ESX 3.5 server connect to?

a. 64

a. 128

b. 254

c. 255

d. 256

Answer: e - An ESX 3.5 server can have a maximum of either 256 iSCSI hardware initiator LUNs or 256 iSCSI software initiator LUNs. It cannot have both iSCSI hardware and software initiator LUNs simultaneously.

10. Your ESX 3.5 server is configured with 4 FC HBAs connected to a FC SAN. A database virtual machine is accessing a raw LUN on the FC SAN. What must you do to configure the ESX 3.5 server to see multiple paths to the FC SAN?

a. Set the mpath variable to "TRUE" in the /etc/msetpath.conf file

b. Create a virtual switch attached to the appropriate subnet

c. Nothing, the ESX 3.5 server will automatically detect multipath to the FC SAN

d. Configure four virtual network cards in the database virtual machine

e. Set the VMkernel port to autodetect in the /etc/autodetect.path file

Answer: c - There are no such files as /etc/msetpath.conf or /etc/autodetect.path. FC HBAs do not require virtual switches or virtual network cards. The VMkernel does not do multipathing by default; instead, it will automatically set the multipathing policy according to the make and model of the array it detects (active/passive = MRU, active/active = Fixed.) An administrator must manually load balance using the Manage Paths button in Properties of a datastore in the Storage link; an ESX Server will only use one path to storage as the 'Active' path, even if there are multiple paths detected.

11. You are trying to connect to your iSCSI server but you believe one of your firewalls is blocking access to it. The ESX 3.5 server uses which of the following TCP ports to communicate with the iSCSI storage device?

a. 2330

b. 2660

c. 3260

d. 3620

e. 6200

Answer: c - You must configure the ESX 3.5 server firewall to use port 3260 as specified in RFC 3720 - Internet Small Computer Systems Interface (iSCSI).

12. You are tasked with setting up the storage for your virtual infrastructure at work. You are trying to determine if you should create a few large LUNs and put a VMFS on each of them or build many LUNS each with a VMFS on them for better disk performance. What is the maximum number of VMFS volumes supported on one ESX 3.5 server?

a. 32

b. 64

c. 128

d. 255

e. 256

Answer: e – Referenced in the VMware Configuration Maximums for VMware Infrastructure 3 document.

13. A blade server is purchased and is to be used as an ESX 3.5 server. The blade does not contain any local hard disk storage. Which of the following are not supported when configuring the blade server to boot from SAN?

a. NFS share

b. iSCSI hardware initiator

c. Fibre Channel HBA

d. iSCSI software initiator

e. CIFS share

Answer: a, d, e - NFS version 3 over TCP is supported only as a means of remote storage. NFS is not supported when booting an ESX 3.5 server. CIFS shares (SMB) is not supported at all. An iSCSI software initiator can be used to access iSCSI SANs, but not to boot an ESX 3.5 server. Fibre Channel HBAs and iSCSI hardware initiators are supported for booting an ESX 3.5 server from a SAN.

14. An ESX 3.5 server is having a problem discovering LUNs on a FC active/active storage array that the SAN administrator has made available to the server. Which of the following can cause the LUNs not to be discovered by the ESX 3.5 server?

a. Improper configuration of the /usr/share/zoneinfo files

b. The LUNs have been administratively masked on the ESX 3.5 server

c. The LUNs are configured with VMFS version 2

d. The virtual switches on the ESX 3.5 server do not have a VMkernel port configured

e. Port numbers 902 and 903 are not open on the ESX 3.5 server

Answer: b - /usr/share/zoneinfo is a directory that contains files used to configure the time zone of an ESX 3.5 server. It is not used in LUN discovery. The version of the VMFS file system does not prevent it from being seen by an ESX 3.5 server. ESX 3.5 servers can access VMFS version 2 LUNs as read only. VMkernel ports are only needed by IP based storage and are not used in a FC SAN. Ports 902 and 903 are used by the VI Client and the Web Access service respectively, these ports are not involved with LUN discovery. An ESX 3.5 server can mask LUNs using the advanced options setting on a ESX server. This practice is not recommended. It is recommended to set LUN masking at the storage processor level as doing so reduces the possibility of misconfigurations between the ESX 3.5 server and the storage array. Therefore, it is generally best to have the SAN administrator configure LUN masking.

LUN masking on an ESX 3.5 server can be performed by navigating to the "Configuration" tab and selecting "Advanced Options" within the "Software"

section. In the Advanced Settings dialog box, select "Disk" from the left window pane and locate "Disk.MaskLUNs" in the right window pane. Enter the LUNs to be masked in the following format:

<adapter>:<target>:<comma separated LUN range list>

15. You are called to investigate an issue with a VM in which the administrator is trying to build a virtual disk and the software is not allowing the disk to be built. Which of the following could prevent the virtual disk from being built?

a. The administrator doesn't have the privileges to add a virtual disk

b. The virtual disk is larger than 256 GB and the VMFS that the disk is trying to be built on was built using the default file size limit

c. The operating system doesn't support a disk that large

d. The VMFS doesn't have enough free space to add the disk file

e. The administrator is using VMplayer to add the virtual hard disk.

Answer: All of the above

16.The SAN administrator configures 5 LUNs on the iSCSI storage array and presents these LUNs to an ESX 3.5 server that is not configured with iSCSI HBA cards. The full path to the LUNs are given to the ESX administrator but the LUNs are not successfully discovered. Which of the following can cause the LUNs to not be discovered?

a. Static discovery method is being used

b. The iSCSI TOE cards need configured

c. The service console port is not able to connect to the iSCSI array

d. Only one iSCSI LUN can be presented at a time

e. The VMkernel port is not configured correctly

Answer: a, c, e - Static discovery method is only applicable for iSCSI hardware initiators. iSCSI TOE (TCP/IP Offload Engine) cards are physical HBA (Host Bus Adapter) cards that are connected to an ESX 3.5 server. This particular server does not contain iSCSI HBAs. Since this ESX server does not contain iSCSI HBAs, the iSCSI software initiator needs to be properly configured. The software initiator requires the Send Targets method of discovery to be used, a service console and VMkernel port to be configured so that each can connect to the iSCSI storage array. More than one iSCSI LUN can be discovered at a time.

17. A CAB (Cluster Across Boxes) is needed using MSCS (Microsoft Cluster Service). Which of the following is required to successfully configure the cluster?

a. Gigabit Ethernet

b. NIC teaming

c. RDM

d. Promiscuous mode set to reject

e. Set rolling failover to Yes

Answer: c – RDM (Raw Device Mapping) files are required when configuring MSCS clusters using virtual machines hosted on two separate ESX servers. Reference the VMware Setup for Microsoft Cluster Service PDF.

18. SAN backups are required for a company's DR (Disaster Recovery) strategy. To meet DR requirements, a raw LUN that the ESX 3.5 server uses is to be backed up using software provided by the SAN vendor. How must the ESX administrator configure access to this raw LUN to fulfill DR requirements?

a. By setting the block size to 8 MB

b. By placing the RDM in physical compatibility mode

c. By having the raw LUN presented as LUN # 0

d. By placing the RDM in virtual compatibility mode

e. By spanning the LUN with at least two extents

Answer: b - The block size setting is not applicable for raw LUNs. The LUN # used to present the LUN to the ESX 3.5 server does not affect backups of raw LUNs. Spanning LUNs is applicable when LUNs are configured with VMFS. RDMs are used to allow ESX 3.5 servers access to raw LUNs. RDMs can be configured in two separate modes, virtual and physical. Virtual compatibility mode is used when it is desired to use the VirtualCenter snapshot manager to take snapshots of the raw LUN. Physical compatibility is used when it is desired to have the raw LUN backed up using software provided by the SAN vendor.

19. During the virtualization planning phase, a company identified the needed functionality to support their business. VMware's VMFS enables the company to utilize which of the following?

a. HA clusters

b. NFS storage

c. DRS clusters

d. Remote Console Access

e. Virtual Machines ACLs (Access Control Lists)

Answer: a, c - NFS storage does not utilize VMFS. VirtualCenter provides remote console access and enforces access to virtual machines. VMFS is a cluster file system that enables both HA and DRS clusters.

20. A virtualization proof of concept project is proposed to the IT department. The ESX administrator is tasked with creating a VMFS LUN for the project.

The LUN is created and presented to the ESX 3.5 server. Which of the following would prevent the VMFS volume from being created?

a. The LUN is located on an iSCSI storage array

b. There is only one HBA card present in the ESX 3.5 server

c. The LUN is 500 MB in size

d. The LUN is located on a FC active/active storage array

e. There is only one network adapter present in the ESX 3.5 server

Answer: c - ESX 3.5 servers can create VMFS volumes on both iSCSI and FC storage arrays. Only one HBA card is required to successfully connect to a storage array however, for redundancy at least two HBAs (N+1) should be present. Only one network adapter is required to connect to an iSCSI storage array when using the iSCSI software initiator. As with FC HBAs, at least two network adapters should be used as a NIC team on a virtual switch when the iSCSI initiator is being used for failover purposes. A LUN that is going to be used as a VMFS volume needs to be at least 1.1 GB in size.

21. A high priority Windows 2003 virtual machine that cannot be powered off requires a second virtual hard disk to be added. The ESX 3.5 server where the LUN used to store this virtual machine is out of free space. What is the feature in VMFS version 3 that supports spanning VMFS volumes across multiple LUNs?

a. LVM (Logical Volume Manager)

b. Hot migration

c. Active/Active storage arrays

d. VMFS sub block architecture

e. VMFS SCSI reservations

Answer: a - Hot migration is also known as VMotion. Hot migrations are used to assign a running virtual machine to another ESX 3.5 server without moving the configuration files of the virtual machine. Active/Active storage arrays improve disk I/O throughput as these storage devices can utilize multiple storage processors simultaneously. VMFS version 3 supports sub block architecture which improves overall LUN storage capacity by not wasting storage at the block level. For example, if a 200 KB file is storage on a VMFS version 3 formatted LUN, it would be possible to store another 800 KB file in the remaining space of the block. VMFS version 2 did not support sub block architecture. VMFS version 3 uses short-lived SCSI reservations to improve LUN access performance. LVM is used in VMFS version 3 to allow VMFS volumes to be extended without the need to power down running virtual machines.

22. A SAN administrator is concerned about security within the FC SAN environment and requires the WWPN (World Wide Port Number) used by all servers connected to the SAN. Which of the following will the ESX server administrator not need to give to the SAN administrator?

a. WWPN of each FC HBA configured in the ESX 3.5 servers

b. iSCSI Qualified Name of each iSCSI HBA configured in the ESX 3.5 servers

c. The IP address of all the NICs configured in the ESX 3.5 servers

d. UUID number of the local storage devices configured in the ESX 3.5 servers

e. The virtual SCSI HBA configured in each virtual machine running on all ESX 3.5 servers

Answer: b, c, d, e - The SAN administrator will not need the IQN (iSCSI Qualified Name) of iSCSI HBAs for security purposes of a Fibre Channel SAN. The IP addresses of NICs, UUID numbers of local storage devices and virtual SCSI HBA details are not needed for securing a Fibre Channel SAN. The virtual SCSI HBAs configured within virtual machines are hidden behind the physical HBAs of the ESX 3.5 server. The WWPN numbers of these physical HBAs are required for securing FC SANs

23. Only one SAN administrator is employed at a company. There is concern that virtualization will place too much of a work load on the SAN administrator. In which of the following ways can VMFS reduce the management tasks of a SAN administrator?

a. By having the ability to store several virtual machines on the same LUN

b. By supporting the use of multiple extents to create VMFS volumes

c. By allowing up to 32 ESX 3.5 servers accessing the same LUN simultaneously

d. By allowing the use of short-lived SCSI reservations

e. By supporting VMFS version 2 volumes as read-only

Answer: a - VMFS can support spanning VMFS volumes across a maximum of 32 LUNs. Spanning VMFS volumes is useful when virtual machines cannot be powered down and more

storage is needed. This places additional work load on the SAN administrator to create and configure each new LUN that is to be spanned.

The ability to support 32 simultaneous ESX 3.5 servers accessing the same LUN is very useful in a DRS cluster where virtual machines are VMotioned to other ESX 3.5 servers. However, the SAN administrator is tasked with the initial setup of correctly presenting each LUN to the intended ESX 3.5 servers. Short-lived SCSI reservations and ESX 3.5 servers having the ability to access VMFS version 2 volumes as read-only, improve the performance of virtual machine access to the LUN and provide backward compatibility respectively but do not reduce a SAN administrators work load. Traditionally, LUNs were assigned to physical machines in a one-to-one relationship. A SAN administrator would typically build a small LUN, perhaps 10 GB in size for the data files of the server's application. In a data center where there can be hundreds of physical machines requiring a separate LUN, the SAN administrator is tasked with configuring new LUNs for all existing physical servers and for the new servers when needed. Within a VI3 environment, now a SAN administrator can build one or two large LUNs, 500 GB in size for example, that several virtual machines can access and share simultaneously. This can significantly reduce the work load of a SAN administrator.

24. Each VMFS volume contains data about the data that is to be stored on the volume. This data is referred to as metadata. During the updating of the metadata on both Fibre Channel and iSCSI storage arrays, which of the following is not used?

a. FC HBAs

b. SCSI Reservations

c. iSCSI HBAs

d. iSCSI software initiator

e. FC Switches

Answer: b - FC HBAs and FC switches are used to connect the ESX 3.5 server to the FC storage device. Both iSCSI HBAs and iSCSI software initiators can be used to connect the ESX 3.5 server to the iSCSI storage target. SCSI reservations are not utilized during metadata updates to the VMFS volume. Short-lived SCSI reservations are part of an ESX 3.5 server's distributed locking protocol.

25. VMware VMFS requirements are being followed as part of a large scale virtualization deployment. The storage system engineers responsible for successfully meeting VMware's storage requirements for VMFS must not implement which of the following?

a. Configure the FC storage array to allow a maximum of 32 ESX 3.5 servers access to the VMFS volume

b. Create the VMFS volume spanning a maximum of 32 extents

c. Configure an ESX 3.5 server to connect to the same LUN in the FC storage array with more than 1 HBA

d. Create a 200 GB VMFS volume

e. Configure two VMFS volumes per LUN

Answer: e - VMFS volumes support up to 32 simultaneous ESX 3.5 servers and a spanning range of up to 32 LUN extents. Multipathing policies are supported by ESX 3.5 servers that utilize more than one HBA. VMFS volumes support a maximum of 2 TB per LUN. VMware requirements state that at most, one VMFS volume per LUN.

26. The backup administrator is researching options to perform backups of the virtual machines. VMware Consolidated Backup is not being used at this time. Which of the following cannot be used as part of the backup solution?

a. VMFS partition on the local SCSI drive within the ESX 3.5 server

b. Remote NFS share

c. Fibre Channel storage LUN

d. Fibre Channel connected tape device

e. iSCSI storage LUN

Answer: d - The local SCSI drives within an ESX 3.5 server, Fibre Channel LUNs, iSCSI LUNs and remote NFS shares are useful for storing virtual machine backups. ESX 3.5 servers do not support the use of Fibre Channel connected tape devices.

27. A standalone ESX 3.5 server is attached to a FC SAN via two HBAs. One HBA is a Emulex and the other is a Qlogic. The ESX 3.5 server is having problems connecting to the target. Which of the following is not a supported configuration?

a. Emulex HBAs are not supported

b. Having two different vendor HBAs accessing the same target is not supported

c. Qlogic HBAs are not supported

d. Two HBAs in the same ESX 3.5 server is not supported

e. Standalone ESX 3.5 servers accessing FC SAN storage is not supported

Answer: b - Emulex and Qlogic HBAs listed in the ESX Server 3.5 I/O Compatibility Guide are supported. Two HBAs in the same ESX 3.5 is supported and is used to implement multipathing. Standalone ESX 3.5 server can access FC SAN storage when configured with supported HBAs and implemented with the appropriate host license. Having two different vendor HBAs accessing the same target is not supported in ESX 3.5 servers.

28. A failure of a FC switch occurred within the FC switch fabric. Although the correct multipathing policy was configured on the ESX 3.5 server which has two HBAs, the ESX 3.5 server did not fail over to the second HBA. Which of the following can cause this to occur?

a. FC active/active storage device was being used with Fixed policy

b. Different LUN numbers were presented to each of the two HBAs in the ESX 3.5 server

c. Only one service console port was configured on the ESX 3.5 server

d. The VirtualCenter service was not running

e. The HA cluster was improperly configured

Answer: b - ESX 3.5 servers should utilize Fixed policy multipathing when connected to FC active/active storage devices. Service console ports, VirtualCenter and HA clusters are not used in accessing FC storage arrays. A SAN administrator should not present the same LUN as two different LUN numbers to each of the HBAs in an ESX 3.5 server. Doing so will cause the mulitpathing capabilities of the ESX 3.5 server to not fail over when a fail over event occurs in the FC switch fabric.

29. Both iSCSI and FC storage arrays are being used in a VI3 environment. An N+1 (Need + 1) configuration is required per service level agreement requirements. The ESX administrator can implement which of the following fail over solutions from the ESX 3.5 server?

a. Fixed policy

b. HA cluster

c. MRU policy

d. Multipathing software running within the virtual machines

e. Multiple NICs when using the iSCSI software initiator

Answer: a, c, e - HA clusters are not a solution for FC, iSCSI storage path failures but rather only deal with the failure of ESX 3.5 servers. Multipathing software running within virtual machines cannot be used for path failure on ESX 3.5 servers. Fixed policy, MRU policy and configuring multiple NICs when using the iSCSI software initiator are fully supported methods in providing storage path redundancy.

30. The SAN administrator inquires about the maximum number of paths to a LUN the ESX 3.5 server supports. The ESX administrator correctly answers the SAN administrator's question with the following response?

a. 32

b. 16

c. 8

d. 4

e. 2

Answer: a - The maximum number of paths to a LUN that an ESX 3.5 server supports is 32.

31. You are asked to configure storage for the storage and operation of 10 new virtual machines. Which of the following storage types can be used to accomplish this task?

a. Fibre Channel storage

b. FTP storage

c. CIFS share

d. iSCSI storage

e. NFS server

Answer: a, d & e - Fibre Channel, iSCSI and NFS storage are supported for the storage of virtual machines. Both FTP and CIFS based storage can be accessed from the ESX 3.5 service console, but cannot be used for the storage and operation of virtual machines.

32. Performance degradation is occurring on a remote storage LUN. Your SAN administrator suspects excessive SCSI reservations may be the root cause. Which types of VMFS metadata updates issue SCSI reservations against the entire LUN?

a. Permissions

b. Ownership

c. Moving a file

d. Renaming a file

e. Accessing the creation and modification times

Answer: All the above. VMFS metadata updates utilize SCSI reservations against the entire LUN when file permissions change, file ownership changes, files are moved, renamed, creation and modification times are accessed.

33. A database server has just been virtualized. The raw LUN that the database server uses was not virtualized. Which of the following allows the newly virtualized database access to the raw LUN?

a. Modification of the /etc/ssh/sshd_config to allow root access

b. RDM file in physical compatibility mode

c. A second service console port configured with the correct default gateway

d. RDM file in virtual compatibility mode

e. RDM file in independent mode

Answer: b & d - Modifications to the /etc/ssh/sshd_config file can be made to allow the service console root account remote log in privileges. Doing so is discouraged as it increases security risks. The service console is not used to access raw LUNs. RDM (Raw Device Mapping) files are used to access raw LUNs when configured in either virtual or physical compatibility modes. Independent mode is not a supported mode for RDM files.

34. A Linux/UNIX administrator recently created 10 NFS servers to be used as remote storage for all the ESX 3.5 virtualization servers. In order for a single ESX 3.5 server to access all NFS servers, which of the following must be done?

a. Open up firewall port 3260

b. Configure NFS servers on the same subnet as the ESX 3.5 servers

c. Increase the NFS.MaxVolumes setting within the Advanced Settings dialog box to 10

d. This can't be done, 8 NFS mounts is the maximum limit

e. Ensure the NFS server accepts only NFS version 4

***Answer: c** - Port 3260 is used as the default port of iSCSI. It is not used for NFS storage. Provided proper routing is implemented within the network infrastructure, the NFS servers do not need to be located on the same subnet as the ESX 3.5 servers. NFS version 4 is not supported on ESX 3.5 servers. Only NFS version 3 over TCP is supported on ESX 3.5 servers. 8 mount points is the default limit for NFS mounts. This can be modified by increasing the NFS.MaxVolumes within the Advanced Settings dialog box. The maximum number of NFS mounted volumes is 32.*

35. While logged into the ESX 3.5 server's service console, an ESX administrator decides to example the metadata of a VMFS volume with the label of MyVMFS. Which of the following commands can be used to accomplish this task?

a. esxcfg-vmhbadevs

b. esxcfg-firewall –q swISCSIClient

c. esxcfg-rescan vmhba40

d. vmkfstools –P –h MyVMFS

e. esxcfg-advcfg -g /NFS/MaxVolumes

***Answer: d** - The esxcfg-vmhbadevs command is used to see which LUNs are available to an ESX host. The esxcfg-firewall –q swISCSIClient command is used to query the software iSCSI Client service to view its current setting. The esxcfg-rescan vmhba32 command is used to rescan for storage devices on vmhba32. The esxcfg-advcfg -g /NFS/MaxVolumes command is used to view the current value for the maximum amount of NFS datastores on the ESX 3.5 server.*

The vmkfstools –P –h MyVMFS command is used to access metadata information on a VMFS volume labeled MyVMFS.

36. The SAN administrator has configured and presented a new iSCSI LUN to your ESX 3.5 server. Using the iSCSI software initiator, you are unable to discover this new LUN. Which of the following daemon can prevent the new LUN from being discovered?

a. vmware-authd

b. vmware-hostd

c. vmkiscsid

d. smbd

e. snmpd

Answer: c - The vmkiscsid daemon is used in the service console to login and authenticate the session to the iSCSI storage array.

Chapter 6

VirtualCenter 2.5

After reading this chapter you should be able to complete the following tasks:

- Explain the functionality that VirtualCenter 2.5 provides
- Describe the components of VirtualCenter 2.5
- Configure the VirtualCenter 2.5 server to access the database
- Install the license server and configure it with a license file
- Describe the best practice guidelines for a VirtualCenter 2.5 installation
- Identify the merits of installing VirtualCenter 2.5 in either a physical system or in a VM
- Install the VirtualCenter 2.5 software
- Configure an ESX 3.5 server to be managed by a VirtualCenter 2.5 server
- Identify the VirtualCenter 2.5 inventory hierarchy components
- Install the VI Client to access VirtualCenter 2.5
- Explore the various VirtualCenter 2.5 tabs and views
- Use the VirtualCenter 2.5 web access method
- Send a remote console link via e-mail
- Troubleshooting common VirtualCenter 2.5 Problems

VirtualCenter 2.5 Overview

VirtualCenter 2.5 is a centralized management tool that allows you to manage multiple ESX 3.5 servers remotely. VirtualCenter 2.5 is installed either on a physical server or in a virtual machine running Windows 2003 server. You must have a VirtualCenter 2.5 server if you intend on using any of the following VMware technologies:

- VMotion
- Storage VMotion
- VMware Distributed Resource Scheduler (DRS)
- VMware High Availability (HA)
- Cloning
- Templates

The VirtualCenter 2.5 software allows you to quickly gather configuration information about your ESX 3.5 servers as well as gather performance information for the previous 365 days. This saves time when doing performance analysis as well as troubleshooting because you won't have to log into each monitored ESX 3.5 server separately.

To get the latest information regarding VirtualCenter 2.5, refer to the ESX Server 3.5 and VirtualCenter 2.5 Release Notes:

http://www.vmware.com/support/vi3/doc/vi3_esx35_vc25_rel_notes.html

What Are the Components of VirtualCenter 2.5?

The VirtualCenter 2.5 product is comprised of the following components:

- A database to store the data collected by the VirtualCenter 2.5 server
- The license server software
- The VirtualCenter 2.5 server software
- The VI Client software
- Converter Enterprise software
- VMware Update Manager software

Supported Databases

Oracle and Microsoft database servers are supported and are recommended in large production environments. SQL Express is the bundled database and recommended for small ESX Server environments only. You will need a username and password to log on to the Oracle or Microsoft SQL database. The supported database versions are listed in the ESX Server 3 Installation Guide:

http://www.vmware.com/pdf/vi3_35/esx_3/r35/vi3_35_25_installation_guide.pdf

VMware provides an Excel spreadsheet to assist in the planning for the sizing of your Microsoft SQL server. The document is the VirtualCenter Database Sizing Calculator for Microsoft SQL Server:

http://www.vmware.com/support/vi3/doc/vc_db_calculator.xls

The License Server Software

The license server software provides central management of the ESX 3.5 server licenses. When the licenses are installed directly on an ESX 3.5 server, the licenses can only be used on that ESX 3.5 server. When a license server is installed and the ESX 3.5 server is configured to use it, then the unused portions of the licenses can be applied to any ESX 3.5 server that is configured to use it. In this manner the licenses essentially "float" from server to server.

The license server software is a Macrovision product. It is their FLEXnet license server software. The license server software is located on the VMware Infrastructure Management Software Installation CD.

The VirtualCenter 2.5 Server Software

The VirtualCenter 2.5 software provides centralized management of multiple ESX 3.5 servers and the virtual machines that run on them. The core services of VirtualCenter 2.5 are:

- Management of the ESX 3.5 servers and VMs
- Statistics logging
- Task scheduler
- Alarm management
- Event management
- Virtual machine provisioning
- Host configuration
- Virtual machine configuration

ESX 3.5 Server and VM Management

VirtualCenter 2.5 organizes all of the ESX 3.5 hosts and the VMs that they contain in the VirtualCenter 2.5 inventory hierarchy. These resources can be organized in a number of ways and managed using the VirtualCenter 2.5 GUI. VirtualCenter 2.5 acts as a proxy for many of the management tasks. In other words VirtualCenter 2.5 forwards the management task request on behalf of the VirtualCenter 2.5 user and it is sent to the appropriate resource to be fulfilled.

Statistics Logging

A database is required to be configured with the VirtualCenter 2.5 server to store data gathered by VirtualCenter 2.5 that can be used to identify performance bottlenecks as well as many other useful pieces of information. Data is also collected on every host and virtual machine, cluster of hosts and resource pools as well as on resource utilization.

Performance data is gathered for CPU, memory, network I/O and disk I/O utilization. Some information is gathered every minute, every 5 minutes and every 15 minutes. Some information is gathered and calculated as an average value over time. Minimum and maximum information is also recorded. Historically data is saved up to one year and can be easily reviewed using the VirtualCenter 2.5 software.

We will cover this process in Chapter 16 - Monitoring And Alerting.

For more detailed information about the data gathering process, read the VMware Tech Note - VirtualCenter Monitoring and Performance Statistics:

http://www.vmware.com/pdf/vi3_monitoring_statistics_note.pdf

Task Scheduler

The task scheduler can be used to schedule specific tasks to be executed at a certain time. For instance you might want to schedule a VM to be cloned during off hours. Cloning a VM is discussed in Chapter 7 – Virtual Machines.

Event Management

VirtualCenter 2.5 can monitor for certain event conditions that occur with a VM, an ESX 3.5 server, a resource pool or a cluster of servers and log the event. We will look at event management in Chapter 16 - Monitoring And Alerting and event logging to aid in troubleshooting throughout the various chapters.

Alarm Management

If an event shows that a resource is over a certain predetermined threshold, VirtualCenter's alarm management warns users on potential resource over-utilization. We will look at alarm management in Chapter 16 - Monitoring And Alerting.

Virtual Machine Provisioning

The process of virtual machine provisioning using cloning or templates provides you with the ability to rapidly deploy multiple near identical VMs. VirtualCenter 2.5 has provisioning wizards to simplify these tasks. We discuss this in Chapter 7 – Virtual Machines.

Host Configuration

VirtualCenter 2.5 can change the various host configuration settings remotely. This allows you to view and change settings on multiple systems without having to log into each one individually.

Virtual Machine Configuration

VirtualCenter 2.5 can change the various VM configuration settings remotely. This allows you to view and change settings on multiple VMs without having to log into each one individually.

VirtualCenter 2.5 Additional Services

User Access Control

VirtualCenter 2.5 provides user and group access controls. Authenticated users can be assigned roles which provide permissions and privileges that provide access to the resources that are managed by the VirtualCenter 2.5 server. We will discuss this in detail in Chapter 10 - Permissions And Rights.

Distributed Services

Distributed services are services that involve more than one ESX 3.5 server. They are:

- VMotion - otherwise known as hot migration or moving a live virtual machine from one ESX 3.5 server to another which will be discussed in Chapter 13 – Virtual Machine Migration
- VMware DRS - the distributed resource scheduler can load balance VMs across multiple ESX 3.5 servers for better performance and reduction of performance bottlenecks which will be discussed in Chapter 14 – Distributed Resource Scheduler
- VMware HA - the high availability product deals with ESX 3.5 server failures and the ability to bring the VMs on the failed server back online on another ESX 3.5 server which will be discussed in Chapter 15 – High Availability

VI API

The VI API provides third party developers the means to connect their management software or applications to VirtualCenter. The use of the VI API enables additional functionality to be added to the virtual infrastructure. For more information review the VMware SDK & API Developer Resources page:

http://www.vmware.com/support/pubs/sdk_pubs.html

Active Directory Interface

Microsoft's active directory product can be configured to provide authentication capabilities for users wishing to access VirtualCenter 2.5.

ESX 3.5 Server Management Interface

The ESX 3.5 server management interface creates a communication path between VirtualCenter 2.5 and your managed ESX 3.5 servers.

Database Interface

The database interface provides a way to connect to the supported databases so that VirtualCenter 2.5 can store the information that it gathers about your hosts, VMs, clusters, resource pools, and other monitored resources.

The VI Client Software

The VI Client software can only be installed on systems running Windows. This GUI based tool allows you to access your ESX 3.5 severs directly or to access them via VirtualCenter 2.5.

The VI Client software is located on the VMware Infrastructure Management Software Installation CD.

VirtualCenter 2.5 Server Database Configuration

The first thing that must be done prior to installing VirtualCenter 2.5 is to configure the VirtualCenter server to connect to the database that will store VirtualCenter's data.

The procedure to do this is as follows:

Step 1. The connection from the VirtualCenter 2.5 server to the database server should be configured prior to the installation of VirtualCenter 2.5. Open the ODBC (Open Database Connectivity) Data Source Administrator application as shown in Figure 6.1.

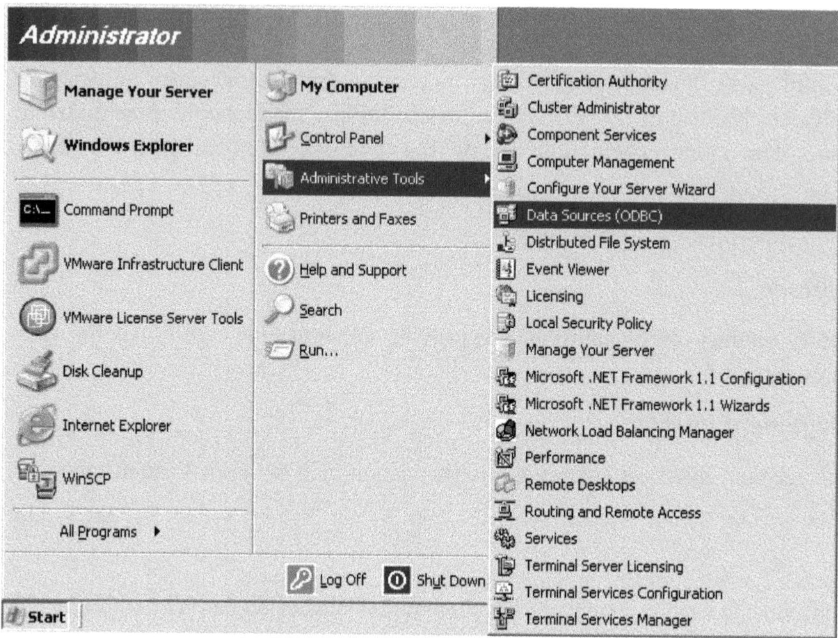

Figure 6.1 Launch ODBC Configuration Application

Step 2. A System DSN (Data Source Name) is required for the VirtualCenter 2.5 Server to access the database server. Select the System DSN tab and click the Add... button as shown in Figure 6.2.

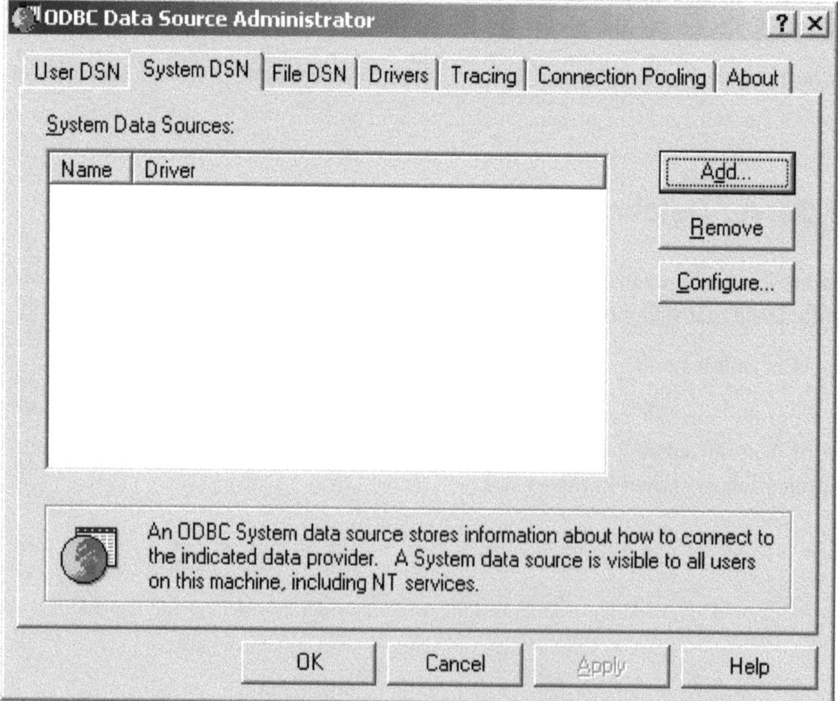

Figure 6.2 Select System DSN Tab

Step 3. The Create New Data Source dialog appears. Select the appropriate driver from the list and click the Finish button as shown in Figure 6.3.

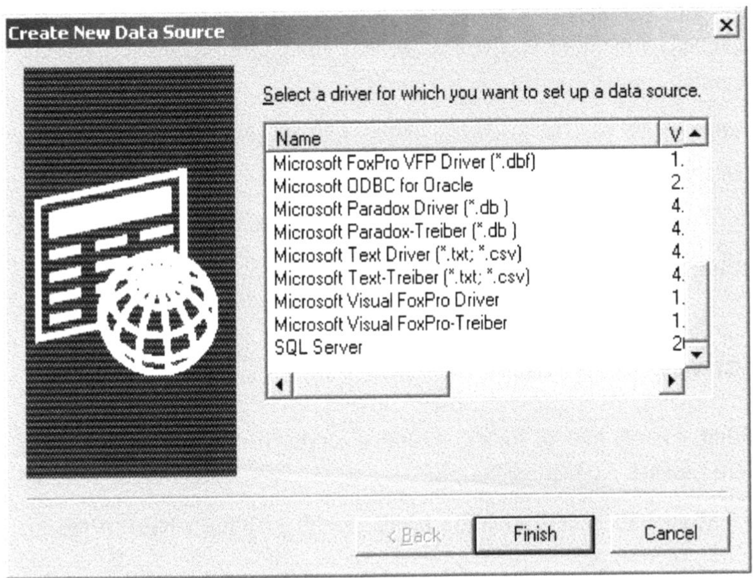

Figure 6.3 Select Appropriate Driver

Step 4. Complete the wizard for the selected driver.

The newly created system data source will be listed in the System DSN tab as shown in Figure 6.4.

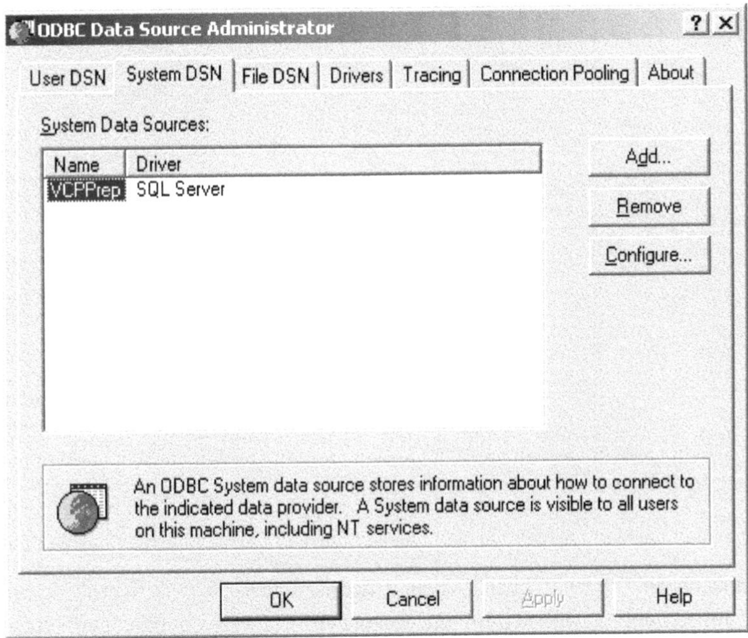

Figure 6.4 Newly Added ODBC Driver

Click OK to close the window.

VMware Server License

You need to purchase the appropriate number of licenses for your virtual infrastructure. VMware prices its licenses on a per socket basis. In other words you are not charged more for a quad-core processor over a single-core processor.

A 32 processor license can be applied for two 16-processor hosts, four 8-processor hosts, eight 4-processor hosts or sixteen 2-processor hosts.

For more information about acquiring licenses go to the VMware Product Licensing Tour:

http://www.vmware.com/support/licensing.html#

The VMware License Activation Portal

You can purchase licenses for either a single host or for a centralized server (the license server). They are available online at the VMware License Activation Portal.

For more information about the VMware License Activation Portal read the "What's New" VMware License Activation Portal FAQ:

http://www.vmware.com/pdf/vi3_license_FAQ.pdf

You can purchase and activate the following VI3 products including:

- ESX 3.5 Server
- VirtualCenter 2.5
- VMotion
- HA
- DRS
- Lab Manager

Licensing Modes

VMware offers two license modes, host-based and license server-based.

Host-based Mode

The license files are located on each ESX server host. When a licensed feature is activated, it is activated on a per host basis. Entitlements reside within the license file stored on that host. The advantage of host-based license mode is having no dependence on a separate license server. An ESX 3.5 server using a host-based license operating in an environment that contains a license server can have modifications made to the license even when the license server is unavailable. A disadvantage of host-based license mode is unused licenses are not automatically distributed to other ESX 3.5 hosts.

There is one host-based license file stored on the ESX 3.5 server and it is located in the following location:

/etc/vmware/vmware.lic

License Server Mode

The license server maintains a pool of licenses simplifying license management. A single license server can retain licenses for a large, dynamic environment. A central license repository handles the check out procedure of a particular license functionality from the pool on an as needed basis. An important advantage of license server mode is when a license key is no longer needed. It is then placed back into the pool ready once again to service other vhost requests.

A 14-day grace period is utilized should the license server become unavailable. Cached licensing configurations are used during this period. Both VirtualCenter 2.5 and ESX 3.5 server hosts retain the cached license configuration even when rebooted. During the grace period, additional ESX 3.5 hosts cannot be added to VirtualCenter 2.5, HA and DRS clusters. Upgrades of any component and removing or adding license keys is not permitted during the grace period. In addition to the restrictions during the grace period, once the grace period has expired, powered on virtual machines continue running but cannot be rebooted. Powered off virtual machines will no longer power on. VMotion migrations are not permitted, therefore DRS will not load balance ESX servers in a DRS cluster. Administrator action is not required when the license server is once again available, hosts will automatically reconnect.

There is one license server-based license file stored on the license server and it is located in the following location:

C:\Program Files\VMware\VMware License Server\vmware.lic

License Editions

VMware provides two license editions for VirtualCenter, Foundation and VirtualCenter.

VirtualCenter Foundation

This edition provides a limited number of ESX servers to manage. The maximum number of ESX servers that can be managed with the Foundation edition is three.

VirtualCenter

The VirtualCenter edition provides the maximum number of ESX servers that can be managed. With this edition, 200 ESX servers and 2,000 virtual machines can be managed.

VMware Infrastructure Management Software Installation and Configuration

The installation of the VMware Infrastructure Management software is accomplished using the following procedure:

Step 1. Insert the VirtualCenter 2.5 installation CD and if autorun is not enabled on your system then launch the autorun program on the CD. The VMware Infrastructure Management software installer window will appear as shown in Figure 6.5.

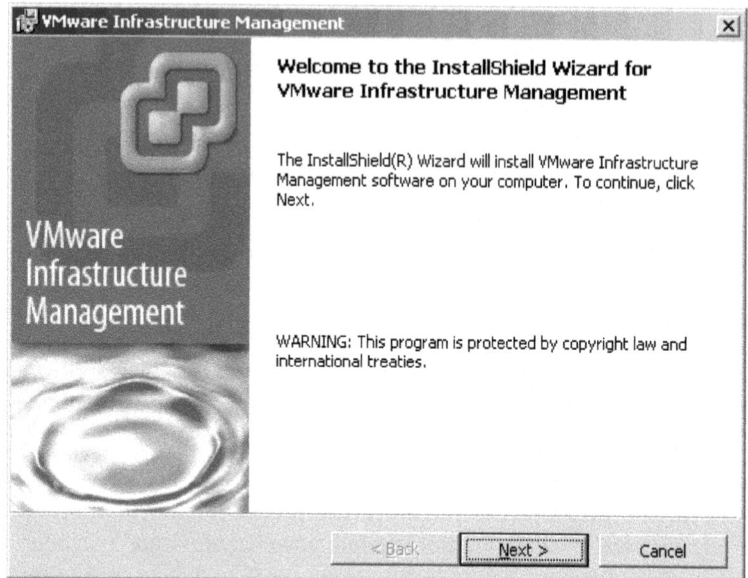

Figure 6.5 VMware Infrastructure Management Installation

Step 2. The first screen you will see is the Introduction screen as shown in Figure 6.6.

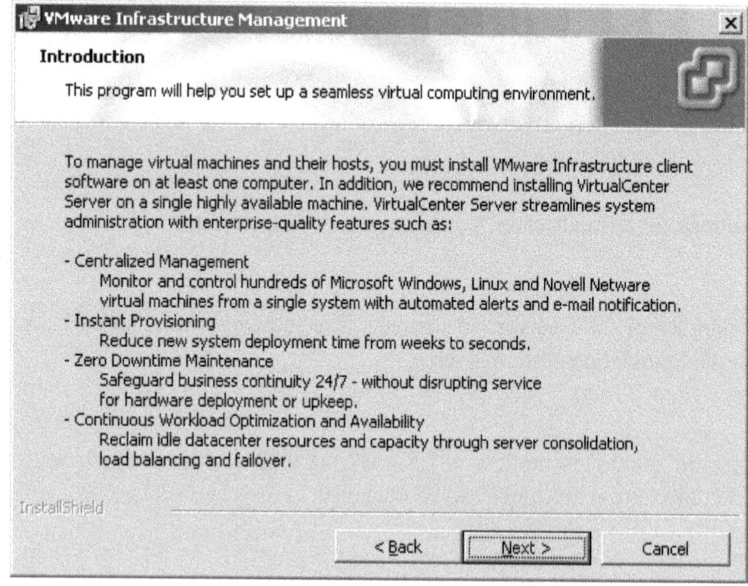

Figure 6.6 VMware Infrastructure Management Introduction

This screen contains information on the benefits of using VirtualCenter 2.5. Click on the Next button to continue.

Step 3. The License Agreement screen will require that you select the radio button that signifies that you accept the license agreement as shown in Figure 6.7

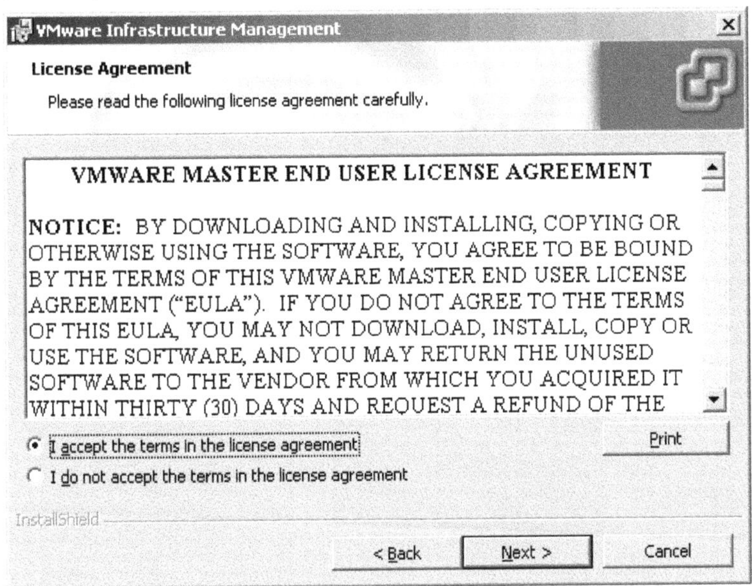

Figure 6.7 VMware Infrastructure Management License Agreement

Click on the Next button to continue.

Step 4. The next screen allows you to enter the username and organization customer information as shown in Figure 6.8.

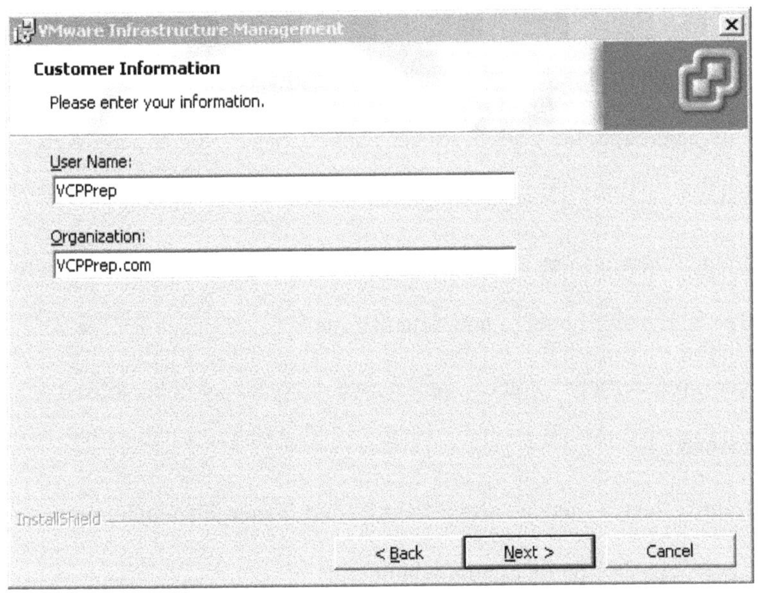

Figure 6.8 VMware Infrastructure Management Customer Information

Click on the Next button to continue.

Step 5. In the next step as shown in Figure 6.9 you can choose to install either the VI Client software, the VirtualCenter 2.5 software or a custom installation that allows you to install all of the software or just parts of it.

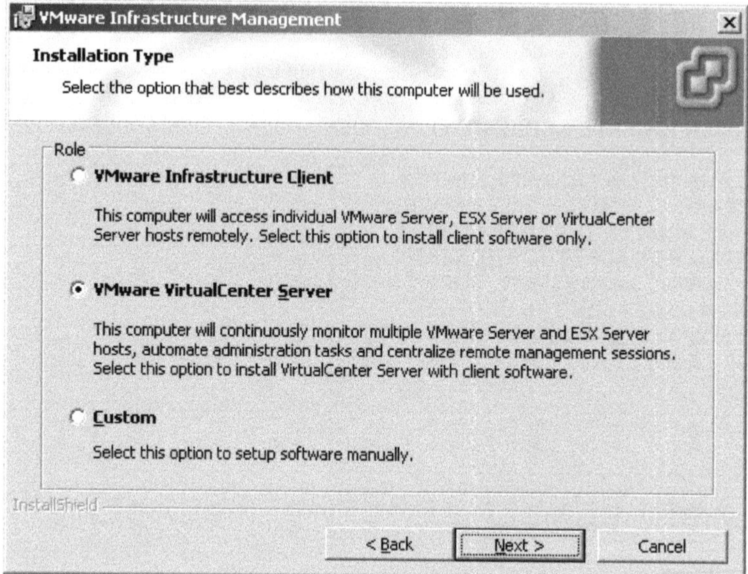

Figure 6.9 VMware Infrastructure Management Installation Type

ESX 3.5 NOTE: Using the Custom option allows you to control the following configuration settings for VirtualCenter 2.5:

- Where you want the program files to be installed
- Configuration of the VirtualCenter 2.5 ports - by default the HTTP web service uses port 80, the HTTPS web service uses port 443, the UDP heartbeat signal uses port 902 and the Web server port uses port 8086.
- VMware Update Manager port settings - by default the SOAP is set to port 8084 and the web port is port 9084. These ports can also be set to non-default ports
- VMware Update Manager proxy settings - you can configure a proxy server to be utilized with the VMware update manager
- VMware Converter Enterprise Server - by default the SOAP is set to port 9085 and the web port is port 9086. These ports can also be set to non-default ports

After you have decided on what installation method you want to use, click on the Next button to continue.

Step 6. Figure 6.10 shows the next screen which allows you to identify which type of database you are going to configure VirtualCenter 2.5 to use and how to connect to it.

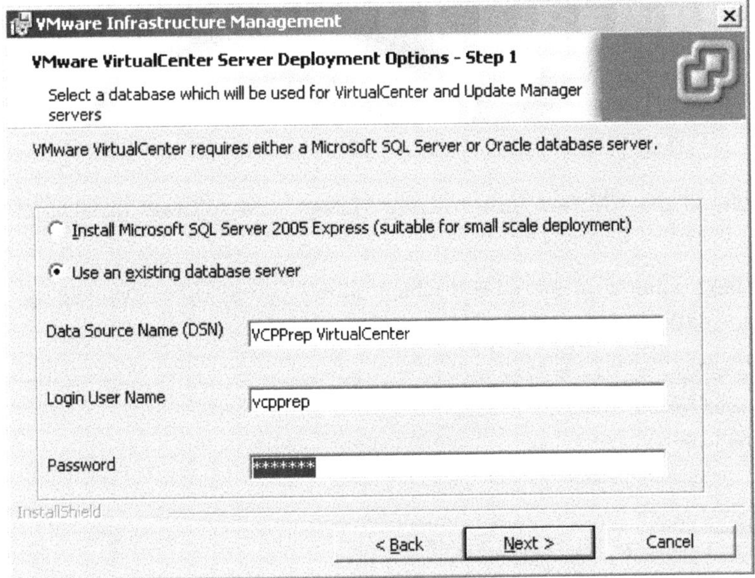

Figure 6.10 VMware Infrastructure Management Database Selection

If you select the upper radio button the installation process will install Microsoft SQL Server 2005 Express which is included on the installation CD. Microsoft SQL Server 2005 Express should only be used for small installations. If you choose the lower radio button you must provide the Data Source Name, the Login User Name and the password to connect to the database that you have already configured earlier. Click on the Next button to continue.

If you are not using the Microsoft SQL Server 2005 Express you will see a warning message box reminding you to make sure the appropriate database agent is running as shown in Figure 6.11.

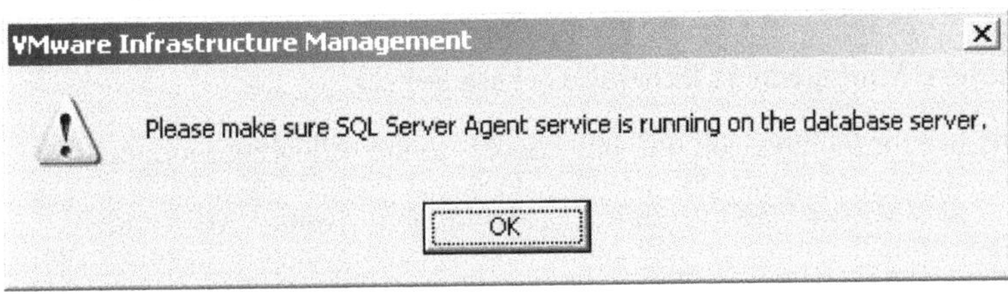

Figure 6.11 SQL Agent Message

Click OK to continue.

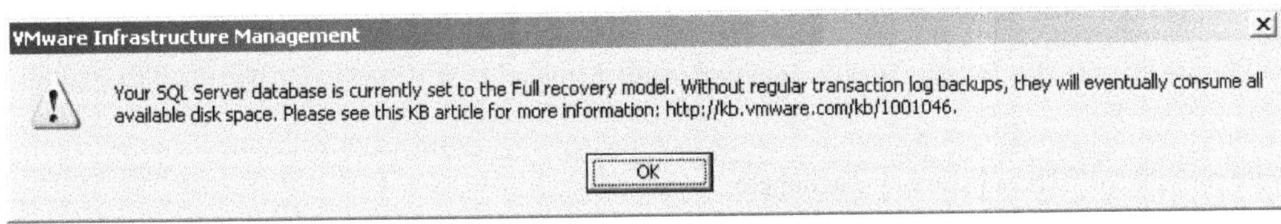

Figure 6.12 SQL Full Recovery Model Message

Figure 6.12 identifies that the Microsoft SQL server used in this example is set to the default of Full recovery model. The message box warns that the the default setting has the potential to consume all available disk space. It references the knowledge base article for more information. Click on the OK button to continue.

Licensing

The next thing that must be done in the VMware Infrastructure Management software installation process is to configure licensing.

Step 7. Figure 6.13 shows the next window in the wizard which allows you to either evaluate the software for free for 60 days or to configure it to use a license server.

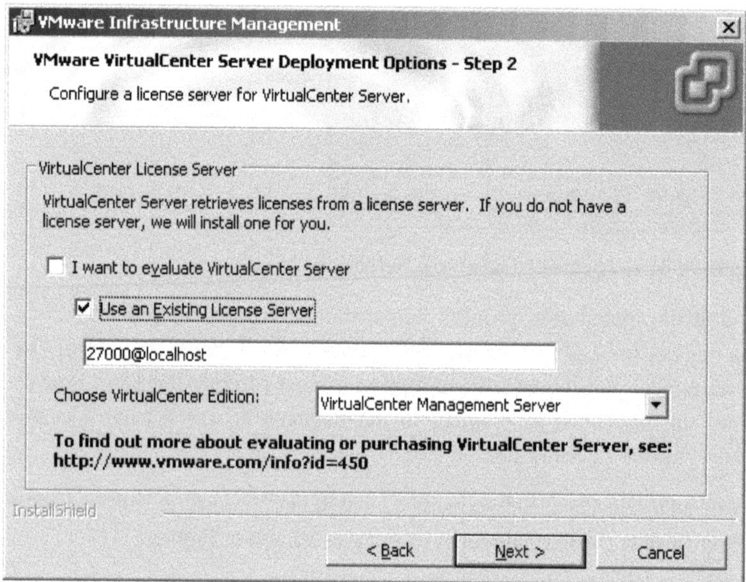

Figure 6.13 VMware Infrastructure Management Existing License Server

If you choose to evaluate the software for 60 days you will have access to the following products:

- VMware ESX Server 3.5 or VMware ESXi version 3.5 (including VMware VMFS and VMware vSMP)
- VMware VirtualCenter 2.5 (including VMware VMotion, VMware DRS, VMware HA and more)
- VMware Consolidated Backup v 1.1

If you choose to use the license server you will need to provide a license file for the installation process.

VMware provides different licensing packages:

- VMware ESXi version 3.5
- VMware Infrastructure Foundation

- VMware Infrastructure Standard
- VMware Infrastructure Enterprise

VMware ESXi Server Version 3.5

This license provides virtualization for a single VMware ESXi Server version 3.5. This license includes support for the following:

- VMware Virtual Machine File System (VMFS)
- VMware Symmetric Multi Processing (vSMP)

This license however will not allow your ESXi Server version 3.5 to work with VirtualCenter 2.5. You would only want to purchase it if you planned on directly managing the servers and weren't going to use any of the technologies that need to be managed by VirtualCenter 2.5.

VMware Infrastructure Foundation

This license would be a good fit for small businesses or branch offices. This license provides similar capabilities of the starter license in the ESX 3.0.x product.

This license includes support for the following:

- VMware ESX Server
- VMware Virtual Machine File System (VMFS)
- VMware Symmetric Multi Processing (vSMP)
- VirtualCenter Agent
- VMware Consolidated Backup
- VMware Update Manager

VMware Infrastructure Standard

This license should be chosen if your infrastructure needs automated failover protection.

This license includes support for the following:

- ESX Server 3
- VirtualCenter 2.5 Agent
- Virtual Machine File System (VMFS)
- VMware Symmetric Multi Processing (vSMP)
- VMware Update Manager
- VMware Consolidated Backup
- VMware High Availability (HA)

VMware Infrastructure Enterprise

This license should be chosen if your infrastructure needs the full set of technologies that work with

VirtualCenter 2.5.

This license includes support for the following:

- VMware ESX Server
- VirtualCenter 2.5 Agent
- VMware Virtual Machine File System (VMFS)
- VMware Virtual Symmetric Multi-Processing (vSMP)
- VMware Update Manager (Guest and Host)
- VMware VMotion + Storage VMotion
- VMware High Availability (HA)
- VMware Distributed Resource Scheduler (DRS)
- VMware Consolidated Backup

All four of the preceding licenses are priced based on the number of processors you intend to manage in your virtual infrastructure as well as the level of support and the number of years of support you have purchased.

Acceleration Kits

VMware also bundles multiple licenses at a discount in "acceleration kits".

The three options are:

- VMware Infrastructure Foundation Acceleration Kit
- VMware Infrastructure Standard High Availability Acceleration Kit
- VMware Infrastructure Midsize Acceleration Kit

VMware Infrastructure Foundation Acceleration Kit includes:

- 3 Licenses of VMware Infrastructure Foundation
- 1 License of VMware VirtualCenter Foundation
- Support and Subscription

VMware Infrastructure Standard High Availability (HA) Acceleration Kit includes:

- 2 Licenses of VMware Infrastructure Standard
- ESX Server 3
    - VirtualCenter 2.5 Agent
    - Virtual Machine File System (VMFS)
    - Virtual Symmetric Multi-Processing (vSMP)
    - VMware Update Manager
    - VMware Consolidated Backup

  - VMware High Availability (HA)
- 1 License of VMware VirtualCenter Foundation
- Support and Subscription (SnS)

The Midsize Acceleration Kit includes:

- 3 Licenses of VMware Infrastructure Enterprise
- 1 License of VirtualCenter Foundation
- 30 Training Credits
- Support and Subscription

For more information about licensing go to:

http://www.vmware.com/vmwarestore/

Once you have decided if you are going to use the temporary license or set up a license server as shown in Figure 6.13, click on the Next button to continue.

Step 8. The next screen in the wizard allows you to select the license file that you received from VMware. It also lets you choose the VirtualCenter Edition from the drop down menu as shown in Figure 6.14.

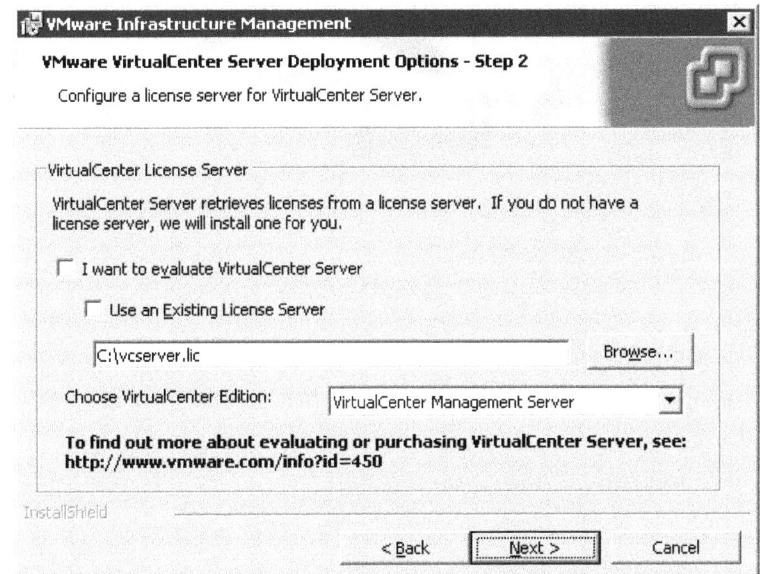

Figure 6.14 VMware Infrastructure Management New License Server

Once you've entered the correct information click on the Next button to continue.

Step 9. Figure 6.15 shows the next screen in the wizard that requires that you enter the IP address of the VirtualCenter 2.5 server, an Administrator account name and password.

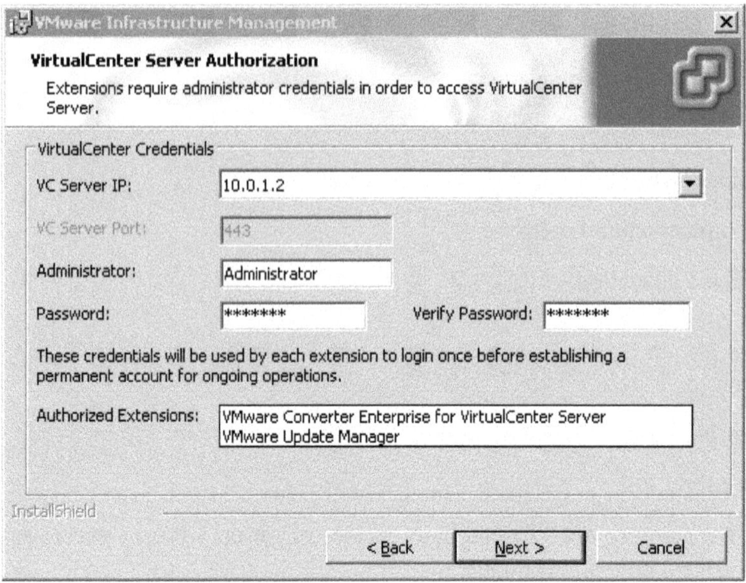

Figure 6.15 VMware Infrastructure Management Credentials

Click on the Next button to continue.

Step 10. The next screen is the Ready to install the program screen as shown in Figure 6.16.

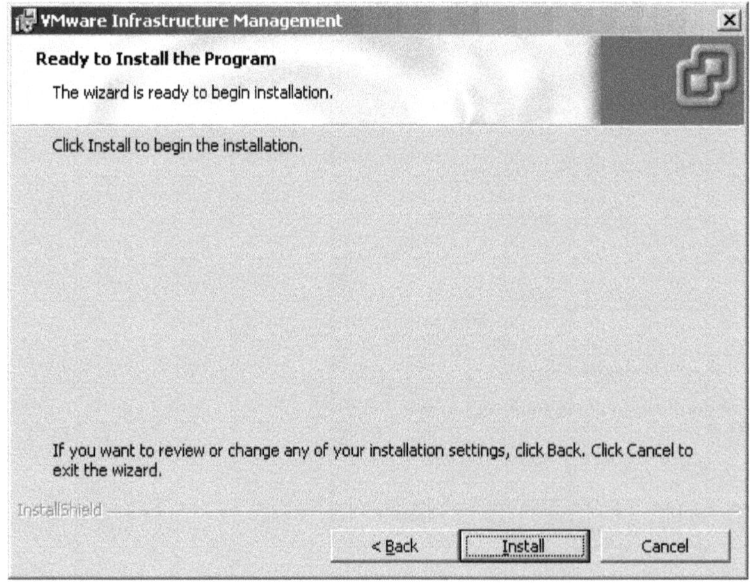

Figure 6.16 VMware Infrastructure Management Ready To Begin Installation

Click on the Next button to continue.

Figure 6.17 and Figure 6.18 show the next two windows in the installation process. Figure 6.17 shows progress and Figure 6.18 warns you that the required .NET Framework 2.0 software needs to be installed on the server.

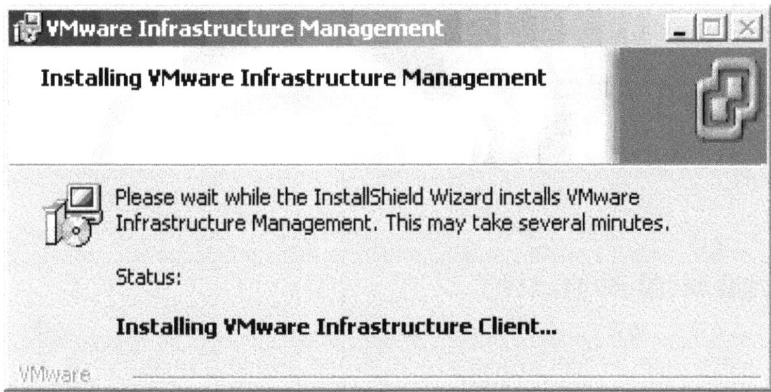

Figure 6.17 Installing VMware Infrastructure Client

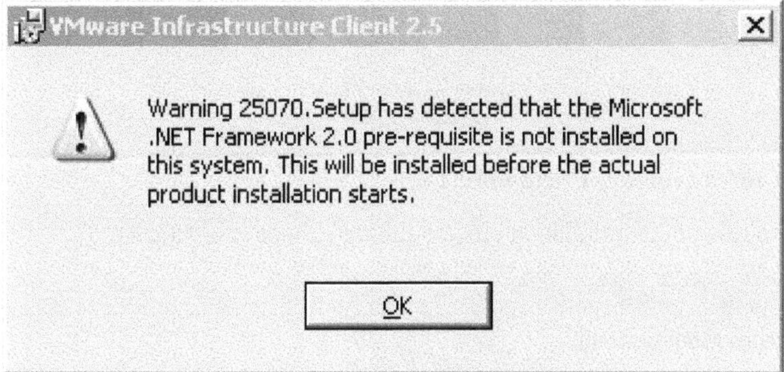

Figure 6.18 Microsoft .NET Framework 2.0 Message

Click the OK button to continue the installation process.

Figure 6.19 shows the installation process.

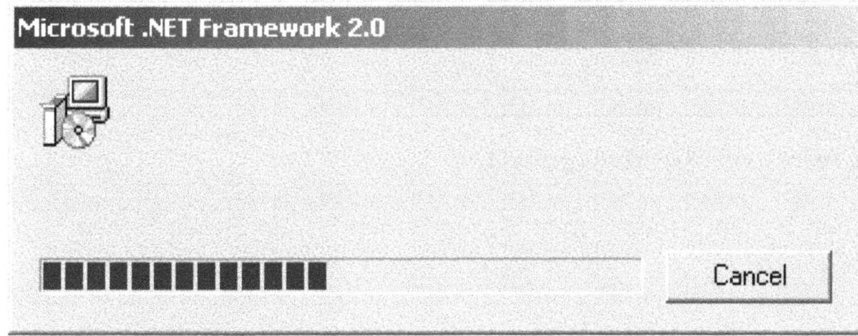

Figure 6.19 Installing Microsoft .NET Framework 2.0

In this example we chose the default full installation option, so the installation process will also install the VI Client software as shown in Figure 6.20.

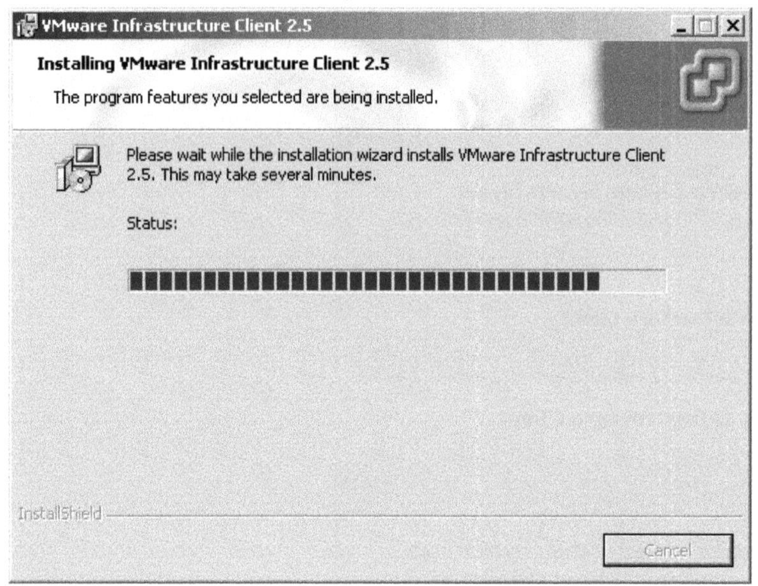

Figure 6.20 Installing VMware Infrastructure Client Status

Figures 6.21 to 6.27 show the progress of the installation process for the various components.

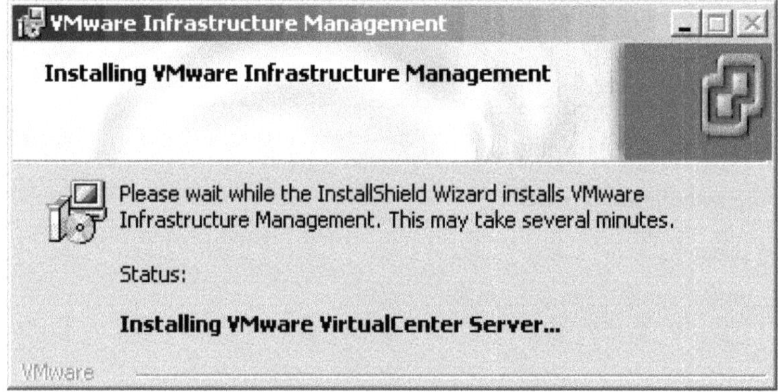

Figure 6.21 Installing VMware Infrastructure Management

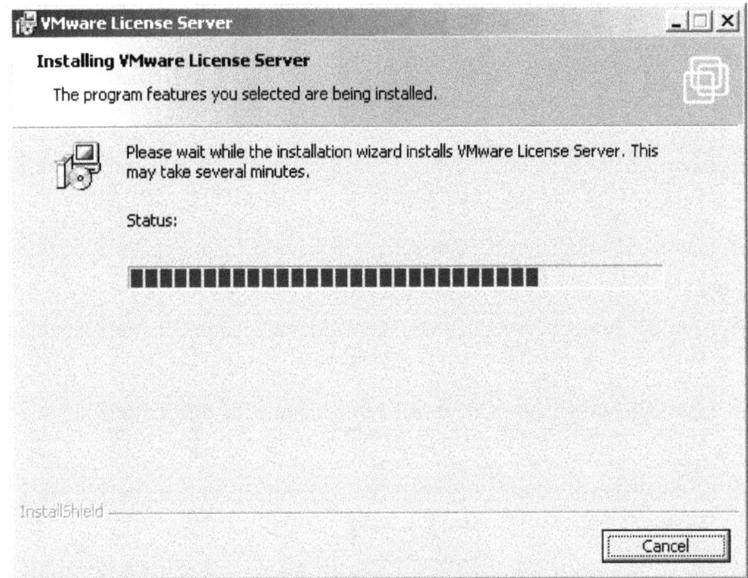

Figure 6.22 Installing VMware License Server

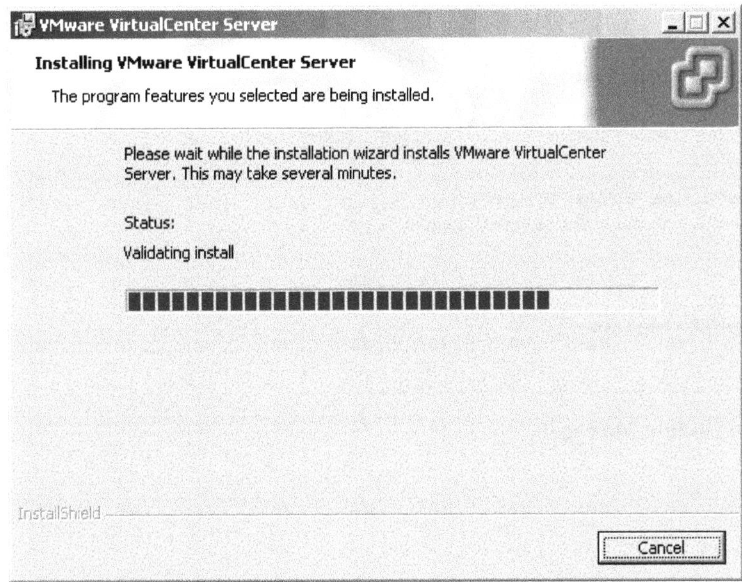

Figure 6.23 Validating VMware VirtualCenter 2.5 Server Installation Status

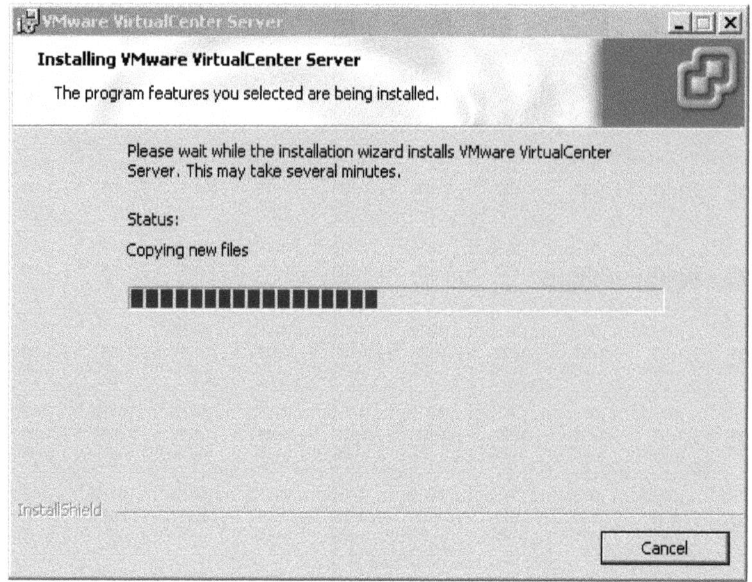

Figure 6.24 Copying VMware VirtualCenter 2.5 Installation Files

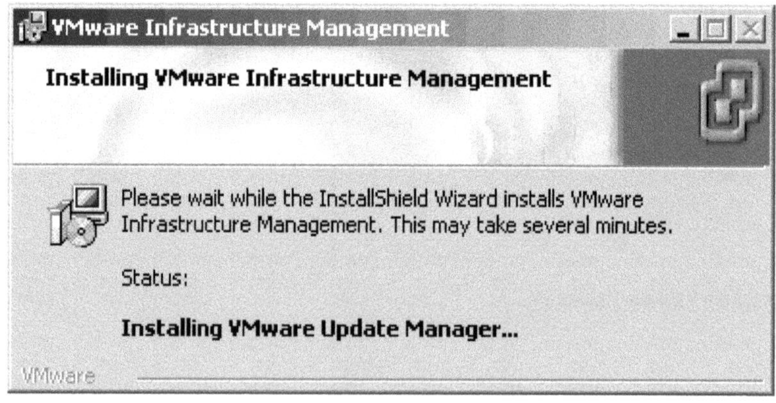

Figure 6.25 Installing VMware Update Manager

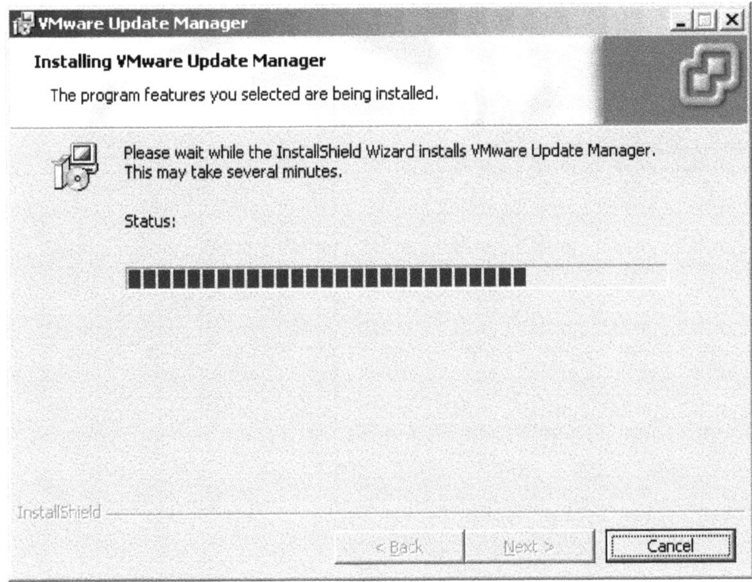

Figure 6.26 Installing VMware Update Manager Status

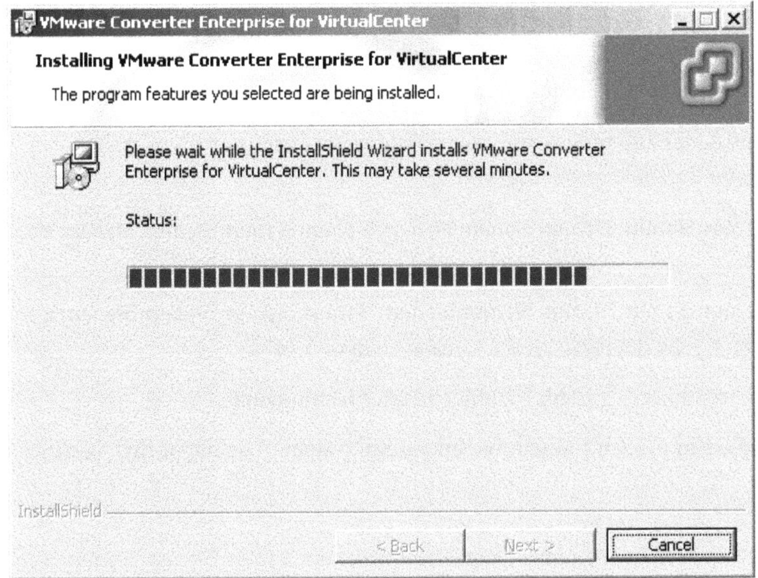

Figure 6.27 Installing VMware Converter Enterprise

Step 11. Once the installation is complete click on the Finish button as shown in Figure 6.28.

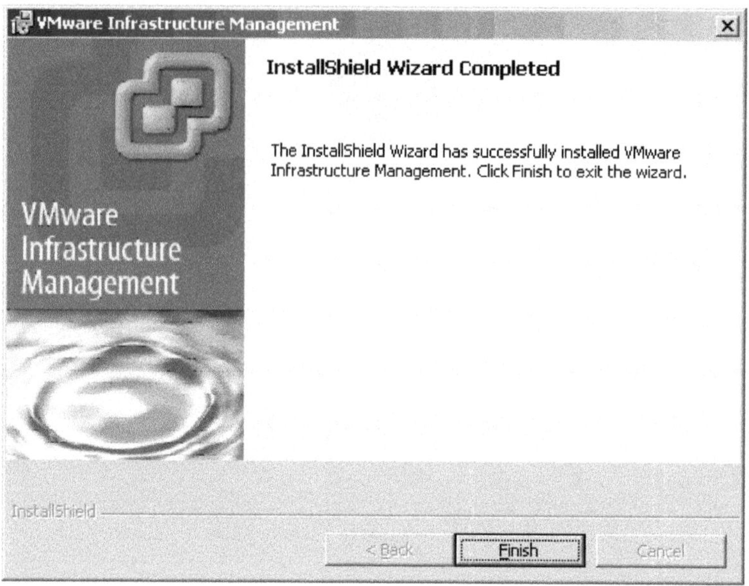

Figure 6.28 VMware Infrastructure Management Installation Complete

VirtualCenter 2.5 Installation Requirements

VirtualCenter 2.5 has the following installation requirements:

- 2 GHz minimum Intel or AMD x86 processor - you should use a faster processor if you plan on running the database on the same system or VM
- 2 GB RAM minimum - you should use more memory if you plan on running the database on the same system or VM
- 560 MB minimum disk storage but 2 GB is recommended - you should provide more storage space if you plan on running the database on the same system or VM
- 10/100 Ethernet adapter minimum - gigabit Ethernet adapter recommended

VirtualCenter 2.5 must be installed in a 32-bit Windows operating system. The supported versions are:

- Windows XP Pro SP2
- Windows 2003 SP1
- Windows 2003 Server R2
- Windows 2000 Server SP4 with Update Rollup 1

Internet Explorer 5.5 or higher is required in order for the VirtualCenter 2.5 installer to run.

VirtualCenter 2.5 server supports the following maximum values if configured with the appropriate hardware resources:

- 200 ESX 3.5 servers
- 2000 virtual machines on those servers

VirtualCenter 2.5 Installation in a Physical System or in a VM

VMware fully supports running VirtualCenter 2.5 in a virtual machine as well as running it on a physical server. The advantages to running VirtualCenter 2.5 in a virtual machine are:

- Server Consolidation: by running VirtualCenter in a VM you don't need to use a physical server which will reduce your data center space requirements, power and cooling requirements.
- Availability: by putting your VirtualCenter VM in a VMware cluster using VMware HA, the VirtualCenter VM will have a much higher level of availability.
- Mobility: you will take advantage of having the VirtualCenter server encapsulated in a virtual machine. You can move it from one ESX 3.5 server to another. You could then do maintenance and other tasks on the ESX 3.5 server that managed it.
- Snapshots: the VirtualCenter virtual machine can be used with the VMware snapshot functionality to backup or archive the VirtualCenter VM.

The reasons for installing VirtualCenter on a physical server deal with the limitations of running it in a VM:

- Some virtual machine management tasks require the VM to be powered off. You cannot perform most of these tasks on the virtual machine that hosts the VirtualCenter server.
- Any other operation which powers down the virtual machine
- Cold-migration
- Cloning
- Editing most of the virtual machine settings, particularly the hardware properties

For more information on choosing to run VirtualCenter in a physical server or in a VM refer to the Running VirtualCenter in a Virtual Machine VMware Technical Note:

http://www.vmware.com/pdf/vi3_vc_in_vm.pdf

Using the VI Client

If you want to access VirtualCenter 2.5 you must install the VI Client software on a windows based system. The VI Client is not supported on non-windows based systems.

You can install the VI Client software without installing any of the other VirtualCenter 2.5 components by selecting the appropriate radio button as shown in Figure 6.9.

After the software is installed you will see a desktop icon as shown in Figure 6.29 that can launch the

VI Client software.

Figure 6.29 VMware Infrastructure Client Icon

Step 1. Click on the Virtual Infrastructure Client icon to launch the program.

The VMware Infrastructure Client Credentials window will appear as shown in Figure 6.30.

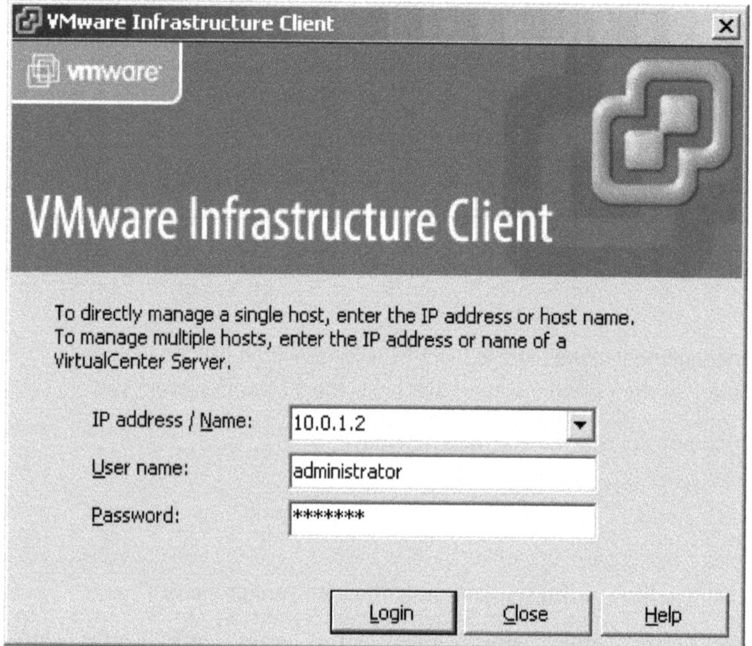

Figure 6.30 VMware Infrastructure Client Credentials

Step 2. Enter the IP address or hostname of the VirtualCenter 2.5 server that you want to connect to as well as the username and password of the account you want to access it with. The account must exist either on the VirturalCenter 2.5 server or you can have the account on a configured Active Directory domain.

Step 3. The VMware Infrastructure Client Security Warning screen will now appear as shown in Figure 6.31.

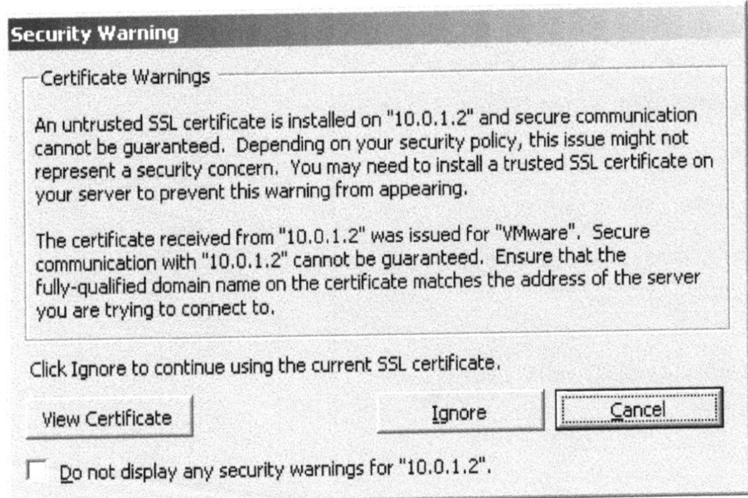

Figure 6.31 VMware Infrastructure Client Security Warning

Click on the View Certificate button to display the SSL certificate information or select the Ignore button to continue the connection process or the Cancel button to stop the connection process. Certificates can be obtained if needed. Please refer to the following document for additional information:

http://www.vmware.com/pdf/vi_vcserver_certificates.pdf

Configuring an ESX 3.5 Server to Be Managed by a VirtualCenter Server

In order to manage an ESX 3.5 server using VirtualCenter you must first add the ESX 3.5 server to the VirtualCenter inventory. The steps to do that are as follows:

Step 1. Right mouse button click a datacenter object in the inventory and select the Add Host command as shown in Figure 6.32. Note, a datacenter object needs to be created prior to performing this step. Datacenter objects will be discussed later in this chapter.

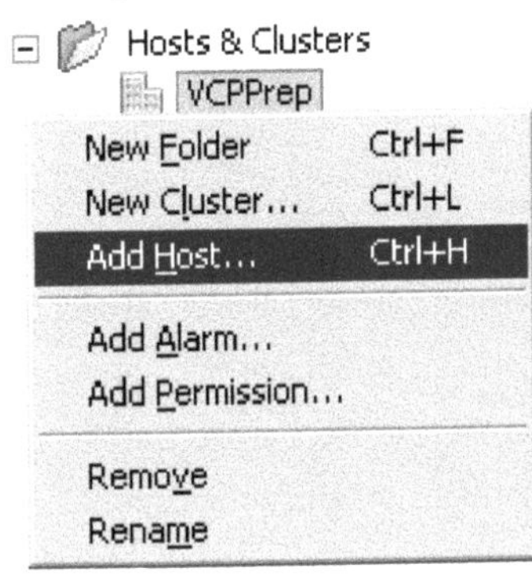

Figure 6.32 Add ESX 3.5 Host Menu

This will launch the Add Host Wizard.

Step 2. The first piece of information required is either the Fully Qualified Domain Name (FQDN) or the IP address of the ESX 3.5 server host as shown in Figure 6.33.

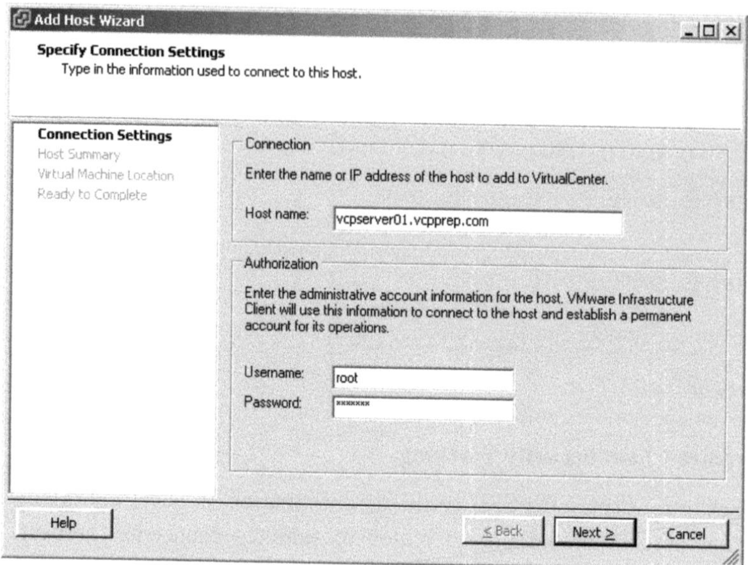

Figure 6.33 Enter ESX 3.5 Host And User Credentials

You must also supply the Administrator (root) account name and password for that account to make the connection to configure the host. After you add the appropriate information, click on the Next button to continue.

Step 3. Figure 6.34 shows the summary screen after VirtualCenter has made it's initial connection with the host.

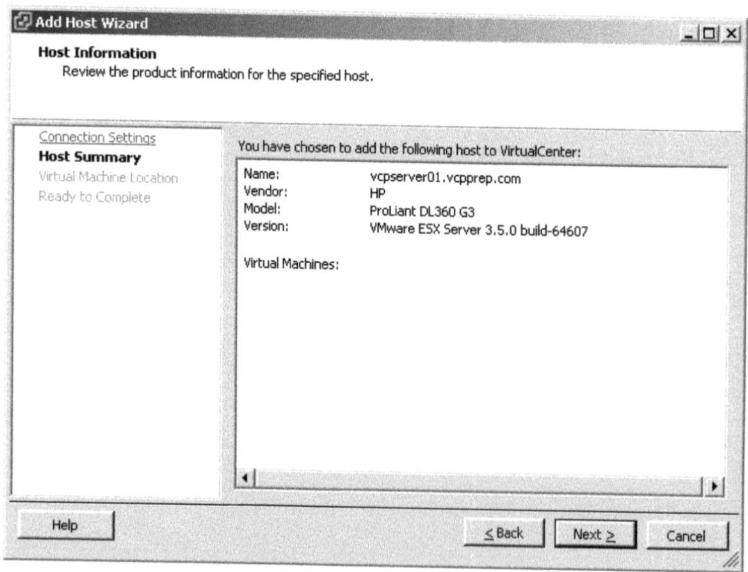

Figure 6.34 ESX 3.5 Host Information

Click on the Next button to continue.

Step 4. Select the location where the virtual machines running on the ESX 3.5 Server being added will be located as shown in Figure 6.35.

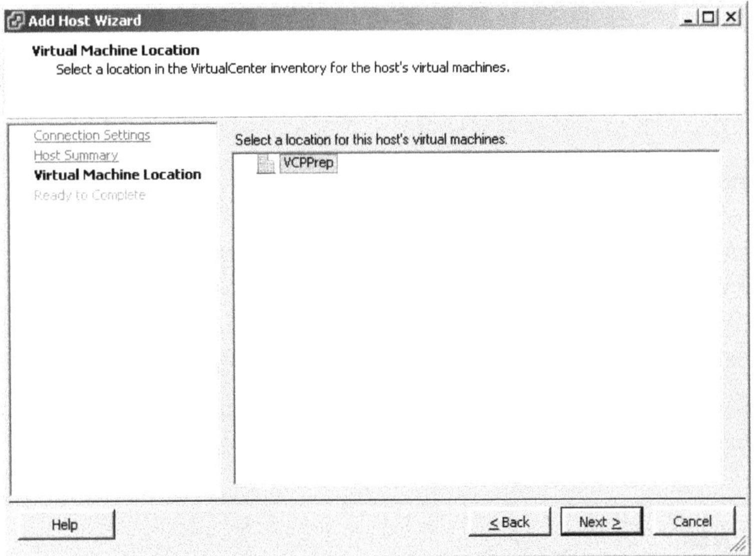

Figure 6.35 Select Location For ESX 3.5 Virtual Machines

Step 5. The last screen in the wizard is the summary screen as shown in Figure 6.36.

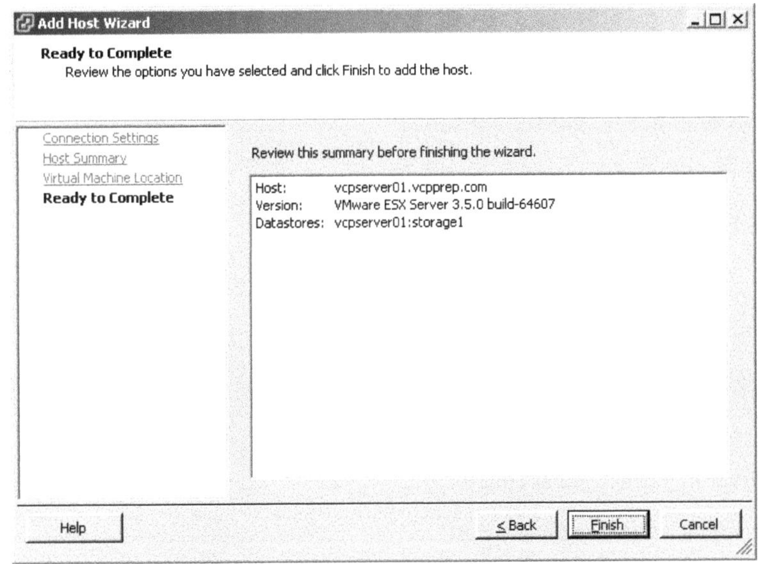

Figure 6.36 Add ESX 3.5 Host Ready To Complete

Click on the Finish button to complete the process.

The ESX 3.5 server will now appear in the list of resources managed by VirtualCenter 2.5 as shown in Figure 6.37.

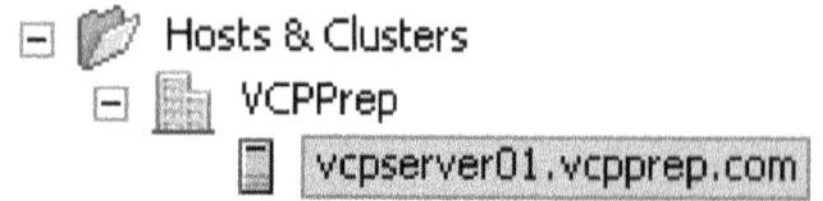

Figure 6.37 New ESX 3.5 Host Added Within VirtualCenter Server

vpxa, hostd and the vpxuser Account

The installation process creates a new background process on the ESX 3.5 server that was added to VirtualCenter's control. This process is called vpxa and the installation process creates a new user account called vpxuser. When VirtualCenter communicates with the ESX 3.5 server it will only communicate using the vpxuser account.

The vpxa process communicates with the hostd process running on the server and these two processes are responsible for the coordination and launching of the tasks requested by VirtualCenter.

Virtual Infrastructure Ports

The following ports are used by the Virtual Infrastructure components to communicate with each other. Please make note to configure your firewalls to allow these ports to be used:

VI Client Ports

- **443/TCP** - VI Client and Web Access to VirtualCenter Server
- **443/TCP** - VI Client and Web Access to ESX 3.5 Server
- **902/TCP** – ESX Server to ESX Server; VC Server to ESX Server
- **903/TCP** - VI Client to ESX 3.5 Server Remote Console

License Server Ports

- **27010/TCP** - License Server to ESX 3.5 Server
- **27000/TCP** - ESX 3.5 Server to License Server

Miscellaneous Ports

- **902/UDP** - ESX 3.5 Server to VirtualCenter Heartbeat
- **8083/TCP** - VMware VirtualCenter Diagnostic Port
- **8086/TCP** - Apache Tomcat Web Server Administration on VirtualCenter Server

The VirtualCenter Inventory

The VirtualCenter inventory is populated with objects that serve a variety of purposes as shown in Figure 6.38.

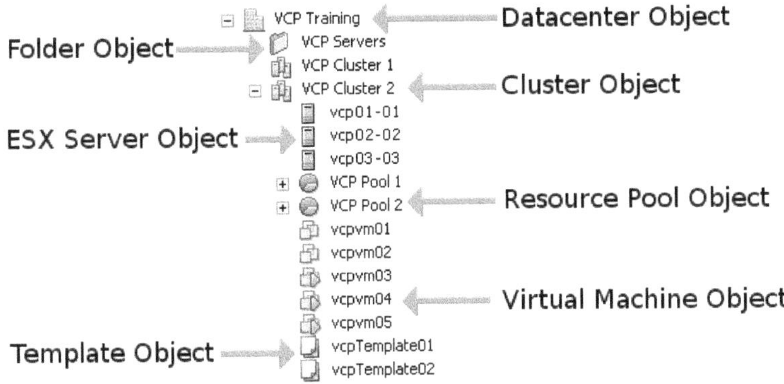

Figure 6.38 VirtualCenter Objects

Datacenter Object - The datacenter is used as the primary organizational object. An administrator can place within a datacenter object ESX 3.5 Server hosts, virtual machines, folders, clusters, networks and datastores. Different datacenter objects can be used simultaneously within the VirtualCenter inventory. The datacenter object can be used to set limitations. Virtual machines located in different datacenter objects cannot be VMotioned to an ESX 3.5 Server in another datacenter object.

Folder Object - Folders are useful objects when organizing objects within a datacenter. Use folder objects to group ESX 3.5 Servers that share the same vendor CPUs, for example, Intel or AMD based servers. Folders can be used to group virtual machines with similar functionality, for example, print and file virtual machines or web server virtual machines. Restricting user access can be accomplished by applying permissions to folder objects.

Cluster Object - Cluster objects are used to balance ESX 3.5 Server workloads and for disaster recovery purposes when configured as a DRS or HA cluster respectively. For more information regarding DRS refer to Chapter 14 – Distributed Resource Scheduler and for information on HA clusters, refer to Chapter 15 – High Availability.

ESX Server Object - ESX Server objects are displayed after the server has been added under the management of VirtualCenter. For more information on adding an ESX host server within VirtualCenter, refer to the Configuring An ESX 3.5 Server To Be Managed By A VirtualCenter Server section earlier in this chapter. Right clicking on an ESX 3.5 Server object allows an ESX Administrator to perform several operations including creating a new virtual machine and rebooting an ESX 3.5 Server.

Resource Pool Object - VirtualCenter provides a means of dividing the memory and CPU resources of a single ESX 3.5 Server or group of ESX 3.5 Servers by using a resource pool object. Resource Pool objects are covered in more detail in Chapter 12.

Virtual Machine Object - Virtual machine objects display the power state of a virtual machine. In Figure 6.38, the virtual machine with the display name vcpvm04 is shown as powered on denoted by the arrow icon in contrast to the vcpvm01 virtual machine icon displayed as powered off. Avoid using special characters and spaces in virtual machine display names.

Template Object - VirtualCenter provides the ability to create a template from a virtual machine for rapid provisioning of new virtual machines. Template objects cannot be powered on. The restriction of disallowing a template object to be powered on is enforced to avoid inadvertent changes to a master template image.

The VirtualCenter Tabs

When you select an ESX 3.5 server from the inventory you will see the following tabs in the window:

- The Host Getting Started Tab
- The Summary Tab
- The Virtual Machines Tab
- The Host Resource Allocation Tab
- The Performance Tab
- The Configuration Tab
- The Tasks & Events Tab
- The Alarms Tab
- The Permissions Tab
- The Maps Tab

The Host Getting Started Tab

This is a new tab in the VirtualCenter 2.5 GUI. Figure 6.39 shows the links that are used to launch two wizards. You can import a virtual appliance or create a new virtual machine with these wizards.

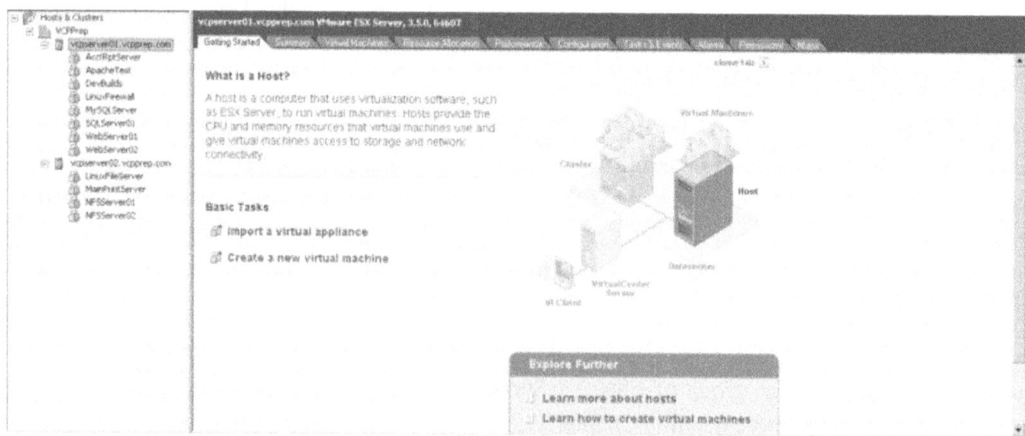

Figure 6.39 Host Getting Started Tab

The Host Summary Tab

VirtualCenter's interface is determined by the object in the inventory that you have selected in the left panel. A set of tabs for that particular object will be displayed on the right hand side of the screen as shown in Figure 6.40.

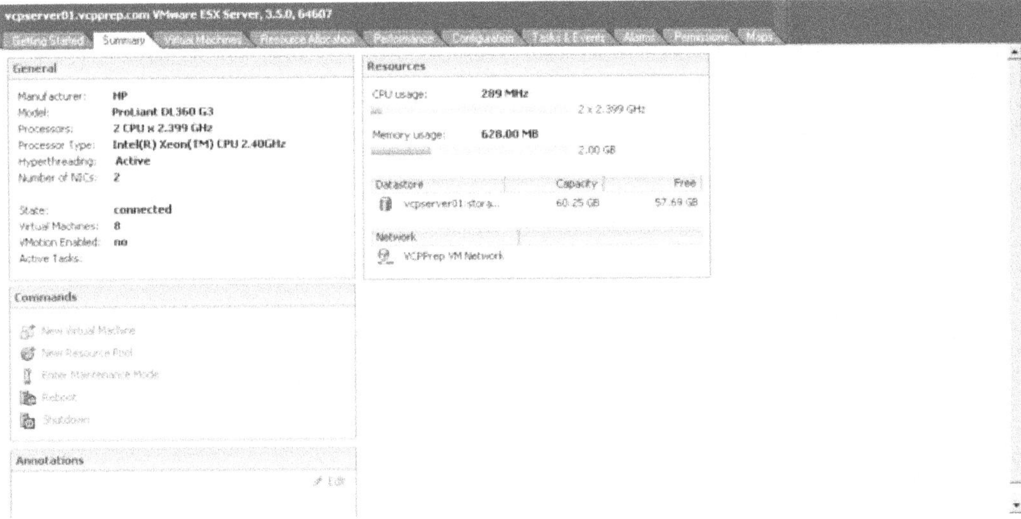

Figure 6.40 Host Summary Tab

For instance when we click on an ESX 3.5 server in the inventory the second tab will be the Summary tab. This tab will display information about the server such as the manufacturer, model and the amount of CPUs and memory that it contains.

It will also show you if hyperthreading is enabled and the number of physical NICs that are installed in the server.

Below that is a Commands section and you can click on the various commands that allow you to add a virtual machine, take the system down to maintenance mode for servicing, reboot or shutdown the server.

The right hand of the display will show you the CPU and memory usage which is useful when troubleshooting performance issues. It also will display all of the datastores that have been configured to be accessed by this server. Below that you will see the virtual networking configured on the server.

The Virtual Machines Tab

The Virtual Machine tab provides information about the configured virtual machines on that ESX 3.5 server as shown in Figure 6.41.

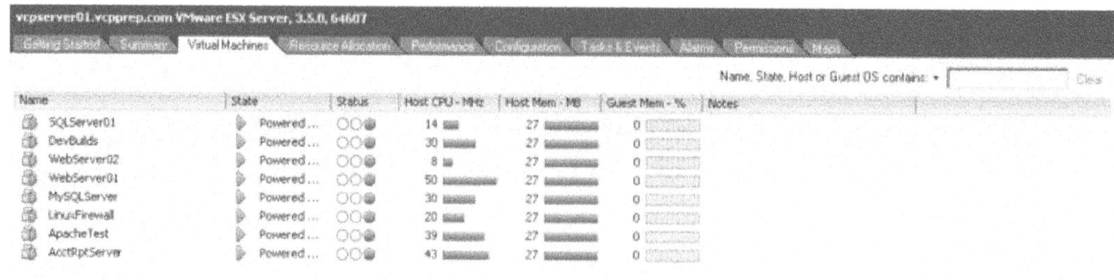

Figure 6.41 Host Virtual Machines Tab

The names of the VMs will be listed as well as their current power state. The status column references if any yellow or red alarms have been triggered. The current CPU usage in MHz and memory usage in MB is also displayed as well as showing the percentage of total memory used and a column for notes is the last field of the display.

The Host Resource Allocation Tab

Figure 6.42 shows the Host Resource Allocation Tab. CPU and Memory utilization is shown for the server as well as for the individual VMs. We will cover how these resources are allocated and how you can control how the resources are distributed in Chapter 11 – Resource Optimization.

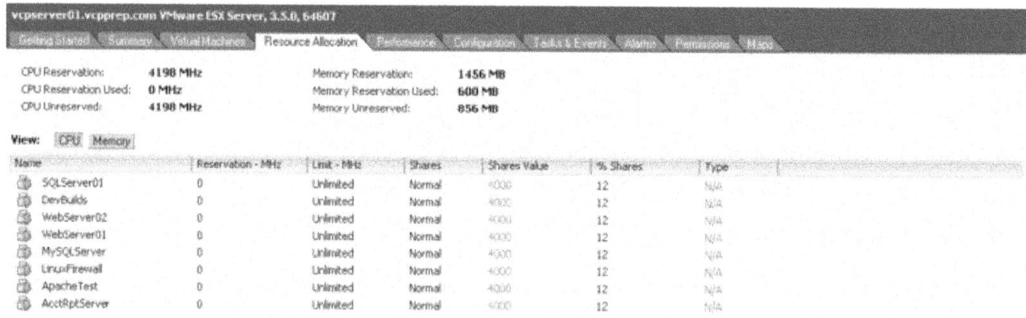

Figure 6.42 Host Resource Allocation Tab

The Performance Tab

The performance tab contains a customizable graph that displays data about the VMs running on the

ESX 3.5 server as shown in Figure 6.43.

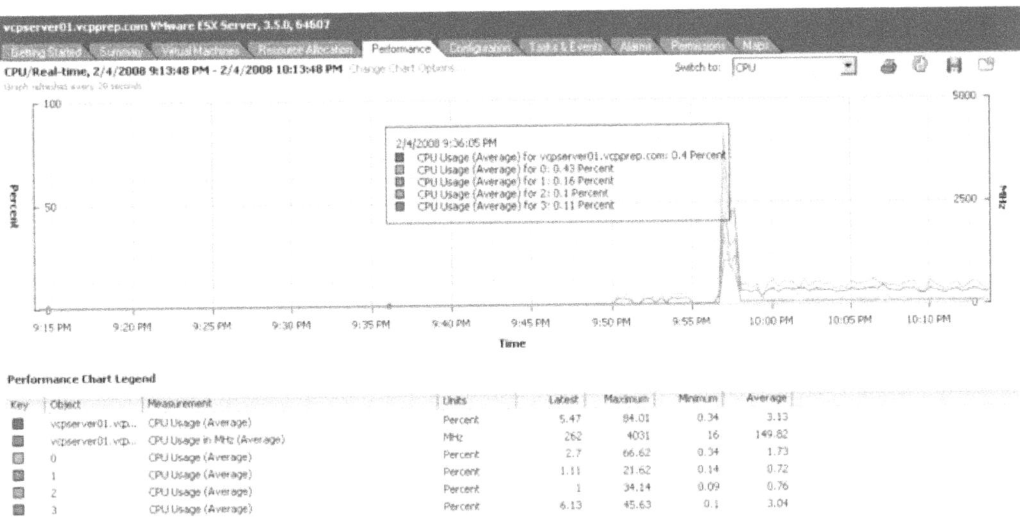

Key	Object	Measurement	Units	Latest	Maximum	Minimum	Average
	vcpserver01.vcp...	CPU Usage (Average)	Percent	5.47	84.01	0.34	3.13
	vcpserver01.vcp...	CPU Usage in MHz (Average)	MHz	262	4031	16	149.82
	0	CPU Usage (Average)	Percent	2.7	66.62	0.34	1.73
	1	CPU Usage (Average)	Percent	1.11	21.62	0.14	0.72
	2	CPU Usage (Average)	Percent	1	34.14	0.09	0.76
	3	CPU Usage (Average)	Percent	6.13	45.63	0.1	3.04

Figure 6.43 Host Performance Tab

The Performance Chart Legend explains what is being displayed as well as the actual data to the right. You can also save this output as an Excel spreadsheet. There are many statistics that can be analyzed. These will be discussed in Chapter 16 - Monitoring and Alerting.

The Configuration Tab

The Configuration tab has a Hardware and Software section to the screen as shown in Figure 6.44.

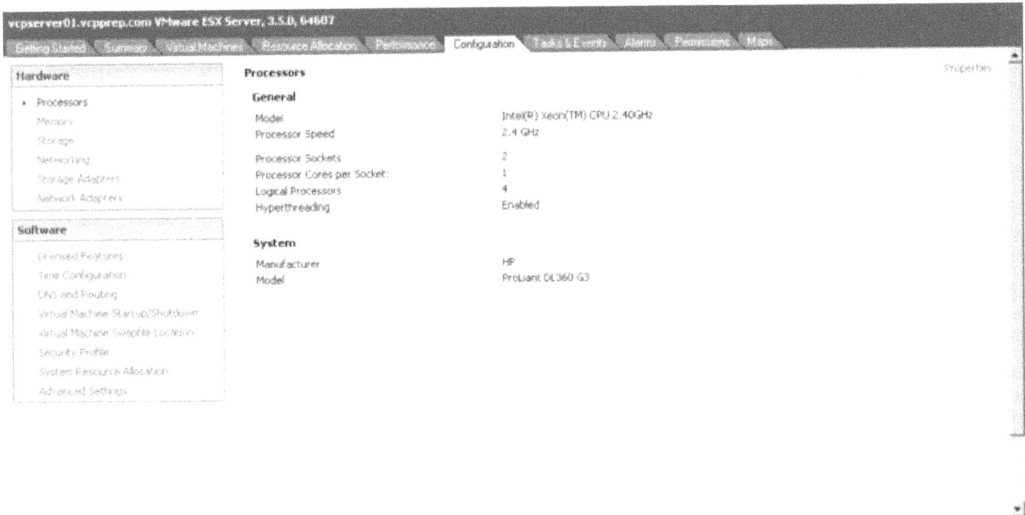

Figure 6.44 Host Configuration Tab

This is the tab where you will do most of your work configuring the ESX 3.5 server. We will explore these links throughout this book.

The Tasks & Events Tab

The Tasks & Events tab provides you with access to a list of the recent tasks as shown in Figure 6.45.

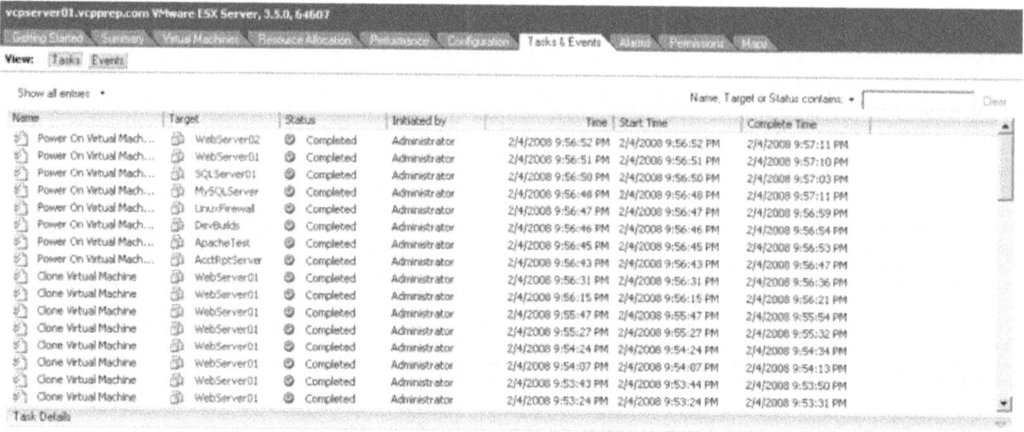

Figure 6.45 Host Tasks & Events Tab

You can see who initiated the task and when it took place. Selecting the Events button in the upper left will display the recent logged events.

The Alarms Tab

The Alarms tab will show you any configured alarms as shown in Figure 6.46.

Figure 6.46 Host Alarms Tab

These can be the default alarms or custom alarms that you create. Default alarms are defined in the Hosts & Clusters folder. You can see the name of the alarm as well as its current status.

The Permissions Tab

Figure 6.47 show the Permissions tab.

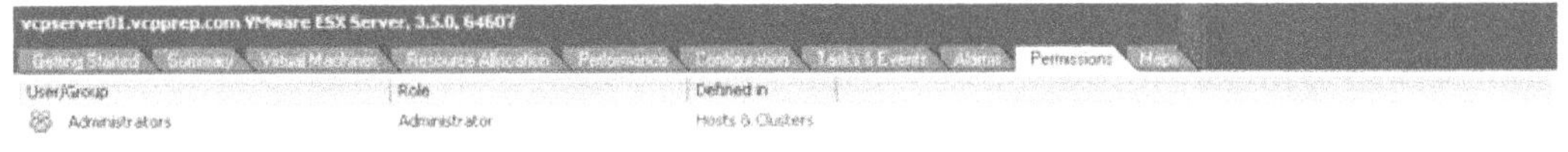

Figure 6.47 Host Permissions Tab

The Permissions tab displays which users or groups are configured to access this ESX 3.5 server. It will also show you the role assigned to the user or group as well as where this permission is defined in the inventory.

The Maps Tab

The Maps tab provides a visual way to see the relationships of the resources on the server as shown in Figure 6.48.

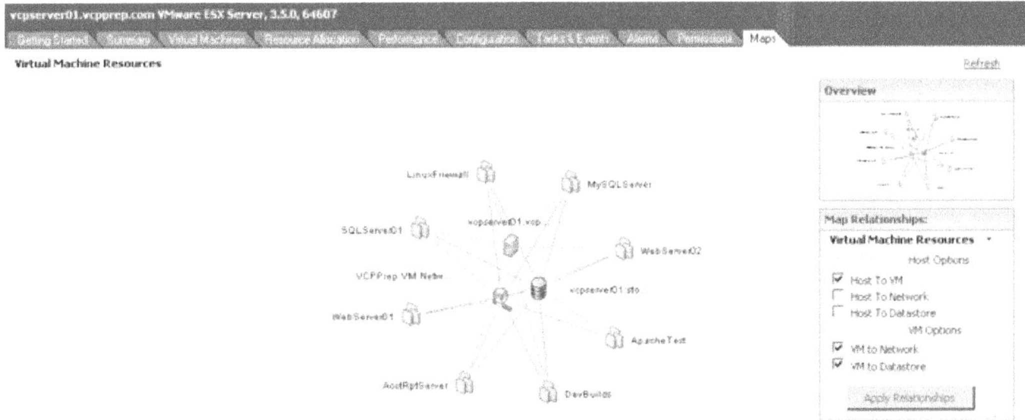

Figure 6.48 Host Maps Tab

A common use of this map is to quickly view VMotion requirements regarding shared datastores and networks. The map can be customized by clicking on the Map Relationships section in the right of the screen.

VirtualCenter Views

VirtualCenter allows you to change the display of the inventory by changing its view as shown in Figure 6.49.

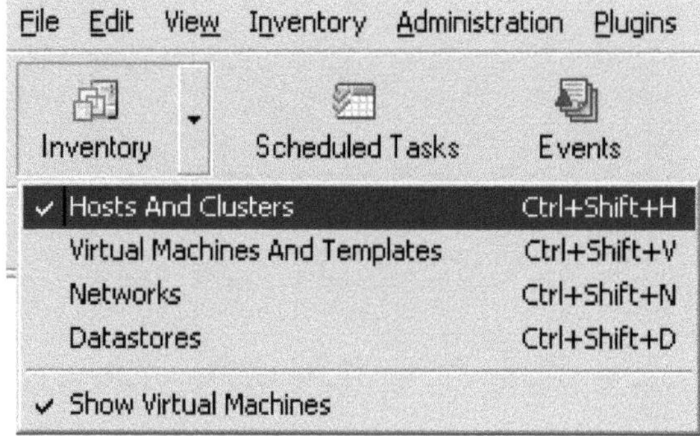

Figure 6.49 Inventory Menu

The drop down menu to the right of the Inventory button displays the various views available:

- Hosts And Clusters
- Virtual Machines And Templates
- Networks
- Datastores

Hosts and Clusters View

Figure 6.50 shows the Hosts and Clusters view which displays all of the ESX 3.5 servers as well as all of the VMware clusters under VirtualCenters control.

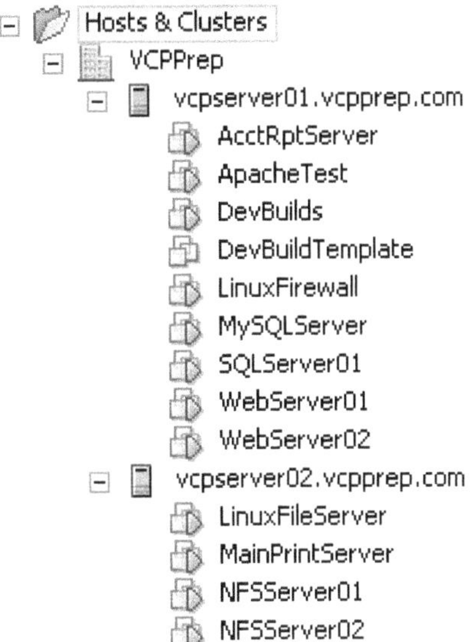

Figure 6.50 Hosts And Cluster View

A VMware cluster is multiple ESX 3.5 servers that are grouped together to support distributed services.

Virtual Machines And Templates View

Figure 6.51 shows the Virtual Machines And Templates view.

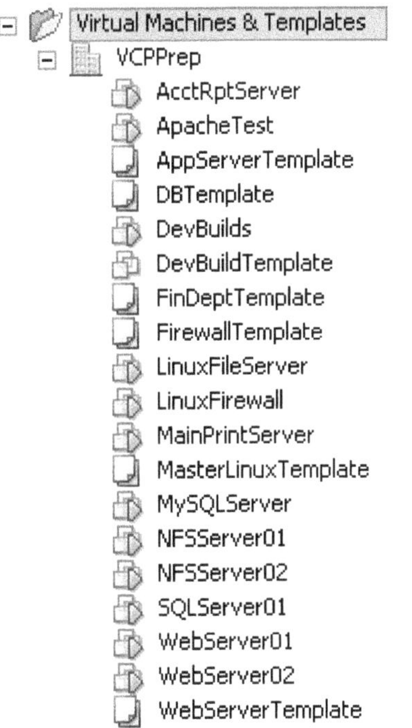

Figure 6.51 Virtual Machines & Templates View

This view displays all of the VMs as well as templates which are VMs designed not to be powered on and are used for rapid provisioning that are managed by VirtualCenter.

Networks View

Figure 6.52 shows the Networks view.

Figure 6.52 Networks View

This view displays the configured virtual switches that are managed by VirtualCenter.

Datastores View

Figure 6.53 shows the Datastores view.

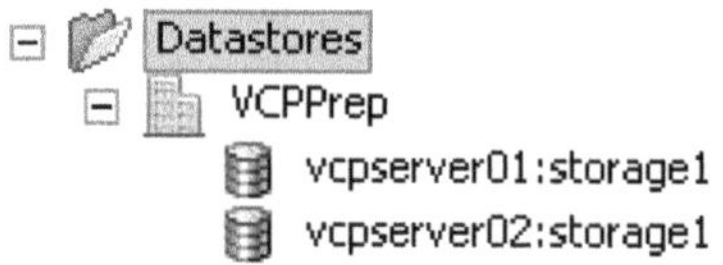

Figure 6.53 Datastores View

This view displays the configured datastores that are managed by VirtualCenter.

Using the VirtualCenter Web Access Method

The VirtualCenter Web Access service can be used to manage virtual machines. Supported Web browsers include the following:

Windows

- Internet Explorer 6.0 or higher
- Netscape Navigator 7.0
- Mozilla 1.X, Firefox 1.0.7 and higher

Linux

- Netscape Navigator 7.0 or later
- Mozilla 1.x
- Firefox 1.0.7 and higher

A key advantage of using Web Access is being able to access virtual machines without requiring the installation of the VI Client. ESX 3.5 Administrators can use Web Access as a method to allow end users access to virtual machines. A user accessing a virtual machine via Web Access can use the client's local floppy or CD/DVD drives to perform software installations, upgrades or accessing user data. Using client devices eliminates the need to use the ESX 3.5 Server host's local floppy and CD/DVD drives.

The following illustrates accessing Web Access:

Step 1. Open a supported web browser and enter either the IP address or the FQDN (Fully Qualified Domain Name) of the ESX 3.5 Server or the VirtualCenter Server. A welcome page is then displayed in the web browser as shown in Figure 6.54.

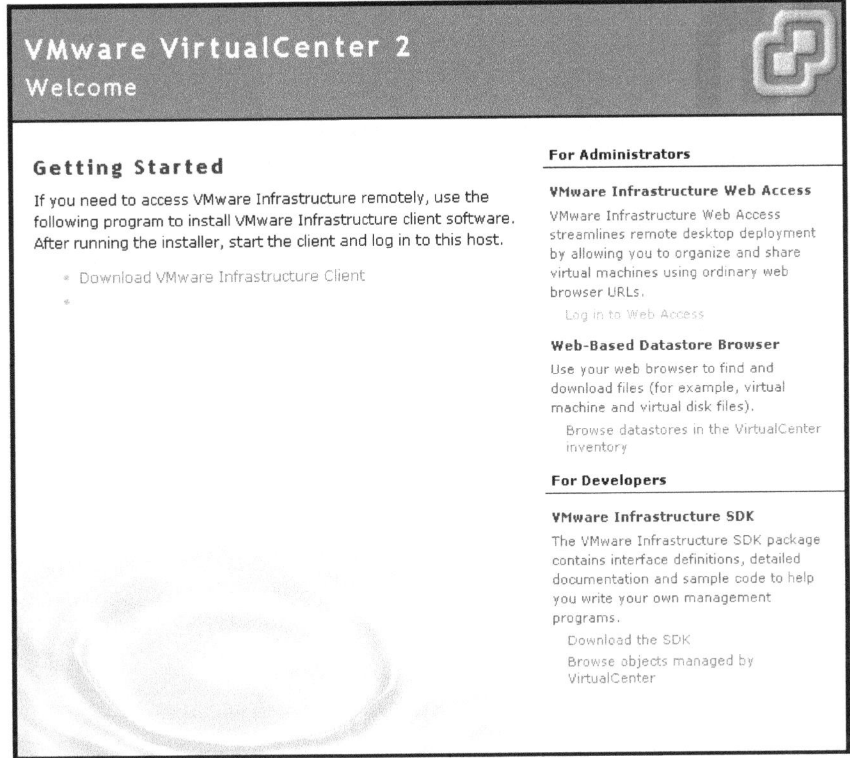

Figure 6.54 Web Access Main Page

To log in to the server, click on the following link on the right of the welcome web page:

Log in to Web Access

Step 2. Enter the correct log in credentials for the Login Name and Password as shown in Figure 6.55.

Figure 6.55 Web Access User Credentials

Double clicking on the Datacenter object within the left window pane will display the list of virtual machines. Selecting a virtual machine displays the Summary tab for the virtual machine as shown in Figure 6.56.

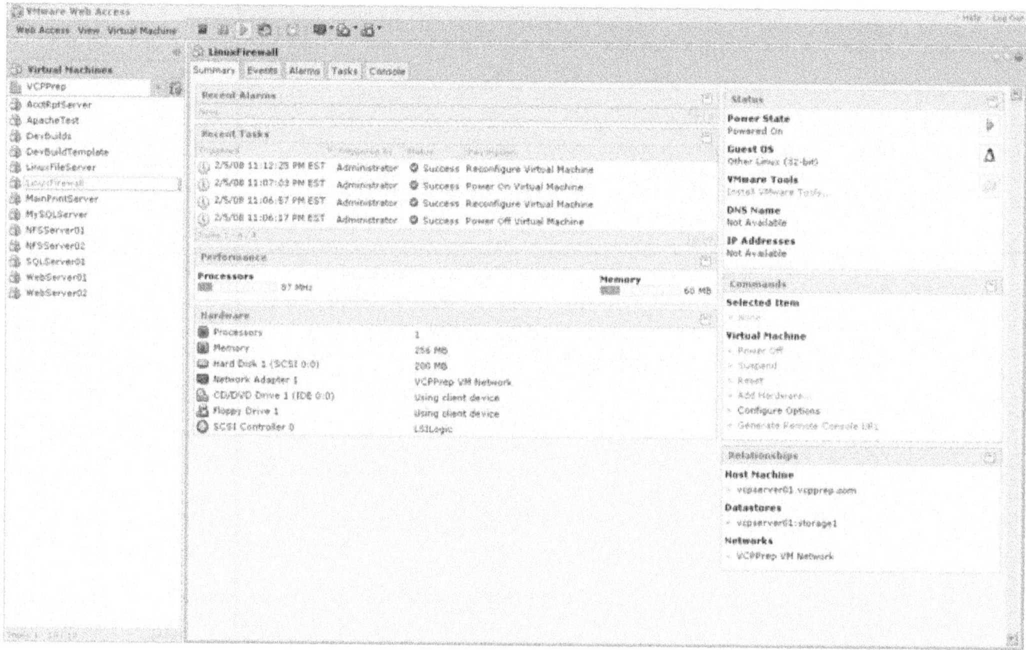

Figure 6.56 Web Access Virtual Machine Summary Tab

The Summary tab contains the Recent Alarms, Recent Tasks and Performance section that can be used for troubleshooting purposes. The Hardware section lists the virtual hardware of the VM. Modifications can be made to the virtual hardware listed by clicking on the virtual hardware item. Doing so causes a new page to load in the web browser that can be used to make the desired changes to the hardware item. Note, most items can only be modified when the virtual machine is in a power off state.

The Status section displays the power state of the virtual machine, the guest OS, state of VMware Tools, DNS name and IP address of the virtual machine. The Commands section can be used to power off, suspend and reset the virtual machine. The Add Hardware... link allows the end user to add virtual hardware. Only virtual hard disks can be added while the virtual machine is powered on. The link to Generate Remote Console URL is discussed in the Remote Console URL section of Chapter 6.

The Relationships section displays the Host Machine name, Datastores and Networks configured for the virtual machine.

To view recent events for the selected virtual machine, click on the Events tab as shown in Figure 6.57.

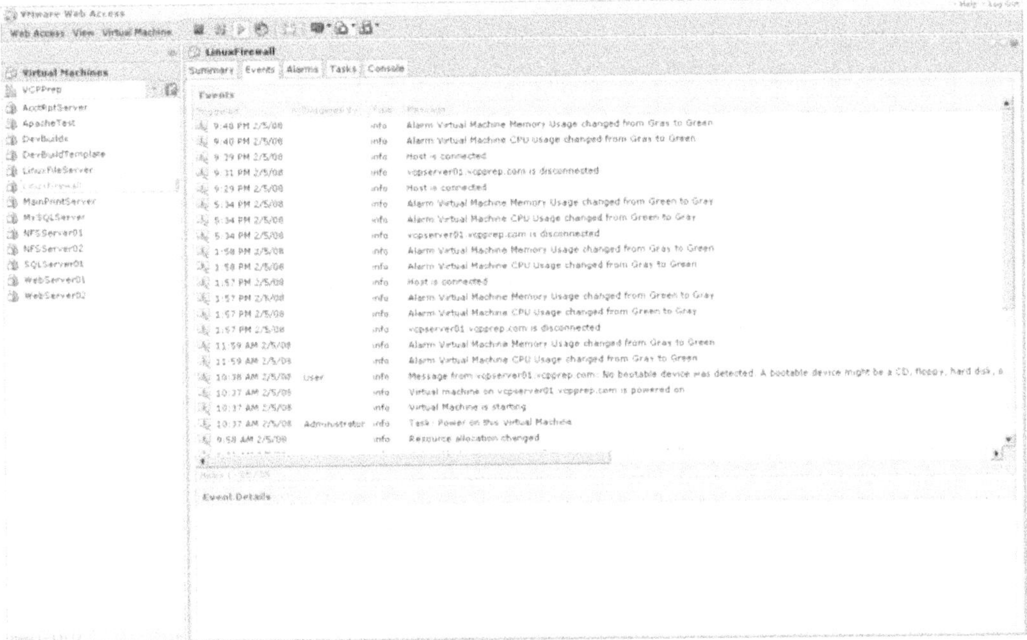

Figure 6.57 Web Access Virtual Machine Events Tab

The Events tab is useful when troubleshooting and diagnosing virtual machine performance issues. Selecting an event in the Triggered column will display additional event information within the Event Details window pane at the bottom of the web page.

To view recent alarms for the selected virtual machine, click on the Alarms tab as shown in Figure 6.58.

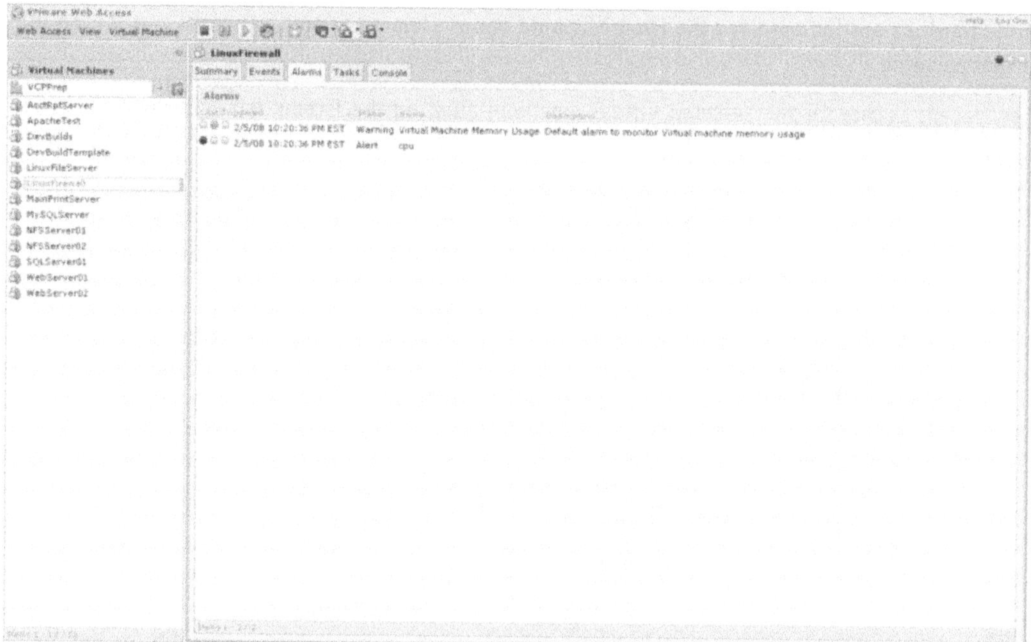

Figure 6.58 Web Access Virtual Machine Alarms Tab

Once an alarm is triggered, the Alarms tab displays the last time the alarm was triggered and status of the alarm whether it is an Alert or Warning. The name of the alarm along with a description is displayed as well.

To view recent tasks for the selected virtual machine, click on the Tasks tab as shown in Figure 6.59.

The Tasks tab is useful when verifying recent task activity of a virtual machine. Selecting a task in the Triggered column will display additional task information within the Task Details window pane at the bottom of the web page.

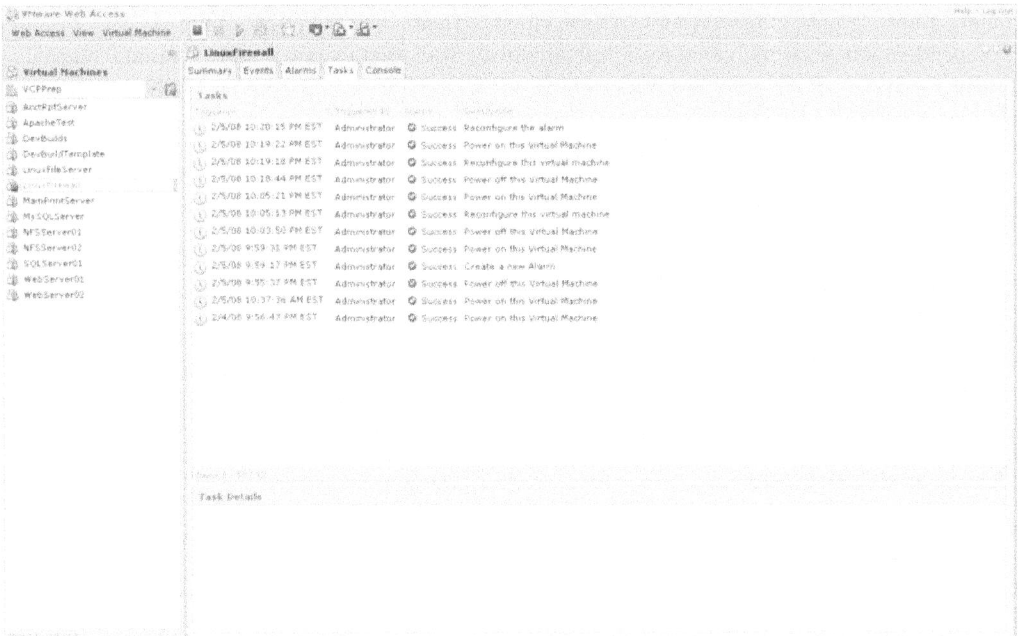

Figure 6.59 Web Access Virtual Machine Tasks Tab

To view the guest OS running within the virtual machine, click on the Console tab as shown in Figure 6.60.

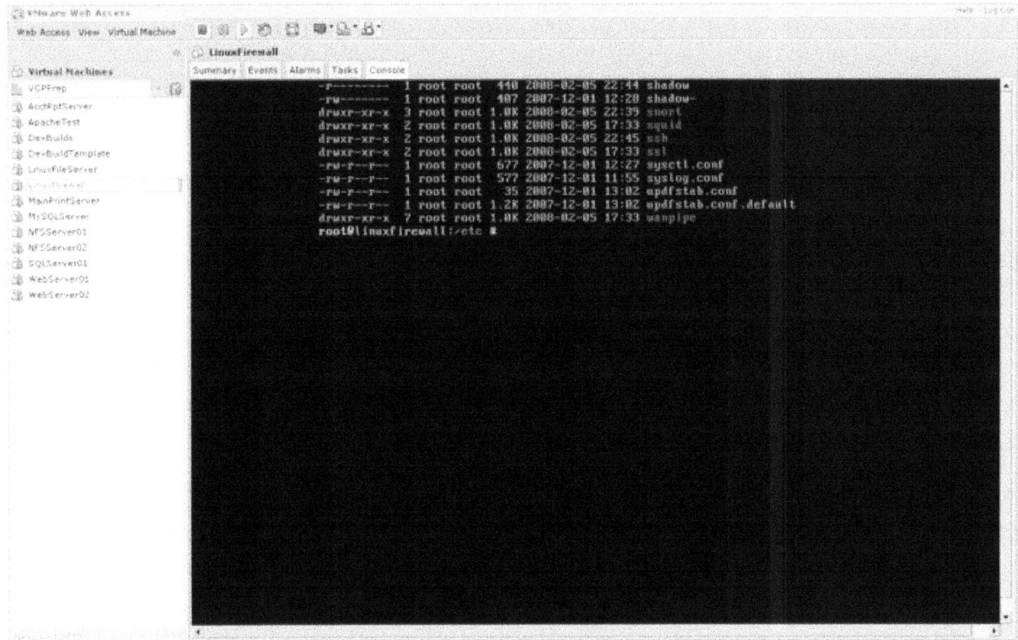

Figure 6.60 Web Access Virtual Machine Console Tab

Figure 6.60 displays a Linux based virtual machine operating in CLI (Command Line Interface) mode. Using the Console tab allows ESX 3.5 administrators and end users the ability to interact with the running guest OS. The performance experienced when interacting with a guest OS via the Console tab is dependent on network connection performance. End users may report a virtual machine performance issue when the slow response time is due to a network connectivity bottleneck or mis-configuration.

Remote Console URL

You can generate a URL link that can be sent via e-mail to give an individual remote access to a virtual machine.

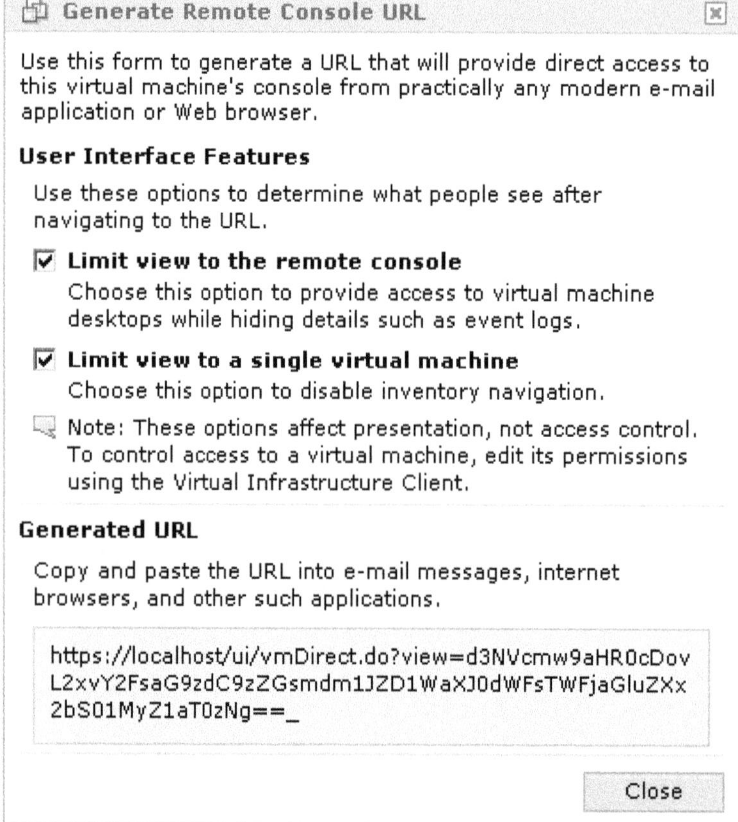

Figure 6.61 Web Access Generate Remote Console URL

The window as shown in Figure 6.61 has two check boxes:

- Limit view to the remote console
- Limit view to a single virtual machine

The first check box will limit the remote viewer to see just the remote console view. The second check box limits the view to just a single VM. The link box at the bottom of the screen contains the URL. Highlight the link and copy and paste it into an e-mail to send it to the VM's remote viewer.

Troubleshooting Common VirtualCenter 2.5 Problems

When troubleshooting VirtualCenter related issues, consult the VirtualCenter log files. VirtualCenter itself runs as a Windows service named vpxd. The log files for the vpxd service are located in the Temp (%Temp%) directory of the user running the vpxd service. Since this user is often the Windows Administrator account, the log files are typically found in the following location:

C:\Windows\Temp\vpx

These log files are named as vpxd-#.log where # is a number in the range of 0-9. Therefore, a total of 10 vpxd log files may be available. The log files rotate each time the vpxd service is started or when a log file becomes 5 MB in size. The currently used vpxd log file is listed in the vpxd-index file. Modifications to the default logging behavior can be made within the following XML (Extensible Markup Language) based file:

%ALLUSERSPROFILE%\Application Data\VMware\VMware VirtualCenter\vpxd.cfg

If VirtualCenter crashes, the crash files will be located in the following directory:

%USERPROFILE%\Application Data\VMware

Since VirtualCenter runs as a Windows Service, it is important to check the Windows event logs as well for clues relating to VirtualCenter's status. In addition, VirtualCenter depends on connectivity to it's database server. If VirtualCenter will not start, check the database server log files. Issues with the ODBC driver may be preventing a successful connection from being made. If the database port number has been changed, this would prevent a connection from the VirtualCenter server. Review any firewall ports that may have been recently blocked if the database server is on a different server from the VirtualCenter server.

The verbosity of VirtualCenter logs can be increased by selecting the Administration menu in the VI Client. Then select VirtualCenter Management Server Configuration to open the dialog box. In the left window pane, the Logging Options should be selected. By doing so, the right window pane will display a drop down box that allows the various logging options to be selected. VirtualCenter also provides the ability to generate a support bundle from within the VI Client using the Export Diagnostics Data option. Alternatively, the "vc-support.wsf" command can be issued on the VirtualCenter server to generate a support bundle. Support bundles can also be created by clicking on the Windows Start button, selecting VMware and then Generate VirtualCenter Server log bundle.

The issue connecting to VirtualCenter may be related to problems with the VI Client. The VI Client log files are located in the following location:

%TEMP%\vpx

NOTE: the Windows %TEMP% environment variable is specific to the logged on user. These log files are also rotated as viclient-#.log file where # is a number in the range 0-9.

Issues with accessing the Web Access component can be found in the following location:

C:\Program Files\VMware\VMware VirtualCenter 2.0\tomcat\logs

Issues with connecting to the guest operating system of a virtual machine via a VirtualCenter remote console are logged in the following location:

%TEMP%\vmware-%USERNAME%\vmware-%USERNAME%-pid.log

It is a good practice to only give the login credentials of the local administrator account on the machine where VirtualCenter is located to authorized individuals. Having the ability to log into the VirtualCenter server as administrator offers complete control over the server. Unauthorized access can potentially affect all hosts and virtual machines being managed by VirtualCenter.

External References

The VMware ESX 3.5 and ESXi Server version 3.5 Documentation Page:

http://www.vmware.com/support/pubs/vi_pubs.html

ESX Server 3.5 and VirtualCenter 2.5 Release Notes:

http://www.vmware.com/support/vi3/doc/vi3_esx35_vc25_rel_notes.html

ESX Server 3 Installation Guide:

http://www.vmware.com/pdf/vi3_35/esx_3/r35/vi3_35_25_installation_guide.pdf

Basic System Administration Guide:

http://www.vmware.com/pdf/vi3_35/esx_3/r35/vi3_35_25_admin_guide.pdf

Server Configuration Guide:

http://www.vmware.com/pdf/vi3_301_201_server_config.pdf

VirtualCenter Database Sizing Calculator for Microsoft SQL Server:

http://www.vmware.com/support/vi3/doc/vc_db_calculator.xls

Virtual Infrastructure Web Access Administrator's Guide:

http://www.vmware.com/pdf/vi3_35/esx_3/r35/vi3_35_25_web_access.pdf

Running VirtualCenter in a Virtual Machine:

http://www.vmware.com/pdf/vi3_vc_in_vm.pdf

VirtualCenter Monitoring and Performance Statistics:

http://www.vmware.com/pdf/vi3_monitoring_statistics_note.pdf

VMware SDK & API Developer Resources page:

http://www.vmware.com/support/pubs/sdk_pubs.html

Sample Test Questions

1. An IT department has virtualized two database servers. These servers are located on two separate ESX 3.5 servers and are required to maintain a high level of uptime. The IT department's decision to implement an HA (High Availability) cluster will require which of the following?

a. DRS (Distributed Resource Scheduler)

b. Six Virtual Switches

c. VirtualCenter 2.5

d. VMotion

e. RDM (Raw Device Mapping)

2. A company's virtualization design team has purchased a physical server that will be used to run the VirtualCenter 2.5 server. This physical machine has 2 CPUs and 3 GB of memory. Which of the following represent the maximum number of virtual machines and ESX 3.5 server hosts that the VirtualCenter 2.5 server can support?

a. 80 hosts and 500 virtual machines

b. 180 hosts and 1400 virtual machines

c. 75 hosts and 600 virtual machines

d. 90 hosts and 700 virtual machines

e. 200 hosts and 2000 virtual machines

3. Within the VI Client, the error message "(not responding)" is being display next to an ESX 3.5 server. The VirtualCenter 2.5 server is unable to make a connection to the ESX 3.5 server. Which of the following services should the IT department verify is actively running on the service console?

a. DRS

b. Apache Tomcat

c. HA

d. vpxa

e. vpxad

4. A lab technician installing a test VI3 environment inquires about the proper sequence of installation. The virtualization support staff respond with the recommended order of installation. Select the correct order of installation from the following list?

a. License Server

b. Database Connection

c. Database Server

d. Virtual Infrastructure Client

e. VirtualCenter 2.5 Server

5. A faulty port on an Ethernet switch has caused the license server to become unavailable. If this network connectivity failure goes unnoticed, how long will the majority of features in the VI3 environment remain unaffected?

a. 7 days

b. 14 days

c. 21 days

d. 28 days

e. 35 days

6. During the virtualization deployment meeting, the license type for the VI3 environment was selected. Which of the following are valid VI3 license types?

a. Static

b. Standard

c. Advanced

d. Base

e. Foundation

7. The Windows Administrator is asked to verify that the VirtualCenter 2.5 services are installed. Within the Windows Control Panel Services application, which of the following services should the Windows Administrator look for?

a. VMware vpdx

b. VMware Virtual Infrastructure Web Access

c. VMware Virtual Mount Manager Extended

d. VMware VirtualCenter 2.5 Server

e. VMware Virtual VMM

8. An organization recently built a secondary datacenter at a remote location. The remote location will include 5 new ESX 3.5 blade servers. The administrator needs to manage the additional ESX 3.5 blade servers with the VirtualCenter 2.5 Server located at the primary datacenter. Which of the following ports should the administrator verify

will be able to pass through the firewall so that the VirtualCenter 2.5 Server can properly manage the new ESX 3.5 blade servers?

a. 801

b. 702

c. 931

d. 8099

e. 902

9. The Database Administrator is tasked with configuring the database server for the VirtualCenter 2.5 Server production environment. Company policies require the use of only supported database servers. Which of the following are supported production databases for VirtualCenter 2.5?

a. Ingres

b. Oracle

c. MySQL

d. MS SQL

e. MSDE

10. The Datacenter object within the VirtualCenter 2.5 inventory is where datastores, networks, ESX 3.5 hosts and virtual machines are configured. Besides being the primary organizational unit of the VirtualCenter 2.5 inventory, which of the following is also true of the Datacenter object?

a. Datacenter object cannot be used when applying permissions

b. VMotion Boundary

c. Datacenter object can only contain a maximum of 6 ESX 3.5 host servers

d. A maximum of 2 VirtualCenter 2.5 Servers can manage the same Datacenter object

e. Datacenter object can only contain a maximum of 8 ESX 3.5 host servers

11. The IT group's Disaster Recovery (DR) policy requires that provisions be made to recover from an ESX 3.5 Server failure. Which of the following does the cluster object provide to meet the DR requirements?

a. DRS

b. MSCS

c. HA

d. VMotion

e. Persistent mode

12. The VI Client when used to connect to a VirtualCenter 2.5 Server can be used for quickly identifying inadequate resource settings, ESX 3.5 host settings and other common mis-configurations and settings. Which of the following are valid VirtualCenter 2.5 inventory views?

a. Datastores

b. Resources

c. Virtual Machines & Templates

d. Networks

e. Hosts & Clusters

13. An ESX 3.5 administrator is surprised to discover that some functionality of the VI3 environment is only possible when accessing the VirtualCenter 2.5 Server with the VI Client. Which of the following can only be accomplished from within VirtualCenter 2.5?

a. Template Creation

b. Firewall Modifications

c. Network Configurations

d. Changing the power state of virtual machines

e. Restarting an ESX 3.5 server host

14. A standalone ESX 3.5 server was recently added under the management of the VirtualCenter 2.5 server. The ESX Administrator is questioning why the VI Client GUI no longer shows the User & Groups tab when accessing the VirtualCenter 2.5 server. Why is this tab no longer available?

a. The vpxd.config file needs to be modified in order to display the User & Groups tab

b. The service console users and groups need synchronize with VirtualCenter 2.5

c. VirtualCenter 2.5 uses both the local machine and Active Directory users and groups

d. The users and groups need to be recreated after adding the ESX 3.5 host to VirtualCenter 2.5

e. The ESX 3.5 host needs to be rebooted after being added to VirtualCenter 2.5

15. The use of folders within the VirtualCenter 2.5 inventory provide a means to properly structure and organize the various objects. Folders can also be used for which of the following purposes?

a. VMotion Boundary

b. Resource Limits

c. Storage Access Management

d. Permissions

e. Customize inventory views

16. A junior administrator is at a remote location when asked to troubleshoot a virtual machine performance issue? The junior administrator does not have the VI Client installed and decides to use VirtualCenter 2.5's Web Access. Which of the following can be performed by the junior administrator using Web Access?

a. Make modifications to the ESX 3.5 server's configuration

b. Clone a virtual machine

c. Access the guest OS of a virtual machine

d. Add virtual hardware to a virtual machine

e. Review the recent events and alarms for a virtual machine

17. You have been tasked to install VirtualCenter 2.5 on a physical server. Which of the following operating systems are not supported to install VirtualCenter 2.5 on?

a. Windows XP Pro SP2 32-bit version

b. Red Hat Linux version 7.0 or newer

c. Windows 2003 64 □bit version

d. Windows 2000 Server SP4 with Update Rollup 1

e. Windows 2003 Server SP1 32-bit version

18. You are planning to install VirtualCenter 2.5 in a VM on one of your existing ESX 3.5 servers. Which of the following should you not do to the VirtualCenter 2.5 VM once it is installed?

a. Power down the VirtualCenter 2.5 virtual machine

b. Snapshot the VirtualCenter 2.5 virtual machine

c. Cold-migrate the VirtualCenter 2.5 virtual machine

d. Clone the VirtualCenter 2.5 virtual machine

e. Edit the VirtualCenter 2.5 virtual machine hardware properties

19. You have been called in to review the CPU usage of a specific ESX 3.5 server over a period of time. Which of the following tabs can show you this information?

a. The Summary Tab

b. The Virtual Machines Tab

c. The Performance Tab

d. The Configuration Tab

e. The Tasks & Events Tab

20. You need to see the various relationships of datastores that the ESX 3.5 servers have access to using VirtualCenter 2.5. Which tab will show you this information?

a. The Configuration Tab

b. The Virtual Machines Tab

c. The Summary Tab

d. The Network Tab

e. The Maps Tab

21. Two add-on license features were purchased for the accounting department's new virtualization project. The accounting department's VI3 environment license type is server-based mode. There are 4 ESX 3.5 servers, one VirtualCenter 2.5 server and one license server. The license department requires regular backups for all license files. How many license files will be needed to be backed up for the accounting departments new VI3 environment?

a. 1

b. 2

c. 3

d. 4

e. 6

22. Two ESX 3.5 servers are purchased for the software development team using host-based license mode. Which of the following will the development team be unable to accomplish?

a. Virtual Machine Creation

b. Virtual Switch Creation

c. VMotion

d. iSCSI storage

e. FC storage

23. Unable to connect to perform administration work on the Apache Tomcat web server running on the VirtualCenter 2.5 server, which of the following ports should the ESX 3.5 administrator verify is not being blocked on the firewall?

a. 9091

b. 448

c. 635

d. 8086

e. 710

24. An ESX administrator returning from a two week vacation is unable to restart any virtual machines. Which of the following should be checked as being a possible root cause of the problem?

a. Web Access service has stopped

b. vpxd service has stopped

c. License server service has stopped

d. VMware Virtual Mount Manager Extended service has stopped

e. VMware VirtualCenter 2.5 service has stopped

25. A VI3 consultant is brought in to evaluate a possible VI3 solution for a company. When asked which core services does VirtualCenter 2.5 provide, the consultant accurately responds with which of the following?

a. Statistics logging

b. Task scheduler

c. Alarm management

d. Event management

e. Virtual machine provisioning

Sample Test Solutions

1. An IT department has virtualized two database servers. These servers are located on two separate ESX 3.5 servers and are required to maintain a high level of uptime. The IT department's decision to implement an HA (High Availability) cluster will require which of the following?

a. DRS (Distributed Resource Scheduler)

b. Six Virtual Switches

c. VirtualCenter 2.5

d. VMotion

e. RDM (Raw Device Mapping)

Answer: c - VirtualCenter 2.5 is required to configure an HA (High Availability) cluster. Once an HA cluster has been configured, it will perform fail over operations without the VirtualCenter 2.5 server currently running.

2. A company's virtualization design team has purchased a physical server that will be used to run the VirtualCenter 2.5 server. This physical machine has 2 CPUs and 3 GB of memory. Which of the following represent the maximum number of virtual machines and ESX 3.5 server hosts that the VirtualCenter 2.5 server can support?

a. 80 hosts and 500 virtual machines

b. 180 hosts and 1400 virtual machines

c. 75 hosts and 600 virtual machines

d. 90 hosts and 700 virtual machines

e. 100 hosts and 1500 virtual machines

Answer: e - A VirtualCenter 2.5 server when configured with 2 CPUs and 3 GB of memory can support a maximum of 200 ESX 3.5 server hosts and 2000 virtual machines.

3. Within the VI Client, the error message "(not responding)" is being display next to an ESX 3.5 server. The VirtualCenter 2.5 server is unable to make a connection to the ESX 3.5 server. Which of the following services should the IT department verify is actively running on the service console?

a. DRS

b. Apache Tomcat

c. HA

d. vpxa

e. vpxad

Answer: d - vpxa is the VirtualCenter 2.5 Agent service responsible for sending task requests from the VirtualCenter 2.5 server to the ESX 3.5 host. The vpxa agent forwards the VirtualCenter 2.5 task requests to the hostd service. The VirtualCenter 2.5 Agent can be restarted with the following command within the service console:

service vmware-vpxa restart

4. A lab technician installing a test VI3 environment inquires about the proper sequence of installation. The virtualization support staff respond with the recommended order of installation. Select the correct order of installation from the following list?

a. License Server

b. Database Connection

c. Database Server

d. Virtual Infrastructure Client

e. VirtualCenter 2.5 Server

Answer: c, b, a, e & d - The recommended order of installation is as follows:

1. ***Database Server***
2. ***Create database connection***
3. ***License Server***
4. ***VirtualCenter 2.5 Server***
5. ***Virtual Infrastructure Client***

5. A faulty port on an Ethernet switch has caused the license server to become unavailable. If this network connectivity failure goes unnoticed, how long will the VI3 environment remain unaffected?

a. 7 days

b. 14 days

c. 21 days

d. 28 days

e. 35 days

Answer: b - A grace period of 14 days is used where the VirtualCenter 2.5 and ESX 3.5 host servers rely on cached licensing configurations that remain effective when these servers are rebooted.

6. During the virtualization deployment meeting, the license type for the VI3 environment was selected. Which of the following are valid VI3 license types?

a. Static

b. Standard

c. Advanced

d. Base

e. Foundation

Answer: b & e - The two license types for VirtualCenter 2.5 are Foundation and Standard.

7. The Windows Administrator is asked to verify that the VirtualCenter 2.5 services are installed. Within the Windows Control Panel Services application, which of the following services should the Windows Administrator look for?

a. VMware vpdx

b. VMware Virtual Infrastructure Web Access

c. VMware Virtual Mount Manager Extended

d. VMware VirtualCenter 2.5 Server

e. VMware Virtual VMM

Answer: b, c & d - The VMware Virtual Infrastructure Web Access service provides the ability to manager virtual machines from a web browser. VMware Virtual Mount Manager Extended is invoked as needed. This service is needed when cloning or deploying a VM from a template within the guest OS customization wizard. The VMware VirtualCenter 2.5 Server service manages all tasks performed on virtual machines and ESX 3.5 host servers.

8. An organization recently built a secondary datacenter at a remote location. The remote location will include 5 new ESX 3.5 blade servers. The administrator needs to managed the additional ESX 3.5 blade servers with the VirtualCenter 2.5 Server located at the primary datacenter. Which of the following ports should the administrator verify will be able to pass through the firewall so that the VirtualCenter 2.5 Server can properly manage the new ESX 3.5 blade servers?

a. 801

b. 702

c. 931

d. 8099

e. 902

Answer: e - Port 902 is used by VirtualCenter 2.5 to manage ESX 3.5 host servers. Ensure this port is open if the VirtualCenter 2.5 Server must pass through a firewall.

9. The Database Administrator is tasked with configuring the database server for the VirtualCenter 2.5 Server production environment. Company policies require the use of only supported database servers. Which of the following are supported production databases for VirtualCenter 2.5?

a. Ingres

b. Oracle

c. MySQL

d. MS SQL

e. MSDE

Answer: b & d - Only Oracle and MS SQL servers are supported in production environments. Check the Installation and Upgrade Guide and the latest Release Notes for the current list of supported databases.

10. The Datacenter object within the VirtualCenter 2.5 inventory is where datastores, networks, ESX 3.5 hosts and virtual machines are configured. Besides being the primary organizational unit of the VirtualCenter 2.5 inventory, which of the following is also true of the Datacenter object?

a. Datacenter object cannot be used when applying permissions

b. VMotion Boundary

c. Datacenter object can only contain a maximum of 6 ESX 3.5 host servers

d. A maximum of 2 VirtualCenter 2.5 Servers can manage the same Datacenter object

e. Datacenter object can only contain a maximum of 8 ESX 3.5 host servers

Answer: b - VMotion is restricted to ESX 3.5 host servers within the same Datacenter object. Proper planning is needed when designing the VI3 environment to ensure the proper functionality is provided.

11. The IT group's Disaster Recovery (DR) policy requires that provisions be made to recover from an ESX 3.5 Server failure. Which of the following does the cluster object provide to meet the DR requirements?

a. DRS

b. MSCS

c. HA

d. VMotion

e. Persistent mode

Answer: c - Cluster objects can be configured as a DRS (Distributed Resource Scheduler) cluster, an HA (High Availability cluster or both. Only the HA cluster functionality provides fail over capabilities to satisfy DR policies.

12. The VI Client when used to connect to a VirtualCenter 2.5 Server can be used for quickly identifying inadequate resource settings, ESX 3.5 host settings and other common mis-configurations and settings. Which of the following are valid

VirtualCenter 2.5 inventory views?

a. Datastores

b. Resources

c. Virtual Machines & Templates

d. Networks

e. Hosts & Clusters

Answer: a, c, d & e - The following are the four inventory views provided by VirtualCenter 2.5:

1. ***Hosts & Clusters***
2. ***Virtual Machines & Templates***
3. ***Networks***
4. ***Datastores***

13. An ESX 3.5 administrator is surprised to discover that some functionality of the VI3 environment is only possible when accessing the VirtualCenter 2.5 Server with the VI Client. Which of the following can only be accomplished from within VirtualCenter 2.5?

a. Template Creation

b. Firewall Modifications

c. Network Configurations

d. Changing the power state of virtual machines

e. Restarting an ESX 3.5 server host

Answer: a - The creation of templates is only available with VirtualCenter 2.5.

14. A standalone ESX 3.5 server was recently added under the management of the VirtualCenter 2.5 server. The ESX Administrator is questioning why the VI Client GUI no longer shows the User & Groups tab when accessing the VirtualCenter 2.5 server. Why is this tab no longer available?

a. The vpxd.config file needs to be modified in order to display the User & Groups tab

b. The service console users and groups need synchronize with VirtualCenter 2.5

c. VirtualCenter 2.5 uses both the local machine and Active Directory users and groups

d. The users and groups need to be recreated after adding the ESX 3.5 host to VirtualCenter 2.5

e. The ESX 3.5 host needs to be rebooted after being added to VirtualCenter 2.5

Answer: c - VirtualCenter 2.5 does not utilize the ESX 3.5 server's service console users and

groups. The users and groups made available to the VirtualCenter 2.5 server are from either the local machine where VirtualCenter 2.5 is installed or from the Active Directory domain.

15. The use of folders within the VirtualCenter 2.5 inventory provide a means to properly structure and organize the various objects. Folders can also be used for which of the following purposes?

a. VMotion Boundary

b. Resource Limits

c. Storage Access Management

d. Permissions

e. Customize inventory views

Answer: d - Folders are used to provide useful organization within the VirtualCenter 2.5 inventory. Applying permissions to a folder that contains a Datacenter object for example can be an easy method of implementing access control for several objects at once.

16. A junior administrator is at a remote location when asked to troubleshoot a virtual machine performance issue? The junior administrator does not have the VI Client installed and decides to use VirtualCenter 2.5's Web Access. Which of the following can be performed by the junior administrator using Web Access?

a. Make modifications to the ESX 3.5 server's configuration

b. Clone a virtual machine

c. Access the guest OS of a virtual machine

d. Add virtual hardware to a virtual machine

e. Review the recent events and alarms for a virtual machine

Answer: c, d & e - Web Access allows access to the guest OS running within a virtual machine. Access to the guest OS is useful for end users needing to perform tasks within the virtual machine. Virtual hardware can be added to a virtual machine from within the Web Access interface. Web Access provides the recent events, alarms and tasks for a virtual machine making it useful for administration and troubleshooting purposes

17. You have been tasked to install VirtualCenter 2.5 on a physical server. Which of the following operating systems are not supported to install VirtualCenter 2.5 on?

a. Windows XP Pro SP2 32-bit version

b. Red Hat Linux version 7.0 or newer

c. Windows 2003 64-bit version

d. Windows 2000 Server SP4 with Update Rollup 1

e. Windows 2003 Server SP1 32-bit version

Answer: b and c - Only Windows XP Pro SP2 32-bit version, Windows 2000 Server SP4 with Update Rollup 1, Windows 2003 Server SP1 32-bit version and Windows 2003 Server R2 32-bit version are supported to install VirtualCenter 2.5.

18. You are planning to install VirtualCenter 2.5 in a VM on one of your existing ESX 3.5 servers. Which of the following should you not do to the VirtualCenter 2.5 VM once it is installed?

a. Power down the VirtualCenter 2.5 virtual machine

b. Snapshot the VirtualCenter 2.5 virtual machine

c. Cold-migrate the VirtualCenter 2.5 virtual machine

d. Clone the VirtualCenter 2.5 virtual machine

e. Edit the VirtualCenter 2.5 virtual machine hardware properties

Answer: a, c, and d - Snapshots and modifying virtual machine hardware properties are allowed on a VirtualCenter 2.5 VM.

19. You have been called in to review the CPU usage of a specific ESX 3.5 server over a period of time. Which of the following tabs can show you this information?

a. The Summary Tab

b. The Virtual Machines Tab

c. The Performance Tab

d. The Configuration Tab

e. The Tasks & Events Tab

Answer: c - this is the only tab that can be configured to show performance data over a time period. Some of the other views can show the current CPU usage but not over a period of time.

20. You need to see the various relationships of datastores that the ESX 3.5 servers have access to using VirtualCenter 2.5. Which tab will show you this information?

a. The Configuration Tab

b. The Virtual Machines Tab

c. The Summary Tab

d. The Network Tab

e. The Maps Tab

Answer: a and e - The Configuration tab can be used to provide this information by selecting the Datastores link in the Hardware Section of the Configuration tab. The maps tab can show relationships between VM's, ESX 3.5 servers, datastores and virtual switches.

21. Two add-on license features were purchased for the accounting department's new virtualization project. The accounting department's VI3 environment license type is server-based mode. There are 4 ESX 3.5 servers, one VirtualCenter 2.5 server and one license server. The license department requires regular backups for all license files. How many license files will need to be backed up for the accounting departments new VI3 environment?

a. 1

b. 2

c. 3

d. 4

e. 6

Answer: a - The license server will contain one license file for the VI3 environment. The default license file will be stored on the license server in the following location:

C:\Program Files\VMware\VMware License Server\Licenses

22. Two ESX 3.5 servers are purchased for the software development team using host-based license mode. Which of the following will the development team be unable to accomplish?

a. Virtual Machine Creation

b. Virtual Switch Creation

c. VMotion

d. iSCSI storage

e. FC storage

Answer: c - VMotion is a feature provided by VirtualCenter 2.5. VirtualCenter 2.5 requires its license type to be the license server-based mode.

23. Unable to connect to perform administration work on the Apache Tomcat web server running on the VirtualCenter 2.5 server, which of the following ports should the ESX 3.5 administrator verify is not being blocked on the firewall?

a. 9091

b. 448

c. 635

d. 8086

e. 710

Answer: d - 8086 is the Apache Tomcat web server administration port used on the VirtualCenter 2.5 server.

24. An ESX administrator returning from a two week vacation is unable to restart any virtual machines. Which of the following should be checked as being a possible root cause of the problem?

a. Web Access service has stopped

b. vpxd service has stopped

c. License server service has stopped

d. VMware Virtual Mount Manager Extended service has stopped

e. VMware VirtualCenter 2.5 service has stopped

Answer: c - The license server has a grace period of 14 days. After the grace period expires, virtual machines will no longer be able to be restarted.

25. A VI3 consultant is brought in to evaluate a possible VI3 solution for a company. When asked which core services does VirtualCenter 2.5 provide, the consultant accurately responds with which of the following?

a. Statistics logging

b. Task scheduler

c. Alarm management

d. Event management

e. Virtual machine provisioning

Answer: a, b, c, d, & e - VirtualCenter 2.5 provides the following core services:

1. ***Management of the ESX 3.5 servers and VMs***
2. ***Statistics logging***
3. ***Task scheduler***
4. ***Alarm management***
5. ***Event management***
6. ***Virtual machine provisioning***
7. ***Host configuration***
8. ***Virtual machine configuration***

Chapter 7

Virtual Machines

After reading this chapter you should be able to complete the following tasks:

- Understand and plan CPU, memory, NIC, and disk requirements for virtual machines
- Explain the purpose of the different VM state files
- Explain the purpose and differences of the disk modes
- Create installation media for virtual machines
- Create a new virtual machine
- Install a guest operating system into a VM
- Install and configure VMware Tools
- Change your VM's existing configuration
- Add an extra disk to your VM
- Add a raw device to your VM
- Setting various virtual machine options
- Understand the various methods to rapidly deploy VM's
- Clone a VM
- Clone a VM to a template
- Cloning A Virtual Machine To Another Datacenter
- Convert a VM to a template
- Deploy a VM from a template
- Deploying A Virtual Machine From A Template To Another Datacenter
- Convert a template to a VM
- Clone a template
- Use the customization wizard
- Troubleshooting common virtual machine problems

Planning CPU, Memory, NIC, And Disk Requirements For Virtual Machines

When planning your virtual machine resource requirements you should look at any existing installations on physical systems when possible for benchmarks. The resources needed to support the operating system and applications on a physical server should equate to similar requirements for your virtual machine. You should have an idea before building your VM as to the following resource requirements to meet your needs:

- Number of virtual processors (choose more than one virtual CPU if your applications support multi-threading)
- Total processing power needed (in MHz) to support OS and application requirements
- Total memory needed (in MBytes) to support OS and application requirements
- Total number of virtual networking adapters to support networking requirements
- Total number of virtual host bus adapters needed (more than one if multi-pathing is needed for redundancy)
- Total number of virtual hard disks and size required to support file systems and storage requirements
- Total number of virtual CDROM devices needed to support OS and application requirements
- Total number of virtual floppy devices needed to support OS and application requirements
- Guest OS licensing requirements

You can reconfigure your virtual machine after it has been built and has an OS installed in it, but only virtual disks can be added while the guest OS is running.

VM State Files

A Virtual Machine when created consists of a set of distinct files located on the local, private or shared storage resources that are configured to be accessed by the ESX 3.5 server. Let's examine the location and purpose of each of these VM state files.

Location of VM State Files

The files can be stored either on a VMFS or NFS datastore. If they are located on

a VMFS, the location would be as follows:

/vmfs/volumes/<Volume Name>/<VM Name>/[VM State Files Here]

For example the location of the state files for a VM named MyVM located on the

VCPvmfs VMFS volume would be:

/vmfs/volumes/VCPvmfs/MyVM/

When you create a VMFS volume, a directory containing a Universal Unique Identifier (UUID) is built. A link to that

directory is created using the name that was given to that datastore.

The following is an example of a path to a virtual machine named MyVM:

/vmfs/volumes/474da1fc-88d1d726-8add-0014c23d3686/MyVM

In the above UUID, the VMkernel creates the UUID as follows:

- 474da1fc- The service console time when the VMFS volume was created
- 88d1d726- The CPU time when the VMFS volume was created
- 8add- Randomly generated value
- 0014c23d3686 - The MAC address of the physical NIC port on the ESX Server that the service console is using

The purpose of the UUID is ensuring that the VMkernel can uniquely identify a VMFS volume. The UUID is stored within the virtual machine configuration file. If the virtual machine files are relocated to another VMFS volume, the virtual machine configuration file will need to be modified with the proper UUID of the VMFS volume it is located on. This process is known as registering a virtual machine.

In the VMFS directory will reside a subdirectory representing the VMs name. The state files will be located there.

On a NFS share they will reside in the shared NFS directory.

Extensions of VM State Files

The following are the various extensions of the VM state files:

- .vmx - virtual machine configuration file
- .vmdk - virtual disk configuration file
- -flat.vmdk - virtual disk data file
- .nvram - virtual machine BIOS file
- .vswp - virtual machine swap file
- vmware.log - virtual machine log file
- vmware-#.log - virtual machine old log files
- .vmsd - virtual machine snapshot file
- -Snapshot#.vmsn - virtual machine snapshot state file
- .vmss - virtual machine suspend state file

The Virtual Machine Configuration File

The VM configuration file ends with the .vmx extension and contains the configuration information for the VM.

The following is an example of a virtual machine configuration file:

MyVM.vmx

#!/usr/bin/vmware

```
config.version = "8"
virtualHW.version = "4"
floppy0.present = "true"
nvram = "MyVM.nvram"
powerType.powerOff = "default"
powerType.powerOn = "default"
powerType.suspend = "default"
powerType.reset = "default"
displayName = "MyVM"
extendedConfigFile = "MyVM.vmxf"
scsi0.present = "true"
scsi0.sharedBus = "none"
scsi0.virtualDev = "lsilogic"
memsize = "256"
scsi0:0.present = "true"
scsi0:0.fileName = "MyVM.vmdk"
scsi0:0.deviceType = "scsi-hardDisk"
ide0:0.present = "true"
ide0:0.clientDevice = "FALSE"
ide0:0.deviceType = "cdrom-image"
ide0:0.startConnected = "true"
floppy0.startConnected = "false"
floppy0.clientDevice = "true"
ethernet0.present = "true"
ethernet0.allowGuestConnectionControl = "false"
ethernet0.networkName = "VCPPREP"
ethernet0.addressType = "vpx"
ethernet0.generatedAddress = "00:50:56:b5:7a:db"
guestOS = "winnetstandard"
uuid.bios = "50 35 a0 6a 02 9b 02 67-0a 71 01 55 17 b3 54 96"
toolScripts.afterPowerOn = "true"
```

toolScripts.afterResume = "true"

toolScripts.beforeSuspend = "true"

toolScripts.beforePowerOff = "true"

ide0:0.fileName = "/vmfs/volumes/c33657ff-3124fc91/CDROM.iso"

floppy0.fileName = "/dev/fd0"

scsi0:0.redo = ""

uuid.location = "56 4d fe 8a cf e2 9e ee-9f 96 bf 4f e6 10 de 6e"

sched.swap.derivedName = "/vmfs/volumes/474da1fc-88d1d726-8add-0014c23d3686/MyVM/MyVM-9868c7cf.vswp"

tools.syncTime = "TRUE"

The Virtual Disk Configuration File

When you create a virtual disk a .vmdk file is created that contains configuration information about the virtual disk. The following is an example of a virtual disk configuration file:

MyVM.vmdk

Disk DescriptorFile

version=1

CID=cb31c634

parentCID=ffffffff

createType="vmfs"

Extent description

RW 4194304 VMFS "MyVM-flat.vmdk"

The Disk Data Base

#DDB

ddb.toolsVersion = "7201"

ddb.adapterType = "lsilogic"

ddb.geometry.sectors = "63"

ddb.geometry.heads = "255"

ddb.geometry.cylinders = "261"

ddb.virtualHWVersion = "4"

The Virtual Disk Data File

The -flat.vmdk file contains the actual virtual disk data. When you choose to make a 10 GB virtual disk for a virtual machine called MyVM for example, this is the file that will be 10 GB in size.

For example: MyVM-flat.vmdk would be the name of the data file created for a virtual disk called MyVM.

Virtual Machine BIOS File

The .nvram file is a binary file that contains the BIOS and the settings for the VM. The default settings can be changed by interrupting the boot process of a VM by pressing the F2 key on the keyboard and editing the BIOS settings.

The Virtual Machine Swap File

The .vswp file gets created when the VM is powered on and deleted when it

is powered off. Its size is the difference between the maximum memory setting

for the VM and its memory reservation setting. Reservations will be discussed in detail in Chapter 11 - Resource Optimization.

For example:

If the VM has a memory reservation of 256 MB and it has a maximum memory setting

of 1024 MB then a 768 MB swap file will be created provided the free space exists

on the file system. If there is not enough free space, the VM will not power on.

The Virtual Machine Log File

The vmware.log file contains log entries generated by the virtual machine. These log entries can be informational messages or contain error information. Every time a VM powers on, a new log file is created.

The Virtual Machine Old Log Entries

Virtual machine log files follow this syntax: vmware-#.log. Up to 6 log files are maintained by default. Logging behavior can be modified for a virtual machine by using the following attributes within the virtual machine's .vmx file.

log.rotateSize - Set the log file size in kilobytes

log.keepOld - Keep old log files

log.filename - Modify the VM log file name

logging - Turn logging on or off

The Virtual Machine Snapshot Dictionary File

The .vmsd file contains the dictionary for the snapshots for that particular virtual machine. We will discuss snapshots and the snapshot manager in Chapter 17 - VMware Consolidated Backup.

The Virtual Machine Snapshot Configuration File

The -Snapshot#.vmsn file contains the virtual machine snapshot state information.

The Virtual Machine Suspend State File

The .vmss file contains the virtual machine suspend state data. When a VM is suspended its memory contents are stored in this file.

What Are Disk Modes?

There are 3 modes that you can configure for your virtual disks in the VMs that you create:

- Independent persistent disk mode
- Independent non-persistent disk mode
- Snapshot disk mode

Independent Persistent Disk Mode

When you set the disk to use the independent persistent mode the changes that are made to files in the guest OS cause the virtual disk files to change as well. Using this mode causes those changes to be made immediately as they occur and are permanently written to the virtual disk file. This mode provides high performance for the virtual disk because of the structure of the VMFS.

Independent Non-persistent Disk Mode

The use of independent non-persistent disk mode is warranted when you don't want any changes to be applied in real time to the virtual disk file. The changes to the virtual disk are discarded when you either power off the VM or revert to a snapshot of the virtual disk. During normal operation all disk writes in the OS files are not written to the virtual disk file but instead are kept in a redo log. When the virtual machine reads from the virtual disk, it must first check the redo log. The redo log tracks the changes to the disk blocks. If the disk block is listed in the log it is then read, if it is not then the read goes to the disk for the virtual machine and reads the appropriate block.

This mode is best suited for non-production VM configurations such as a test or development environment that you want to be able to reset back to its initial state when you powered it on. By powering off the VM you will be asked to save the changes in the redo log or discard them. Using this mode will cause poor disk performance.

Snapshot Disk Mode

Snapshot disk mode is useful to capture the entire state of the VM at the time the snapshot was taken. The snapshot will contain the following:

- The configuration settings of the VM
- The memory state of the VM
- The disk states of the VM

Reverting the VM to a snapshot causes all of the VM settings and memory and virtual disks state to be restored at the time you took that snapshot. This is the default mode for virtual disk files.

Creating Installation Media for Virtual Machines

Software installations on virtual machines can be performed using physical media such as CDROMs and floppy disks. A downside to using such physical media is that physical media can be misplaced or lost. Physical servers may be located in a remote location making the use of physical media difficult or not feasible. Longer installation times are often incurred due to the limiting speeds of physical CDROM and floppy devices.

It is possible to make a file that contains the entire contents of a physical CD/DVD or floppy disk. This type of image is often referred to as an ISO image and stored on a hard disk that can be accessed by several different machines via a network share. An ISO image is saved in ISO-9660 format. ISO images contain the individual files along with the track and sector information of the physical media. Whereas physical media is inserted into a physical drive, an ISO image is mounted as a file system.

ISO images of floppy and CD/DVD disks can be created using the dd command within the ESX 3.5 server's service console. The following describes how to make an ISO image of a CD/DVD or floppy device:

Create a CD/DVD ISO Image

Place the CD/DVD media into the physical drive, but do not manually mount it. If it automatically mounts, unmount the disk using the umount command. For example, umount /dev/cdrom

Next, issue the following command:

dd if=/dev/cdrom of=/tmp/cdisoimage.iso

In the above command, the letters (if) specify the input file, in this case this is /dev/cdrom. The letters (of) specify the output file, in this case this is tmp/cdisoimage.iso

Create a Floppy ISO Image

Place the CD/DVD media into the physical drive, but do not manually mount it. If it automatically mounts, unmount the disk using the umount command. For example, umount /dev/floppy

Next, issue the following command:

dd if=/dev/floppy of=floppyisoimage.flp bs=512

Create an ISO image from Files on a Hard Drive:

You can also make an ISO using existing files on your hard drive.

First create a directory to hold the files you want created as an ISO image. For example, to create a directory within the /tmp directory called isofiles, enter the following command from the ESX 3.5 server's service console:

mkdir /tmp/isofiles

Then use the mkisofs command to create the ISO image as follows:

mkisofs -o /tmp/isofiles.iso /tmp/isofiles/

This results in a file called isofiles.iso within the /tmp which contains all the files and directories in /tmp/isofiles/.

Creating a New Virtual Machine

Creating a virtual machine provides the framework to install a guest operating system. The following steps illustrate how to build a virtual machine.

Step 1. Right mouse button click on the ESX 3.5 server that you want to build a VM on. Select the New Virtual Machine option from the pop up menu as shown in Figure 7.1.

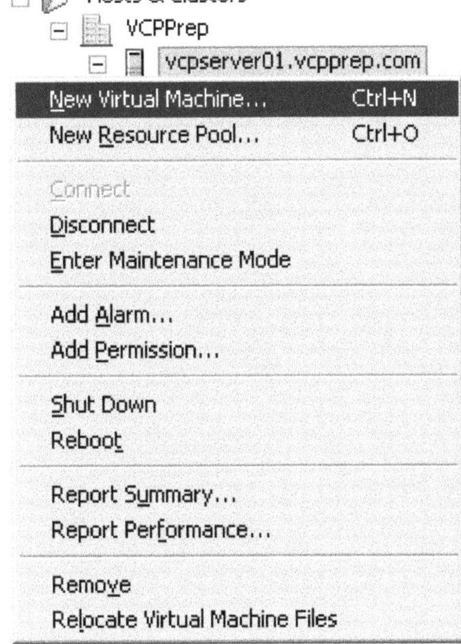

Figure 7.1 Create New Virtual Machine Menu

The New Virtual Machine Wizard will now start as shown in Figure 7.2.

Step 2. You can select either the Typical or Custom radio button in this window. The Typical option uses the default settings while the Custom option allows you to pick and choose the various custom configuration options.

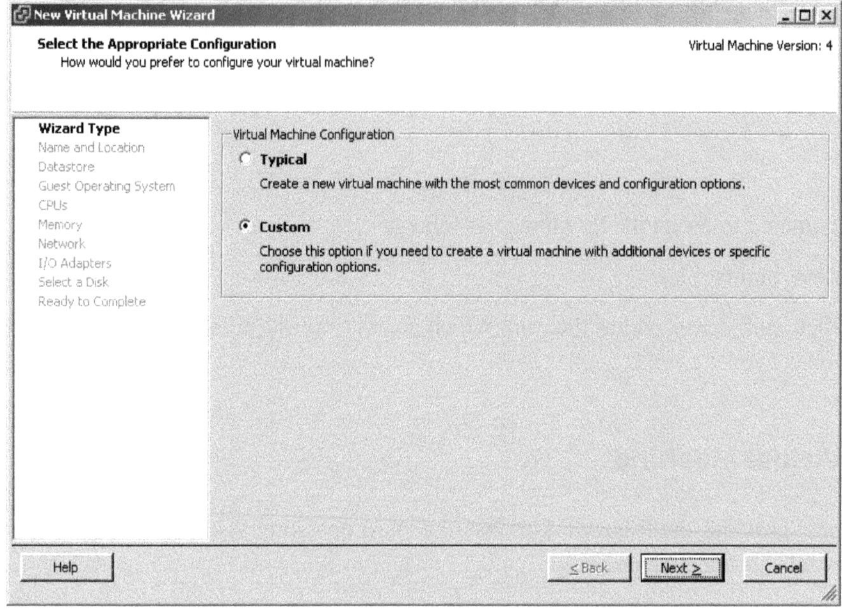

Figure 7.2 New Virtual Machine Wizard Custom Configuration

Choose the appropriate radio button and click the Next button to continue.

Step 3. The next thing you need to do is to create a name for your VM as shown in Figure 7.3. Do not use spaces in the name. This can cause issues with the ESX 3.5 server when attempting to manage the VM using the CLI and requiring the VM name as an argument, due to space characters in the VM name. Remember that the labels are case sensitive.

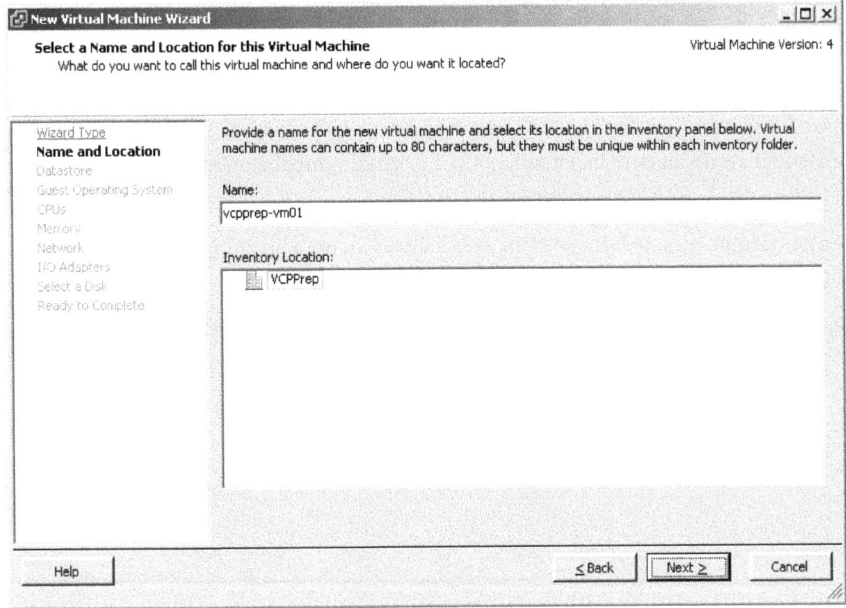

Figure 7.3 New Virtual Machine Wizard Name And Location

After you input the name click on the Next button to continue.

Step 4. Now you must select the datastore that to hold the VM state files as shown in Figure 7.4.

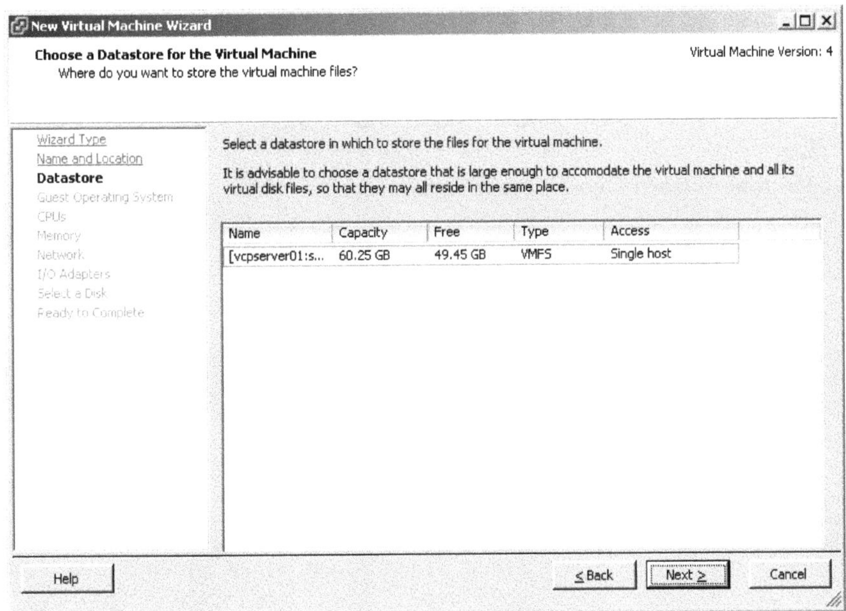

Figure 7.4 New Virtual Machine Wizard Datastore

Be sure that you choose a datastore that has enough free space to support all the files of the new VM as well as providing enough free space for the VM swap files to be created when any of the VMs on that datastore are powered on. You should also take into consideration whether the datastore is a private or local datastore. If it is you will not be able to move the VM off of the server while it is running since VMotion requires that the source and destination servers both have access to the VM state files. The new ESX Server 3.5 feature of Storage VMotion allows for the movement of files of a powered on VM to a shared datastore, so that the VM can subsequently be VMotioned to an alternate ESX Server. Storage VMotion is discussed in Chapter 13 – Virtual Machine Migration. After you select the appropriate datastore click on the Next button to continue.

Step 5. You can now choose which supported guest operating system you want to install in the virtual machine as shown in Figure 7.5.

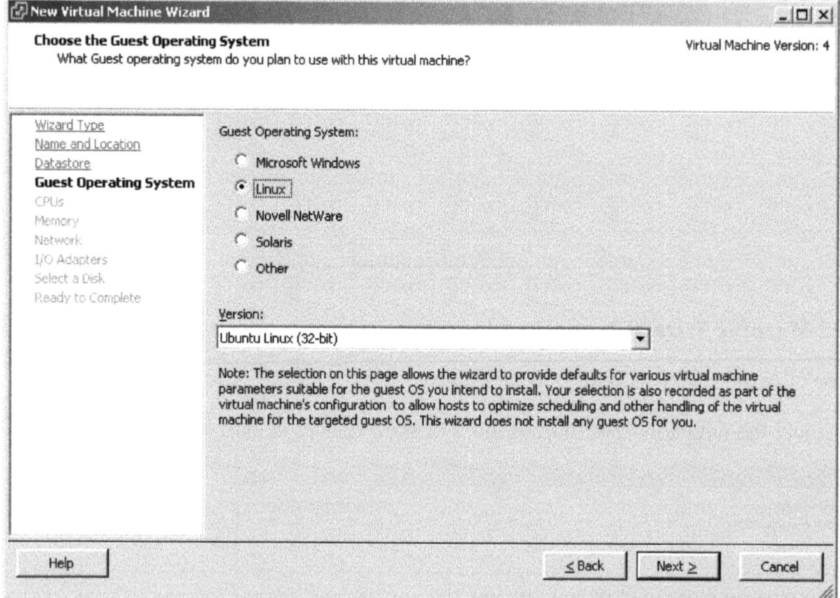

Figure 7.5 New Virtual Machine Wizard Guest Operating System

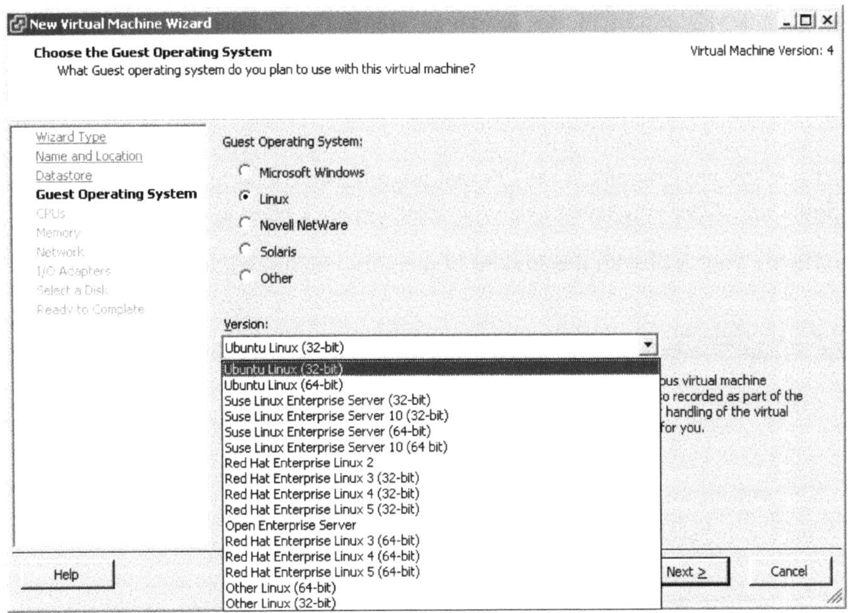

Figure 7.6 New Virtual Machine Wizard Guest Operating System List

Step 6. Select the appropriate radio button and use the drop down menu to choose the version of that OS as shown in Figure 7.6.

After you have made your selection click the Next button to continue.

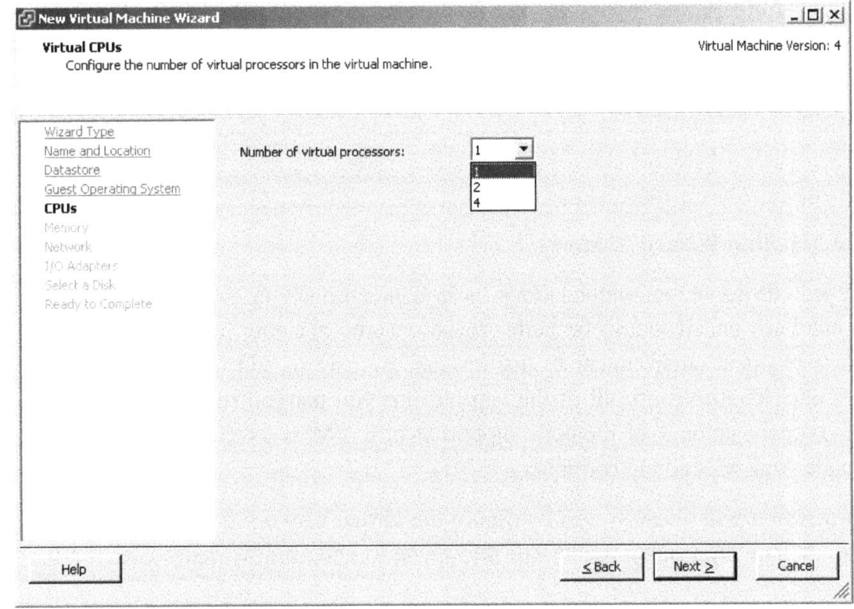

Figure 7.7 New Virtual Machine Wizard CPUs

Step 7. The wizard will now prompt you to configure the number of virtual processors you want in your VM. You can choose either 1, 2 or 4 vCPUs as shown in Figure 7.7. A 3 vCPU configuration is not supported.

You must have a VMware SMP license installed in order to operate the VM if you decide to choose 2 or 4 virtual processors in your configuration. It will be a waste of CPU resources if you choose more than one vCPU and don't run any applications in the OS that are multi-threaded to take advantage of the multiple vCPU configuration. After you have made your selection click Next to continue.

Step 8. You can now configure your VM with the amount of memory you think it will need as shown in Figure 7.8.

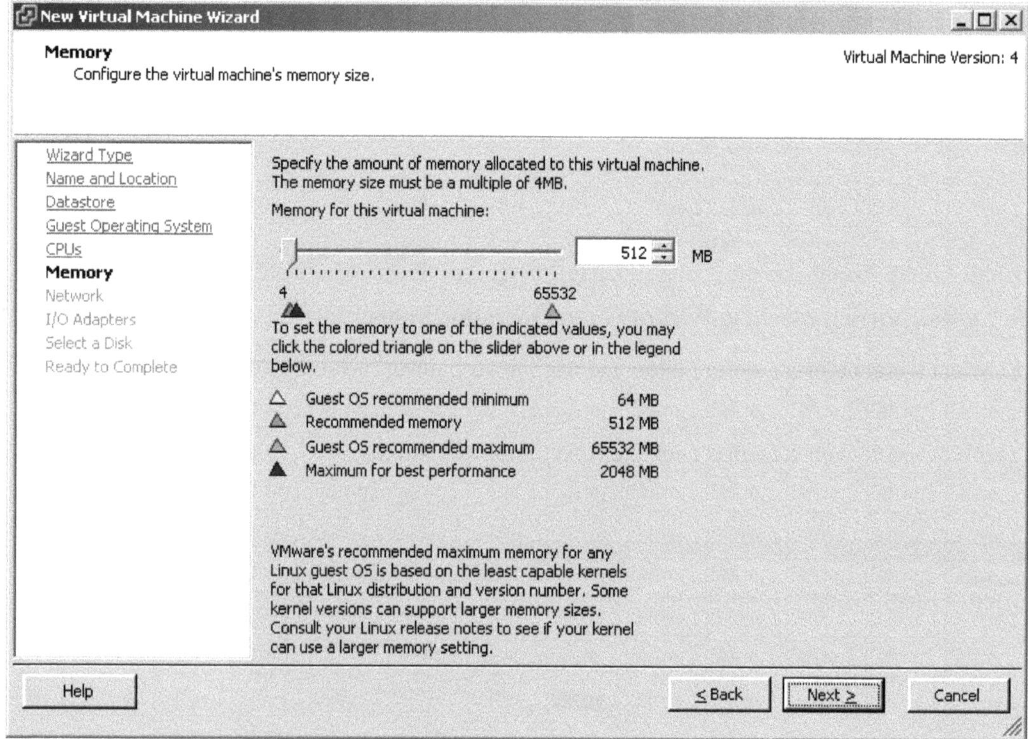

Figure 7.8 New Virtual Machine Wizard Memory

The wizard screen will provide some recommendations on how much memory the guest OS should need. These are just guidelines and it would be better to have some accurate benchmarks from a similar configuration in a physical environment to use instead. Be sure to add to the OS memory requirements how much additional memory all of the applications you plan on running in the guest OS will require. The maximum amount of memory supported in a VM is 64 GB. Click the Next button after you have made your selection to continue.

Step 9. This next wizard screen will allow you to configure the virtual network devices in the guest OS as shown in Figure 7.9. The drop down menu will allow you to choose how many virtual NICs you want to configure.

- Vlance — This network adapter is not optimized but will work will a wide variety of guest operating systems, except Windows Vista.

- vmxnet — This network adapter is optimized. It requires that VMware tools be installed within the guest operating system.
- Flexible — This network adapter is able to be used with or without VMware tools being installed within the guest operating system. Without VMware tools or an older version of VMware tools installed, it uses the Vlance adapter. With newer versions of VMware tools, the vmxnet adapter is used.
- e1000 — This network adapter is widely supported by guest operating systems. It's performs in the range between the Vlance adapter and the vmxnet adapter.
- Enhanced vmxnet — This is a high-performance network adapter. It supports the use of jumbo frames and TCP/IP Segmentation Offload (TSO). However, it only has limited guest operating system support.

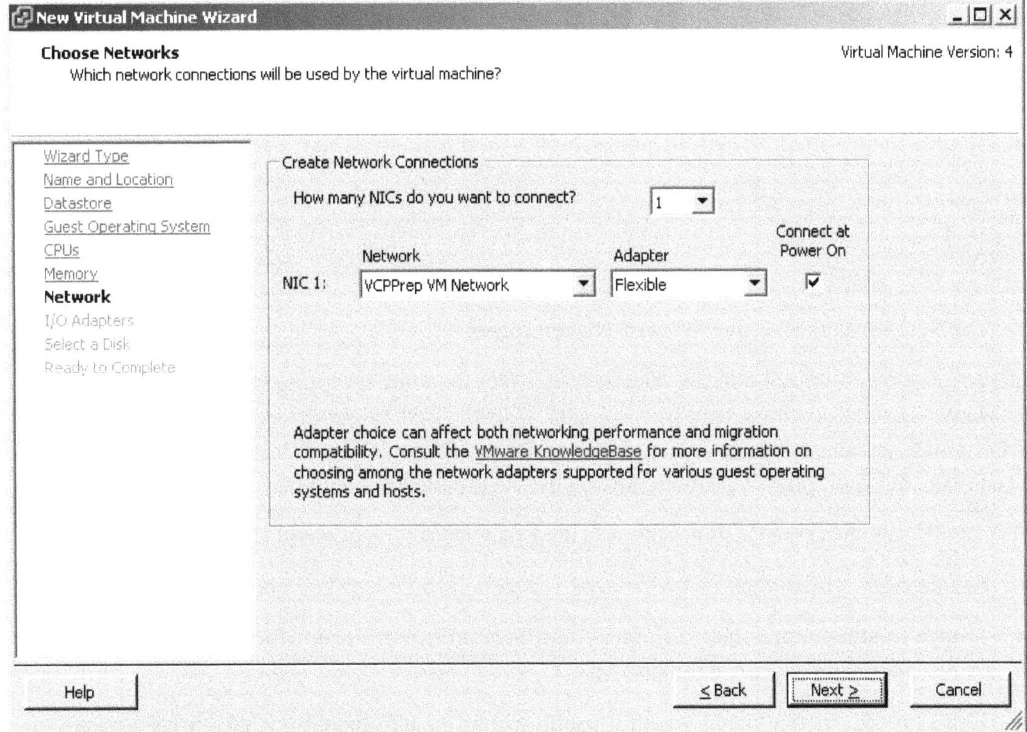

Figure 7.9 New Virtual Machine Wizard Network

For each NIC you choose you must select the appropriate virtual switch to connect it to. You also must click the check box if you want the virtual NIC to be connected to that virtual switch when the VM is powered on. Click the Next button after you have made your selections.

If you selected the Custom option in the first wizard screen you will be prompted to choose the I/O adapters next as shown in Figure 7.10.

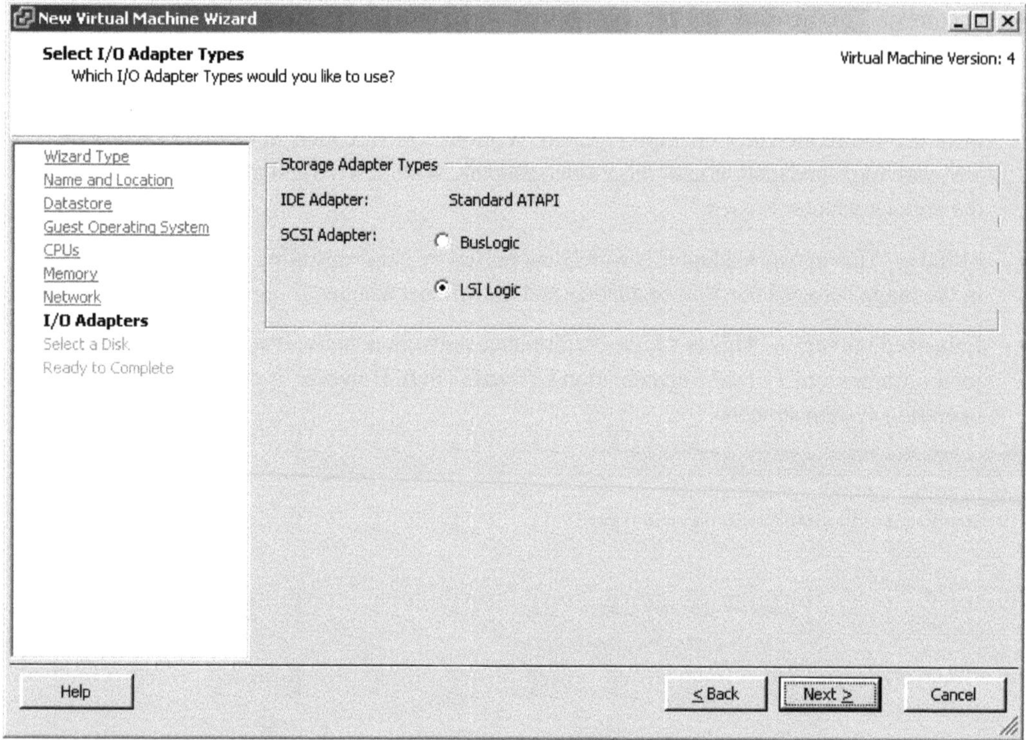

Figure 7.10 New Virtual Machine Wizard I/O Adapters

The LSI Logic is an optimized adapter. The default driver for some operating systems is the BusLogic driver. Many versions of Linux tend to run better with the LSI Logic driver. Consult the VMware Guest OS Guide for more information concerning which driver is better suited for your guest OS. After you make the appropriate selection click on the Next button to continue.

The next step if you chose the Custom option in the first wizard screen would allow you to:

- Create a new virtual disk - which allows you to build a new disk as shown in Figure 7.11
- Use an existing virtual disk - this lets you choose an existing disk which is handy if you want to recover data files from another VM
- Use a raw device mapping - which is useful when you are giving your VM direct access to a SAN
- Do not create a virtual disk

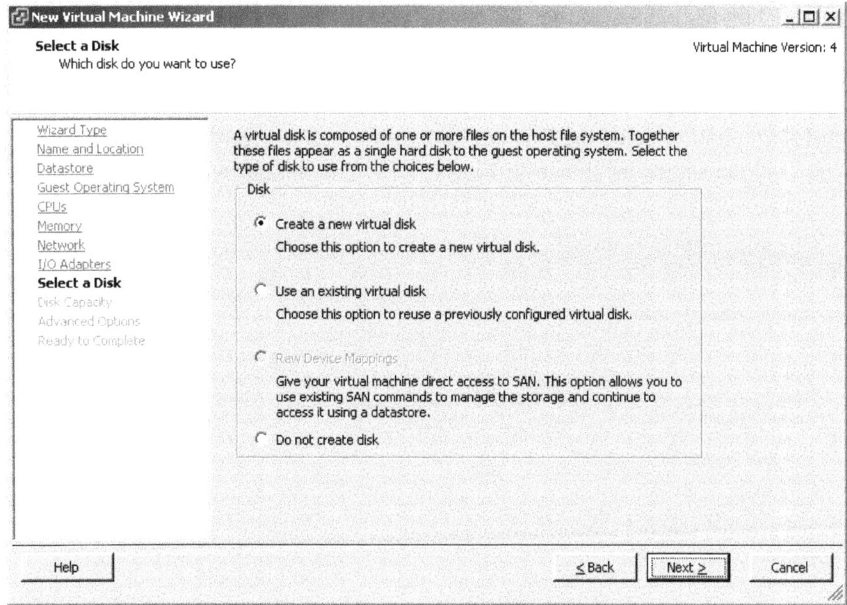

Figure 7.11 New Virtual Machine Wizard Select A Disk

After you make the appropriate selection click on the Next button to continue.

Step 10. The virtual machine requires at least one virtual disk at least 1 MB in size. Figure 7.12 shows the next wizard screen which will allow you to set the virtual machines disk size. You also can choose to locate the virtual disk on either the same datastore as the rest of the VM state files that will be created for the VM or on a different datastore if needed for performance reasons.

Figure 7.12 New Virtual Machine Wizard Disk Capacity

Select the up and down arrow buttons to change the size or just click in the box and enter the number. You can also choose if the number is in megabytes or gigabytes. After you have configured the virtual disk size click the Next button to continue.

At this point of the wizard if you had selected the Custom option in the first wizard screen you would get the Custom Advanced Options screen as shown in Figure 7.13. The default wizard process does not offer this option.

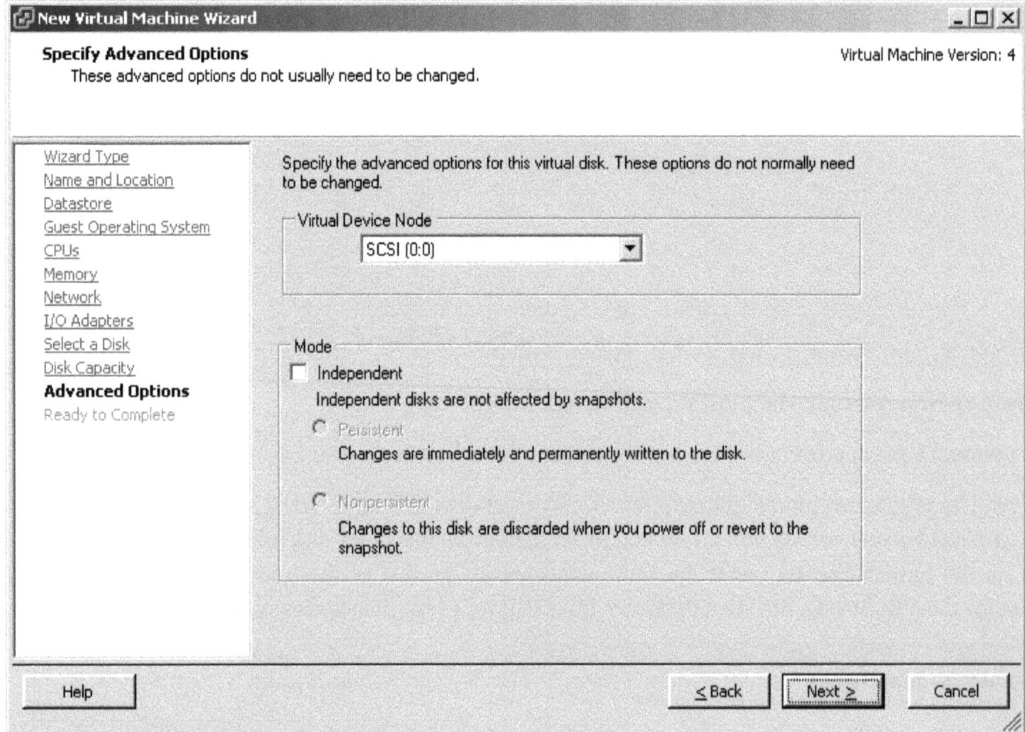

Figure 7.13 New Virtual Machine Wizard Advanced Options

You can set the Virtual Device Node which sets the SCSI device target assigned to the virtual disk as shown in Figure 7.13. You also can set if the virtual disks are affected by snapshots and if they are set to persistent and nonpersistent mode. These settings were discussed in the previous section of this chapter. After you make the appropriate selection click on the Next button to continue.

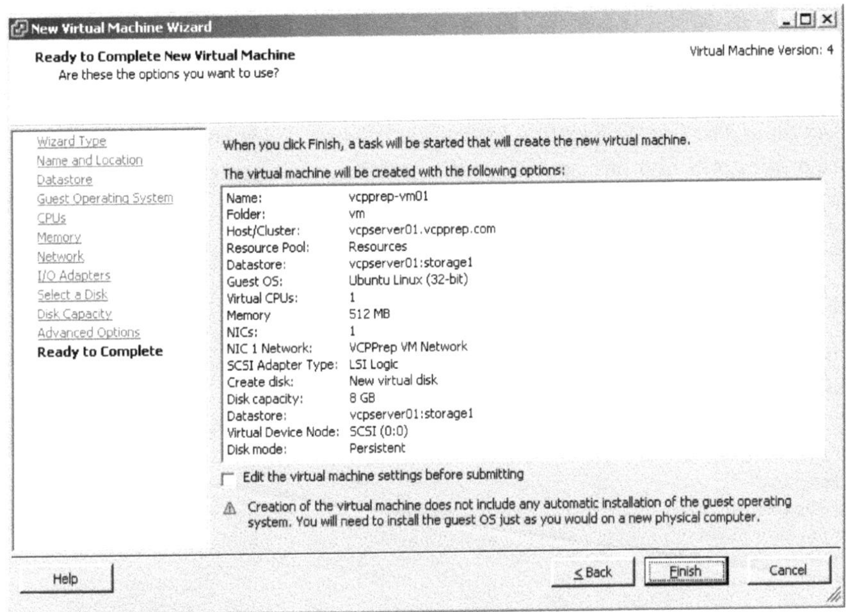

Figure 7.14 New Virtual Machine Wizard Ready To Complete

Step 11. The next screen is a summary of your configuration choices as shown in Figure 7.14

If all choices are satisfactory click on the Finish button to complete the wizard.

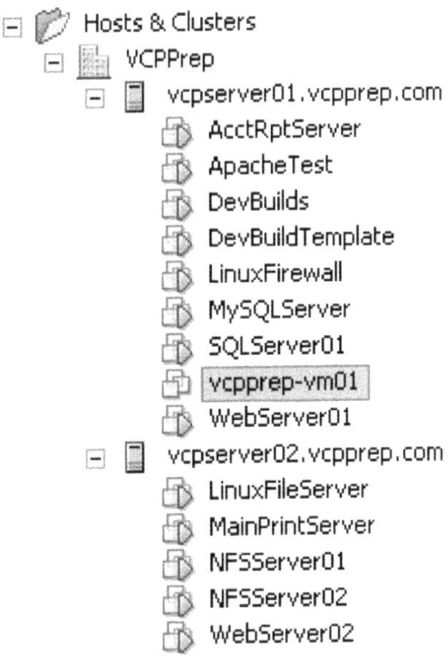

Figure 7.15 New Virtual Machine Listed Within The VirtualCenter Inventory

Your new VM will now appear in the inventory under the ESX 3.5 server you had chosen as shown in Figure 7.15.

Virtual Machine Operating System Installation

Once the virtual hardware devices are configured for your virtual machine, you can proceed to install the guest operating system on it. The Guest Operating System Installation Guide contains information specific to each supported guest OS and any special configuration requirements. You can get the Guest Operating System Installation Guide at:

http://www.vmware.com/pdf/GuestOS_guide.pdf

To install a guest OS on your VM use the following procedure:

Step 1: Select the VM that you want to install the OS on to and right mouse button click to select the Edit Settings menu option.

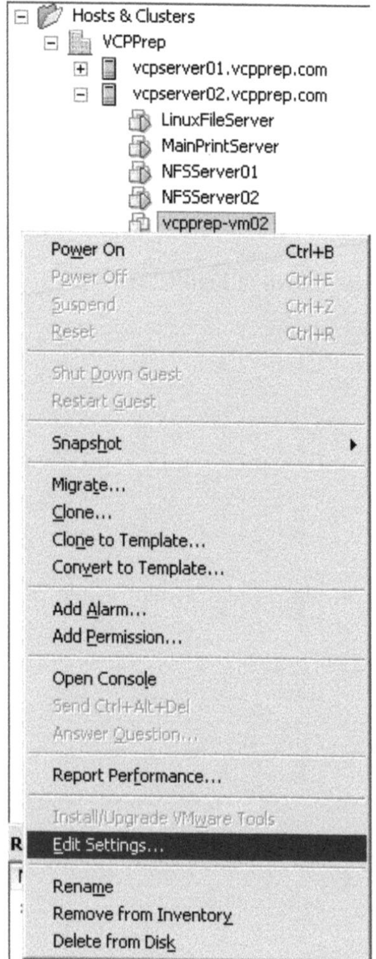

Figure 7.16 Edit Settings for Virtual Machine

Step 2: Choose the device that contains the installation media as shown in Figure 7.17.

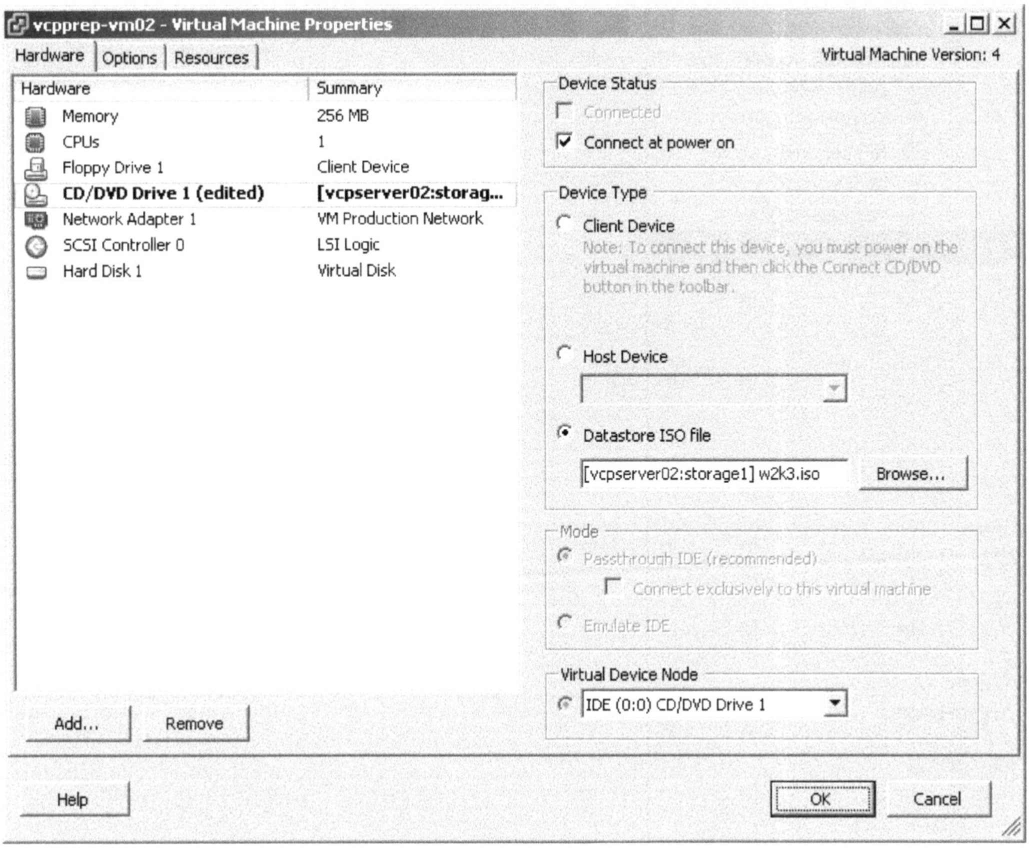

Figure 7.17 Virtual Machine Properties Configuration For CD/DVD Drive

You can use either your local CD/DVD device by selecting the Client Device radio button in the Device Type section of the window, the CD/DVD device on the ESX 3.5 server by selecting the Host Device radio button or an ISO image of the installation media located on a datastore accessible by the ESX 3.5 server by selecting the Datastore ISO File radio button. You can use the Browse button to locate the appropriate ISO image.

You should also make sure that the Connect at power on check box is selected. This will make the installation media accessible at boot time. Once all of the configuration settings are selected click on the OK button to continue.

Step 3. Select the VM icon in the inventory and right mouse button click and select the Power On option to start the virtual machine as shown in Figure 7.18.

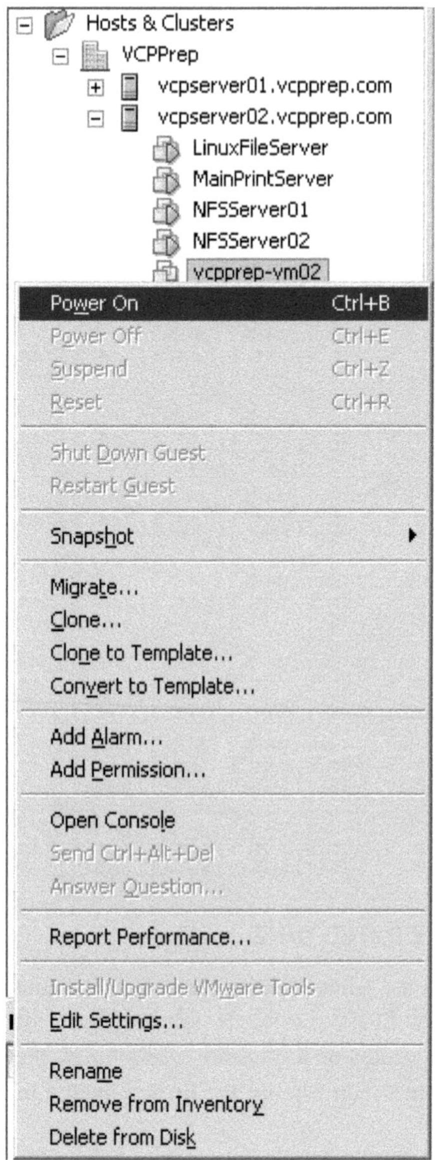

Figure 7.18 Power On Virtual Machine

The virtual machine will now power on. You can also use the Ctrl + B keyboard combination shortcut to accomplish this task as well.

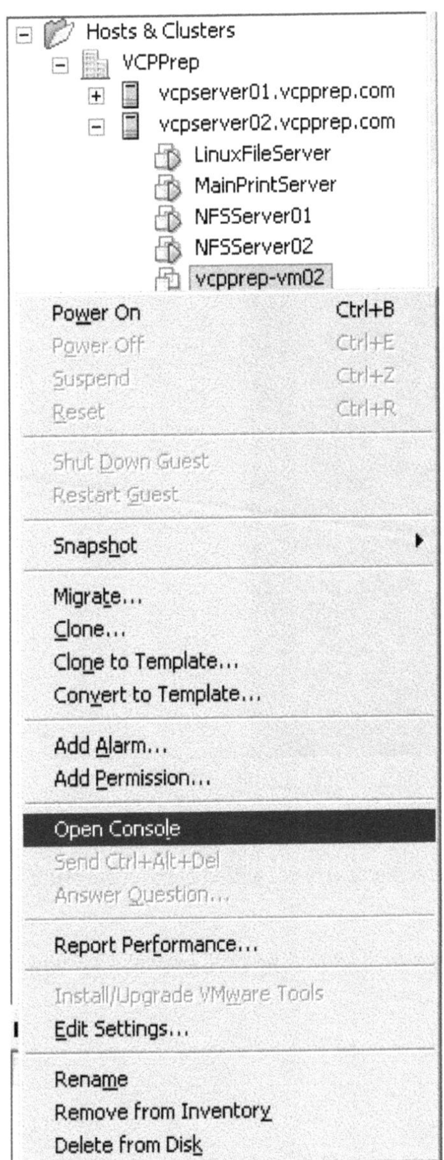

Figure 7.19 Open Virtual Machine Console

Step 4. Select the VM icon in the inventory and right mouse button click and select the Open Console command as shown in Figure 7.19.

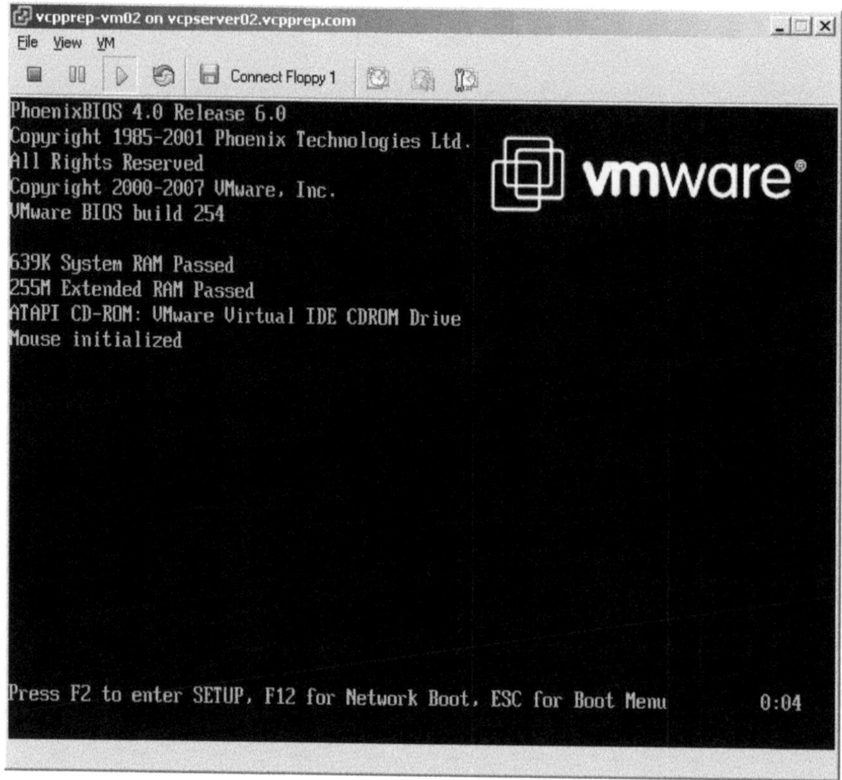

Figure 7.20 Virtual Machine Power On Self Test

The VM console window will show the virtual machine powering and you will see the VM BIOS screen start up as shown in Figure 7.20

The installation of the operating system at this point is the same as it would be on a physical system. Follow the OS installation procedure to complete the task.

Installing and Configuring VMware Tools

It is recommended to install VMware tools after the guest OS has been installed. When logging into a supported Windows operating system, use the Ctrl+Alt+Ins key sequence to access the user credentials log in dialog box. The VMware tools software is installed into the guest OS just like any other application. VMware Tools will provide the following to your virtual machine:

- Memory management enhancements - these enhancements will be discussed in Chapter 11 - Resource Optimization
- An accelerated mouse driver - for faster mouse response
- An optimized SCSI driver - for faster I/O performance
- An accelerated video driver - for faster video refresh
- Support for quiescing the guest OS - used with the VMware consolidated backup software

Step 1. You can start the installation of the VMware tools using the following methods:

- Select the VM from the inventory and select the Add VMware Tools option from the VI Client or VirtualCenter screen option
- Select the VM from the inventory and right mouse button click on it and select Install VMware Tools from the menu
- Some guest operating systems let you install the tools manually in the guest OS. Refer to the Guest Operating System Installation Guide for specific instructions for the procedure
- Select the VM from the inventory and launch the VM's console window and select the VM menu option and select the Install VMware Tools option as shown in Figure 7.21
-

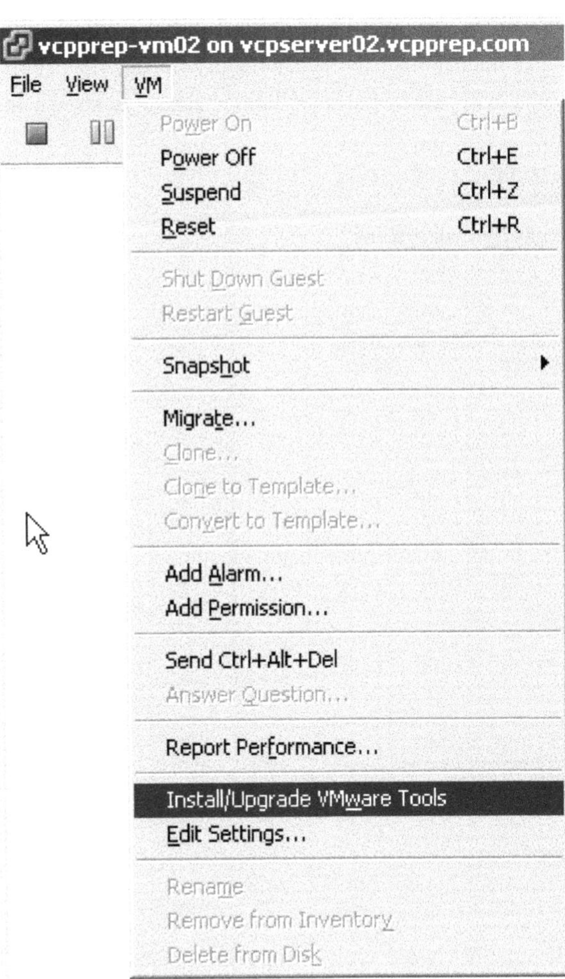

Figure 7.21 Install/Upgrade VMware Tools Menu

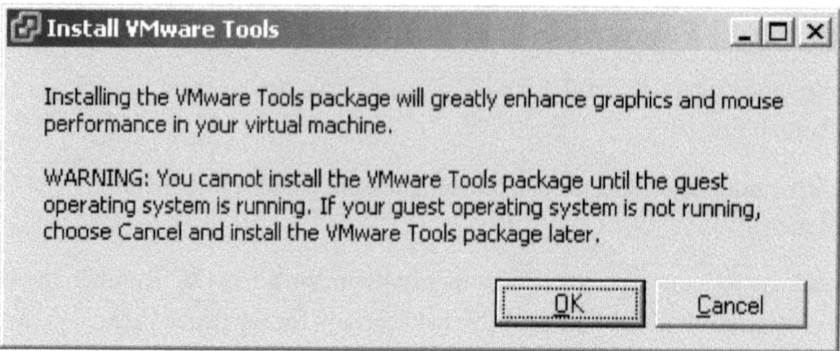

Figure 7.22 Install VMware Tools Installation Warning Message

Step 2. The Install Tools window will appear as shown in Figure 7.22.

The Virtual Machine must be powered on and the guest OS must be running in order to install the VMware tools software. Click on the OK button to continue.

Step 3. The welcome screen is the next screen you will see in the installation wizard as shown in Figure 7.23.

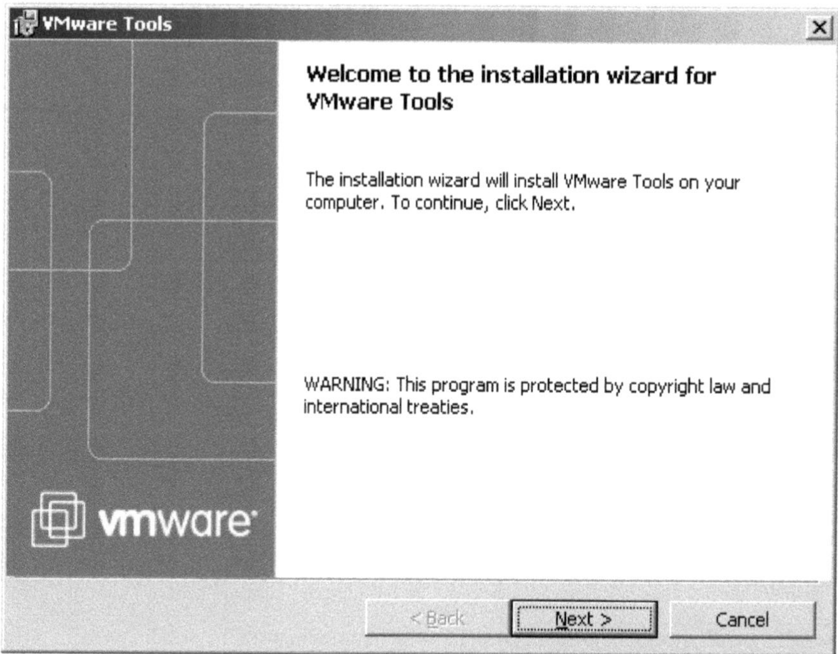

Figure 7.23 VMware Tools Installation Wizard

Click on the Next button to continue.

Step 4. You can now choose if you want the Typical VMware tools components installed for the current VMware product. For this VM, the Typical radio button is selected as shown in Figure 7.24.

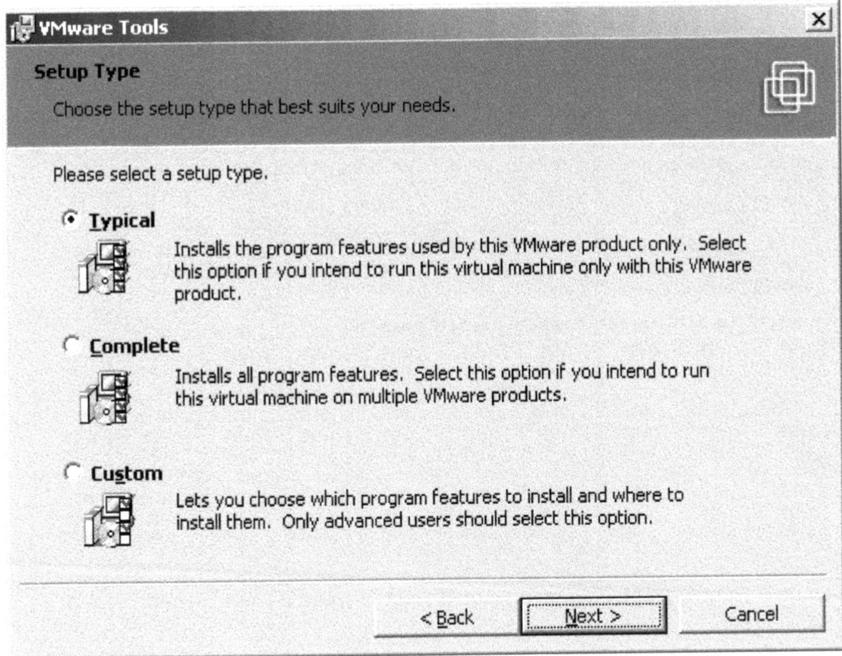

Figure 7.24 VMware Tools Installation Wizard Typical Settings

The Complete option installs all of the features supported by the VMware tools software. You can also pick and choose what parts of the software you want installed by choosing the Custom radio button. After you have made your selection click on the Next button to continue.

Step 5. The Ready to Install the Program screen is the final one in the installation process as shown in Figure 7.25.

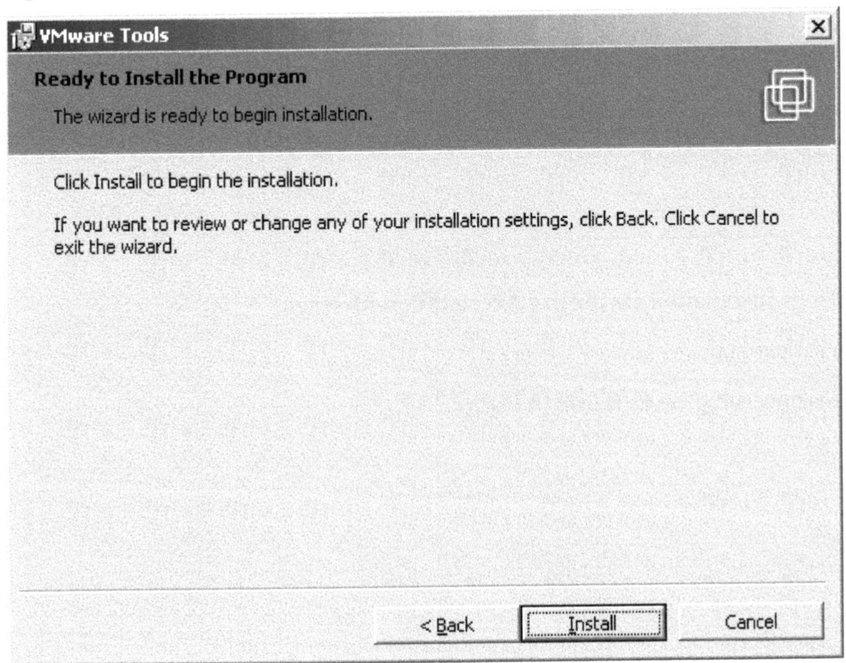

Figure 7.25 VMware Tools Installation Wizard Ready To Install

Click on the Install button to complete the process.

The software will now install and you will see the progress in the next screen as shown in Figure 7.26.

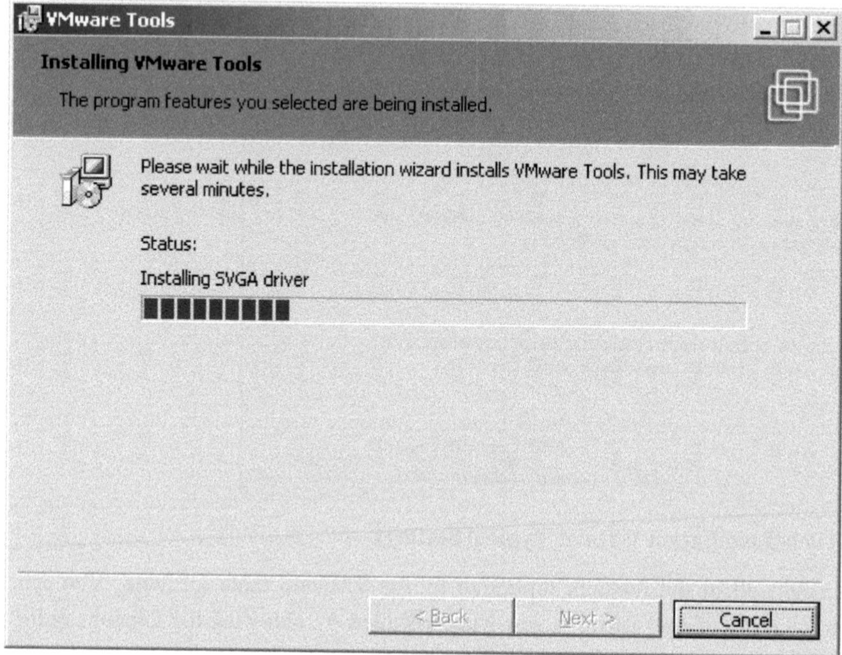

Figure 7.26 VMware Tools Installation Status

You will be prompted to configure your hardware acceleration settings in the guest OS as shown in Figure 7.27.

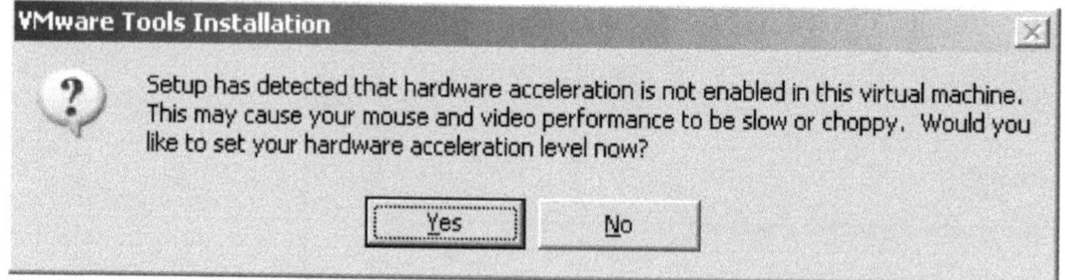

Figure 7.27 VMware Tools Installation Hardware Acceleration Message

Click on the Yes button to continue.

The installation process is now complete as shown in Figure 7.28.

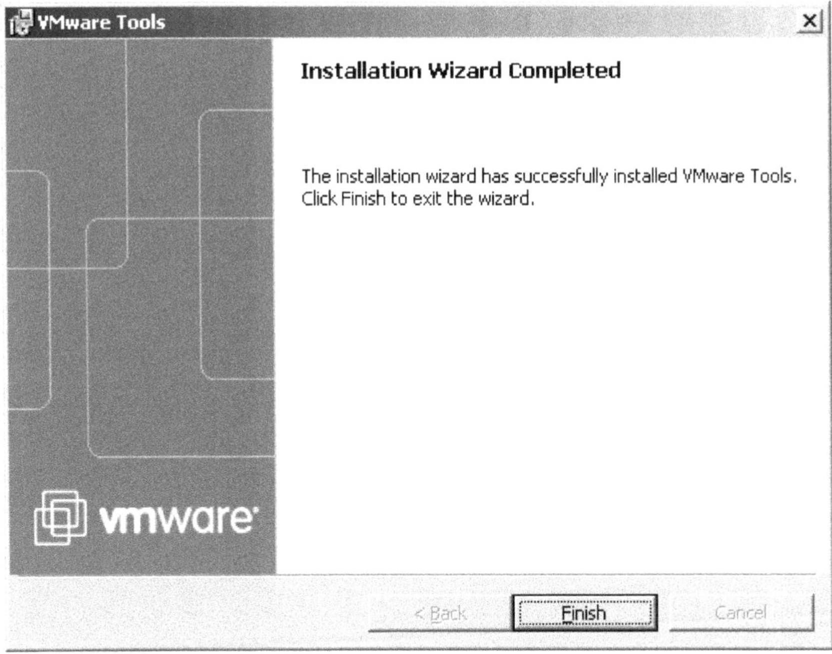

Figure 7.28 VMware Tools Installation Wizard Finished

Click on the Finish button to close the wizard window.

You will be prompted to restart your guest OS as shown in Figure 7.29.

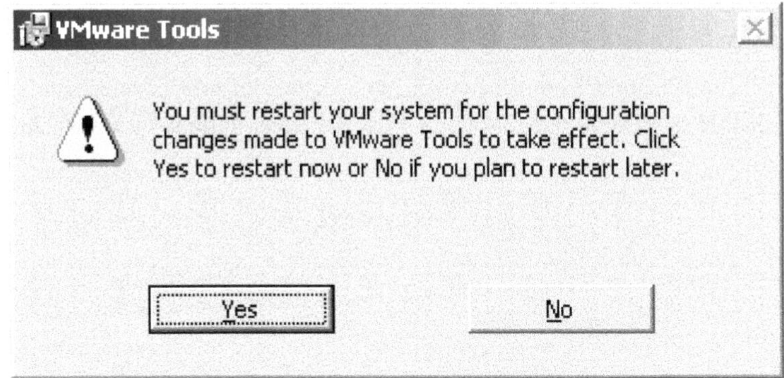

Figure 7.29 VMware Tools Installation Reboot Message

Click on the Yes button to restart the guest OS.

If the guest OS has the VMware tools installed you will see the VMware tools icon in its title bar as shown in Figure 7.30.

Figure 7.30 VMware Tools System Tray Icon

If you right mouse button click on the icon you can select the Open VMware Tools command from the menu as shown in Figure 7.31.

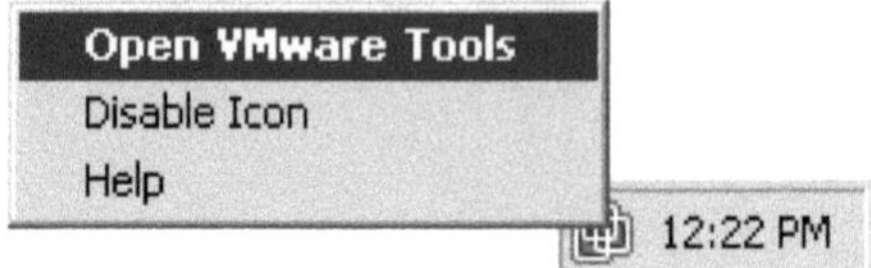

Figure 7.31 VMware Tools System Tray Icon Menu

This will allow you to configure the VMware tools options.

Setting Virtual Machine Options

The VMware Tools Properties has five tabs:

- Options
- Devices
- Scripts
- Shared Folders
- Shrink
- About

The Options Tab

The Options tab allows you to enable or disable the following Miscellaneous options as shown in Figure 7.32.

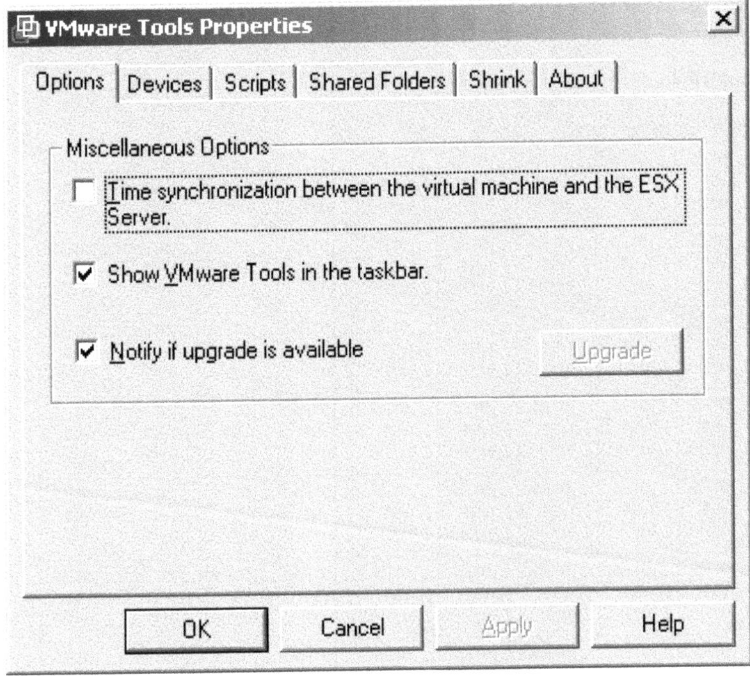

Figure 7.32 VMware Tools Properties Options Tab

- Time synchronization between the virtual machine and the host operating system - when this check box is enabled, every second the guest operating system time is checked to see if it is lagging behind the ESX 3.5 server operating system time. If the time is lagging behind, the guest operating system time is set to match the host operating system time
- Show VMware Tools in the taskbar - when this check box is enabled, the VMware Tools icon will appear in the taskbar
- Notify if upgrade is available - a notification is issued when a newer version of VMware tools is available

The Devices Tab

The Devices tab allows you to connect or disconnect a virtual disk, virtual floppy disk, or virtual NIC to the VM as shown in Figure 7.33.

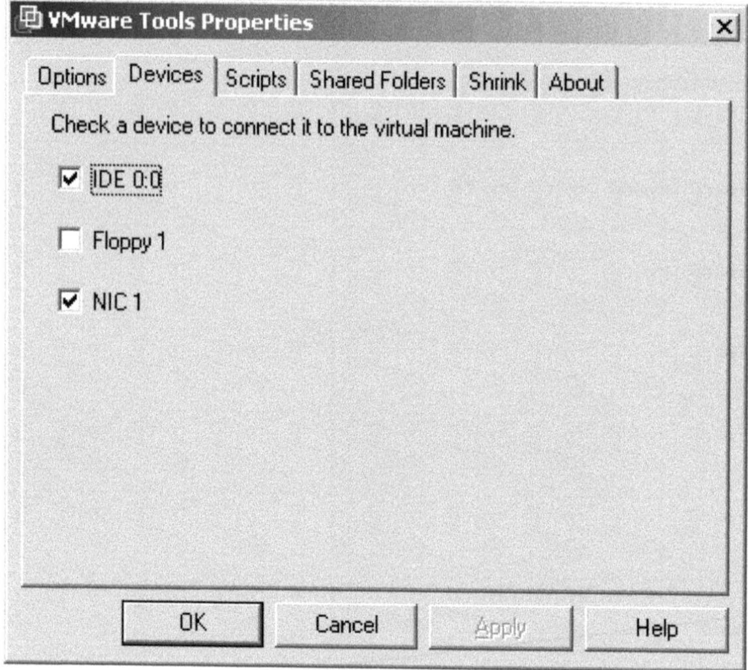

Figure 7.33 VMware Tools Properties Devices Tab

The Scripts Tab

As shown in Figure 7.34 the Scripts tab allows you to configure the VMware Tools scripts configuration that can help automate guest operating system operations when you change the virtual machine's power state.

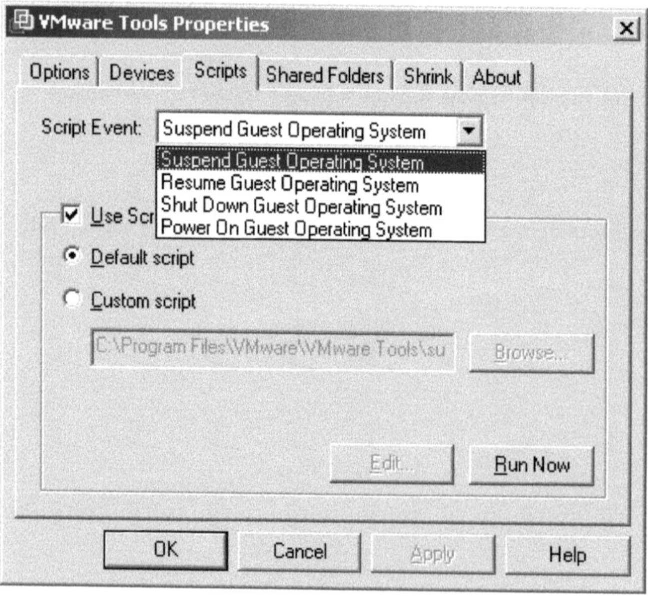

Figure 7.34 VMware Tools Properties Scripts Tab

There are default scripts for each power state included in VMware Tools. In a Windows guest OS the scripts are located in C:\Program Files\VMware. The default scripts for each of the power change options are:

- Suspend the guest operating system: suspend-vm-default.bat
- Resume the guest operating system: resume-vm-default.bat
- Power off the guest operating system: poweroff-vm-default.bat
- Power on the guest operating system: poweron-vm-default.bat

You can also use custom scripts that can be run for each power state change.

The Shared Folders Tab

The shared folders tab is a feature of the VMware Workstation product (See Figure 7.35). It is disabled in ESX 3.5.

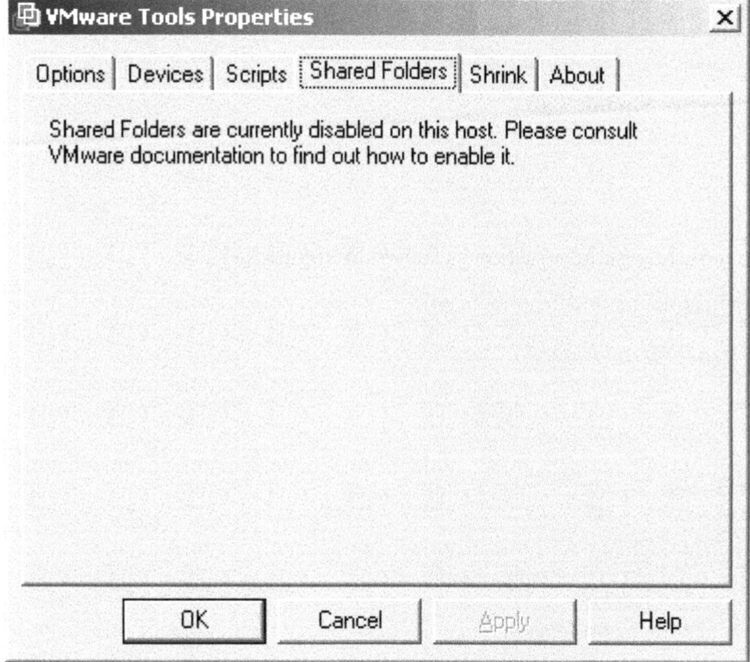

Figure 7.35 VMware Tools Properties Shared Folders Tab

The Shrink Tab

A virtual disk can have its unused space reclaimed by using shrinking. This process reduces the amount of space the virtual disk uses on the host drive. Not all disk modes will allow this process. Also note according to VMware's documentation that the ESX Server 3.5 does not support shrinking virtual disks as shown in Figure 7.36.

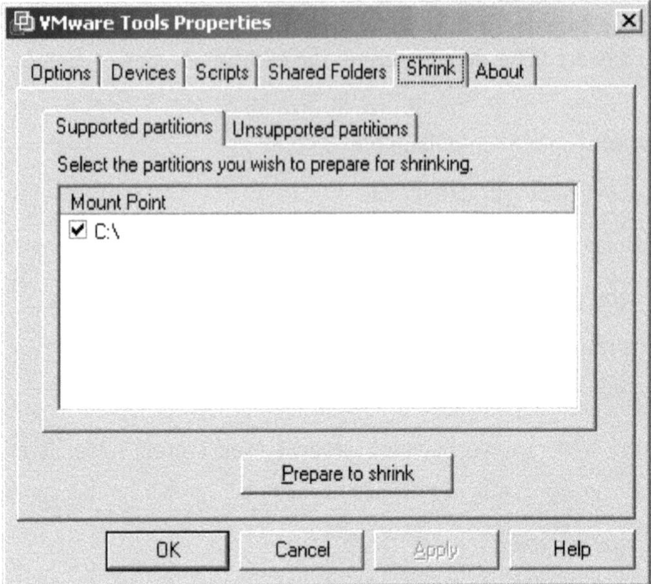

Figure 7.36 VMware Tools Properties Shrink Tab

The About Tab

The About tab displays VMware tools release information as shown in Figure 7.37.

Figure 7.37 VMware Tools Properties About Tab

Click on the OK button to close the window.

Changing Your VM's Existing Configuration

As you monitor the performance or configuration of your virtual machine you might determine that you need to change the configuration of its resources.

The only device that can be configured while the VM is powered on are the virtual disks. They can only be added while the guest OS is running. They cannot be removed. All other devices cannot be changed while the virtual machine is running. To edit the properties of a powered off VM do the following:

Step 1. Right mouse button click on the VM in the inventory that you want to configure and select the Edit Settings option in the pop up menu, as shown in Figure 7.38.

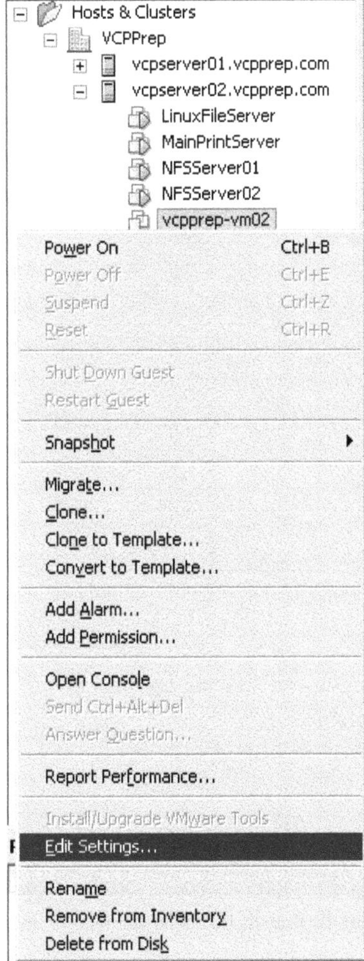

Figure 7.38 Virtual Machine Edit Settings Menu Option

Step 2. The Hardware tab will show you the current Virtual Machine Properties.

Changing Memory Settings

If you click on the Memory icon you can change the memory allocated to the virtual machine as shown in Figure 7.39.

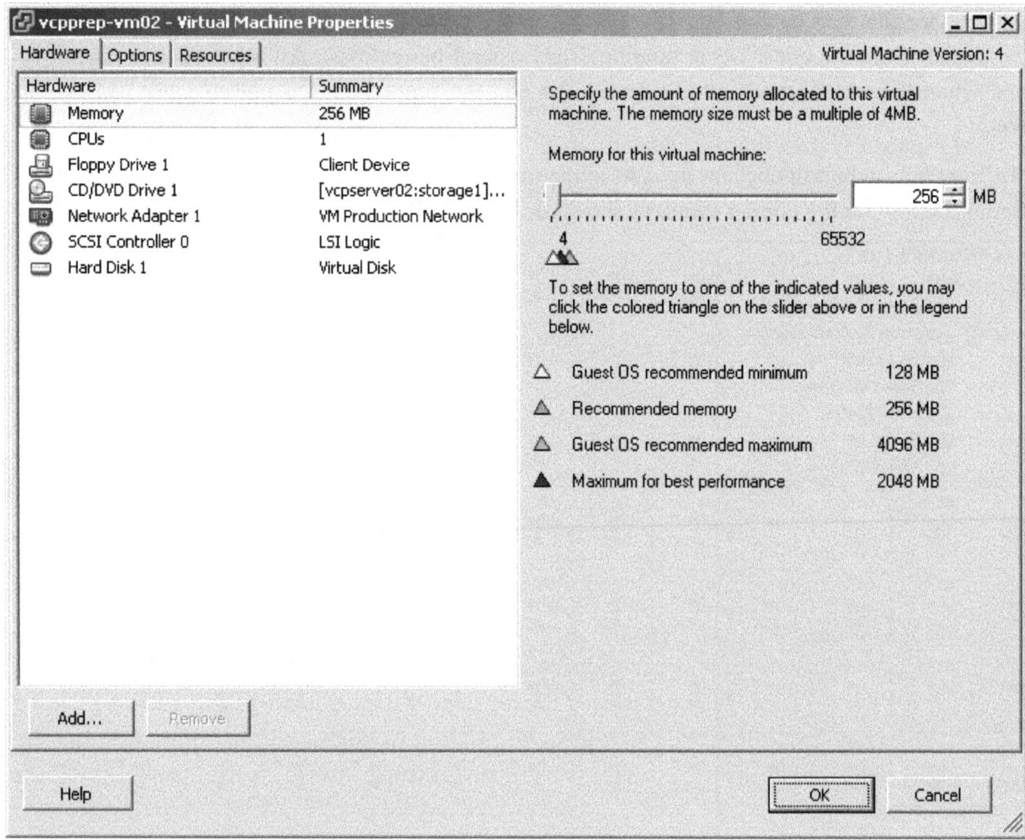

Figure 7.39 Virtual Machine Properties Hardware Tab Memory

The screen will give you recommendations for the operating system. You can allocate up to 64 GB of memory for your VM. Click on the OK button if all settings are acceptable.

Changing vCPU Settings

If you want to change the VMs number of virtual CPUs, click on the CPUs icon and click on the drop down menu on the right to select the number of vCPUs that you want to use in the VM as shown in Figure 7.40. Notice the warning on the screen!

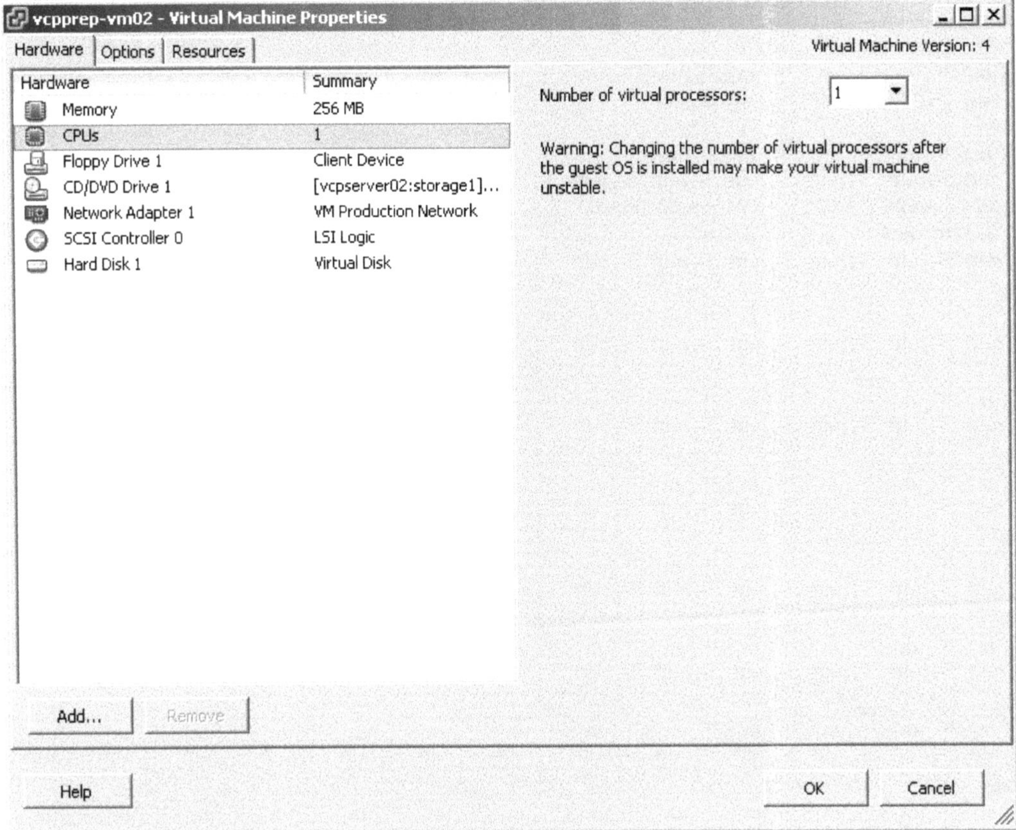

Figure 7.40 Virtual Machine Properties Hardware Tab CPUs

You can configure the VM with 1, 2 or 4 vCPUs providing the server will support that configuration. You must have a VMware SMP license in order to operate a 2 or 4 vCPU configured VM. Click on the OK button if all settings are acceptable.

Changing Floppy Drive Settings

You can select the Floppy Drive icon if you want to change its configuration as shown in Figure 7.41. You can also add one additional virtual floppy device to your VM by clicking on the Add button on the bottom left of the screen.

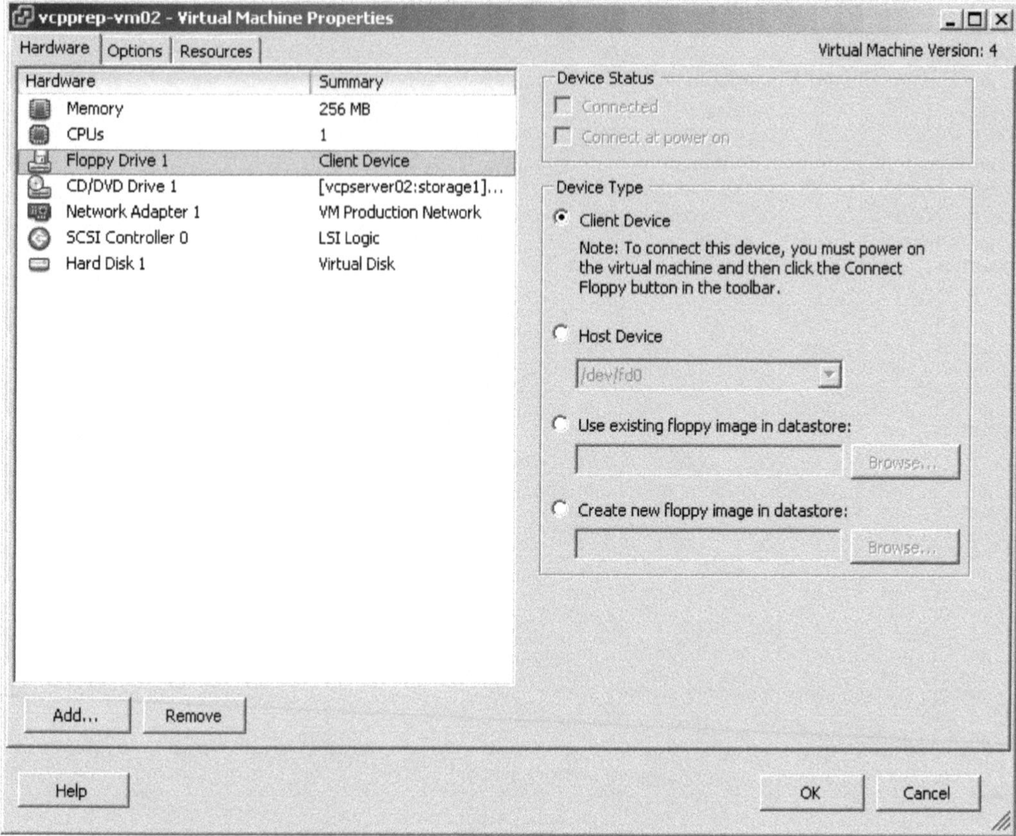

Figure 7.41 Virtual Machine Properties Hardware Tab Floppy Drive

If you are modifying the existing virtual floppy device you have the option to connect it to:

- The client device which is the device at the physical machine where the user is running the VI Client
- The physical floppy device, which must be present in the ESX 3.5 server
- An existing virtual floppy file (ends with a .flp extension) in an existing datastore
- Or create a new floppy file in a datastore

You also can control if the device is to be connected when the VM is powered on. When the VM is running you can connect or disconnect access to the virtual floppy device by selecting the check boxes on the top of the screen. Click on the OK button if all settings are acceptable.

Changing CD/DVD Drive Settings

You can select the CD/DVD Drive icon if you want to change its configuration as shown in Figure 7.42. You can configure a VM with a total of four virtual CD/DVD devices by clicking on the Add button on the bottom left of the screen.

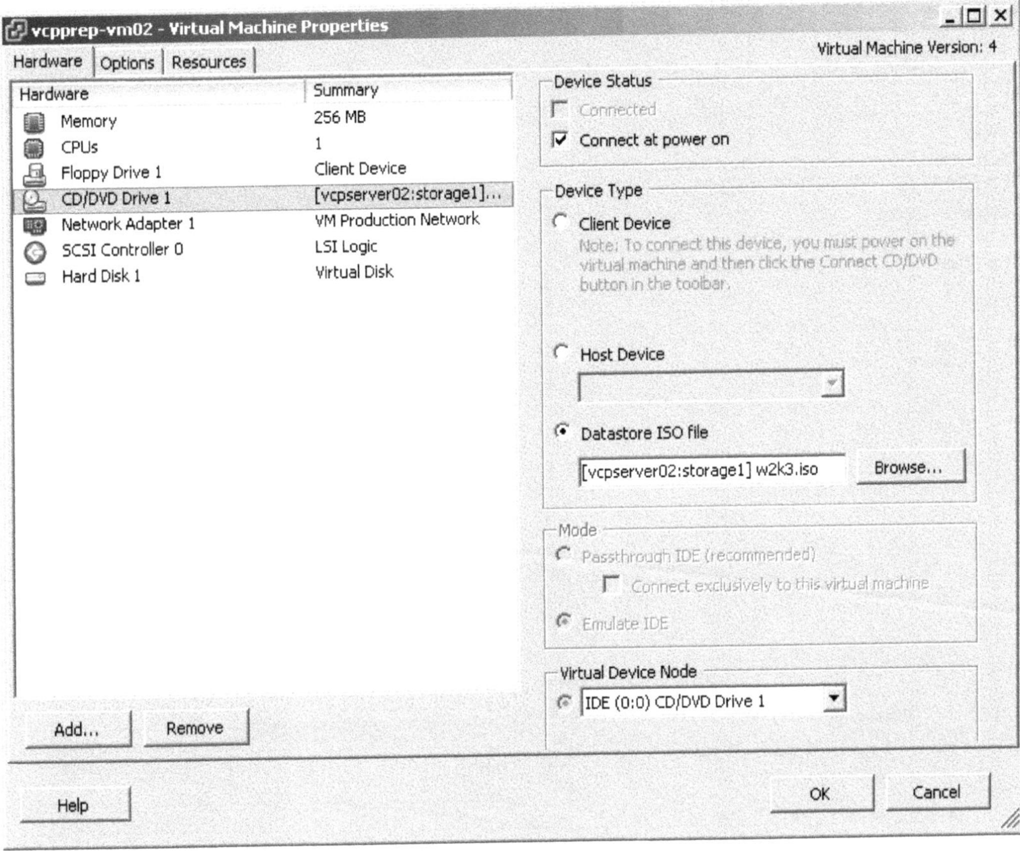

Figure 7.42 Virtual Machine Properties Hardware Tab CD/DVD Drive

If you are modifying the existing CD/DVD device you have the option to connect it to:

- The client device which is the device at the physical machine where the user is running the VI Client
- The physical CD/DVD device, which must be present in the ESX 3.5 server
- An existing virtual CD/DVD file (ends with a .iso extension) in an existing datastore

You also can control if the device is to be connected when the VM is powered on. When the VM is running you can connect or disconnect access to the virtual CD/DVD device by selecting the check boxes on the top of the screen.

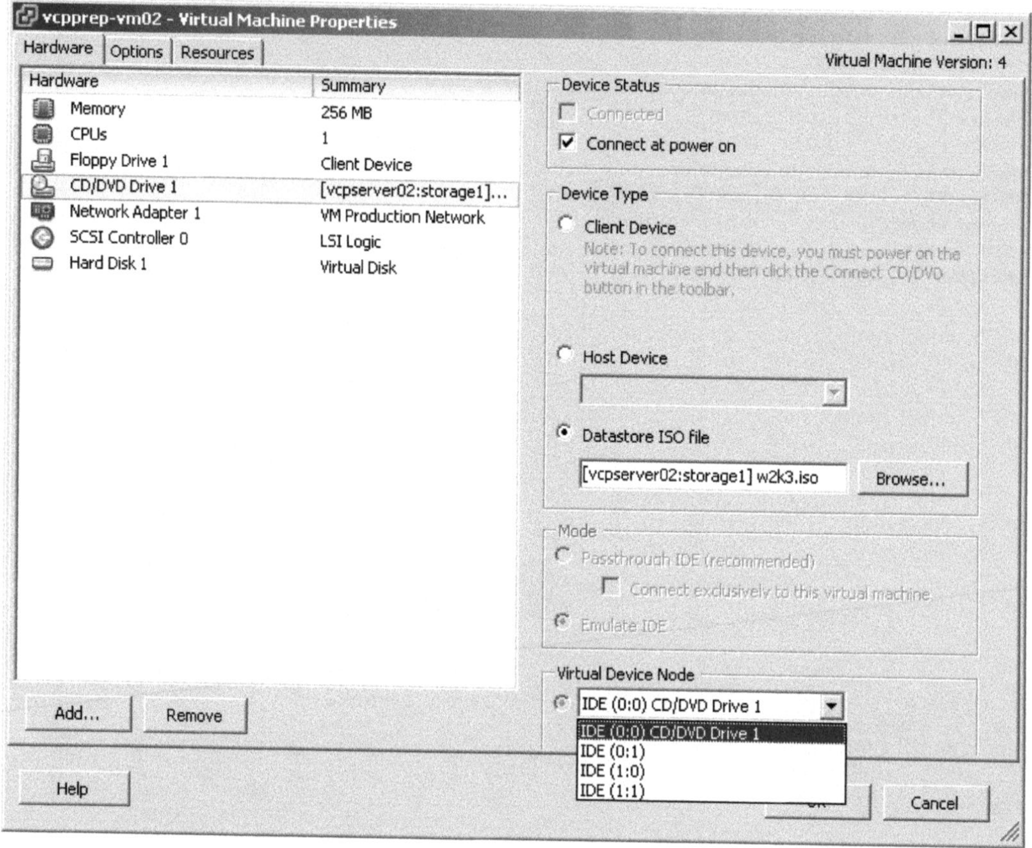

Figure 7.43 Virtual Machine Properties Hardware Tab CD/DVD Drive Virtual Device Node List

The virtual device node option as shown in Figure 7.43 identifies the IDE bus the CD/DVD device will appear to be on in the guest OS as well as if it is the first or second device on that bus. The virtual device nodes are as follows:

- IDE 0:0 is the Primary IDE Bus - Master device
- IDE 0:1 is the Primary IDE Bus - Slave device
- IDE 1:0 is the Secondary IDE Bus - Master device
- IDE 1:1 is the Secondary IDE Bus - Slave device

You can set the drive to an unused virtual device node if the guest OS needs the CD/DVD to be one of the other IDE devices. Click on the OK button if all settings are acceptable.

Changing Network Adapter Settings

You can select the Network Adapter icon if you want to change its configuration as shown in Figure 7.44. You can configure a VM with a total of four virtual network devices by clicking on the Add button on the bottom left of the screen.

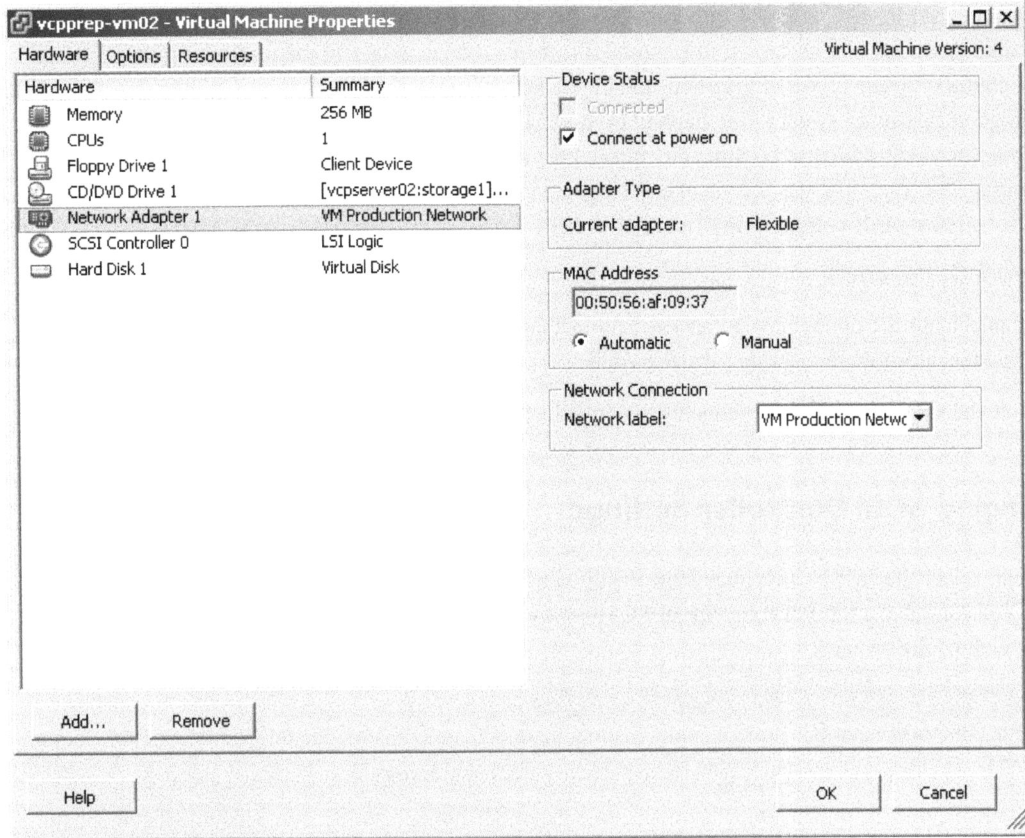

Figure 7.44 Virtual Machine Properties Hardware Tab Network Adapter

Device Status

You can select whether the virtual network adapter should be connected when you power on the virtual machine.

Adapter Type

The Flexible network adapter is able to be used with or without VMware tools being installed within the guest operating system. Without VMware tools or an older version of VMware tools installed, it uses the Vlance adapter. With newer versions of VMware tools, the vmxnet adapter is used.

MAC Address

A virtual machine's MAC address is a six-byte number. VMware has its own unique three-byte prefix known as a Organizationally Unique Identifier (OUI). When an ESX 3.5 server automatically generates a MAC address for a virtual machine, the OUI will be 00:0C:29 if the VM was created through the MUI on ESX 2.5, as this was defined as the dynamically-generated MAC address prefix. In 3.x, all VM MACs and virtual switch ports are assigned the 00:50:56 prefix. The remaining 3 bytes are generated by using the path to the virtual machine's state and configuration files along with the ESX server's SMBIOS UUID. A virtual machine will receive a new MAC address if the location of its files are changed on the same ESX host or moved to another host. Vmotion migration does not change the MAC address of a virtual machine due to files remaining in the same location during migration.

To manually set a MAC address, either modify the virtual machines .vmx configuration file or use the Edit Settings dialog box as shown in Figure 7.44. It may be necessary to manually set a MAC address when conflicts occur or when a virtual machine files has been relocated. Some applications running within guest operating system may depend on a MAC address for licensing purposes. When manually assigning a MAC address, be sure the range of values in the fourth octet is between 00 and 3f. Exceeding that range in the fourth octet will potentially conflict with dynamically-generated MAC addresses (backwards compatibility issues with ESX 2.5 VMs created through the MUI).

Network Connection

You can change the connection to an existing virtual switch by clicking on the drop down menu and selecting the appropriate existing virtual switch.

Click on the OK button if all settings are acceptable.

Changing SCSI Controller Settings

You can select the SCSI Controller icon if you want to change its configuration as shown in Figure 7.45. You can have a total of four virtual SCSI controller devices by clicking on the Add button on the bottom left of the screen.

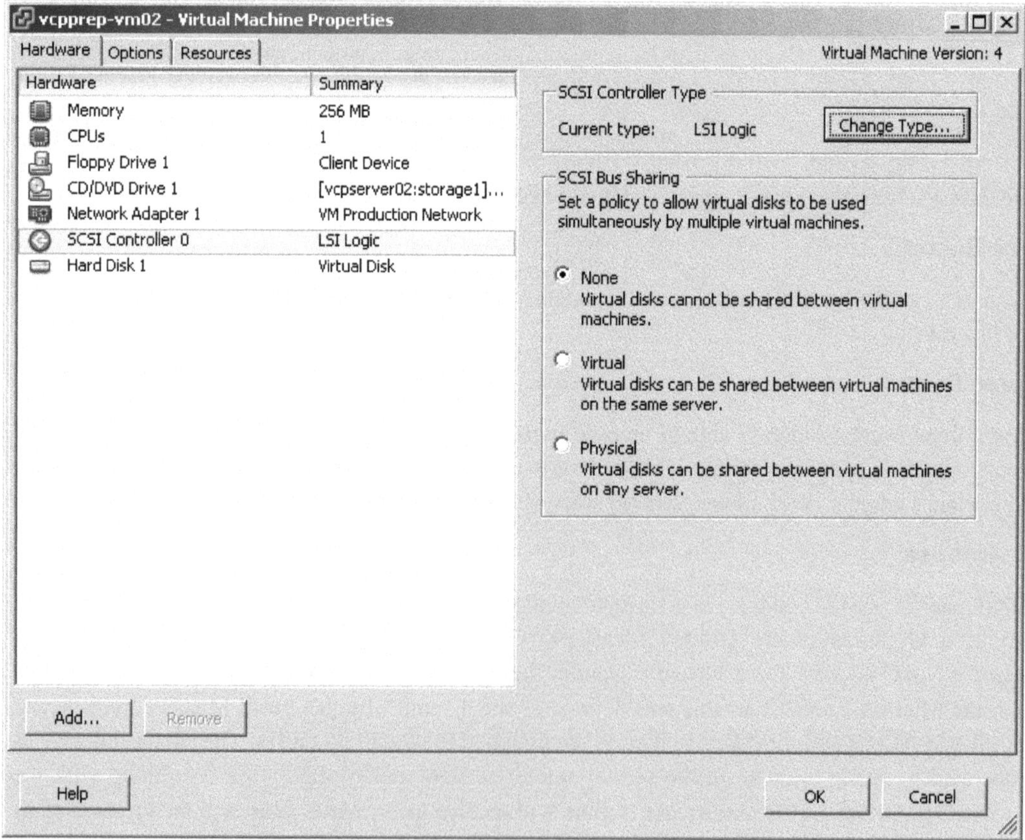

Figure 7.45 Virtual Machine Properties Hardware Tab SCSI Controller

SCSI Bus Sharing

You can also set the policy to control if other virtual machines can access this virtual disk by selecting on of the radio buttons in the SCSI Bus Sharing section of the screen. This is useful when you want to cluster the VM with another VM. Select the Virtual option when clustering VMs in the same ESX 3.5 server or select the Physical option when clustering virtual machines across two ESX 3.5 servers.

Each virtual SCSI controller can control up to 15 SCSI devices. The devices can be virtual SCSI hard disks or connected to physical SCSI devices attached to the ESX 3.5 server like a SCSI tape drive for instance. By clicking on the Change Type button in the SCSI Controller Type section in the upper right of the screen as shown in Figure 7.46 you can change the controller driver to either a Buslogic or LSI Logic virtual controller device. Some guest operating systems work better with a specific driver. Check the VMware Guest Operating System Installation Guide for more details.

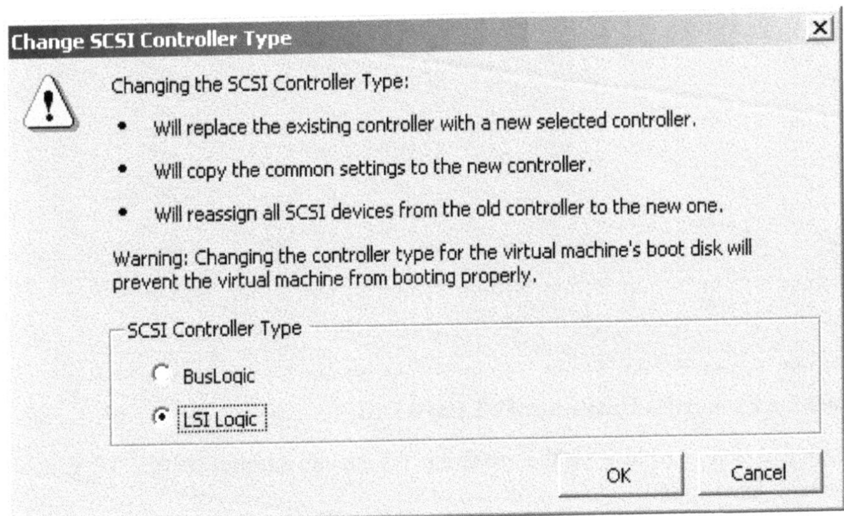

Figure 7.46 Virtual Machine Properties Hardware Tab SCSI Controller Type

Click on the OK button to close the Change SCSI Controller Type pop up window and then click on the OK button if all settings are acceptable.

Changing Virtual Hard Disk Settings

You can select the Hard Disk icon if you want to change its configuration as shown in Figure 7.47. You can have up to 60 virtual hard disk devices per VM. They can be added to your VMs configuration by clicking on the Add button on the bottom left of the screen.

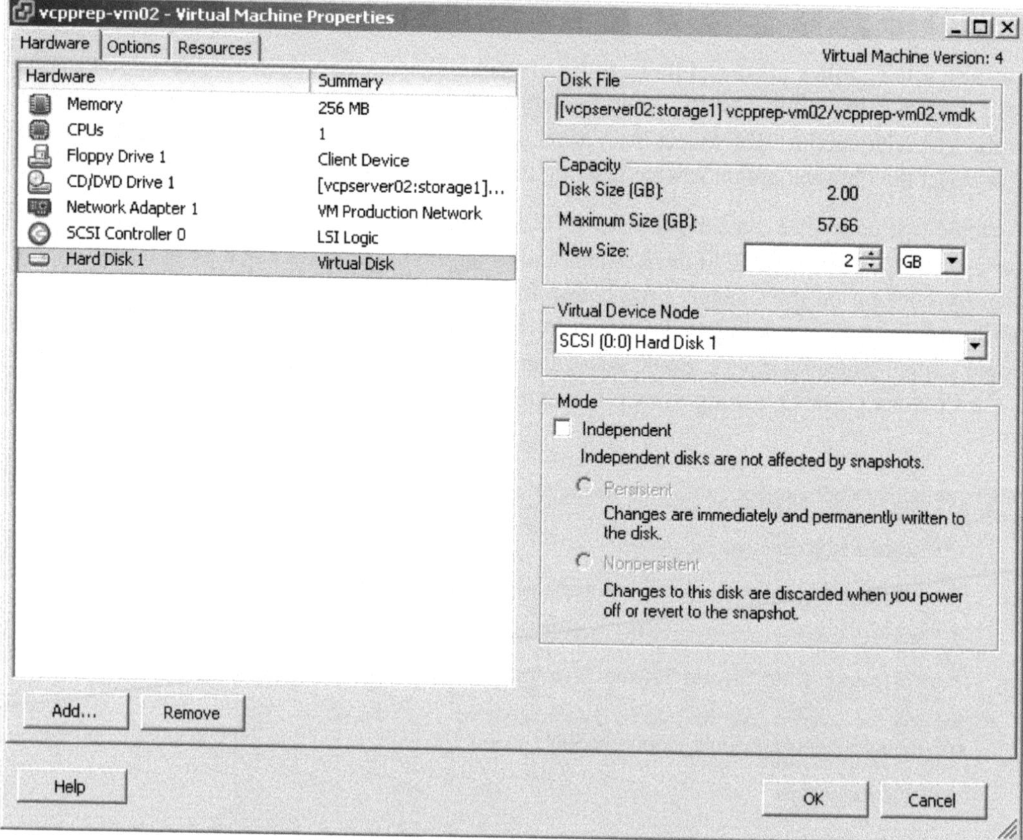

Figure 7.47 Virtual Machine Properties Hardware Tab Hard Disk

The largest disk size supported is limited to what the operating system can support up to 2 TB which is the largest file size a VMFS can support.

You can also add up to 15 additional virtual hard disk devices per controller to your VM by clicking on the Add button on the bottom left of the screen.

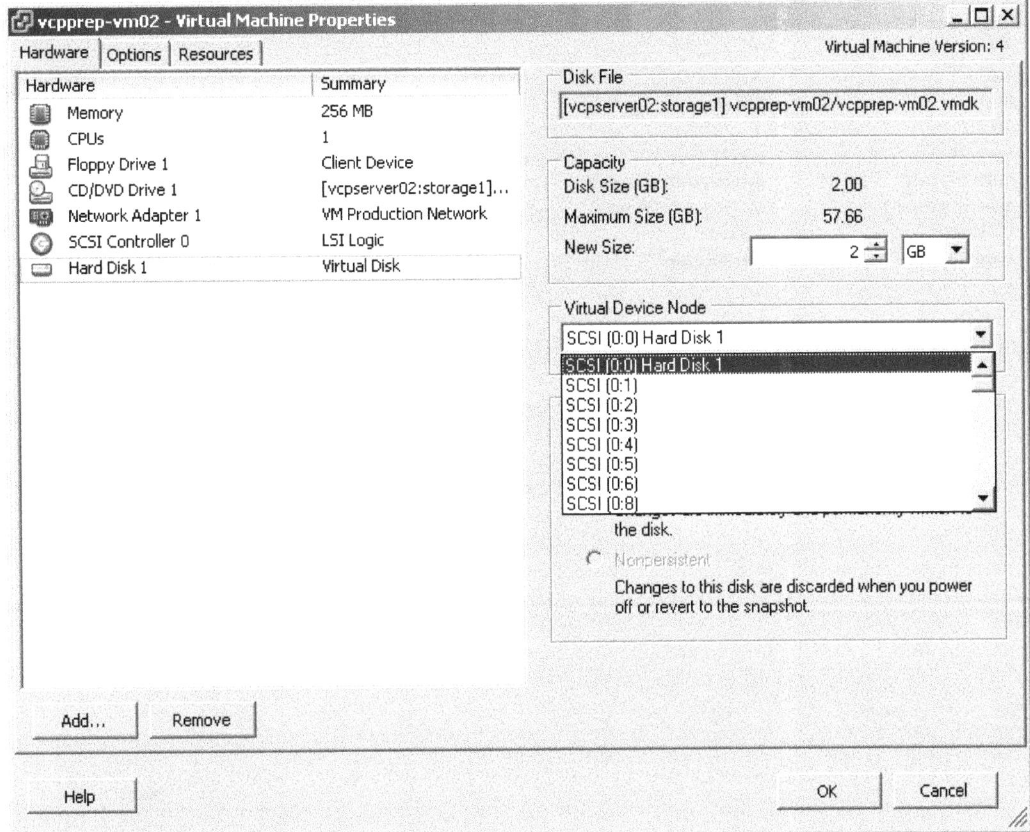

Figure 7.48 Virtual Machine Properties Hardware Tab Hard Disk Virtual Device Node List

You can change the virtual device node designation by selecting the drop down menu in the Virtual Device Node section as shown in Figure 7.48. This is useful if you must make the SCSI virtual hard disk appear to the guest OS as a different target number.

You can set the disk mode for your virtual hard disk in the Mode section of the screen as shown in Figure 7.49. You can set the disk mode to Persistent or Nonpersistent. The disk modes were discussed earlier in this chapter.

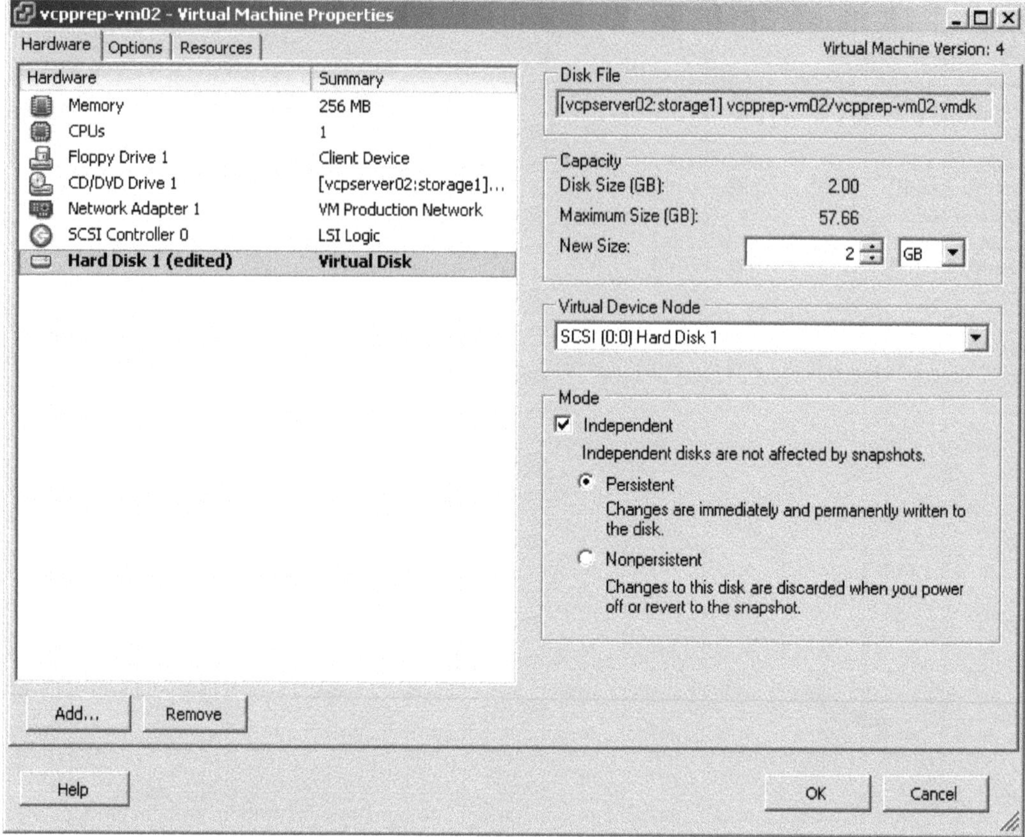

Figure 7.49 Virtual Machine Properties Hardware Tab Hard Disk Independent Mode

Click on the OK button if all settings are acceptable.

Adding a New Extra Disk to Your Virtual Machine

You may find that a virtual machine's virtual disk is getting close to capacity and you need more space for files. You can easily add additional virtual disks to your VM. Virtual disks can be added while the VM is running.

To add a virtual hard disk to an existing VMs configuration do the following steps:

Step 1. Right mouse button click on the VM in the inventory and select the Edit properties option in the pop up menu. Click on the Add device button which will start the Add Hardware Wizard as shown in Figure 7.50.

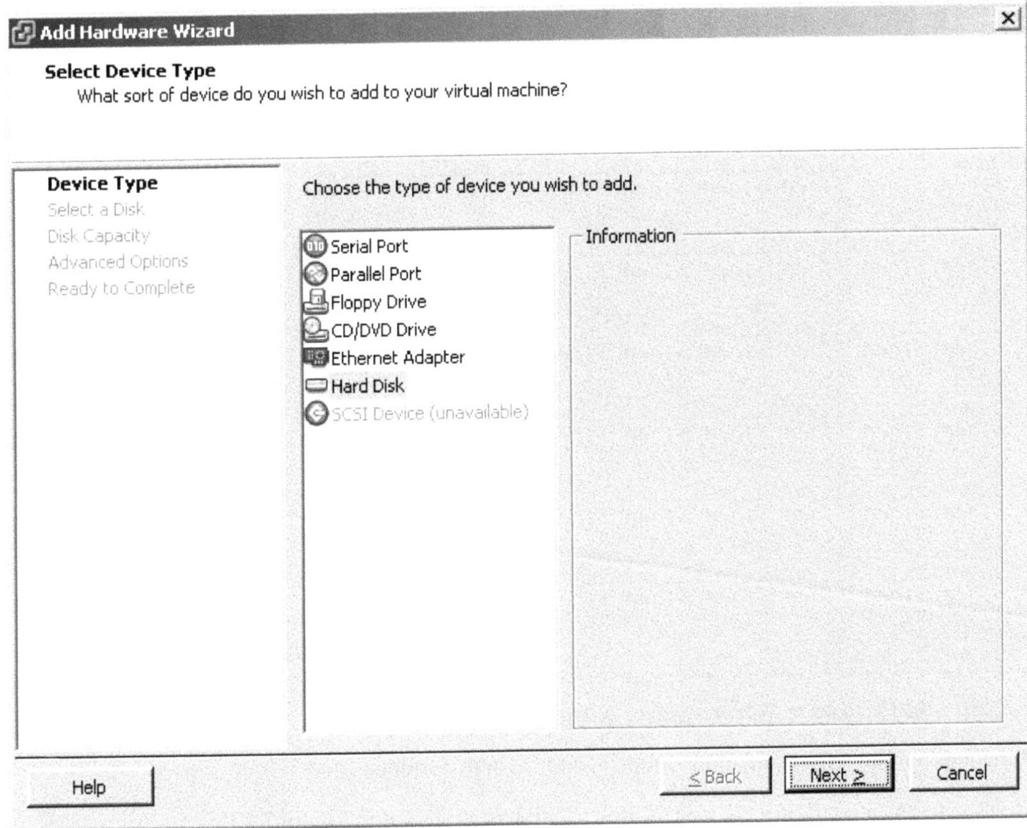

Figure 7.50 Add Hardware Wizard Hard Disk

Select the Hard Disk icon and click on the Next button to continue.

Step 2. Figure 7.51 shows that you can now select a disk from the following options:

- Create a new virtual disk - which allows you to build a new disk
- Use an existing virtual disk - this lets you choose an existing disk which is useful if you want to recover data files from another VM
- Raw Device Mappings - which are useful when you are giving your VM direct access to a SAN LUN. RDM files were discussed in Chapter 5 - ESX 3.x Server Storage Configurations

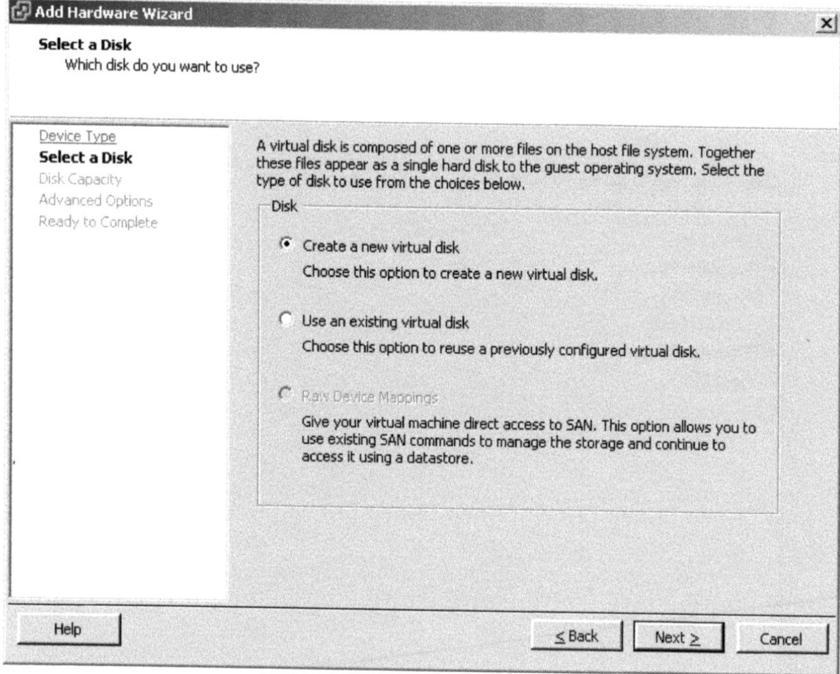

Figure 7.51 Add Hardware Wizard Select A Disk

Select the appropriate option and click on the Next button to continue.

Step 3. Now you can configure the size of the virtual disk as shown in Figure 7.52.

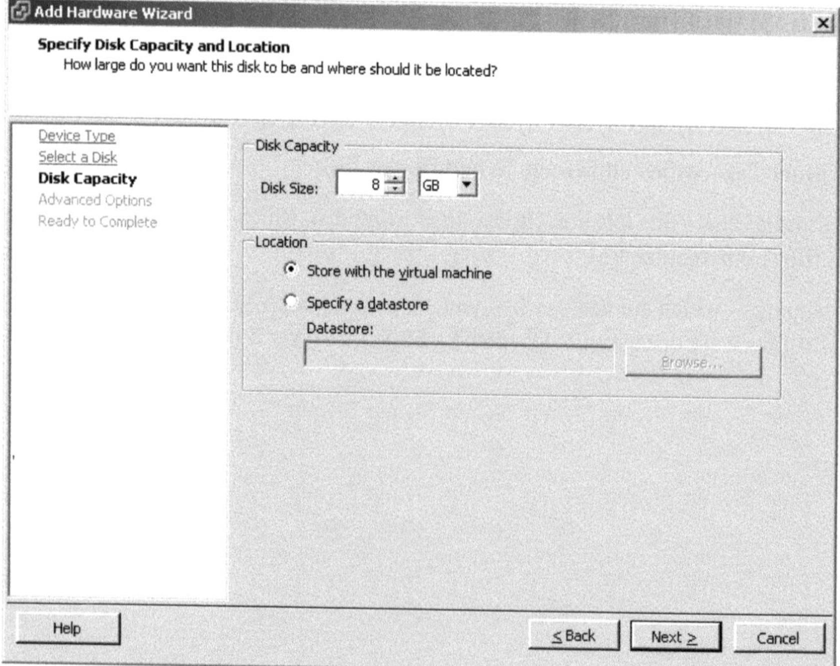

Figure 7.52 Add Hardware Wizard Disk Capacity

By default the virtual disk files are stored in the same location as the other VM state files. You can select a different location by selecting the Specify a location radio button in the Location section of the window. Use the browse button to select a different datastore for the virtual disk files. Click on the Next button to continue.

Step 4. The final screen of the Add Hardware Wizard shows a summary of your previous choices as shown in Figure 7.53.

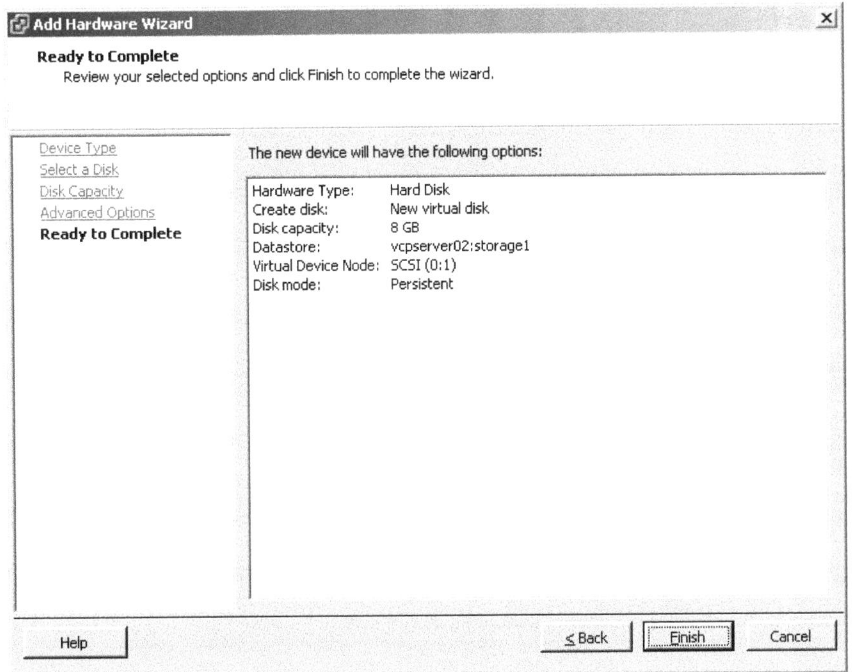

Figure 7.53 Add Hardware Wizard Ready To Complete

Click on the Finish button to complete the process.

Adding an Existing Disk to Your Virtual Machine

Step 1. Right mouse button click on the VM in the inventory and select the Edit properties option in the pop up menu. Click on the Add device button which will start the Add Hardware Wizard as shown in Figure 7.54.

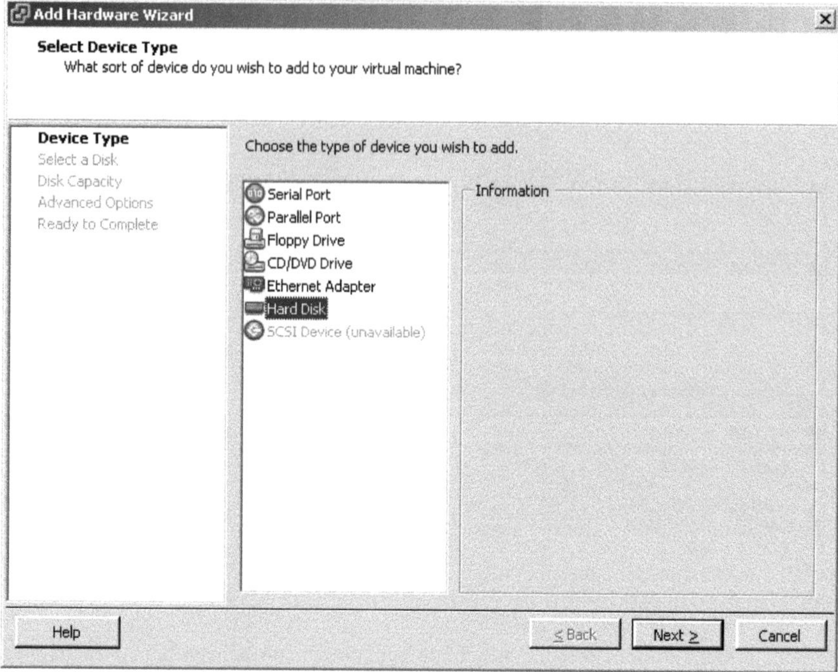

Figure 7.54 Add Hardware Wizard Hard Disk

Select the Hard Disk icon and click on the Next button to continue.

Step 2. The add hardware wizard gives the option to reuse an existing disk as shown in Figure 7.55.

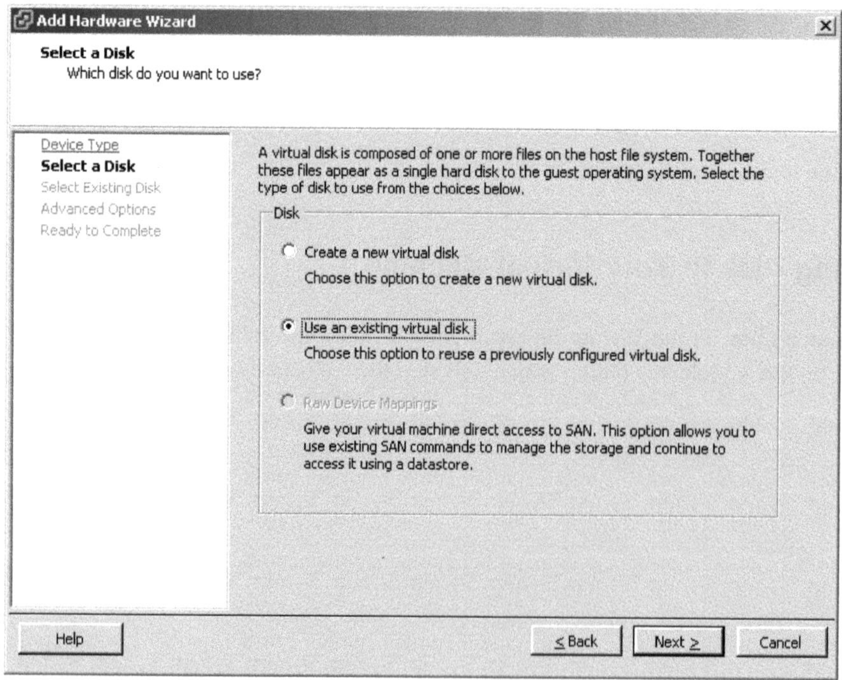

Figure 7.55 Add Hardware Wizard to Use an Existing Virtual Disk

Select the Use the existing virtual disk radio button and select the Next button to continue the process.

The Select Existing Disk screen allows you to choose which existing virtual disk you want to reuse as shown in Figure 7.56.

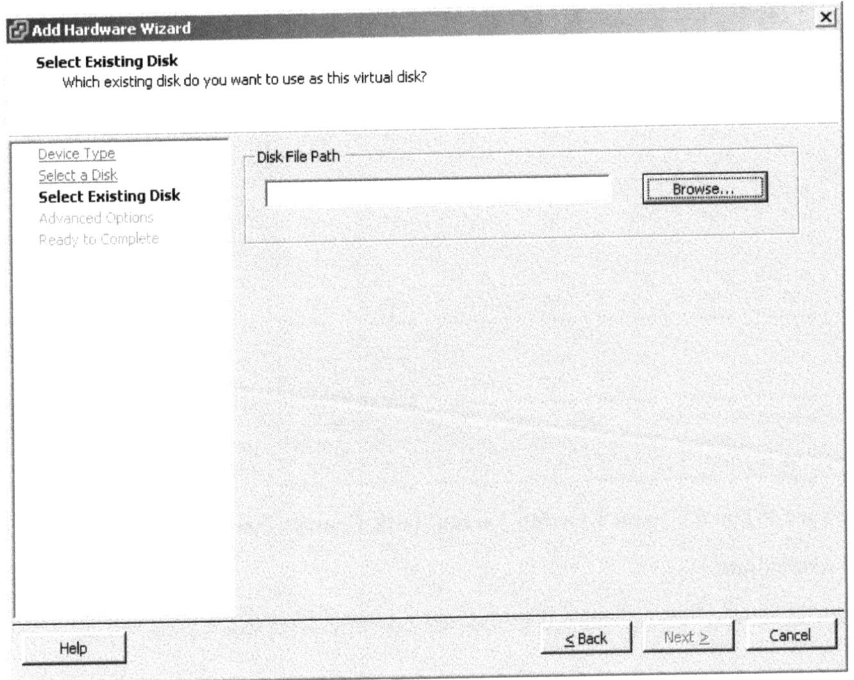

Figure 7.56 Add Hardware Wizard Use An Existing Virtual Disk Browse Button

Click on the Browse button to select the appropriate virtual disk file that you wish to reuse as shown in Figure 7.57. This could have been a virtual disk that was used in another VM that you want configured into a different VM.

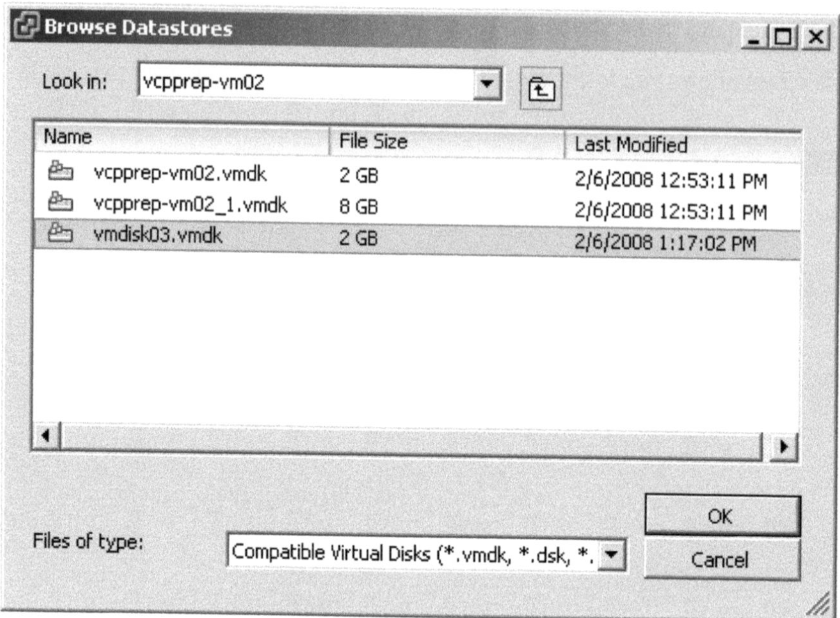

Figure 7.57 Add Hardware Wizard Use an Existing Virtual Disk Browse Datastores

Click on the OK button to continue.

The datastore name and filename will be displayed in the text box after you make your selection as shown in Figure 7.58.

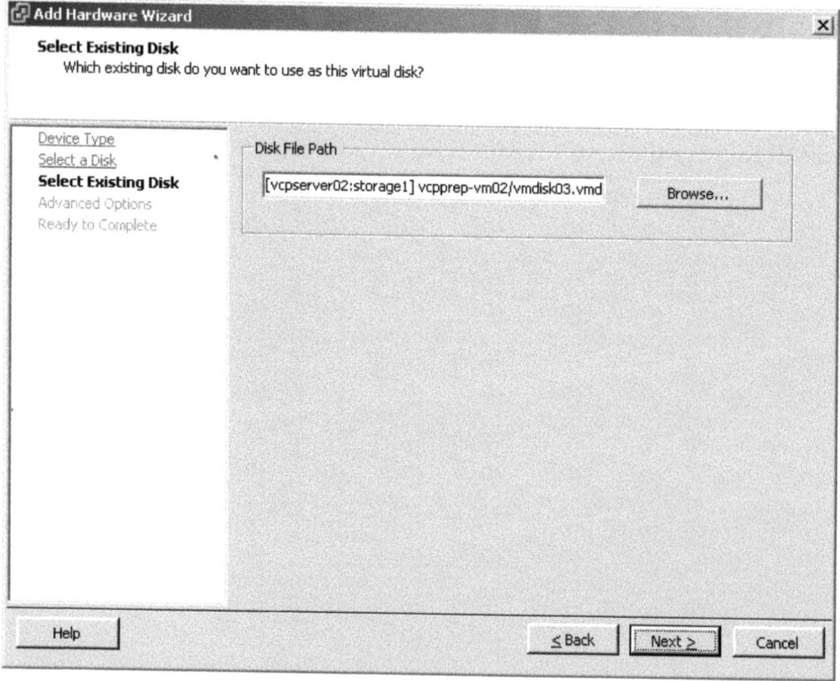

Figure 7.58 Add Hardware Wizard Use an Existing Virtual Disk File Path

Click on the Next button to continue.

Step 3. You can also change the virtual disk node as shown in Figure 7.59.

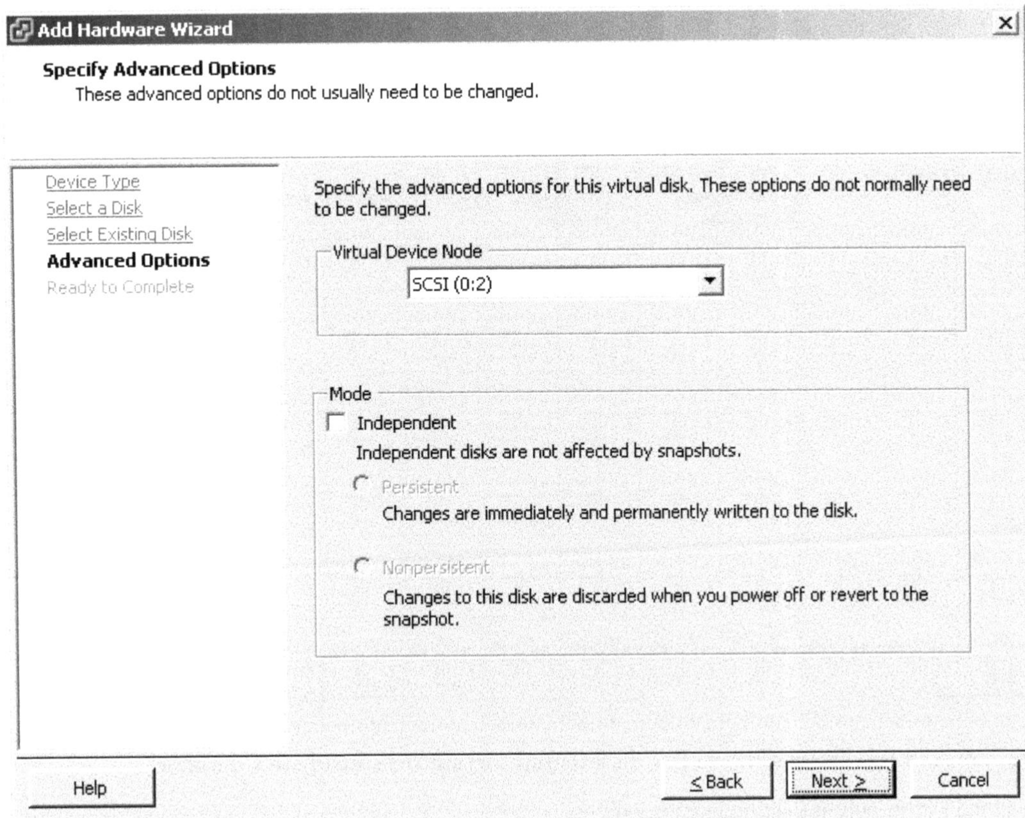

Figure 7.59 Add Hardware Wizard Use An Existing Virtual Disk Advanced Options

Click on the Next button to continue.

Step 4. The final screen of the Add Hardware Wizard shows a summary of your previous choices as shown in Figure 7.60.

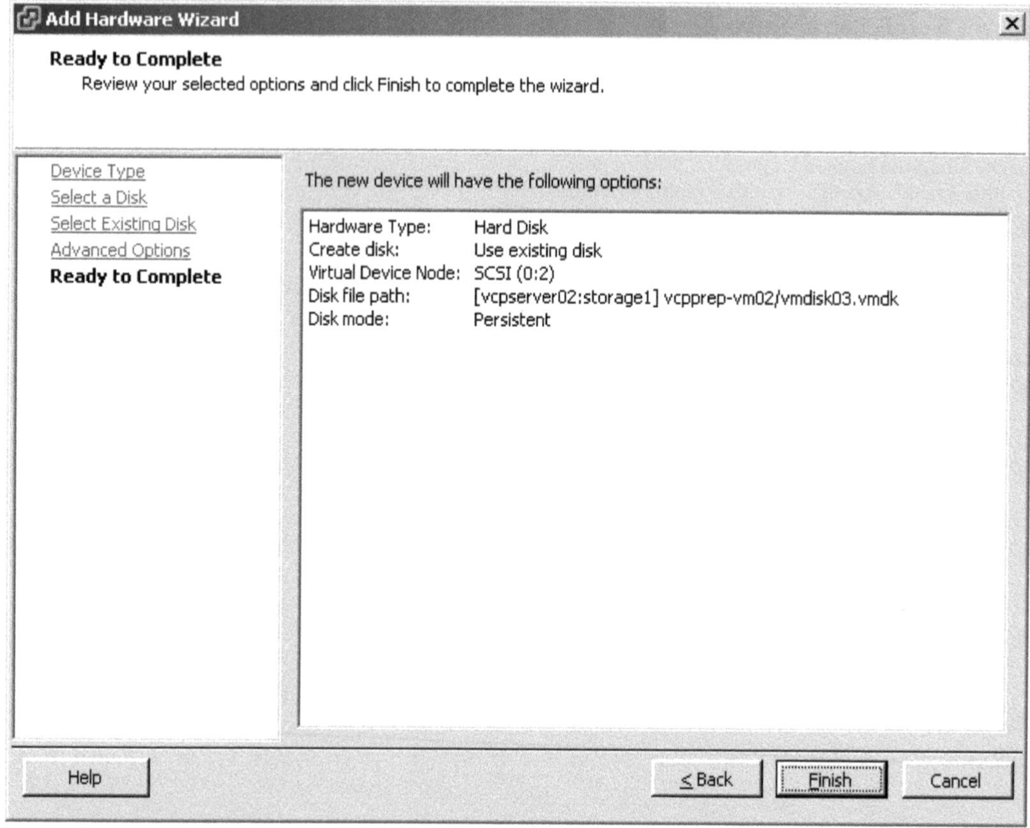

Figure 7.60 Add Hardware Wizard Use an Existing Virtual Disk Ready to Complete

Click on the Finish button to complete the process.

Adding Raw Device Mapping to Your Virtual Machine

In Chapter 5 - ESX 3.x Server Storage Configurations, we discussed the use of RDM files to point to a raw device for use with clustering.

To add Raw Device Mapping to an existing VMs configuration do the following steps:

Step 1. Right mouse button click on the VM in the inventory and select the Edit properties option in the pop up menu. Click on the Add device button which will start the Add Hardware Wizard as shown in Figure 7.61.

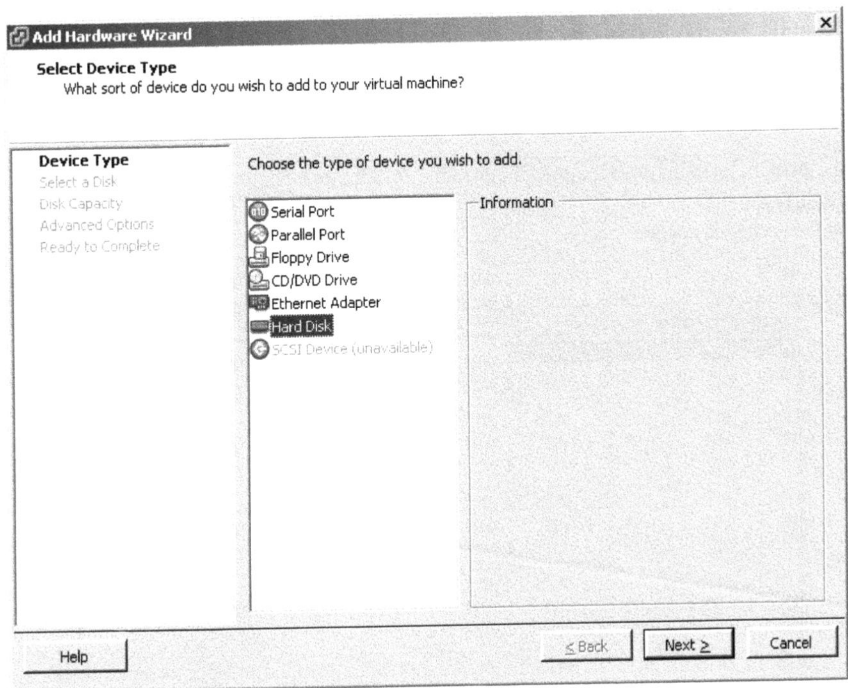

Figure 7.61 Add Hardware Wizard Hard Disk

Select the Hard Disk icon and click on the Next button to continue.

Step 2. The add hardware wizard gives the option to add a raw device mapping; see Figure 7.62.

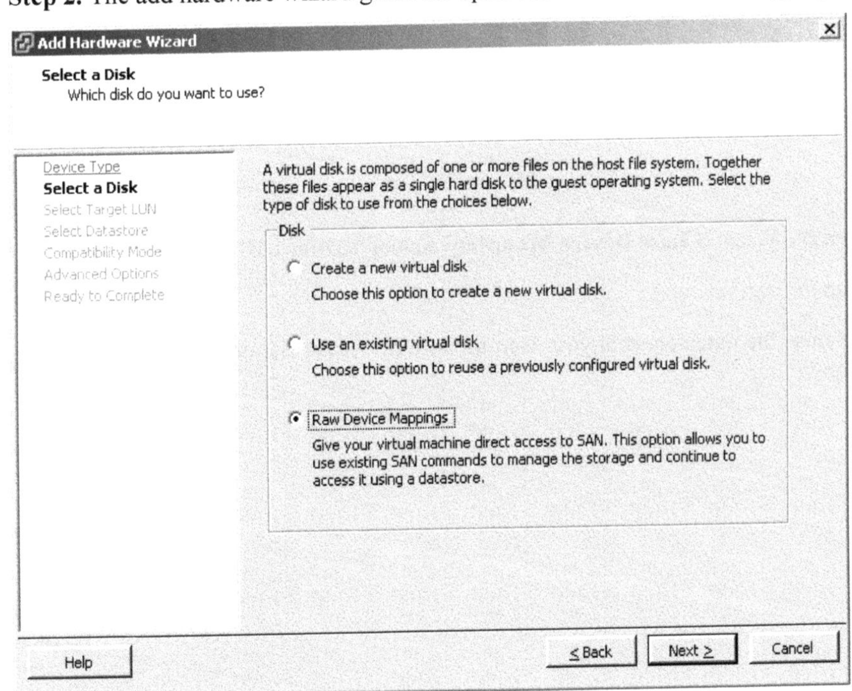

Figure 7.62 Add Hardware Wizard Raw Device Mappings

Select the Add Device Mappings radio button and select the Next button to continue the process.

Step 3. The next step is to select and configure a raw LUN. The LUNs that are available to the ESX 3.5 server will be listed in this screen. Click on the one that you want to use as shown in Figure 7.63.

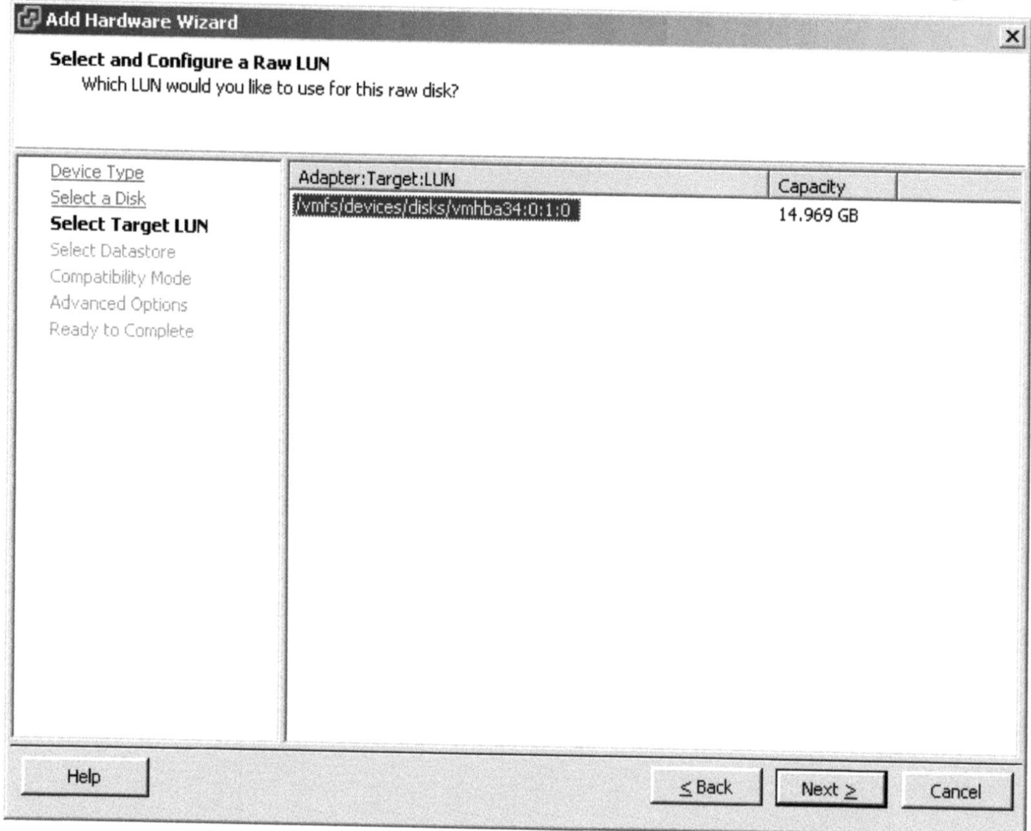

Figure 7.63 Add Hardware Wizard Raw Device Mappings Select Target LUN

Click on the Next Button to continue.

Step 4. You now can choose the datastore that you want to store the RDM file on as shown in Figure 7.64.

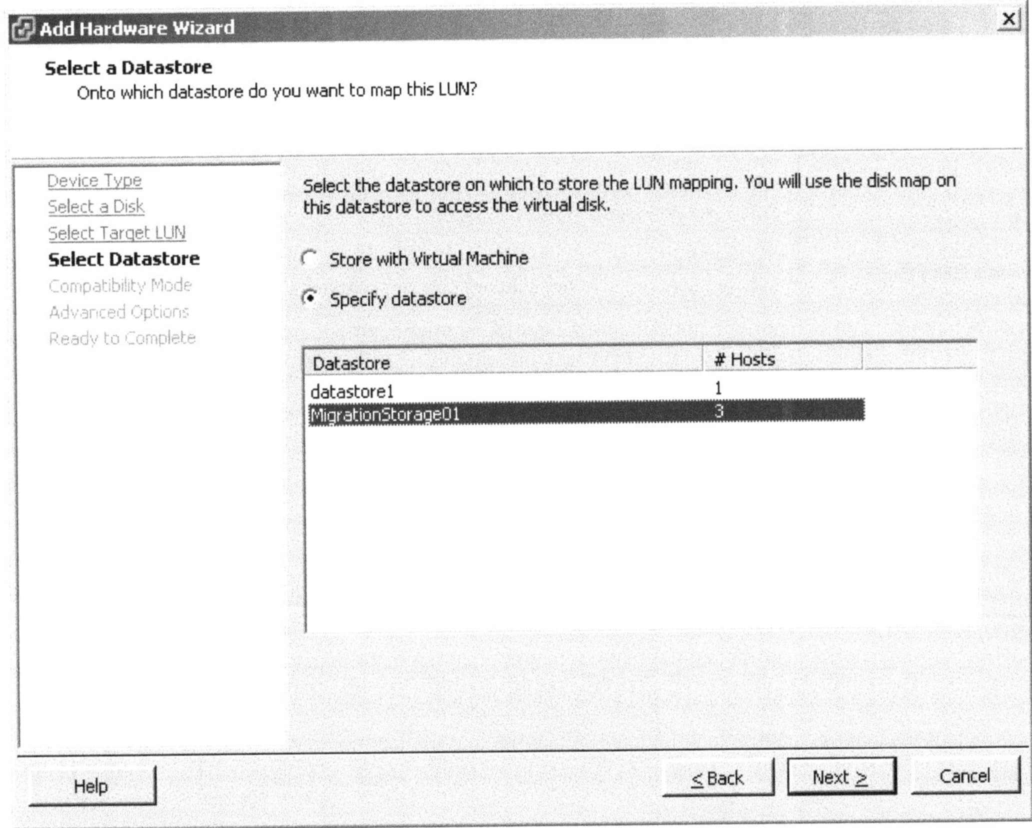

Figure 7.64 Add Hardware Wizard Raw Device Mappings Select Datastore

Click on the Next Button to continue.

Step 5. Now you can choose the compatibility mode for this RDM as shown in Figure 7.65. Choose the Physical radio button if you want to do a cluster-across-boxes (recommended) cluster or a physical to virtual cluster configuration. Physical compatibility mode is also useful when using SAN management tools from within a virtual machine. Snapshots cannot be used on RDMs in physical mode. Choose the Virtual radio button when you want to configure a cluster in a box environment. Snapshots can be taken when using RDMs in virtual mode.

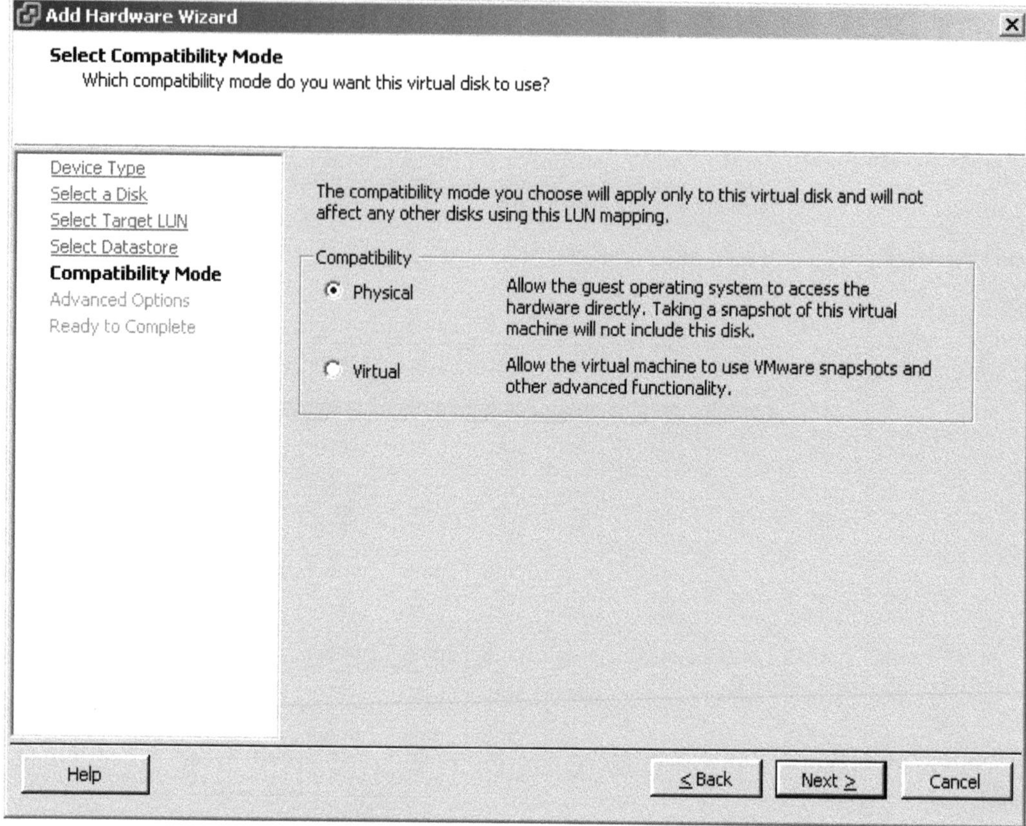

Figure 7.65 Add Hardware Wizard Raw Device Mappings Compatibility Mode

Click on the Next Button to continue.

Advanced Option

You can configure the Virtual Device Node if you want it to use a non default assigned node number as shown in Figure 7.66.

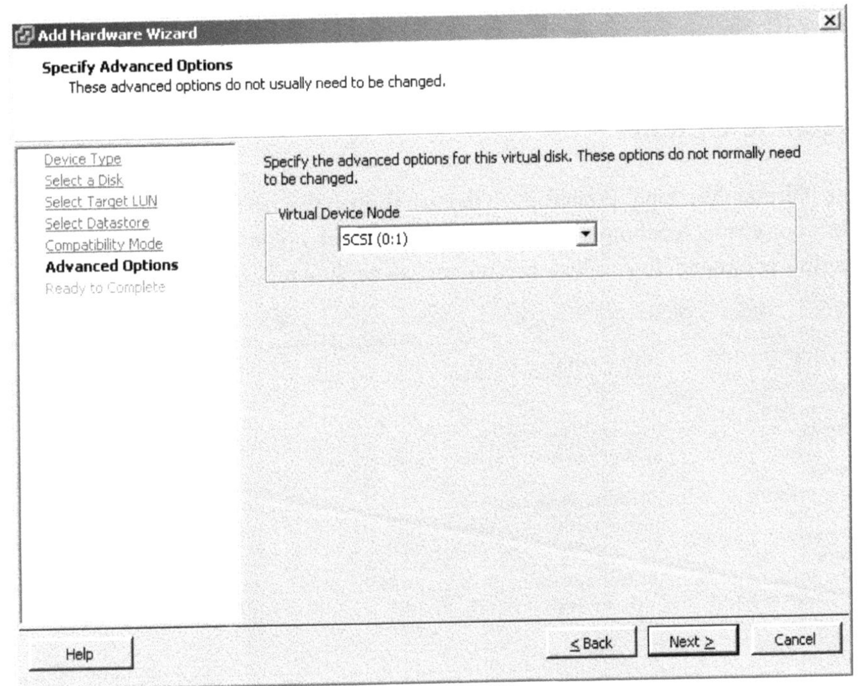

Figure 7.66 Add Hardware Wizard Raw Device Mappings Advanced Options

Click on the Next button to continue.

Step 6. The final screen of this Wizard, shown in Figure 7.67, summarizes your previous choices.

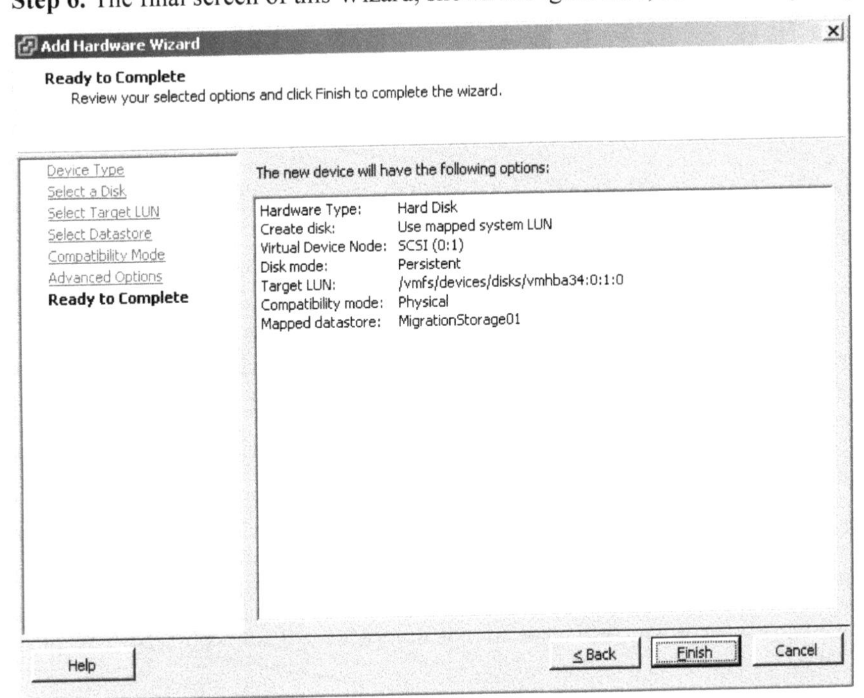

Figure 7.67 Add Hardware Wizard Raw Device Mappings Ready To Complete

Click on the Finish button to complete the process.

Setting Virtual Machine Options

The Options tab in the Virtual Machine Properties window allows you to set some additional configuration options for your virtual machines. Right mouse button click on the VM in the inventory and select the Edit Properties command, then select the Options tab as shown in Figure 7.68.

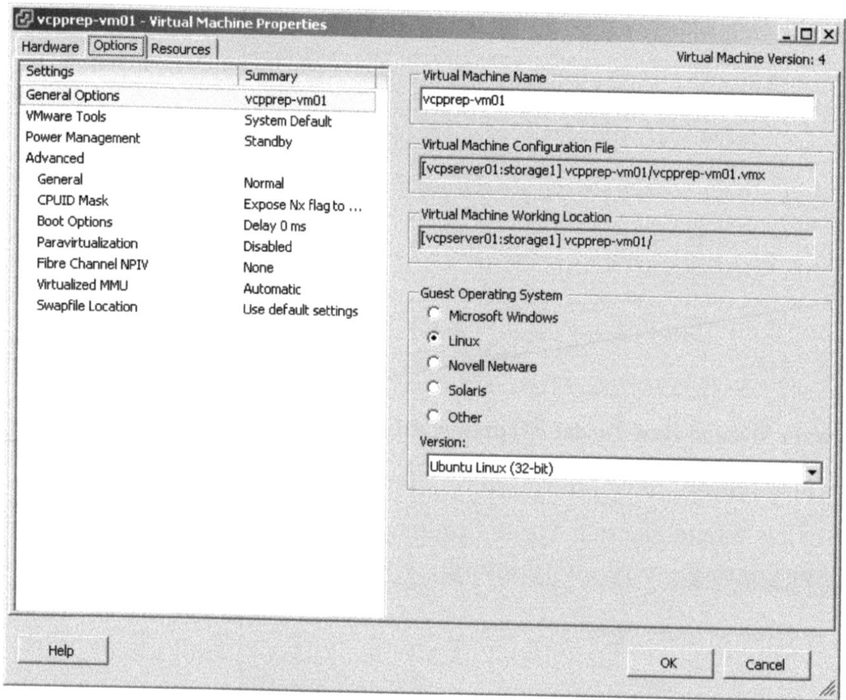

Figure 7.68 Virtual Machine Properties Options Tab General Options

The General settings will display the following:

- The virtual machine name - This is the display name for the VM. The display name assigned to the VM during creation is used as the name of the directory where the VM will be located and for the files that make up the virtual machine. If at a later time, the original display name is modified, the original directory name and file names will still be used. New files, such has virtual hard disks, will be named with the modified display name.
- The virtual machine configuration file and the datastore it is located on
- The virtual machine working location
- The guest operating system that was installed in the VM and what version was used

The second choice that you can select in the Settings section is the VMware Tools option as shown in Figure 7.69.

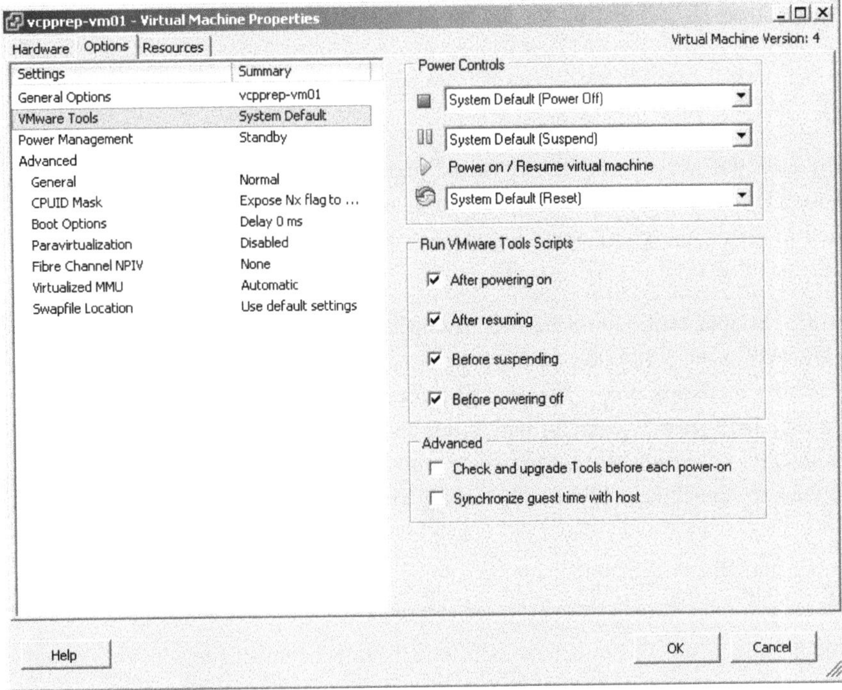

Figure 7.69 Virtual Machine Properties Options Tab VMware Tools

The VMware Tools Power Controls section provides the ability to redefine the default power state icons as follows:

Red Square Icon

- Power Off
- Shut Down Guest

By default, the Red square icon will immediately power off a virtual machine possibly leaving the guest operating system's file system in an inconsistent state, often referred to as a "crash-consistent" state. Changing this icon to the Shut Down Guest option will gracefully shut down the guest operating system in an orderly manner using VMware Tools.

Pause Icon

- Suspend
- Put Guest on Standby

The Pause icon default setting is to place the virtual machine in a suspended state. This default behavior can be changed to having the guest operating system placed in standby mode.

Power Icon

The green triangle power icon is not configurable. This icon can be used to power on a powered off virtual machine or resume a virtual machine that has been suspended.

Red and Green Arrows Icon:

- Reset
- Restart Guest

The red and green arrow icon will reset (reboot) the virtual machine by default. Resetting a virtual machine in this manner may leave the guest operating system in an inconsistent state. The behavior of this icon can be modified to restart the guest operating system in an orderly manner using VMware Tools.

In the Run VMware Tools Scripts section, select the appropriate check boxes to enable whether VMware Tools will be allowed to run scripts for each power state event as shown in Figure 7.69. The value of these settings within this dialog box is that the VM does not have to be powered on to alter whether or not a script is run. This can prove useful within test and development configurations where several virtual machines interact with each other. Modifying start up scripts is often necessary in such environments. The following are the choices of when to run a VMware Tools Script:

- After power on
- After resuming
- Before suspending
- Before powering off

The Advanced section allows you to configure the VM to check to see if a newer version of VMware tools is available. You can also synchronize the VM's time and date to that of the ESX 3.5 server.

Once you have made your selections, click OK to save your changes.

The third screen is the Power Management settings, as shown in Figure 7.70.

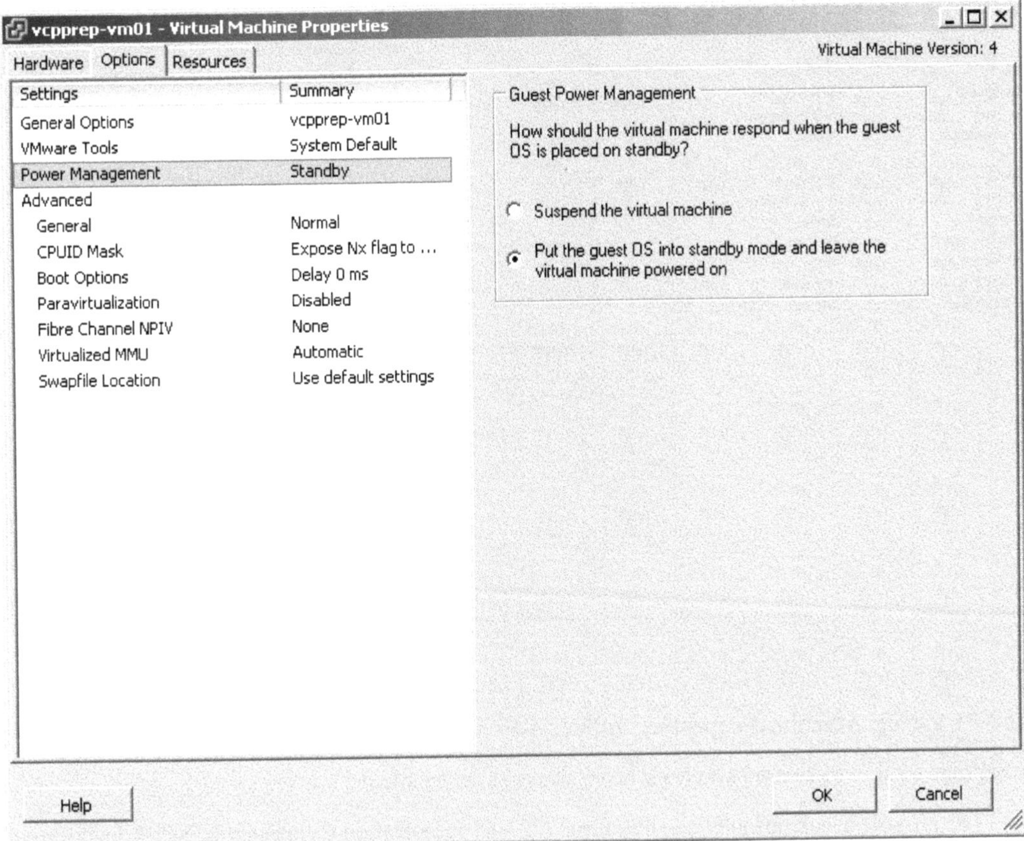

Figure 7.70 Virtual Machine Properties Options Tab Power Management

You can control the behavior of the guest OS when it is put in standby mode. The "Suspend the virtual machine" radio button should be selected when you want the VM's guest OS to be put in a suspended state. This will cause the guest OS to be paused and the contents of what was in memory will be written to the VMs suspend state files. The VM then would be powered off.

The second option is the "Put the guest OS into standby mode and leave the VM powered on" radio button. This option requires support from the guest operating system. When is standby mode, the guest operating system can be resumed via a Wake-on-LAN packet.

The Advanced settings screen as shown in Figure 7.71 displays a number of advanced configuration options that should only be changed when needed.

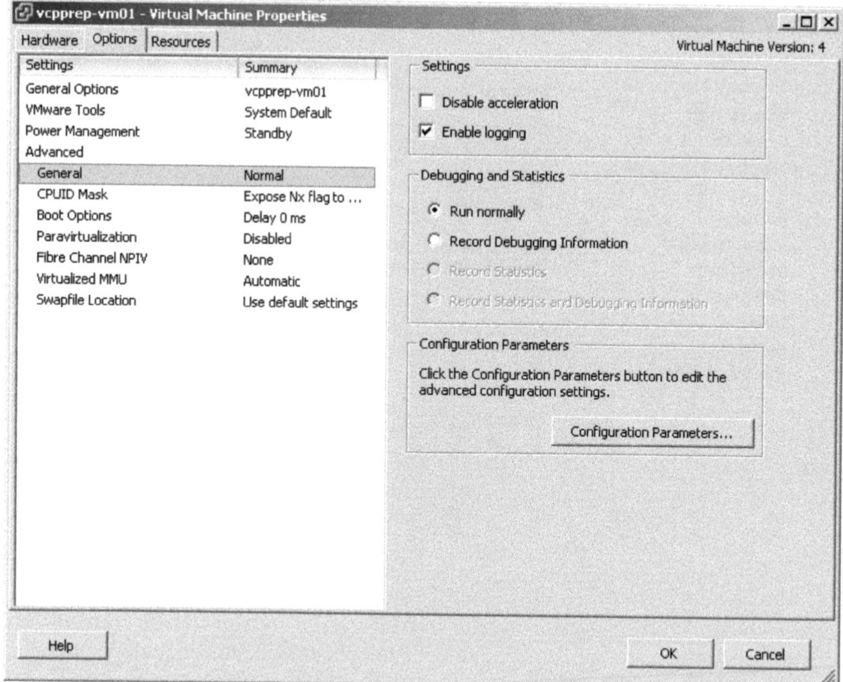

Figure 7.71 Virtual Machine Properties Options Tab Advanced General

In the Settings section there are two check boxes that can be enabled:

- The Disable acceleration check box turns off VM acceleration technologies. When installing or running software within a virtual machine, the application may appear to hang. To try and resolve this problem, this option temporarily disables acceleration in the virtual machine. If disabling acceleration resolves the problem, you may re-enable acceleration once the application is successfully running so that the virtual machine performance is no longer degraded.
- The Enable debugging information check box creates virtual machine log files that are useful when troubleshooting VM operational problems.

The Debugging and Statistics section is new for Virtual Center 2.5 and allows you to control the verbosity of messages within the virtual machine log files. By default, standard messages are logged. By selecting the Record Debugging Information, detail debug messages are logged. This option is useful when providing documentation to VMware support personnel.

The CPU Identification Mask section allows you to set whether or not the NX flag will be hidden from the guest OS.

AMD processors use the NX flag and Intel processors use the XD flag to do basically the same thing which is to lock a certain part of memory after data has been loaded into it by the boot process for the storage of processor instructions or the storage of data. The reason to do this is to prevent malicious code from changing the data stored in those memory locations after the OS has been started. Setting this setting can prevent buffer overflow attacks.

You might have to disable this setting temporarily in order to get the VMotion process to work properly. We will discuss this in more detail in Chapter 13 - Virtual Machine Migration.

If you click on the Advanced button in the CPU Identification Mask section as shown in Figure 7.72 you will be able to control the NX flag from being seen by the VM as well as setting a CPU identification mask. If changing this setting, the virtual machine will need to be rebooted in order for the guest operating system to utilize the modified setting.

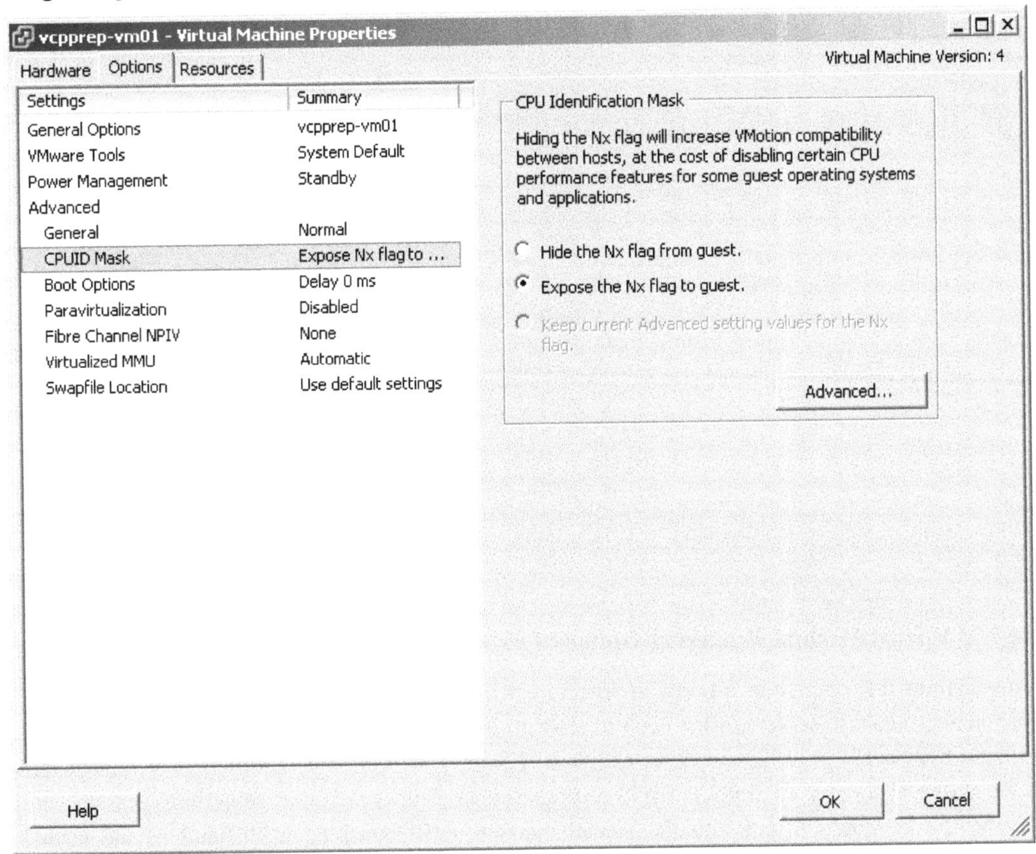

Figure 7.72 Virtual Machine Properties Options Tab Advanced CPUID Mask

Click on the Advanced button within the CPU Identification Mask section and enter information there only when directed by either VMware's support or your ESX 3.5 server vendor's support personnel. Incorrect settings can cause the system to not function properly.

Once all of the advanced options are set then you can select the OK button to close the window and accept the settings.

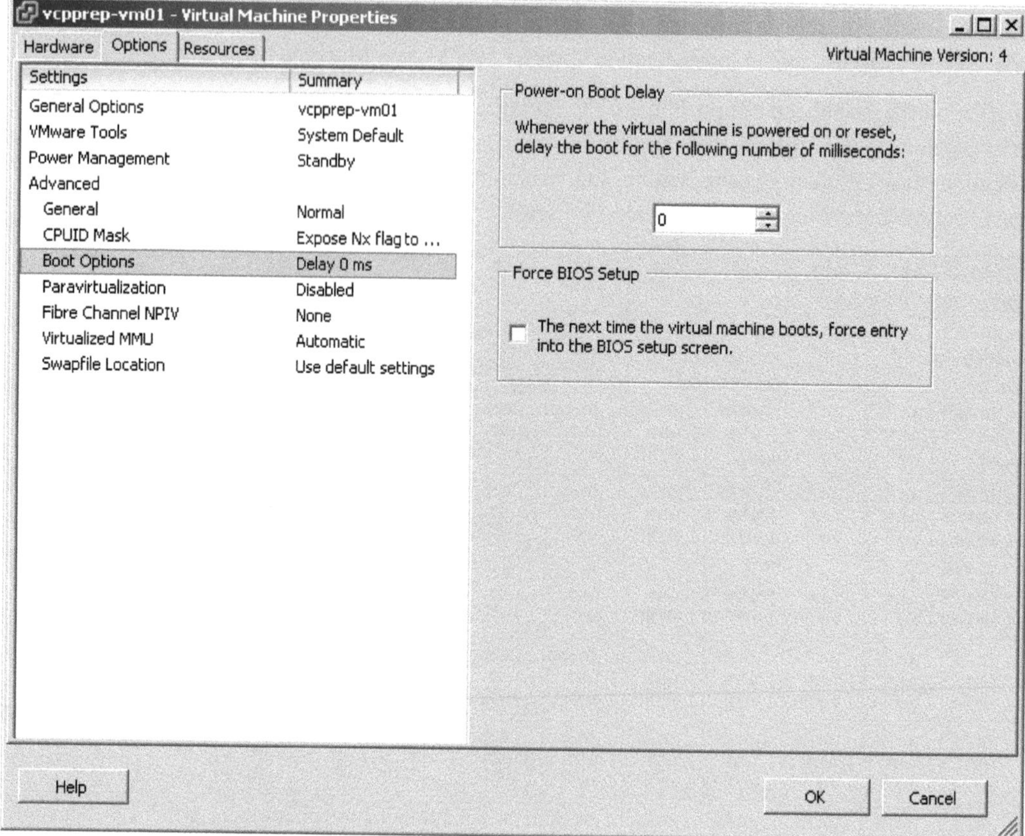

Figure 7.73 Virtual Machine Properties Options Tab Advanced Boot Options

Virtual machines that operate in a tiered architecture with other virtual machines, for example, web, application and database servers, often need to start up in a specific order. This can be accomplished by setting a boot delay in milliseconds as shown in Figure 7.73. One nice addition to VirtualCenter 2.5 is the ability to force a VM into its BIOS settings screen. This is useful as sometimes pressing the F2 key on the keyboard to get into the virtual machine's BIOS screen is difficult as the virtual machines tend to boot very quickly.

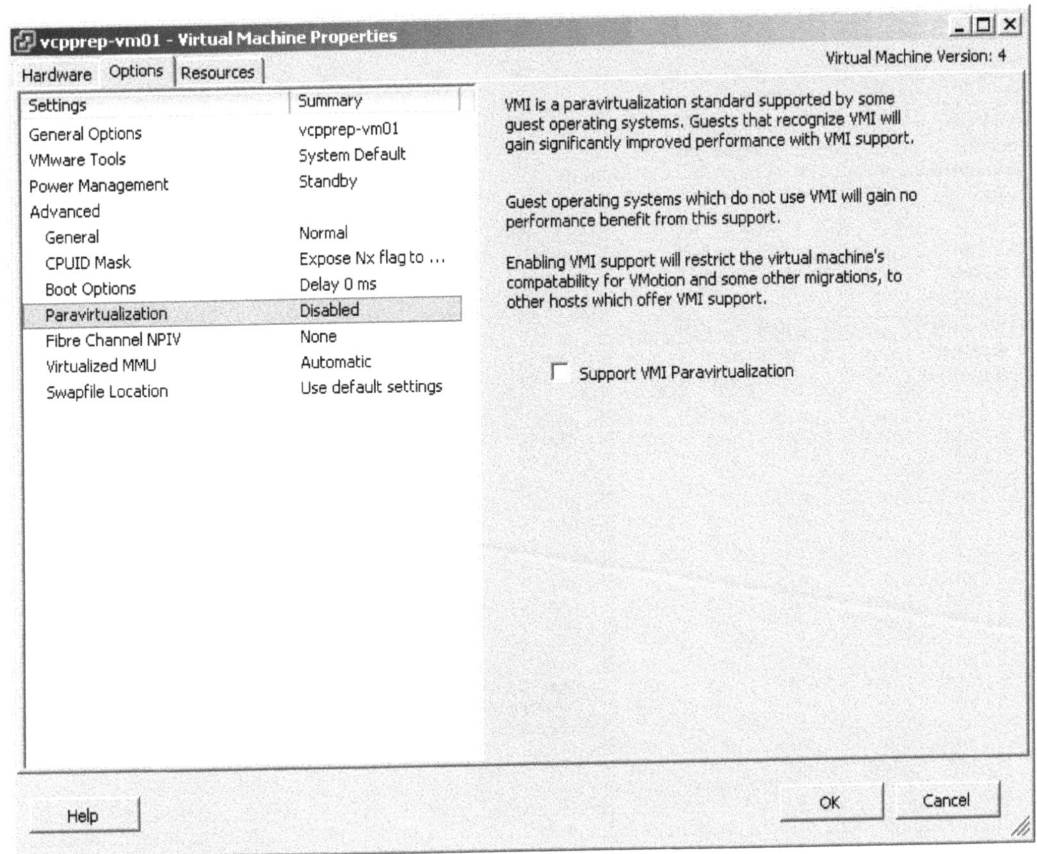

Figure 7.74 Virtual Machine Properties Options Tab Advanced Paravirtualization

A paravirtualized guest operating system is an operating system that has been modified to enhance performance and lower overhead in a virtualized environment. Only virtual machines that adhere to the VMware Virtual Machine Interface (VMI) 3.0 open standards interface can take advantage of the paravirtualization feature as shown in Figure 7.74. VMI was developed by VMware in junction with the Linux community. As of version 2.6.22 of the Linux kernel, VMI has been integrated into the Linux kernel.

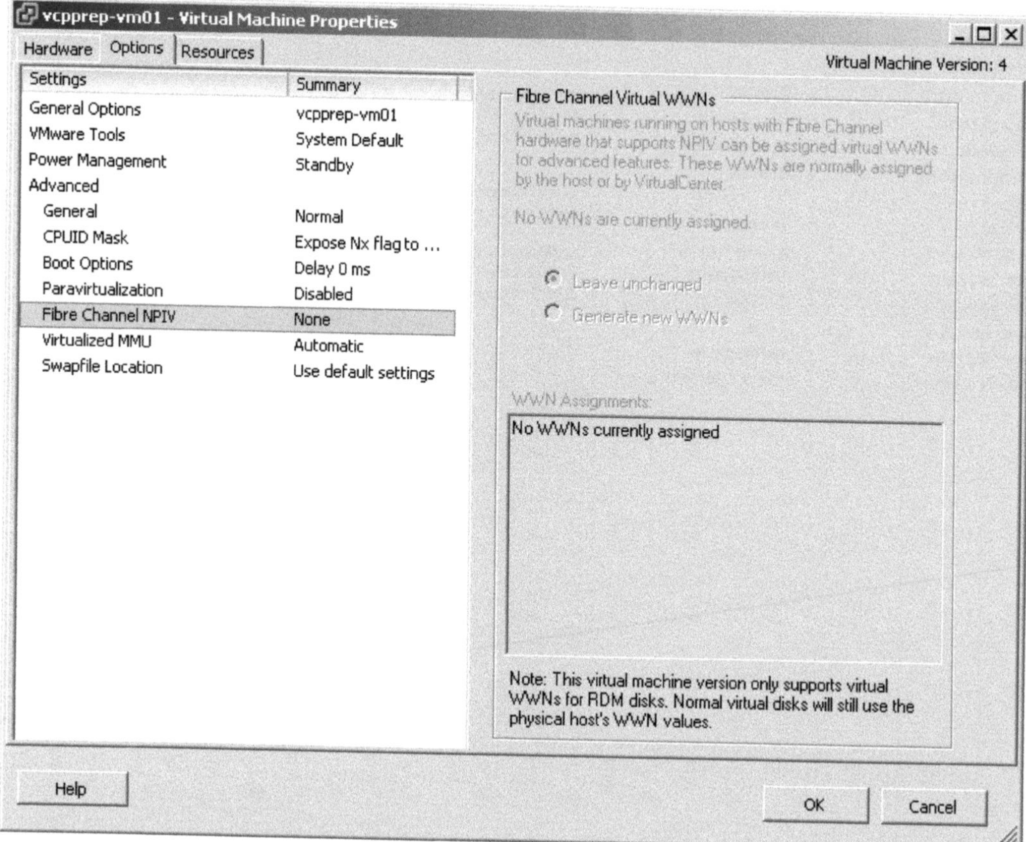

Figure 7.75 Virtual Machine Properties Options Tab Advanced Fibre Channel NPIV

N_Port ID Virtualization (NPIV) (see Figure 7.75) provides a virtual machine with its own WWN. This allows a SAN administrator to map to a virtual machine as opposed to an ESX 3.5 server. The HBA card within the ESX server must support this feature. Most newer HBAs now support NPIV. A virtual machine can now be zoned and masked to enhance security. With NPIV, the SAN team can now more closely monitor a virtual machines performance and use of a LUN. The virtual machine can still only access the virtual hard disk file stored on the LUN.

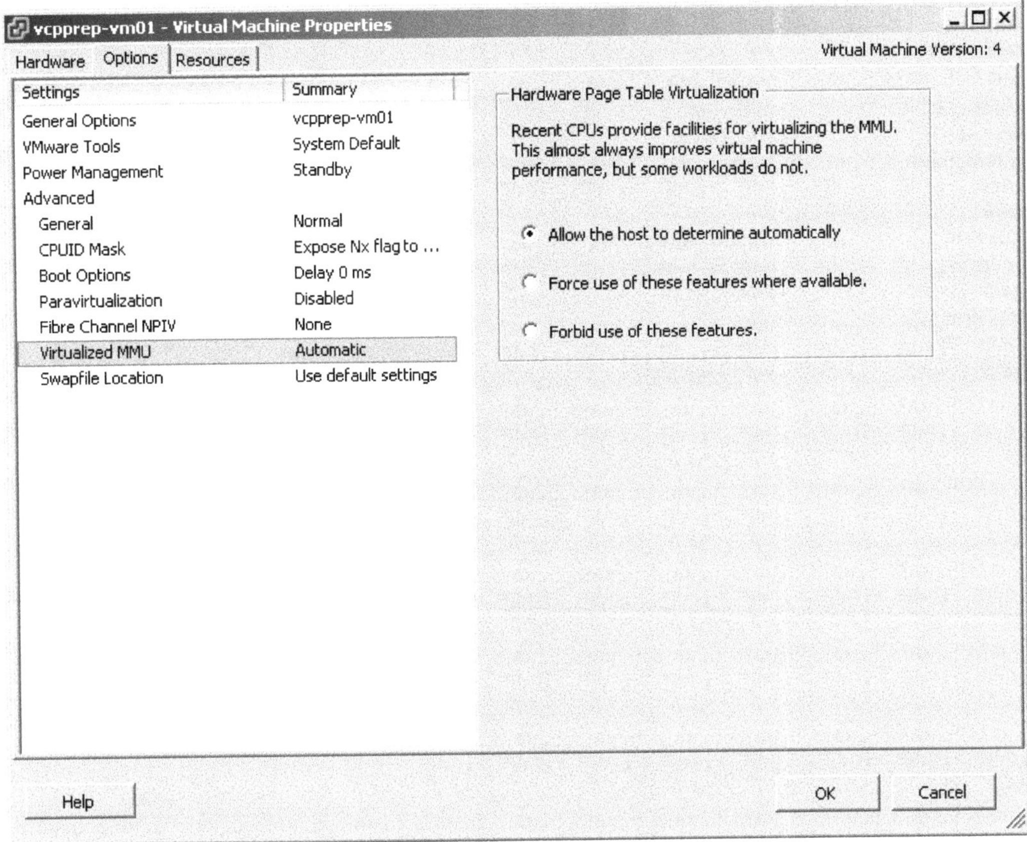

Figure 7.76 Virtual Machine Properties Options Tab Advanced Virtualized MMU

Prior to Memory Management Unit (MMU) virtualization, the VMkernel was responsible for the mapping of memory between the guest operating system and the machine pages of the physical machine. With newer CPUs that support hardware assisted Extended Page Table processor extensions; now the guest operating system can manage its own page tables. This capability can improve virtual machine memory performance. Refer to Figure 7.76.

.

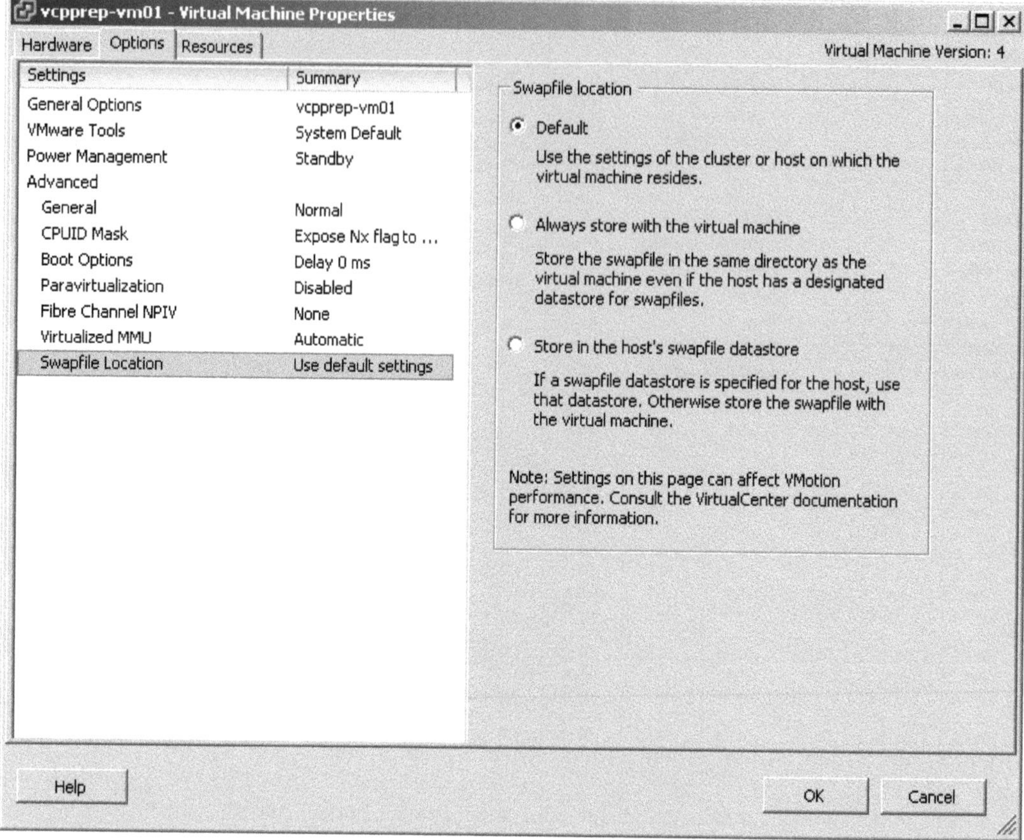

Figure 7.77 Virtual Machine Properties Options Tab Advanced Swapfile Location

VirtualCenter 2.5 now supports placing the virtual machine swap file in different locations. The default setting is to store the swap file as defined at the cluster or host level. If the virtual machine is not located within a VirtualCenter cluster (i.e. DRS or HA cluster), the host location is used. The default can be overridden by specifying either the virtual machine location or host location. It is ideal to store the swap file in a location with adequate storage space and if the VM is participating within a cluster, stored on shared storage. Sufficient storage space reduces virtual machine power on errors. Shared storage eliminates the need to move the swap file during fail over in a HA cluster for example.

Rapid Virtual Machine Deployment

Physical servers take time to rack mount and configure. You need to make sure the firmware is up to date on the server, the drives and the host bus adapters. You must also make sure that there are drivers for all of the hardware in the server so that the OS can communicate with the devices. All of these tasks take a lot of time and effort.

One of the benefits of using virtual machines is the ability to rapidly deploy them. A VM is just a set of encapsulated files and is easy to replicate. There are a number of ways to rapidly deploy your virtual machines:

- Clone a virtual machine
- Clone a virtual machine to a template
- Convert a virtual machine to template
- Deploying a virtual machine from a template
- Clone a template

Cloning a Virtual Machine

A virtual machine that needs to be duplicated can be cloned. Clones can be used to do testing of software updates such as service packs or upgrades to the latest revision of a software application. A clone of a virtual machine can also serve as a backup of a virtual machine.

Cloning a Virtual Machine to a Template

A virtual machine that meets the organizations compliance standards for example, can serve as the source configuration of a template. If the source virtual machine is needed to continue in operation as a powered on virtual machine, you can choose to use the virtual machine as the source of the template.

Converting a Virtual Machine to Template

You can update your virtual machine with the appropriate software applications, patches and security fixes and then convert it to a template. A template is a VM designed not to be powered on. It can be used to rapidly deploy multiple identically configured VMs quickly.

Deploying a Virtual Machine from a Template

The value of taking the time to create templates is seen when it comes time to deploy several new virtual machines. Integration with Microsoft Sysprep software or the built in Linux tool (in VirtualCenter) enables rapid provisioning of unique virtual machines with little effort. Templates are prevented from being powered on and altered. This insures that the source image is consistent each time a new virtual machine is deployed.

Cloning A Template

Templates can also be cloned. This is a useful feature if you want to keep a backup copy of the template because you plan on updating it and you still want the original configuration stored. You might want to make additional copies to keep on other storage devices for redundancy or for higher availability if the template gets accessed a lot.

Be aware that you cannot clone a VM on a standalone ESX 3.5 server. You must use VirtualCenter 2.5 to manage the process. Let's examine the steps to the various rapid deployment methods.

Cloning a Virtual Machine

The following steps illustrate how to clone a virtual machine.

Step 1. Right mouse button click on the virtual machine that you want to clone. Select the Clone Option from the pop up menu as shown in Figure 7.78.

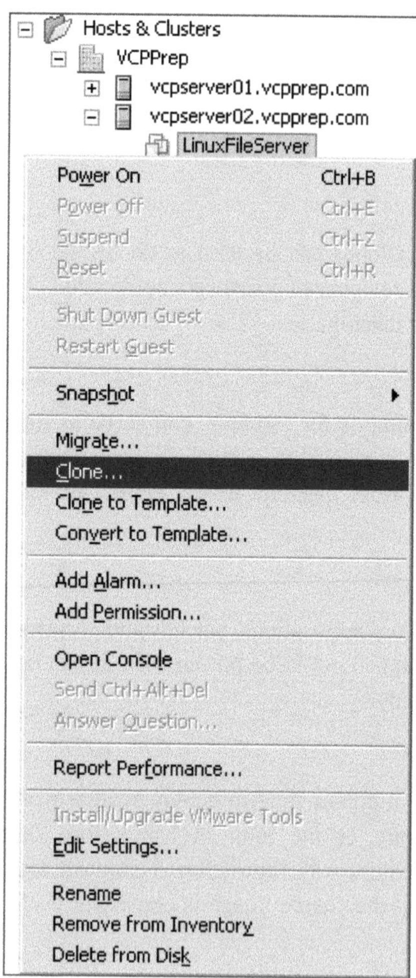

Figure 7.78 Clone Virtual Machine Menu Option

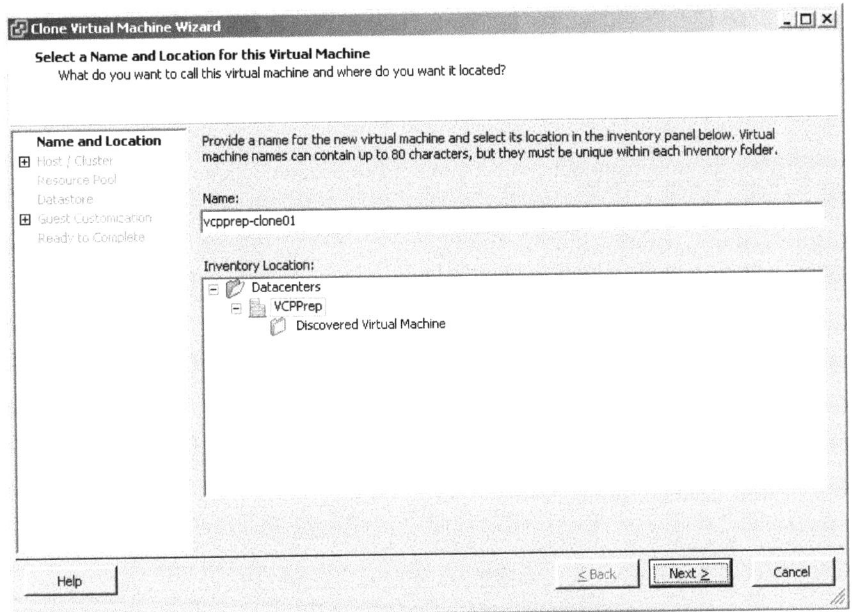

Figure 7.79 Clone Virtual Machine Wizard Name And Location

Step 2. Choose a name and a location for this cloned virtual machine as shown in Figure 7.79.

Step 3. Choose an appropriate ESX server host or cluster of ESX servers that will run this cloned virtual machine as shown in Figure 7.80.

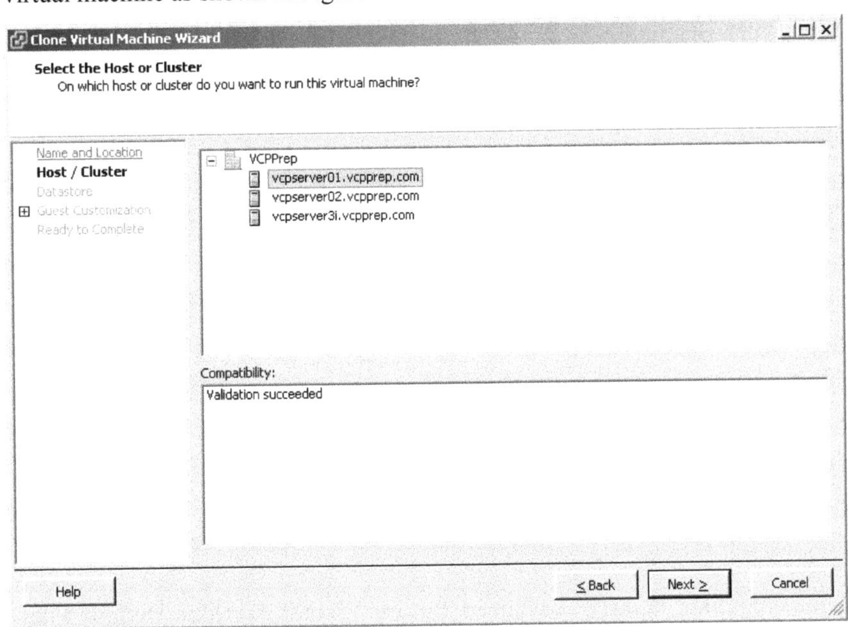

Figure 7.80 Clone Virtual Machine Wizard Host / Cluster

Step 4. Choose the location that will be used to store this cloned virtual machine as shown in Figure 7.81.

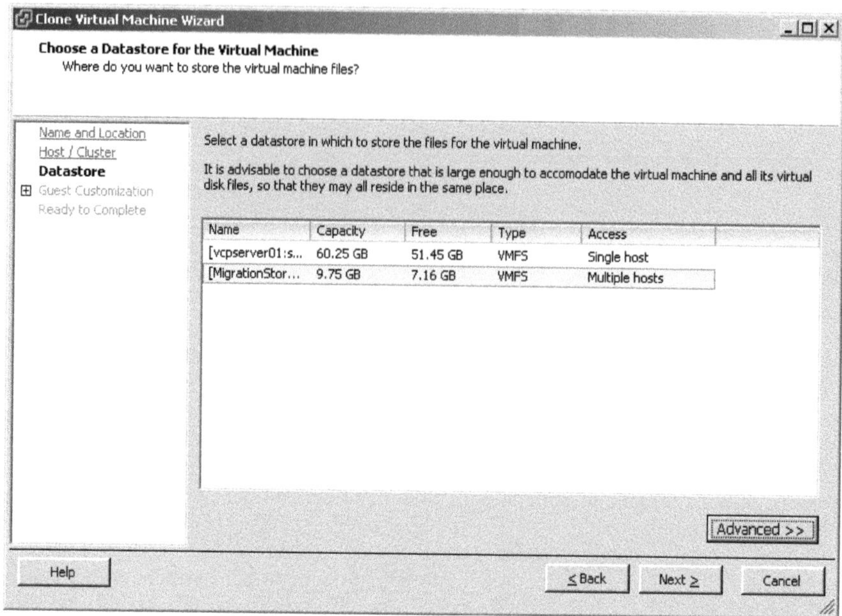

Figure 7.81 Clone Virtual Machine Wizard Datastore Advanced Button

Step 5. Select the Advanced button if needing to choose a separate configuration file and or hard drive file location as shown in Figure 7.82.

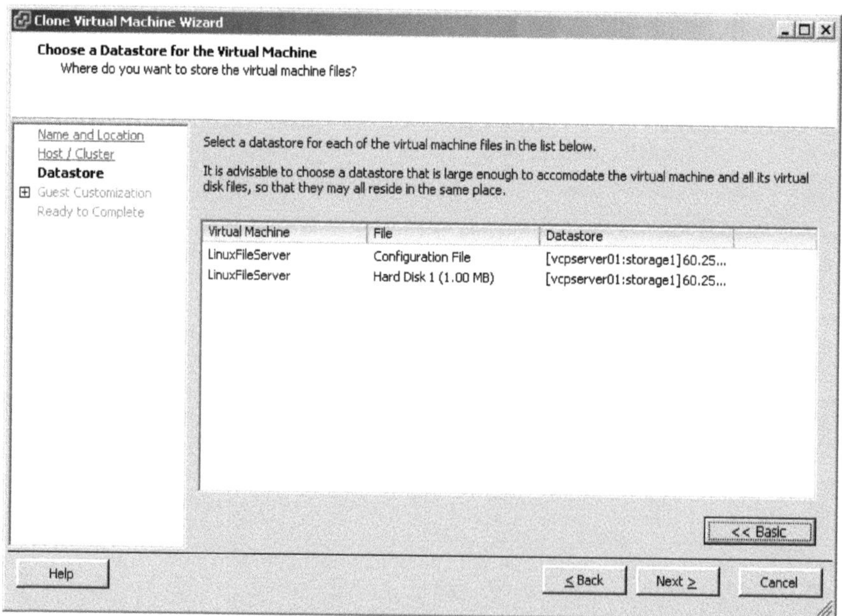

Figure 7.82 Clone Virtual Machine Wizard Advanced Button Virtual Machine Default Files Location

Step 6. Select the drop down selection to choose another location for the cloned virtual machine's configuration file as shown in Figure 7.83.

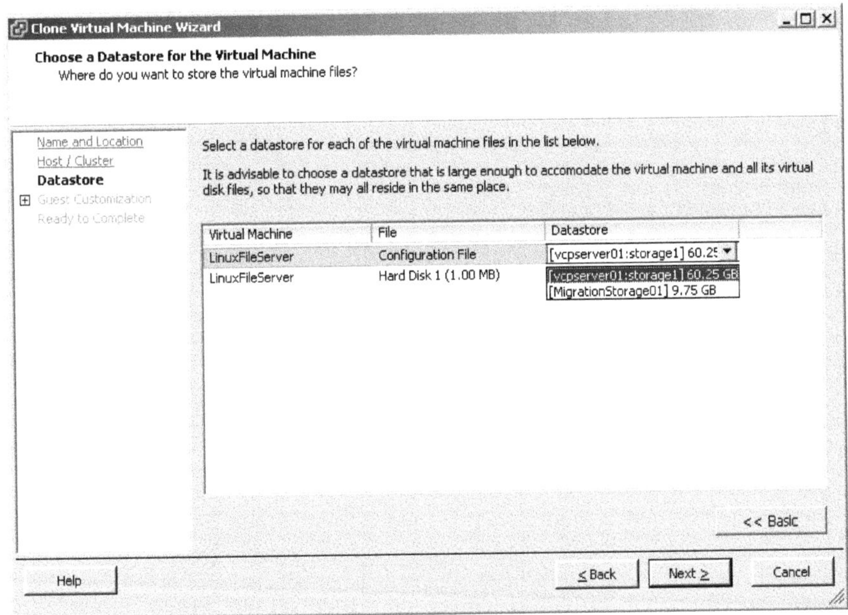

Figure 7.83 Clone Virtual Machine Wizard Advanced Button Virtual Machine Configuration File

Step 7. Select the drop down selection to choose another location for the cloned virtual machine's hard drive file as shown in Figure 7.84.

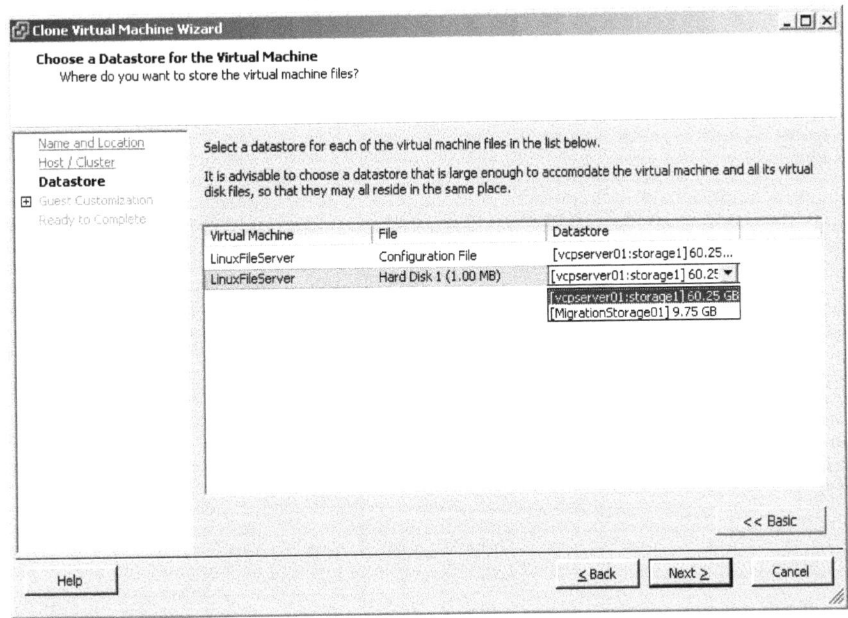

Figure 7.84 Clone Virtual Machine Wizard Advanced Button Virtual Machine Hard Disk File

Step 8. Select the Do not customize radio button if the guest customization wizard is not desired as shown in Figure 7.85.

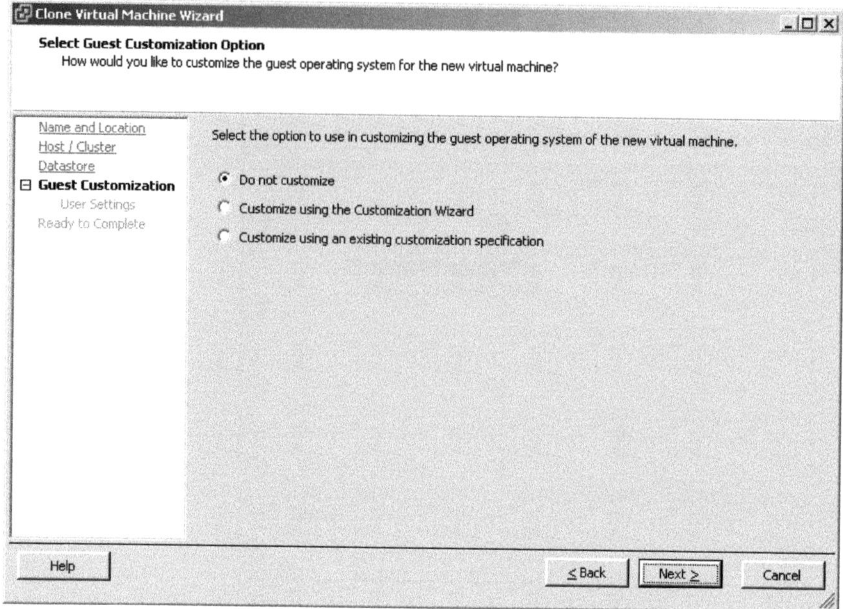

Figure 7.85 Clone Virtual Machine Wizard Do Not Customize

Step 9. Select the Finish button to complete the cloning a virtual machine wizard as shown in Figure 7.86.

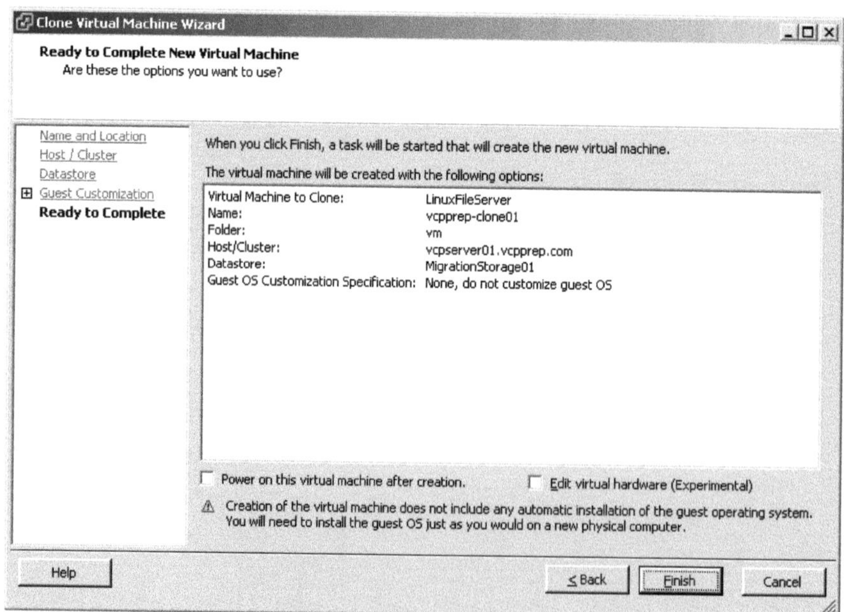

Figure 7.86 Clone Virtual Machine Wizard Ready To Complete

Cloning a Virtual Machine to a Template

Step 1. Right mouse button click on the virtual machine that you want to use as the source configuration for the template. Select the Clone to Template Option from the pop up menu as shown in Figure 7.87.

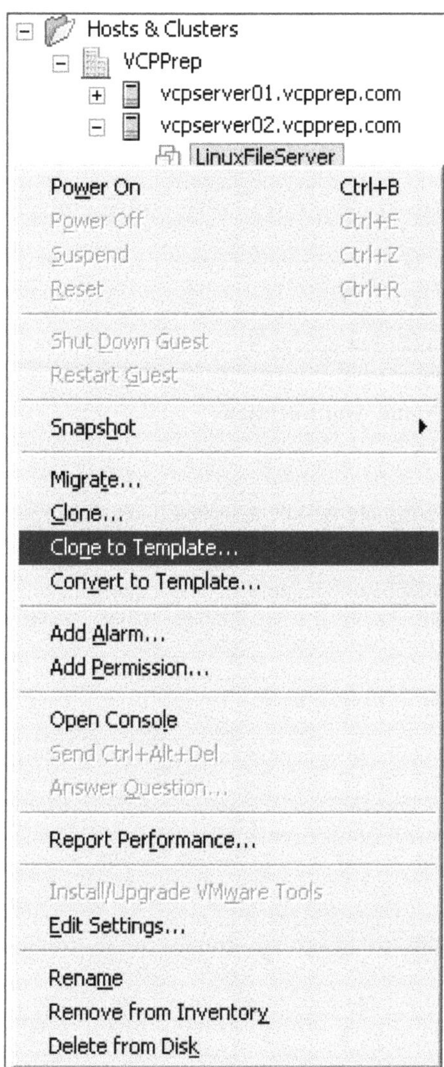

Figure 7.87 Clone To Template Menu Option

Step 2. Assign the template a descriptive name and a location to place the template within the VirtualCenter inventory as shown in Figure 7.88.

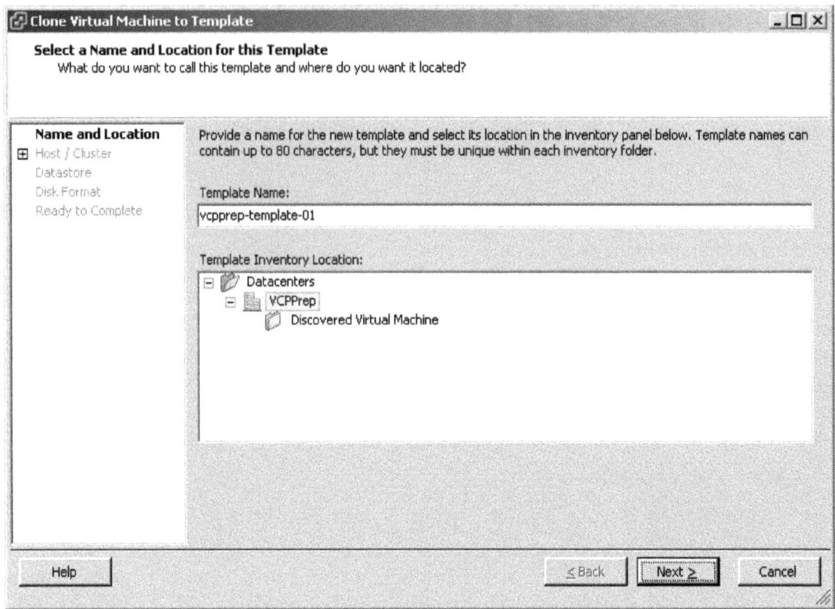

Figure 7.88 Clone Virtual Machine To Template Wizard Name And Location

Click on the Next button to continue.

Step 3. Select the ESX host or cluster of ESX hosts that the template will be assigned to as shown in Figure 7.89.

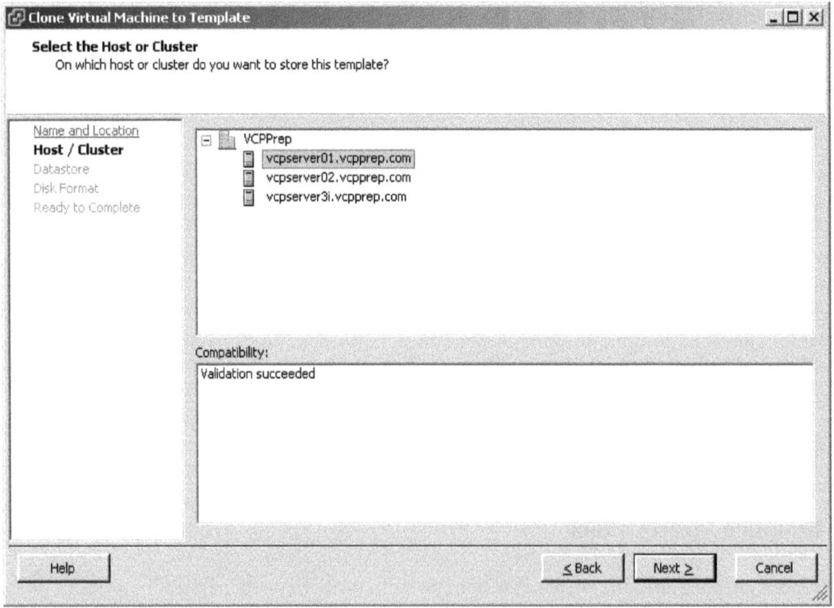

Figure 7.89 Clone Virtual Machine To Template Wizard Host / Cluster

Click on the Next button to continue.

Step 4. Choose the datastore where the template files will be placed. To choose a different location other than the specified datastore, select the Advanced button in the lower right corner of the Clone Virtual Machine to Template dialog box as shown in Figure 7.90.

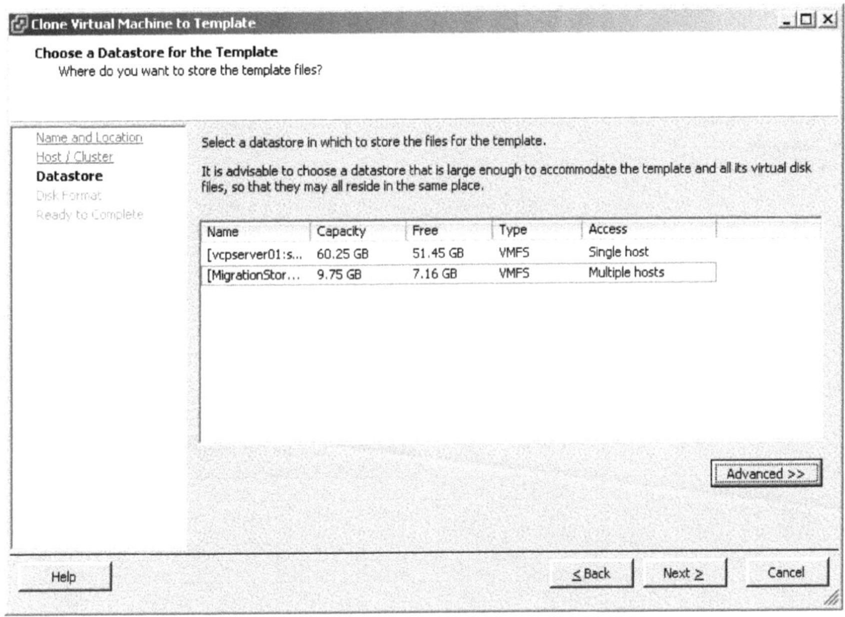

Figure 7.90 Clone Virtual Machine To Template Wizard Datastore Advanced Button

Step 5. Click on the Current Location text under the Datastore column to specify a separate storage location for the Configuration and Hard Disk files as shown in Figure 7.91.

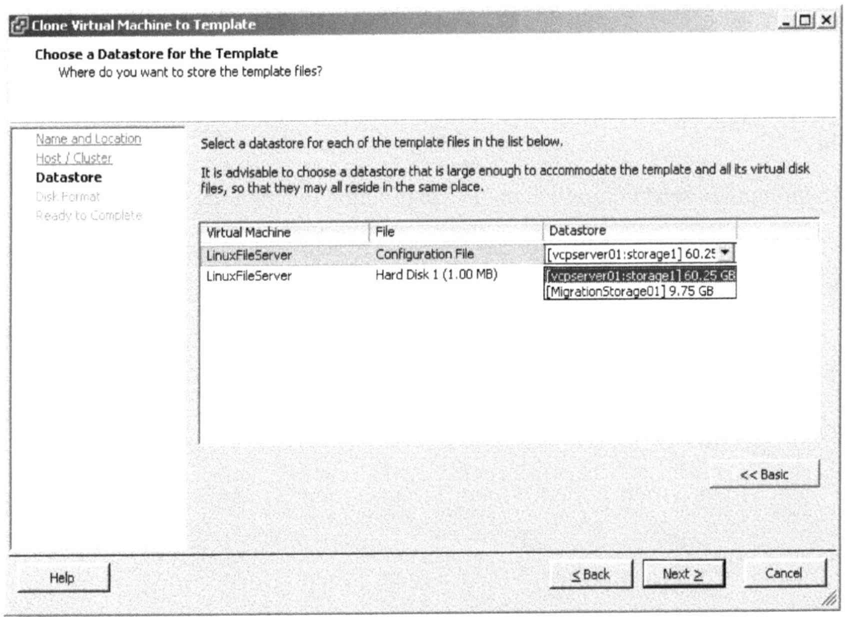

Figure 7.91 Clone Virtual Machine To Template Wizard Datastore Advanced Button Virtual Machine Configuration File

The configuration file can be stored in any of the displayed locations under the Current Location drop-down box.

Step 6. The virtual Hard Disk file can also be stored in any of the displayed locations under the Current Location drop-down box as shown in Figure 7.92.

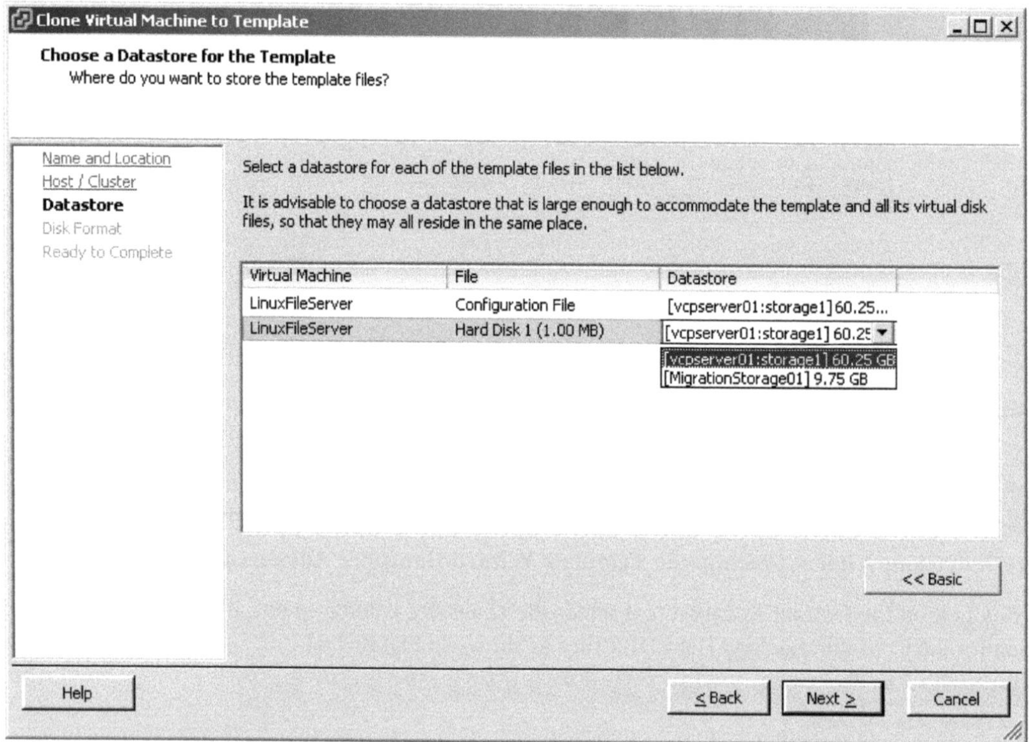

Figure 7.92 Clone Virtual Machine to Template Wizard Datastore Advanced Button Virtual Machine Hard Disk File

Once you have made the appropriate selections, click on the Next button to continue.

Step 7. Select the disk format for the template. Normal format will leave the virtual hard disk the same size whereas the Compact format takes up less storage space.

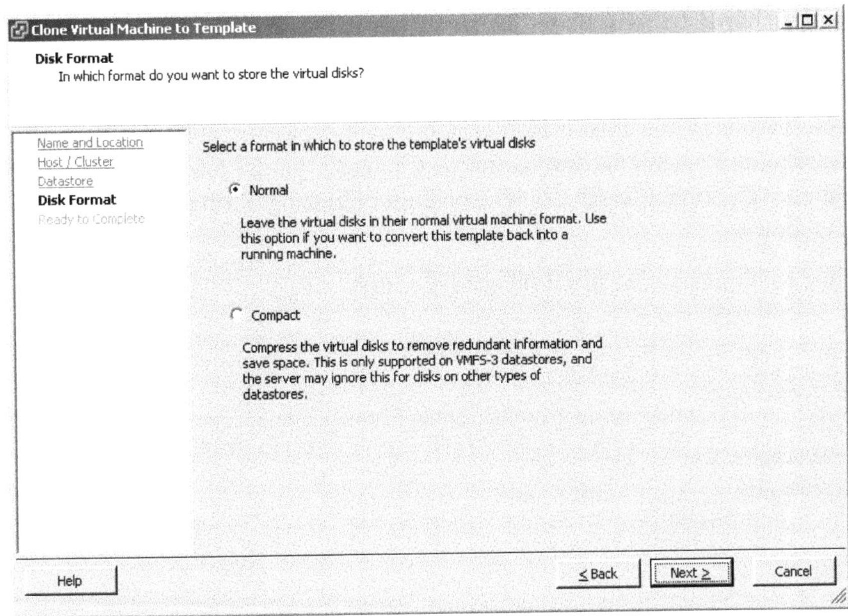

Figure 7.93 Clone Virtual Machine To Template Wizard Disk Format

Choose the appropriate disk format and click the Next button as shown in Figure 7.93.

Step 8. Review the selected options. If any options need modified, click the Back button and locate the appropriate step in the wizard.

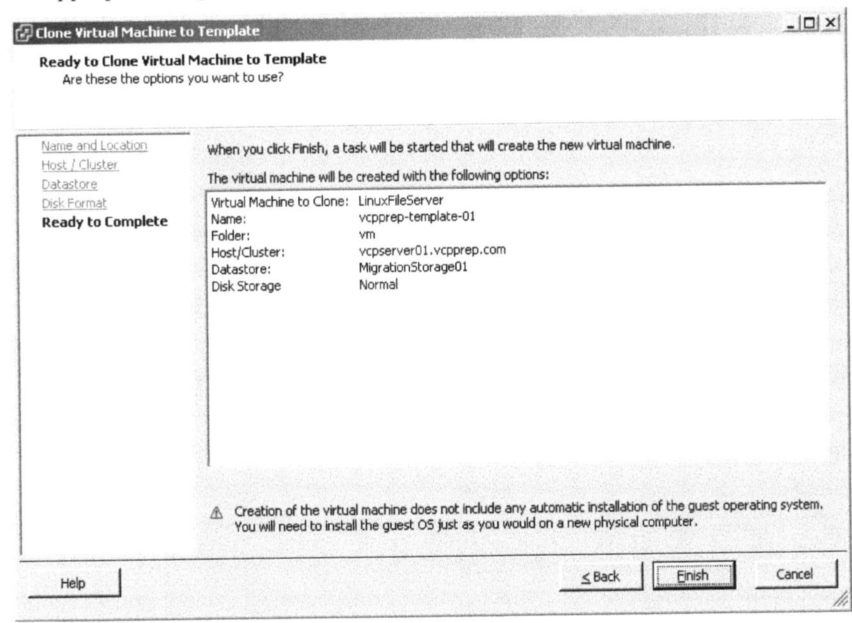

Figure 7.94 Clone Virtual Machine To Template Wizard Ready To Complete

Once the options have been confirmed, click the Finish button to complete the Clone Virtual Machine to Template wizard as shown in Figure 7.94.

Cloning a Virtual Machine to another Datacenter

We will see in Chapter 10 that the Datacenter object in the VirtualCenter 2.5 inventory is the highest level management object. Placement of virtual machines in different datacenter objects will impact who will be able to manage and control its configuration. Cloning a virtual machine to another datacenter is a new feature with VirtualCenter 2.5. The process of cloning a virtual machine to a different datacenter is as follows:

Step 1: Select the VM that you want to clone to a different datacenter.

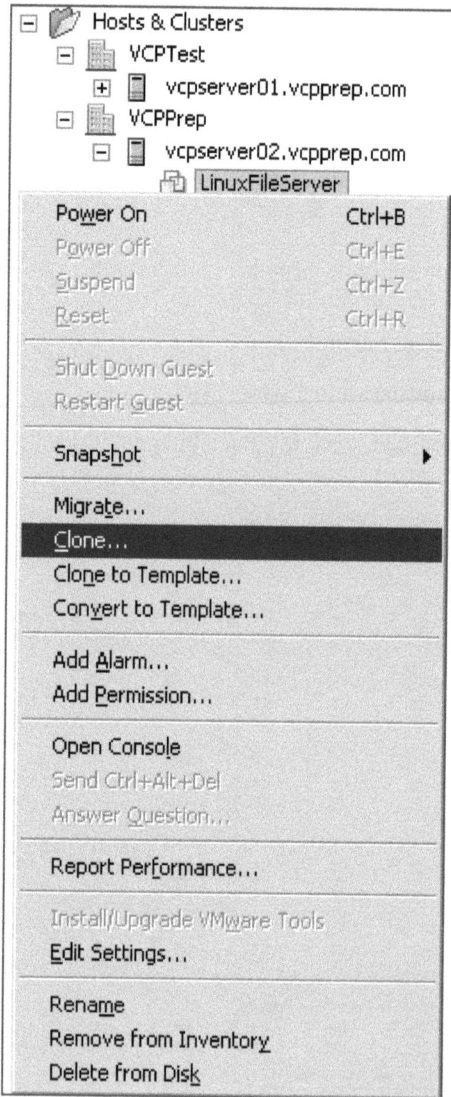

Figure 7.95 Clone Virtual Machine Menu Option

Figure 7.95 shows that we have right mouse button clicked on a VM called LinuxFileServer that is in the VCPPrep datacenter and selected the Clone command. This launches the Clone Virtual Machine Wizard.

Step 2: Select a Name and Location for this Virtual Machine screen.

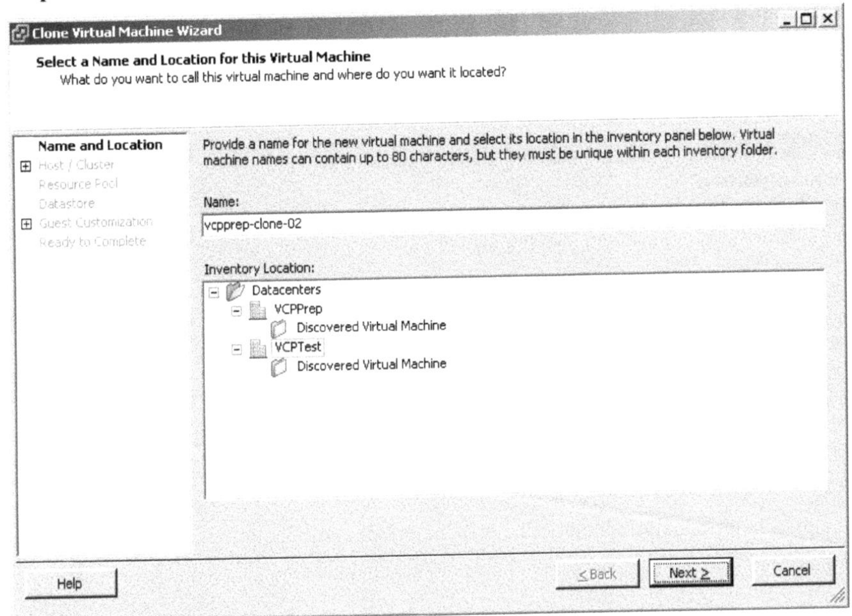

Figure 7.96 Clone Virtual Machine Wizard Name And Location

The next step in the process requires that you name the new virtual machine and select the datacenter that it will reside in as shown in Figure 7.96. Notice in this example that we have selected a different datacenter (VCPTest). After you have made your choice, click on the Next button to continue.

Step 3: Select the Host or Cluster screen.

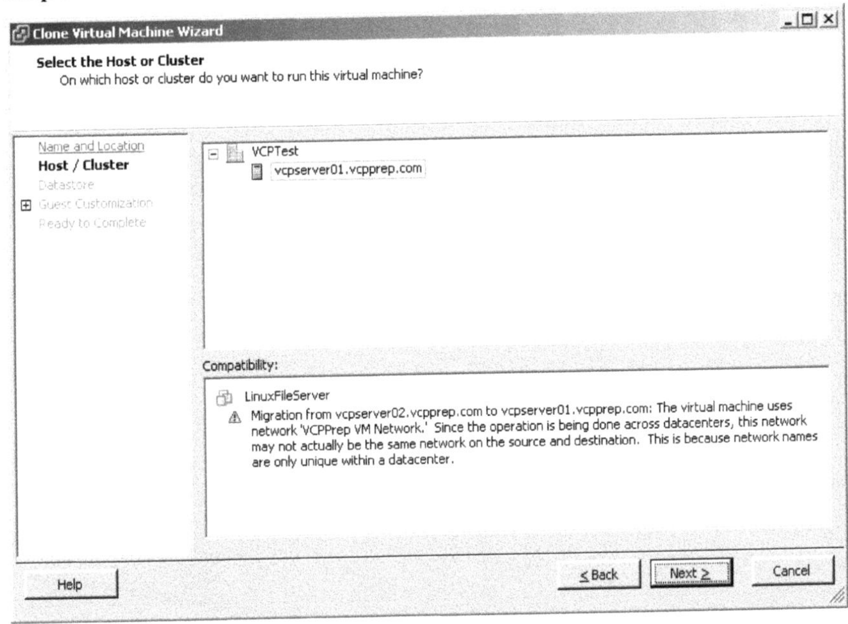

Figure 7.97 Clone Virtual Machine Wizard Host / Cluster

The next step requires that you select the specific host or VMware cluster that you want to control the new cloned VM. In this example in Figure 7.97, we have selected the vcpserver01.vcpprep.com ESX 3.5 server. After you have made your selection, click on the Next button to continue.

Step 4: Choose a Datastore for the Virtual Machine screen.

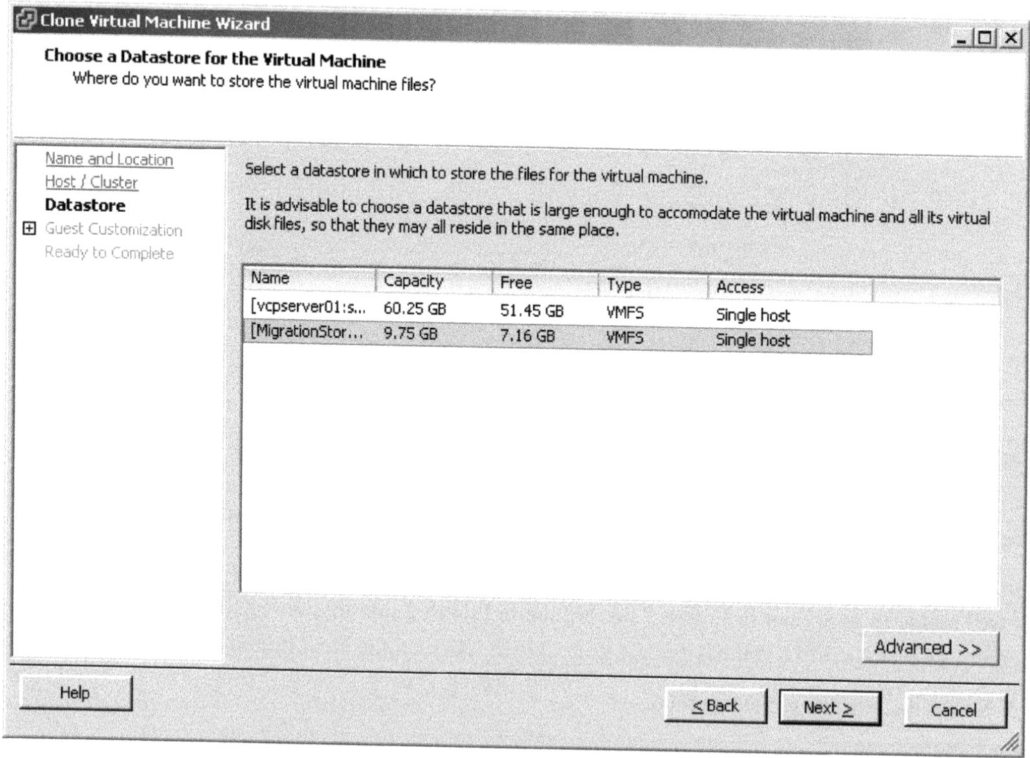

Figure 7.98 Clone Virtual Machine Wizard Datastore

The new VMs state files will be created on a datastore during the cloning process. Figure 7.98 shows that we have chosen the MigrationStorage01 datastore. As we discussed in Chapter 5 - ESX 3.x Server Storage Configuration, placement of these files on poorly configured storage devices can impact the performance of the VM. Once you have made your selection, press the Next button to continue.

Step 5: Select Guest Optimization Option screen.

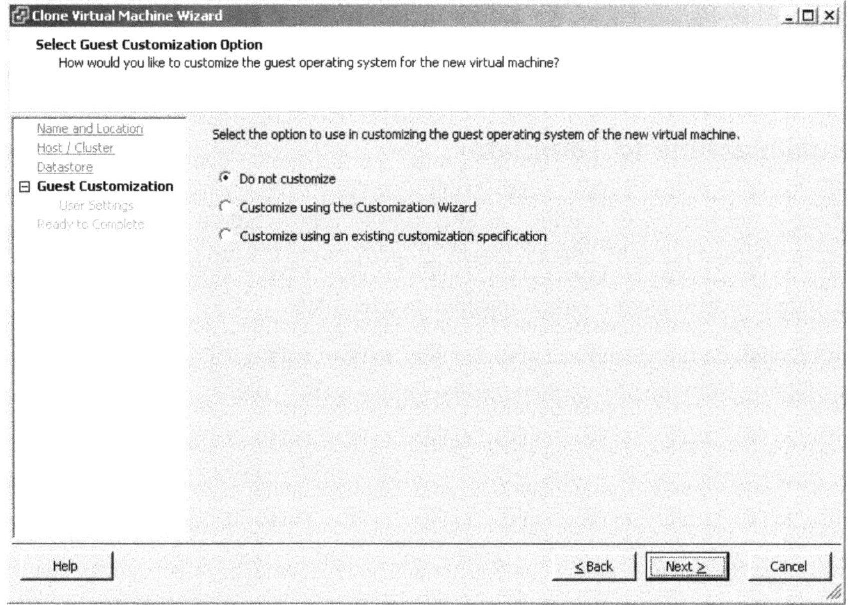

Figure 7.99 Clone Virtual Machine Wizard Do Not Customize

The next step requires that we select if the VM is to be customized or not. Use of the Customization Wizard will be discussed later in this chapter. In this example we are not going to customize the guest OS. After you have made the selection as shown in Figure 7.99, click on the Next button to continue.

Step 6: Ready to Complete New Virtual Machine screen.

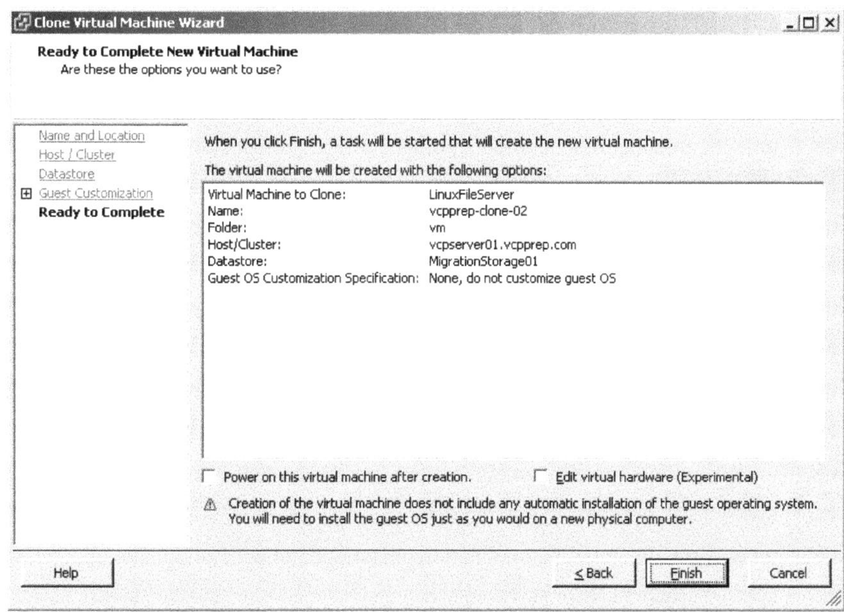

Figure 7.100 Clone Virtual Machine Wizard Ready To Complete

The final screen as shown in Figure 7.100 provides a summary of your choices. If you discover that you want to change an incorrect choice, click on the Back button to make the changes. Select the Finish button to start the cloning process.

Converting a Virtual Machine to Template

If a source virtual machine is not needed to continue in operation as a powered on virtual machine, you can choose to convert the virtual machine into a template by performing the following steps:

The following steps illustrate how to convert a virtual machine to a template.

Step 1. Right mouse button click on the virtual machine that you want to convert to a template. Select the Convert To Template Option from the pop up menu as shown in Figure 7.101.

Figure 7.101 Convert To Template Menu Option

If the current VirtualCenter view being used is the Host And Clusters view, it will be necessary to change the view as templates are not displayed within the Host And Clusters view.

Step 2. To change the view, click the Inventory button at the upper left top of the VI Client and select the Virtual Machines And Templates view option from the drop down list as shown in Figure 7.102.

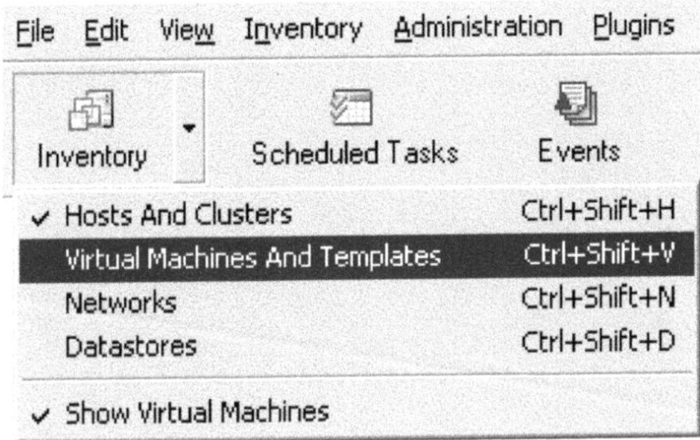

Figure 7.102 Inventory Menu Virtual Machines And Templates View

You can also use the keyboard sequence of Ctrl+Shift+V to select the Virtual Machines And Templates view.

The newly created template is now displayed within the Virtual Machines And Templates view as shown in Figure 7.103.

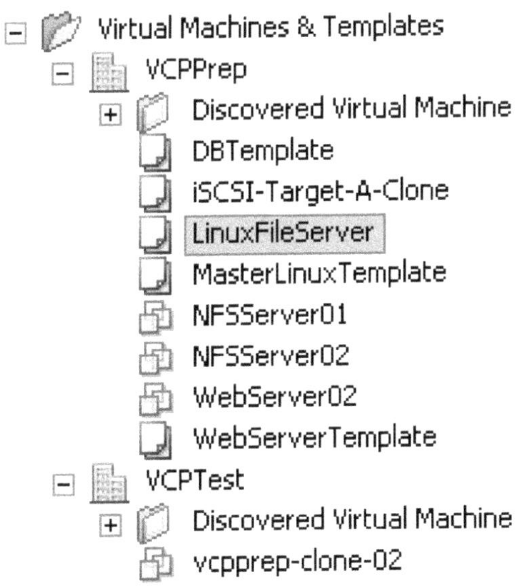

Figure 7.103 Virtual Machines And Templates View

Deploying a Virtual Machine from a Template

The following steps illustrate how to deploy a virtual machine from a template.

Step 1. Right mouse button click on the template to use to deploy a virtual machine. Select the Deploy Virtual Machine from this Template option from the pop up menu as shown in Figure 7.104.

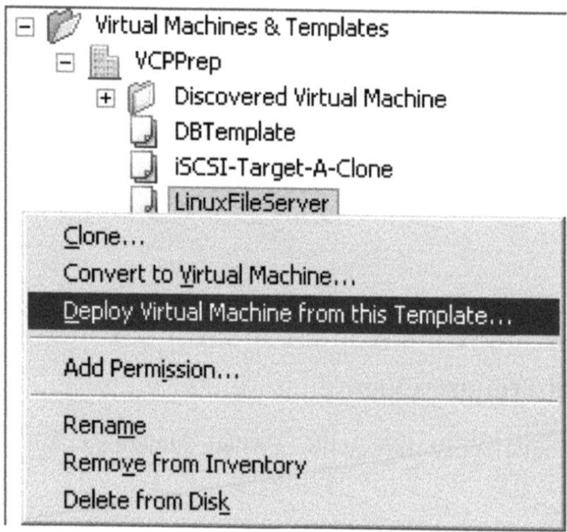

Figure 7.104 Deploy Virtual Machine From This Template Menu Option

The Deploy Template Wizard will now launch.

Step 2. Select a Name and Location for this Virtual Machine screen.

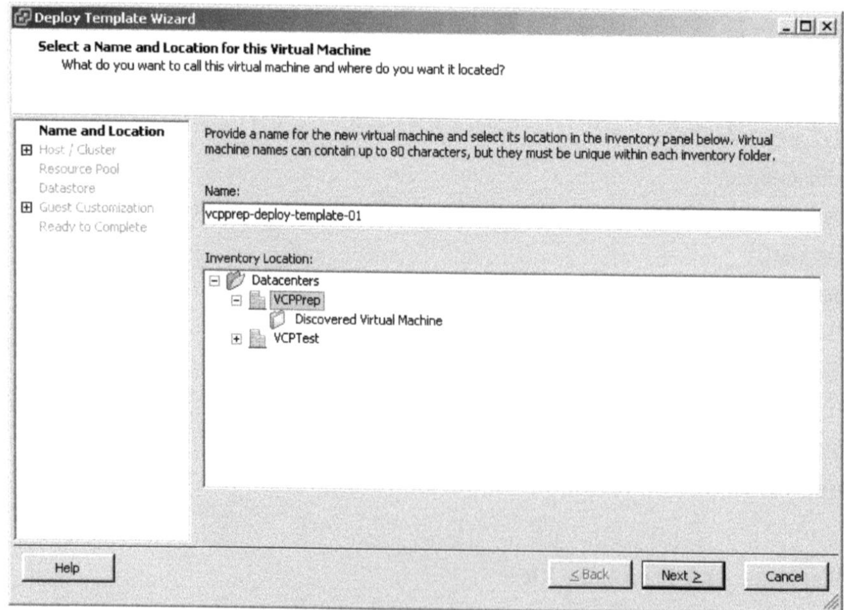

Figure 7.105 Deploy Template Wizard Name And Location

Assign the virtual machine a descriptive name and a location to place the virtual machine within the VirtualCenter inventory as shown in Figure 7.105. The chosen virtual machine name will be used as the display name within the VirtualCenter inventory. Click the Next button to continue.

Step 3. Select the Host or Cluster screen.

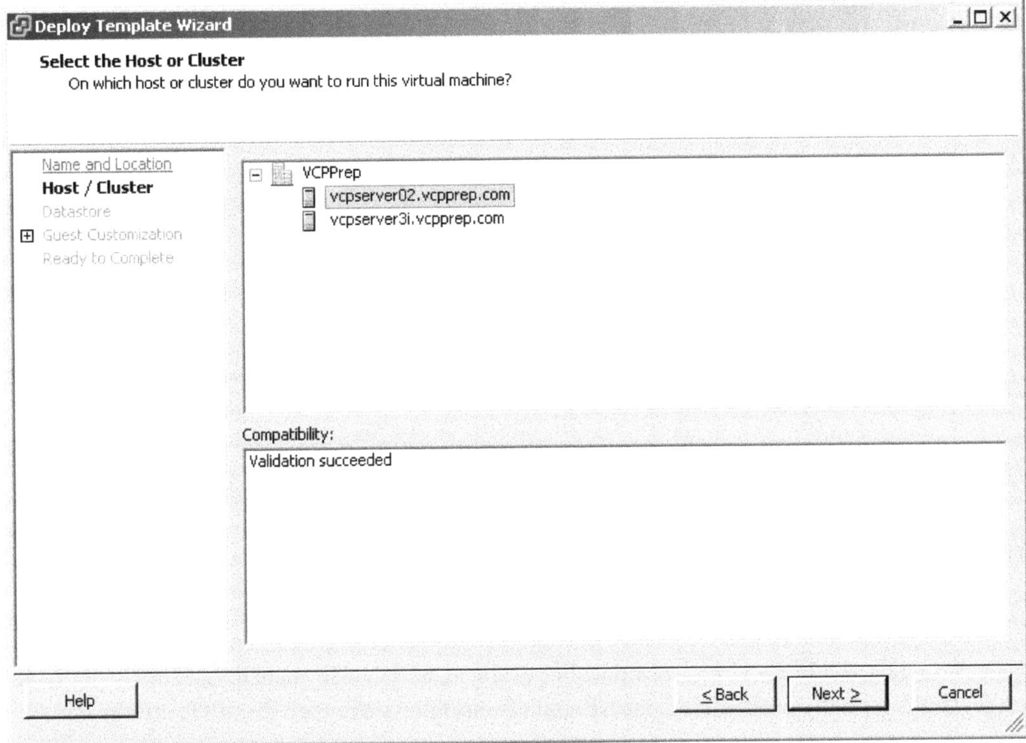

Figure 7.106 Deploy Template Wizard Host or Cluster

Choose an appropriate ESX server host or cluster of ESX servers that will run this virtual machine as shown in Figure 7.106. The virtual machine will be assigned to the selected ESX server or cluster of ESX servers. A validation check occurs to verify compatibility of the virtual machine and host. Validation failure could be for example, selecting an older version ESX server as a host when deploying a version 4 virtual machine. The validation in this example was successful, click the Next button to continue.

Step 4. Choose a Datastore for the Virtual Machine screen.

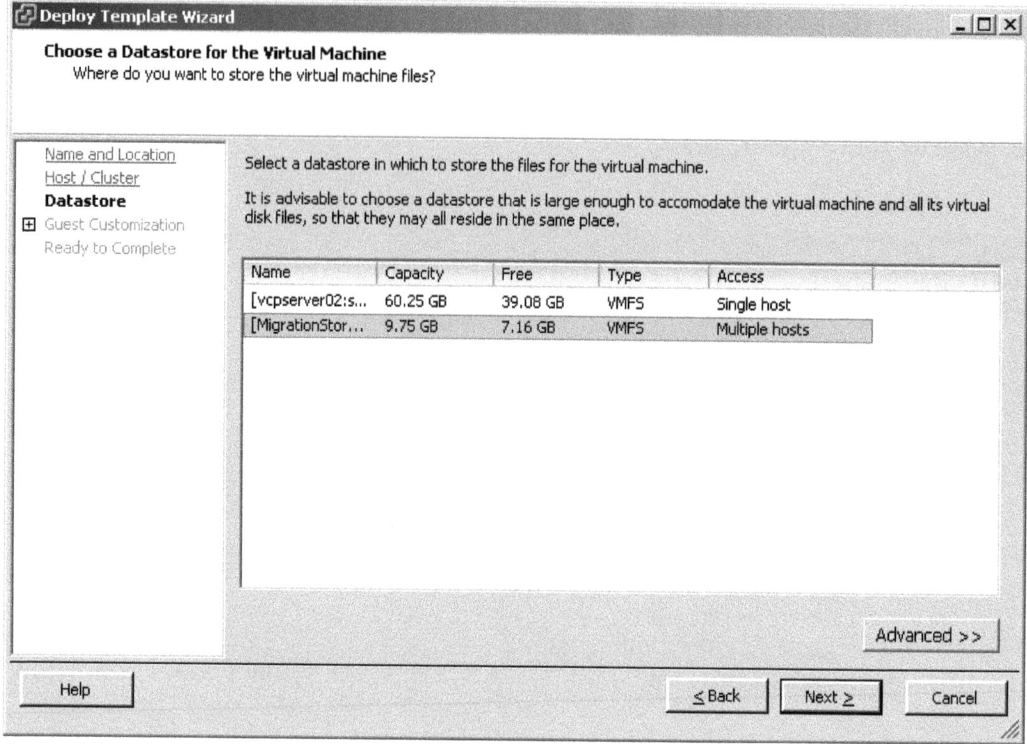

Figure 7.107 Deploy Template Wizard Datastore

Choose the location that will be used to store the state files for this virtual machine as shown in Figure 7.107. The virtual machine should be located on a storage device configured to meet the needs of the applications running within the virtual machine. For example, a LUN that encompasses many physical storage devices is typically desired for database applications to improve their disk I/O performance.

NOTE: Select the Advanced button if needing to choose a separate configuration file and or hard drive file location.

Click the Next button to continue.

Step 5. Select Guest Customization Option screen.

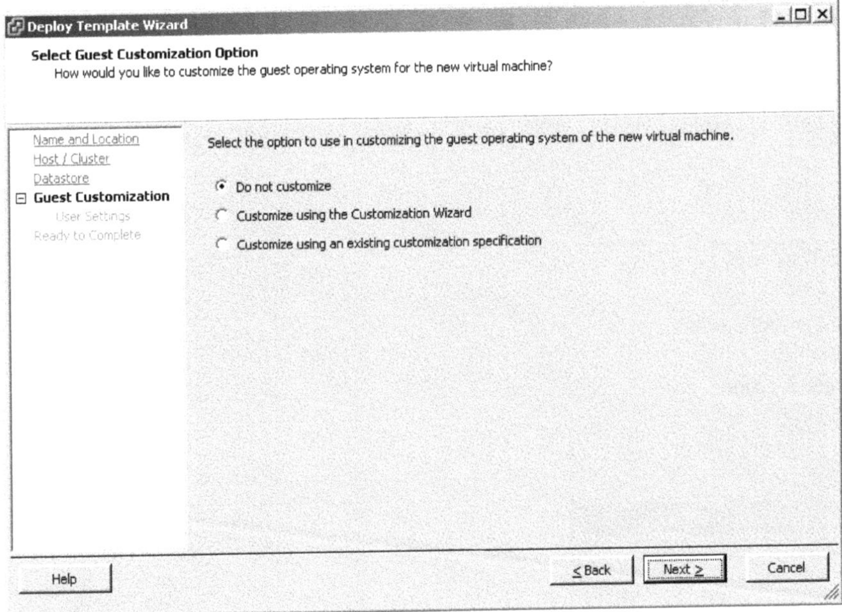

Figure 7.108 Deploy Template Wizard Do Not Customize

Select the Do not customize radio button if the guest customization wizard is not desired as shown in Figure 7.108. Select the Next button to continue.

Step 6. Ready to Complete new Virtual Machine screen.

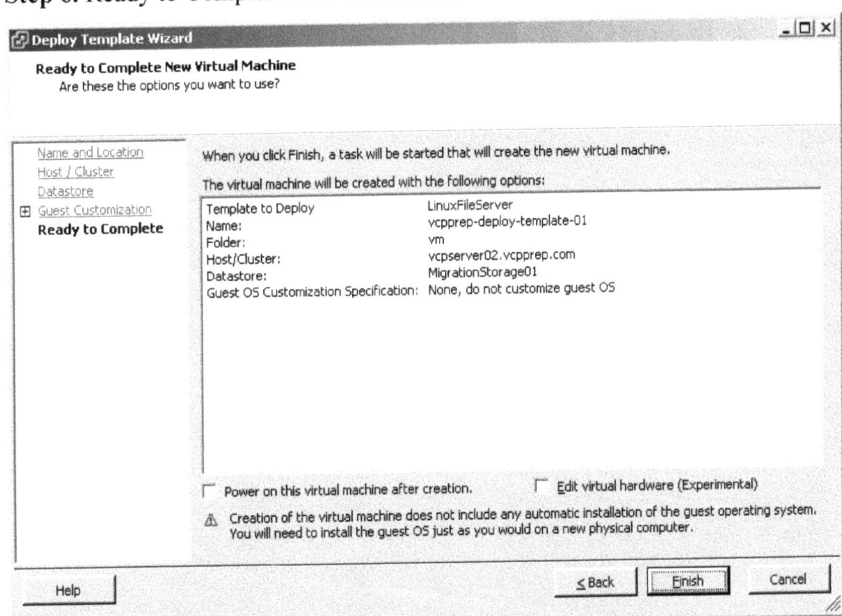

Figure 7.109 Deploy Template Wizard Ready To Complete

Select the Finish button to complete the deployment of a virtual machine wizard from a template as shown in Figure 7.109. The new VM will now appear in the inventory.

Deploying a Virtual Machine from a Template to another Datacenter

Deploying a virtual machine from a template to another datacenter is a new feature in VirtualCenter 2.5. You can use templates to rapidly deploy VMs on a different datacenter as illustrated in the following example:

Step 1: Launching the wizard.

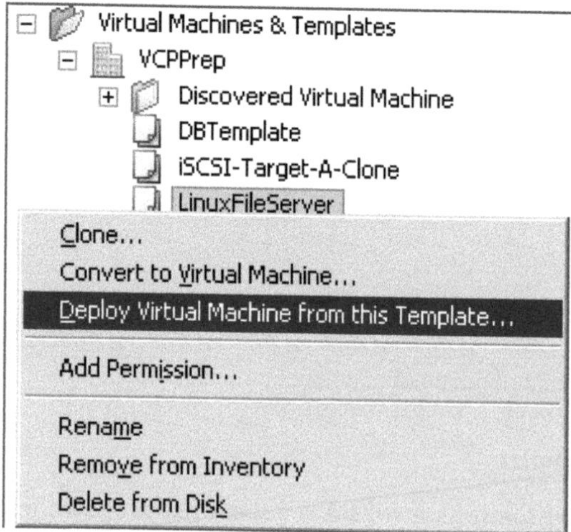

Figure 7.110 Deploy Virtual Machine From This Template Menu Option

Right mouse button click on the template in the inventory that you want to clone and select the Deploy Virtual Machine from this Template option in the pop-up menu as shown in Figure 7.110.

Step 2: Select a Name and Location for this Virtual Machine screen.

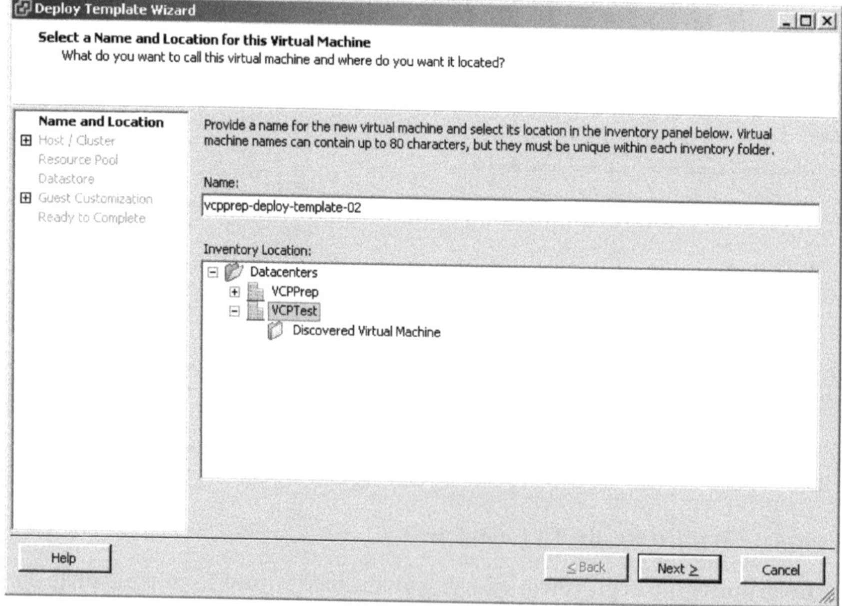

Figure 7.111 Deploy Template Wizard Name And Location

Assign the virtual machine a descriptive name and select the datacenter that you want to manage the VM from the VirtualCenter inventory as shown in Figure 7.111. Click the Next button to continue.

Step 3: Select the Host or Cluster screen.

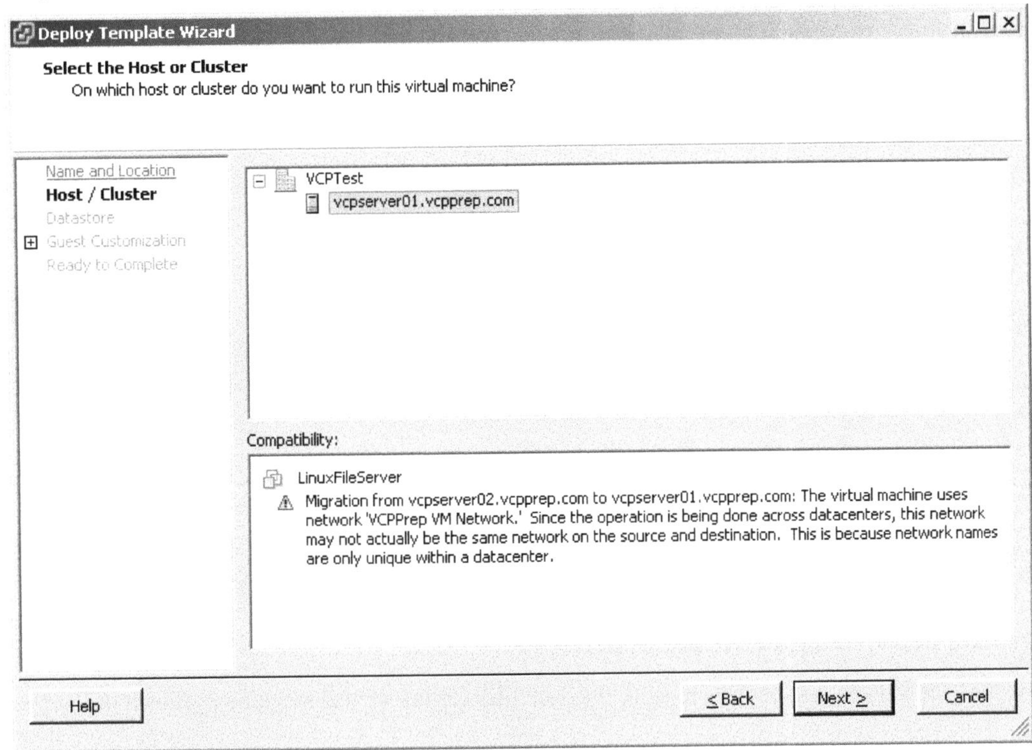

Figure 7.112 Deploy Template Wizard Host / Cluster

This is the same screen we saw in earlier examples. In Figure 7.112, we selected the ESX server in the different datacenter to deploy the VM in. Notice the warning in the Compatibility section. The wizard will analyze the configuration of the VM that will be built and alert you to any compatibility issues that it discovers. If everything is ok with the compatibility check then click on the Next button to continue.

Step 4: Choose a Datastore for the Virtual Machine screen.

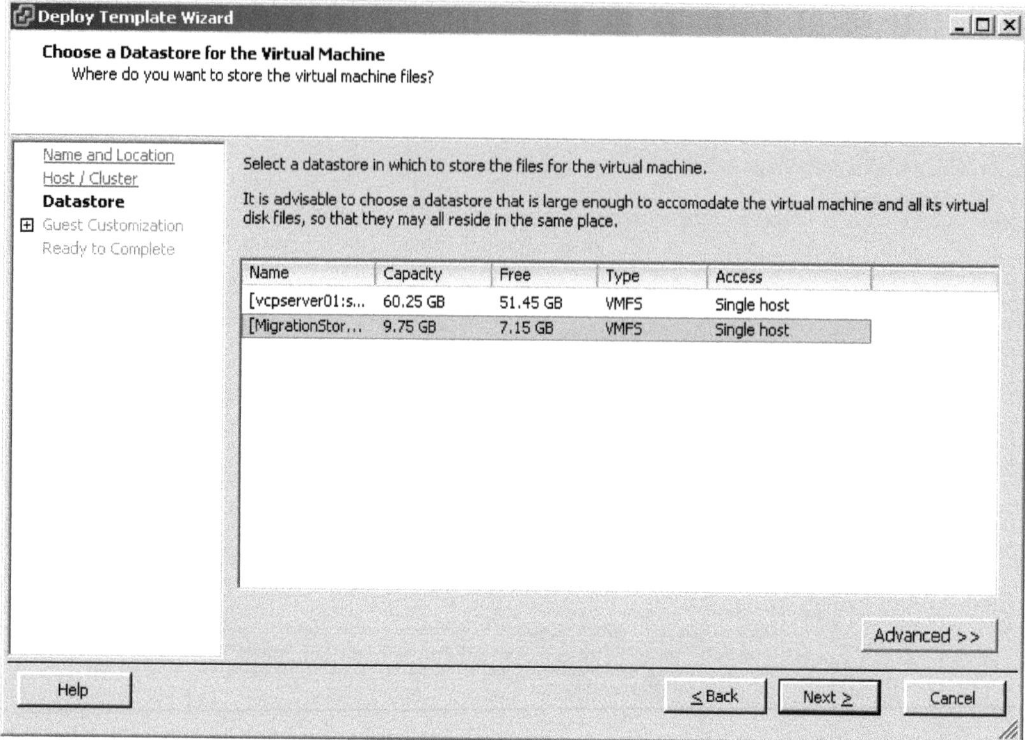

Figure 7.113 Deploy Template Wizard Datastore

Choose the location that will be used to store the state files for this virtual machine as shown in Figure 7.113.

NOTE: Select the Advanced button if needing to choose a separate configuration file and or hard drive file location.

Click the Next button to continue.

Step 5: Select Guest Customization Option screen.

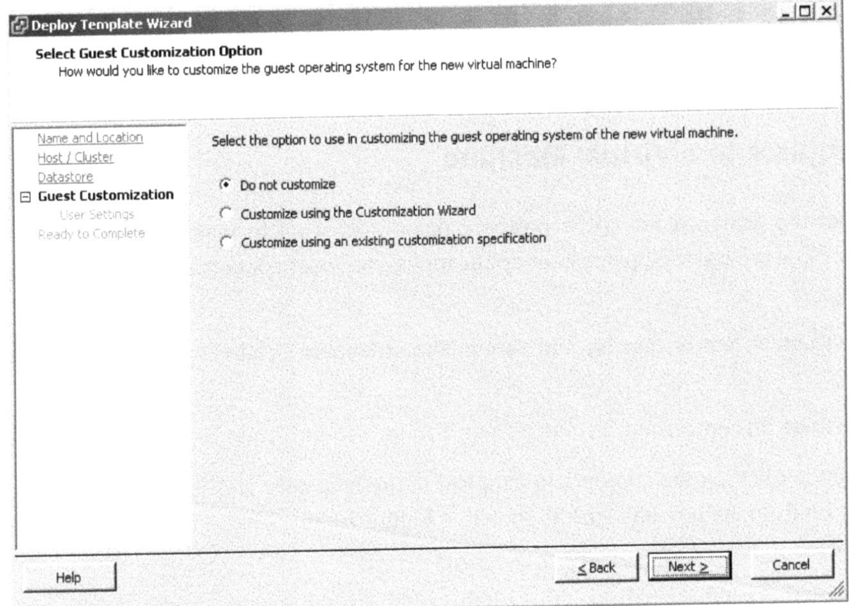

Figure 7.114 Deploy Template Wizard Do Not Customize

Select the Do not customize radio button if the guest customization wizard is not desired as shown in Figure 7.114. Select the Next button to continue.

Step 6: Ready to Complete New Virtual Machine screen.

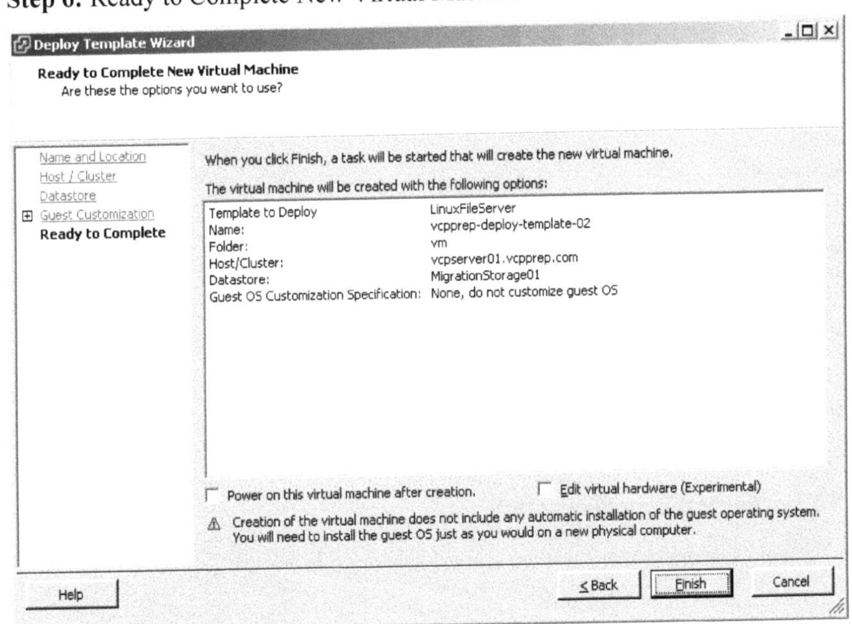

Figure 7.115 Deploy Template Wizard Ready To Complete

Select the Finish button to complete the deployment of a virtual machine wizard from a template as shown in Figure 7.115.

The new VM will now appear in the inventory in the datacenter that does not contain the original template.

Converting a Template to a Virtual Machine

Templates are VMs that are designed not to be powered on. If you want to manually update the template by installing new service packs, patches or applications you must convert the template to a VM.

NOTE: The new VirtualCenter Server feature, VMware Update Manager (VUM) updates templates automatically.

The following steps illustrate this process:

Step 1. Right mouse button click on the appropriate template in the inventory and select the Convert To Virtual Machine option from the pop up menu as shown in Figure 7.116.

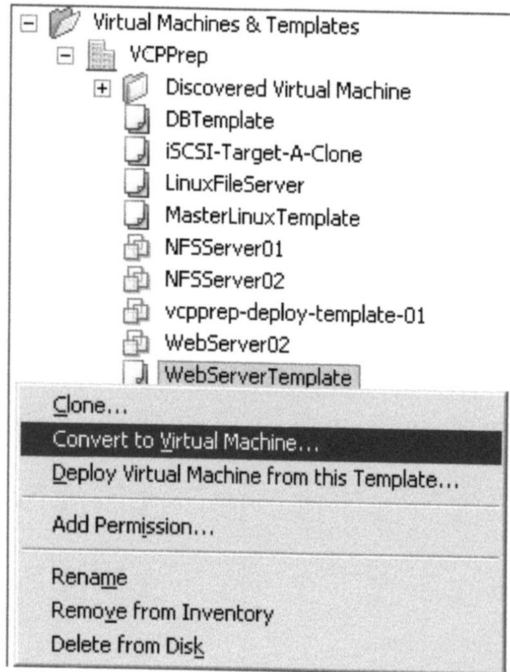

Figure 7.116 Convert To Virtual Machine Menu Option

Step 2. The Convert To Virtual Machine wizard will be started as shown in Figure 7.117.

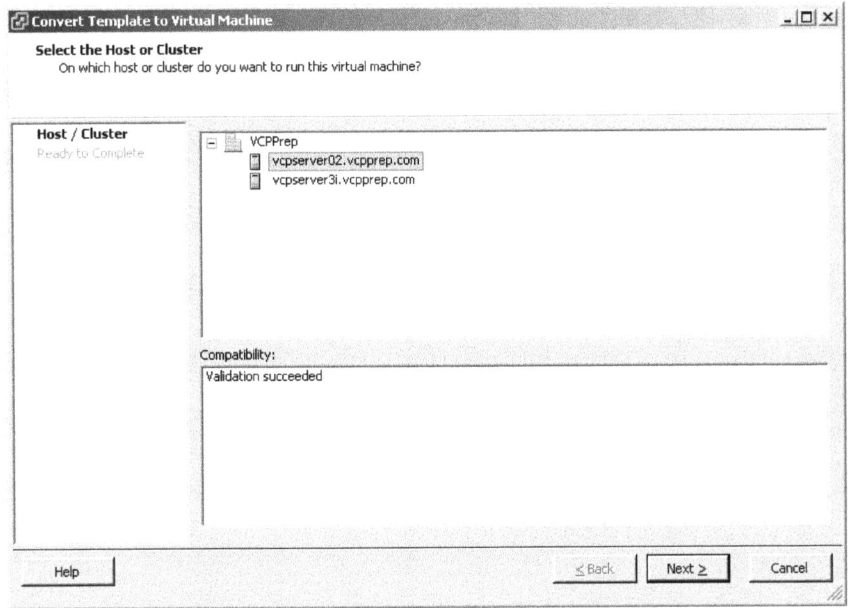

Figure 7.117 Convert Template To Virtual Machine Wizard Host or Cluster

Select the appropriate host or cluster that you want to run the VM and click on the Next button.

Step 3. The Ready to Complete New Virtual Machine screen is the final screen in the wizard as shown in Figure 7.118.

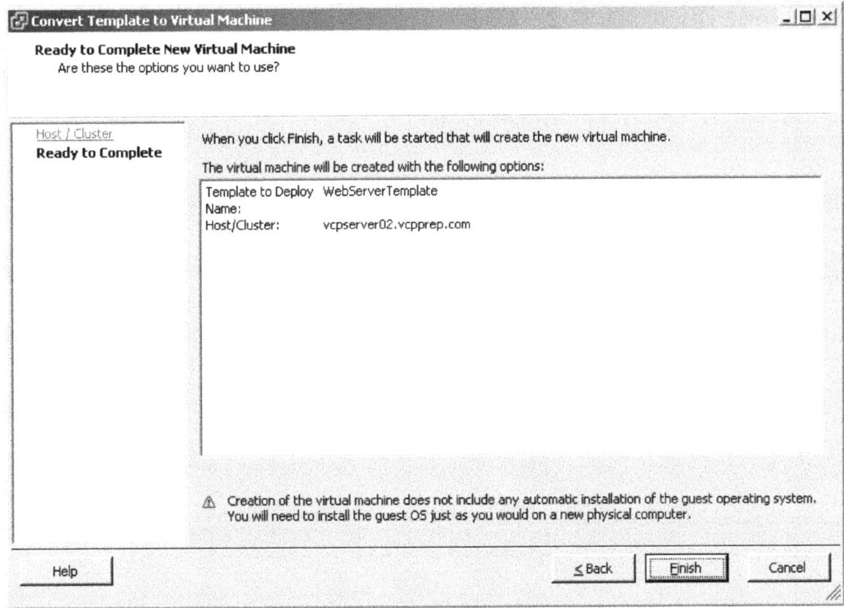

Figure 7.118 Convert Template To Virtual Machine Wizard Ready To Complete

The template will now be converted to a VM that can be powered on. After you have updated the VM you can convert it back to a template.

Cloning a Template

You can clone a template in VirtualCenter 2.5 by doing these steps:

Step 1. Right mouse button click on the template that you want to clone. Select the Clone... Option from the pop up menu as shown in Figure 7.119.

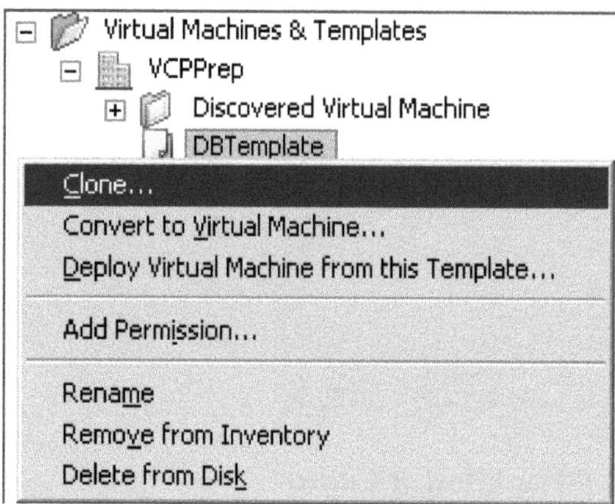

Figure 7.119 Clone Template Menu Option

Step 2. Select a Name and Location for this Template screen.

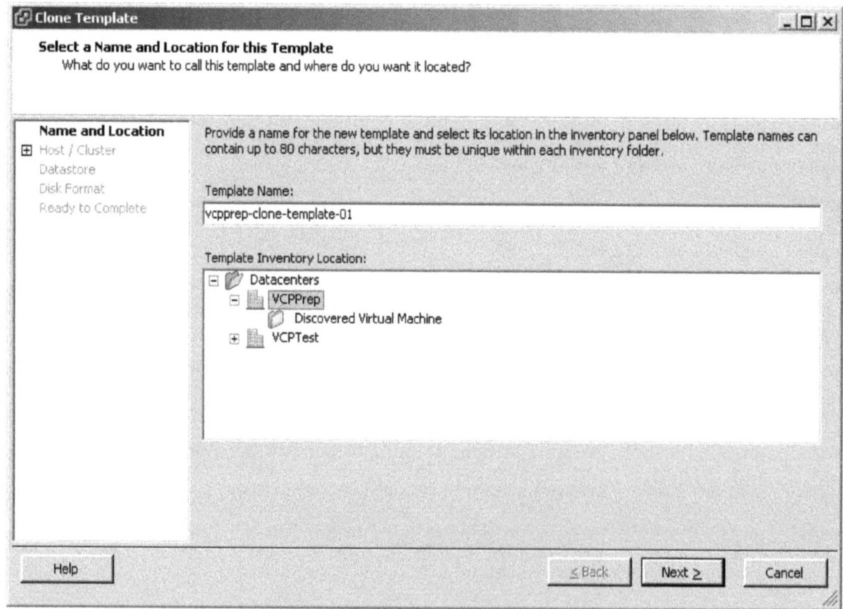

Figure 7.120 Clone Template Wizard Name And Location

Assign the template a descriptive name and a location within the VirtualCenter inventory as shown in Figure 7.120. Click on the Next button to continue.

Step 3. Select the Host or Cluster screen.

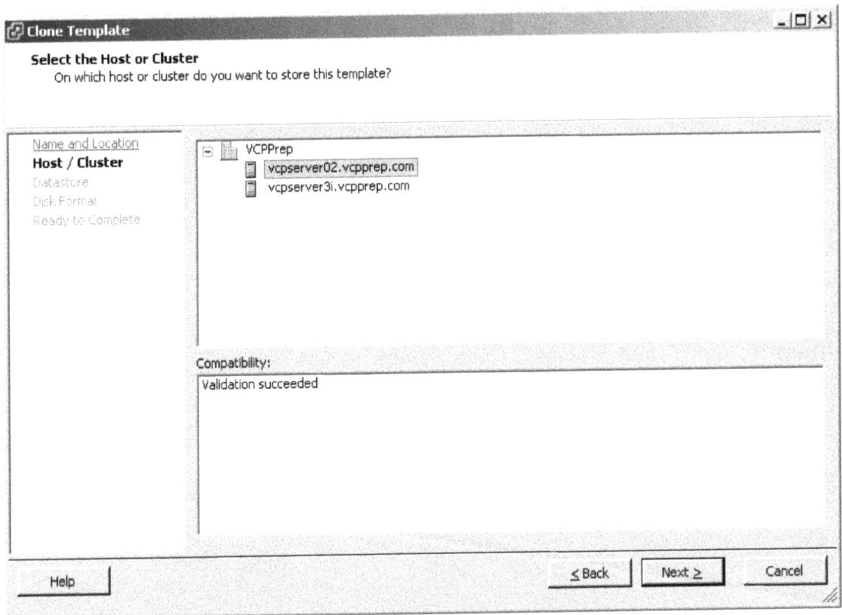

Figure 7.121 Clone Template Wizard Host / Cluster

Select the ESX host or cluster of ESX hosts that the template will be assigned to as shown in Figure 7.121. Click on the Next button to continue.

Step 4. Choose a Datastore for the Template screen.

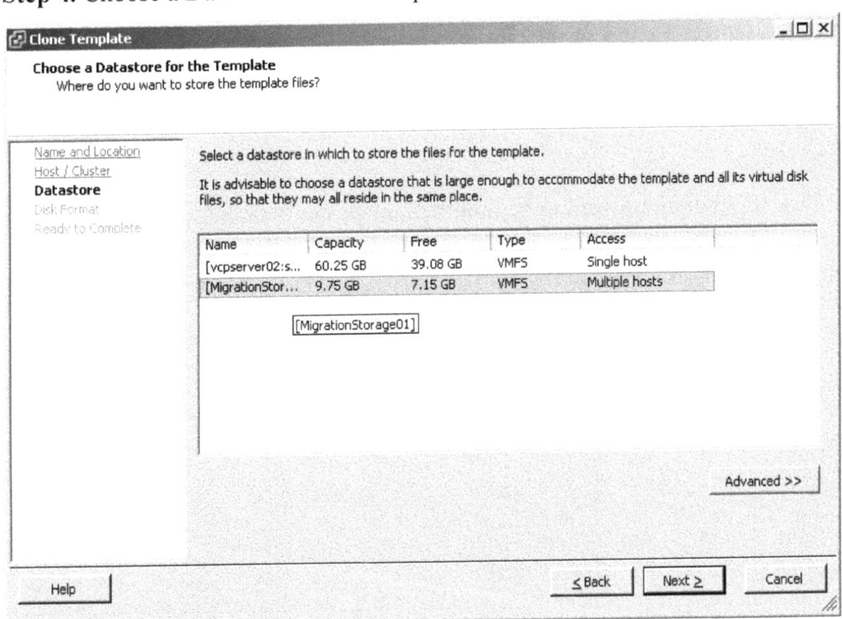

Figure 7.122 Clone Template Wizard Datastore

Choose the datastore where the template files will be placed. To choose a different location other than the specified datastore, select the Advanced button in the lower right corner of the Clone Virtual

Machine to Template dialog box as shown in Figure 7.122. Click on the Next button to continue.

Step 5. Disk Format screen.

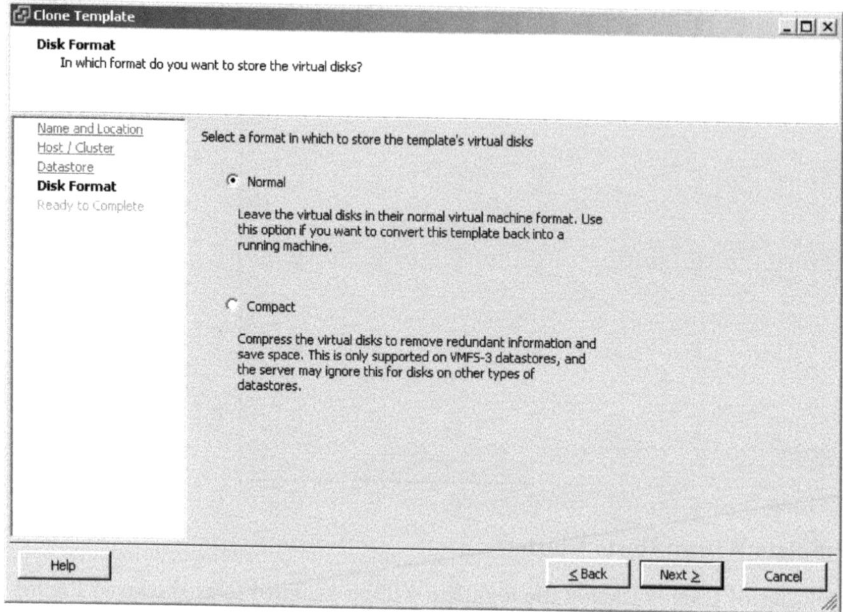

Figure 7.123 Clone Template Wizard Disk Format

You can format the virtual machine's virtual disk in either normal or compact mode as shown in Figure 7.123. Use normal mode if you want to be able to convert the template back into a running virtual machine. Use compact mode which compresses the virtual disk and therefore saves space on your storage device. Click on the Next button to continue.

Step 6. Ready to Clone screen.

Review the selected options. If any options need to be modified, click the Back button and locate the appropriate step in the wizard. Once the options have been confirmed, click the Finish button to complete the Clone Template wizard as shown in Figure 7.124.

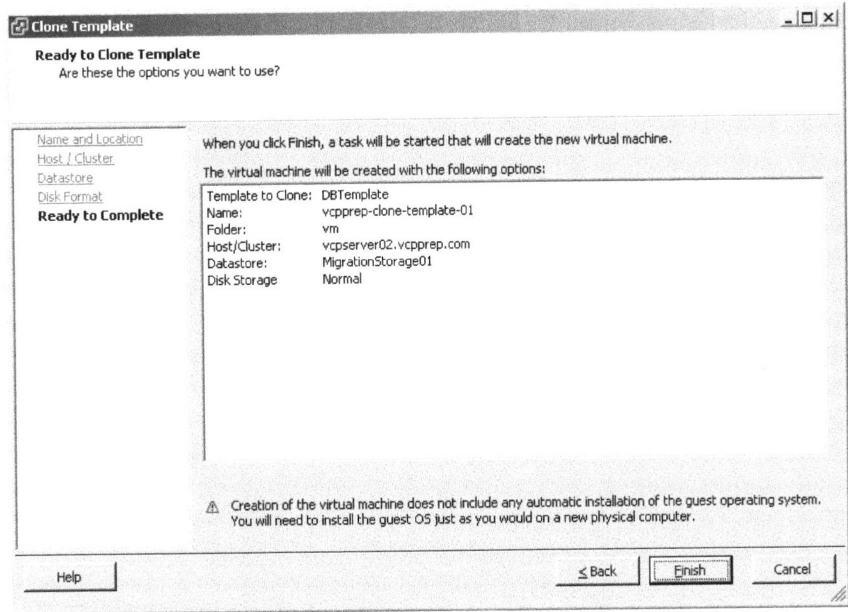

Figure 7.124 Clone Template Wizard Ready To Complete

Using the Customization Wizard

VirtualCenter provides the capability of rapid deployment of virtual machines. This is accomplished by using a virtual machine that has been built and configured as a master image suitable for serving as a source image. Newly deployed virtual machines can be exact copies of the master image. This may be desirable if testing is to be done on a copy of the master image so as not to modify the original master copy.

An exact copy of the master image may not always be desirable. This may be the case for a newly deployed virtual machine that will be put into a production environment. Multiple virtual machines with the same Microsoft Windows host name, Security Identifier (SID) and network settings will cause conflicts within the network. To avoid such problems and still have rapid provision capabilities with little administration work when cloning a virtual machine or deploying a virtual machine from a template, the guest customization wizard can be used.

When using the guest customization wizard with Microsoft Windows virtual machines, the Sysprep files need to be extracted to the proper Windows version directory within the following directory on the VirtualCenter server:

C:\Documents and Settings\All Users\Application Data\VMware\VMware VirtualCenter\sysprep\1.1

NOTE: There are Windows version-specific sub-folders for each version of Windows that the Sysprep files must be extracted to; this is new as of VirtualCenter Server 2.5.

The following steps illustrate using the guest customization wizard:

Step 1. Select Guest Customization Option screen.

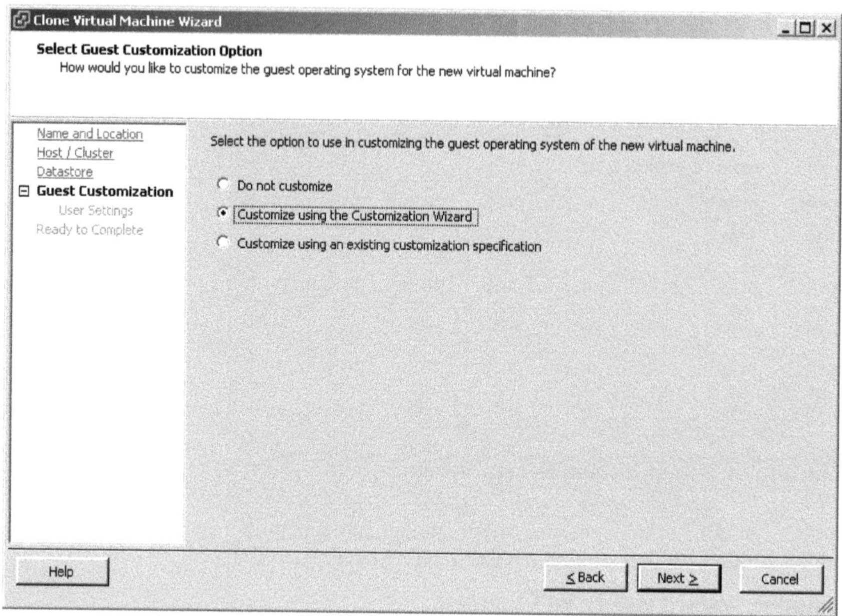

Figure 7.125 Clone Virtual Machine Wizard Customize Using The Guest Customization Wizard

We have already started the cloning wizard as demonstrated previously starting with Figures 07-104, 07-110 and 07-119. When you get to this step in the wizard, select the Customize using the Customization Wizard radio button to begin the guest customization wizard as shown in Figure 7.125. Click on the Next button to continue.

Step 2. Registration Information screen.

Figure 7.126 Guest Customization Wizard Registration Information

Enter the virtual machine owner's name and organization for the registration information as shown in Figure 7.126. Click on the Next button to continue.

Step 3. Computer Name screen.

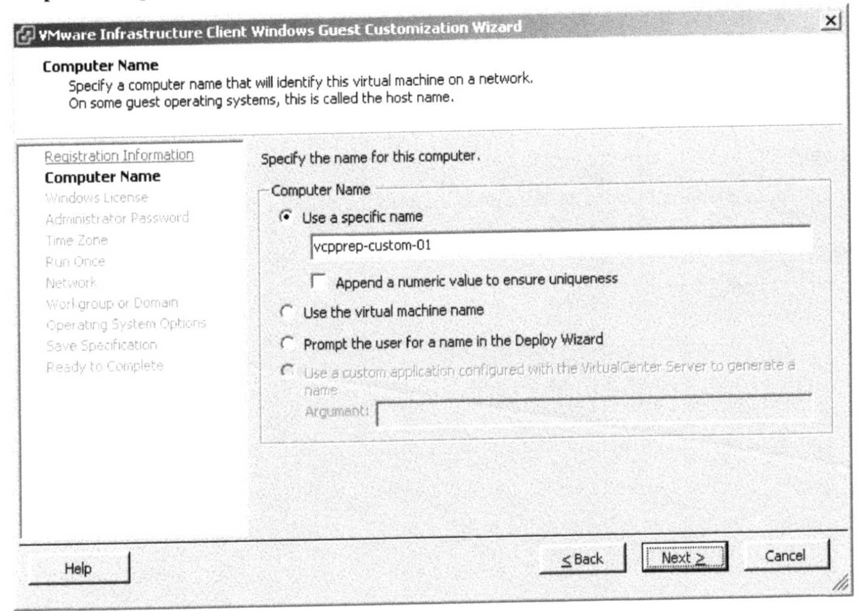

Figure 7.127 Guest Customization Wizard Computer Name

Enter the host name that will be used to uniquely identify this virtual machine as shown in Figure 7.127. Click on the Next button to continue.

Step 4. Windows License screen.

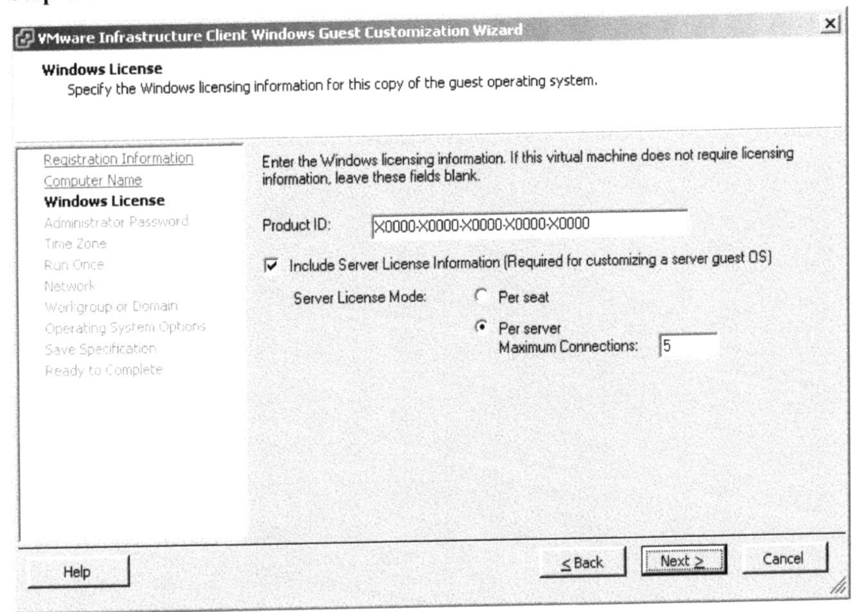

Figure 7.128 Guest Customization Wizard Windows License

Enter the licensing information for the Windows guest operating system that will be running within this virtual machine as shown in Figure 7.128. Click on the Next button to continue.

Step 5. Administrative Password screen.

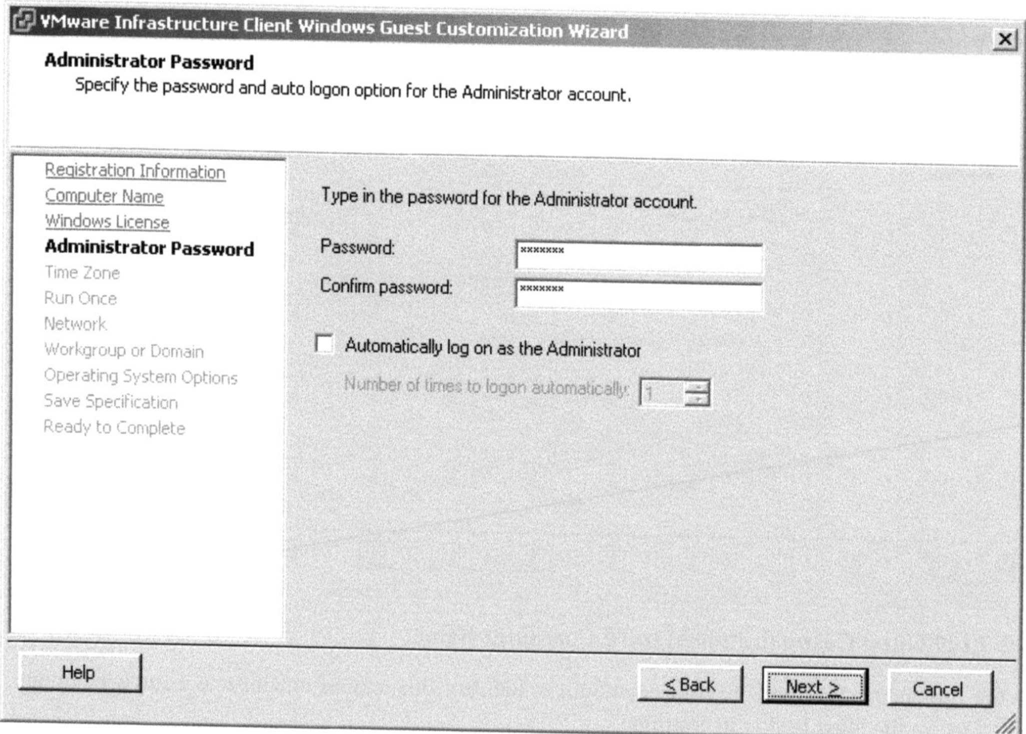

Figure 7.129 Guest Customization Wizard Administrator Password

Choose the administrative password. It is good practice to use a minimum password length of 6 characters. In addition, security is enhanced when using a combination of uppercase and lowercase characters and numbers. The option to have the administrator account automatically log on is available as well as shown in Figure 7.129. Click on the Next button to continue.

Step 6. Time Zone screen.

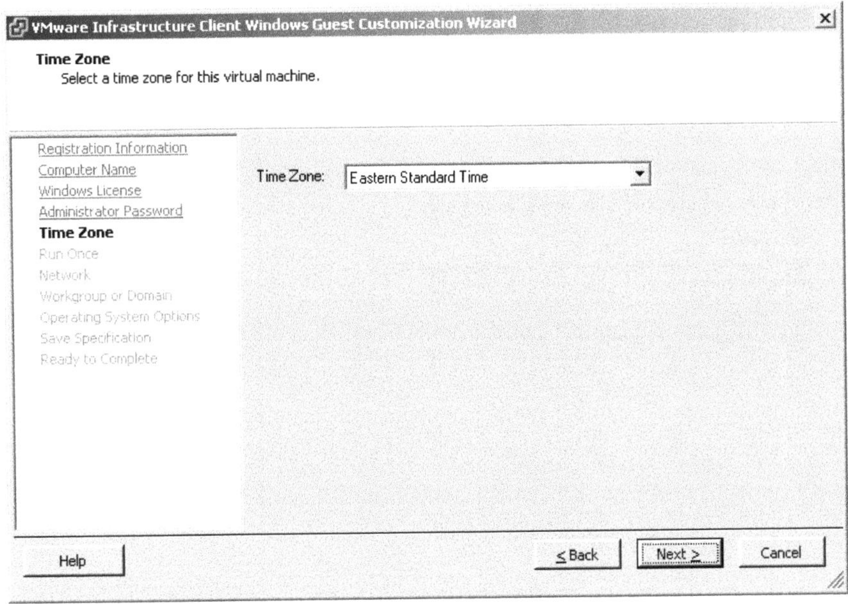

Figure 7.130 Guest Customization Wizard Time Zone

Select the appropriate time zone for this virtual machine as shown in Figure 7.130. Click on the Next button to continue.

Step 7. Run Once screen.

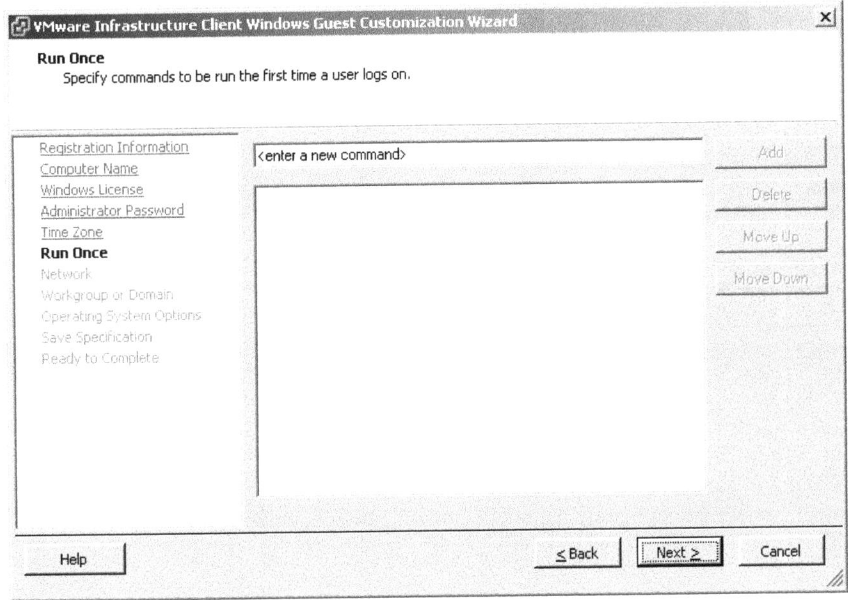

Figure 7.131 Guest Customization Wizard Run Once

Commands can be entered and executed the first time a user logs on, such as downloading virus definition files or creating UNC mapped drives. Type the command in the text box <enter a new command> then click the Add button as shown in Figure 7.131. Click on the Next button to continue.

Step 8. Network Interface Settings screen.

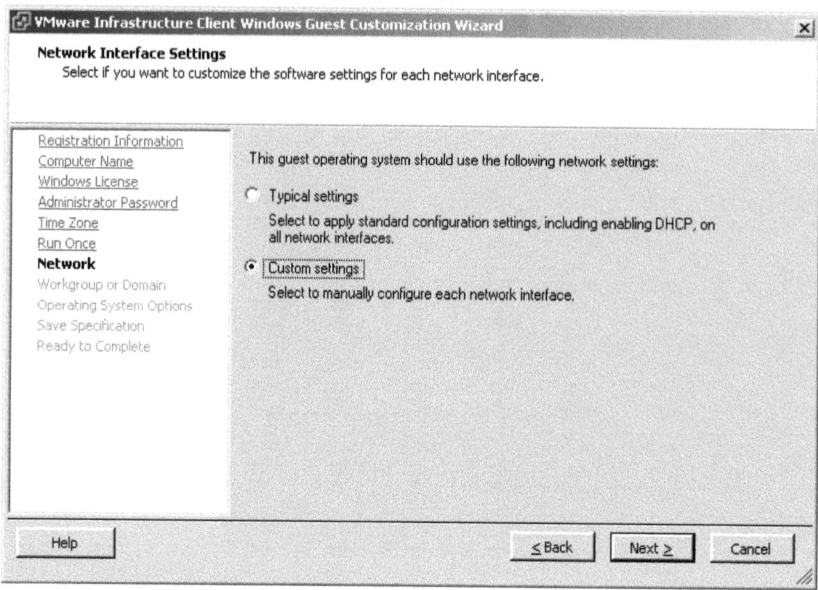

Figure 7.132 Guest Customization Wizard Network Custom Settings

A choice of network settings is presented. The Typical settings automatically use DHCP for all the network interfaces within the virtual machine. The Custom settings allow the individual configuration of each network interface within the virtual machine. Select the appropriate type of network settings for this virtual machine and click the Next button. In this example we have selected the Custom Settings radio box and clicked the Next button as shown in Figure 7.132.

Step 9. Network Interface Customizations screen.

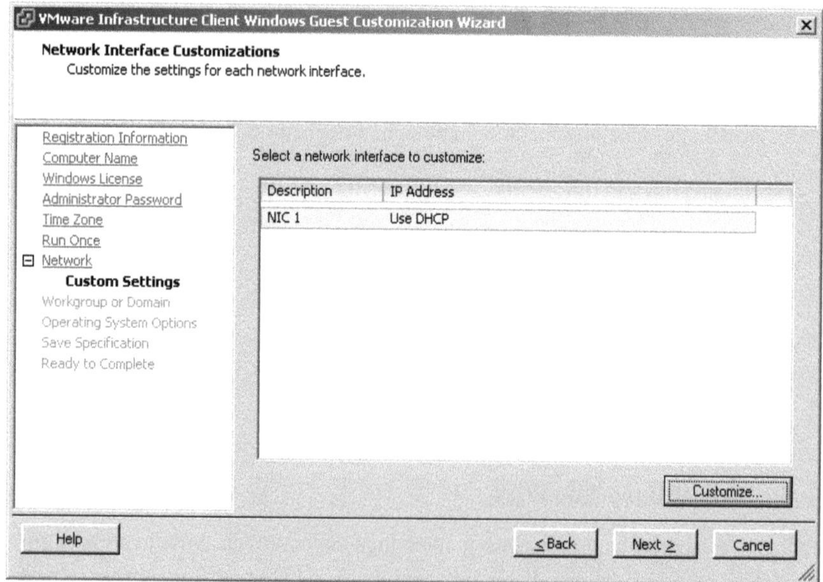

Figure 7.133 Guest Customization Wizard Network Customize Button

Select the network interface to configure and click the Customize... button as shown in Figure 7.133.

Step 10. Network Properties window.

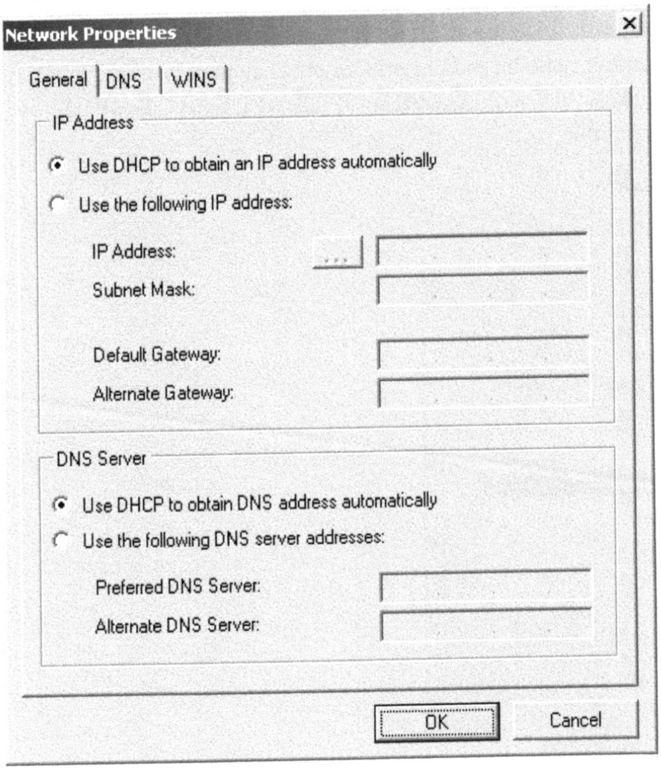

Figure 7.134 Guest Customization Wizard Network Properties General Tab

To set the network interface to DHCP, select the Use DHCP to obtain an IP address automatically radio button as shown in Figure 7.134. To configure the network interface with a static IP address, select the Use the following IP address radio button and click the button with the three dots (...).

Step 11. Static IP Address Selection window.

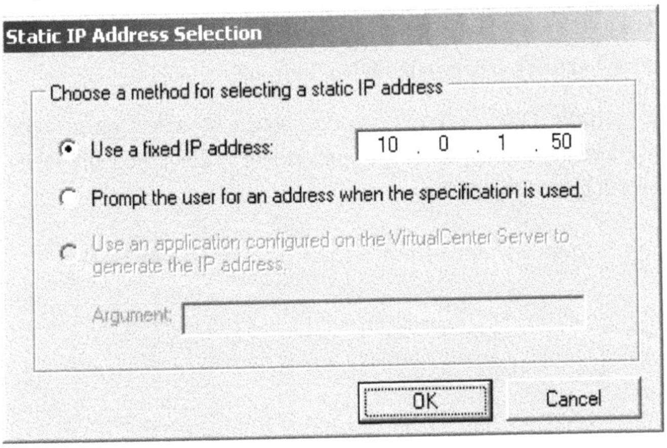

Figure 7.135 Guest Customization Wizard Static IP Address Selection

Select the Use a fixed IP address radio button and enter the desired static IP address as shown in Figure 7.135. There are two other choices for setting the IP address. Selecting the Prompt the user for an address when the specification is used radio button will prompt the user for an IP address when a user chooses the customization specification. Selecting the Use an application configured on the VirtualCenter server to generate the IP address radio button requires an absolute path be entered in the Argument text field for the custom application that will generate an IP address. Select the IP address option to use and click the OK button to continue.

Step 12. Network Properties DNS tab window.

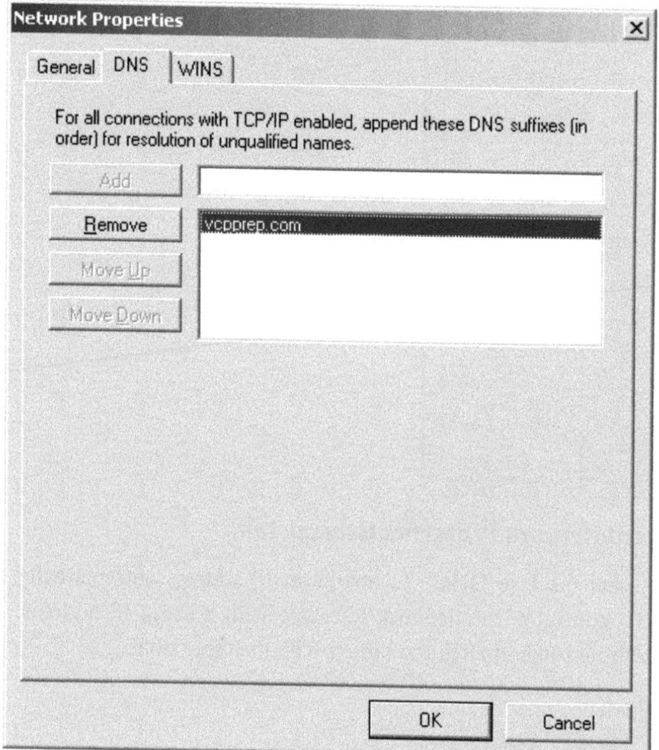

Figure 7.136 Guest Customization Wizard Network Properties DNS Tab

The order in which virtual machines use multiple DNS suffixes can be chosen by selecting a DNS suffix then clicking the Move Up and Move Down buttons to set the appropriate order. Enter the DNS suffix to use as shown in Figure 7.136 then click the OK button.

Step 13. Network Properties WINS tab window.

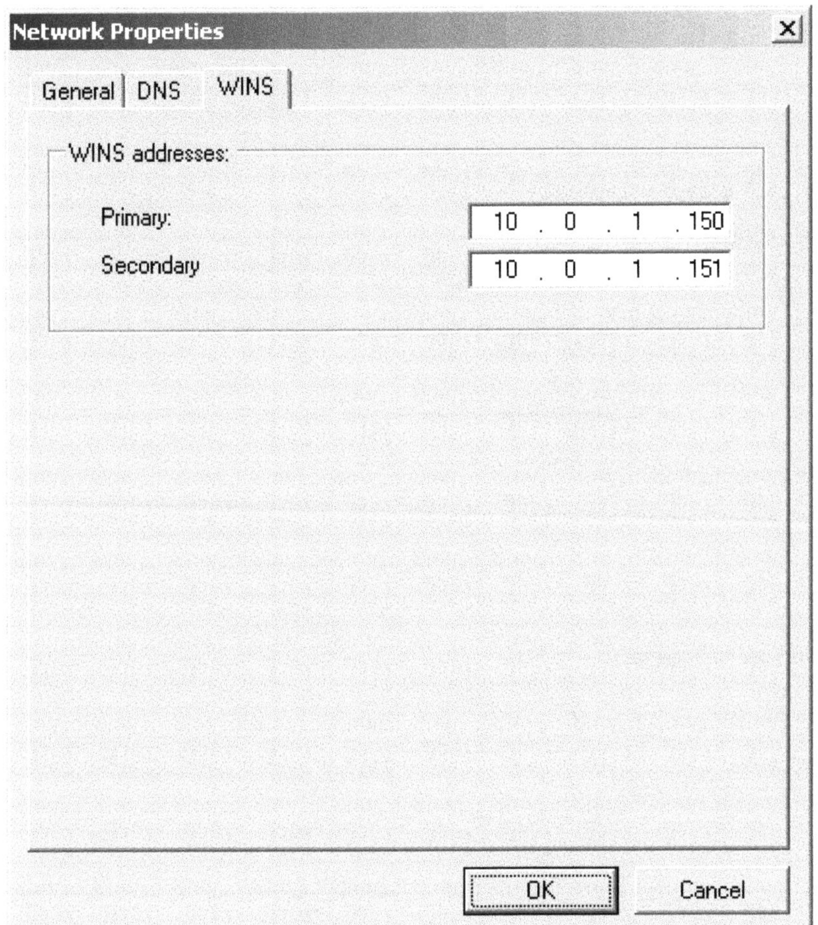

Figure 7.137 Guest Customization Wizard Network Properties WINS Tab

Enter the IP addresses in the entry boxes to specify the primary and secondary WINS addresses as shown in Figure 7.137. Click OK to continue.

Step 14. Network Properties General tab window.

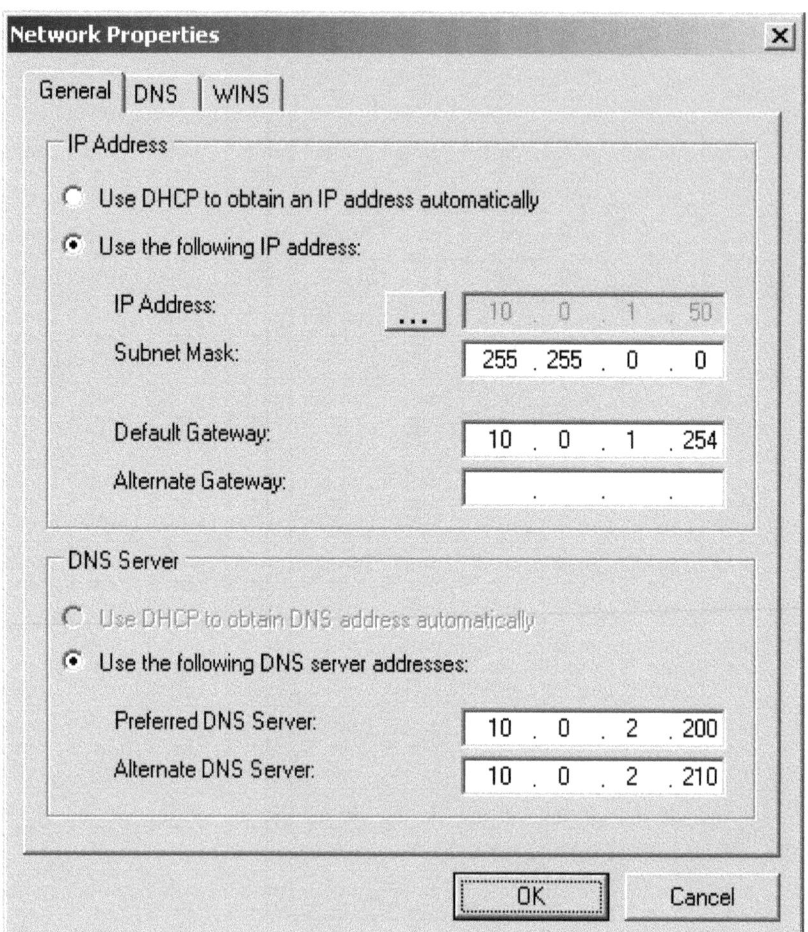

Figure 7.138 Guest Customization Wizard Network Properties IP Configuration

Enter the appropriate subnet mask, default and alternate gateways as shown in Figure 7.138. Click OK to continue.

Step 15. Network Interface Customizations screen.

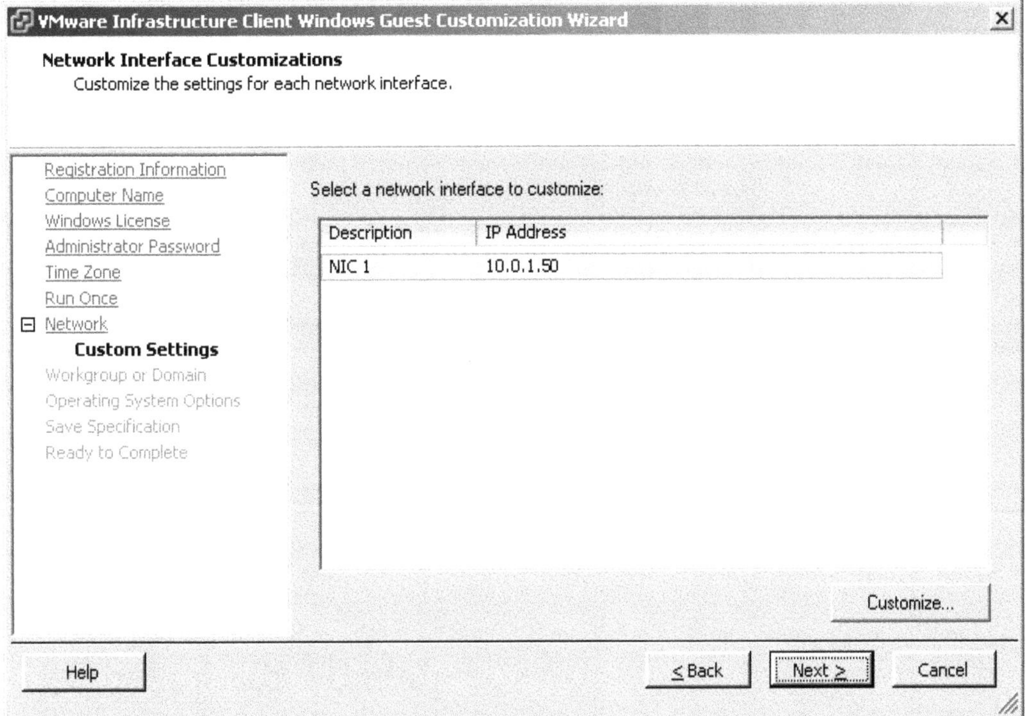

Figure 7.139 Guest Customization Wizard Network Interfaced Customized

Verify that the displayed IP address is correct and click the Next button as shown in Figure 7.139.

Step 16. Workgroup or Domain screen.

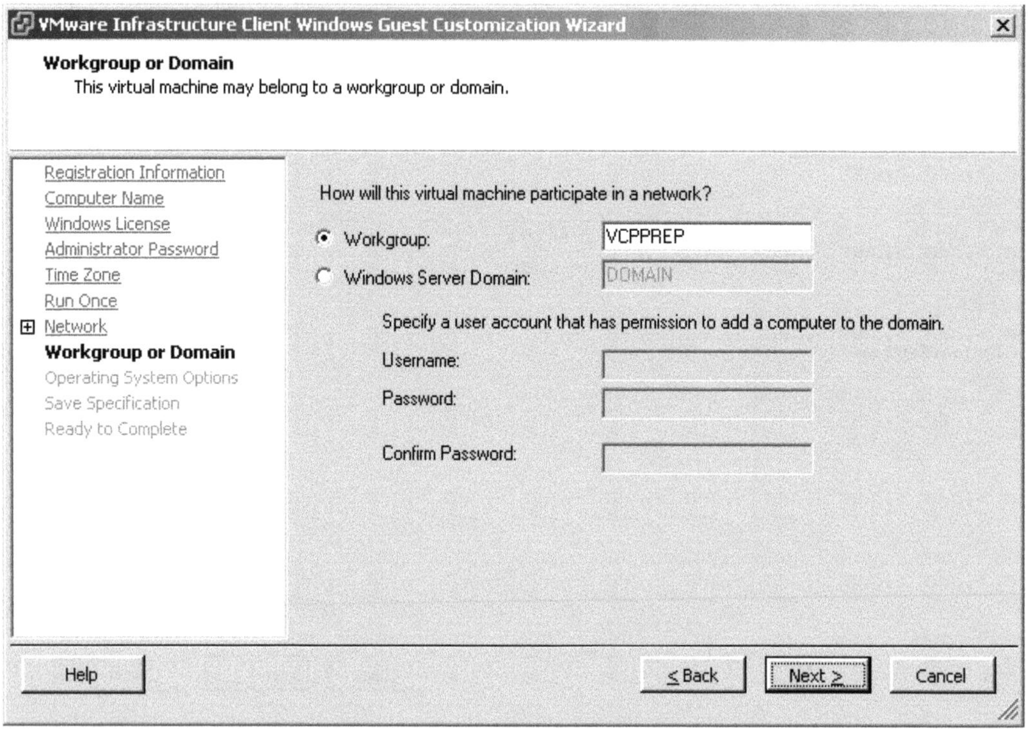

VMware Infrastructure Client Windows Guest Customization Wizard

Workgroup or Domain
This virtual machine may belong to a workgroup or domain.

Registration Information
Computer Name
Windows License
Administrator Password
Time Zone
Run Once
Network
Workgroup or Domain
Operating System Options
Save Specification
Ready to Complete

How will this virtual machine participate in a network?

Workgroup: VCPPREP
Windows Server Domain: DOMAIN

Specify a user account that has permission to add a computer to the domain.

Username:
Password:
Confirm Password:

Help | < Back | Next > | Cancel

Figure 7.140 Guest Customization Wizard Workgroup Or Domain

Specify whether this virtual machine will be apart of a Windows Workgroup or Windows Server Domain then enter the correct Workgroup or Domain name. When choosing to join a Windows Server Domain, both the username and password with the proper permissions to join the Windows Server Domain must be correctly entered. Select the desired method for how this virtual machine will participate in the network and click the Next button as shown in Figure 7.140.

Step 17. Operating Systems Options screen.

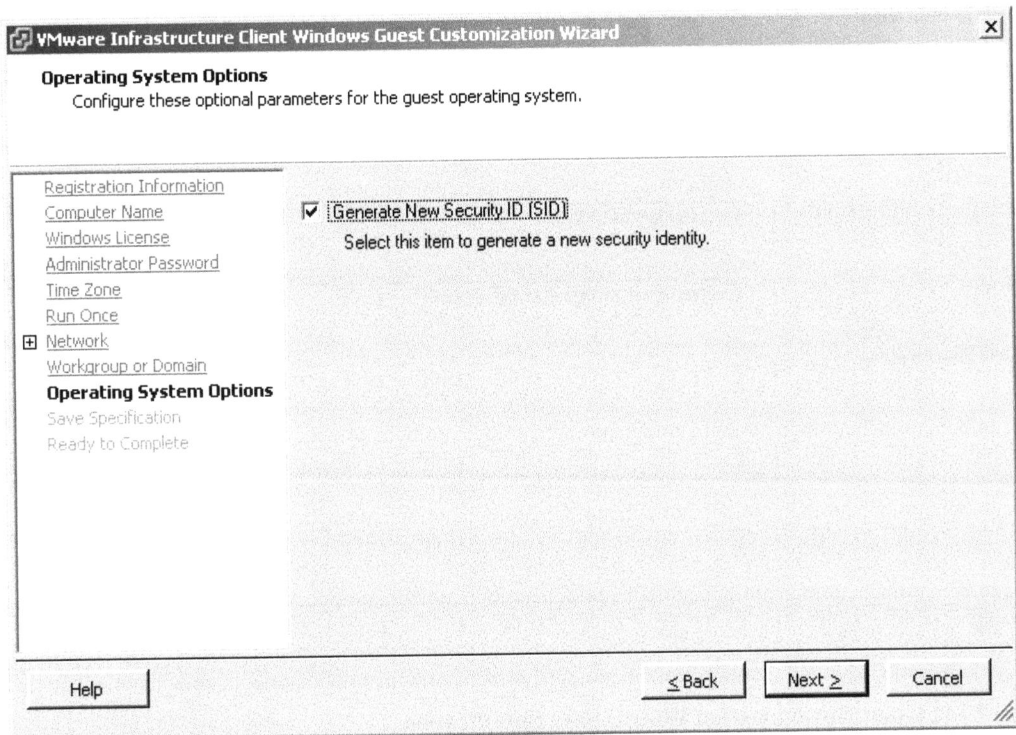

Figure 7.141 Guest Customization Wizard Operating System Options

A Windows clone by default will have the same security identifier (SID) as the source virtual machine being used to clone from. Having the same SID on the same Windows network will cause access and permission problems for both the source and cloned virtual machines. If the clone will be used on the same network as the source virtual machine, select the Generate New Security ID (SID) check box. If desired, all existing user accounts for the cloned virtual machine can be deleted. This can be useful if the administrator account on the source virtual machine is non-empty and will be modified for the cloned virtual machine. Select the desired options for this virtual machine as shown in Figure 7.141.

Step 18. Save Specification screen.

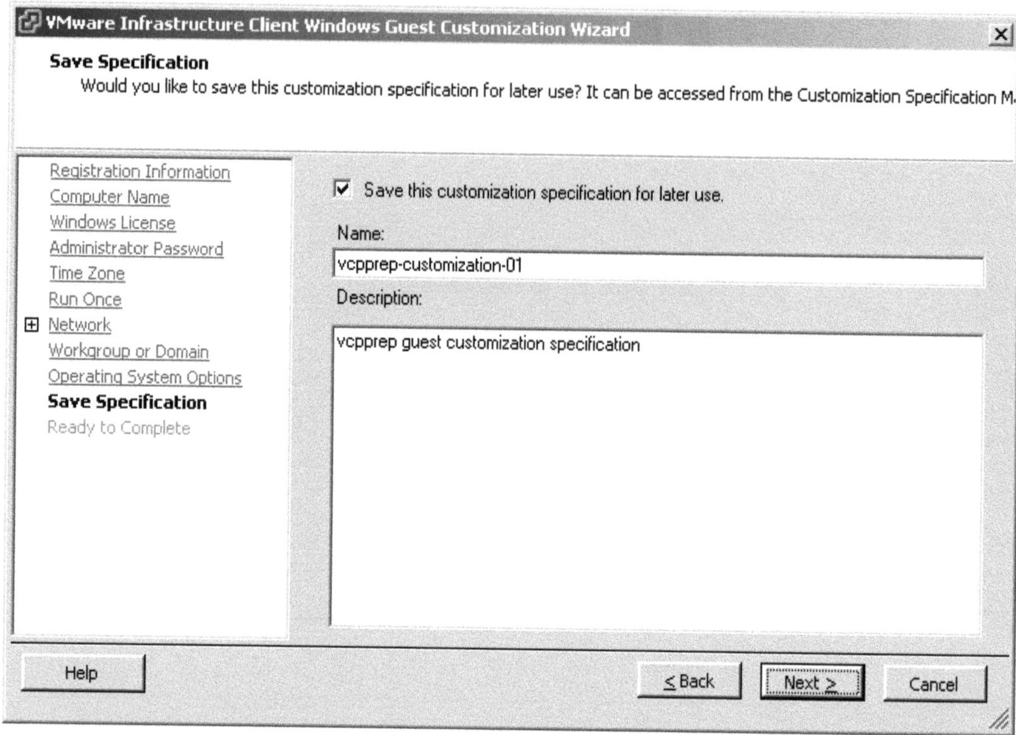

Figure 7.142 Guest Customization Wizard Save Specification

The choices that were made for the previous nine steps can be saved for later use as a customization specification file. Customization specification files can be accessed by selecting the Edit menu in the VirtualCenter menu bar and selecting the Customizations Specifications... menu option. This will display the Customization Specification Manager that can be used to manage existing specification files. To create a customization specification file, select the Save this customization specification for later use check box. Next, enter a name and description for the customization specification file as shown in Figure 7.142.

Step 19. Ready to Complete screen.

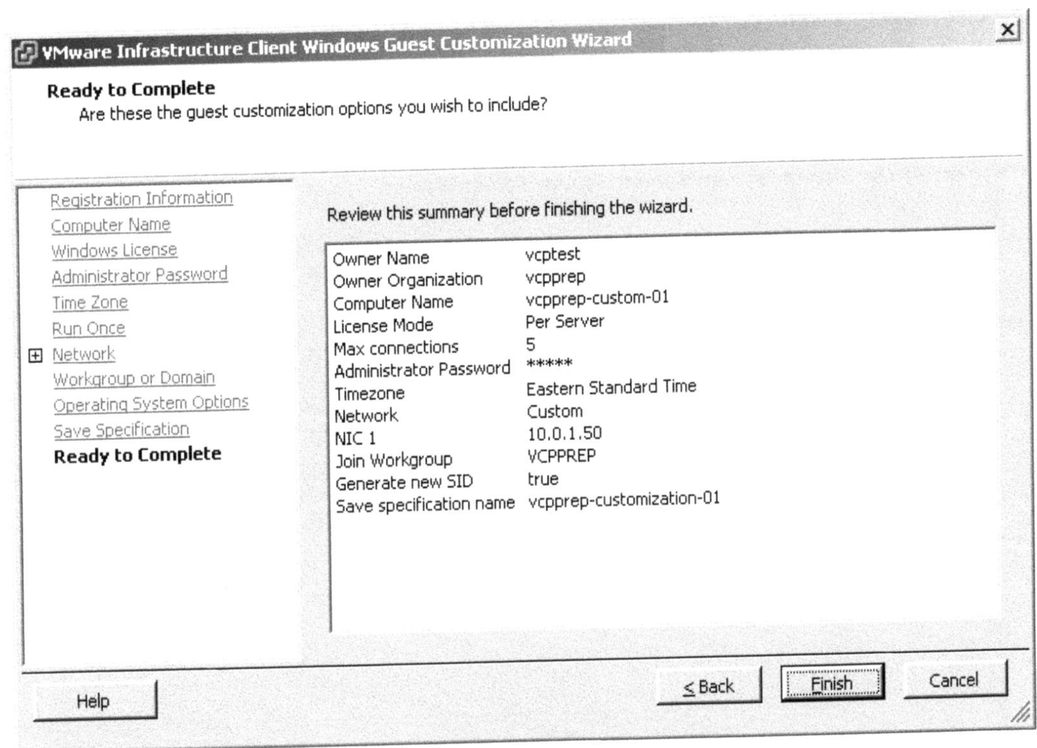

Figure 7.143 Guest Customization Wizard Ready To Complete

Confirm the configuration options. If changes are needed, select the Back button to navigate to the appropriate configuration to modify. Once the options are confirmed select the Finish button as shown in Figure 7.143.

Once a customization specification file has been created, it can be chosen during the Deploy Template Wizard by selecting the Customize using an existing customization specification.

Step 1. Select Guest Customization Option screen.

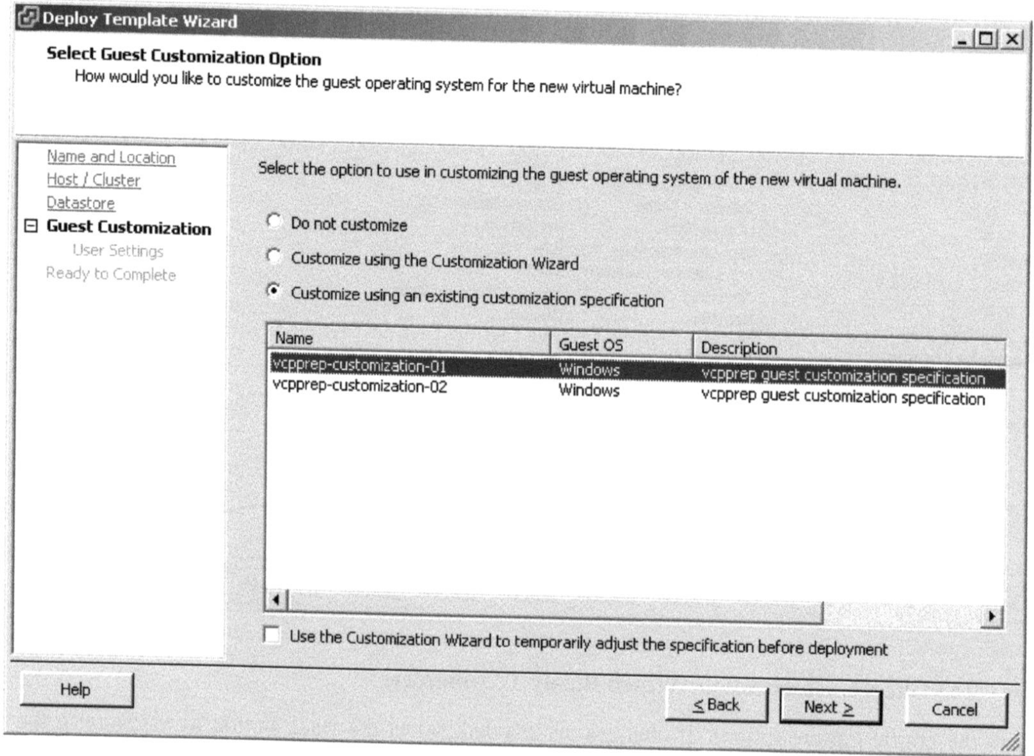

Figure 7.144 Guest Customization Wizard Customize Using An Existing Customization Specification

Choose the Customize using an existing customization specification radio button to select an existing customization specification file. The Use the Customization Wizard to temporarily adjust the specification before deployment check box can be selected to alter the pre-defined options for the selected customization specification file. Click the Next button to continue as shown in Figure 7.144.

Step 2. Ready to Complete New Virtual Machine screen.

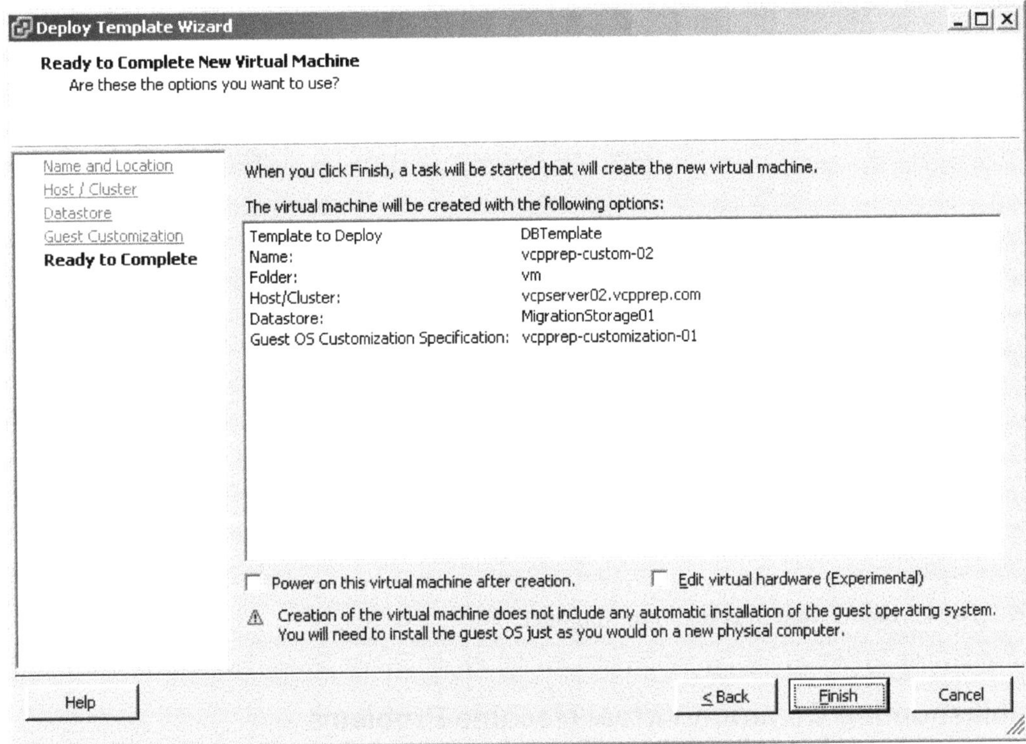

Figure 7.145 Guest Customization Wizard Customize Using An Existing Customization Specification Ready To Complete

Review the customization options. Optionally, the virtual machine can be powered on by selecting the check box for the Power on the new virtual machine after creation option. Confirm the customization options and select the Finish button as shown in Figure 7.145.

To create, modify or delete a customization specification file, select the Edit menu from within the VI Client and chose the Customizations Specifications... option as shown in Figure 7.146.

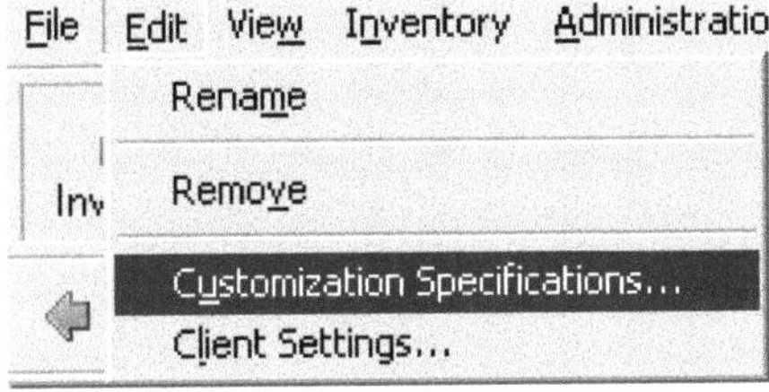

Figure 7.146 Customization Specifications Menu Option

The customization specification manager dialog box, shown in Figure 7.147 allows for the creation, modification and deletion of customization specification files. A export feature is provided as well. This is useful when transporting customization specification files to another VirtualCenter server.

Once exported, the file can be imported on another VirtualCenter server by selecting the Import button in the top left menu as shown in Figure 7.147.

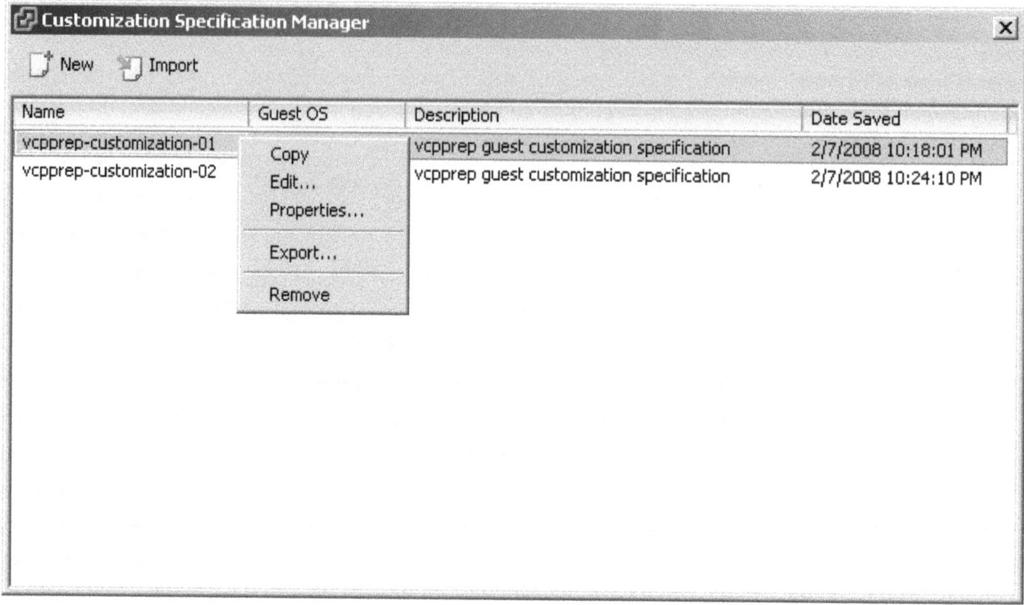

Figure 7.147 Customization Specification Manager

Troubleshooting Common Virtual Machine Problems

Troubleshooting virtual machines typically concerns resource issues. Does the virtual machine have enough memory and CPU cycles to perform its workload? Performance issues will be looked at further in Chapter 16 - Monitoring and Alerting. But what if the virtual machine crashes? An ESX administrator would want to review the virtual machine log files. These log files are located in the directory where the virtual machine state files are located. Every time a virtual machine powers on, a new log file is created. Virtual machine log files follow this syntax: vmware-#.log. Up to 6 log files are maintained by default. Logging behavior can be modified for a VM by using the following attributes within the virtual machine .vmx file:

log.rotateSize - Set the log file size in kilobytes

log.keepOld - Keep old log files

log.filename - Modify the VM log file name

logging - Turn logging on or off

As shown previously in Figure 7.71, the Disable acceleration check box turns off VM acceleration technologies. When installing or running software within a virtual machine, the application may appear to hang. To try and resolve this problem, this option temporarily disables acceleration in the virtual machine. If disabling acceleration resolves the problem, you may re-enable acceleration once the application is successfully running so that the virtual machine performance is no longer degraded.

Also shown in Figure 7.71, the Enable debugging information check box creates virtual machine log files that are useful when troubleshooting virtual machine operational problems. The Debugging and Statistics section is new for Virtual Center 2.5 and allows you to control the verbosity of messages within the virtual machine log files. By default, standard messages are logged. By selecting the Record Debugging Information, detail debug messages are logged. This option is useful when providing documentation to VMware support personnel.

External References

The VMware ESX 3.5 and ESXi Server version 3.5 Documentation Page:

http://www.vmware.com/support/pubs/vi_pubs.html

Guest Operating System Installation Guide:

http://www.vmware.com/pdf/GuestOS_guide.pdf

Performance Tuning Best Practices for ESX Server 3:

http://www.vmware.com/pdf/vi_performance_tuning.pdf

Performance Characteristics of VMFS and RDM:

http://www.vmware.com/files/pdf/vmfs_rdm_perf.pdf

Open Virtual Machine Format (OVF):

http://www.vmware.com/appliances/learn/ovf.html

Setup for Microsoft Cluster Service:

http://www.vmware.com/pdf/vi3_301_201_mscs.pdf

Sample Test Questions

1. A request is made to increase the memory of a virtual machine named Dev_Test_01. The ESX administrator does not have access to the VI Client software or a web browser. The only access is to the service console via a SSH remote connection. Which file should the ESX administrator modify to alter the memory allocated to the VM?

a. Dev_Test_01.vmdk

b. Dev_Test_01.vswp

c. Dev_Test_01-flat.vmdk

d. Dev_Test_01.vmx

e. Dev_Test_01.log

2. A newly purchased application is to be installed within a virtual machine. The application requires 8 GB of memory to function properly. The ESX administrator is consulted and asked what the maximum amount of memory that can be assigned to a virtual machine. The ESX administrator responds with which of the following?

a. 10 GB

b. 8 GB

c. 16 GB

d. 64 GB

e. 32 GB

3. A junior ESX administrator is asked to update a master template image used for the accounting department. Which of the following will need to be performed first to accomplish this task?

a. Clone the template first

b. Convert the template to a VM

c. Merge the snapshot files first

d. Deploy the template to a VM

e. Templates cannot be updated

4. Jessica is the Virtualization Architect asked to create a virtual machine to serve as a firewall for other virtual machines hosted on the same ESX server. The firewall VM is to be connected to two virtual switches. Which of the following is the maximum number of virtual network cards that a VM can contain?

a. 4

b. 2

c. 8

d. 6

e. 1

5. During the initial creation of a virtual machine named Test_05, the ESX administrator selects to configure the virtual machine with 256 MB of memory and keeps the default for all other settings. Once the new virtual machine is powered on, the ESX administrator notices that there is a Test_05.vswp file located in the new virtual machine's directory with a file size of 256 MB. Which of the following memory limits will the guest OS running inside the Test_05 virtual machine have access to?

a. 272 MB

b. 1 GB

c. 512 MB

d. 500 MB

e. 256 MB

6. A software developer is using a virtual machine to run several code tests but does not want to permanently alter the guest operating system. The developer does not have the user permissions needed to take snapshots. Which of the following modes can the developer place the virtual disk in to complete the code tests?

a. Independent - persistent

b. Read-only

c. Independent - non-persistent

d. Normal - persistent

e. Normal - non-persistent

7. When attempting to install a guest operating system within a virtual machine, the operating system installation fails due to not being able to find a hard disk. Which of the following should be modified?

a. Virtual Network Adapter

b. Virtual Storage Adapter

c. The storage setting within the .vmx file

d. The virtual disk mode

e. The boot order in the nvram file

8. A virtual machine is to be used as a file server. The files are all stored on multiple CDROM ISO images. What is the maximum CDROM ISO images this virtual machine can be configured with?

a. 2

b. 4

c. 6

d. 8

e. 10

9. A user has started a Windows 2003 virtual machine remotely through VirtualCenter. Which of the following is the correct keyboard sequence to issue in order to log into the Windows virtual machine?

a. Ctrl+Alt+Del

b. Ctrl+Alt+Shift

c. Ctrl+Alt+Ins

d. Ctrl+Shift+Del

e. Ctrl+Shift+Ins

10. A newly built virtual machine was created by a Junior ESX administrator. The operator of this virtual machine has opened a help desk ticket stating the performance of the VM is very slow. Which of the following should the Junior ESX administrator check first?

a. Investigate the network configuration of the end users machine

b. Allocate additional memory to the VM

c. Allocate another virtual processor to the VM

d. Allocate another virtual network card to the VM

e. Install VMware tools if it is not installed

11. The physical DHCP server machine was recently converted to a virtual machine. A few days later, the DHCP server administrator notices that the time zone is correct but the time within this VM is not correct. What steps should be taken to prevent this from occurring?

a. Readjust the virtual machine's time within the guest operating system

b. Verify VMware tools is installed

c. Set the tools.syncTime to the value of "TRUE" within the .vmx file for this VM

d. Verify that the time synchronization check is select in VMware tools

e. Readjust the time on the VirtualCenter server

12. A junior administrator noticed that a VM called Test_06 had a 128 MB .vswp file that was created when the VM was powered on. They noticed that VM Test_05 had a 256 MB .vswp file. Both VMs were given 256 MB of memory when created and were configured using the same version of a Windows guest OS. What would cause this?

a. The difference is due to the applications loaded into the VM

b. The difference is due to the lack of service packs installed

c. The difference was due to the reservation settings

d. The difference was due to location of the VMFS and the underlying RAID level

e. The difference was due to the SCSI reservation settings on the VMFS

13. A technician configures a training class room to use virtual machines for a custom class. The technician is interested in modifying the virtual hardware of the virtual machines in order to add additional network cards and SCSI controllers. The technician consults the ESX administrator regarding the maximum number of PCI slots available in a virtual machine. The ESX administrator responds with the following answer:

a. 3

b. 5

c. 6

d. 2

e. 16

14. A database administrator is implementing a proof-of-concept project involving a physical to virtual conversion of a database server. The database application is multi-thread capable. The database administrator inquires about the maximum vCPUs a virtual machine can contain. Which of the following are available vCPU configurations?

a. 4

b. 1

c. 2

d. 3

e. 6

15. A file server virtual machine requires an additional virtual hard drive to be added. In order to verify that the second virtual hard drive was successfully added, the VM administrator should look for the existence of which files?

a. A file ending with a .vmx file extension

b. Two files containing -flat.vmdk in the name

c. A file ending with a .vswp file extension

d. Two files ending with a .vmdk file extension

e. A file ending with a .vmsd file extension

16. To take advantage of VirtualCenter's rapid provisioning capabilities, three virtual machines have been created to serve as templates. Just before converting the VMs to templates, you discover that there is limited space on the storage device that will be used to store the templates. Which of the following formats should be used to conserve storage space?

a. Normal

b. Compressed

c. Zipped

d. Optimized

e. Compact

17. A junior ESX administrator involved with implementing a VDI deployment is tasked with the creation of the accounting and financial virtual machine templates. Which two methods can be used by the junior administrator to create the templates?

a. Convert to Template

b. Copy to Template

c. Template Quick Mode

d. Template Full Mode

e. Clone to Template

18. A recent service pack was released that contains important security patches. The ESX administrator needs to apply this service pack to an existing server template. When right clicking on the template, which of the following is an available option in the pop up menu that can be used to update the template with the needed service pack?

a. Template Update

b. Template Sync

c. Convert To Virtual Machine

d. Merge to Virtual Machine

e. Template Merge

19. When deploying a Windows virtual machine from a template, the guest operating system customization wizard is not available. What must the ESX administrator do in order to be able to utilize the guest customization wizard?

a. Install the guest customization software from VMware

b. Ensure Microsoft Sysprep has been extracted in the proper directory

c. Guest Customization Wizard is only available for non-Windows operating systems

d. Add the "guest customization" option to the template's .vmx file

e. Verify that the guest customization license has not expired

20. The marketing department virtual machine used for file and print sharing requires that another virtual hard disk be added to the VM. The remote SAN storage LUN where this VM resides does not contain enough spare storage space for the addition of the second virtual hard disk. Which of the following can be performed to resolve this problem?

a. VMotion the VM to another LUN that contains sufficient disk space

b. Create the second virtual hard disk in compact mode

c. Nothing can be done to resolve this

d. Perform a cold migration of the VM using the option to move the VM state files

e. Create the second virtual hard disk in non-persistent mode

21. The software development team is ready to perform a series of code tests against a newly developed application. This new application is currently installed and operating within a VM. Each test will drastically alter the VMs configuration. The software developers want to use snapshots to quickly revert back to a known good state after each test. Which of the following tools provides snapshot capabilities?

a. Snapshot Creator

b. Snapshot Manager

c. Snapshot Capture

d. Snapshot Maker

e. Snapshot Taker

22. The intranet web server is running within a virtual machine. During 9 to 5 working hours, this virtual machine cannot be powered off. At 11:00 am, the web developers request that the virtual machine have additional virtual hardware added to address several insufficient resource issues. Which of the following virtual hardware cannot be added while the VM is powered on?

a. Ethernet Adapter

b. SCSI Controller

c. Parallel Port

d. DVD/CDROM

e. Floppy Drive

23. The disaster recovery plans include clustering physical servers with virtual servers. During the creation and configuration of the virtual machines, which of the following must be added to the virtual machine in order to accomplish this task?

a. Virtual hard disk in independent persistent mode

b. Virtual hard disk in independent non-persistent mode

c. RDM file in virtual compatibility mode

d. RDM file in physical compatibility mode

e. Virtual hard disk in normal snapshot mode

24. An organization is currently in the late planning stages of a virtualization deployment. The ESX servers, networking, disaster recovery and storage plans have been completed. The plan called for using very descriptive text for the virtual machine display names within VirtualCenter. Which of the following is recommended to avoid using for VM display names?

a. A mixture of numbers and characters

b. All uppercase characters

c. All lowercase characters

d. The use of special characters and spaces

e. Display names less than 5 characters in length

25. A heavily used FTP server running within a virtual machine requires more virtual hard drives to meet the demands of end users. The FTP server administrator asks the ESX administrator for the maximum number of SCSI controllers that a single virtual machine can support. Which of the following is the correct response the ESX administrator should give?

a. 1

b. 8

c. 6

d. 2

e. 4

26. You are asked to configure a virtual machine so that it can support a bidirectional printer, a scanner and a dongle. The virtual machine settings included options to add parallel ports that will be needed for this configuration. How many parallel ports can a single virtual machine support?

a. 3

b. 4

c. 2

d. 1

e. 6

27. The service console on a ESX server contains the dd command that can be used to create CDROM or Floppy drive images. An ESX administrator creates multiple Floppy drive images that end in a .flp file extension. What is the maximum physical or floppy .flp image files that a virtual machine can be configured with?

a. 2

b. 0

c. 4

d. 6

e. 1

28. Seth is the Director of Technology, he is concerned that the ESX administrator has built both high priority and low priority virtual machines on the same ESX server. When asked about how the ESX server uses physical memory efficiently, the ESX administrator responds by stating that VMware tools installed in the guest operating systems of all virtual machines assists in memory management. Which of the following drivers does VMware tools provide to ensure efficient use of physical memory?

a. The Expandable Driver

b. The vmmemctl Driver

c. The Memory Switch Driver

d. The Inflate Driver

e. The Bubble Driver

29. A software developer is planning on using a virtual serial port in a virtual machine to send its output to a file on the host computer for debugging purposes. This technique is used within the development group when capturing the data of a program running in the virtual machine and sending via the virtual serial port as a way to transfer a file from the guest operating system to the host. How many virtual serial ports can the developer configure a single virtual machine with?

a. 4

b. 6

c. 3

d. 1

e. 2

30. A new user of virtualization technology has just successfully built their first virtual machine. The next step is the installation of the selected guest operating system. Which of the following can be used to install the guest operating system software?

a. Physical Floppy Drive

b. Physical DVD/CDROM Drive

c. ISO image

d. USB Drive

e. CIFS Share

Sample Test Solutions

1. A request is made to increase the memory of a virtual machine named Dev_Test_01. The ESX administrator does not have access to the VI Client software or a web browser. The only access is to the service console via a SSH remote connection. Which file should the ESX administrator modify to alter the memory allocated to the VM?

a. Dev_Test_01.vmdk

b. Dev_Test_01.vswp

c. Dev_Test_01-flat.vmdk

d. Dev_Test_01.vmx

e. Dev_Test_01.log

Answer: d - The .vmx file is the main configuration file for a VM. It is an ASCII text file that can be modified using a command line editor such as VI or Nano to make changes to the virtual machines memory settings. Virtual Machine files with a .vmdk file extension are used for the virtual hard disk. The .vswp file extension is used for the VMkernel swap file. The .log file extension is used to record logging information for a virtual machine.

2. An newly purchased application is to be installed within a virtual machine. The application requires 8 GB of memory to function properly. The ESX administrator is consulted and asked what the maximum amount of memory that can be assigned to a virtual machine. The ESX administrator responds with which of the following?

a. 8 GB

b. 12 GB

c. 16 GB

d. 64 GB

e. 32 GB

Answer: d - A virtual machine can be configured with a maximum memory size of 64 GB. Applications requiring more than 64 GB of memory are not good virtualization candidates. The ESX 3.0.x server product supported a maximum of 16 GB of memory.

3. A junior ESX administrator is asked to update a master template image used for the accounting department. Which of the following will need to be performed first to accomplish this task?

a. Clone the template first

b. Convert the template to a VM

c. Merge the snapshot files first

d. Deploy the template to a VM

e. Templates cannot be updated

Answer: b -Templates cannot be powered on. The template must first be converted to a VM. Once the template has been converted back to a VM, it is good practice to isolate it from the network to avoid any unintended access to the template image which could potentially corrupt the template image. You can then power it on, update the operating system with new programs or patches/service packs and then convert it back to a template.

4. Jessica is the Virtualization Architect asked to create a virtual machine to serve as a firewall for other virtual machines hosted on the same ESX server. The firewall VM is to be connected to two virtual switches. Which of the following is the maximum number of virtual network cards that a VM can contain?

a. 4

b. 2

c. 8

d. 6

e. 1

Answer: a - A virtual machine can contain a maximum of four virtual network cards.

5. During the initial creation of a virtual machine named Test_05, the ESX administrator selects the option to configure the virtual machine with 256 MB of memory and keeps the default for all other settings. Once the new virtual machine is powered on, the ESX administrator notices that there is a Test_05.vswp file located in the new virtual machine's directory with a file size of 256 MB. Which of the following memory limits will the guest OS running inside the Test_05 virtual machine have access to?

a. 272 MB

b. 1 GB

c. 512 MB

d. 500 MB

e. 256 MB

Answer: e - The Test_05 virtual machine will have access to a maximum of 256 MB of memory as configured during the initial virtual machine creation wizard. The VMkernel creates the Test_05.vswp file when the Test_05 virtual machine is first powered on. The VMkernel will use the Test_05.vswp when necessary if physical memory is unavailable. When the Test_05 virtual machine is powered off, the Test_05.vswp file will be deleted.

6. A software developer is using a virtual machine to run several code tests but does not want to permanently alter the guest operating system. The developer does not have the user permissions needed to take snapshots. Which of the following modes can the developer place the virtual disk in to complete the code tests?

a. Independent - persistent

b. Read-only

c. Independent - non-persistent

d. Normal - persistent

e. Normal - non-persistent

Answer: c - Independent - non-persistent mode will allow a virtual machine operator to make non permanent changes to a virtual machine. Any changes made to the guest operating system are saved if the virtual machine is rebooted but these changes are lost once the virtual machine is powered off.

7. When attempting to install a guest operating system within a virtual machine, the operating system installation fails due to not being able to find a hard disk. Which of the following should be modified?

a. Virtual Network Adapter

b. Virtual Storage Adapter

c. The storage setting within the .vmx file

d. The virtual disk mode

e. The boot order in the nvram file

Answer: b - Virtual machines support the LSILogic and BusLogic virtual storage adapters. When a virtual machine is created, the guest operating system that is to be installed is selected which results in the correct virtual storage adapter for that guest operating system. If another operating system is being installed or if the virtual storage adapter setting has been modified, the guest operating system may not be able to communicate with the virtual hard disk.

8. A virtual machine is to be used as a file server. The files are all stored on multiple CDROM ISO images. What is the maximum CDROM ISO images this virtual machine can be configured with?

a. 2

b. 4

c. 6

d. 8

e. 10

Answer: b - A virtual machine can be configured with a maximum of four virtual CDROM drives.

The virtual CDROM drives can attached to either physical CDROM drives, CDROM ISO images or a combination of both.

9. A user has started a Windows 2003 virtual machine remotely through VirtualCenter. Which of the following is the correct keyboard sequence to issue in order to log into the Windows virtual machine?

a. Ctrl+Alt+Del

b. Ctrl+Alt+Shift

c. Ctrl+Alt+Ins

d. Ctrl+Shift+Del

e. Ctrl+Shift+Ins

Answer: c - The correct key sequence to issue to log into a Windows 2003 virtual machine is Ctrl+Alt+Ins

10. A newly built virtual machine was created by a Junior ESX administrator. The operator of this virtual machine has opened a help desk ticket stating the performance of the VM is very slow. Which of the following should the Junior ESX administrator check first?

a. Investigate the network configuration of the end users machine

b. Allocate additional memory to the VM

c. Allocate another virtual processor to the VM

d. Allocate another virtual network card to the VM

e. Install VMware tools if it is not installed

Answer: e - VMware tools provides performance enhancements to virtual machines. Optimized drivers for the virtual mouse, video, SCSI controller and memory can be utilized by the virtual machine once VMware tools is installed.

11. The physical DHCP server machine was recently converted to a virtual machine. A few days later, the DHCP server administrator notices that the time zone is correct but the time within this VM is not correct. What steps should be taken to prevent this from occurring?

a. Readjust the virtual machine's time within the guest operating system

b. Verify VMware tools is installed

c. Set the tools.syncTime to the value of "TRUE" within the .vmx file for this VM

d. Verify that the time synchronization check is select in VMware tools

e. Readjust the time on the VirtualCenter server

Answer: b, c, d - VMware tools provides time synchronization between a virtual machine and the

ESX host server the VM is running on. Once VMware tools is installed, either open the VMware tool application, select the "Options" tab and select the time synchronization box or modify the .vmx file of the VM and verify that the tools.syncTime attribute is set as follows:

tools.syncTime = "TRUE"

12. A junior administrator noticed that a VM called Test_06 had a 128 MB .vswp file that was created when the VM was powered on. They noticed that VM Test_05 had a 256 MB .vswp file. Both VMs were given 256 MB of memory when created and were configured using the same version of a Windows guest OS. What would cause this?

a. The difference is due to the applications loaded into the VM

b. The difference is due to the lack of service packs installed

c. The difference was due to the reservation settings

d. The difference was due to location of the VMFS and the underlying RAID level

e. The difference was due to the SCSI reservation settings on the VMFS

Answer: c - The size of the .vswp file created when the VM is powered on is determined by subtracting the memory reservation value from the maximum memory given to the VM. Test_05 had a reservation of 0 MB and a maximum value of 256 MB which causes the creation of a 256 MB .vswp file. Test_06 had a reservation of 128 MB and a maximum value of 256 MB which causes the creation of a 128 MB .vswp file. More information on how the swap files are used is covered in Chapter 11 – Resource Optimization.

13. A technician configures a training class room to use virtual machines for a custom class. The technician is interested in modifying the virtual hardware of the virtual machines in order to add additional network cards and SCSI controllers. The technician consults the ESX administrator regarding the maximum number of PCI slots available in a virtual machine. The ESX administrator responds with the following answer:

a. 3

b. 5

c. 6

d. 2

e. 16

Answer: b - Virtual machines have a maximum of 6 PCI slots. One of these PCI slots is dedicated to the virtual VGA graphics card. The remaining 5 PCI slots can be used as needed.

14. A database administrator is implementing a proof-of-concept project involving a physical to virtual conversion of a database server. The database application is multi-thread capable. The database administrator inquires about the maximum vCPUs a virtual machine can contain. Which of the following are available vCPU

configurations?

a. 4

b. 1

c. 2

d. 3

e. 6

Answer: a, b, c - Virtual machines can contain either 1, 2 or 4 vCPUs. When more than 1 vCPU is used, a virtual SMP license must be purchased.

15. A file server virtual machine requires an additional virtual hard drive to be added. In order to verify that the second virtual hard drive was successfully added, the VM administrator should look for the existence of which files?

a. A file ending with a .vmx file extension

b. Two files containing -flat.vmdk in the name

c. A file ending with a .vswp file extension

d. Two files ending with a .vmdk file extension

e. A file ending with a .vmsd file extension

Answer: b, d - Virtual hard disks consist of two files. A metadata file is used to describe the virtual disk attributes and this file has a file extension of .vmdk. The actual virtual hard disk contains a -flat.vmdk within the file name.

16. To take advantage of VirtualCenter's rapid provisioning capabilities, three virtual machines have been created to serve as templates. Just before converting the VMs to templates, you discover that there is limited space on the storage device that will be used to store the templates. Which of the following formats should be used to conserve storage space?

a. Normal

b. Compressed

c. Zipped

d. Optimized

e. Compact

Answer: e - Compact is a format that can be chosen when converting a VM to a template. This format will zero out any unused virtual hard disk space so that less disk space will be needed to store the template image.

17. A junior ESX administrator involved with implementing a VDI deployment is tasked with the creation of the accounting and financial virtual machine templates.

Which two methods can be used by the junior administrator to create the templates?

a. Convert to Template

b. Copy to Template

c. Template Quick Mode

d. Template Full Mode

e. Clone to Template

Answer: a,e - A template can be created when right clicking on a virtual machine and choosing either "Convert to Template" or "Clone to Template" from the pop up menu option. When converting a virtual machine to a template, the virtual machine will no longer be able to power on. When cloning a virtual machine to a template, the virtual machine can still be powered on and used.

18. A recent service pack was released that contains important security patches. The ESX administrator needs to apply this service pack to an existing server template. When right clicking on the template, which of the following is an available option in the pop up menu that can be used to update the template with the needed service pack?

a. Template Update

b. Template Sync

c. Convert To Virtual Machine

d. Merge to Virtual Machine

e. Template Merge

Answer: c - A template cannot be powered on. It must first be converted back to a virtual machine in order to update the guest operating systems with the latest service pack. It is a good practice to place the template on an isolated network when converting it back to a virtual machine so that any unexpected modifications to the template image do not occur.

19. When deploying a Windows virtual machine from a template, the guest operating system customization wizard is not available. What must the ESX administrator do in order to be able to utilize the guest customization wizard?

a. Install the guest customization software from VMware

b. Ensure Microsoft Sysprep has been extracted in the proper directory

c. Guest Customization Wizard is only available for non-Windows operating systems

d. Add the "guest customization" option to the template's .vmx file

e. Verify that the guest customization license has not expired

Answer: b - The guest customization wizard requires that Microsoft Sysprep has been properly extracted to the correct directory within the VirtualCenter server. A common cause of the guest customization wizard being unavailable is extracting Microsoft Sysprep to the incorrect directory.

The following is the correct path to extract the Sysprep files on the VirtualCenter server:

C:\Documents and Settings\All Users\Application Data\VMware\VMware VirtualCenter\sysprep\1.1

There are Windows version-specific sub-folders for each version of Windows that the Sysprep files must be extracted to; this is new as of VirtualCenter Server 2.5.

20. The marketing department virtual machine used for file and print sharing requires that another virtual hard disk be added to the VM. The remote SAN storage LUN where this VM resides does not contain enough spare storage space for the addition of the second virtual hard disk. Which of the following can be performed to resolve this problem?

a. VMotion the VM to another LUN that contains sufficient disk space

b. Create the second virtual hard disk in compact mode

c. Nothing can be done to resolve this

d. Perform a cold migration of the VM using the option to move the VM state files

e. Create the second virtual hard disk in non-persistent mode

Answer: d - Performing a cold migration provides the option to leave the VM state files in their current location or physically move the VM state files to an alternate storage location. However, as of ESX 3.5/VC Server 2.5, storage VMotion could be used to move the VM's files to a larger datastore, with no downtime.

21. The software development team is ready to perform a series of code tests against a newly developed application. This new application is currently installed and operating within a VM. Each test will drastically alter the VMs configuration. The software developers want to use snapshots to quickly revert back to a known good state after each test. Which of the following tools provides snapshot capabilities?

a. Snapshot Creator

b. Snapshot Manager

c. Snapshot Capture

d. Snapshot Maker

e. Snapshot Taker

Answer: b - Snapshot Manager is the tool to use that enables multiple snapshots to be taken. Snapshot Manager captures the entire state of a virtual machine at the point in time the snapshot is taken. Once the snapshot has been taken, the state of the virtual machines memory, the state of the virtual machines virtual disks and the configuration settings of the VM are recorded. Capturing the state of memory is optional. With Snapshot Manager, the captured state of a VM can be returned to repeatedly.

22. The intranet web server is running within a virtual machine. During 9 to 5 working hours, this virtual machine cannot be powered off. At 11:00 am, the web developers request that the virtual machine have additional virtual hardware added to address several insufficient resource issues. Which of the following virtual hardware cannot be added while the VM is powered on?

a. Ethernet Adapter

b. SCSI Controller

c. Parallel Port

d. DVD/CDROM

e. Floppy Drive

Answer: a,b,c,d,e - The only supported device that can be added while a virtual machine is powered on is a virtual hard disk. These devices are the only "hot-pluggable" devices. Although virtual hard disks can be added to a powered on virtual machine, they cannot be removed unless the virtual machine is in a powered off state. Note, RDM files can are treated as virtual hard disks and can be added while the VM is powered on as well.

23. The disaster recovery plans include clustering physical servers with virtual servers. During the creation and configuration of the virtual machines, which of the following must be added to the virtual machine in order to accomplish this task?

a. Virtual hard disk in independent persistent mode

b. Virtual hard disk in independent non-persistent mode

c. RDM file in virtual compatibility mode

d. RDM file in physical compatibility mode

e. Virtual hard disk in normal snapshot mode

Answer: d - RDM files created in physical compatibility mode are needed when clustering physical machines to virtual machines.

24. An organization is currently in the late planning stages of a virtualization deployment. The ESX servers, networking, disaster recovery and storage plans have been completed. The plan called for using very descriptive text for the virtual machine display names within VirtualCenter. Which of the following is recommended to avoid using for VM display names?

a. A mixture of numbers and characters

b. All uppercase characters

c. All lowercase characters

d. The use of special characters and spaces

e. Display names less than 5 characters in length

Answer: d - The use of special characters and spaces within display names of virtual machines is not recommended. The service console running on an ESX server is Linux-based. Within Linux environments, problems may occur when processing virtual machine display names that contain special characters and spaces.

25. A heavily used FTP server running within a virtual machine requires more virtual hard drives to meet the demands of end users. The FTP server administrator asks the ESX administrator for the maximum number of SCSI controllers that a single virtual machine can support. Which of the following is the correct response the ESX administrator should give?

a. 1

b. 8

c. 6

d. 2

e. 4

Answer: e - A virtual machine can support a maximum of 4 SCSI controllers. Each SCSI controller can contain 1-15 devices each.

26. You are asked to configure a virtual machine so that it can support a bidirectional printer, a scanner and a dongle. The virtual machine settings included options to add parallel ports that will be needed for this configuration. How many parallel ports can a single virtual machine support?

a. 3

b. 4

c. 2

d. 1

e. 6

Answer: c - The maximum amount of parallel ports that a single virtual machine can contain is two. Therefore, the bidirectional printer, scanner and dongle cannot be configured simultaneously within the same virtual machine.

27. The service console on a ESX server contains the dd command that can be used to create CDROM or Floppy drive images. An ESX administrator creates multiple Floppy drive images that end in a .flp file extension. What is the maximum physical or floppy .flp image files can a virtual machine be configured with?

a. 2

b. 0

c. 4

d. 6

e. 1

Answer: a - Virtual machines can make use of both physical floppy drives as well as floppy image files. A virtual machine can contain one or two floppy images, physical devices or a combination of both at the same time.

28. Seth is the Director of Technology, he is concerned that the ESX administrator has built both high priority and low priority virtual machines on the same ESX server. When asked about how the ESX server uses physical memory efficiently, the ESX administrator responds by stating that VMware tools installed in the guest operating systems of all virtual machines assists in memory management. Which of the following drivers does VMware tools provide to ensure efficient use of physical memory?

a. The Expandable Driver

b. The vmmemctl Driver

c. The Memory Switch Driver

d. The Inflate Driver

e. The Bubble Driver

Answer: b - The vmmemctl driver is responsible for reclaiming idle physical memory. It does so by reclaiming those pages that are considered least valuable by the guest operating system. It does not dictate which memory pages to write to disk, just how much memory. The technique in which the vmmemctl driver accomplishes this task is proprietary and referred to as ballooning.

29. A software developer is planning on using a virtual serial port in a virtual machine to send its output to a file on the host computer for debugging purposes. This technique is used within the development group when capturing the data of a program running in the virtual machine and sending via the virtual serial port as a way to transfer a file from the guest operating system to the host. How many virtual serial ports can the developer configure a single virtual machine with?

a. 4

b. 6

c. 3

d. 1

e. 2

Answer: e - A virtual machine can contain a maximum of two virtual serial ports. Virtual serial ports are often used as a quick method of transferring data between a guest operating system and the physical host that it is running on.

30. A new user of virtualization technology has just successfully built their first virtual machine. The next step is the installation of the selected guest operating system. Which of the following can be used to install the guest operating system software?

a. Physical Floppy Drive

b. Physical DVD/CDROM Drive

c. ISO image

d. USB Drive

e. CIFS Share

Answer: a,b,c - Virtual machines support the use of physical floppy and DVD/CDROM drives when performing guest operating system installations. ISO images of CDROM is also supported as is floppy disk images. ISO images are generally preferred as these can be copied to various locations on the network and easily accessed. Since ISO images are stored on physical hard drives, guest operating system installations are installed more quickly than when using physical floppy or DVD/CDROM drives. Both USB drives and CIFS shares are not supported for the installation of guest operating systems within a virtual machine.

Chapter 8

Converter Enterprise

After reading this chapter you should be able to complete the following tasks:

- Install Converter Enterprise
- Understand Converter Enterprise components
- Perform a hot clone import of a physical machine
- Perform a cold clone import of physical machine
- Customize imported physical machines
- Troubleshoot failed cloning operations

Converter Enterprise

Chapters 1 through 7 detailed building a virtualization solution from the ground up. The installations of ESX 3.5, ESXi Server version 3.5, and VirtualCenter server were explained. We discussed configuring ESX 3.5 server storage and networking. We've seen the process of creating virtual machines from scratch and walked through rapidly deploying virtual machines using templates. These products do not address existing physical machines in the datacenter. Many organizations are faced with the challenge of moving operating systems and applications housed on existing physical machines into the virtualized environment. VMware has a solution to address this issue, VMware Converter Enterprise.

VMware Converter Enterprise has many capabilities. It is a tool that can be used to perform physical to virtual (P2V) conversions. Such conversions are useful within test and development environments. For example, a converted physical machine can be deployed as a virtual machine to verify successful service pack update installations. Disaster recovery operations can also benefit from P2V conversions. A remote datacenter can be configured with virtual machines created via Converter Enterprise and serve as a disaster recovery solution.

VMware Converter Enterprise can be used to perform:

- Hot Cloning (Remote And Local)
- Cold Cloning
- Virtual To Virtual (V2V) Cloning
- Export Virtual Machines
- VMware Consolidated Backup Restores
- Reconfiguration Of Systems

Let's take a look at each of these capabilities.

Hot Cloning

A physical machine can be running while Converter Enterprise is performing its conversion operations. Conversions performed in this manner are referred to as hot cloning. A hot clone operation can be performed by downloading the standalone version of VMware Enterprise Converter from the VMware website and installing it on the machine that is to be cloned. Hot cloning can also be performed remotely. That is, by using a VMware Enterprise server to clone a physical machine remotely across the network. When hot cloning a physical machine, the following Windows operating systems can be converted:

- Windows NT 4 Workstation/Server SP4+
- Windows 2000 Professional
- Windows 2000 Server
- Windows 2000 Advanced
- Windows XP Professional (32 - bit and 64 - bit)
- Windows 2003 Standard (32 - bit and 64 - bit)
- Windows 2003 Web (32 - bit and 64 - bit)
- Windows 2003 Enterprise (32 - bit and 64 - bit)
- Windows Vista (32 - bit and 64 - bit)

To successfully convert a running physical machine, several conversion processes need to be performed. First, a user needs to launch the Import Wizard. The Import Wizard can be launched by several methods. Right clicking on a cluster, host or resource pool inventory object. The pop up menu will contain the Import Machine menu option. Right clicking on a folder from within the Virtual Machines and Templates view and selecting the Import Machine menu option. VI Client scheduled tasks can also be used to launch the Import Wizard. Once the Import Wizard has been completed, the converter agent is then installed on the target physical machine. In order for the agent to install properly, the correct user credentials need to be supplied during the Import Wizard. In addition, the Windows firewall service should be stopped if applicable and the following ports need to be open on the target machine:

- 139
- 445

Any firewalls between the Converter Enterprise server, VirtualCenter server and target machine will need to have the above two ports open and the following two ports open:

- 902
- 443

The agent is responsible for invoking the Windows Volume Shadow Copy service to take a snapshot of the target machine's hard disk(s). The following are the two forms of disk cloning using Converter Enterprise:

- Volume-Based Cloning - Cloning performed on a block level basis
- Disk-based Cloning - Cloning performed on a sector by sector basis

Volume-Based Cloning

In Volume-Based cloning, the target machines disk(s) must be basic volumes. Windows basic disks contain basic volumes such as primary partitions and extended partitions. Hot cloning only supports volume-based cloning. The volumes can be resized when using volume-based cloning. If resizing the disk to a smaller size than the original, copying is performed on a file-level basis. This may cause the conversion process to take more time to complete.

Disk-based Cloning

Disk-based cloning supports both basic and dynamic disks. Dynamic disks contain dynamic volumes. Dynamic volumes can be mirrored volumes, spanned volumes, striped volumes, RAID-5 volumes or just simple volumes. Cloning using disk-based does not support resizing of the disk volumes. Disk-based cloning can be used when performing a cold clone or when importing a virtual machine. Cold cloning and virtual machine importing will be discussed later in this chapter.

After the agent has completed the disk snapshot, a new virtual machine is created on the destination ESX server. The disk snapshots are then copied over to the destination ESX server. Converter Enterprise needs to reconfigure the virtual machine by replacing drivers so that the new virtual machine will be able to successfully boot. Using the Import Wizard, options may have been chosen to assign a new name or IP address to the converted virtual machine. Any such optional configuration changes are then applied. Snapshot(s) are then deleted from the target machine. The last step is removing the Converter Enterprise Agent. The removal of the agent is done automatically by default. This behavior can be changed to have the agent set to be manually removed if desired.

Cold Cloning

If hot cloning is not possible, an alternative is cold cloning. Cold cloning is performed by using the VMware Converter Enterprise boot disk. The boot disk initializes the physical system by using the Windows Preinstallation Environment (WinPE) operating system. WinPE is a scaled down version of Windows XP and it is often used in deploying systems. Once the system is initialized, the converter enterprise application is automatically started. The boot disk can be obtained from the following URL:

http://www.vmware.com/download/vi/

The above link is the main VMware download page. Locate the VMware Converter download link and select it to access the Converter download page. The boot CD is provided as a zip file that contains an ISO image file. First, extract the ISO image from the zip file. If cold cloning a physical system, it will be necessary to create a CD from the Converter ISO image. If cold cloning a virtual machine, the ISO image can simply be mounted to the virtual machine's CD/DVD drive.

When cold cloning a physical machine, the following Windows operating systems can be converted:

- Windows NT 4 Workstation/Server SP4+
- Windows 2000 Professional
- Windows 2000 Server
- Windows 2000 Advanced
- Windows XP Professional (32 - bit and 64 - bit)
- Windows 2003 Standard (32 - bit and 64 - bit)
- Windows 2003 Web (32 - bit and 64 - bit)
- Windows 2003 Enterprise (32 - bit and 64 - bit)
- Windows Vista (32 - bit and 64 - bit)
- Windows XP Home

NOTE: For Linux operating systems, P2V conversions using the cold clone method only has experimental support when the source physical machine has SCSI disks.

To begin the cold clone process, place the Converter Enterprise boot CD into the physical machine and reboot the system. During the initial boot phase, the system networking settings can be set along with setting any mapped drives. At this time, the temporary and log files location can be specified. Once the system has been booted and the Standalone Converter Enterprise application has been started, the network settings can still be modified but the location of the temporary and log files cannot. These files are stored in the RAM disk by default.

The cold cloning process is similar to the hot cloning process. However, with hot cloning, multiple conversions can be launched simultaneously. With cold cloning, only one conversion takes place at a time. Now that the system has been booted, the Import Wizard can be launched from the Standalone Converter Enterprise application. When the Import Wizard is finished, converter enterprise begins its processes without the need to install an agent. First it begins copying the selected source volume(s) into a RAM disk. A new virtual machine is created on the destination ESX server and the disk volume(s) are copied to the destination ESX server. Appropriate drivers are installed within the guest operating system so that the new virtual machine can be booted. Next, any customizations selected during the Import Wizard are performed, such as configuring the virtual machine name or networking modifications. Finally the Converter Enterprise boot CD is removed and the system can be powered off or restarted.

VMware includes the peTool with the Converter download image. This tool can be used to add both storage and network drivers to the Converter Enterprise boot CD. It can also be used for several other modifications such as disabling the WinPE firewall, adding software packages and specifying a temporary directory. Modifying the converter boot CD ISO image by adding a storage driver to it for example, can be accomplished by issuing the following command:

```
peTool -i <Converter_boot_cd.iso> -d <storage_driver_folder_path>
```

Several other options are possible when using the peTool command. To obtain a help menu for the peTool, issue the following command:

peTool -h

Virtual To Virtual (V2V) Cloning

The target machine does not have to be a physical machine. It is possible to hot or cold clone a virtual machine using VMware Enterprise Converter. Cloning virtual machines is useful for testing and development as well as disaster recovery purposes. V2V is also useful to import a virtual machine created in another virtualization product. Virtual machines created using any of the following products can be used during a V2V cloning operation:

- VMware Player
- VMware Workstation
- VMware ACE
- VMware Fusion
- VMware Server
- VMware GSX Server
- VMware ESX Server
- Virtual PC
- Microsoft Virtual Server

This can be a flexible solution when needing to take an existing virtual machine created in VMware Workstation on a laptop, and being able to import it into a VirtualCenter 2.5 managed host environment, for example. Using converter in this manner opens up numerous possibilities for using virtual machines on a variety of platforms.

Export Virtual Machines

A virtual machine hosted on an ESX 3.5 server does not have to permanently reside in that environment. V2V can be performed to export virtual machines from a VirtualCenter 2.5 managed host environment to another virtualization product. The following are supported hosted destinations that can be exported to:

- VMware Player
- VMware Workstation
- VMware ACE
- VMware Fusion
- VMware Server
- VMware GSX Server

The export functionality in combination with the import capability provides a means to seamlessly move virtual machines across platforms as needed. Support and quality assurance personnel can use the import / export features when working with customers and software developers. System administrators can implement "what if" scenarios with cloned production virtual machines running in VMware Workstation. This offloads the system resources from the ESX server so that production virtual machines can run unaffected.

VMware Consolidated Backup Restores

VMware Converter Enterprise can also be used to restore virtual machines that were backed up using VMware Consolidated Backup. When using Converter Enterprise to restore virtual machines, the virtual machines can be placed into a resource pool, host or datacenter objects within the VirtualCenter 2.5 inventory. With Converter Enterprise, most virtual machines are restored with the same hostname and virtual disk configurations. There are some guest operating systems where the backed up virtual machine can have its volumes resized and modifications made to its identity. This is possible if the guest operating system is one of the following:

- Windows XP Professional 32-bit
- Windows XP Professional 64-bit
- Windows 2003 32-bit
- Windows 2003 64-bit
- Windows 2000

A VMware Consolidated Backup job creates a catalog file for the virtual machine. The catalog file is an ASCII text file that contains specific information about the virtual machine. VMware Converter Enterprise does not read this file during restoration. It may be necessary to review the catalog file if placing the virtual machine in its original datastore and using its original hostname. The catalog file will provide such information if needed. Converter Enterprise will not restore any virtual machine log files or the virtual machine BIOS (.nvram) file. If these files are needed, they will need to be manually copied to the virtual machine restored location.

Some virtual hardware settings are not preserved when restoring a virtual machine using Converter Enterprise. The defaults settings for serial and parallel ports are used. Floppy and CD/ROM drive defaults are used. Network settings are not preserved either. The MAC address used is generated from the destination ESX server. The destination host also generates a new value for both the uuid.location and uuid.bios values for the virtual machine.

VMware Converter Enterprise can also import the following third party images of Windows operating systems:

- Norton Ghost - Must be version 9 and higher
- Symantec Backup Exec System Recovery
- Acronis True Image
- StorageCraft ShadowProtect

Reconfiguration of Systems

Another useful feature of Converter Enterprise is the ability to reconfigure an existing virtual machine. By right clicking on a virtual machine and selecting Reconfigure from the pop up menu, a Windows based virtual machine can have its network information, Security Identifier (SID),time zone and license information reconfigured using the built in integration with Microsoft Sysprep.

Converter Enterprise Components

VMware Converter Enterprise consists of the following three components:

- Converter Enterprise Server - This server provides the ability to perform P2V, V2V and both importing and exporting of virtual machines.
- Converter Enterprise Agent - The agent is responsible for preparing the target machine for conversion.
- Converter Enterprise CLI - Connects to a Converter Enterprise Server using a command line interface. Provides a facility in which to automate conversions by scripting of conversion tasks.

VMware Converter Enterprise is installed by default with the installation of VirtualCenter 2.5. The default installation may be satisfactory if an occasional conversion is performed. The default installation of Enterprise Converter was shown in chapter 6 - VirtualCenter 2.5. The decision to perform a default installation really depends upon the workload placed upon the VirtualCenter 2.5 server. In cases where the VirtualCenter 2.5 server is heavily used or a large number of conversions are scheduled to be performed, the default installation may not be appropriate.

The Converter Enterprise installation can be performed on a separate, standalone server. This can be accomplished by launching the VirtualCenter 2.5 installer and selecting the Custom option. This option provides the ability to just install the VMware Converter Enterprise for VirtualCenter server software. The installation requires the specification of a VirtualCenter 2.5 server and login credentials to access this server.

Converter Enterprise Plugin Installation

The functionality of VMware Converter Enterprise is not enabled by default. It is first necessary to install the Converter Enterprise plugin. The installation of the Converter Enterprise plugin is done by doing the following:

Step 1. VirtualCenter Plugins Menu

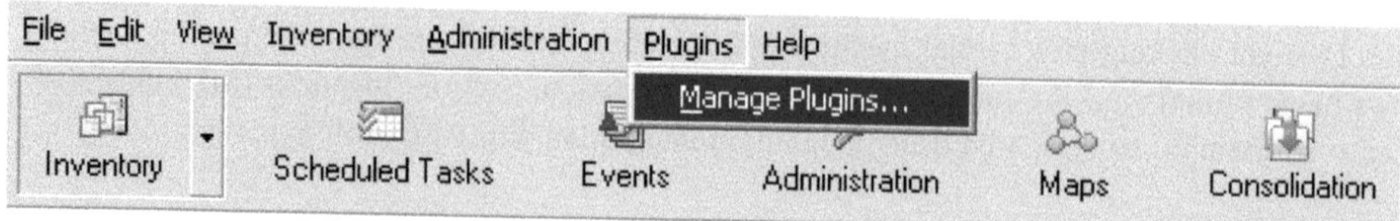

Figure 8.1 VirtualCenter Plugins Menu

Select the Manage Plugins command from the Plugins pull down menu as shown in Figure 8.1. This will launch the Plugin manager screen. If you use the VI Client from any machine other than the VirtualCenter 2.5 server, the plug-ins need to be installed so that the additional features are available within the VI Client. In other words, once the plugin is downloaded from the VirtualCenter 2.5 server and enabled, additional menu options are available when right clicking on inventory objects such as the Reconfigure menu option and new buttons appear on the top menu bar.

Step 2. The Plugin Manager screen.

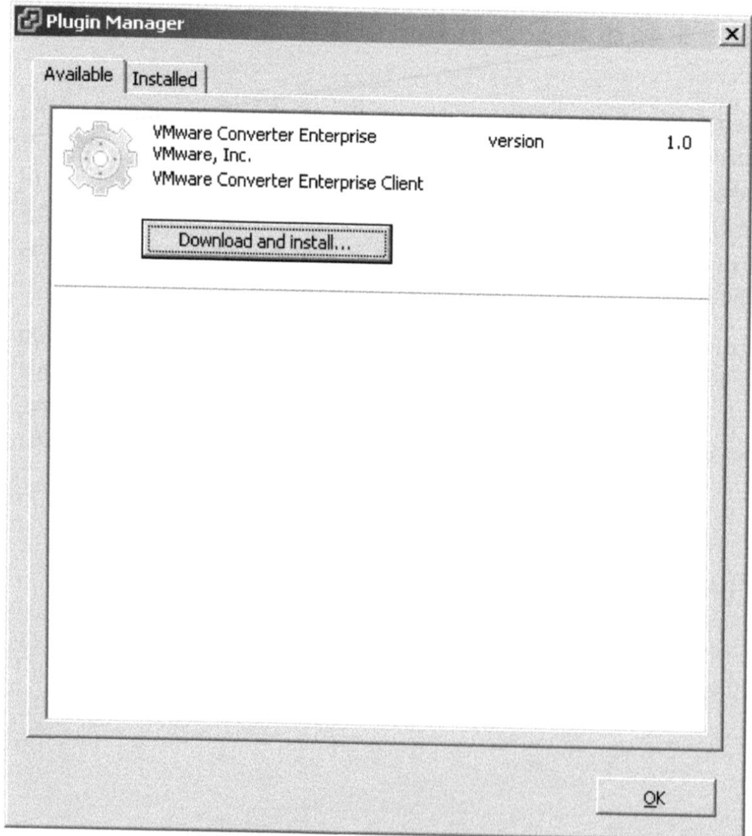

Figure 8.2 VirtualCenter Plugin Manager

The Available tab in the Plugin Manager screen shown in Figure 8.2 will list the available plug-ins for this VirtualCenter 2.5 server. Click on the Download and Install button to get the plugin from the

VirtualCenter 2.5 server logged into by the VI Client.

Step 3. The Plugin Manager screen.

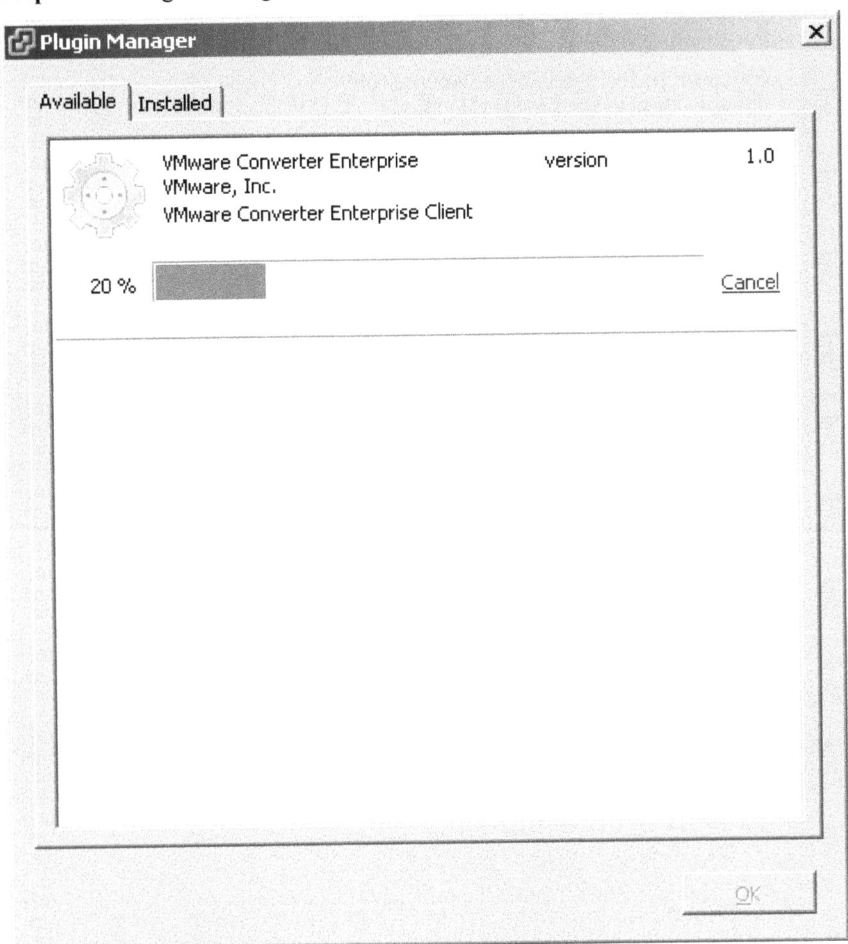

Figure 8.3 Downloading Converter Enterprise Client

Figure 8.3 illustrates that you will see the progress of the download in this screen.

Step 4. The Installation wizard screen.

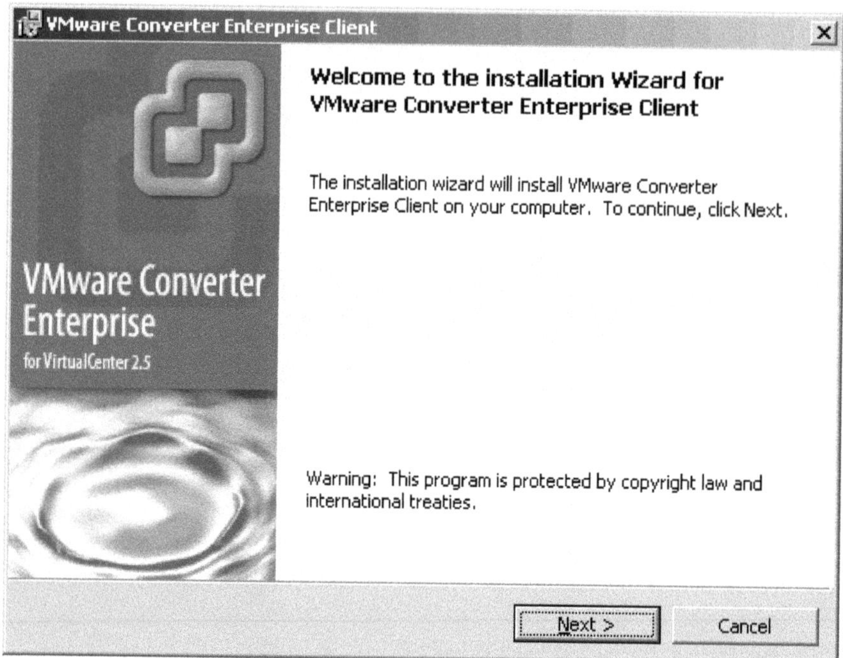

Figure 8.4 Converter Enterprise Client Installation

Once the download of the software is completed the Install wizard for the product will launch as shown in Figure 8.4. Click on the Next button to continue.

Step 5. Ready to Install the Program screen.

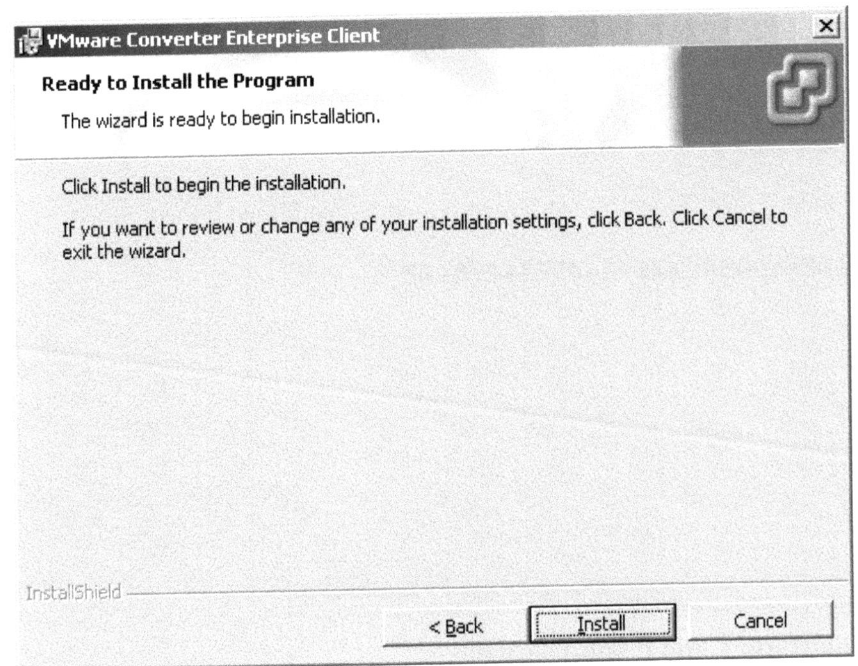

Figure 8.5 Converter Enterprise Client Ready To Install

Figure 8.5 shows that the wizard has initialized and is ready to start the installation process. Click on the Install button to continue.

Step 6. Installing VMware Converter Enterprise Client screen.

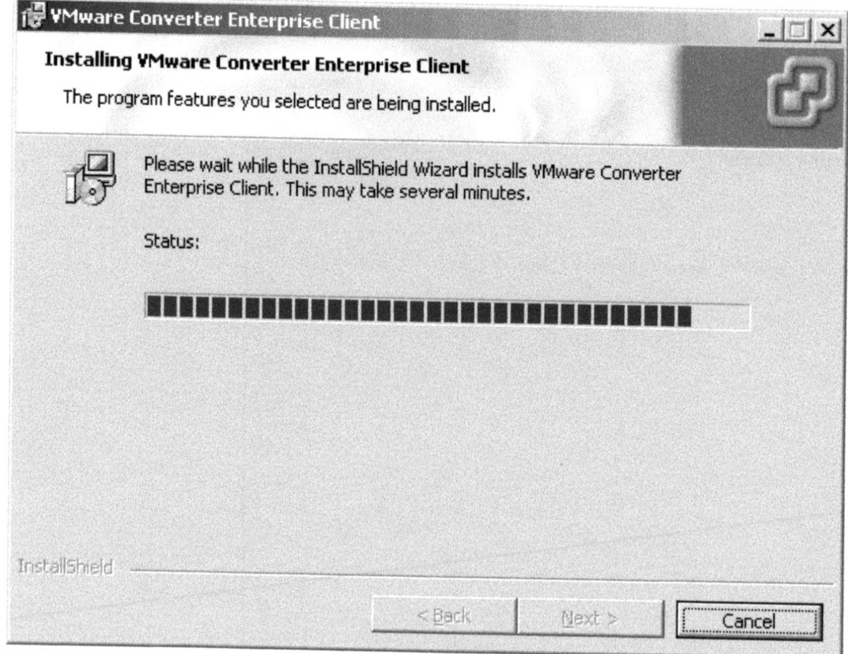

Figure 8.6 Converter Enterprise Client Installation Status

Figure 8.6 shows you the installation progress.

Step 7. Installation Completed screen.

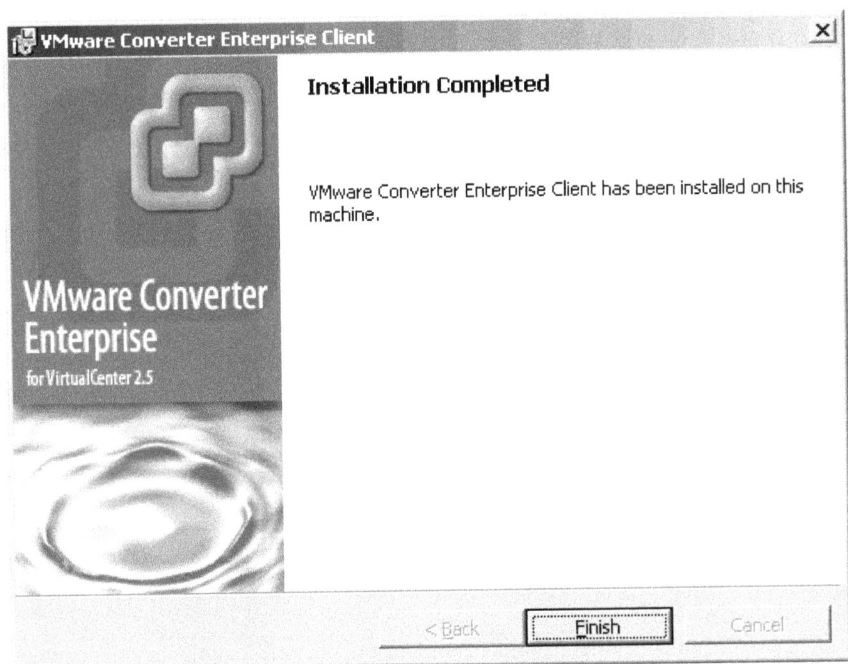

Figure 8.7 Converter Enterprise Client Installation Finished

Once the installation is completed, click on the Finish button as shown in Figure 8.7 to close the installation wizard.

The Plugin Manager still needs to configure the plugin as shown in Figure 8.8. This may take a few minutes.

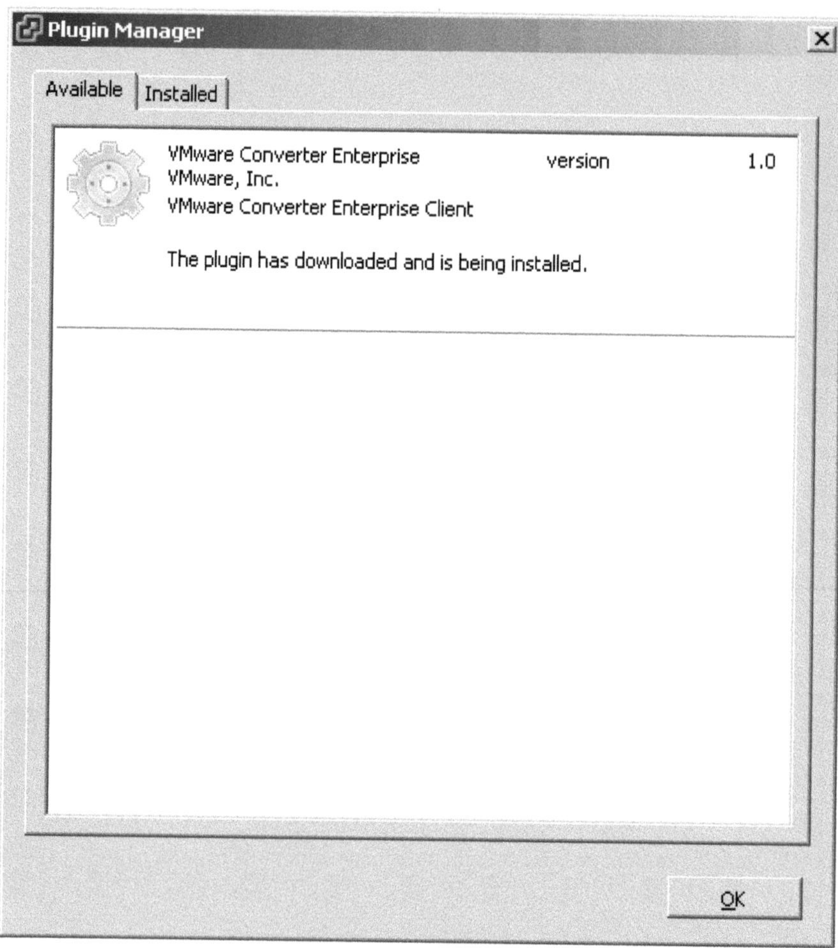

Figure 8.8 Converter Enterprise Client Plugin Installation

The Plugin Manager window shown in Figure 8.9 now confirms that the Plugin Manager has completed the VMware Converter Enterprise Client software installation and it is now available.

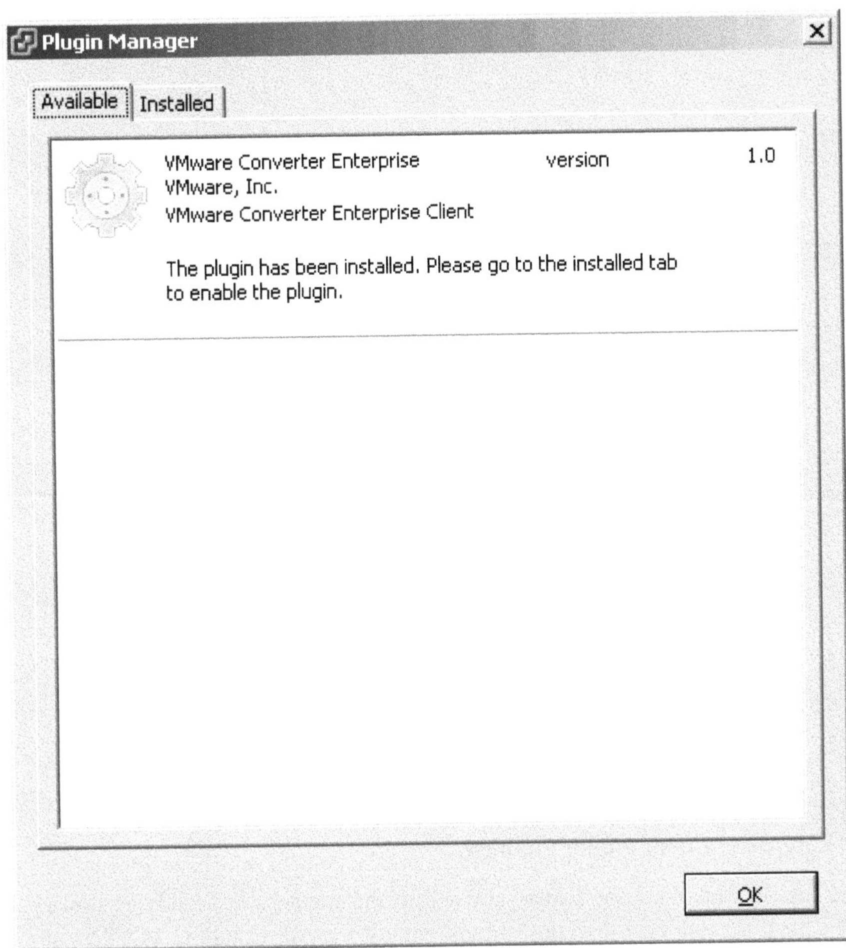

Figure 8.9 Converter Enterprise Client Plugin Installed

To use the new Converter Enterprise plugin, it must first be enabled as shown in Figure 8.10. Select the Installed tab and select the check box next to the Enabled option to enable the plugin. Select the Ok button to complete the plugin installation process.

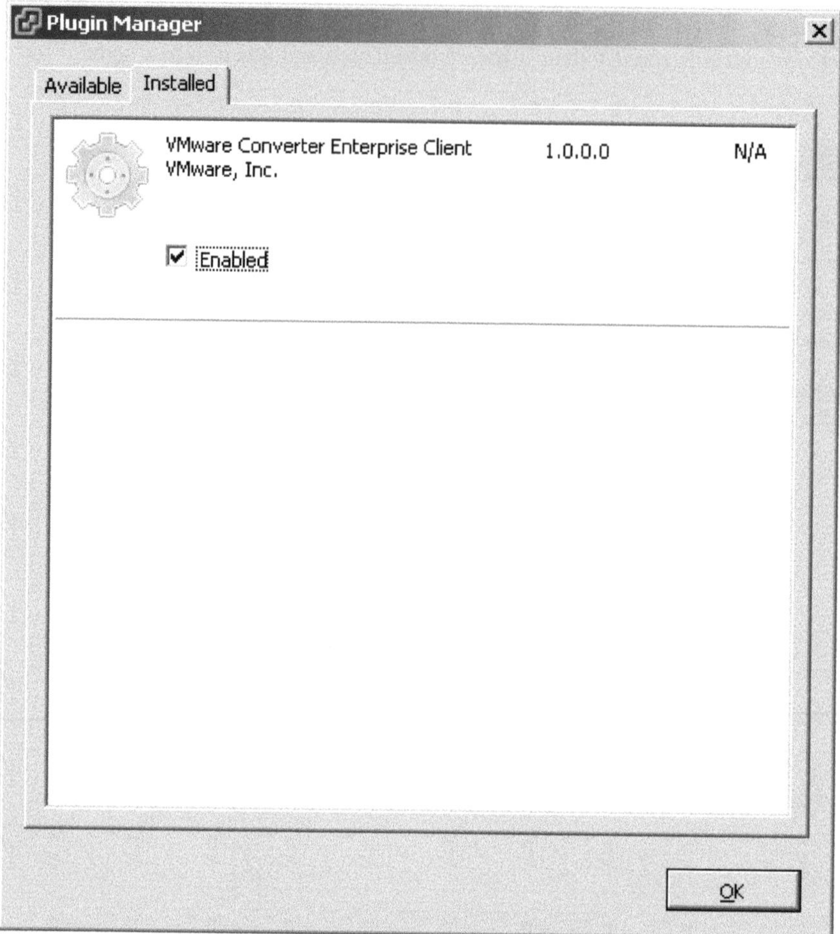

Figure 8.10 Converter Enterprise Client Plugin Enabled

Note, that sometimes the Installed tab does not display any text. If this happens, it usually is resolved by logging out of the VI Client, logging back into the VirtualCenter 2.5 server using the VI Client and using the Plugin Manager once more to enable the plugin.

Hot Clone Import of a Physical Machine

A hot clone import of a physical machine running the supported Windows operating systems is performed using the following steps:

Step 1. Launch the wizard.

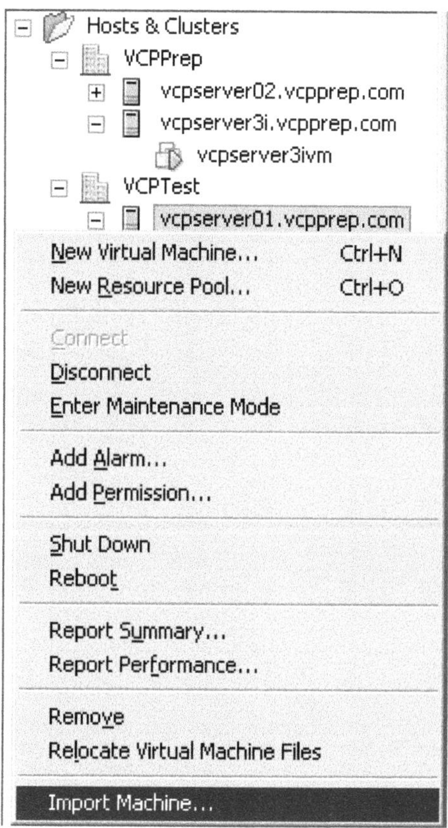

Figure 8.11 Converter Enterprise Import Machine Menu Option

You must right mouse button click on the ESX server that you want to use to operate the new VM that will be built by this process. Select the Import Machine command from the pop-up menu as shown in Figure 8.11. You could also have selected a cluster or resource pool inventory object to build the new VM in.

Step 2. Source screen.

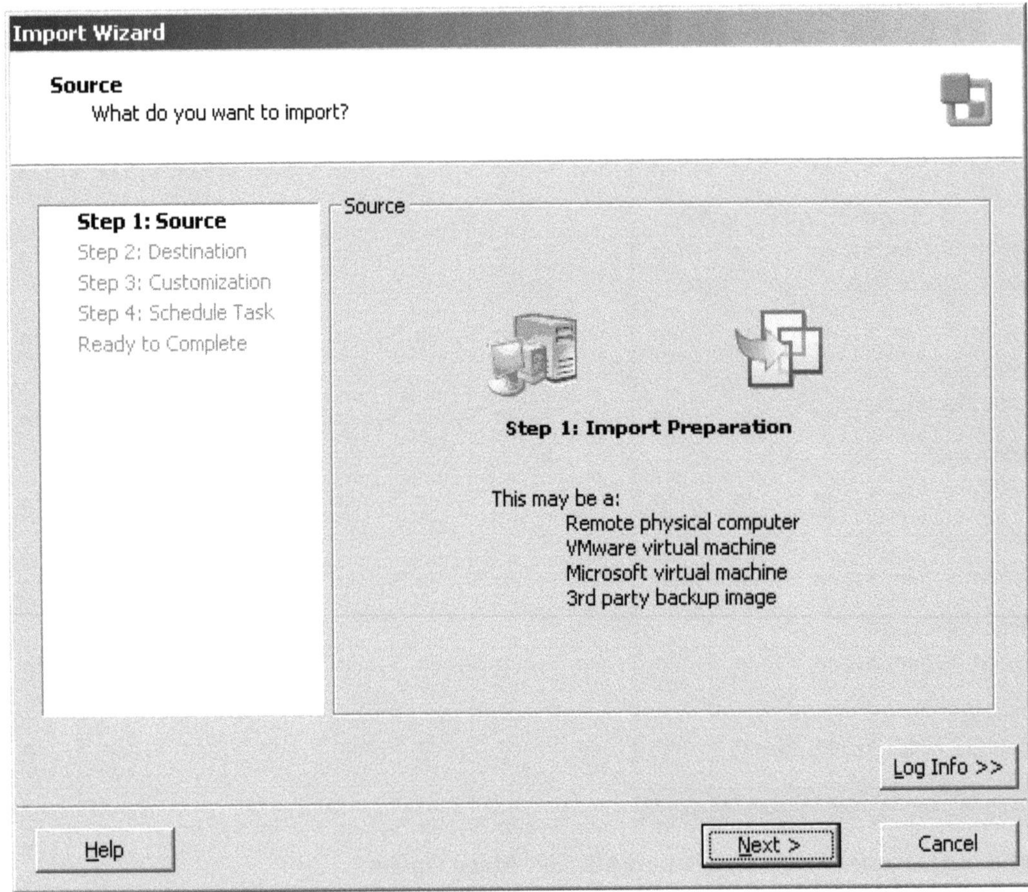

Figure 8.12 Converter Enterprise Import Wizard Select Source

Figure 8.12 shows the first screen will list the steps that will be taken by the wizard to complete the process.

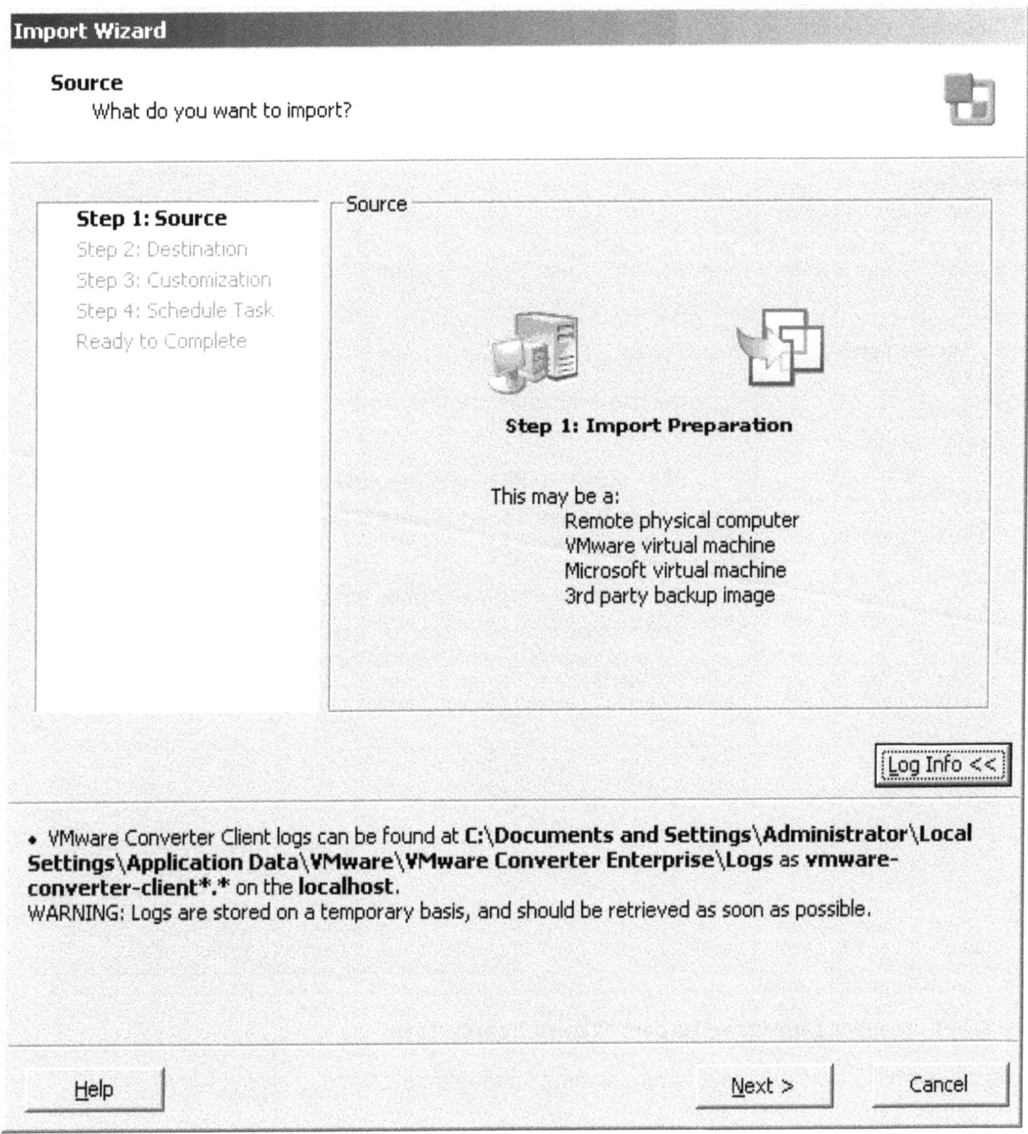

Figure 8.13 Converter Enterprise Import Wizard Log Information

By clicking on the Log button as shown in Figure 8.13 you can display information about the log files that get generated by the process. If something goes wrong with the hot cloning process you should review the log file for more details. Click on the Next button to continue.

Step 3. Source Type screen.

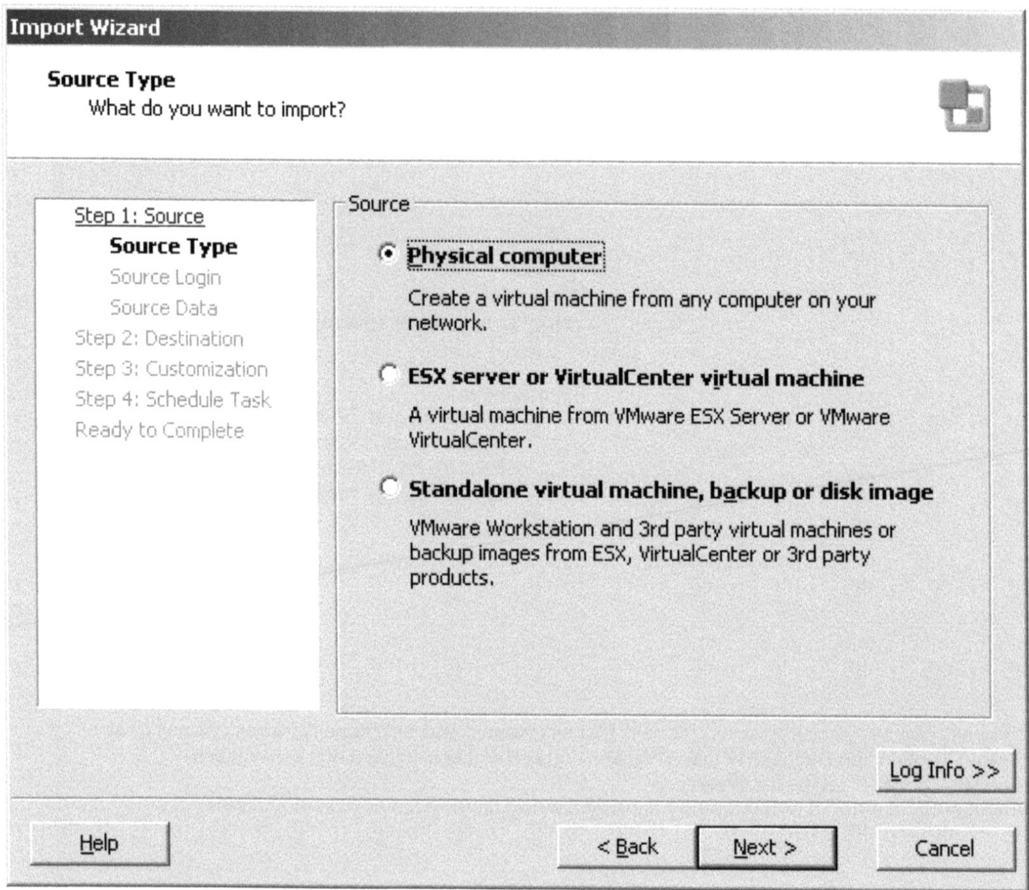

Figure 8.14 Converter Enterprise Import Wizard Source Type

You can choose from the following sources as shown in Figure 8.14:

- Physical Computer - be aware that you can only convert Windows based physical servers with this product.
- ESX server or Virtual Center virtual machines - existing VMs located on these resources.
- Standalone virtual machine, backup or disk image. Refer to the Virtual To Virtual (V2V) Cloning section earlier in this chapter for the supported virtual machines created in another virtualization product. Refer to the VMware Consolidated Backup Restores section earlier in this chapter for the supported backups that can be converted to a virtual machine. Refer to the VMware Consolidated Backup Restores section earlier in this chapter for the supported disk images that can be used as the basis for a new VM.

Step 4. Source Login screen

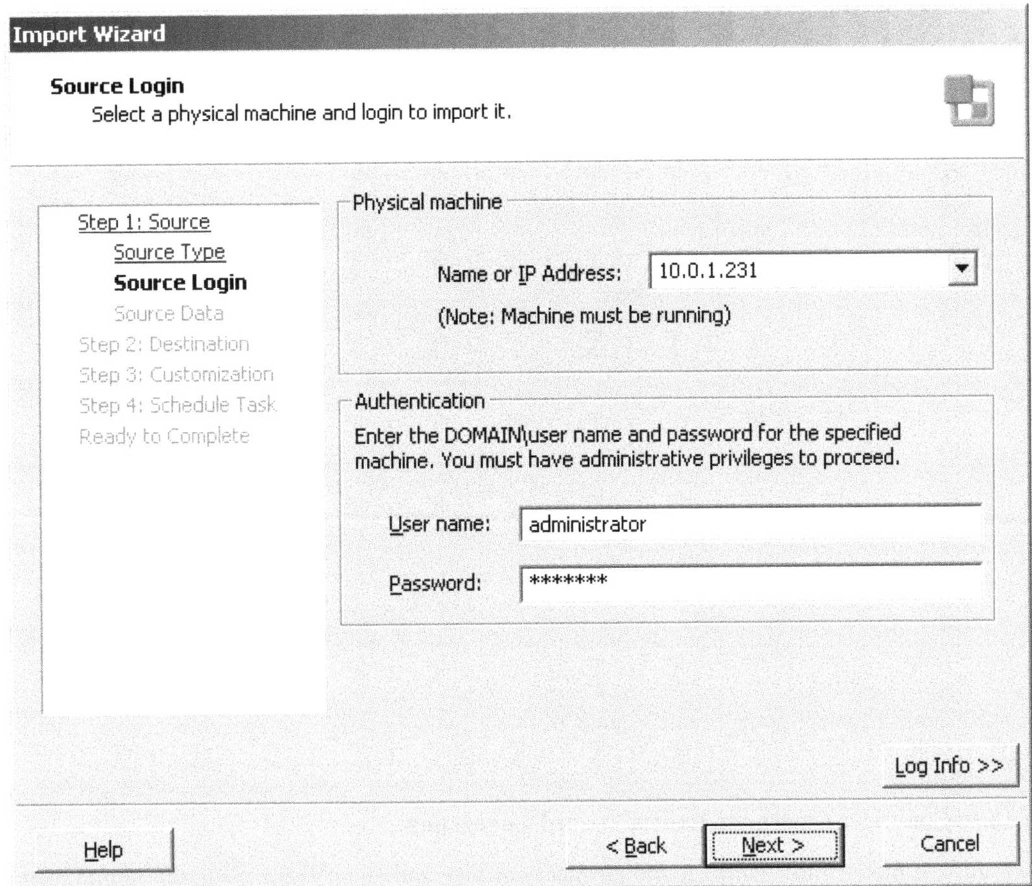

Figure 8.15 Converter Enterprise Import Wizard Source Login

In Figure 8.15 you must provide in the Source Login screen the IP address or a resolvable hostname as well as an administrator account name and password on the physical machine that you want to hot clone. Click on the Next button to continue.

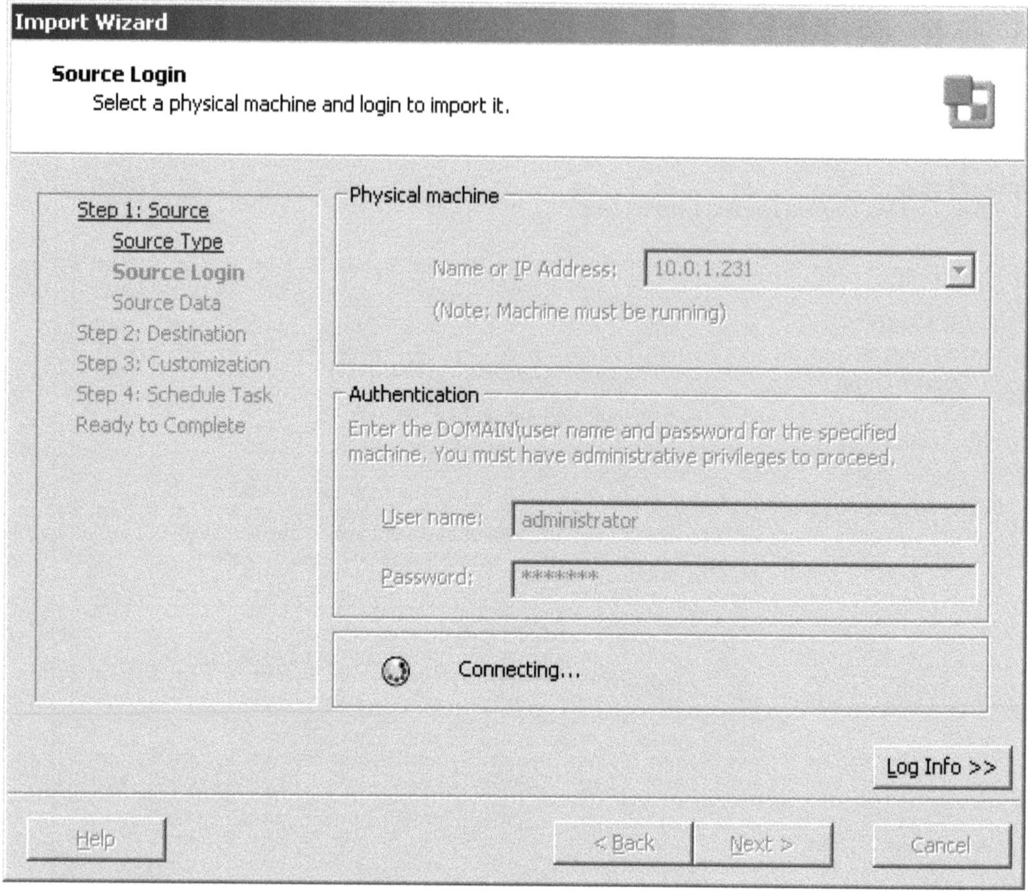

Figure 8.16 Converter Enterprise Import Wizard Connecting

The wizard will then try to connect to the physical machine and authenticate using the information you provided as shown in Figure 8.16.

Step 5. Warning: Remote Installation Required screen.

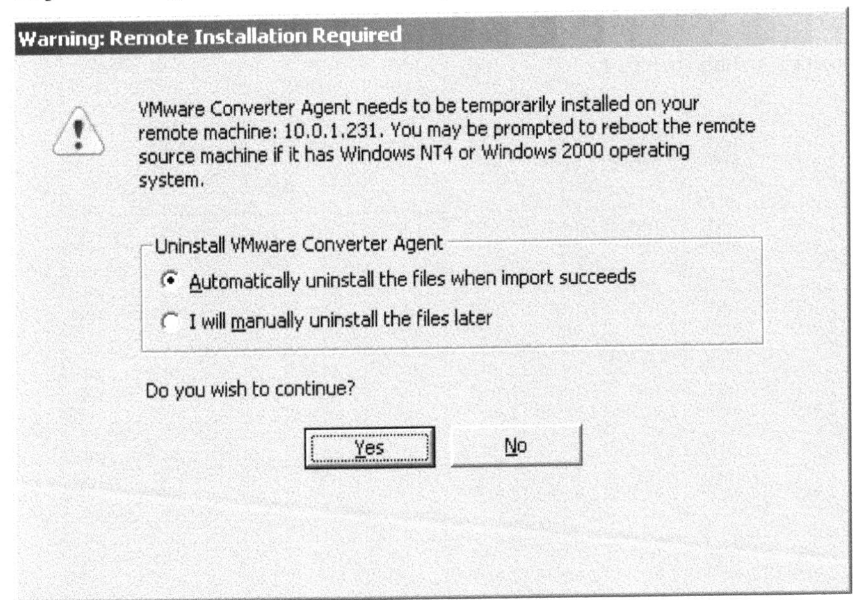

Figure 8.17 Converter Enterprise Import Wizard Agent Installation Warning

Figure 8.17 illustrates how the wizard will now prompt you to install the VMware Converter Agent on the machine. The radio buttons offer you the choice of automatically or manually removing the VMware Converter Agent after the process has completed. Click on the Yes button to continue.

You will now see that the agent is being installed. This may take some time.

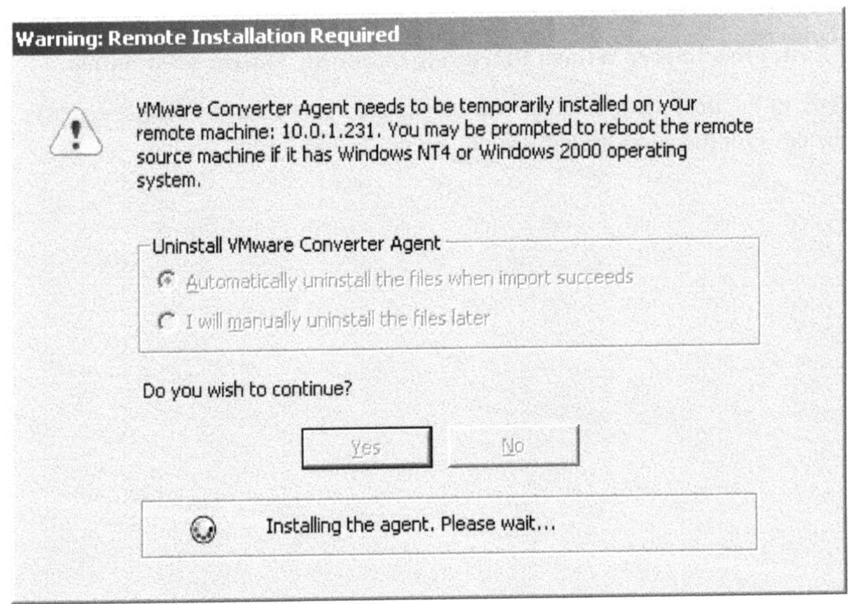

Figure 8.18 Converter Enterprise Import Wizard Agent Installation

The wizard will now retrieve information about the operating system as shown in Figure 8.18.

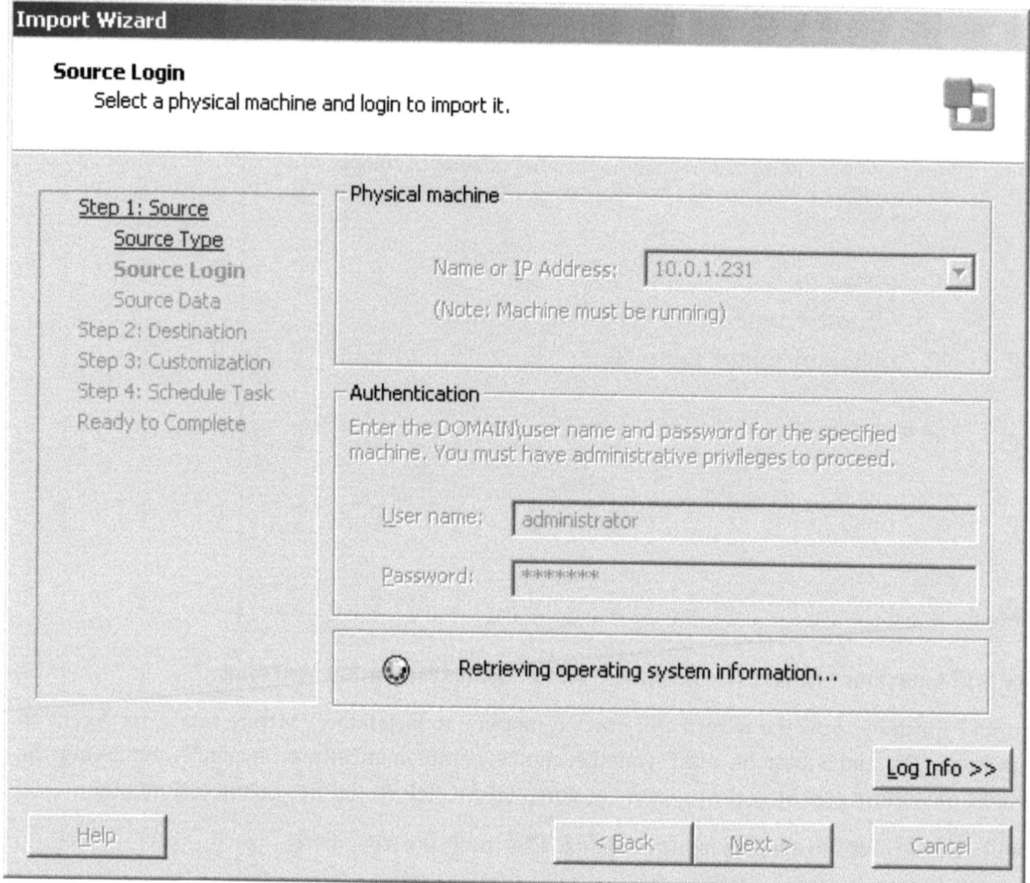

Figure 8.19 Converter Enterprise Import Wizard Retrieving Operating System Information

Figure 8.19 shows the size of the disk partitions that will be gathered as well as the Windows drive letters that are used as the basis for the new virtual disks.

Step 6. Source Data screen.

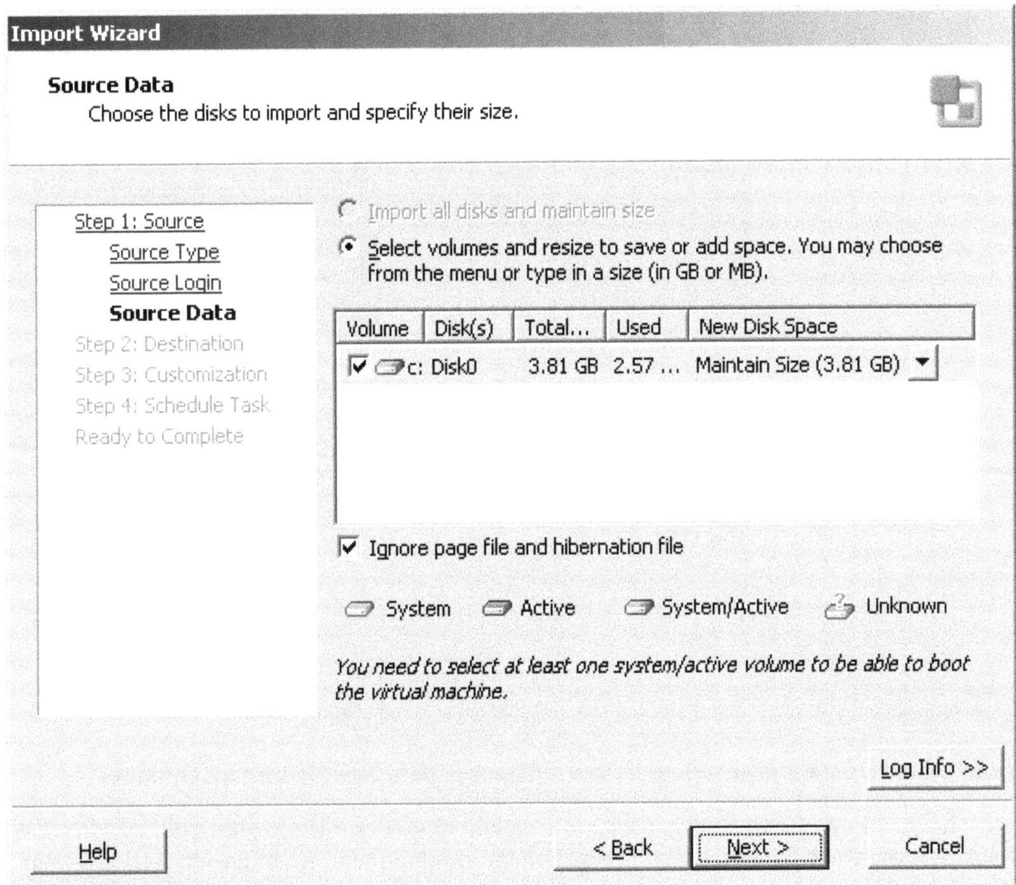

Figure 8.20 Converter Enterprise Import Wizard Source Data

In Figure 8.20 you can select the physical disks that you want to be converted to be the virtual disks for your VM. If the physical system has more than one physical disk you can select these individually as needed. Notice the check box to ignore the page file and hibernation file. This option is selected by default as both the page and hibernation files do not contain data that is typically needed when being cloned.

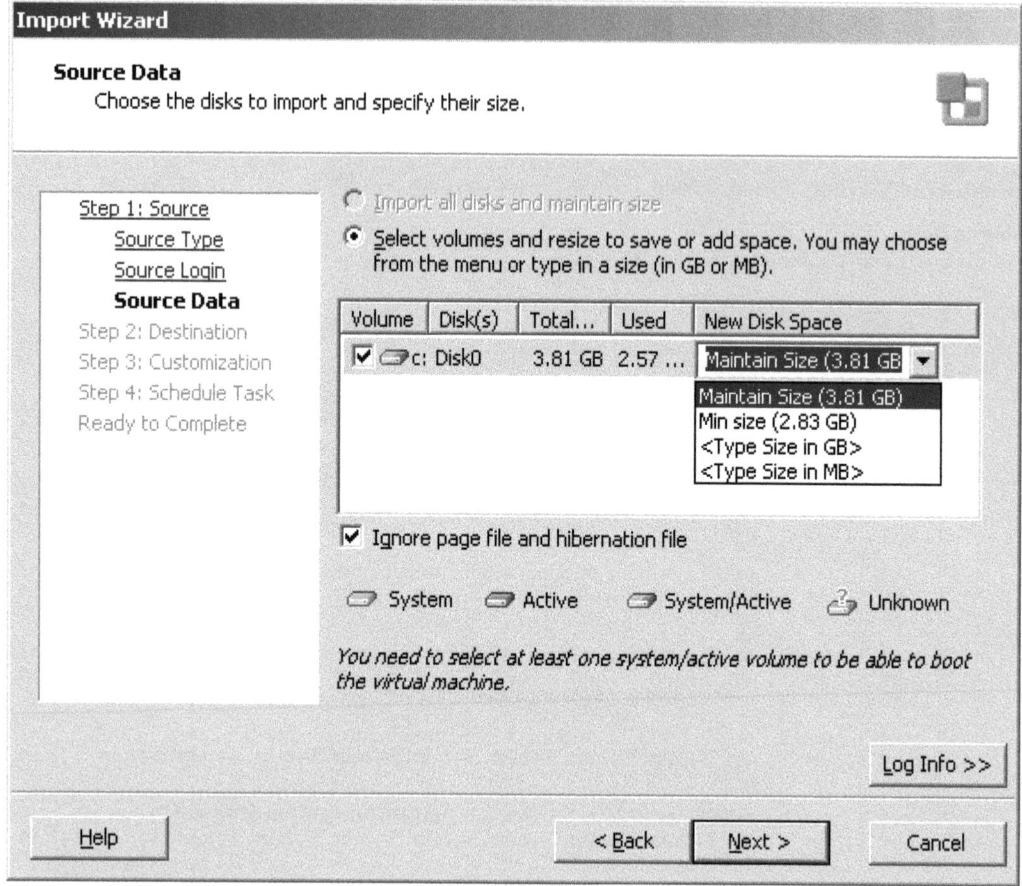

Figure 8.21 Converter Enterprise Import Wizard Source Data New Disk Space Options

In Figure 8.21 you can chose to resize the size of the virtual disk. The wizard will calculate the smallest size it can make the disk which is based on the existing file usage of the physical disk. You can also manually set the size using the drop-down menu options. Once you have sized the disks, select the Next button to continue.

Step 7. Destination screen.

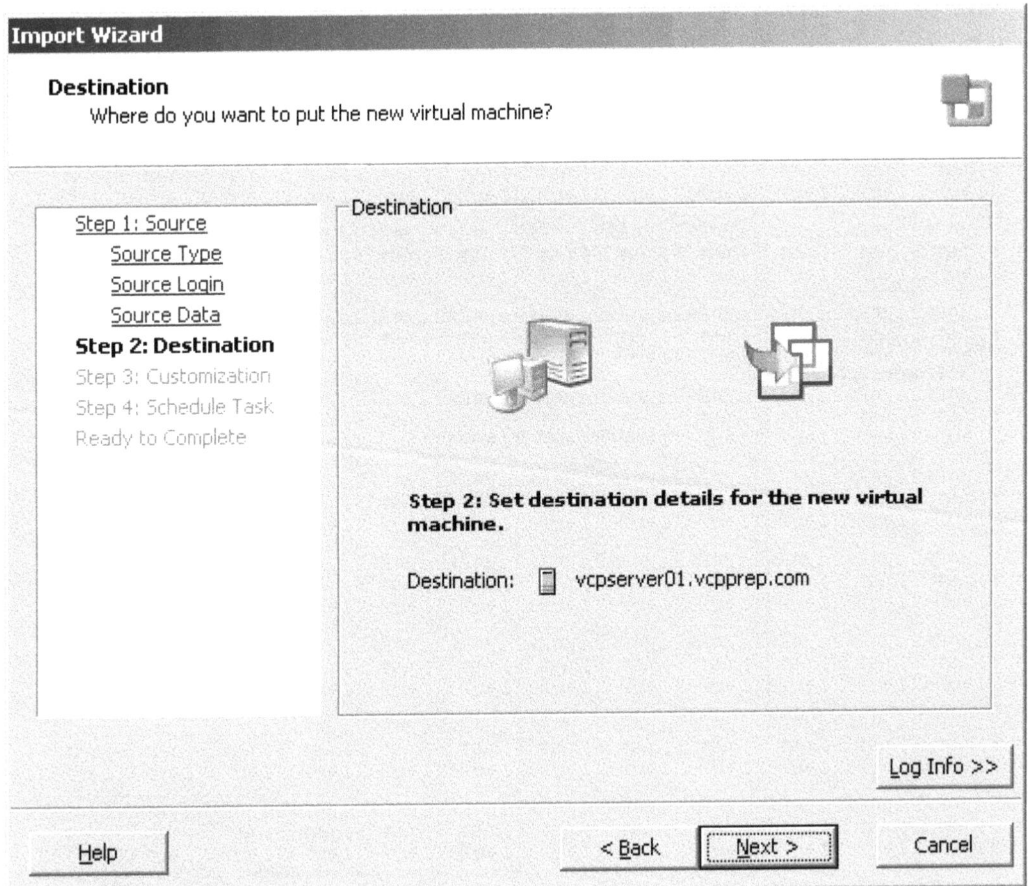

Figure 8.22 Install Converter Enterprise Import Wizard Destination

The next phase of the wizard process requires that you select a destination for your VM's state files as shown in Figure 8.22. In Figure 8.11 we had selected the vcpserver01.vcpprep.com ESX 3.5 server and the screen shows the server hostname. Click on the Next button to start this process.

Step 8. Virtual Machine Name and Folder screen.

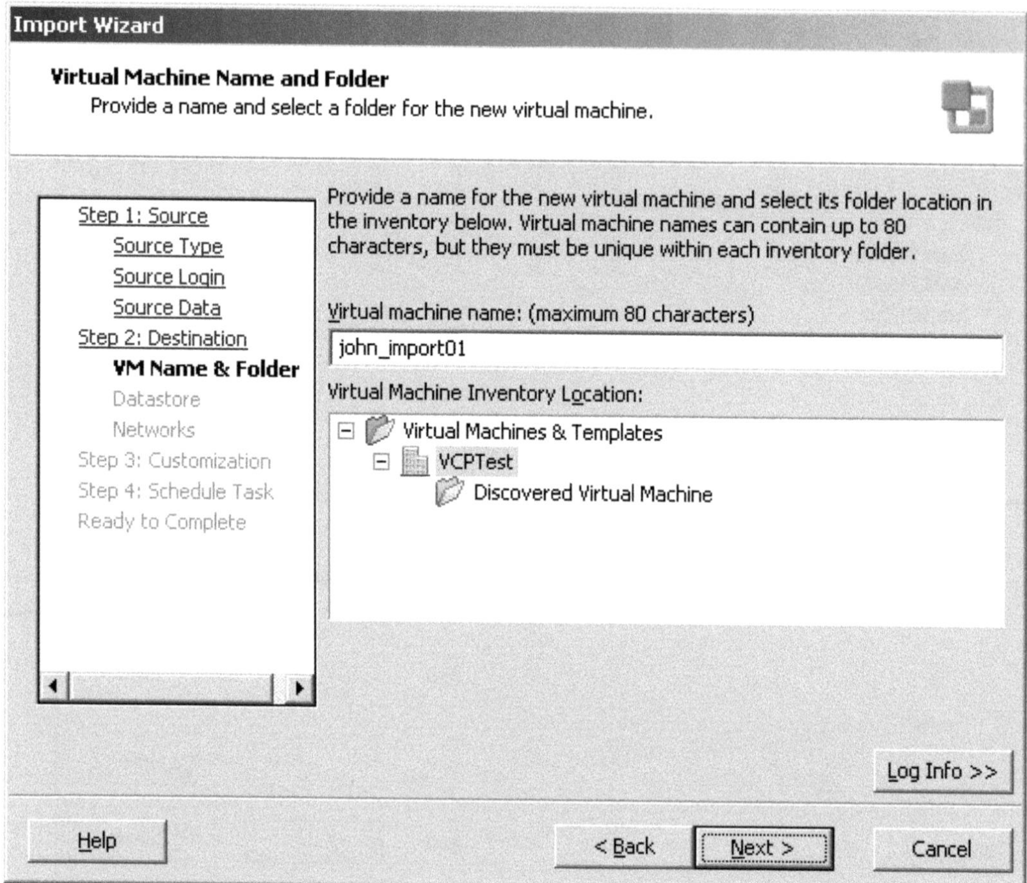

Figure 8.23 Converter Enterprise Import Wizard Virtual Machine Name And Folder

In Figure 8.23 you will provide the VM name and location of where you want the new VM to appear in the VirtualCenter 2.5 inventory. Placement of the VM in the inventory affects who can access it based on the permissions that get applied to the VM. We will discuss this in more detail in Chapter 10 - Permissions and Rights. Resource requirements of the newly converted virtual machine should also be considered when choosing an ESX server destination host. Once you have made your selection, click on the Next button to continue.

Step 9. Datastore screen.

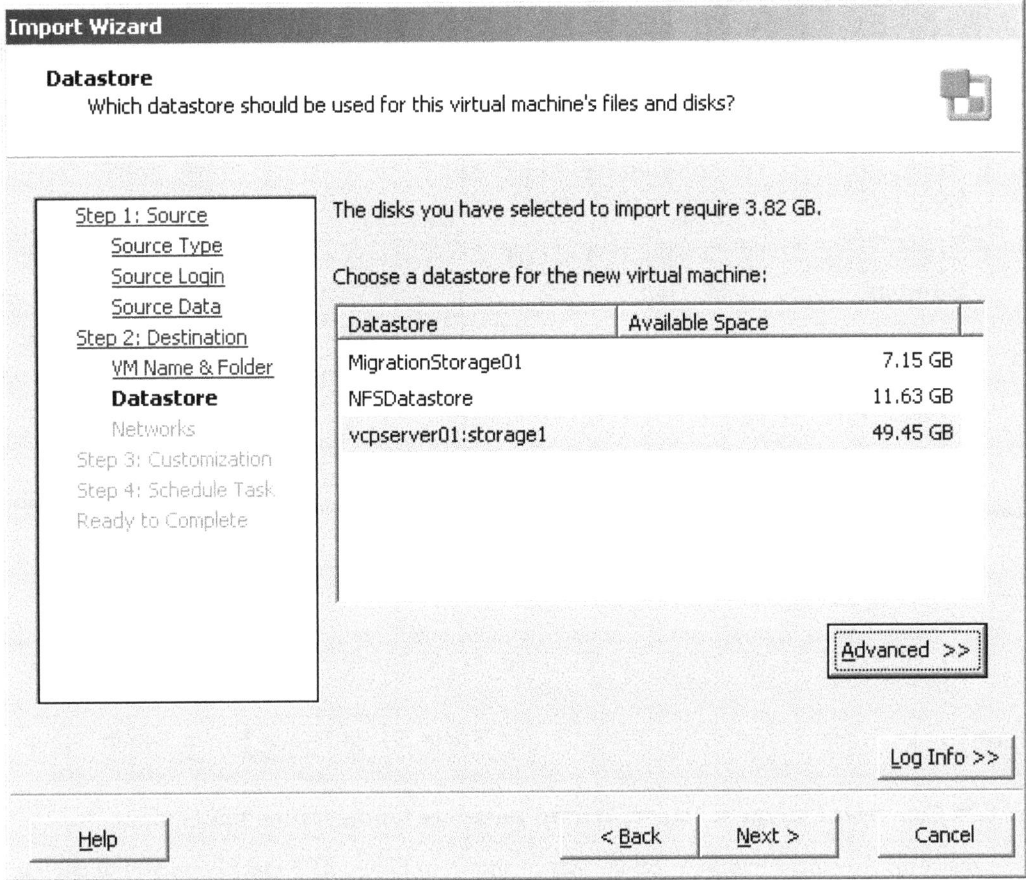

Figure 8.24 Converter Enterprise Import Wizard Datastore

In Figure 8.24 you will choose the datastore that you want to store the VM's state files on.

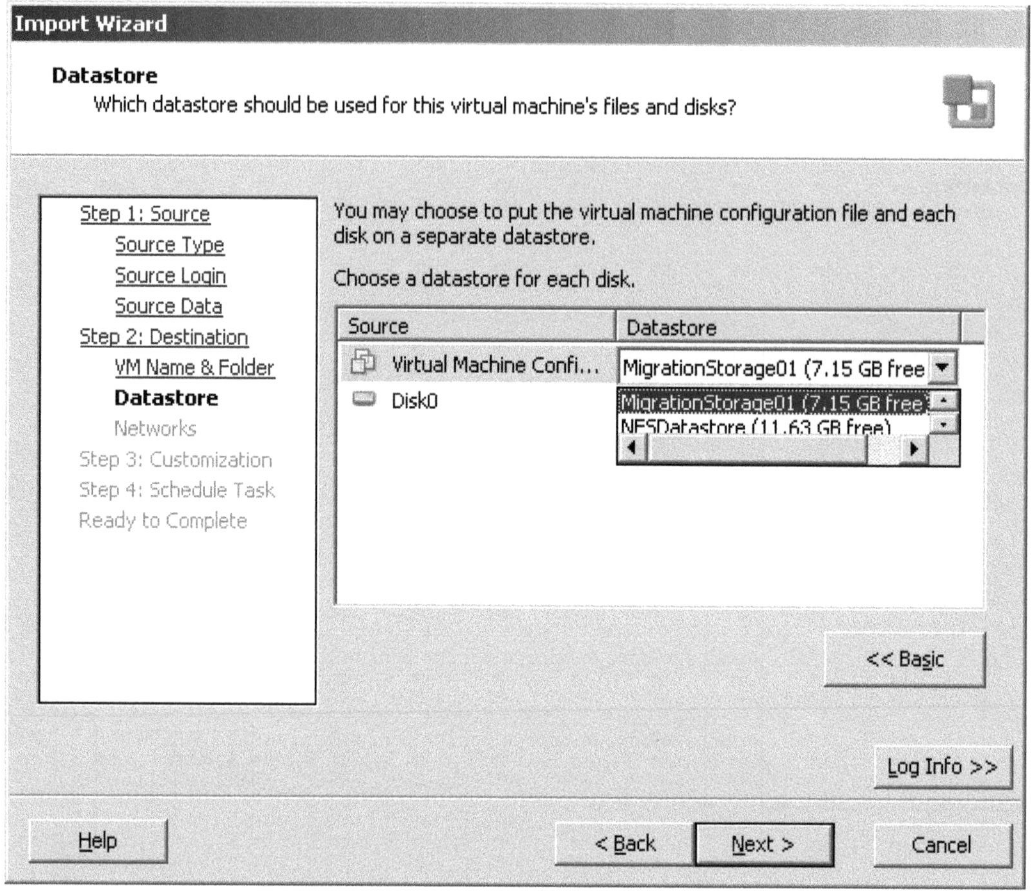

Figure 8.25 Converter Enterprise Import Wizard Datastore Configuration File Options

You can select the Advanced button to get the screen shown in Figure 8.25 that allows you to choose a separate location for the VM's virtual disk and configuration files.

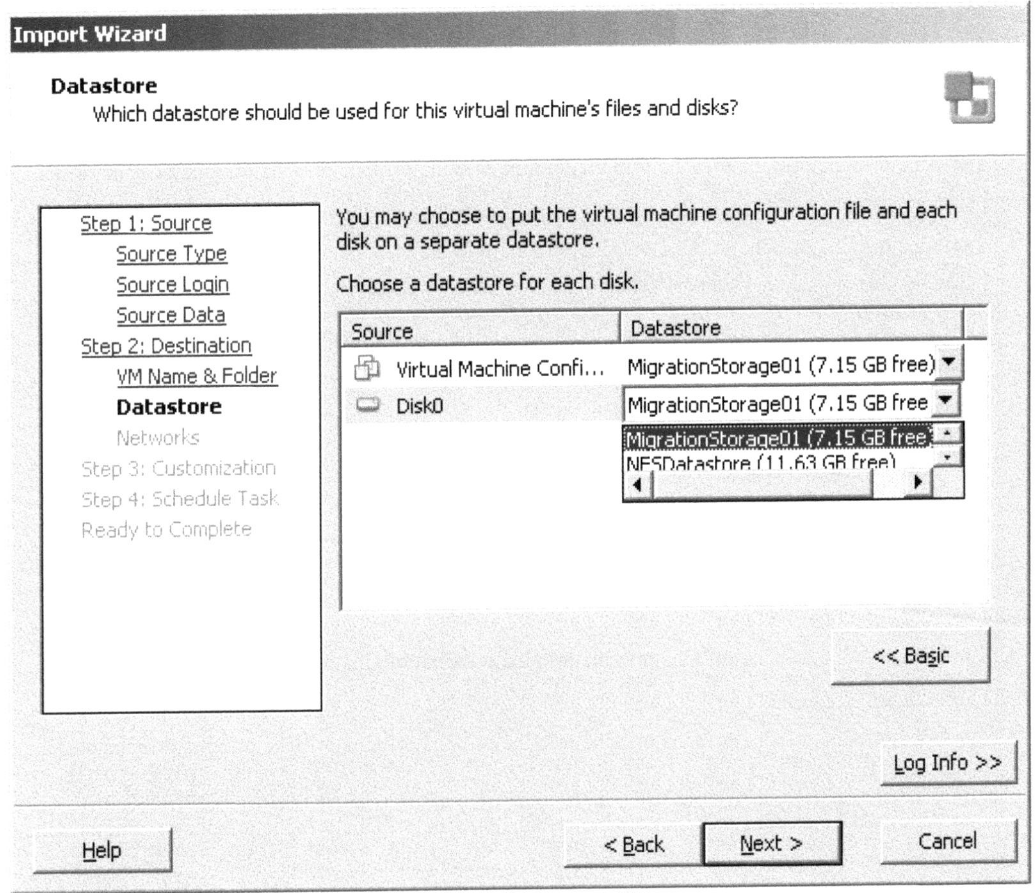

Figure 8.26 Converter Enterprise Import Wizard Datastore Hard Disk File Options

Figure 8.26 shows setting the virtual disk to a different datastore.

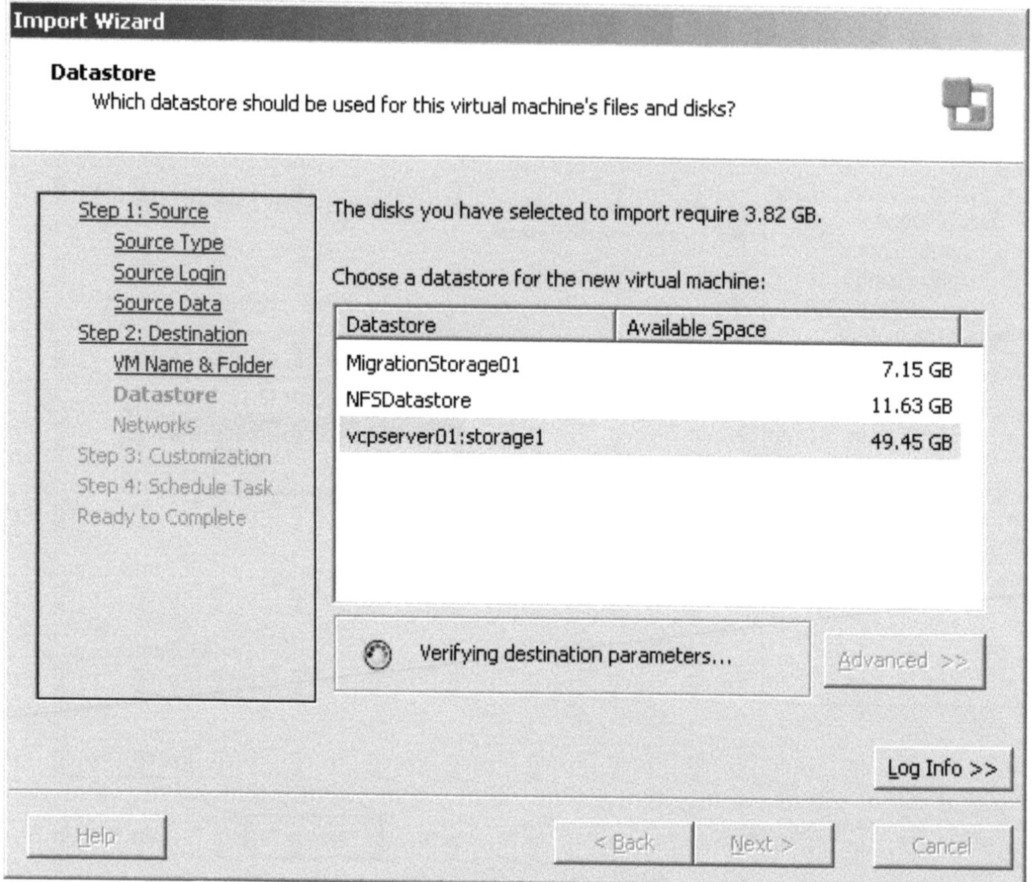

Figure 8.27 Converter Enterprise Import Wizard Verify Destination Parameters

Once you have made your selection, the wizard checks the datastore configuration to make sure that there is enough space for the new files as shown on Figure 8.27. Click on the Next button to continue.

Step 10. Networks screen.

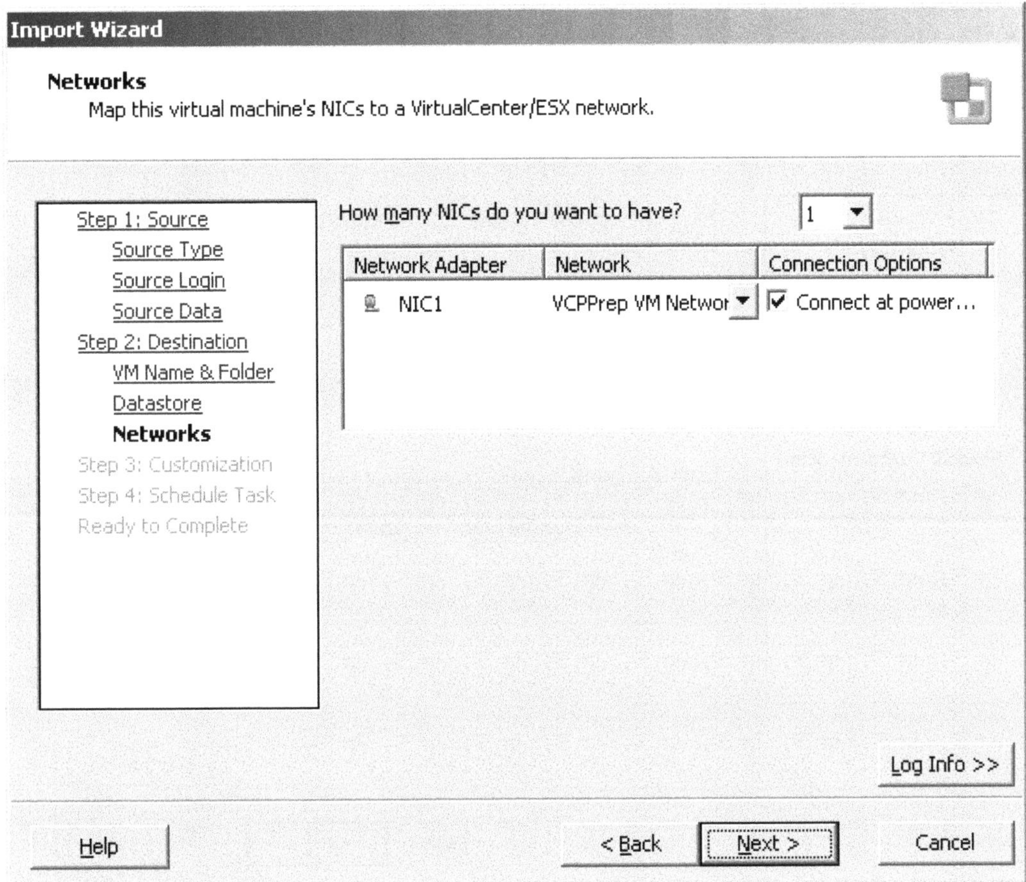

Figure 8.28 Converter Enterprise Import Wizard Networks

You will then be prompted to configure the number of virtual NICs to be used by the new VM. Figure 8.28 illustrates the options in this step. Take into consideration any VMotion, DRS and HA networking requirements when making your choices. We will cover these topics in later chapters. Click on the Next button to continue.

Step 11. Customization screen.

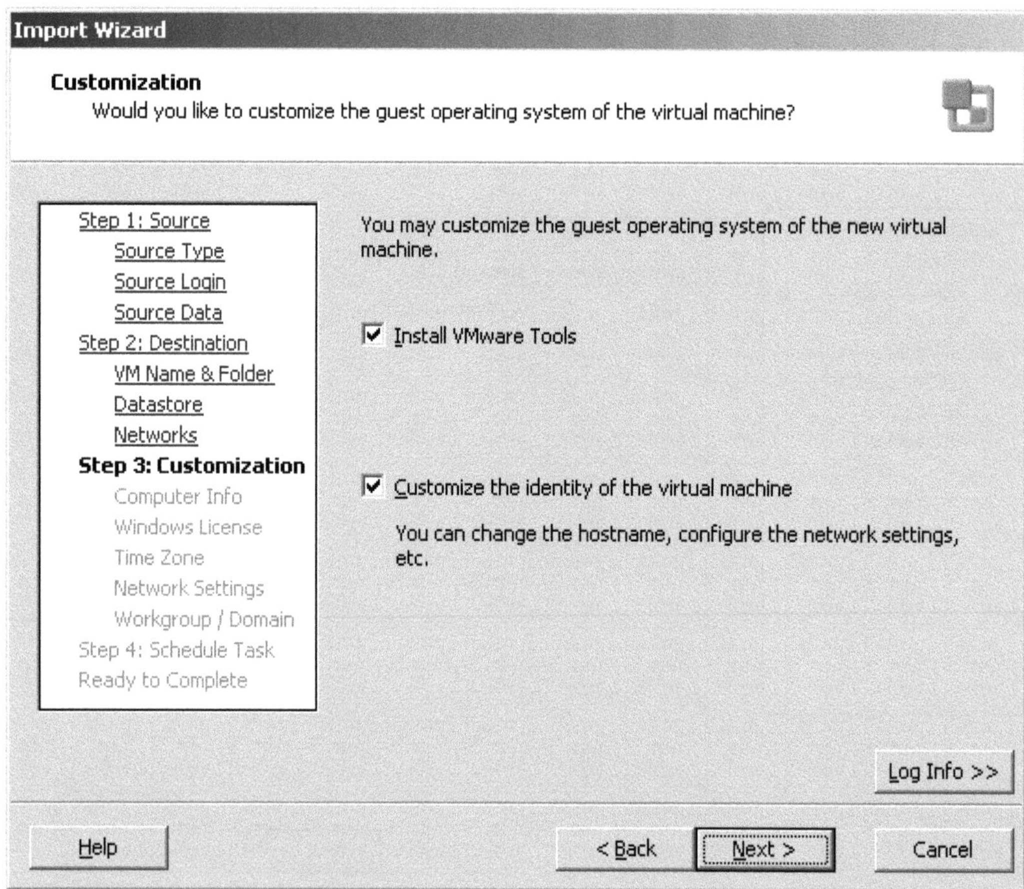

Figure 8.29 Converter Enterprise Import Wizard Customization

The next screen allows you to customize the guest OS. Since the only currently supported OS's for this process are Windows operating systems, you can install the VMware tools and prep the OS to have a unique identity as shown in Figure 8.29. Click on the Next button to continue.

Step 12. Computer Information screen.

Import Wizard

Computer Information

Specify computer information for identifying this virtual machine on a network.

Step 1: Source
Source Type
Source Login
Source Data
Step 2: Destination
VM Name & Folder
Datastore
Networks
Step 3: Customization
Computer Info
Windows License
Time Zone
Network Settings
Workgroup / Domain
Step 4: Schedule Task
Ready to Complete

Computer Name: john_import01

Owner Name: John

Organization: VCPPrep.com

Generate New Security ID (SID)

☑ Select this item to generate a new security identity.

Log Info >>

Help < Back Next > Cancel

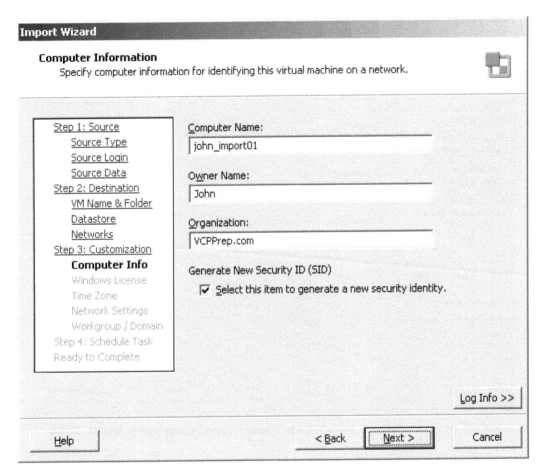

Figure 8.30 Converter Enterprise Import Wizard Customization Computer Information

Figure 8.30 shows the Computer Information screen which allows you to input the Computer Name, Owner and Organization information for the new VM. The check box allows the process to build a new SID for the VM as well. After you have put in the needed information, click on the Next button to continue.

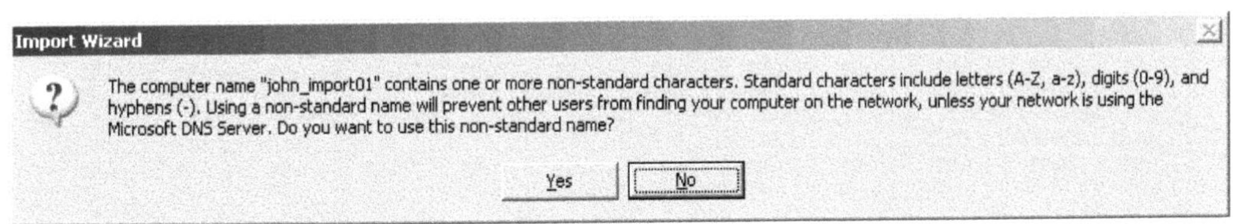

Figure 8.31 Converter Enterprise Import Wizard Customization Computer Name Warning

Figure 8.31 shows a warning if you use non-standard characters in the VM's name. Click on the No button to go back to the previous screen to make a change.

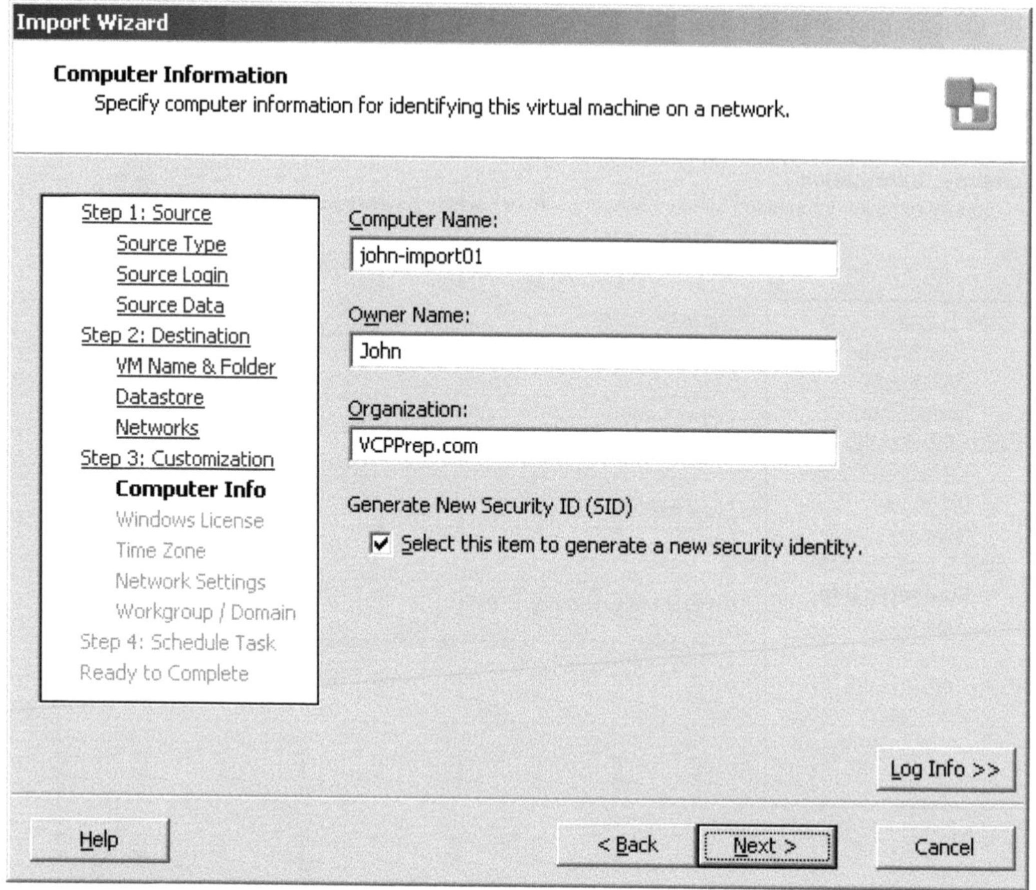

Figure 8.32 Converter Enterprise Import Wizard Customization Computer Name Modified

Figure 8.32 shows that we changed the underscore character to a hyphen. Click on the Next button to continue.

Step 13. Windows License screen.

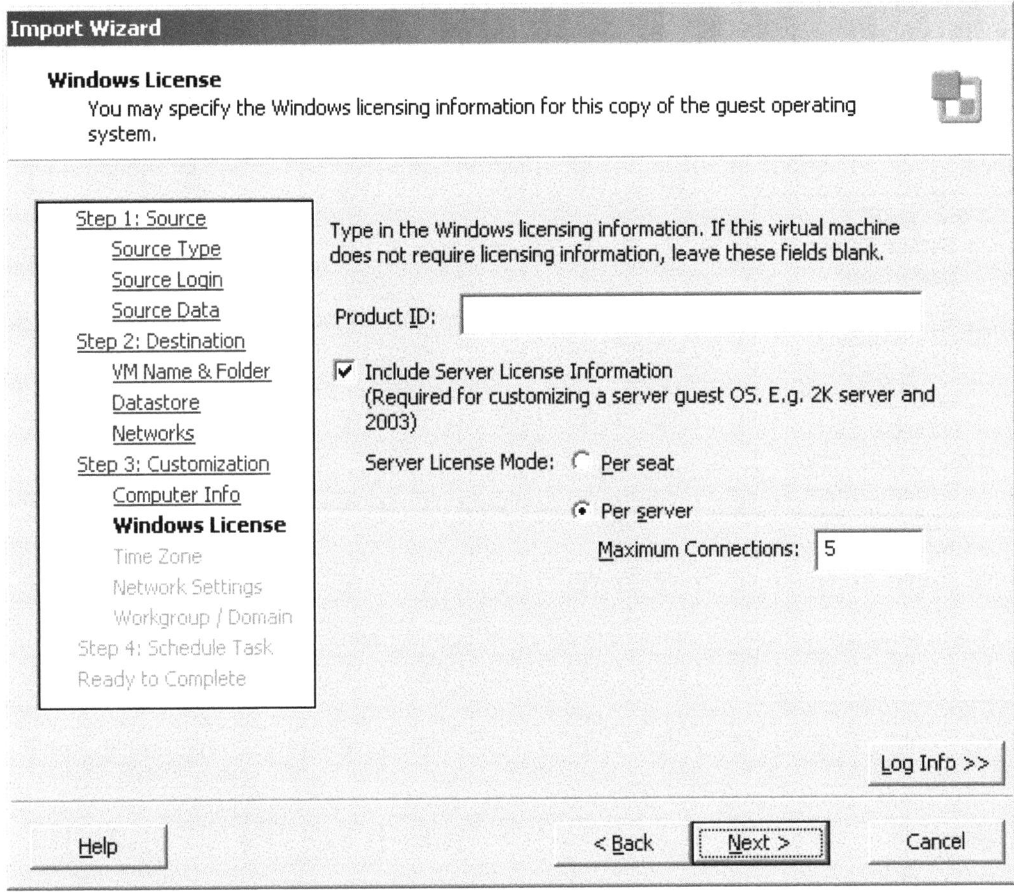

Figure 8.33 Converter Enterprise Import Wizard Customization Operating System License

The next step allows you to input a valid windows license. If your VM does not require a license or you plan on adding it later then you should leave the box blank. You can also configure the License server information on this screen as shown in Figure 8.33. Click on the Next button to continue.

Step 14. Time Zone screen.

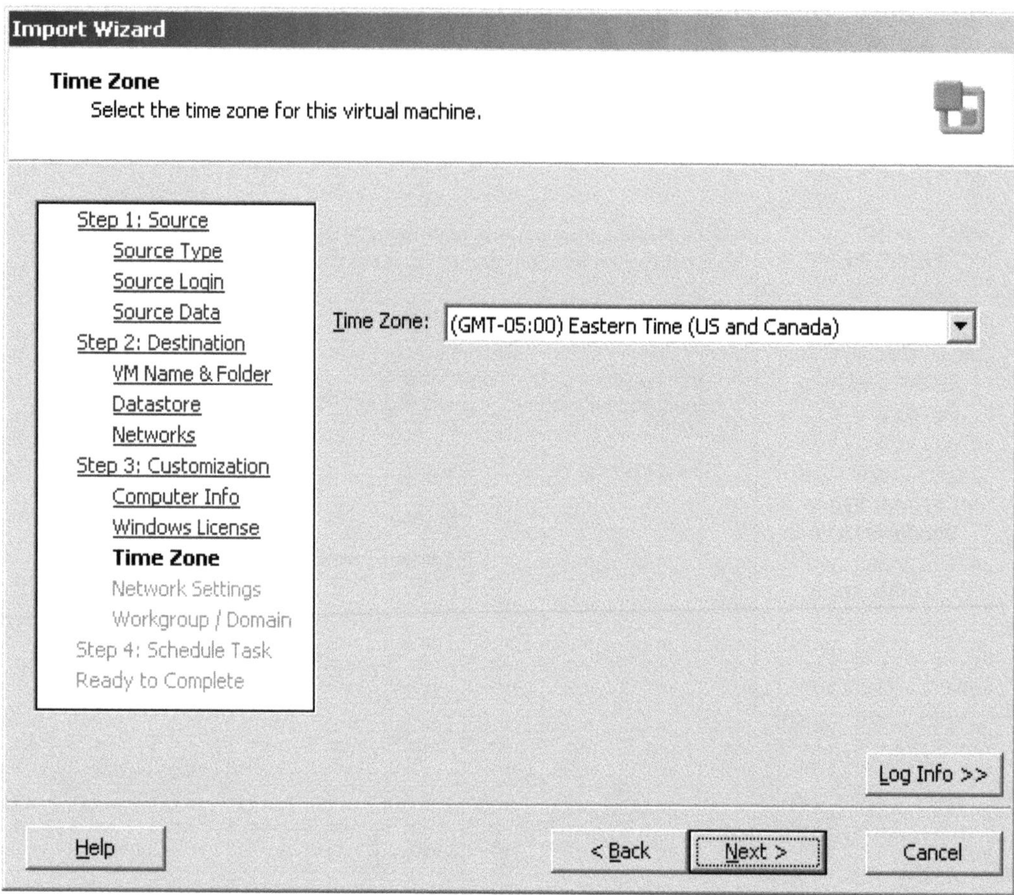

Figure 8.34 Converter Enterprise Import Wizard Customization Time Zone

Figure 8.34 illustrates the time zone drop down menu that you should set for the new VM. Click on the Next button to continue.

Step 15. Network Interface Settings screen.

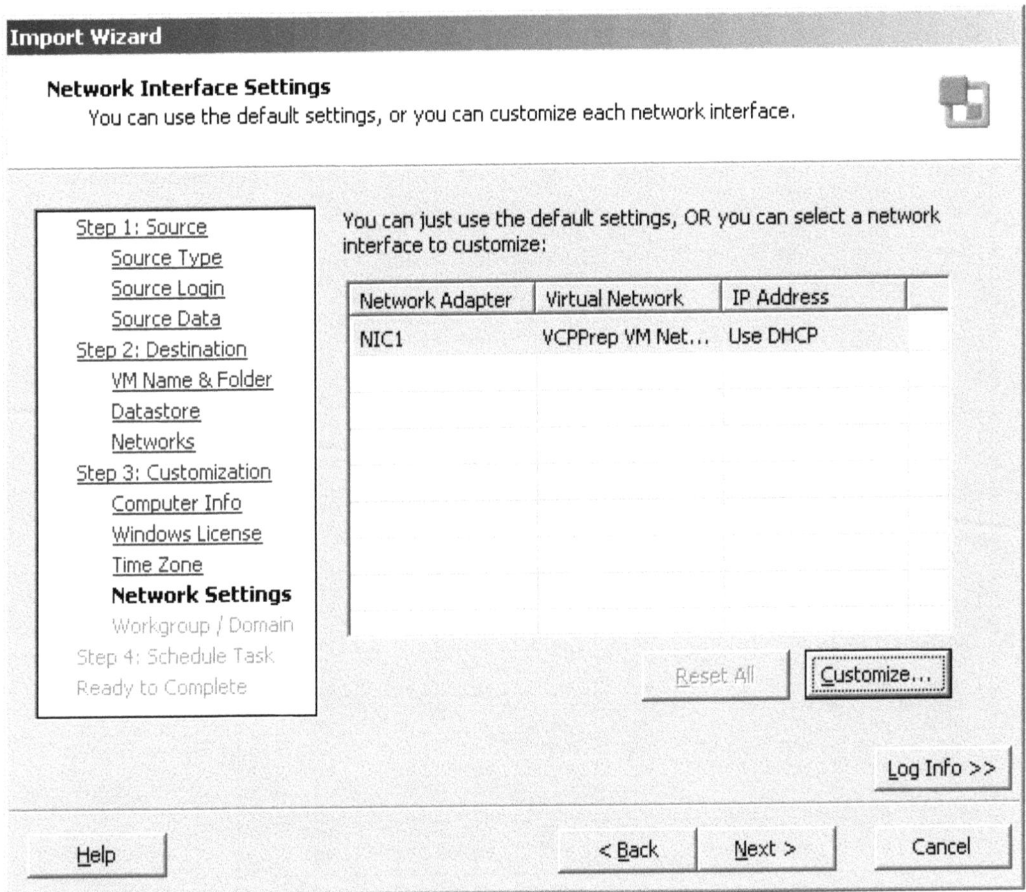

Figure 8.35 Converter Enterprise Import Wizard Customization Network Settings

You can set the configuration for the VM's network interface in the Network Interface Settings screen as shown in Figure 8.35. Click on the Customize button if you don't want the VM to get it's network configuration via DHCP.

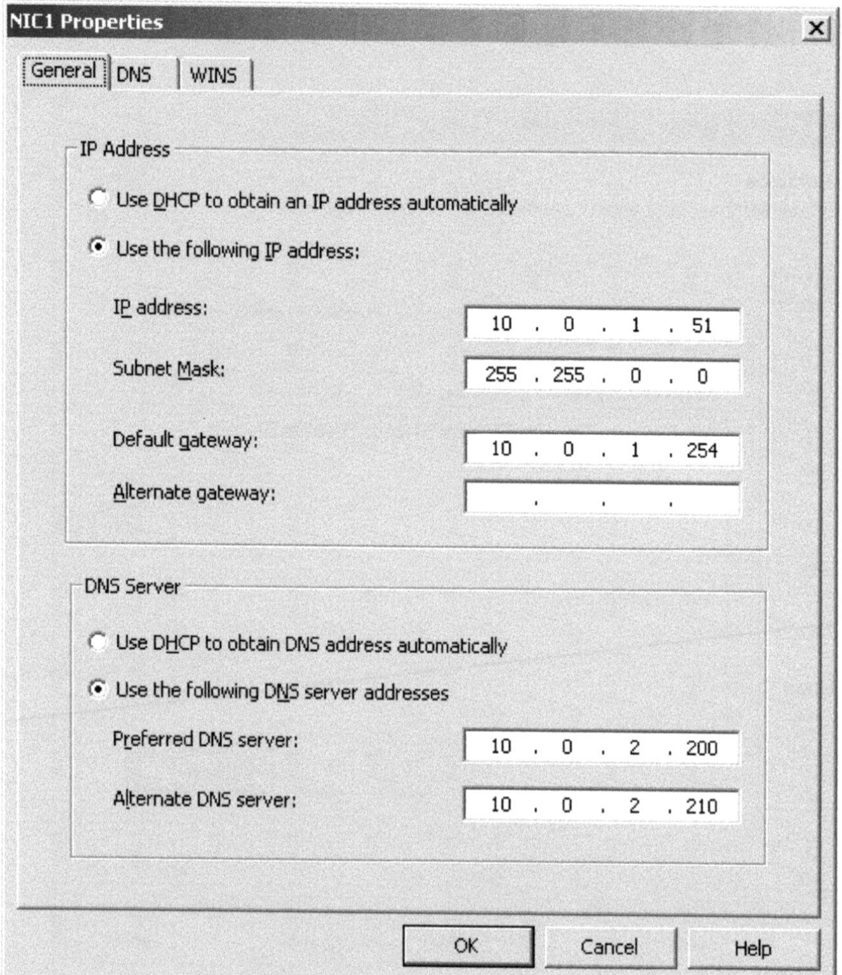

Figure 8.36 Converter Enterprise Import Wizard Customization Network Settings General Tab

The Properties window for the virtual NIC will now appear and you can configure the IP address settings as well as configuring the DNS server settings as shown in Figure 8.36. Click on the OK button to return to the previous screen.

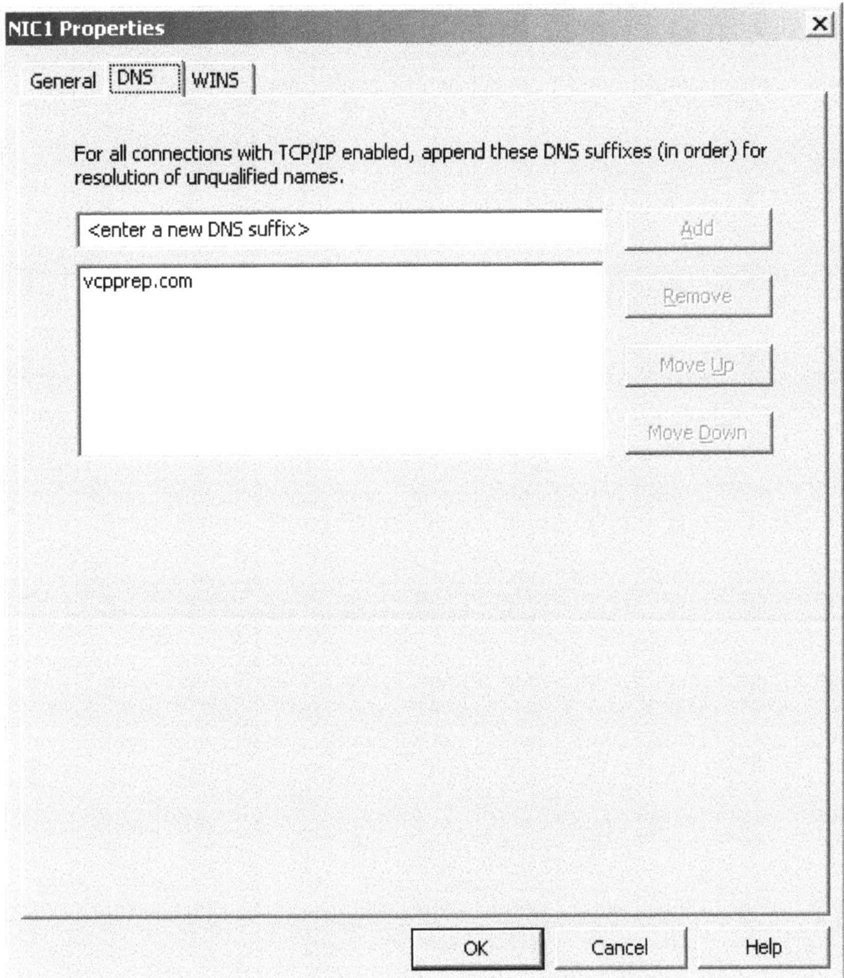

Figure 8.37 Converter Enterprise Import Wizard Customization Network Settings DNS Tab

By selecting the DNS tab in the NIC Properties window as shown in Figure 8.37, you can set the guest OS's DNS configuration information.

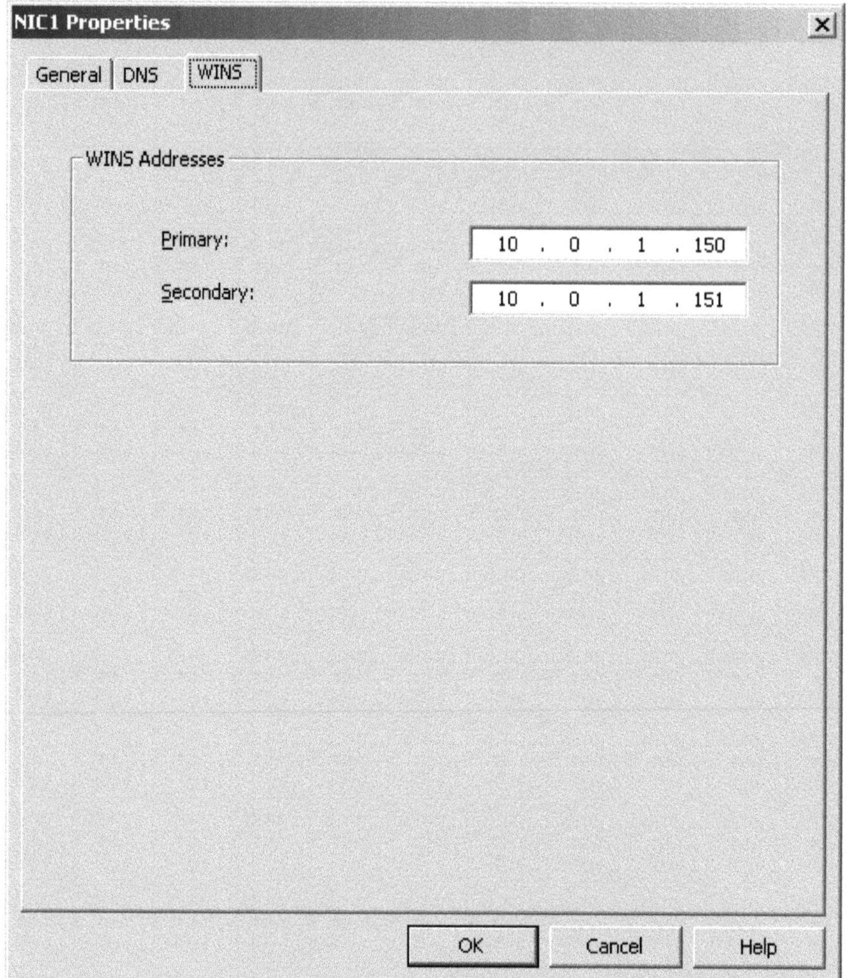

Figure 8.38 Converter Enterprise Import Wizard Customization Network Settings WINS Tab

By selecting the WINS tab in the NIC Properties window as shown in Figure 8.38, you can set the guest OS's WINS addresses. Click on the OK button to return to the previous screen.

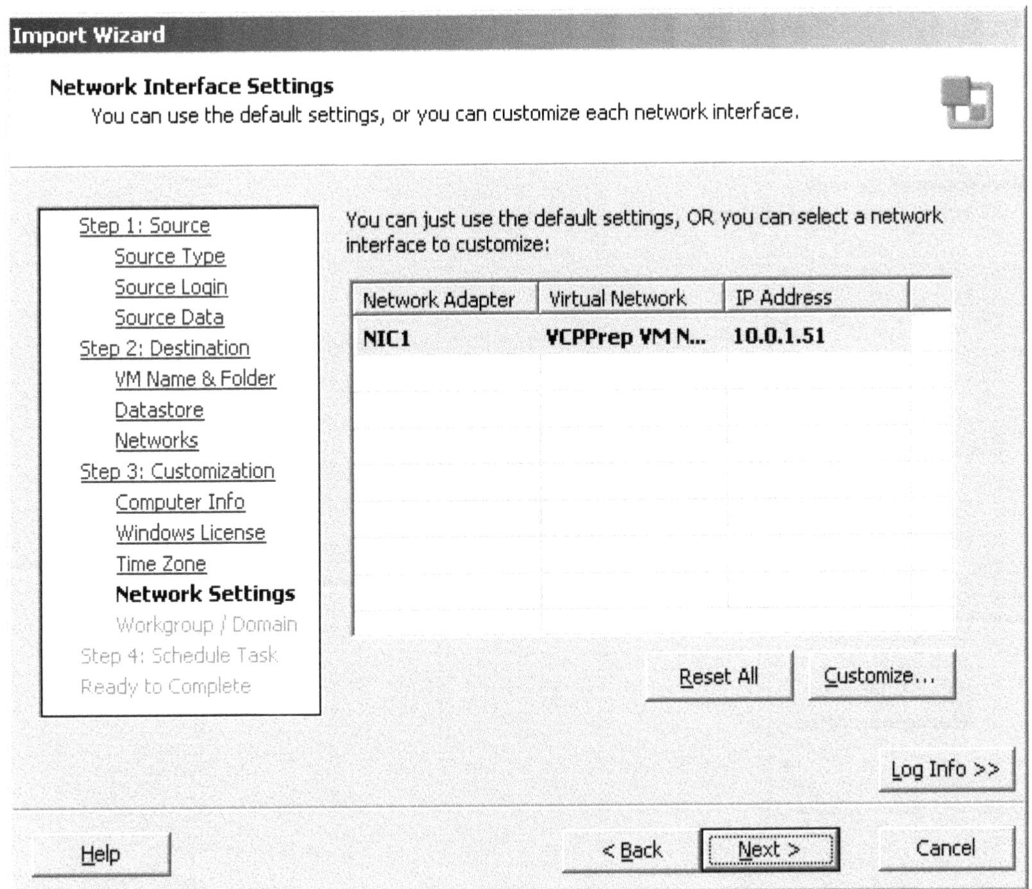

Figure 8.39 Converter Enterprise Import Wizard Customization Network Settings Modified

The settings you set in the Properties window will appear in this screen as shown in Figure 8.39. Click on the Next button to continue.

Step 16. Workgroup or Domain screen.

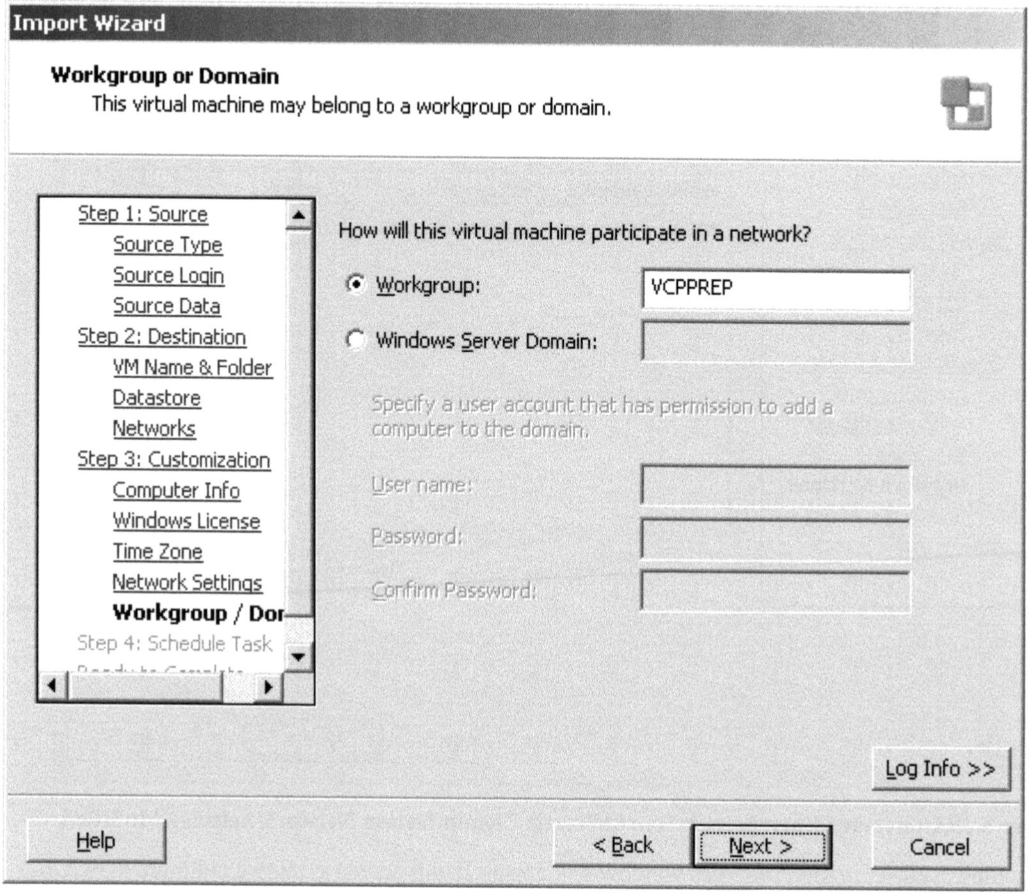

Figure 8.40 Converter Enterprise Import Wizard Customization Workgroup Or Domain

You can set the Windows OS Workgroup name or the name of the Windows Server Domain that the VM will be a part of. Click on the Next button to continue.

Step 17. Scheduled Task screen.

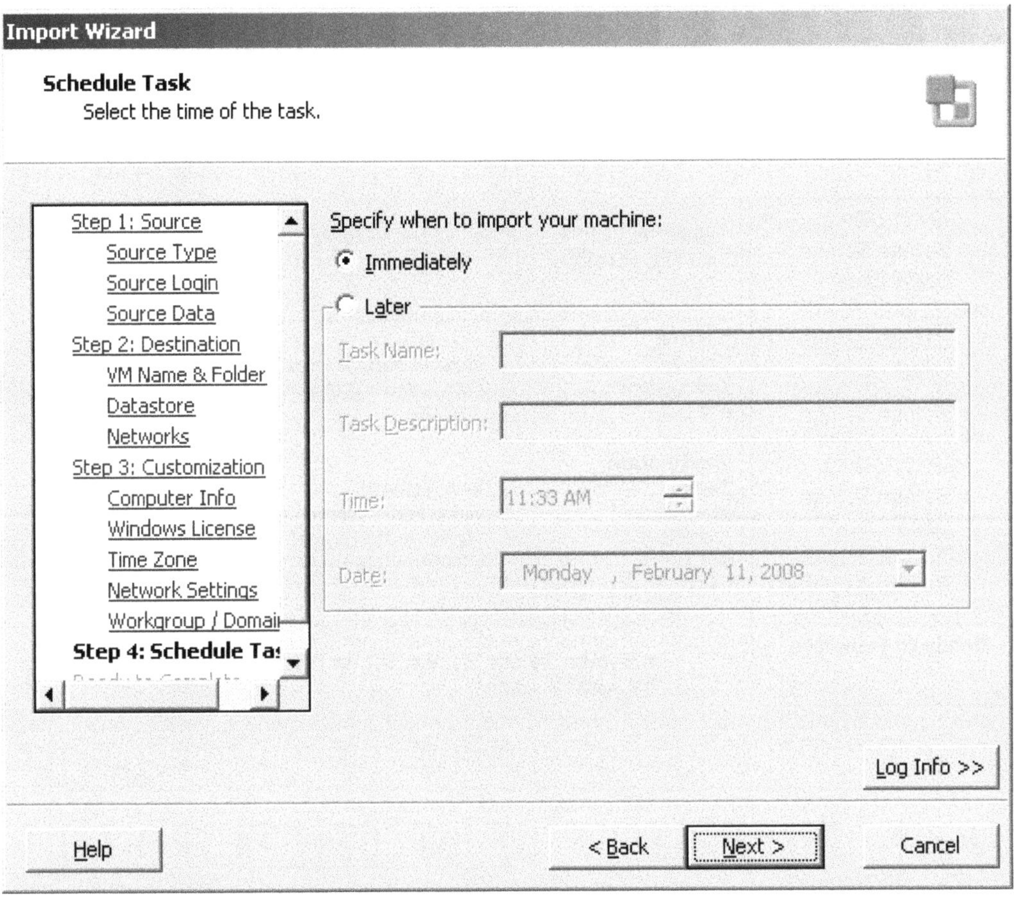

Figure 8.41 Converter Enterprise Import Wizard Customization Scheduled Task

If you don't want the hot cloning to start immediately you can schedule the process in the Scheduled Task screen. Figure 8.41 shows the options to configure the scheduled task. Click on the Next button to continue.

Step 18. Ready to Complete screen.

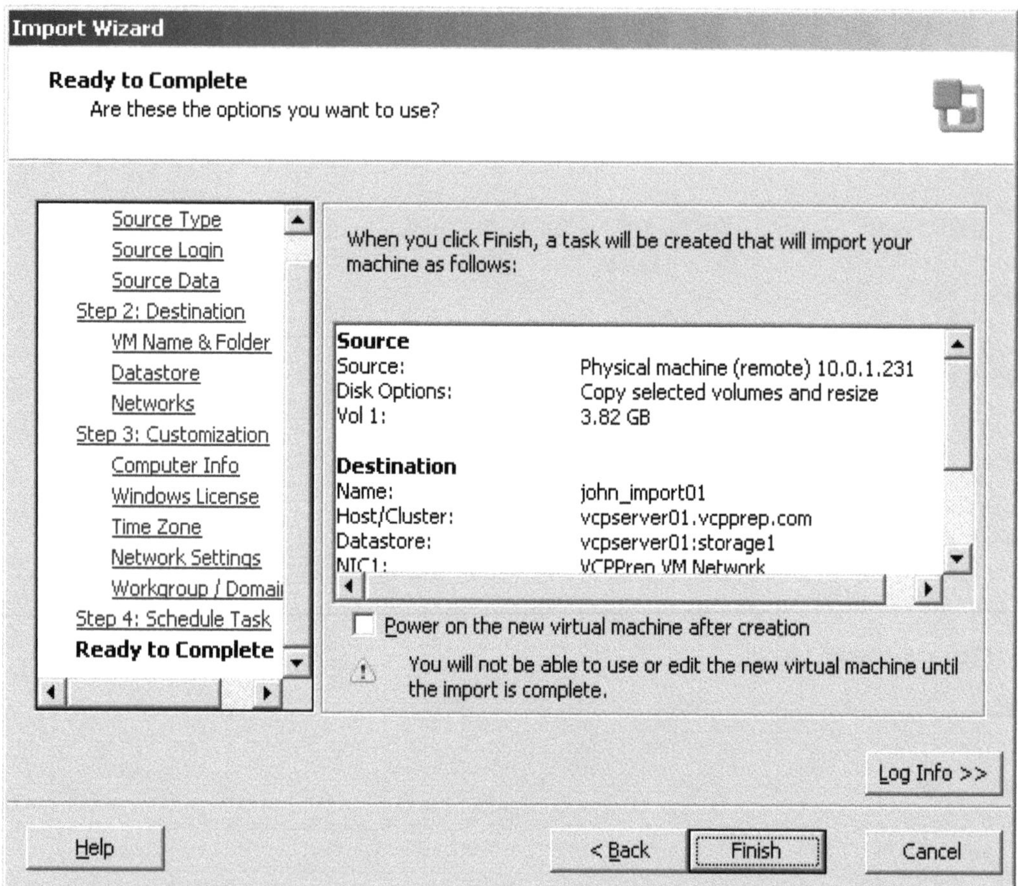

Figure 8.42 Converter Enterprise Import Wizard Customization Ready To Complete

You will see a summary of all of your choices in the hot cloning wizard process in this screen as shown in Figure 8.42. You can also select the check box to power on the new VM after it has been created. Click on the Finish button to continue.

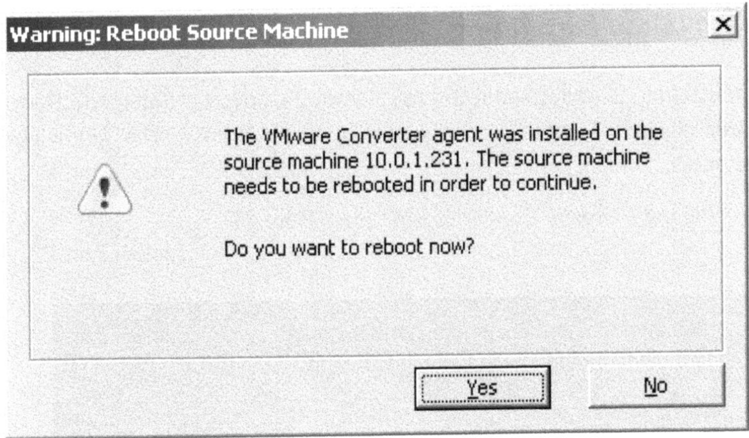

Figure 8.43 Converter Enterprise Import Wizard Reboot Source Machine Message

The source machine might have to be rebooted in order for the cloning process to continue as shown in Figure 8.43. Windows NT and Windows 2000 require a successful reboot. Click on the Yes button to reboot the physical server.

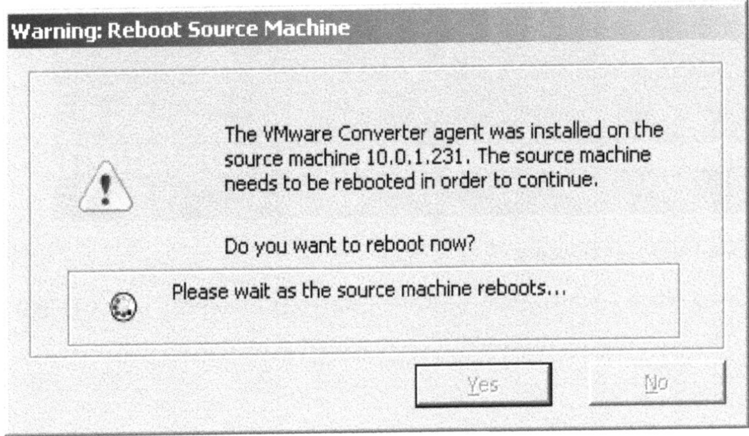

Figure 8.44 Converter Enterprise Import Wizard Reboot Source Machine Message Waiting To Reboot

Figure 8.44 shows the message while the physical server is rebooting.

Figure 8.45 Converter Enterprise Import Process Status

In VirtualCenter 2.5 you will be able to see the progress of the hot cloning task in the Recent Tasks pane.

Cold Clone Import of a Physical Machine

A cold clone import of a physical machine is performed using the VMware Converter Enterprise Boot CD as discussed previously in this chapter. The boot CD operates by using WinPE. The following steps illustrate the cold cloning process:

Step 1. Boot the physical server using the VMware Converter Enterprise Boot CD.

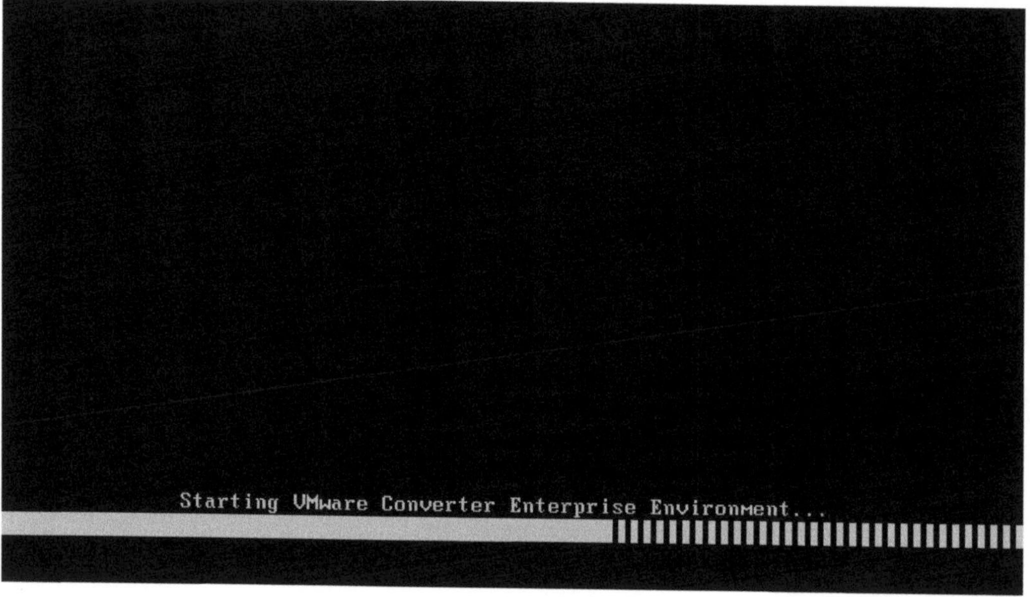

Figure 8.46 Converter Enterprise Boot CD Booting

Figure 8.46 shows the boot up screen when you place the VMware Converter Enterprise boot CD into the physical machine.

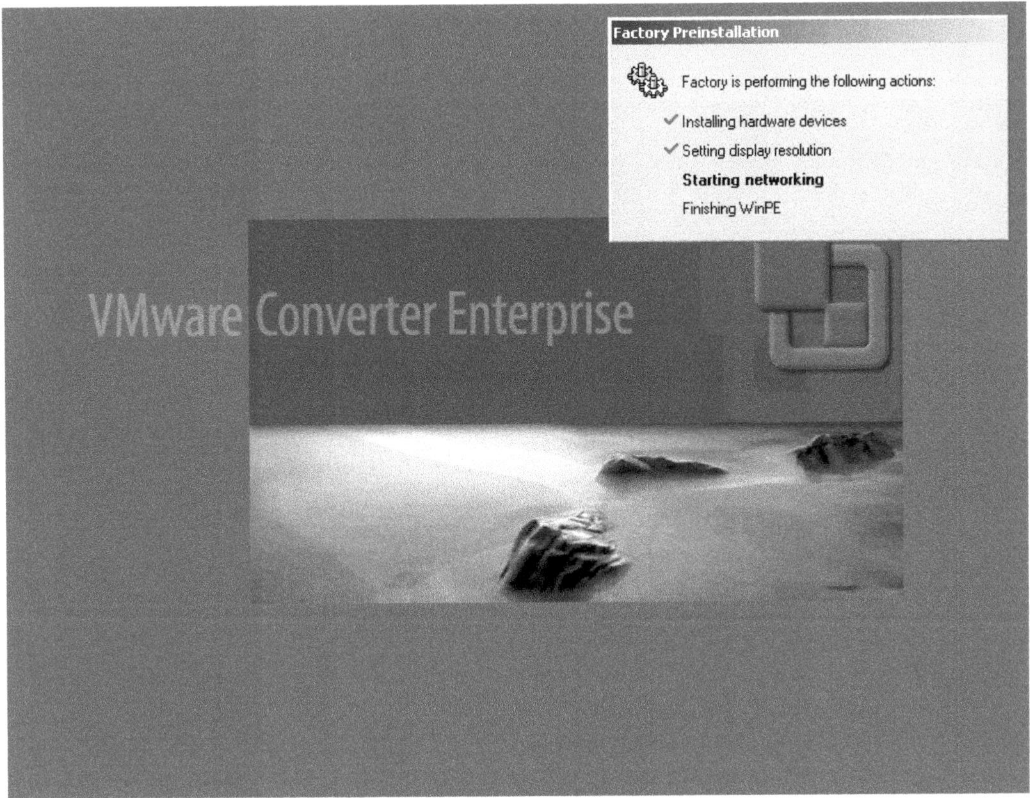

Figure 8.47 Converter Enterprise Boot CD Factory Preinstallation

Figure 8.47 shows the Factory Preinstallation screen. The WinPE environment is being initialized so that the standalone Converter Enterprise application can be loaded.

Step 2. Converter Enterprise Boot CD License Agreement screen.

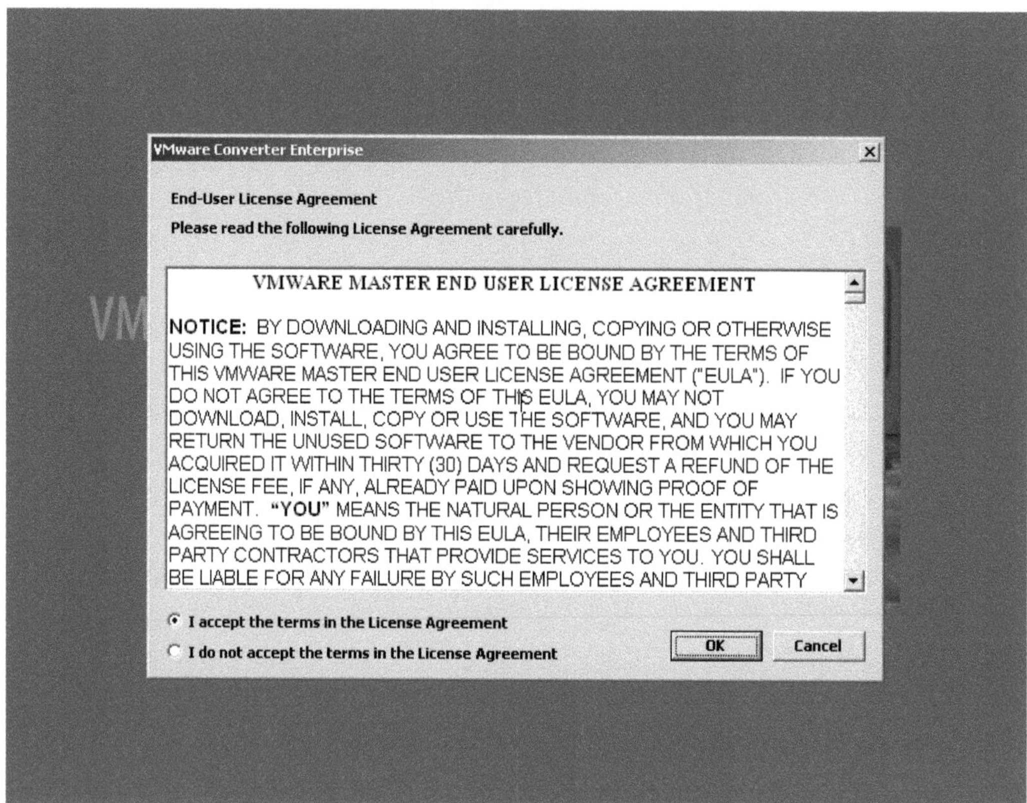

Figure 8.48 Converter Enterprise Boot CD License Agreement

Once the WinPE environment is initialized you will see the license window as shown in Figure 8.48. Click on the radio button to accept the license agreement and select the OK button to continue.

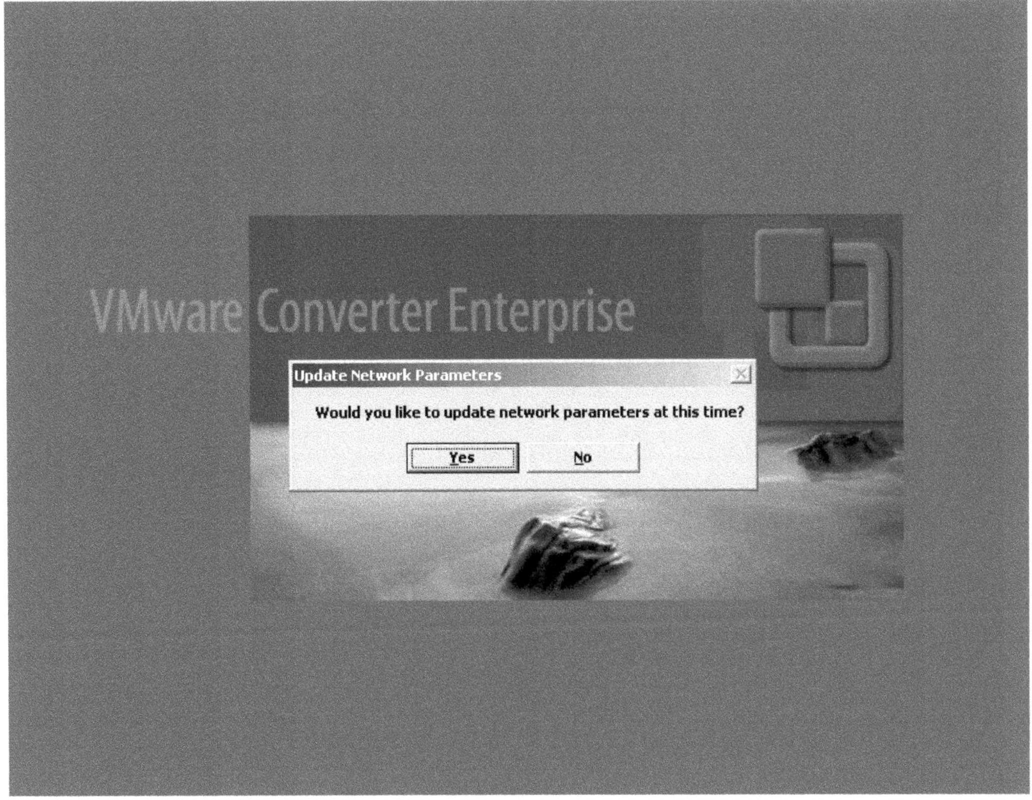

Figure 8.49 Converter Enterprise Boot CD Update Network Parameters Dialog Box

The next thing you will see is a window requesting a change to the network parameters for the new VM as shown in Figure 8.49. Selecting the No button allows the WinPE environment to obtain it's network settings via DHCP. If you want to modify the network settings of the WinPE environment select the Yes button to continue.

Step 3. Network Configuration screen.

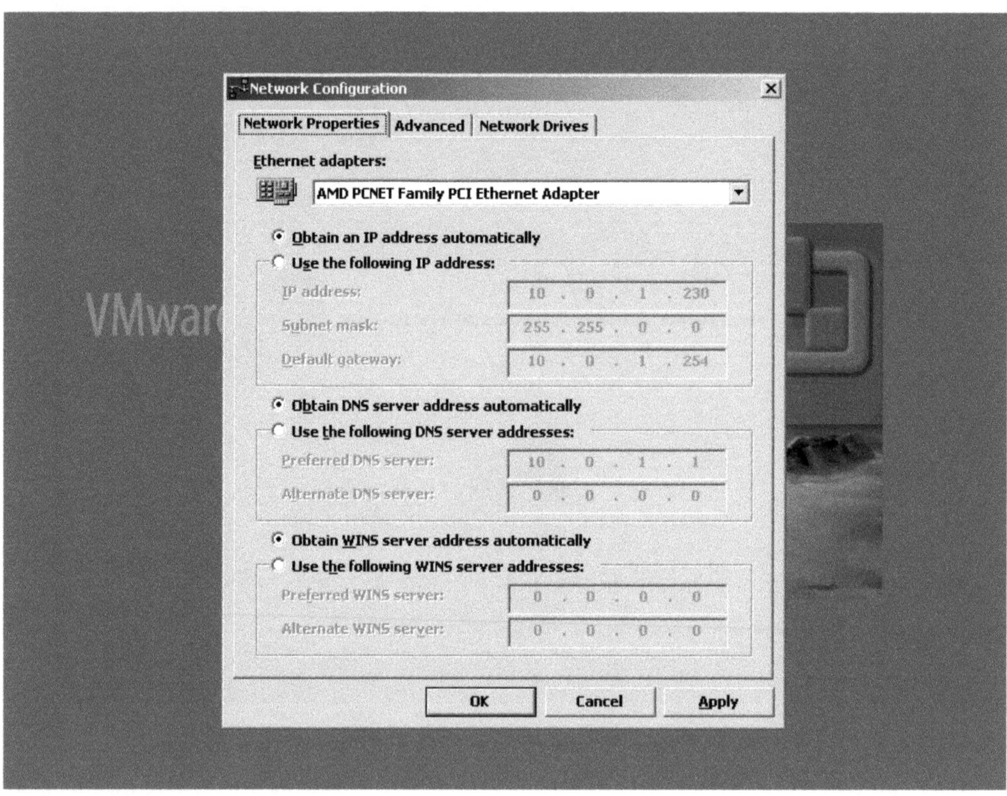

Figure 8.50 Converter Enterprise Boot CD Update Network Configuration Network Properties

Figure 8.50 shows the network configuration options that you can set so that the converter software can copy the files via network file copy (NFC) over to the destination ESX server. Input the appropriate information.

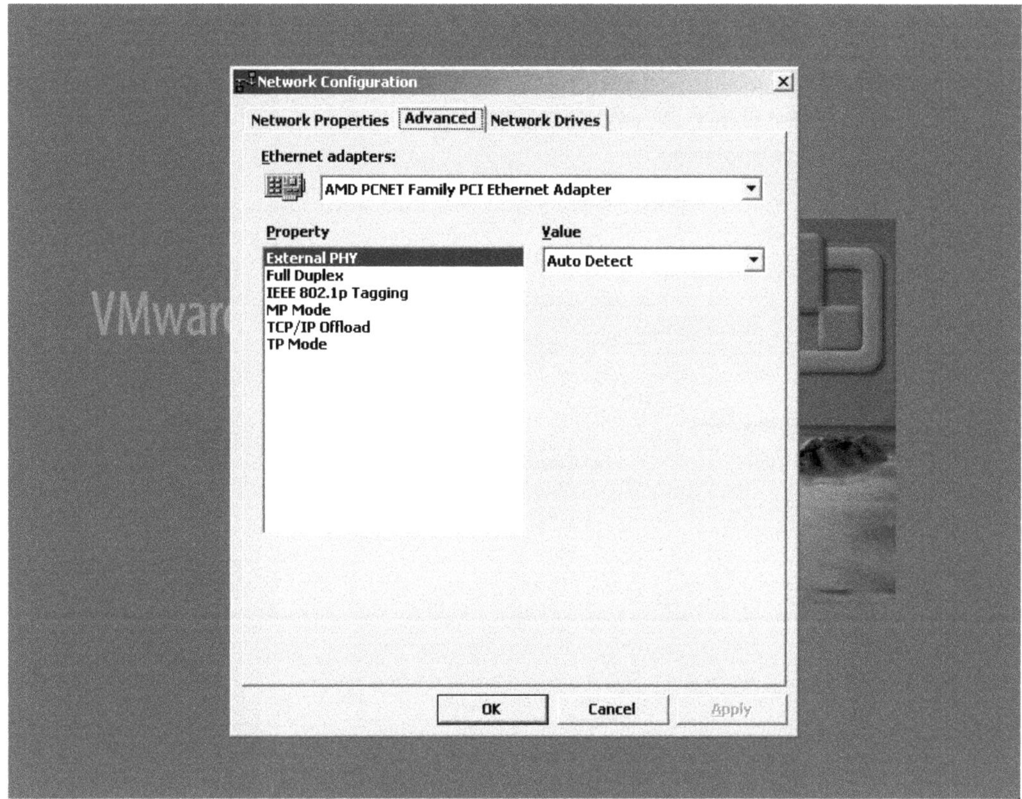

Figure 8.51 Converter Enterprise Boot CD Update Network Configuration Advanced

You can select the Advanced tab in the Network Configuration screen as shown in Figure 8.51 to set the specific Ethernet adapter settings on the physical server.

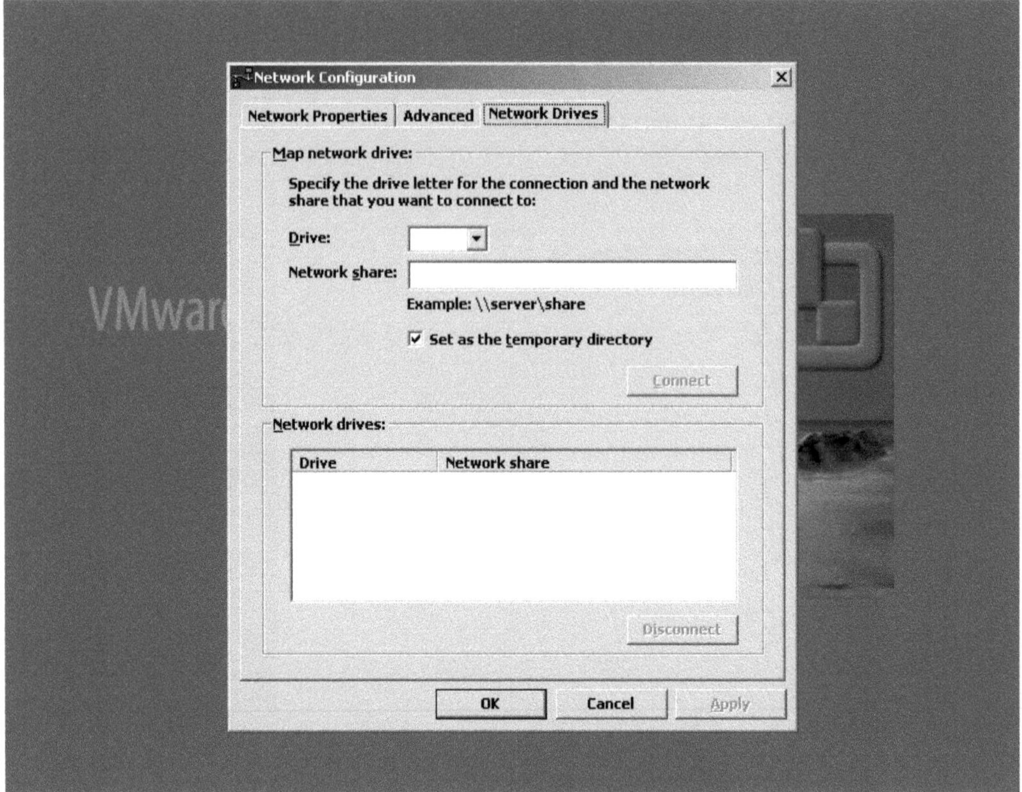

Figure 8.52 Converter Enterprise Boot CD Update Network Configuration Network Drives

As shown in Figure 8.52, a mapped drive can be used as the temporary directory for the conversion operation. Specify the correct domain username and password to connect to the share.

Step 4. Converter Enterprise Boot CD Interface screen.

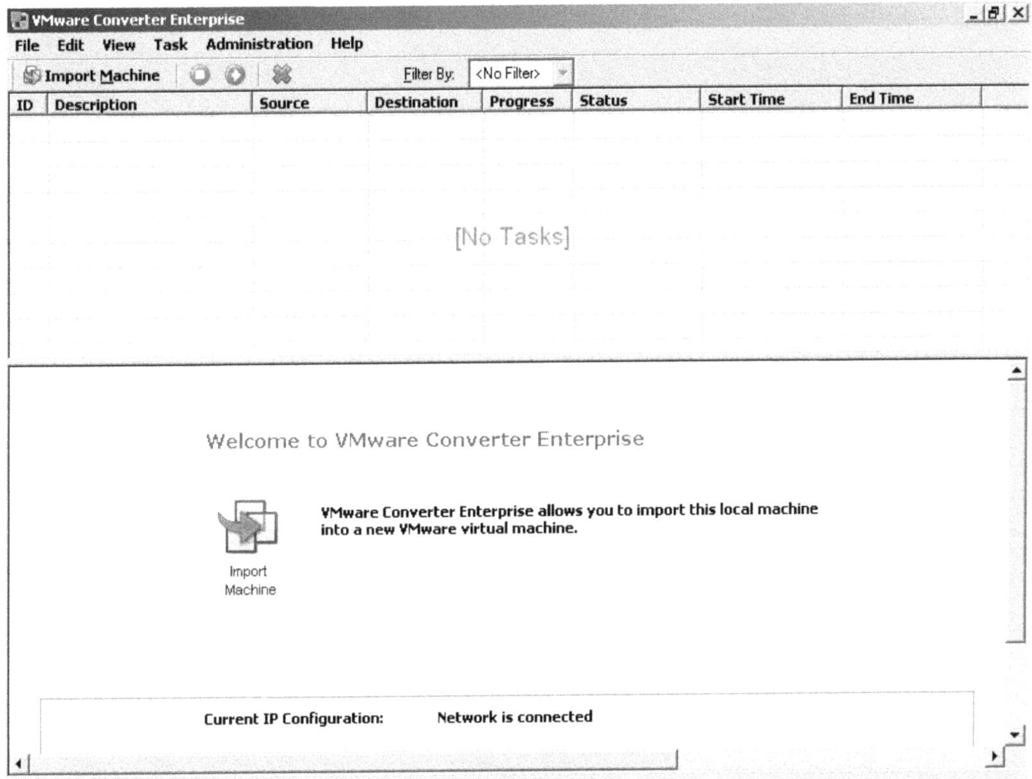

Figure 8.53 Converter Enterprise Boot CD Interface

Once the Converter Enterprise software is loaded you will see the screen shown in Figure 8.53. You can click on the Import Machine icon to launch the Import Wizard.

Step 5. Import Wizard screen.

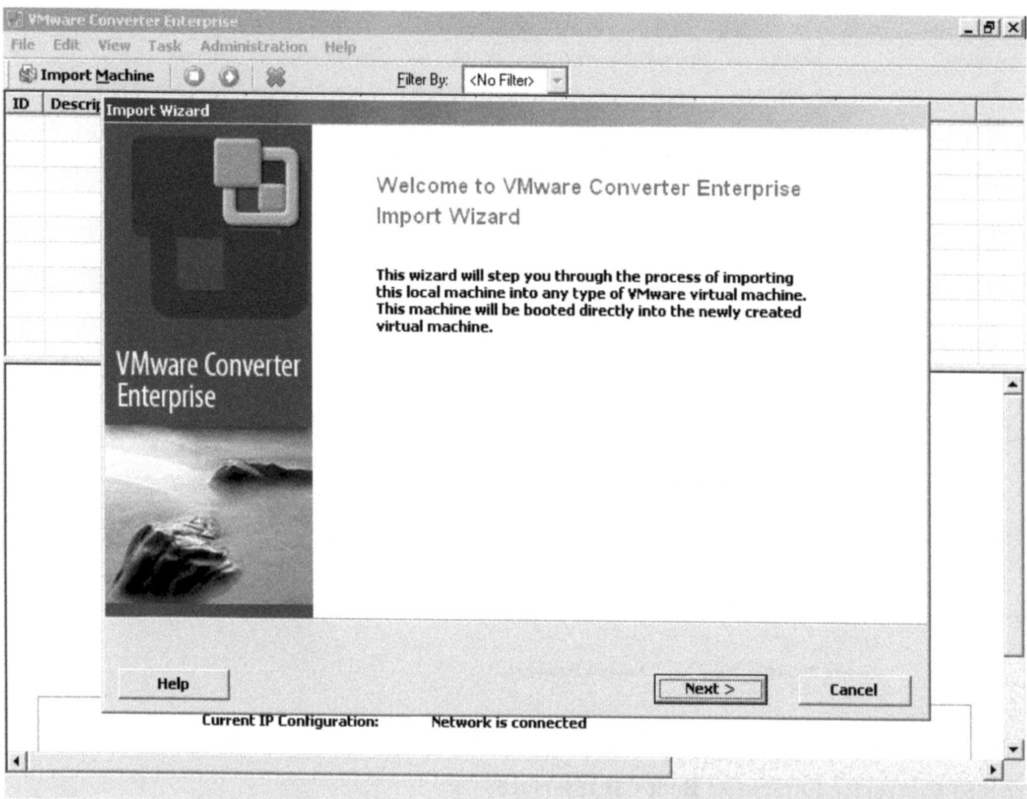

Figure 8.54 Converter Enterprise Boot CD Import Wizard

The first screen of the wizard introduces the process as shown in Figure 8.54. Click on the Next button to continue.

Step 6. Source screen.

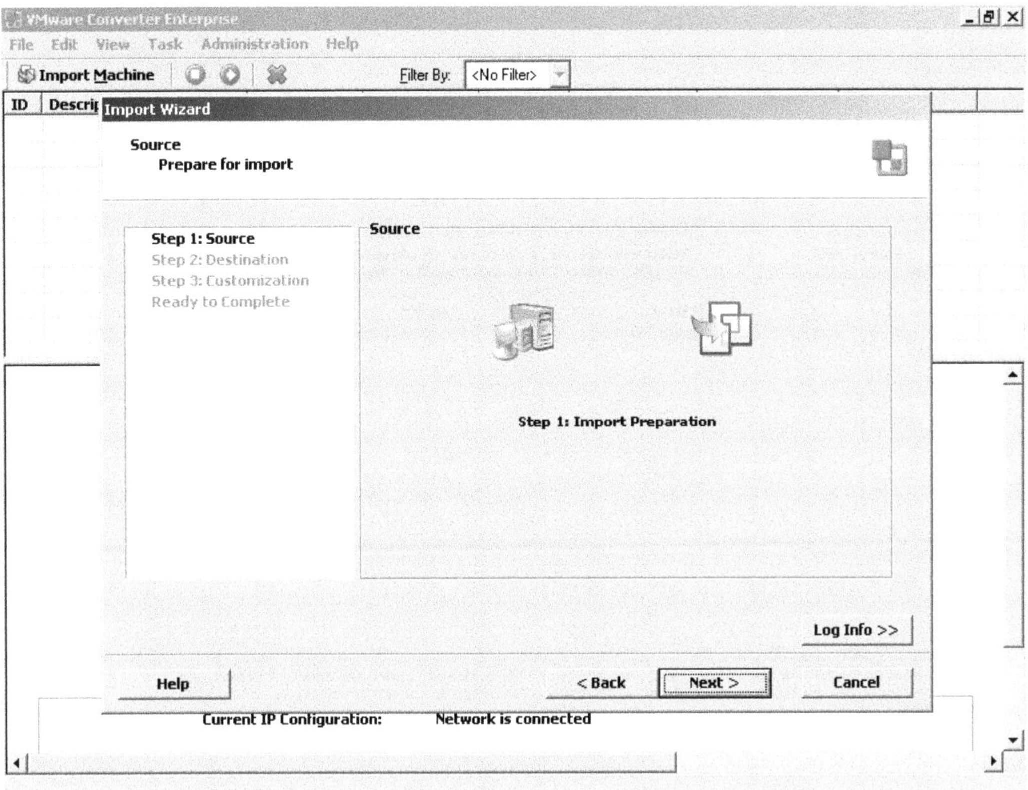

Figure 8.55 Converter Enterprise Boot CD Import Wizard Source

Figure 8.55 shows the first screen that lists the steps that will be taken by the wizard to complete the process. Click on the Next button to continue.

Step 7. Source Data screen.

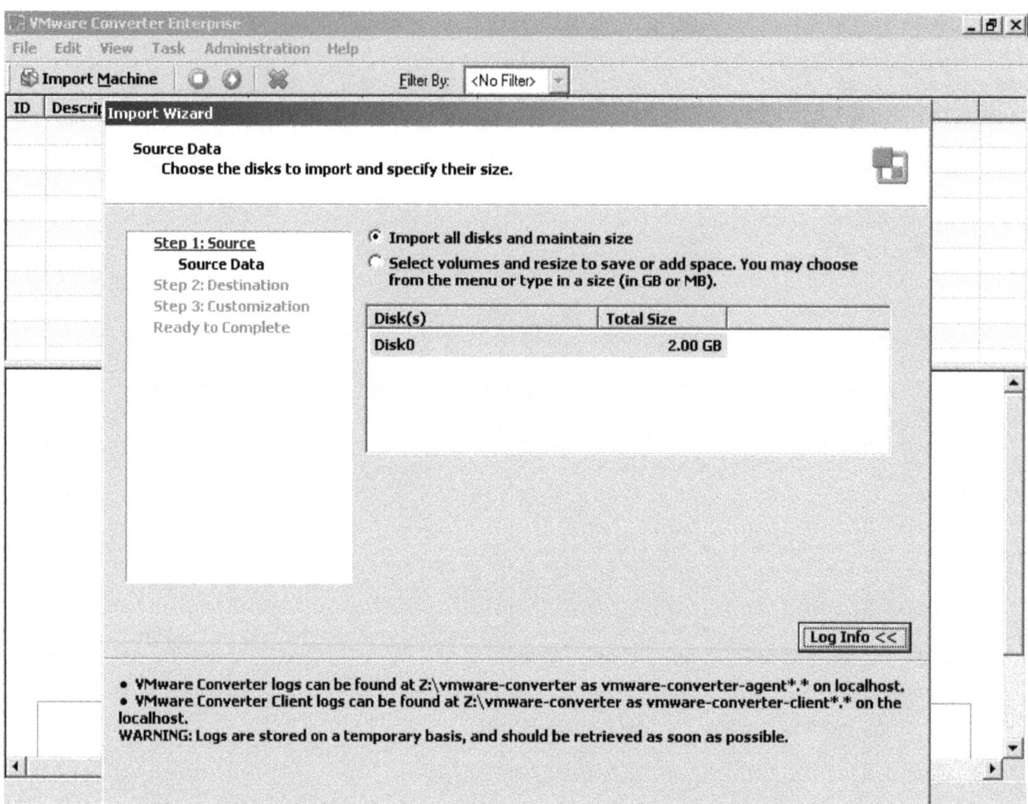

Figure 8.56 Converter Enterprise Boot CD Import Wizard Source Data

In Figure 8.56 you can import all of the physical disks that you want to be converted to be the virtual disks for your VM. You can also resize the disks by selecting the second radio button.

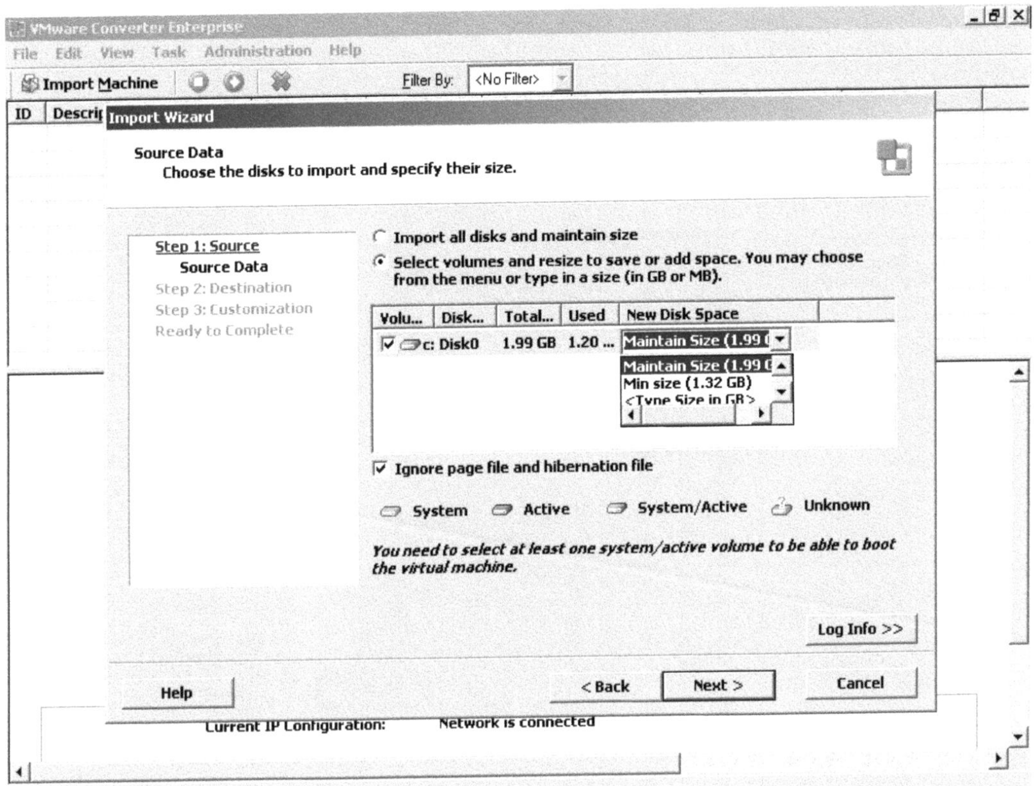

Figure 8.57 Converter Enterprise Boot CD Import Wizard Source Data New Disk Space Options

In Figure 8.57 we have selected the second radio button and decided to maintain the size of the original disk. Click on the Next button to continue.

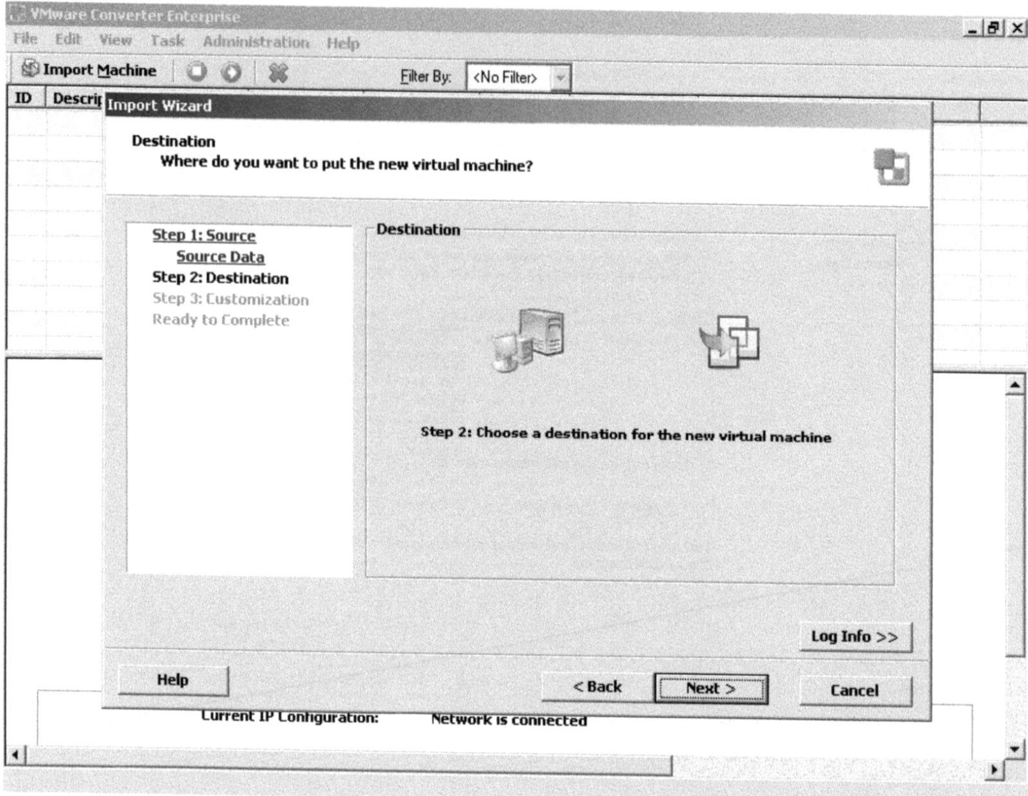

Figure 8.58 Converter Enterprise Boot CD Import Wizard Destination

The next phase of the wizard process requires you to select a destination for your VM's state files as shown in Figure 8.58. Click on the Next button to start this process.

Step 8. Destination Type screen.

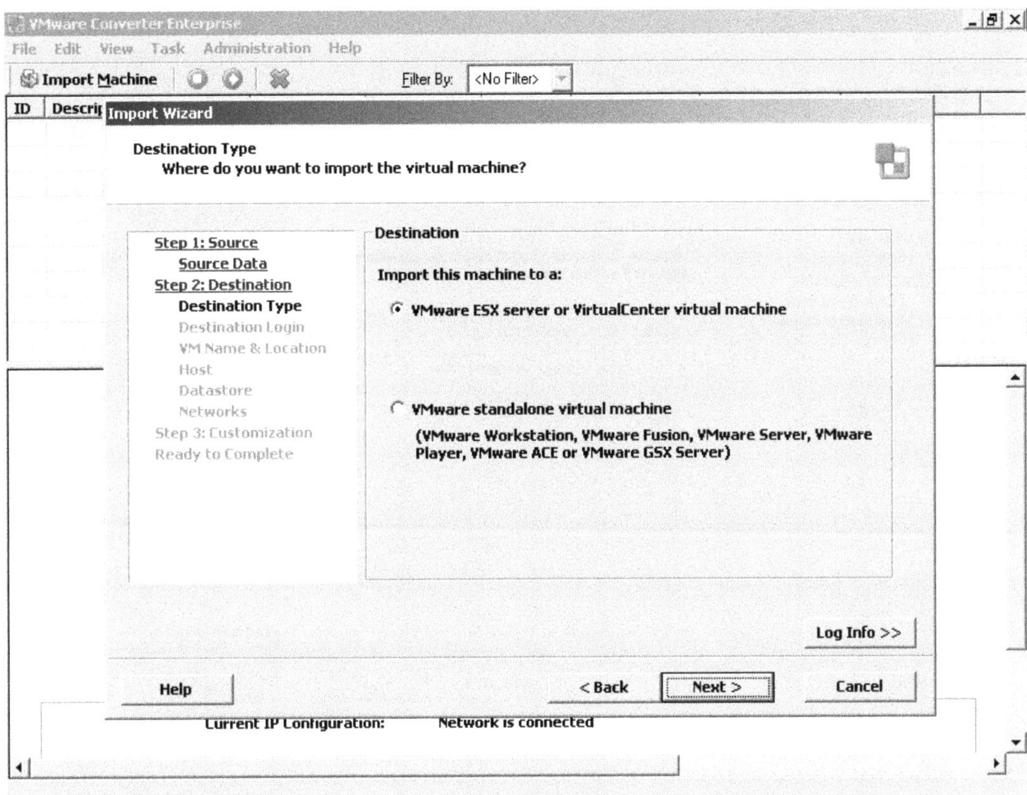

Figure 8.59 Converter Enterprise Boot CD Import Wizard Destination Type

In Figure 8.59 you can choose to import the VM to an existing ESX server or to a VirtualCenter server by selecting the upper radio button. You can also make the VM work with the other VMware products listed on the screen. Click on the Next button to continue.

Step 9. Destination Login

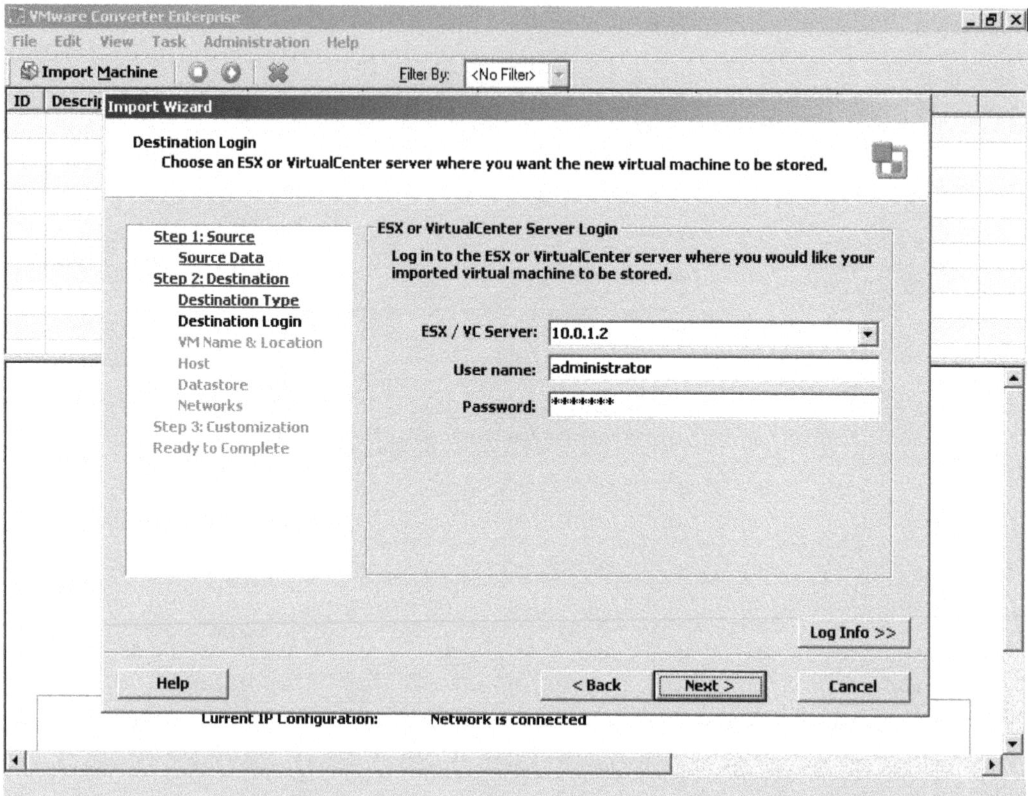

Figure 8.60 Converter Enterprise Boot CD Import Wizard Destination Login

You will need to provide the login information to the ESX server or VirtualCenter server that you are logging into. Click on the Next button to continue.

Step 10. Virtual Machine Name and Folder screen.

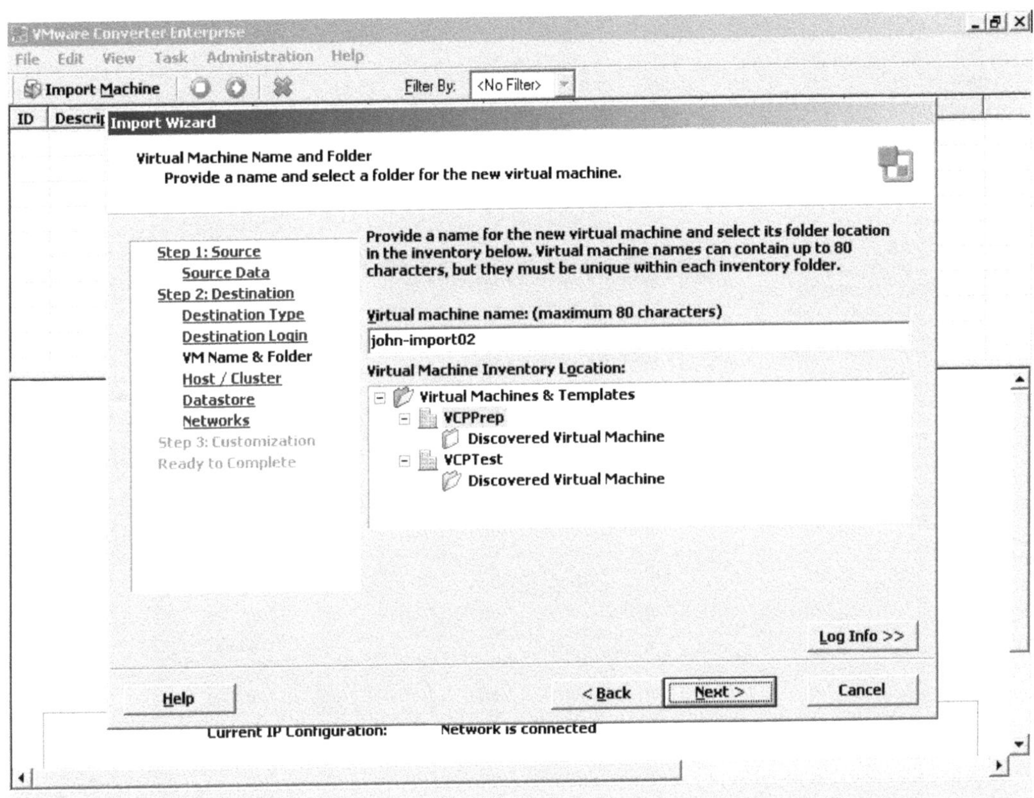

Figure 8.61 Converter Enterprise Boot CD Import Wizard Virtual Machine Name And Location

In Figure 8.61 you will provide the VM name and location of where you want the new VM to appear in the virtual infrastructure inventory. Placement of the VM in the inventory affects who can access it based on the permissions that get applied to the VM. We will discuss this in more detail in Chapter 10 - Permissions and Rights. In this example we have selected the VCPPrep Datacenter object. Once you have made your selection, click on the Next button to continue.

Step 11. Host or Cluster screen.

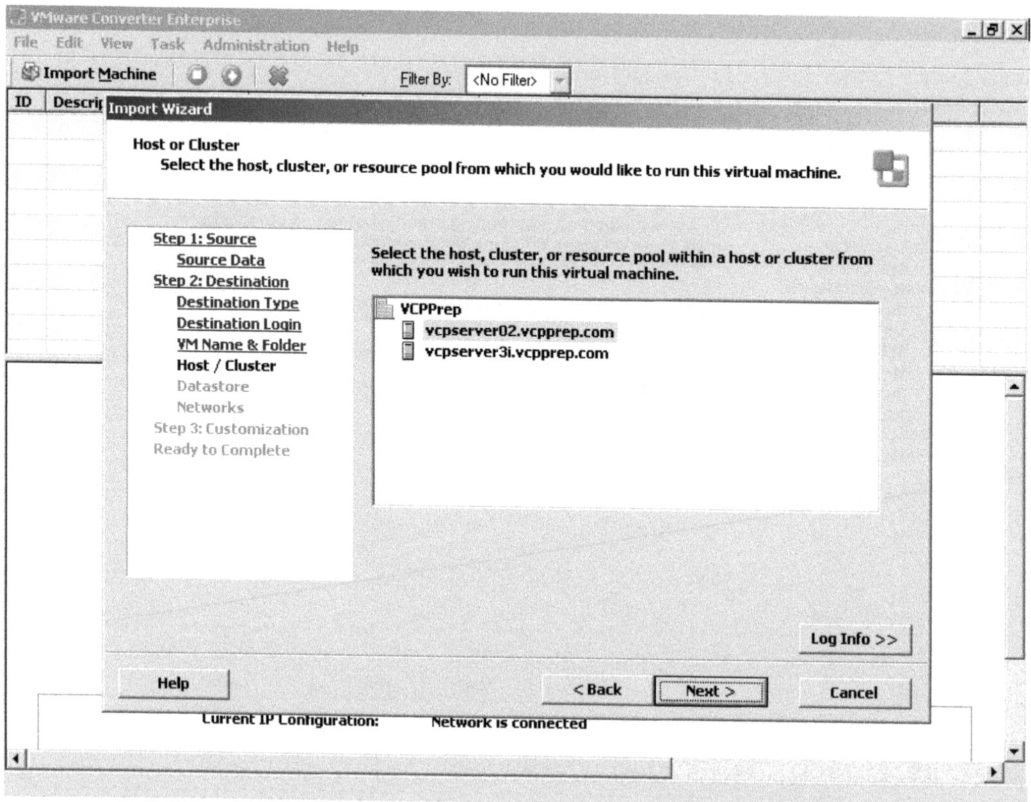

Figure 8.62 Converter Enterprise Boot CD Import Wizard Host Or Cluster

In the previous screen we selected a Datacenter object, so we will now select the ESX server that resides in that Datacenter as shown in Figure -62. Click on the Next button to continue.

Step 12. Datastore screen.

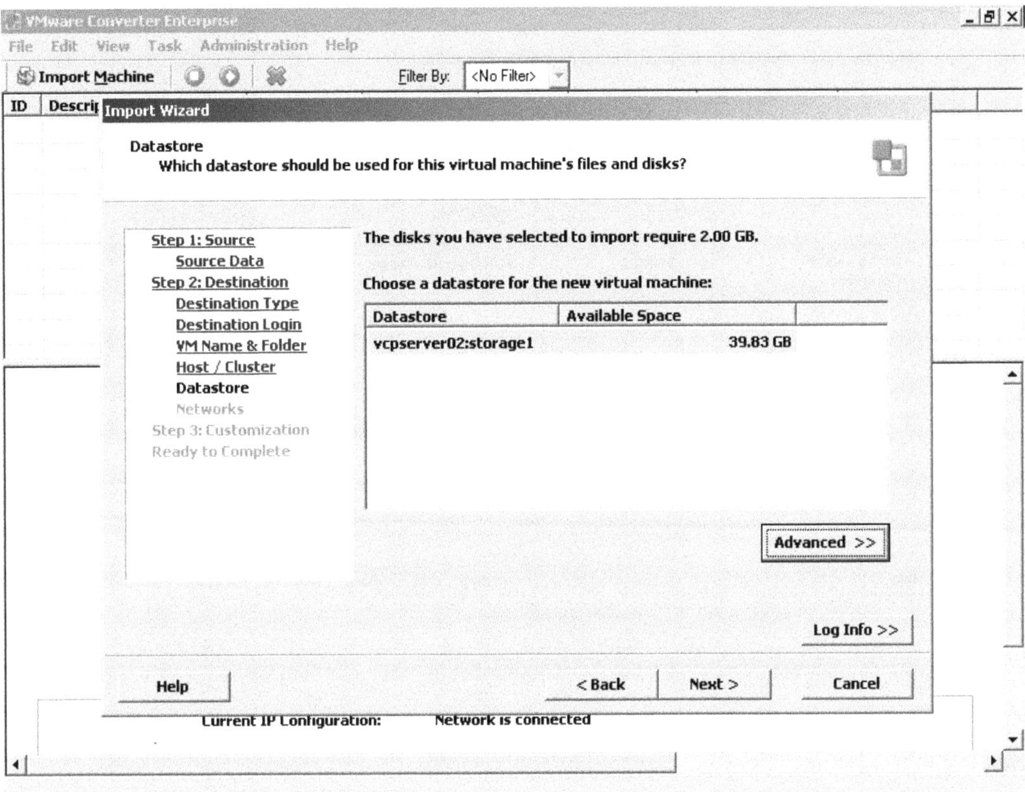

Figure 8.63 Converter Enterprise Boot CD Import Wizard Datastore

Figure 8.63 shows that you can choose the datastore that you want to store the VM's state files on. Be sure to consider the storage characteristics of the datastore because it can affect performance of the VM. Click on the Next button to continue.

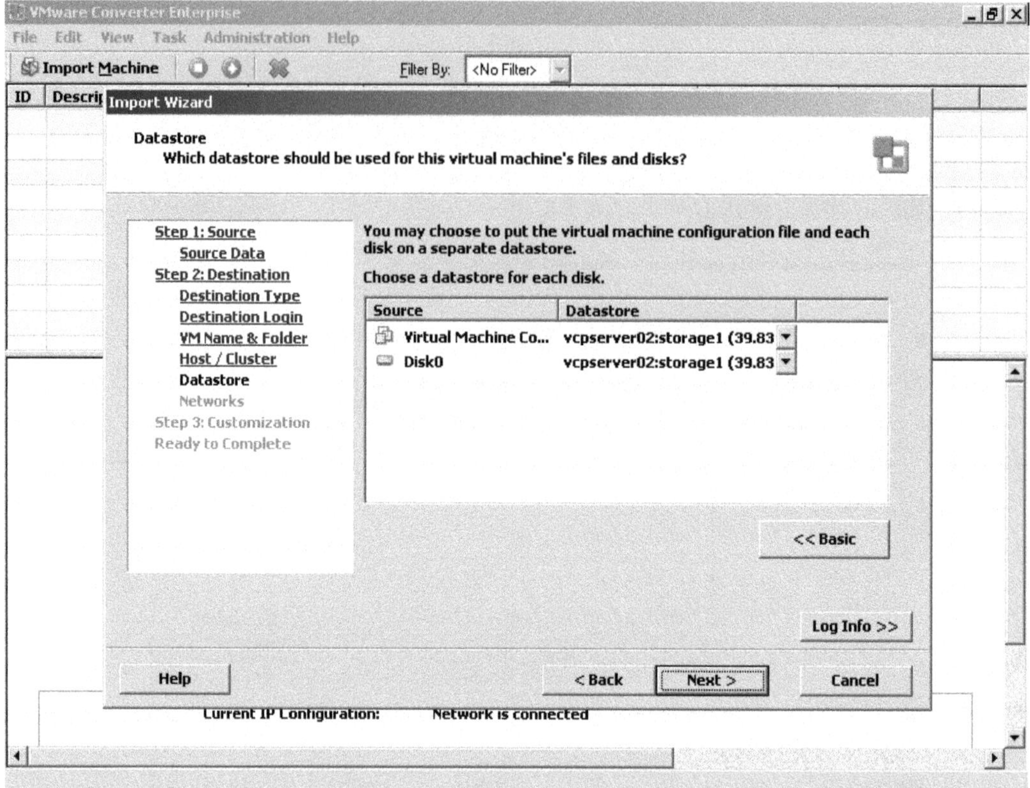

Figure 8.64 Converter Enterprise Boot CD Import Wizard Datastore Virtual Machine File Locations

You can select the Advanced button to get the screen shown in Figure 8.64 that allows you to choose a separate location for the VM's virtual disk and configuration files. Click on the Basic button to return to the previous screen.

Step 13. Networks screen.

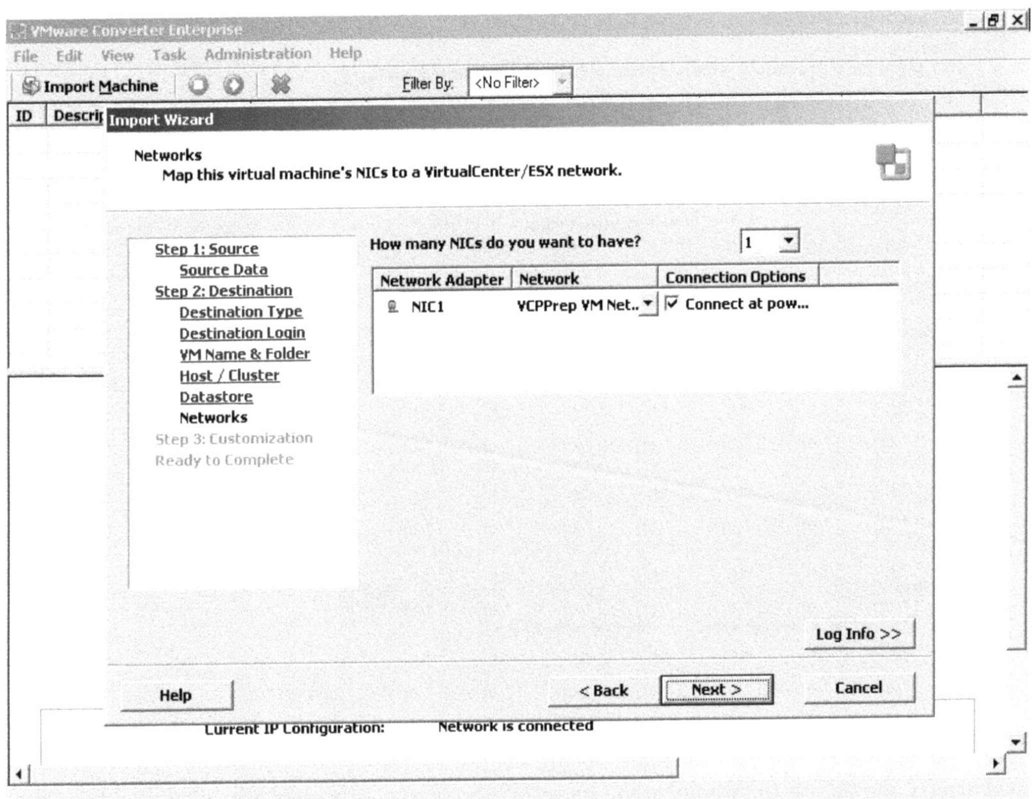

Figure 8.65 Converter Enterprise Boot CD Import Wizard Networks

You will then be prompted to configure the number of virtual NICs to be used by the new VM. Figure 8.65 illustrates the options in this step. Take into consideration any VMotion, DRS and HA networking requirements when making your choices. We will cover these topics in later chapters. Click on the Next button to continue.

Step 14. Customization screen.

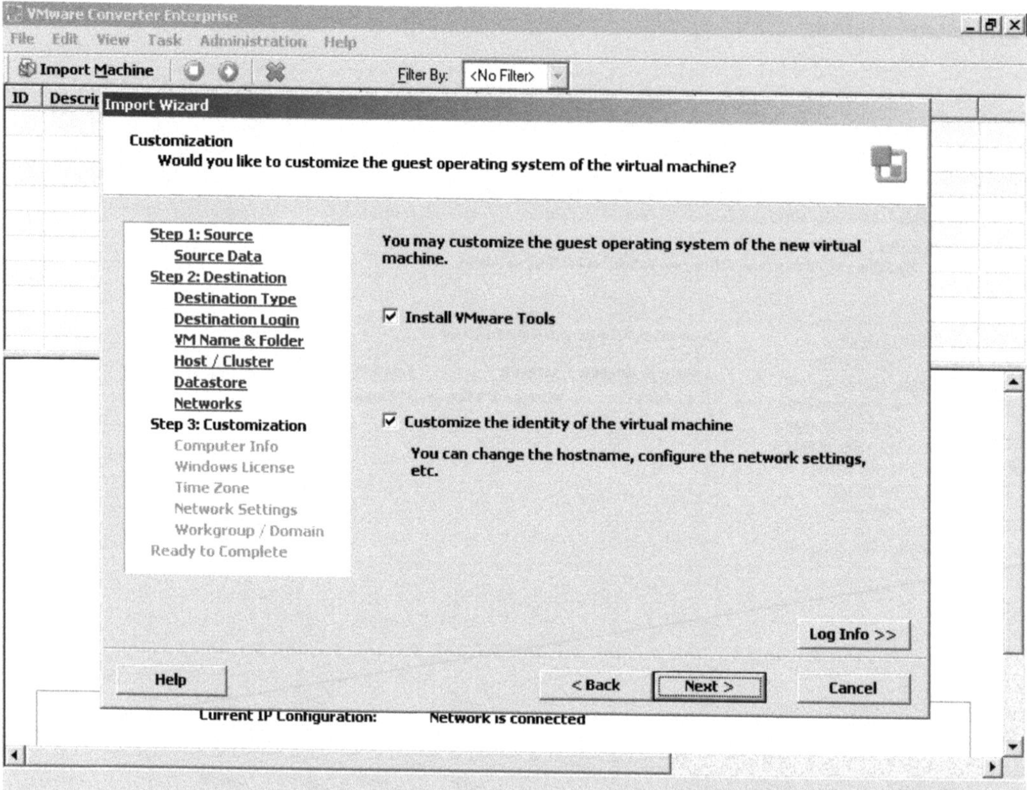

Figure 8.66 Converter Enterprise Boot CD Import Wizard Customization

The next screen allows you to customize the guest OS. Since the only currently supported OS's for this process are Windows operating systems, you can install the VMware tools and prep the OS to have a unique identity as shown in Figure 8.66. Click on the Next button to continue.

Step 15. Computer Information screen.

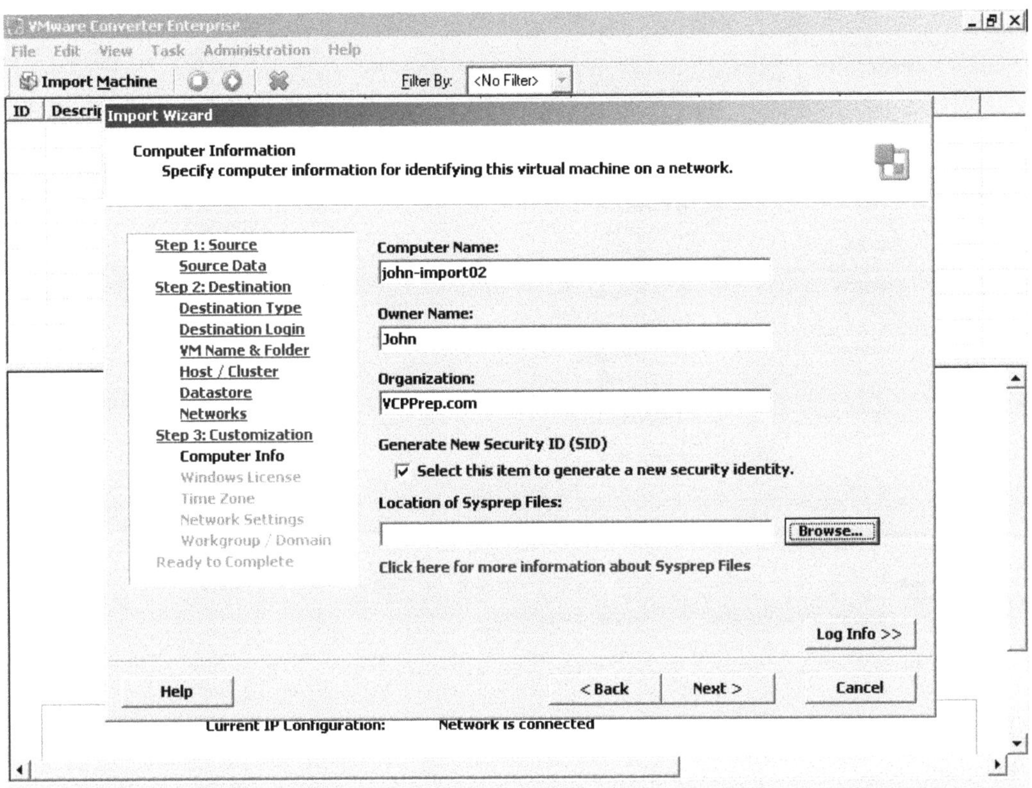

Figure 8.67 Converter Enterprise Boot CD Import Wizard Customization Computer Information

Figure 8.67 shows the Computer Information screen which allows you to input the Computer Name, Owner and Organization information for the new VM. The check box allows the process to build a new SID for the VM as well. After you have put in the needed information, click on the Next button to continue.

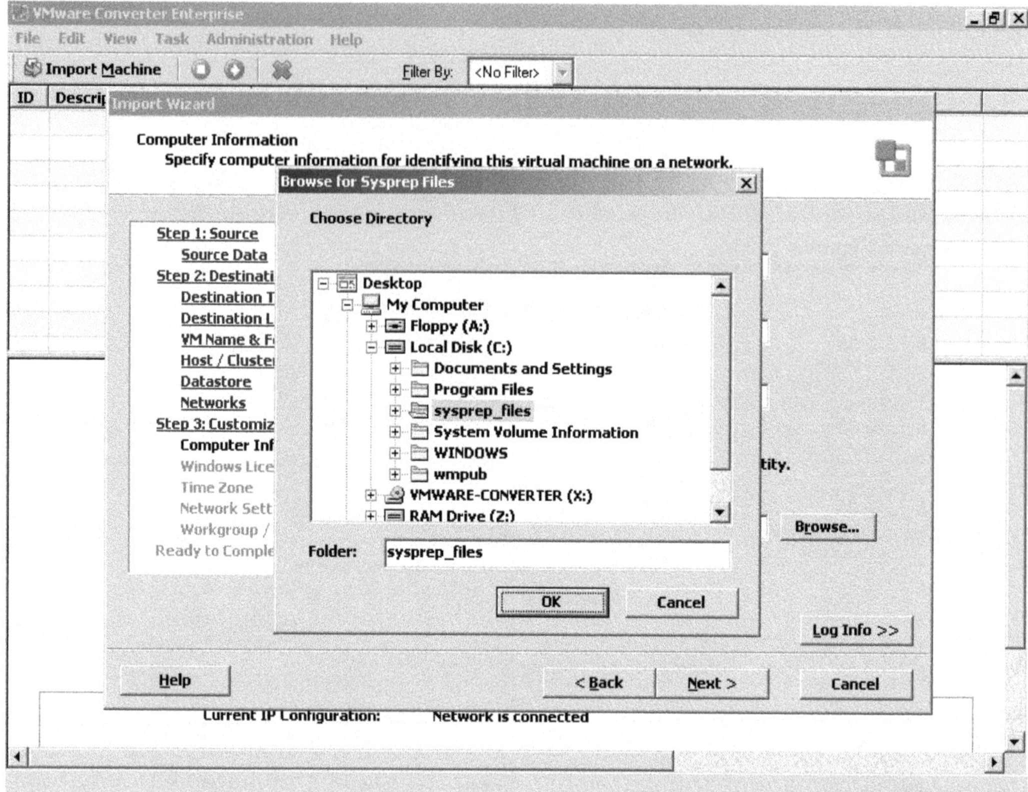

Figure 8.68 Converter Enterprise Boot CD Import Wizard Customization Browse For Sysprep Files Location

Figure 8.68 requires that you select the location of the sysprep files. After locating the directory select OK to continue.

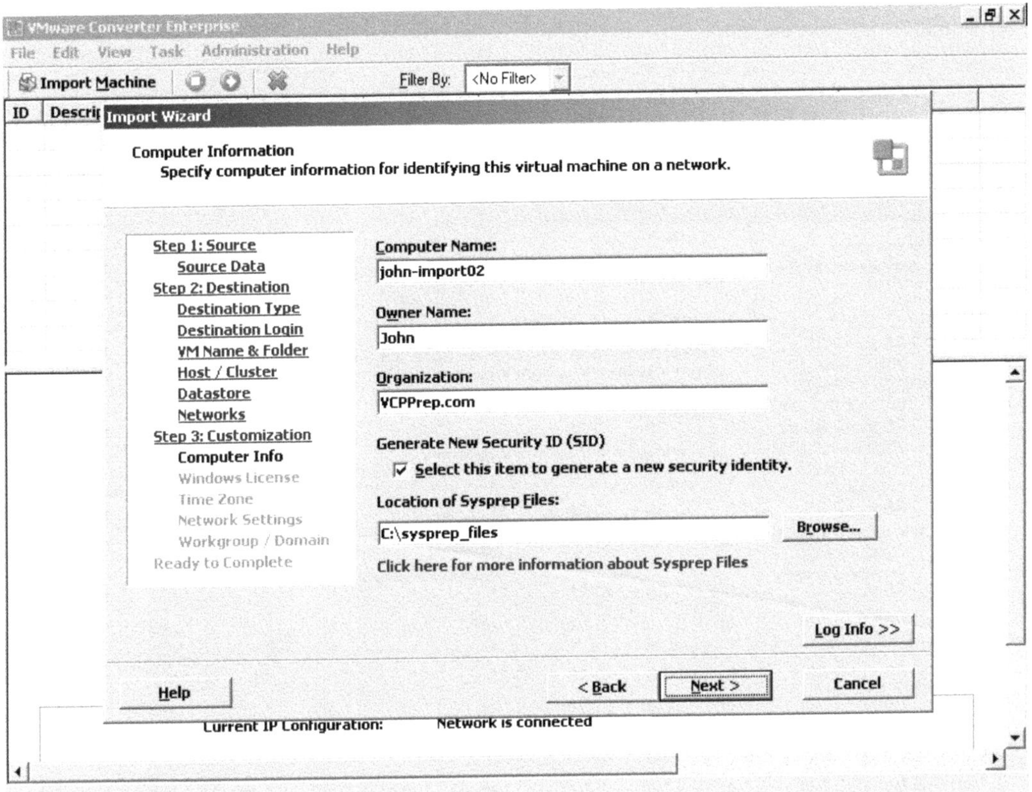

Figure 8.69 Converter Enterprise Boot CD Import Wizard Customization Sysprep Files Location

After all of the requested information is input into the appropriate text boxes, click on the Next button to continue.

Step 16. Windows License screen.

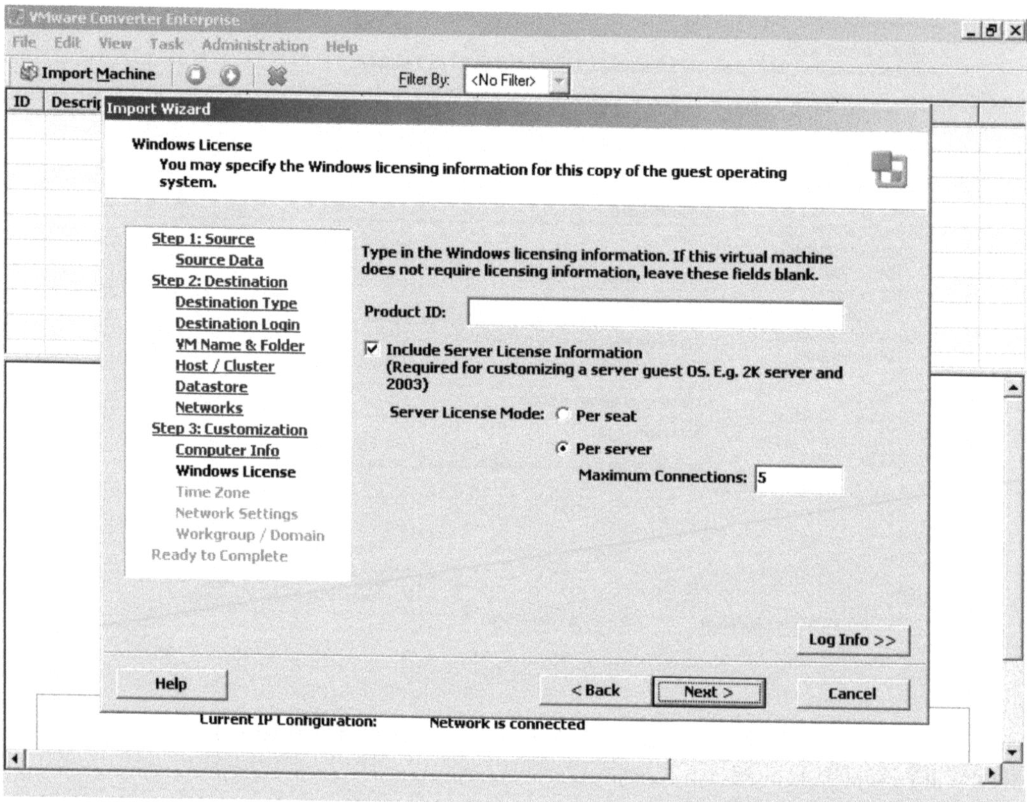

Figure 8.70 Converter Enterprise Boot CD Import Wizard Customization License Information

The next step allows you to input a valid windows license. If your VM does not require a license or you plan on adding it later then you should leave the box blank. You can also configure the License server information on this screen as shown in Figure 8.70. Click on the Next button to continue.

Step 17. Time Zone screen.

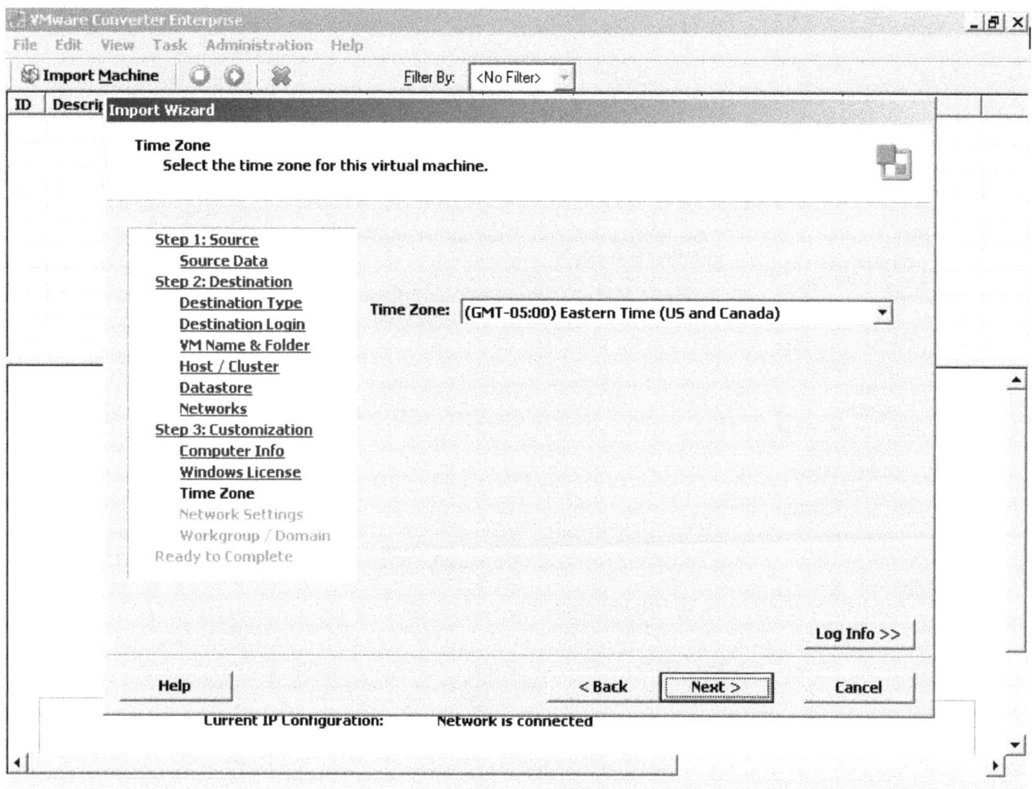

Figure 8.71 Converter Enterprise Boot CD Import Wizard Customization Time Zone

Figure 8.71 illustrates the time zone drop down menu that you should set for the new VM. Click on the Next button to continue.

Step 18. Network Interface Settings screen.

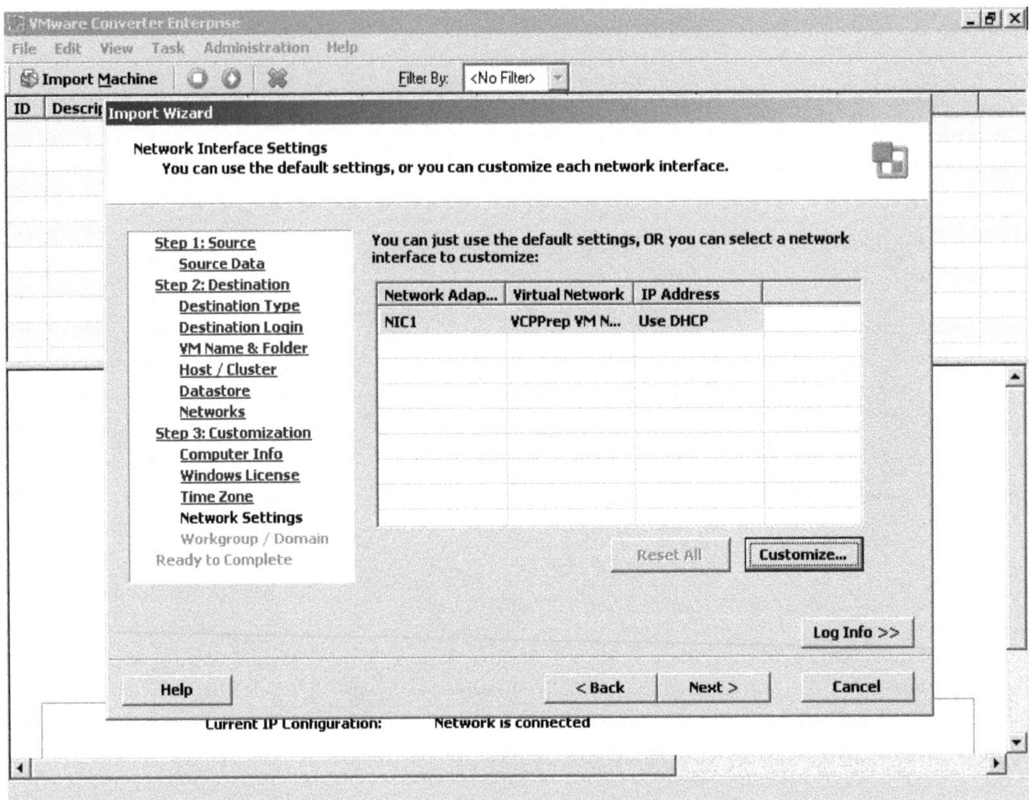

Figure 8.72 Converter Enterprise Boot CD Import Wizard Customization Network Settings

You can set the configuration for the VM's network interface in the Network Interface Settings screen as shown in Figure 8.72. Click on the Customize button if you don't want the VM to get its network configuration via DHCP.

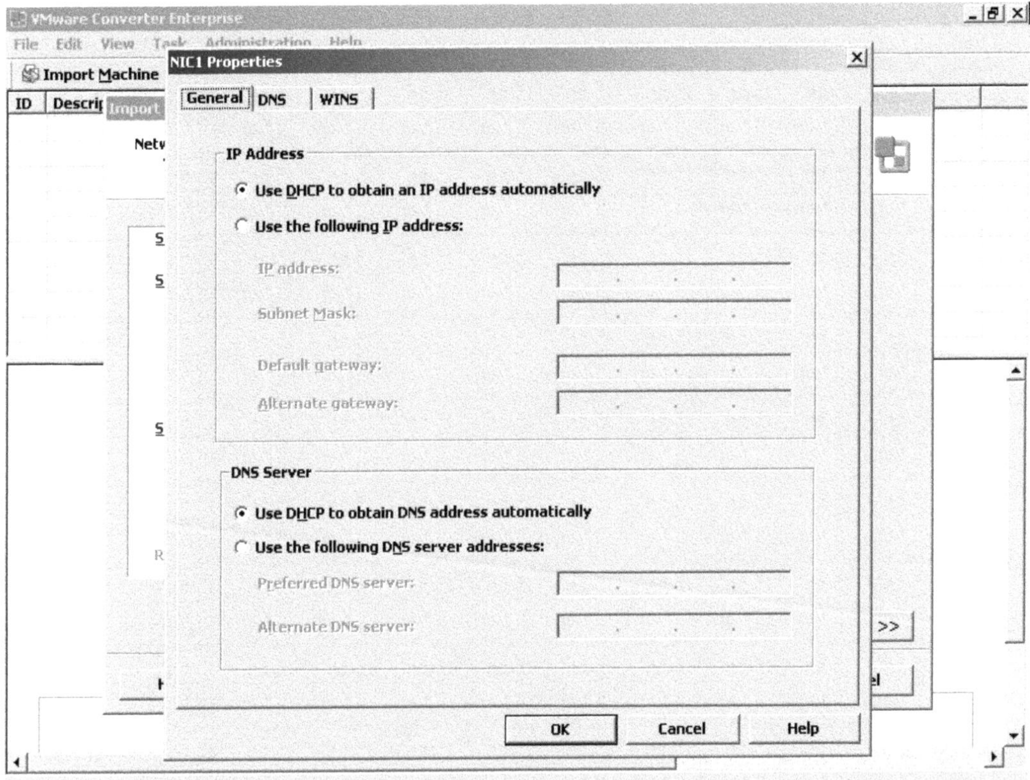

Figure 8.73 Converter Enterprise Boot CD Import Wizard Customization Network Settings General Tab

The Properties window for the virtual NIC will now appear and you can configure the IP address settings as well as configuring the DNS server settings as shown in Figure 8.73. Click on the OK button to return to the previous screen.

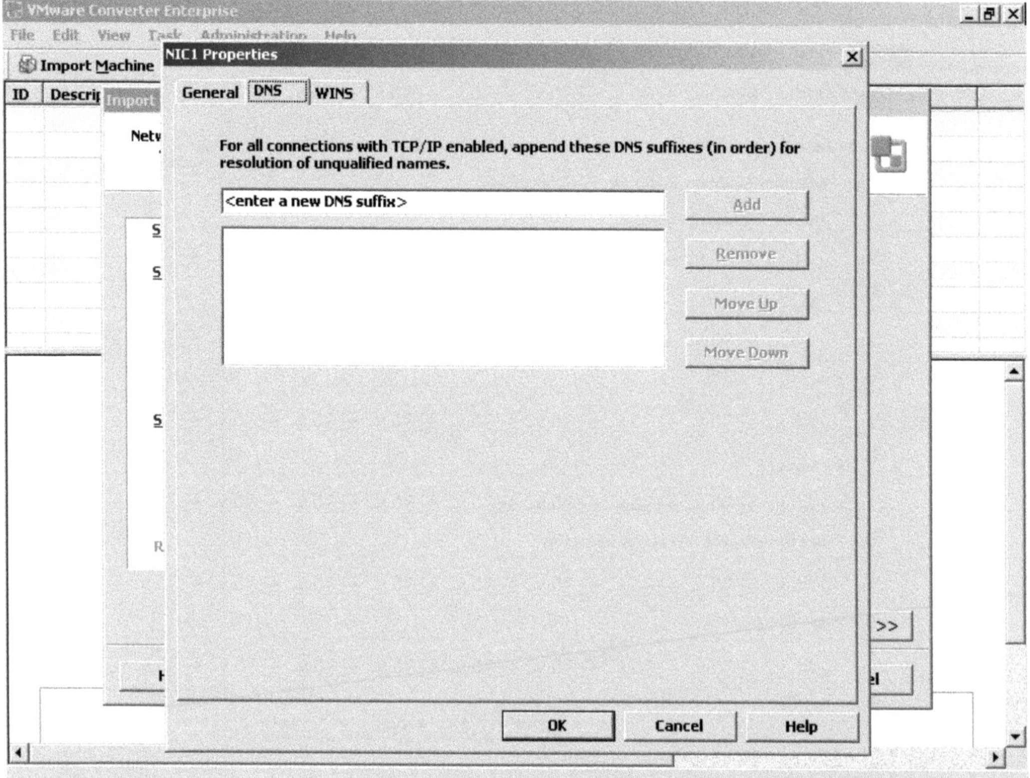

Figure 8.74 Converter Enterprise Boot CD Import Wizard Customization Network Settings DNS Tab

By selecting the DNS tab in the NIC Properties window as shown in Figure 8.74, you can set the guest OS's DNS configuration information.

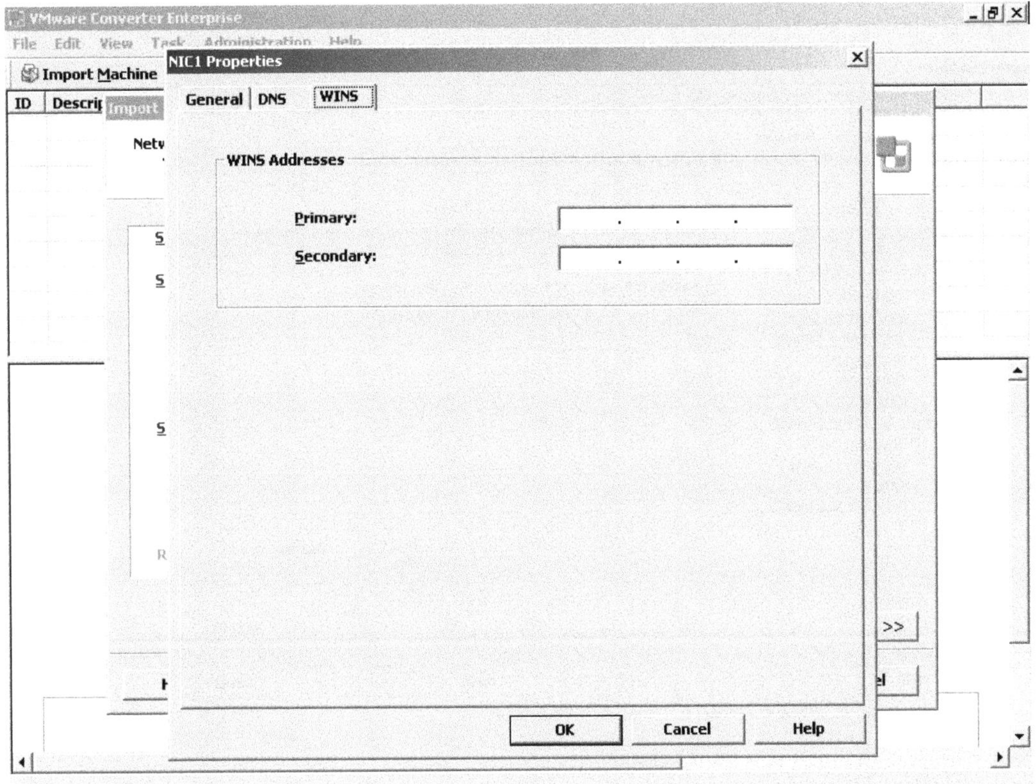

Figure 8.75 Converter Enterprise Boot CD Import Wizard Customization Network Settings WINS Tab

By selecting the WINS tab in the NIC Properties window as shown in Figure 8.75, you can set the guest OS's WINS addresses. Click on the OK button to return to the previous screen.

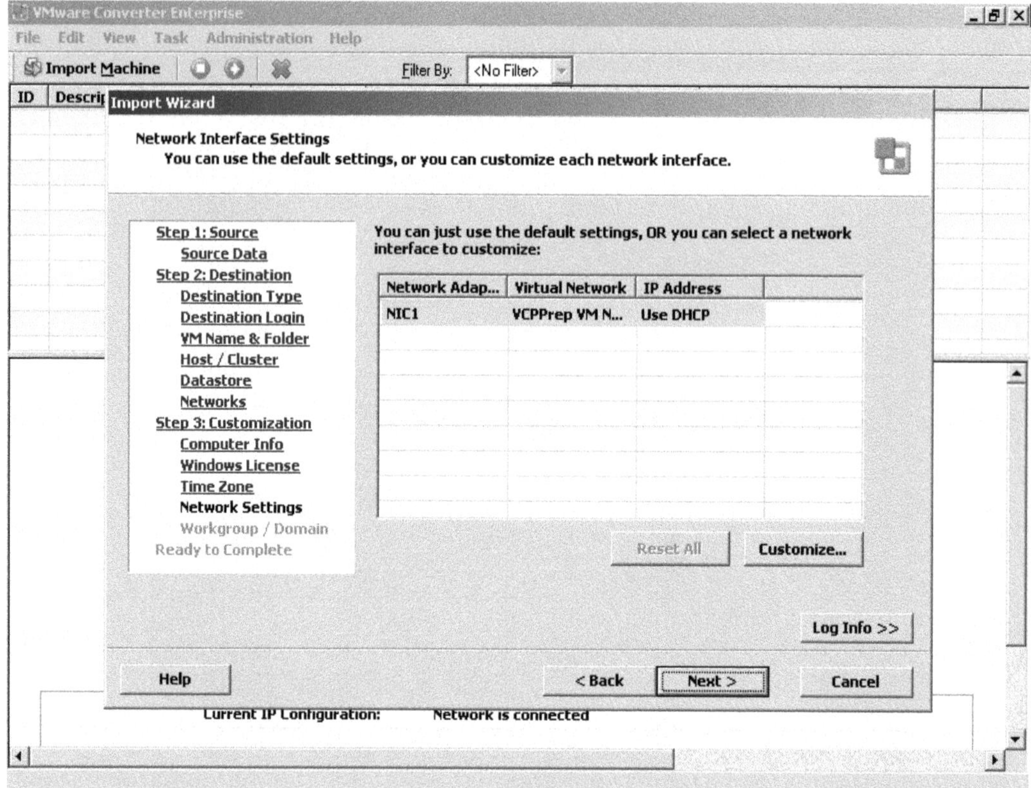

Figure 8.76 Converter Enterprise Boot CD Import Wizard Customization Network Settings Modified

The settings you set in the Properties window will appear in this screen as shown in Figure 8.76. Click on the Next button to continue.

Step 19. Workgroup or Domain screen.

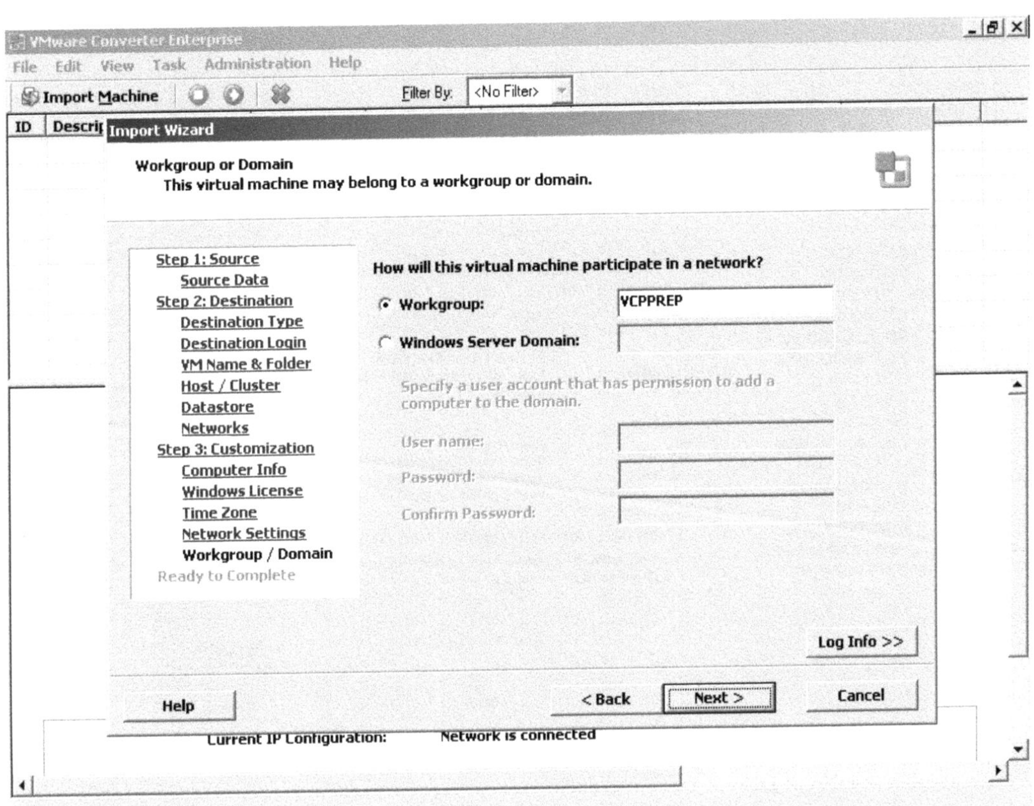

Figure 8.77 Converter Enterprise Boot CD Import Wizard Customization Workgroup Or Domain

You can set the Windows OS Workgroup name or the name of the Windows Server Domain that the VM will be a part of. Click on the Next button to continue.

Step 20. Ready to Complete screen.

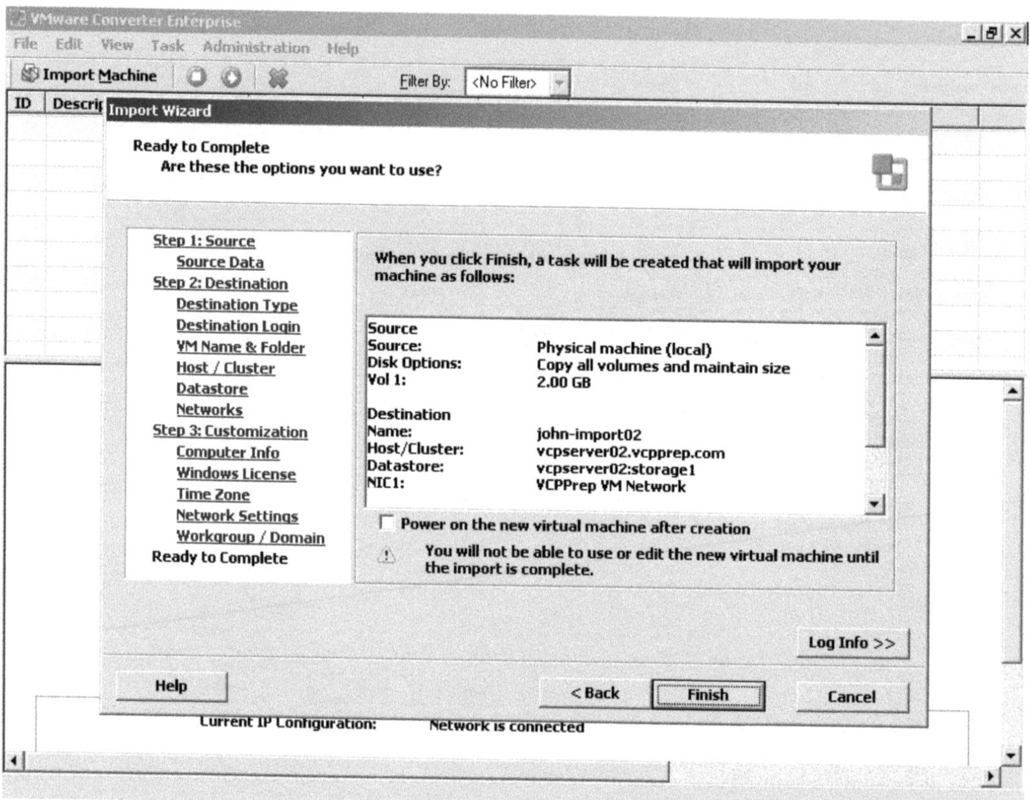

Figure 8.78 Converter Enterprise Boot CD Import Wizard Customization Ready To Complete

You will see a summary of all of your choices in the cold cloning wizard process in this screen as shown in Figure 8.78. You can also select the check box to power on the new VM after it has been created. Click on the Finish button to continue.

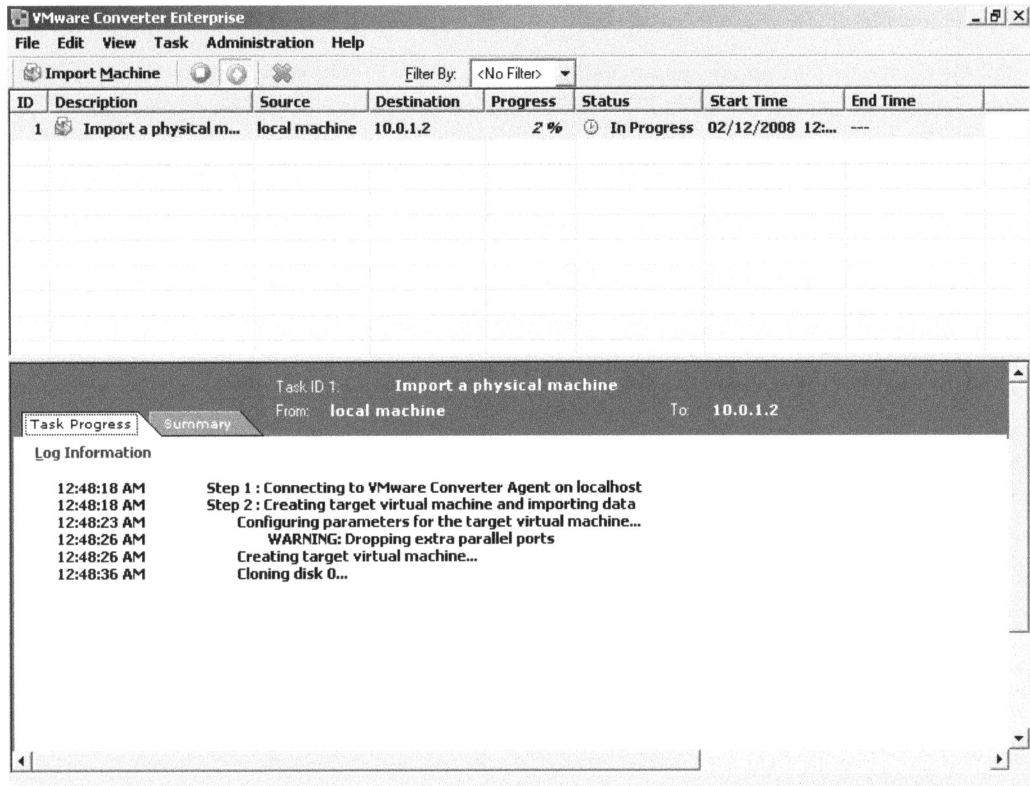

Figure 8.79 Converter Enterprise Boot CD Virtual Machine Import Task Progress

You will be able to see the progress of the cold clone in the VMware Converter Enterprise Task Progress tab.

Converter Enterprise CLI

The Converter Enterprise CLI is automatically installed using the default options when installing VirtualCenter 2.5. It can also be installed on a separate Windows or Linux machine that has access to Converter Enterprise server. To install Converter Enterprise CLI on a Windows machine, start the Converter installation executable and select the Custom option. This will allow an installation for just the CLI Converter tool which requires 36 MB of free space. The following Windows operating systems are supported:

- Windows Vista 32 - bit
- Windows Vista 64 - bit
- Windows XP Professional 32 - bit
- Windows XP Professional 64 - bit
- Windows 2003 32 - bit
- Windows 2003 64 - bit

- Windows 2000

To install the Converter CLI on a Linux operating system, 195 MB of storage space is required. The Converter Enterprise installer is Windows based so it cannot be used for Linux installations. A separate download is available that contains the Linux installer. It can be obtained from the following URL:

http://www.vmware.com/download/vi/

The following Linux operating systems are supported:

- SUSE Linux Enterprise Server version 10
- Red Hat Enterprise Linux version 5

After the installation is complete, the converter-tool command can be used to submit reconfiguration, import and export jobs. Authenticating to a Converter Enterprise server is necessary. Jobs submitted using the converter-tool are described in XML files that are based on the p2v.xsd XML schema. There are sample XML files provided by the installation process. Sample XML files are provided for different types of conversion jobs such as importing, exporting or reconfigurations and the different types of sources and destinations. Issuing the converter-tool command without any arguments produces the following output on the command line:

C:\converter-tool

converter-tool version 4.0.0 build-62386

--help This help page.

--jE arg

--jobExec arg jobDescription.xml Execute a job synchronously.

--jS arg

--jobSubmit arg jobDescription.xml Submit a job to a Converter Server to run asynchronously.

--jQ arg

--jobQuery arg jobId Query the status of a job.

--jC arg

--jobCancel arg jobId Cancel a job.

--jW arg

--jobWait arg jobId Wait for an asynchronous job to complete before returning.

--jG

--jobGetAll Return a list of all jobs for the current user.

--jV arg

--jobValidate arg jobDescription.xml Validate a job without running it.

--jI arg

--jobSourceInspect arg jobDescription.xml Retrieve extended information on a source machine.

--oS arg

--ovrSourceCreds arg user[:password] Override / Specify credentials for a source machine.

--oT arg

--ovrTargetCreds arg user[:password] Override / Specify credentials for a target machine.

--oD arg

--ovrDomainCreds arg user[:password] Override / Specify credentials for a Windows Domain (used for customization only).

--oF arg

--ovrOutputFile arg output.xml Redirect XML output to a file instead of the console.

--vH arg

--vcHost arg hostname[:port] Specify a VC host.

--vC arg

--vcCreds arg user[:password] Specify credentials for a VC host.

Additional command reference information can be found in the following location:

http://www.vmware.com/pdf/vi3_vec_10_admin_guide.pdf

Troubleshooting Converter Enterprise

Conversions performed with Converter Enterprise can incur problems due to hardware details being modified from the physical machine to the virtual machine. Some applications may be dependent on physical hardware attributes such as manufacture or serial numbers. After the conversion process, disk devices can have different model information, network adapters can be different as well as the MAC address. Graphics card and CPU device information can be altered too. These changes may effect applications that are licensed based off of hardware specific information.

Some of the common errors during hot cloning operations are Windows NT and Windows 2000 physical machines not rebooting. These two operating systems require a reboot after the Converter Agent has been installed. If the reboot fails, the conversion will not be successful. Also, the Windows Volume Shadow Copy service is needed in order to successfully snapshot the physical machine's drive(s). Without this service, the conversion operation fails. The proper ports need to be opened on the target machine. These are port 139 and 445. In addition, ports 902 and 443 need to be opened on any firewalls between the Converter Enterprise server and the VirtualCenter server. Networking mis-configurations in the physical environment such as DNS errors or routing errors can cause remote cloning operations to fail.

The logs for the conversion process are found by clicking on the Log Info button shown in the lower right of the window as shown in Figure 8.14. These logs are not permanently stored so they should be reviewed as soon as conversion problems occur.

VMware Converter Enterprise can import to a DRS enabled cluster only if its settings are set to manual. Partially automated or fully automated DRS settings are not supported.

If the installation of the Converter Enterprise server hangs, check to see if the VirtualCenter 2.5 server that the failed installation is using is not already configured to use an existing Converter Enterprise server. A VirtualCenter 2.5 server can only have one Converter Enterprise server configured to use it.

Review the VMware Converter Enterprise release notes for the most up to date information regarding known issues. The release notes can be found at the following URL:

http://vmware.com/support/vi3/doc/vi3_vec_10_rel_notes.html

External References

VMware Converter Download page:

http://www.vmware.com/products/converter/get.html

VMware Converter 3.x Documentation:

http://www.vmware.com/support/pubs/converter_pubs.html

Sample Test Questions

1. An organization hires a consultant to perform a virtualization analysis of their datacenter. Twenty physical machines are identified as good virtualization candidates. The consultant will use VMware Converter Enterprise to perform the consolidation tasks. Which of the following cloning methods will be possible?

a. Local Cloning

b. Encrypted Cloning

c. Hot Cloning

d. Secure Cloning

e. Cold Cloning

2. An attempt to cold clone a physical machine using VMware Converter Enterprise Boot CD has failed. The error is suspected to be a driver problem with the local storage device. Which tool provided by VMware can be used to make modifications to the Converter Enterprise Boot CD image?

a. winpe-patch

b. converter-tool

c. update-boot

d. peTool

e. vmboot

3. VMware Converter Enterprise consists of several components. Which of the following are components of VMware Converter Enterprise?

a. Converter Enterprise CLI

b. Converter Enterprise Analysis Service

c. Converter Enterprise Agent

d. Converter Enterprise Server

e. Converter Enterprise Reporting Service

4. A remote hot cloning operation has failed. The system administrator suspects that the necessary ports are not open on the target physical machine. Which of the following ports should the administrator verify are open?

a. 449

b. 445

c. 139

d. 131

e. 802

5. A physical database server is planned to be cold cloned using VMware Enterprise Converter. When providing the Import Wizard the necessary information to clone the machine, which of the following disk cloning methods can be used?

a. sparse-based cloning

b. volume-based cloning

c. monolithic-based cloning

d. raw-based cloning

e. disk-based cloning

6. Support personnel are inquiring about third party backup images being converted into virtual machines. The ESX administrator responds by providing the supported third party images that can be converted using VMware Converter Enterprise. Which of the following are the supported third party images?

a. Symantec Backup Exec System Recovery

b. Acronis True Image

c. Norton Ghost - Must be version 9 and higher

d. DriveImage XML

e. StorageCraft ShadowProtect

7. Tina is the ESX administrator tasked with converting several physical machines on the network. The VirtualCenter 2.5 server is also a VMware Converter Enterprise server. She has just installed the VI Client to the local workstation and logged onto the VirtualCenter 2.5 server. Which of the following additional steps must be performed prior to beginning the physical to virtual conversions?

a. Reboot the local workstation

b. Download and install the VI Client Converter plugin

c. Start the conversion service on the local workstation

d. Enable the VI Client Converter plugin

e. Register the local workstation with the Converter Enterprise server

8. A physical machine containing a RAID-5 volume will be converted using VMware Converter Enterprise. Which method of cloning will need to be used in order to accomplish this task?

a. Hot cloning

b. Cold cloning

c. Remote cloning

d. Local cloning

e. Standalone cloning

9. A software developer suggests using an existing virtual machine for troubleshooting a support issue. This would save time in resolving the issue however, the virtual machine was created with a hosted application. Testing would need to be done within a managed VI3 environment in order to properly reproduce the support issue. Which of the following hosted application virtual machines can be converted and used in a ESX environment?

a. VMware Player

b. VMware Workstation

c. VMware ACE

d. VMware Fusion

e. VMware Server

f. VMware GSX Server

10. Having the VI Client enabled with the Converter Enterprise plugin will provide which of the following menu options within the VirtualCenter 2.5 inventory?

a. Reconfigure

b. Hot clone

c. Cold clone

d. Convert

e. P2V

Sample Test Solutions

1. An organization hires a consultant to perform a virtualization analysis of their datacenter. Twenty physical machines are identified as good virtualization candidates. The consultant will use VMware Converter Enterprise to perform the consolidation tasks. Which of the following cloning methods will be possible?

a. Local Cloning

b. Encrypted Cloning

c. Hot Cloning

d. Secure Cloning

e. Cold Cloning

Answer: a, c and e - Local cloning is possible in the above scenario using VMware Converter Enterprise. The standalone version of Converter Enterprise can be downloaded from VMware's website and installed onto the physical machine that is to be converted. Hot cloning can be performed on a running physical machine either locally or remotely across the network. Cold cloning can be performed using the VMware Converter Enterprise Boot CD. This method requires downtime of the physical machine but may be the preferred method when file system consistency is a concern. Cloning operations using VMware Converter Enterprise does not include security mechanisms such as encryption.

2. An attempt to cold clone a physical machine using VMware Converter Enterprise Boot CD has failed. The error is suspected to be a driver problem with the local storage device. Which tool provided by VMware can be used to make modifications to the Converter Enterprise Boot CD image?

a. winpe-patch

b. converter-tool

c. update-boot

d. peTool

e. vmboot

Answer: d - peTool can be used to make modifications to the VMware Converter Enterprise Boot CD image. A listing of the arguments that can be passed to this tool can be obtained by issuing the following command from a command prompt on the VMware Converter Enterprise server:

peTool -h

3. VMware Converter Enterprise consists of several components. Which of the following are components of VMware Converter Enterprise?

a. Converter Enterprise CLI

b. Converter Enterprise Analysis Service

c. Converter Enterprise Agent

d. Converter Enterprise Server

e. Converter Enterprise Reporting Service

Answer: a, c and d - VMware Converter Enterprise consists of the following three components:

- ***Converter Enterprise Server***
- ***Converter Enterprise Agent***
- ***Converter Enterprise CLI***

The VMware Converter Enterprise server facilitates that conversions process and communicates with the VirtualCenter 2.5 server. The Converter Enterprise Agent is responsible for initiating the snapshot of the target machine disk volume(s), preparing the virtual machine on the destination ESX server and copying the snapshot volume(s) to the destination ESX server. Converter Enterprise CLI is a component that can be used to initiate conversion tasks from the command line. This tool can be installed on a separate system from the VMware Converter Enterprise server.

4. A remote hot cloning operation has failed. The system administrator suspects that the necessary ports are not open on the target physical machine. Which of the following ports should the administrator verify are open?

a. 449

b. 445

c. 139

d. 131

e. 802

Answer: b and c - Ports 139 and 445 are necessary for cloning operations to successfully succeed. Port 445 is used for Server Message Block (SMB) protocol over TCP. SMB is typically used for file sharing in Windows 2003 server, Windows XP and Windows 2000 environments. Port 139 in a Windows NT environment is used to implement SMB on top of NetBT (NetBIOS over TCP/IP).

5. A physical database server is planned to be cold cloned using VMware Enterprise Converter. When providing the Import Wizard the necessary information to clone the machine, which of the following disk cloning methods can be used?

a. sparse-based cloning

b. volume-based cloning

c. monolithic-based cloning

d. raw-based cloning

e. disk-based cloning

Answer: b and e - When cold cloning, the import wizard allows either disk-based or volume-based cloning. The following two radio buttons are provided during the Import Wizard in order to chose the disk cloning method as shown in Figure 8.56:

- *Import all disks and maintain size (Disk-based)*
- *Select volumes and resize to save or add space (Volume-based)*

6. Support personnel are inquiring about third party backup images being converted into virtual machines. The ESX administrator responds by providing the supported third party images that can be converted using VMware Converter Enterprise. Which of the following are the supported third party images?

a. Symantec Backup Exec System Recovery

b. Acronis True Image

c. Norton Ghost - Must be version 9 and higher

d. DriveImage XML

e. StorageCraft ShadowProtect

Answer: a, b, c and e - Symantec Backup Exec System Recovery and Norton Ghost version 9 or higher, Acronis True Image and StorageCraft ShadowProtect can be converted to virtual machine format using VMware Converter Enterprise.

7. Tina is the ESX administrator tasked with converting several physical machines on the network. The VirtualCenter 2.5 server is also a VMware Converter Enterprise server. She has just installed the VI Client to the local workstation and logged onto the VirtualCenter 2.5 server. Which of the following additional steps must be performed prior to beginning the physical to virtual conversions?

a. Reboot the local workstation

b. Download and install the VI Client Converter plugin

c. Start the conversion service on the local workstation

d. Enable the VI Client Converter plugin

e. Register the local workstation with the Converter Enterprise server

Answer: b and d - The VI Client on the local workstation will require the Converter Enterprise plugin to be downloaded, installed and enabled prior to performing conversions. Doing so enables the VI Client to display the necessary options in the GUI menus for conversion operations.

8. A physical machine containing a RAID-5 volume will be converted using VMware Converter Enterprise. Which method of cloning will need to be used in order to accomplish this task?

a. Hot cloning

b. Cold cloning

c. Remote cloning

d. Local cloning

e. Standalone cloning

Answer: c - Cold cloning would be necessary. This is due to the RAID-5 volume. This type of volume requires disk-based cloning which is only available with cold cloning.

9. A software developer suggests using an existing virtual machine for troubleshooting a support issue. This would save time in resolving the issue however, the virtual machine was created with a hosted application. Testing would need to be done within a managed VI3 environment in order to properly reproduce the support issue. Which of the following hosted application virtual machines can be converted and used in a ESX environment?

a. VMware Player

b. VMware Workstation

c. VMware ACE

d. VMware Fusion

e. VMware Server

f. VMware GSX Server

Answer: a,b,c,d,e and f - Several hosted application based virtual machines can be converted using VMware Converter Enterprise's V2V capabilities. The following is the list of supported hosted applications:

- ***VMware Player***
- ***VMware Workstation***
- ***VMware ACE***
- ***VMware Fusion***
- ***VMware Server***
- ***VMware GSX Server***
- ***VMware ESX Server***
- ***Virtual PC***
- ***Microsoft Virtual Server***

10. Having the VI Client enabled with the Converter Enterprise plugin will provide which of the following menu options within the VirtualCenter 2.5 inventory?

a. Reconfigure

b. Hot clone

c. Cold clone

d. Convert

e. P2V

Answer: a - The VI Client when properly configured with the Converter Enterprise plugin, provides a menu option to Reconfigure virtual machines. This menu option can be used to configure existing virtual machines with new settings such as networking, time zone, license information and SID.

Chapter 9

Guided Consolidation

After reading this chapter you should be able to complete the following tasks:

- Understand Guided Consolidation components
- Configure Guided Consolidation services
- Perform Guided Consolidation discovery
- Understand Guided Consolidation analysis
- Understand Guided Consolidation and Converter Enterprise integration

Guided Consolidation Components

Guided Consolidation is a new feature in VirtualCenter 2.5. It is a subset of functionality found in VMware's Capacity Planner service. The benefit it provides is in facilitating the process of virtualizing physical servers in the datacenter for small to medium sized organizations. A step-by-step process is followed to guide new users with the tasks of consolidating the physical servers in the datacenter. There is no need to perform a separate installation as Guided Consolidation is included as part of the default installation process of VirtualCenter 2.5. Guided Consolidation uses the following two services:

- Capacity Planner Service
- VMware Converter Enterprise Service

The Capacity Planner service is used to collect usage information of the discovered physical machines. Usage data is collected once an hour. The VMware Converter Enterprise service is used to perform the planned consolidation tasks (i.e. physical to virtual conversions.) A detailed discussion of VMware Converter Enterprise can be found in Chapter 8 – Converter Enterprise.

Using Guided Consolidation from within the VI Client simply entails following a three step procedure. The following are the three essential steps performed when using Guided Consolidation:

- Discovery
- Analyze
- Consolidate

Let's take a look at each of these three steps:

Discovery

During the discovery step, physical systems need to be selected and added to the analysis list. This step is not possible unless at least one datacenter object exists in the VirtualCenter inventory. In addition, at least one ESX host needs to be registered with VirtualCenter.

The list of machines to discover is provided by Microsoft LAN Manager or an Active Directory server. Without either of these implemented within the Windows network environment, discovery cannot perform its tasks. It is not possible to discover machines located in multiple Active Directory sources. The target machines must be located within domains from a single Active Directory source. There is no facility in which to filter machines being discovered. Once discovered, this information is cached so that subsequent lists are built more quickly. The list can be sorted if needed. The system queries for new systems every half hour and new domains every 24 hours. A large amount of cached information can adversely impact the performance of the VirtualCenter server. VMware recommends not running Guided Consolidation on more than 20,000 systems without clearing the cache. We will discuss how to clear the cache in the troubleshooting section at the end of this chapter.

Analysis

The analysis process involves the collection of resource metrics, which are stored on the VirtualCenter 2.5 server. No agent is required to be installed on the discovered physical machines to accomplish this task. The information is collected by using Windows Management Instrumentation (WMI) and Remote Registry. WMI provides an interface for collecting data from Windows systems. Remote Registry is a Windows service that allows access to Windows registry settings. A maximum of 100 systems can be analyzed at the same time. It is necessary to have the following ports open on the physical system where data is being collected:

- 445
- 139
- 138
- 137
- 135

Guided Consolidation samples usage metrics for CPU, memory and disk I/O along with the number of physical NICs in the target system. Collected statistics are used to determine which ESX server to place the virtual machine on once the physical system has been consolidated. Guided Consolidation offers a confidence metric rating based off of the time period of the collected data to help users choose an ESX destination server to host the newly converted virtual machine. The longer the time frame for collecting information, the higher the confidence rating. A high confidence rating may occur even after only collecting data for a 24 hour period. The time frame used to analyze the physical systems should be determined by the individual workloads placed on the physical system by its running applications. Some applications may only require a day, some a week and others a month or longer depending on the workload cycles of the applications. In other words, it is important to obtain not only the average workload but also the bigger picture including the low and high peak usage periods as well.

Consolidate

The plan consolidation button is used to begin the consolidation process. VMware Converter Enterprise is used to accomplish the conversion tasks. Converter Enterprise can be installed on the VirtualCenter 2.5 server or on a separate server. It is recommended to only perform one consolidation process at a time due to system resources and storage capacity. Virtual disks may be resized during the conversion process to conserve datastore space. A consolidated machine will never have a virtual disk size smaller than 4GB. Guided Consolidation conversions can only be performed on Windows machines. Refer to Chapter 8 – Converter Enterprise, to obtain a list of supported guest operating systems.

Guided Consolidation Services Configuration

Administrator privileges are needed on the VirtualCenter host. The collector service needs to run with local administrator privileges and must also be granted the Logon as a service privilege. These privileges are necessary to access both WMI and the Remote Registry service on the discovered physical systems. If Active Directory is deployed on the network, the credentials to run the collector service must have domain privileges to query the Active Directory database. This is necessary for both analysis and consolidation (converter) operations.

The first time using Guided Consolidation, the user will be prompted for the consolidation settings. A VirtualCenter Consolidation Initial Setup Wizard is launched that guides the user through the process of configuring authentication credentials. The Service Credentials (used during analysis) and Default Credentials (used when no credentials are entered when adding machines to be analyzed) can be defined in this wizard.

These authorization credentials can also be set or modified without the Consolidation Initial Setup Wizard. To do so, configure the Guided Consolidation Services as follows:

Step 1. Select the Consolidation Settings option from the Administration pull-done menu (Figure 9.1).

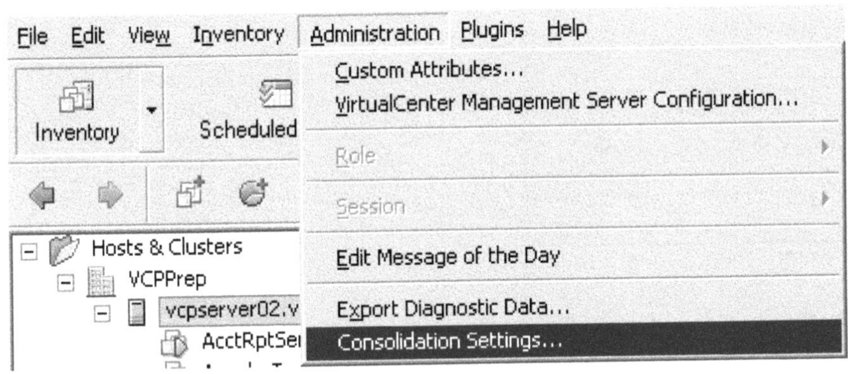

Figure 9.1 Guided Consolidation Configuration Settings Menu Option

Step 2. In the Consolidation Configuration window Credentials tab, select the Change button to configure the service. (Figure 9.2)

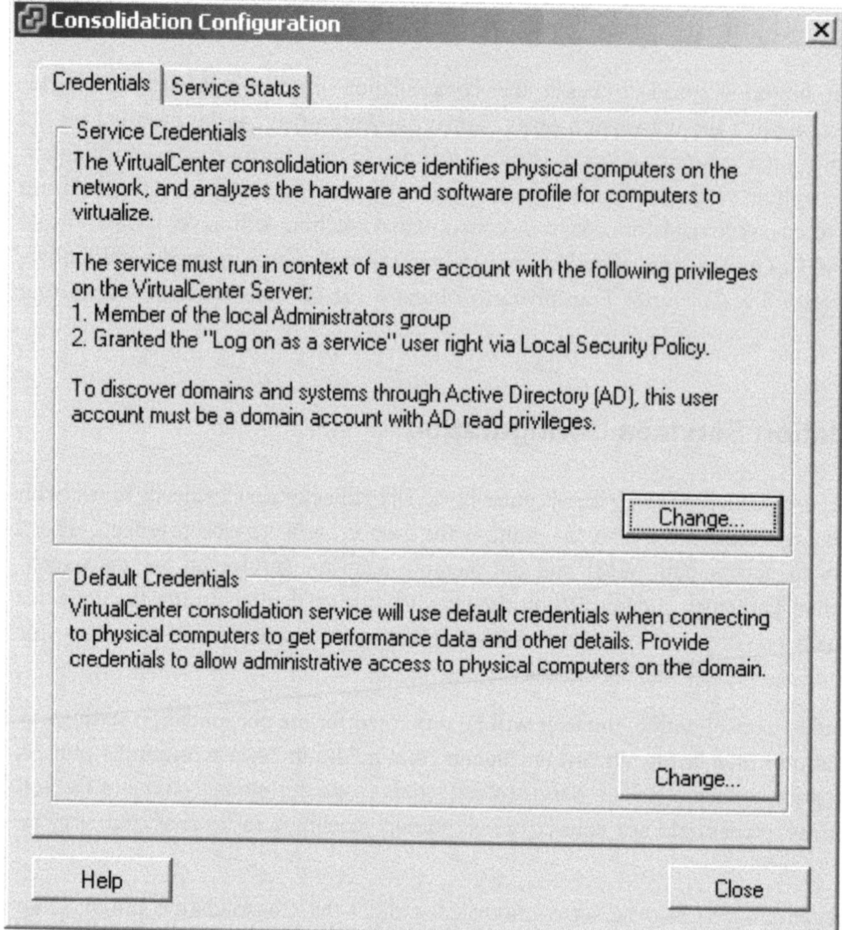

Figure 9.2 Guided Consolidation Configuration Credentials Tab

Step 3. In the Enter Credentials window you will need to provide the username of an account in the Administrators group, and enter the account's password.

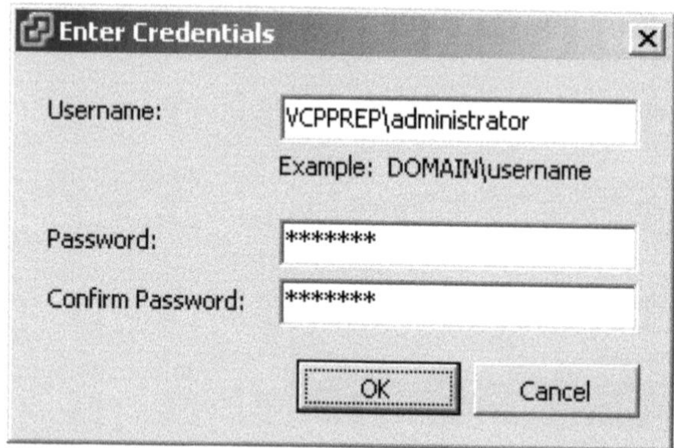

Figure 9.3 Guided Consolidation Enter Credentials Tab

Click on the OK button to continue (Figure 9.3).

Step 4. By clicking on the Service Status tab in the Consolidation Configuration window you will see what consolidation services are currently running in the VirtualCenter 2.5 server.

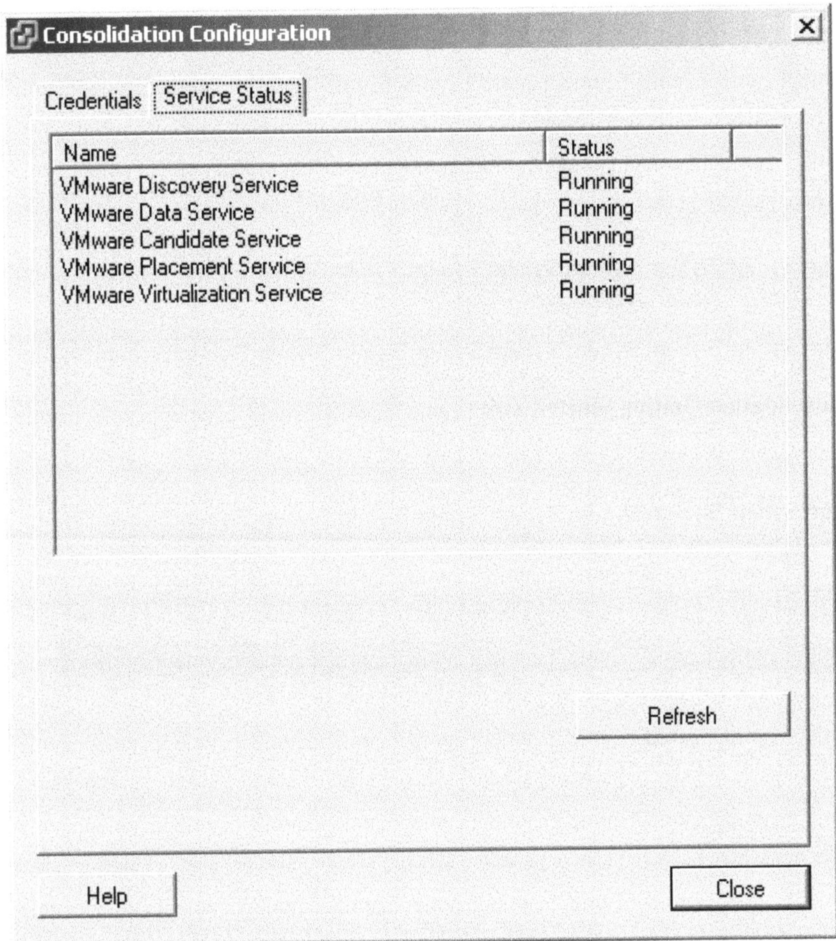

Figure 9.4 Guided Consolidation Configuration Service Status Tab

Click on the Close button to finish (Figure 9.4).

Guided Consolidation Discovery Process

To start the Guided Consolidation Discovery Process, do the following:

Step 1. In the Getting Started tab select the Learn more about Consolidation link to bring up the online help.

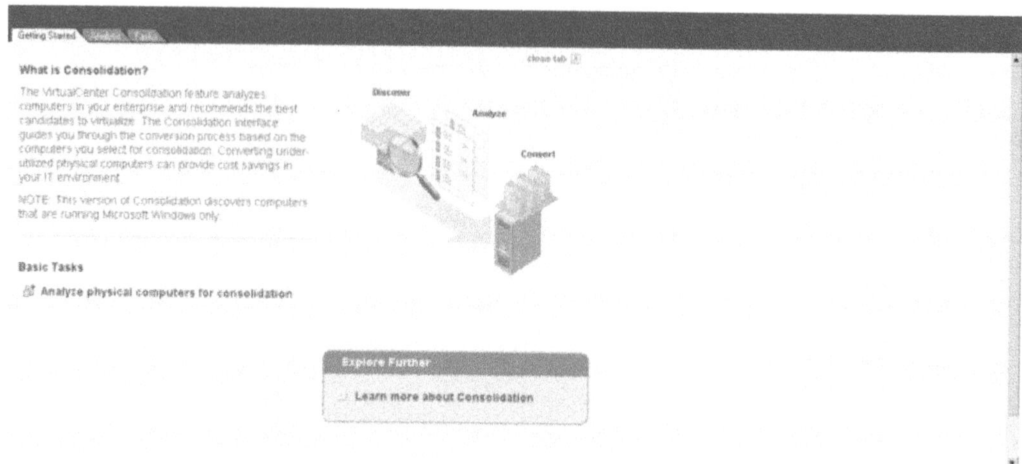

Figure 9.5 Guided Consolidation Getting Started Tab

Step 2. Select the Analysis tab (Figure 9.5).

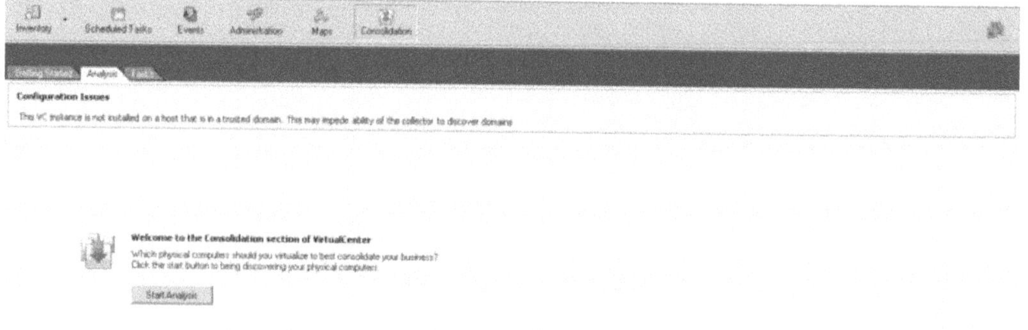

Figure 9.6 Guided Consolidation Getting Analysis Tab

Click on the Start Analysis button to start the process (Figure 9.6).

Step 3. In the Add to Analysis window select the domains that contain systems that you want to be analyzed. (Figure 9.7)

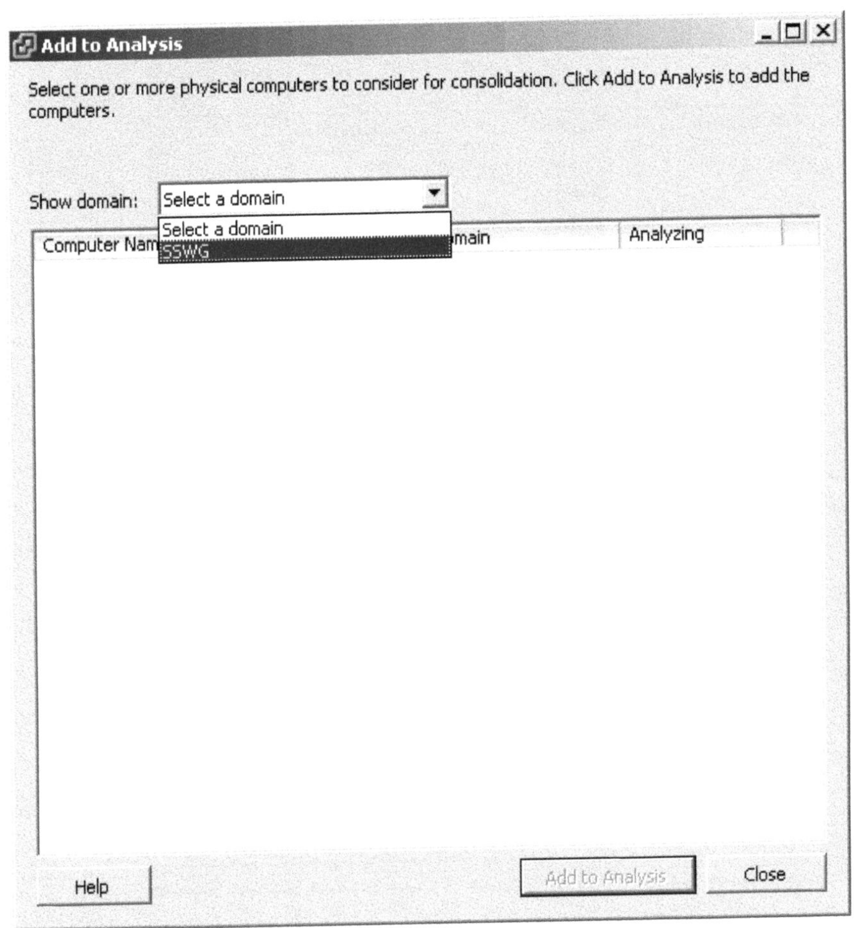

Figure 9.7 Guided Consolidation Add To Analysis Domain Selection

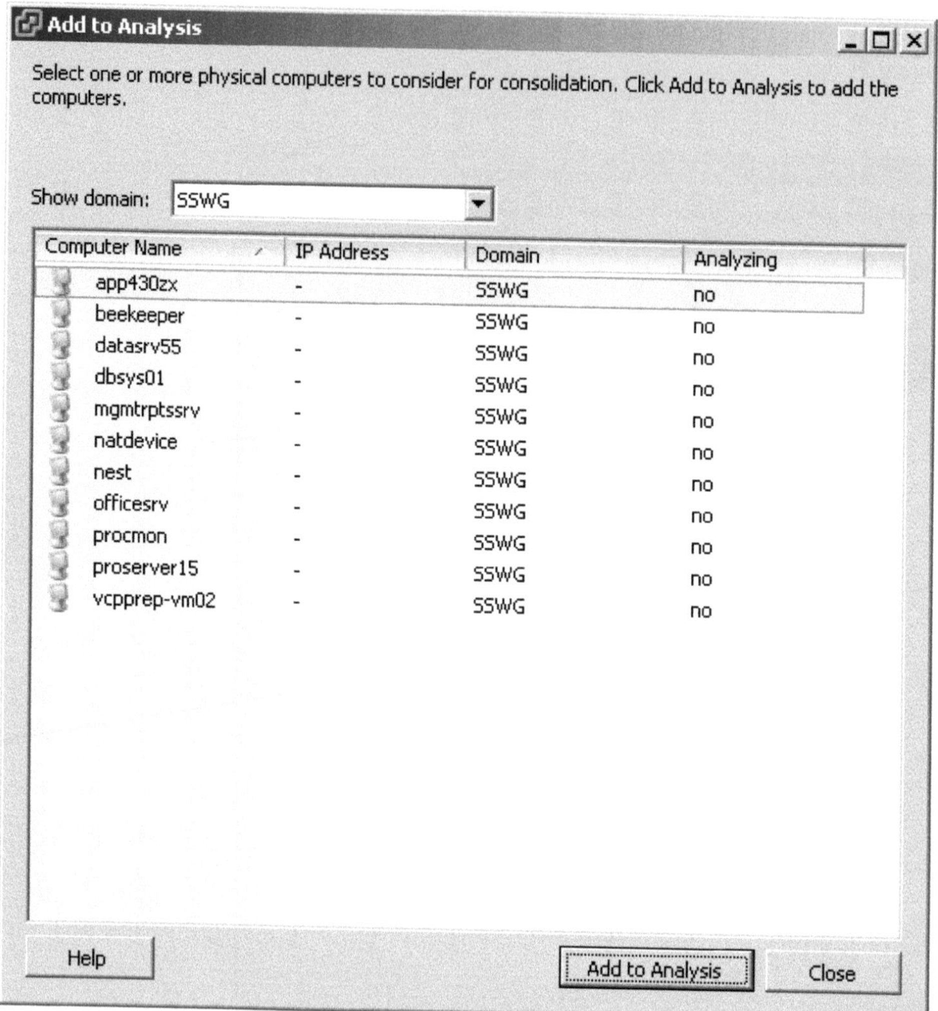

Figure 9.8 Guided Consolidation Add To Analysis

Step 4. Select the systems that you want the analysis process to determine if it is a candidate for virtualization. After selecting the system in the list, click on the Add to Analysis button (Figure 9.8).

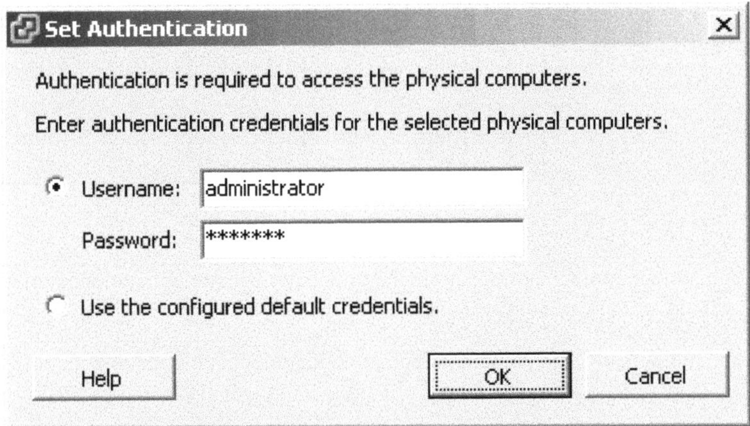

Figure 9.9 Guided Consolidation Add To Analysis Set Authentication

Step 5. In the Set Authentication window, provide the authentication information to access the selected systems. Click on the OK button to continue (Figure 9.9).

Guided Consolidation Analysis

Once the guided consolidation analysis process is under way you can view the progress in the Analysis as shown in Figure 9.10.

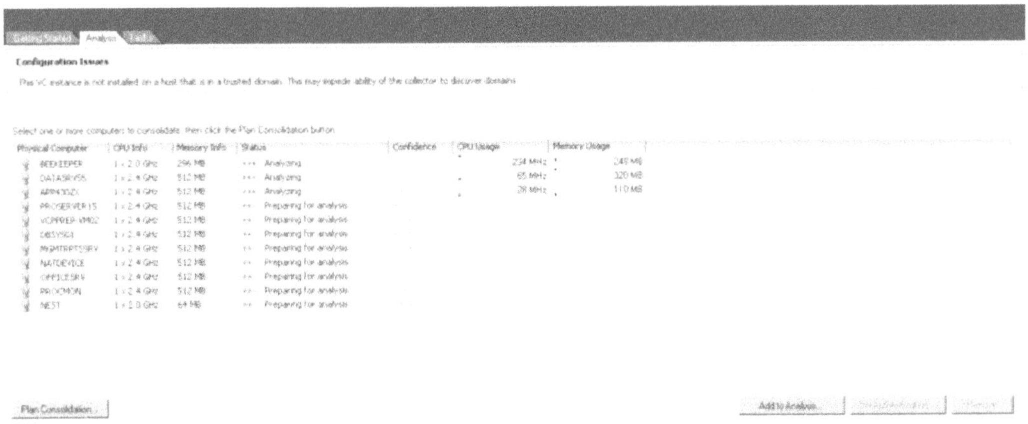

Figure 9.10 Guided Consolidation Analysis Tab Preparing To Analyze

The physical systems that have been designated to be analyzed are listed along with information about the CPUs and memory as well as usage information on these resources. The status of the process is also shown.

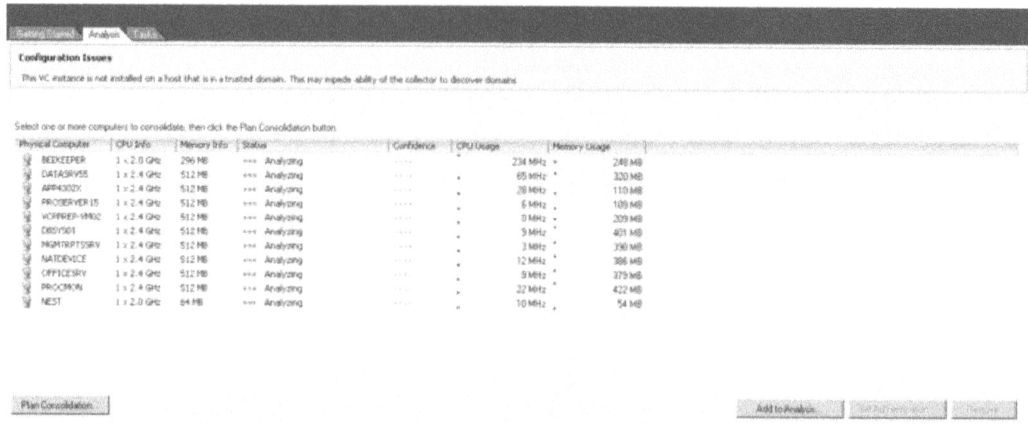

Figure 9.11 Guided Consolidation Analysis Tab Analyzing

Figure 9.11 shows that all systems are currently being analyzed.

Figures 9.12, 9.13 and 9.14 show the output of the Analysis tab as the analysis process progresses. The Low, Medium and High confidence values are displayed in the output. The higher the confidence value, the more accurate the resource estimates will be.

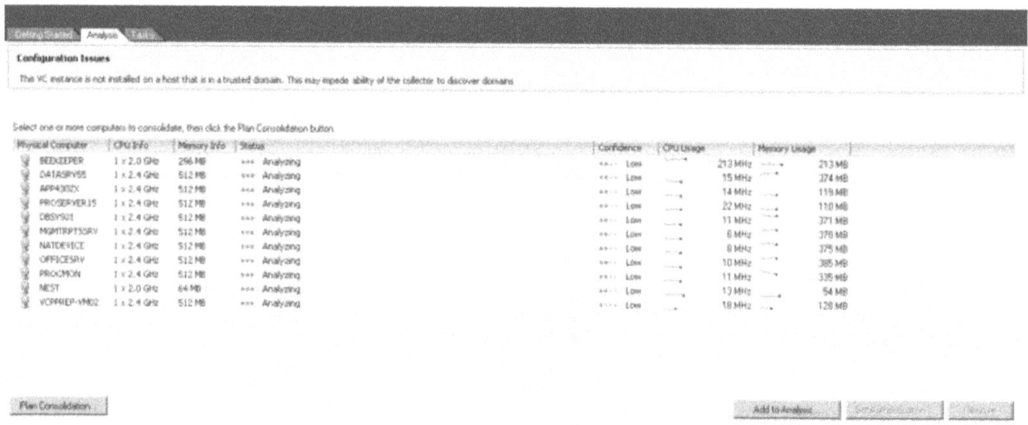

Figure 9.12 Guided Consolidation Analysis Tab Confidence Rating Low

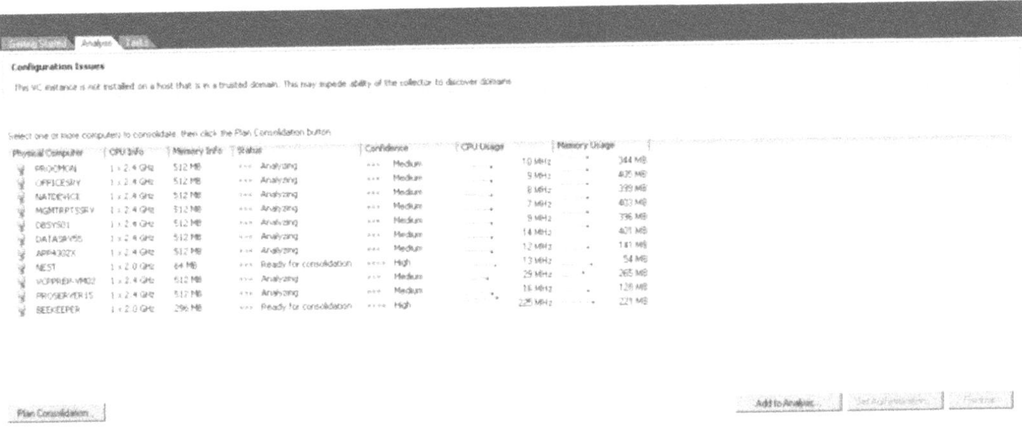

Figure 9.13 Guided Consolidation Analysis Tab Confidence Rating Medium

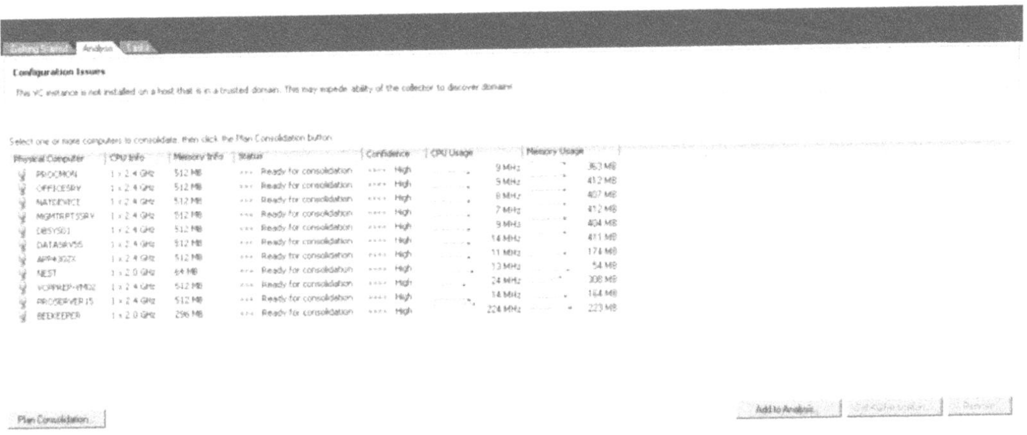

Figure 9.14 Guided Consolidation Analysis Tab Confidence Rating High

Guided Consolidation and Converter Enterprise Integration

After you have run the analysis process and determined the resource needs for the VMs that you want to create, the Consolidation Plan window will list the physical servers and the proposed ESX 3.5 servers to place the new VMs on as shown in Figure 9.15.

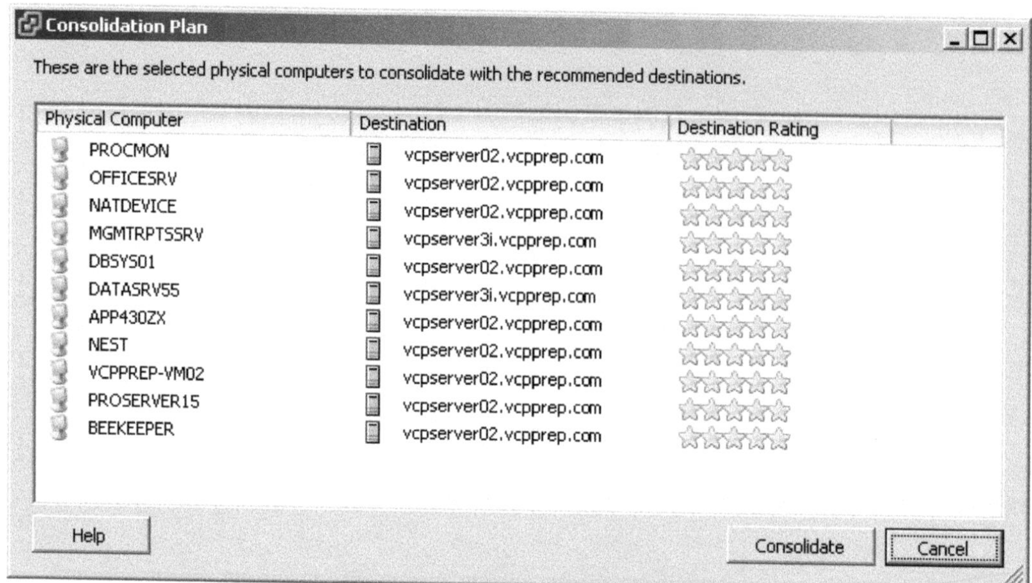

Figure 9.15 Guided Consolidation Plan for Multiple Physical Machines

The Analysis tab shows the status of all of the physical servers that are now ready to consolidate into a new VM. The Status column shown in Figure 9.16 shows that they are all ready to consolidate. Click on the physical server and then click the Consolidation Plan button to start the consolidation process for that physical server.

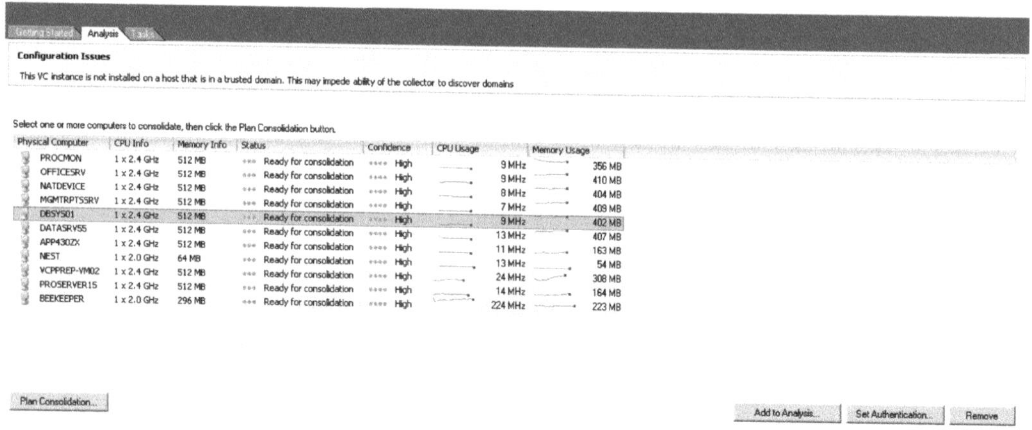

Figure 9.16 Guided Consolidation Analysis Tab Select Physical Machine To Consolidate

Figure 9.17 shows the Consolidation Plan window. In Figure 9.15 the physical server named "DBSYS01" was selected and now it is listed in the Consolidation Plan window. The ESX servers that are deemed a good candidate for the placement of the new VM to be created are listed in the drop-down menu. Make your selection and click on the Consolidate button.

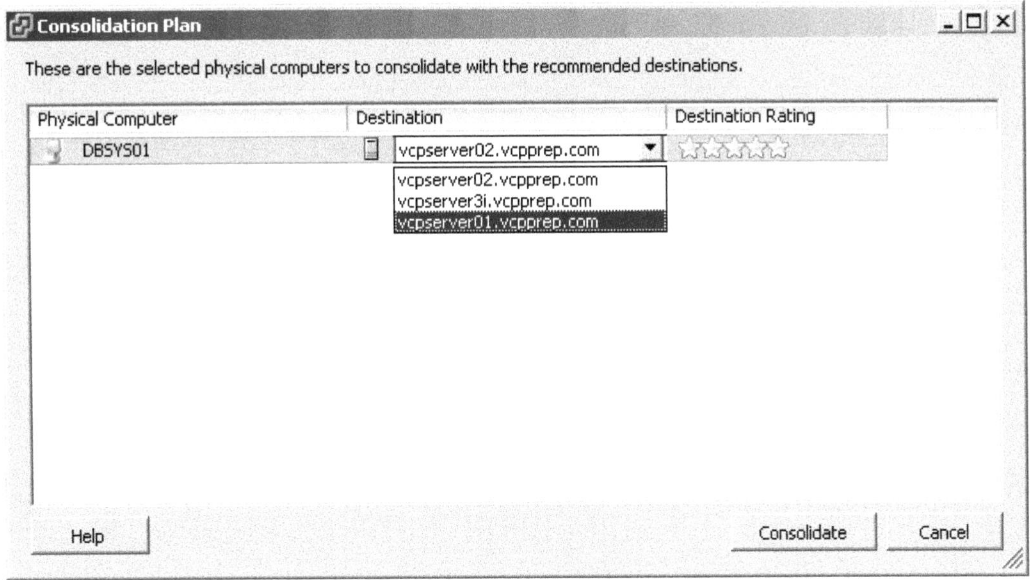

Figure 9.17 Guided Consolidation Plan

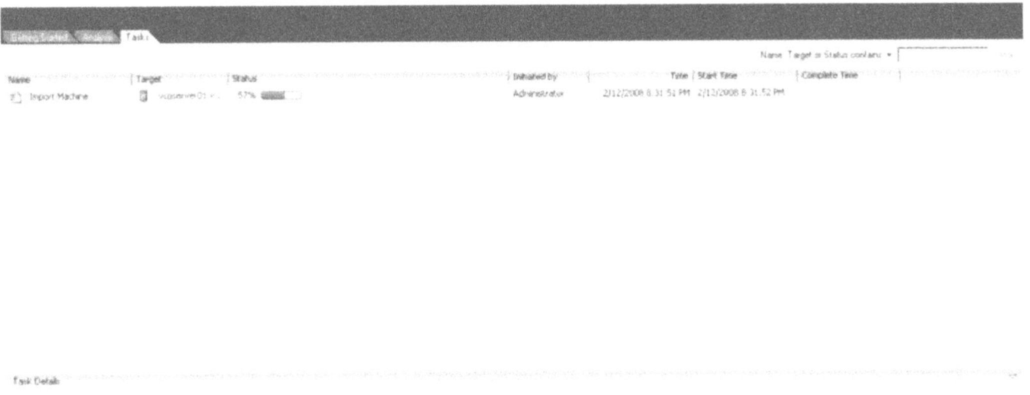

Figure 9.18 Guided Consolidation Tasks Tab Import Progress Status

The tasks tab shown in Figure 9.18 show the current consolidation tasks and their progress .

Once the process is completed the Tasks tab will reflect that in the Status column. The new VM will now be able to be managed using VirtualCenter or accessed directly on the ESX server (see Figure 9.19).

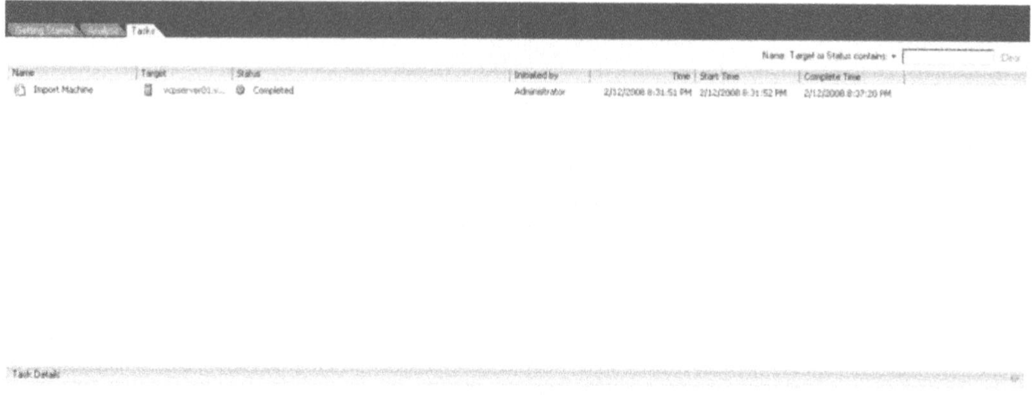

Figure 9.19 Guided Consolidation Tasks Tab Import Completed

Troubleshooting Guided Consolidation

It is important to identify for which of the three steps the error is occurring; discovery, analysis or consolidation the problem is occurring in. Doing so should reduce the time to identify the root cause of the problem. Discovery issues can occur from improper user credentials provided for the Capacity Planner service. Mis-configurations within the switched network could present connectivity issues. Name resolution errors may prevent discovery or inconsistencies within the directory service.

Analysis issues may be caused by inadequate permissions as well. Proper ports need to be opened on the target system and possibly on firewall residing in between the VirtualCenter server and the target systems. These ports include the following:

- 445
- 139
- 138
- 137
- 135

Check to ensure that both WMI and Remote Registry are available on the target system.

Consolidation errors with VMware Converter Enterprise may result for example from insufficient authorization, necessary ports not open or blocked by a firewall and network misconfigurations. Please refer to the troubleshooting section in Chapter 8 – Converter Enterprise for more information.

VMware recommends not running Guided Consolidation on more than 20,000 systems without clearing the cache as this may degrade VirtualCenter performance. To clear the Guided Consolidation cache and disable this service, from within the VI Client, select the Administration menu option in the top menu bar. Then select the VirtualCenter Management Server Configuration menu option. Next, select Advanced Options and click the Add Row button. The following should be entered into the Key field:

dontStartConsolidation

The value placed into the Value field should be as follows:

true

Once this has been performed, the VirtualCenter server should be restarted. To disable Consolidation without clearing the cache, uninstall the collector service. There is no need to restart the VirtualCenter Server.

External References

Details of What's New and Improved in VMware Infrastructure 3 version 3.5:

http://www.vmware.com/support/vi3/doc/whatsnew_esx35_vc25.html

Basic System Administration - ESX Server 3.5, ESXi version 3.5, VirtualCenter 2.5:

http://www.vmware.com/pdf/vi3_35/esx_3/r35/vi3_35_25_admin_guide.pdf

Sample Test Questions

1. Jaclyn is the senior systems engineer for a small start up company that has recently implemented a VI3 virtualization environment. She notices that when attempting to use Guided Consolidation, the analysis of the physical machines fails. Which of the following services does Guided Consolidation use?

a. Capacity Planner Service

b. RemoteVI Service

c. Capacity Enterprise Service

d. VMware Converter Enterprise Service

e. VMware Discovery Service

2. Guided Consolidation consists of a series of steps to complete the process. Which of the following steps is a part of Guided Consolidation?

a. Report Generation

b. Consolidation

c. Discovery

d. Identification

e. Analysis

3. A physical machine that is converted by Guided Consolidation will not create a virtual disk with a size less than which of the following?

a. 5 GB

b. 6 GB

c. 3 GB

d. 2 GB

e. 4 GB

4. The data collection that is performed by Guided Consolidation is set to occur at which of the following intervals?

a. 5 minute

b. 60 minute

c. 25 minute

d. 15 minute

e. 15 minute

5. A problem has occurred with a physical accounting system being analyzed with Guided Consolidation. The ESX administrator suspects the root cause is related to the firewall application running on the target system. Which of the following ports are required to be open when using Guided Consolidation?

a. 445

b. 137

c. 139

d. 135

e. 138

Sample Test Solutions

1. Jaclyn is the senior systems engineer for a small start up company that has recently implemented a VI3 virtualization environment. She notices that when attempting to use Guided Consolidation, the analysis of the physical machines fails. Which of the following services does Guided Consolidation use?

a. Capacity Planner Service

b. RemoteVI Service

c. Capacity Enterprise Service

d. VMware Converter Enterprise Service

e. VMware Discovery Service

Answer: a and d - The following are the two services utilized by Guided Consolidation:

- ***Capacity Planner Service***
- ***VMware Converter Enterprise Service***

The Capacity Planner service is used to collect usage information of the discovered physical machines. Usage data is collected once an hour. The VMware Converter Enterprise service is used to perform the planned consolidation tasks (i.e. physical to virtual conversions.) A detailed discussion of VMware Converter Enterprise can be found in Chapter 8 – Converter Enterprise.

2. Guided Consolidation consists of a series of steps to complete the process. Which of the following steps is a part of Guided Consolidation?

a. Report Generation

b. Consolidation

c. Discovery

d. Identification

e. Analysis

Answer: b, c and e - Using Guided Consolidation from within the VI Client simply entails following a three step procedure. The following are the three essential steps performed when using Guided Consolidation:

- ***Discovery***
- ***Analyze***
- ***Consolidate***

3. A physical machine that is converted by Guided Consolidation will not create a virtual disk with a size less than which of the following?

a. 5 GB

b. 6 GB

c. 3 GB

d. 2 GB

e. 4 GB

Answer: e - A consolidated machine will never have a virtual disk size smaller than 4GB.

4. The data collection that is performed by Guided Consolidation is set to occur at which of the following intervals?

a. 5 minute

b. 60 minute

c. 25 minute

d. 15 minute

e. 15 minute

Answer: b - Data collection occurs once every 60 minutes.

5. A problem has occurred with a physical accounting system being analyzed with Guided Consolidation. The ESX administrator suspects the root cause is related to the firewall application running on the target system. Which of the following ports are required to be open when using Guided Consolidation?

a. 445

b. 137

c. 139

d. 135

e. 138

Answer: a, b, c, d, and e - It is necessary to have the following ports open on the physical system where data is being collected:

- ***445***
- ***139***
- ***138***
- ***137***
- ***135***

Chapter 10

Permissions and Rights

After reading this chapter you should be able to complete the following tasks:

- Access methods for the Virtual Infrastructure
- Understand and configure VirtualCenter authentication
- Understand VirtualCenter predefined roles and associated privileges
- Configure users and groups to access VirtualCenter
- Building custom roles
- Understand privilege propagation in the VirtualCenter inventory
- Understand and configure ESX 3.5 Server authentication
- Understand ESX 3.5 Server predefined roles and associated privileges
- Configure users and groups to access an ESX 3.5 Server
- Building custom roles
- Understand privilege propagation in an ESX 3.5 Server
- Troubleshooting Common Permissions and Rights problems

Virtual Infrastructure Access Methods

There are five ways to access your virtual infrastructure:

1. Using the VI Client to access the ESX 3.5 server directly
2. Using the CLI interface to access the ESX 3.5 server directly
3. Using the web interface to access the ESX 3.5 server directly
4. Using the VI Client to access the ESX 3.5 server using VirtualCenter
5. Using the web interface to access the ESX 3.5 server using VirtualCenter

VirtualCenter Authentication

In order to be able to access VirtualCenter you must have either a user account on the Windows system or Windows VM or be authenticated using Microsoft Active Directory services. Once the user account exists in the Windows environment, it can be configured to access VirtualCenter.

For more information on authenticating using AD read Enabling Active Directory Authentication with

ESX Server: http://www.vmware.com/pdf/esx3_esxcfg_auth_tn.pdf

VirtualCenter Predefined Roles and Associated Privileges

VirtualCenter includes nine predefined roles. The collection of a given set of privileges constitutes a role. Roles are a convenient method of assigning privileges to single users and groups of users. An ESX administrator equipped with an understanding of the purpose of each of the predefined roles will be able to quickly and efficiently apply access permissions within the VirtualCenter inventory.

VirtualCenter provides two types of roles, system and sample. System roles and their privileges are permanent; these cannot be modified or removed. The following are the system roles:

- No Access
- Read-Only
- Administrator

Sample roles serve as examples of common privilege sets. The sample roles can be modified or removed as needed. The following are the sample roles:

- Virtual Machine User
- Virtual Machine Power User
- Virtual Machine Administrator
- Resource Pool Administrator
- Datacenter Administrator
- VMware Consolidated Backup User

The predefined roles are built from a set of categories. Each category has a set of associated privileges. Some categories contain subcategories. VirtualCenter provides the following thirteen categories and subcategories of privileges:

- Global
- Folder
- Datacenter
- Datastore
- Network
- Host
    - Inventory
    - Configuration
    - Local Operations
    - CIM
- Virtual Machine
    - Inventory
    - Interaction

    - Configuration
    - State
    - Provisioning

- Resource
- Alarms
- Scheduled Task
- Sessions
- Performance
- Permissions
- Extension
- VMware Update Manager
    - Configure
    - Manage Updates
    - Manage Baseline

The following describes the predefined roles and their complete set of privileges:

No Access Role

Users assigned the No Access system role on an object are unable to view or modify the object. In addition, users will not be able to view content in the VI Client tabs associated with the object. This role is the default role for all users with the exception of those users in the Administrators group.

Read-Only Role

Users assigned the Read-Only system role will be able to view the state and details of an object. VI Client menus and toolbar actions are disabled. All tabs within the VI Client are accessible except the console tab.

Administrator Role

Users assigned the Administrator system role are given all privileges for all the objects within the VirtualCenter inventory. This is the default role for users of the Administrators group. The following lists the entire privilege set for the Administrator role:

Global Category:

- Manage Custom Attributes
- Set Custom Attribute
- Log Event
- Cancel Task
- Licenses

- Diagnostics
- Settings
- VC Server

Folder Category:

- Create Folder
- Delete Folder
- Rename Folder
- Move Folder

Datacenter Category:

- Create Datacenter
- Remove Datacenter
- Rename Datacenter
- Move Datacenter

Datastore Category:

- Rename File
- Remove Datastore
- Browse Datastore
- Remove File

Network Category:

- Remove

Host Inventory Subcategory:

- Add Standalone Host
- Create Cluster
- Add Host To Cluster
- Remove Host
- Move Cluster/Standalone Host
- Rename Cluster
- Remove Cluster
- Modify Cluster
- Move Host

Host Configuration Subcategory:

- Connection
- Maintenance
- Virtual Machine Auto-start Configuration

- HyperThreading
- Storage Partition Configuration
- Security Profile and Firewall
- Memory Configuration
- Network Configuration
- Advanced Settings
- System Resource Allocation
- Change SNMP settings

Host Local Operations Subcategory:

- Add host to VirtualCenter
- Manage User Groups
- Create Virtual Machine
- Delete Virtual Machine

Host CIM Subcategory:

- CIM Interaction

Virtual Machine Inventory Subcategory:

- Create
- Remove
- Move

Virtual Machine Interaction Subcategory:

- Power On
- Power Off
- Suspend
- Reset
- Answer Question
- Console Interaction
- Device Connection
- Configure CD Media
- Configure Floppy Media
- Tools Install

Virtual Machine Configuration Subcategory:

- Rename
- Add Existing Disk
- Add New Disk
- Remove Disk
- Raw Device
- Change CPU Count

- Memory
- Add or Remove Device
- Modify Device Settings
- Settings
- Change Resource
- Upgrade Virtual Hardware
- Reset Guest Information
- Advanced
- Disk Lease

Virtual Machine State Subcategory:

- Create Snapshot
- Revert To Snapshot
- Remove Snapshot
- Rename Snapshot

Virtual Machine Provisioning Subcategory:

- Customize
- Clone
- Create Template From Virtual Machine
- Deploy Template
- Clone Template
- Mark As Template
- Mark As Virtual Machine
- Read Customization Specifications
- Modify Customization Specification
- Allow Disk Access
- Allow Read-only Disk Access
- Allow Virtual Machine Download
- Allow Virtual Machine Files Upload

Resource Category:

- Assign Virtual Machine To Resource Pool
- Apply Recommendation
- Create Pool
- Rename Pool
- Modify Pool
- Move Pool
- Remove Pool
- Migrate
- Relocate
- Query VMotion

Alarms Category:

- Create Alarm
- Remove Alarm
- Modify Alarm

Scheduled Task Category:

- Create Tasks
- Remove Task
- Run Task
- Modify Task

Sessions Category:

- View and Terminate Sessions
- Global Message

Performance Category:

- Modify Interval

Permissions Category:

- Modify Role
- Reassign Role Permissions
- Modify Permission

Extension Category:

- Register
- Update
- Unregister

VMware Update Manager Category:

- Configure
- Manage Updates
- Manage Baseline

Virtual Machine User Role

End users who perform actions only on virtual machines can be assigned to the Virtual Machine User sample role. A user assigned this role can interact with virtual machines but cannot modify the virtual machine configuration. The following lists the entire privilege set for the Virtual Machine User role.

Global Category:

- Cancel Task

Virtual Machine Interaction Subcategory:

- Power On
- Power Off
- Suspend
- Reset
- Answer Question
- Console Interaction
- Device Connection
- Configure CD Media
- Configure Floppy Media
- Tools Install

Scheduled Task Category:

- Create Tasks
- Remove Task
- Run Task
- Modify Task

Virtual Machine Power User Role

An end user needing to perform actions on virtual machines and resource objects can be assigned to the Virtual Machine Power User sample role. This role enables the user to interact and modify several virtual machine configuration settings. The following lists the entire privilege set for the Virtual Machine Power User role:

Global Category:

- Cancel Task

Datastore Category:

- Browse Datastore

Virtual Machine Interaction Subcategory:

- Power On
- Power Off
- Suspend
- Reset

- Answer Question
- Console Interaction
- Device Connection
- Configure CD Media
- Configure Floppy Media
- Tools Install

Virtual Machine Configuration Subcategory:

- Rename
- Add Existing Disk
- Add New Disk
- Remove Disk
- Change CPU Count
- Memory
- Add or Remove Device
- Modify Device Settings
- Settings
- Change Resource
- Upgrade Virtual Hardware
- Reset Guest Information
- Advanced
- Disk Lease

Virtual Machine State Subcategory:

- Create Snapshot
- Revert To Snapshot
- Remove Snapshot
- Rename Snapshot

Scheduled Task Category:

- Create Tasks
- Remove Task
- Run Task
- Modify Task

Virtual Machine Administrator Role

An end user requiring administrator capabilities for virtual machines within VirtualCenter can be assigned the Virtual Machine Administrator role. This role is a highly privileged role that assigns all privileges except for the privileges in the Permissions category. The following lists the entire privilege set for the Virtual Machine Administrator role.

Global Category:

- Manage Custom Attributes
- Set Custom Attribute
- Log Event
- Cancel Task
- Licenses
- Diagnostics
- Settings
- VC Server

Folder Category:

- Create Folder
- Delete Folder
- Rename Folder
- Move Folder

Datacenter Category:

- Create Datacenter
- Remove Datacenter
- Rename Datacenter
- Move Datacenter

Datastore Category:

- Rename File
- Remove Datastore
- Browse Datastore
- Remove File

Network Category:

- Remove

Host Inventory Subcategory:

- Add Standalone Host
- Create Cluster
- Add Host To Cluster
- Remove Host
- Move Cluster/Standalone Host
- Rename Cluster
- Remove Cluster
- Modify Cluster
- Move Host

Host Configuration Subcategory:

- Connection
- Maintenance
- Virtual Machine Auto-start Configuration
- HyperThreading
- Storage Partition Configuration
- Security Profile and Firewall
- Memory Configuration
- Network Configuration
- Advanced Settings
- System Resource Allocation
- Change SNMP settings

Host Local Operations Subcategory:

- Add host to VirtualCenter
- Manage User Groups
- Create Virtual Machine
- Delete Virtual Machine

Virtual Machine Inventory Subcategory:

- Create
- Remove
- Move

Virtual Machine Interaction Subcategory:

- Power On
- Power Off
- Suspend
- Reset
- Answer Question
- Console Interaction
- Device Connection
- Configure CD Media
- Configure Floppy Media
- Tools Install

Virtual Machine Configuration Subcategory:

- Rename
- Add Existing Disk
- Add New Disk
- Remove Disk
- Raw Device

- Change CPU Count
- Memory
- Add or Remove Device
- Modify Device Settings
- Settings
- Change Resource
- Upgrade Virtual Hardware
- Reset Guest Information
- Advanced
- Disk Lease

Virtual Machine State Subcategory:

- Create Snapshot
- Revert To Snapshot
- Remove Snapshot
- Rename Snapshot

Virtual Machine Provisioning Subcategory:

- Customize
- Clone
- Create Template From Virtual Machine
- Deploy Template
- Clone Template
- Mark As Template
- Mark As Virtual Machine
- Read Customization Specifications
- Modify Customization Specification
- Allow Disk Access
- Allow Read-only Disk Access
- Allow Virtual Machine Download
- Allow Virtual Machine Files Upload

Resource Category:

- Assign Virtual Machine To Resource Pool
- Apply Recommendation
- Create Pool
- Rename Pool
- Modify Pool
- Move Pool
- Remove Pool
- Migrate
- Relocate
- Query VMotion

Alarms Category:

- Create Alarm
- Remove Alarm
- Modify Alarm

Scheduled Task Category:

- Create Tasks
- Remove Task
- Run Task
- Modify Task

Sessions Category:

- View and Terminate Sessions
- Global Message

Performance Category:

- Modify Interval

Resource Pool Administrator Role

An administrator responsible for assigning ESX 3.5 server CPU and memory resources can be assigned the Resource Pool Administrator sample role. This role allows a VirtualCenter user the ability to perform actions on several inventory objects including resource delegation. The following lists the entire privilege set for the Resource Pool Administrator role:

Global Category:

- Set Custom Attribute
- Log Event
- Cancel Task

Folder Category:

- Create Folder
- Delete Folder
- Rename Folder
- Move Folder

Datastore Category:

- Browse Datastore

Virtual Machine Inventory Subcategory:

- Create
- Remove
- Move

Virtual Machine Interaction Subcategory:

- Power On
- Power Off
- Suspend
- Reset
- Answer Question
- Console Interaction
- Device Connection
- Configure CD Media
- Configure Floppy Media
- Tools Install

Virtual Machine Configuration Subcategory:

- Rename
- Add Existing Disk
- Add New Disk
- Remove Disk
- Raw Device
- Change CPU Count
- Memory
- Add or Remove Device
- Modify Device Settings
- Settings
- Change Resource
- Upgrade Virtual Hardware
- Reset Guest Information
- Advanced
- Disk Lease

Virtual Machine State Subcategory:

- Create Snapshot
- Revert To Snapshot
- Remove Snapshot
- Rename Snapshot

Virtual Machine Provisioning Subcategory:

- Customize

- Clone
- Create Template From Virtual Machine
- Deploy Template
- Clone Template
- Mark As Template
- Mark As Virtual Machine
- Read Customization Specifications
- Modify Customization Specification
- Allow Disk Access
- Allow Read-only Disk Access
- Allow Virtual Machine Download
- Allow Virtual Machine Files Upload

Resource Category:

- Assign Virtual Machine To Resource Pool
- Create Pool
- Rename Pool
- Modify Pool
- Move Pool
- Remove Pool
- Migrate
- Relocate
- Query VMotion

Alarms Category:

- Create Alarm
- Remove Alarm
- Modify Alarm

Scheduled Task Category:

- Create Tasks
- Remove Task
- Run Task
- Modify Task

Permissions Category:

- Modify Permission

Datacenter Administrator Role

An administrator needing to configure datacenter objects can be assigned to the Datacenter Administrator sample role. A user assigned this role can perform actions on several inventory objects needed to set up a datacenter but will have limited interaction with virtual machines. The following lists the entire privilege set for the Datacenter Administrator role:

Global Category:

- Set Custom Attribute
- Log Event
- Cancel Task

Folder Category:

- Create Folder
- Delete Folder
- Rename Folder
- Move Folder

Datacenter Category:

- Create Datacenter
- Remove Datacenter
- Rename Datacenter
- Move Datacenter

Datastore Category:

- Rename File
- Remove Datastore
- Browse Datastore
- Remove File

Network Category:

- Remove

Host Inventory Subcategory:

- Add Standalone Host
- Create Cluster
- Add Host To Cluster
- Remove Host
- Move Cluster/Standalone Host
- Rename Cluster
- Remove Cluster
- Modify Cluster
- Move Host

Host Configuration Subcategory:

- Connection
- Maintenance
- HyperThreading
- Security Profile and Firewall
- Memory Configuration
- Advanced Settings
- System Resource Allocation
- Change SNMP settings

Virtual Machine Inventory Subcategory:

- Read Customization Specifications
- Modify Customization Specification

Resource Category:

- Assign Virtual Machine To Resource Pool
- Apply Recommendation
- Create Pool
- Rename Pool
- Modify Pool
- Move Pool
- Remove Pool
- Migrate
- Relocate
- Query VMotion

Alarms Category:

- Create Alarm
- Remove Alarm
- Modify Alarm

Scheduled Task Category:

- Create Tasks
- Remove Task
- Run Task
- Modify Task

VMware Consolidated Backup User Role

The VMware Consolidated Backup User sample role allows a user with this role assignment to use the built-in GUI tool, and Snapshot Manager to do VM snapshots. Performing backup operations for

VMs using VCB requires administrative (admin or admin group access on the Windows VCB Proxy Server, or root access on the ESX Server directly, or root privileges through sudo) privileges, as VCB backups are CLI on the Windows Proxy Server and/or ESX Server, not the GUI. Role-based access/privileges are related to GUI operations only with the VI Client through the VC Server. The VMware Consolidated Backup User sample role is a VC Server pre-defined role.

Virtual Machine Configuration Subcategory:

- Disk Lease

Virtual Machine State Subcategory:

- Create Snapshot
- Remove Snapshot

Virtual Machine Provisioning Subcategory:

- Allow Read-only Disk Access
- Allow Virtual Machine Download

VirtualCenter User and Group Access

You must add permissions for users or groups of users to access an object and the objects below it in the inventory hierarchy. The steps to do this process are as follows:

Step 1. Click on the object in the VirtualCenter inventory that you want to add permissions to as shown in Figure 10.1 and select the Add Permission command.

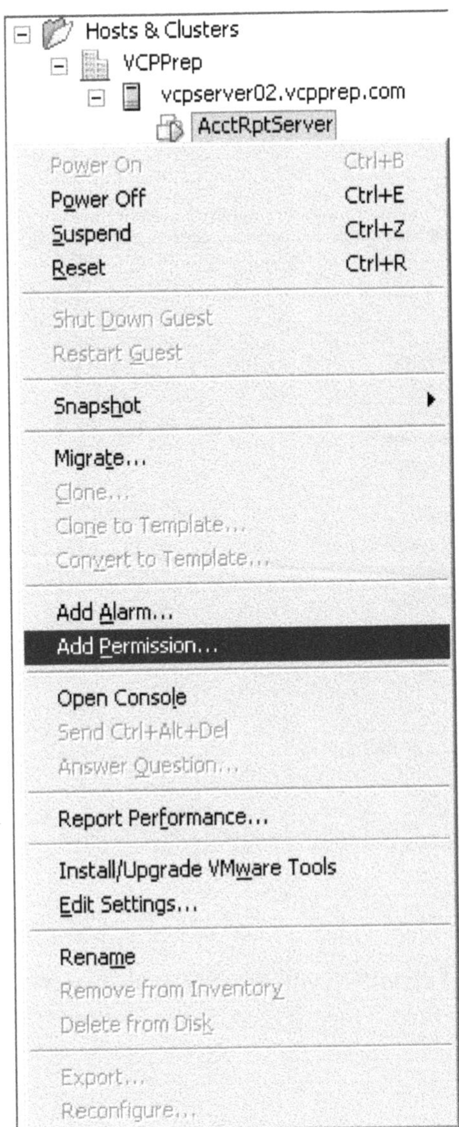

Figure 10.1 Add Permission Menu

If the object is a parent object in the inventory, be aware that the permissions can (by default) propagate downward to children objects from that parent in the inventory.

Step 2. Figure 10.2 shows the Add Permission window which allows you to select the users and groups that will be given these permissions.

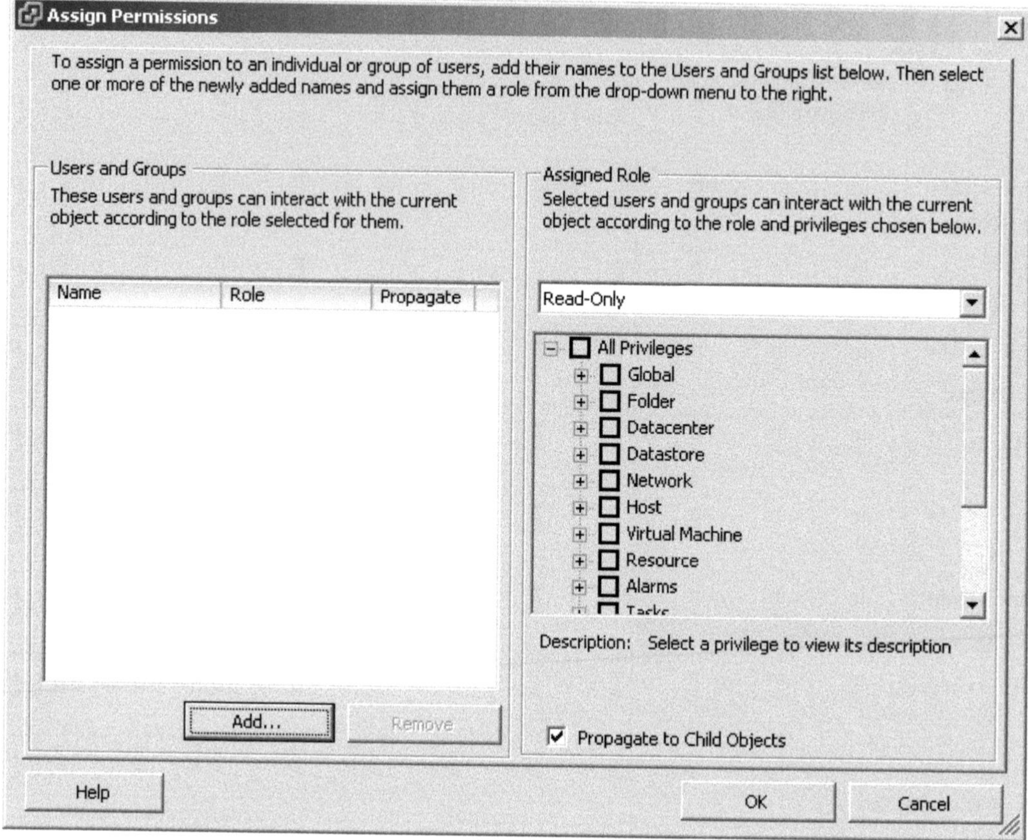

Figure 10.2 Assign Permissions Dialog Box

You click on the Add button and select the Windows user and group accounts that you want to set the permissions for on this object.

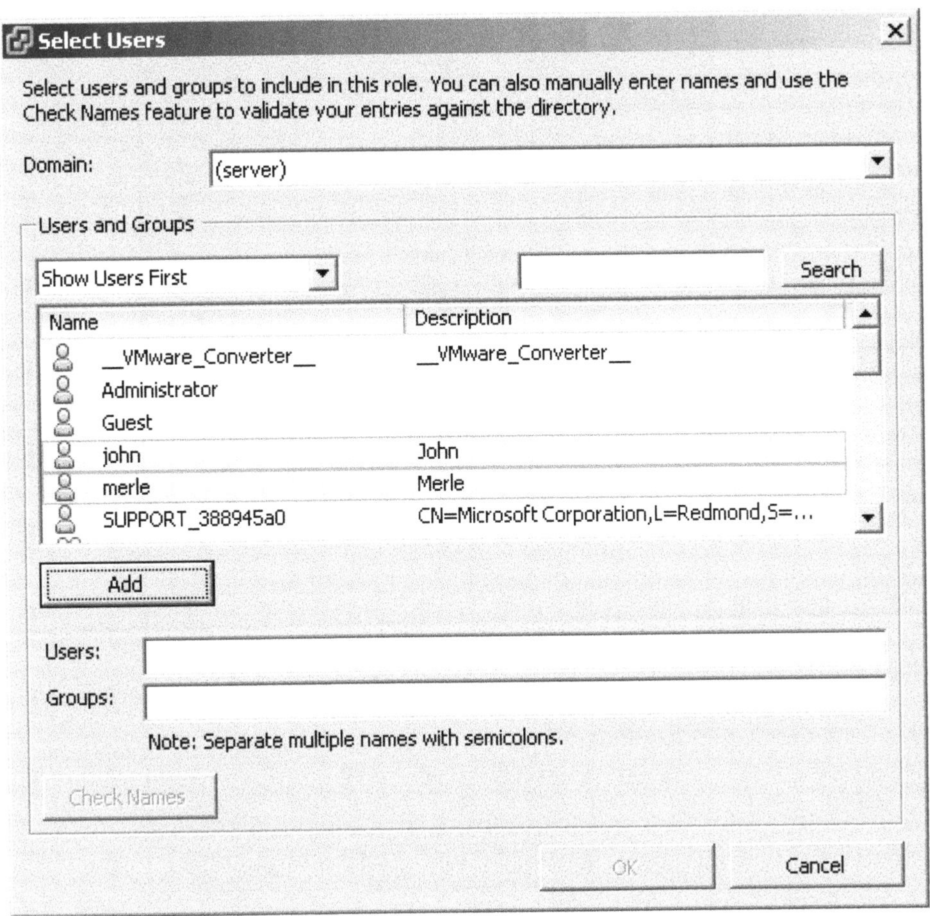

Figure 10.3 Select Users Dialog Box

Figure 10.3 shows the Select Users window.

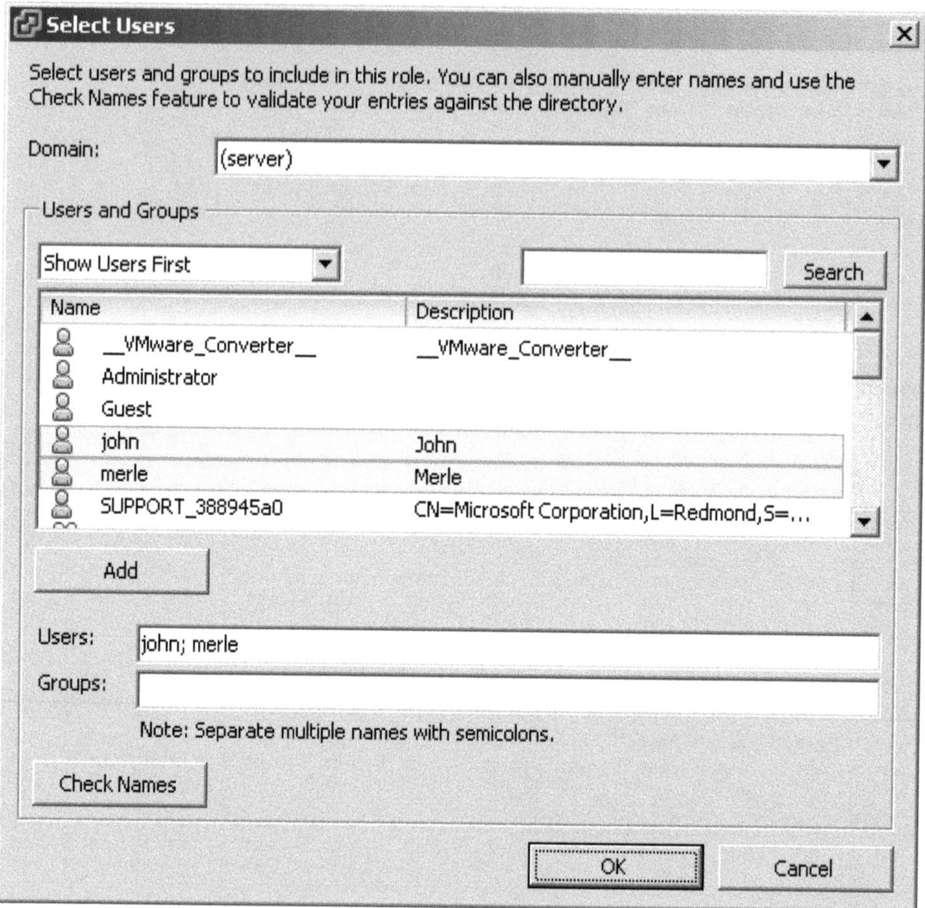

Figure 10.4 Select Users Dialog Box Add Button

The Windows users accounts that are configured for this system or are configured using Active Directory are visible in this window. You can organize the display by using the sort pull down menu to display users or groups first as shown in Figure 10.4.

You can also search for the user or group or enter the name of the user or group in the appropriate text box at the bottom of the window. You can also check the names to verify if it is a valid user name or group name. Select the OK button once you have the user or group that you want to set the permissions to.

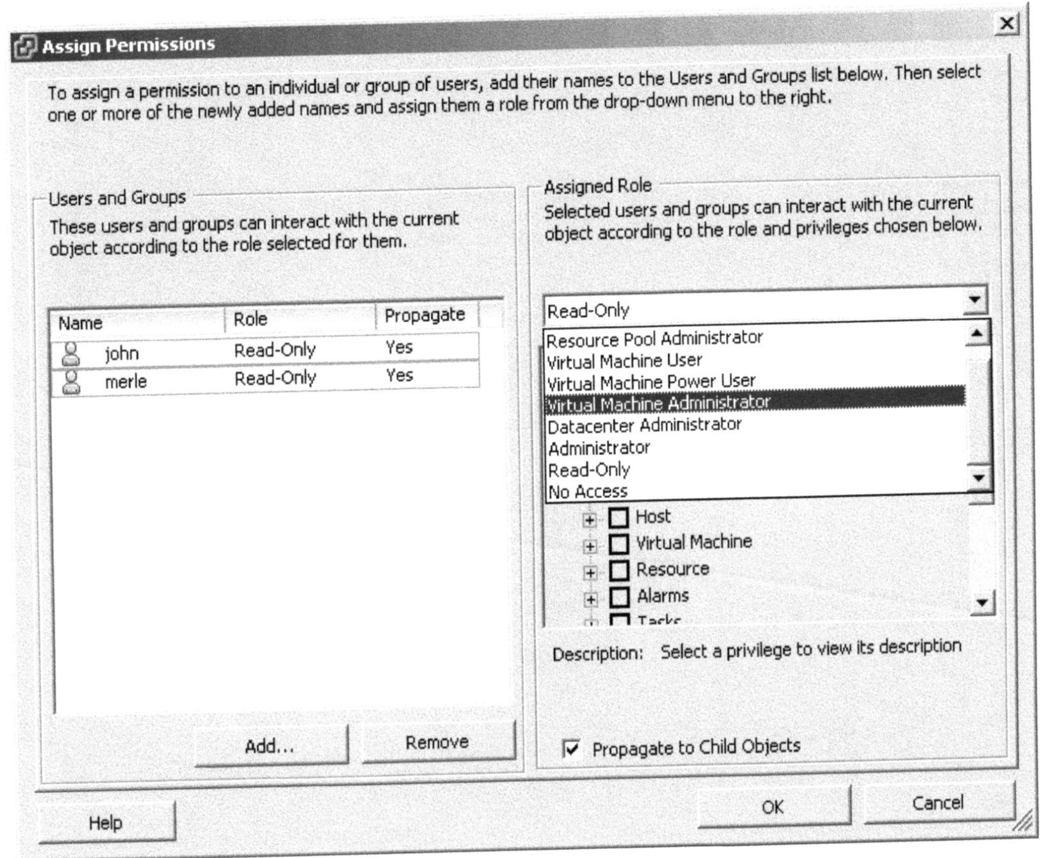

Figure 10.5 Assign Permissions Dialog Box Assign Role

Step 3. Figure 10.5 shows the Assign Permissions window.

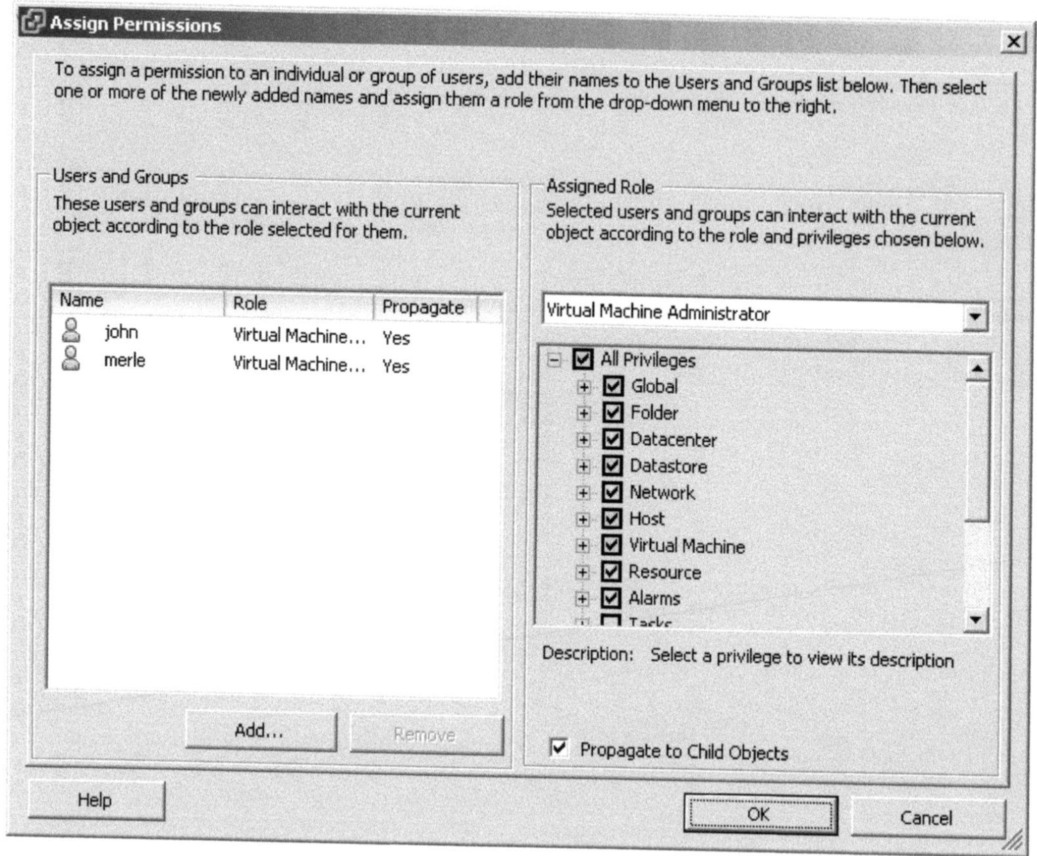

Figure 10.6 VirtualCenter Permissions View Current Role Assignment

By clicking on the drop down menu in the Assigned Roles section of the window you can apply one of the predefined roles for the users or groups listed on the left side of the window. The Propagate to Child Object check box when checked causes these permissions to be set for all child objects in the inventory. You have now set a role for a user or group.

Figure 10.6 shows the user and group entries in the Permissions tab for that object.

You can determine what role has been assigned to the user or group as well as what object the role was propagated from.

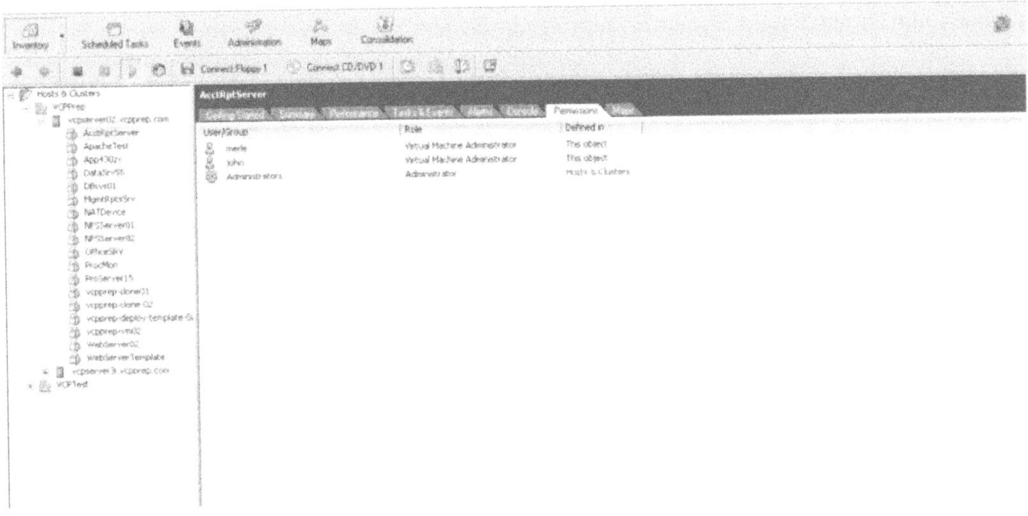

Figure 10.7 VirtualCenter Permissions Tab

Changing an Existing User/Group Role

Select the object you want to modify permissions for and click on the Permissions tab as shown in Figure 10.7.

We will examine how to edit the properties by selecting the Properties command from the pop up menu.

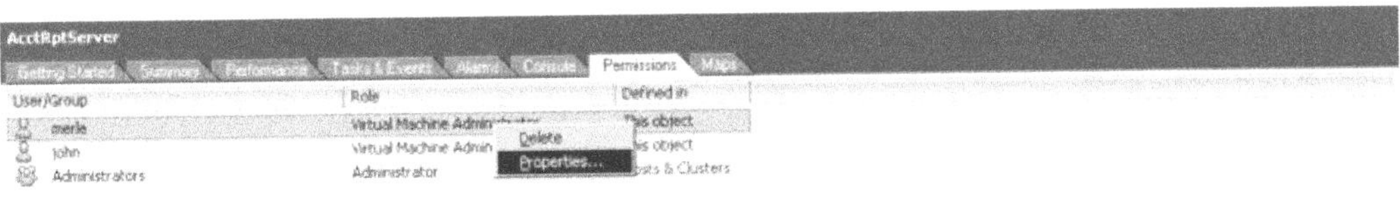

Figure 10.8 VirtualCenter User/Group Menu

If you right mouse button click on a user or group entry as shown in Figure 10.8, you can either delete the entry or edit its properties.

Selecting the Properties menu option launches the Change Access Rule dialog box as shown in Figure 10.9. This window allows you to change the role or turn off propagation for the user or group entry.

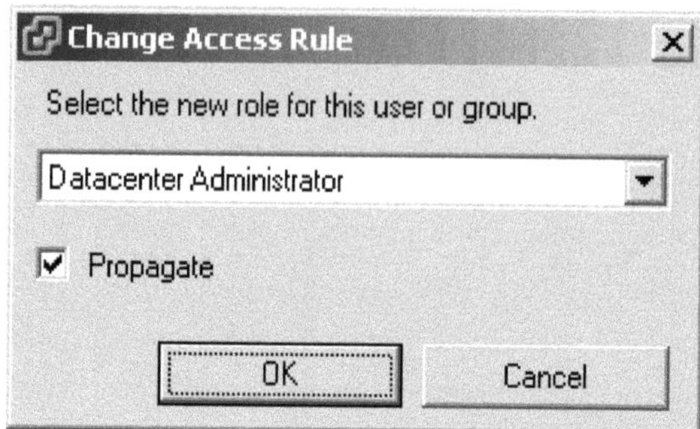

Figure 10.9 Change Access Rule Dialog Box

Click on the drop down menu as shown in Figure 10.10 to select one of the other roles that are configured on this VirtualCenter server. Once you have made your selection click on the OK button to close the window.

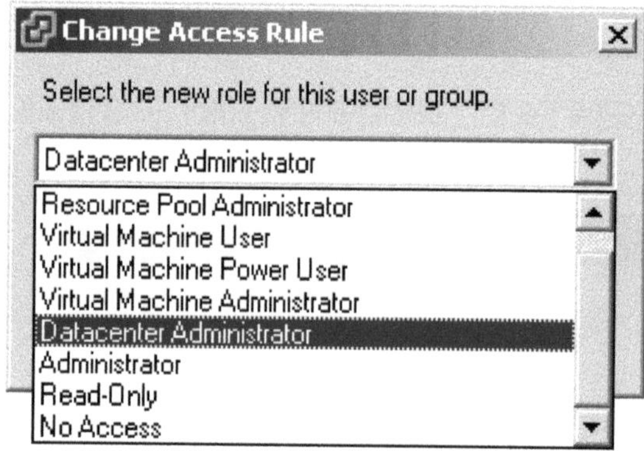

Figure 10.10 Access Rule Dialog Box Selection

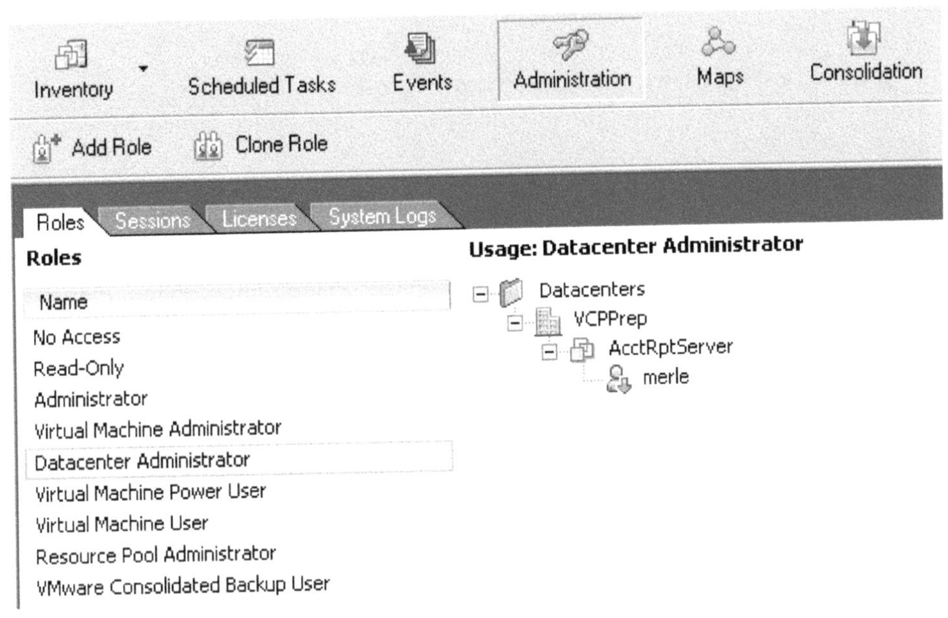

Figure 10.11 VirtualCenter Roles Tab

VirtualCenter Custom Roles

You can build custom roles for VirtualCenter to add to the 9 pre-built roles. You can build these custom roles with any of the over 110 available role privileges.

The Admin Button

Figure 10.11 shows the tabs that are displayed when you click on the Admin button. You need to click on the roles tab to view and configure custom roles.

The Roles Tab

The Roles tab shows you all of the configured VirtualCenter roles.

When you click on a role on the left of the tab it will display where the role was applied in the inventory.

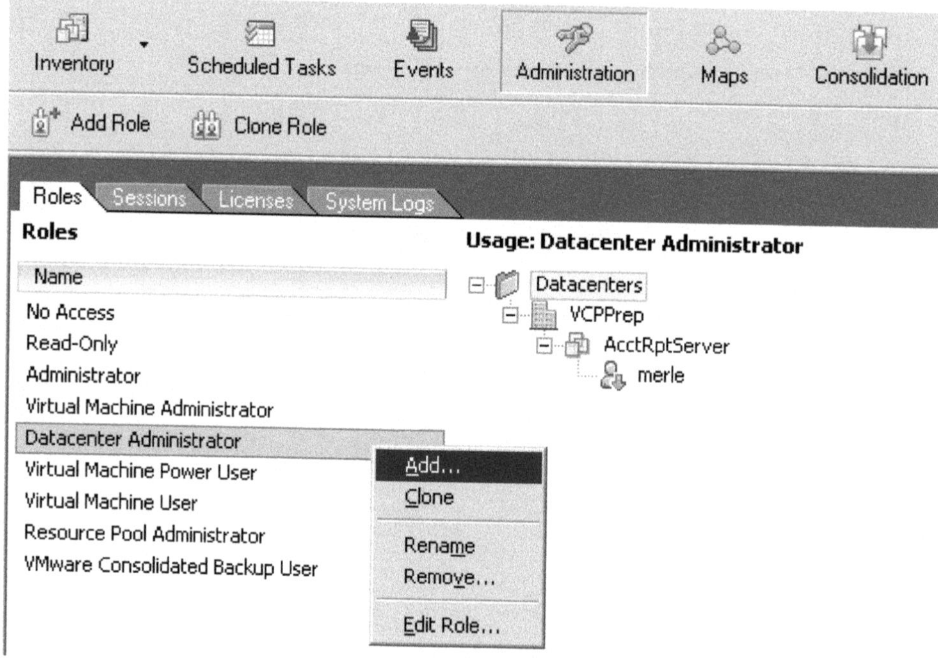

Figure 10.12 VirtualCenter Roles Tab Add Role Menu

Creating a Custom Role

You can right mouse button click to bring up the pop up menu and select the Add command to add a new role to VirtualCenter as shown in Figure 10.12.

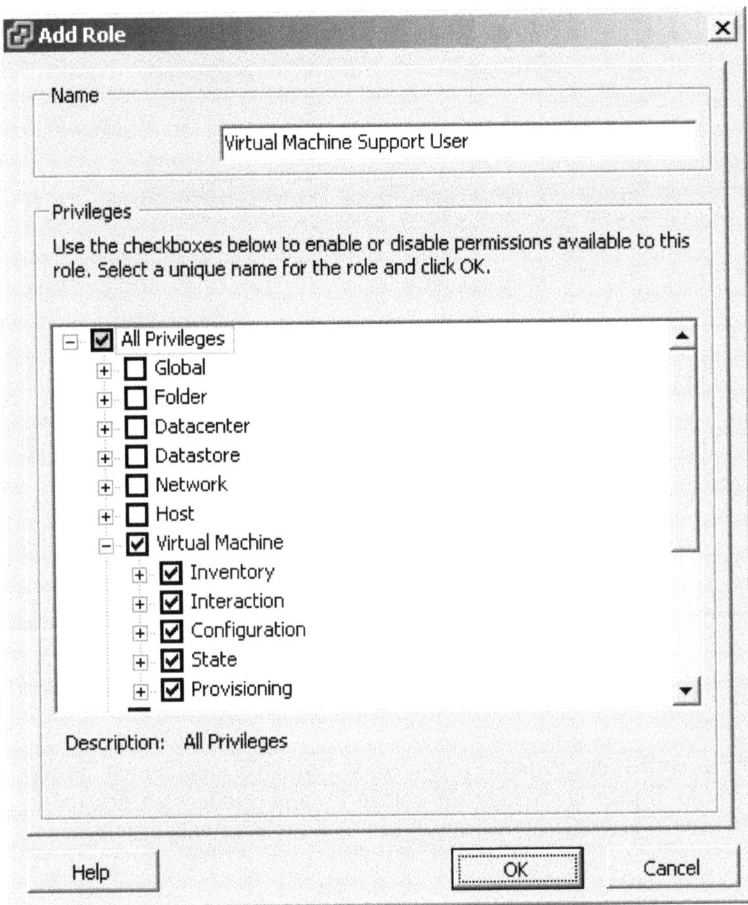

Figure 10.13 Add Role Dialog Box

Selecting the add command will bring up the Add Role dialog box as shown in Figure 10.13.

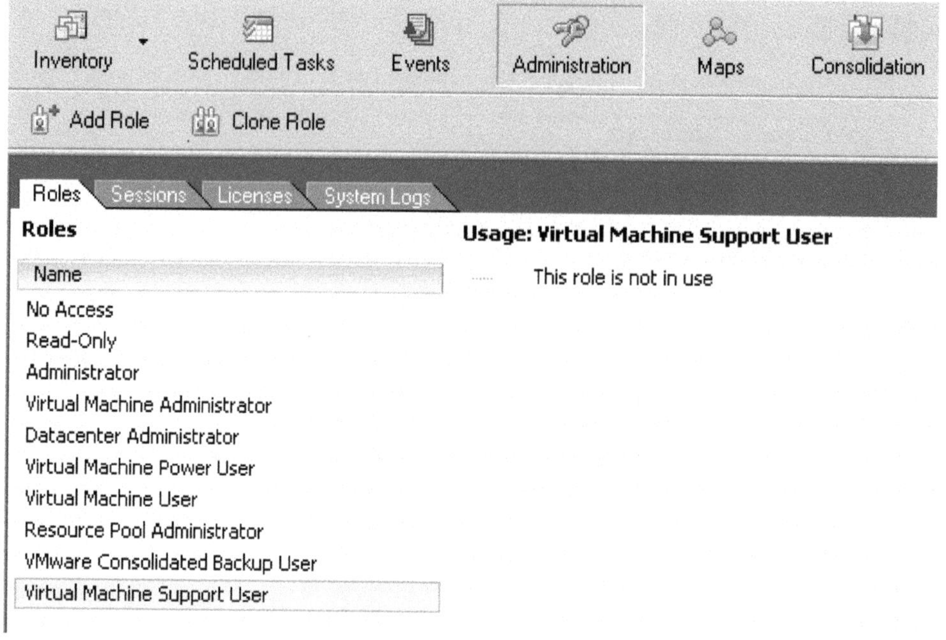

Figure 10.14 VirtualCenter Roles Tab New Role

You will enter a custom role name as well as selecting the privileges for this role. Clicking on the plus symbols expands out the categories to display the hidden sub-categories and privileges. Click on the OK button when completed. The newly created role now appears in the list of roles as shown in Figure 10.14.

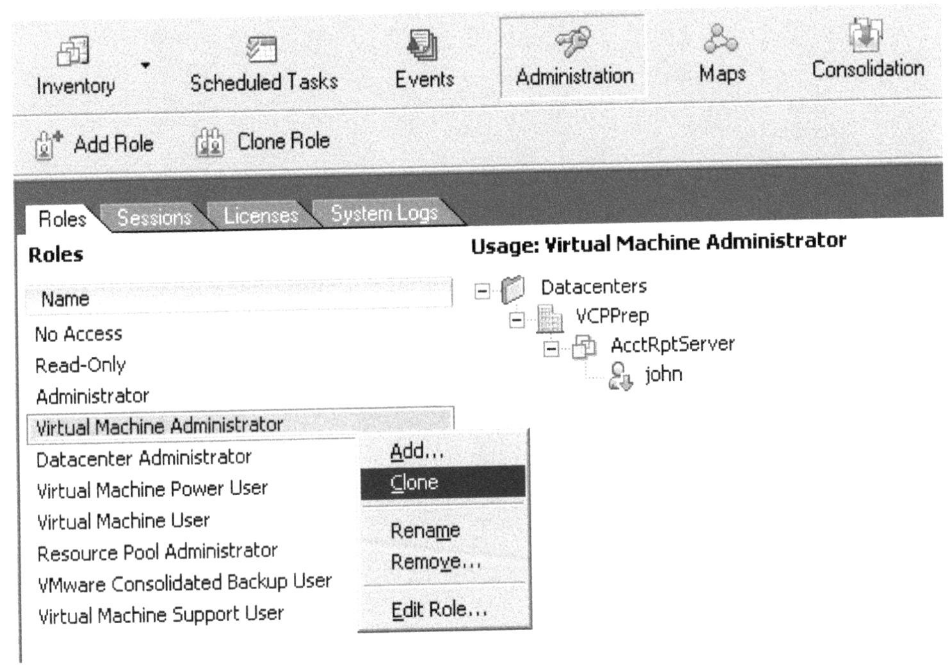

Figure 10.15 VirtualCenter Roles Tab Clone Role Menu

Cloning a Role

You can clone a role by right mouse button clicking on the role that you want to clone as shown in Figure 10.15.

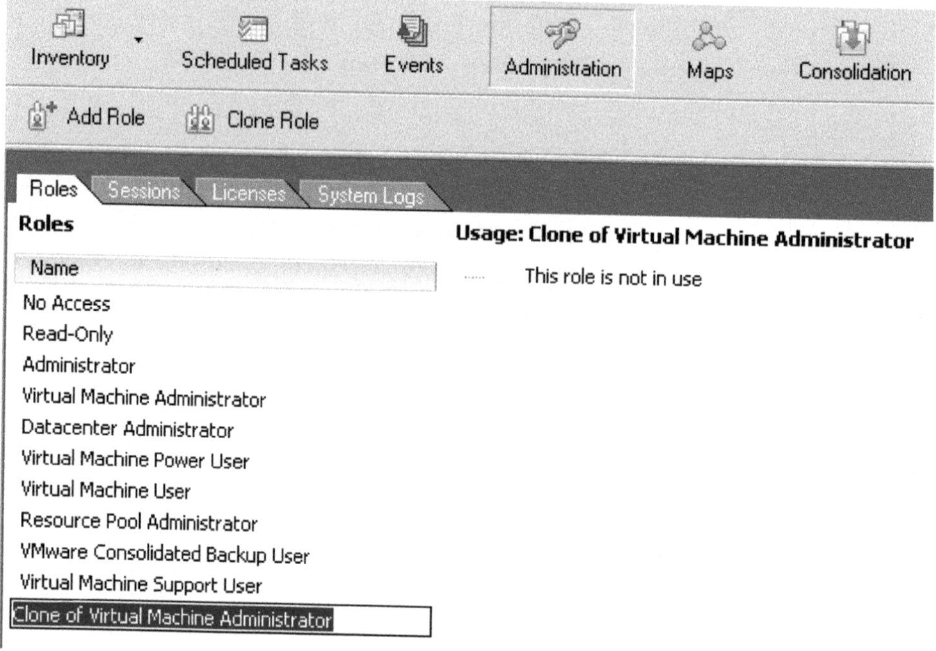

Figure 10.16 VirtualCenter Roles Tab Clone Role Name Assignment

The cloned role will now appear in the display as shown in Figure 10.16. The cloned role can now be given a label.

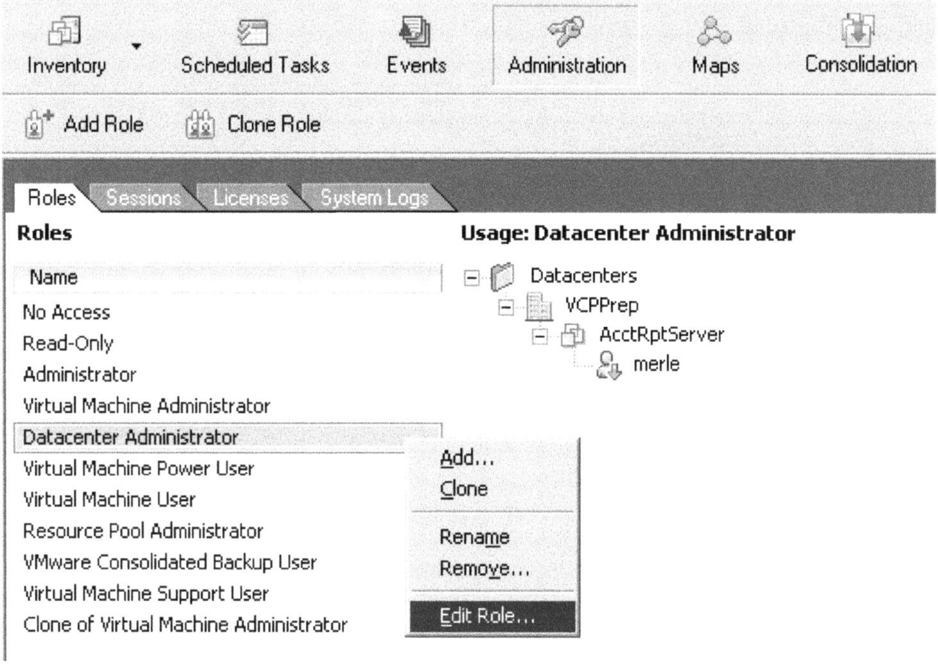

Figure 10.17 VirtualCenter Roles Tab Edit Role Menu

Editing a Role

If you right mouse button click on a role as shown in Figure 10.17 you can edit the role. The Edit Role window will appear and you can edit the roles privileges in this window as shown in Figure 10.18.

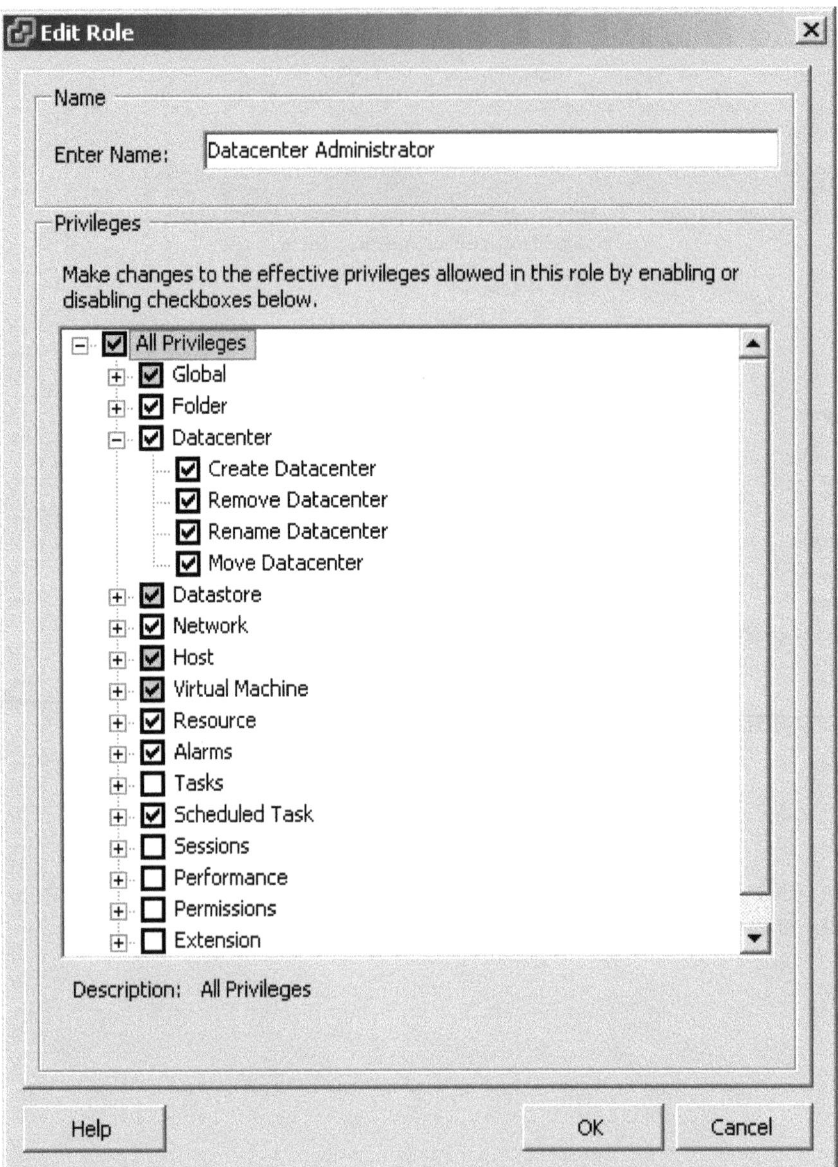

Figure 10.18 VirtualCenter Roles Tab Edit Role Dialog Box

When you are done editing the privileges click on the OK button to complete the task.

Privilege Propagation in the VirtualCenter Inventory

VirtualCenter permissions are implemented by combining a user or group with a role and assigning them to an object in the inventory. It is important where in the inventory permission assignments occur. The default behavior is that the permission assignment propagates from the parent object, such as a folder or cluster, to its child object, such as templates or virtual machines.

Propagating permissions to child objects can simplify permission assignments. By default, a permission granted to a folder will give the user or group the assigned permissions to all current and future child objects. The default permission propagation behavior can be disabled by removing the check box next to the Propagate to Child Objects selection within the Assign Permissions dialog box as shown previously in Figure 10.2.

The rules for assigning permissions are as follows:

Rule 1: A user that **is a member of multiple groups with permissions on different objects**

When the groups are assigned permissions on different objects, it is equivalent to the user account being assigned permissions to the different objects directly.

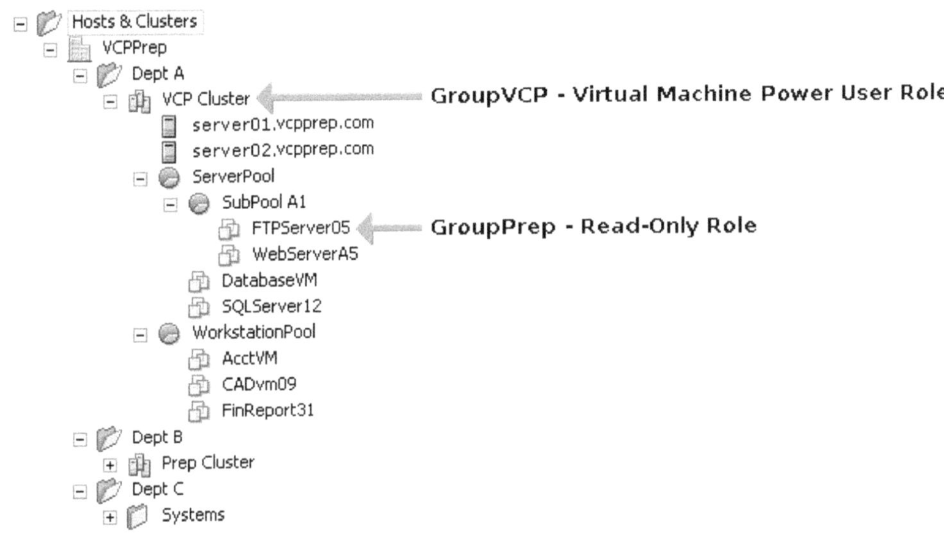

Figure 10.19 VirtualCenter Multiple Group Permissions on Different Objects

In Figure 10.19, a user assigned to both the GroupVCP and GroupPrep groups will have Virtual Machine Power User role permission over all objects within the VCP Cluster parent object except the FTPSever05 virtual machine. The user will be assigned the Read-Only role for the FTPServer05 virtual machine.

Rule 2: (First Example) A user that is a member of multiple groups having permissions on the same object with non-conflicting roles

When the groups are assigned permissions on the same object, the user account is assigned the union of all privileges assigned to both groups.

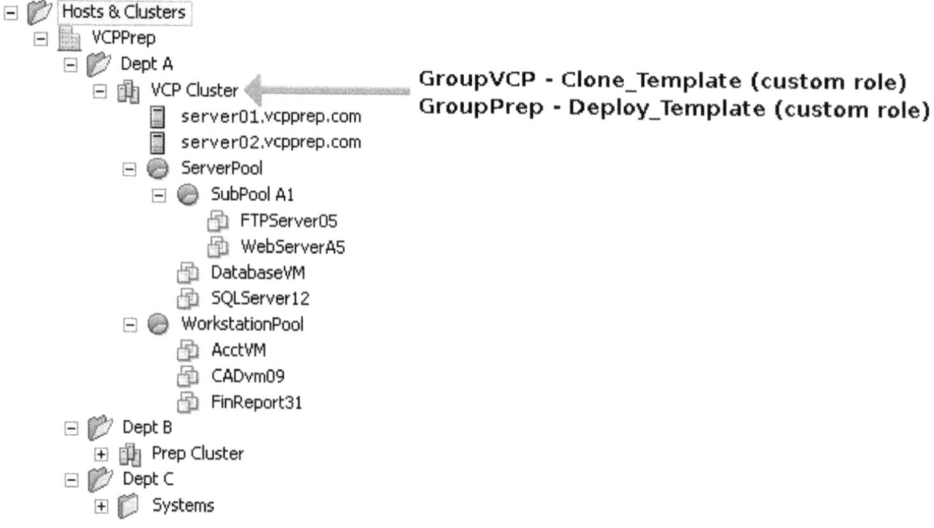

Figure 10.20 VirtualCenter Multiple Group Permissions On Different Objects

In Figure 10.20, a user assigned to both the GroupVCP and GroupPrep groups will have the union of privileges from both the Clone_Template and Deploy_Template custom roles over all objects within the VCP Cluster parent object.

Rule 2: (Second Example) A user that is a member of multiple groups having permissions on the same object with conflicting roles

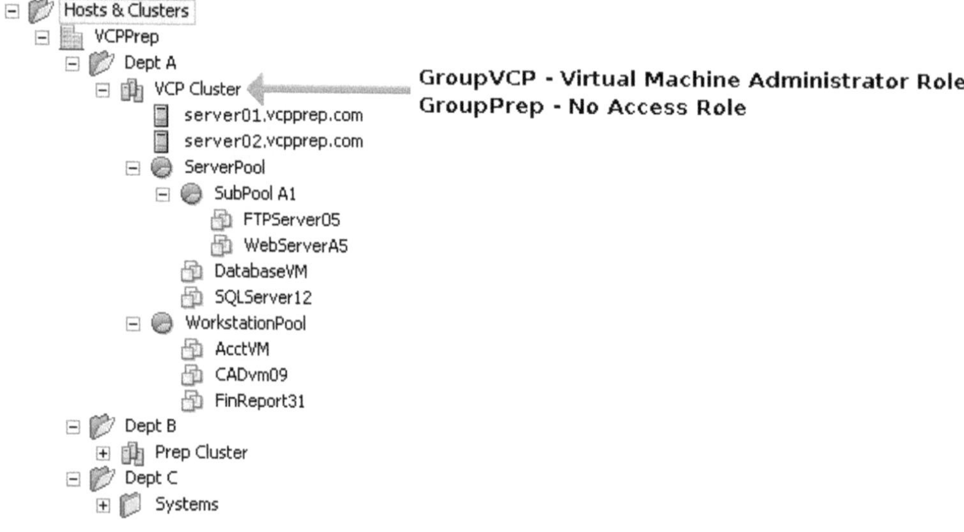

Figure 10.21 VirtualCenter Multiple Group Permissions On Different Objects

In Figure 10.21, the user is assigned to both GroupVCP and GroupPrep, which have the Virtual Machine Administrator and No Access roles respectively. The union of both role privileges gives the user the Virtual Machine Administrator role thereby negating the No Access role.

Rule 3: A user account **takes precedence over group permissions**

When a user that is a member of a group where both the group and user account have assigned permissions on the same object, the user account permissions will take precedence. User account permissions applied on a different object further down in the inventory take precedence over group permissions.

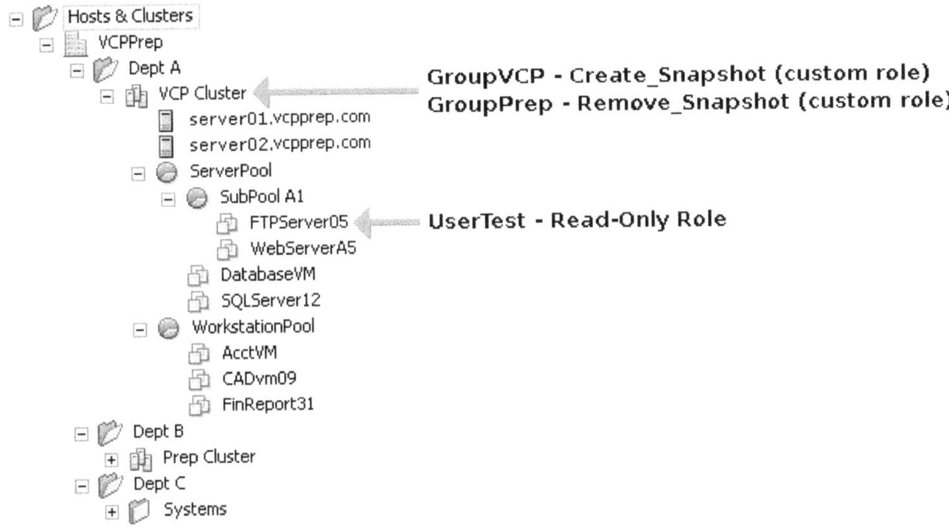

Figure 10.22 VirtualCenter Multiple Group Permissions On Different Objects

In Figure 10.22, the UserTest account assigned to both the GroupVCP and GroupPrep groups will have the union of privileges from both the Create_Snapshot and Remove_Snapshot custom roles over all objects within the VCP Cluster parent object except the FTPServer05 virtual machine. The UserTest account will be assigned the Read-Only role for the FTPServer05 virtual machine.

Rule 4: A user account with directly applied permissions takes precedence over propagated permissions

When a user **account** has both propagated and directly assigned permissions on the same object, the directly assigned permissions take precedence.

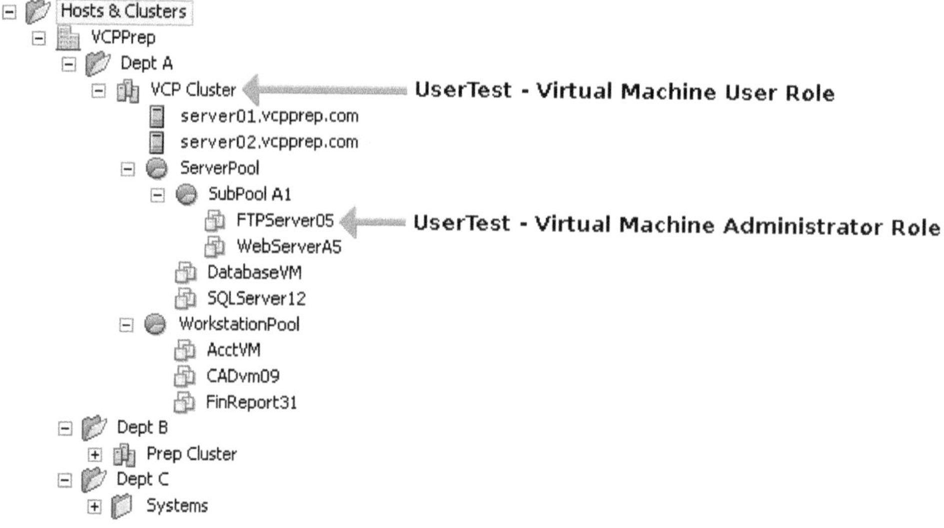

Figure 10.23 VirtualCenter Multiple Group Permissions On Different Objects

In Figure 10.23, the UserTest account is assigned the Virtual Machine User role at the VCP Cluster parent object. The UserTest account will have Virtual Machine User role privileges over all objects within the VCP Cluster object except the FTPServer05 virtual machine. The UserTest account will be assigned the Virtual Machine Administrator role for the FTPServer05 virtual machine.

ESX 3.5 Server Authentication

In order to be able to access an ESX 3.5 server directly you must have a user account on the ESX 3.5 server.

Once the user account exists in the ESX 3.5 server you can log into it using either:

- The VI Client
- The Web Access interface
- A service console session (not directly available on an ESXi or ESXi Server version 3.5)

Be aware that there is no attempt to reconcile the accounts on the ESX 3.5 server and the accounts on the VirtualCenter server. So a user John on the ESX 3.5 server is considered a different account and can be configured with different privileges than a user John on the VirtualCenter server.

VMware recommends that you only use VirtualCenter to manage your ESX 3.5 servers once they have been put under VirtualCenter's control.

ESX 3.5 Server Predefined Roles and Associated Privileges

ESX 3.5 server includes three predefined roles. These are system roles. System roles and their privileges are permanent; these cannot be modified or removed.

The following are the system roles:

- No Access
- Read-Only
- Administrator

Additional VirtualCenter roles are defined but not used on a stand-alone ESX 3.5 server. They are defined in case the ESX 3.5 server is later added to the VirtualCenter inventory.

No Access Role

Users assigned the No Access system role on an object are unable to view or modify the object. In addition, users will not be able to view content in the VI Client tabs associated with the object. This role is the default role for all users with the exception of those users in the Administrators group.

Read-Only Role

Users assigned the Read-Only system role will be able to view the state and details of an object. VI Client menus and toolbar actions are disabled. All tabs within the VI Client are accessible except the console tab.

Administrator Role

User assigned the Administrator system role are given all privileges for all the objects within the ESX 3.5 server inventory. This is the default role for the root and vpxuser accounts. The following lists the entire privilege set for the Administrator role:

NOTE: Several of the listed privileges are not applicable to a standalone VI Client directly accessing a standalone ESX server, as provisioning (templates and cloning) is only available through VC Server, and cluster configurations are only for VC Server licensed features of DRS and HA.

Global Category:

- Manage Custom Attributes
- Set Custom Attribute
- Log Event
- Cancel Task
- Licenses
- Diagnostics

- Settings
- VC Server

Folder Category:

- Create Folder
- Delete Folder
- Rename Folder
- Move Folder

Datacenter Category:

- Create Datacenter
- Remove Datacenter
- Rename Datacenter
- Move Datacenter

Datastore Category:

- Rename File
- Remove Datastore
- Browse Datastore
- Remove File

Network Category:

- Remove

Host Inventory Subcategory:

- Add Standalone Host
- Create Cluster
- Add Host To Cluster
- Remove Host
- Move Cluster/Standalone Host
- Rename Cluster
- Remove Cluster
- Modify Cluster
- Move Host

Host Configuration Subcategory:

- Connection
- Maintenance
- Virtual Machine Auto-start Configuration
- HyperThreading

- Storage Partition Configuration
- Security Profile and Firewall
- Memory Configuration
- Network Configuration
- Advanced Settings
- System Resource Allocation
- Change SNMP settings

Host Local Operations Subcategory:

- Add host to VirtualCenter
- Manage User Groups
- Create Virtual Machine
- Delete Virtual Machine

Virtual Machine Inventory Subcategory:

- Create
- Remove
- Move

Virtual Machine Interaction Subcategory:

- Power On
- Power Off
- Suspend
- Reset
- Answer Question
- Console Interaction
- Device Connection
- Configure CD Media
- Configure Floppy Media
- Tools Install

Virtual Machine Configuration Subcategory:

- Rename
- Add Existing Disk
- Add New Disk
- Remove Disk
- Raw Device
- Change CPU Count
- Memory
- Add or Remove Device
- Modify Device Settings
- Settings
- Change Resource

- Upgrade Virtual Hardware
- Reset Guest Information
- Advanced
- Disk Lease

Virtual Machine State Subcategory:

- Create Snapshot
- Revert To Snapshot
- Remove Snapshot
- Rename Snapshot

Virtual Machine Provisioning Subcategory:

- Customize
- Clone
- Create Template From Virtual Machine
- Deploy Template
- Clone Template
- Mark As Template
- Mark As Virtual Machine
- Read Customization Specifications
- Modify Customization Specification
- Allow Disk Access
- Allow Read-only Disk Access
- Allow Virtual Machine Download
- Allow Virtual Machine Files Upload

Resource Category:

- Assign Virtual Machine To Resource Pool
- Apply Recommendation
- Create Pool
- Rename Pool
- Modify Pool
- Move Pool
- Remove Pool
- Migrate
- Relocate
- Query VMotion

Alarms Category:

- Create Alarm
- Remove Alarm
- Modify Alarm

Scheduled Task Category:

- Create Tasks
- Remove Task
- Run Task
- Modify Task

Sessions Category:

- View and Terminate Sessions
- Global Message

Performance Category:

- Modify Interval

Permissions Category:

- Modify Role
- Reassign Role Permissions
- Modify Permission

ESX 3.5 Server User and Group Access

The Users and Groups Tab

The Users & Groups tab lists all of the ESX 3.5 server users and groups. These users and groups are used for accessing the ESX 3.5 server service console and for direct access to an ESX server through VI Client, thus are not accessible by the VirtualCenter server. The Users & Groups tab contains two buttons, the Users and Groups buttons listed in the View: section. Click on the Users button to display the users currently defined within the ESX 3.5 service console as shown in Figure 10.24.

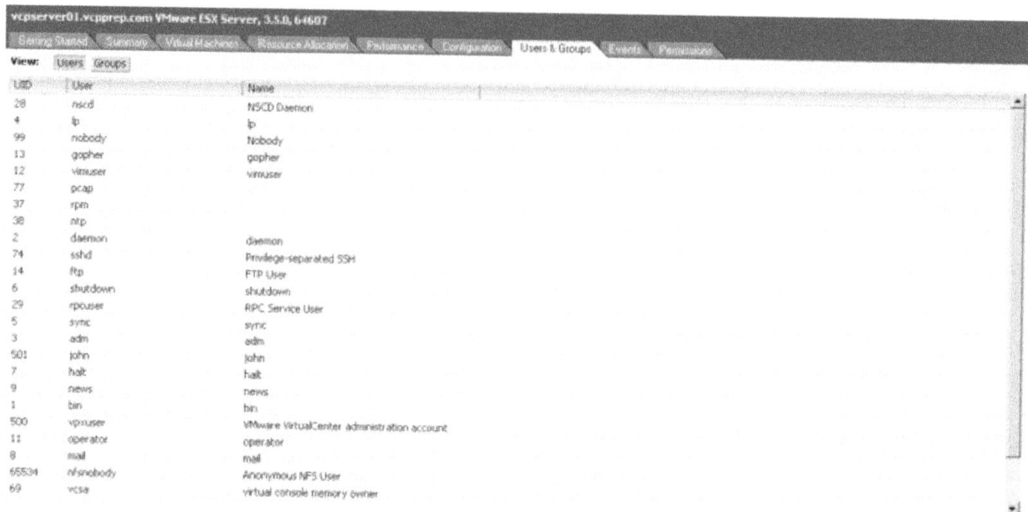

Figure 10.24 ESX 3.5 Server Users & Groups Tab Users List

By default, there are 23 users defined on the ESX 3.5 server service console.

To add a new user to the service console, right click within the Users & Groups tab and select Add from the popup menu as shown in Figure 10.25.

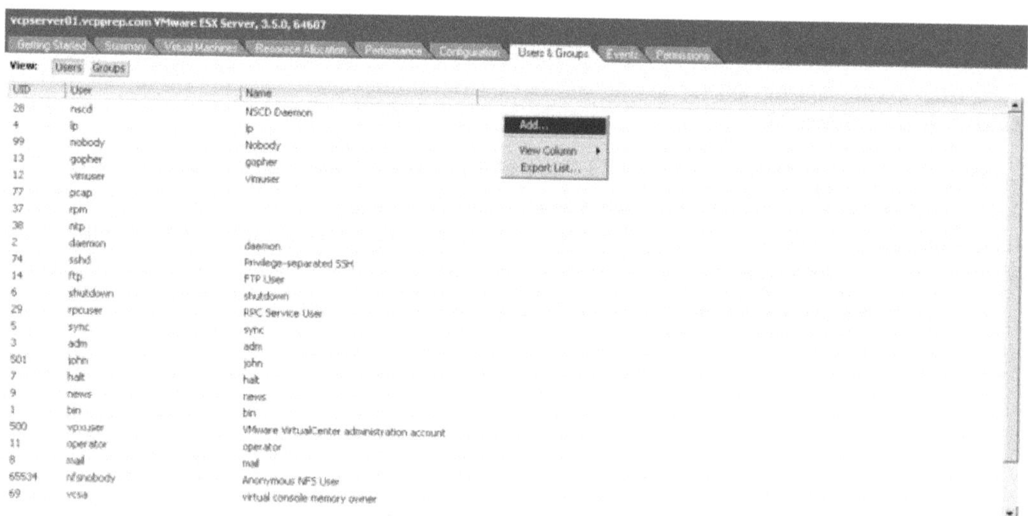

Figure 10.25 ESX 3.5 Server Users & Groups Tab Users Add Menu

Within the User Information section of the Add New User dialog box, enter the new user, case-sensitive log in name in the Login name text field. Optionally, enter the UID (User Identification number) and User Name. Enter the new user's password in both the Password and Confirm text boxes within the Enter Password section. For this new user to be able to log in to the service console, the Grant shell access to this user check box should be selected within the Shell Access section. The

Group Membership section can be used to add the new user into a group. Select the OK button to add the new user as shown in Figure 10.26.

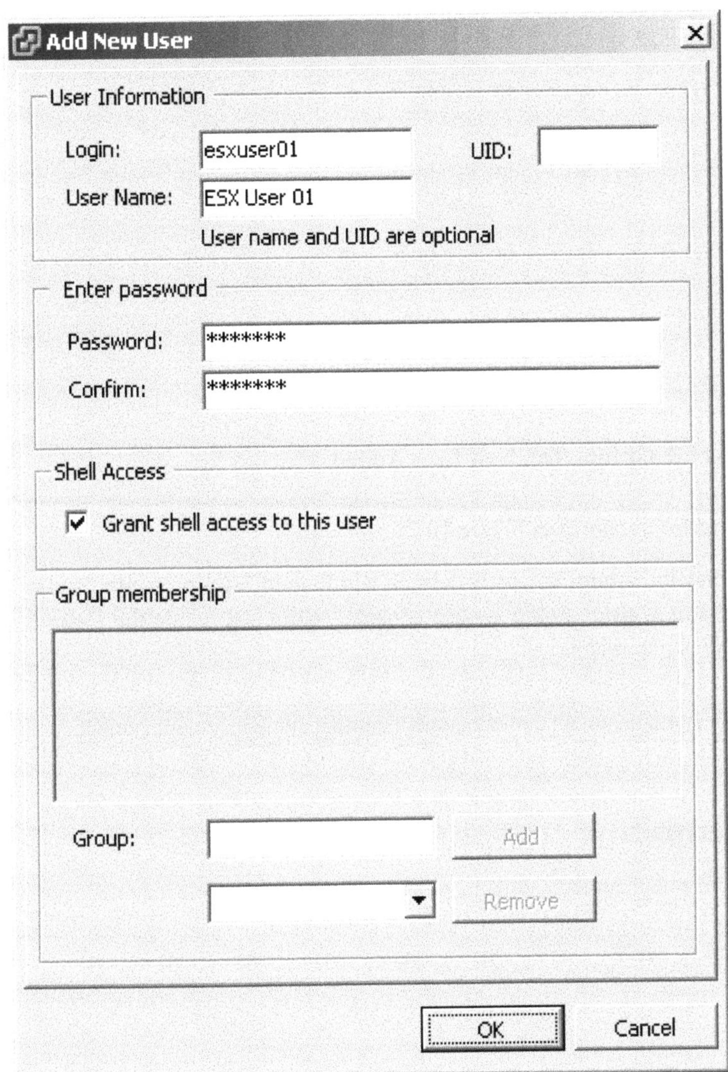

Figure 10.26 ESX 3.5 Server Users & Groups Tab Add New User Dialog Box

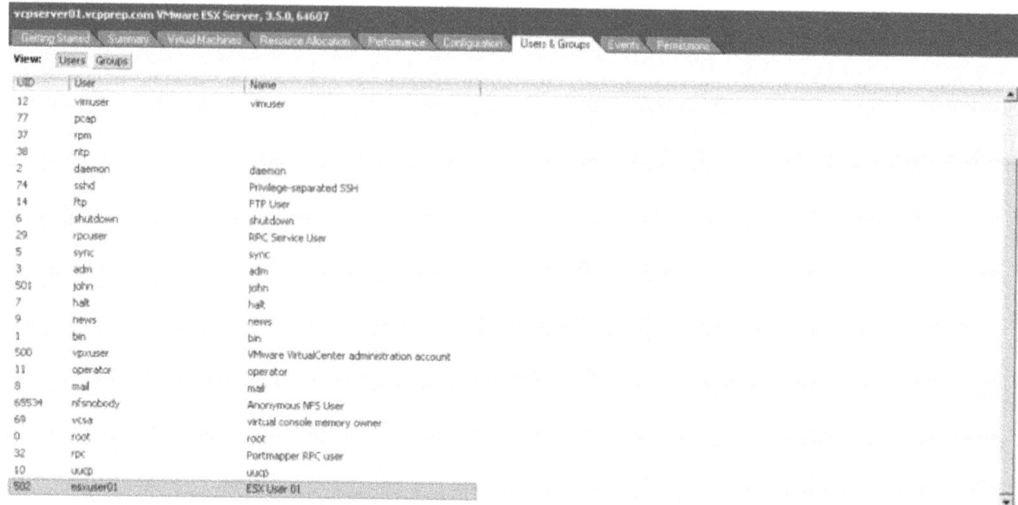

Figure 10.27 ESX 3.5 Server Users & Groups Tab New User Added

The new user esxuser01 has been added as shown in Figure 10.27.

Click on the Groups button to display the groups currently defined within the ESX 3.5 service console as shown in Figure 10.28. To add a new group to the service console, right click within the Users & Groups tab and select Add from the popup menu.

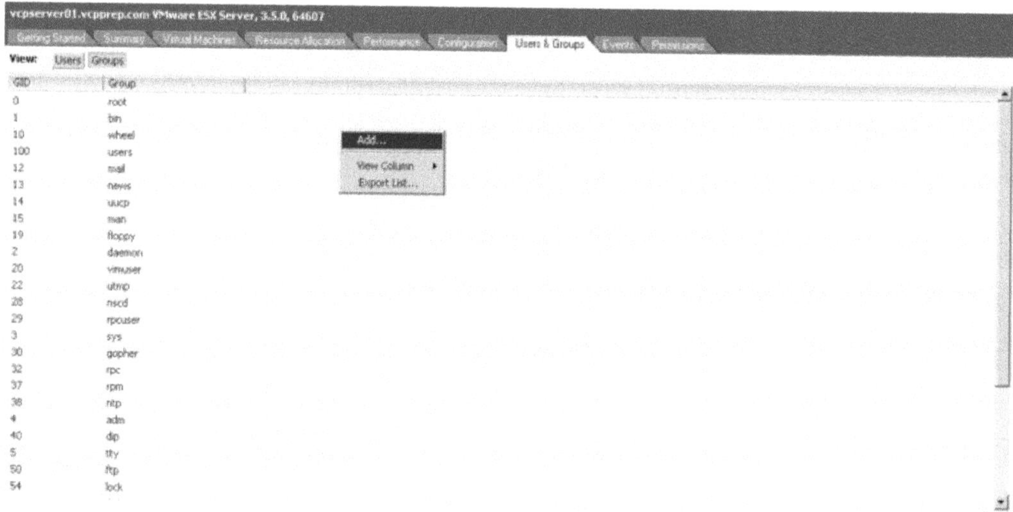

Figure 10.28 ESX 3.5 Server Users & Groups Tab Groups List

By default, there are 31 groups defined on the ESX 3.5 server service console.

Within the Group Information section of the Create New Group dialog box, enter the new group name in the Group name text field. Optionally, enter the GID (Group Identification number) for the new group. The Users in this group section can be used to add users into the new group. Select the OK button to create the new group as shown in Figure 10.29.

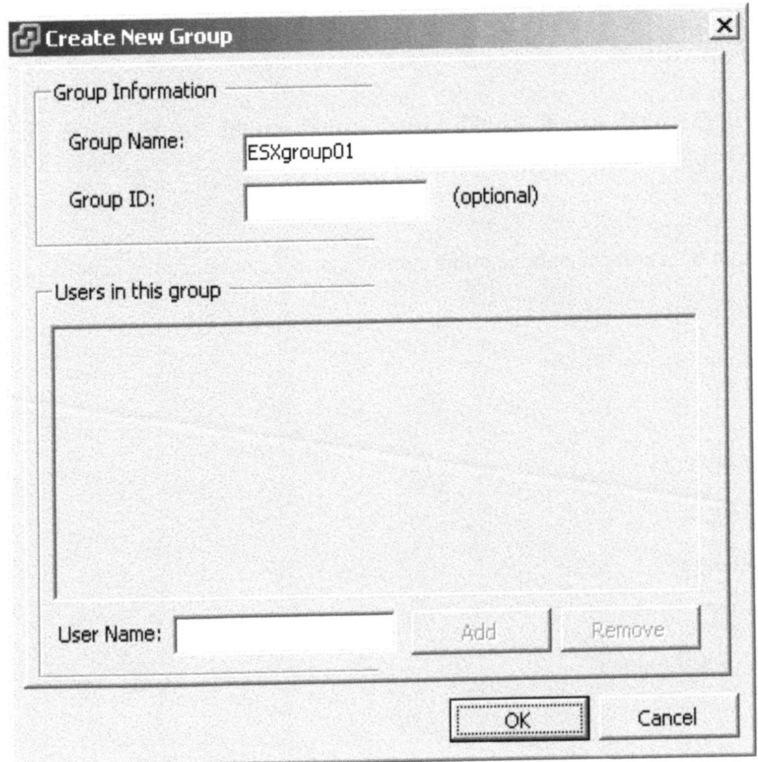

Figure 10.29 ESX 3.5 Server Users & Groups Tab Create New Group Dialog Box

The new group ESXgroup01 has been created as shown in Figure 10.30.

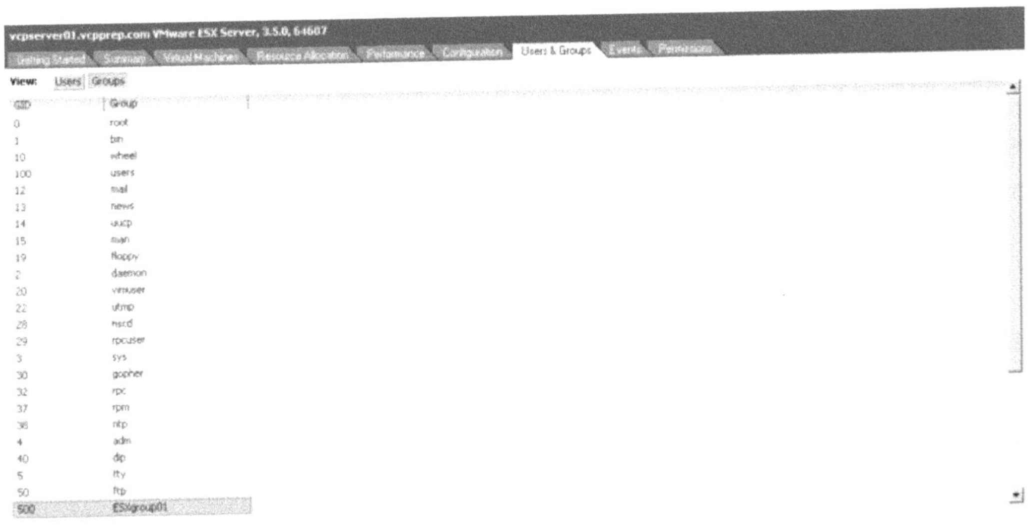

Figure 10.30 ESX 3.5 Server Users & Groups Tab New Group Added

The ESX 3.5 service console uses Linux user account and group configuration settings.

Service Console User Accounts

The user accounts are defined in the /etc/passwd file. To view the contents of this file, enter the following command from the ESX 3.5 server CLI:

cat /etc/passwd

The following is an example output of issuing the above command:

```
root@vcpserver01 etc]# cat /etc/passwd
root:x:0:0:root:/root:/bin/bash
bin:x:1:1:bin:/bin:/sbin/nologin
daemon:x:2:2:daemon:/sbin:/sbin/nologin
adm:x:3:4:adm:/var/adm:/sbin/nologin
lp:x:4:7:lp:/var/spool/lpd:/sbin/nologin
sync:x:5:0:sync:/sbin:/bin/sync
shutdown:x:6:0:shutdown:/sbin:/sbin/shutdown
halt:x:7:0:halt:/sbin:/sbin/halt
mail:x:8:12:mail:/var/spool/mail:/sbin/nologin
news:x:9:13:news:/etc/news:
uucp:x:10:14:uucp:/var/spool/uucp:/sbin/nologin
operator:x:11:0:operator:/root:/sbin/nologin
gopher:x:13:30:gopher:/var/gopher:/sbin/nologin
ftp:x:14:50:FTP User:/var/ftp:/sbin/nologin
nobody:x:99:99:Nobody:/:/sbin/nologin
nscd:x:28:28:NSCD Daemon:/:/sbin/nologin
vcsa:x:69:69:virtual console memory owner:/dev:/sbin/nologin
ntp:x:38:38::/etc/ntp:/sbin/nologin
sshd:x:74:74:Privilege-separated SSH:/var/empty/sshd:/sbin/nologin
rpc:x:32:32:Portmapper RPC user:/:/sbin/nologin
pcap:x:77:77::/var/arpwatch:/sbin/nologin
rpm:x:37:37::/var/lib/rpm:/sbin/nologin
vimuser:x:12:20:vimuser:/sbin:/sbin/nologin
```

VcpEsxUser01:x:500:100:VCP ESX User 01:/home/VcpEsxUser01:/bin/bash

Service Console User Passwords

A hash of the encrypted user passwords are stored in the /etc/shadow file. To view the contents of this file, enter the following command from the ESX 3.5 server CLI:

cat /etc/shadow

The following is an example output of issuing the above command:

```
[root@vcpserver01 etc]# cat /etc/shadow
root:$1$Svs1IUzR$8sKIfudCRMiLw9cNKjee00:13877:0:-1:7:::
bin:*:13877:0:90:7:::
daemon:*:13877:0:90:7:::
adm:*:13877:0:90:7:::
lp:*:13877:0:90:7:::
sync:*:13877:0:90:7:::
shutdown:*:13877:0:90:7:::
halt:*:13877:0:90:7:::
mail:*:13877:0:90:7:::
news:*:13877:0:90:7:::
uucp:*:13877:0:90:7:::
operator:*:13877:0:90:7:::
gopher:*:13877:0:90:7:::
ftp:*:13877:0:90:7:::
nobody:*:13877:0:90:7:::
nscd:!!:13877:0:90:7:::
vcsa:!!:13877:0:90:7:::
ntp:!!:13877:0:90:7:::
sshd:!!:13877:0:90:7:::
rpc:!!:13877:0:90:7:::
pcap:!!:13877:0:90:7:::
rpm:!!:13877:0:90:7:::
vimuser:*:13877:0:90:7:::
```

VcpEsxUser01:$1$6rokpYUW$3WheNNj9gzCNJUB4ZLoBu.:13877:0:-1:7:::

Service Console Group Accounts

The group accounts are stored in the /etc/group file. To view the contents of this file, enter the following command from the ESX 3.5 server CLI:

cat /etc/group

The following is an example output of issuing the above command:

[root@vcpserver01 etc]# cat /etc/group

root:x:0:root

bin:x:1:root,bin,daemon

daemon:x:2:root,bin,daemon

sys:x:3:root,bin,adm

adm:x:4:root,adm,daemon

tty:x:5:

disk:x:6:root

lp:x:7:daemon,lp

mem:x:8:

kmem:x:9:

wheel:x:10:root

mail:x:12:mail

news:x:13:news

uucp:x:14:uucp

man:x:15:

gopher:x:30:

dip:x:40:

ftp:x:50:

lock:x:54:

nobody:x:99:

users:x:100:VcpEsxUser01

nscd:x:28:

floppy:x:19:

vcsa:x:69:

ntp:x:38:

utmp:x:22:

sshd:x:74:

rpc:x:32:

pcap:x:77:

rpm:x:37:

vimuser:x:20:

VcpEsxGroup01:x:500:

The ESX 3.5 server stores role settings in the /etc/vmware/hostd/authorization.xml file. To view the contents of this file, enter the following command from the ESX 3.5 server CLI:

cat /etc/vmware/hostd/authorization.xml

The following is an example output of issuing the above command on the default authorization.xml file:

```
[root@vcpserver01]# cat /etc/vmware/hostd/authorization.xml
<ConfigRoot>
<ACEData id="10">
<ACEDataEntity>ha-folder-root</ACEDataEntity>
<ACEDataId>10</ACEDataId>
<ACEDataIsGroup>false</ACEDataIsGroup>
<ACEDataPropagate>true</ACEDataPropagate>
<ACEDataRoleId>-1</ACEDataRoleId>
<ACEDataUser>root</ACEDataUser>
</ACEData>
<NextAceId>11</NextAceId>
</ConfigRoot>
```

When you create role settings for users or groups directly on the ESX 3.5 server the /etc/vmware/hostd/authorization.xml file gets updated.

The following is an example output of the /etc/vmware/hostd/authorization.xml file after a permission has been assigned to a service console user:

```
[root@vcpserver01 hostd]# cat /etc/vmware/hostd/authorization.xml
<ConfigRoot>
```

<ACEData id="10">
<ACEDataEntity>ha-folder-root</ACEDataEntity>
<ACEDataId>10</ACEDataId>
<ACEDataIsGroup>false</ACEDataIsGroup>
<ACEDataPropagate>true</ACEDataPropagate>
<ACEDataRoleId>-1</ACEDataRoleId>
<ACEDataUser>root</ACEDataUser>
</ACEData>
<ACEData id="11">
<ACEDataEntity>16</ACEDataEntity>
<ACEDataId>11</ACEDataId>
<ACEDataIsGroup>false</ACEDataIsGroup>
<ACEDataPropagate>true</ACEDataPropagate>
<ACEDataRoleId>-2</ACEDataRoleId>
<ACEDataUser>VcpEsxUser01</ACEDataUser>
</ACEData>
<ACEData id="12">
<ACEDataEntity>ha-folder-root</ACEDataEntity>
<ACEDataId>12</ACEDataId>
<ACEDataIsGroup>false</ACEDataIsGroup>
<ACEDataPropagate>true</ACEDataPropagate>
<ACEDataRoleId>-2</ACEDataRoleId>
<ACEDataUser>VcpEsxUser01</ACEDataUser>
</ACEData>
<NextAceId>13</NextAceId>
<NextRoleId>12</NextRoleId>
<PrivSet id="11">
<Priv id="Alarm.Create">Alarm.Create</Priv>
<Priv id="Alarm.Delete">Alarm.Delete</Priv>
<Priv id="Alarm.Edit">Alarm.Edit</Priv>
<Priv id="Authorization.ModifyPermissions">Authorization.ModifyPermissions</Priv>

```
<Priv id="Authorization.ModifyRoles">Authorization.ModifyRoles</Priv>
<Priv id="Authorization.ReassignRolePermissions">Authorization.ReassignRolePermissions</Priv>
<Priv id="Datacenter.Create">Datacenter.Create</Priv>
<Priv id="Datacenter.Delete">Datacenter.Delete</Priv>
<Priv id="Datacenter.Move">Datacenter.Move</Priv>
<Priv id="Datacenter.Rename">Datacenter.Rename</Priv>
<Priv id="Datastore.Browse">Datastore.Browse</Priv>
<Priv id="Datastore.Delete">Datastore.Delete</Priv>
<Priv id="Datastore.DeleteFile">Datastore.DeleteFile</Priv>
<Priv id="Datastore.Rename">Datastore.Rename</Priv>
<Priv id="Folder.Create">Folder.Create</Priv>
<Priv id="Folder.Delete">Folder.Delete</Priv>
<Priv id="Folder.Move">Folder.Move</Priv>
<Priv id="Folder.Rename">Folder.Rename</Priv>
<Priv id="Global.CancelTask">Global.CancelTask</Priv>
<Priv id="Global.Diagnostics">Global.Diagnostics</Priv>
<Priv id="Global.Licenses">Global.Licenses</Priv>
<Priv id="Global.LogEvent">Global.LogEvent</Priv>
<Priv id="Global.ManageCustomFields">Global.ManageCustomFields</Priv>
<Priv id="Global.SetCustomField">Global.SetCustomField</Priv>
<Priv id="Global.Settings">Global.Settings</Priv>
<Priv id="Global.VCServer">Global.VCServer</Priv>
<Priv id="Host.Config.AdvancedConfig">Host.Config.AdvancedConfig</Priv>
<Priv id="Host.Config.AutoStart">Host.Config.AutoStart</Priv>
<Priv id="Host.Config.Connection">Host.Config.Connection</Priv>
<Priv id="Host.Config.HyperThreading">Host.Config.HyperThreading</Priv>
<Priv id="Host.Config.Maintenance">Host.Config.Maintenance</Priv>
<Priv id="Host.Config.Memory">Host.Config.Memory</Priv>
<Priv id="Host.Config.NetService">Host.Config.NetService</Priv>
<Priv id="Host.Config.Network">Host.Config.Network</Priv>
<Priv id="Host.Config.Resources">Host.Config.Resources</Priv>
```

```
<Priv id="Host.Config.Snmp">Host.Config.Snmp</Priv>
<Priv id="Host.Config.Storage">Host.Config.Storage</Priv>
<Priv id="Host.Inventory.AddHostToCluster">Host.Inventory.AddHostToCluster</Priv>
<Priv id="Host.Inventory.AddStandaloneHost">Host.Inventory.AddStandaloneHost</Priv>
<Priv id="Host.Inventory.CreateCluster">Host.Inventory.CreateCluster</Priv>
<Priv id="Host.Inventory.DeleteCluster">Host.Inventory.DeleteCluster</Priv>
<Priv id="Host.Inventory.EditCluster">Host.Inventory.EditCluster</Priv>
<Priv id="Host.Inventory.MoveCluster">Host.Inventory.MoveCluster</Priv>
<Priv id="Host.Inventory.MoveHost">Host.Inventory.MoveHost</Priv>
<Priv
id="Host.Inventory.RemoveHostFromCluster">Host.Inventory.RemoveHostFromCluster</Priv>
<Priv id="Host.Inventory.RenameCluster">Host.Inventory.RenameCluster</Priv>
<Priv id="Host.Local.CreateVM">Host.Local.CreateVM</Priv>
<Priv id="Host.Local.DeleteVM">Host.Local.DeleteVM</Priv>
<Priv id="Host.Local.InstallAgent">Host.Local.InstallAgent</Priv>
<Priv id="Host.Local.ManageUserGroups">Host.Local.ManageUserGroups</Priv>
<Priv id="Network.Delete">Network.Delete</Priv>
<Priv id="Performance.ModifyIntervals">Performance.ModifyIntervals</Priv>
<Priv id="Resource.ApplyRecommendation">Resource.ApplyRecommendation</Priv>
<Priv id="Resource.AssignVMToPool">Resource.AssignVMToPool</Priv>
<Priv id="Resource.ColdMigrate">Resource.ColdMigrate</Priv>
<Priv id="Resource.CreatePool">Resource.CreatePool</Priv>
<Priv id="Resource.DeletePool">Resource.DeletePool</Priv>
<Priv id="Resource.EditPool">Resource.EditPool</Priv>
<Priv id="Resource.HotMigrate">Resource.HotMigrate</Priv>
<Priv id="Resource.MovePool">Resource.MovePool</Priv>
<Priv id="Resource.QueryVMotion">Resource.QueryVMotion</Priv>
<Priv id="Resource.RenamePool">Resource.RenamePool</Priv>
<Priv id="ScheduledTask.Create">ScheduledTask.Create</Priv>
<Priv id="ScheduledTask.Delete">ScheduledTask.Delete</Priv>
<Priv id="ScheduledTask.Edit">ScheduledTask.Edit</Priv>
```

<Priv id="ScheduledTask.Run">ScheduledTask.Run</Priv>

<Priv id="Sessions.GlobalMessage">Sessions.GlobalMessage</Priv>

<Priv id="Sessions.TerminateSession">Sessions.TerminateSession</Priv>

<Priv id="VirtualMachine.Config.AddExistingDisk">VirtualMachine.Config.AddExistingDisk</Priv>

<Priv id="VirtualMachine.Config.AddNewDisk">VirtualMachine.Config.AddNewDisk</Priv>

<Priv id="VirtualMachine.Config.AddRemoveDevice">VirtualMachine.Config.AddRemoveDevice</Priv>

<Priv id="VirtualMachine.Config.AdvancedConfig">VirtualMachine.Config.AdvancedConfig</Priv>

<Priv id="VirtualMachine.Config.CPUCount">VirtualMachine.Config.CPUCount</Priv>

<Priv id="VirtualMachine.Config.DiskLease">VirtualMachine.Config.DiskLease</Priv>

<Priv id="VirtualMachine.Config.EditDevice">VirtualMachine.Config.EditDevice</Priv>

<Priv id="VirtualMachine.Config.Memory">VirtualMachine.Config.Memory</Priv>

<Priv id="VirtualMachine.Config.RawDevice">VirtualMachine.Config.RawDevice</Priv>

<Priv id="VirtualMachine.Config.RemoveDisk">VirtualMachine.Config.RemoveDisk</Priv>

<Priv id="VirtualMachine.Config.Rename">VirtualMachine.Config.Rename</Priv>

<Priv id="VirtualMachine.Config.ResetGuestInfo">VirtualMachine.Config.ResetGuestInfo</Priv>

<Priv id="VirtualMachine.Config.Resource">VirtualMachine.Config.Resource</Priv>

<Priv id="VirtualMachine.Config.Settings">VirtualMachine.Config.Settings</Priv>

<Priv id="VirtualMachine.Config.UpgradeVirtualHardware">VirtualMachine.Config.UpgradeVirtualHardware</Priv>

<Priv id="VirtualMachine.Interact.AnswerQuestion">VirtualMachine.Interact.AnswerQuestion</Priv>

<Priv id="VirtualMachine.Interact.ConsoleInteract">VirtualMachine.Interact.ConsoleInteract</Priv>

<Priv id="VirtualMachine.Interact.DeviceConnection">VirtualMachine.Interact.DeviceConnection</Priv>

<Priv id="VirtualMachine.Interact.PowerOff">VirtualMachine.Interact.PowerOff</Priv>

<Priv id="VirtualMachine.Interact.PowerOn">VirtualMachine.Interact.PowerOn</Priv>

<Priv id="VirtualMachine.Interact.Reset">VirtualMachine.Interact.Reset</Priv>

<Priv id="VirtualMachine.Interact.SetCDMedia">VirtualMachine.Interact.SetCDMedia</Priv>

<Priv

id="VirtualMachine.Interact.SetFloppyMedia">VirtualMachine.Interact.SetFloppyMedia</Priv>

<Priv id="VirtualMachine.Interact.Suspend">VirtualMachine.Interact.Suspend</Priv>

<Priv id="VirtualMachine.Interact.ToolsInstall">VirtualMachine.Interact.ToolsInstall</Priv>

<Priv id="VirtualMachine.Inventory.Create">VirtualMachine.Inventory.Create</Priv>

<Priv id="VirtualMachine.Inventory.Delete">VirtualMachine.Inventory.Delete</Priv>

<Priv id="VirtualMachine.Inventory.Move">VirtualMachine.Inventory.Move</Priv>

<Priv id="VirtualMachine.Provisioning.Clone">VirtualMachine.Provisioning.Clone</Priv>

<Priv id="VirtualMachine.Provisioning.CloneTemplate">VirtualMachine.Provisioning.CloneTemplate</Priv>

<Priv id="VirtualMachine.Provisioning.CreateTemplateFromVM">VirtualMachine.Provisioning.CreateTemplateFromVM</Priv>

<Priv id="VirtualMachine.Provisioning.Customize">VirtualMachine.Provisioning.Customize</Priv>

<Priv id="VirtualMachine.Provisioning.DeployTemplate">VirtualMachine.Provisioning.DeployTemplate</Priv>

<Priv id="VirtualMachine.Provisioning.DiskRandomAccess">VirtualMachine.Provisioning.DiskRandomAccess</Priv>

<Priv id="VirtualMachine.Provisioning.DiskRandomRead">VirtualMachine.Provisioning.DiskRandomRead</Priv>

<Priv id="VirtualMachine.Provisioning.GetVmFiles">VirtualMachine.Provisioning.GetVmFiles</Priv>

<Priv id="VirtualMachine.Provisioning.MarkAsTemplate">VirtualMachine.Provisioning.MarkAsTemplate</Priv>

<Priv id="VirtualMachine.Provisioning.MarkAsVM">VirtualMachine.Provisioning.MarkAsVM</Priv>

<Priv id="VirtualMachine.Provisioning.ModifyCustSpecs">VirtualMachine.Provisioning.ModifyCustSpecs</Priv>

<Priv id="VirtualMachine.Provisioning.PutVmFiles">VirtualMachine.Provisioning.PutVmFiles</Priv>

<Priv id="VirtualMachine.Provisioning.ReadCustSpecs">VirtualMachine.Provisioning.ReadCustSpecs</Pr

```
iv>
<Priv id="VirtualMachine.State.CreateSnapshot">VirtualMachine.State.CreateSnapshot</Priv>
<Priv id="VirtualMachine.State.RemoveSnapshot">VirtualMachine.State.RemoveSnapshot</Priv>
<Priv id="VirtualMachine.State.RenameSnapshot">VirtualMachine.State.RenameSnapshot</Priv>
<Priv id="VirtualMachine.State.RevertToSnapshot">VirtualMachine.State.RevertToSnapshot</Priv>
<PrivRoleId>11</PrivRoleId>
</PrivSet>
<RoleData id="11">
<RoleId>11</RoleId>
<RoleName>Clone of Administrator</RoleName>
</RoleData>
</ConfigRoot>
```


ESX 3.5 Server Custom Roles

You can build custom roles directly on a stand-alone ESX 3.5 server by using the following steps:

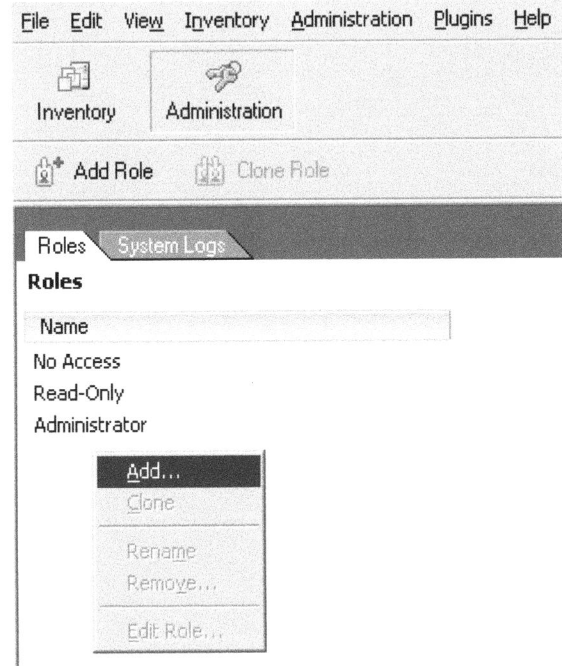

Figure 10.31 ESX 3.5 Server Roles Tab Add Role Menu

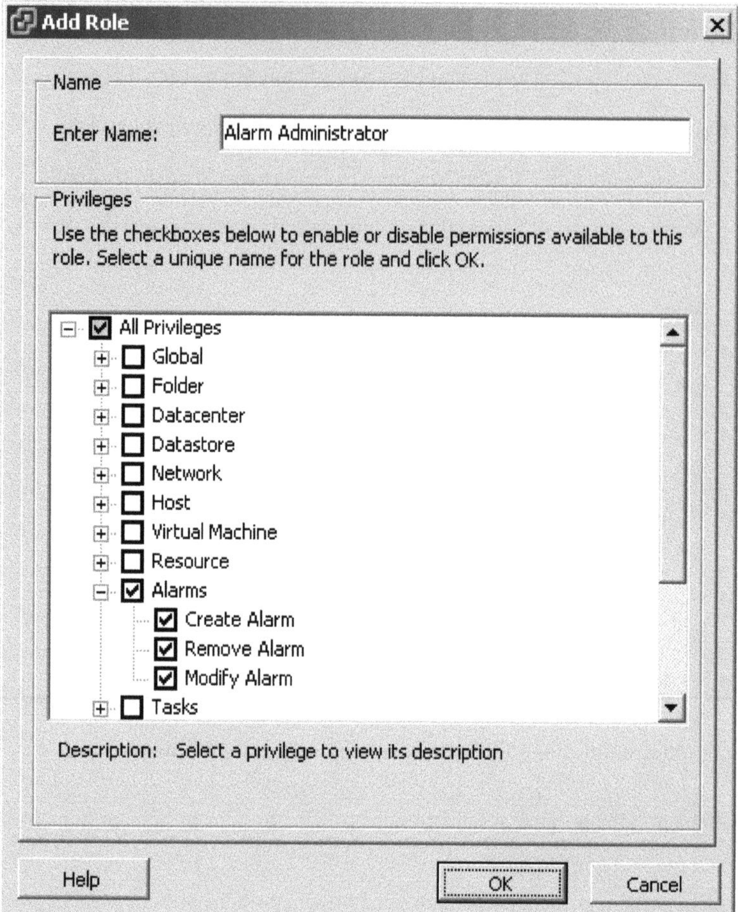

Figure 10.32 ESX 3.5 Server Add Role Dialog Box

Selecting the add command will bring up the Add Role dialog box as shown in Figure 10.32. Click the OK button to continue.

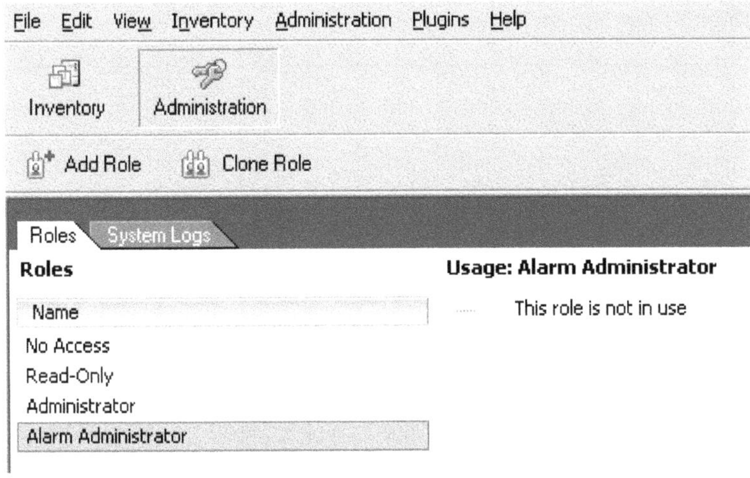

Figure 10.33 Alarm Administrator Custom Role

The newly added Alarm Administrator custom role has been added as shown in Figure 10.33.

Right clicking on a role and selecting the Edit Role... menu option will bring up the Edit Role dialog box as shown in Figure 10.34.

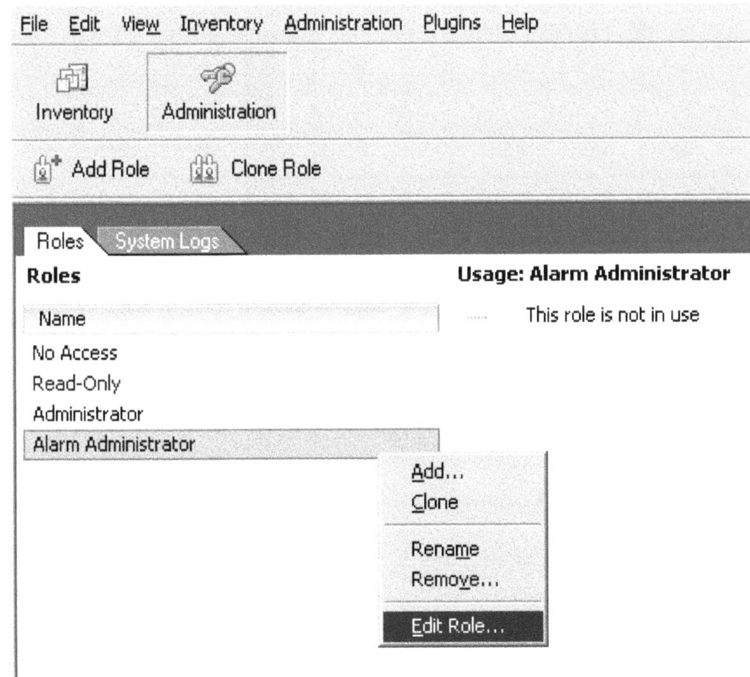

Figure 10.34 ESX 3.5 Server Edit Role Menu Option

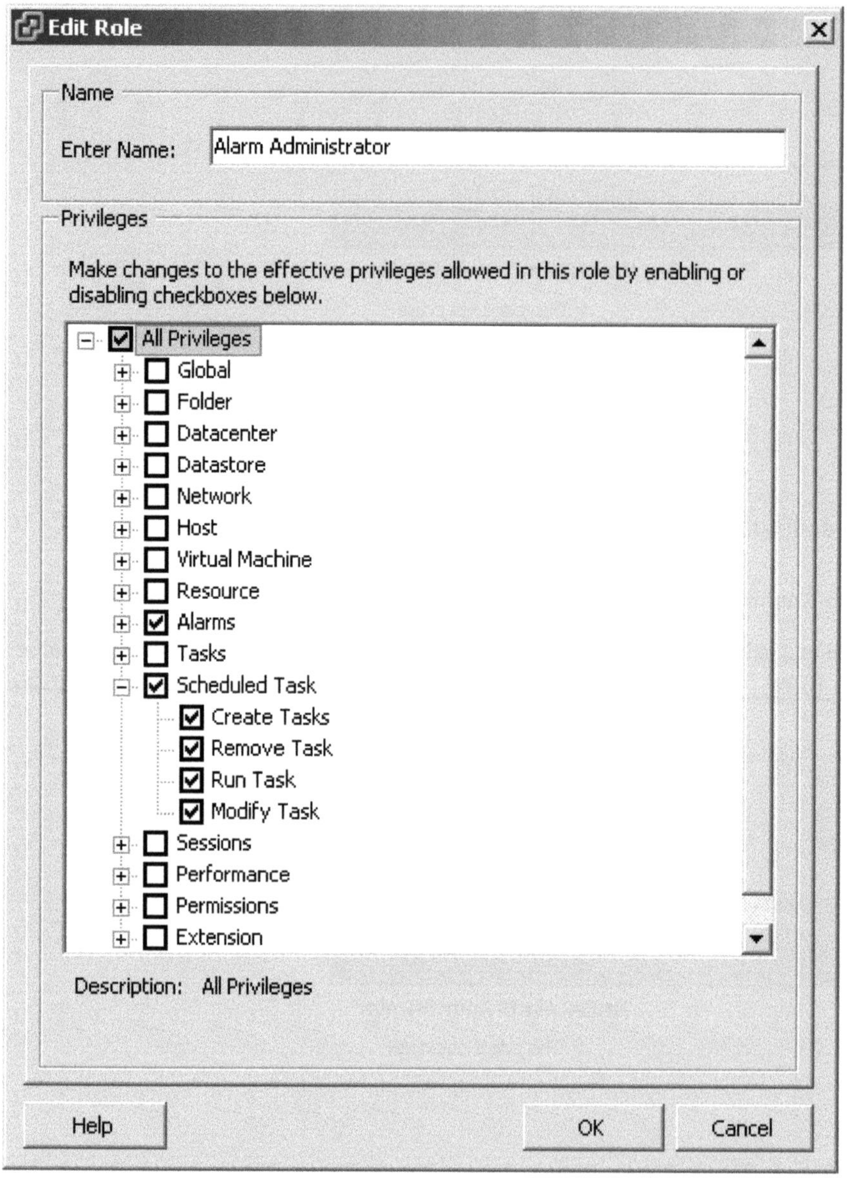

Figure 10.35 ESX 3.5 Server Edit Role Dialog Box

Make the appropriate modifications to the role and select the OK button as shown in Figure 10.35.

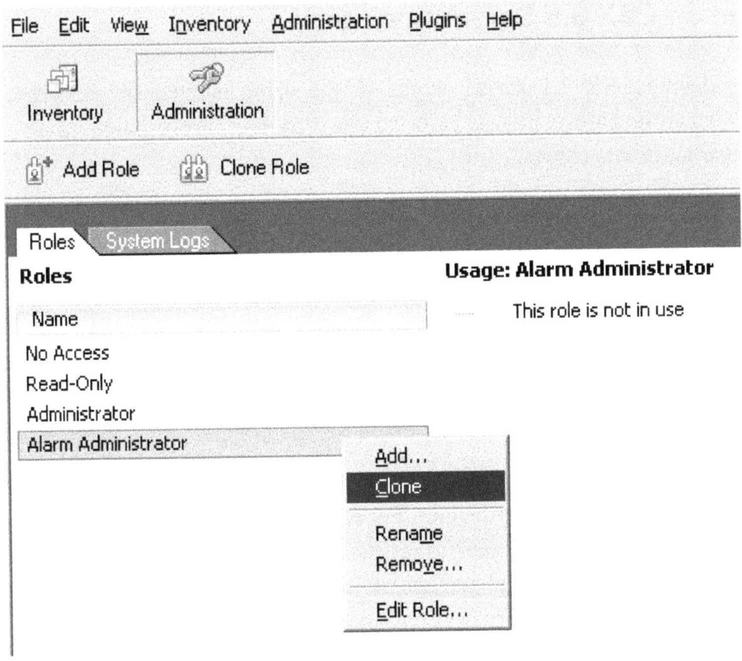

Figure 10.36 ESX 3.5 Server Clone Role Menu Option

Right clicking on a role and selecting the Clone command will clone the role as shown in Figure 10.36.

Enter the name of the cloned role or press enter to accept the default as shown in Figure 10.37.

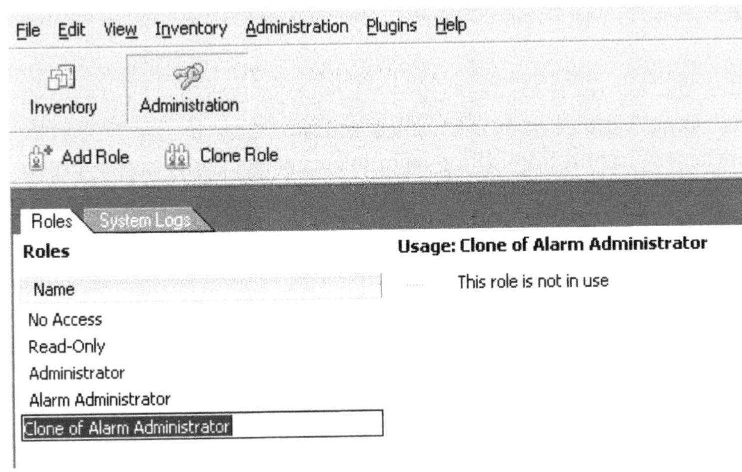

Figure 10.37 ESX 3.5 Server Cloned Role

Privilege Propagation in an ESX 3.5 Server Inventory

Privilege propagation on a standalone ESX 3.5 server works in the same manner as privilege propagation within the VirtualCenter inventory. Please refer to the Privilege Propagation in the VirtualCenter Inventory section earlier in this chapter.

Troubleshooting Common Permissions and Rights Problems

Possible problems with permissions can occur from incorrectly applying permissions on an object with the default propagate to child objects setting in place. In such circumstances, a user may obtain more permissions than desired. It is important to keep in mind that permissions by default propagate downward in the VirtualCenter inventory. When using the default settings, apply more restrictive access further down the inventory hierarchy to restrict user access.

VirtualCenter views may also cause permission inconsistencies. For example, applying permissions to a folder called VMProduction in the Hosts & Clusters view to restrict virtual machine access may not completely remove the user's ability to access the virtual machine. In this example, the VMProduction folder contains the ESX server that hosts the Web Server virtual machine. A user without access to the VMProduction folder in the Hosts & Clusters view will not be able to access the Web Server virtual machine in this view. If the user changes to the Virtual Machine & Templates view, the VMProduction folder may not exist in this view. This would allow the user to access the Web Server virtual machine.

Verify the correct permissions are applied on the inventory object by selecting the object and clicking on the Permissions tab. Review the User/Group, Role and Defined in columns. The Permissions tab displays all permissions applied to this object whether directly or indirectly (i.e. inherited). It may also be necessary to review any sample or custom roles to verify the correct privileges are being used in the role.

When logging onto VirtualCenter, the log on credentials can be integrated with the local system accounts on the Windows server where VirtualCenter is installed and also from within the Active Directory domain that the VirtualCenter server resides. If log on problems occur, verify proper log on credentials are being used either by logging directly onto the Windows server where VirtualCenter is installed or logging onto the Active Directory domain.

Problems logging onto the ESX server using the VI Client could be improper log on credentials being used or possibly the vmware-hostd service is not running. To verify if the vmware-hostd service is running, log on to the ESX host either using the local console or via SSH, switch to the root user and issue the following command:

service mgmt-vmware status

The output should be as follows if the vmware-hostd service is running: (Note, the Process Identification (PID) number may vary)

vmware-hostd (pid 1433) is running...

External References

The VMware ESX 3.5 and ESXi Server version 3.5 Documentation Page:

http://www.vmware.com/support/pubs/vi_pubs.html

Installation and Upgrade Guide:

http://www.vmware.com/pdf/vi3_301_201_installation_guide.pdf

Basic System Administration Guide:

http://www.vmware.com/pdf/vi3_301_201_admin_guide.pdf

Server Configuration Guide:

http://www.vmware.com/pdf/vi3_301_201_server_config.pdf

Managing VMware VirtualCenter Roles and Permissions:

http://www.vmware.com/pdf/vi3_vc_roles.pdf

Enabling Active Directory Authentication with ESX Server:

http://www.vmware.com/pdf/esx3_esxcfg_auth_tn.pdf

Sample Test Questions

1. Which three are ESX Server pre-defined system roles?

a. Virtual Machine Power User

b. Administrator

c. Read Only

d. Virtual Machine Administrator

e. No Access

2. You work as an administrator in your company. You are using VirtualCenter to manage multiple ESX 3.5 servers and you create a new user account and assign this user Administrator Privileges. Assuming you have not changed the default user privileges settings for the account created, which privileges will that user have on the ESX Server cluster in which this server resides?

a. No Access

b. ESX Server User

c. None

d. Virtual Machine Administrator

e Administrator

3. You need to connect to your resources in your virtual infrastructure. Which way is not a supported method to connect?

a. Using the VI Client to access the ESX 3.5 server directly

b. Using the CLI interface to access the ESX 3.5 server directly

c. Using the web interface to access the ESX 3.5 server directly

d. Using the CLI interface to access the ESX 3.5 server using VirtualCenter

e. Using the VI Client to access the ESX 3.5 server using VirtualCenter

f. Using the web interface to access the ESX 3.5 server using VirtualCenter

4. What ESX 3.5 server accounts by default have administrator access?

a. vpxauser

b. administrator

c. root

d. hostd

e. vpxuser

5. There are thirteen categories of privileges. Which are not one of the 13 categories?

a. Local

b. Global

c. Folder

d. Datacenter

e. Datastore

f Network

g. Virtual Switch

h. Host

i. Cluster

j. Virtual Machine

k. Resource

l. Alarms

m. Events

m. Scheduled Task

o. Sessions

p. Performance

q. Permissions

6. You want to restrict a user's capabilities of access to your virtual resources so you give them the No Access role. Which of the following describes what privileges the No Access role has?

a. Users assigned the No Access system role will be able to view the state and details of an object. VI Client menus and toolbar actions are disabled.

b. Users assigned the No Access system role will not be able to log into an ESX 3.5 server.

c. Users assigned the No Access system role on an object are unable to view or modify the object. In addition, users will not be able to view content in the VI Client tabs associated with the object.

d. Users assigned the No Access system role on an object are unable to modify the account password.

e. Users assigned the No Access system role on an object are unable to access only VirtualCenter. Access is still allowed via the CLI.

7. Which of the following default VirtualCenter roles can be modified?

a. Resource Pool Administrator

b. Administrator

c. Virtual Machine Administrator

d. Read-Only

e. None of the above - default roles cannot be modified.

8. Ann Marie is the security administrator that is working on trying to determine why a user does not have access to the console of a virtual machine. She discovers that they have administrator access which is propagated to the VM in question. What could cause them not getting access to that VM?

a. They have the No Access role directly assigned to that VM.

b. They have the Read Only role directly assigned to that VM.

c. They have the No Access role directly assigned to the parent object of the VM.

d. They have the Read Only role directly assigned to the parent object of the VM.

e. They don't have a user account on that VM.

9. Which of the following are types of roles used in VirtualCenter?

a. Simple

b. Custom

c. State

d. Sample

e. Site

f. System

10. You are going to create a custom role for one of your user accounts. How many different privileges are available for you to configure the custom role?

a. 8

b. 24

c. 56

d. 64

e. 110

Sample Test Solutions

1. Which three are ESX Server pre-defined system roles?

a. Virtual Machine Power User

b. Administrator

c. Read Only

d. Virtual Machine Administrator

e. No Access

Answer: b, c and e - Virtual Machine Power User and Virtual Machine Administrator are VirtualCenter sample roles.

2. You work as an administrator in your company. You are using VirtualCenter to manage multiple ESX 3.5 servers and you create a new user account and assign this user Administrator Privileges. Assuming you have not changed the default user privileges settings for the account created, which privileges will that user have on the ESX Server cluster in which this server resides?

a. No Access

b. ESX Server User

c. None

d. Virtual Machine Administrator

e. Administrator

Answer: e - Administrator privileges give a user all privileges for all objects in the inventory.

3. You need to connect to your resources in your virtual infrastructure. Which way is not a supported method to connect?

a. Using the VI Client to access the ESX 3.5 server directly

b. Using the CLI interface to access the ESX 3.5 server directly

c. Using the web interface to access the ESX 3.5 server directly

d. Using the CLI interface to access the ESX 3.5 server using VirtualCenter

e. Using the VI Client to access the ESX 3.5 server using VirtualCenter

f. Using the web interface to access the ESX 3.5 server using VirtualCenter

Answer: d - There is no CLI interface for VirtualCenter.

4. What ESX 3.5 server accounts by default have administrator access?

a. vpxauser

b. administrator

c. root

d. hostd

e. vpxuser

***Answer:** c and e - The ESX 3.5 server does not have an administrator account like a Windows server does. hostd is a process and there isn't a vpxauser account.*

5. There are thirteen categories of privileges. Which are not one of the 13 categories?

a. Local

b. Global

c. Folder

d. Datacenter

e. Datastore

f. Network

g. Virtual Switch

h. Host

i. Cluster

j. Virtual Machine

k. Resource

l. Alarms

m. Events

n. Scheduled Task

o. Sessions

p. Performance

q. Permissions

***Answer:** a, g, i, and m - these are not privilege categories.*

6. You want to restrict a user's capabilities when access your virtual resources so you give them the No Access role. Which of the following describes what privileges the No Access role has?

a. Users assigned the No Access system role will be able to view the state and details of an object. VI

Client menus and toolbar actions are disabled.

b. Users assigned the No Access system role will not be able to log into an ESX 3.5 server.

c. Users assigned the No Access system role on an object are unable to view or modify the object. In addition, users will not be able to view content in the VI Client tabs associated with the object.

d. Users assigned the No Access system role on an object are unable to modify the account password.

e. Users assigned the No Access system role on an object are unable to access only VirtualCenter. Access is still allowed via the CLI.

Answer: c

7. Which of the following default VirtualCenter roles can be modified?

a. Resource Pool Administrator

b. Administrator

c. Virtual Machine Administrator

d. Read-Only

e. None of the above - default roles cannot be modified.

Answer: a and c - the 5 sample roles that can be modified: Resource Pool Administrator, Virtual Machine Administrator, Virtual Machine User, Virtual Machine Power User and Datacenter Administrator.

8. Ann Marie is the security administrator that is working on trying to determine why a user does not have access to the console of a virtual machine. She discovers that they have administrator access which is propagated to the VM in question. What could cause them not getting access to that VM?

a. They have the No Access role directly assigned to that VM.

b. They have the Read Only role directly assigned to that VM.

c. They have the No Access role directly assigned to the parent object of the VM.

d. They have the Read Only role directly assigned to the parent object of the VM.

e. They don't have a user account on that VM.

Answer: a and b - When a user account has both propagated and directly assigned permissions on the same object, the directly assigned permissions take precedence.

9. Which of the following are types of roles used in VirtualCenter?

a. Simple

b. Custom

c. State

d. Sample

e. Site

f. System

Answer: b, d and f - the other choices are not valid types.

10. You are going to create a custom role for one of your user accounts. How many different privileges are available for you to configure the custom role?

a. 8

b. 24

c. 56

d. 64

e. 110

Answer: e - There are 110 different privileges.

Chapter 11

Resource Optimization

After reading this chapter you should be able to complete the following tasks:

- Understand resource consumption
- Understand CPU utilization
- Understand and configure processor affinity
- Configure CPU utilization for a virtual machine
- Understand memory utilization
- Configure memory utilization for a virtual machine
- Understand network utilization
- Configure network I/O utilization for a virtual machine
- Understand disk I/O utilization
- Configure disk I/O utilization for a virtual machine
- Troubleshooting common resource optimization problems

Resource Consumption

The operating system and applications in a physical server have exclusive access to all of the CPU, memory, network I/O and disk I/O resources. As long as the OS and applications don't attempt to utilize more resources than the system has there shouldn't be any performance issues on that system.

The same is true for an ESX 3.5 server. As long as the total aggregate CPU, memory, network I/O and disk I/O utilization of all the VMs running on that server do not exceed its capacity then there shouldn't be any performance issues on that ESX 3.5 server.

Resource Utilization

One of the biggest benefits of virtualization is to get better resource utilization out of the physical servers. It is possible to over commit those resources and create performance bottlenecks in any of the four resource categories:

- CPU utilization
- Memory utilization
- Network I/O utilization
- Disk I/O utilization

We will examine in this chapter how virtual machines utilize these four resources and how to configure and manage the resource consumption on an ESX 3.5 server.

We will see that we can set the following configuration settings for vCPUs and memory resources:

- Limits
- Reservations
- Shares

We will also see how the VMkernel manages these resources based on those configuration settings. We also examine how to configure disk I/O shares and how to limit the network outbound traffic.

How Are Virtual CPUs Utilized in a Virtual Machine?

In a physical system the operating system has exclusive access to all process power provided by the CPUs. In a virtualized environment the CPU resources are shared between multiple guest operating systems installed in the VMs on the ESX 3.5 server. The first thing we need to look at is how the ESX 3.5 server shares the CPU resources.

Virtual CPUs

Virtual machines when built can be configured with 1, 2 or 4 virtual CPUs as shown in Figure 11.1.

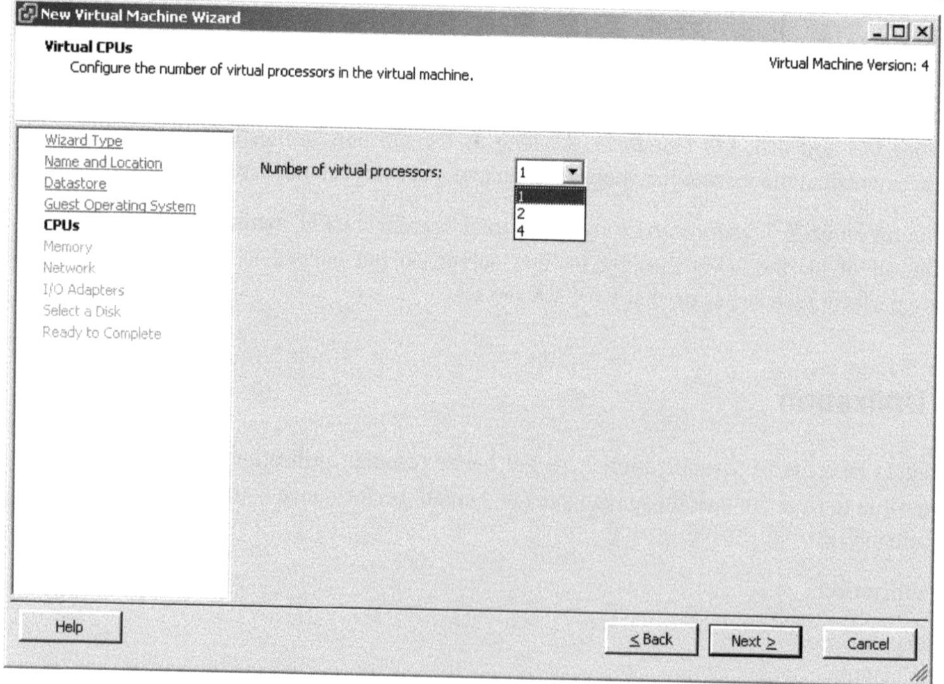

Figure 11.1 New Virtual Machine Virtual CPU

As we learned in Chapter 7 – Virtual Machines, we can control the number of virtual CPUs as well as the total MHz of processing power that can be assigned to those virtual CPUs.

CPU Time

When we create a VM we can decide how many vCPUs the VM is to have. It is important to note that the number of vCPUs configured in a VM is the total number of processors the guest OS thinks it has. Remember that a guest OS does not realize that it is in a virtual environment when using a full virtualization product like the VMware VI 3 product. So the virtualization process has to operate like a physical server from the VMs perspective.

It is also important to note that running your guest OS with multiple vCPUs will not necessarily increase your OS or application performance. The guest OS and application needs to be able to support multi-threaded operations to take advantage of the multiple vCPUs. In some cases it would be better just to have one vCPU and give it more CPU time. CPU time is the total amount of processing power given to the virtual machine.

CPU time is calculated as follows:

[Total number of sockets] times [total number of cores per socket] times [core speed in MHz] equals [CPU time in MHz]

Sockets

A socket is the physical connector the actual processor chip in the server is placed into. AMD and Intel have a number of different CPU chips that are supported in an ESX 3.5 server. These chips are able to execute one computational process per cycle which explains why processor speeds have risen over the past decades dramatically. The only way the chip vendors could get their processor to do more work was to make it be able to run at a faster speed thus increasing the amount of cycles and increasing the amount of work the processor could do.

The downside with increasing speed is that the chips need to access the data in memory and over the years this process has taken more and more cycles to accomplish. Also the chip design has got a lot smaller and this increased the chance of having path delays when accessing the circuitry on the chip. This issue required more error correction circuitry which required more transistors in the chip. The increase in transistor count required more power for the CPU which in turn generated more heat. The increase in heat required more cooling in the server and server room. It became a vicious cycle! 1993 era Intel Pentium processors had approximately 3 million transistors. Today's processors have over a billion transistors!

Cores

In 2004 Intel joined AMD, IBM and Sun Microsystems in announcing that it wasn't feasible to try to continue building processors with higher clock speeds. Instead they decided on a different approach, to build multiple instances of the processor on the same socket. Multicore CPUs are more power efficient because they use a slower clock speed and require less transistors. Total processing power increased since each core can process data independently of the other cores.

Core Speed

Core speed is measured in MHz. A 2 GHz core speed is equal to 2,000 MHz. 2,000 MHz is equal to 2,000 million cycles and a core can execute one instruction per cycle.

CPU Time Examples

Let's take a look at a few examples on calculating CPU time for an ESX 3.5 server.

Example 1:

If the system had two single core processors running at 3.2 GHz the CPU time would be equal to:

2 sockets times 1 cores per socket times 3,200 MHz core speed equals 6,400 MHz CPU time

Example 2:

If the system had 4 dual core processors running at 2.6 GHz the CPU time would be equal to:

4 sockets times 2 cores per socket times 2,600 MHz core speed equals 20,800 MHz CPU time

Example 3:

If the system had 8 quad core processors running at 2.4 GHz the CPU time would be equal to:

8 sockets times 4 cores per socket times 2,400 MHz core speed equals 76,800 MHz CPU time

ESX 3.5 Server Maximums

- The maximum number of virtual CPUs supported in an ESX 3.5 server configuration is 128
- The maximum amount of sockets supported in an ESX 3.5 server configuration is 32. ESX supports a maximum of 32 proc threads; thus, if there are 32 sockets on a server, each can only be occupied by a single core proc, as the system would be at the supported maximum
- The maximum amount of cores per socket in an ESX 3.5 server configuration is 8 (at the time of writing no AMD or Intel processor has more than 4 cores per socket.) 8 vCPUs is the maximum per core for ESX Server. Virtual Desktop Infrastructure (VDI) maximum is 11 vCPUs

Hyper-Threading Technology (HTT)

Intel created and supports the hyper-threading technology for a number of its processors:

- Intel® Itanium® Processor
- Intel® Xeon® Processor

- Intel® Pentium® 4 Processor Extreme Edition Supporting Hyper-Threading Technology
- Intel® Pentium® 4 Processor

An Intel processor with Hyper-Threading enabled is treated by the guest operating system in an ESX 3.5 server as two processors instead of one. These two hyper-threads are considered to be two logical CPUs (LCPUs) and therefore appear to the ESX 3.5 server as two LCPUs.

NOTE: vCPUs are what are scheduled by the VMkernel, as the processors for the VMs.

For an in-depth look at how the hyper-threading technology works read the *Intel Technology Journal* Volume 06 Issue 01 Published February 14, 2002 ISSN 1535766X: ftp://download.intel.com/technology/itj/2002/volume06issue01/vol6iss1_hyper_threading_technology .pdf

The VMkernel Scheduler

The VMkernel scheduler is responsible to allocate the CPU time to the virtual machines. It does not give out the cycles based on a first come first serve basis. Instead it looks at the amount of cycles requested by the VMs every 20 milliseconds and calculates what it can give each VM based on the configured constraints applied to each VM.

We will now examine these constraints.

Processor Affinity

When you build your VM you can decide to allocate it 1, 2 or 4 vCPUs. By default the VMkernel can schedule a VMs request for a virtual processor on any available LCPU in the server. You can however configure your VM to use specific LCPUs in the system.

Figure 11.2 shows the Virtual Machine Properties screen. The Resources tab is selected and the Advanced CPU Settings has been selected.

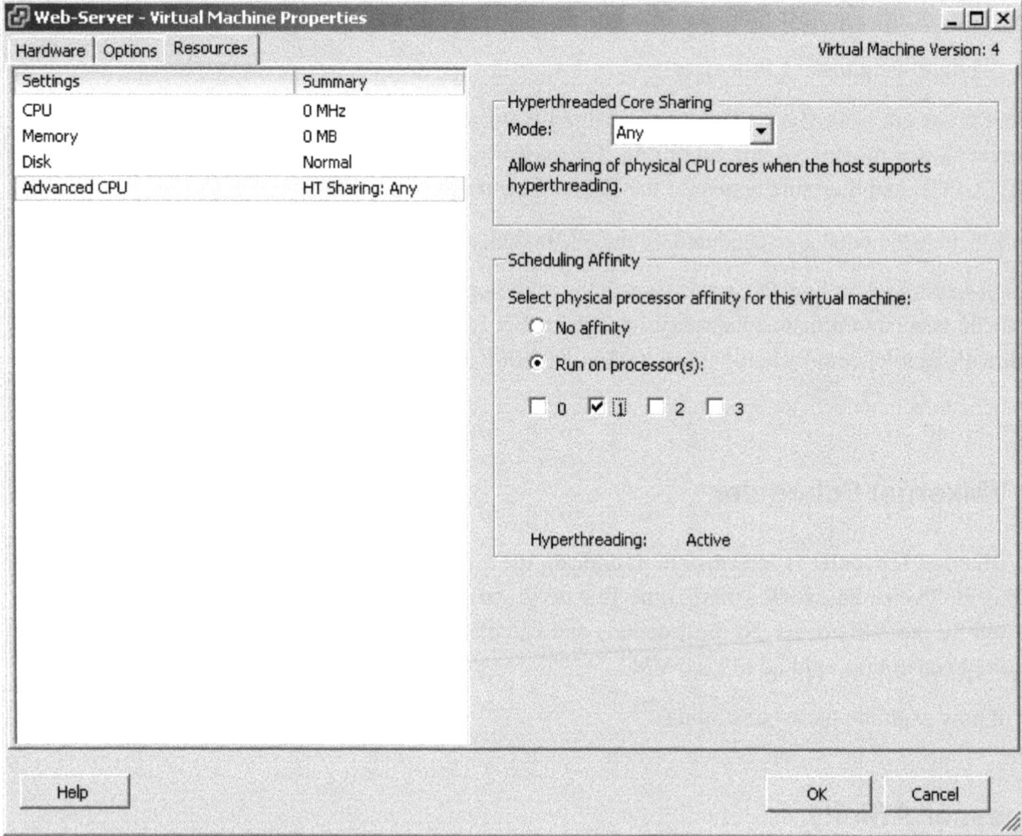

Figure 11.2 CPU Affinity Settings

You typically do not need to edit any of the settings on this screen. The only time you would do it is to improve performance on critical virtual machines. Assigning a vCPU to a physical CPU via processor affinity requires the virtual machine to be powered off then back on for the change to take affect.

Hyper-threading Sharing

You can set the Hyper-threading Sharing Mode in this screen. The supported modes are:

- Any - which is the default mode which will allow the VMkernel to schedule this VM to use any of the hyper-threads on any core available on the ESX 3.5 server.
- None - this setting will cause the VMkernel to schedule this VM to have exclusive use of a processor core whenever it is scheduled to it. When the virtual machine is using the core the other hyper-thread of the core is "halted".
- Internal - if this setting is chosen for a virtual machine with exactly two virtual processors, the two virtual processors are allowed to share one physical core. This functionality is at the discretion of the ESX 3.5 server scheduler. The virtual machine never shares a core with any other virtual machines on the ESX 3.5 server when this option is selected. If this virtual

machine is configured with one or four vCPUs then this setting is the same as the None setting.

NOTE: Be aware that you will not see these options if the VM is in a fully automated DRS cluster or when the ESX 3.5 server has only one processor core and no hyper-threading.

Scheduling Affinity

The Scheduling Affinity settings control how the virtual machine vCPUs are distributed across the ESX 3.5 server's physical cores and hyper-threads if hyper-threading is enabled.

NOTE: If the virtual machine resides in a fully automated DRS cluster then this option is not allowed. If the virtual machine is cold migrated to a new host then the settings are cleared as VMotion is not allowed for a VM with processor scheduling affinity set.

If hyper-threading is disabled the check boxes for the individual processors represent physical cores. If hyper-threading is enabled the check boxes for the individual processors represent logical cores which is two per physical core.

NOTE: If you put checks in all the boxes that is the same as not applying any affinity. You must provide at least as many processor affinities as the number of virtual CPUs configured in the virtual machine.

Configure Virtual Machine CPU Utilization

When we examine CPU resource utilization we must consider that there are many resource settings that can influence the VMkernel's scheduler and how it allocates the CPU cycles available in the ESX 3.5 server. Let's look at a scenario that can help better explain these resource settings and how the VMkernel scheduler implements those settings on the ESX 3.5 stand alone system.

We will examine the following virtual machine CPU performance and management technologies:

- CPU reservations
- Service console CPU reservation
- CPU limits
- Admission control
- CPU shares

In our first scenario an ESX administrator is in charge of implementing a standalone ESX server to be used for the company's first virtualization project involving four physical servers in the datacenter.

The following are the four physical servers and the applications that they provide:

- Web Server - The web server is the main production web server for the company. It experiences heavy traffic between 10am - 5pm.
- Application Server - The application server is used in conjunction with the web server to

process user requests from the web site.

- Database Server - The database server is the back end transaction engine and services data requests from the application server.
- Firewall Server - The firewall server is responsible for filtering requests from outside the corporate network in order to preserve the integrity of the web, application and database servers.

Capacity Planning

Without having monitored the physical systems actual CPU usage, there would be no way to size the virtual machines short of guessing the values. It is extremely important to gather this data prior to building your ESX server.

In our scenario, after monitoring the performance of each physical server for two weeks to gather baseline information, the ESX administrator presented the baseline performance charts to the IT administrators that maintained the physical servers. The CPU and memory requirements to operate the four physical servers were a total of 8,000 MHz for CPU processing power and 8 GB of memory.

The ESX administrator then purchased a system that is listed on the VMware hardware compatibility list. It is configured with dual sockets and dual cores with each core operating at 2,125 MHz. It also is configured with 8 GB of memory.

The ESX administrator built the first virtual machine to be used to run the web server application in the guest OS. The physical server was configured with one CPU. The baseline information showed that the web server required between 250 MHz and 500 MHz processing power to meet its workload requirements. The ESX administrator noted that the physical server had a single one core CPU operating at 2,000 MHz. The ESX administrator decided to use VMware Enterprise Converter to convert the physical machine into a virtual machine.

CPU Reservations

In order to configure the web server VM so it can meet its normal workload, the ESX server administrator decided to build the VM with one vCPU and give the VM a CPU reservation of 500 MHz. CPU reservations are 0 (zero) by default. CPU reservations are a guarantee that the scheduler will be able to give the VM the processing power if it requires it. If the VM doesn't need the full amount of CPU cycles defined in its CPU reservation then the remaining CPU cycles can be allocated to other VMs on the ESX 3.5 server.

Service Console CPU Reservation

The service console reserves 8% of CPU capacity time in the ESX 3.5 server. In our scenario this would calculate to be 8% of 8,500 MHz which equals 680 MHz. This is an important number to know because this 680 MHz is not available for use by virtual machines.

NOTE: The service console is always scheduled to use CPU 0.

Admission Control

The purpose of admission control is to determine whether or not a VM can be powered on. Another way to look at admission control for a VM is whether the VMkernel will "press the virtual power button" on the VM or not. To make this determination, the admission control process subtracts the total reservations of all running VMs from the total available resources to determine if there are enough additional resources to meet the reservation of the VM that is being powered on. For example, let's take a look at how the admission control process may function on an ESX system with 2,000 MHz available for virtual machine use and 6 virtual machines configured but powered off. Our six virtual machines are labeled VM1, VM2, VM3, VM4, VM5 and VM6. Each has a CPU reservation of 200 MHz. These virtual machines are powered on one at a time as shown below:

VM1 - Powered on using 100 MHz - 400 MHz Reserved

VM2 - Powered on using 100 MHz - 400 MHz Reserved

VM3 - Powered on using 100 MHz - 400 MHz Reserved

VM4 - Powered on using 100 MHz - 400 MHz Reserved

VM5 - Powered on using 100 MHz - 400 MHz Reserved

Total CPU used equals 500 MHz. Total CPU reserved equals 2,000 MHz

As VM6 with its 200 MHz attempts to power on, it fails with insufficient resources as the cause of the failure. Even though there is only 500 MHz being used leaving 1500 MHz unused, the total CPU reservation on the ESX server is 2,000 MHz. Therefore, since a reservation is a guarantee by the VMkernel that it can always provide the reservation value of a powered on virtual machine, admission control denies the sixth virtual machine the ability to power on. We will discuss admission control as it relates to memory later in this chapter.

In our scenario as shown in Figure 11.3 we see the service console has 1 vCPU and its CPU reservation is 680 MHz. By subtracting the current reservation of the service console from the ESX system which in our example is 8,500 MHz, a remainder of 7,820 MHz is left for virtual machine use. Since the service console is started before any virtual machines are started, the service console resources are already subtracted from the total available CPU time. Hence, when reviewing unreserved CPU capacity from within the VI Client, the value stated as unreserved is the total value available for virtual machines.

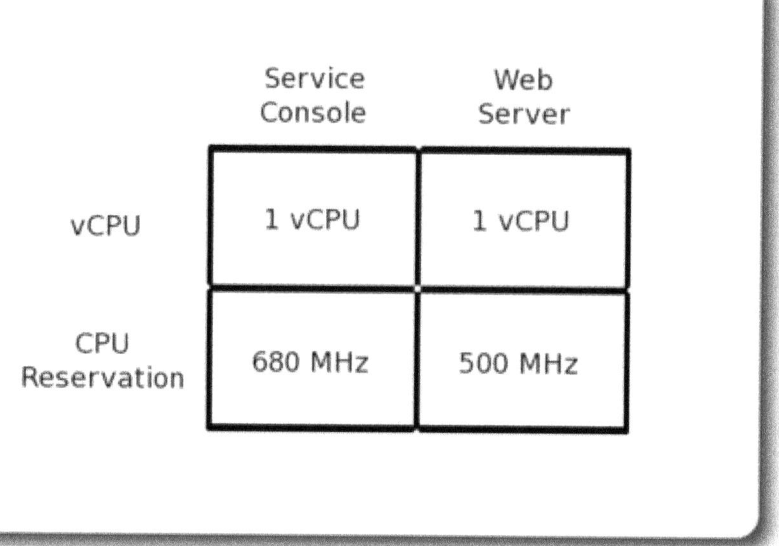

Figure 11.3 Service Console and Web Server VM

We noted previously that the web server VM has one vCPU and a CPU reservation of 500 MHz. When this VM is powered on, admission control subtracts the web server's reservation of 500 MHz from the system's total unreserved CPU time for virtual machines. This VM can be powered on as it only requires a reservation value of 500 MHz and the system currently has 7,820 MHz unreserved.

CPU Limits

When you build a VM you can set the CPU limit which is the total amount of CPU cycles in MHz that the VM is allowed to have. This is what the guest operating system thinks it has. A virtual machine by default has its limit set as unlimited which equals the total number of vCPUs configured for the VM times the CPU core speed of the ESX host.

NOTE: The unlimited value represents the total CPU time in the ESX server minus 8% reservation for the service console.

For example: In our scenario the ESX 3.5 server is configured with dual sockets and dual cores with each core operating at 2,125 MHz. Unlimited would be as follows:

- On a one vCPU VM it would represent 2,125 MHz
- On a two vCPU VM it would represent 4,250 MHz
- On a four vCPU VM it would represent 7,820 MHz (8,500 MHz minus the 680 MHz service console reservation)

The ESX administrator can edit this value after the VM is built by editing its properties as shown in Figure 11.4.

NOTE: Changing the VMs limit setting can be done while the VM is running. The VM however doesn't realize that it no longer has what it thinks it has.

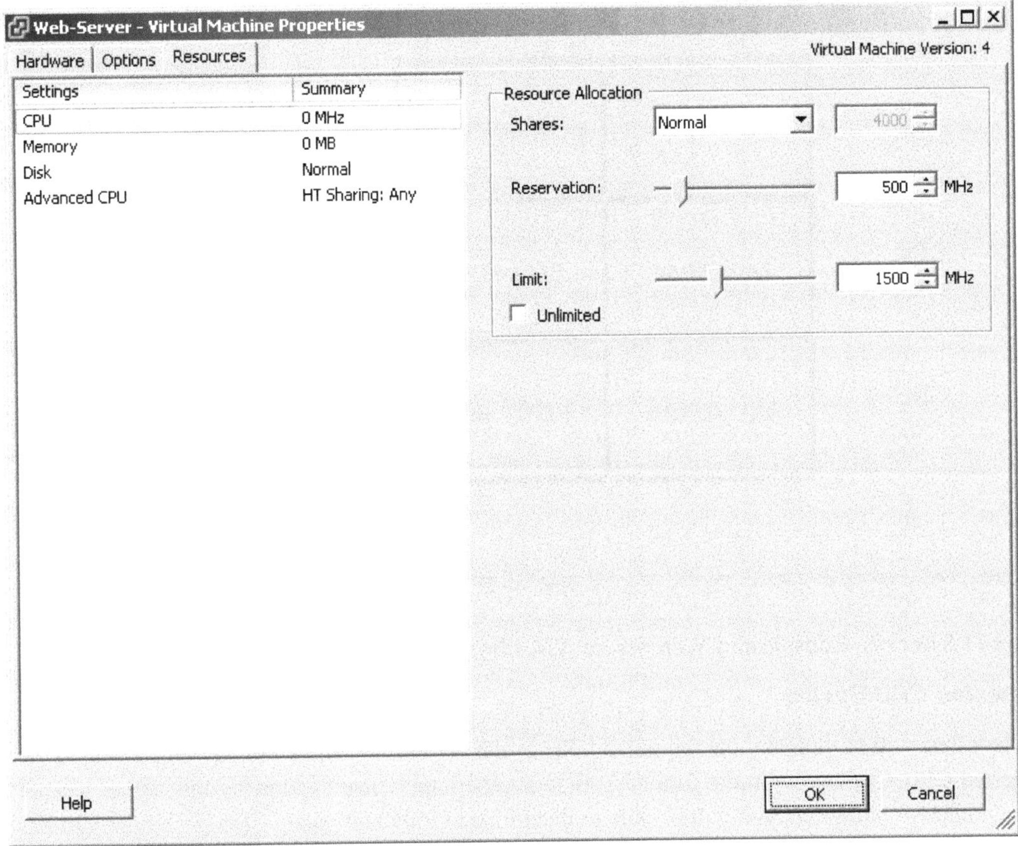

Figure 11.4 Service Console and Web Server VM

NOTE: The CPU limit is divided by the number of vCPUs configured in the VM. For example, in a VM with four vCPUs and a limit of 1,000 MHz, the guest OS would see four 250 MHz processors. If that same VM were configured with just one vCPU the guest OS would see it as one 1,000 MHz processor. If the application in the VM is not programmed to take advantage of multiple processors then the four vCPU configuration could actually cause a performance bottleneck.

In our scenario the web server VM has one vCPU. The ESX administrator configured it with a CPU limit of 1,500 MHz as shown in Figure 11.4. This value was set based on the baseline information gathered from the physical server that previously ran the application. If you don't have a baseline then you will need to make an educated guess. The CPU limit can be adjusted later if needed.

We can see in Figure 11.5 that the service console has a CPU limit set at the default of unlimited.

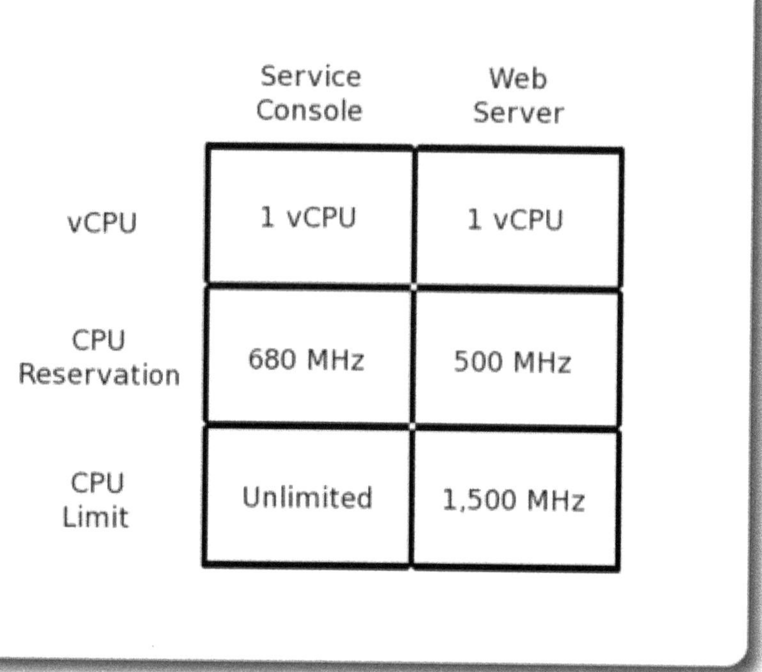

Figure 11.5 Service Console and Web Server VM Limits

Requested CPU Cycles

For clarity we will be showing the requested CPU cycles for each VM and the service console in the Requested CPU Cycles row in the following figures. The importance to showing this is that when a VM is properly configured, you will be able to determine exactly how many CPU cycles the VM has requested from the VMkernel scheduler and what it received. You can get this information using the VI client, the CLI command esxtop or using tools from within the guest OS.

If however, the VM needs more CPU cycles than the VM has been configured to allow it to have or the ESX 3.5 server does not have enough resources to fulfill the request then you would not be able to determine how much more capacity the VM would need.

The web server VM has been configured with a CPU limit of 1,500 MHz. In a physical system, if the OS and applications tried to request more than 1,500 MHz, the OS would report that it was running at 100% CPU utilization. We would see that the same scenario is true for a virtual machine. It is important to set the limit to a reasonable value. If it is set too low it will affect the performance of the VM.

We can see in Figure 11.6 that after the web server VM was started that it requested from the VMkernel scheduler 250 MHz of CPU time.

	Service Console	Web Server
vCPU	1 vCPU	1 vCPU
CPU Reservation	680 MHz	500 MHz
CPU Limit	Unlimited	1,500 MHz
Requested CPU Cycles	160 MHz	250 MHz

Current Requested Server Workload = 410 MHz

Figure 11.6 Service Console and Web Server Requested CPU Cycles

We also see that the service console is requesting 160 MHz of CPU time. The ESX administrator now builds the application server VM with one vCPU. The CPU reservation is configured to 500 MHz and the CPU limit is configured to 1,100 MHz based on the baseline information. The ESX administrator builds the database server VM with four vCPUs. The CPU reservation is configured to 1,000 MHz and the CPU limit was left at the default which is unlimited.

The ESX administrator now powers on the application server VM and then the database server VM. Admission control allows both VMs to power on because the total CPU reservations do not exceed the total CPU time of the server as shown in Figure 11.7.

	Service Console	Web Server	Application Server	Database Server
vCPU	1 vCPU	1 vCPU	1 vCPU	4 vCPU
CPU Reservation	680 MHz	500 MHz	500 MHz	1,000 MHz
CPU Limit	Unlimited	1,500 MHz	1,100 MHz	Unlimited
Requested CPU Cycles	160 MHz	250 MHz	Powering On	Powering On

Current Requested Server Workload = 410 MHz

Figure 11.7 Scenario Values

The guest OS and applications are now installed in both of the new VMs. The application server VM's requested CPU cycles is 1,100 MHz and the database server VM's CPU usage is 1,000 MHz. The total CPU workload for the service console and three running VMs is 2,510 MHz as shown in Figure 11.8.

	Service Console	Web Server	Application Server	Database Server
vCPU	1 vCPU	1 vCPU	1 vCPU	4 vCPU
CPU Reservation	680 MHz	500 MHz	500 MHz	1,000 MHz
CPU Limit	Unlimited	1,500 MHz	1,100 MHz	Unlimited
Requested CPU Cycles	160 MHz	250 MHz	1,100 MHz	1,000 MHz

Current Requested Server Workload = 2,510 MHz

Figure 11.8 Three Running VMs

The final VM that needs to be built is the firewall server VM. Based on the baseline information it requires 1 vCPU, a 500 MHz CPU reservation and a CPU limit configured at 2,000 MHz. The ESX administrator based the limit for this VM on how much processing power the physical server had as shown in Figure 11.9.

	Service Console	Web Server	Application Server	Database Server	Firewall Server
vCPU	1 vCPU	1 vCPU	1 vCPU	4 vCPU	1 vCPU
CPU Reservation	680 MHz	500 MHz	500 MHz	1,000 MHz	500 MHz
CPU Limit	Unlimited	1,500 MHz	1,100 MHz	Unlimited	2,000 MHz
Requested CPU Cycles	160 MHz	250 MHz	1,100 MHz	1,000 MHz	Powered Off

Current Requested Server Workload = 2,510 MHz

Figure 11.9 The fourth VM Configured

The ESX administrator now powers on the firewall server VM as shown in Figure 11.10. Admission control allows the firewall VM to power on because the total CPU reservations do not exceed the total CPU time of the server. (680 MHz + 500 MHz + 500 MHz + 1,000 MHz + 500 MHz = 3,180 MHz). After the guest OS and application is installed in the firewall VM, we see that its workload adds 1,900 MHz to the CPU load on the ESX 3.5 server. The total workload in our scenario calculates to 160 MHz + 250 MHz + 1,100 MHz + 1,000 MHz + 1,900 MHz = 4,410 MHz. The ESX 3.5 server can support up to 8,500 MHz. The total workload has not put the server into an over-committed state.

	Service Console	Web Server	Application Server	Database Server	Firewall Server
vCPU	1 vCPU	1 vCPU	1 vCPU	4 vCPU	1 vCPU
CPU Reservation	680 MHz	500 MHz	500 MHz	1,000 MHz	500 MHz
CPU Limit	Unlimited	1,500 MHz	1,100 MHz	Unlimited	2,000 MHz
Requested CPU Cycles	160 MHz	250 MHz	1,100 MHz	1,000 MHz	1,900 MHz

Current Requested Server Workload = 4,410 MHz

Figure 11.10 Full ESX 3.5 Server Workload

CPU Over-commitment

In our scenario two weeks later, the ESX administrator gets a frantic call from the web server VM administrator. The performance of the web server is terrible. The company's sales managers are all trying to send in their end of the month sales report data and it has caused the ESX 3.5 server to go into an over-committed state.

The sales managers had never seen an issue with performance before on the physical web, application or database servers. They can't understand why the VMs perform so poorly. They deduce that it must be the software and it is the ESX administrators fault for talking them into virtualizing their environment.

The ESX administrator looks at the ESX 3.5 server to determine what the CPU resource utilization is. The database server VM thinks it has four CPUs running at 1,955 MHz. Here's the math:

[total CPU time] minus [service console reservation]divided by [number of vCPUs] equals vCPU core speed.

8,500 MHz - 680 MHz / 4 = 1,955 MHz per vCPU

It is reporting that it is running at 49% CPU utilization. Here's the math:

[VM workload] divided by ([total CPU time] minus [service console reservation)equals CPU utilization percentage.

3,800 MHz / (8,500 MHz - 680 MHz) = 48.59%

The database server VM really wants 3,900 MHz but it can't have it. This is due to increasing workloads of the other virtual machines as shown in Figure 11.11.

The ESX administrator observes in the guest operating systems of the web server and application server VMs that they are reporting that their current CPU usage is at 100%. The ESX administrator understands that on a physical server when the OS and applications require more processing power than the processors can provide the OS will show that it is at 100% CPU utilization. There is no way to determine what the actual amount of processing power to meet that need really is (short of adding additional processors if that is supported on the physical server). The only practical way to determine what the true demand would be on the physical server would be to shut down each application, determine what the OS by itself required and then one by one start up each application and look at the workload it generates on the system. Then you would total up all of the workloads to determine how much additional resources the system needs.

The same thing is true in a virtual machine. The ESX administrator will have to shut down some of the VM's to get the ESX 3.5 server out of an over-committed state to figure out what the workload truly is for each VM. The problem that the ESX administrator has in this scenario is that the web server VM provides services for the application server VM. The web server VM also forwards the data from the application server to the database server VM. The only VM that can be shut down in this scenario is the firewall server VM which reduces the workload by 1,900 MHz and takes the server out of an over-committed state.

	Service Console	Web Server	Application Server	Database Server	Firewall Server
vCPU	1 vCPU	1 vCPU	1 vCPU	4 vCPU	1 vCPU
CPU Reservation	680 MHz	500 MHz	500 MHz	1,000 MHz	500 MHz
CPU Limit	Unlimited	2,000 MHz	2,000 MHz	4,000 MHz	2,000 MHz
Requested CPU Cycles	200 MHz	1,900 MHz	1,860 MHz	3,900 MHz	1,900 MHz

Current Requested Server Workload = 9,760 MHz

Figure 11.11 Full ESX 3.5 Server in an Over-committed State

The ESX administrator now powers off the firewall server VM and sees however that the web server and application server VMs are still reporting that their current requested CPU cycles are at 100%.

The database server however is now not showing 100% CPU utilization. The ESX administrator sees that it is using 3,900 MHz as shown in Figure 11.11. The ESX administrator decides to set the limit for the database server VM to 4,000 MHz. Then the ESX administrator raises the limits for both the web and application server VMs and through trial and error determines that both VMs should have the CPU limit set to 2,000 MHz. The web server VM needs 1,900 MHz and the application server VM needs 1,860 MHz to meet its workload. The ESX administrator also sees that the service console's CPU usage has risen to 200 MHz due to the increased workload of the ESX 3.5 server.

The ESX administrator has observed the degraded performance when the ESX 3.5 server went into an over-committed state. Good capacity planning involves a clear understanding of the purpose of each VM, how they interact and what their peak workloads can be. The performance problem however isn't solved yet for these VMs by just changing the limits. Figure 11.12 shows the total workload generated by the service console and each VM after the firewall server VM was powered off.

	Service Console	Web Server	Application Server	Database Server	Firewall Server
vCPU	1 vCPU	1 vCPU	1 vCPU	4 vCPU	1 vCPU
CPU Reservation	680 MHz	500 MHz	500 MHz	1,000 MHz	500 MHz
CPU Limit	Unlimited	2,000 MHz	2,000 MHz	4,000 MHz	2,000 MHz
Requested CPU Cycles	200 MHz	1,900 MHz	1,860 MHz	3,900 MHz	Powered Off

Current Requested Server Workload = 7,860 MHz

Figure 11.12 Total CPU Workloads

It would take 9,760 MHz to provide enough CPU cycles to satisfy the workloads of all four VMs when they are powered on. The combined workload cannot be fulfilled by the CPU time of this ESX 3.5 server. The ESX administrator has the following options to address the CPU time shortage:

1. Remove one of the VMs to free up the CPU resources that it is using. The firewall server would be the only choice in this scenario because the other three VMs are part of a three-tiered configuration. Moving any of these to a different standalone ESX system would incur downtime. In addition, since these three virtual machines currently communicate using the same virtual switch, moving any of these to a different ESX system increases the traffic on the physical network.

2. Set the limits lower on one or more of the VMs to selectively reduce performance on those VMs. This will reduce the total workload because the VMs with a lower limit will not be given more CPU cycles than what the limit is set for. This option can take the system out of an over-committed state. The new limit value can be set dynamically and take effect without requiring the VM to be rebooted.

3. Raise the reservation of the VMs to give them a higher guaranteed level of CPU cycles. The downside with this option is that it also requires a reboot of the VMs that had their reservations changed. This option does not prevent the system from being in an over-committed state.

4. Use CPU shares so that the VM will win competitions for CPU time more often. This option can be set dynamically and does not require the VMs to be rebooted.

CPU Shares

CPU Shares are used to give CPU time to the virtual machines that need it the most. A VM administrator can give the VM one of the four following shares settings:

- Low – 2,000 shares
- Normal – 4,000 shares (default setting)

- High – 8,000 shares
- Custom - any amount of shares you decide up to 1,000,000 shares

NOTE: Figure 11.4 shows that the default setting for Shares in the Resource Allocation section is set to Normal which is 4,000 shares.

As shown in Figure 11.13, the ESX administrator used custom values for the share settings, so each VM received the value of 1,000 shares and the service console is set to 2,000 shares.

	Service Console	Web Server	Application Server	Database Server	Firewall Server
vCPU	1 vCPU	1 vCPU	1 vCPU	4 vCPU	1 vCPU
CPU Reservation	680 MHz	500 MHz	500 MHz	1,000 MHz	500 MHz
CPU Limit	Unlimited	2,000 MHz	2,000 MHz	4,000 MHz	2,000 MHz
Requested CPU Cycles	200 MHz	1,900 MHz	1,860 MHz	3,900 MHz	Powered Off
CPU Shares	2,000 Shares	1,000 Shares	1,000 Shares	1,000 Shares	1,000 Shares

Current Requested Server Workload = 7,860 MHz

Figure 11.13 Default Share Allocations

The ESX administrator now powers on the firewall server VM. This action puts the ESX 3.5 server into an over-committed state. The VMkernel scheduler uses CPU shares to allocate any remaining CPU cycles after each VM gets its CPU reservation (if needed). CPU shares only affect CPU allocation when the ESX 3.5 server is in an over-committed state.

In our example the VMkernel scheduler computations would work out like this:

Total CPU time in the ESX 3.5 server: 8,500 MHz

Total CPU reservations required by VMs: 2,500 MHz

The service console only requires 200 MHz of its reservation: 200 MHz

Total unreserved CPU cycles: 8,500 MHz - 2,500 MHz - 200 MHz = 5,800 MHz unreserved CPU time

The 5,800 MHz are left over after each VM gets what it has been guaranteed to get from the VMkernel scheduler. These are the cycles that are to be divided up by using CPU shares. CPU shares are relative. In other words, a VM with 1,000 CPU shares has the same relative claim to the unreserved CPU cycles as another VM that also has 1,000 CPU shares. In our scenario, all of the VMs require the use of their CPU reservations. Therefore, they all will need to contend for some of the unreserved CPU cycles. Since all of the VMs have the same number of CPU shares they will all get an equal amount of unreserved CPU cycles allocated by the VMkernel scheduler as shown in Figure 11.14.

	Service Console	Web Server	Application Server	Database Server	Firewall Server
vCPU	1 vCPU	1 vCPU	1 vCPU	4 vCPU	1 vCPU
CPU Reservation	680 MHz	500 MHz	500 MHz	1,000 MHz	500 MHz
CPU Limit	Unlimited	2,000 MHz	2,000 MHz	4,000 MHz	2,000 MHz
Requested CPU Cycles	200 MHz	1,900 MHz	1,860 MHz	3,900 MHz	1,900 MHz
CPU Shares	2,000 Shares	1,000 Shares	1,000 Shares	1,000 Shares	1,000 Shares

Current Requested Server Workload = 9,760 MHz

Figure 11.14 Equal Share Allocations

In Figure 11.15 notice that the service console has 2,000 CPU shares but will not receive any of the unreserved CPU cycles. This is because it still has CPU reservation cycles available. This would also be true if any of the VMs requested CPU cycles was less than its reservation.

The VMkernel scheduler will do the following calculations to determine what the CPU share allocation percentage is:

[VM CPU shares] divided by [total CPU shares on all resources contending for unreserved CPU cycles]= CPU share allocation %

All four of the VMs on this system are contending for those unreserved CPU cycles, in our scenario the calculations for each VM would be:

1,000 CPU shares divided by 4,000 CPU shares = 25% CPU share allocation.

	Service Console	Web Server	Application Server	Database Server	Firewall Server
vCPU	1 vCPU	1 vCPU	1 vCPU	4 vCPU	1 vCPU
CPU Reservation	680 MHz	500 MHz	500 MHz	1,000 MHz	500 MHz
CPU Limit	Unlimited	2,000 MHz	2,000 MHz	4,000 MHz	2,000 MHz
Requested CPU Cycles	200 MHz	1,900 MHz	1,860 MHz	3,900 MHz	1,900 MHz
CPU Shares	2,000 Shares	1,000 Shares	1,000 Shares	1,000 Shares	1,000 Shares
CPU Share Allocation Percentage	0 %	25 %	25 %	25 %	25 %

Current Requested Server Workload = 9,760 MHz

Figure 11.15 Equal Share Allocations

In our scenario, 25 % of the total unreserved CPU cycles is 1,450 MHz. If the VM does not require the full allotment it is entitled to, then the remaining unreserved CPU cycles are divided amongst the remaining VMs that are contending for them. If the VMs' CPU limit has been met by the VMs' CPU share allotment and its CPU reservation, then the remaining unreserved CPU cycles are also divided amongst the remaining VMs that are contending for them. The calculations made by the VMkernel scheduler are shown in Figure 11.16.

	Web Server	Application Server	Database Server	Firewall Server
CPU Requested Cycles	- 1,900 MHz	- 1,860 MHz	- 3,900 MHz	- 1,900 MHz
CPU Reservation	+ 500 MHz	+ 500 MHz	+ 1,000 MHz	+ 500 MHz
CPU Cycles Needed From Shares	- 1,400 MHz	- 1,360 MHz	- 2,900 MHz	- 1,400 MHz
CPU Share Allocation Total	+ 1,450 MHz	+ 1,450 MHz	+ 1,450 MHz	+ 1,450 MHz
CPU Cycles Needed / Not Needed	+ 50 MHz	+ 90 MHz	+ 1,450 MHz + 50 MHz + 90 MHz + 50 MHz	+ 50 MHz
CPU Cycles Still Needed By Database Server			- 1,260 MHz	

Figure 11.16 Equal Share Calculations

The total CPU allocation for each VM is shown in Figure 11.17. As we can see only the database server VM still requires more CPU time. The problem is that if the database server VM does not get enough processing power then the updating of the sales managers data slows dramatically. The ESX administrator needs to change the default share settings to correct this problem.

	Service Console	Web Server	Application Server	Database Server	Firewall Server
vCPU	1 vCPU	1 vCPU	1 vCPU	4 vCPU	1 vCPU
CPU Reservation	680 MHz	500 MHz	500 MHz	1,000 MHz	500 MHz
CPU Limit	Unlimited	2,000 MHz	2,000 MHz	4,000 MHz	2,000 MHz
Requested CPU Cycles	200 MHz	1,900 MHz	1,860 MHz	3,900 MHz	1,900 MHz
CPU Shares	2,000 Shares	1,000 Shares	1,000 Shares	1,000 Shares	1,000 Shares
CPU Share Allocation Percentage	0 %	25 %	25 %	25 %	25 %
CPU Share Allocation	0 MHz	1,400 MHz	1,360 MHz	1,640 MHz	1,400 MHz
CPU Share Allocation Total	200 MHz	1,900 MHz	1,860 MHz	2,640 MHz	1,900 MHz

Current Requested Server Workload = 9,760 MHz

Figure 11.17 CPU Share Allocation Total

The ESX administrator can adjust the CPU shares and the changes will take place immediately. If the database server's CPU shares were raised from 1,000 to 2,000 shares and the firewall server's CPU shares were lowered from 1,000 to 500 shares it would change the CPU share allocation total as shown in Figure 11.18.

	Service Console	Web Server	Application Server	Database Server	Firewall Server
vCPU	1 vCPU	1 vCPU	1 vCPU	4 vCPU	1 vCPU
CPU Reservation	680 MHz	500 MHz	500 MHz	1,000 MHz	500 MHz
CPU Limit	Unlimited	2,000 MHz	2,000 MHz	4,000 MHz	2,000 MHz
Requested CPU Cycles	200 MHz	1,900 MHz	1,860 MHz	3,900 MHz	1,900 MHz
CPU Shares	2,000 Shares	1,000 Shares	1,000 Shares	2,000 Shares	500 Shares
CPU Share Allocation Percentage	0 %	22.22 %	22.22 %	44.44 %	11.11 %
CPU Share Allocation	0 MHz	1,289 MHz	1,289 MHz	2,578 MHz	644 MHz
CPU Share Allocation Total	200 MHz	1,789 MHz	1,789 MHz	3,578 MHz	1,144 MHz

Current Requested Server Workload = 9,760 MHz

Figure 11.18 Revised CPU Share Shares

Notice that the web server would now get a 22.22% share allocation (1,000 shares divided by 4,500 shares) of the unreserved CPU cycles for a total 1,289 MHz. The application server would also get 1,289 MHz. The database server would now get 44.44% share allocation (2,000 shares divided by 4,500 shares) of the unreserved CPU cycles for a total of 2,578 MHz. The firewall server would now get 11.11% share allocation (500 shares divided by 4,500 shares) of the unreserved CPU cycles for a total of 644 MHz.

Scenario Summary

The lessons that the ESX administrator has learned is that there are multiple configuration settings that can affect the performance of the VMs running on the ESX 3.5 server. The ESX administrator now has to determine if the degraded performance for the three day period at the end of the month warrants moving the firewall server VM to another ESX 3.5 server.

CPU Scheduling Issues

Another performance issue that the ESX administrator needs to consider is the possibility of unused CPU cycles.

Consider this scenario:

You have built four VMs called VM1, VM2, VM3 and VM4 each with four vCPUs. They are installed in a two socket, two core, 2 GHz per core ESX 3.5 server. Each core generates 2,000 million cycles per second that can be used by the server. The VMkernel scheduler must evaluate each VMs workload and determine how to schedule those CPU cycles to the virtual machines.

In Figure 11.19 we see that the scheduler has scheduled VM1 on cycle 1.

	vCPU 0	vCPU 1	vCPU 2	vCPU 3
Cycle 1	VM 1	VM 1	VM 1	VM 1
Cycle 2	VM 2	VM 2	VM 2	VM 2
Cycle 3	VM 3	VM 3	VM 3	VM 3
Cycle 4	VM 4	VM 4	VM 4	VM 4

Figure 11.19 Cycle 1-4

It also scheduled VM2 on cycle 2, VM3 on cycle 3 and VM4 on cycle 4. What happens when the service console needs to use a processor?

Remember earlier in the book we noted that the service console can only be scheduled on CPU 0. On cycle 5 it gets scheduled on vCPU 0 as shown in Figure 11.20.

	vCPU 0	vCPU 1	vCPU 2	vCPU 3
Cycle 1	VM 1	VM 1	VM 1	VM 1
Cycle 2	VM 2	VM 2	VM 2	VM 2
Cycle 3	VM 3	VM 3	VM 3	VM 3
Cycle 4	VM 4	VM 4	VM 4	VM 4
Cycle 5	Service Console	X	X	X

Figure 11.20 Cycle 5

The problem with this configuration is that the scheduler cannot schedule any other VM to use the available cycles on vCPUs 2, 3 and 4. In a physical server configured with two sockets and two cores per socket the OS would think it has 4 CPUs. If one of those four CPUs failed the OS would crash. The same thing is true for our four vCPU VMs. The scheduler must have enough vCPUs available each cycle to meet the VMs requirements.

NOTE: None of the other LCPUs would be available during this cycle if the VMs are all dual-proc VMs due to the non-sharing of the same core for each vCPU of a dual-proc VM.

Best Practices for VM Configurations

VMware recommends that if you have just two CPUs in your system then only build one vCPU VMs in your ESX 3.5 server. If you have four CPUs in your ESX system only build one or two vCPU configured VMs in your ESX 3.5 server. If you have more than four CPUs in your ESX 3.5 server then the scheduler can better accommodate four vCPU VMs.

How Is Memory Utilized In A Virtual Machine?

In a physical system the operating system has exclusive access to all of the physical memory in the system. In a virtualized environment the memory resources are shared between multiple guest operating systems installed in the VMs on the ESX 3.5 server. The first thing we need to clarify is how memory is defined when referring to a VI3 environment. Memory in the form of physical Dual In-line Memory Module (DIMM) chips, is referred to as machine memory. The memory that the VMkernel provides to both the service console and virtual machines is referred to as physical memory. Memory provided to the applications running within the guest operating system is referred to as virtual memory. Next we need to understand how the ESX 3.5 server shares the memory resources.

Memory resource utilization settings are similar to the CPU settings that we've seen previously, such as shares, reservations and limits. These settings can influence the VMkernel's memory management and how it allocates the physical memory in the ESX 3.5 server. An important distinction between memory and CPU is that since CPU cycles are provided exclusively from the physical CPU chips in the system, once the physical CPU chips are fully utilized, there is no other facility to provide additional cycles; whereas memory does not have to be provided solely by the physical DIMM chips within the ESX server. Memory can also be provided by paging out to the physical hard drives. Doing so is not desired due to the physical access speeds of hard drives being much slower than DIMM chips. Having this paging out option with memory does allow the ESX system one of several methods in which memory can be over committed. By over committed, we mean that more memory can be assigned to the virtual machines than physically is installed via DIMM chips in the ESX 3.5 server.

Memory Management

The ESX administrator should be equipped with the memory baseline information of the virtual machine prior to placing the virtual machine into a production environment. Memory workloads may span daily, weekly or even on monthly cycles. Capturing such data is very helpful in configuring the memory settings of the virtual machine. Having the memory workload requirements at hand can reduce potential performance problems once the virtual machine is placed into production. Memory allocation to a virtual machine is controlled by an ESX administrator using the following settings:

- Memory Limits
- Memory Reservations
- Memory Shares

Memory Limits

A virtual machine's memory limit is set during the initial virtual machine creation wizard as shown in Figure 11.21.

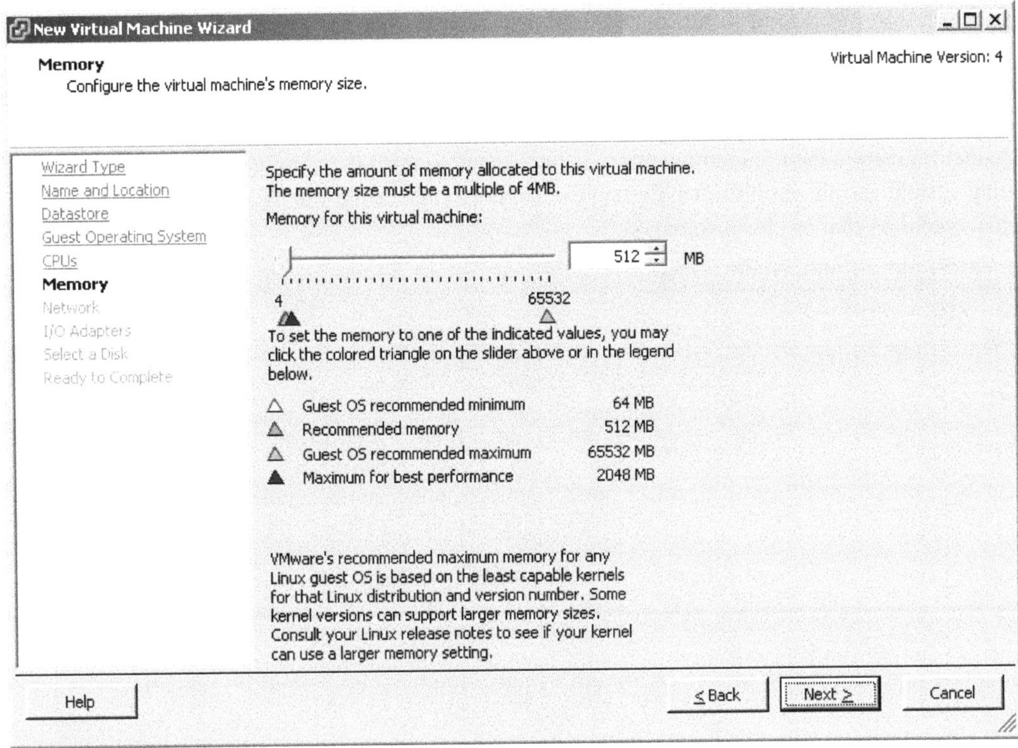

Figure 11.21 New Virtual Machine Virtual Memory Configuration

By default, 256 MB is assigned as the memory limit. The maximum limit that can be set is 64 GB. This value should be set according to the memory workload of the virtual machine. On a new ESX 3.5 system configured with 16 GB of memory, setting the first several virtual machines memory limits to 2 GB may make the operators of these virtual machines quite content. However, after eight such virtual machines are up and running, memory contention may occur and the operators experience may not be as it once was. In situations where the memory working set is unknown prior to being placed into production, setting the limit lower then incrementally raising it after collecting and analyzing performance data may be a helpful strategy. In other words, having user expectations set lower than gradually increasing performance is often better than setting the performance expectations high and having to later degrade performance at a later time due to memory constraints.

Memory Reservations

As with CPU reservations, memory reservations are a guarantee by the VMkernel that the value assigned as a memory reservation to a virtual machine will always be available physically to a virtual machine. This reservation value guarantee is enforced using the admission control process. The memory reservation is 0 (zero) by default as shown in Figure 11.22. To modify the reservation value, move the slider bar to the right or type a value in the text box. The reservation value can never be greater than the limit setting. The VMkernel will not allow a virtual machine to power on if the unreserved memory reservation on the ESX host is not large enough to satisfy the virtual machine's reservation value. As with CPU, a running total of the currently powered on virtual machines memory reservation is stored and used to make the admission control decisions. There is one key difference with memory and CPU admission control. The difference being with memory admission control, the reservation value and the memory overhead value are used to determine whether or not the virtual machine can be powered on. The decision to set reservations for memory is often recommended to be a value that represents the minimum memory value needed to meet the memory demands of the guest operating system and its applications. Setting the memory reservation too high can limit the number of virtual machines that can be powered on.

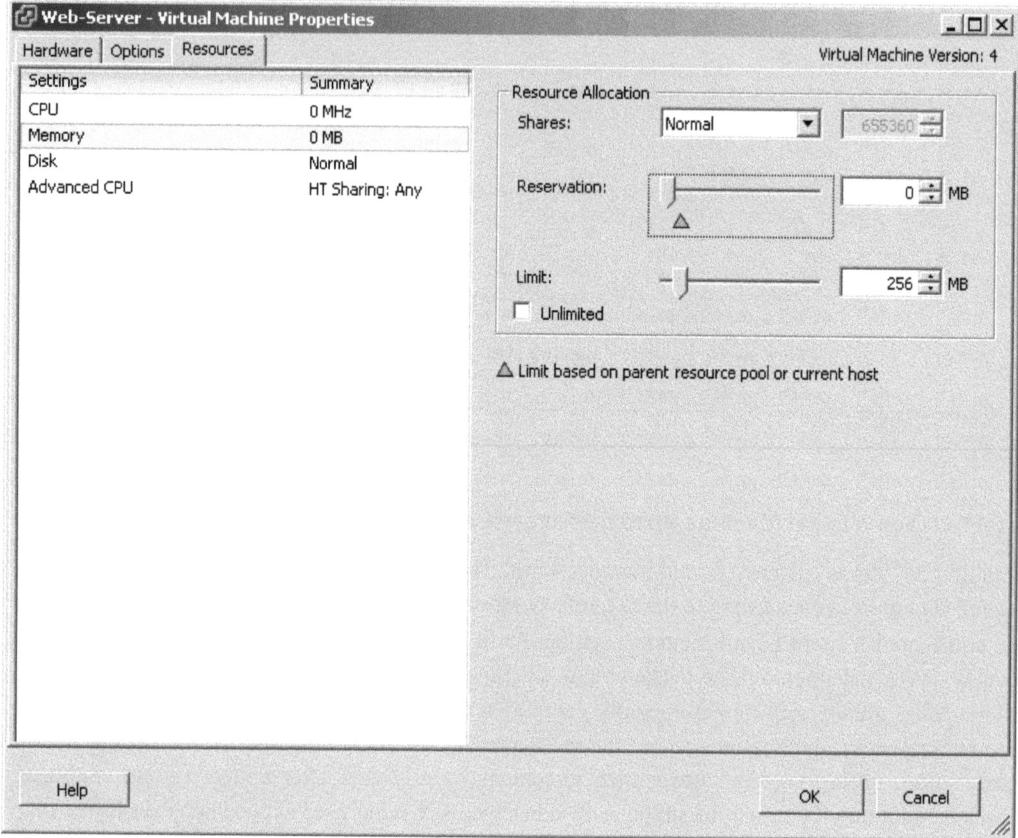

Figure 11.22 Virtual Machine Memory Reservation Configuration

Memory overhead per virtual machine is part of the virtualization overhead incurred in order for the VMkernel to manage the virtual machine. How much overhead per virtual machine depends upon the configuration of the virtual machine. A virtual machine with a 1024 MB memory limit will have a larger memory overhead value than a virtual machine with a 256 MB memory limit. The more vCPUs the VM has, the more memory overhead needed to manage the VM. A 64-bit guest operating system requires more memory overhead than does a 32-bit guest operating system. For example, with the default setting of 256 MB of memory and one vCPU using a 32-bit operating system, the memory overhead would be approximately 87 MB. The overhead value is not static. It varies throughout the duration of time the virtual machine is powered on. Adding a second vCPU to this virtual machine would increase the overhead to 108 MB. Keeping the 256 MB memory limit and two vCPUs, installing a 64-bit guest operating system would increase the memory overhead to 146 MB. Removing the second vCPU would decrease the memory overhead when using a 64-bit guest operating system to 107 MB. A complete table of virtual machine memory overhead configurations can be found in the Resource Management Guide located at the following URL:

http://www.vmware.com/pdf/vi3_35/esx_3/r35/vi3_35_25_resource_mgmt.pdf

The overhead value can also be seen using the VI client as shown in Figure 11.23.

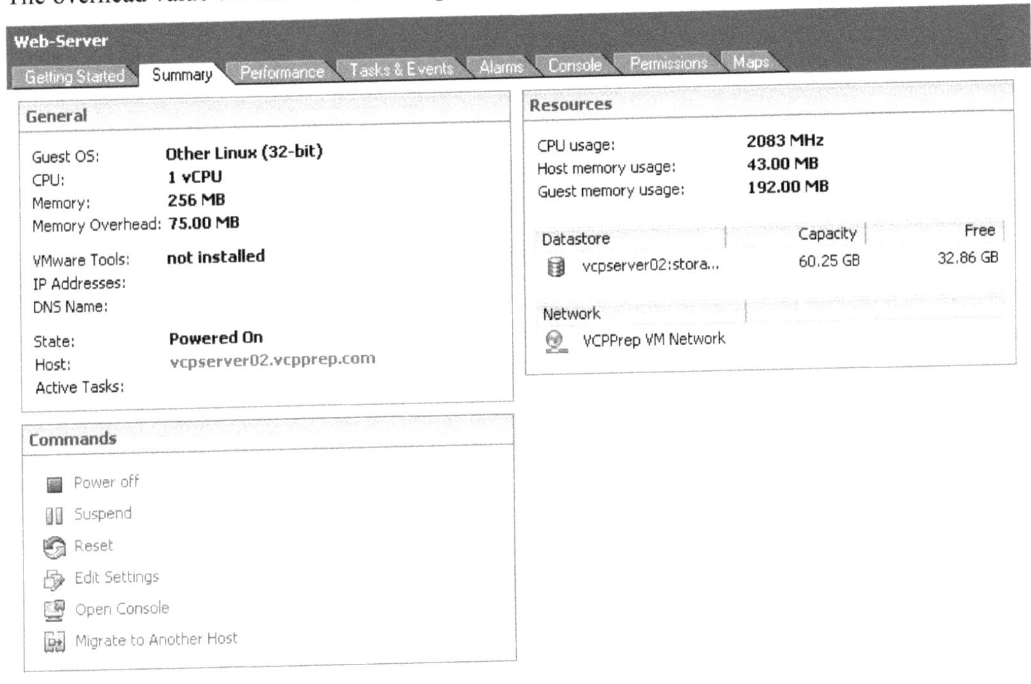

Figure 11.23 Virtual Machine Memory Overhead

Memory Shares

On an ESX system that has exhausted all of its physical memory, the shares mechanism discussed earlier with CPU resources comes into play for memory resources as well. A virtual machine is guaranteed to have all of its reserved memory available if a reservation value other than the default 0 (zero) has been set. Shares compete in the range between the reservation value and the limit. Unused reserved memory may be given to other virtual machines if they need it.

Shares are assigned the following default values:

- Low - 5 times the memory limit
- Normal - 10 times the memory limit
- High - 20 times the memory limit
- Custom - Any amount of shares you decide on

Low, Normal (Default) and High values are used as a multiplier.

For example, the default Normal is 10 times the configured memory maximum of the guest; thus, if the configured memory maximum for the guest is the 256, then the amount of memory shares for this VM is 2,560.

Shares for memory can be set by modifying the virtual machine properties as shown in Figure 11.24.

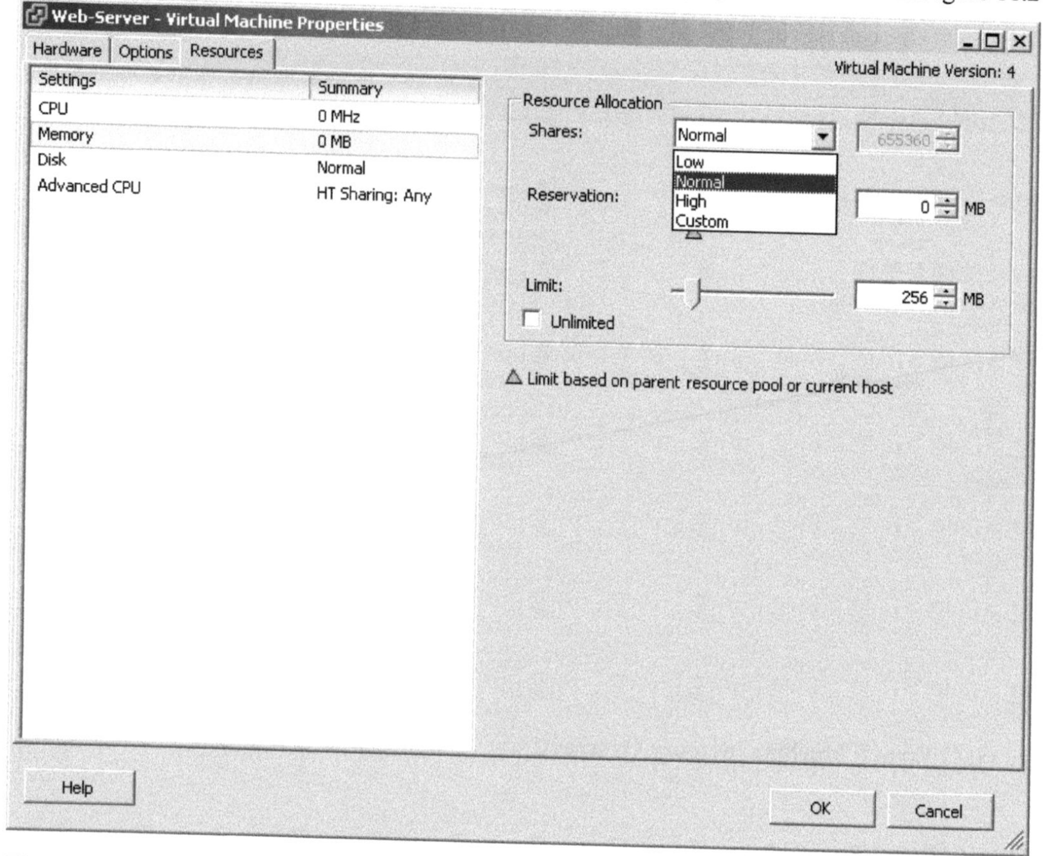

Figure 11.24 Virtual Machine Memory Shares Configuration

The VMkernel also provides additional memory management tools. They are:

- Transparent Page Sharing (TPS)
- vmmemctl (Ballooning)
- VMkernel Swap

Transparent Page Sharing (TPS)

A way to think of the TPS process would be for example, an IT department recently purchased ten identical physical servers. Then installed the exact same Linux operating system on each of the physical servers. Once the operating system has been installed and the machines booted up, if we were able to look into the memory pages of each machine, we would see a lot of redundant memory pages due to the same operating system code being used and the same drivers being loaded for the same hardware devices. In the physical world, this redundant memory usage is wasted. Not so in a VI3 environment.

Transparent Page Sharing (TPS) is a mechanism used by the VMkernel to provide as much physical memory as possible to the virtual machines running on an ESX 3.5 system. TPS is enabled by default. This process works by scanning machine memory and searching for duplicate pages of memory. It is able to make a read-only copy of the duplicate memory and free up the rest of the duplicate pages. Therefore, when memory is scarce on an ESX host, grouping virtual machines with the same operating system version on that ESX host will offer a greater amount of memory that can be reclaimed by the VMkernel. In addition, if possible, grouping not only the same operating system version but also the same applications as well, for example, all Web servers on the same ESX host can greatly aid in reclaiming duplicate machine memory. TPS uses processing power to accomplish its task. The process by default takes approximately one hour to completely scan for new pages and uses one GHz of processing power to scan four MB of memory per second. These values can be modified via the service console CLI. To obtain the value for how often machine pages are scanned, issue the following command from the command line:

esxcfg-advcfg -g /Mem/ShareScanTime

The default value is 60 minutes. Setting this value to 0 (zero) effectively disables TPS.

Issue the following command to obtain the processing power used to scan for duplicate machine pages:

esxcfg-advcfg -g /Mem/ShareScanGHz

The default value is 4 GHz

The -g (minus g) option to the esxcfg-advcfg command gets the current assigned value. Use a -s (minus s) to set a new value.

In circumstances where more memory is available than CPU processing power (unlikely as that may be) it is possible to disable TPS per virtual machine by setting the following virtual machine attribute to a value of FALSE:

sched.mem.pshare.enable

This is accomplished by selecting the Configuration Parameters button from within the virtual machine's Edit Settings Options tab. We will see in Chapter 16 - Monitoring and Alerting, how to determine how much machine memory is being freed up by TPS.

NOTE: Although it is possible to disable TPS, it is generally not necessary to do so.

vmmemctl (Ballooning)

The VMkernel monitors physical memory pages used with the ESX 3.5 server. It has the ability to place pressure on a virtual machine to page a given amount of memory to the virtual machines page file if the guest operating system is Windows based or to the virtual machine swap partition if the guest operating system is Linux/UNIX based. This is accomplished with the help of the vmmemctl driver which is often referred to as the balloon driver. This driver is installed within the guest operating system whenever VMware tools is installed. It is used to reclaim physical memory from a virtual machine when the amount of available physical memory is low within the ESX 3.5 server. The VMkernel does not tell the guest operating system in this situation, which physical pages of memory to page out to disk, but rather how much physical memory to page. This is done as the guest operating system knows best which pages should paged out to disk. The balloon driver is also used to reclaim physical memory that has not be used by the guest operating system for a while. In such cases, such idol physical memory can be given to other virtual machines that will actively use it.

VMkernel Swap

Each virtual machine upon powering on, has a swap file created for its own exclusive use. The guest operating system is not aware of this swap file. The VMkernel makes use of this file as a last resort when physical memory is unavailable. The swap file is created when a virtual machine is powered on and deleted once the virtual machine is powered off. The size of this swap file is determined by the difference between the virtual machine's reservation value and the virtual machine's memory limit. By default, this swap file is 256 MB in size. If upon powering on a virtual machine, there is not enough spare storage space available to create the swap file, the virtual machine will be unable to successfully power on. The location of the swap file by default is defined at the cluster or host on which the virtual machine is located. Typically the swap location is the directory where the virtual machine configuration and state files are located. This location can be modified if necessary as shown in Chapter 7 - Virtual Machines, in Figure 7.77. If the virtual machine resides on an NFS server and the VMkernel requires the use of the swap file for this virtual machine, paging reads and writes may be considerably slow. In such situations, it may be useful to move the swap file to a higher performing storage datastore. Setting the reservation memory value to equal the memory limit for a VM will avoid the use of the swap file altogether. Although, doing so affects admission control and available physical memory for other virtual machines as discussed previously in this chapter.

The following is the order in which the VMkernel utilizes memory:

1. Uses virtual machine reserved memory

2. Uses any available physical memory between the reservation value and memory limit

3. Uses balloon driver (memmctl)

4. Uses the VMkernel swap file

Network I/O Resource Utilization

It is important to keep in mind that the VMkernel requires CPU cycles to accomplish all virtual machine networking. In order to optimize network I/O, consider the types of virtual machines that will reside on the same ESX host. Virtual machines that require high CPU time, such as a heavily used report generating application running inside a virtual machine will be competing for the same CPU resources as a heavily used FTP server virtual machine. In addition, the overall physical network has an impact on virtual machine network performance. Good network design is just as important for virtual machines as physical machines. With this in mind, proper planning and monitoring of the physical network environment is critical for network optimization. In Chapter 16 - Monitoring and Alerting, we discuss network monitoring tools that can help isolate network bottlenecks.

Providing there is adequate CPU resources on an ESX host system, the use of internal virtual switches can help increase communication performance amongst virtual machines. ESX administrators can use TSO and jumbo frames to help offset the amount of CPU cycles needed to perform network operations. ESX server uplink ports default to auto negotiation. It may be necessary to manually set the speed and duplex setting of these physical NICs on the ESX server to properly utilize the full bandwidth as some NIC and switch combinations do not auto negotiate properly. Installing VMware tools inside the guest operating system provides improved paravirtualized network drivers that increase performance and reduce network latency. Other options such as NIC teaming and Traffic Shaping can also help optimize network performance. Please refer to Chapter 4 - ESX 3.x Server Networking Configurations for a detailed discussion of virtual networking topics.

Disk I/O Resource Utilization

Disk I/O optimization is primarily determined by the type of hardware being used and the overall SAN design. It is imperative to align the proper storage characteristics to the applications running within the guest operating system. For example, applications that read data more often than write data may benefit from the use of a mirrored drive configuration. Modifications to the host bus adapter card settings may improve disk I/O performance. For example, a host bus adapter's queue depth settings can be increased. The queue depth is the number of I/O operations that can be run in parallel on a host bus adapter. This value can be modified for a QLogic card for example, from 32 to 64 by issuing the following from the service console CLI:

```
esxcfg-module -s ql2maxqdepth=64 qla2300_707_vmw
```

It is recommended to contact VMware support and your storage vendor for recommended settings prior to making such modifications. An ESX administrator can also affect disk I/O performance by assigning disk share values to virtual machines as shown if Figure 11.25.

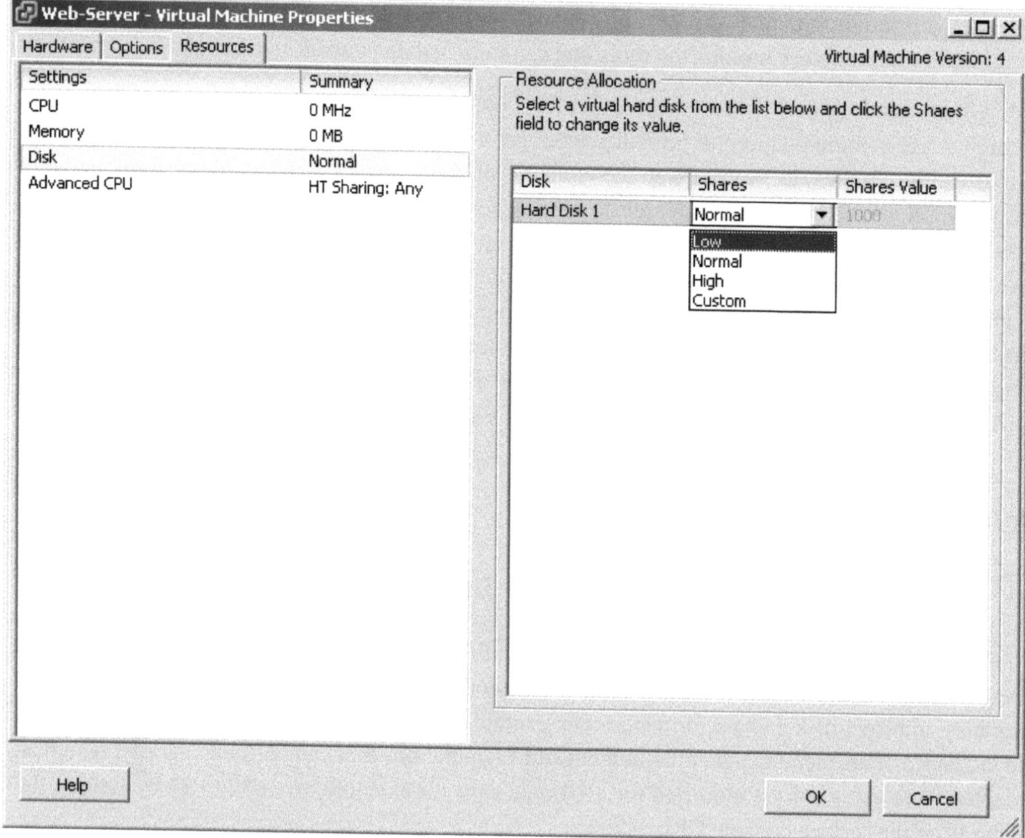

Figure 11.25 Virtual Machine Disk Shares

Setting disk shares allows an ESX administrator to set a higher disk I/O priority to virtual machines requiring more access to storage devices. The default values for disk shares are as follows:

- Low - 500 shares
- Medium - 1,000 shares (default setting)
- High - 2,000 shares
- Custom - any amount of shares you decide on up to 1,000,000

Please refer to Chapter 5 - ESX 3.x Server Storage Configurations for a detailed discussion of virtual machine storage topics.

Troubleshooting Common Resource Usage Problems

Common resource usage issues typically concern insufficient resources to provide adequate performance. As documented in this chapter, issues with CPU and memory contention can be resolved by proper planning using performance benchmark information. As additional virtual machines are hosted on an ESX system, it may be necessary to distribute CPU and memory resources using a combination of shares, reservations and limits. To provide higher priority virtual machines additional resource capacity, it is often necessary to lower the shares, reservations and limits of lower priority virtual machines. It some cases, it may even be necessary to power off the lower priority virtual machines. When this is not an option, if another ESX server is available, it may be possible to re-assign some virtual machines to another ESX server without powering off the virtual machine using VMware's VMotion technology. VMotion is covered later in this book in Chapter 13 – Virtual Machine Migration. In some cases, it may be necessary to add more physical resources such as additional memory, network cards and host bus adapters.

External References

The VMware ESX 3.5 and ESXi Server version 3.5 Documentation Page

: http://www.vmware.com/support/pubs/vi_pubs.html

VMware ESX Server 3 Ready Time Observations White Paper:

http://www.vmware.com/pdf/esx3_ready_time.pdf

A Performance Comparison of Hypervisors:

http://www.vmware.com/pdf/hypervisor_performance.pdf

Multi-NIC Performance in ESX 3.0.1 and XenEnterprise 3.2.0:

http://www.vmware.com/pdf/Multi-NIC_Performance.pdf

Performance Tuning Best Practices for ESX Server 3:

http://www.vmware.com/pdf/vi_performance_tuning.pdf

Intel Technology Journal ***Volume 06 Issue 01 Published February 14, 2002 ISSN 1535766X:***

ftp://download.intel.com/technology/itj/2002/volume06issue01/vol6iss1_hyper_threading_technology.pdf

Sample Test Questions

1. A VM administrator reported a problem with starting up a virtual machine. The error that is displayed states the VM cannot start due to a memory error. Which of the following could cause this problem?

a. The memory limit was set too low on the VM

b. The memory reservation was set to low on the VM

c. The memory reservation was set to zero on the VM

d. Admission control is preventing the VM from starting up due to lack of memory to meet the VMs reservation

e. The permissions were changed on the VM preventing the administrator from powering on the VM

2. The IT department personnel held a meeting to determine resource priority for the newly created virtual machines. It was decided that three of the default share settings would be used. Which of the following is not an available share setting for a virtual machine?

a. Medium

b. Low

c. Normal

d. High

e. Upper

3. A virtual machine was created with the default settings for a newly hired end user. The end user had unintentionally downloaded a virus that consumed all available CPU usage for the virtual machine. What is the default setting for CPU limit?

a. 1,000 MHz

b. 2,500 MHz

c. Unlimited

d. Limited

e. 50 %

4.Three virtual machines were built for the support organization to be used for troubleshooting different severity levels of support issues. The ESX administrator has assigned each virtual machine a different pre-defined share value. Which of the following is not a pre-defined share value on an ESX 3.5 server?

a. 2000

b. 3,000

c. 4,000

d. 1,000

e. 8,000

5. Ten new virtual machines were created, six of these are using the default settings and four have the memory reservation modified. The reservation values of these four VMs are preventing one of the four modified VMs from starting. What is the default memory and CPU reservation values?

a. 500

b. 0

c. 1,000

d. 600

e. 2,000

6. A virtual machine running the Apache web server application is used as the source VM when cloning nine additional web server VMs. The ten web server virtual machines are powered on and left running over the weekend. On Monday, the ESX administrator notices the CPU utilization being reported for each VM's guest operating system is 100% but there still is 2,500 MHz of unused CPU cycles on the host ESX 3.5 server. What could cause this to happen?

a. Virtual machine reservation values have not been satisfied

b. CPU failure on ESX 3.5 host server

c. Hyperthreading is not enabled on the ESX 3.5 host server

d. The CPU limit setting for each VM is set lower than what the guest OS requires

e. There are not enough virtual SMP licenses

7. One of the four standalone ESX 3.5 servers in production is suffering from poor performance. This server contains a mix of both high, normal and low priority VMs. One possible solution is to set the higher priority VMs with the default High share value. What is the ratio between the default share values?

a. 8:5

b. 6:3

c. 4:1

d. 10:4

e. 4:2:1

8. Which of the following allows the ESX 3.5 server to reclaim physical memory from a virtual machine?

a. vmmex driver

b. memctrl driver

c. numamem driver

d. vmmemctl driver

e. memmanager driver

9. When a virtual machine is powered on, the standalone ESX 3.5 server checks the amount of CPU and memory resources that have not been reserved. The server takes into account the available unreserved resources to determine if it can guarantee the reservation for which the virtual machine has been configured. Which of the following defines this process?

a. Admission Control

b. Power On Test

c. Reservation Control

d. Resource Monitor

e. Service Level

10. A junior ESX administrator is reviewing the configuration settings for all virtual machines on the production ESX 3.5 server. Not sure of the meaning of share values, the junior administrator asks how these values are used. The senior ESX administrator correctly responds with which of the following?

a. The share values are used during the admission control process

b. Share values are only used when the ESX 3.5 server is in an over committed state

c. Share values are used individually as needed by guest operating system applications

d. The share values are constantly in use to determine resource entitlement

e. Share values are used to determine the restart priority of a VM when an ESX 3.5 server powers on

Sample Test Solutions

1. A VM administrator reported a problem with starting up a virtual machine. The error that is displayed states the VM cannot start due to a memory error. Which of the following could cause this problem?

a. The memory limit was set too low on the VM

b. The memory reservation was set to low on the VM

c. The memory reservation was set to zero on the VM

e. Admission control is preventing the VM from starting up due to lack of memory to meet the VMs reservation

f. The permissions were changed on the VM preventing the administrator from powering on the VM

Answer: d - Setting the limit too low will just make the VM run more slowly. If the memory reservation was set too low it would cause the VM to have to contend to get the memory it might need, but that would not prevent it from powering on. Setting the memory reservation to zero insures that admission control will turn on the VM, but the VM will have no guarantee for memory and will have to contend for the memory it needs. The permissions can prevent access to a VM, but you will not get a memory error because of incorrect permissions.

2. The IT department personnel held a meeting to determine resource priority for the newly created virtual machines. It was decided that three of the default share settings would be used. Which of the following is not an available share setting for a virtual machine?

a. Medium

b. Low

c. Normal

d. High

e. Upper

Answer: a and e - The following are the default share settings:

1. High

2. Normal

3. Low

4. Custom

3. A virtual machine was created with the default settings for a newly hired end user. The end user had unintentionally downloaded a virus that consumed all available CPU usage for the virtual machine. What is the default setting for CPU limit?

a. 1,000 MHz

b. 2,500 MHz

c. Unlimited

d. Limited

e. 50 %

Answer: c - When you build a VM you can set the CPU limit which is the total amount of CPU cycles in MHz that the VM is allowed to have. This is what the guest operating system thinks it has. A virtual machine by default has its limit set as unlimited which equals the total number of vCPUs configured for the VM times the CPU core speed.

NOTE: If the unlimited value represents the total CPU time in the server you must subtract the 8% reservation for the service console.

For example: An ESX 3.5 server configured with dual sockets and dual cores with each core operating at 2,125 MHz. Unlimited would be as follows:

- ***On a one vCPU VM it would represent 2,125 MHz***
- ***On a Two vCPU VM it would represent 4,250 MHz***
- ***On a four vCPU VM it would represent 7,820 MHz (8,500 MHz minus the 680 MHz service console reservation)***

4. Three virtual machines were built for the support organization to be used for troubleshooting different severity levels of support issues. The ESX administrator has assigned each virtual machine a different pre-defined share value. Which of the following is not a pre-defined share value?

a. 2000

b. 3,000

c. 4,000

d. 1,000

e. 8,000

Answer: - b and d - The following lists the pre-defined share values:

1. High = 8,000

2. Normal = 4,000

3. Low = 200

5. Ten new virtual machines were created, six of these are using the default settings and four have the memory reservation modified. The reservation values of these four VMs are preventing one of the four modified VMs from starting. What is the default memory and CPU reservation values?

a. 500

b. 0

c. 1,000

d. 600

e. 2,000

Answer: b - By default, a virtual machines reservation value for both memory and CPU is 0. This default value will cause minimal impact on the unreserved capacity of the ESX server.

6. A virtual machine running the Apache web server application is used as the source VM when cloning nine additional web server VMs. The ten web server virtual machines are powered on and left running over the weekend. On Monday, the ESX administrator notices the CPU utilization being reported for each VM's guest operating system is 100% but there still is 2,500 MHz of unused CPU cycles on the host ESX 3.5 server. What could cause this to happen?

a. Virtual machine reservation values have not been satisfied

b. CPU failure on ESX 3.5 host server

c. Hyperthreading is not enabled on the ESX 3.5 host server

d. The CPU limit setting for each VM is set lower than what the guest OS requires

e. There are not enough virtual SMP licenses

Answer: d - The original web server virtual machine was configured with a CPU limit value that is not able to properly handle the necessary CPU workload of the guest operating system's application requirements. Since this virtual machine was used to clone the nine other web server VMs, the problem of insufficient CPU capacity within the guest operating system has been replicated. The total of all the CPU limits placed on the ten VMs is 2,500 MHz less than what the ESX 3.5 host currently has available. To resolve this problem, the ESX administrator needs to isolate one of the web server VMs to obtain an accurate CPU baseline so that the correct CPU limit can be used that will provide each VM the necessary CPU cycles.

7. One of the four standalone ESX 3.5 servers in production is suffering from poor performance. This server contains a mix of both high, normal and low priority VMs. One possible solution is to set the higher priority VMs with the default High share value. What is the ratio between the default share values?

a. 8:5

b. 6:3

c. 4:1

d. 10:4

e. 4:2:1

Answer: e - The share ratio for the default share values is 4:2:1. Thus, setting a VM with the High share default value of 8,000 shares will give it twice the entitlement of resources than a VM with the Normal default value of 4,000 shares. The Normal default share value is twice as much as the Low default share value of 2,000.

8. Which of the following allows the ESX 3.5 server to reclaim physical memory from a virtual machine?

a. vmmex driver

b. memctrl driver

c. numamem driver

d. vmmemctl driver

e. memmanager driver

Answer: d - The vmmemctl driver is installed into a VM guest operating system when VMware tools is installed. This driver is often referred to as the memory balloon driver and is used by the VMkernel to reclaim memory from a virtual machine.

9. When a virtual machine is powered on, the standalone ESX 3.5 server checks the amount of CPU and memory resources that have not been reserved. The server takes into account the available unreserved resources to determine if it can guarantee the reservation for which the virtual machine has been configured. Which of the following defines this process?

a. Admission Control

b. Power On Test

c. Reservation Control

d. Resource Monitor

e. Service Level

Answer: a - Admission control is the process by which the ESX 3.5 server uses to determine whether or not a virtual machine reservation value can be guaranteed at initial power on. The server calculates the sum of reservation values of all currently powered on VMs. If the difference between this sum and the total available memory or CPU resources is more than the set reservation value of the virtual machine attempting to power on, it will successfully power on. If the sum and the total available memory or CPU resources is less than the set reservation value, the VM will not power on.

10. A junior ESX administrator is reviewing the configuration settings for all virtual machines on the production ESX 3.5 server. Not sure of the meaning of share values, the junior administrator asks how these values are used. The senior ESX administrator correctly responds with which of the following?

a. The share values are used during the admission control process

b. Share values are only used when the ESX 3.5 server is in an over committed state

c. Share values are used individually as needed by guest operating system applications

d. The share values are constantly in use to determine resource entitlement

e. Share values are used to determine the restart priority of a VM when an ESX 3.5 server powers on

Answer: - b - Share values come into play only when the ESX 3.5 server is in an over committed state for either memory, CPU or disk I/O resources.

Chapter 12

Resource Pools

After reading this chapter you should be able to complete the following tasks:

- Describe the function of a resource pool
- Create a resource pool
- Explain how resources are allocated when shares are used
- Explain how expandable reservations work

Resource Pools

Resource pools allow you to control the distribution of CPU and memory resources on ESX servers or in VMware clusters. The benefit of resource pools is that you can assure standards of performance of the VMs where needed. You can also constrain VM administrators and not allow them to use more resources than they are entitled to.

Example 1 - Resource Pools on Stand-Alone ESX Servers

Matt and Joel are administrators in the same company but they work for different departments. Neither one of them had enough money in their budget to buy their own ESX server. They decided to combine their money and share a server. Each of them has contributed 50% of the total cost of the server. Matt sets up the server and starts creating VMs. When Joel finally builds his first VM he notices that its performance is poor. Using the monitoring tools (that will be covered in Chapter 16 – Monitoring And Alerting), Joel discovers that the server is in an over committed state. The total workload of all of Matt's VMs exceed what the server can handle.

Joel then creates two resource pools, one for his department and one resource pool for Matt's department. He allocates 50% of the CPU and memory resources to each of the resource pools to correspond to the amount their departments contributed to the purchase of the system. He assigns his VM to his resource pool and all of Matt's VMs to his pool. Joel's VMs now have access to the resources they are entitled to. Matt will need to scale back the VMs or they will suffer poor performance. Matt's pool only contains the resources that he has been allocated.

NOTE: Be aware that the overhead for the service console must be taken into consideration. The service console is allocated 272 MB of memory and is guaranteed at least 8 % of the CPU resources in the server. The VMkernel is also guaranteed memory and CPU cycles. The RAM for the VMkernel is approximately 50 MB and its CPU cycles scheduled on CPU 0.

Example 2 - Resource Pools in VMware Clusters

Matt realizes that he must acquire additional servers to meet his VMs resource requirements. He convinces the purchasing department to buy an additional ESX server. He configures the new server as well as the original one in a VMware cluster configuration. Now the total resources on both machines can be grouped together and sliced up as needed. Matt adds the resources from the second server to his resource pool. The important thing to note here is that even though Joel's department is only given access to 50 % of the resources of the first server, his VMs do not have to reside on that server. That is because both systems are now in the same VMware cluster so their resources are considered combined for management purposes.

Create a Resource Pool

The process of creating a resource pool is as follows:

Step 1. Select the ESX 3.5 server or cluster of servers that you want to create a resource pool on. In our example in Figure 12.1 we have selected the ESX server vcpserver01.vcpprep.com.

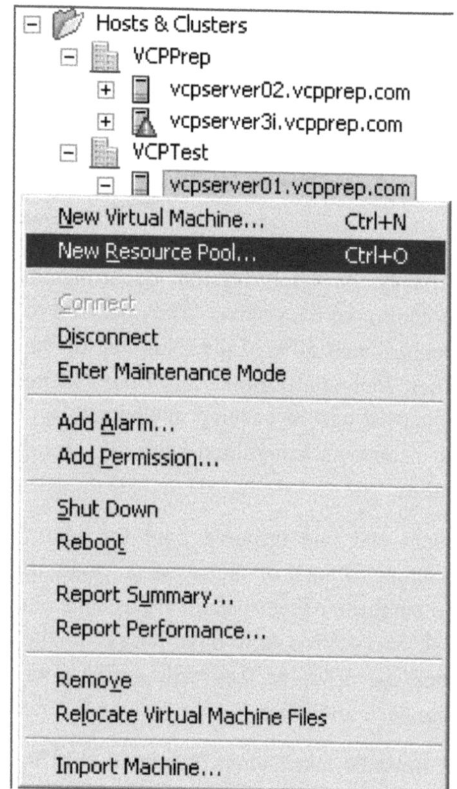

Figure 12.1 New Resource Pool Menu Option

Step 2. In the Create Resource Pool Dialog Box input the name of the new resource pool as shown in Figure 12.2.

You can set the CPU Reservation by either adjusting the value using the slider or entering the value in the box on the right. The Expandable check box can be set to allow an expandable reservation for the resource pool.

The Limit setting controls the limit of CPU resources in the resource pool. The Limit check box can be set to allow an unlimited amount of CPU resources to be available for the resource pool. The term "unlimited" implies up to the maximum amount of CPU cycles the ESX server's physical processors can offer.

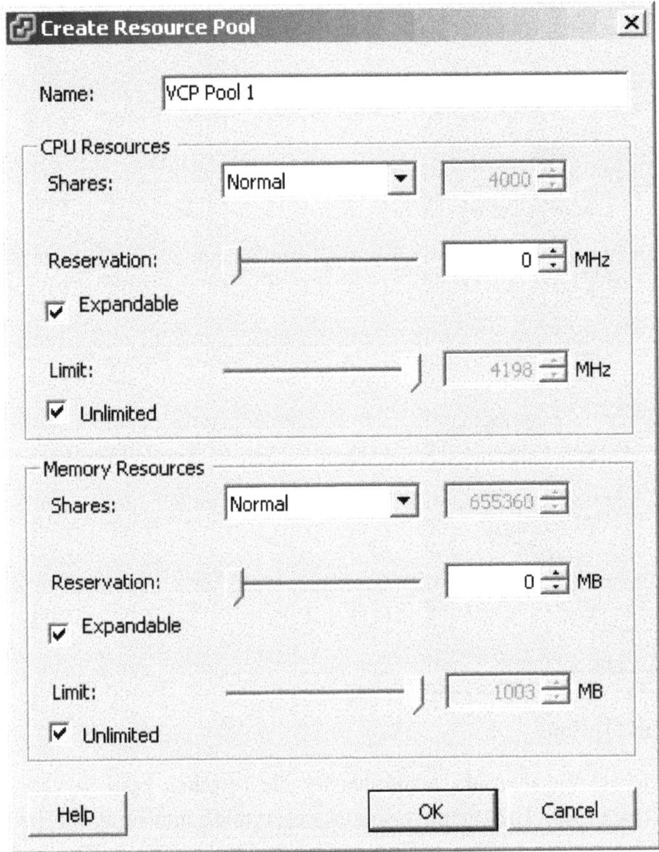

Figure 12.2 Create Resource Pool Dialog Box

In the CPU Resources box you can set the amount of CPU shares to one of the default settings as shown in Figure 12.3:

- Low = 2,000 shares
- Normal = 4,000 shares
- High = 8,000 shares
- Custom allows you to set the value to a non default value by changing the number of shares in the box on the upper right.

NOTE: New in ESX 3.5, CPU share values for both resource pools and virtual machines are the same.

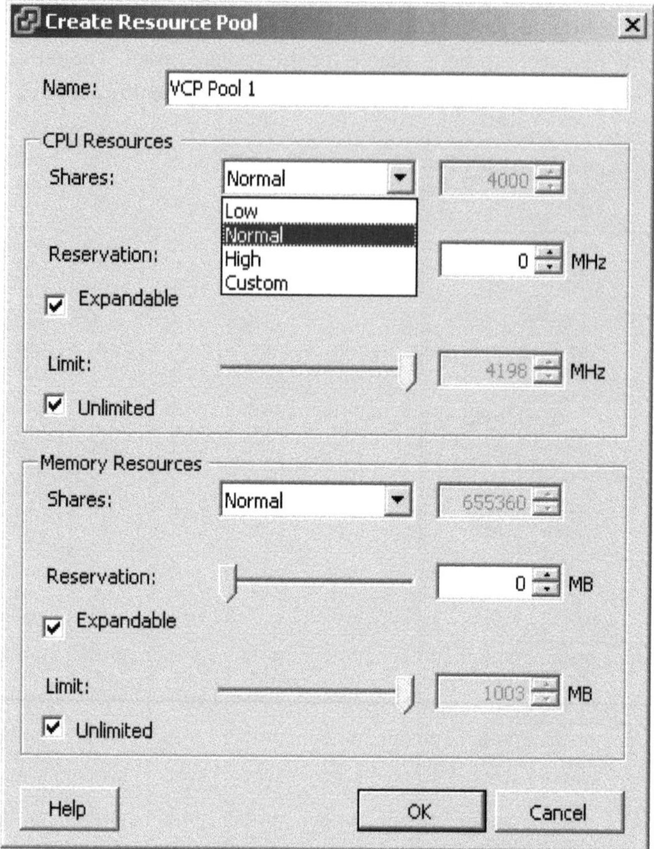

Figure 12.3 Create Resource Pool Shares Options

The Memory Resource box allows you to set the memory resources for the resource pool in very much the same way as was set for CPU resources. The memory shares, reservation and limit can be set in this part of the window.

Share Utilization

Resource shares are only utilized when the resource is in an over committed state.

On the VMs

CPU and memory shares are considered when the VMs in the resource pool are requesting more resources than the resource pool has available. For example, if the resource pool has 4,000 MHz CPU resources allocated for its VMs use and the aggregate CPU utilization on all running VMs in the pool exceeds 4,000 MHz, then the CPU shares assigned to the individual VMs will be considered.

On the Resource Pools

The CPU or memory shares allocated to the resource pools are considered when the total aggregate resource utilization of all VMs or child resource pools in all resource pools on the ESX server or in the cluster have exceeded the total amount of resources available. Shares are used when the pool's reservations (guaranteed minimums) are exhausted/fully-committed and when there is no more unreserved capacity. When the resource pool needs more of the particular resource it can have an amount up to its limit, but not exceeding its limit, if available from the parent/root resource pool. If other resource pools are competing for the resource, shares are used for 'fair share allocation,' the pool with the higher shares winning more frequently and allocated the resource being competed for.

Resources Allocation in Resource Pools

To look at the resource allocation of your resource pools do the following:

Step 1. In the Getting Started tab, you can select the links to either edit the resource pool settings or create a new resource pool as shown in Figure 12.4.

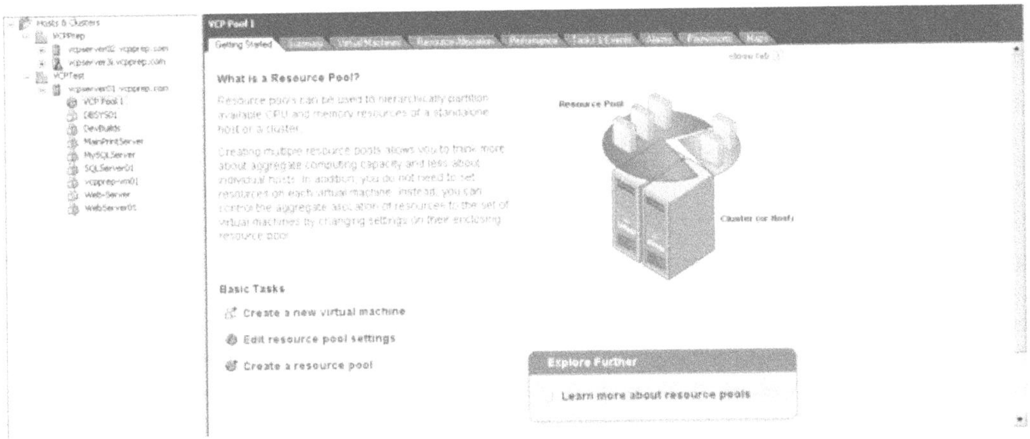

Figure 12.4 Resource Pool Getting Started Tab

If you just want to look at the existing configuration of the resource pool, select the pool from the inventory and then click on the Summary tab to view the current configuration. Figure 12.5 shows that we chose the pool named VCP Pool 1.

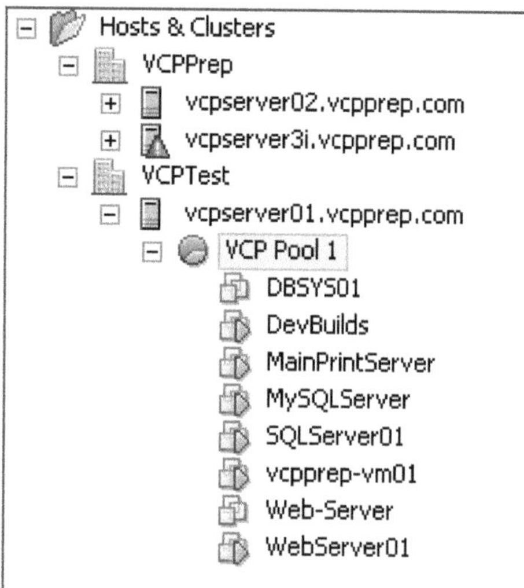

Figure 12.5 Resource Pool With Virtual Machines

Step 2. The Resource Pool Summary tab provides information about the resource pool. Figure 12.6 shows on the General box the number of VMs that are part of this resource pool as well as how many of them are actually operational at this moment in time. It also will show if there are any child resource pools to this pool.

The Resources box shows current CPU and memory usage of the pool.

The CPU box shows the Shares, Reservation, Type, and Limit settings for the pool. It also shows how much of the CPU usage for available processors is unreserved. This is a useful number to examine to see if there are any available resources if you need to raise the reservation of the pool.

The Memory box shows the Shares, Reservation, Type, and Limit settings for the pool. It also shows how much of the memory usage is unreserved.

The Commands box provides a useful shortcut to some common tasks such as creating a new virtual machine.

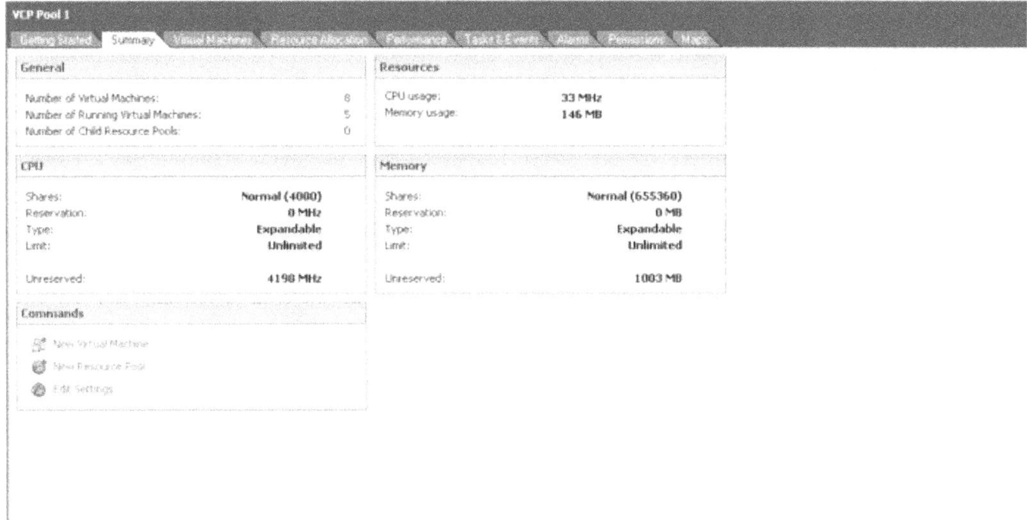

Figure 12.6 Resource Pool Summary Tab

Step 3. The Resource Pool Virtual Machines tab provides resource usage information for the virtual machines that are part of this resource pool. Figure 12.7 shows an example of this tab.

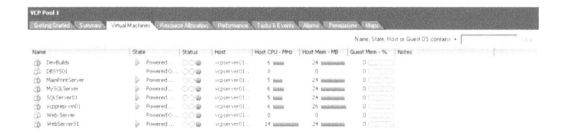

VCP Pool 1

Virtual Machines

Name, State, Host or Guest OS contains

Name	State	Status	Host	Host CPU - MHz	Host Mem - MB	Guest Mem - %	Notes
DevBuilds	Powered ...		vcpserver01...	6	24	0	
DBSYS01	Powered O...		vcpserver01...	0	0	0	
MainPrintServer	Powered ...		vcpserver01...	5	24	0	
MySQLServer	Powered ...		vcpserver01...	6	24	0	
SQLServer01	Powered ...		vcpserver01...	5	24	0	
vcpprep-vm01	Powered ...		vcpserver01...	6	26	0	
Web-Server	Powered O...		vcpserver01...	0	0	0	
WebServer01	Powered ...		vcpserver01...	14	24	0	

Figure 12.7 Resource Pool Virtual Machines Tab

Expandable Reservations

Expandable reservations allow a resource pool to be allocated CPU or memory resources from their parent pools. The reservation taken from the parent will not be given back when not needed, which is why expandable reservations decisions should be carefully planned. The expandable reservation check box should be selected as shown in Figure 12.2 in order for this feature to be enabled for the resource pool. As discussed in Chapter 11 – Resource Optimization, reservation settings are a guarantee that the virtual machine will have access to the reserved amount of CPU and or memory. Once a resource pool has used expandable reservations and given these resources to a virtual machine, a virtual machine may use these resources as needed, when needed. In other words, the reservation is still a guarantee at the time of power on and these resources will be made available to a virtual machine until the virtual machine is powered off. The ESX server's CPU and memory resources are considered the root resource pool. A virtual machine with reservation values set, that is not within a resource pool would have the admissions control process verify that the ESX server's unreserved capacity is able to meet the virtual machines reservation values in order to power on the virtual machine. The unreserved capacity in this case would be the root resource pool.

Consider a resource pool that has the default settings of its CPU limit set to unlimited, expandable reservations set to enabled and both CPU and memory reservations set to 0 (zero). This resource pool has one virtual machine in it that has a CPU reservation of 250 MHz. As long as the root resource pool has at least 250 MHz CPU unreserved, this virtual machine will be allowed to power on due to expandable reservations. If we disable CPU expandable reservations for this pool and once again attempt to power on the virtual machine, the power on process will fail with an error stating "Insufficient CPU resources". This is because the resource pool itself does not have any reserved CPU resources. Simply assigning this resource pool a CPU reservation value of 250 MHz will allow the virtual machine to power on.

Now let's consider memory. This same resource pool now has its memory reservation set to 512 MB and its memory expandable reservation value has been disabled. The virtual machine inside this resource pool now has its memory reservation set to 512 MB. When we attempt to power on this virtual machine, we will once again receive an error message. This time the error message will state "Insufficient memory resources". The reason powering on this virtual machine fails is due to the memory overhead discussed in Chapter 11 – Resource Optimization. This virtual machine has approximately 72 MB of memory overhead. By raising the resource pool memory reservation an additional 73 MB, to 585 MB, the virtual machine can now be powered on. The additional 73 MB of memory assigned to the resource pool memory reservation was needed in our example due to the memory overhead of the virtual machine of approximately 72 MB to 73 MB. *Note, just like a virtual machine, the CPU and memory reservation values of a resource pool can never be more than the CPU and memory limit values.

You can confirm the configuration of expandable reservations by viewing the Resource Allocation tab for the resource pool in question. In Figure 12.8 we can see that expandable reservations are enabled for both CPU and memory resources on pool VCP Pool 1. The CPU button has been selected to show each VMs CPU resource consumption.

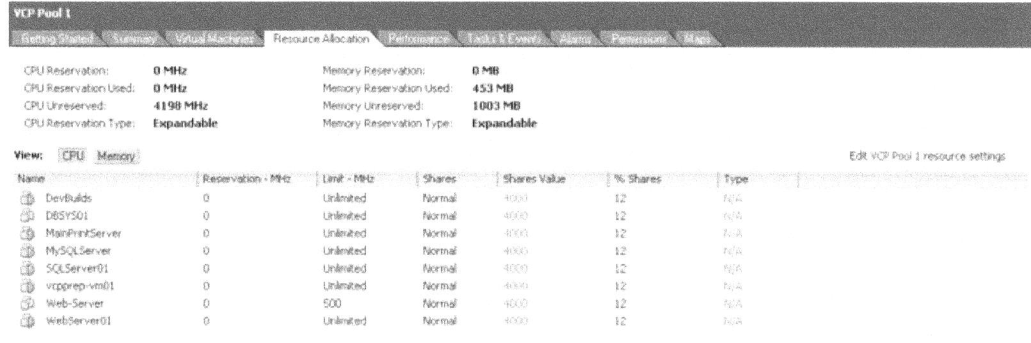

Figure 12.8 Resource Pool Resource Allocation Tab CPU

Figure 12.9 shows the memory button is selected showing the VMs memory consumption.

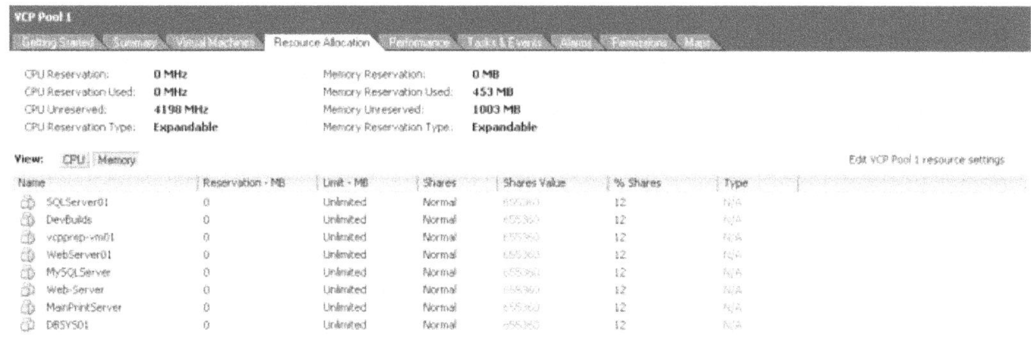

Figure 12.9 Resource Pool Resource Allocation Memory

Troubleshooting Resource Pools

Resource pool issues are typically caused by the following problems:

- Insufficient CPU resources in the resource pool
- Insufficient memory resources in the resource pool
- Misconfigured CPU limits in the resource pool

- Misconfigured memory limits in the resource pool
- Misconfiguration of the expandable reservation setting

To view a resource pool utilization and performance metrics, select the Performance tab as shown in Figure 12.10.

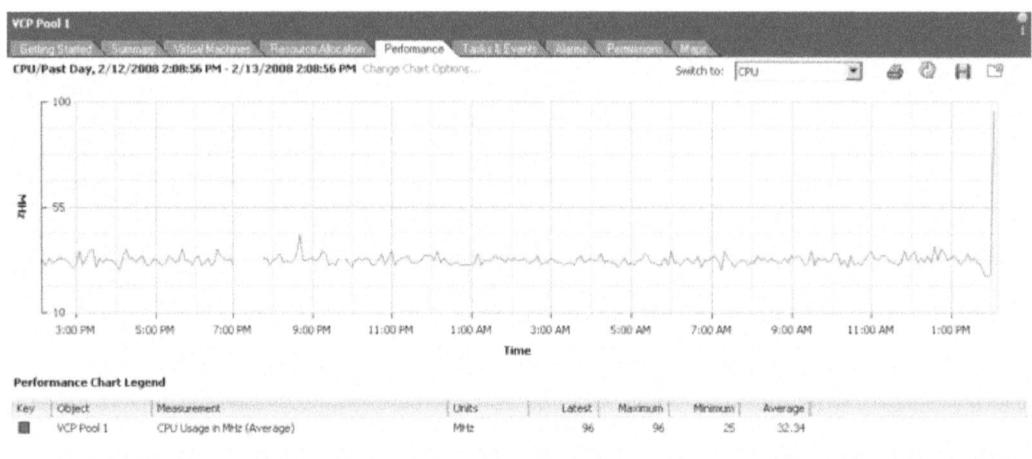

Figure 12.10 Resource Pool Performance Tab

The Performance Chart Legend at the bottom of the screen in Figure 12.10 provides details as to what is being charted. It also provides numerical data as well. In this example we can see a spike in CPU usage around 2 p.m. By observing the performance information we can determine if the combined workloads of the VMs in the pool are reaching the full capacity of the pool.

The Tasks & Events tab displays information useful for analyzing the resource pool activity. There are two different views provided, the Tasks view and the Events view. The Tasks button is selected and located in the upper left hand corner of the screen as shown in Figure 12.11. We can see the virtual machine state changes and the associated time of the task for the VCP Pool 1 resource pool.

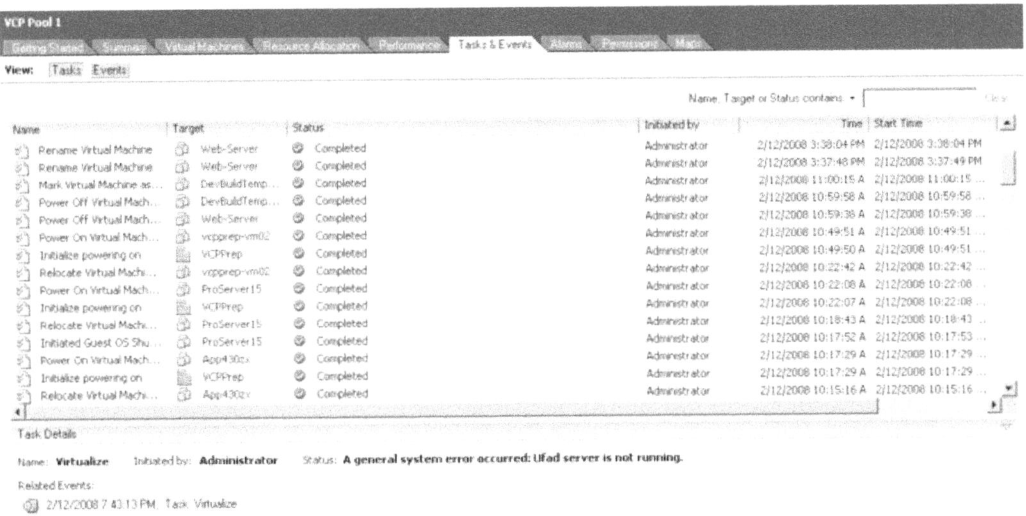

Figure 12.11 Resource Pool Tasks & Events Tab Tasks

The Events button is selected and located in the upper left hand corner of the screen as shown in Figure 12.12. We can see the virtual machine information messages and the associated time of the event for the VCP Pool 1 resource pool.

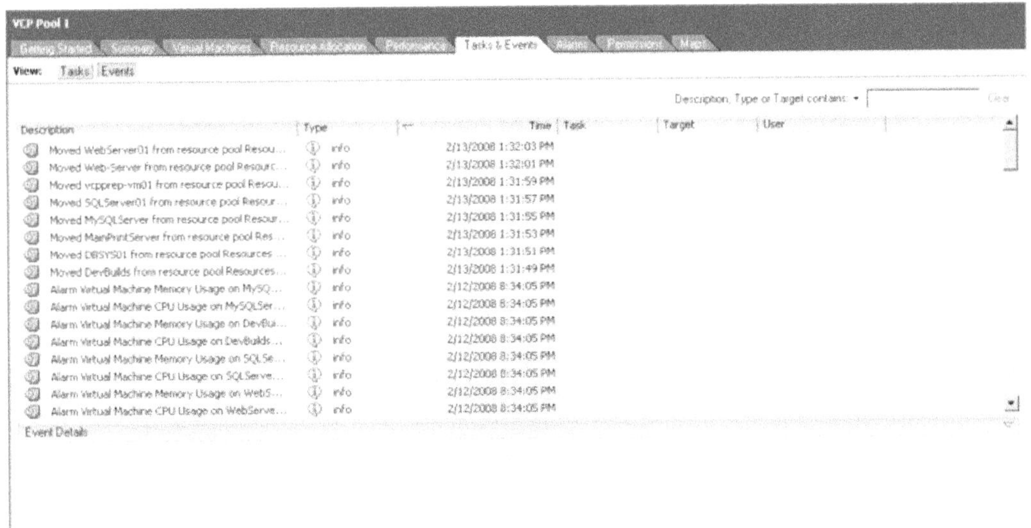

Figure 12.12 Resource Pool Tasks & Events Tab Events

The Alarms tab has two views, the Triggered Alarms view and the Definitions view. The Triggered Alarms button is selected and located in the upper left hand corner of the screen as shown in Figure 12.13. We can see the status of the alarm, the alarm name and when the alarm was triggered from this view.

Figure 12.13 Resource Pool Alarms Tab Triggered Alarms

The Definitions button is selected and located in the upper left hand corner of the screen as shown in Figure 12.14. Use this view to obtain a description of the triggered alarms.

Figure 12.14 Resource Pool Alarms Tab Definitions

Improper permissions on the resource pool may have allowed a user to modify the resource pool settings. Such unauthorized changes can alter virtual machine resource access causing performance degradation and jeopardizing any Service Level Agreements (SLAs) that may be associated with the resource pool. Use the Permissions tab as shown in Figure 12.15 to verify that the correct permissions are assigned to the proper user accounts.

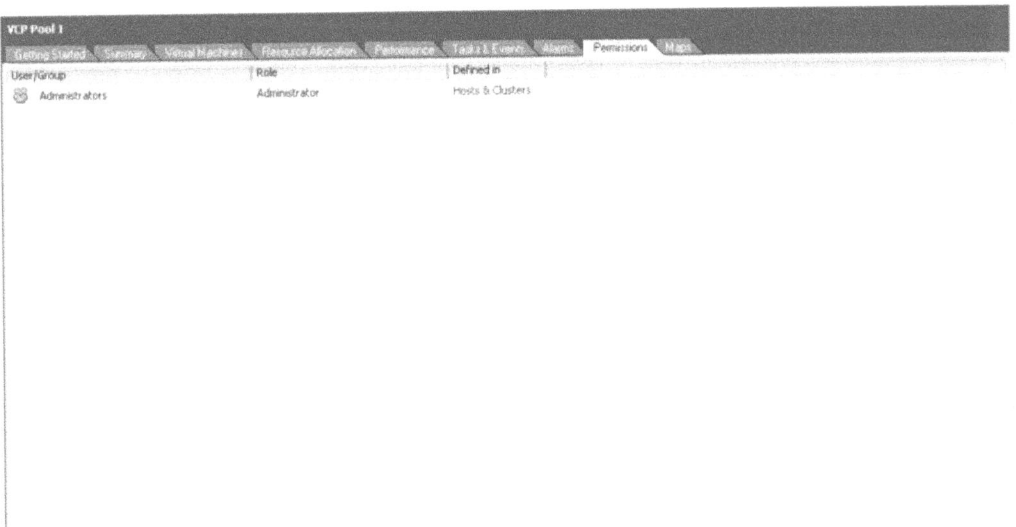

Figure 12.15 Resource Pool Permissions Tab

The Maps tab as shown in Figure 12.16 can provide an ESX administrator quick access for viewing the various relationships between virtual machines, networks and storage. Maps can be altered by simply selecting the various choices within the Map Relationships section. Limiting the maps view to a narrow scope can often aid in troubleshooting configurations issues.

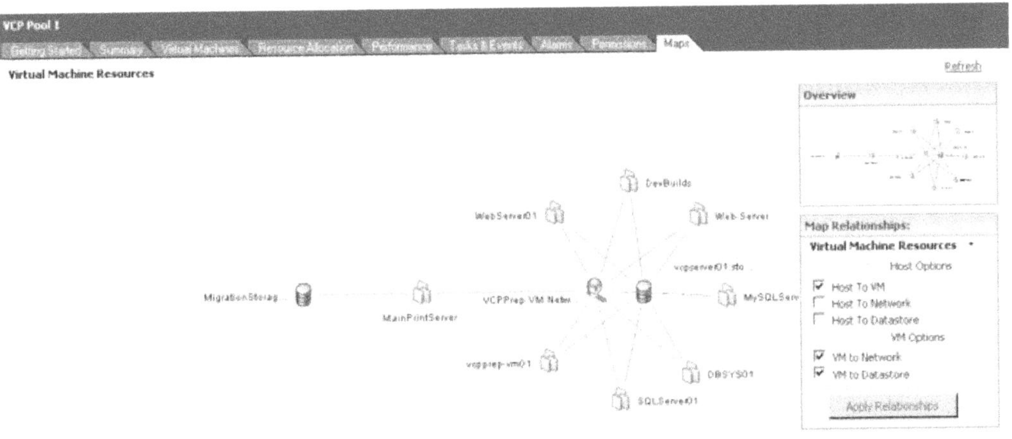

Figure 12.16 Resource Pool Maps Tab

In Figure 12.17, we see an example of parent and child resource pools. Further dividing resource pool resources allows fine tuning a given set of computational CPU and memory capacity. However, sub pools and virtual machines that are at the same hierarchy level will compete for resources. For example, a sub pool that has a memory reservation value of 500 MB is essentially like an always powered on virtual machine as far as admission control is concerned. If we tried to power on a virtual machine that also required 500 MB of memory reservation, the power on process would fail if the parent resource pool did not have 500 MB of unreserved memory or expandable reservation enabled where its parent resource pool or the root resource pool did not have 500 MB of unreserved memory.

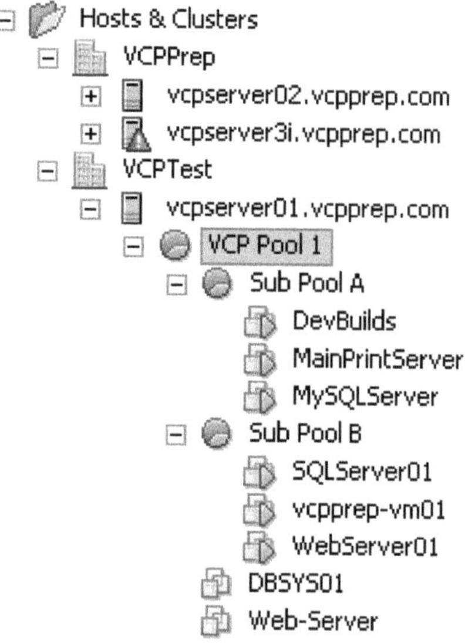

Figure 12.17 Resource Pool With Sub Pools

External References

The VMware ESX 3.5 and ESXi Server version 3.5 Documentation Page:

http://www.vmware.com/support/pubs/vi_pubs.html

Basic System Administration - ESX Server 3.5, ESXi Server version 3.5, VirtualCenter 2.5:

http://www.vmware.com/pdf/vi3_35/esx_3/r35/vi3_35_25_admin_guide.pdf

Sample Test Questions

1. Your company leases virtual machines to small start-up companies. You decide to create a resource pool for each client. Some pools have only one VM in them, while others have many. Which of the following configuration settings will provide the client with a guaranteed minimal amount of resources in their resource pool?

a. Expandable reservation disabled

b. The limit set to a small value

c. The reservation set to a value equal to what the VMs normally will need

d. Expandable reservation enabled

e. Unlimited set for the limit

2. A virtual machine is unable to power on within a resource pool. The administrator checks the resource pool settings and sees that some of the default settings have been modified. Which of the following resource pool settings affect admission control?

a. Resource pool CPU share value

b. Resource pool expandable memory reservation value

c. Resource pool memory share value

d. Resource pool expandable CPU reservation value

e. Resource pool swap file

3. Three new web server virtual machines have been placed into the WebServer resource pool. These new virtual machines have been able to successfully power on. However, the IT department has received several calls concerning poor performance of the new virtual machines. Which of the following within the VI Client provides the information needed for quick analysis of resource distribution?

a. Tasks & Events tab

b. Performance tab

c. Resource Allocation tab

d. Summary tab

e. Maps tab

4. A resource pool has pre-defined CPU share values available in order for the resource pool to obtain CPU resources during resource contention. Which of the following are the pre-defined CPU share values of a resource pool?

a. High - 8,000

b. High - 10,000

c. Low - 500

d. Custom - 1,500

e. Normal - 4,000

5. Resource pools are useful by providing which of the following benefits?

a. Load balancing

b. Resource allocation

c. High availability

d. Easier management

e. Access control

Sample Test Solutions

1. Your company leases virtual machines to small start-up companies. You decide to create a resource pool for each client. Some pools have only one VM in them, while others have many. Which of the following configuration settings will provide the client with a guaranteed minimal amount of resources in their resource pool?

a. Expandable reservation disabled

b. The limit set to a small value

c. The reservation set to a value equal to what the VMs normally will need

d. Expandable reservation enabled

e. Unlimited set for the limit

Answer: c - The reservation is a guaranteed amount of resources for the pool. This value must be available in order for the pool to be created.

2. A virtual machine is unable to power on within a resource pool. The administrator checks the resource pool settings and sees that some of the default settings have been modified. Which of the following resource pool settings affect admission control?

a. Resource pool CPU share value

b. Resource pool expandable memory reservation value

c. Resource pool memory share value

d. Resource pool expandable CPU reservation value

e. Resource pool swap file

Answer: b and d - The resource pool CPU and memory share values are not considered by the admission control process. Resource pools do not have a swap file like virtual machines do. Both CPU and memory expandable reservation values are used by the admission control process at the time a virtual machine is powered on.

3. Three new web server virtual machines have been placed into the WebServer resource pool. These new virtual machines have been able to successfully power on however, the IT department has received several calls concerning poor performance of the new virtual machines. Which of the following within the VI Client provides the information needed for quick analysis of resource distribution?

a. Tasks & Events tab

b. Performance tab

c. Resource Allocation tab

d. Summary tab

e. Maps tab

Answer: c - The resource allocation tab should be consulted when needing to ascertain virtual machine resource consumption within a resource pool.

4. A resource pool has pre-defined CPU share values available in order for the resource pool to obtain CPU resources during resource contention. Which of the following are the pre-defined CPU share values of a resource pool?

a. High - 8,000

b. High - 10,000

c. Low - 500

d. Custom - 1,500

e. Normal - 4,000

Answer: a and e - A resource pool has default share values assigned to it. These values are as follows:

- ***Low = 2,000 shares***
- ***Normal = 4,000 shares***
- ***High = 8,000 shares***
- ***Custom = 0***

The custom setting allows an administrator to set the value to a non default value if needed.

5. Resource pools are useful by providing by enabling which of the following benefits?

a. Load balancing

b. Resource allocation

c. High availability

d. Easier management

e. Access control

Answer: b, d and e - Resource pools do not provide load balancing or high availability benefits. These are obtained by using VMware DRS and HA clusters respectively. Resource pools do offer a means to effectively allocate CPU and memory resources to virtual machines. An ESX administrator can reduce their management activities by placing a group of virtual machines with the same resource priorities into a resource pool.

In such a configuration, the resource assignment task need only be performed at the resource pool level just once. This allows the virtual machine resources to be managed as a group. Access permission can be applied to resource pools objects. This increases access security to virtual machines while reducing the security management tasks as access permissions just need to be applied at the resource pool level.

Chapter 13

Virtual Machine Migration

After reading this chapter you should be able to complete the following tasks:

- Using Cold Migration
- Describe VMotion
- Describe VMotion Requirements
- Using VMotion
- Using Storage VMotion Migration
- Troubleshooting Virtual Machine Migrations

The ability to re-assign the CPU, memory and storage resources required by virtual machines from one ESX server to another is one of the unique benefits that VMware's VI3 environment offers. This ability enables system administrators to minimize virtual machine downtime as well as manually or automatically balance resource utilization of the physical ESX host systems. VirtualCenter 2.5 provides different methods to migrate virtual machines between ESX hosts. We will examine the following three methods in this chapter:

- Cold Migration
- VMotion (Hot Migration)
- Storage VMotion Migration

Initiating a Cold Migration

It may be necessary at times to move a virtual machine's configuration and state files from one storage location to another or from one ESX Host to a different type of ESX Host, one with a different type of CPU. One method of accomplishing this is with cold migration. A cold migration is simply a migration that occurs while the virtual machine is either in suspend mode or powered off. The following are the steps used from within the VI Client to accomplish a cold migration.

Figure 13.1 Migrate Menu Option

Step 1. Select the virtual machine to cold migrate and right click on it. In this example, we have chosen the MgmtRptsSrv virtual machine that is currently hosted on the vcpserver02 ESX server. This will display the pop up menu as shown in Figure 13.1. Select the Migrate... menu option to invoke the Migrate Virtual Machine Wizard.

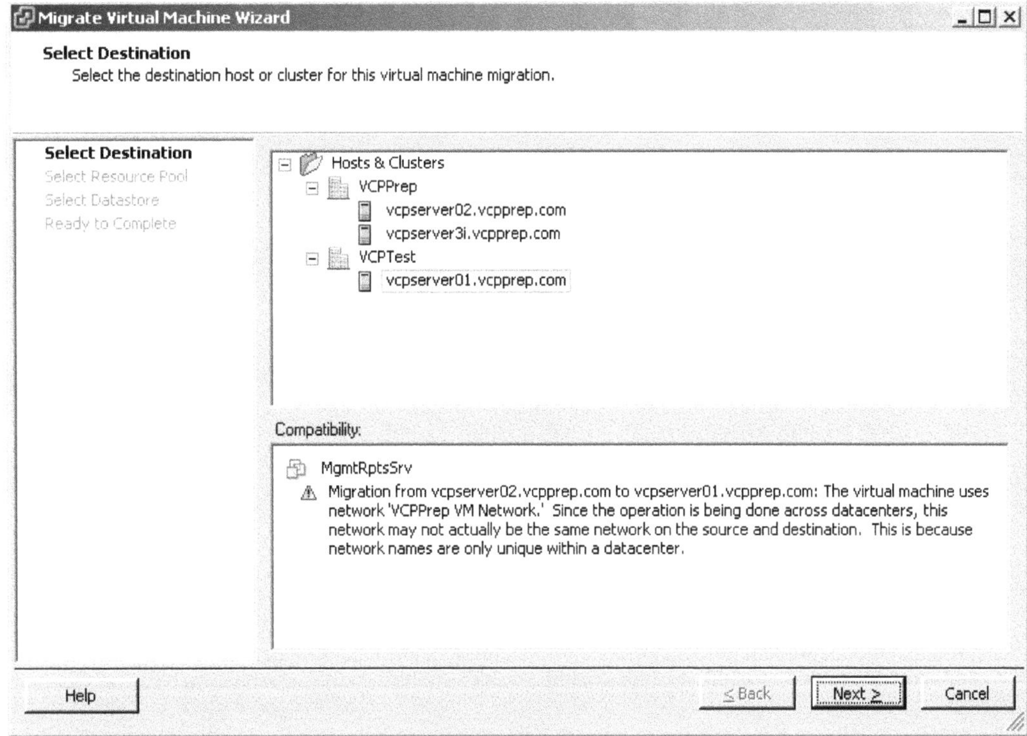

Figure 13.2 Migrate Virtual Machine Wizard Dialog Box

Step 2. The Migrate Virtual Machine Wizard allows the choice of the destination ESX host. It is possible to choose the ESX host server that is currently hosting the virtual machine being migrated. Doing so would allow the virtual machine's configuration and state files to be moved while the virtual machine is not relocated to another ESX host. Select an ESX host destination as shown in Figure 13.2 and click the Next button.

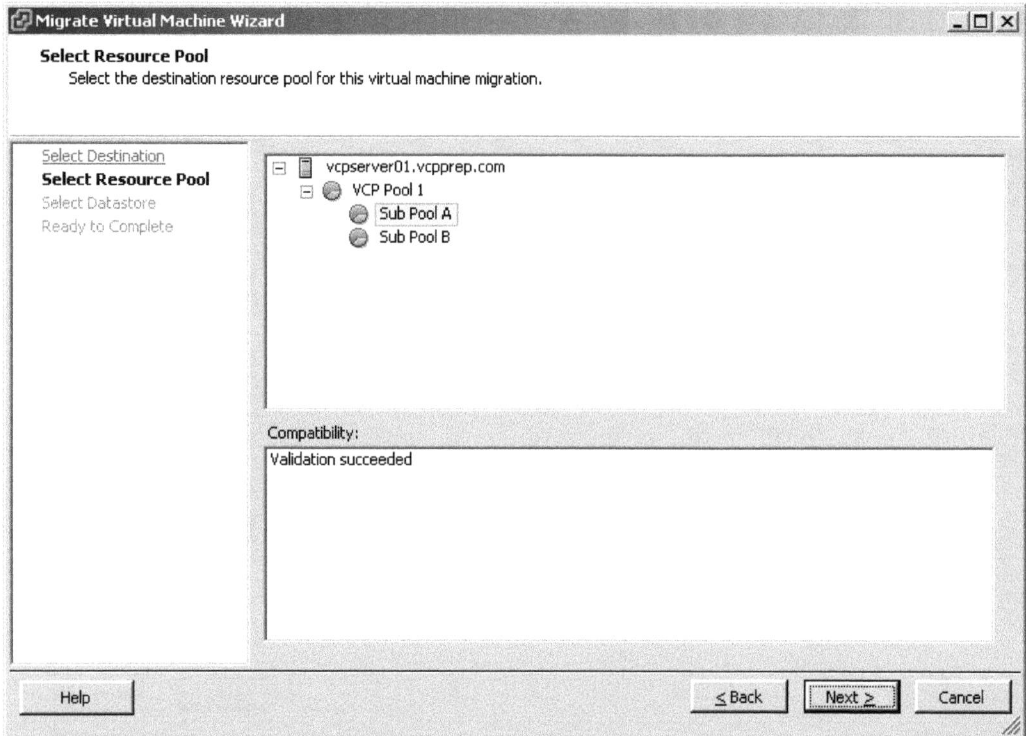

Figure 13.3 Migrate Virtual Machine Wizard Select Resource Pool

Step 3. If any resource pools exist, the destination resource pool can be selected. As shown in Figure 13.3, the Sub Pool A resource pool has been selected. Make the appropriate selection and click the next button to continue.

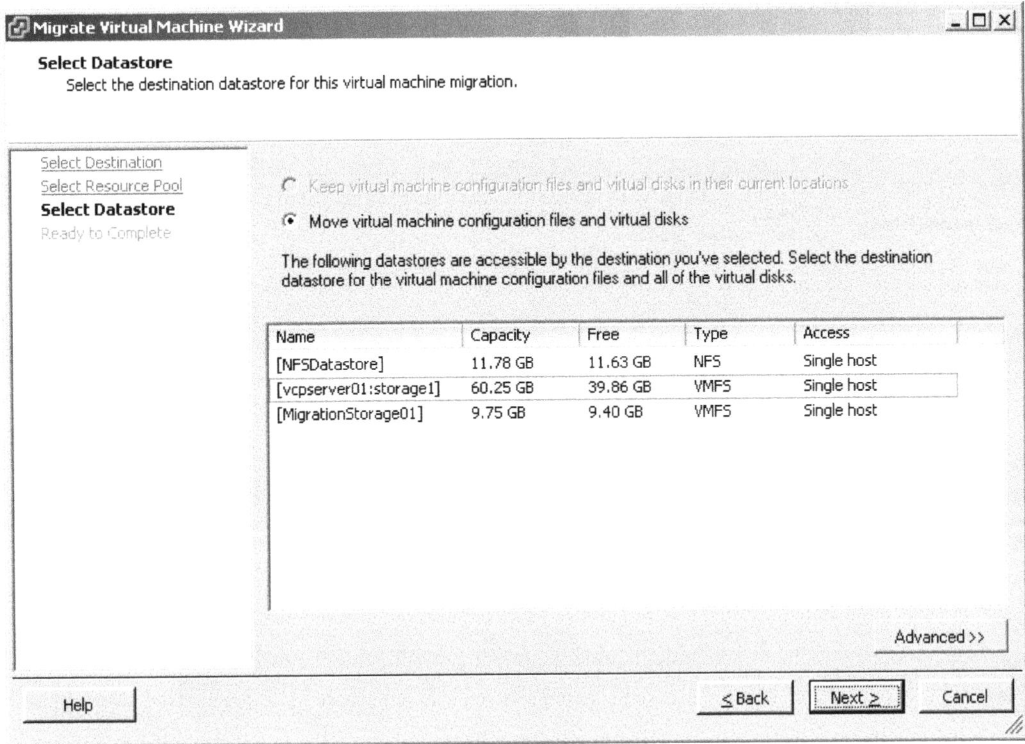

Figure 13.4 Migrate Virtual Machine Wizard Select Datastore

Step 4. The virtual machine configuration and state files can be moved to another storage location if desired. If the virtual machine configuration and state files are located on shared storage, it is not necessary to move these files as it is possible to leave these files as is and only re-assign the virtual machine to a new ESX host by selecting a different ESX host as previously shown in Figure 13.2. It is possible to not move the virtual machine state files or select a new destination host but doing so is not a very practical exercise. Since this virtual machine's state files are stored on the local storage of the vcpserver02 ESX server, the option to leave these files without moving them is not available due to the destination ESX server not having access to the local storage of the vcpserver02 ESX server. Selecting the advanced button shown in Figure 13.4 allows a separate location to be specified for both the configuration and state files. Once the appropriate choices have been made, select the Next button to continue.

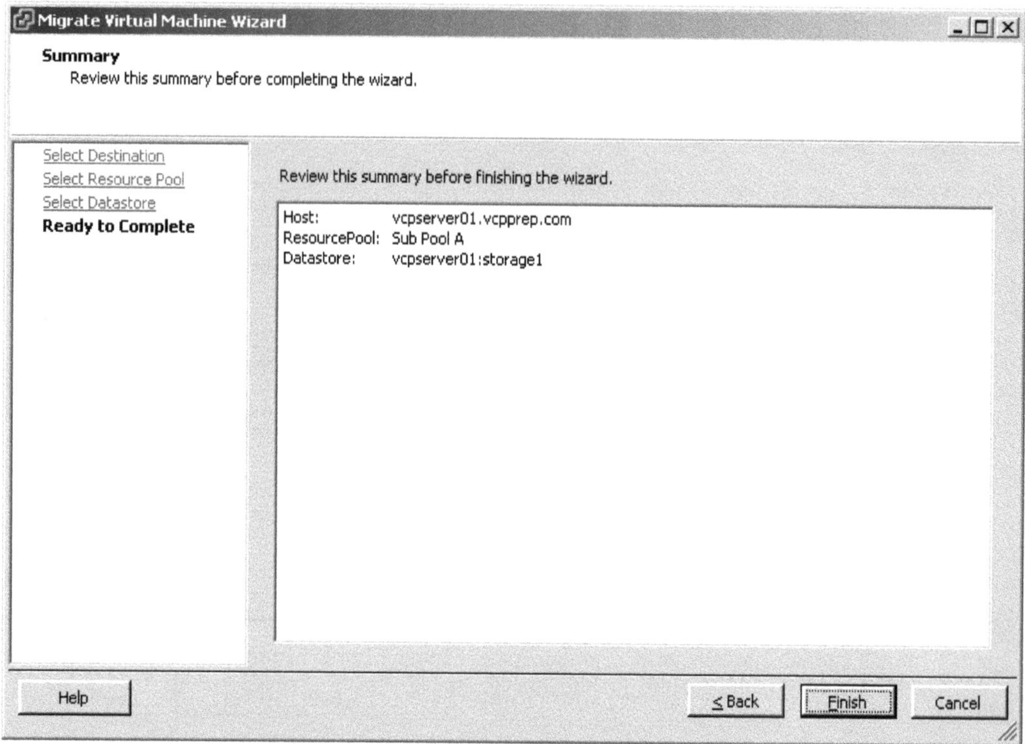

Figure 13.5 Migrate Virtual Machine Wizard Ready To Complete

The final summary screen is displayed as shown in Figure 13.5. Verify the correct host, resource pool and datastore have been chosen and select the Finish button to initiate the cold migration process.

The status of the cold migration can be observed from within the Recent Tasks window pane located at the bottom of the VI Client window screen as shown in Figure 13.6. The length of time it takes to complete a cold migration depends on a number of factors, such as the size of the files being copied, available bandwidth and current storage device work load. It is often best to perform cold migrations during off peak hours if possible to reduce the extra work load placed on the network and storage devices.

Figure 13.6 Migrate Virtual Machine Status

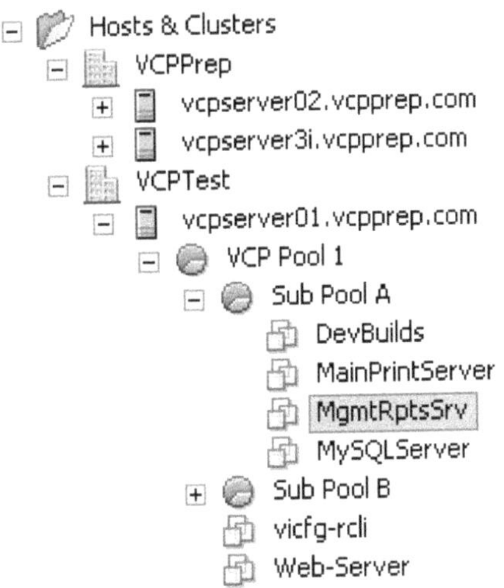

Figure 13.7 Virtual Machine Migrated To New Destination

As shown in Figure 13.7, once the cold migration process has finished, the MgmtRptsSrv virtual machine is now being hosted on the vcpserver01 ESX server within the Sub Pool A resource pool.

The VMotion Technology

Having to either suspend or power down may not be an option for production virtual machines. Providing that the proper requirements have been met, a virtual machine can be re-assigned to another ESX host system without the need to suspend or power off the virtual machine. This can be accomplished via the VMotion technology VMware provides in a VI3 environment. VMotion is also referred to as a hot or live migration. This is because it provides real-time re-assignment from one ESX host to another. Such virtual machine migrations off of an ESX host that is required to be powered off for scheduled maintenance will keep the virtual machines up and running without disruption. VMotion technology also allows the ESX administrator the ability to manually balance CPU and memory resources across a group of ESX hosts. Automatic CPU and memory resource balance across ESX hosts is also possible using VMotion technology within a Dynamic Resource Scheduler (DRS) cluster. DRS clusters are discussed in Chapter 14 – Distributed Resource Scheduler.

The primary activity that takes place during a VMotion migration concerns the transfer of virtual machine memory data from the source ESX host to the destination ESX host. This memory transfer operation is carried out using several steps. The VMotion migration is initiated via the Migrate Virtual Machine Wizard launched using the VI Client. The VMotion process first pre-copies the virtual machine's memory from the source to the destination ESX host via the Gigabit Ethernet network. Since the virtual machine is currently powered on, all memory changes now need to be tracked. This is accomplished by the creation of a memory bitmap on the source ESX host that records the address location of all memory changes that have taken place after the initial pre-copying of memory. The virtual machine is now briefly paused so that its device state and the memory bitmap can be transferred to the destination ESX host. The memory locations recorded in the memory bitmap file are now copied over to the destination host. Now the virtual machine is resumed on the destination host. To avoid any network latency issues with the virtual machine, a RARP (Reverse Address Resolution Protocol) is sent over the subnet so that its MAC address within the physical switches forwarding tables will be correctly sent out the new switch port. The virtual machine MAC and IP address do not change during the VMotion migration. The original virtual machine instance on the source ESX host is kept until the new instance is resumed on the destination host just in case the new instance cannot be resumed. Once the new instance has resumed on the destination host, the original virtual machine instance is deleted.

Let's take a look at the requirements that need to be met for a successful VMotion across ESX host systems.

VMotion Requirements

The VMotion process requires several compatibilities between the ESX hosts involved in the live migration. Certain CPU characteristics have to match across ESX hosts or else the VMotion process will fail. The CPU vendor must match. VMotion will not be successful if attempting to migrate from an Intel based ESX server to an AMD based ESX server. CPU's of the ESX hosts must also be within the same CPU vendor family (i.e. P3, P4).

AMD introduced the NX (No eXecute) bit to separate sections of memory that are used for either processor instructions or for the purpose of storing application data. Intel has the same feature in their CPUs and is known as the XD (eXecute Disable) bit. Using the NX bit helps to prevent malicious software from accessing and writing code to the memory allocated to application data where it can then be executed. If there is a NX bit mismatch between the ESX hosts preventing VMotions from occurring, the use of the NX bit can be masked by the ESX administrator. To mask the NX bit, right click on the virtual machine from within the VI Client and select the "Edit Settings" menu option. Next, select the "Options" tab and click on the "CPUID Mask" option. Choose the "Hide the NX flag from guest" radio button and click on the "OK" button to save the changes. The virtual machine will need to be rebooted for the modification to take effect. Figure 7.72 in Chapter 7 - Virtual Machines, shows the NX flag configuration setting.

In 2005, CPU vendors began adding hardware assist technology into their CPUs in order to enhance virtualization performance. Intel introduced the IVT (Intel Virtualization Technology) and AMD introduced the AMD-V (AMD Virtualization) CPU extensions. VMware uses its binary translation method for 32-bit guest operating systems, thereby not requiring an exact match between Intel based ESX hosts. For 64-bit guest operating systems hosted on Intel based ESX hosts, an exact match in hardware assist technologies is required.

Another potential CPU mismatch can occur across ESX hosts with Streaming SIMD Extensions 3 (SSE3) and cause the hot migration to fail. SSE3 uses Single Instruction, Multiple Data (SIMD) to enhance the multimedia capabilities of the CPU. It is a requirement that the SSE3 capabilities match exactly. An exact match is also required for Supplemental Streaming SIMD Extension 3 (SSSE3). SSSE3 adds additional instructions to SSE3 capabilities.

VMware also requires a Gigabit Ethernet network to be used for the VMotion process. Ideally, a dedicated Gigabit Ethernet backplane to enhance both performance and security. Although a 100 MB network may work for VMotion, it is considered an unsupported configuration. It is necessary to create a virtual switch with a VMkernel port enabled for VMotion on all ESX hosts participating in the VMotion process. These switches need to be identically labeled as well. Please refer to Chapter 4 - ESX 3.x Server Networking Configurations for additional information on virtual switches. Each ESX host involved in the hot migration process will be required to access the same physical network. These ESX hosts will also be required to access the shared storage datastore of each virtual machine that is being migrated using the VMotion process. The reason for this is that the virtual machine configuration and state files do not move during the live migration.

Initiating a VMotion Migration

Prior to initiating a VMotion migration, a VMkernel port needs to be configured. Recall from Chapter 4 - ESX 3.x Server Networking Configurations, that a VMkernel port is used for IP based storage access and VMotion migrations. In Figure 13.8, we can see a VMkernel port has been created with the label of iSCSIa01. In this example setup, this VMkernel port is going to be used to perform a VMotion migration.

Step 1. To verify the VMkernel port is VMotion enabled, select the Properties link next to the virtual switch that contains the VMkernel port.

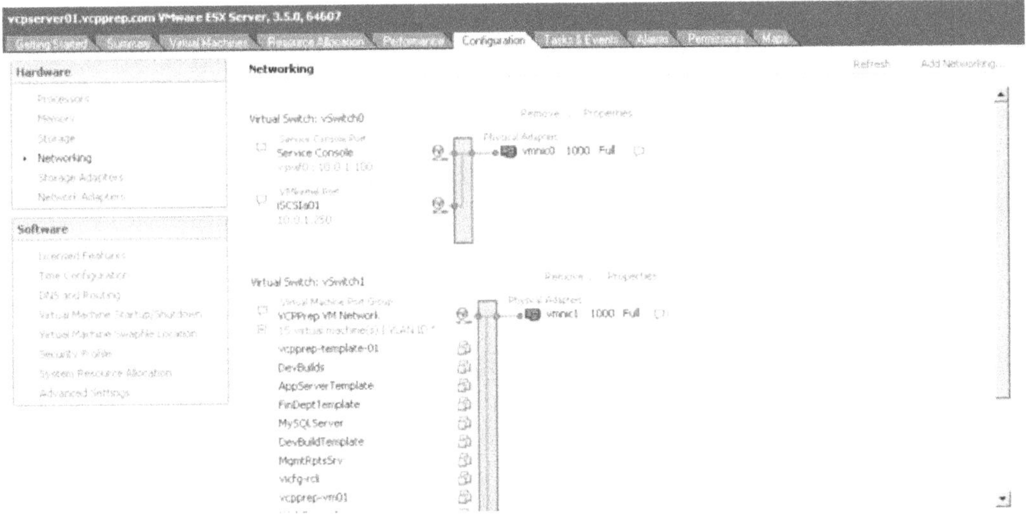

Figure 13.8 Configuration Tab Networking

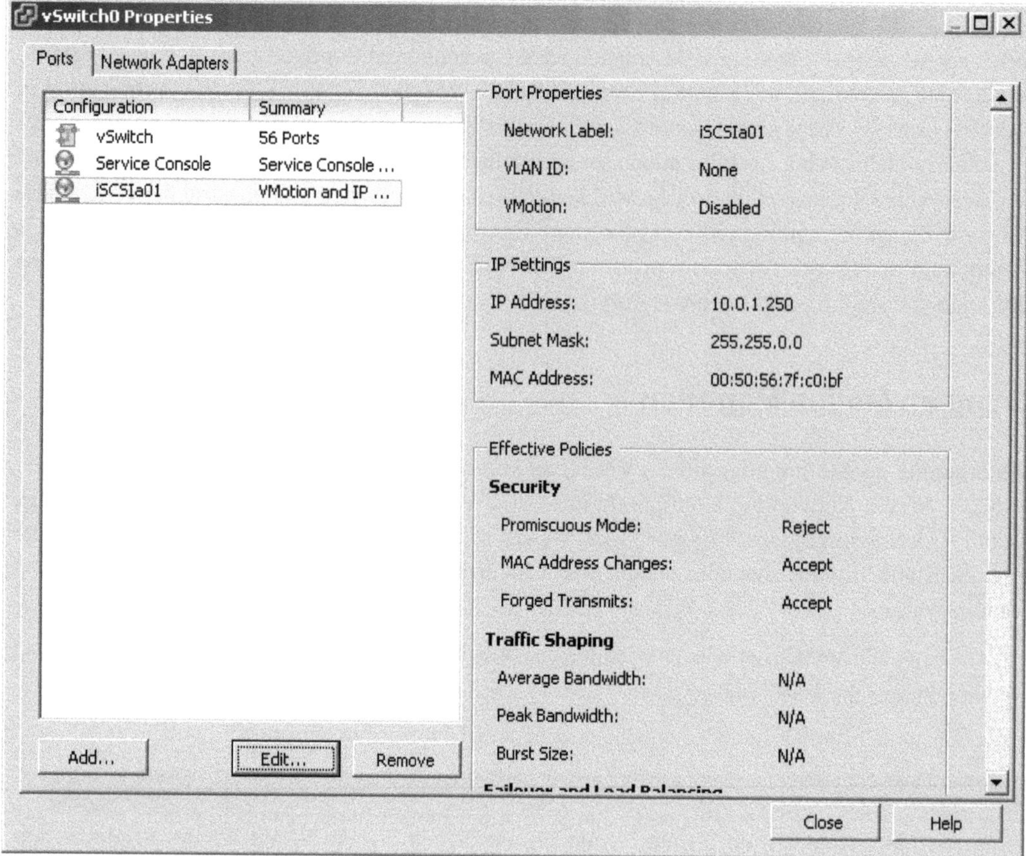

Figure 13.9 vSwitch0 Properties

Step 2. The virtual switch properties dialog box is displayed as shown in Figure 13.9. The Port Properties section shows that VMotion is currently disabled. Select the iSCSIa01 VMkernel port and click on the Edit button to view its configuration.

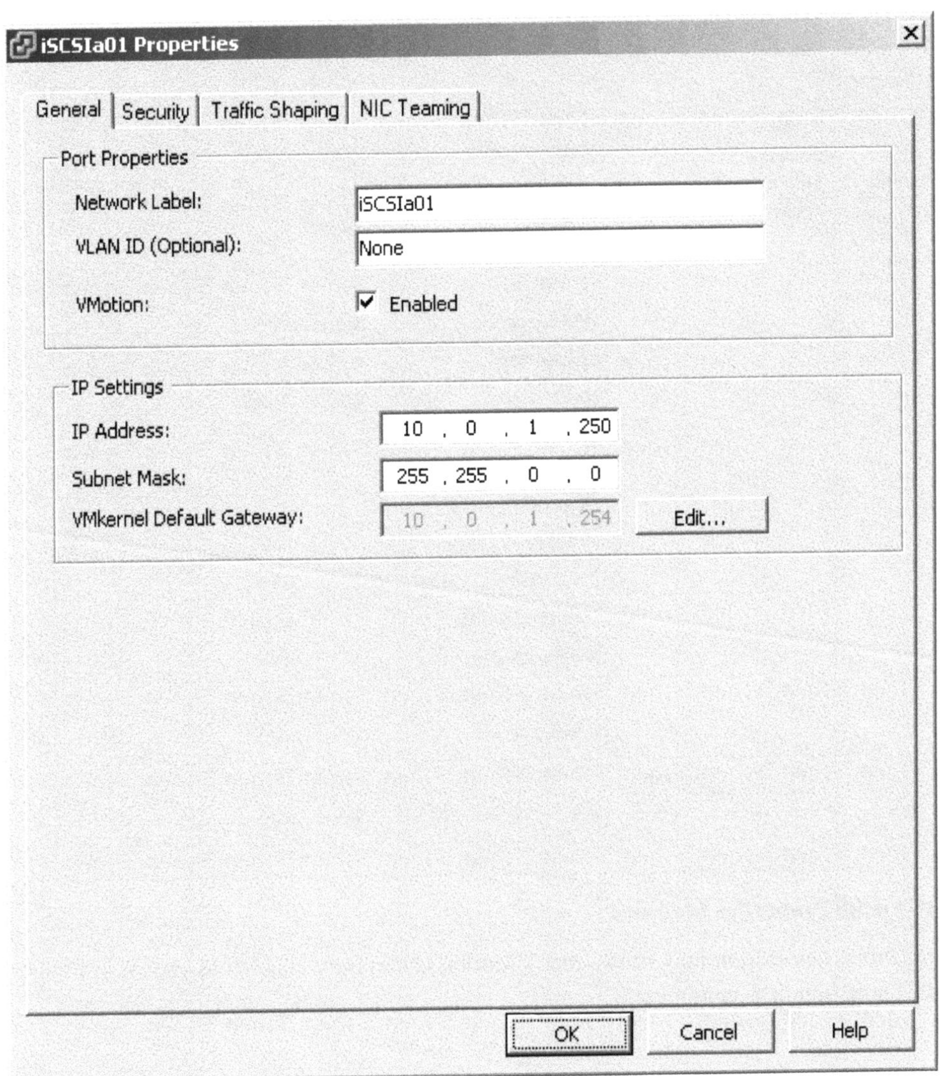

Figure 13.10 iSCSI VMkernel Properties

Step 3. The General tab displays the Port Properties section that contains the VMotion Enabled check box. Select this check box to enable the VMkernel port for VMotion. It is only possible to have one VMkernel port per ESX host enabled for VMotion. If another VMkernel port is currently VMotion enabled, select this check box will automatically deselect the other VMkernel port from being VMotion enabled. Click the OK button to continue (See Figure 13.10).

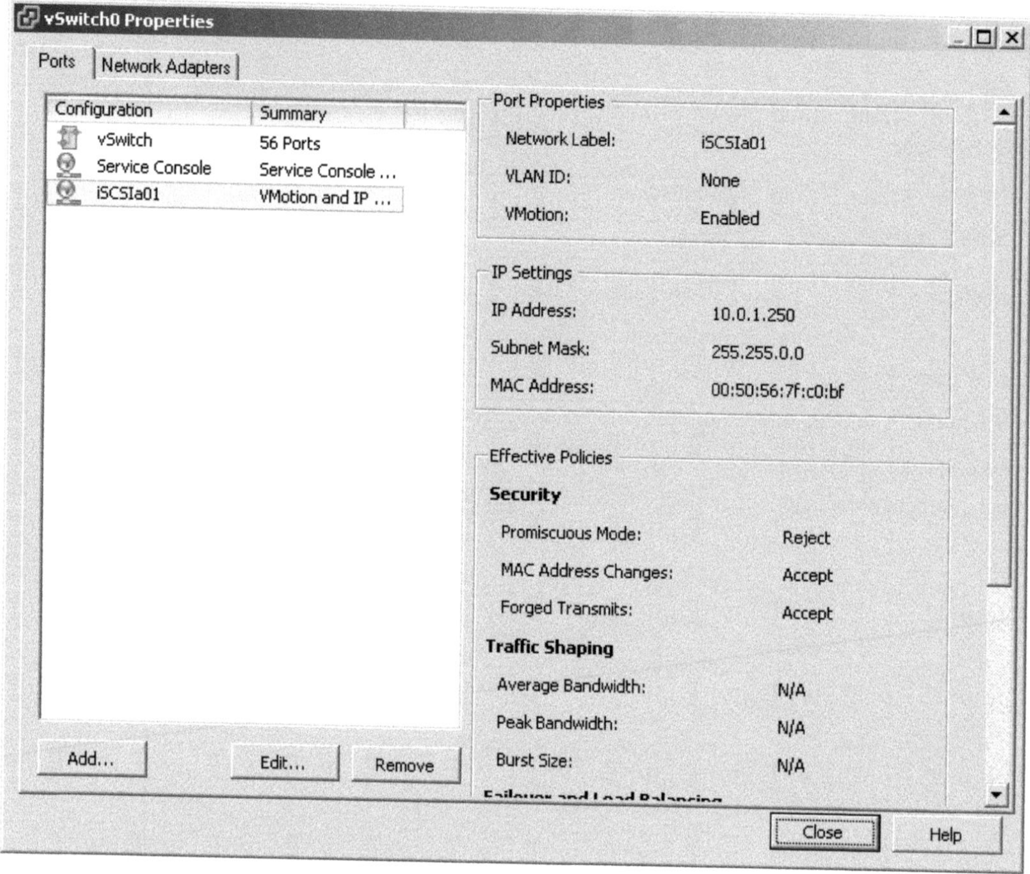

Figure 13.11 vSwitch0 Properties Modified

Step 4. The Port Properties section now shows that VMotion is currently enabled as shown in Figure 13.11. Select the Close button to continue.

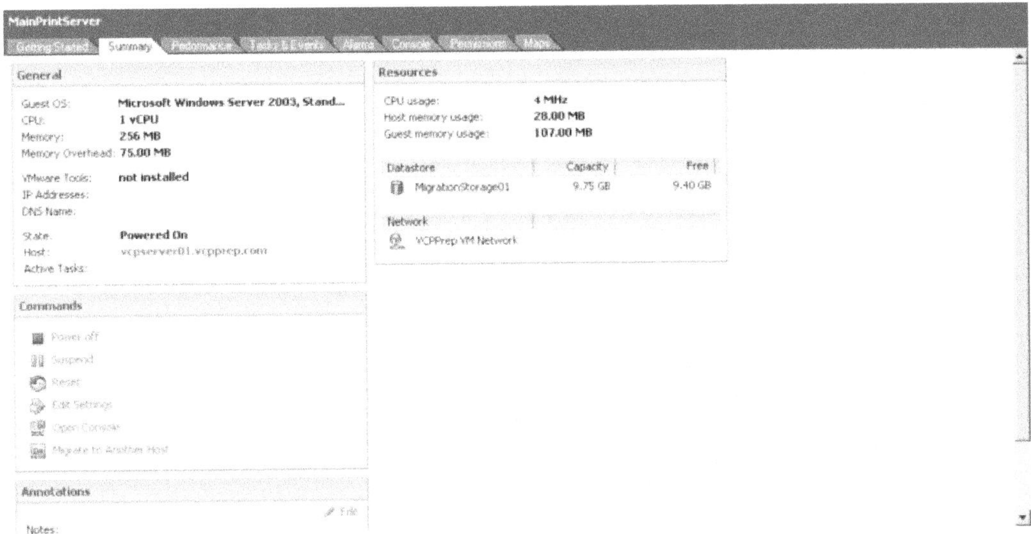

Figure 13.12 Virtual Machine Summary Tab

Step 5. Choose a virtual machine to migrate. Figure 13.12 displays the summary tab for the MainPrintServer virtual machine. The General section lists this virtual machine as currently powered on and hosted by the vcpserver01.vcpprep.com ESX host system. This virtual machine is also connected to the VCPPrep VM Network virtual machine port group. This port group uses the vmnic1 physical uplink port as shown in Figure 13.8. A virtual machine must not be connected to an internal virtual switch. If it is, the VMotion process will fail the validation check of the VMotion Manual Migration Wizard. The MainPrintServer virtual machine will be used to perform a live migration.

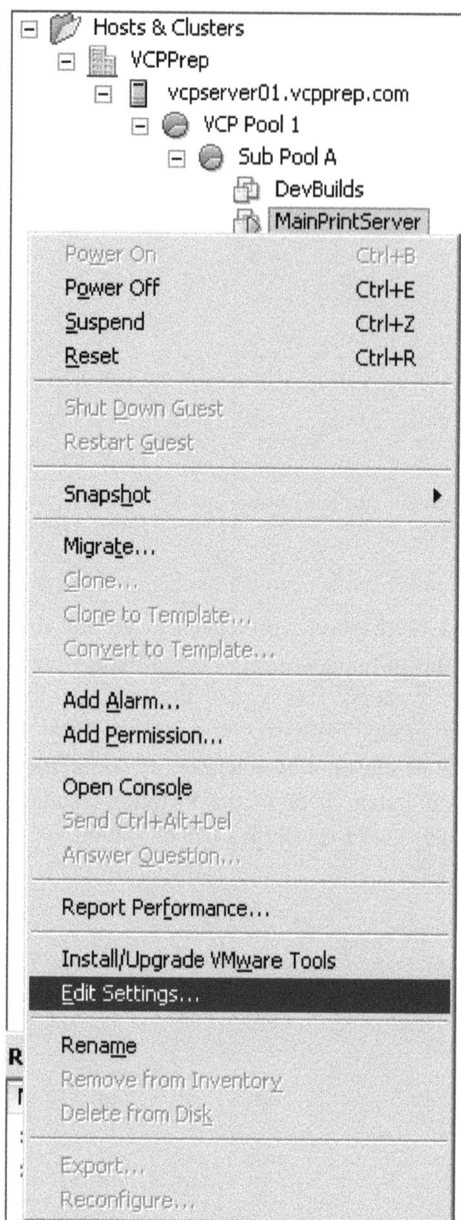

Figure 13.13 Virtual Machine Edit Settings Menu Option

Step 6. A quick inspection of the virtual machine device configuration should be performed prior to initiating the VMotion migration. To do so, right click on the virtual machine to be migrated and select the Edit Settings... menu option as shown in Figure 13.13.

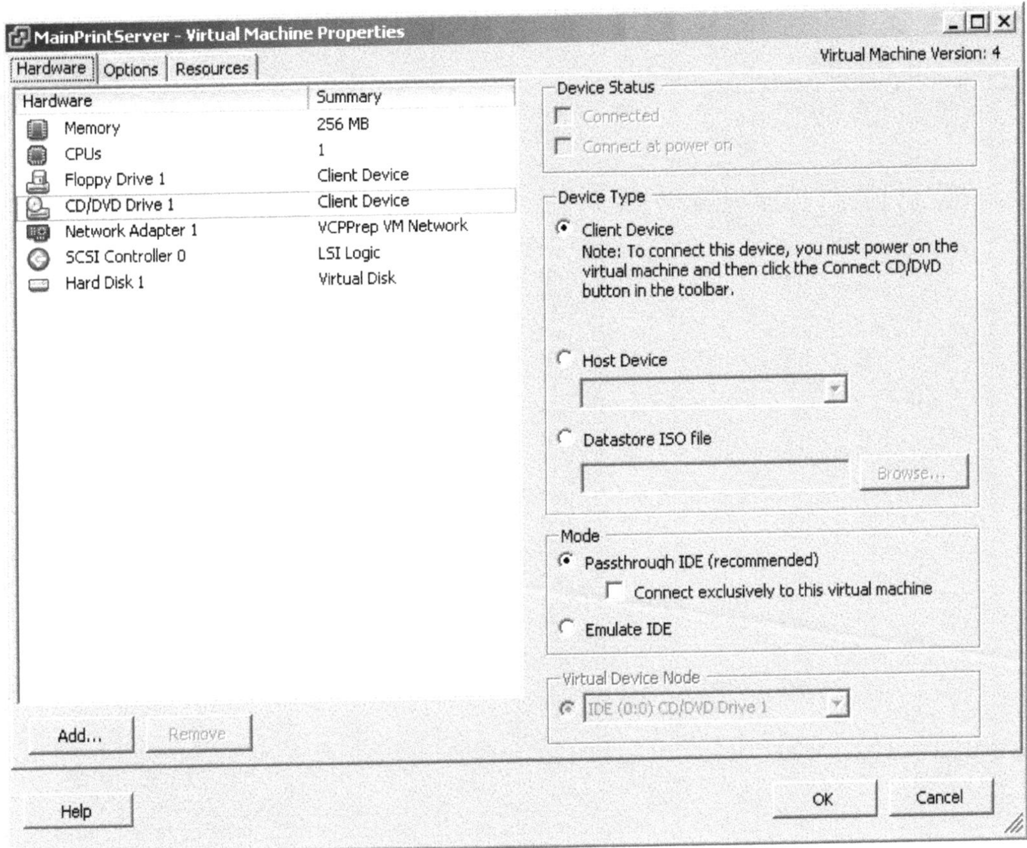

Figure 13.14 Virtual Machine Properties CD/DVD Drive

Step 7. Verify that the virtual machine is not currently configured to use the ESX host's CD/DVD drive. In Figure 13.14, the Hardware tab was chosen and the CD/DVD drive selected. Doing so reveals the current configuration for this device. This device is not currently connected to the ESX host's physical CD/DVD drive. If it were, this would prevent the VMotion process from proceeding.

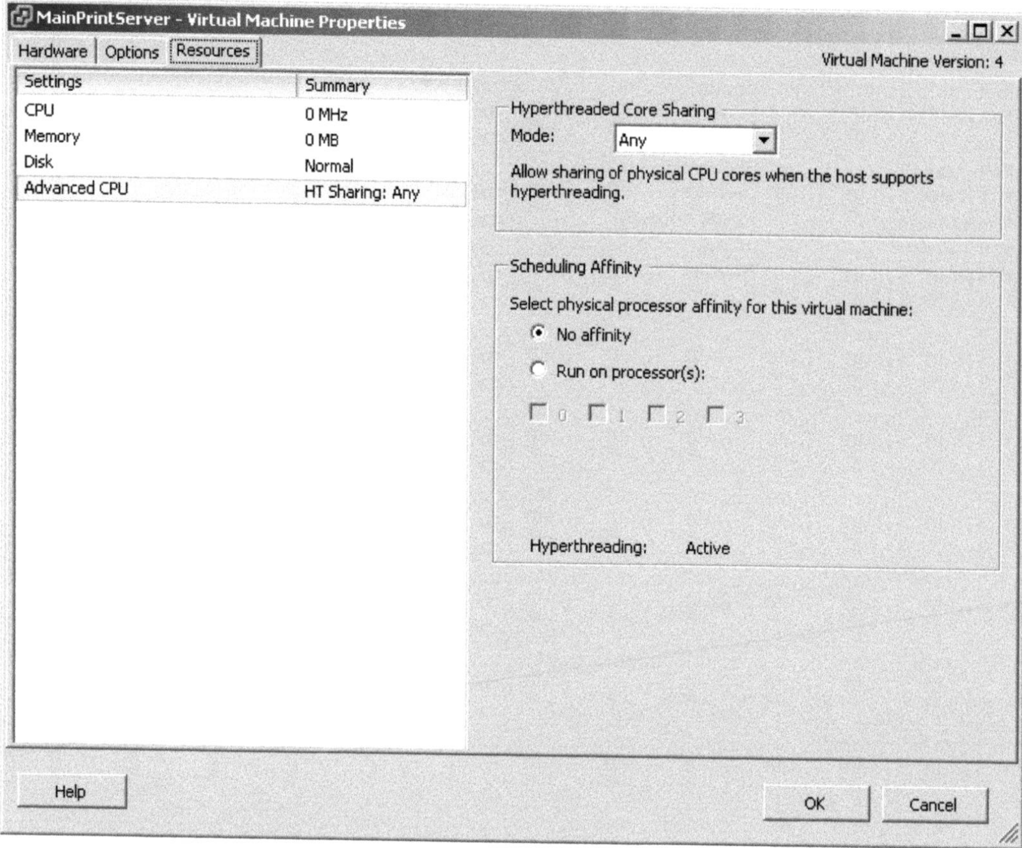

Figure 13.15 Virtual Machine Properties Resources Tab

Step 8. Select the Resources tab as shown in Figure 13.15 to verify if this virtual machine is configured to use processor affinity. The Scheduling Affinity section reveals that this virtual machine is not configured to use processor affinity. If it were, this would prevent the VMotion process from proceeding. Click the Cancel button to close the Virtual Machine Properties dialog box.

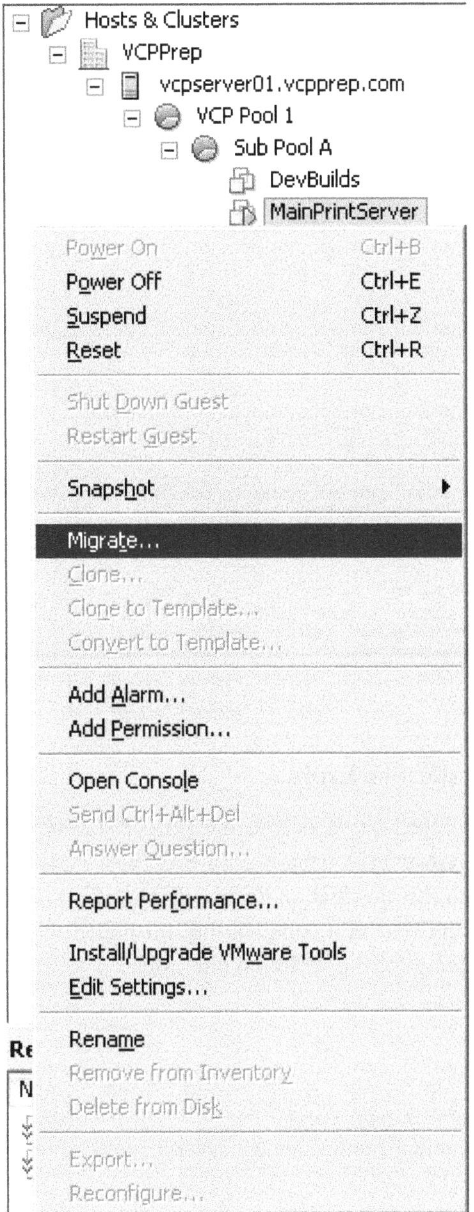

Figure 13.16 Virtual Machine Migrate Menu Option

Step 9. To launch the Migrate Virtual Machine Wizard, right click the virtual machine and select the Migrate... menu option as shown in Figure 13.16.

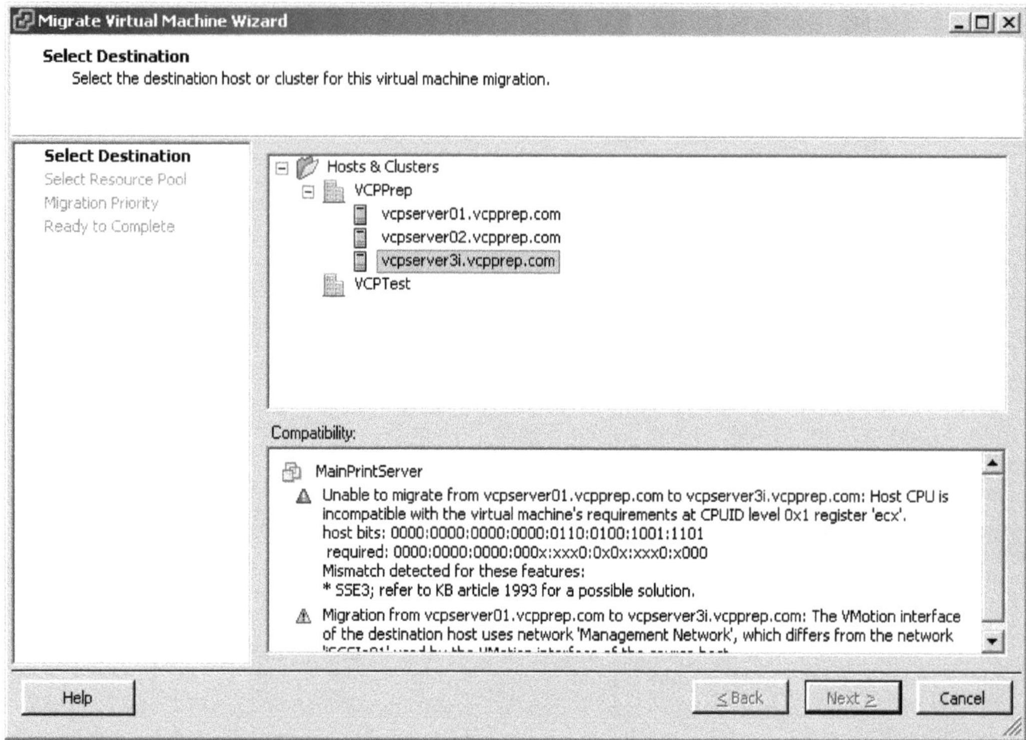

Figure 13.17 Migrate Virtual Machine Wizard Select Destination Error

Step 10. The Migrate Virtual Machine Wizard is launched. Select a new destination ESX host system for this virtual machine. In Figure 13.17, we see that the vcpserver3i.vcpprep.com ESX host system was selected. A problem with CPU compatibility exists with this destination host as displayed within the Compatibility section. The root cause of the error is identified as a compatibility mismatch with SSE3. Another ESX host system will need to be chosen to complete the VMotion migration.

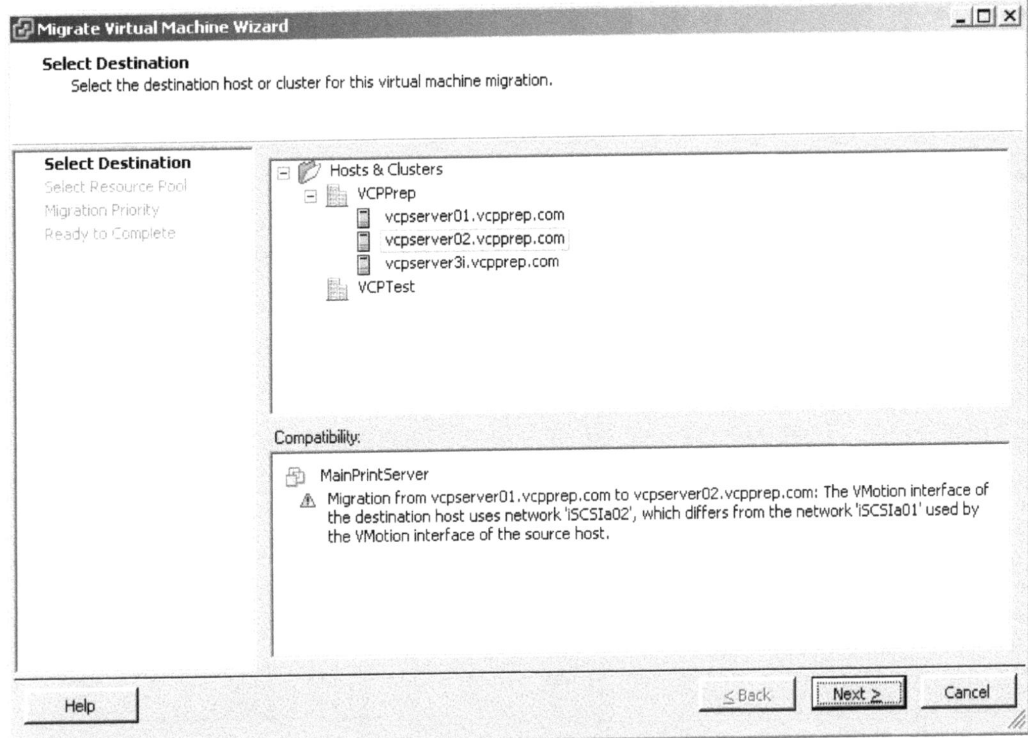

Figure 13.18 Migrate Virtual Machine Wizard Select Destination

Step 11. The vcpserver02.vcpprep.com ESX host has been selected as shown in Figure 13.18. Within the Compatibility section, a warning regarding the differences in name for the source and destination ESX hosts VMkernel port. It is good practice to keep a consistent naming convention for virtual switch ports however, the difference in VMkernel port names will not prevent the VMotion migration from completing. Click the Next button to continue.

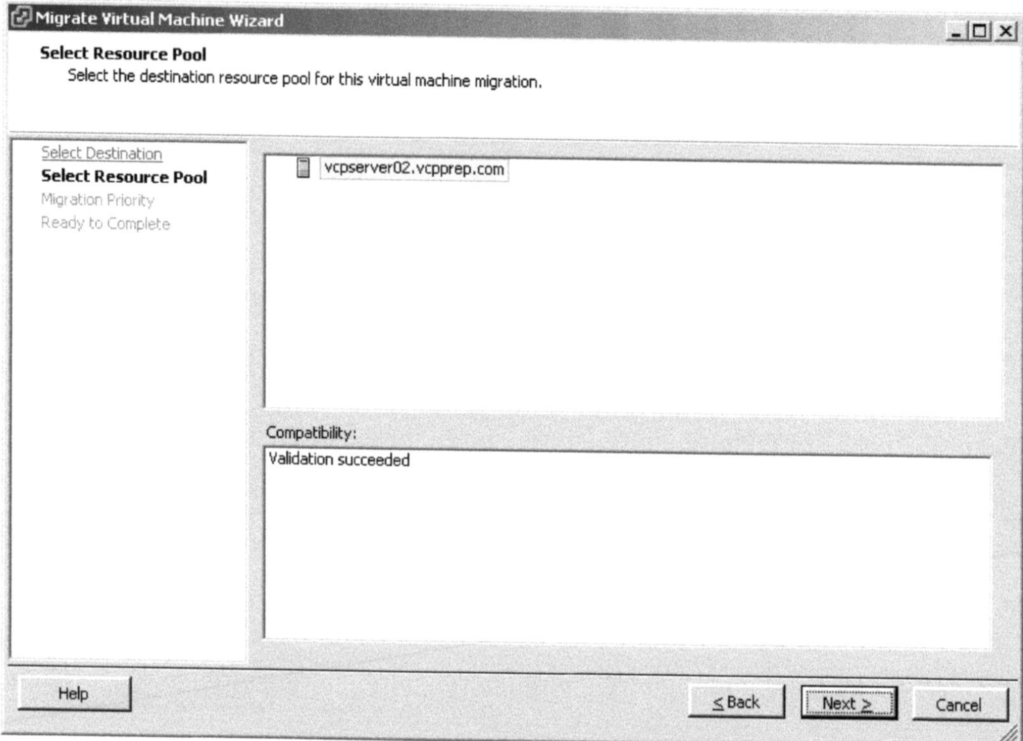

Figure 13.19 Migrate Virtual Machine Wizard Select Resource Pool

Step 12. The destination resource pool should now be selected. In this example as shown in Figure 13.19, no resource pools exist on the vcpserver02.vcpprep.com ESX host. By simply selecting the host, the root resource pool is used. Please refer to Chapter 12 – Resource Pools, for more information regarding resource pools.

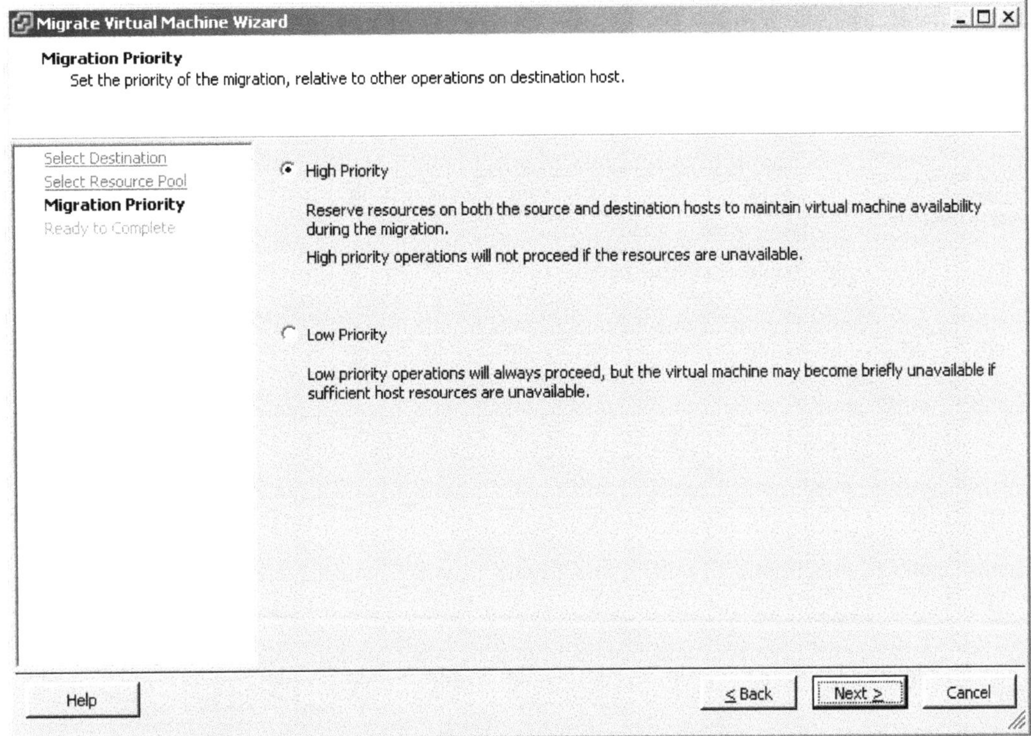

Figure 13.20 Migrate Virtual Machine Wizard Migration Priority

Step 13. A priority can be assigned to the VMotion migration. If re-assigning the virtual machine to another ESX host is critical and sufficient resources exist on both the source and destination ESX hosts, select the High Priority radio button as shown in Figure 13.20. This selection can provide the virtual machine ample resources during the migration so that it remains accessible by those currently working within its guest operating system. However, if there are not sufficient resources, the migration may not succeed. Select the Low Priority radio button when operator accessibility is not a great concern. This option can help to ensure the migration will succeed when resources are scarce. Once the priority has been chosen, select the Next button to continue.

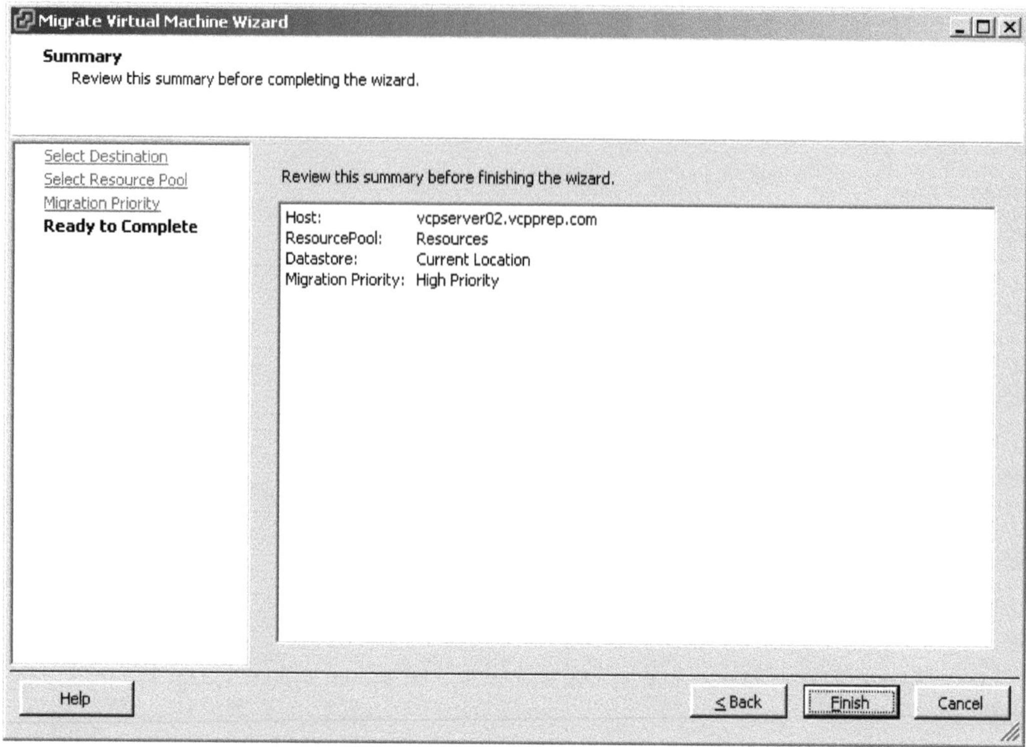

Figure 13.21 Migrate Virtual Machine Wizard Ready To Complete

Step 14. The Ready to Complete screen is displayed as shown in Figure 13.21. Review the summary of choices made. If any changes need to be made, select the Back button to make the necessary modifications. After the choices have been verified, select the Finish button to initiate the VMotion migration.

The progress of the VMotion migration can be observed within the Recent Tasks pane located at the bottom of the VI Client screen as shown in Figure 13.22. Note, if using the Tasks & Events tab to locate VMotion activity, you can enter the search string of "migrate" in the search filter. A search using the string of "VMotion" will not return any results.

Figure 13.22 Migrate Virtual Machine Status

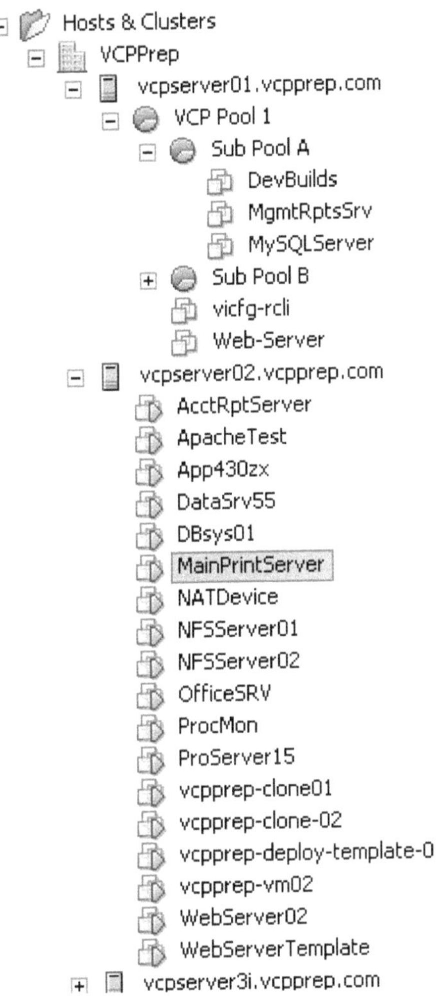

Figure 13.23 Virtual Machine New Destination

Figure 13.23 displays the new location of the MainPrintServer virtual machine within the inventory hierarchy.

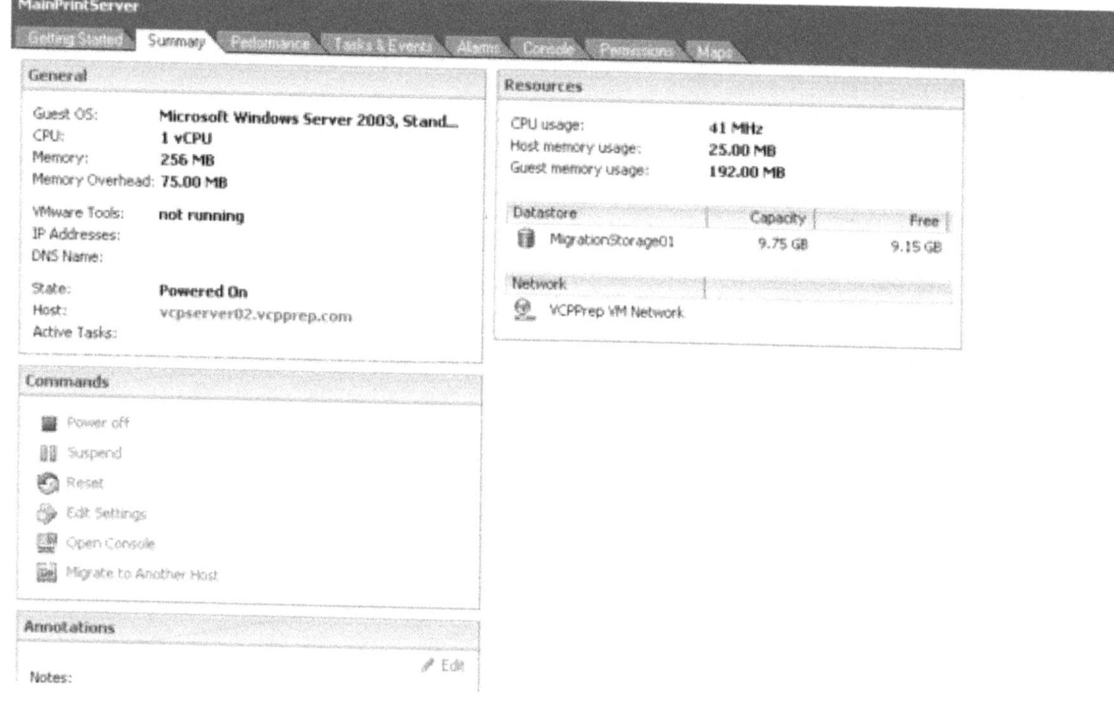

Figure 13.24 Virtual Machine Summary Tab

Figure 13.24 displays the summary tab of the MainPrintServer virtual machine. The General section now lists this virtual machine as being hosted by the vcpserver02.vcpprep.com ESX host.

Initiating a Storage VMotion Migration

With VirtualCenter 2.5 and ESX 3.5, it is now possible to perform a live migration of the virtual machine configuration and state files while the virtual machine is powered on. This new feature is called storage VMotion. Unlike a normal VMotion, a storage VMotion does not re-assign the virtual machine to another ESX host. The VMotion process actually performs a self-VMotion to the same ESX host. Doing so requires a doubling of the virtual machine CPU and memory resources including memory reservations and overhead. It is often best to perform storage VMotions during non peak periods such as evenings or weekends.

Storage VMotion is useful when needing to move a virtual machine from one SAN storage array to another. Now when decommissioning an older SAN storage array, or re-assigning it from production to test and development use, the virtual machines residing on this storage array do not have to experience any service disruptions. Eliminating this downtime is also helpful if moving a virtual machine hosted on a slower performing storage array to a higher performance storage array. Another use case for storage VMotion is having the ability to move the files of a running virtual machine off of a LUN with limited storage space to a larger capacity LUN.

Certain restrictions apply when performing a storage VMotion. For example, the virtual machine must have all snapshots committed prior to performing the storage VMotion. The storage VMotion process utilizes VMware's snapshot technology by creating a child disk (write buffer) before the migration operation copies the configuration and state files. During the copy operation which takes about as long as a cold migration would take, users can be actively using the virtual machine. Any new write operations would be committed to the child disk however, read operations can be performed on both the child and parent disk(s). After the copy operation is completed, the child disk is merged (re-parented) back into the original parent (base) disk. Only a single storage VMotion migration is supported per datastore at any time. As with normal VMotion, a VMotion license must be purchased. Also like normal VMotion, virtual machines with connections to internal virtual switches cannot participate in storage VMotion.

The storage VMotion process cannot be performed using the VI Client or the ESX service console's CLI. To perform storage VMotions, VMware has provided the Remote Command Line Interface (RCLI). The RCLI is also the primary management interface for ESXi servers. There are three different environments in which to use the RCLI. A windows installation binary, Linux installation binary and a virtual appliance with the RCLI already installed. Each of these can be obtained at the following location:

http://www.vmware.com/download/download.do?downloadGroup=VI-RCLI

A log on is required to access the files for download. The files are listed on the download page as follows:

- Virtual appliance for the VMware Infrastructure Remote CLI - Binary (.zip)
- Windows installer for VMware Infrastructure Remote CLI - Binary (.exe)
- Linux installer for VMware Infrastructure Remote CLI - Binary (.tar.gz)

In our example, we are going to demonstrate performing a storage VMotion by using the RCLI virtual appliance. Upon first boot of the RCLI appliance, you will need to accept the license agreement and enter a password for the root account. The RCLI appliance is based off of Linux. It also may be necessary to set a configuration option for the keyboard in order to prevent multiples of the same character from being entered on the screen when they are typed. If this is occurring, power down the RCLI appliance. Right click on the RCLI appliance from within the VI Client and select the Edit Settings menu option. Next select the Options tab and then General under the Advanced category. Click the Configuration Parameters... button. Add a row using the following attribute / value pair:

attribute - keyboard.Typematic.MinDelay

value - 1000000

Next save the settings and exit the Virtual Machines Properties dialog box by clicking the OK button. The next time the RCLI appliance is powered on, the typed characters should no longer be repeated numerous times on the output display.

The RCLI appliance should automatically be assigned an IP address if a DHCP server is available. If not, a static IP address can be configured if needed logging onto the RCLI appliance as user "network" and using the same password assigned to the root account.

Step 1. Log on as root as shown in Figure 13.25.

```
Virtual Infrastructure CLI (0.1.64557)

Current Network Configuration for eth0

IP Address:      10.0.1.219
Broadcast:       10.0.1.255
Netmask:         255.255.0.0
Gateway:         10.0.1.254
Hostname:        vcprcli.vcpprep.com
DNS Servers:     10.0.2.200, 10.0.2.200
Proxy Server:    :

These parameters have been manually set to a static IP Address.
To use a DHCP server instead, or to change any of these values,
please browse to https://10.0.1.219:8080 or log in as the user
"network" (same password as root).

Appliance home page:    http://10.0.1.219
vcprcli.vcpprep.com login: root
Password: _
```

Figure 13.25 Remote CLI User Credentials

Step 2. The storage VMotion process can be performed by either entering all at once the required information needed by the svmotion command or by using the interactive method. Be aware that entries provided for the svmotion command are case-sensitive. In this example, the interactive method is being used as shown in Figure 13.26 by entering the following command: svmotion --interactive

```
Virtual Infrastructure CLI (0.1.64557)

Current Network Configuration for eth0

IP Address:      10.0.1.219
Broadcast:       10.0.1.255
Netmask:         255.255.0.0
Gateway:         10.0.1.254
Hostname:        vcprcli.vcpprep.com
DNS Servers:     10.0.2.200, 10.0.2.200
Proxy Server:    :

These parameters have been manually set to a static IP Address.
To use a DHCP server instead, or to change any of these values,
please browse to https://10.0.1.219:8080 or log in as the user
"network" (same password as root).

Appliance home page:    http://10.0.1.219
vcprcli.vcpprep.com login: root
Password:
Linux 3(NXDOMAIN) 2.4.27-2-386 #1 Wed Aug 17 09:33:35 UTC 2005 i686 GNU/Linux
vcprcli:~# svmotion --interactive_
```

Figure 13.26 Storage VMotion Command

Step 3. The interactive process prompts for the information to access the VirtualCenter server that manages the ESX host where the virtual machine to be migrated is located as shown in Figure 13.27.

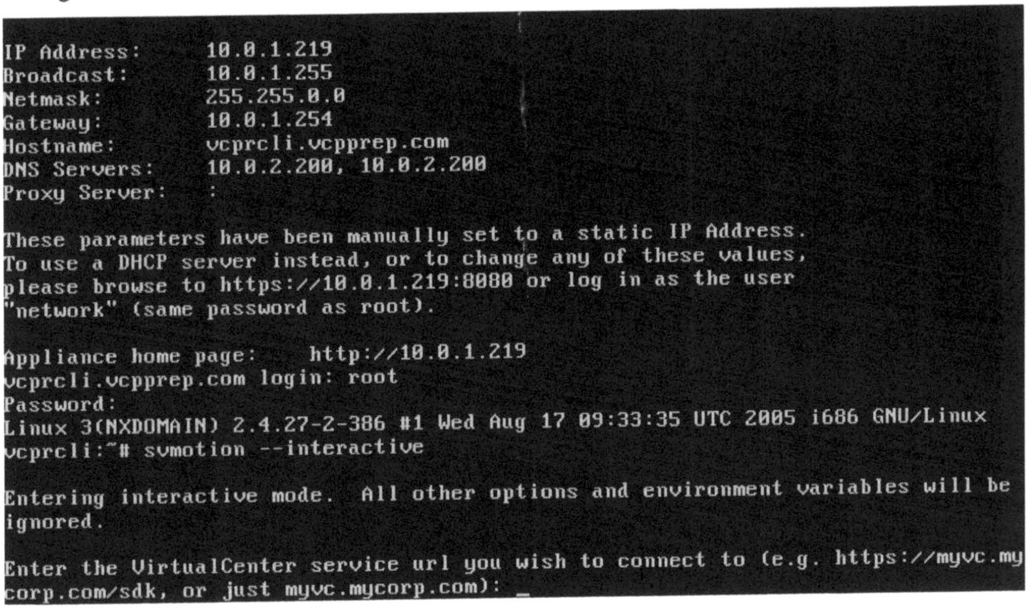

```
IP Address:      10.0.1.219
Broadcast:       10.0.1.255
Netmask:         255.255.0.0
Gateway:         10.0.1.254
Hostname:        vcprcli.vcpprep.com
DNS Servers:     10.0.2.200, 10.0.2.200
Proxy Server:    :

These parameters have been manually set to a static IP Address.
To use a DHCP server instead, or to change any of these values,
please browse to https://10.0.1.219:8080 or log in as the user
"network" (same password as root).

Appliance home page:    http://10.0.1.219
vcprcli.vcpprep.com login: root
Password:
Linux 3(NXDOMAIN) 2.4.27-2-386 #1 Wed Aug 17 09:33:35 UTC 2005 i686 GNU/Linux
vcprcli:~# svmotion --interactive

Entering interactive mode.  All other options and environment variables will be
ignored.

Enter the VirtualCenter service url you wish to connect to (e.g. https://myvc.my
corp.com/sdk, or just myvc.mycorp.com): _
```

Figure 13.27 Storage VMotion Command VirtualCenter Information Prompt

Step 4. Enter the VirtualCenter fully qualified domain name or IP address as shown in Figure 13.28.

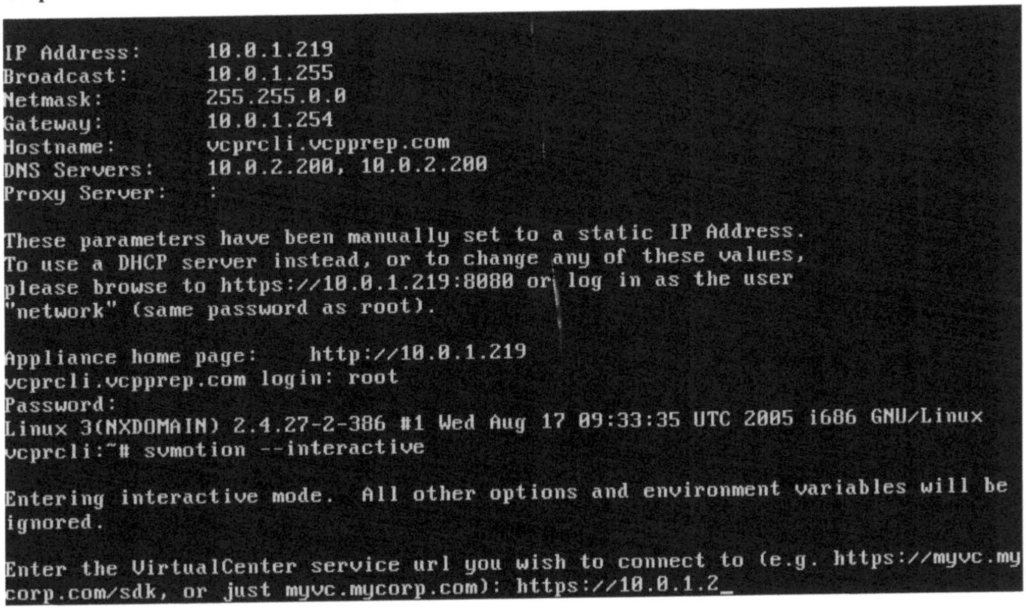

```
IP Address:      10.0.1.219
Broadcast:       10.0.1.255
Netmask:         255.255.0.0
Gateway:         10.0.1.254
Hostname:        vcprcli.vcpprep.com
DNS Servers:     10.0.2.200, 10.0.2.200
Proxy Server:    :

These parameters have been manually set to a static IP Address.
To use a DHCP server instead, or to change any of these values,
please browse to https://10.0.1.219:8080 or log in as the user
"network" (same password as root).

Appliance home page:    http://10.0.1.219
vcprcli.vcpprep.com login: root
Password:
Linux 3(NXDOMAIN) 2.4.27-2-386 #1 Wed Aug 17 09:33:35 UTC 2005 i686 GNU/Linux
vcprcli:~# svmotion --interactive

Entering interactive mode.  All other options and environment variables will be
ignored.

Enter the VirtualCenter service url you wish to connect to (e.g. https://myvc.my
corp.com/sdk, or just myvc.mycorp.com): https://10.0.1.2_
```

Figure 13.28 Storage VMotion Command VirtualCenter Information

```
Broadcast:          10.0.1.255
Netmask:            255.255.0.0
Gateway:            10.0.1.254
Hostname:           vcprcli.vcpprep.com
DNS Servers:        10.0.2.200, 10.0.2.200
Proxy Server:       :

These parameters have been manually set to a static IP Address.
To use a DHCP server instead, or to change any of these values,
please browse to https://10.0.1.219:8080 or log in as the user
"network" (same password as root).

Appliance home page:    http://10.0.1.219
vcprcli.vcpprep.com login: root
Password:
Linux 3(NXDOMAIN) 2.4.27-2-386 #1 Wed Aug 17 09:33:35 UTC 2005 i686 GNU/Linux
vcprcli:~# svmotion --interactive

Entering interactive mode.  All other options and environment variables will be
ignored.

Enter the VirtualCenter service url you wish to connect to (e.g. https://myvc.my
corp.com/sdk, or just myvc.mycorp.com): https://10.0.1.2
Enter your username: administrator
Enter your password: _
```

Figure 13.29 Storage VMotion Command VirtualCenter User Credentials

Step 5. Next, provide the log on credentials to the VirtualCenter server as shown in Figure 13.29.

Step 6. The datacenter name where the virtual machine resides in the inventory is required. In this example, the datacenter name is VCPPrep as shown in Figure 13.30.

```
Proxy Server:       :

These parameters have been manually set to a static IP Address.
To use a DHCP server instead, or to change any of these values,
please browse to https://10.0.1.219:8080 or log in as the user
"network" (same password as root).

Appliance home page:    http://10.0.1.219
vcprcli.vcpprep.com login: root
Password:
Linux 3(NXDOMAIN) 2.4.27-2-386 #1 Wed Aug 17 09:33:35 UTC 2005 i686 GNU/Linux
vcprcli:~# svmotion --interactive

Entering interactive mode.  All other options and environment variables will be
ignored.

Enter the VirtualCenter service url you wish to connect to (e.g. https://myvc.my
corp.com/sdk, or just myvc.mycorp.com): https://10.0.1.2
Enter your username: administrator
Enter your password:

Attempting to connect to https://10.0.1.2/sdk.
Connected to server.

Enter the name of the datacenter: VCPPrep_
```

Figure 13.30 Storage VMotion Command Datacenter Information

```
These parameters have been manually set to a static IP Address.
To use a DHCP server instead, or to change any of these values,
please browse to https://10.0.1.219:8080 or log in as the user
"network" (same password as root).

Appliance home page:    http://10.0.1.219
vcprcli.vcpprep.com login: root
Password:
Linux 3(NXDOMAIN) 2.4.27-2-386 #1 Wed Aug 17 09:33:35 UTC 2005 i686 GNU/Linux
vcprcli:~# svmotion --interactive

Entering interactive mode.  All other options and environment variables will be
ignored.

Enter the VirtualCenter service url you wish to connect to (e.g. https://myvc.my
corp.com/sdk, or just myvc.mycorp.com): https://10.0.1.2
Enter your username: administrator
Enter your password:

Attempting to connect to https://10.0.1.2/sdk.
Connected to server.

Enter the name of the datacenter: VCPPrep
Enter the datastore path of the virtual machine (e.g. [datastore1] myvm/myvm.vmx
): [MigrationStorage01]MainPrintServer/MainPrintServer.vmx_
```

Figure 13.31 Storage VMotion Command Datastore Path Of Virtual Machine

Step 7. As shown in Figure 13.31, the datastore path of the virtual machine is needed. In this example, the datastore path is as follows:

[MigrationStorage01] MainPrintServer/MainPrintServer.vmx

Correct syntax is critical. The values entered are case-sensitive, and the square brackets around the source datastore are required.

```
To use a DHCP server instead, or to change any of these values,
please browse to https://10.0.1.219:8080 or log in as the user
"network" (same password as root).

Appliance home page:    http://10.0.1.219
vcprcli.vcpprep.com login: root
Password:
Linux 3(NXDOMAIN) 2.4.27-2-386 #1 Wed Aug 17 09:33:35 UTC 2005 i686 GNU/Linux
vcprcli:~# svmotion --interactive

Entering interactive mode.  All other options and environment variables will be
ignored.

Enter the VirtualCenter service url you wish to connect to (e.g. https://myvc.my
corp.com/sdk, or just myvc.mycorp.com): https://10.0.1.2
Enter your username: administrator
Enter your password:

Attempting to connect to https://10.0.1.2/sdk.
Connected to server.

Enter the name of the datacenter: VCPPrep
Enter the datastore path of the virtual machine (e.g. [datastore1] myvm/myvm.vmx
): [MigrationStorage01]MainPrintServer/MainPrintServer.vmx
Enter the name of the destination datastore: vcpserver02:storage1_
```

Figure 13.32 Storage VMotion Command Destination Datastore

Step 8. Next, provide the name of the destination datastore as shown in Figure 13.32. In this example, the destination datastore is as follows:

vcpserver02:storage1

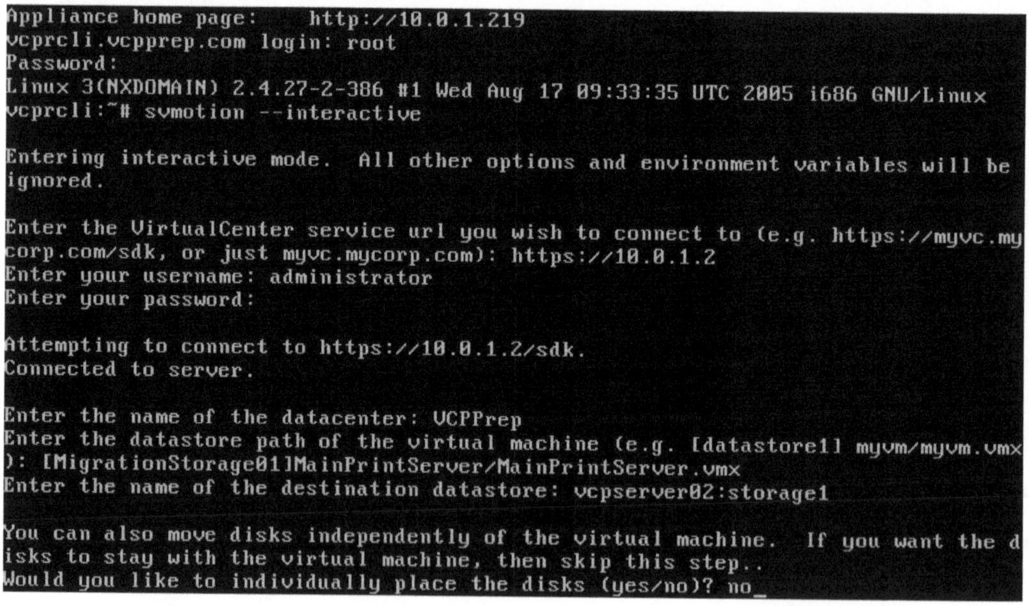

```
Appliance home page:    http://10.0.1.219
vcprcli.vcpprep.com login: root
Password:
Linux 3(NXDOMAIN) 2.4.27-2-386 #1 Wed Aug 17 09:33:35 UTC 2005 i686 GNU/Linux
vcprcli:~# svmotion --interactive

Entering interactive mode.  All other options and environment variables will be
ignored.

Enter the VirtualCenter service url you wish to connect to (e.g. https://myvc.my
corp.com/sdk, or just myvc.mycorp.com): https://10.0.1.2
Enter your username: administrator
Enter your password:

Attempting to connect to https://10.0.1.2/sdk.
Connected to server.

Enter the name of the datacenter: VCPPrep
Enter the datastore path of the virtual machine (e.g. [datastore1] myvm/myvm.vmx
): [MigrationStorage01]MainPrintServer/MainPrintServer.vmx
Enter the name of the destination datastore: vcpserver02:storage1

You can also move disks independently of the virtual machine.  If you want the d
isks to stay with the virtual machine, then skip this step..
Would you like to individually place the disks (yes/no)? no_
```

Figure 13.33 Storage VMotion Command Individually Place Disks Prompt

Step 9. The interactive process queries to determine whether or not you would like to move the virtual disks to separate datastores. It is common practice to have for example in a Windows based VM, a C: drive for the operating system and a D: drive for application data. The storage VMotion process can move such virtual disks to different datastores if needed. In this example, only one virtual disk exists for this virtual machine, therefore the correct response entered is "no" as shown in Figure 13.33.

```
Entering interactive mode.  All other options and environment variables will be
ignored.

Enter the VirtualCenter service url you wish to connect to (e.g. https://myvc.my
corp.com/sdk, or just myvc.mycorp.com): https://10.0.1.2
Enter your username: administrator
Enter your password:

Attempting to connect to https://10.0.1.2/sdk.
Connected to server.

Enter the name of the datacenter: VCPPrep
Enter the datastore path of the virtual machine (e.g. [datastore1] myvm/myvm.vmx
): [MigrationStorage01]MainPrintServer/MainPrintServer.vmx
Enter the name of the destination datastore: vcpserver02:storage1

You can also move disks independently of the virtual machine.  If you want the d
isks to stay with the virtual machine, then skip this step..
Would you like to individually place the disks (yes/no)? no

Performing Storage VMotion.
0% |----------------------------------------------------------------------------
------------------------| 100%
    ##############################_
```

Figure 13.34 Storage VMotion Command Status

The svmotion command outputs its progress as shown in Figure 13.34.

Once the storage VMotion operation has successfully completed, the svmotion command will display this as shown in Figure 13.35.

```
corp.com/sdk, or just myvc.mycorp.com): https://10.0.1.2
Enter your username: administrator
Enter your password:

Attempting to connect to https://10.0.1.2/sdk.
Connected to server.

Enter the name of the datacenter: VCPPrep
Enter the datastore path of the virtual machine (e.g. [datastore1] myvm/myvm.vmx
): [MigrationStorage01]MainPrintServer/MainPrintServer.vmx
Enter the name of the destination datastore: vcpserver02:storage1

You can also move disks independently of the virtual machine.  If you want the d
isks to stay with the virtual machine, then skip this step..
Would you like to individually place the disks (yes/no)? no

Performing Storage VMotion.
0% |----------------------------------------------------------------------------
------------------------| 100%
    ############################################################################
###############
Storage VMotion completed successfully.

Disconnecting.
vcprcli:~# _
```

Figure 13.35 Storage VMotion Command Completed Successfully

Figure 13.36 Storage VMotion Recent Tasks Status

As with normal VMotions, it is also possible to observe the storage VMotion operation from with the VI Client interface by viewing the Recent Tasks pane as shown in Figure 13.36.

To confirm that the virtual machine files have been successfully relocated, view the virtual machine summary tab as shown in Figure 13.37. We can see within the Datastore section that the virtual machine files have been moved from the MigrationStorage01 datastore to the vcpserver:storage1 datastore.

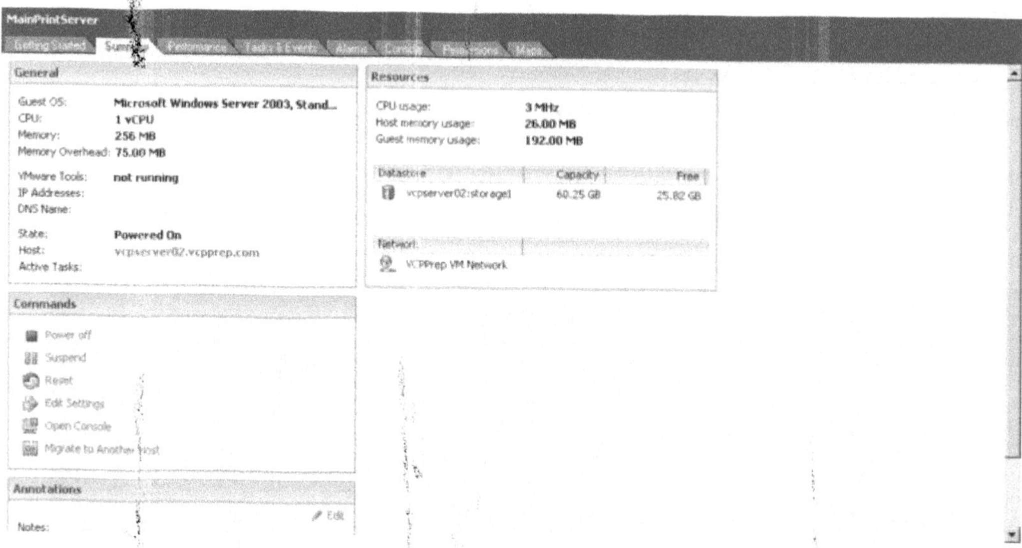

Figure 13.37 Virtual Machine Summary Tab

Troubleshooting Virtual Machine Migrations

It is important to have a clear understanding of what is taking place during the VMotion process. We've discussed that the virtual machine memory is copied across a Gigabit Ethernet network from the source to the destination ESX host. Troubleshooting time is often reduced by first eliminating network related issues. Verify that the VMkernel port is enabled for VMotion. Check the virtual switch labels on each ESX host involved in the VMotion operation. Connectivity can be confirmed by using the vmkping command from within the ESX service console as discussed in Chapter 4 - ESX 3.x Server Networking Configurations.

The virtual machine must not be actively connected to the ESX host's Floppy or CD/DVD drive. A connection to an internal virtual switch will cause the VMotion validation test to fail, precluding a

VMotion until the error is resolved. A virtual machine configured in a MSCS cluster relationship cannot be used in a hot migration. The virtual machine used in the live migration must not have CPU affinity set. Processor information can be viewed by issuing the following command from the service console CLI:

```
[root@vcpserver01 root]#cat /proc/cpuinfo

processor : 0

vendor_id : GenuineIntel

cpu family : 15

model : 4

model name : Intel(R) Xeon(TM) CPU 3.40GHz

stepping : 10

cpu MHz : 3400.260

cache size : 2048 KB

fdiv_bug : no

hlt_bug : no

f00f_bug : no

coma_bug : no

fpu : yes

fpu_exception : yes

cpuid level : 5

wp : yes

flags : fpu vme de pse tsc msr pae mce cx8 apic sep mtrr pge mca cmov pat pse36 clflush dts acpi mmx fxsr sse sse2 ss tm lm

bogomips : 6789.52
```

Snapshots of the virtual machine must be committed prior to performing a virtual machine storage VMotion. The Storage VMotion operation requires doubling of CPU and memory resources.

```
ignored.

Enter the VirtualCenter service url you wish to connect to (e.g. https://myvc.my
corp.com/sdk, or just myvc.mycorp.com): https://10.0.1.2
Enter your username: administrator
Enter your password:

Attempting to connect to https://10.0.1.2/sdk.
Connected to server.

Enter the name of the datacenter: VCPPrep
Enter the datastore path of the virtual machine (e.g. [datastore1] myvm/myvm.vmx
): [MigrationStorage01]MainPrintServer/MainPrintServer.vmx
Enter the name of the destination datastore: vcpserver02:storage1

You can also move disks independently of the virtual machine.  If you want the d
isks to stay with the virtual machine, then skip this step..
Would you like to individually place the disks (yes/no)? no

Performing Storage VMotion.
0% |----------------------------------------------------------------------------
------------------------| 100%

Received an error from the server: Insufficient memory resources.
vcprcli:~# _
```

Figure 13.38 Storage VMotion Command Error

If sufficient resources do not exist, an error message, such as the one displayed in Figure 13.38 will be reported.

External References

The VMware ESX 3.5 and ESXi Server version 3.5 Documentation Page:

http://www.vmware.com/support/pubs/vi_pubs.html

The VMware RCLI download page:

http://www.vmware.com/download/download.do?downloadGroup=VI-RCLI

Sample Test Questions

1. One of the ESX servers in the datacenter is operating under a heavy CPU workload. This situation has caused the shares mechanism to come into play on this host. This ESX server hosts these production virtual machines that cannot be powered down. All virtual machines in this datacenter are located on a shared SAN datastore. Two other ESX servers in the datacenter with access to all shared datastores have ample CPU resources. What can the administrator do to provide additional resources to the production virtual machines?

a. Power down some of the virtual machines.

b. Cold migrate the virtual machines.

c. Use Storage VMotion to migrate the virtual machines.

d. Use VMotion migration to migrate the virtual machines.

e. Increase CPU reservations.

2. Several unsuccessful attempts have been made to perform a storage VMotion on the PrintServer virtual machine. Which of the following prevents storage VMotions from successfully completing?

a. Virtual machine connected to an internal virtual switch.

b. Virtual machine has snapshots.

c. Virtual machine with two or more virtual hard disks.

d. Virtual machine with two or more CD/DVD drives.

e. Virtual machine operating within a MSCS configuration.

3. Which of the following commands issued from the service console CLI provides CPU information that can aid in troubleshooting the VMotion process?

a. cpustat

b. catproc

c. cat /proc/info

d. cat /proc/iostat

e. cat /proc/cpuinfo

4. Which of the following can prevent a successful VMotion operation?

a. Having more than 512 MB of memory assigned to a virtual machine.

b. A virtual machine that is actively connected to the host's CD/DVD drive.

c. A virtual machine configured to use processor affinity.

d. A virtual machine with snapshots.

e. A virtual machine configured with four virtual NICs.

5. A mismatch in which of the following will prevent a successful VMotion operation?

a. SSE3

b. SSSE3

c. CPU vendor

d. CPU family

e. NX bit

Sample Test Solutions

1. One of the ESX servers in the datacenter is operating under a heavy CPU workload. This situation has caused the shares mechanism to come into play on this host. This ESX server hosts these production virtual machines that cannot be powered down. All virtual machines in this datacenter are located on a shared SAN datastore. Two other ESX servers in the datacenter with access to all shared datastores have ample CPU resources. What can the administrator do to provide additional resources to the production virtual machines?

a. Power down some of the virtual machines.

b. Cold migrate the virtual machines.

c. Use Storage VMotion to migrate the virtual machines.

d. Use VMotion migration to migrate the virtual machines.

e. Increase CPU reservations.

Answer: d - Powering down production virtual machines is not acceptable in this situation. Cold migration requires the virtual machines to either be in suspend mode or powered off. Storage VMotion only relocates the virtual machine configuration files and state files. It does not address the CPU contention issue. Increasing CPU reservations in this situation would not help as it will require the virtual machines to be powered off in order to raise the CPU reservation. Performing a VMotion allows the ESX administrator the ability to reassign the virtual machine to another ESX host that has ample CPU cycles without requiring the virtual machine to be powered off.

2. Several unsuccessful attempts have been made to perform a storage VMotion on the PrintServer virtual machine. Which of the following prevents storage VMotions from successfully completing?

a. Virtual machine connected to an internal virtual switch.

b. Virtual machine has snapshots.

c. Virtual machine with two or more virtual hard disks.

d. Virtual machine with two or more CD/DVD drives.

e. Virtual machine operating within a MSCS configuration.

Answer: a, b and e - Virtual machines with two or more CD/DVD or virtual hard drives will not cause storage VMotion to fail. A virtual machine connected to a internal virtual switch, configured in a MSCS cluster configuration or that has snapshots will cause storage VMotion to fail.

3. Which of the following commands issued from the service console CLI provides CPU information that can aid in troubleshooting the VMotion process?

a. cpustat

b. catproc

c. cat /proc/info

d. cat /proc/iostat

e. cat /proc/cpuinfo

Answer: e - Issuing the "cat /proc/cpuinfo" command from the service console CLI provides specific CPU information that can aid in troubleshooting VMotion migrations. Answers a, b, c, d are fictitious commands.

4. Which of the following can prevent a successful VMotion operation?

a. Having more than 512 MB of memory assigned to a virtual machine.

b. A virtual machine that is actively connected to the host's CD/DVD drive.

c. A virtual machine configure to use processor affinity.

d. A virtual machine with snapshots.

e. A virtual machine configured with four virtual NICs.

Answer: b and c - Virtual machines with 512 MB of memory, snapshots and four NICs will not prevent a successful VMotion operation. A virtual machine with processor affinity set on its vCPU(s) or being actively connected to a host's floppy or CD/DVD drives will cause VMotion to fail.

5. A mismatch in which of the following will prevent a successful VMotion operation?

a. SSE3

b. SSSE3

c. CPU vendor

d. CPU family

e. NX bit

Answer: a, b, c, d, e - A mismatch in SSE3 and SSSE3 versions can cause the VMotion operation to fail. CPU vendor and family must match. A mismatch with the NX bit can prevent a VMotion operation from completing, however it is possible to mask the NX bit to resolve the inconsistency.

Chapter 14

Distributed Resource Scheduler

After reading this chapter you should be able to complete the following tasks:

- Explain the purpose, features and benefits of using DRS
- Explain how to set up and configure DRS
- Troubleshoot common Distributed Resource Scheduler problems

Overview of the Distributed Resource Scheduler

In non-virtualized datacenters, several different applications are often needed for each operating system to obtain measured performance statistics. System administrators spend time analyzing charts and reports generated by these applications to determine if the CPU, memory, disk I/O and network I/O resources of their physical servers are adequate. Often, a physical server will only be taxed on one resource. For example, a server may be running low on memory while still having plenty of CPU resources unused. These unused CPU cycles are wasted resources, reducing a company's ROI (Return On Investment) expectations.

A virtualized datacenter implementing VMware's VI3 solution, can reduce the potential of unused CPU and memory resources. VirtualCenter provides the ESX administrator the ability to create a cluster object within its inventory. A cluster object can be populated with up to thirty two ESX servers. Grouping ESX hosts within a cluster object enables an ESX administrator to utilize VMware's Distributed Resource Scheduler (DRS). DRS is a VirtualCenter feature that can be used to automatically analyze the CPU and memory resources across a range of ESX hosts. The workload placed on these ESX hosts can then be balanced by employing the use of the VMotion process. For example, an ESX host under heavy memory contention can have one or more of the virtual machines it is hosting automatically migrated to another ESX host within the DRS cluster that has sufficient memory resources currently unused.

Let's take a look at how to create a DRS cluster and the various configuration choices it offers.

Creating the Distributed Resource Scheduler Cluster

The process to create a DRS cluster is performed by using the New Cluster Wizard.

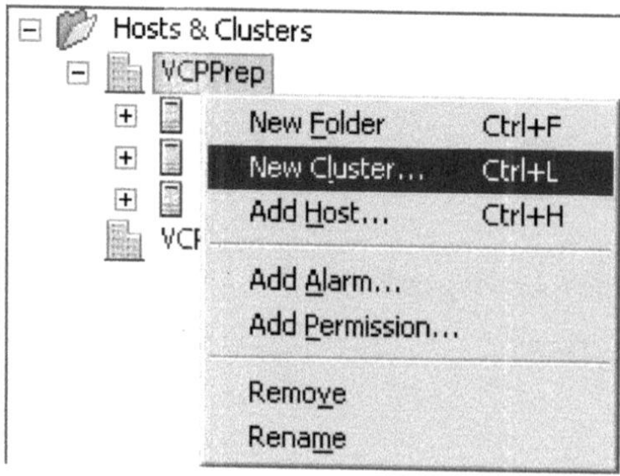

Figure 14.1 New Cluster Menu Option

Step 1. Right click on a datacenter object and select the New Cluster... menu option as shown is Figure 14.1.

Step 2. The New Cluster Wizard displays as shown in Figure 14.2. A cluster object can be defined as either a HA (High Availability) cluster, a DRS cluster or both. HA clusters are discussed in Chapter 15 – High Availability. To create a DRS cluster, enter a name in the Name text box then choose the VMware DRS check box. In this example, the DRS cluster has been assigned the name DRSCluster. Click the Next button to continue.

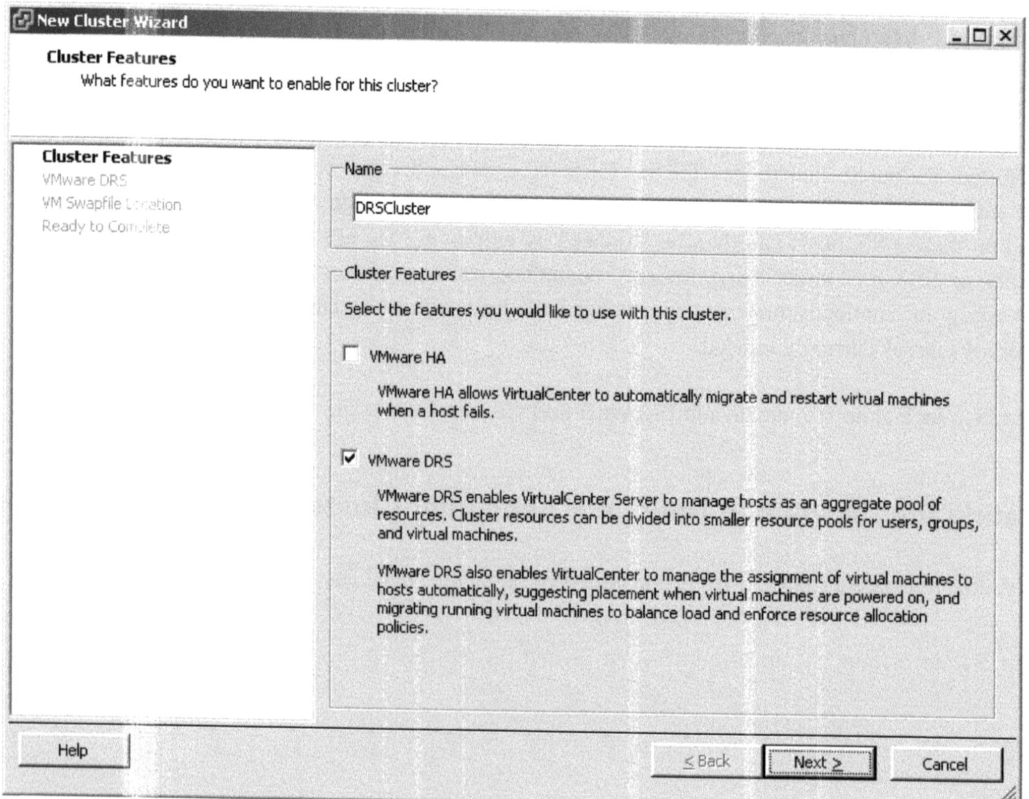

Figure 14.2 New Cluster Wizard Dialog Box

Step 3. The DRS automation level can be set to one of the following values:

- Manual - When set to manual automation, the DRS cluster will provide a list of ESX servers that can be used to host the virtual machine that is being powered on. The virtual machine will not power on until an ESX host server is chosen from the list. Any DRS migration recommendations made to balance the DRS cluster will need to be approved prior to the virtual machine being VMotioned to another ESX host.
- Partially Automated - Using the partially automated setting allows the DRS cluster to determine which ESX host in the cluster to place the virtual machine when it is being powered on. Any DRS migration recommendations made to balance the DRS cluster will need to be approved prior to the virtual machine being VMotioned to another ESX host.
- Fully Automated - A DRS cluster working in fully automated mode provides automatic virtual machine placement at power on. Virtual machines that are VMotion compliant can be automatically migrated as needed to balance the workload of each ESX host within the DRS cluster.

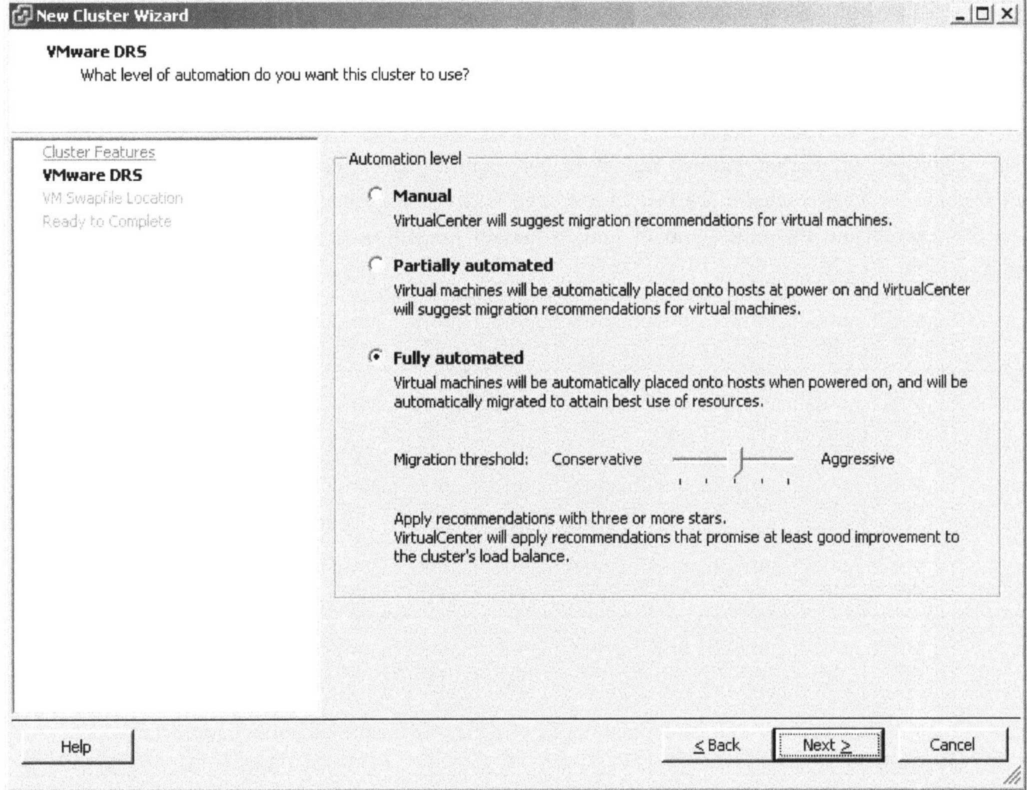

Figure 14.3 New Cluster Wizard Automation Level

The migration threshold can be used to determine how often migrations occur to balance the resources of the cluster. There are five levels of migration thresholds that can be set, each with having its own star based rating. Setting the value all the way to the left (most conservative) places the threshold at level one. At this level, it will require a five star rating for a migration recommendation to occur. A five star rating must be performed to comply with affinity rules. Setting affinity rules will be discussed later in this chapter.

A level two recommendation generates a four star rating. This level is set by sliding the migration threshold bar to the second tick mark from the left. This level is considered moderately conservative in the frequency of migration recommendations. Applying four star recommendations can greatly improve resource imbalances in the cluster.

Level three is the default setting, it is the midpoint in the migration threshold slider bar. This level requires a three star rating to occur. Applying three star migration recommendations will provide a good improvement to the overall resource balance of the cluster.

Sliding the migration threshold setting to the fourth tick mark from the left, sets the level to four. At this level, migration recommendations are considered moderately aggressive, requiring a two star rating. A moderate improvement in the cluster resource balance can be achieved by applying any two star migration recommendations.

The migration threshold, when positioned all the way to the right, sets the migration threshold to level five. Any one star rated migration recommendations applied can slightly improve the cluster resource balance.

Each level includes all recommendations from previous levels. For example, level two includes all five star migration recommendations and level five applies all migration recommendations. The default settings for a DRS cluster are fully automated with the migration threshold set to level three. Choose the appropriate automation level and threshold migration then select the Next button to continue.

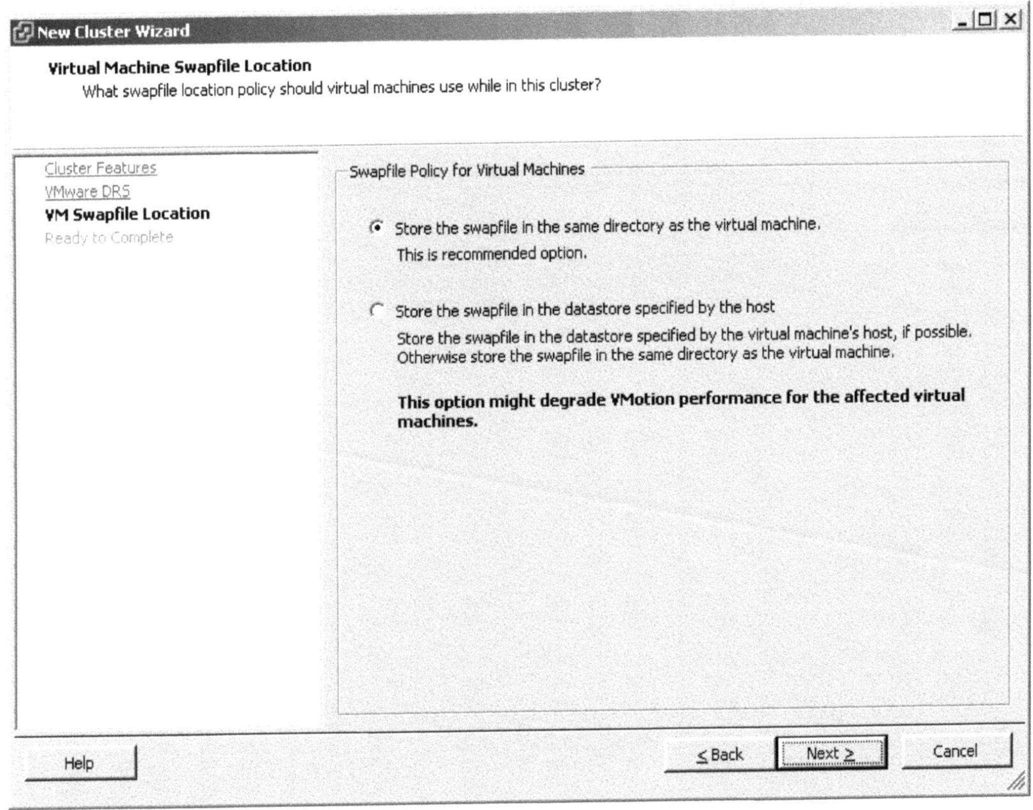

Figure 14.4 New Cluster Wizard VM Swapfile Location

Step 4. There are two swap file policies that can be chosen as shown in Figure 14.4.. This swap file is the VMkernel swap file that is created when a virtual machine is powered on. The size of this file is the difference between the virtual machine's memory reservation value and its memory limit. Typically, this file is located in the directory where the virtual machine was created. A new option in VirtualCenter 2.5 allows a swap file location to be set at the ESX host level. Choosing to set the swap file location at the host level might be done for example, if the virtual machine files are located on slower performing datastore. Placing the swap file on a faster performing datastore may improve the virtual machine performance. Select the appropriate swap file policy and click the Next button to continue.

Step 5. The last step of the wizard is to verify all the choices made. As shown in Figure 14.5, review the Ready to Complete screen. The Back button can be used to make any necessary changes. If no changes are needed, select the Finish button to complete the New Cluster Wizard.

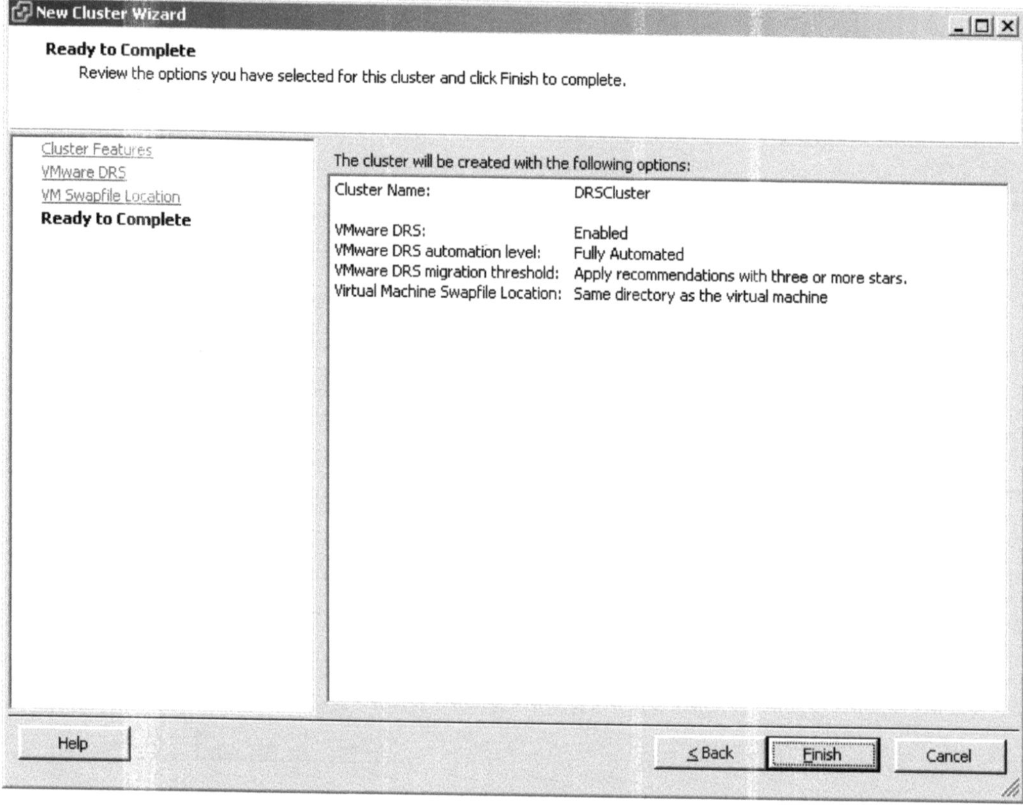

Figure 14.5 New Cluster Wizard Ready To Complete

Adding an ESX Server to a Distributed Resource Scheduler Cluster

Figure 14.6 displays the Getting Started tab for the newly created DRSCluster object. Also shown are three ESX servers, vcpserver01, vcpserver02 and vcpserver03. We are going to see how to add the vcpserver01 ESX server to the DRS cluster.

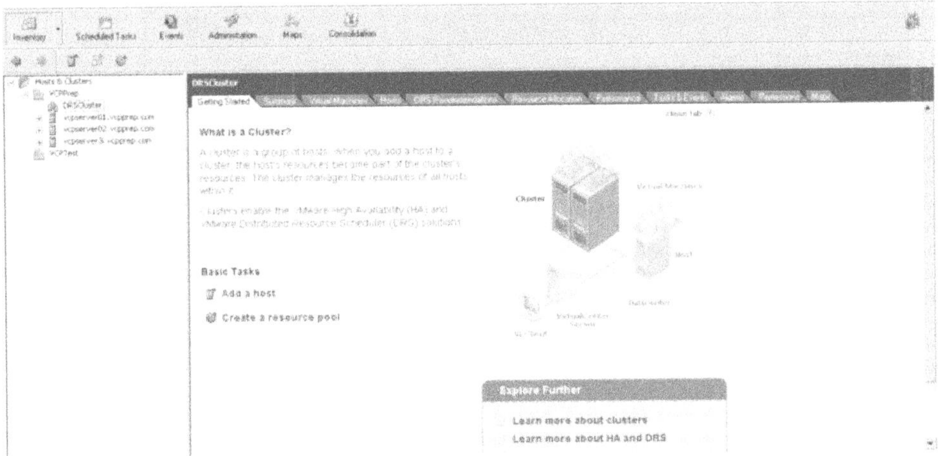

Figure 14.6 DRS Cluster Getting Started Tab

Step 1. Select one of the following to add an ESX server to a DRS cluster:

- Dragging the ESX host over top of the cluster object
- Right clicking on the DRS cluster and selecting the Add Host menu option
- Selecting the DRS cluster object. Then select the Getting Started tab and clicking the Add Host link.

The Add Host link was used to in this example to launch the Add Host Wizard as shown in Figure 14.7.

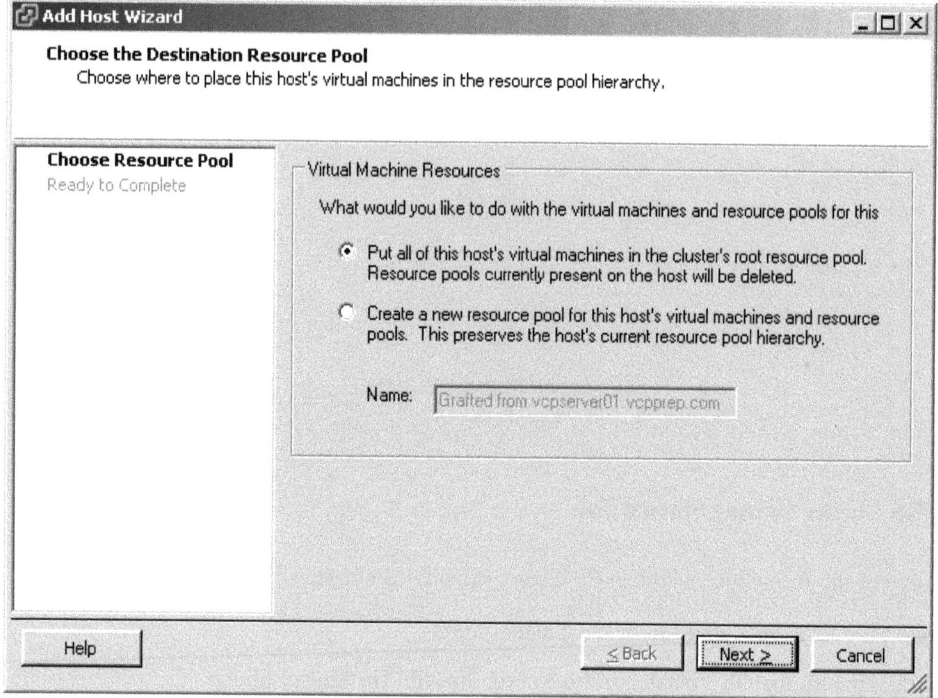

Figure 14.7 Add Host To DRS Cluster Choose Resource Pool

Step 2. An ESX server that has been configured with resource pools can either have these moved into the DRS cluster or deleted. The default is to delete any existing pools on the ESX host. To retain any resource pools, select the radio button that creates a new resource pool for the host's virtual machines and resource pools. Doing so in this example would create a new resource pool that would be labeled "Grafted from vcpserver01.vcpprep.com". Any existing virtual machines and resource pools would be placed into the "Grafted from vcpserver01.vcpprep.com" resource pool. Select the appropriate choice and click the Next button to continue.

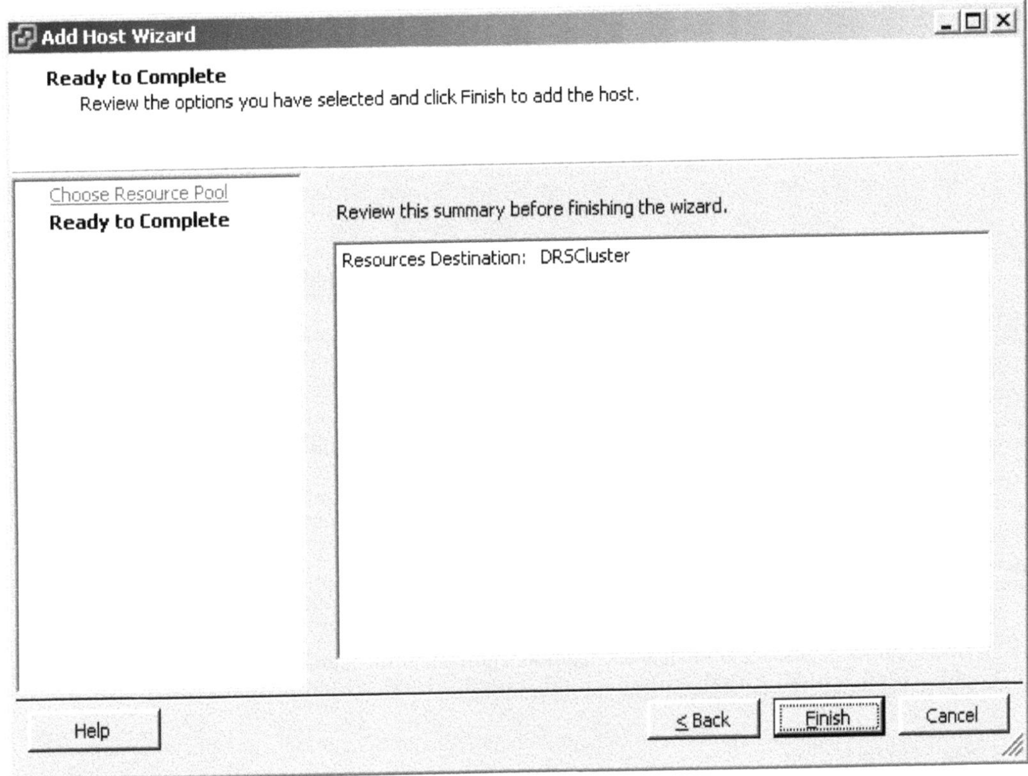

Figure 14.8 Add Host To DRS Cluster Ready To Complete

Step 3. As shown in Figure 14.8, the Ready to Complete screen is the final step in adding the vcpserver01 host to the DRSCluster object. Any changes that need to be made can be done by selecting the Back button. To complete the Add Host Wizard, select the Finish button.

Configuring Distributed Resource Scheduler

Accepting the DRS cluster defaults during creation might be common practice. Most of the time the defaults may work just fine. ESX administrators may find it necessary from time to time to place a DRS cluster in manual mode so that they can control the initial placement and migrations of virtual machines. Migration recommendations can be viewed by clicking on the DRS cluster object then selecting the DRS Recommendations tab as shown in Figure 14.9. New to VirtualCenter 2.5 is the Generate Recommendations button. It may be necessary to manually generate a DRS recommendation for example, when testing the DRS cluster functionality. Migration history can be observed by reviewing the DRS Action History section at the bottom of Figure 14.9. This section displays the DRS actions along with the time these actions occurred.

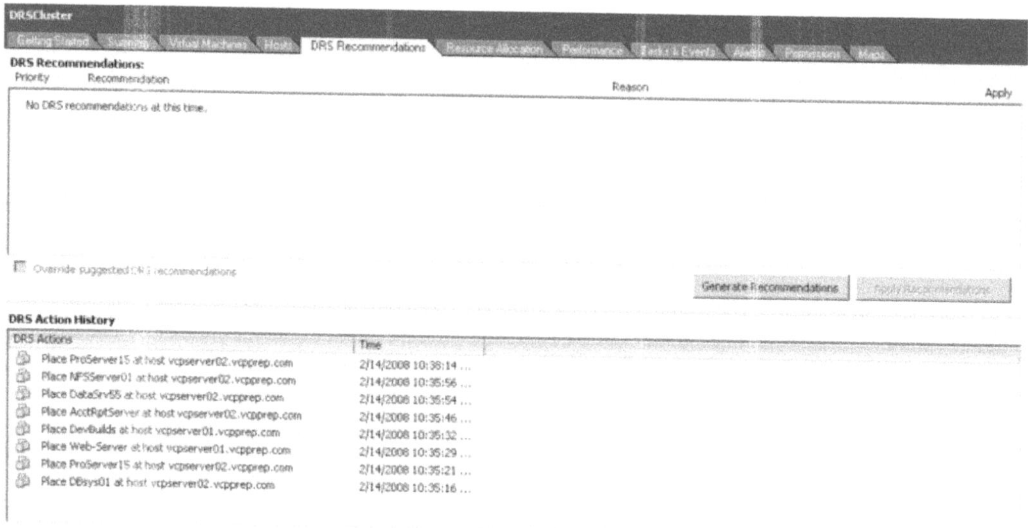

Figure 14.9 DRS Recommendations Tab

Step 1. When changes to the DRS cluster are needed, right click on the DRS cluster object as shown in Figure 14.10 and select the Edit Settings... menu option.

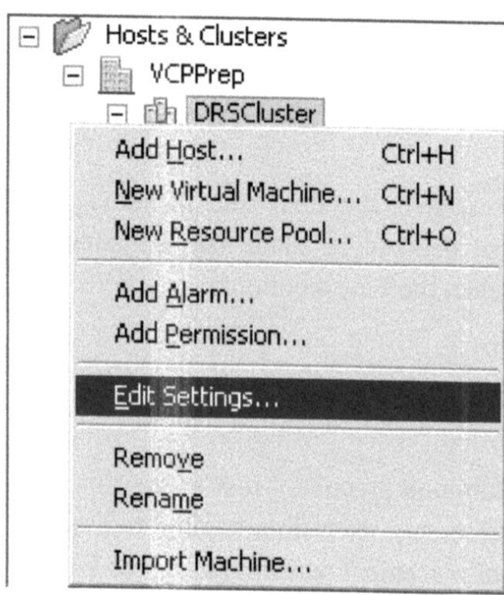

Figure 14.10 Cluster Edit Settings Menu Option

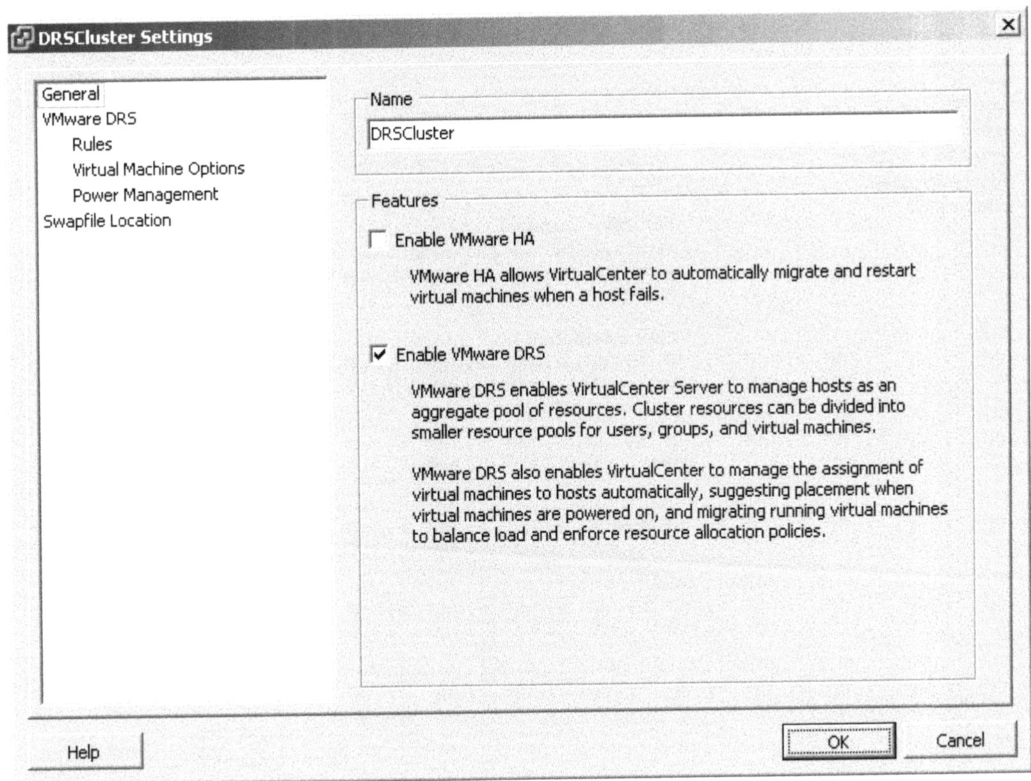

Figure 14.11 DRS Cluster Settings General Option

Step 2. Within the General option, as shown in Figure 14.11, placing or removing a check in the Enable VMware DRS check box enables or disables the DRS cluster respectively. In this example, we are going to leave the DRS cluster enabled and select the VMware DRS option in the upper left hand corner of Figure 14.11 to continue.

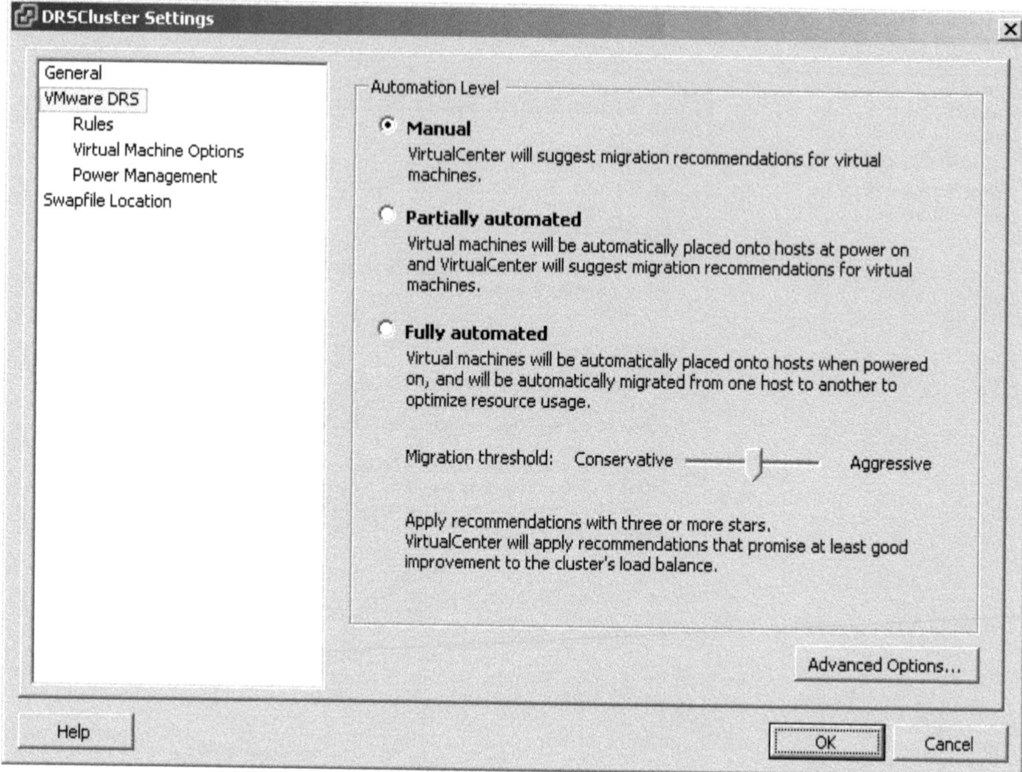

Figure 14.12 DRS Cluster Settings Manual Automation Level

Step 3. The default automation level as mentioned earlier for a DRS cluster is to have it set at fully automated. In this example, we are going to set the DRS cluster to manual automation by selecting the Manual radio button as shown in Figure 14.12. To continue modifying the DRS cluster, select the Rules option in the upper left hand corner of Figure 14.12.

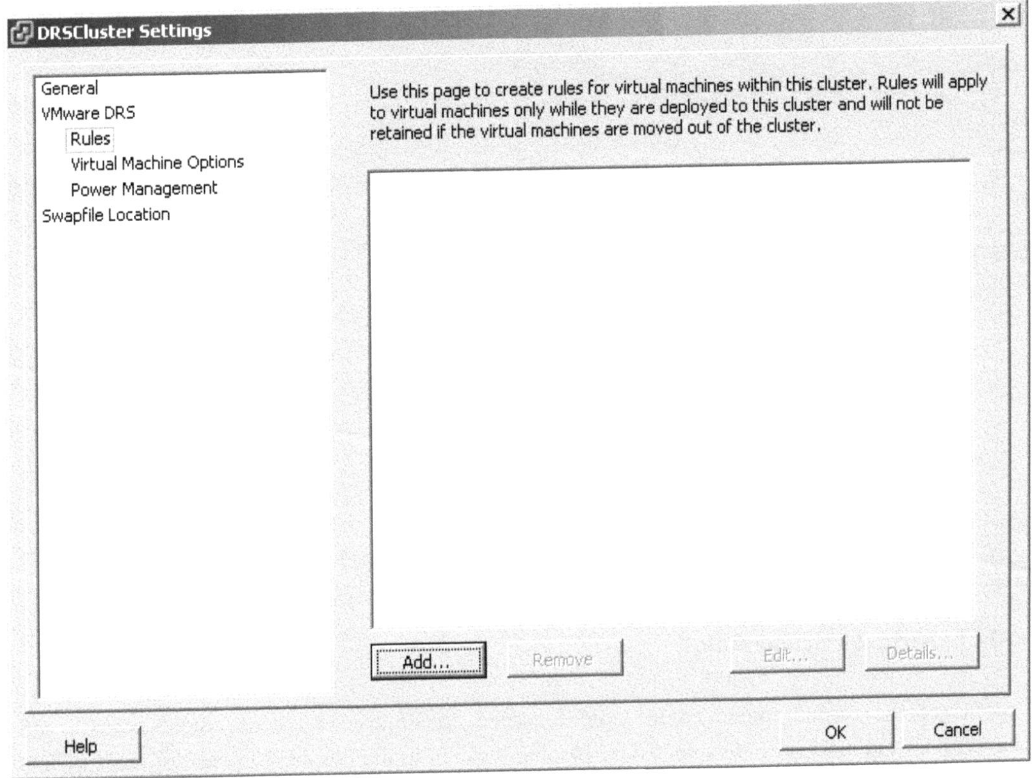

Figure 14.13 DRS Cluster Settings Rules Option

Step 4. Rules can be created in a DRS cluster to control whether virtual machines are always kept together on an ESX host or kept on different ESX host systems. To create these rules, select the Add button as shown in Figure 14.13.

Step 5. The Virtual Machine Rule dialog box is used to create the following rule types:

- Affinity Rule - Keeps virtual machines together on the same ESX host. This type of rule is often used for performance reasons. Virtual machines such as an application and database servers that often exchange information together can increase network communication performance when kept on the same ESX host.
- Anti-Affinity Rule - Separate virtual machines on different ESX hosts. This rule type is often used to increase availability. For example, using an anti-affinity rule for a primary and secondary domain controller ensures that if one of the ESX system hosting either controller goes down, the other virtual machine will be available for service. A maximum of two virtual machines can be sleeted for an anti-affinity rule.

In this example, we give the rule the name of SameHostRule as we are going to create an affinity rule by selecting the drop down box option to Keep Virtual Machines Together as shown in Figure 14.14. Next select the Add button to select the virtual machines to include in this rule.

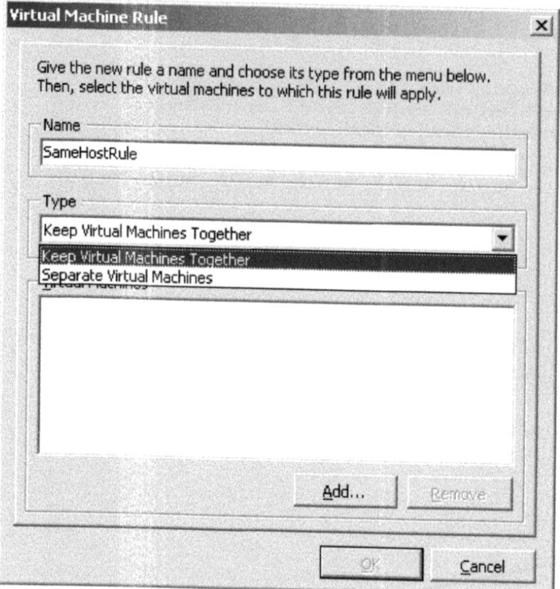

Figure 14.14 Virtual Machine Rule

Step 6. Select the virtual machines to keep together. In Figure 14.15, the SQLServer01 and WebServer01 virtual machines are selected by placing a check in the box next to each of these virtual machines. Select the OK button to continue.

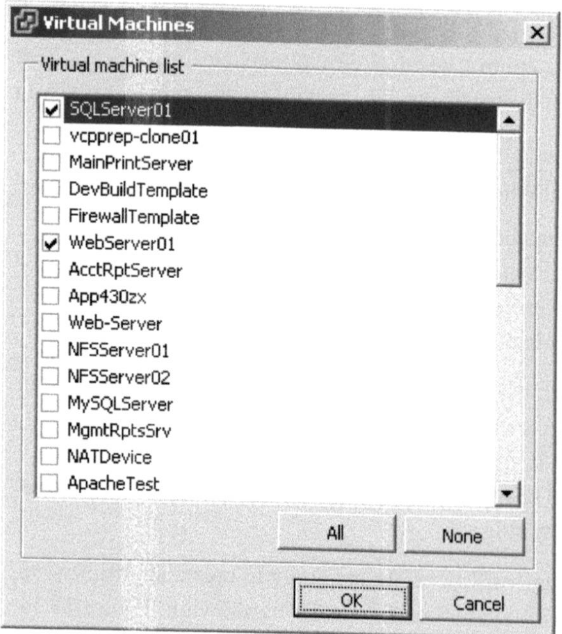

Figure 14.15 Virtual Machine List

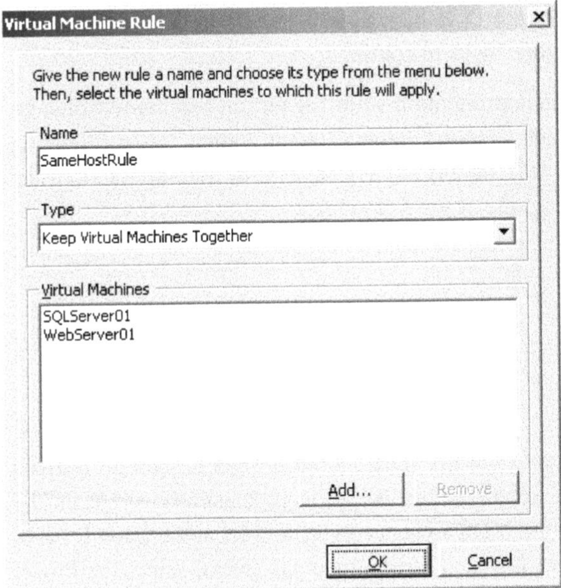

Figure 14.16 Virtual Machine Rule Created

Step 7. The Virtual Machines section now contains the two virtual machines we selected as shown in Figure 14.16. Select the OK button once more to complete the creation of the rule.

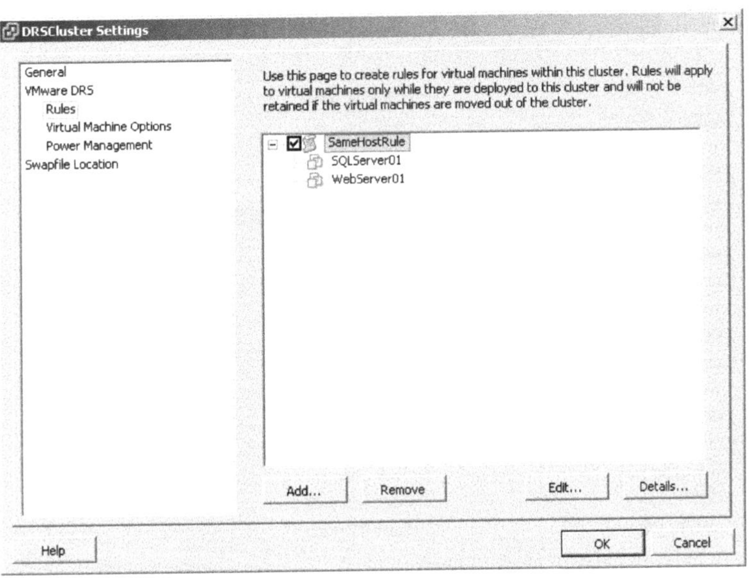

Figure 14.17 Virtual Machine Rule Added

Step 8. In Figure 14.17, we can see the new SameHostRule listed along with the virtual machines contained in the rule. A virtual machine cannot be included in multiple affinity rules. New rules can be added, existing rules deleted or modified using the Add... Remove or Edit... buttons respectively.

To view information about the listed rules, select the Details... button. Select the Virtual Machine Options option in the upper left hand corner of Figure 14.17 to continue.

Step 9. A DRS cluster that did not allow individual automation rules for virtual machines would be very limiting. Fortunately, VMware provides such granular control by providing the Automation Level drop down selection as shown in Figure 14.18. Therefore, you can set how an individual virtual machine participates in the DRS cluster by selecting one of the following:

- Fully Automated
- Partially Automated
- Manual
- Disabled

Selecting the Disabled option can be useful if the virtual machine should always remain on a given host. For example, a virtual machine that is CPU intensive can be set to permanently reside on the ESX host with the most available CPU cycles within a DRS cluster by setting its automation level to Disabled. Choose the appropriate automation level for each virtual machine. Next, select the Power Management option in the upper left hand corner of Figure 14.18 to continue.

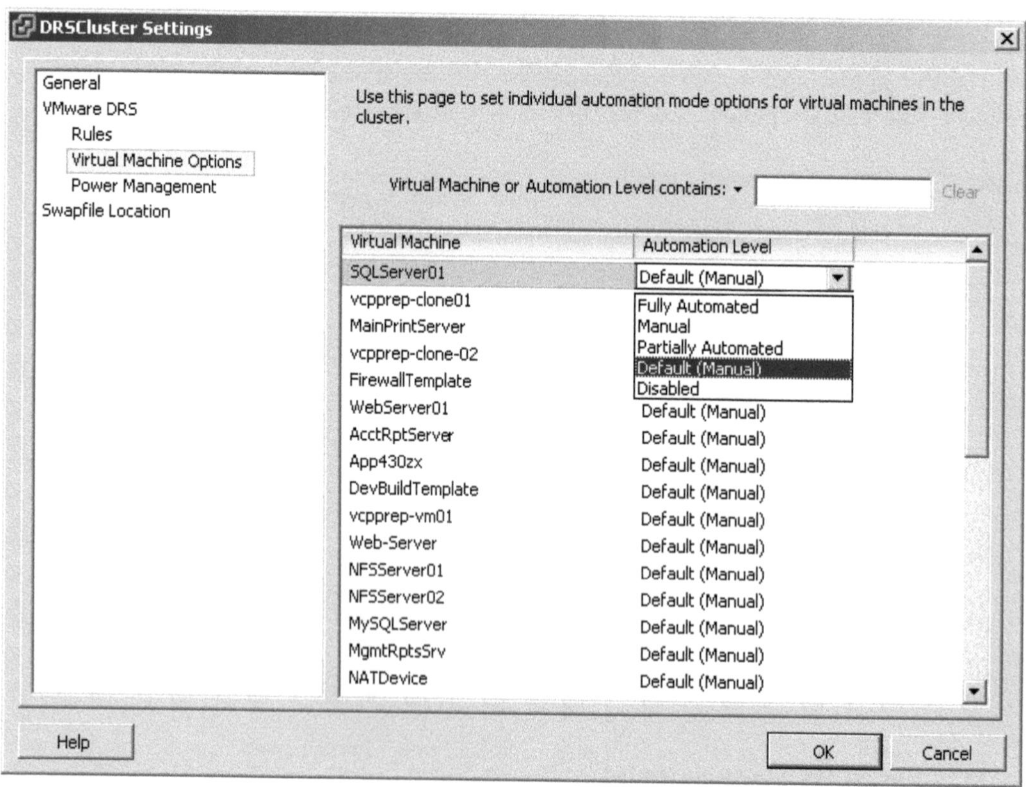

Figure 14.18 DRS Cluster Settings Virtual Machine Options

Step 10. Distributed Power Management (DPM) is an experimentally supported feature with

VirtualCenter 2.5 servers. DPM is a feature that works in conjunction with a DRS cluster. Its purpose is to determine whether the resources of an ESX host are currently needed to satisfy virtual machine needs. If not, it can make recommendations to place an ESX host in standby mode. When placed in Manual mode, an ESX administrator can view the DPM recommendations and chose whether to apply these recommendations or not. Setting the DPM to the Automatic mode, ESX hosts can be automatically placed into standby mode. If at a later time, the resource of the ESX host that has been placed into standby mode is needed, DPM can send the ESX host a Wake-On-LAN packet. This will cause the ESX host to once again become available. Reasons that cause DPM to bring a host back into service include not only increasing resource demands of already powered on virtual machines but also of powered off machines. DPM will bring the host back into service in order to meet admission control reservation requests. In our example, the DPM setting is in the Off mode as shown in Figure 14.19. Select the Swapfile Location option in the upper left hand corner of Figure 14.19 to continue.

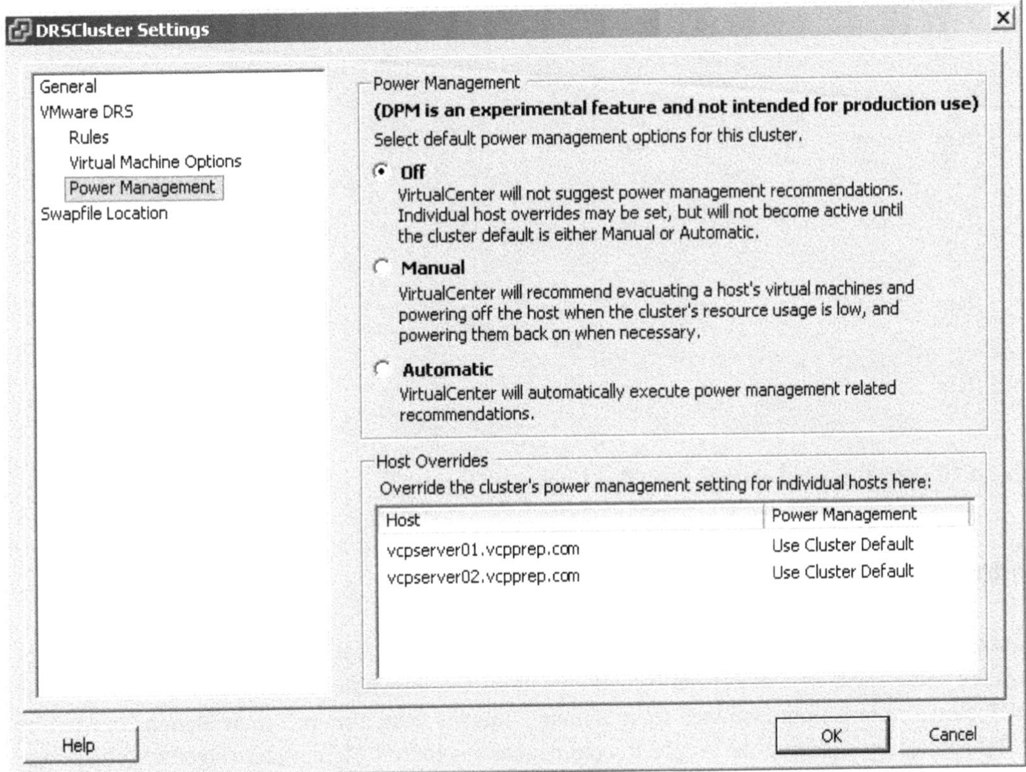

Figure 14.19 DRS Cluster Settings Power Management Option

Step 11. There are two swap file policies that can be chosen as shown in Figure 14.20. This swap file is the VMkernel swap file that is created when a virtual machine is powered on. The size of this file is the difference between the virtual machine's memory reservation value and its memory limit. Typically, this file is located in the directory where the virtual machine was created. A new option in VirtualCenter 2.5 allows a swap file location to be set at the ESX host level. Choosing to set the swap file location at the host level might be done for example, if the virtual machine files are located on slower performing datastore. Placing the swap file on a faster performing datastore may improve the virtual machine performance. Select the appropriate swap file policy and click the OK button to complete the modification of the DRS cluster.

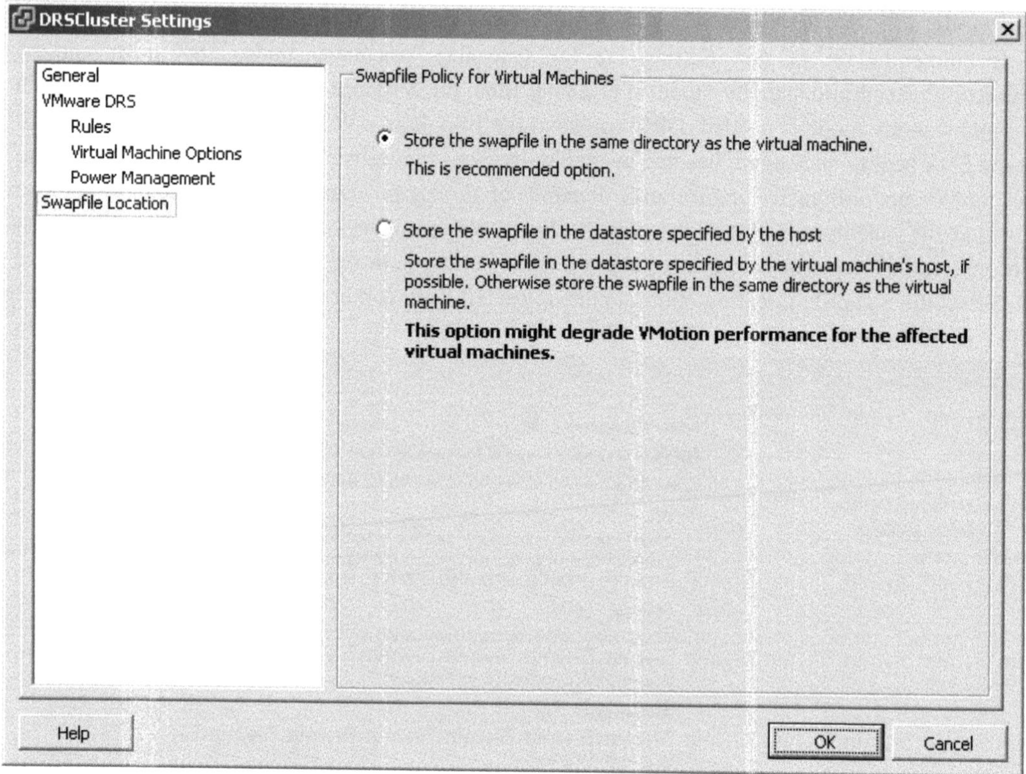

Figure 14.20 DRS Cluster Settings Swapfile Location Option

Monitoring Distributed Resource Scheduler

Monitoring the activity migrations is necessary in determining that the appropriate DRS cluster settings are being used. Two migration recommendations are shown in Figure 14.21. In this example, the DRS cluster automation level was set to manual, thus the migration recommendations need to be manually applied by selecting the Apply Recommendations button. A four star (level two) and three star (level three) migration recommendation have been made as noted in the Priority column. The Recommendation column contains information about the virtual machine to be migrated, its current host and the host that it is to be migrated to. The Reason column contains the motive behind the recommendation. In this case, the recommendation is an attempt to balance the memory load of the DRS cluster.

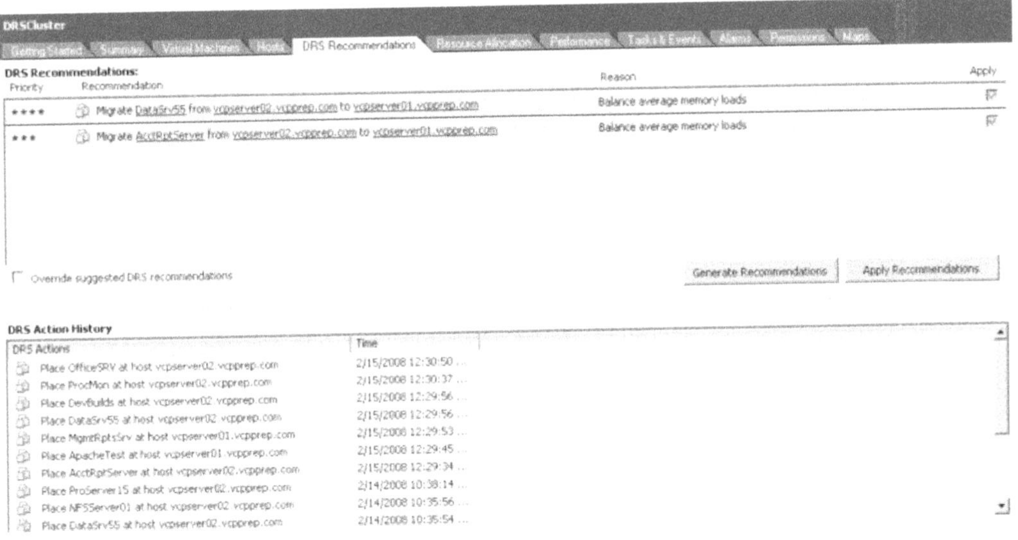

Figure 14.21 DRS Migration Recommendations

The VI Client offers summary information and graphs for monitoring the DRS cluster. To view this information, select the DRS cluster object and then select the Summary tab as shown in Figure 14.22. The VMware DRS section displays the cluster setting. The VMware DRS Resource Distribution section displays two graphs. The top graph is used to monitor the effectiveness of the DRS cluster in balancing both CPU and memory resources across all ESX hosts. When viewing the graphs in the VI Client, the vertical bars in the graph are different colors. CPU bars are blue and memory bars are orange. In this example, the two vertical bars in the 10-20 and 20-30 ranges are the CPU bars. The two vertical bars in the 60-70 and 80-90 ranges are the memory bars. This graphs depicts that the DRS cluster is not balanced in its CPU usage. One ESX server is using between 10-20 percent of its CPU capacity and the other is using between 20-30 percent. The memory is not balanced either. One ESX server is using between 60-70 percent of its available memory and the other is using between 80-90 percent of its available memory. If it were balanced, there would be one CPU vertical bar and one memory bar.

The bottom graph displays the percentage of resources received when requested by the virtual machines. In this example, virtual machines received the requested CPU cycles between 90-100 percent of the time. The virtual machines on one of the ESX hosts received memory resource requests between 80-90 percent of the time and another host serviced memory resource requests between 90-100 percent of the time. The shares, limits and reservation values of both virtual machines and resource pools are taking into consideration in determining an ESX hosts ability to provide resources.

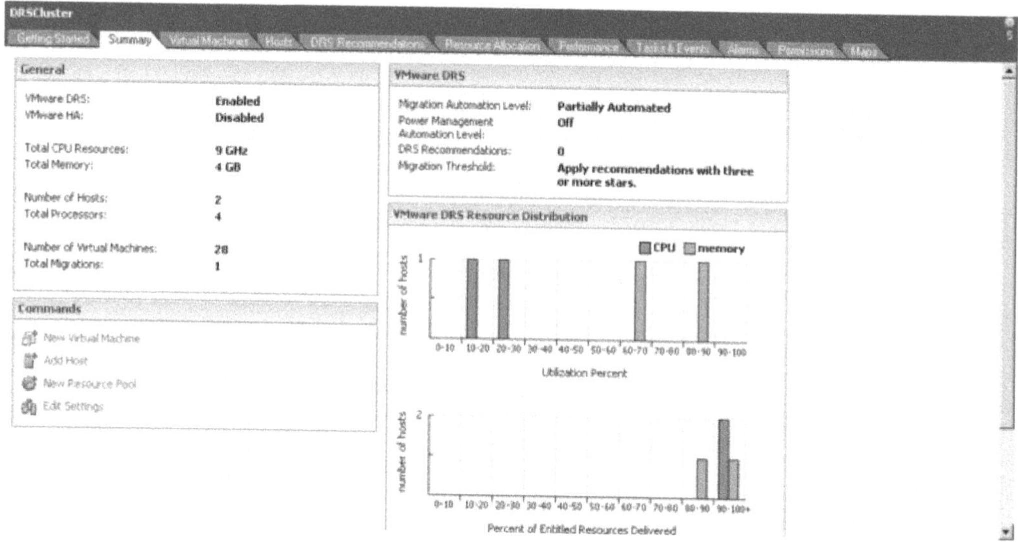

Figure 14.22 DRS Cluster Summary Tab

Removing an ESX Server from a Distributed Resource Scheduler Cluster

Step 1. To remove an ESX host from a DRS cluster, right click on the ESX host and select the Remove menu option as shown in Figure 14.23.

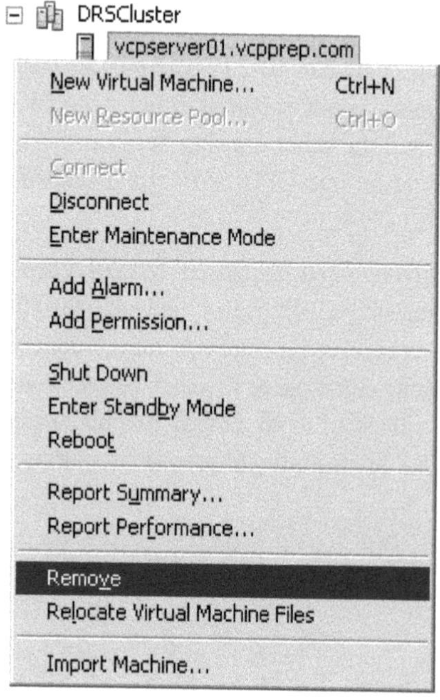

Figure 14.23 ESX Host Remove Menu Option

Step 2. A pop up dialog box is displayed as shown in Figure 14.24, noting that the ESX host needs to be in maintenance mode before it can be removed from the DRS cluster. Maintenance mode allows the ESX host to be put into a state where it can be patched or brought down completely to do physical upgrades for example. All virtual machines must be evacuated off a ESX host before it can operate in maintenance mode. We will take a look at how to place a ESX host into maintenance mode. Select the OK button to continue.

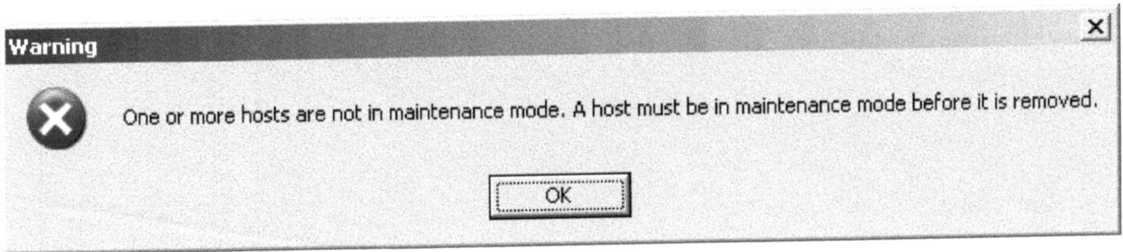

Figure 14.24 Maintenance Mode Warning Dialog Box

Step 3. To place an ESX host into maintenance mode, right click the ESX host and select the Enter Maintenance Mode menu option as shown in Figure 14.25.

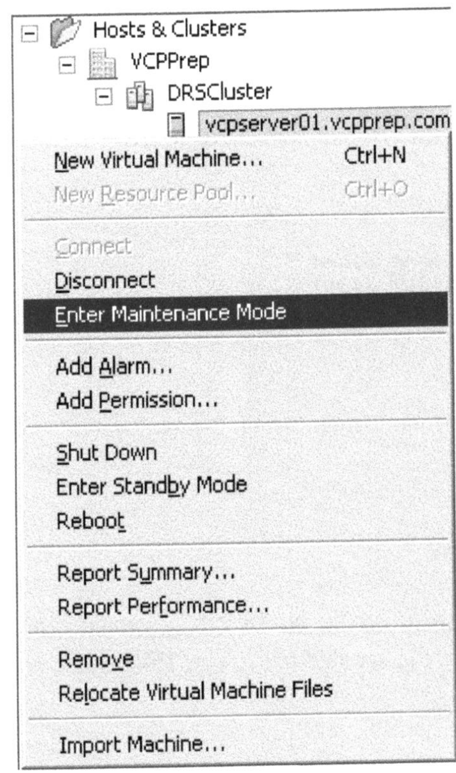

Figure 14.25 Enter Maintenance Mode Menu Option

Step 4. The dialog box in Figure 14.26 prompts to continue entrance into maintenance mode.

Selecting the Yes button will allow the DRS cluster to move any powered on or suspended virtual machines to another ESX host. Click the Yes button to continue.

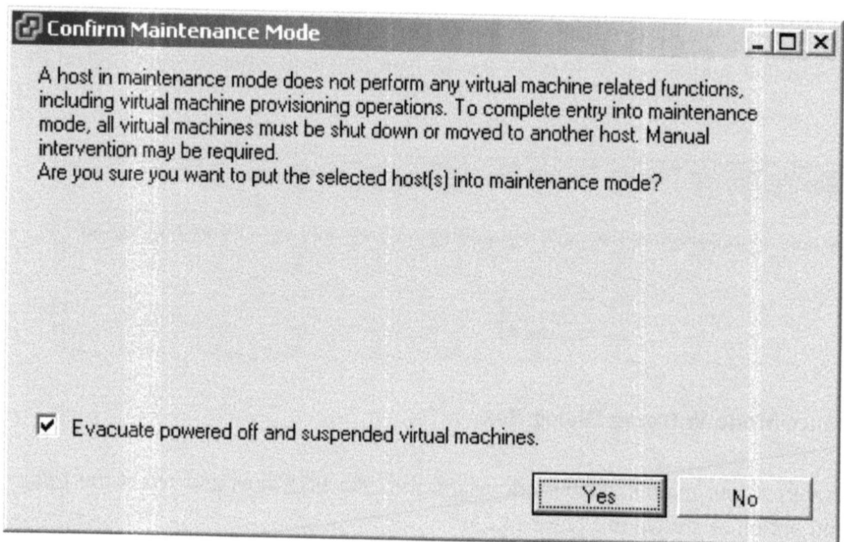

Figure 14.26 Enter Maintenance Mode Confirmation Dialog Box

Step 5. The dialog box shown in Figure 14.27 provides a warning that virtual machines will need to be moved to complete entrance into maintenance mode. Click the OK button to continue.

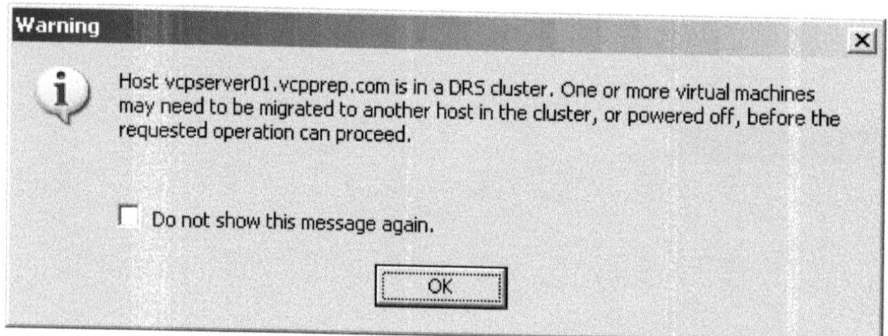

Figure 14.27 Enter Maintenance Mode Warning Dialog Box

To monitor the maintenance mode progress, select the Summary tab for the ESX host as shown in Figure 14.28. In the General section of the Summary tab, we can see that the Active Tasks value is listed as Enter Maintenance Mode.

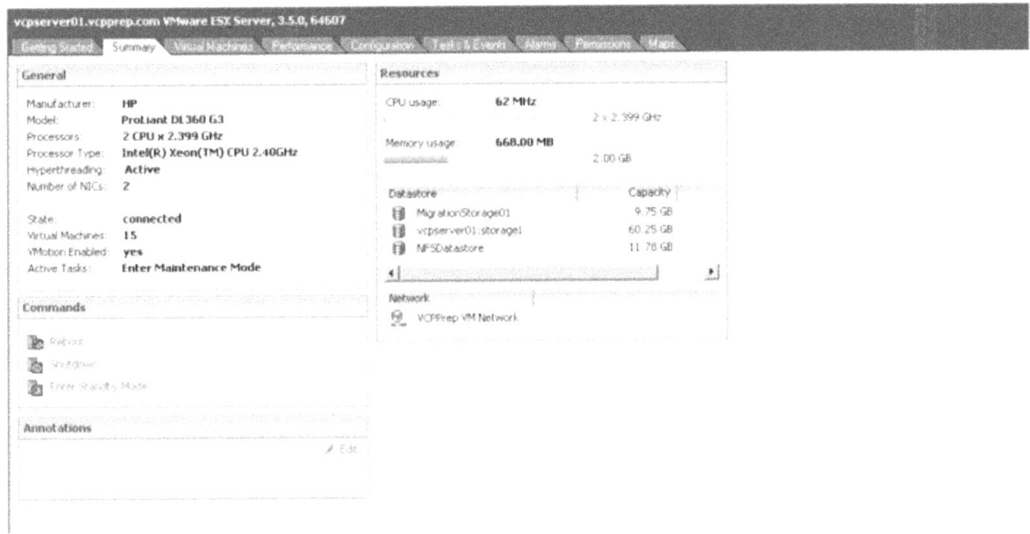

Figure 14.28 ESX Server 3.5 Summary Tab

To observe the powered on virtual machines of the host entering maintenance mode, select the host's Virtual Machines tab as shown in Figure 14.29. We can see that there are currently two virtual machines still hosted by this ESX server.

vcpserver01.vcpprep.com VMware ESX Server, 3.5.0, 64607

Getting Started | Summary | Virtual Machines | Performance | Configuration | Tasks & Events | Alarms | Permissions | Maps

Name, State, Host or Guest OS contains: •

Name	State	Status	Host CPU - MHz	Host Mem - MB	Guest Mem - %	Notes
vcpprep-template-01	Powered O...		0	0	0	
AppServerTemplate	Powered O...		0	0	0	
FinDeptTemplate	Powered O...		0	0	0	
test3i	Powered O...		0	0	0	
DevBuildTemplate	Powered O...		0	0	0	
DBsys01	Powered O...		0	0	0	
ProServer15	Powered O...		0	0	0	
MgmtRptsSrv	Powered ...		12	124	1	
vicfg-rcli	Powered O...		0	0	0	This appliance provides an environ...
vcpprep-vm01	Powered O...		0	0	0	
WebServer01	Powered O...		0	0	0	
Web-Server	Powered O...		0	0	0	
MainPrintServer	Powered O...		0	0	0	
vicfg-rcli2	Powered ...		13	119	1	This appliance provides an environ...
FirewallTemplate	Powered O...		0	0	0	

Figure 14.29 ESX Server 3.5 Virtual Machines Tab

Step 6. Review the Summary tab once again to confirm that the ESX host is now in maintenance mode. We can now see that the Active Tasks value is listed as connected (maintenance mode) as shown in Figure 14.30. This ESX host can now be removed from the DRS cluster by right clicking the ESX host and selecting the Remove menu option.

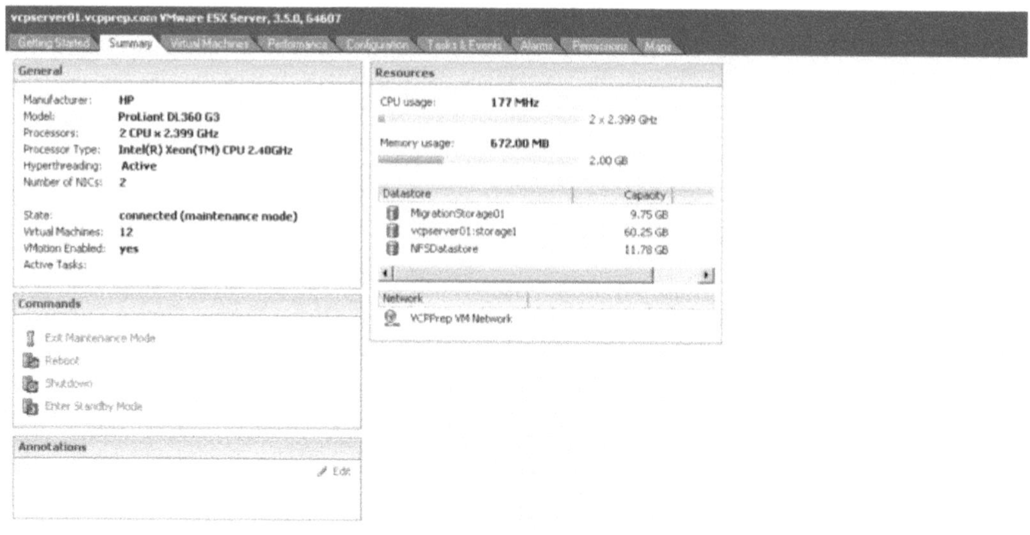

Figure 14.30 ESX Server 3.5 Summary Tab

ESX Server Maintenance Mode

The vcpserver01.vcpprep.com ESX host has been successfully removed from the DRS cluster as shown in Figure 14.31. The ESX host is in maintenance mode therefore, no virtual machines can be powered on or VMotioned to this host. A common use of maintenance mode is when applying software patches to the ESX service console. Some patches require a reboot to the service console. Let's take a look at rebooting an ESX server while in maintenance mode.

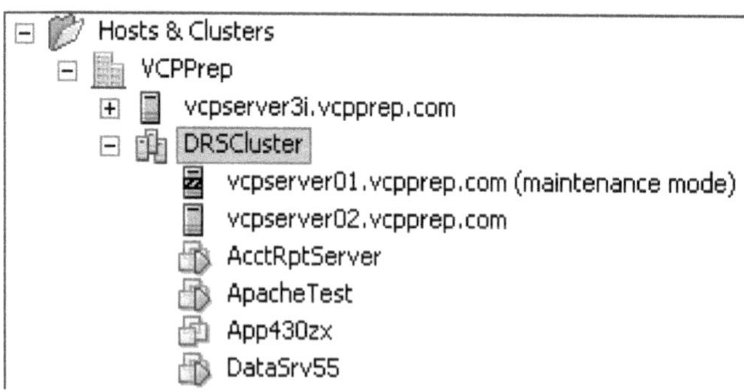

Figure 14.31 ESX Server 3.5 Maintenance Mode

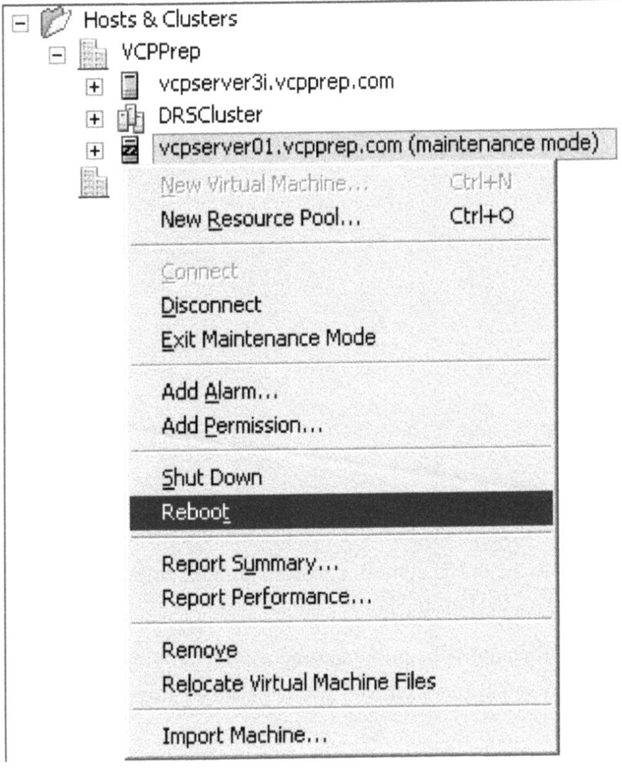

Figure 14.32 ESX Server 3.5 Reboot Menu Option

Step 1. To reboot the ESX server, right click the ESX host and select the Reboot option as shown in Figure 14.32.

Step 2. Provide a purpose for the reboot and select the OK button to continue as shown in Figure 14.33.

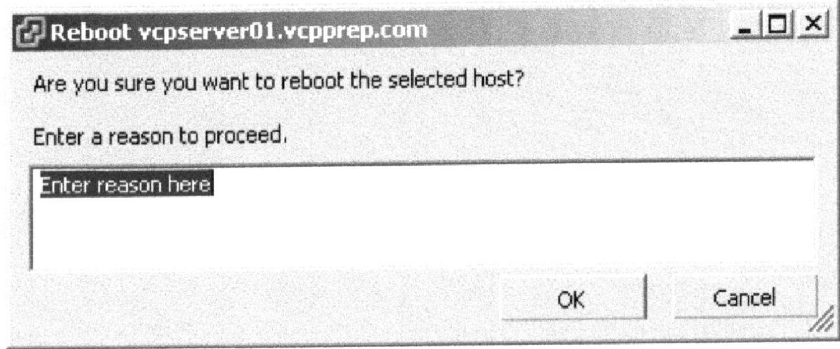

Figure 14.33 Reboot Server Enter Reason To Proceed Dialog Box

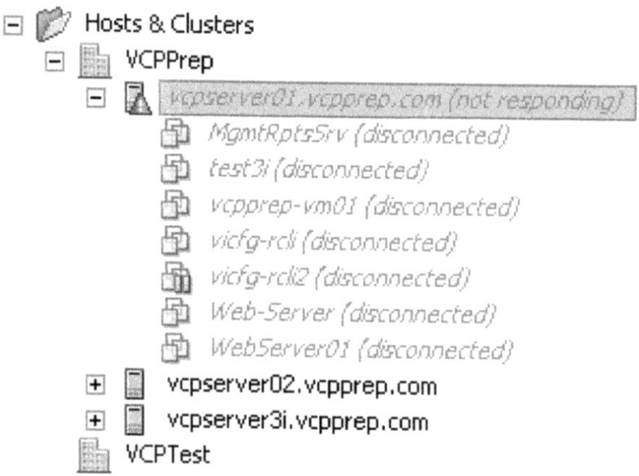

Figure 14.34 ESX Server Not Responding

During the reboot process, the ESX host status in the VI Client is reported as not responding and virtual machines on this host listed as disconnected as shown in Figure 14.34.

Step 3. Upon successful reboot, an ESX server still remains in maintenance mode. To place the ESX host back into service, right click the ESX host and select the Exit Maintenance Mode menu option as shown in Figure 14.35.

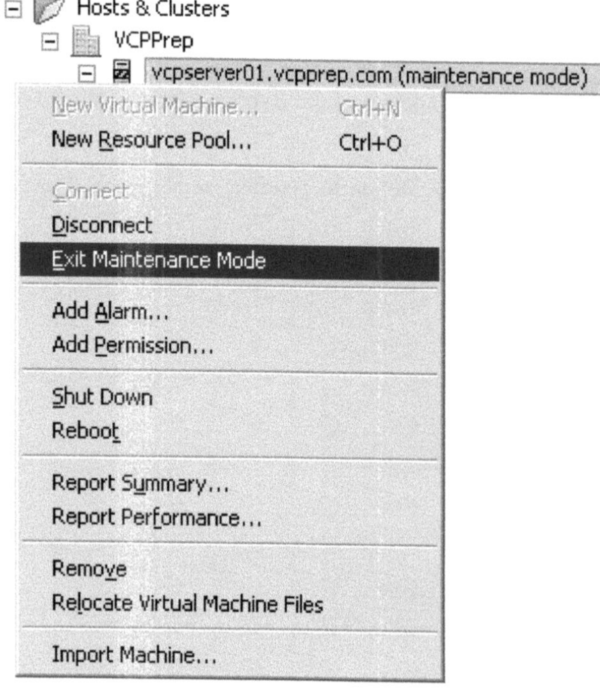

Figure 14.35 ESX Server Exit Maintenance Mode

Removing a Distributed Resource Scheduler Cluster

Step 1. A DRS cluster can be removed from the VirtualCenter inventory simply by right clicking on the DRS cluster and selecting the Remove menu option as shown in Figure 14.36.

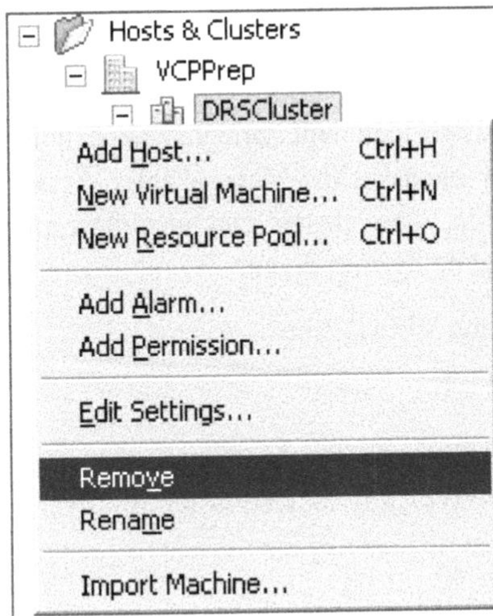

Figure 14.36 Remove Cluster Warning Dialog Box

Step 2. A pop up dialog box is displayed as shown in Figure 14.37 that asks for confirmation to remove the DRS cluster. Answering Yes to this dialog box removes the DRS cluster including the ESX hosts and virtual machines contained in the cluster from the VirtualCenter inventory. In our example, we are going to select No to avoid removing the cluster.

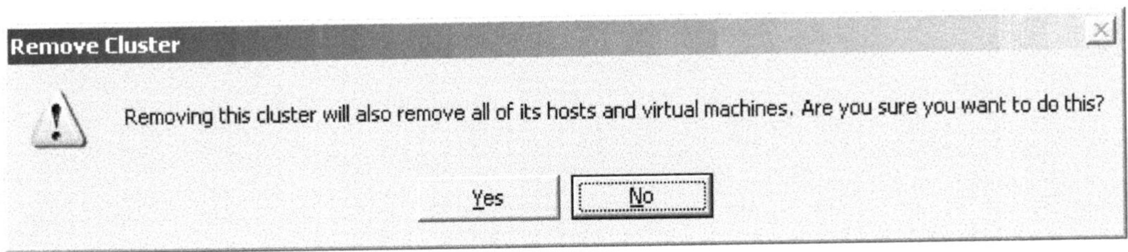

Figure 14.37 Remove Cluster Error Dialog Box

Troubleshooting Distributed Resource Scheduler

Troubleshooting DRS clusters can be done by using the Resource Allocation tab within the VI Client. This tab can be used to check the CPU and memory total available reservation values, Reservation Used and Reservation Unreserved values. These values can help in quickly determining if a DRS cluster is in an over committed state or if the appropriate reservation values for resource pools and virtual machines are being used.

A DRS cluster may become internally inconsistent if an administrator bypasses the VirtualCenter server and makes resource pool changes at the ESX host level. Virtual machines that would not otherwise be able to power on when accessed via the VirtualCenter server may be permitted to power on causing an inconsistent state for the DRS cluster. The following message has been observed in the Recent Tasks section of the VI Client when a virtual machine is allowed to power on when directly connected to the ESX host even though the VirtualCenter would not permit it due to CPU admission control:

A specified parameter was not correct. spec.cpuAllocation.overheadLimit

When in this state, the DRS cluster icon turns red. A DRS cluster icon will turn yellow if it is overcommitted. This could happen once again if an administrator bypasses the VirtualCenter server and makes reservation changes to virtual machines for example. The cluster can also become overcommitted due to a loss of resources, for example, an ESX host being shut down.

DRS dump files are placed by default in the following location on the VirtualCenter server:

C:\WINDOWS\Temp\vpx\drmdump\cluster#

Where cluster# is the number of the DRS cluster. For example, cluster5. The log files are mostly cryptic and probably best used by VMware support. These files are typically labeled in the following manner:

12123459283453-proposeActions.dump

12123454002406-mapVm.dump

External References

The VMware ESX 3.5 and ESXi Server version 3.5 Documentation Page:

http://www.vmware.com/support/pubs/vi_pubs.html

Sample Test Questions

1. A DRS cluster can be used to balance which of the following resources?

a. CPU

b. Disk I/O

c. Network I/O

d. Memory

2. The automation level of a DRS cluster can be administratively set to which of the following settings?

a. Partially Automated

b. Fully Manual

c. Manual

d. Partially Manual

e. Fully Automated

3. The swap file policy of a DRS cluster can be set to which of the following?

a. As specified by the resource pool policy

b. Stored in the same directory as the virtual machine

c. As specified by the datacenter policy

d. Stored in the datacenter specified by the host

e. As specified by the Hosts & Clusters view

4. DPM can be used experimentally to achieve which of the following:

a. Better use of physical network I/O resources

b. More efficient use of physical disk I/O resources

c. Energy efficiency

d. Virtual machine fault tolerance

e. Improved VMotion migrations

5. DRS clusters can be configured to enforce rules created by the ESX administrator. Which of the following rule types can be configured with a DRS cluster?

a. Anti-Affinity rule

b. Multi-Group rule

c. Single-Group rule

d. Anti-Member rule

e. Affinity rule

Sample Test Solutions

1. A DRS cluster can be used to balance which of the following resources?

a. CPU

b. Disk I/O

c. Network I/O

d. Memory

Answer: a and d - DRS clusters monitor the CPU and memory resource utilization of all ESX hosts placed into the cluster. Network and disk I/O resources are not taken into consideration by DRS but can be adjusted accordingly by an ESX administrator. Refer to Chapter 4 - ESX 3.x Server Networking Configurations and Chapter 5 - ESX 3.x Server Storage Configurations for adjusting network and disk I/O respectively.

2. The automation level of a DRS cluster can be administratively set to which of the following settings?

a. Partially Automated

b. Fully Manual

c. Manual

d. Partially Manual

e. Fully Automated

Answer: a, c and e - The automation level of a DRS cluster can be set by an administrator to the following three settings:

- ***Manual***
- ***Partially Automated***
- ***Fully Automated***

3. The swap file policy of a DRS cluster can be set to which of the following?

a. As specified by the resource pool policy

b. Stored in the same directory as the virtual machine

c. As specified by the datacenter policy

d. Stored in the datacenter specified by the host

e. As specified by the Hosts & Clusters view

Answer: b and d - There are two swap file policies that can be chosen when creating a DRS cluster. The swap file of the virtual machine can be located in the directory where the virtual machine was

created. A new option in VirtualCenter 2.5 allows a swap file location to be set at the ESX host level. Choosing to set the swap file location at the host level might be done for example, if the virtual machine files are located on slower performing datastore. Placing the swap file on a faster performing datastore may improve the virtual machine performance.

4. DPM can be used experimentally to achieve which of the following:

a. Better use of physical network I/O resources

b. More efficient use of physical disk I/O resources

c. Energy efficiency

d. Virtual machine fault tolerance

e. Improved VMotion migrations

Answer: c - Distributed Power Management (DPM) is an experimentally supported feature with VirtualCenter 2.5 servers. DPM is a feature that works in conjunction with a DRS cluster. Its purpose is to determine whether the resources of an ESX host are currently needed to satisfy virtual machine needs.

5. DRS clusters can be configured to enforce rules created by the ESX administrator. Which of the following rule types can be configured with a DRS cluster?

a. Anti-Affinity rule

b. Multi-Group rule

c. Single-Group rule

d. Anti-Member rule

e. Affinity rule

Answer: a and e - The following are the two rules that can be configured with DRS clusters:

Affinity Rule - Keeps virtual machines together on the same ESX host. This type of rule is often used for performance reasons. Virtual machines such as an application and database servers that often exchange information together can increase network communication performance when kept on the same ESX host.

Anti-Affinity Rule - Separate virtual machines on different ESX hosts. This rule type is often used to increase availability. For example, using an anti-affinity rule for a primary and secondary domain controller ensures that if one of the ESX systems hosting either controller goes down, the other virtual machine will be available for service. A maximum of two virtual machines can be sleeted for an anti-affinity rule.

Chapter 15

High Availability

After reading this chapter you should be able to complete the following tasks:

- Describe the purpose, features and benefits of using VMware's High Availability technology
- Configure ESX servers within a HA cluster
- Configure virtual machines within a HA cluster
- Monitor High Availability failover events
- Use the ESX standby mode
- Use Microsoft Cluster Service (MSCS) with virtual machines
- Troubleshooting High Availability problems

Overview of VMware High Availability

Achieving high uptime with physical servers can be burdensome for traditional datacenters. High availability clusters with physical servers are costly due to the additional second or even third servers that are required. More physical servers consume a larger amount of power, driving up the operational costs. Other expenses include the clustering software and licenses that are needed. VMware's High Availability (HA) solution can reduce the cost and configuration of traditional clustering solutions. Applications that cannot be clustered when operating on physical machines can benefit from VMware's HA solution when run within a virtual machine. The disaster recovery options available to datacenters using VMware ESX hosts continues to be one of the most compelling reasons to adopt virtualization.

VMware HA clusters support the failure of the physical ESX hosts. A single ESX host failure will cause all virtual machines running on the host to be powered off. A failed ESX host placed into a VMware HA cluster can have its virtual machines that were running on the failed host automatically restarted on another ESX host that is also within the same HA cluster. A maximum of 32 ESX hosts can be within an HA cluster. Lets start by taking a look at how to create an HA cluster.

Creating the High Availability Cluster

The process to create a HA cluster is performed by using the New Cluster Wizard.

Step 1. Right click on a datacenter object and select the New Cluster... menu option as shown is Figure 15.1.

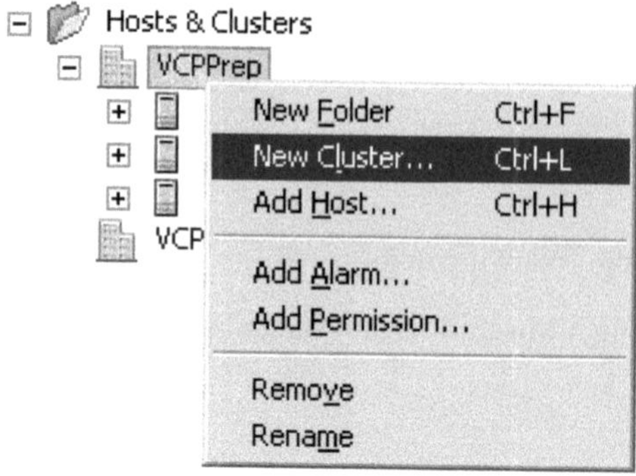

Figure 15.1 New Cluster Menu Option

Step 2. The New Cluster Wizard displays as shown in Figure 15.2. A cluster object can be defined as either a HA (High Availability) cluster, a DRS cluster or both. DRS clusters were discussed in Chapter 14 – Distributed Resource Scheduler. To create a HA cluster, enter a name in the Name text box then choose the VMware HA check box. In this example, the HA cluster has been assigned the name HACluster. Click the Next button to continue.

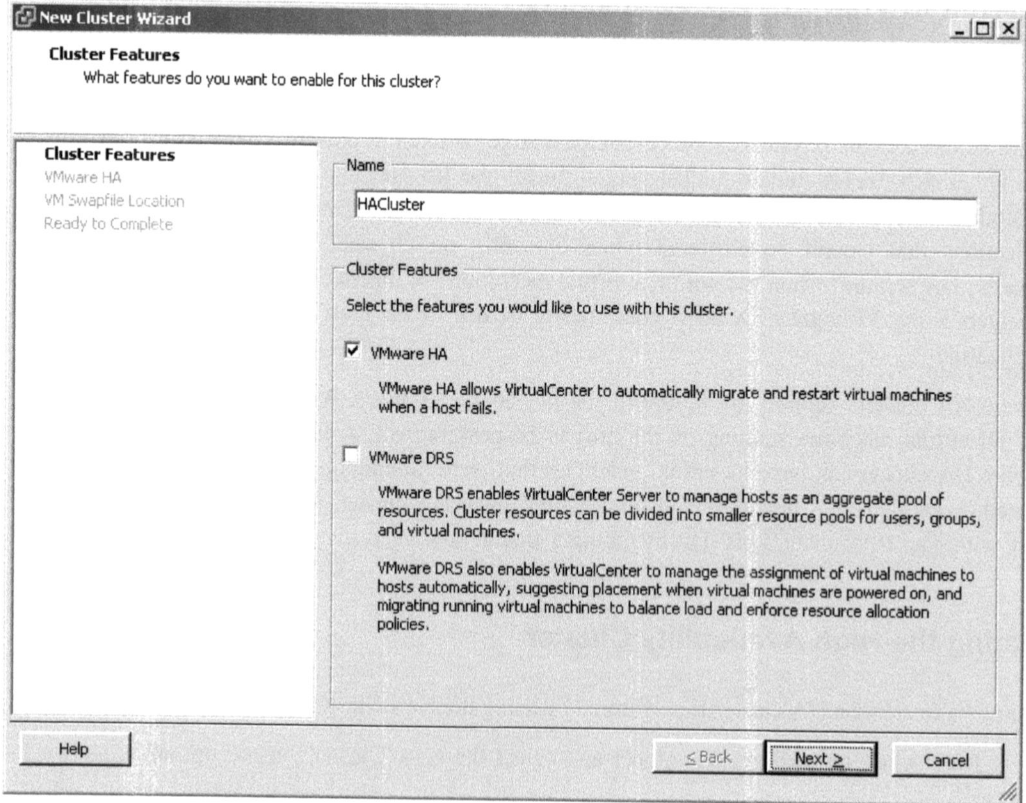

Figure 15.2 New Cluster Wizard Cluster Features

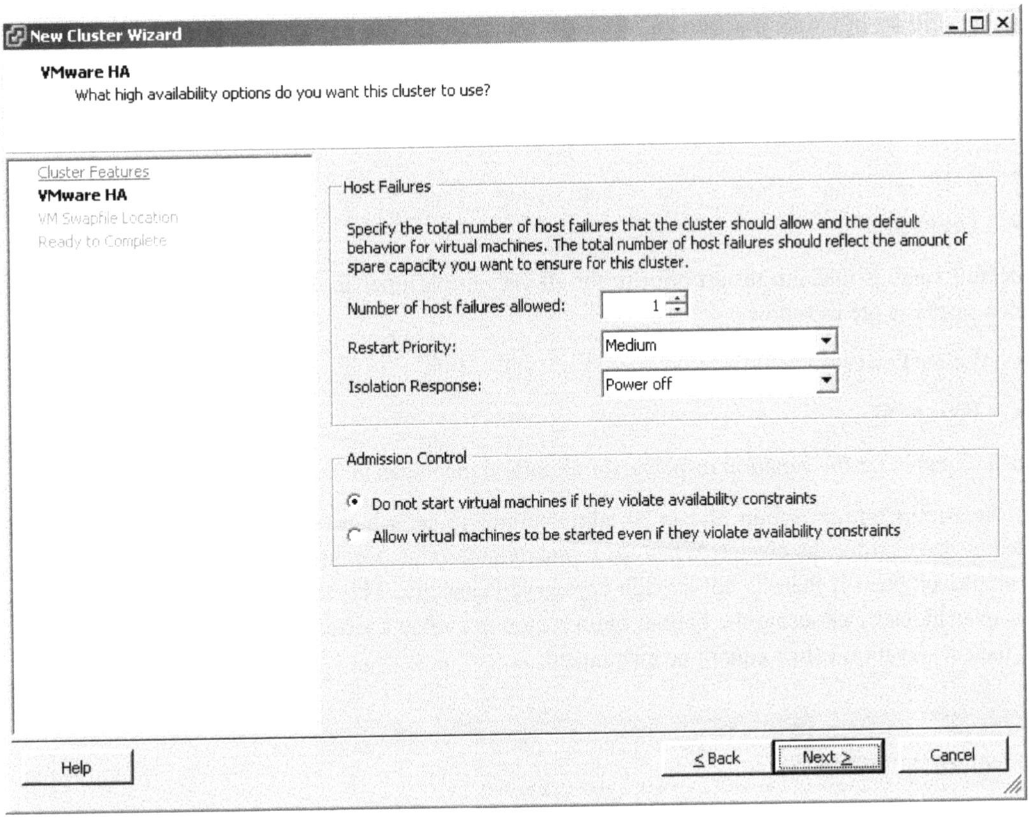

New Cluster Wizard

VMware HA

What high availability options do you want this cluster to use?

Cluster Features
VMware HA
VM Swapfile Location
Ready to Complete

Host Failures

Specify the total number of host failures that the cluster should allow and the default behavior for virtual machines. The total number of host failures should reflect the amount of spare capacity you want to ensure for this cluster.

Number of host failures allowed: 1

Restart Priority: Medium

Isolation Response: Power off

Admission Control

Do not start virtual machines if they violate availability constraints

Allow virtual machines to be started even if they violate availability constraints

Help < Back Next > Cancel

Figure 15.3 New Cluster Wizard High Availability Features

Step 3. The Hosts Failures section displayed in Figure 15.3 is an important configuration setting. The value chosen for the "Number of failures allowed" option will be used by the HA cluster in determining how many host failures can occur and still have enough spare resources in the cluster to power on the virtual machines hosted by all failed ESX servers. The maximum value that can be set is four. Setting this value requires a solid understanding of the available physical resources of each ESX host configured within the HA cluster as well as the computing demands of all virtual machines. The number of virtual machines that can be powered on is dependent upon the number of available slots. The HA cluster calculates the number of slots based on the CPU and memory reservations of the VMs that need to be restarted. In the absence of reservations settings where the default reservation settings for both CPU and memory values of 0 are used, HA assumes a slot of 256 MHz CPU and 256 MB memory for each VM that needs to be restarted within the cluster.

ESX hosts placed into the HA cluster are either primary or secondary servers. There is always one more primary server than the value set for "Number of failures allowed". The maximum primary HA servers in a cluster is five. Primary servers are responsible for synchronizing the messages that are used to maintain the cluster state and to facilitate failover events. The first host added to the cluster becomes a primary server. The cluster determines which role, either primary or secondary a host will be assigned. In the event that a primary server fails, the cluster will promote a secondary server to primary status.

The restart priority of virtual machines after an ESX host failure can be set to the following:

- High
- Medium
- Low
- Disabled

The default value is medium restart priority for all virtual machines in the cluster. The values for the isolation response are as follows:

- Leave Powered On
- Power Off

The default value for the isolation response for all virtual machines in the cluster is set to power off.

The Admission Control section allows an administrator to set whether or not admission control is enabled or disabled for the cluster. When set to the default value, virtual machines will not be started after a failover event if there is not enough unreserved capacity. This strict admission control policy can be overridden by choosing the bottom radio button that allows virtual machines to power on even when their reservation values cannot be guaranteed.

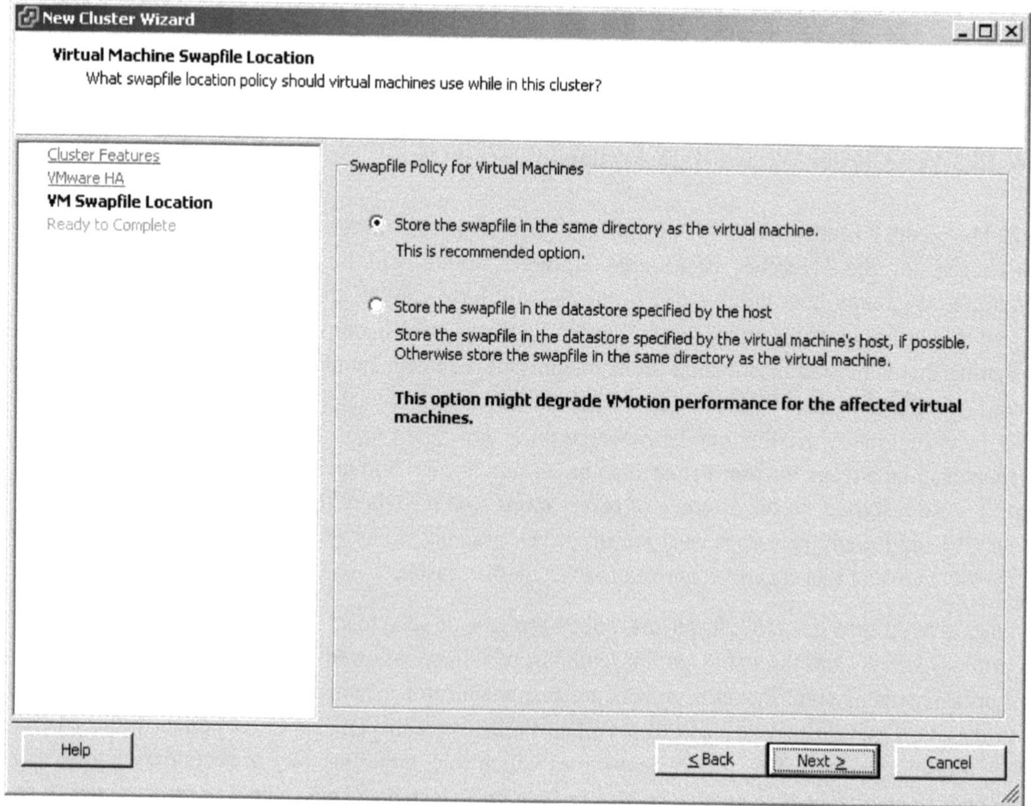

Figure 15.4 New Cluster Wizard VM Swapfile Location

Step 4. There are two swap file policies that can be chosen as shown in Figure 15.4. This swap file is the VMkernel swap file that is created when a virtual machine is powered on. The size of this file is the difference between the virtual machine's memory reservation value and its memory limit. Typically, this file is located in the directory where the virtual machine was created. A new option in VirtualCenter 2.5 allows a swap file location to be set at the ESX host level. Choosing to set the swap file location at the host level might be done for example, if the virtual machine files are located on a slower performing datastore. Placing the swap file on a faster performing datastore may improve the virtual machine performance. Select the appropriate swap file policy and click the Next button to continue.

Step 5. The last step of the wizard is to verify all the choices made. As shown in Figure 15.5, review the Ready to Complete screen. The Back button can be used to make any necessary changes. If no changes are needed, select the Finish button to complete the New Cluster Wizard.

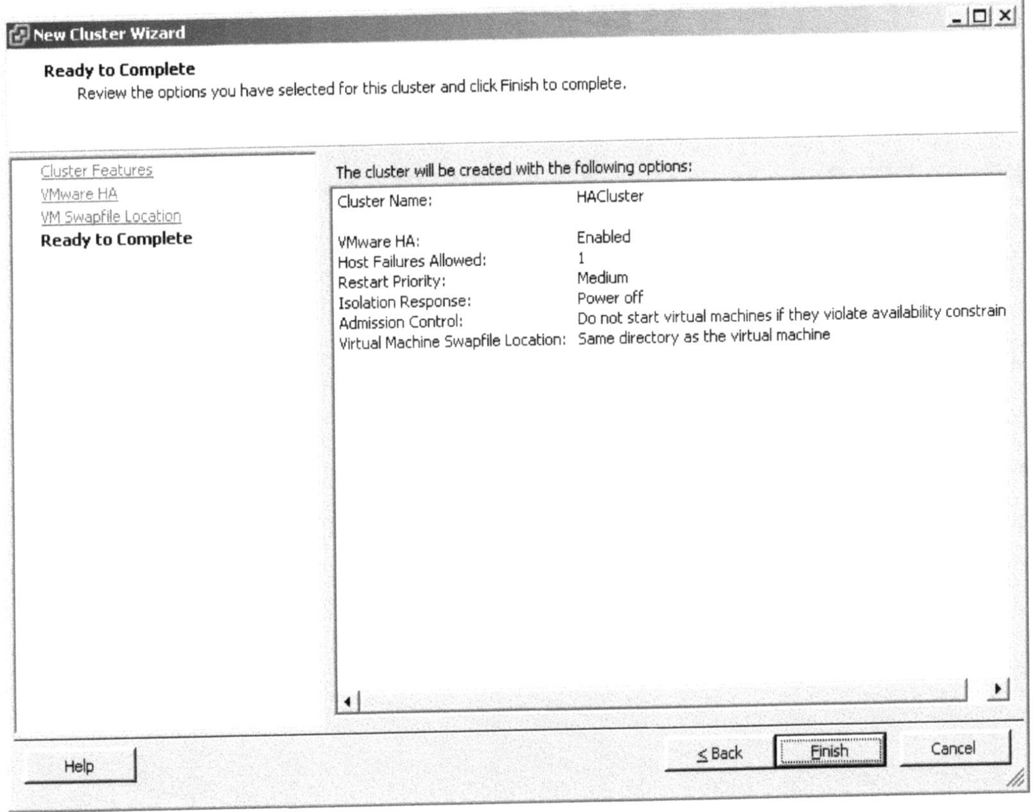

Figure 15.5 New Cluster Wizard Ready To Complete

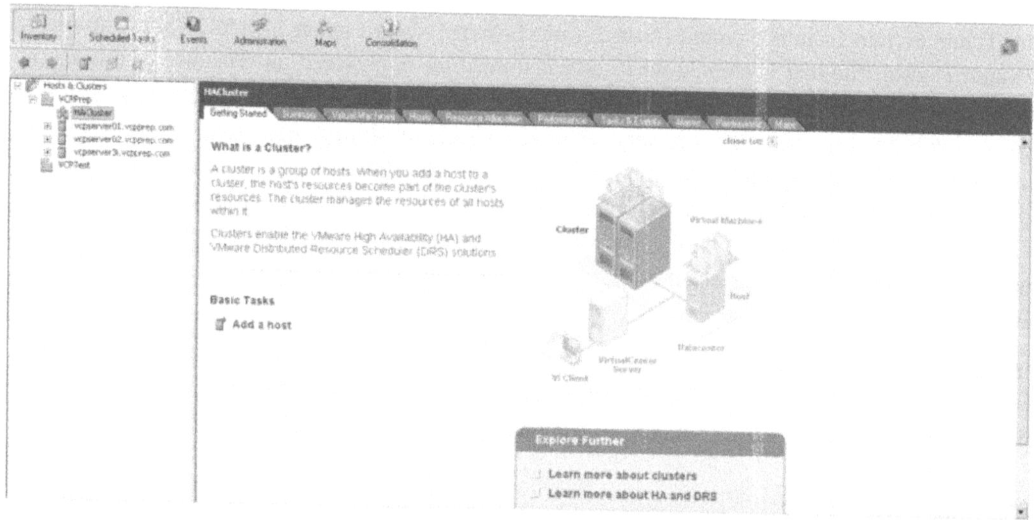

Figure 15.6 HA Cluster Getting Started Tab

Adding an ESX Server to a High Availability Cluster

Figure 15.6 displays the Getting Started tab for the newly created HACluster object. Also shown are three ESX servers, vcpserver01, vcpserver02 and vcpserver03. We are going to see how to add the vcpserver01 ESX server to the HA cluster.

Step 1. Select one of the following to add an ESX server to a HA cluster:

- Dragging the ESX host over top of the cluster object
- Right clicking on the HA cluster and selecting the Add Host menu option
- Selecting the HA cluster object. Then select the Getting Started tab and clicking the Add Host link.

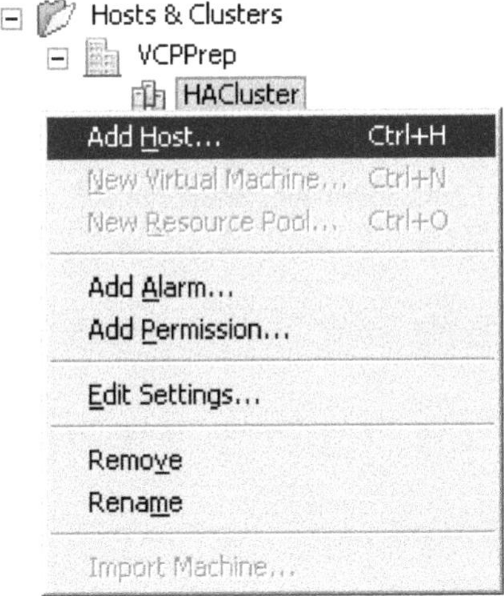

Figure 15.7 Adding An ESX Server To HA Cluster Recent Tasks Status

Step 2. Right click on the HA cluster and select the Add Host menu option to launch the Add Host Wizard as shown in Figure 15.7.

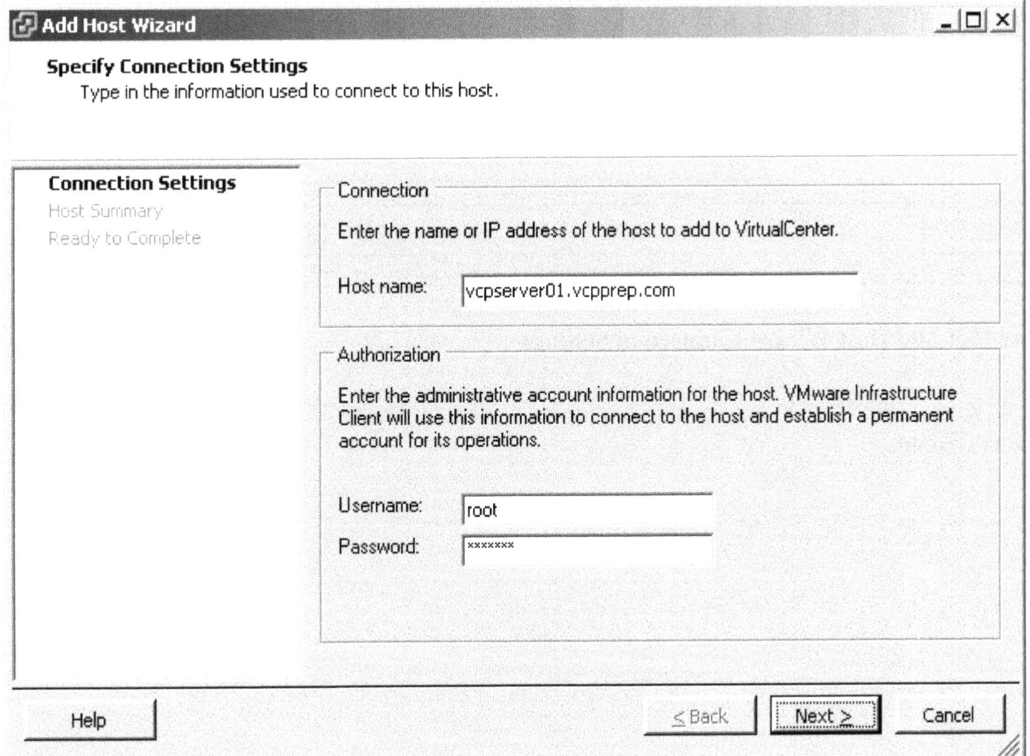

Figure 15.8 Add Host Menu Option

Step 3. In the Connection section shown in Figure 15.8, enter the Fully Qualified Domain Name (FQDN) of the ESX host. Entering the ESX host's IP address instead of its FQDN can cause problems within the HA cluster. It is very important to have a solid DNS enabled environment. VMware HA needs to be able to resolve both long and short hostnames, forward and reverse to work properly. In the Authorization section, enter the ESX host service console's root username and password. The authorization credentials are case-sensitive.

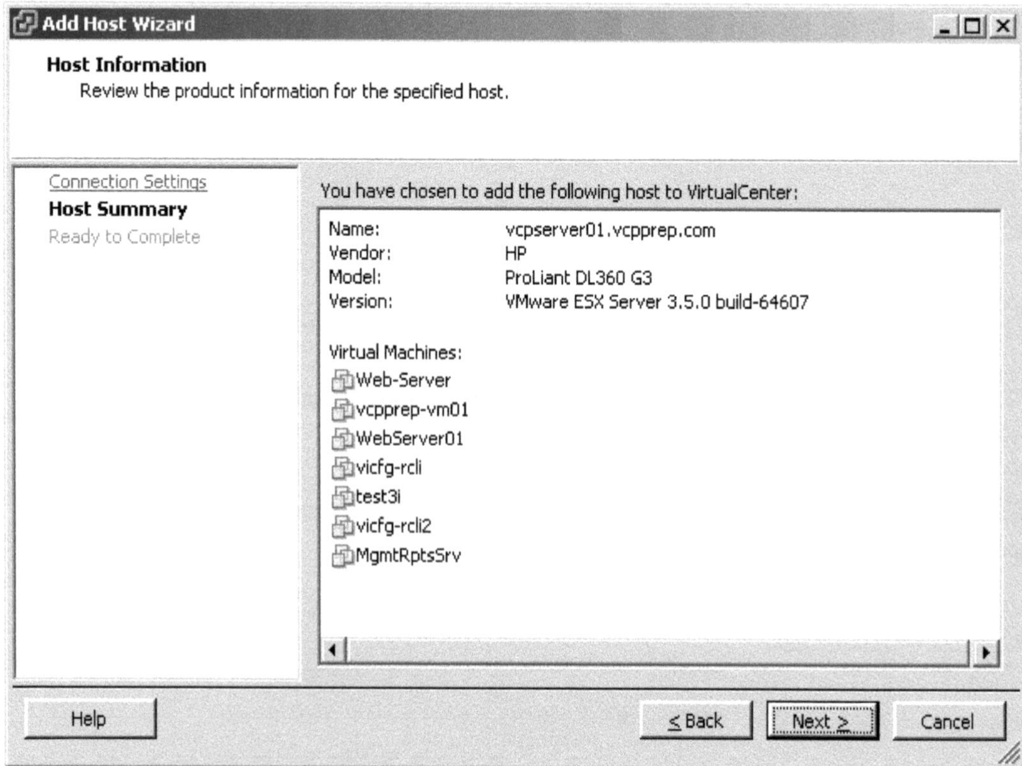

Figure 15.9 Add Host Wizard Connection Settings

Step 4. Review the Host Summary information as shown in Figure 15.9, and then click the Next button to continue.

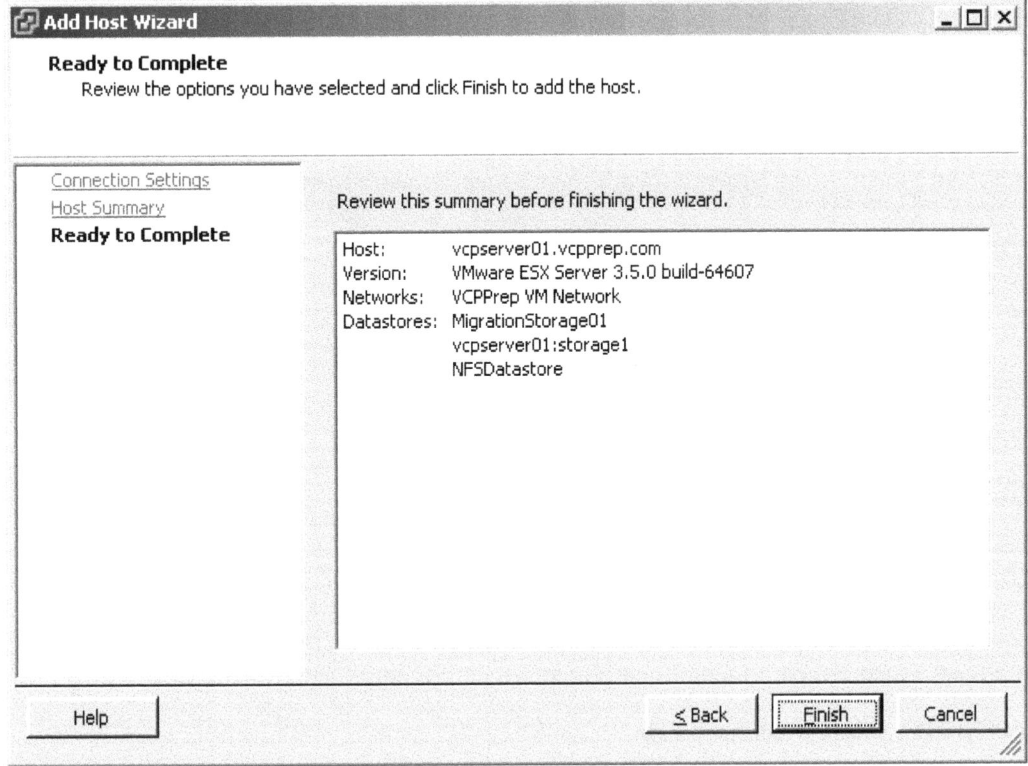

Figure 15.10 Add Host Wizard Host Information

Step 5. As shown in Figure 15.10, the Ready to Complete screen is the final step in adding the vcpserver01 host to the HACluster object. Any changes that need to be made can be done by selecting the Back button. To complete the Add Host Wizard, select the Finish button.

The status of adding the ESX host to the HA cluster can be observed by viewing the Recent Tasks window pane located at the bottom of the VI Client window screen as shown in Figure 15.11. Adding a host to the cluster may fail for some reasons. For example, if there are inconsistencies in DNS name resolution or if the host cannot ping a default gateway.

Figure 15.11 Add Host Wizard Ready to Complete

In Figure 15.12, we can see that the HA cluster is now enabled as listed in the General section. We have also added a second server, vcpserver02 to the HA cluster. In the VMware HA section, the current failover capacity is two and the configured failover capacity is one. These values signify that there is enough current capacity to satisfy the resources needed if one of the ESX hosts fail. As long as the current failover capacity is at least equal to the configured capacity, HA should be able to restart all virtual machines that were running on the failed host. A configured capacity greater than current capacity means HA will not be able to restart all virtual machines that were running on the failed host.

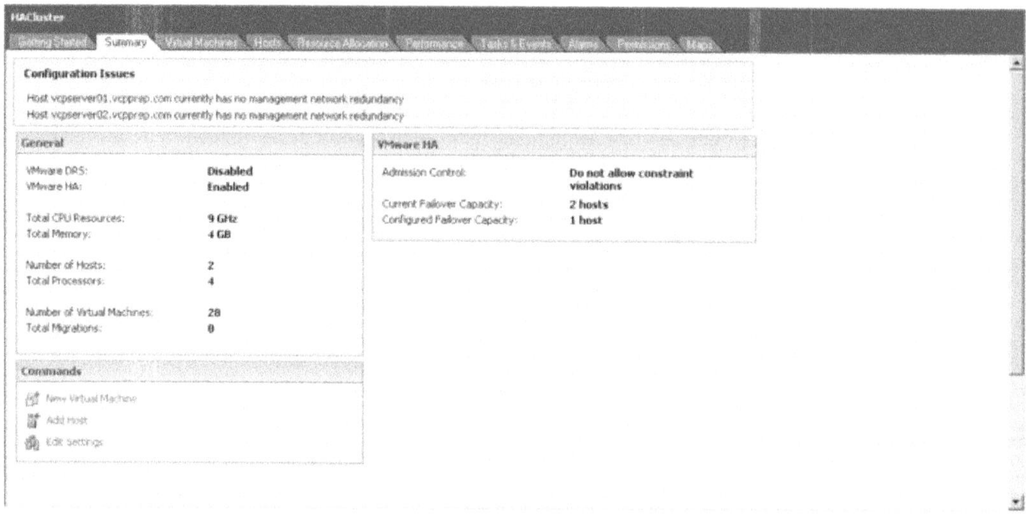

Figure 15.12 HA Cluster Summary Tab

Figure 15.12 also lists two configurations issues in the upper left hand corner of the screen. Both issues are caused by each of the ESX hosts having only one service console. An HA agent is installed on the ESX host when it is added to an HA cluster. The HA agent communicates with other HA agents via the service console port to coordinate the active and passive nodes. This communication is called the HA heartbeat which occurs at five second intervals. The heartbeat incoming traffic uses TCP/UDP with ports 8042-8045 and for outgoing traffic it uses TCP/UDP with ports 2050-2250. The service console port is also used for the state synchronization of the HA cluster.

Configuring Networking for High Availability Clusters

Redundant networking between ESX hosts is a best practice and can be accomplished either by creating two service console ports or by the use of NIC teaming. In our example configuration, there is only one service console port located on vSwitch0 as shown in Figure 15.13. We are going to create a second service console port on vSwitch1 for redundancy within the HA cluster.

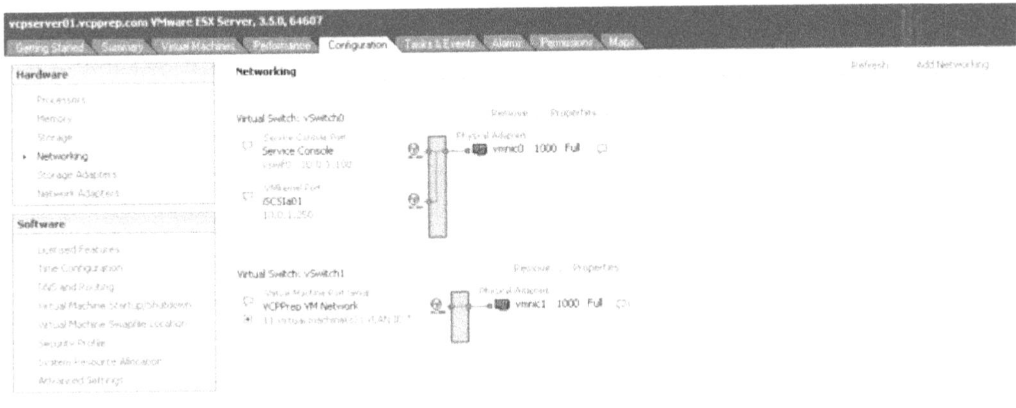

Figure 15.13 Configuration Tab Networking

Step 1. Select the Properties link for vSwitch1. Click the Add button. The Add Network Wizard displays, as shown in Figure 15.14. Select the Service Console radio button and. click the Next button.

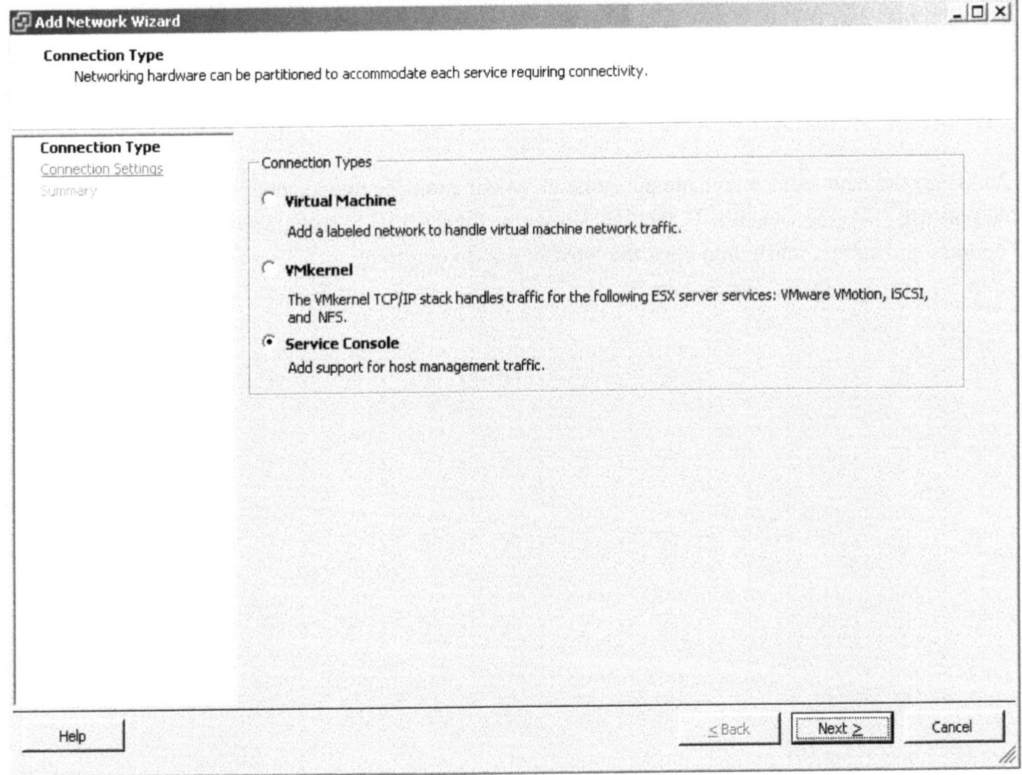

Figure 15.14 Add Network Wizard Connection Type

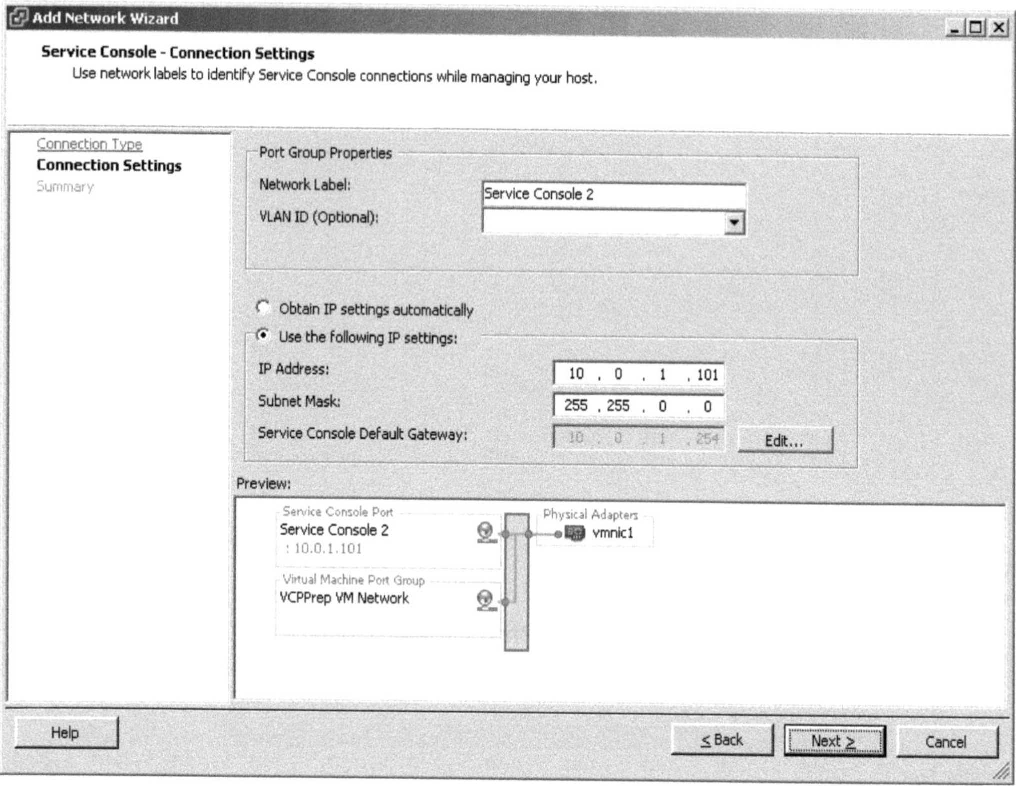

Figure 15.15 Add Network Wizard Connection Settings

Step 2. Assign the new service console port a label. In our example, we have assigned the new service console port the "Service Console 2" label as shown in Figure 15.15. Assign the service console port an IP address and subnet mask then click the Next button to continue.

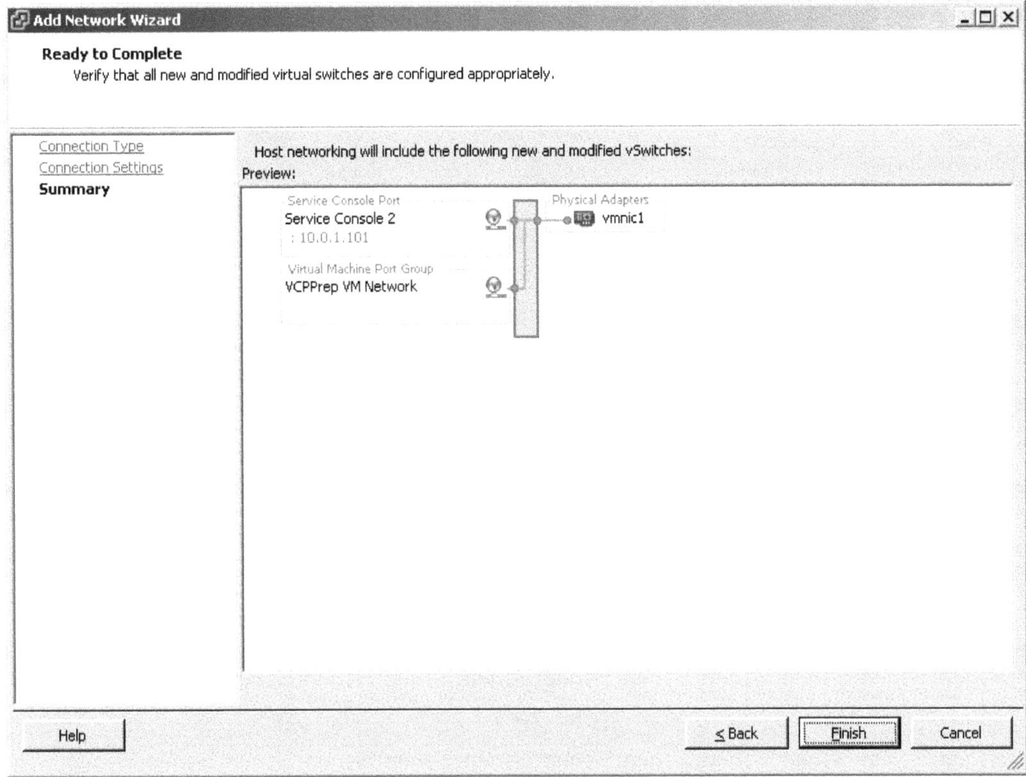

Figure 15.16 Add Network Wizard Connection Summary

Step 3. As shown in Figure 15.16, the Ready to Complete screen is the final step in adding the new service console port to vSwitch1. Any changes that need made can be done by selecting the Back button. To complete the Add Host Wizard, select the Finish button.

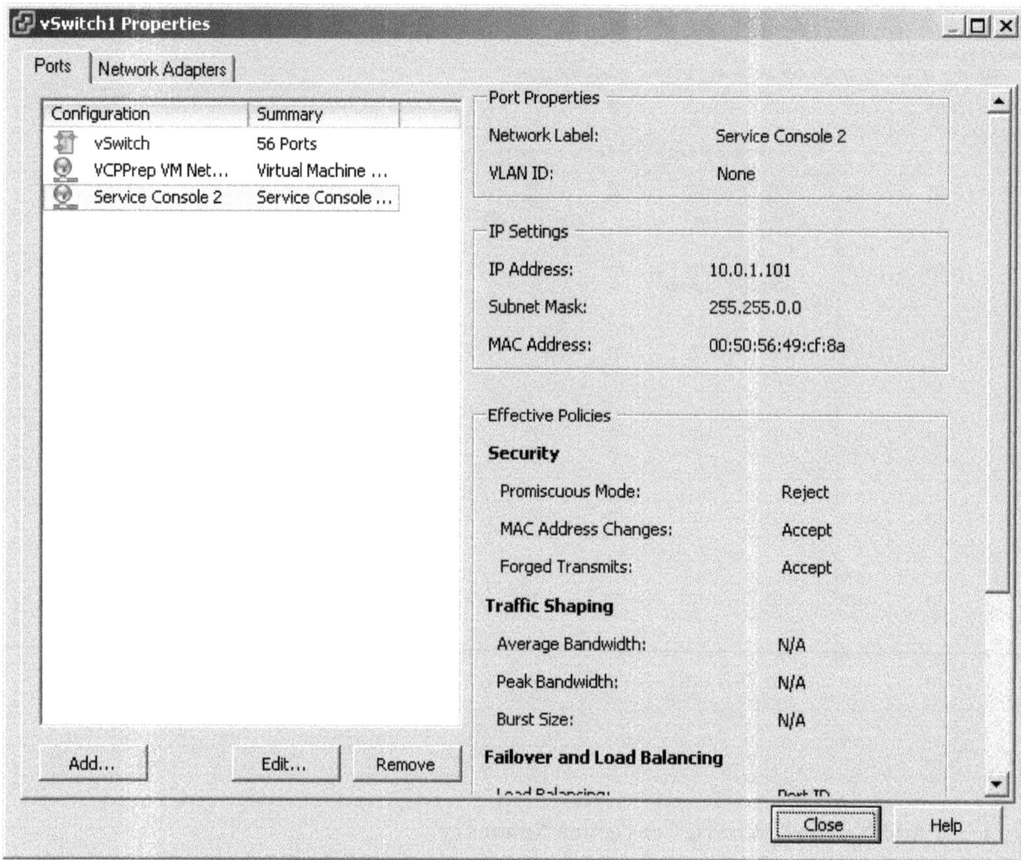

Figure 15.17 vSwitch1 Properties

Step 4. The Service Console 2 port now appears within the Ports tab as shown in Figure 15.17. In our example, we added the new service console port to an existing virtual switch that contains a virtual machine port group. The Port Properties section lists none for the VLAN ID for the new service console port. We did not place this new service console port within a VLAN. In a production environment, it is a good practice to keep service console ports isolated from virtual machine traffic either by physical separation or with the use of a VLAN.

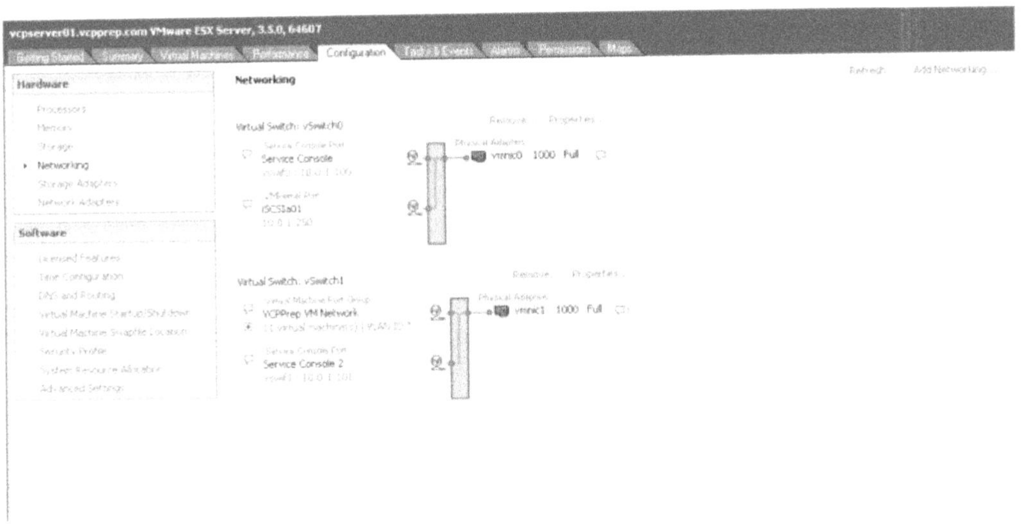

Figure 15.18 Configuration Tab Networking

Figure 15.18 displays the new service console port configured on vSwitch1. This configuration offers our HA cluster network redundancy. Be sure to connect each physical uplink port to a separate physical switch to avoid a single point of failure at the physical switch level. Note, in some configurations, there have been issues with the heartbeat traffic when using this type of service console network configuration. If this configuration experiences problems, use just one service console port on a virtual switch that is configured with a NIC team.

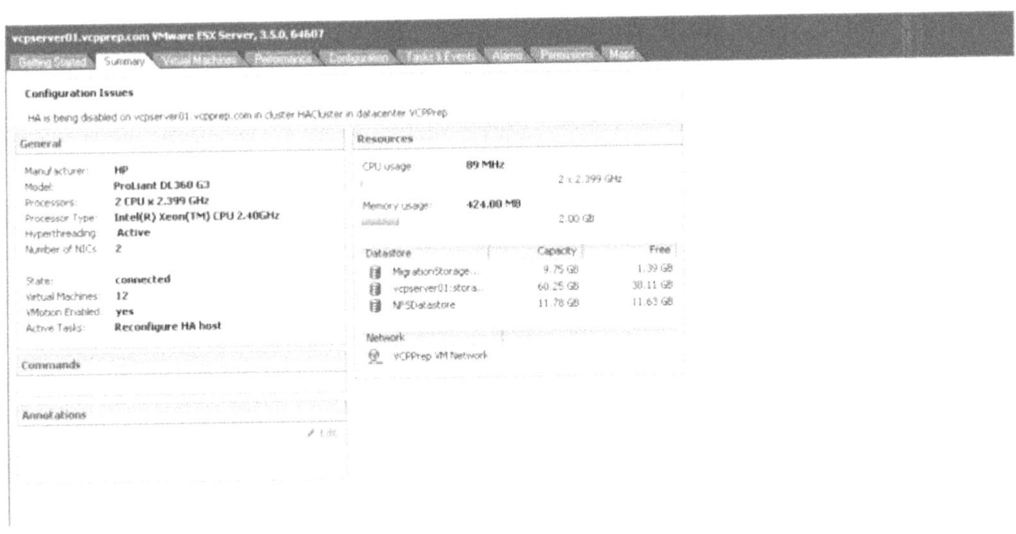

Figure 15.19 ESX Server Summary Tab Reconfigure HA Host

Now that the second service console port has been successfully added, we must reconfigure each ESX host for HA. To do so, right click on the ESX host and select the Reconfigure for VMware HA menu option. Figure 15.19 displays within the General section the Active Tasks value as Reconfigure HA host. Once the reconfiguration process has completed, the service console redundancy issue should be resolved.

Monitoring High Availability Failover Events

To demonstrate a failover event, we are going to manually shutdown the vcpserver02 ESX host in the HA cluster. First, let's see which virtual machines are currently running on this host by selecting the host in the VirtualCenter inventory then clicking on the Virtual Machines tab as shown in Figure 15.20. We can see that the following four virtual machines are currently running on the vcpserver02 host:

- AcctRptServer
- DevBuilds
- DataSrv55
- NFSServer01

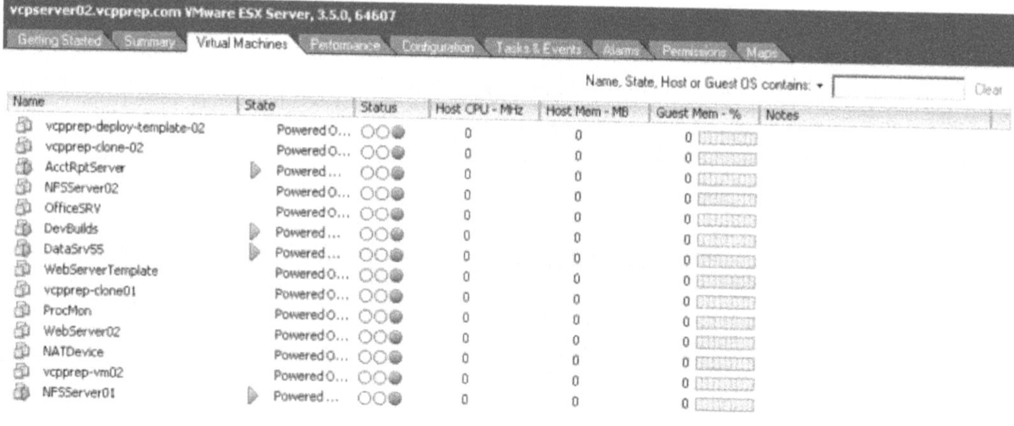

Figure 15.20 ESX Server Virtual Machine Tab

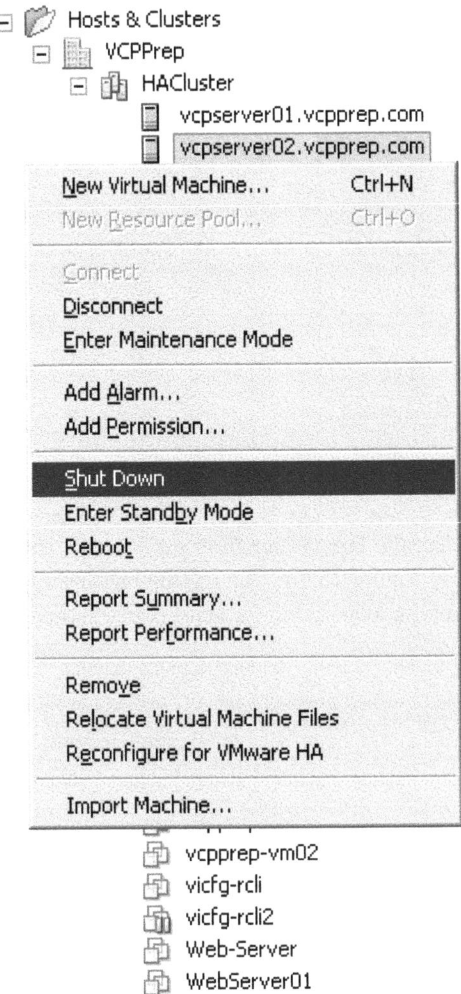

Figure 15.21 Shut Down Menu Option

We right click on the vcpserver02 and select the Shutdown menu option as shown in Figure 15.21.

Since we want to simulate a host failover event, we select the Yes button to confirm the shutdown, as in Figure 15.22.

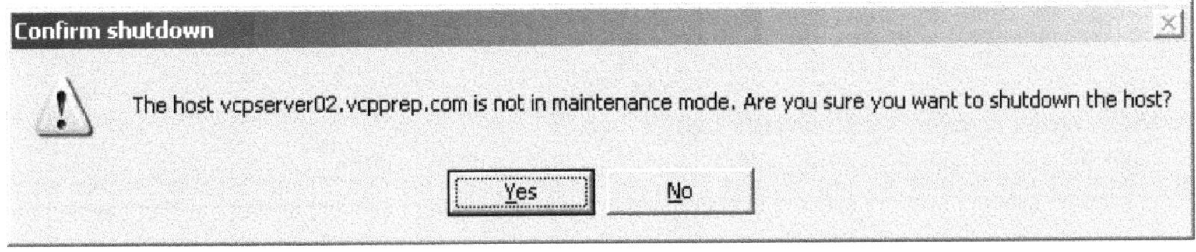

Figure 15.22 Confirm Shutdown Dialog Box

VirtualCenter prompts for a reason to shutdown the host. We accepted the default text and clicked the OK button to continue. Refer to Figure 15.23.

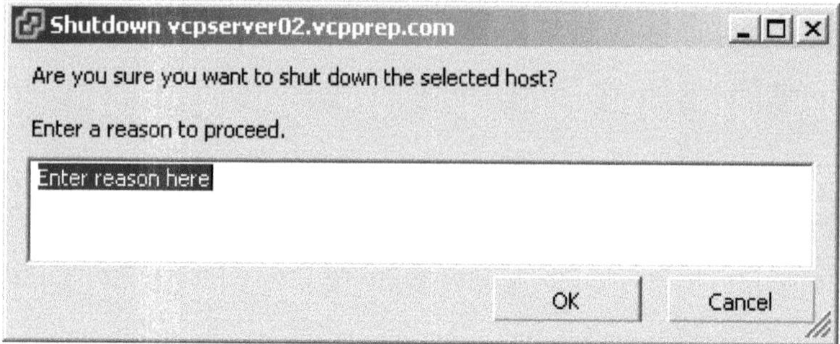

Figure 15.23 Shut Down Enter Reason Dialog Box

To review the events that are related to the HA cluster, select the HA cluster from the VirtualCenter inventory and click on the Tasks & Events tab as shown in Figure 15.24. The Events button in the upper left hand corner was selected. We can see that the Shutdown operation for vcpserver02 has been logged.

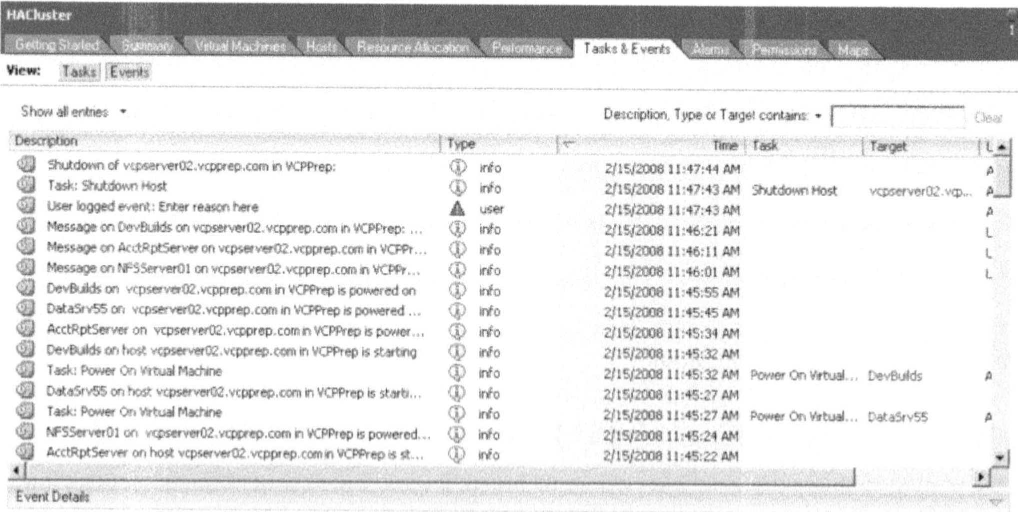

Figure 15.24 Tasks & Events Tab Events List

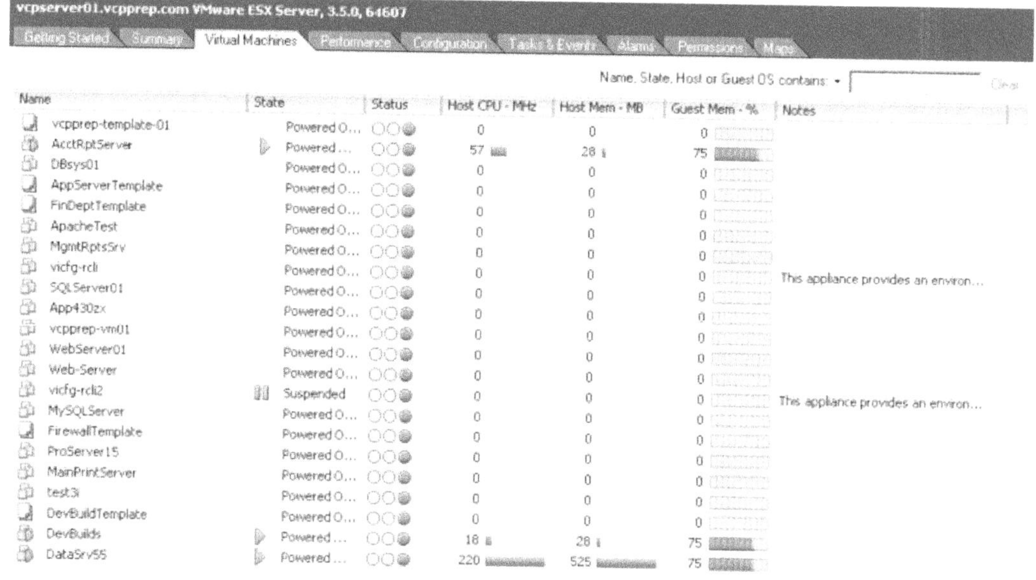

Figure 15.25 ESX Server Virtual Machines Tab

Now that the vcpserver02 host is powered off, select the vcpserver01 host from the VirtualCenter inventory and click on the Virtual Machines tab. As seen in Figure 15.25, we can see that the following virtual machines have been automatically restarted on this host:

- AcctRptServer
- DevBuilds
- DataSrv55

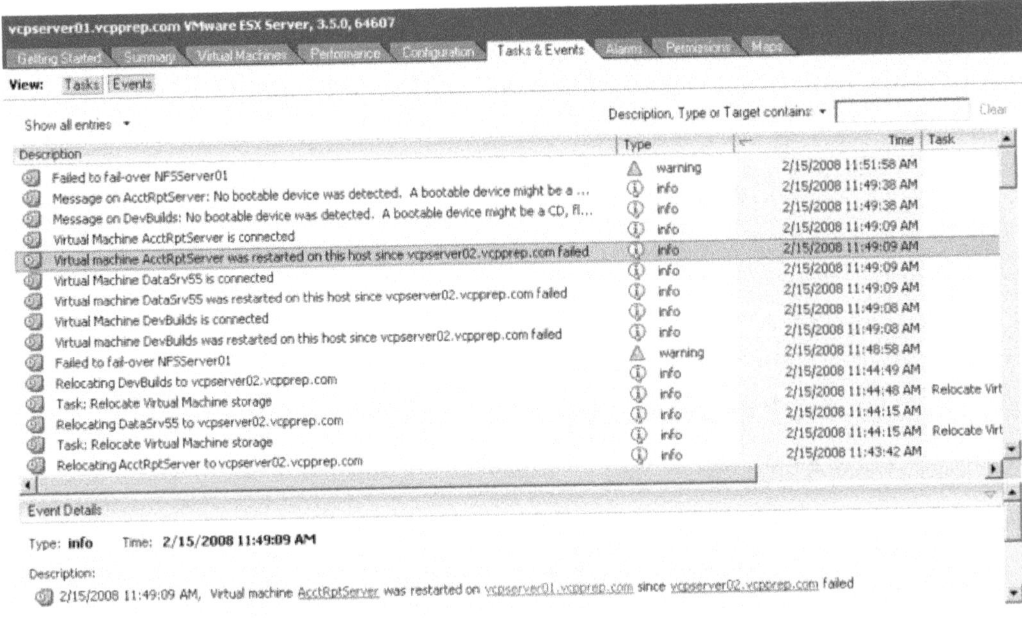

Figure 15.26 Tasks & Events Tab Events List

Selecting the Tasks & Events tab for the vcpserver01 host and clicking on the Events button reveals that each of these virtual machines are now running on the vcpserver01 host due to the failure of vcpserver02. Refer to figure 15.26.

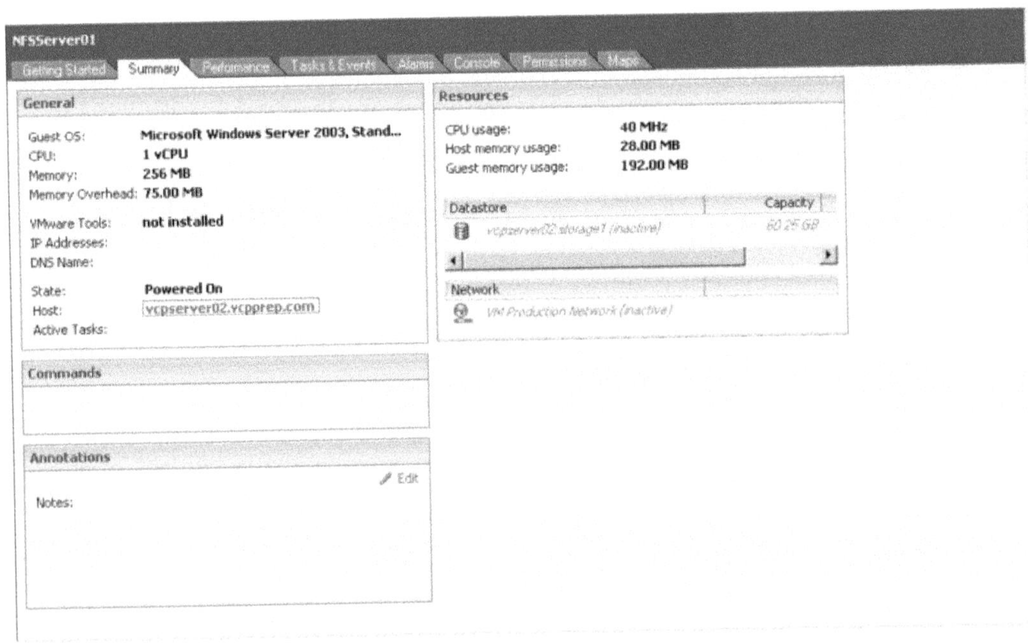

Figure 15.27 Virtual Machine Summary Tab

But what happened to the NFSServer01 virtual machine? It was not automatically restarted on the vcpserver01 host. We begin to investigate by selecting the NFSServer01 virtual machine from the VirtualCenter inventory and clicking the Summary tab as shown in Figure 15.27. The Datastore section displays that this virtual machine is located on the vcpserver02:storage1 datastore. This is the local SCSI drive of the vcpserver02 host. Since this datastore is not accessible by the vcpserver01 host, HA was not able to restart this virtual machine on this host. All ESX hosts participating in an HA cluster need to be able to access the shared storage where the virtual machine configuration and state files reside. If not, as we've seen in this example, HA will not restart the virtual machines.

Configuring High Availability

The default values available during the initial HA cluster creation wizard may be acceptable. If at a later time, changes to the HA cluster are needed, the cluster can be modified using the following steps.

Step 1. Right click on the HA cluster object as shown in Figure 15.28 and select the Edit Settings... menu option.

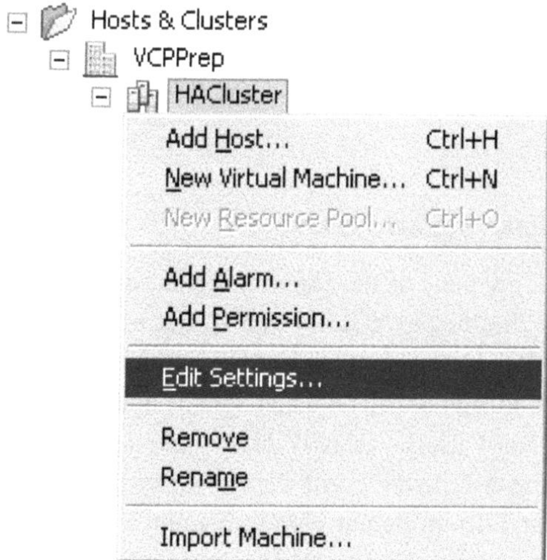

Figure 15.28 Edit Settings Menu Option

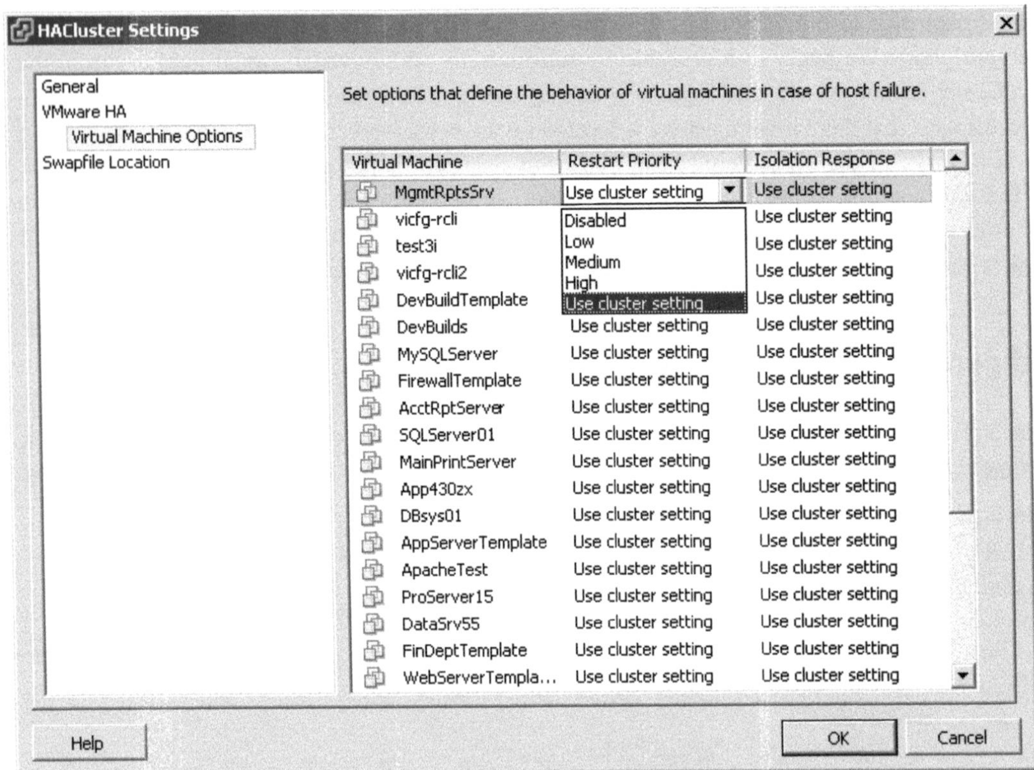

Figure 15.29 HA Cluster Settings Virtual Machine Options Restart Priority

Step 2. Select the Virtual Machine Options in the left window pane of the HA Cluster Settings dialog box as shown in Figure 15.29. As mentioned previously, the restart priority can be set to different options. The value selected during the initial creation of the HA cluster can be used by choosing the Use cluster setting option in the drop down box as shown in Figure 15.29. Each virtual machine can have its own individual restart priority setting. This is very useful as it is often necessary to be selective as to which virtual machines are restarted during a failover event due to limited resource capacity within the cluster. For example, if there are test and development virtual machines, these are often set at a the Low priority setting or even set to the Disabled setting so that the production virtual machines will have more physical resources available to them. Setting Low or Disabled restart priorities is also useful when there is redundancy in server functionality, for example with primary and secondary domain controllers or DNS servers that have anti-affinity rules set through DRS.

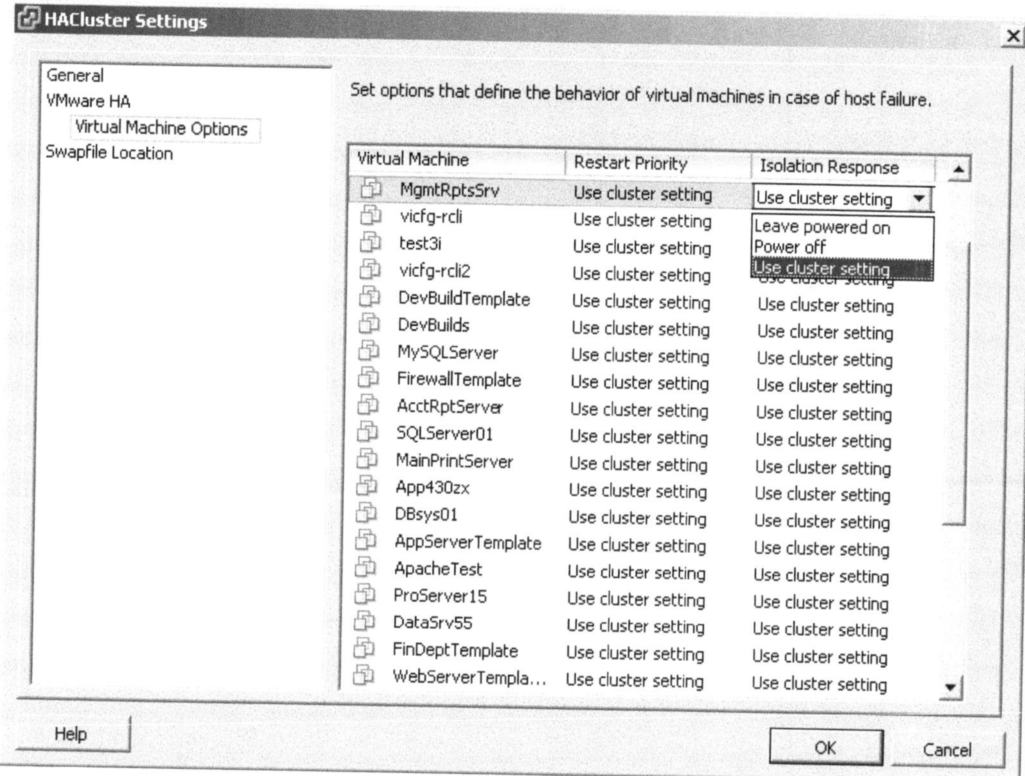

Figure 15.30 HA Cluster Settings Virtual Machine Options Isolation Response

Step 3. The Isolation Response value can also be set per VM. Refer to figure 15.30. This value is used when an ESX host within the HA cluster can no longer receive heartbeat messages through its service console. The default isolation response is to power off the virtual machines. Before the virtual machines start to power off, the isolated host will attempt to ping its default gateway for fifteen seconds. If still unable to successfully ping, the virtual machines power off. Virtual machines that do not use the same physical uplink port as the service console may still be actively servicing users. Consider changing the isolation response to leave powered on. If however, a virtual machine's configuration and state files are stored on, for example, an iSCSI datastore and the ESX server is configured to use the iSCSI software initiator, consider powering off these virtual machines if the service console loses network connectivity since the service console is needed to access this type of storage.

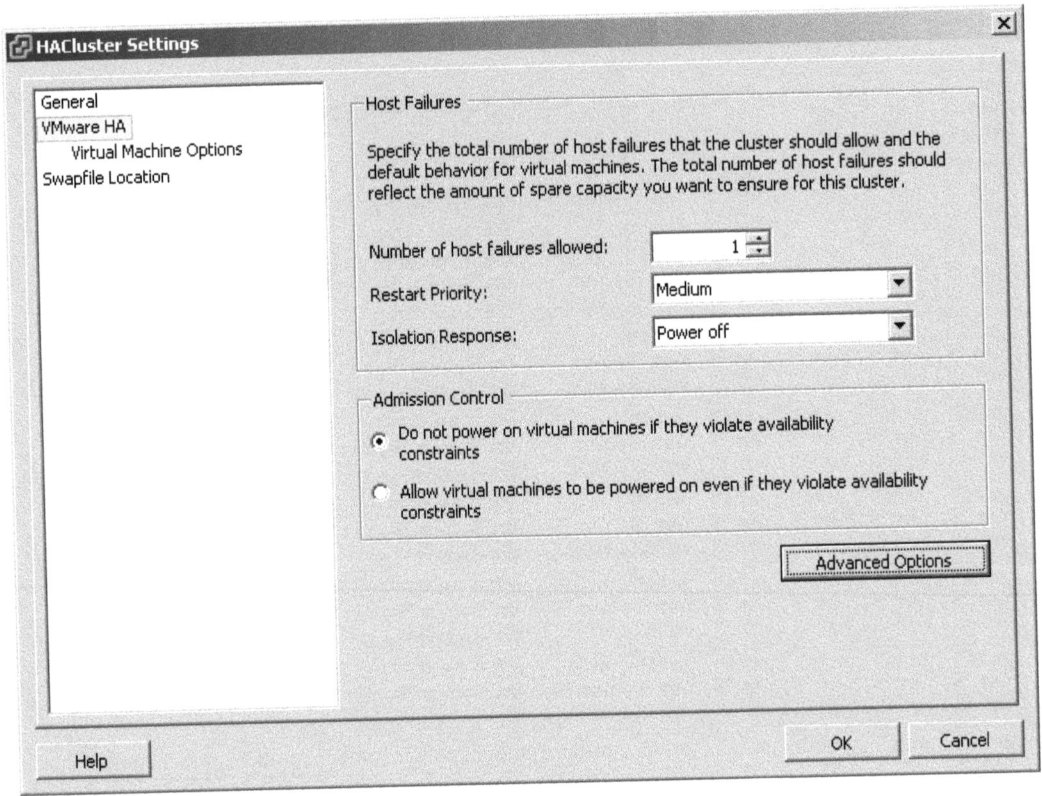

Figure 15.31 HA Cluster Settings Advanced Options Button

Step 4. Select the VMware HA option in the upper left window pane. Refer to Figure 15.31.The number of hosts failures allowed should be set according to the spare resource capacity of the ESX hosts in the cluster. The values for the restart priority and isolation response entered here set the default for all virtual machines in the cluster. As previously mentioned, the Admission Control section allows an administrator to set whether or not admission control is enabled or disabled for the cluster.

The Advanced Options button can be used to modify some of the HA cluster's default behavior. For example, to modify the failure detection time that is used to determine when to begin the isolation response settings for each virtual machine to a value of one minute, click on the Advanced Options button and enter the following attribute / value pair:

das.failuredetectiontime = 60000

The value is set in milliseconds.

If the service console's default gateway is set to not respond to ICMP requests, the address that is used to ping can also be modified using the Advanced button. For example, to set this value to 10.0.1.150, enter the following attribute / value pair:

das.isolationaddress = 10.0.1.150

The Advanced button can also be used to implement VMware's experimental support for virtual machine failure monitoring. This is a new capability with VirtualCenter 2.5. Virtual machines configured with VMware tools can be monitored within an HA cluster. If the virtual machine fails, it can be restarted. The attribute / value pairs that are used for virtual machine failure monitoring are shown in Figure 15.32.

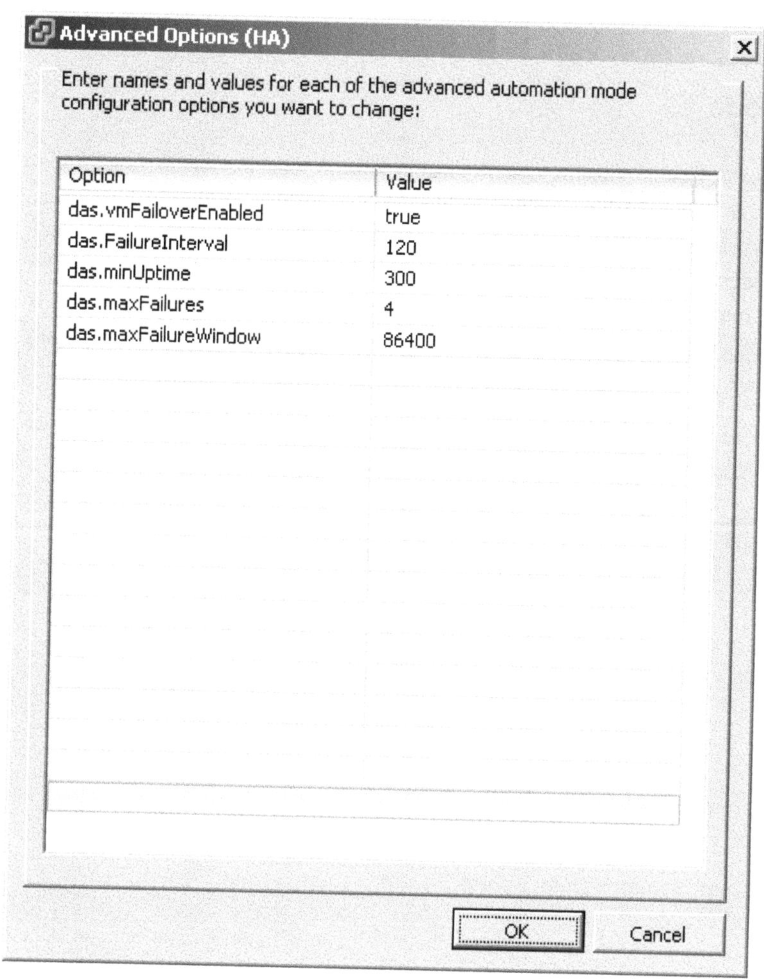

Figure 15.32 HA Cluster Settings Advanced Options

- das.vmFailoverEnabled - When set to true, the entire cluster is enabled for virtual machine failure monitoring.
- das.FailureInterval - Sets the number of seconds before a virtual machine is considered failed when no heartbeat is received.
- das.minUptime Integer - Identifies the number of seconds once a virtual machine has been started to allow its heartbeats to become stable.
- das.maxFailures Integer - Total number of failures and restarts allowed within the time specified by maxFailureWindow.
- das.maxFailureWindow Integer - Number of seconds based on das.maxFailures before

automatic responses stop..

Refer to the VMware Virtual Machine Failure Monitoring at the following location:

http://www.vmware.com/pdf/vi3_35_25_vmha.pdf

ESX Server Standby Mode

An ESX server within an HA cluster that is entering standby mode will not cause a HA failover event to occur. Virtual machines actively running on a host that is placed into standby mode must be either VMotioned to another host, suspended or manually powered off. The host will wait to fully enter standby mode until all virtual machines are no longer powered on. While it is waiting, it will not be possible to power on any virtual machines currently hosted on this ESX server. However, if while it is waiting to fully enter standby mode, another ESX host in the HA cluster fails, virtual machines from the failed host can be restarted on the ESX host that is currently waiting to fully enter standby mode.

To place an ESX host in standby mode, choose the ESX host, select the Summary tab and click on the Enter Standby Mode in the Commands section as shown in Figure 15.33.

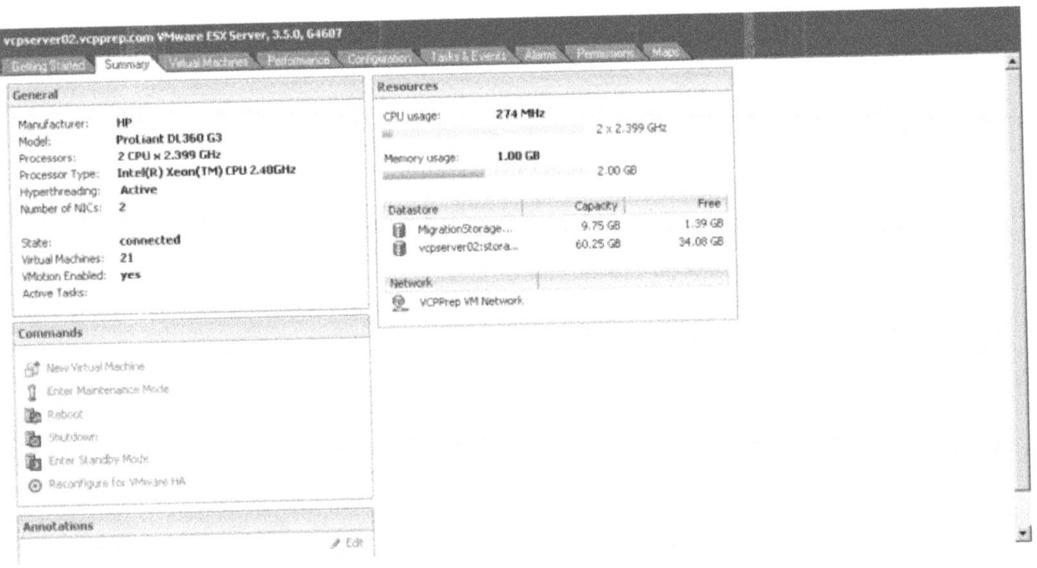

Figure 15.33 ESX Server Summary Tab Enter Standby Mode

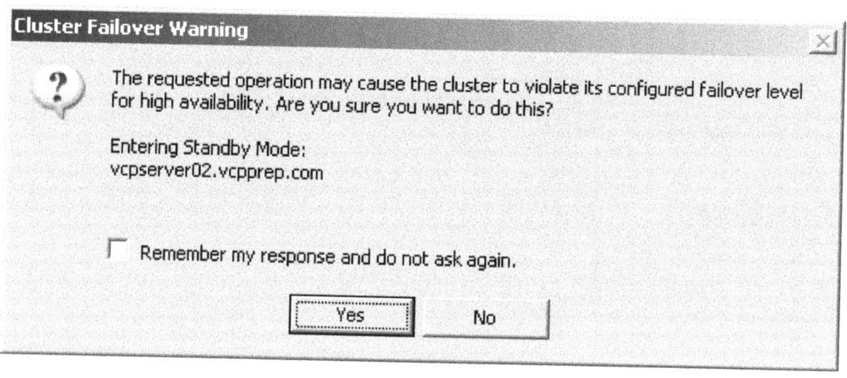

Figure 15.34 Cluster Failover Warning Dialog Box

The Cluster Failover Warning dialog box will be displayed as shown in Figure 15.34. Select the Yes button to continue.

The Confirm Standby dialog box is displayed next as shown in Figure 15.35. As this dialog box states, an ESX host in standby mode is considered a powered off host. The host must support the Wake-on-LAN technology. This can be verified by viewing the host's network adapters from the Configuration tab. Select the Yes button to continue.

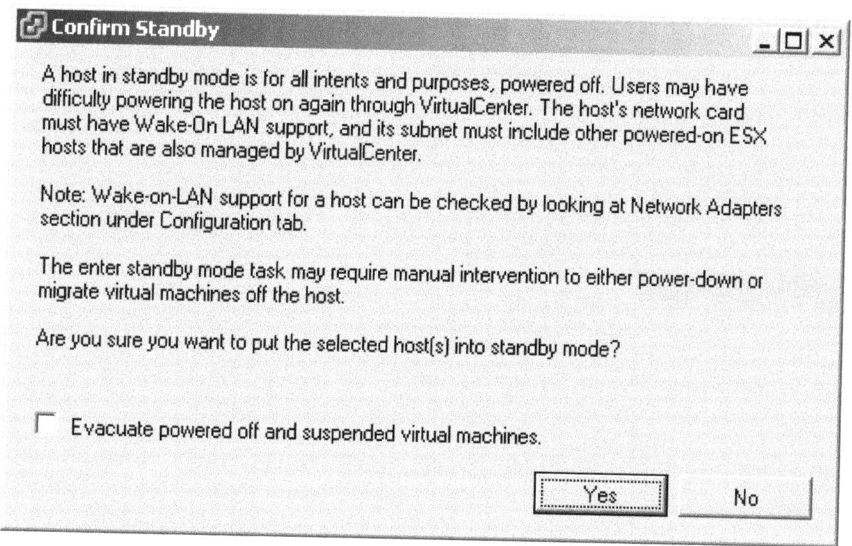

Figure 15.35 Confirm Standby Dialog Box

The Warning dialog box shown in Figure 15.36 informs that the host be placed into standby mode has actively running virtual machines. These machines will need to be VMotioned to another host, suspended or manually powered off before the host can fully enter standby mode. Click the OK button to continue.

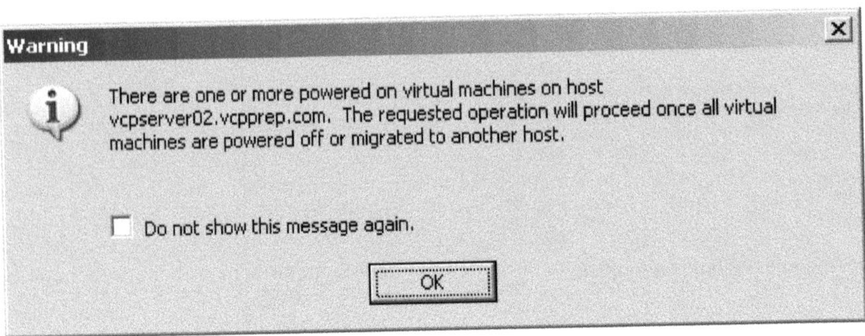

Figure 15.36 Warning Dialog Box

The VI Client displays the (standby mode) text next to the ESX host in the VirtualCenter inventory once the host has fully entered standby mode. To exit standby mode, right click on the host and select the Power On menu option as shown in Figure 15.37.

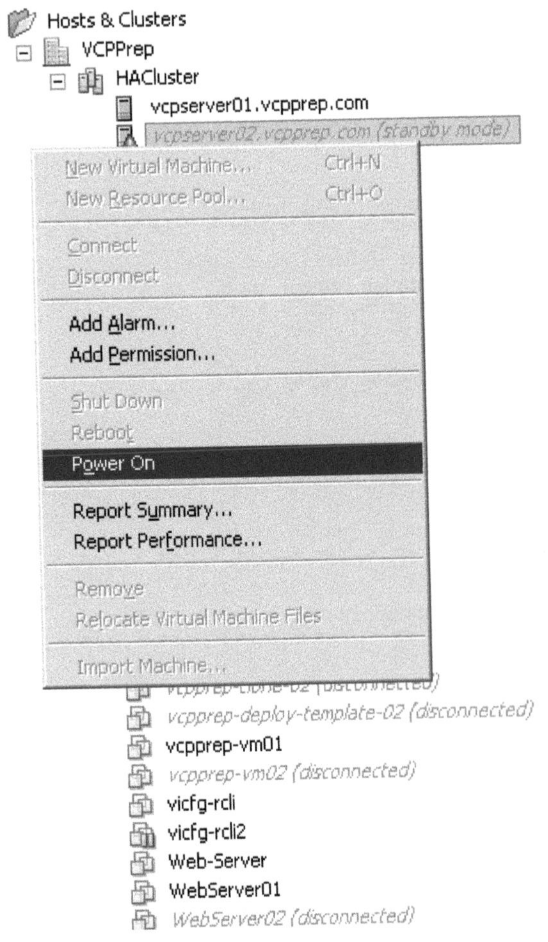

Figure 15.37 Power On Menu Option

NOTE: If there isn't another ESX host that is currently powered on, the host in standby mode will display the following error "Failed to find a peer host to wake up this host". As a result, the host will remain in standby mode (this situation could occur if there was another host available at the time a host was placed in standby mode, but that host is no longer available when attempting to take the host out of standby mode.) Once a host is fully in standby mode and it is then powered off, it does not remain in standby mode once it has been powered back on. This behavior is different than maintenance mode as the host remains in maintenance mode even if its power has been cycled.

Using Microsoft Clustering Service in Your Virtual Infrastructure

Microsoft Clustering Service (MSCS) is supported with ESX 3.5 hosts running VMware ESX 3.5 Update 1. This update is located at the following location: http://www.vmware.com/download/vi/

The following are the three different supported MSCS cluster configurations:

- Cluster In a Box (CIB) - In this cluster configuration, each of the clustered virtual machines are located on the same ESX host.
- Cluster Across Boxes (CAB) - In this cluster configuration, each of the clustered virtual machines are located on a different ESX host.
- Physical to Virtual Clusters - In this cluster configuration, a virtual machine on an ESX host is clustered with a physical server.

VMware supports each of the three cluster types in two-node configurations. The three cluster types require that each of the two virtual machines in the MSCS cluster be configured with two virtual NICs. One virtual NIC is used as the public network and the other is for the private communications between the two virtual machines. It is an unsupported configuration to have these virtual NICs attached to a virtual switch that is configured as a NIC team.

Each virtual machine in the cluster needs to have a total of three virtual disks. One of these virtual disks will be private to the virtual machine as it will be its C: drive. The other two virtual disks are shared among the two clustered virtual machines. One of these virtual disks is used as the quorum disk (logging) and the other is used as the data disk.

With CIB clusters, all of the virtual disks can be local on the same ESX host. In a CAB cluster, the two shared disks are required to be on a shared datastore and accessed via RDMs either in virtual or physical compatibility mode. A physical to virtual cluster also requires the two shared disks to be on a shared datastore and accessed only via a RDM in physical compatibility mode. In all three MSCS Cluster Configurations, it is also required that each cluster VM node's system disk (C:drive the guest is utilizing) use local storage only, as it was found that SAN failures were causing guest failures if all virtual disks were on shared storage.

Troubleshooting Common High Availability Problems

A common problem with HA clusters is mis-configurations in name resolution. Inconsistencies with DNS servers can be reviewed from the service console by issuing the nslookup command. The output of this command in our example environment is as follows:

[root@vcpserver01 root]# nslookup vcpserver02

Server: 10.0.2.200

Address: 10.0.2.200#53

Name: vcpserver02.vcppprep.com

Address: 10.0.1.102

Consult the network administrator to resolve any name resolution errors.

The following files should be reviewed and verified to be correct. These files can be used when the DNS server is unavailable.

FT_HOSTS

[root@vcpserver01 root]# cat /etc/FT_HOSTS

Auto-generated FT_HOSTS file. Timestamp: Fri May 23 22:18:55 2008

10.0.1.100 vcpserver01

10.0.2.200 vcpserver02

The FT_HOSTS file is created when the ESX host is added to the HA cluster.

resolv.conf

[root@vcpserver01 root]# cat /etc/resolv.conf

search vcpprep.com

nameserver 10.0.2.200

nameserver 10.0.3.210

/etc/hosts

[root@vcpserver01 root]# cat /etc/hosts

Do not remove the following line, or various programs

that require network functionality will fail.

127.0.0.1 localhost.localdomain localhost

10.0.1.100 vcpserver01.vcpprep.com vcpserver01

10.0.2.200 vcpserver02.vcpprep.com vcpserver02

10.0.1.2 vcserver01.vcpprep.com vcserver01

Note: It is a good practice to include an entry for all ESX hosts as well as the VirtualCenter server in the hosts file. The log files for each host in the cluster are located in the following location:

/var/log/vmware/aam/

External References

VMware Virtual Machine Failure Monitoring documentation:

http://www.vmware.com/pdf/vi3_35_25_vmha.pdf

VMware ESX 3.5 Update 1 is located at the following location:

http://www.vmware.com/download/vi/

The VMware ESX 3.5 and ESXi Server version 3.5 Documentation Page:

http://www.vmware.com/support/pubs/vi_pubs.html

Sample Test Questions

1. An HA cluster is populated with fourteen ESX blade server hosts. The cluster settings have been configured to allow four hosts failures. In this configuration, how many primary HA servers will there be?

a. 4

b. 14

c. 6

d. 5

e. 1

2. Which of the following can be set for the isolation response option of an HA cluster?

a. Leave Powered On

b. Power Off

c. Disabled

d. Suspend

e. Snapshot

3. An ESX administrator creates a cluster of virtual machines using MSCS in a cluster across boxes (CAB) configuration. What is the maximum number of virtual machines that can be clustered together in this configuration?

a. 5

b. 6

c. 2

d. 3

e. 4

4. An ESX administrator is unable to successfully add an ESX host to an HA cluster. Which of the following is required to successfully add a host to an HA cluster?

a. VirtualCenter administrator username

b. VirtualCenter administrator password

c. ESX service console root username

d. ESX service console root password

e. ESX serial number

5. For ESX hosts placed into an HA cluster, which of the following is a good practice to perform concerning host configuration?

a. Creating two VMkernel ports on each host in the HA cluster

b. Populating the /etc/hosts with name resolution for each ESX host in the cluster

c. Setting the "Number of failures allowed" option to five

d. Creating two service console ports on each host in the HA cluster

e. Verifying that the /etc/resolv.conf file is correctly populated

Sample Test Solutions

1. An HA cluster is populated with fourteen ESX blade server hosts. The cluster settings have been configured to allow four hosts failures. In this configuration, how many primary HA servers will there be?

a. 4

b. 14

c. 6

d. 5

e. 1

Answer: d - The HA cluster setting "Number of failures allowed" in this cluster was set to four. There are a total of fourteen ESX hosts in this cluster. The total primary HA hosts is always one more than the value set for the "Number of failures allowed" option. Therefore, the first five ESX hosts added to the cluster will be primary HA servers within this cluster. If the blade chassis in this example is serviced by two separate power sources, it would be good practice to populate the HA cluster by alternating the ESX host blade servers so that the first five do not all have the same power source.

2. Which of the following can be set for the isolation response option of an HA cluster?

a. Leave Powered On

b. Power Off

c. Disabled

d. Suspend

e. Snapshot

Answer: a and b - The isolation response value can be set per VM in the HA cluster. This value is used when an ESX host within the HA cluster can no longer receive heartbeat messages through its service console. The default isolation response is to power off the virtual machines. If virtual machine operations are unaffected by failure of the service console port, consider setting the isolation response for these virtual machines to leave powered on.

3. An ESX administrator creates a cluster of virtual machines using MSCS in a cluster across boxes (CAB) configuration. What is the maximum number of virtual machines that can be clustered together in this configuration?

a. 5

b. 6

c. 2

d. 3

e. 4

Answer: c - VMware supports each of the following three cluster types in two-node configurations:

- ***Cluster In a Box (CIB)***
- ***Cluster Across Boxes (CAB)***
- ***Physical to Virtual Clusters***

4. An ESX administrator is unable to successfully add an ESX host to an HA cluster. Which of the following is required to successfully add a host to an HA cluster?

a. VirtualCenter administrator username

b. VirtualCenter administrator password

c. ESX service console root username

d. ESX service console root password

e. ESX serial number

Answer: c and d - To successfully add the ESX host to the HA cluster, the service console's root username and password are required. The authorization credentials are case-sensitive.

5. For ESX hosts placed into an HA cluster, which of the following is a good practice to perform concerning host configuration?

a. Creating two VMkernel ports on each host in the HA cluster

b. Populating the /etc/hosts with name resolution for each ESX host in the cluster

c. Setting the "Number of failures allowed" option to five

d. Creating two service console ports on each host in the HA cluster

e. Verifying that the /etc/resolv.conf file is correctly populated

Answer: b, d and e - It is a good practice to include an entry for all ESX hosts as well as the VirtualCenter server in the hosts file in case of DNS server failure. Redundant networking between ESX hosts is a best practice and can be accomplished either by creating two service console ports or by the use of NIC teaming. The HA agent communicates with other HA agents via the service console port to coordinate the active and passive nodes. A common problem with HA clusters is mis-configurations in name resolution. The /etc/resolv.conf file is used to correctly identify the domain and DNS servers for the ESX host.

Chapter 16

Monitoring and Alerting

After reading this chapter you should be able to complete the following tasks:

- Configuring the VirtualCenter collection intervals
- Using performance charts
- Creating alarms
- Monitoring alarms
- Using the esxtop command
- Troubleshooting performance and alarm issues

Fixing problems is often easy. Finding the root cause of the problem is usually more time consuming and difficult. Third party tools can be used such as Iometer and Wireshark to assist in analysis and troubleshooting. These tools can be located at the following URLs:

Iometer:

http://www.iometer.org

Wireshark:

http://www.wireshark.org

At the ESX host level, an ESX administrator can use command line based tools to monitor various metrics. ESX hosts also offer numerous log files that can be reviewed when troubleshooting performance issues. VirtualCenter provides very useful information when diagnosing resource consumption issues. Using the VI Client allows an ESX administrator to quickly analyze ESX host and virtual machine CPU, memory, network I/O and disk I/O. Lets take a look at how to configure VirtualCenter's ability to collect statistical information.

Configuring the VirtualCenter Collection Intervals

VirtualCenter offers several collection interval and statistics level settings that can be modified as needed. These values can be changed using the following procedure:

File Edit View Inventory Administration Plugins Help
Custom Attributes...
VirtualCenter Management Server Configuration...
Role
Session
Edit Message of the Day
Export Diagnostic Data...
Consolidation Settings...
Inventory
Scheduled
Hosts & Clusters
VCPPrep
VCPTest

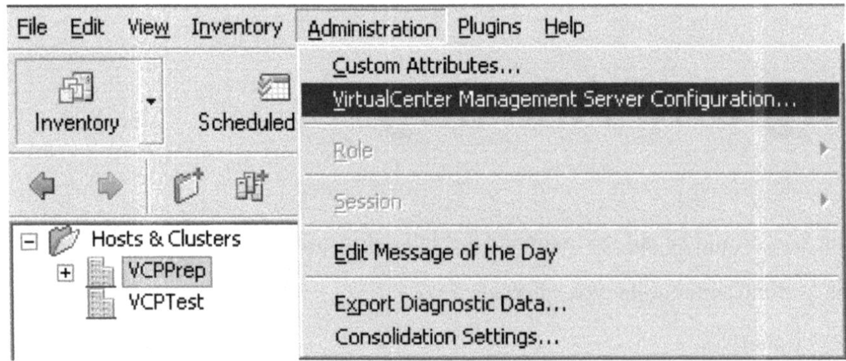

Figure 16.1 VirtualCenter Management Server Configuration

Step 1. Select the Administration menu option and click on the VirtualCenter Management Server Configuration... menu option as shown in Figure 16.1.

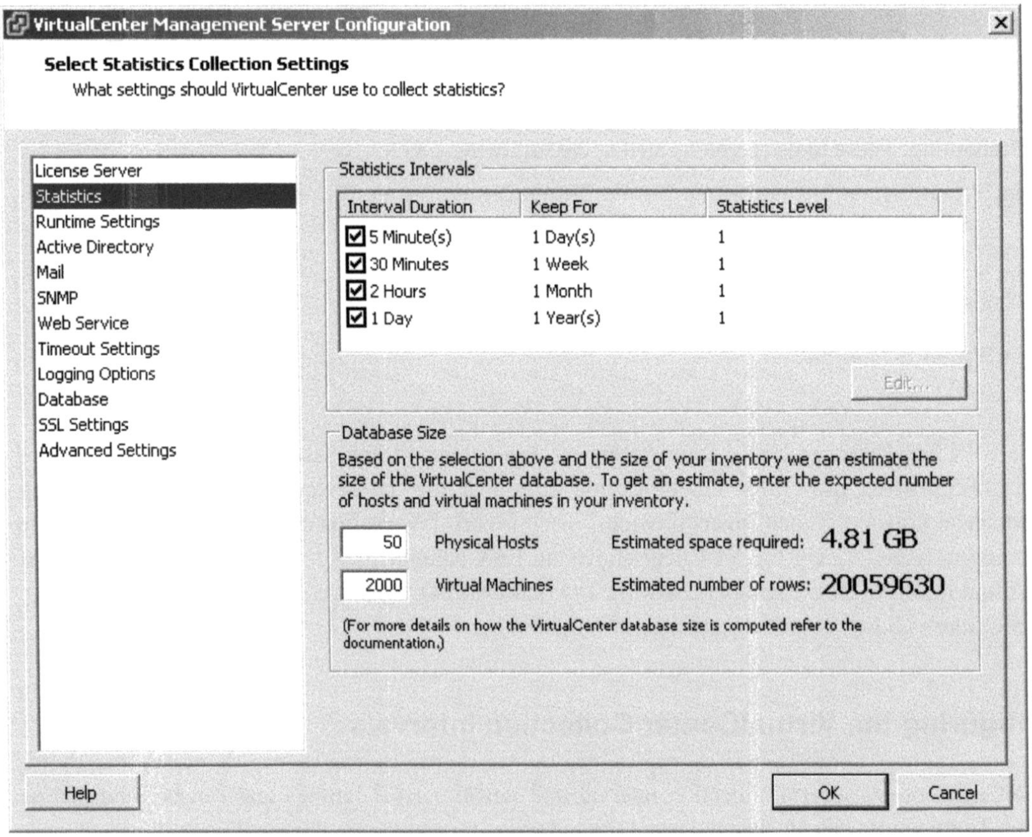

VirtualCenter Management Server Configuration
Select Statistics Collection Settings
What settings should VirtualCenter use to collect statistics?
License Server
Statistics
Runtime Settings
Active Directory
Mail
SNMP
Web Service
Timeout Settings
Logging Options
Database
SSL Settings
Advanced Settings
Statistics Intervals
Interval Duration
Keep For
Statistics Level
5 Minute(s)
1 Day(s)
1
30 Minutes
1 Week
1
2 Hours
1 Month
1
1 Day
1 Year(s)
1
Edit...
Database Size
Based on the selection above and the size of your inventory we can estimate the size of the VirtualCenter database. To get an estimate, enter the expected number of hosts and virtual machines in your inventory.
50
Physical Hosts
Estimated space required: 4.81 GB
2000
Virtual Machines
Estimated number of rows: 20059630
(For more details on how the VirtualCenter database size is computed refer to the documentation.)
Help
OK
Cancel

Figure 16.2 VirtualCenter Management Server Configuration Dialog Box

Step 2. The VirtualCenter Management Server Configuration dialog box is launched as shown in Figure 16.2. The left hand window pane contains twelve options that allow various VirtualCenter functionality to be modified. Select the Statistics option. The bottom right window pane provides a database size tool. By entering the number of ESX hosts and virtual machines configured in the VirtualCenter inventory, an estimated value for the number of rows and size of the database needed by VirtualCenter can be obtained. The right upper window pane contains the Statistics Intervals section. The four interval durations that can be set are:

- 5 Minute(s)
- 30 Minutes
- 2 Hours
- 1 Day

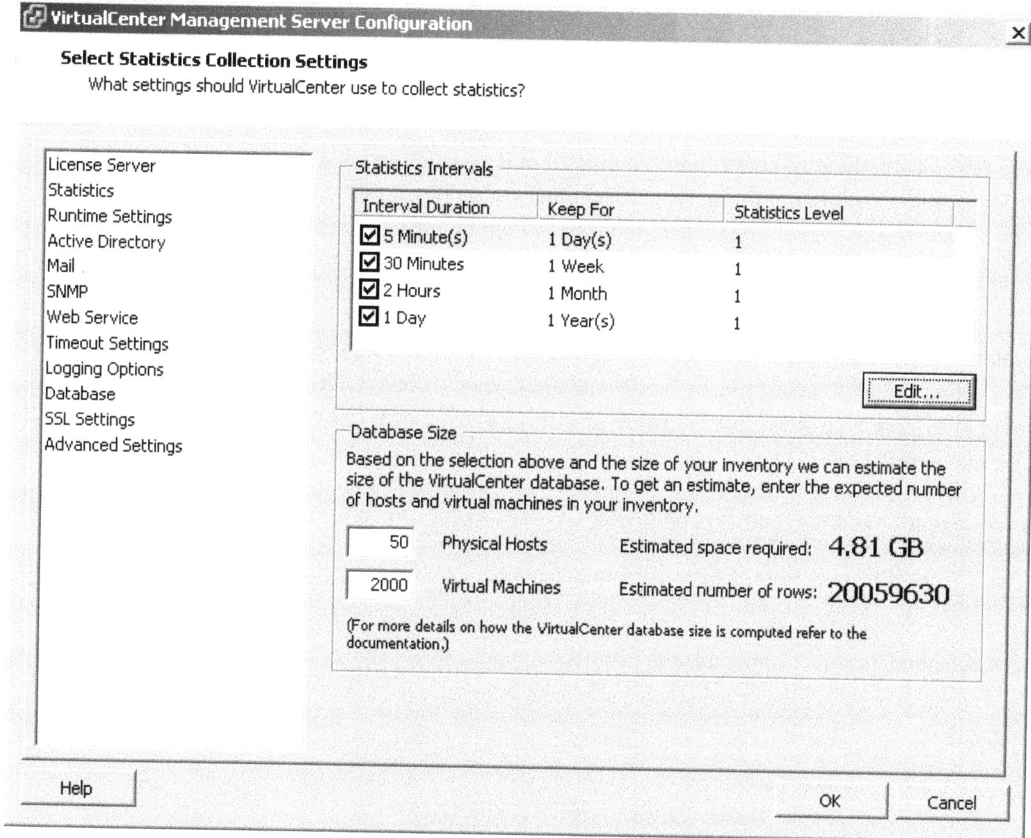

Figure 16.3 VirtualCenter Management Server Configuration

Step 3. A check box next to the interval duration identifies it as being enabled. A interval duration can be disabled by removing the check in the check box. Note that longer durations automatically include shorter duration intervals. In other words, if all intervals are disabled and a check is placed in the 2 Hours interval duration, both the 5 and 30 minutes interval durations will automatically be enabled while the 1 Day interval duration will be left disabled. To modify one of these, select the interval duration and select the Edit button as shown in Figure 16.3.

Step 4. The Edit Statistics Interval dialog box is displayed as shown in Figure 16.4. Selecting the Statistics Interval drop down box allows the values of 1,2,3 and 5 minutes to be set. Four minute interval is not an option. The values for the Keep Samples for drop down box are 1,2,3,4 and 5 days. The Statistics Level drop down box allows the following values to be set:

- Level 1 - General utilization information provides high level view. Average usage metrics are included in this level for CPU, memory, disk and network. Very little VirtualCenter and ESX resources used to collect level 1 information. This is the default level.
- Level 2 - Includes all information collected in level 1 and additional counters for CPU, memory, network and disk. Level 2 uses more VirtualCenter and ESX resources to collect information than it does to collect level 1 information. Monitoring more than ten ESX hosts can use a significant amount of resources on the VirtualCenter server.
- Level 3 - Includes all information collected in levels 1 and 2. Collects device based metrics. This level is useful in determining the usefulness of virtual SMP (Symmetric multiprocessing) for virtual machines configured with multiple virtual CPUs.
- Level 4 - Includes all information collected in levels 1,2, and 3. This level adds the additional maximum / minimum rollup types. The other rollup types are Summation, Average and Latest. Use this level to gain detailed information on virtual machine CPU usage or when diagnosing device performance problems. Operating a VirtualCenter server for several days at this level can quickly populate its database server.

Changes to the statistics level takes affect immediately however, changes will not appear until the next collection interval takes place. Some statistics levels don't collect every metric type. It is important to discern a collected metric value of 0 from a value of 0 due to no collection taking place at all for that metric type.

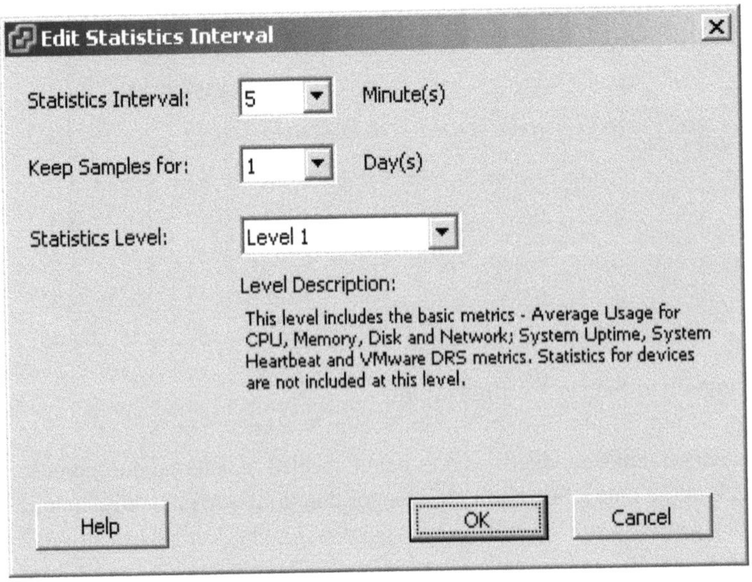

Figure 16.4 Edit Statistics Interval Dialog Box

Selecting the various collection levels provides information about what is collected for the selected level as shown in Figure 16.4. Make the appropriate changes and select the OK button to continue.

Step 4. VirtualCenter can be configured to send email alerts. Clicking on the Mail option in the left window pane will display the Mail section in the upper right window pane as shown in Figure 16.5. Enter the SNMP server and email account that will be used to identify who the email is from.

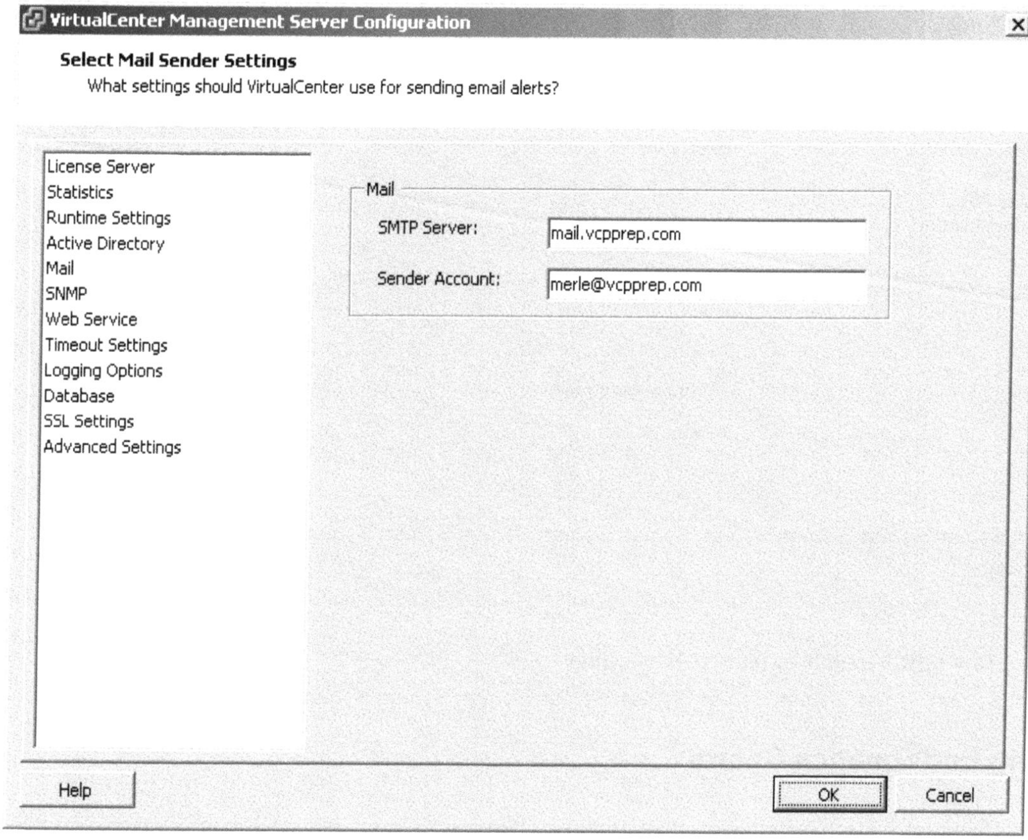

Figure 16.5 Edit VirtualCenter Mail Settings

Step 5. VirtualCenter can be configured to use the Simple Network Management Protocol (SNMP) to send messages. Clicking on the SNMP option in the left window pane will display the SNMP Receivers section in the upper right window pane as shown in Figure 16.6. Enter the host to send the SNMP traps to along with the port and community string to use. VirtualCenter uses SNMP version 1 for event alarm notifications. We will discuss VirtualCenter alarms later in this chapter.

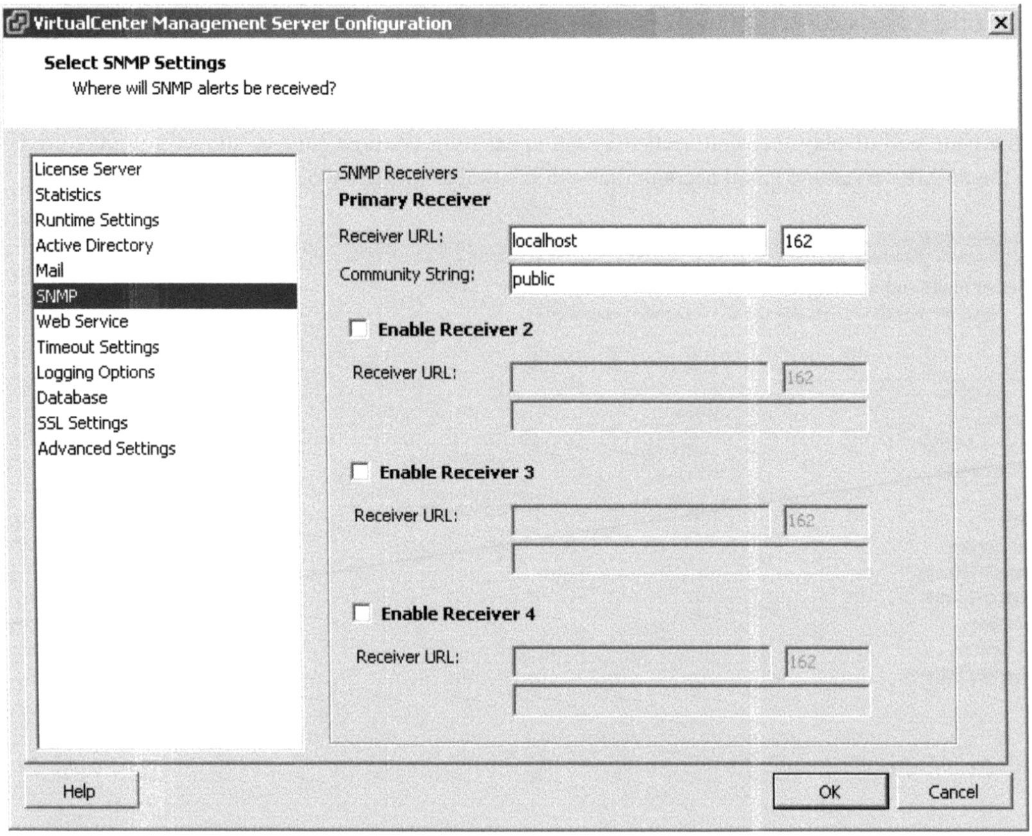

Figure 16.6 Edit VirtualCenter SNMP Settings

Using Performance Charts

VirtualCenter provides performance charts that can be used to view collected metric values of ESX hosts and virtual machines. Performance information for resource pools, DRS and HA clusters can also be viewed. In Figure 16.7, the DataSrv55 virtual machine was chosen from within the VirtualCenter inventory and the Performance tab was selected. The data in the chart is refreshed every twenty seconds. Performance charts can be printed, refreshed, exported in several different graphic formats or as an Microsoft Excel file using the icons in the upper right hand corner of the chart. The Switched to drop down box can be used to quickly change the metric type displayed. This drop down box is a new addition in VirtualCenter 2.5.

The legend is displayed at the bottom of the performance chart. The Key column identifies the color that is associated to a given metric. When clicked on, the corresponding charted data points are highlighted in the performance chart. Also listed in the legend is the object being monitored, the measured metric, units used, the latest, maximum, minimum and average values.

To view another metric type, click on the Change Chart Options... link in the upper left hand of the performance chart.

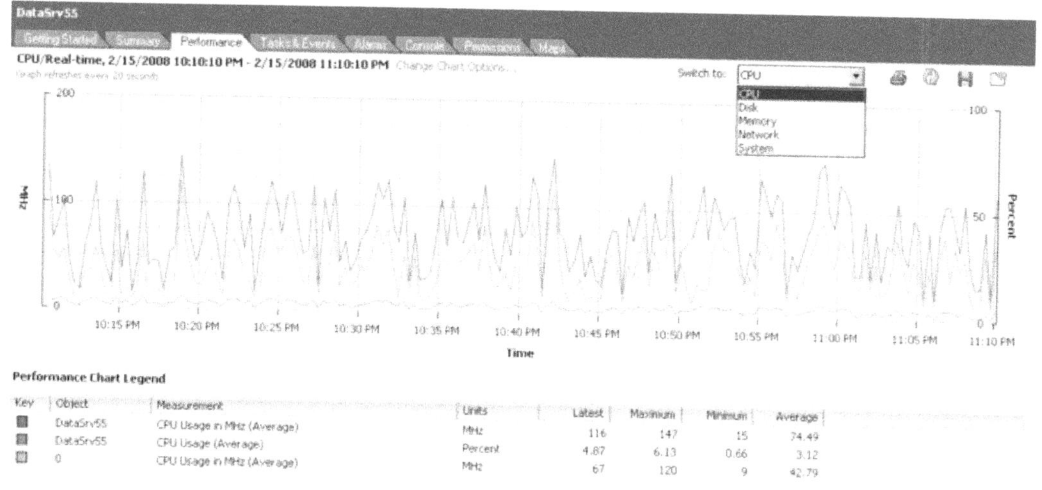

Figure 16.7 Performance Chart Switch To Drop Down Box

The Customize Performance Chart dialog box is launched as shown in Figure 16.8. The Chart Options section is used to modify the time frame for displaying data. The available metrics are for CPU, memory, network I/O, disk I/O and system. System allows an ESX administrator to monitor the number of VMware tools heartbeat and the uptime value of the virtual machine. Current data can be viewed by selecting the Real-Time option. Historical data points collected can be viewed for the past day, week, month and year. A custom time frame can be chosen by selecting the Custom... option. This will allow you to enter the desired time range. The Last and From radio boxes are used to set the custom option.

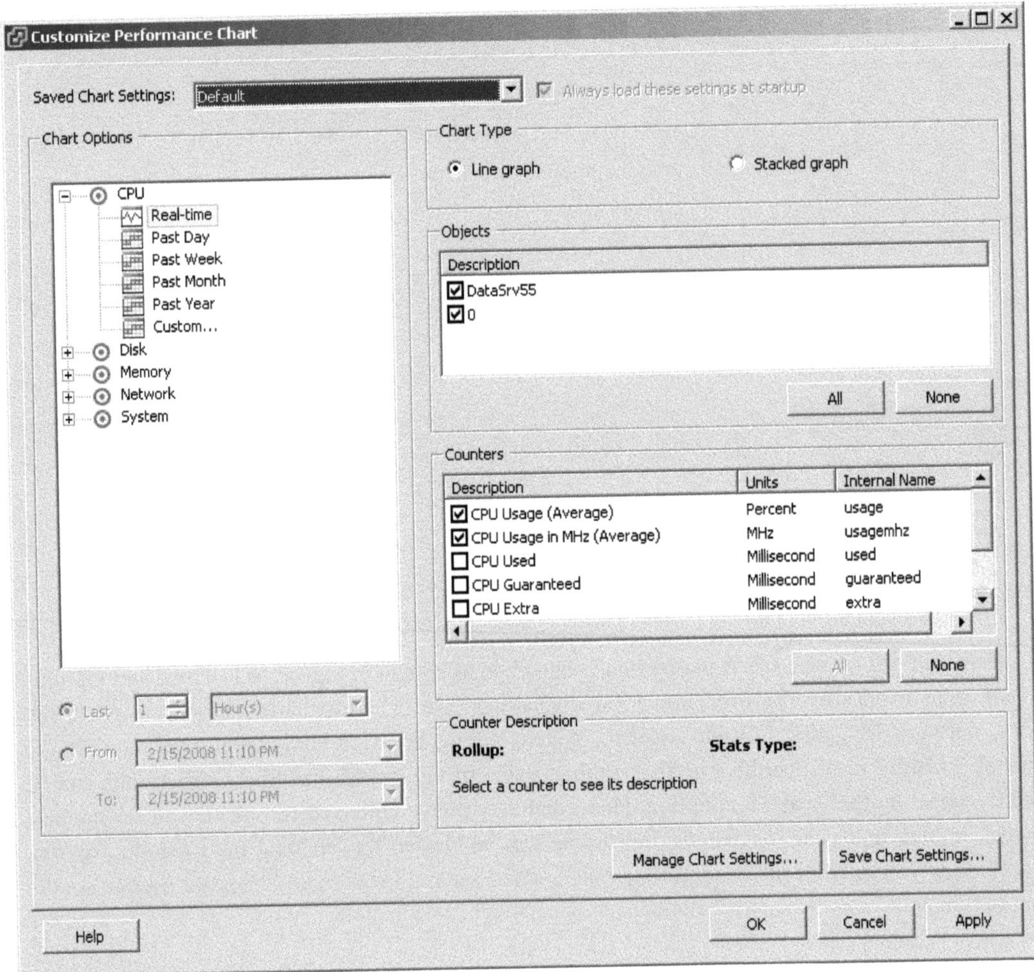

Figure 16.8 Customize Performance Chart Dialog Box

Selecting a time range for one of the metric types in the Chart Options section will make available the Chart Type section that can be used to choose between viewing a Line graph or a Stacked graph. This choice is essentially a personal preference. The Objects section can be used to select object to monitor on the performance chart. The Counters Section allows the various counters for the metric type to be chosen.

Any changes made in the Customize Performance Chart dialog box can be saved for as a custom chart. To save a custom chart, click the Save Chart Settings... button as shown in Figure 16.9.

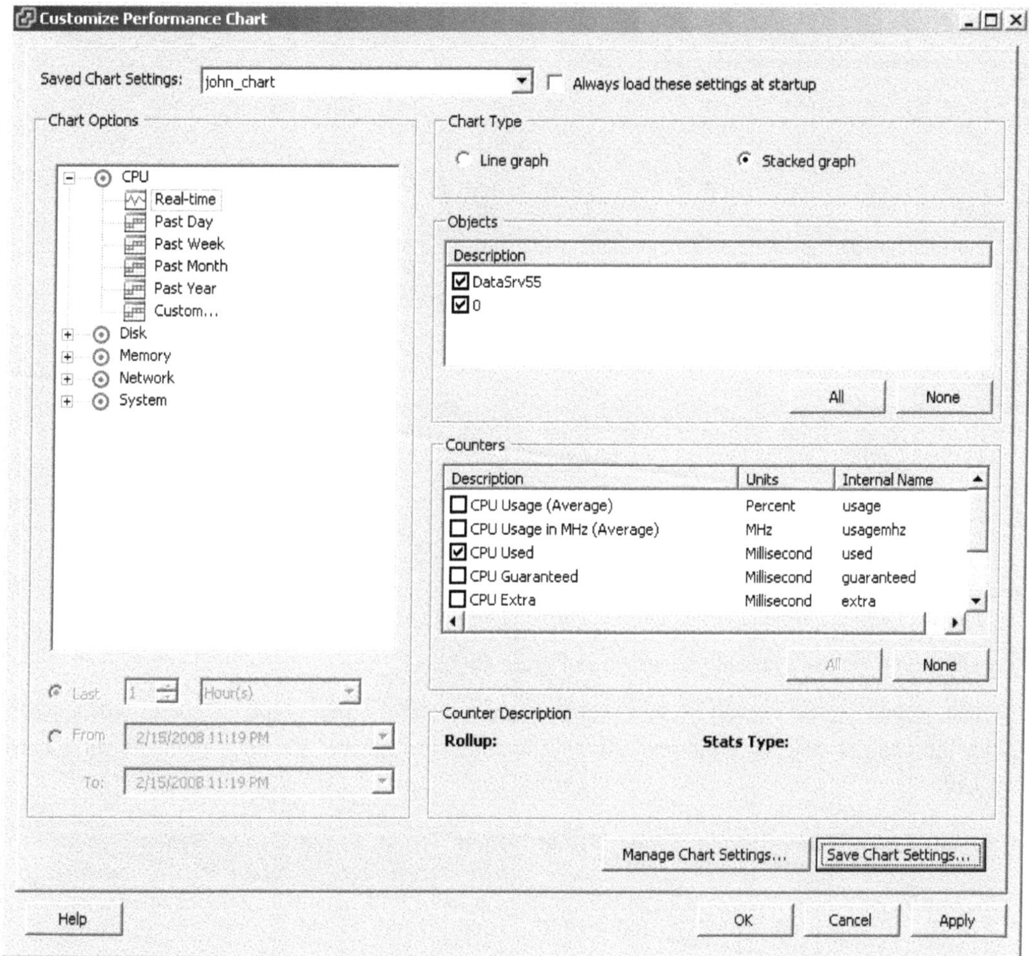

Figure 16.9 Customize Performance Chart Dialog Box Custom Chart

The Save Selection dialog box is displayed as shown in Figure 16.10. Enter a new chart name and click the OK button.

Save Selection
Save selected options
Enter a name for the selected settings: john_chart
OK Cancel

Figure 16.10 Save Selection Dialog Box

Figure 16.11 Custom Chart Selection

The new chart type is now available as shown in Figure 16.11.

Specific data points can be viewed by mousing over any part of the line graph. A popup will appear displaying the charted objects, their respective values and the time of the data point as shown in Figure 16.12.

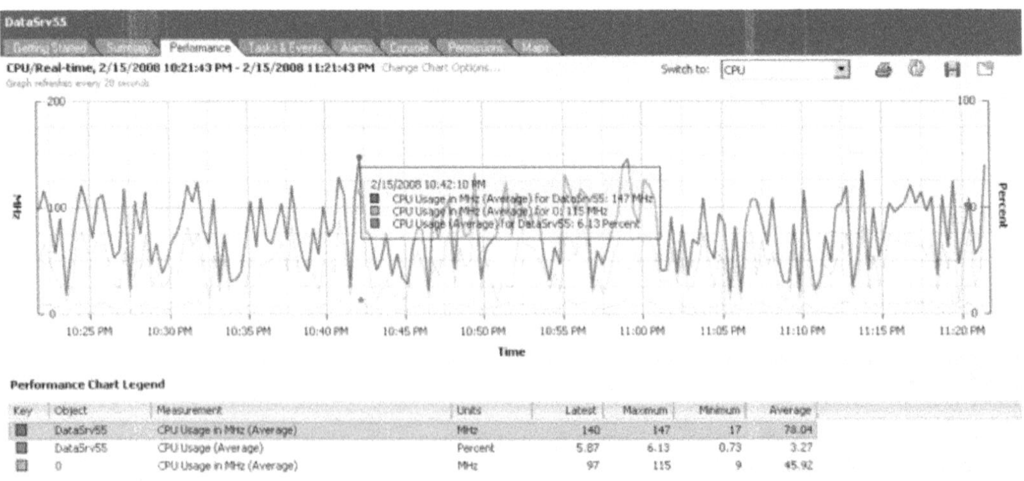

Figure 16.12 Popup of Specific Data Points

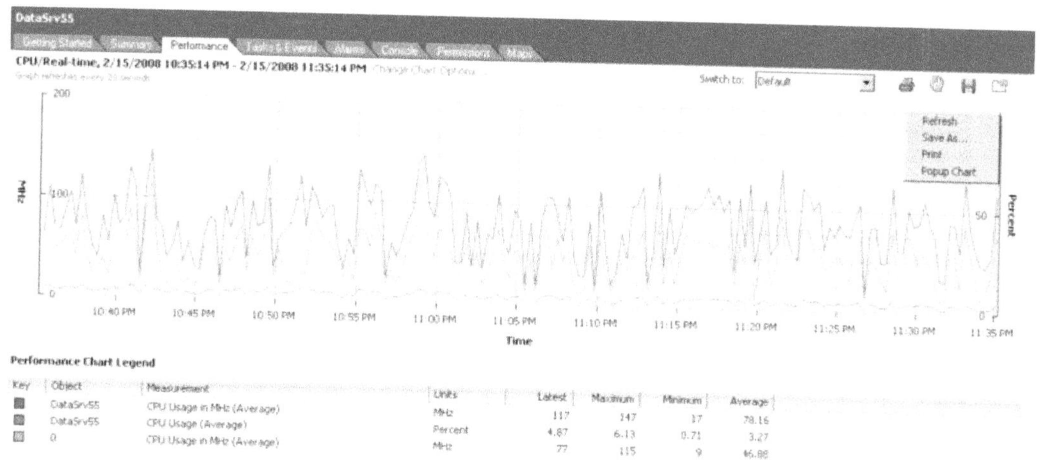

Figure 16.13 Performance Chart Right Click Menu

A shortcut menu is available by right clicking anywhere within the graph area as shown in Figure 16.13.

Creating Alarms

VirtualCenter can be configured to trigger alarms on objects in the inventory when a threshold has been crossed. Alarms can help an ESX administrator maintain acceptable performance levels on ESX hosts and virtual machines. It is often useful to set an alarm on a folder object as opposed to setting alarms on individual virtual machines for example. Let's take a look at how an alarm can be placed on an object in the VirtualCenter inventory.

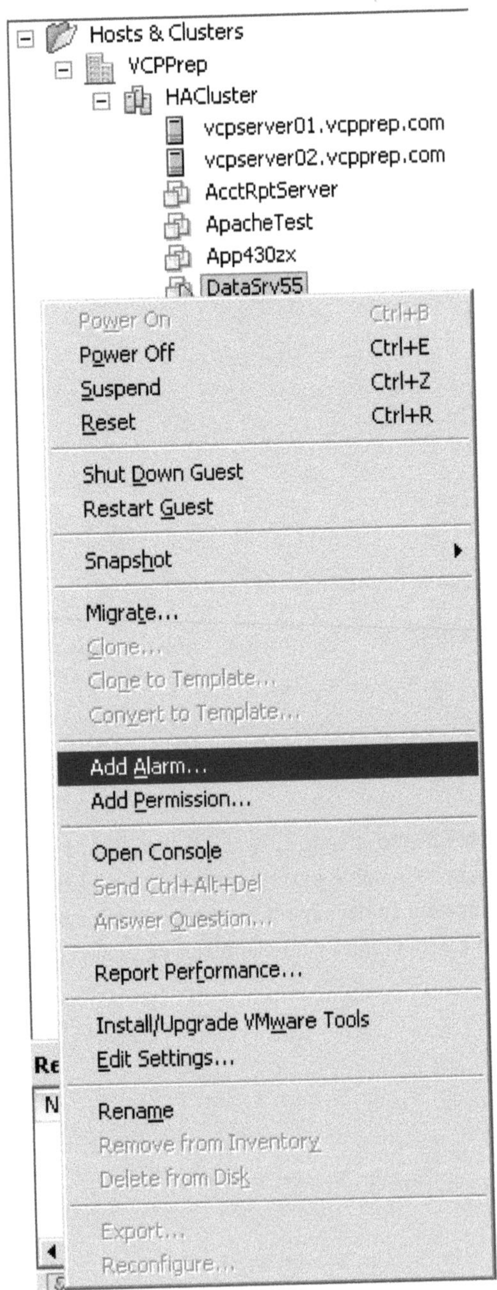

Figure 16.14 Add Alarm Menu Option

Step 1. To create a new alarm, chose the object, right click on it and select the Add Alarm... menu option as shown in Figure 16.14.

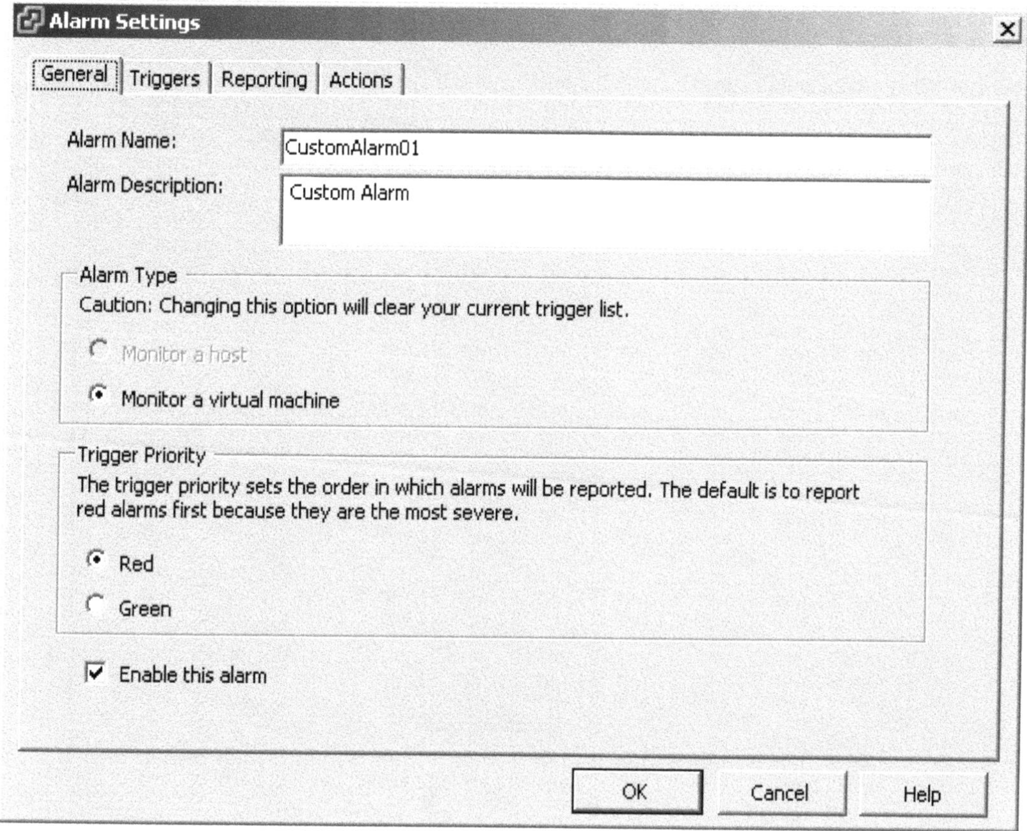

Figure 16.15 Alarm Settings Dialog Box

Step 2. The Alarm Settings dialog box is displayed as shown in Figure 16.15. Use the General tab to give the alarm a name and description. In this example, since we selected a virtual machine object to create an alarm for, we can see that Alarm Type section has the Monitor a virtual machine radio button selected. The Trigger Priority section can be set to either Red or Green. Red alarms are the default and are reported first due to indicating a more severe condition. An alarm can be disabled by removing the check in the check box next to the Enable this alarm option.

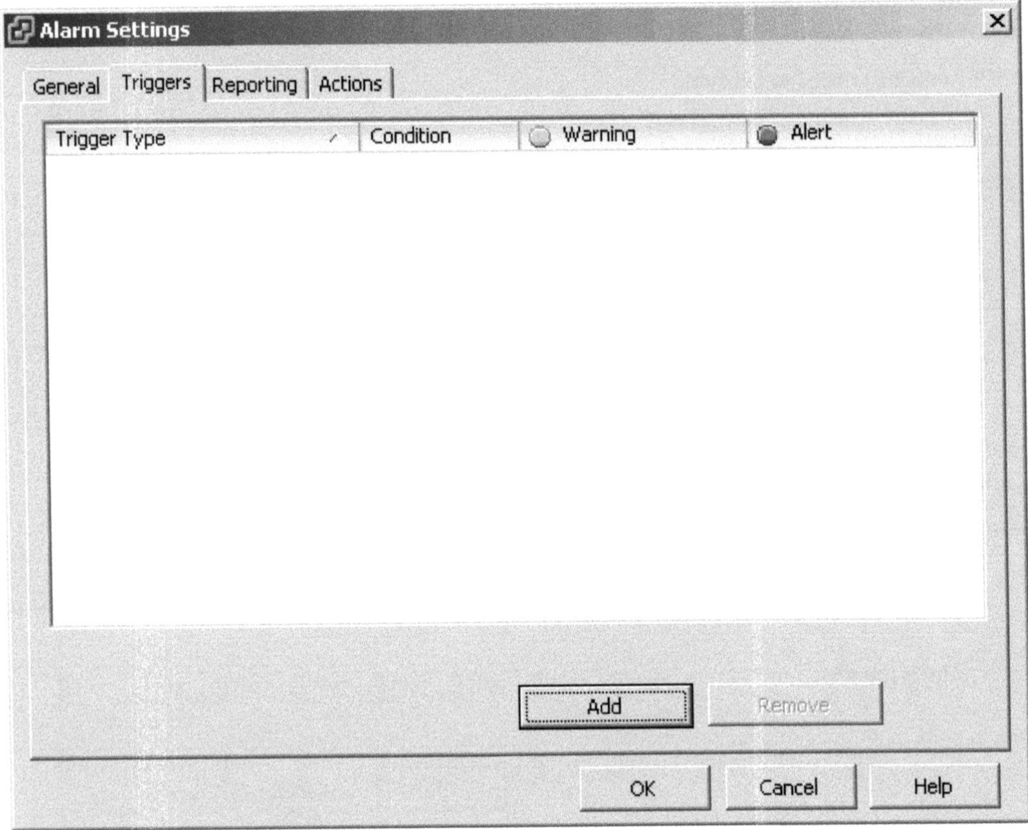

Figure 16.16 Alarm Settings Dialog Box Add Button

Step 3. Select the Triggers tab and click on the Add button as shown in Figure 16.16 to add a new trigger.

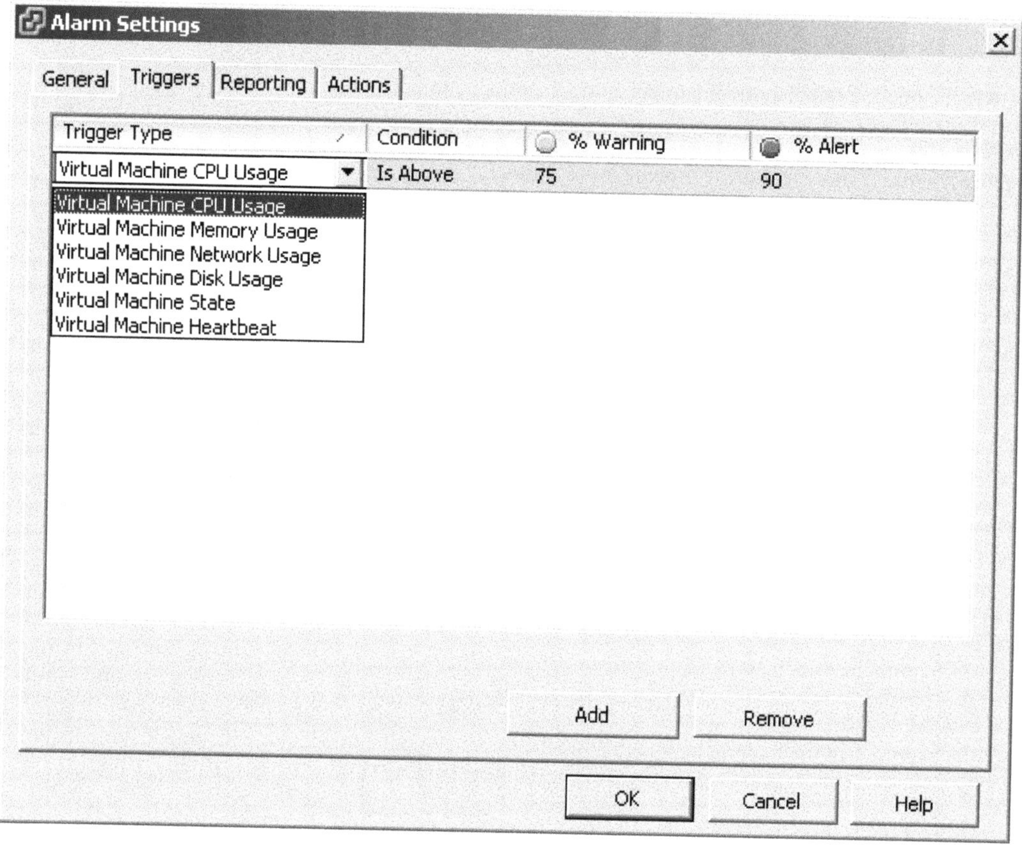

Figure 16.17 Alarm Settings Dialog Box Triggers Tab

Step 4. Click on the Trigger Type column as shown in Figure 16.17 and select a trigger type from the drop down list. In this example, we have selected the Virtual Machine CPU Usage trigger type.

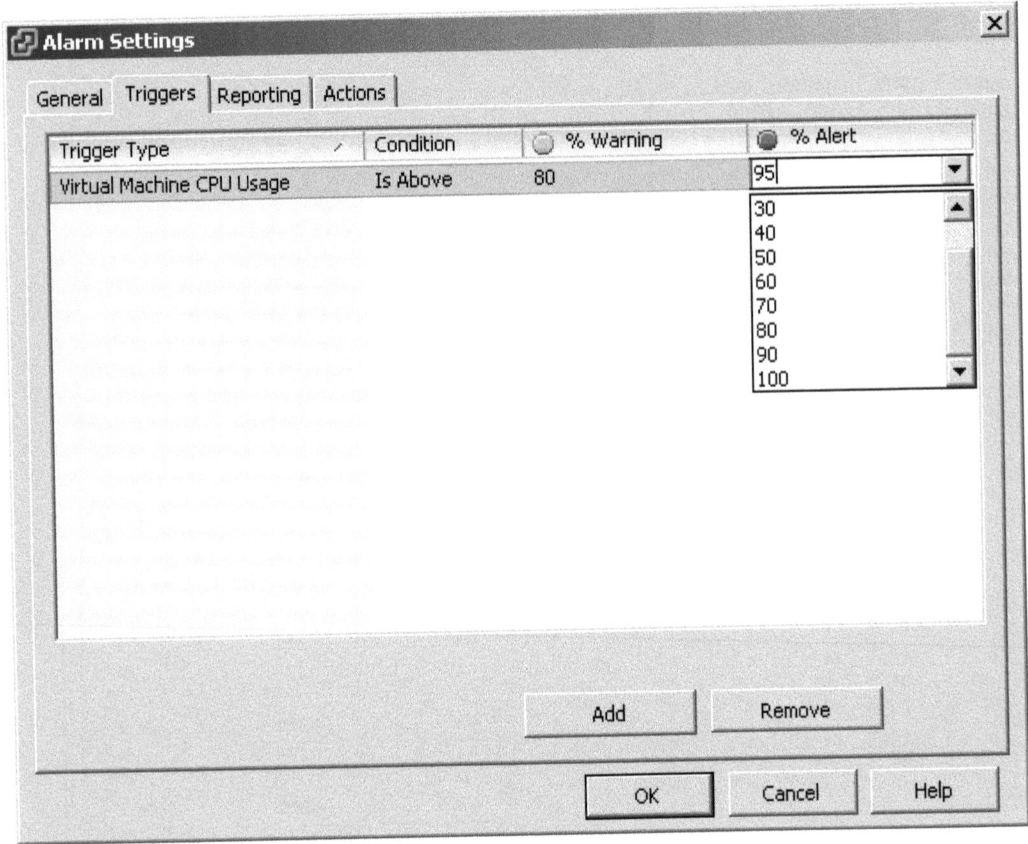

Figure 16.18 Alarm Settings Dialog Box Alert Value

Step 5. For this trigger type, the Condition column can be set to either Is Above or Is Below. To modify this column or any of the other columns listed, double click in the space just below the column title. The % Warning column has been set to 80 so that when the virtual machine has reached 80% of its CPU usage, a warning alarm will be created. The % Alert column has been set to 95 so that when the virtual machine has reached 95 % CPU usage an alert alarm will be created. Refer to Figure 16.18.

NOTE: The value set for the warning alarm cannot be equal to or greater than the value set for the alert alarm.

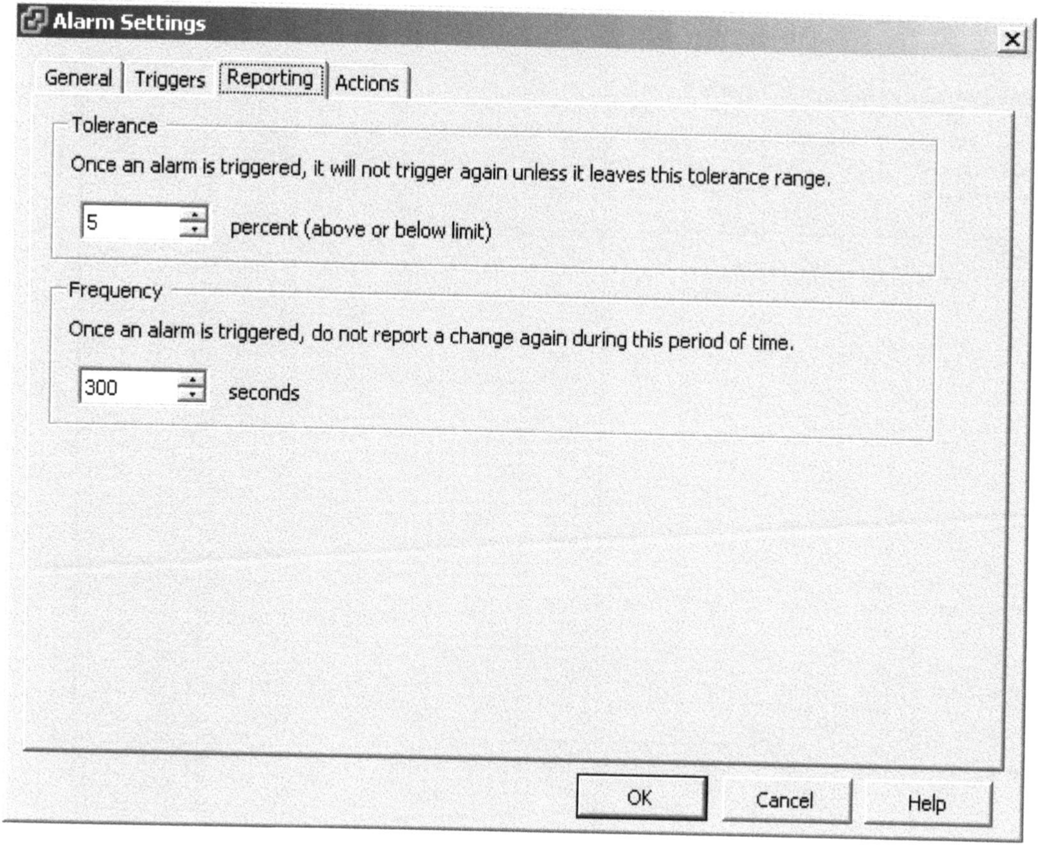

Figure 16.19 Alarm Settings Dialog Box Reporting Tab

Step 6. The Reporting tab is used to set a tolerance range. In this example, as shown in Figure 16.19, an alarm will not be triggered again until it has decreased or increased 5 % above either the warning or alert values set in the Triggers tab. How often an alarm is triggered can also be set by using the Frequency section. In this example, another alarm will not be triggered until five minutes have elapsed.

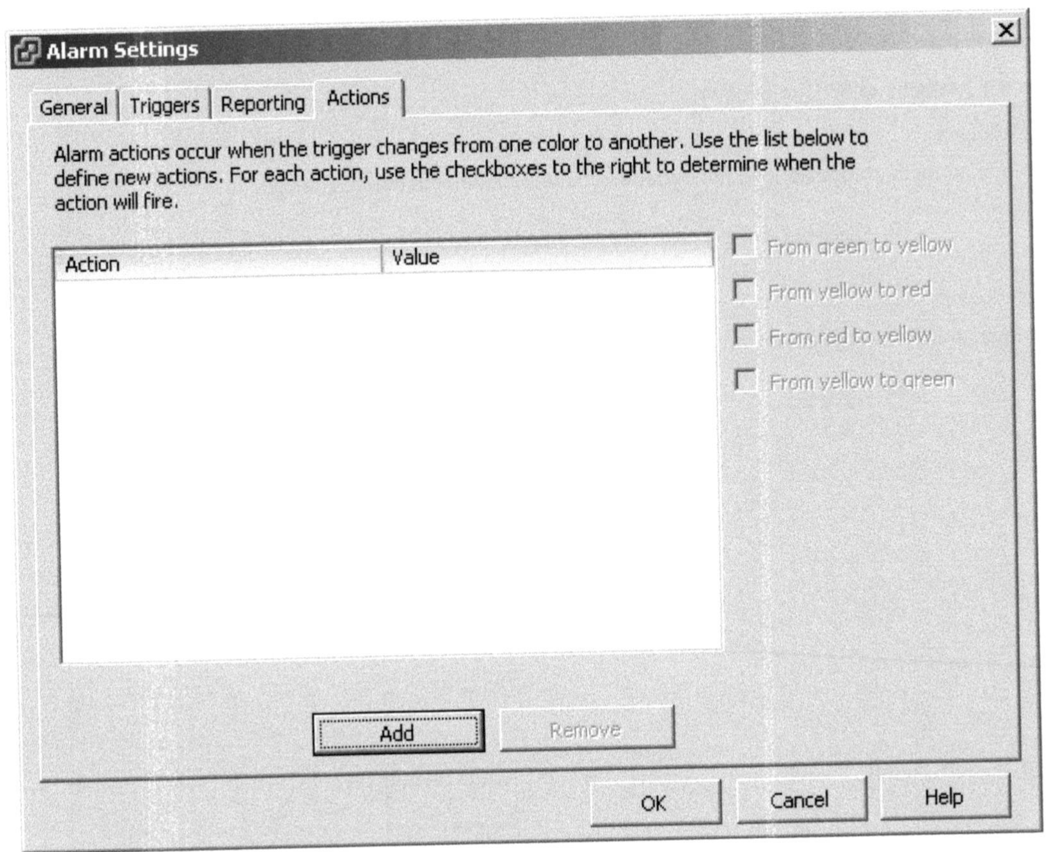

Figure 16.20 Alarm Settings Dialog Box Actions Tab

Step 7. The Actions tab shown in Figure 16.20 shows the Actions tab. To configure an action for the alarm, click on the Add button.

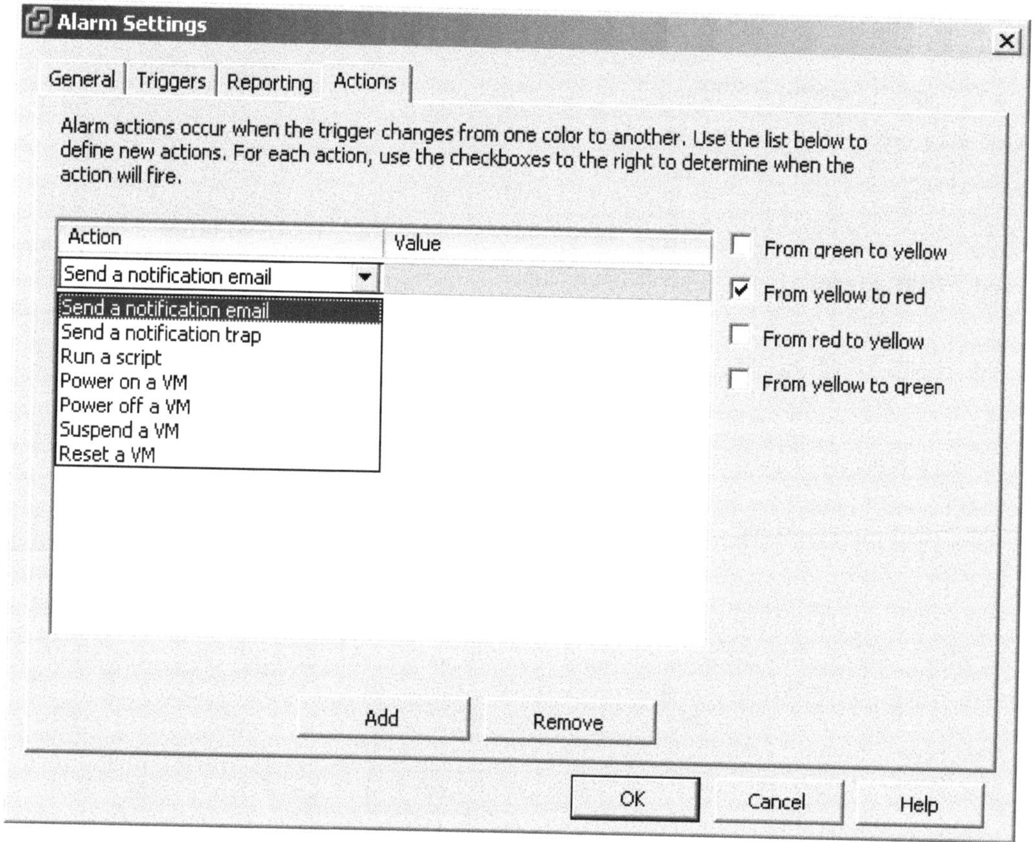

Figure 16.21 Alarm Settings Dialog Box Actions Tab Action Value

Step 8. The drop down box is displayed under the Action tab as shown in Figure 16.21. Select an action to continue.

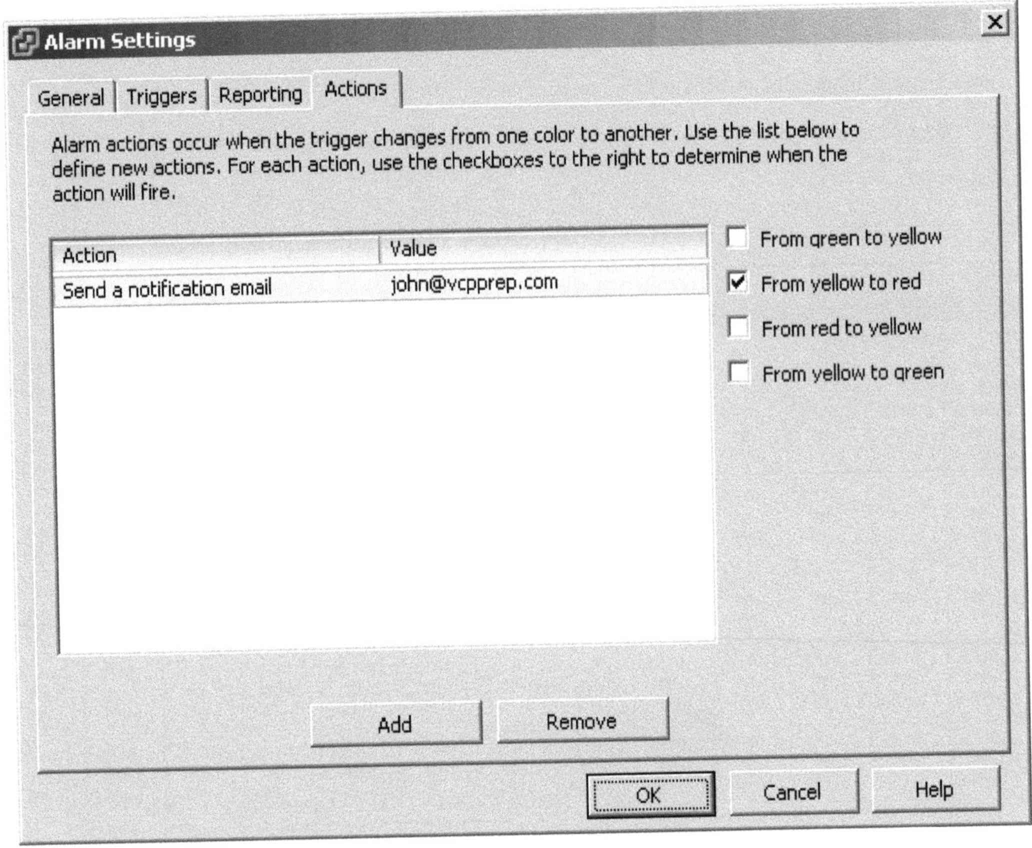

Figure 16.22 Alarm Settings Dialog Box Alarm Created

Step 9. In this example, the Send a notification email action was selected. Enter a value to send the email notification to as shown in Figure 16.22. The condition that the email is to be sent under can be controlled by selecting one of the following icon status changes:

- From green to yellow
- From yellow to red
- From red to yellow
- From yellow to green

Choose the desired condition changes and select the OK button to create the custom alarm.

Monitoring Alarms

There are default alarms that are created when VirtualCenter is installed. These alarms are created on the Hosts & Clusters and Virtual Machines & Templates folders. You cannot modify or change these default alarms unless you are modifying the alarms directly on these objects. Let's take a look at how to view alarms information in the VI Client.

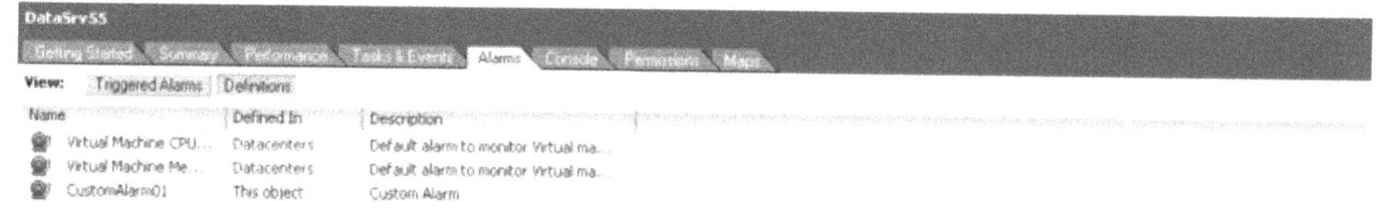

Figure 16.23 Virtual Machine Alarms Tab

Step 1. Chose a virtual machine in the VirtualCenter inventory and select the Alarms tab as shown in Figure 16.23. To view information about the already defined alarms, click the Definitions button. The Defined In column identifies where in the inventory the alarm was assigned. This is important as the object that was used to originally assign the alarm to be the object that can be used to make any modifications to the alarm.

Step 2. The VI Client makes it very easy to identify generated alarms by making a visual change in the object's icon in the inventory as shown in Figure 16.24. We can see that the DataSrv55 virtual machine has an triangle with an exclamation point icon. This icon if yellow, represents a warning alarm. If this icon is red, it represents an alert alarm.

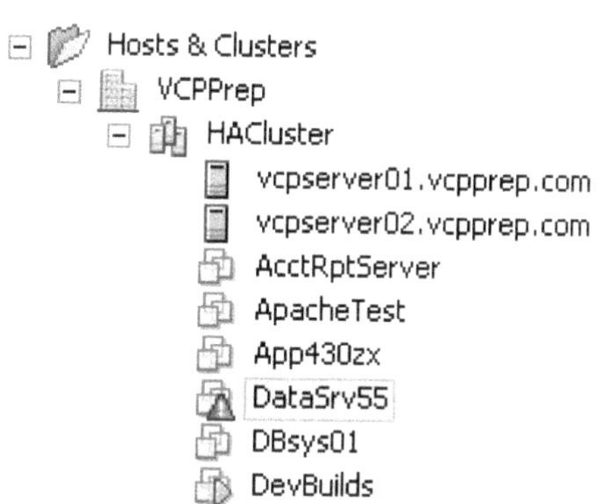

Figure 16.24 Virtual Machine Alarms Icon Change

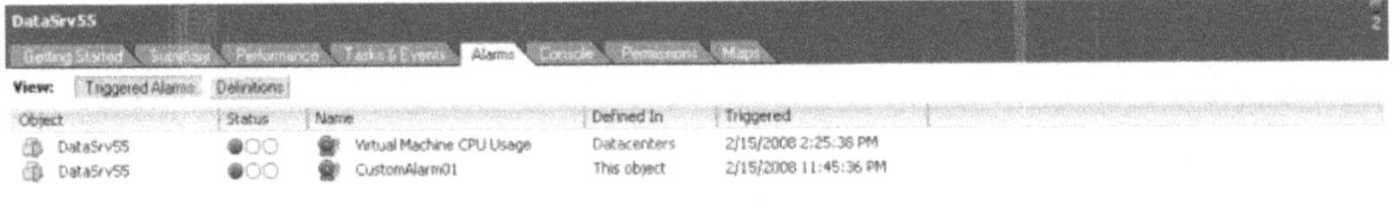

Figure 16.25 Virtual Machine Triggered Alarms

Step 3. Once again, select the virtual machine's Alarm tab as shown in Figure 16.25. Click on the Triggered Alarms button to view information about generated alarms.

Using the esxtop Command

The esxtop command is available when logged into the ESX host's service console. It can be used to monitor the resource usage of an ESX host. To invoke esxtop, enter the following command from the service console CLI:

```
[root@vcpserver01 root]# esxtop
```

Four different modes can be used for the esxtop command:

- CPU
- Memory
- Disk
- Network

Figure 16.26 displays the default CPU mode. To change into another mode, press the M key to enter Memory mode, the D key for Disk mode, the N key for Network mode and press the C key to enter CPU mode. A key metric to observe while in CPU mode is the % RDY column. The values listed there identify how long a virtual machine has had to wait to have one of its threads executed on a physical core. The % USED column is another key CPU performance indicator. It identifies how much a virtual machine has used of its CPU capacity. Having both high usage and ready time values can lead to a severe performance degradation with virtual machines running on the host.

```
12:00:14am up 14:47, 70 worlds; CPU load average: 0.38, 0.49, 0.28
PCPU(%):  41.64,  45.02 ;  used total:  43.33
LCPU(%):  35.48,   6.16,  36.16,   8.86
CCPU(%):   0 us,   0 sy,  99 id,   1 wa ;        cs/sec:    132

  ID    GID NAME                 NWLD   %USED    %RUN    %SYS    %WAIT    %RDY
   1      1 idle                    4  114.10  176.39    0.00     0.00  200.00
   2      2 system                  6    0.06    0.01    0.02   600.00    0.00
   6      6 helper                 22    0.05    0.02    0.00  2200.00    0.09
   7      7 drivers                19    0.14    0.73    0.47  1899.15    0.56
   8      8 vmotion                 1    0.00    0.00    0.00   100.00    0.00
   9      9 console                 1    0.99    1.50    0.01    98.04    0.48
  18     18 vmware-vmkauthd         1    0.00    0.00    0.00   100.00    0.00
  23     23 ReConSrv                5    2.23    1.75    0.00   497.51    0.81
  24     24 DataSrv55               6   78.45   78.13    1.17   516.32    5.63
  25     25 DevBuilds               5    2.22    0.78    0.00   499.11    0.20
```

Figure 16.26 ESXTOP CPU Mode

```
12:01:00am up 14:48, 70 worlds; MEM overcommit avg: 0.00, 0.00, 0.00
PMEM  /MB:  2047   total:   272     cos,   153 vmk,     734 other,    887 free
VMKMEM/MB:  1725 managed:   103 minfree,   355 rsvd,   1264 ursvd,  high state
COSMEM/MB:    12    free:   541  swap_t,   541 swap_f:   0.00 r/s,   0.00 w/s
PSHARE/MB:   468  shared,    68  common:   400 saving
SWAP  /MB:     0    curr,     0  target:
                                                         0.00 r/s,   0.00 w/s
MEMCTL/MB:     0    curr,     0  target,   665 max

   GID NAME              NWLD    MEMSZ    SZTGT     TCHD %ACTV %ACTVS %ACTVF %A
    18 vmware-vmkauthd      1     5.59     5.59     1.91     0      0      0
    23 ReConSrv             5   512.00   205.20    20.48     3      1      2
    24 DataSrv55            6   512.00   596.95   378.88    31     10     23
    25 DevBuilds            5   256.00   325.81     0.00     0      0      0
```

Figure 16.27 ESXTOP Memory Mode

Figure 16.27 displays the Memory mode. This mode is useful when determining how much memory TPS (Transparent Page Sharing) is freeing up. The PSHARE/MB row lists 468 MB being identified by TPS as duplicate memory. The 68 MB value is the amount of memory of identical content, common memory between the VMs on this ESX Server shared as read-only pages. By reducing the 468 MB of memory down to 68 MB, TPS was able to save 400 MB of physical memory.

12:01:41am up 14:49, 70 worlds; CPU load average: 0.14, 0.38, 0.29

ADAPTR	CID	TID	LID	WID	NCHNS	NTGTS	NLUNS	NVMS	AQLEN	LQLEN	WQLEN	ACTV	QUED	%U
vmhba0	-	-	-	-	1	1	1	12	128	0	0	-	-	
vmhba32	-	-	-	-	1	3	3	29	4096	0	0	-	-	

Figure 16.28 ESXTOP Disk Mode

Figure 16.28 displays the Disk mode. Use this mode when troubleshooting HBA (Host Bus Adapter) latency and performance issues.

12:02:14am up 14:49, 70 worlds; CPU load average: 0.09, 0.33, 0.29

PORT ID	UPLINK	USED BY	DTYP	DNAME	PKTTX/s	MbTX/s
16777217	Y	vmnic0	H	vSwitch0	10.53	0.02
16777218	N	0:NCP	H	vSwitch0	0.00	0.00
16777219	N	0:CDP	H	vSwitch0	0.00	0.00
16777220	N	0:vmk-tcpip-10.0.1.2	H	vSwitch0	3.97	0.00
16777221	N	0:vswif0	H	vSwitch0	6.56	0.01
33554433	Y	vmnic1	H	vSwitch1	0.60	0.00
33554434	N	0:NCP	H	vSwitch1	0.00	0.00
33554435	N	0:CDP	H	vSwitch1	0.00	0.00
33554436	N	0:vswif1	H	vSwitch1	0.00	0.00
33554451	N	1103:ReConSrv	H	vSwitch1	0.00	0.00
33554454	N	1112:DevBuilds	H	vSwitch1	0.00	0.00
33554456	N	1107:DataSrv55	H	vSwitch1	0.60	0.00
50331649	N	0:CDP	H	vSwitch2	0.00	0.00

Figure 16.29 ESXTOP Network Mode

Figure 16.29 displays the Network mode. Use this mode when troubleshooting NIC performance, identifying bottlenecks and determining latency issues.

Figure 16.30 displays the help screen. The help screen can be reached by entering an H while running the esxtop command.

```
space    - update display
h or ?   - help; show this text
q        - quit

Interactive commands are:

fF       Add or remove fields
oO       Change the order of displayed fields
s        Set the delay in seconds between updates
#        Set the number of instances to display
W        Write configuration file ~/.esxtop3rc
e        Expand/Rollup Disk World Statistics
p        Expand/Rollup Disk Path Statistics
t        Expand/Rollup Disk Partition Statistics

Sort by:
         r:READS/s       w:WRITES/s
         R:MBREAD/s      T:MBWRTN/s
         N:Default
Switch display:
         c:ESX cpu       m:ESX memory     d:ESX disk adapter      v:ESX disk VM   n
:ESX nic

Hit any key to continue:
```

Figure 16.30 ESXTOP Help Screen

Troubleshooting Performance and Alarm issues

If alarms are not triggering, verify that the correct thresholds have been set for the alarms. It is also important to be certain that the appropriate resources have been assigned to the virtual machines. Physical firewalls can block ports needing to be open in order to facilitate communications between an ESX host and a VirtualCenter server. Port 902 is used for communications between the VirtualCenter server and the ESX host. If port 902 is blocked, information that is normally sent and used for alarm triggers may not be available.

VirtualCenter and the ESX host provide useful log files when troubleshooting communication issues between these servers. The VirtualCenter log files are located in the following location on the VirtualCenter server:

C:\Windows\Temp\vpx

The VirtualCenter agent running on the ESX host has its log files located in the following location on the ESX host:

/var/log/vmware/vpx

It is recommended to configure the ESX 3.5 servers to use a Network Time Protocol (NTP) server to synchronize the server's time and date settings to a consistent common time source. By having a consistent time across ESX hosts, troubleshooting is enhanced by having accurate time/date stamps in system log files across ESX hosts. Guest operating systems running inside virtual machines can have their system time synchronized to the system time of the ESX hosts they are operating on. This is an important configuration as it allows consistent task scheduling and accurate performance statistics to be recorded when the ESX 3.5 host is under the management of a VirtualCenter server.

External References

The VMware ESX 3.5 and ESXi Server version 3.5 Documentation Page:

http://www.vmware.com/support/pubs/vi_pubs.html

Installation and Upgrade Guide:

http://www.vmware.com/pdf/vi3_301_201_installation_guide.pdf

Basic System Administration Guide:

http://www.vmware.com/pdf/vi3_301_201_admin_guide.pdf

Server Configuration Guide:

http://www.vmware.com/pdf/vi3_301_201_server_config.pdf

VirtualCenter Monitoring and Performance Statistics:

http://www.vmware.com/pdf/vi3_monitoring_statistics_note.pdf

Iometer:

http://www.iometer.org

Wireshark:

http://www.wireshark.org

VMware SDK & API Developer Resources page:

http://www.vmware.com/support/pubs/sdk_pubs.html

Configuring Management Agents for ESX Server 3.0.1:

http://www.vmware.com/pdf/esx30_cfg_mgmt_tools.pdf

Sample Test Questions

1. VirtualCenter contains several levels of data collection. Which of the following is the maximum data collection level?

a. 3

b. 5

c. 4

d. 2

e. 6

2. Which of the following are valid alarm trigger actions for a virtual machine?

a. Send a notification trap

b. Send a notification email

c. Restart the vpxd service

d. Restart the vmware-hostd service

e. Run a script

3. Which objects are default alarms defined in?

a. Datacenter

b. HA Cluster

c. DRS Cluster

d. Hosts & Clusters Folder

e. Virtual Machines & Templates Folder

4. Which of the following, when viewed using the esxtop command is a key indicator of CPU resource constraints?

a. High % USED value

b. Low % RDY value

c. Low % SYS value

d. High % RDY value

e. Low % USED value

5. Which of the following chart types are available when using the performance tab in the VI Client?

a. Bar graph

b. Line graph

c. Pie graph

d. Stacked graph

e. Histogram

Sample Test Solutions

1. VirtualCenter contains several levels of data collection. Which of the following is the maximum data collection level?

a. 3

b. 5

c. 4

d. 2

e. 6

Answer: c - VirtualCenter offers the following data collection levels:

- ***Level 1 - General utilization information provides high level view. Average usage metrics are included in this level for CPU, memory, disk and network. Very little VirtualCenter and ESX resources used to collect level 1 information. This is the default level.***
- ***Level 2 - Includes all information collected in level 1 and additional counters for CPU, memory, network and disk. Level 2 uses more VirtualCenter and ESX resources to collect information than it does to collect level 1 information. Monitoring more than ten ESX hosts can use a significant amount of resources on the VirtualCenter server.***
- ***Level 3 - Includes all information collected in levels 1 and 2. Collects device based metrics. This level is useful in determining the usefulness of virtual SMP (Symmetric multiprocessing) for virtual machines configured with multiple virtual CPUs.***
- ***Level 4 - Includes all information collected in levels 1,2, and 3. This level adds the additional maximum / minimum rollup types. The other rollup types are Summation, Average and Latest. Use this level to gain detailed information on virtual machine CPU usage or when diagnosing device performance problems. Operating a VirtualCenter server for several days at this level can quickly populate its database server.***

2. Which of the following are valid alarm trigger actions for a virtual machine?

a. Send a notification trap

b. Send a notification email

c. Restart the vpxd service

d. Restart the vmware-hostd service

e. Run a script

Answer - a, b and e - The following are the alarm trigger actions for a virtual machine:

- ***Send a notification email***
- ***Send a notification trap***
- ***Run a script***
- ***Power on a VM***
- ***Power off a VM***
- ***Suspend a VM***
- ***Reset a VM***

3. Which objects are default alarms defined in?

a. Datacenter

b. HA Cluster

c. DRS Cluster

d. Hosts & Clusters Folder

e. Virtual Machines & Templates Folder

Answer: d and e - There are default alarms that are created when VirtualCenter is installed. These alarms are created on the Hosts & Clusters and Virtual Machines & Templates folders. You cannot modify or change these default alarms unless you modify the alarms directly on these objects.

4. Which of the following, when viewed using the esxtop command is a key indicator of CPU resource constraints?

a. High % USED value

b. Low % RDY value

c. Low % SYS value

d. High % RDY value

e. Low % USED value

Answer: d - A key metric to observe while in CPU mode is the % RDY column. The values listed there identify how long a virtual machine has had to wait to have one of its threads executed on a physical core. The % USED column is another key CPU performance indicator. It identifies how much a virtual machine has used of its CPU capacity. Having both high usage and ready time values can lead to a severe performance degradation with virtual machines running on the host.

5. Which of the following chart types are available when using the performance tab in the VI Client?

a. Bar graph

b. Line graph

c. Pie graph

d. Stacked graph

e. Histogram

Answer: - b and d - The performance graphs support line and stacked graphs.

Chapter 17

VMware Consolidated Backup

After reading this chapter you should be able to complete the following tasks:

- Understand what VCB offers
- Requirements for using VCB
- VCB Installation
- VCB commands

What Is VMware Consolidated Backup?

Several methods exist for performing file level and full image backups of virtual machines. Third party backup tools can be used in the same manner as they are used to perform backup jobs on physical machines. These tools often employ the use of agents installed in the guest operating system. Agents provide the benefit of automating the backup job. Refer to the Backup Software Compatibility Guide for ESX Server 3.5 and ESXi for a list of the supported third party tools. This document can be found at the following location:

http://www.vmware.com/pdf/vi35_backup_guide.pdf

The downside of using agents is cost. An average cost per agent is typically between $500 to $1,000. This can become quite costly when backing up a large number of virtual machines. Agents also require the virtual machine to be up and running for the agent to perform its backup operation.

Another disadvantage of using agents is that with these installed in the virtual machines or in the ESX service console, they consume resources that the ESX server could otherwise use to service the virtualized environment. VMware developed a software framework called VMware Consolidated Backup (VCB) to offload the backup workload placed on an ESX host to another physical machine. A machine that has VCB installed on it is referred to as the VCB proxy server. The VCB framework is not a full blown backup solution. It does not offer a GUI interface where backup jobs can be configured and scheduled. It makes use of VCB commands that are part of the framework to perform both file level and full image virtual machine backups. The VMware Infrastructure Foundation, Standard and Enterprise editions all include the VCB framework.

The VCB framework offers the following advantages when backing up virtual machines:

- 24/7 backup window - Virtual machines can be backed up whether powered on or off. This provides flexibility and enables backups to be performed on a consistent basis.
- ESX workload reduced - Having a separate physical machine operating as the VCB proxy server removes the backup job resource consumption off of the ESX host. Virtual machines will have more resources available to satisfy their workload demands.

- LAN free backups - The VCB proxy server can be configured to access the same LUNs on the storage array that the ESX servers use. Backup jobs can take place completely off of the network freeing up bandwidth for other applications when backing up SAN-based VMs
- Agentless - VCB does not require an agent to be installed on the ESX service console or within the guest operating system of the virtual machine. This can provide a substantial cost savings for backup operations.

The VCB proxy server can perform full image backups for any supported guest operating system. It can perform file level backups only of supported Windows operating systems.

Requirements for using VCB

VCB version 1.1 released with ESX 3.5 / VC 2.5 can be installed within a virtual machine. Doing so, places the workload back on the ESX host and eliminates being able to perform LAN free backups. Backups performed with the VCB proxy running in a virtual machine either are performed over the network to a network share or an iSCSI storage array.

The VCB proxy server requires one of the following operating systems to be installed:

- Microsoft Windows Server 2003 Service Pack 1 - 32 - bit
- Microsoft Windows Server 2003 Service Pack 1 - 64 - bit
- Microsoft Windows Server 2003 R2 - 32 - bit
- Microsoft Windows Server 2003 R2 - 64 - bit

The physical VCB proxy server needs to be configured with at least one NIC and a HBA card if accessing Fibre channel storage. Let's take a look at the installation process of the VCB proxy server.

VCB Installation

Except for Windows 2003 Enterprise Edition and Windows 2003 Datacenter Edition, all versions of Windows will assign drive letters to every FAT and NTFS volume it sees. The first step in configuring the VCB proxy host is to remove any unused assigned drive letters. To accomplish this, either mask all LUNs from the VCB proxy server containing RDMs or VMFS volumes or shutdown it down and disconnect it from the SAN. Restart the VCB proxy if needed and using the administrator account perform the following from the command line:

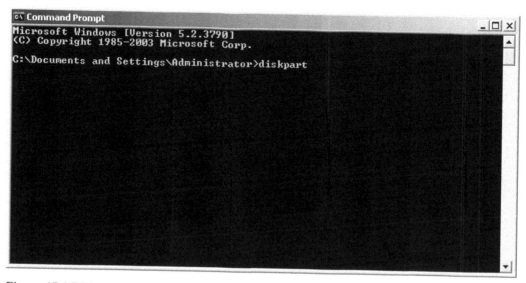

Figure 17.1 Diskpart command

Step 1. Type the diskpart command as shown in Figure 17.1. This command will display the diskpart command line.

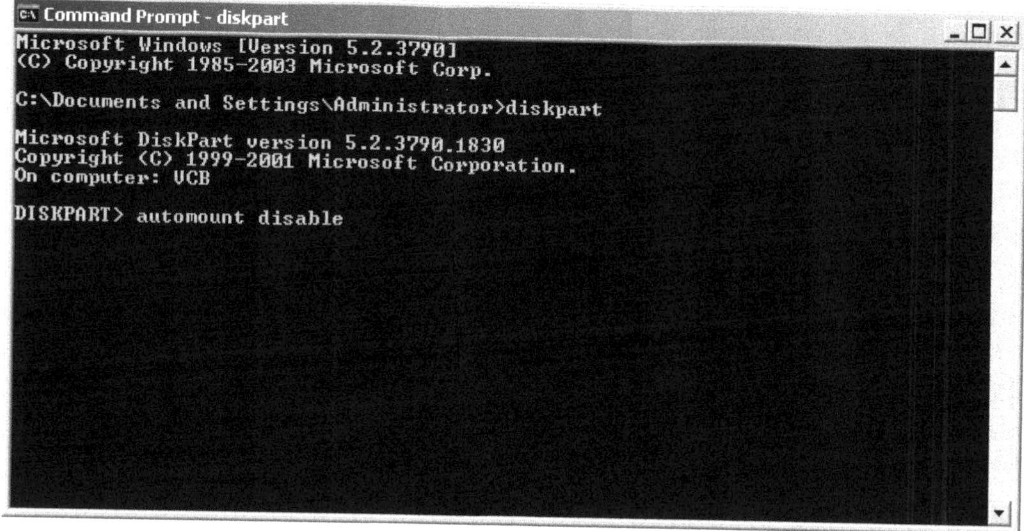

Figure 17.2 Automount Disable Command

Step 2. Enter the automount disable command as shown in Figure 17.2. This command is used to disable automatic drive letter assignment.

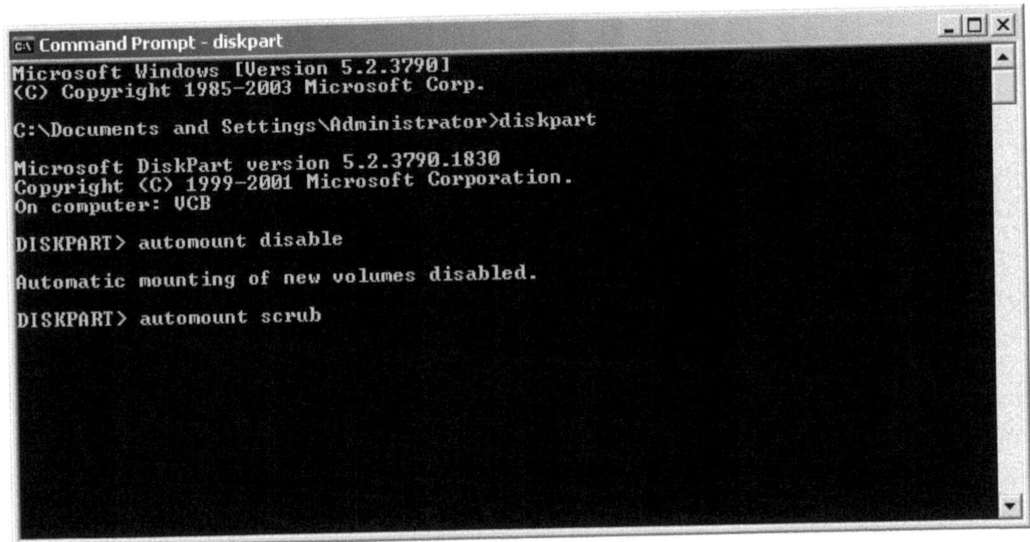

Figure 17.3 Automount Scrub Command

Step 3. Enter the automount scrub command as shown in Figure 17.3 to delete entries of mounted volumes stored in the registry.

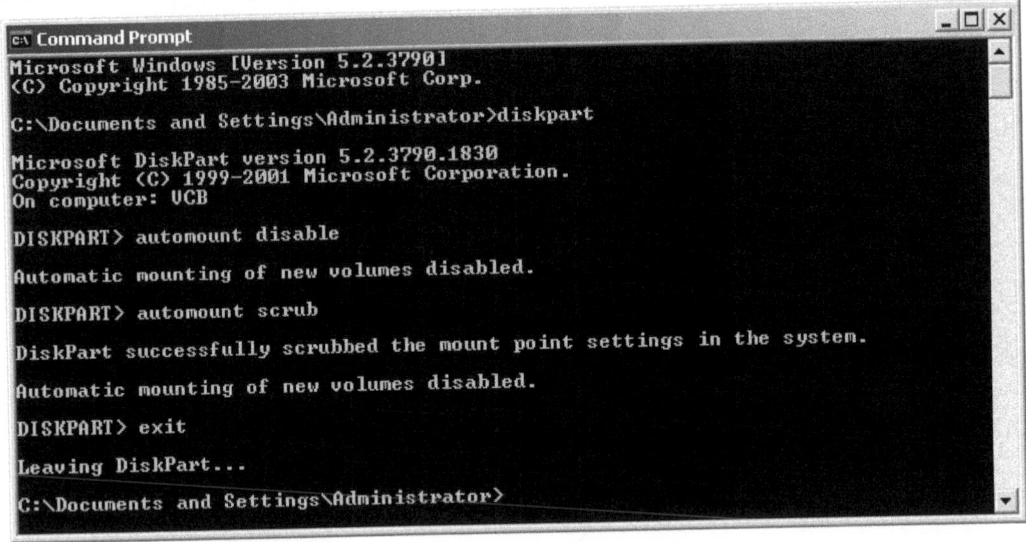

Figure 17.4 Exiting Diskpart

Step 4. Exit diskpart by entering exit as shown in Figure 17.4.

Once again, power down the VCB proxy host and unmask any FAT or NTFS volumes previously masked or reconnect the server to the SAN if needed. Power on the VCB proxy and log in as administrator.

The VCB framework installation is relatively quick. The size of the installer is approximately 10 MB. The installer is named "VMware Consolidated Backup Framework.msi". To install VCB, perform the following steps:

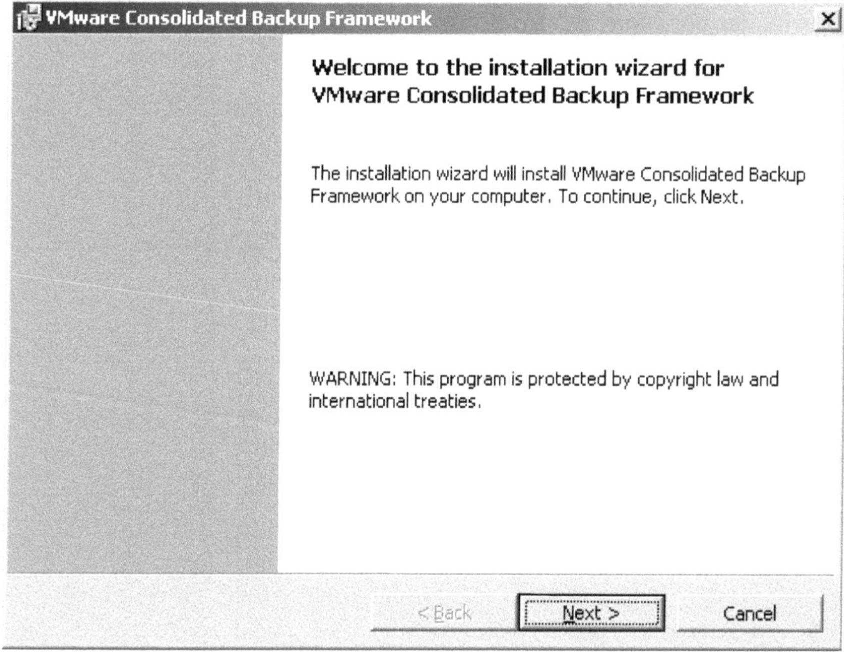

Figure 17.5 VMware Consolidated Backup Framework Installer Dialog Box

Step 1. Double click on the "VMware Consolidated Backup Framework.msi" installer file. This will launch the VMware Consolidated Backup Framework installer as shown in Figure 17.5. Click the Next button to continue.

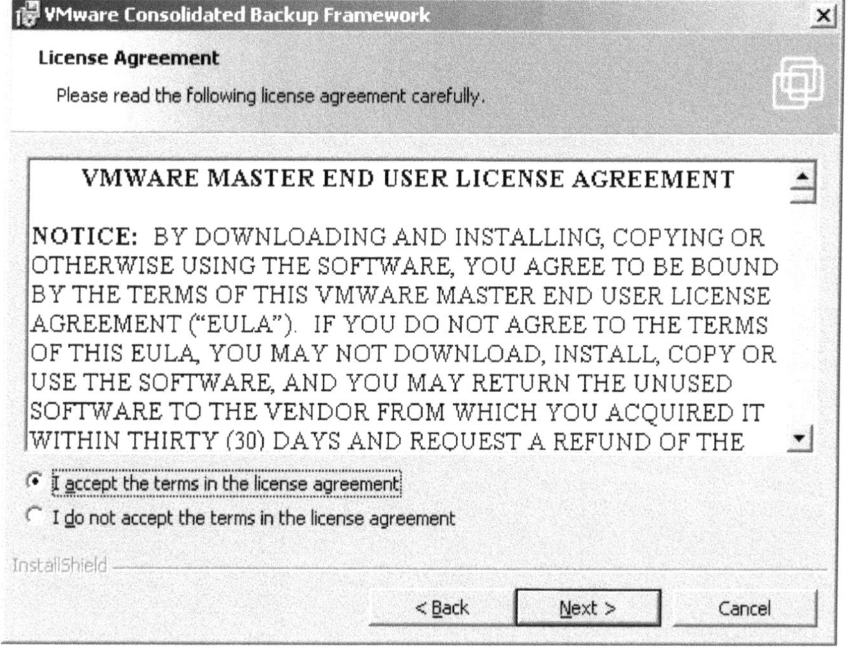

Figure 17.6 HA VMware Consolidated Backup Framework Installer License Agreement

Step 2. Review the license information. To continue the installation, chose the "I accept the terms in the license agreement" radio box as shown in Figure 17.6. Click the Next button to continue.

Step 3. Choose the destination for the VCB framework installed files as shown in Figure 17.7. The default installation path is as follows:

C:\Program Files\VMware\VMware Consolidated Backup Framework\

Click the Change button to modify the default installation path if needed. Click the Next button to continue.

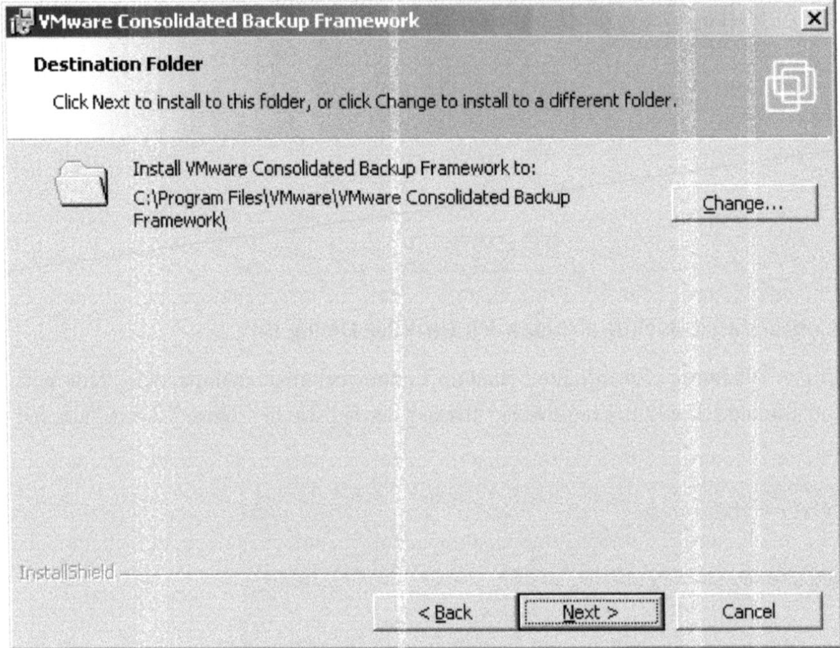

Figure 17.7 VMware Consolidated Backup Framework Installer Destination Folder

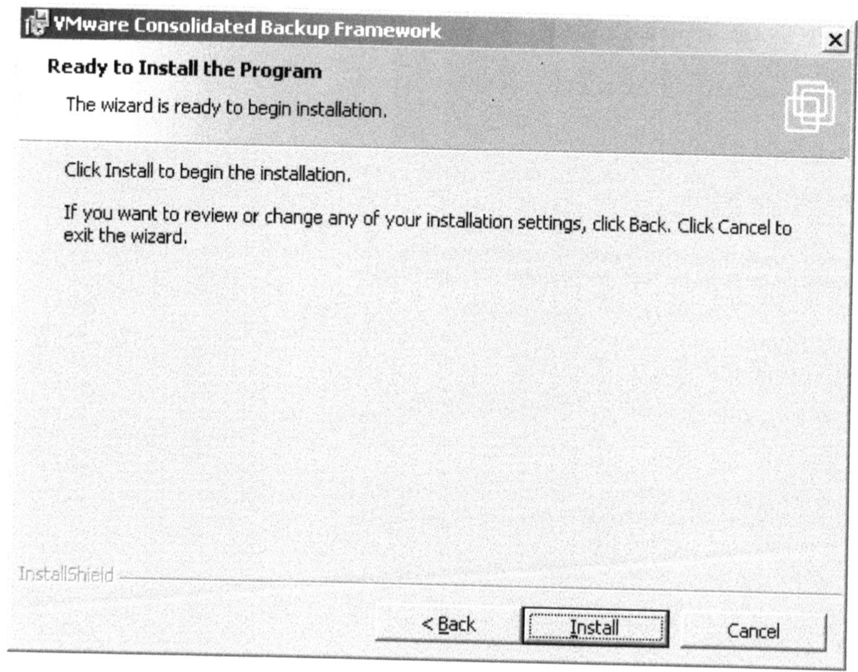

Figure 17.8 VMware Consolidated Backup Framework Installer Ready To Begin

Step 4. The wizard is now ready to begin the installation as shown in Figure 17.8. Click the Install button to continue.

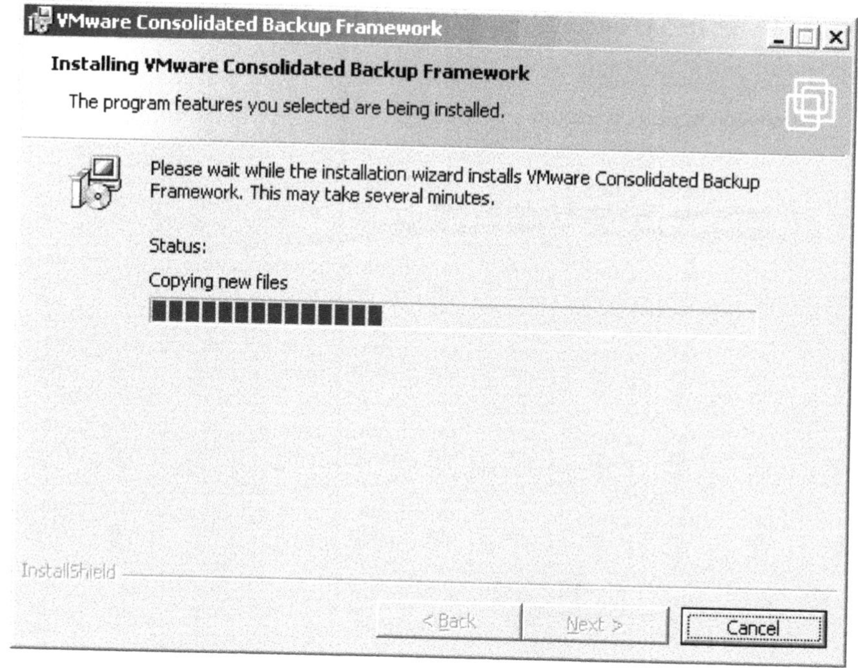

Figure 17.9 VMware Consolidated Backup Framework Installer Status

The installer displays the status as it installs the necessary files as shown in Figure 17.9. The VCB framework typically installs in a short period of time.

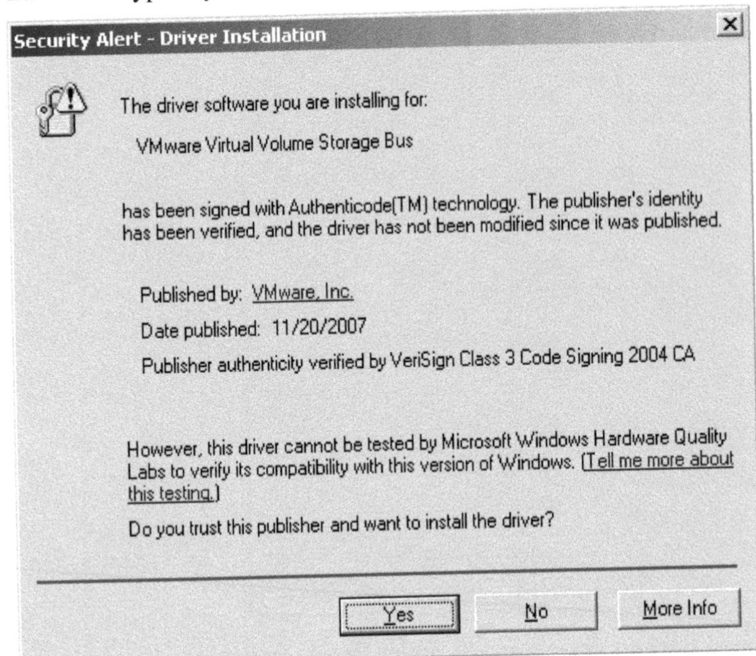

Figure 17.10 VMware Consolidated Backup Framework Installer Security Alert

Step 5. The VMware Virtual Volume Storage Bus driver causes a security alert dialog box to be displayed as shown in Figure 17.10. To continue with the installation, select the Yes button.

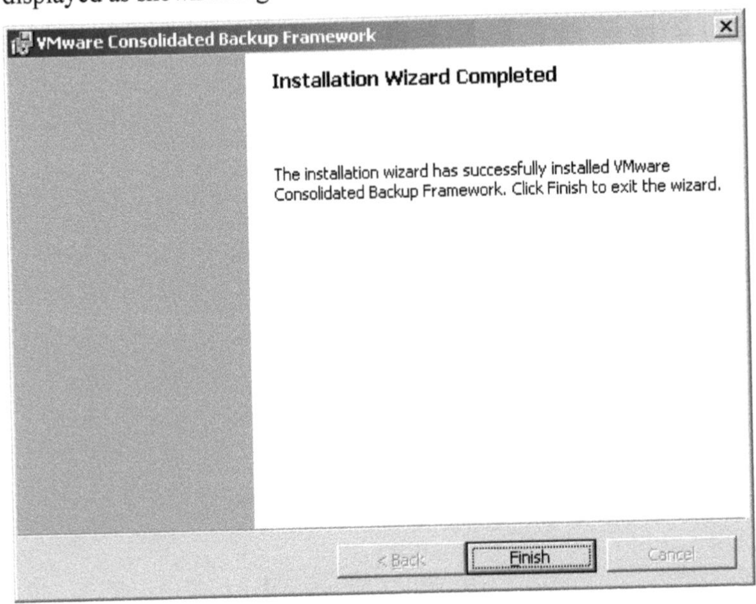

Figure 17.11 VMware Consolidated Backup Framework Installer Completed

Step 6. The VCB framework installation is now complete as shown in Figure 17.11. Click the Finish button to continue.

VCB Commands

The VCB framework provides eight commands that allow both backup and restore jobs to be performed. Some of the commands are only available on either the ESX service console or VCB proxy server while others are available on both the service console and the VCB proxy server. Commands that are executed on the service console are case-sensitive; commands issued on the VCB proxy server are not, with the exception of options and arguments to the commands on the Windows VCB Proxy Server. It is necessary to run these commands with administrator privileges. You can create a separate Windows account and assign it to a custom VirtualCenter role that contains the following privileges in order to use the GUI Snapshot Manager for creating snapshots when preparing to perform backups:

- Disk Lease
- Allow Virtual Machine Download
- Create Snapshot
- Delete Snapshot
- Allow Read-only Disk Access

In order for a regular user account to execute the commands on the Windows Proxy Server, the user needs to belong to the Administrator's group; on the ESX Server, the user will need to have sudo configured for execution of the ESX-bundled VCB commands.

All of the available commands and their descriptions are listed below:

vcbVmName - Use this command from either the service console or VCB proxy server to gather configuration information about virtual machines. Entering the following will output the command's usage information:

vcbVmName -h

vcbMounter - This command can be invoked from either the service console or VCB proxy server to perform backup jobs. When ran from the service console, it can only perform full virtual machine backups. When ran from the VCB proxy server, it can perform both full and file level backups. It will only backup a virtual machine that is configured with a single virtual disk. If a virtual machine is configure with multiple virtual disks, the virtual machine's configuration file (.vmx) will need to be modified by setting all by one of the virtual machine's virtual disks to active. Entering just the command without any arguments will output the command's usage information.

vcbSnapshot - This command creates, deletes and retrieves information about virtual machine snapshots. It can be issued on both the service console and the VCB proxy server. Entering just the command without any arguments will output the command's usage information.

vcbExport - This command can be ran from both the service console and VCB proxy server to make a backup of a virtual machine's virtual disk. It is often used injunction with the vcbSnapshot command. Entering just the command without any arguments will output the command's usage information.

vcbRestore - This command is only available on the service console. It can be used to restore full image backup of a virtual machine that was created by VCB. Entering just the command without any arguments will output the command's usage information.

mountvm - This command can only be invoked on the VCB proxy server. It is used to mount a virtual machine's disk typically when performing a file level backup on a Windows based virtual machine. Entering just the command without any arguments will output the command's usage information.

vcbCleanup - This command is only available on the VCB proxy server and is used to cleanup if a backup operation has failed. Entering just the command without any arguments will output the command's usage information.

vcbUtil - This command is only available from the service console and is used to gather information about a virtual machine's placement in the VirtualCenter inventory and includes resource pool information. Entering just the command without any arguments will output the command's usage information.

Troubleshooting Common VMware Consolidate Backup Problems

Performing backup jobs can place a heavy demand on available resources. Ensure that the storage array has enough storage space and available storage processor capacity to perform backups. When performing full image backups from the VCB proxy server, ensure there is enough storage space available. The VCB proxy server communicates with the VirtualCenter server to obtain necessary backup information about the virtual machine. It then uses this information to locate the virtual machine's virtual disk(s). A copy of these virtual disks is then made. Virtual disks larger than 2 GB will be divided in size to just under 2 GB in size. When performing a file level backup, the VCB proxy server only needs to remotely mount the virtual machine's virtual disk(s) which does not require a large amount of storage space.

The log level for the VCB proxy server can be increased to obtain additional troubleshooting information. Open up the config.js file located in the following location:

C:\Program Files\VMware\VMware Consolidated Backup Framework\config

The log level values can be set in the range of 0-6. When set to 0, the least amount of information is logged. Level 6 is the most verbose. The default value is 3.

Search the config.js file and locate the following line:

// LOGLEVEL=6;

Remove the "//" and set the value as needed.

Consult the following log files when troubleshooting VCB issues:

- C:\Windows\temp\vmware-vlun.log - located on the VCB Proxy server
- C:\Windows\temp\vmware-vmount.log - located on the VCB Proxy server

- /var/log/vmware/hostd.log - located on the ESX service console

External References

Backup Software Compatibility Guide for ESX Server 3.5 and ESXi Server version 3.5:

http://www.vmware.com/pdf/vi35_backup_guide.pdf

The VMware ESX 3.5 and ESXi Server version 3.5 Documentation Page:

http://www.vmware.com/support/pubs/vi_pubs.html

Sample Test Questions

1. Which of the following operating systems can be used by the VCB framework software?

a. Windows 2000 Professional

b. Windows NT

c. MAC OS

d. SUSE Linux

e. Microsoft Windows Server 2003 Service Pack 1 - 64 - bit

2. Which of the following can be used on both the service console and VCB proxy server to retrieve information about a virtual machine's configuration?

a. diskpart

b. vcbExport

c. vcbVmName

d. mountvm

e. esxcfg-info

3. Automatic drive letter assignment can cause problems with the VCB proxy server. Which of the following operating systems do not require modifications to be made to avoid drive letter assignment issues?

a. Windows 2003 Enterprise Edition

b. Windows 2003 Datacenter Edition

c. Windows 2003 Standard Edition

d. Windows 2003 Web Edition

4. Which of the following benefits can be realized when using the VCB framework?

a. LAN free backups

b. Cost savings due to agentless backups

c. ESX workload reduced

d. GUI based scheduler

e. 24/7 backup window

5. Which of the following operating systems can file level backups be performed using the VCB proxy server?

a. Solaris

b. Netware

c. Windows

d. Red Hat Linux

e. Ubuntu Linux

Sample Test Solutions

1. Which of the following operating systems can be used by the VCB framework software?

a. Windows 2000 Professional

b. Windows NT

c. MAC OS

d. SUSE Linux

e. Microsoft Windows Server 2003 Service Pack 1 - 64 - bit

Answer: e - VMware supports the following operating systems on the VCB Proxy Server:

- ***Microsoft Windows Server 2003 Service Pack 1 - 32 - bit***
- ***Microsoft Windows Server 2003 Service Pack 1 - 64 - bit***
- ***Microsoft Windows Server 2003 R2 - 32 - bit***
- ***Microsoft Windows Server 2003 R2 - 64 - bit***

2. Which of the following can be used on both the service console and VCB proxy server to retrieve information about a virtual machine's configuration?

a. diskpart

b. vcbExport

c. vcbVmName

d. mountvm

e. esxcfg-info

Answer: c - The vcbVmName command can be used either from the service console or the VCB proxy server to gather configuration information about virtual machines.

3. Automatic drive letter assignment can cause problems with the VCB proxy server. Which of the following operating systems do not require modifications to be made to avoid drive letter assignment issues?

a. Windows 2003 Enterprise Edition

b. Windows 2003 Datacenter Edition

c. Windows 2003 Standard Edition

d. Windows 2003 Web Edition

Answer: a and b - Except for Windows 2003 Enterprise Edition and Windows 2003 Datacenter Edition, all versions of Windows will assign drive letters to every FAT and NTFS volume it sees.

4. Which of the following benefits can be realized when using the VCB framework?

a. LAN free backups

b. Cost savings due to agentless backups

c. ESX workload reduced

d. GUI based scheduler

e. 24/7 backup window

Answer: a, b, c and e - The VCB framework is not a full blown backup solution. It does not offer a GUI interface where backup jobs can be configured and scheduled. The VCB framework offers the following advantages when backing up virtual machines:

- ***24/7 backup window - Virtual machines can be backed up whether powered on or off. This provides flexibility and enables backups to be performed on a consistent basis.***
- ***ESX workload reduced - Having a separate physical machine operating as the VCB proxy server removes the backup job resource consumption off of the ESX host. Virtual machines will have more resources available to satisfy their workload demands.***
- ***LAN free backups - The VCB proxy server can be configured to access the same LUNs on the storage array that the ESX servers use. Backup jobs can take place completely off of the network freeing up bandwidth for other applications.***
- ***Agentless - VCB does not require an agent to be installed on the ESX service console or within the guest operating system of the virtual machine. This can provide a substantial cost savings for backup operations.***

5. Which of the following operating systems can file level backups be performed using the VCB proxy server?

a. Solaris

b. Netware

c. Windows

d. Red Hat Linux

e. Ubuntu Linux

Answer: c - Windows is the only supported operating system for performing file level backups. Full image backups can be performed on any supported operating system.

Index

D

E

N

O

T

U

V

Milton Keynes UK
Ingram Content Group UK Ltd.
UKHW020828141024
449569UK00008B/590